1 MONTH OF FREE READING

at

www.ForgottenBooks.com

By purchasing this book you are eligible for one month membership to ForgottenBooks.com, giving you unlimited access to our entire collection of over 1,000,000 titles via our web site and mobile apps.

To claim your free month visit: www.forgottenbooks.com/free925848

* Offer is valid for 45 days from date of purchase. Terms and conditions apply.

ISBN 978-0-260-07137-8
PIBN 10925848

This book is a reproduction of an important historical work. Forgotten Books uses state-of-the-art technology to digitally reconstruct the work, preserving the original format whilst repairing imperfections present in the aged copy. In rare cases, an imperfection in the original, such as a blemish or missing page, may be replicated in our edition. We do, however, repair the vast majority of imperfections successfully; any imperfections that remain are intentionally left to preserve the state of such historical works.

Forgotten Books is a registered trademark of FB &c Ltd.
Copyright © 2018 FB &c Ltd.
FB &c Ltd, Dalton House, 60 Windsor Avenue, London, SW19 2RR.
Company number 08720141. Registered in England and Wales.

For support please visit www.forgottenbooks.com

THE COMMONHEALTH

Volume 24-26   Jan.-Feb.-Mar.
No. 1   1937

FINAL REPORT
OF THE
MASSACHUSETTS
PNEUMONIA STUDY AND SERVICE
1931-1935

RODERICK HEFFRON, M.D.

Field Director of Study; Formerly Field Director, Pneumonia Study and Service, Massachusetts Department of Health

ELLIOTT S. ROBINSON, M.D.

Director of Antitoxin and Vaccine Laboratory, Massachusetts Department of Public Health

MASSACHUSETTS
DEPARTMENT OF PUBLIC HEALTH

THE COMMONHEALTH
QUARTERLY BULLETIN OF THE MASSACHUSETTS DEPARTMENT OF
PUBLIC HEALTH

Sent Free to any Citizen of the State

Entered as second class matter at Boston Postoffice.

M. LUISE DIEZ, M.D., DIRECTOR OF DIVISION OF CHILD HYGIENE, EDITOR.
1 Beacon Street, Boston, Mass.

CONTENTS

	PAGE
Foreword	4
Report of Field Director of Study:	
Introduction	6
General Statement	7
Outline of Program and of Report	8

Section:
I. Epidemiological 10
    Respiratory Disease Deaths 10
    Pneumonia in Hospitals 13
    Reporting Current Cases and Deaths . . 15
    Cases, Contacts, and Carriers . . . 16
    Newer Types of Pneumococci . . . 19
    Home-Treated Cases 22

II. Educational 25
    Graduate Courses 26
    Pneumonia Meetings in Areas Chosen for Intensive
      Work 27
    District Medical Society Meetings . . 28
    Addresses Before State Medical Society . 28
    Addresses Before National Medical Societies . 29
    Other Meetings 29
    Printed Matter 30

III. Clinical—Pneumonia Areas Organized . . 31
    Organization of Collaborator Areas . . 31
    Collaborator Areas 32
      Population Served 32
    Organization of New Type Areas . . . 33
    Training Technicians 34
    Comparison of Typing Methods . . . 36
    Increase in Pneumococcus Typing . . 38

IV. Results Obtained in Serum-Treated Cases	39
Total Cases	39
Type I Cases	40
Type II Cases	44
Lives Saved	47
Type III Cases	47
Group IV Cases	47
Miscellaneous Cases	48
Pneumococcus Meningitis	48
Serum Reactions	48
V. Result of Plan for Decentralizing Service	50
VI. Budget and Personnel	53
VII. Summary	53
Conclusions	57
VIII. Recommendations	57
Report of Director, Antitoxin and Vaccine Laboratory:	
IX. Work Carried on at Antitoxin and Vaccine Laboratory	62
Production of Therapeutic Serums	62
Production of Diagnostic Serums	63
Investigation and Improvement of Methods for Producing Therapeutic Serums	63
Investigation of Other Problems	66
Skin Tests in Horses and Rabbits	67
Pneumococcus Bibliography and Monograph	67
Plans for Continuation of Study	67
Bibliography of Articles Emanating from Study	68
Appendix:	
Pneumonia Collaborators	69
Laboratories for Typing and Serum Distribution	71
Report of Division of Food and Drugs, October, November, December, 1936	73

FOREWORD

HENRY D. CHADWICK, M.D.

Commissioner of Public Health
Massachusetts Department of Public Health

The Massachusetts pneumonia study had two objectives, the evaluation of pneumonia serum under the conditions of the general practice of medicine, and the development of plans for the distribution of this serum for the treatment of those patients who might reasonably be expected to benefit from its use. It thus embraced problems of scientific research as well as of administrative procedure. That the study could be carried through to a successful conclusion with so few departures from the original plans was a real tribute to the foresight and vision of those who developed it, the late Dr. George H. Bigelow, then Commissioner of Public Health and Dr. Benjamin White, then Director of the Antitoxin and Vaccine Laboratory.

The development of such a program looking forward to the eventual statewide distribution of pneumonia serum was recognition of the fact that even though a health department may be unable to prevent the spread of certain infections, it can nevertheless do much to reduce the resultant loss of life. Long before it was possible to control diphtheria through immunizing procedures, health departments distributed antitoxin and thereby achieved a decrease in the deaths even if not in the cases of diphtheria. If the concentrated pneumonia serum as developed by Felton was capable of reducing the fatality rate for certain types of lobar pneumonia, why should not the State, through its official health agency, make the same services available for this disease which claims almost two thousand victims each year as had so long prevailed for diphtheria which had formerly numbered its victims in the hundreds. Such was the basic guiding thought behind the Massachusetts pneumonia study.

Before any plans for general serum distribution might be considered it was necessary to show that the serum could be used effectively in home practice and in the small hospitals. This was essentially a problem of field research. These early findings showed that, with proper instructions, the general practitioner could use serum as effectively as could the large metropolitan hospital centers. Such a conclusion was important inasmuch as the number of pneumonia patients who reached these large hospitals early enough to benefit much from serum was but a small fraction of the total number of cases in Massachusetts.

The coincidental development of the Neufeld method of sputum typing provided rapid and simple laboratory procedures which were within the reach of any laboratory employing adequately trained personnel. Equally important was the elimination of the long delays that formerly attended most type determinations. The introduction of the Neufeld method furnished the key to the problem of controlled serum distribution in that it made it possible to limit the serum to those who might reasonably be expected to profit from its use. Such a limitation was essential if so expensive a serum was to be distributed at public expense. That the plan so evolved was administratively sound has been well shown by over two years' experience.

Improvements in the methods of serum production were equally essential to the success of the Massachusetts program. These improvements were realized both as a part of and independently of the study, so that the serum as distributed today is a more refined and more effective product than was the serum generally available in 1931.

The study would have been but a partial success had it merely demonstrated certain administrative principles or elicited certain scientific truths. Its true success must be measured by the extent to which its findings could be applied in practice. It is, therefore, significant to note that with the completion of the five years of formal study, financed by the Commonwealth Fund, the Department of Public Health was able to take over as an essential part of its program these services which had been found to be essential for the continued manufacture and use of pneumonia serum. Thus the distribution of this serum has become as integral a part of the public health program of the State as is the distribution of other sera or the supervision of the milk or water supplies. The serum is now readily available in all parts of the Commonwealth. The study has thus accomplished the ends for which it was designed.

Whatever success may have attended this study was due in large measure to the wise counsel of the Advisory Committee and to the hearty cooperation of the collaborating clinicians. In even larger measure was its success due to the skill and ability of Dr. Roderick Heffron, who served as field director throughout the five years of the study.

In presenting at this time the complete report of the Massachusetts pneumonia study, the Department of Public Health hopes that through this record others may profit from what the Department has learned. It is the Department's hope that through this study some small contribution may have been made to the serious problem of reducing the present high death rate from lobar pneumonia. If through this study human lives may be saved and the principles developed may be applied to similar problems in other states, the results will have well rewarded the labor attendant upon the study.

FINAL REPORT OF MASSACHUSETTS PNEUMONIA STUDY AND SERVICE

Introduction

In 1930, lobar pneumonia had for ten years been seventh, eighth, or ninth among the commonest causes of death in Massachusetts. Each year approximately 4,000 cases and nearly 2,000 deaths due to this disease were reported. There was reason to believe that only about one-half of the cases that occurred were reported. Little was known of the manner in which the disease was spread, and no satisfactory method was available for its prevention or control. Hundreds of young adults of the greatest economic value to the community died from the disease each year. A great multiplicity of methods was in use for the treatment of cases, and each had its advocates. The efficacy of most of these methods rested on unsupported claims. One method, however, had adherents who pointed to an impressive experimental, clinical, and statistical proof of its value. This was the treatment of patients with type-specific antipneumococcic serum, which resulted, for the first time in history, in a regular and definitely measurable saving of lives.

Antipneumococcic serum, in both its unconcentrated and concentrated forms, had been used over a period of years for the treatment of many hundred cases of Type I and Type II pneumococcus lobar pneumonia. These cases, and more especially those treated early in their illness, showed a marked lowering of their expected fatality rates. Such cases, however, had nearly all been treated under fairly optimal conditions in a few large medical centers and hospitals.

After years of controversy the fact emerged that the Type I and Type II immune serum available was type-specific in action and produced the desired response only when used in cases having pneumococcus Type I or II infections. It was known that, in general, about one-half of all cases of lobar pneumonia were due to infection with either of these two types. To be certain of the identity of the organism causing the pneumonia, however, it was necessary to obtain sputum or other material from each patient for laboratory examination and bacteriologic diagnosis. Thus it was only by the application of suitable laboratory procedures that the proper cases could be selected for treatment. Facilities for carrying out such laboratory procedures were not generally available in Massachusetts in 1930. Further, the great expense of the therapeutic serum militated against its being generally used.

Thus there was known a method of treatment which, when instituted early in the proper cases, would save scores of lives yearly. But, due to the technical difficulties of obtaining an early bacteriologic diagnosis, the expense of the therapeutic serum, and the lack of precise information concerning its administration, it was not generally used. In addition, whether this somewhat complex method of treatment could be carried out with success in the numerous smaller hospitals and in patients' homes over an area as large as this State was not known.

This, then, was the problem that presented itself in Massachusetts at the end of 1930. Its challenge to ingenuity was accepted, and, after careful consideration, a plan for attacking it was devised by Doctor

George H. Bigelow, then Commissioner of the Department of Public Health, and Doctor Benjamin White, then Director of the Antitoxin and Vaccine Laboratory of this Department. The purposes of this plan, conceived in. genius and dedicated to humanity, were (quoting from the original):

"1. To study the epidemiology of lobar pneumonia in the State.
2. To promote more prompt diagnosis of the disease.
3. To encourage and facilitate earlier and more general serum treatment.
4. To study and improve methods for serum production.
5. To correlate the studies on serum production with the results following its clinical use.
6. To devise procedures for the future prevention, serum treatment, and control of the disease."

The procedures to be followed in carrying out this work were laid down in detail in the original plan dated January 6, 1931. It was apparent that the successful conclusion of such a program might bring to light information of great value, not only to this State but to other communities as well. In consequence, and due to the extent of the proposed program, it appeared advisable to request aid from some large foundation whose funds were frequently devoted to investigations of a similar nature. This was done, and financial assistance was obtained from the Commonwealth Fund of New York.

General Statement

The Pneumonia Study and Service in Massachusetts was begun in 1931. Purchases of animals and necessary additional supplies were started in January. By early March the Field Director and his secretary were at work and detailed plans of organization were being prepared. The Commonwealth Fund promised its support for three years and agreed to continue such aid for two additional years if reasonable accomplishments were being made. The work of the Study was continued for five years, during which time it became apparent that the original plan of procedure was clearly and ably prepared, for it has not been necessary to deviate from it in any important part, and even the provisions for continuing future work are being put into effect as proposed over six years ago. In considerable measure the success attending the progress of this Study resulted from the care with which the original plan was prepared.

The activities of the Pneumonia Program were developed and prosecuted under the guidance of a Pneumonia Advisory Committee. This was composed of representatives of Boston University, Harvard, and Tufts medical schools, the profession at large, and interested public health workers. In 1931 the general personnel of this committee was as follows:

1. Dr. E. S. Calderwood, Professor of Medicine, Boston University Medical School
2. Dr. Arthur A. Cushing, Brookline, general practitioner
3. Dr. Roger I. Lee, member of Public Health Council, State Department of Public Health

4. Dr. Edwin A. Locke, Professor of Medicine, Harvard University Medical School
5. Dr. Frederick T. Lord, Professor of Medicine, Harvard University Medical School
6. Dr. Robert N. Nye, Department of Bacteriology, Harvard University Medical School
7. Dr. A. E. Parkhurst, Beverly, general practitioner
8. Dr. Joseph Pratt, Professor of Medicine, Tufts College Medical School
9. Dr. Milton J. Rosenau, Professor of Preventive Medicine and Hygiene, Harvard University Medical School
10. Dr. Wilson G. Smillie, Professor of Public Health Administration, Harvard University School of Public Health.

One change in the personnel of this committee was made in 1934 when Doctor Cushing resigned and Doctor Channing Frothingham, formerly Assistant Professor of Medicine, Harvard University Medical School, and now associated with the Faulkner Hospital, Boston, was appointed in his place.

Other members of the committee were the Commissioner and Deputy Commissioner of the State Department of Public Health and the Director of the Antitoxin and Vaccine Laboratory. In addition, as guests of the Committee, the Assistant Director and Dr. L. A. Barnes of the Antitoxin and Vaccine Laboratory, Professor E. B. Wilson (Professor of Vital Statistics, Harvard University School of Public Health), Doctors L. D. Felton, W. D. Sutliff, M. Finland, and occasionally other interested physicians were invited to meet with this group. Meetings of the Committee were held once and sometimes twice yearly. At such gatherings the Field Director of the Study and the Director of the Antitoxin and Vaccine Laboratory reviewed the progress of the Study up to that point. Discussion was open, and decisions were made at the meetings which had an important bearing on the further progress of the work.

The Advisory Committee was extremely cooperative and rendered assistance of great value to the conduct of the Study. The last meeting of this group was held the latter part of December 1935, following which the Committee was dissolved.

General Outline of Pneumonia Study and of Present Report

In general, matters of interest concerning the Pneumonia Study and Service may be considered under the following nine sections:

I. Epidemiologic studies were made. Normal persons and patients with pneumonia and their contacts were investigated bacteriologically. A study was made of the prevalence of lobar pneumonia and of cases and deaths resulting from it. Information was gathered on the occurrence of the various types of pneumococci in respiratory diseases, and their frequency and distribution over the State was noted. These investigations have added importantly to our knowledge of the epidemiology of pneumonia.

II. Activities of an educational nature were confined almost exclusively to the medical profession. For this purpose meetings were held, articles published, and charts, slides, and exhibits shown at various medical meetings. The literature on pneumonia was extensively reviewed and a handbook on serum treatment published (15). Two large monographs, one dealing with Pneumonia in its various phases and the other with the Pneumococcus, are in preparation.

III. Work of a clinical nature was slowly and carefully expanded. During the first three years selected areas were organized, and in them facilities made available for rapid and accurate pneumococcus typing in centrally located laboratories. Concentrated Type I and Type II antipneumococcic serum was made available for the treatment of cases. Certain physicians were appointed as consultants (later referred to as collaborators) to assist in confirming the clinical diagnosis and initiating the serum treatment of patients with lobar pneumonia. Late in 1933 a review of the several hundred cases thus treated showed that physicians in general practice could use serum as satisfactorily as those in the large metropolitan hospitals or in medical centers. Further, typing methods were investigated and a new method introduced which greatly shortened the time formerly required for bacteriologic diagnosis. In consequence by December 1933 the next step was taken. This was to begin, in the areas previously organized, an alteration of the plan in use in order to do away with the consultant system. By this variation and the inclusion of new districts, it was hoped to make serum equally available, with certain restrictions, to all physicians. This was successful, and by the end of 1935 serum was available to all physicians in the State for use only in their patients with Type I or II infections who had not been ill longer than four days. Thus the problem was solved for restricting the distribution of this serum and yet having it generally available for cases of the proper type at the time they are most likely to benefit from its administration.

IV. By the end of 1935 data were obtained on the fatality rates of over 1,600 typed cases of pneumococcus lobar pneumonia. Nearly 1,000 of these received varying amounts of antiserum (*). Records of serum-treated cases were analyzed, and the results obtained were correlated with the dose of serum administered both in cubic centimeters and in units.

V. The effectiveness of the plan for decentralizing the control of serum treatment has been reviewed.

VI. The budget has been tabulated by years, listing the amounts granted for this work and the amounts actually expended, and the personnel engaged in the Study has been noted.

VII. The conclusions and general findings of the Study have been summarized.

VIII. A set of general recommendations, including plans for the future and the continuation of certain activities, has been prepared.

IX. The Antitoxin and Vaccine Laboratory has produced both typing and therapeutic antipneumococcic serum in increasing amounts since the Study began in 1931. Research on problems relating to this work has been instituted. In many instances such work has been carried through to conclusion, and in certain others additional work is being continued. Studies have been made of some aspects of immunity to the

---

(*) This figure is now over 1,000. See Results of Serum Treatment, page 39.

pneumococcus and of the most satisfactory schedule for immunizing animals for the production of diagnostic and therapeutic serum. Methods of concentration have been investigated and improved, and procedures for testing the potency of serum studied. A test for the identification of lots of serum likely to give rise to chill reactions in humans has been devised.

The above is a brief review of the undertakings of this Pneumonia Study. A somewhat detailed discussion of these and of the findings of the Study follows. In conclusion, a bibliography is presented of articles dealing with this Study and its results.

I — EPIDEMIOLOGICAL

Data of epidemiologic significance have been accumulated from several sources.

(1) Respiratory Disease Deaths

During the summer of 1931, two and sometimes three workers were occupied in transferring information found on original death certificates to Pneumonia Mortality Code Sheets. Over 60,000 sheets were filled out for all patients dying of any form of respiratory infection, whether primary or secondary, during the eight years 1892, 1902, 1912, 1921, 1922, 1928, 1929, and 1930, representing over 60,000 deaths. The information contained on these sheets was transferred to punch cards. One worker spent nearly full time and four others spent some two months at this task. The cards were sorted and a statistical analysis was made by Doctor Herbert L. Lombard, Director, Division of Adult Hygiene. The findings obtained from the analysis of this large group of deaths are presented below. With one or two exceptions most of the findings were regarded as of relatively little significance.

Probably the most important finding was that the rate per 100,000 population for all respiratory disease deaths exhibited a downward trend for the years studied. It was impossible to prepare rates for lobar and bronchopneumonia separately over long periods of time as changes in the classification of these diseases made conclusions concerning them inaccurate. In consequence, all deaths from pneumonia, bronchitis, and influenza were considered in a single group for the study of the trend of rates over a long period.

The finding of the downward trend of the rate for all respiratory diseases coincides with the observations made by Doering and Lombard in their study of "Influenza in Massachusetts" (Boston M. & S. J., 195:405, August 26, 1926). They determined the rates for influenza, pneumonia, and bronchitis by months from 1843 to 1925. This finding is also in accord with the results of a study completed in September 1935 by Miss Angeline D. Hamblen, Principal Statistical Clerk of this Department, of the trend of death rates per 100,000 population for pneumonia of all forms in the ten original registration states since 1900 and in Massachusetts since 1900. In both instances the rates show a slight but significant downward trend throughout the period in question; the trend from 1900 through 1932 for the ten original registration states being

-2.39 ± 0.7 units yearly, while in Massachusetts from 1900 through 1934 the trend was -2.88 ± 0.7 units yearly. (Figures for 1918 are included in both groups.)

The other general findings resulting from the study of data obtained from the death certificates of patients dying of respiratory diseases are shown below. In occasional instances figures relating to the rates for recent years are included.

1. An analysis was made of the respiratory disease deaths by age and place of death. This revealed that the largest proportion of the deaths that occurred in hospitals and institutions was in the age group 20 to 40 years (58 to 59 per cent in 1930).

2. From the high hospitalization rates in the young adult groups a gradual decline appeared in both directions, and the lowest rates were in the under 1 and over 80-year-old groups. (The proportions in the latter groups were 38 and 24 per cent respectively in 1930.)

3. Deaths from respiratory disease in hospitals greatly increased between 1892 and 1930. In the former year 11.2 per cent of the deaths from respiratory disease occurred in hospitals, while in 1930 the figure was 43.1 per cent. Throughout the period covered the proportion of such deaths in hospitals was higher in males than in females (48.1 per cent for males and 37.6 per cent for females in 1930).

4. Hospitalization for respiratory diseases in Massachusetts apparently varied in the different nativity groups, and in the earlier years individuals born in the United States had smaller percentages of deaths in hospitals from the respiratory diseases than did those from most foreign countries. In later years the percentage of such deaths in individuals born in the United States increased until in 1930 there was practically no difference between the rates for the various nativity groups, with the exception of individuals born in Russia-Poland. In most of the years studied the Russia-Poland group had a higher percentage of respiratory disease deaths in hospitals than any of the six other nativity groups investigated. The hospitalization rate, by sex, for the nativity groups showed that males had higher rates than females for all nativity groups. (The nativity groups studied were: United States, England, Ireland, Russia-Poland, Italy, Canada, and All Others.)

5. The hospitalization of respiratory diseases occurred to a greater extent among individuals living in the larger cities. It was also greater in those living near the ocean (probably due to Metropolitan Boston and nearness to a medical center).

6. The age distribution of respiratory disease death rates per 100,000 population showed the highest rate in the over 80-year-old group (rate 2895 in 1930) with the under-1-year-old group second (rate 1702 in 1930), and the lowest rate in the 10-19-year-old group (rate 21 in 1930). From the latter age group the rates increased in both directions. Males had significantly higher rates than females in the

under-1 group (rates 1778 versus 1624 in 1930) and between 30 and 60 years of age (rates 82 to 291 versus 50 to 181 in 1930). In all other age groups the rates were similar for the two sexes.

7. The colored had considerably higher death rates per 100,000 population for respiratory diseases than the white (rates 307 versus 190 in 1930). This was true for both sexes.

8. Complications of respiratory disease, such as empyema, pericarditis, meningitis, lung abscess, and peritonitis, were studied by months. The percentage of individuals dying of respiratory diseases with a complication did not vary appreciably in the respective months.

9. Respiratory disease death rates per 100,000 population were determined by conjugal state for all individuals over the age of fifteen. Single individuals (rate 110 in 1930) had lower rates than the married (rate 166 in 1930); the married had lower rates than the divorced (rate 285 in 1930); and the widowed had the highest rates (rate 810 in 1930). Probably the age distribution would account for a large part but possibly not all of these differences. In the married, divorced, and widowed, the males had higher rates than the females.

10. A comparison of the hospitalization rates for deaths from lobar pneumonia and from bronchopneumonia in recent years showed higher rates for lobar pneumonia in 1921 and 1922 and no difference in the rates in 1929 and 1930.

    Subdivided by nativity in 1921 and 1922, the rates per 100 deaths were greater for the hospitalization of lobar pneumonia among individuals born in the United States than elsewhere and were higher for bronchopneumonia among males born in Canada. In 1929 and 1930 there were no differences in the rates with the exception that they were higher in Irish females with bronchopneumonia than with lobar pneumonia.

11. Subdividing the deaths from pneumonia in hospitals and institutions by age, the proportion of deaths attributed to lobar pneumonia or to bronchopneumonia was the same in the younger age groups, while in the older age groups the proportion was higher for bronchopneumonia.

    In 1921 and 1922 a slightly larger proportion of the deaths in both sexes in hospitals occurred from lobar pneumonia than from bronchopneumonia, while in 1929 and 1930 the proportion (46 and 47 per cent) was the same.

12. Conjugal state—rates for 1929 and 1930: The death rates per 100,000 population for both lobar pneumonia and bronchopneumonia in persons over fifteen years of age were lowest among single individuals (rates 38 and 57 respectively), were higher among the married (rates 59 and 79), and highest among the divorced (rates 99 and 167) and the widowed (rates 177 and 484). Single females had higher rates for bronchopneumonia (rate 63) than single males (rate 52). The married (rate 95), divorced (rate 260), and widowed (rate 594) males had higher rates for bronchopneumonia than the females (rates 63, 102, and 440 respectively). The male

rates for lobar pneumonia (rates 46, 75, 135, and 230) were higher than rates for the females in all four groups (rates 29, 43, 75, 155).

The colored had higher rates than the whites for both bronchopneumonia (rates 204 versus 110) and lobar pneumonia (rates 90 versus 52). The rates for bronchopneumonia were higher than for lobar pneumonia in both sexes and in both colors.

13. Average of lobar pneumonia and bronchopneumonia death rates per 100,000 population for 1921 and 1922 compared with average for 1928, 1929, and 1930 by age and sex: The rates for lobar pneumonia did not differ between 1921 and 1930, while in bronchopneumonia the age group 1-4 years had a higher rate in 1921 and 1922 and the age groups over 60 years had higher rates in 1930. In the younger age groups and in the old age groups the rates were higher for bronchopneumonia than for lobar pneumonia in both sexes. In middle life lobar pneumonia exceeded bronchopneumonia in 1921 and 1922, but the rates were similar in 1929 and 1930. Males had higher rates for bronchopneumonia than females under the age of 1 year (average rate in 1928-30, 1495 versus 1239) and higher rates for lobar pneumonia than females between the ages of 40 to 60 years. (Average rates for 1928-30 were 73 for males and 40 for females 40-49 years of age and 114 for males and 63 for females 50-59 years of age.)

(2) Pneumonia in Hospitals

During the summer of 1931, a second group of nine workers was occupied in going to fifty-seven hospitals in this State to review the case record of every patient who had pneumonia of any form in those institutions during the years 1928, 1929, and 1930. Eighteen of the hospitals were of over 150-bed capacity, twenty-three had between 75 and 150 beds, and sixteen had 75 or less beds.

The data obtained were transferred to epidemiologic sheets and during the spring of 1932 to punch cards, which were made available for sorting purposes. Records of approximately 8,850 cases of pneumonia were represented by this group. These data were also analyzed statistically by Doctor H. L. Lombard. Due to the limited extent to which bacteriologic diagnosis and pneumococcus typing had been used throughout the State, the marked differences in the completeness of the records in various hospitals, and numerous other contributing factors, the information obtained from the hospital records of patients with pneumonia proved of limited value.

The findings of this investigation are summarized below:

1. The case fatality rate varied from 12 per cent to 55 per cent with an average of 38 per cent. In the larger hospitals the average rate was 44 per cent, in the medium-sized hospitals 38 per cent, and in the smaller hospitals 32 per cent. The differences appeared significant in indicating higher fatality rates in the larger institutions. Complications were also recorded more frequently in the larger hospitals, the figures being 6.3 per cent in the large hospitals, 5.0 per cent in the medium-sized, and 5.2 per cent in the small hospitals.

2. A study of the recorded incidence of 32 various causes which were associated with or might possibly have contributed to the occurrence of pneumonia revealed that cases in large hospitals had more contributory causes than those in the medium-sized and small hospitals, the figures being 50.3 per cent, 33.6 per cent, and 28.2 per cent respectively. The more adequate records kept by large hospitals might account for part of this difference, but inasmuch as pregnancy, fractures, and "other traumas" showed no difference in incidence in the various groups, it is possible that individuals with certain types of disease are apt to choose the larger hospitals or, conversely, that individuals residing in the region of the larger hospitals are, in some instances, subject to more unfavorable conditions.

3. A study of the duration of illness in cases diagnosed as lobar pneumonia or bronchopneumonia or simply as "pneumonia", and all other pneumonias by day of admission to the hospital showed that the fatality rate was about the same for each variety of pneumonia irrespective of the duration of the disease when the patient entered the hospital. No evidence was obtained that early hospitalization favorably affected the outcome.

4. While the fatality rates of all cases considered as a single group were greater in the large hospitals, when cases were subdivided into varieties of pneumonia the situation was different. The fatality rates for lobar pneumonia were the same in small, medium, and large hospitals. However, the rates for bronchopneumonia and "pneumonia" increased with the size of the hospital, the rates in small, medium, and large-sized hospitals being 33.3 per cent, 39.6 per cent, and 56.7 per cent respectively for the former and 32.6 per cent, 34.5 per cent, and 42.7 per cent for the latter; the rates for all other pneumonias being 37.1 per cent, 65.2 per cent, and 53.9 per cent respectively.

5. Cases of post-operative pneumonia were recorded more frequently in the larger-sized hospitals and were found nearly three times (14.1 per cent) as often in such institutions as in small hospitals (5.6 per cent). These figures were doubtless influenced by the more adequate records in the larger institutions. Sixteen per cent of the bronchopneumonias and 5.7 per cent of the lobar pneumonias were post-operative, as was 20.7 per cent of pneumonia, variety undefined. The average case occurred four days after operation.

6. Necropsy was done on 25.2 per cent of the patients dying of pneumonia in large hospitals, on 10.7 per cent of those in medium-sized hospitals, and on 1.6 per cent of those in small hospitals.

7. The incidence of empyema and meningitis as complications of pneumonia was determined. Empyema was more commonly encountered in lobar (6.2 per cent) than in bronchopneumonia (2.6 per cent), while meningitis was more frequent in pneumonia of the latter variety (1.4 per cent) than in that of the former (0.6 per cent). Both empyema (11.8 per cent) and meningitis (1.8 per cent) were most frequent in pneumonia, variety undefined.

8. A study of the recorded incidence of 32 various causes which were associated with or might have contributed to the occurrence of pneumonia was made by the variety of pneumonia encountered. Heart disease was reported as the largest single contributory factor and had a rate per 100 cases of 5.3 in lobar pneumonia and 14.2 in bronchopneumonia as well as 6.5 in pneumonia undefined and 18.1 in all other pneumonias. About one-quarter of the cases of lobar pneumonia and over one-half of all the pneumonias of other varieties had contributory causes.

In post-operative pneumonia appendicitis was given as the most frequent contributory cause with diseases of the gall bladder second. The figures were doubtless influenced by the relative frequency of operations for these two conditions.

9. Studies on recurrences of pneumonia in the same patient suggested that pneumonia is more liable to occur in individuals who have once had pneumonia than it is in others lacking this experience.

(3) Reporting Current Cases and Deaths

As in a few other states in this country, lobar pneumonia in Massachusetts is a reportable disease. The available facts suggest, however, that only about one-half of the cases which occur each year are reported. The attention of physicians in nearly every part of the State has been called to this matter and there has perhaps been some improvement in the number of cases reported. Nevertheless, it seems unlikely that all cases will ever be reported unless something specific in the way of a reward, such as information, serum, and so forth, is offered physicians in return for their reporting cases. At present this hardly seems advisable or necessary.

The record for lobar pneumonia in Massachusetts during the past seventeen years is as follows:

LOBAR PNEUMONIA ONLY

Year	Number of cases	Case rate**	Number of deaths	Death rate**	Fatality rate
1920	5,558	143.2	2,750	70.7	49.5
1921	4,080	103.7	1,749	44.4	42.9
1922	5,194	130.1	2,238	56.1	43.1
1923	4,759	117.6	2,166	53.5	45.5
1924	4,552	111.0	1,817	44.3	39.9
1925	5,544	133.3	2,274	54.7	41.0
1926	5,134	123.1	2,315	55.5	45.1
1927	4,279	102.1	1,909	45.5	44.6
1928	4,785	113.6	2,106	50.0	44.0
1929	5,287	124.9	2,154	50.9	40.7
1930	4,333	101.8	1,816	42.7	41.9
1931*	3,873	90.6	1,717	40.2	44.3
1932*	4,028	93.7	1,688	39.3	41.9
1933*	4,277	99.0	1,825	42.3	42.7
1934*	3,976	91.6	1,601	36.9	40.3
1935*	4,369	100.2	1,731	39.7	39.6
1936	5,459	124.6	1,944	44.4	35.6

* Years during which the Pneumonia Study was in progress.
** Rates per 100,000 population.

(4) Cases, Contacts, and Carriers

During the winters of 1931-32 and 1932-33, Doctor Wilson G. Smillie carried out certain epidemiologic studies with the financial assistance of the Massachusetts Pneumonia Study. The first of these studies, made during 1931-32, was carried through the summer, fall, winter, and spring seasons to determine the incidence of various types of pneumococci in the nasopharynx of normal people and to compare these findings with the incidence of such types occurring in patients ill with lobar pneumonia and in the nasopharynx of persons in contact with these cases. Pneumococci obtained from sputum and cultures from such individuals were typed out through Type XIX. A laboratory technician and a field worker were employed to assist in this study. A complete report of this study was given by Doctor Smillie before the annual meeting of the American Medical Association in June 1933 and was published in the journal of that society (7). The important conclusions of this work were:

1. In answer to the question of whether any one specific type of the more than twenty types of pneumococci was more prevalent in the immediate family contacts of a case of lobar pneumonia due to that particular type than in the population at large, it was found that Types I and II occurred more frequently in contacts of cases due to these two types than in the population at large.

2. A difference in the epidemiologic behavior of the different types of pneumococci was found.

3. Except for Types I and II, certain specific types of pneumococci which are more or less prevalent in the normal population do not pass more readily from the sick to the well than from normal person to normal person.

4. Efforts were made to determine whether there were any measurable environmental factors, such as economic or social status, seasonal variations, and so forth, which might influence the ready transfer of specific pneumococci from the patient to his immediate contacts. The carrier rate of pneumococci was found to be definitely influenced by seasonal variations, being lowest in summer and highest in winter and early spring, but was not observably altered by poor economic conditions with resultant overcrowding except possibly in the case of Types III and V.

5. No evidence was found that contacts having a common cold at the time of contact with a case of pneumococcus lobar pneumonia harbored pneumococci in general more frequently than other contacts not having colds. Nevertheless, in some instances epidemics of acute colds in a family appeared to be a factor in the finding of a high prevalence of Types I and II in contacts.

General discussion: Typing was carried out on all the pneumococci obtained from the examination of 173 patients with pneumococcus lobar pneumonia and from 493 controls and 582 contacts of the cases which were examined. In the latter two groups pneumococci were found in 43 per cent and 59.6 per cent respectively. A very general distribution of pneumococci was found in both the control and contact groups. Excluding Types I and II, all types from III to XIX inclusive showed an almost equal prevalence of each type in the controls and contacts. Excluding Types I and II, the remainder of the data represented, therefore, the normal distribution of pneumococci in the community during the year.

The finding of pneumococci of Types III to XIX inclusive about as frequently in contacts as in controls indicated that such organisms had little tendency to be passed from the sick to the well. The findings in regard to the occurrence of Type I and Type II carriers were in great contrast to this, for Type I was *twenty times* more prevalent in the immediate family contacts of patients with Type I lobar pneumonia than in the population at large, and Type II was *ten times* more prevalent in its contacts. The only pneumococci which appeared to have a very definite epidemiologic significance were those of Types I and II.

From the evidence accumulated in this study it seemed probable that pneumococci of the higher types, which are responsible for about one-third of the cases of lobar pneumonia, have no epidemiologic significance. There were exceptions to this generalization, of course, possibly related to poor economic conditions and overcrowding or to other factors. As most of the deaths from lobar pneumonia are caused by virulent pneumococci of Types I or II, their presence was of definite epidemiologic significance. The findings indicated the advisability of conducting a more detailed study of the immediate family contacts of Type I and Type II cases as well as of the production of carriers of these types and, if possible, of small epidemics of pneumonia in addition.

The true significance of the above study is not apparent on the surface. It lies primarily in the fact that many years ago epidemiologic studies made by Dochez and Avery and by Stillman clearly showed that Type I and Type II carriers might represent an important means of spreading infection with these organisms; but, inasmuch as types of pneumococci above III could not be individually identified during the period when their work was done, it was not possible for these early investigators to ascertain the relative importance of Type I and Type II as compared with the importance of some of the higher types. This Doctor Smillie has done and, for the first time, has clearly shown that, of all types, Types I and II are the ones of the greatest epidemiologic significance. This particular study fills a gap in our knowledge which has existed for over fifteen years and is of fundamental importance.

During the winter of 1932-33, Doctor Smillie's second study was carried out, and a detailed survey was made of the carriers produced by contact with cases of lobar pneumonia due to Types I and II and some other types of pneumococci. In addition, he was fortunate enough to secure valuable data from a small epidemic of pneumonia occurring in an institution for feeble-minded children. Doctor Leeder assisted in this work, and the intensive study was extended into the summer of 1933. A preliminary report of this work was given by Doctors Smillie and Leeder before the American Epidemiological Society in Washington, D. C., in May 1933. The final report was published later (8).

In this study, typing was carried out through the full thirty-two known types. Whenever a Type I or II case was reported in Boston, efforts were made to obtain nasopharyngeal cultures from all the individuals in the families of such patients. Also, when Type I or II cases were to be hospitalized, cultures were first taken from patients in the ward into which the pneumonia patient was to be placed and from the doctors, nurses, and orderliés in attendance. This culturing was repeated at intervals after the patient was introduced into this new environment. Investigation revealed two things of importance: the first was that, whereas about 20 per cet of the *family contacts* with Type I or II cases were carriers of pneumococci of these types, only about 2 per cent of *hospital contacts* (either patients or professional attendants) became carriers of these types. This suggested that if the ordinary infectious precautions used in caring for pneumonia cases in hospitals were carried out, there might be no especial danger in keeping pneumonia patients on the open wards in a general hospital. (This finding is at variance with that of Cruickshank, Milroy Lectures, Lancet, 1:563, 621, 680, March and April 1933, who found that the incidence of such types may rise as high in patients and nurses in contact with Type I and Type II cases as 16 per cent and 18 per cent respectively. The reasons for the differences between the findings in Smillie's and Cruickshank's investigations are as yet unknown.)

The finding of the high incidence of carriers of Type I and Type II pneumococci in family contacts was of importance and was further studied. This led to the second important finding by Doctors Smillie and Leeder that some *additional* factor other than simple contact determined the transfer of Type I and Type II pneumococci from patients with lobar pneumonia to healthy contacts, and this additional factor appeared to be the presence in the contact of a mild upper respiratory infection such as the common cold. Persons with colds who were in contact with Type I or II cases were very likely to become carriers of those organisms. Once acquired, the carrier condition might persist for many weeks or months. It was quite possible that such carriers might, under adverse conditions, come down with pneumonia due to either of these types. In any event, this work further served to focus attention on the importance of upper respiratory infections to the pneumonia problem.

About the time this study was finished, Dochez and his collaborators in New York published a report of a study carried out by them which attacked the problem in a different way but which tended to confirm Doctors Smillie and Leeder's finding that upper respiratory infections may play a role of prime importance in the spread of pneumonia (J.A.M.A. 101:1441, November 4, 1933).

Additional work is needed along these lines, but it may be said that notable progress toward the solution of this most complex epidemiologic problem has been made.

Before the final answer becomes apparent, it would seem necessary to determine whether or not pneumococci may change type under natural conditions. It has been suggested that "rough" pneumococci, or pneumococci of some type with little invasive power, which may be resident in the nasopharynx of an individual, might under adverse environmental conditions become changed into virulent pneumococci of a different type and under the proper circumstances give rise to pulmonary infection. If this occurred, the isolation of cases or contacts could do little to reduce the spread of pneumonia. While it is possible experimentally to change a pneumococcus of one type into that of another, proof is still lacking that a similar change may occur spontaneously in nature (see also page 66.)

There is another problem relating to epidemiology which is of great importance from the public health aspect. This is to establish whether a given type of pneumococcus, such as Type I for instance, may get into a family and be spread to various members of it, thus producing carriers, before one peculiarly susceptible individual happens to come down with pneumonia due to that type; or whether one person in a family may acquire a Type I infection and pneumonia, subsequently spread pneumococcus Type I to other members of the family, and produce Type I carriers in that fashion. It is obvious from the standpoint of pneumonia control that this problem must be solved, for if the members of a family are all carriers before one individual becomes ill with pneumonia, it would do but little good to isolate the patient after he becomes ill.

(5) The Newer Types of Pneumococci

In order that accurate information as to the geographical and numerical occurrence of the various newer types of pneumococci (Types IV through XXXII) as a cause of pneumonia might be obtained, it was advised during the first three years of the Study that cultures of all Group IV pneumococci obtained from sputums received by the various outlying hospital laboratories over the State who were cooperating in this Study be sent to the State Bacteriologic Laboratory in Boston. There such cultures could be typed out to the full thirty-two known types. The sending in of Group IV cultures was carried out fairly regularly during the first three years, but during the last two years of the Study the number of such cultures received rapidly decreased inasmuch as the methods of typing in use in the outlying laboratories had changed and, as mice were seldom being employed, it was no longer possible to get these organisms in relatively pure culture. In all, 803 cultures of this nature were received and examined. The distribution of such specimens by type was as shown in Table 1.

TABLE 1 — DISTRIBUTION OF TYPES AMONG 803 CULTURES RECEIVED FROM OUTLYING LABORATORIES

Type	Number of Cases	Type	Number of Cases
I	34*	XVIII	24
II	14*	XIX	31
III	34*	XX	14
IV	23	XXI	17
V	38	XXII	6
VI	16	XXIII	7
VII	44	XXIV	3
VIII	65	XXV	1
IX	17	XXVI	3
X	18	XXVII	3
XI	6	XXVIII	5
XII	6	XXIX	10
XIII	12	XXX	8
XIV	14	XXXI	7
XV	—	XXXII	—
XVI	4	Group IV and no pneu-	
XVII	7	mococci	312
		Total	803

* Many of these were sent in as Type I, II, or III; others were missed on the initial typing in the outlying laboratories.

As was demonstrated by the findings in these and other typings done at the State Bacteriologic Laboratory, the occurrence of pneumococci of the types found was widespread over the State; and, except for the fact, as is mentioned later, that some types were encountered more frequently than others, no unusual geographical prevalence of the types found was noted. Occasional instances of multiple cases of pneumonia in a single family due to some one type occurred but were not common.* (Small outbreaks of pneumonia were investigated by Doctor Smillie in a school for feeble-minded children and in the Veterans' Hospital in Bedford. A small outbreak of Type I pneumococcus infection including pneumonia occurred in the town of Colrain and was investigated by Doctors Anderson and Gilman. The latter likewise investigated an outbreak of Type I pneumonia occurring in a family in Boston.)

At this point it is of interest to survey the available records as to the findings obtained from the total number of typings carried out in this State since September 1931. (See Table 2.) Probably only about one-half of these specimens were obtained from patients with lobar pneumonia.

List A—Typings at State Bacteriologic Laboratory. This lists typings carried out on specimens sent in between September 1, 1931 and January 1, 1936. It does not include typings

*During 1936, after the conclusion of the Study, additional small outbreaks of pneumococcus infection were encountered in families or communities with startling frequency and regularity. This did not appear entirely due to the increased prevalence of pneumonia which occurred in the early part of that year. Everything considered, it seemed probable that similar small outbreaks have occurred fairly regularly in the past but, for the most part, they have passed unnoticed. It appeared that their recognition in 1936 resulted from the widespread bacteriologic examination of cultures and sputums, facilities for such examinations then being generally available in all sections of the State.

It seems probable that such outbreaks will continue to be recognized from time to time. This opens up possibilities for further epidemiologic investigation which might prove profitable. For this Department to take full advantage of the opportunity offered may be difficult unless additional personnel be employed.

on 803 Group IV cultures (see Table 1) sent in from outside laboratories and counted in their totals, 8 urines typed, 414 typings on cultures from Colrain, nor 40 cultures from a family outbreak of pneumococcus infection.

List B—Typings at all other cooperating laboratories from the fall of 1931 to September 20, 1935, with the exception of the results obtained at the Boston City Hospital during the year 1931 and the spring of 1932, which were not available.

List C—Total of Lists A and B.

TABLE 2 — INCIDENCE OF PNEUMOCOCCI BY TYPE, IN SPECIMENS FROM PATIENTS WITH RESPIRATORY DISEASE IN MASSACHUSETTS, 1931-1935

Type	List A Typings at State Bacteriologic Laboratory		List B Typings at all other laboratories	List C Total
	Number	Per cent of pneumococci among strains found	Number	Number
I	534	17.0	951	1485
II	140	4.4	238	378
III	439	13.9	583	1022
IV	92	2.9	61	153
V	139	4.4	145	284
VI	99	3.1	47	146
VII	136	4.3	102	238
VIII	310	9.8	186	496
IX	95	3.0	41	136
X	50	1.6	60	110
XI	63	2.0	28	91
XII	33	1.0	29	62
XIII	50	1.6	26	76
XIV	61	1.9	47	108
XV	23	0.7	9	32
XVI	31	1.0	12	43
XVII	54	1.7	31	85
XVIII	117	3.7	55	172
XIX	98	3.1	59	157
XX	57	1.8	56	113
XXI	77	2.4	30	107
XXII	37	1.2	23	60
XXIII	49	1.6	6	55
XXIV	14	0.4	9	23
XXV	6	0.2	3	9
XXVI	7	0.2	11	18
XXVII	10	0.3	—	10
XXVIII	40	1.3	6	46
XXIX	38	1.2	12	50
XXX	35	1.1	10	45
XXXI	23	0.7	8	31
XXXII	4	0.1	2	6
Group IV	189	6.0		
No pneumococci	1190		2,511	3,890
Total	4340		5397	9737

As seen in Table 2, the Pneumonia Study experience with pneumococcus typing embraces the results obtained from the examination of nearly 10,000 specimens from patients with lobar pneumonia and bronchopneumonia and a few other varieties of respiratory disease. If all specimens had come from patients with lobar pneumonia, doubtless Type I and Type II pneumococci would have been found more frequently. It is important to note that the six most common types found in this large group were Types I, III, VIII, II, V, and VII, in the order named (See Table 3). These types were found in 3,903 or 41 per cent of all the specimens examined, and made up 67 per cent of all the specimens containing pneumococci which could be typed.

TABLE 3 — SIX COMMONEST TYPES OF PNEUMOCOCCI FOUND IN THE EXAMINATION OF 9,737 SPECIMENS FROM PATIENTS WITH RESPIRATORY DISEASE

Type	Number	Type	Number
I	1,485	II	378
III	1,022	V	284
VIII	496	VII	238
		Total	3,903

In 1933 Sutliff and Finland (J.A.M.A. 101:1289, October 21, 1933) reported a series of 770 typed cases of pneumococcus lobar pneumonia from the Boston City Hospital. In this series Types I, II, III, VIII, V, and VII, in the order named, were the commonest and were responsible for 84 per cent of the cases. List C, as given in Table 2, also includes most of the typing figures from the Boston City Hospital. List A, however, includes no specimens typed at the Boston City Hospital, and reference to that list will likewise show that Types I, III, VIII, II, V, and VII, in the order named, were again the six most common types and were found in 53.8 per cent of the specimens examined at the State Laboratory. Further, a comparison of the findings obtained from typing the 803 Group IV cultures mentioned earlier in this section, as shown in Table 1, reveals that in the outlying districts of the State, Types VIII, VII, and V were the commonest of the higher types encountered.

These figures are important and show that the six types above mentioned are uniformly the commonest types encountered in pneumonia, not only in Boston but in other parts of the State as well; and, because of that, they assume especial significance. In New York City, in 1,000 consecutive cases of typed pneumococcus lobar pneumonia reported by Bullowa (J.A.M.A. 105:1512, November 9, 1935), seven types—Types I, III, VIII, II, VII, IV, and V, in the order named—were the commonest types and were responsible for 74 per cent of the cases.

(6) Home Treated Cases

There are nowhere available in the literature figures giving the case fatality rate of large series of patients with lobar pneumonia (typed or untyped) who were cared for at home but not treated with specific immune serum or vaccine. For the purpose of comparing the fatality rates of cases treated with and without antiserum in the home, it appeared of interest that such a series be obtained, and attempts were made to gather a representative group of such home-treated cases (see Table 4).

TABLE 4 — NUMBER AND PERCENTAGE INCIDENCE OF CASES AND NUMBER OF DEATHS FROM LOBAR PNEUMONIA IN PATIENTS TREATED AT HOME OR IN HOSPITALS WITHOUT VACCINE OR SPECIFIC SERUM THERAPY, BY PNEUMOCOCCUS TYPE

Type	Home Cases			Hospital Cases		
	Cases	Died	Per Cent Fatality Rate	Cases	Died	Per Cent Fatality Rate
I	84	21	25.0	106	29	27.4
II	18	3	16.7	33	8	24.2
III	51	21	41.2	53	19	35.8
IV	10	4	40.0	11	2	18.2
V	12	3	25.0	32	8	25.0
VI	4	2		6	2	
VII	20	2	10.0	21	—	—
VIII	33	1	3.0	33	7	21.2
IX	11	2		2	1	
X	3	—		4	1	
XI	6	1		2	—	
XII	6	1		3	—	
XIII	3	1		1	—	
XIV	5	—		9	3	
XV	1	—		1	1	
XVI	3	—		—	—	
XVII	2	—		4	1	
XVIII	8	1		11	—	
XIX	6	—		6	1	
XX	1	—		4	—	
XXI	4	—		3	—	
XXII	4	—		—	—	
XXIII	3	—		—	—	
XXIV	2	—		1	—	
XXV	1	—		—	—	
XXVI	—	—		—	—	
XXVII	—	—		—	—	
XXVIII	—	—		1	—	
XXIX	2	—		1	—	
XXX	3	—		2	1	
XXXI	1	—		1	—	
XXXII	—	—		—	—	
Group IV	3	2		5	—	
Miscellaneous	6	2		—	—	
No pneumococci	22	3		11	1	
Total	338	70	20.7	367	85	23.2
(All cases due to pneumococci above Type III together	157	20	12.7	164	28	17.1*)

* This case fatality rate is considerably lower than that of 28.2 per cent found in the total 493 cases (139 deaths) in adults due to infection with the various types from IV to XXVI inclusive, reported by Bullowa (Med. & Surg. Year Book, Physicians' Hospital, Plattsburg, 1:3, 1929), Park (J. State Med. 39:187, April 1931), and Sutliff and Finland (J.A.M.A. 101:1289, October 21, 1933). Their cases were cared for at the Harlem Hospital in New York City and at the City Hospital in Boston and were not given specific serum treatment.

It appears obvious from the findings in the collected series listed in Table 4 that the true situation has not been disclosed. The reason for this belief is that the fatality rates of cases due to some of the types of pneumococci appear far lower (even in the hospital-treated cases) than in other cases not receiving specific treatment due to these same types as reported in the literature. While the fatality rate of cases treated at home may, due to various reasons, be expected to be somewhat lower than that of others cared for in hospitals, when such rates are as low as, for instance, that shown by the Type II cases in this group, they must be regarded with open suspicion. With the exception of Type I, and possibly Type III, the number of cases due to each of the other types is too small to be of significance. It would be highly desirable if figures on a large group of typed cases of pneumonia cared for at home but not treated with specific immune serum could be obtained which were truly representative.

The series shown in Table 4 was collected through the aid of the District Health Officers of this Department, who sent sputum for typing to the State Bacteriologic Laboratory from cases of lobar pneumonia treated at home in various regions of the State. In addition to this, a small group of cases was obtained from Doctor Smillie's series; and during the summers of 1932, 1933, 1934 and 1935, data on a third group were gathered by members of the Study. In addition to including cases treated at home, information was gathered on a considerable number of cases treated without anti-serum or vaccine in the small, medium, and large-sized hospitals throughout the State. Nearly all cases were in adults. Medical students were employed during several summers to assist in gathering this information and in analyzing the results in cases treated with and without specific serum therapy.

A summary of the findings in Table 4 is given in Table 5.

TABLE 5 — NUMBER OF CASES AND DEATHS, AND PERCENTAGE FATALITY RATE OF PATIENTS WITH LOBAR PNEUMONIA NOT GIVEN VACCINE OR SPECIFIC SERUM THERAPY, BY PLACE OF TREATMENT

	Cases	Died	Per cent Fatality Rate
Home cases	338	70	20.7
Hospital cases	367	85	23.2
Total	705	155	22.0

Among the groups listed in Table 4 which were treated without vaccine or specific antiserum, there are 190 Type I cases of which 50 or 26.3 per cent ended fatally. This is of interest and a contrast to the unusually low fatality rate of 21.6 per cent shown by the 51 Type II cases. Of course, the number of cases in the Type II series is very small and represents the accumulation of only 10 or 12 cases a year. Enough selection may have been exercised in gathering such cases so as to yield this extraordinarily low fatality rate. This seems almost certain in view of the procedures used, especially by District Health Officers, for the collection of about one-half of these cases. The inclusion of cases obtained from the epidemiologic study of Doctor Smillie is open to the same criticism. It is recognized, for example, that both Type II and Type V cases have a high incidence of bacteremia, and a high fatality

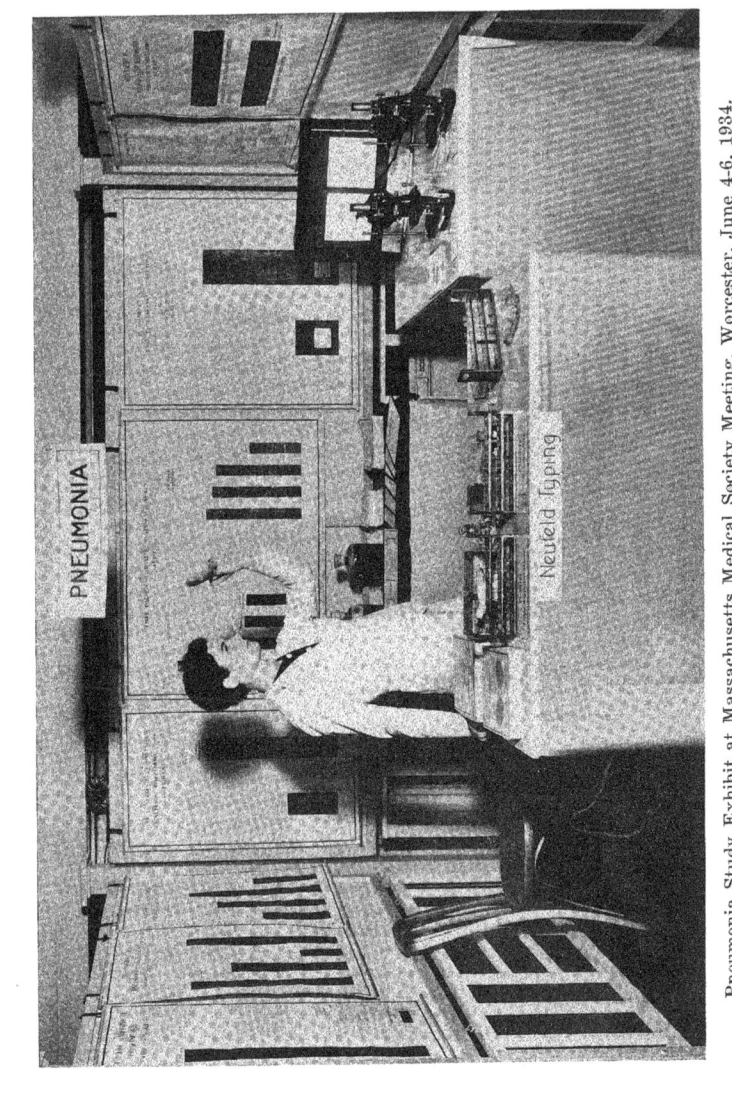

Pneumonia Study Exhibit at Massachusetts Medical Society Meeting, Worcester, June 4-6, 1934.

rate, and that death often occurs early in the illness. Where data are gathered on cases relatively late in their illness (favorable cases), as often occurred in the present series, patients dying early are completely missed. At all events, the low fatality rate in the Type II cases listed in Table 4 is certainly at variance with that of 41.0 per cent shown by a series of 992 Type II cases treated without specific serum with 407 deaths which have been reported in the American and Canadian literature (15). This latter figure, it is believed, more correctly illustrates the usual fatality rate from Type II lobar pneumonia and, even though high, is somewhat lower than the 51 per cent fatality rate of 148 Type II cases not receiving antiserum and cared for at the Boston City Hospital from 1930-35 inclusive (personal communication from Doctor M. Finland of the Boston City Hospital).

II — EDUCATIONAL

Because of the rapid advances in the newer methods of pneumococcus typing and serum production and concentration, with resulting change in the procedures used in the serum treatment of patients ill with pneumococcus pneumonia, it was found that the average physician was unable to fully cooperate in the Pneumonia Study without further education along these lines. Various means were employed to spread all available sound information regarding these matters, and repeated attempts were made to call them to the attention of every physician in the State, both individually and collectively. The media used to spread this propaganda were numerous. It may be conservatively stated that at least a majority of the physicians in Massachusetts heard of the Pneumonia Study and from a sufficient number of angles to realize that a serious attempt was made to do something about this disease. Judging from the attendance at meetings held throughout the State, it was possible to reach directly approximately 75 per cent or more of the physicians outside of Metropolitan Boston. Within Metropolitan Boston, however, it was felt that a much smaller proportion of the practicing physicians were reached directly. In addition, of course, all physicians in the State were circularized a number of times and sent various notices and reprints of work being carried out.

There has been a steady increase in the demand for pneumococcus typing since the inauguration of this Study. The demand for therapeutic pneumonia serum has likewise increased, and this especially so during the latter part of 1935, by which time serum was available on an equal basis to all physicians in the State.

In the past physicians were often hesitant to use antipneumococcic serum because of the possibility that a reaction, either of an allergic or thermal nature, might result from its injection. The fear of such reactions has constituted and to a certain extent still does constitute a considerable handicap to the more widespread use of specific serum therapy. In many instances, however, such fears were grossly exaggerated, and educational efforts leading to a better understanding of the proper selection of cases for treatment resulted in a considerable improvement in this situation. Through improvements in the serum produced were also of aid in reducing fear of reactions, there is still much to be done along the line of improving the serum. In fact, at the conclusion of the Study this remained one of the most difficult problems to solve and still is in need of intensive investigation.

From the educational standpoint one of the most important problems yet remaining is that of increasing physicians' understanding of when to use and when not to use antipneumococcic serum and to improve their technic of its administration.

The following is a list of the efforts, methods, and material used to stimulate the interest of physicians in this work.

(1) Graduate Courses

An intensive one-day course covering various aspects of the epidemiology, diagnosis, specific and non-specific treatment, and treatment of surgical complications of lobar pneumonia, with a review of the Pneumonia Program, was organized by and given through the Graduate School of the Harvard Medical School. This course was given twice in Boston, once in October 1931 and again in the spring of 1932, and once in the spring of 1933 in Worcester. Every physician cooperating in the Study as a pneumonia collaborator in the chosen pneumonia areas in and outside of Boston up to the spring of 1933 was present at some one of these courses. In addition, at the course in Worcester, of the more than 150 physicians present, only about 20 represented pneumonia collaborators. This meeting in particular did a great deal to stimulate interest in pneumonia in the area around Worcester. It is felt that courses of this type do great good and are valuable in calling attention to the problems offered by pneumonia.

The programs of these meetings were essentially similar each time, though the personnel giving them varied. Each graduate course lasted about five hours. The following is an example of a typical program of one of these meetings.

Time of meeting: 9:30 a.m. to 4 p.m.

Subjects

1. Epidemiology
2. Diagnosis and Non-specific Treatment
3. Surgical Treatment of Intrathoracic Complications of Pneumonia
4. Typing: Methods and Significance
5. Serum Administration and Reactions
6. Pneumonia Program in Massachusetts

In the fall of 1933 the Massachusetts Medical Society formed a Committee on Courses for Graduates, and in the winter of 1933-34 offered a large number of graduate courses to its constituent medical societies in the State. That winter Doctor F. T. Lord was in charge of the graduate work on pneumonia for the Medical Society. He was assisted by Doctor W. D. Sutliff and the Field Director of the Study. In all, some fourteen or fifteen one-hour talks on pneumonia were given in various parts of the State. Eight of these were given by the Field Director. In each of these, of course, the serum treatment of pneumonia and the Massachusetts Pneumonia Program were discussed. During the winter of 1934-35 no graduate courses on pneumonia were given. In the fall of 1935 the courses on pneumonia were again revived and, under the chairmanship of Doctor Joseph Pratt with the assistance of Doctor D. King and Doctor M. Finland, many additional talks of this nature were given. In essentially all of these the Massachusetts Pneumonia Program was mentioned.

As a result of the activities of the Committee on Graduate Courses of the Massachusetts Medical Society, it was not felt necessary to undertake any further graduate courses on pneumonia under the auspices of the Harvard Medical School.

(2) Pneumonia Meetings in Areas Chosen for Intensive Work

A large number of meetings were held in areas especially designated by the Advisory Committee for carrying out an intensive pneumonia study. All but two or three of these meetings were symposiums lasting from two to three hours each, at which from two to four speakers appeared. Many of these meetings were addressed by leading internists and surgeons, the latter speaking on the treatment of empyema, as well as by the Commissioner or Deputy Commissioner of this Department; and all were addressed by the Field Director of the Study. In some instances more than one meeting was held in a given area. Where this occurred, the interval between meetings was usually a year or more. The official pneumonia meetings addressed were in the following communities:

1931. Beverly, Newton, Great Barrington, Pittsfield.
1932. Worcester, Ayer, Malden, Chelsea, New Bedford, Natick.
1933. Fall River, Springfield, Salem, Clinton.
1934. Lowell, Lawrence, Haverhill, Fall River, Great Barrington, Newburyport.

Subsequent to changing the method of organizing areas for the treatment of pneumonia, several pneumonia meetings were held in 1935 in additional areas organized under the new plan. These meetings were in various towns, as follows: two in Greenfield, and one each in Peabody, Lynn, Chelsea, Southbridge, Attleboro, and Taunton. All these meetings were addressed by the Field Director of the Study, and at Attleboro and Taunton by Doctor F. T. Lord as well.

From time to time requests were received from hospitals and medical groups in various communities to have the Field Director address a group of physicians on pneumonia and the Massachusetts Pneumonia Study. The following were among the places where these meetings were held:

1932. Everett, Whidden Memorial Hospital;
Marlboro, Marlboro Hospital.
1933. Chelsea, Chelsea Naval Hospital;
Cambridge, Cambridge Medical Improvement Society.
1934. Everett, Whidden Memorial Hospital;
Boston, annual meeting of Massachusetts Associated Boards of Health.
1935. Winthrop, Community Memorial Hospital;
Chelsea, Chelsea Naval Hospital.

At all the meetings in the above groups, especially those in the outlying towns, the attendance was excellent. The subject of pneumonia and its serum treatment was discussed in detail, and physicians were informed of the organization set up in their communities so that serum might be available for their use.

(3) District Medical Society Meetings

The organization and purposes of the Pneumonia Program were outlined to most of the District Medical Societies of the State at some one of their regular meetings. Many of these meetings were symposiums lasting from one and one-half to three hours and devoted entirely to pneumonia. The society meetings addressed were as follows:

1931
Pittsfield   Berkshire District Medical Society
1932
New Bedford   Bristol South District Medical Society
Andover   Essex North District Medical Society
Greenfield   Franklin District Medical Society
Springfield   Hampden District Medical Society
Northampton   Hampshire District Medical Society
Braintree   Norfolk South District Medical Society
Boston   Suffolk District Medical Society
Worcester   Worcester District Medical Society
Leominster   Worcester North District Medical Society
1933
Winchester   Middlesex East District Medical Society
Springfield   Hampden District Medical Society
1934
Roxbury   Norfolk District Medical Society
Boston   Suffolk District Medical Society
1935
Northampton   Hampshire District Medical Society
Palmer   Hampden District Medical Society
Danvers   Essex South District Medical Society

Special pneumonia meetings were not held by the following District Medical Societies: Middlesex North and South, Plymouth, Bristol North, and Barnstable. In some of these, however, graduate courses (of the Massachusetts Medical Society) on pneumonia were given.

(4) Addresses Before State Medical Society

The Massachusetts Medical Society was addressed in June 1931 by Doctor G. H. Bigelow, who delivered a paper on lobar pneumonia and its serum treatment and outlined the proposed Pneumonia Program (1).

In 1932 a paper was delivered by the Field Director of the Study at the annual meeting of this Society, outlining the whole program and the accomplishments of the Study up to that time (3).

In 1934 and again in 1935 scientific exhibits were shown at the annual meetings of the State Medical Society, illustrating the materials needed for serum treatment and the results of the Massachusetts Pneumonia Program to date, and demonstrating the Neufeld method of typing. A photograph of a typical exhibit is shown in the accompanying illustration.

(5) Addresses Before National Medical Societies

In 1932, through the courtesy of Doctor Lord, the Field Director addressed the Association of American Physicians in Atlantic City, calling their attention to the Pneumonia Program in Massachusetts. Doctor Smillie brought this matter to the attention of the American Medical Association at its annual meeting in New Orleans, and the Field Director spoke of it to the American Society of Bacteriologists and Pathologists.

In 1933 Doctor Smillie addressed the American Epidemiological Society in Washington in May, giving a preliminary report of the study conducted by Doctors Smillie and Leeder and calling attention to the Massachusetts Pneumonia Program. In June of that year he also addressed the American Medical Association in Milwaukee. The Field Director delivered a paper before the American Public Health Association in Washington, D. C., on pneumococcus typing. Doctor Anderson spoke before the American Medical Association in Milwaukee, giving a report on the Pneumonia Program up to that time.

(6) Other Meetings

The attention of physicians in various parts of the country, especially in New England, and in New York, and Pennsylvania was called to the Massachusetts Pneumonia Program. This was done by various physicians here. The following is a list of the communities in which such meetings were known to have occurred. There were doubtless other meetings in other localities about which no information is available.

1931-33

Doctors Lord and Locke spoke in New Jersey, New York City, Pennsylvania, Maine, and Vermont.

1932

Doctor Heffron; Springfield, Illinois.

1934

Doctor Lord; Maine, Vermont, and Chicago, Illinois.
Doctors Locke and Felton; Philadelphia.
Doctor Heffron; Hartford, Manchester, and Bristol, Connecticut.
Doctor Donald King; New Hampshire.

1935

Doctor Felton; Springfield, Illinois.
Doctor Lord; Saratoga Springs, New York.
Doctor Finland; Syracuse, New York.
Doctor Rosenau; Philadelphia.

Also in 1935, at the request of the New York Academy of Medicine, an exhibit was shown in New York City giving the results of serum treatment as obtained in the Massachusetts Pneumonia Study.

(7) Printed Matter

Reprints concerning the Massachusetts Pneumonia Study: In 1931, 6500 copies of Doctor Bigelow's address (1) before the State Medical Society were obtained. One was sent to each physician in the State. Some 13,500 copies of the Department's quarterly bulletin, *The Commonhealth* (2), were obtained of an issue devoted almost entirely to a complete discussion of lobar pneumonia. One of these was sent to each physician in the State. Some 400 copies of a set of directions giving the technic to be used for pneumococcus typing were mimeographed and copies sent to all interested and collaborating bacteriologists and technicians. In 1932, 8000 copies of the Field Director's preliminary report (3) of the Study before the Massachusetts Medical Society were obtained. One of these was sent to each physician in the State. In 1933, 6500 copies of a paper by Doctors Heffron and Anderson on the two-year report of the Pneumonia Study (6), presented to the American Medical Association, were obtained. A copy was sent to each physician in the State. In 1935, 200 copies of an article by Doctors Anderson and Heffron on the Present Status of the Pneumonia Problem (14), which appeared in the Public Health Nursing Journal, were obtained. A copy was sent to each of our former pneumonia collaborators.

Special Sheets: In 1931, 500 copies of a sheet listing the conditions under which pneumonia serum would be given out were obtained and were distributed to physicians. Some 15,000 "flyers" listing the precautions to be taken and the technic of serum treatment were obtained and were later distributed to physicians and interested laboratory workers. About 3,000 record blanks were printed for recording the results in the cases treated with serum. These were all used up. Several thousand cards for the use of laboratory workers for recording the results of sputum examination and typing were printed and widely distributed.

From 1931 through 1933, 3000 copies each of two sheets illustrating graphically the Krumwiede, Mouse, and Urine methods of typing were obtained. The bulk of these were distributed to medical students, physicians, and laboratory workers.

In 1934 the record blanks were reprinted and 3000 obtained, most of which were distributed for use. Also 5000 sheets illustrating diagrammatically the technic of the Neufeld method of typing were obtained. Over half of these were distributed. In the latter part of 1934 a new brief record form was drawn up and several hundred copies were made on the multigraph. In 1935 these were again multigraphed. In 1934 and again in 1935 several hundred cards were multigraphed and distributed for keeping a record in the cooperating laboratories of the amount of serum given out to various physicians.

In 1935 several thousand sheets listing the precautions to be used prior to serum administration were obtained for distribution, and some 5000 new flyers were printed giving the details of the technic of serum treatment and the dosage advised.

Special Articles for Collaborators and Other Interested Physicians: Reprints were obtained of seven of the best available articles dealing with the experience of numerous investigators in New York and

Boston with specific serum therapy. These were obtained either directly from the authors or were reprinted with the permission of the authors and the editors of the various journals in which they appeared. Copies of such articles were sent to all physicians cooperating in the Pneumonia Study as collaborators, and in certain instances to especially interested physicians in some of the newer areas. Further, reprints of three articles dealing with pneumococcus typing were sent to hospital technicians as well as to collaborators and interested physicians.

In addition to the above educational efforts, a small handbook on Lobar Pneumonia and Serum Therapy, with Special Reference to the Massachusetts Pneumonia Study (15) was written by Doctors Lord and Heffron. Two large monographs are in preparation, one on the pneumococcus and the other on various aspects of lobar pneumonia.

During the course of the Study other efforts were also made to gain the attention of the medical profession and to impart to them some of the newer information regarding typing and the serum treatment of patients with pneumonia. For this purpose numerous lantern slides were prepared for use at various meetings. Many wall charts were likewise made and used at lectures and exhibits.

III — CLINICAL—PNEUMONIA AREAS ORGANIZED

One of the most important items in the original plan of the Pneumonia Study was that of attempting to determine whether or not concentrated antipneumococcic serum could be used satisfactorily in the small hospitals and homes throughout the State. To accomplish this purpose, it was desired to select circumscribed areas in various parts of the State for intensive efforts in this direction. These areas were chosen to embrace urban, rural, residential, industrial, seashore, and upland regions: in a word, to encompass districts characteristic of the various conditions existing in the State. In all, some seventeen selected areas were organized outside of Boston, embracing a population of about one-half that of the State.

(1) Organization of Collaborator Areas

With advice and guidance from the Advisory Committee, some two or more physicians locally prominent in the practice of medicine were designated as pneumonia collaborators in each of the areas organized (see Appendix). The Field Director of the Study interviewed these physicians and discussed the problem with them; and upon their agreement to act as collaborators they were furnished with reprints of the best articles then available on the serum treatment of pneumonia. After a period of three or four weeks allowed for study of these reprints, a dinner was usually held some place within the area to which these collaborators were invited, and the entire evening was spent discussing the various aspects of pneumonia and its serum treatment. Later, arrangements were made to have all collaborators attend, at the expense of the Study, one of the Graduate Courses arranged for through the Harvard Medical School (see page 26). All physicians acting as collaborators up to the spring of 1933 attended at least one of these courses. In addition to preparing the collaborators for their work, arrangements were also made so that the technicians in one or more centrally located hospitals of each area could be given a week's training in Boston in pneumococcus typing.

Concentrated bivalent Type I and II antipneumococcic serum was supplied to the collaborators in the special districts for use in cases of lobar pneumonia which they might see in consultation or in their own private practice and wish to treat with serum. After completing the necessary arrangements for such an organization in each area, the other local physicians in the nearby towns were invited to a special meeting and informed of the organization at their disposal for the bacteriologic diagnosis and the serum treatment of patients with pneumonia. At that time the Pneumonia Program and its aims was outlined to them. Physicians were informed that if any of them had a patient with pneumonia that they wished to treat with serum, they might call in consultation any one of the collaborators in that area. The latter individual would confirm the clinical diagnosis, either begin the initial serum treatment of the patient or show the physician how to do it, and take care of having the case typed. In this manner the first doses of immune serum were ordinarily given before the type of pneumococcus infection was known. After giving the third dose, no further serum was given such patients until the type of infection was determined. If the patient proved to have a Type I or II pneumonia and still appeared ill, additional serum might be given; but if the infection was caused by pneumococci of Type III or one of the higher types, or by some other organism, no further serum was given.

(2) Collaborator Areas

The seventeen areas organized outside of Boston functioned for periods of from about one to nearly four years and were as follows:

Area	Number of Towns Included	Approximate Population Served*
1. Beverly	10	75,839
2. Malden	5	204,044
3. Newton	7	178,641
4. Brockton	1	63,797
5. New Bedford	5	137,919
6. Ayer (Nashoba Health District)	12	20,143
7. Worcester	28	316,161
8. Pittsfield	10	60,614
9. Great Barrington (Southern Berkshire Health District)	14	18,186
10. Chelsea Naval Reserve	—	—
11. Fall River	5	130,677
12. Salem	5	85,306
13. Springfield	13	273,383
14. Clinton	9	31,722
15. Lowell	6	129,233
16. Lawrence	5	123,719
17. Haverhill	10	88,903
Total		1,984,103

*Based on census of 1930. Population of State in 1930 was 4,249,614.

In these areas there were, in all, twenty-eight hospitals, in which typing was carried out by thirty trained technicians, and seventy-eight physicians who acted as pneumonia collaborators.

In addition to the above areas with their one or more hospitals, serum was available in Boston from eight different hospitals. Each of these had one or more properly designated physicians in charge of the serum for that institution, and all but the Boston Dispensary had one or more laboratory workers for carrying out typing. These hospitals were the

1. Peter Bent Brigham
2. Boston City
3. Massachusetts General
4. Boston Dispensary*
5. Beth Israel
6. Carney
7. New England Deaconess
8. Massachusetts Memorial

* Typings from the Boston Dispensary were done at the Boston City Hospital or at the State Bacteriologic Laboratory.

Typing was also done at the State Bacteriologic Laboratory, State House, Boston.

(3) Organization of New Type Areas

In the plan originally outlined for the Pneumonia Study, it was contemplated that, if the results of serum treatment proved satisfactory, the State would doubtless take over the cost of continuing the production and distribution of pneumonia serum. If this occurred and money from State funds was used to produce serum, it would, of course, have to be made equally available to all physicians. By 1934 a review of the experience of the State Bacteriologic Laboratory with the then new Neufeld method of typing showed it to be simple, rapid, and reliable. The use of this procedure usually reduced the time required for typing from many hours to a few minutes. The fatality rates of cases treated with specific serum in the early part of the Study in Massachusetts, and the results previously reported by physicians elsewhere in this country, clearly showed that the maximum benefit of serum therapy was obtained when such treatment was begun within the first four days of illness. Further, the serum available was useful for combatting only Type I and Type II infections. Just how the distribution of this serum might be restricted to patients with Type I or Type II pneumonia who had not been ill longer than four days constituted a problem of great importance.

The solution to this problem was supplied by Doctor G. W. Anderson, Deputy Commissioner of this Department, who suggested a likely plan for distributing serum to all physicians in the State who wished to use it. Physicians were to be informed that they could obtain serum from the laboratory of the one or more centrally located hospitals in their district (the technicians from such laboratories having previously been trained in typing) providing the following conditions were fulfilled. These were:

1. Sputum or other material from the patient shall first be typed and shown to contain Type I or II pneumococci.
2. The physician must be willing to certify that his patient has not been ill with pneumonia longer than four days (96 hours).
3. The physician must agree to fill out and return to this Depart-

ment, when his patient is discharged, a brief questionnaire which will be furnished to him with the serum.

Upon meeting these requirements satisfactorily, physicians would receive from the typing laboratory an average dose of serum for each Type I or Type II case.

An examination of the records of treated cases revealed that the occurrence of certain conditions increased the fatality rate of patients experiencing them. It seemed desirable, therefore, to make provision for distributing an additional amount of serum to certain cases. This was done, and arrangements were made to distribute an extra amount of serum to any patient whose temperature failed to fall below 101°F. by mouth within eighteen hours of the beginning of treatment; or, if having fallen, it again rose above this level within forty-eight hours. This extra amount of serum was also made available for patients having a pneumococcus Type I or Type II bacteremia or who were pregnant or had been delivered within the previous seven days.

This plan seemed entirely feasible, and experience has shown that physicians are willing to accept the above restrictions to the distribution of serum. This must be regarded as an important finding. With such an arrangement the services of physicians who formerly acted as pneumonia collaborators would no longer be required, and serum would be equally available to all physicians in the State.

In order that this new type of organization might be tried out in a nearby area and in one which had previously had some experience with the use of serum, it was thought best to reorganize one of the old collaborator areas. Thus, in November 1933, this new plan was put into effect in the area around Newton. Very little pneumonia occurred there during the first winter after this reorganization, but there was enough to show that this system of distributing serum could function successfully. Following this, the older collaborator areas in the State were changed over to this new type of organization, and many new districts organized along the new plan were included. In consequence, by the end of 1935 serum was available to *all* physicians throughout the State from their nearby hospitals, each of which had one or more properly trained technicians. It was not until the end of 1935, however, that the final arrangements in many of these hospitals throughout the State were completed. Until that time, of course, serum was not equally available to all physicians in the State. The Study ended at that point and without any official lay publicity being given to the use of serum in pneumonia. At that time sixty-six laboratories widely scattered over the State were prepared to carry out pneumococcus typing.

A complete list of the hospitals in Massachusetts which do typing and dispense antipneumococcic serum to physicians under the conditions outlined above is given in the appendix. Typing is also done and serum is available from the State Bacteriologic Laboratory, State House, Boston.

(4) Training Technicians

In 1931, in view of the fact that pneumococcus typing was being done regularly in only two or three of the hospitals in Boston and, so far as known, in none elsewhere in the State, it was apparent that the technicians from a large number of hospitals throughout the State would have to be trained in the methods of typing. It was thought advisable to give such training to all technicians in hospitals cooperating in this work, even though a few such individuals already knew something of the procedures used. This was done to secure uniformity of technic and for the opportunity it offered to acquaint these laboratory workers with the Pneumonia Program and its aims. For training in typing, technicians were brought to Boston. Their travel and their living expenses while here were paid but not their salaries, if these were continued during that period. Hospital authorities were glad to cooperate in this matter.

At the beginning of the Study arrangements for giving this training were still incomplete at the State Bacteriologic Laboratory. Consequently, the first technicians brought to Boston were trained under Doctor W. D. Sutliff at the Boston City Hospital. These are mentioned below.

In July 1931 an extra bacteriologist began work at the State Bacteriologic Laboratory. She devoted full time to pneumococcus typing work. During the winter of 1931-32 the demand for typing at this laboratory practically doubled, and an assistant was employed for the winter and was re-employed during the winters of 1932-33 and 1933-34. The original bacteriologist left the laboratory here in the fall of 1934, and at that time her assistant was employed nearly full time and continued to work up to the end of December 1935.

In 1931 six technicians from outlying laboratories were trained in pneumococcus typing at the Boston City Hospital. By the end of 1932 a total of thirteen technicians had received training in typing at that hospital. In that year the training of technicians was also begun under the bacteriologists at the State Bacteriologic Laboratory. From twenty to forty technicians were subsequently trained each year at this laboratory. In all, more than ninety hospital technicians received training in pneumococcus typing. This included one each from Hartford, Connecticut; Newport, Rhode Island; Brattleboro, Vermont; Portsmouth, New Hampshire; and Cincinnati, Ohio, the remainder being from Massachusetts hospitals. In addition, there were numerous visitors who spent one or two hours or more in the laboratory at various times learning the Neufeld technic of typing. With the exception of these, all other technicians trained received from two to five and one-half days' work in the laboratory, the average being about four days.

After training the technicians in the outlying laboratories in the methods of pneumococcus typing and supplying them with diagnostic serum, cards for keeping their reports, and pamphlets giving the detailed technic of pneumococcus typing, it was desirable that some supervision be exercised over them. This could only be done in an advisory capacity. In consequence, it was thought best for one of the bacteriologists from the State Laboratory to visit each of the outlying laboratories once or twice a year and at times to request that technicians in these laboratories spend a day at the State Laboratory in Boston discussing typing work in general and whatever problems they might have. The following visits were made: in the spring of 1932, 1933, 1934, and 1935 one of the Pneumonia Study bacteriologists made a short visit to each of the cooperating laboratories. In the fall of 1932 all technicians were brought to the State Laboratory for a one-day discussion and review. In the fall of 1933 all technicians were again brought to this laboratory in small groups for one day each and taught the Neufeld method of typing. In the fall of 1934 and 1935 the outlying laboratories were again visited.

It is quite obvious that the bacteriologist's visits to outlying laboratories and the visits of technicians to the State Bacteriologic Laboratory were extremely successful and stimulating from many points of view. Significantly, the technicians soon realized the importance of their position and that they formed an integral part of the whole Pneumonia Study. This matter was stressed and particular pains were taken by the Field Director of the Study to show them the many ways in which they might assist the physicians in their various communities with the bacteriologic diagnosis and serum treatment of patients with pneumonia. The realization of their importance to the proper conclusion of the Pneumonia Study and the willingness of members of the Study not only to admit but to emphasize this has in considerable measure been responsible for the excellent degree of cooperation obtained from these individuals.

The last new procedure taught technicians was the Neufeld method of typing. Instruction in this began in the fall of 1933, and during 1934 and 1935 instruction in typing was largely limited to this, for by that time the method had been found so successful that the older and slower methods of typing were largely displaced. On direct questioning, all cooperating technicians in the State have stated that they prefer the Neufeld to any other method of typing, for it is not only accurate but extremely simple and rapid.

(5) Comparison of Typing Methods

During the course of the Study a detailed investigation was made of the accuracy, efficiency, or inadequacies of seven methods of typing. The following is a list of the methods studied:
1. Krumwiede
2. Sabin
3. Tube agglutination
4. Precipitin
5. Urine
6. Rosenthal and Sternberg
7. Neufeld

Conclusions drawn from typing over 700 specimens by two, three, or more of the first five above methods were presented in 1932 to the Laboratory Section of the American Public Health Association (4). At that time the Sabin method of typing was relatively new, and the most important finding of this work was that the method was reliable and accurate and required only five to seven hours for its completion. Later, the Neufeld method of typing was introduced and thoroughly investigated. This method was found to be as accurate as any other method of typing, much simpler, and a great deal more rapid. In November 1934 Miss E. A. Beckler, Director of the State Bacteriologic

Laboratory, and Mrs. P. MacLeod, of that laboratory, reported (12) the results of typing 760 specimens by the Neufeld and one, two, three, or more other methods as well. A comparison was made of the findings obtained by the use of the Neufeld and these other methods of typing. Subsequently, comparisons were also made on an additional number of specimens, bringing the total number so examined to over 1500.

These investigations revealed that the Neufeld is extremely rapid, requiring only from five to thirty minutes to perform; it is the simplest of all typing methods and is accurate. This finding is of great practical importance in that the use of this method greatly facilitates early serum treatment. The general adoption of the Neufeld method of typing as a routine procedure permits typing cases first and limiting serum treatment to those patients having infections due to a type of pneumococcus for which a specific serum is available. In the laboratory it saves time and expense for help needed. In the field it speeds treatment and saves serum, and consequently money, for its use eliminates the need of treating cases before typing in order to save time and thus does away with the possible danger of reactions occurring during the treatment of cases with infections other than those for which specific serums are available.

A comparison was made of the results obtained by the Neufeld method with those of other methods of typing. This led to the decision that the Neufeld be adopted as a routine procedure and that in the future it would no longer be necessary to check the results of a Neufeld typing by carrying out other procedures on the specimen when such results were positive. It was advised, however, that whenever a Type III or one of the Group IV's was found in a specimen, a second specimen be obtained from the same patient within twelve to twenty-four hours and retyped. This was done because of the possibility that the first specimen contained nothing but mouth organisms, which are commonly Type III or Group IV pneumococci, and a Type I or II infection might otherwise be missed.

(6) Increase in Pneumococcus Typing

After beginning the Study there was a steady increase in the number of typings done in the State each year. The number of typings performed at the State Bacteriologic Laboratory is shown in Table 6.

TABLE 6.—NUMBER OF SPECIMENS SENT TO STATE BACTERIOLOGIC LABORATORY FOR TYPING*

Month	Before Beginning Pneumonia Study		After Beginning Pneumonia Study				
	1929	1930	1931	1932	1933	1934	1935**
January	115	55	94	138	288	157	218
February	76	55	103	144	126	129	113
March	82	90	58	210	123	131	120
April	58	66	41	160	118	99	125
May	43	36	43	76	61	78	119
June	26	19	17	40	45	59	57
July	15	10	11	11	29	27	38
August	19	12	9	24	47	33	32
September	18	12	22	49	36	39	46
October	20	27	44	85	55	90	72
November	26	36	44	63	103	89	78
December	57	47	72	111	167	113	188
Total	555	465	558	1111	1198	1044	1206

* Does not include the typing of 414 cultures from Colrain or 40 cultures from a family outbreak of pneumococcus infection.
** During 1936, the year following the termination of the Pneumonia Study, 1451 typings were done at the State Laboratory.

In addition to the typings shown in Table 6, several thousand others were done in the sixty-five cooperating laboratories in the various areas of the State, only two or three of which previous to the beginning of the Study were doing typing. The yearly number of typings done in outside laboratories (including Boston hospitals) is listed in Table 7.

TABLE 7.— TOTAL NUMBER OF TYPINGS DONE IN OUTSIDE LABORATORIES, INCLUDING THE BOSTON HOSPITALS, FROM SEPTEMBER 1931, TO AUGUST 1, 1935, BY TWELVE-MONTH PERIODS*

Period	Number of Typings
1931-1932 (11-month period)	521**
1932-1933	1,337
1933-1934	1,506
1934-1935	2,033
Total	5,397

* Typings done since August 1, 1935 not included as some of the data is inadequate.
** Boston City Hospital figures for this year not included.

Dividing the typings carried out at the State Bacteriologic Laboratory (Table 6) by similar twelve-month periods and combining the figures with those performed in other laboratories (Table 7), the total number of typings done in this State since 1931 on which information is available may be listed as shown in Table 8.

TABLE 8.— TOTAL NUMBER OF TYPINGS DONE IN ALL LABORATORIES IN STATE FROM 1931 THROUGH 1935, BY VARIOUS PERIODS

Period	State Laboratory	All other laboratories	Total done in State
Jan.-Aug. 31, 1931	376	—	376
1931-1932	789	521	1,310
1932-1933	882	1,337	2,219
1933-1934	1,117	1,506	2,623
1934-1935	1,122	2,033	3,155
Sept.-Dec. 31, 1935	420	—*	420
Total Group IV Cultures	803**	—	803
Totals	5,509***	5,397	10,906***

* Adequate data not available for typings done since Aug. 1, 1935.
** Also counted in typings done in All Other Laboratories; cultures were sent to State Laboratory where they were typed out to Type XXXII.
*** Does not include 414 cultures from Colrain nor 40 cultures typed at State Laboratory.

At the present rate, approximately 3000 specimens are being typed in this State each year. This is three or four times as many as were being typed here prior to the beginning of the Pneumonia Study. The number of typings done annually may continue to increase for some time.

IV — RESULTS OBTAINED IN SERUM TREATED CASES OF LOBAR PNEUMONIA 1931 THROUGH DECEMBER 12, 1935

The following is a tabulation of the cases which received treatment with Type I and II concentrated antipneumococcic serum. Cases are divided into various groups for purposes of comparison. Only the most important of the more than two hundred tables prepared are presented below.

The results shown below represent the combined efforts of nearly 400 Massachusetts physicians located in 98 towns, who treated 213 patients in their homes and 742 patients in 80 hospitals throughout the State. Cases were treated in every district of the State. The results obtained may doubtless be regarded as typical of what the medical profession may do in any similar area where typing facilities and antipneumococcic serum are generally available.

Table 9 lists the total number of cases treated with antiserum from January 1931 through December 12, 1935, when the last major detailed analysis of the treated cases was made.

TABLE 9.—TOTAL NUMBER OF CASES TREATED WITH TYPE I AND II ANTIPNEUMOCOCCIC SERUM DURING THE PNEUMONIA STUDY, BY YEAR

Year	Total Cases	Type I or II Only
1931	104	79
1932	228	127
1933	226	181
1934	214	192
1935	184*	177*
Grand Total	956	756

* In addition, at least 51 other cases were treated later in 1935, 50 of which were Type I or II. During 1936 more than 306 cases were treated, of which at least 304 were Type I or II.

It is apparent that there has been a progressive increase in the number of Type I and Type II cases given specific serum therapy since the inauguration of the Study.

A division of the 956 treated cases by place of treatment and pneumococcus type is given in Table 10.

TABLE 10.—TOTAL NUMBER OF CASES TREATED WITH TYPE I AND II ANTISERUM, BY PLACE OF TREATMENT AND PNEUMOCOCCUS TYPE

Type	Hospital cases	Home cases	Total
I	468	130	598
II	128	29	157
III	19	9	28
Group IV	97	31	128
Miscellaneous	9	5	14
Organism not stated	21	9	30
Total	742	213 (22 per cent)	955
1 Type I case, not stated where treated			1
Grand Total			956

Of the group of 956 cases, 213 or 22 per cent received serum treatment in their homes, and the remainder or 78 per cent were treated in various hospitals throughout the State.

The total 599 Type I cases and 157 Type II cases shown in Table 10 have been subdivided to facilitate analysis, as shown below. In each instance those Type I and Type II cases treated with 16 cc. or more of the specific Type I and II concentrated antiserum in which such treatment was begun within the first four days (96 hours from the time of onset) of illness have been considered as separate groups and are referred to as "Special Group" cases. The results obtained in these Special Group cases have proved of the greatest interest and significance.

Type I Cases

The analysis of the Type I cases may be presented first. A comparison of the fatality rates of Special Group and other Type I cases is shown in Table 11.

TABLE 11.—NUMBER OF CASES AND DEATHS AND FATALITY RATE OF SPECIAL GROUP AND OTHER TYPE I CASES

	Cases	Died	Per cent fatality rate
Special Group*	504	56	11.1
Others—received less serum or treated later than cases above	95	31	32.6
Total	599	87	14.5

* As of December 1936, the number of Special Group Type I cases was 724 with 79 or 10.9 per cent of deaths.

Three things are of especial interest concerning the cases in Table 11. First, the total group of 599 cases is one of the largest single series of Type I cases (treated with or without serum) ever reported. Second, the fatality rate of 11 per cent in the Special Group cases compares favorably with that of 10.5 per cent reported by Cole (J.A.M.A.

93:741, September 7, 1929) for 371 Type I cases treated with specific serum over a sixteen-year period at the Hospital of the Rockefeller Institute for Medical Research. Third, the 11 per cent fatality rate is markedly lower (56 per cent) than in Type I cases not treated with serum, as shown by the 25 per cent fatality rate found in 1614 cases with 403 deaths reported in the American and Canadian literature since 1913 (15).

Age: The 504 Type I Special Group cases may be divided into age groups and the fatality rates in each group compared with the fatality rates of the series of 190 Massachusetts Type I cases, similarly divided, which did not receive serum (see Table 12). This latter series of cases is listed elsewhere under the section on Epidemiology (see page 23).

TABLE 12.—TYPE I CASES TREATED WITH AND WITHOUT SPECIFIC SERUM. NUMBER AND PERCENTAGE OF DEATHS BY AGE GROUP

	10 to 49 years of age			50 years of age and over		
	Cases	Deaths	Per cent Fatality rate	Cases	Deaths	Per cent Fatality rate
Treated with serum*	432	36	8.3	65	20	30.8
Not treated with serum**	149	32	21.5	32	18	56.3

* 7 cases not included as age unknown.
** 9 cases not included as age unknown or under 10 years old.

As shown in Table 12, early specific serum treatment decreases the fatality rate of Type I cases in all age groups studied, but the most marked saving of lives occurs in the younger patients. (Most Type I pneumonias occur in young persons, as will be noted below.)

Bacteremia: Of the 504 Type I Special Group cases, blood cultures were made in 259 or 51.4 per cent. Ordinarily such cultures were taken only once and this was done prior to serum administration. In 5 cases the cultures were not satisfactory; of the 254 remaining, 61 or 24 per cent were positive. Patients with positive cultures had a fatality rate about five times as high as those with negative cultures, as shown in Table 13.

TABLE 13.—TYPE I SPECIAL GROUP CASES. NUMBER AND PERCENTAGE OF DEATHS IN CASES WITH AND WITHOUT BACTEREMIA

	Cases	Died	Per cent fatality rate
Negative blood cultures	193	10	5.2
Positive blood cultures	61	16	26.2
Total	254		

Empyema: Of the 504 Type I Special Group cases, 37 or 7.4 per cent developed empyema. This complication was about three times as frequent in patients with positive blood cultures as in those whose cultures were sterile, as shown in Table 14.

TABLE 14.—TYPE I SPECIAL GROUP CASES. INCIDENCE OF EMPYEMA
IN CASES WITH AND WITHOUT BACTEREMIA

	Number of cases	Empyema Number	Per cent
Negative blood cultures	193	12	6.2
Positive blood cultures	61	12	19.7

Time: The fatality rate in pneumonia is shown above to vary markedly with age and the presence or absence of bacteremia. The time of beginning specific serum treatment is also of great importance, as may be seen in Table 15.

TABLE 15.—TYPE I SPECIAL GROUP CASES. NUMBER AND PERCENTAGE OF
DEATHS BY DAY ON WHICH SERUM TREATMENT WAS BEGUN

Day of illness treatment begun	Cases	Died	Per cent fatality rate
1	50	3	6.0
2	162	16	9.9
3	165	13	7.9
4	127	24	18.9
Total	504	56	11.1

The advantage of early treatment is apparent.

Other Data: The average age of the total 599 Type I cases was 34.3 years, 87 per cent occurred in patients 10 to 49 years of age, and 69 per cent were in males.

Dosage: The *average* dose of specific serum in cubic centimeters given the 504 Type I Special Group cases was 74 cc. per patient. An increasing serum potency and a better understanding of the use of serum has permitted a steady decrease in the volume of serum used per patient, with a resultant reduction in the cost per patient. In 1931 the average dose was 99 cc. per patient, and by 1935 this had been lowered to 54 cc. per patient, a reduction of over 40 per cent.

Dosage in Units: Within the past few years the National Institute of Health set a standard for the unit of antipneumococcic serum. On reviewing the 504 Special Group Type I cases, it was found that the dose in terms of the present unit (taking N.I.H. serum P11 as a standard) could be determined in 429 cases and averaged 95,976 units per patient. Dividing such cases into groups by the number of units of serum given shows that, though the average dose in cubic centimeters was decreased by nearly one-half, the number of units given in the smaller volume of serum used in 1935 was actually as much as or more than that given in the early part of the Study.

Additional analysis of these 429 cases which received serum of known potency suggests that the average dosage, at least for many cases, may be still further reduced without harm, as illustrated by the results shown in Table 16. A reduction in the dosage should probably be limited to uncomplicated cases in young patients with negative blood cultures whose serum treatment is begun early in their illness.

TABLE 16.—TYPE I SPECIAL GROUP CASES. NUMBER AND PERCENTAGE OF
DEATHS BY DOSE OF SERUM GIVEN IN UNITS

Serum dosage in units	Cases	Died	Per cent Fatality rate	Average dose in units
12,000-80,000	164	16	9.8	54,412
81,000-150,000	218	20	9.2	101,906
151,000 and over*	47	11	23.4	212,653
Total	429	47	11.0	95,976

* The higher dosage of serum used in the patients here was due to the fact that nearly every patient in this group had some serious complicating condition, and many had bacteremia as well. Note the high fatality rate in this group.

A more detailed analysis of the 429 Type I Special Group cases in which the dosage of serum in units was known is given in Table 17. This presents the dosage used both by volume of serum given and the average dose in units, as well as the fatality rates of the cases by years. The decrease in the average volume of serum given yearly is shown, as is the change of the dose in units. While there is an indication of a gradual increase in the fatality rate, it is probably unsafe to lay too much stress upon the fatality rates of individual years, as shown in Table 17, for it has long been known that such rates may vary markedly from year to year.* In considering the optimum dose of antibody in units, it would seem best to refer to Table 16.

TABLE 17.—TYPE I SPECIAL GROUP CASES. NUMBER AND PERCENTAGE OF
DEATHS BY DOSE OF SERUM BY VOLUME AND NUMBER OF UNITS
GIVEN IN DIFFERENT YEARS

Year	Total cases	Number died	Per cent fatality rate	Average dose in cc.	Total amount serum given in units	Average dose in units
1931	8	—	0.0	74.8	681,720	85,215
1932	78	5	6.4	76.2	4,821,825	61,818 }*
1933	119	10	8.4	82.4	10,996,450	92,407
1934	122	17	13.9	68.1	14,467,000	118,582
1935	102	15	14.7	54.0	10,206,900	100,068
Total	429	47	11.0	70.5	41,173,895	95,976 Average

* 327 cases with 32 deaths = 9.8 per cent fatality rate with 94,700 units average.

At present the routine initial dosage advised is 60,000 units for Type I cases and 100,000 units for Type II cases (see subsequent tables for Type II cases). Arrangements have been made to dispense an additional 60,000 units to such Type I or II cases who have a bacteremia, a poor temperature response, or are pregnant or have been delivered within the previous seven days. This dosage for Type I or II cases may later be found to be somewhat too low, but there is reason to believe that for average cases, and especially those treated early, it will be found satisfactory.

At the termination of this Study in 1935 it appeared from the results obtained and from those reported by the Therapeutic Trials Committee of the Medical Research Council in Great Britain (Lancet, 1:290, February 10, 1934) that for the first time the dose of serum required,

* The fatality rate of 10.9 per cent of the total 724 Special Group Type I cases at hand December 1936 indicates that the apparent steady rise in the fatality rates by years as shown in Table 17 has not been maintained.

within moderate limits, for the usual Type I or II case could be stated in units. It seemed probable, as is since becoming apparent, that this would do much to lower the cost of serum treatment per case and place this mode of therapy on a sounder basis.

Type II Cases

The number of Type II Special Group cases on which data are available is still so small that the results shown in some of the following tables must be viewed with caution.

TABLE 18.—NUMBER OF CASES AND DEATHS AND FATALITY RATE OF SPECIAL GROUP AND OTHER TYPE II CASES

	Cases	Died	Per cent fatality rate
Special Group*	136	37	27.2
Others—received less serum or treated later than cases above	21	8	38.1
Total	157	45	28.6

* As of December 1936, the number of Special Group Type II cases was 191 with 45 or 23.6 per cent of deaths.

Of interest in connection with the cases in Table 18 is the fact that the series of 136 Special Group Type II cases is the largest series of early-treated cases of this type ever reported and one of the largest single series of serum-treated Type II cases to be reported. The fatality rate of 27.2 per cent in the early treated group compares favorably with that of 30.6 per cent for 670 Type II cases treated with serum at various periods during their illness as reported in the American and Canadian literature since 1913, and with that of 41 per cent for 992 cases of this type not given serum collected from the American and Canadian literature (15).

Age: A division of the 136 Type II Special Group cases into age groups is shown in Table 19. A fatality rate of 21.4 per cent in the younger patients as compared with a rate of 46.7 per cent in the older ones indicates the importance of age in influencing the prognosis in such cases. No suitable series of cases not given serum is available for comparison with the results in treated cases. As remarked above in the section on Epidemiology (see page 23), the 49 Massachusetts Type II cases not receiving serum, here shown in Table 19, cannot be regarded as illustrating the usual outcome for Type II cases. They are included here, however, for the sake of completion.

TABLE 19.—TYPE II CASES TREATED WITH AND WITHOUT SPECIFIC SERUM. NUMBER AND PERCENTAGE OF DEATHS BY AGE GROUP

	10 to 49 years of age			50 years of age and over		
	Cases	Deaths	Per cent fatality rate	Cases	Deaths	Per cent fatality rate
Treated with serum*	103	22	21.4	30	14	46.7
Treated without serum**	38	5	13.2	11	6	54.5

* 3 cases not included: 1 under 10 years old, and age not stated in 2.
** 2 cases not included as under 10 years old.

Bacteremia: Of the 136 Type II Special Group cases, blood cultures were made in 80 or 59 per cent. In 2 the cultures were not satisfactory. Of the 78 remaining, 24 or 31 per cent were positive. Patients with positive cultures had a fatality rate over three times as high as those with negative cultures.

TABLE 20.—TYPE II SPECIAL GROUP CASES. NUMBER AND PERCENTAGE OF DEATHS IN CASES WITH AND WITHOUT BACTEREMIA

	Cases	Died	Per cent fatality rate
Negative blood cultures	54	9	16.7
Positive blood cultures	24	13	54.2
Total	78		

Empyema: Of the 136 Type II Special Group cases, 9 or 6.6 per cent developed empyema. The incidence of this complication was about three times as high in cases with positive blood cultures as in others whose cultures were sterile.

TABLE 21.—TYPE II SPECIAL GROUP CASES. INCIDENCE OF EMPYEMA IN CASES WITH AND WITHOUT BACTEREMIA

	Number of cases	Empyema Number	Per cent
Negative blood cultures	54	3	5.6
Positive blood cultures	24	4	16.7

Time: The time of beginning specific serum treatment is known to be an important factor in influencing the case fatality rate. This is not clearly shown in Table 22, probably because the individual groups considered are too small to be significant.

TABLE 22.—TYPE II SPECIAL GROUP CASES. NUMBER AND PERCENTAGE OF DEATHS BY DAY ON WHICH SERUM TREATMENT WAS BEGUN

Day of illness treatment begun	Cases	Died	Per cent fatality rate
1	21	7	33.3
2	45	13	28.9
3	42	9	21.4
4	28	8	28.6
Total	136	37	27.2

Other Data: The average age of the total 157 Type II cases was 37.4 years, 78 per cent occurred in patients 10 to 49 years of age, and 80 per cent were in males.

Dosage: The average dose of specific serum given the 136 Type II Special Group cases was 113 cc. per patient. The volume of serum given per patient decreased 45 per cent, or from 142 cc. used in 1931 to the 1935 average of 78 cc. per patient.

Dosage in Units: Due to fluctuations which apparently occurred in the serums used as a standard against which all lots of the serum used during the Study were tested, it is impossible to be strictly accurate concerning the exact number of units of antibody given the Type II cases.

(Workers elsewhere than in this State have experienced a similar difficulty. This was commented on by Hartley and Smith, League of Nations Quarterly Bulletin of the Health Organization, Special Number, pp. 48, 65, January 1935.) The average dosage below stated for Type II cases is the *minimum* such patients received, and it is possible that the serum given them was even more potent than the figures indicate. This would mean that the average dose per case, as stated, may be somewhat too low.

Of the 136 Type II Special Group cases treated, the dose in units could be calculated in 115. These averaged 53,456 units per case. (Allowing for the discrepancy noted above, the average per case may actually have been from 1.5 to 5 times this amount.) When the dose for Type II cases averages or exceeds the minimum of 100,000 units now advised, it is probable that the fatality rate will be lowered considerably below the present figure of 27.2 per cent for the Special Group cases.*

A division of the 115 Special Group cases in which the dose in units could be calculated into groups treated with varying numbers of units of antibody is of some interest, though the groups are still small. This is shown in Table 23.

TABLE 23.—TYPE II SPECIAL GROUP CASES. NUMBER AND PERCENTAGE OF DEATHS BY DOSE OF SERUM GIVEN IN UNITS

Dose in units	Cases	Died	Per cent fatality rate	Average dose in units
1,280-40,000	60	14	23.3	19,471
41,000-100,000	37	12	32.4	70,676
101,000-150,000	15	3	20.0	117,473
151,000 and over**	3	2	66.7	200,667
Total	115	31	27.0	53,456

** This larger dosage was given a few patients who had a persistent bacteremia or other complicating factor present. The severity of the cases is reflected in their high fatality rate.

An additional analysis of the cases in Table 23 is shown in Table 24. This presents the dosage used both by volume of serum given and the average dose in units, with the fatality rates of the cases by years. The decrease in the average volume of serum given yearly is shown, as is the change of the dose in units. It is probably unsafe to lay too much emphasis on the fatality rates obtained in individual years, for the number of cases treated in any year is small, and the fatality rate of pneumonia due to the different types of pneumococci may vary spontaneously from year to year. In attempting to determine the optimum dose of antibody in units, it is believed that the figures for 1935 in Table 24 are the most satisfactory ones for the purpose. Even so, the number of cases treated in that year is too small to give significant findings. In this respect, however, when the British figures (mentioned on page 43) for Type II cases are also considered, more weight is lent to the belief that an average of 100,000 units should be considered a minimum for the treatment of such cases. Doubtless results better than those thus

* Evidence is now at hand in the shape of Type II Special Group cases treated subsequent to the analysis of the above cases in December 1935 that the use of an average dose more nearly approaching that advised is yielding a lower case fatality rate. Such data, however, are limited to cases treated during the course of one year, and, in consequence, additional information is necessary to confirm this view. The findings of Finland and Dowling (Am. J. M. Sc. 191:658, May 1936) also suggests the effectiveness of larger doses of specific antibody in Type II pneumonia.

far obtained in Type II cases will result from the use of an even larger amount of antibody. The larger doses appear especially needed by patients who have complicating conditions present, such as pregnancy, or have an unusually severe infection or bacteremia, or are treated late in their illness, and by patients who are fifty or more years of age.

TABLE 24.—TYPE II SPECIAL GROUP CASES. NUMBER AND PERCENTAGE OF DEATHS BY DOSE OF SERUM BY VOLUME AND NUMBER OF UNITS GIVEN IN DIFFERENT YEARS

Year	Total cases	Number died	Per cent fatality rate	Average dose in cc.	Total amount serum given in units	Average dose in units
1931	3	—	0.0	80.0	14,800	4,933
1932	14	5	35.7	143.0	367,140	26,224 |*
1933	33	7	21.2	127.8	834,250	25,280
1934	28	8	28.6	107.7	1,564,000	55,857
1935	37	11	29.7	81.7	3,367,200	91,005
Total	115	31	27.0	108.7	6,147,390	53,456 Average

* 78 cases with 20 deaths = 25.6 per cent fatality rate with 35,643 units average.

Lives Saved

It is possible to estimate the number of lives saved during the course of this Study by the adequate early use of serum in Type I and II cases. The usual fatality rate without serum therapy is 25 per cent for Type I and 41 per cent for Type II cases. These rates may be applied to the number of cases in the Type I and II Special Groups and the resulting figures compared with those obtained in these treated cases. This is shown in Table 25.

TABLE 25.—TYPE I AND II SPECIAL GROUP CASES. EXPECTED AND ACTUAL NUMBER OF DEATHS AND ESTIMATED NUMBER OF LIVES SAVED

Type	Number of Special Group cases	Expected deaths	Actual deaths	Estimated number of lives saved
I	504	126	56	70
II	136	56	37	19
Total	640	182	93	89

It has been estimated that the widespread use of specific antipneumococcic serum in pneumonia due to pneumococci of Types I and II alone might save in the neighborhood of 18,000 lives a year in this country (Heffron: New England J. Med. 214:222, January 30, 1936).

Type III Cases

In all, 28 Type III cases received varying amounts of the Type I and Type II antiserum used with 7 or 25 per cent of deaths. No evidence of a specific or non-specific therapeutic response was noted in this small group of cases. In these 28 cases, blood cultures were made in 15 or 53.6 per cent. Of these 15, 3 or 20 per cent were positive.

Group IV Cases

In all, 128 Group IV cases received varying amounts of the Type I and Type II specific serum used with 23 or 18 per cent of deaths. In a few of these cases some clinical improvement apparently occurred after serum administration. Such results, however, were scarce and not reproducible in successive cases. Errors in typing might, of course, have been the explanation. Blood cultures were done in 76 or 59.4 per cent of the cases. In 3 of these the results were not satisfactory. Of the remaining 73, 9 or 12.3 per cent were positive.

Miscellaneous Cases

In all, 44 cases in this group received varying amounts of the Type I and Type II antiserum used. Either no typing was done in these cases or else bacteriologic examination of the sputum showed the patient to be infected with some organism other than a pneumococcus. These cases were of no special interest or value.

Pneumococcus Meningitis

Records were obtained of 17 cases of pneumoccocus meningitis (see Table 26), all of which were given varying amounts of the Type I and Type II antiserum in use.

TABLE 26.—CASES OF PNEUMOCOCCUS MENINGITIS BY PNEUMOCOCCUS TYPE

Type	Number of cases
I	6
II	2
III	3
Group IV	5
Type undetermined	1
Total	17

Only 2 of the 17 cases listed in Table 26 recovered. One of the recovered cases was a Type I and received 150 cc. of serum, and the other, which received 125 cc. of serum, was due to a pneumococcus of undetermined type.

Serum Reactions

Patients with known or demonstrable sensitivity to horse serum were almost invariably excluded from the groups treated with specific serum.

Deaths: Among the 956 cases receiving varying amounts of concentrated antipneumococcic serum, 4 or 0.4 per cent died probably as a result of a serum reaction.* One of these deaths followed an immediate allergic reaction, and the remaining three followed chill reactions. These latter deaths occurred before the monkey test for detecting lots of serum likely to give rise to chill reactions in patients under treatment was introduced. This test, incidentally, has proved of great value and is further discussed in the Antitoxin and Vaccine Laboratory section of this report (see page 66).

---

* No additional deaths of this nature have occurred in cases treated subsequent to the analysis of the 956 cases here noted in December 1935. As of December 1936, at least 1313 cases have received varying amounts of serum since the beginning of 1931. Basing the proportion of fatal serum accidents (4 in all) upon this larger number of cases, their incidence has decreased to 0.3 per cent.

Allergic Reactions: Reactions of this nature occurred in 77 or 8.1 per cent of the 956 cases treated with specific serum. The large majority of these were mild or moderate and were easily controlled by the use of epinephrine.

Chill Reactions: These include all reactions in which a chill occurred and were reported in 196 or 20.5 per cent of the total 956 cases treated. They have been less severe and only about half as frequent since the monkey test has been routinely used to detect those lots of serum likely to be chill-producing. Such lots are withheld from general distribution.

It has been said, and some believe, that the occurrence of a chill reaction is beneficial in pneumonia and aids in decreasing the case fatality rate. For years Cole has contended that this is not so, but no figures available have any bearing on the matter. When the Type I Special Group cases were analyzed in July 1935, there were found to be 406 Type I cases in that group. A division of these into cases with or without chill reactions and their corresponding fatality rates are of interest (see Table 27).

TABLE 27.—TYPE I SPECIAL GROUP CASES TO JULY 1935. CASE FATALITY RATE BY THE PRESENCE OR ABSENCE OF A CHILL REACTION

	Cases	Per cent fatality rate
Having chill reactions	75	9.3
Without chill reactions	325	9.8
Total	400*	

* Does not include 6 cases in which no statement was made as to whether chill reaction occurred or not.

The difference between the fatality rate of 9.3 per cent for cases having chill reactions and that of 9.8 per cent for those without such reactions is small and insignificant. These figures give substance to the statement that chill reactions appear to have no definite value and probably do not decrease the case fatality rate of patients experiencing them.

From the clinical standpoint, one of the biggest problems confronting the more general use of specific serum for the treatment of pneumonia is the frequently encountered fear of untoward reactions. It is doubtful whether it will be possible to greatly reduce the incidence of allergic reactions unless new sensitivity tests are devised; but it is possible that with improvements in the serum the incidence of chill reactions may be markedly decreased. This would be of great value, for it would facilitate a more widespread use of serum with the result that many more lives would be saved each year. Many lots of antipneumococcic serum are practically free of chill-producing properties.

Serum Sickness: Serum sickness or serum disease has been mild and was reported as occurring in 163 or 17.5 per cent* of the 956 cases treated. Cases which received the largest doses of serum had serum sickness oftenest, as is shown in Table 28, which lists data on *recovered* cases up to July 1935.

* The figure of 22.1 per cent for the incidence of serum sickness as shown in Table 28 is probably more nearly accurate as it is based upon recovered cases only.

TABLE 28.—INCIDENCE OF SERUM SICKNESS IN RECOVERED CASES OF
PNEUMONIA TREATED WITH SERUM, BY DOSE OF SERUM USED

Dose of serum used	Recovered cases	Cases with serum sickness reported Number	Per cent
1-15 cc.	21	1	4.8
16-45 cc.	98	17	17.3
46-75 cc.	350	74	21.1
76-105 cc.	83	24	28.9
106-150 cc.	58	15	25.9
151 cc. and over	43	13	30.2
Total	653	144	22.1

V—RESULT OF PLAN FOR DECENTRALIZING SERVICE

In pneumonia, early bacteriologic diagnosis and early specific serum treatment involve the prompt cooperation of physicians and laboratory workers. In the past, to obtain this cooperation early, when most needed, was usually impossible outside of Boston and was seldom easy even in this city. The whole process of typing and serum treatment is a somewhat complex procedure. It had previously been carried out successfully only under centralized control in a few large hospitals; but most patients arrived at these hospitals too late to obtain the maximum benefit of this form of treatment.

For the people, then, to obtain the greatest value of this form of treatment, it was necessary to make it available in the smaller hospitals of the State and to patients in their homes. This meant a decentralization of service. Whether this could be accomplished without impairing the quality of the diagnostic and therapeutic service necessary was unknown. There is now reason to believe that this has been accomplished and with a considerable degree of success.

As discussed above under the section on Education (page 25), it was found possible to get the personal attention of a larger proportion of the physicians in the State outside of Metropolitan Boston than in that area. Apparently more physicians in the outlying districts belong to their local District Medical Societies and attend meetings of these than is the case in and around Boston. As a result, by speaking before the District Medical Societies, a much larger proportion of the physicians in the State was reached directly in the outlying districts than in Boston.

In the operation of the collaborator or consultant system, which was used exclusively for the first three years in carrying out the Pneumonia Study, it was necessary for the ordinary physician, in order to obtain specific serum for his patients, to call in consultation one of the designated collaborators in his area. The duties of the collaborator called were to confirm the clinical diagnosis, institute serum treatment or instruct the physician how to do this, and send sputum or other material for typing to the laboratory of the nearby hospital, whose technician had been especially trained in typing. The collaborator was also responsible for returning to this Department a complete record of the case treated.

In some respects this was a precarious system, and much depended on the local situation, medical and otherwise, and the popularity, quality, and integrity of the physicians designated as collaborators. The Advisory Committee on Pneumonia rendered essential service in assisting in the selection of the collaborators. Even so, some criticism of the whole plan was aroused. In some instances other physicians feared losing their patients to the collaborator called. Actually, however, such an occurrence was rare. The necessity for the collaborator system was explained in detail at various meetings, and the need of obtaining records more complete than the general physician could be asked for was pointed out. The fact that the project was of an experimental nature and afforded many physicians the opportunity of taking part in it aided the progress of the Study.

In some areas organized for this work the plan was very successful and collaborators were freely called. In other areas individual collaborators were freely used while other collaborators in the same area were never called. And in a few districts almost the only cases treated were those occurring in the private practice of the collaborators themselves. The majority of collaborators treated one or more cases. They were called in consultation by 229 other physicians and, together with these, were responsible for treating 540 cases.

As originally planned, if patients could pay for the collaborator's services, they were expected to do so; but if patients were unable to pay their fee, it was agreed that $15 and six or eight cents a mile for mileage should be paid to collaborators from the Pneumonia Study budget for each case seen. It is of interest that of the 540 cases treated in conjunction with a collaborator's services, such fees were paid for 403 cases (about 75 per cent). Figures relating to these fees are shown in Table 29.

TABLE 29.—FEES PAID COLLABORATORS DURING PNEUMONIA STUDY, BY YEARS

Year	Cases treated	Amount for mileage	Consultant fees	Total
1931	5	$ 0.84	$ 75.00	$ 75.84
1932	92	85.77	1380.00	1465.77
1933	111	62.04	1665.00	1727.74*
1934**	128	83.22	1920.00	2003.22
1935	67	27.12	1005.00	1032.12
Total	403	$258.99	$6045.00	$6304.69

* Telephone, 70 cents.
** In this year reorganization of collaborator areas was begun on a large scale, and by the end of 1935 the collaborator system was, no longer in use.

The largest number of cases treated by any collaborator was 60. with 55, 42, 25, and 24 the next largest numbers. Smaller numbers of cases were treated by many other collaborators, and 26 apparently treated no cases. Many of the latter, however, were associated with other collaborators who did treat cases, and in many *known* instances supplied sound advice at critical moments. In consequence, it is impossible to clearly separate those treating and those not treating cases, as essentially every one had a finger in the pie some place. Further, some of the last collaborator areas formed in 1933 were in existence as such but a relatively short time when they were reorganized on the new plan and serum was made available to all physicians equally.

In any event, of the total 956 records of cases treated from January 1931 through December 12, 1935, the distribution by physicians known to be directly concerned in their serum treatment was as shown in Table 30.

TABLE 30.—MASSACHUSETTS PHYSICIANS CONCERNED IN THE SERUM TREATMENT OF 956 CASES OF PNEUMONIA

Physicians calling collaborators	229
Collaborators called	53
Boston consultants called	8
Physicians treating cases alone	96
Total	386

As seen in Table 30, 386 Massachusetts physicians were concerned directly in the treatment of the 956 cases. Also, of the total number of cases, several hundred were treated on the wards of large hospitals. The number of physicians who observed the treatment and progress of these cases is unknown.

The distribution of cases treated in Boston hospitals was as listed in Table 31.

TABLE 31.—CASES OF PNEUMONIA TREATED IN BOSTON HOSPITALS WITH VARYING AMOUNTS OF SERUM, BY HOSPITAL

Hospital	Cases Treated
Boston City	219
Massachusetts General	44
Peter Bent Brigham	21
Beth Israel	5
Carney	1
Total	290

A few other cases were treated in some of the smaller Boston hospitals. A tabulation of the total 956 cases shows that over 65 per cent were treated outside of the large Boston hospitals. Nearly all of these were treated in homes or hospitals outside of Boston.

In the old collaborator areas the number of Type I and Type II cases treated averaged about 10 per cent of the *estimated* number of cases of these types ocurring there. This figure varied greatly, however; and in some areas the bulk of the Type I and Type II cases was treated, while in others a very small percentage was treated. In view of the results obtained, the collaborator system might possibly be regarded as only 10 per cent effective. This, however, is somewhat of a delusion, for the proportion of the Type I and Type II cases occurring in any considerable area which might be treated if serum were generally available was not and still is not known. Then, too, the intensive educational work concentrated on collaborators has taken time for digestion, but information as to the value of treatment with specific serum has been spread and is obviously seeping into other physicians in their communities. This, like-

wise, takes time. Additional periodic stimuli are needed to keep alive
and progressing the interest aroused. On the whole, it would appear
that the collaborator system has been fairly successful.

VI—BUDGET AND PERSONNEL

The amount of money granted by the Commonwealth Fund to
support this Study and the total amounts actually spent in the course of
work are listed in Table 32.

TABLE 32.—AMOUNT OF MONEY GRANTED BY THE COMMONWEALTH FUND
AND THE AMOUNT SPENT DURING THE PNEUMONIA STUDY, BY YEARS

Year	Amount Granted	Amount Spent
1931	$36,000	$28,441.15
1932	36,000	33,212.54
1933	36,000	29,780.76
1934	34,000	28,371.28
1935	30,000	23,301.66
Total	$172,000	$143,107.39

During the Pneumonia Study generous use was made of various
members of the State Department of Public Health as well as of numerous
of the facilities of this Department. The entire Study was conducted under
the Divisions of Communicable Diseases and Biologic Laboratories. The
additional full-time personnel employed to carry out the Study consisted
of a Field Director and a secretary, a senior bacteriologist, two junior
bacteriologists, two laboratory helpers, and an animal man. A junior
bacteriologist was employed part time, as were a few medical students.

Beginning as early as the fall of 1934, various items on the budget were taken over by this Department. By the latter part of 1935 all
items on the budget which were to continue following the termination of
the Study were taken over by the Department. This gradual take-over
of essential items onto the Department budget facilitated the continuance
of typing work and the production of serum without undue sudden strain
and confusion at the end of 1935 such as might otherwise have occurred.

VII—GENERAL SUMMARY AND CONCLUSIONS

The Pneumonia Study in Massachusetts was begun in January
1931 and ended December 31, 1935. Information of value to laboratory
workers, physicians, and departments of health has been obtained.

The important findings of the Study are considered under several
headings below.

(1) Epidemiological

Over 60,000 death certificates of patients dying of various forms
of respiratory disease were examined. The data obtained yielded information of but little value. This was also true of the data obtained from
the examination of over 8,000 hospital records of patients having pneumonia. Epidemiologic studies were made of cases, carriers, and contacts.
Typing was carried out through most of the higher types, and for the

first time it was clearly shown that, of all the types, only Type I and Type
II were of special epidemiologic significance. Type I was found twenty
times as prevalent in immediate family contacts of Type I cases as in
the population at large, and Type II ten times as prevalent in its contacts.
Investigation of cases showed that about 20 per cent of family contacts
with Type I or II cases became carriers of these types, while only about
2 per cent of hospital contacts became carriers of such types. It was
found that some factor in addition to contact alone was needed to determine the transfer of Type I or II pneumococci from patients to contacts,
and this factor appeared to be the presence in such contacts of upper
respiratory infections such as the common cold. Persons with colds in
contact with Type I or II cases were likely to become carriers of these
types, and the carrier state might persist for weeks.

A study of the incidence of all thirty-two types of pneumococci
in the specimens sent for examination from patients with respiratory
disease showed that, in nearly 10,000 such specimens examined, Types I,
III, VIII, II, V, and VII, in this order, were the six commonest and made
up 67 per cent of all specimens containing pneumococci which could be
typed. Data were gathered on the case fatality rates by types of 333
cases of lobar pneumonia cared for at home and of 367 others treated in
hospitals. None of these 705 cases received specific serum or vaccine
treatment.

(2) Educational

Efforts were made to acquaint physicians with the newer information available regarding pneumococcus typing, serum concentration
and its relation to dosage, and the technic of treating patients with serum. Graduate courses, many special meetings, chiefly symposiums, and
District Medical Society meetings were held in nearly all parts of the
State to present these matters to the profession and to acquaint them
with the Pneumonia Program. In addition, some similar groups in
various other states were addressed, and several state and national medical societies were informed of this work. In several instances reprints
of articles emanating from this Study were sent to all physicians in the
State, and at times articles from other sources giving a more detailed
discussion of the specific serum treatment of pneumonia were sent to
pneumonia collaborators and to interested physicians. Instruction sheets
were supplied to cooperating laboratory technicians, who were also furnished cards upon which to record the findings of their typing work.
Instruction sheets and record blanks were given physicians responsible
for the serum treatment of cases. Lantern slides and wall charts were
made and used for lectures. Exhibits were held at State Medical Society
meetings. A handbook on Lobar Pneumonia and Serum Therapy, with
Special Reference to the Massachusetts Pneumonia Study (15) was published. Two large monographs, one on the pneumococcus and one on lobar pneumonia, are being prepared.

(3) Clinical

During the first three years of the Study, seventeen especially
selected areas were organized for intensive work. In these, typing was

done in twenty-eight hospitals by thirty especially trained technicians, and serum was available through seventy-eight collaborators in these areas. In addition, there were eight hospitals in Boston from which serum was available, and typing was done in seven of these. This organization served approximately one-half the population of the State.

During the course of the whole Study, over ninety technicians were trained in typing. A thorough investigation of the various methods of typing was made. The important result of this was that the Neufeld method was found simple, rapid, and accurate, and was advised as a routine method of typing. This reduced the time required for typing in most cases to a matter of a few minutes.

In 1934 it was obvious that by the end of the Study in 1935, if the State took over the production and distribution of serum, it would have to be equally available to all physicians. It became apparent then that some new plan would have to be developed whereby the distribution of the serum dispensed could be restricted for use only in early Type I and Type II cases. Such a plan was evolved and has worked successfully. By the end of 1935 serum was equally available to all physicians in the State through the State Bacteriologic Laboratory and eight hospitals in Boston, as well as from fifty-seven hospitals outside of Boston, making a total of sixty-six depots in all.

There has been a continual increase in the number of typings done in this State since 1931. Typings are now being done in areas where previously none were being done. At the present rate, about three to four times as many typings are being done in the State annually as in 1931.

(4) Results In Treated Cases

From January 1931 through December 12, 1935, a total of 956 records of cases of lobar pneumonia treated with the Type I and Type II antiserum used were obtained and analyzed. Importantly, the results showed conclusively that serum can be used successfully by physicians in general practice throughout the State.

Large series of early treated Type I and Type II cases were collected. Of 504 Type I cases treated within the first four days of illness, only 56 or 11.1 per cent died. Of 136 Type II cases also treated early, 37 or 27.2 per cent died. A comparison of the fatality rates of these treated cases with the expected fatality rate of cases of the same type not receiving serum showed that the early use of serum brought about a considerable reduction in the fatality rate of the treated cases. It was estimated that the lives of eighty-nine patients were saved.

Further analysis of the cases showed that their fatality rates varied markedly with the age of the patient, the presence or absence of bacteremia, and the day of illness on which specific serum treatment was begun. During the course of the Study the average volume of serum used per patient decreased by nearly one-half, with a consequent lowering in the cost of the serum used per patient. The dose in units was calculated, and for the first time it was possible to state the dose in units required for the average Type I or Type II case when such treatment was begun within the first four days of illness. Information on the serum reactions occurring in the treated patients was obtained and studied. At the Antitoxin and Vaccine Laboratory a test was devised for using monkeys to detect lots of serum likely to give rise to chill reactions in humans.

(5) Decentralization of Service

In pneumonia, early bacteriologic diagnosis and early treatment are necessary if the maximum benefit of specific serum treatment is to be obtained. Whether or not this somewhat complex procedure could be carried out on a large scale without impairing the quality essential to success was unknown. Experience has shown, however, that this can be done fairly successfully. Pneumonia collaborators were used exclusively for the first three years of the Study. During the last two years a reorganization was carried out so that collaborators would not be necessary, and by the end of 1935 the services of collaborating physicians were entirely dispensed with and serum was made equally available to all physicians in the State. During the Study most of the seventy-eight collaborators treated one or more cases. They were called by 229 other physicians and, together with these, treated 540 cases. In addition, 96 other physicians also treated cases. A total of 386 physicians located in 98 towns in Massachusetts were responsible for the 956 cases treated; 213 patients (22 per cent) received treatment in their homes, and 742 in eighty hospitals of the State. (In one additional case the place of treatment was not stated.) In all, over 65 per cent of the cases were treated outside of the large Boston hospitals, and nearly all of these were treated in homes and hospitals elsewhere in the State.

(6) Budget

In none of the five years was the total amount of money annually granted by the Commonwealth Fund for this work spent. Items on the budget essential to the continuance of typing at the State Bacteriologic Laboratory and the production and distribution of serum by the Antitoxin and Vaccine Laboratory were taken over by the State before the end of 1935.

(7) Future Plans

The production and distribution of concentrated antipneumococcic serum for the treatment of Type I and Type II cases, and research allied to this, will be continued. Records of treated cases will continue to be collected and analyzed. Special attention will be given to the fatality rates of treated cases and to the optimum dose of serum needed in units. In addition, the State Bacteriologic Laboratory will continue to do routine typing for all thirty-two types and to give instruction in typing methods to interested technicians.* Outbreaks of pneumococcus infection will be investigated epidemiologically when the occasion affords.

---

* Typing will doubtless also continue to be done for all thirty-two types at the Boston City Hospital. It is likely that that hospital and the State Bacteriologic Laboratory will be the only places in the State in which such extensive typing will be carried out routinely. In several instances, however, typing may be carried on for some of the commoner of the higher types in other places as well.

Conclusions

Important discoveries have been made concerning the epidemiology of pneumococcus pneumonia. Extensive educational activities have been carried out and are bearing fruit in this and other states. Since the beginning of this Study, programs dealing with the study and serum treatment of pneumonia have been instituted in Connecticut, New York, Maine, and Michigan.*

Though no adequate measures for the prevention or control of pneumonia have yet been developed, physicians throughout Massachusetts are rapidly coming to the conclusion that something real is being offered for the treatment of current cases. The use of the collaborator system has shown that a decentralization of administrative control can be accomplished without great sacrifice of quality. A satisfactory plan has been evolved for distributing serum to all physicians for the treatment of their early cases of the proper type.

The specific serum treatment of patients in their homes and in hospitals throughout the State has resulted in a marked decrease in the expected fatality rate of early Type I and Type II cases of pneumococcus pneumonia. It has been demonstrated that serum can be successfully used by physicians in general practice.

The study and serum treatment of pneumococcus pneumonia on a large scale is a community problem and jointly concerns laboratory workers, physicians, and departments of health.

Further information is needed on the epidemiology of this disease, on the dose of specific serum required for its treatment, on the value of serum for the treatment of cases due to types other than I or II, and for the development of more satisfactory methods of serum production and concentration so as to yield a more potent serum as free as possible from chill-producing properties.

VIII—RECOMMENDATIONS

(1) Epidemiological

Every effort should be made to continue and to support the epidemiologic investigation of cases, contacts, and carriers. Outbreaks of pneumococcus infection should be investigated. Typing at the State Bacteriologic Laboratory should continue to be carried out for the thirty-two known types. In this way the occurrence of the various types of pneumococci in a large group of pneumonias and other respiratory infections can be followed month by month. This is particularly important in view of the fact that during the Study Types V, VII, and VIII were the three commonest higher types found, and evidence is accumulating (Bullowa and Wilcox: Type V paper, J. Clin. Investigation, 15:711, November 1936; Finland and Tilghman: Type V, New England J. Med. 215:1211, December 24, 1936; Bullowa: Type VII, Libman Anniversary Volume, Vol. I, N. Y., International Press, 1932, p. 283; Bullowa: Type VIII,

---

* During the course of 1936 it became apparent that the interest in pneumonia is widespread in this country, and investigations of various sorts are now in progress or are being contemplated by several other states as well.

J.A.M.A. 102:1560, May 12, 1934; Bullowa: Type VIII, Am. J. M. Sc.
190:65, July 1935) that specific serum is of value for the treatment of
pneumonia caused by any one of these types. The Department should
consider the possibility of supplying typing and therapeutic serum for
some of these types.*

(2) Educational

Some physician in the Division of Communicable Diseases should
keep in touch with the pneumonia work and maintain a record of the frequency of reactions and the fatality rate in the serum-treated cases (see
Clinical section, page 59). Periodic stimulation of the medical profession in regard to the problem of pneumonia and its treatment is needed.
For this purpose the official cooperation of the Massachusetts Medical
Society would be of great aid. That society should be requested to
appoint a special pneumonia committee and through it, if possible, official
sponsorship should be obtained for the use of specific serum in pneumonia. The medical profession should then be informed of this sponsorship by a notice sent to all District Medical Societies and published in the
New England Journal of Medicine.

A pneumonia committee of the Massachusetts Medical Society
could cooperate with representatives of the Department in many ways
and assist in obtaining suitable lay and professional publicity. During
the course of the Study no official lay publicity was given the fact that
the fatality rate of pneumonia due to certain types of pneumococci may
be reduced by the early adequate use of potent specific serum. It would
be desirable that a fair amount of carefully thought out lay publicity be
given this matter.

The special committee of the Massachusetts Medical Society, in
cooperation with representatives of this Department could assist in
spreading the best information available as to the value and proper use
of the various therapeutic agents and procedures advocated for the treatment of pneumonia. It could keep in touch with the current literature;
and, when especially valuable articles and real advances in our knowledge
concerning pneumonia and its treatment are available, the committee
should, through a letter to the New England Journal or by other suitable means, call the attention of the profession to such matters. The committee could arrange for and conduct scientific exhibits at various meetings, including the annual meeting of the Massachusetts Medical Society.

The medical profession, in general, was to a certain extent
aroused by the Pneumonia Study carried out during the five years of
1931 through 1935, and to a considerable degree is beginning to realize
that something can be done for pneumonia. It would be a great waste,
both of opportunity and of lives, if stimulation of this interest abruptly
ceases. While the Department alone could do much to keep this interest
alive, it would be far more satisfactory to have the official cooperation of
the State Medical Society in this work.

---

* As may be noted in the following report of the Antitoxin and Vaccine Laboratory, preparations are now under way in Massachusetts to produce and distribute specific serum for Types V, VII, and VIII.

(3) Clinical

The records returned to the Department of all cases treated should be kept in one place and made the responsibility of one individual. It would seem best to have such records cared for by someone at the Antitoxin and Vaccine Laboratory. In this way the Laboratory would be in constant touch with the results being obtained in the patients receiving serum.

Each record should be carefully looked over *as it comes in;* and if any important information is missing from it, a letter should at once be written to the responsible physician with a request that the additional information be supplied. From time to time questions appear on these records. It is important in continuing the interest of the physicians in the field that such questions be answered at once as adequately as is possible.

Experience has shown that when physicians are convinced that someone is really interested in the record forms they are asked to fill out and return to the Department, they are willing to cooperate and, where omissions occur, will gladly supply the information needed. If, however, the physicians believe that such records are simply a matter of red tape and nothing is done with them after they are received by the Department, their interest at once lags, with the result that the records are either filled out incompletely or not at all.

A plan was devised by Doctor Robinson, Director, Antitoxin and Vaccine Laboratory, for checking up physicians who receive serum from the various typing laboratories in the State but who do not send in records of the cases they treat. This plan was put into operation at the termination of the Study, and whenever a physician receives serum from the various cooperating laboratories, a note is made on a special card provided for that purpose and the card mailed at once to the Antitoxin and Vaccine Laboratory. If, within a reasonable period (say, four or five weeks), a record of the case treated is not received by the Laboratory, a letter is sent to the physician requesting information on the case. If this does not produce results, the physician's name is turned over to the proper District Health Officer who is to interview him and obtain the necessary information. In this way it should be possible to obtain approximately 95 per cent of the records of the cases treated each year in this State.

The records of the treated cases should be analyzed twice yearly, preferably in midwinter and in summer. Special attention should be given the total case fatality rate and variations of this with age, day of beginning serum treatment, and the presence or absence of bacteremia. The incidence of reactions and the dose of serum in units should be watched. Large numbers of cases will be dealt with, and experience has clearly shown that it is almost impossible to analyze the necessary data accurately if written in longhand on various work sheets. By far the simplest way of analyzing the treated cases is to fill out an especially prepared code sheet (a supply of these is available) for each record and to make a punch card from this. These cards can then be sorted mechanically and suitable tables prepared. Every year or two it would be advisable to publish the results obtained from the use of serum in the treated cases.

Hospitals: It would seem advisable to eliminate some of the smaller hospitals in areas close to larger ones from the list of those doing typing and giving out serum for the treatment of cases. The inclusion of some of these smaller hospitals, which may do only half a dozen typings or so a year, means a needless duplication of resources and a waste of the therapeutic serum inasmuch as each typing laboratory keeps its own supply of serum on hand.

Hospital Technicians: Experience has shown that among the hospitals in the State having laboratory technicians about 5 to 10 per cent change technicians each year. Some plan should be evolved for finding out at least twice a year which hospitals doing typing have employed new technicians. This information could easily be obtained through District Health Officers. Arrangements should be made to train the new technicians in pneumococcus typing and to inform them of the various bacteriologic procedures which can be used to assist physicians in the treatment of their cases and of the need of accurate bacteriologic work and proper records. The Department might offer to pay the transportation of such technicians to and from Boston if the hospital (or the technician) pays their expenses while they are here reviewing typing procedures at the State Bacteriologic Laboratory. It would seem, however, that the benefit to each community resulting from this training and the serum made available there would be sufficient to justify each local hospital in paying all expenses for its technician's training in typing. A period of three days at the State Laboratory is probably sufficient for training most technicians. Occasionally an exceptional technician is encountered who may need only a one-day review at the laboratory. This contact with the State Bacteriologic Laboratory is much more valuable than is at once apparent, for technicians are not only instructed in the proper methods of typing, but they also become acquainted with the personnel of the laboratory and obtain a bird's-eye view of what can be accomplished by the use of serum for the treatment of pneumonia.

It would seem highly desirable, for the time being at least, to refuse to send therapeutic antipneumococcic serum for distribution from hospitals whose technicians have not been trained in typing at the State Bacteriologic Laboratory. It is possible that in the future many of those schools which train technicians will place more emphasis on pneumococcus typing, with the result that their graduates may be more adequately trained in typing than they are at present. It would seem advisable to continue to supply technicians in the cooperating laboratories with instruction sheets listing the proper technic of the various methods of typing and from time to time with either reprints of or references to articles pertinent to typing work which may appear in the current literature.

(4) Antitoxin and Vaccine Laboratory

This laboratory should continue to supply Type I and II typing serum and also therapeutic antipneumococcic serum for cases of these types in which pneumonia has not been present longer than four days (see report of Antitoxin and Vaccine Laboratory, page 62). A new system for recording the amount of therapeutic serum sent out, used, and returned to the laboratory should be developed. At a later date, when the value of therapeutic serums for Types V, VII, and VIII, and perhaps some of the other types, has been clearly demonstrated, it might be advisable for this laboratory to undertake to obtain and distribute typing and therapeutic serum for such types. Unless a special study is conducted for the purpose of determining the value of serum for some of these higher types, it would seem advisable to wait until adequate proof of the value of such serums had been obtained before undertaking their production and distribution.*

The investigation of immunizing antigens begun during the Study should be continued with the hope of discovering a more satisfactory preparation, the use of which might yield a more potent and still cheaper therapeutic serum.

Probably the most important immediate challenge to the Laboratory, other than the continued production and distribution of the serums now in use, is that of making a serious attempt to investigate the properties of serum responsible for chill reactions. The occurrence of such reactions in from 10 to 20 per cent of pneumonia patients treated is unfortunate. This high incidence of chill reactions in treated cases, coupled with the fact that in some patients death has apparently resulted from the reaction, constitutes an extremely serious situation. The three deaths among the serum-treated cases (see page 48) which followed chill reactions occurred early in the Study before the monkey test was routinely used. Since then there have been no deaths attributable to chill reactions. Nevertheless, chill reactions continue to occur and are a cause of anxiety to many physicians. Every effort should be made to reduce the frequency of these reactions.

As investigation of a chemical nature has not identified the property of serum responsible for chill reactions, it appears of value to attack this problem from another angle. This might be done by finding a serum which would produce severe chills in monkeys and injecting a sufficient amount into such animals to cause death if possible. Careful and complete pathological examination of monkeys sacrificed in this manner might bring to light information of value which at present is not available. Insight into either the nature of the reacting material or proper methods for treating such reactions when they occur might thus be obtained.

In a review of the physiology of the nuclei of the hypothalmus, Fulton (New England J. Med. 207:60, July 14, 1932) reported some interesting animal experiments. Various animals were injected via different routes with pituitrin, pilocarpine, and atropine. The symptoms occurring during reactions to some of these drugs were not greatly different from those shown by certain patients experiencing chill reactions

---

* Because of the frequency with which pneumococci of Types V, VII, or VIII, are encountered in patients with respiratory disease, including pneumonia, as earlier mentioned, and as the result of accumulating evidence of the value of serums specific for these types for the treatment of pneumonia caused by them, preparations are now being made to produce and distribute such serums (see page 67).

following the exhibition of concentrated antipneumococcic serum. The effect of drugs for the prevention or treatment of chill reactions in monkeys might be investigated with profit.

These and similar investigations of this problem are sorely needed. Their conduct would probably require many experimental animals, adequate working facilities, and the cooperation of immunologists, pathologists, and pharmacologists. It is realized that the facilities at present available at the Antitoxin and Vaccine Laboratory do not appear adequate for carrying out these studies on such an extensive scale. The problem, however, is badly in need of solution, and encouragement should be offered to all who wish to tackle it.

IX—REPORT OF WORK CARRIED ON AT THE ANTITOXIN AND VACCINE LABORATORY 1931-1935

Under the original plans for the Massachusetts Pneumonia Study and Service, the Antitoxin and Vaccine Laboratory was given the following duties :
1) to produce therapeutic serums active against Types I and II pneumococci;
2) to produce diagnostic serums;
3) to investigate and improve methods for the production of therapeutic serums;
4) to investigate such other problems involving pneumococcus as are of interest to the purpose of the study; and
5) to assist in evaluating the results of serum therapy.

It is under these headings that the work of the years 1931-1935 will be described.

1. The Production of Therapeutic Serums

Prior to the beginning of the Study, small amounts of concentrated therapeutic serums active against Type I and Type II pneumococci had been produced in this laboratory and used in the State. Enough had been done to justify a belief that such serums were of value and to indicate that the methods then in use were open to improvement in nearly every process of manufacture. The changes introduced will be discussed more fully below.

At the beginning of the Study, eleven horses were under immunization. Enough horses were added to maintain a group of not less than fifteen and from these enough serum was obtained to furnish the following amounts of serum for distribution:

1931 ... 1,392 vials   1933 .... 2,849 vials   1935 ... 3,717 vials
1932 .... 2,591 vials   1934 .... 2,382 vials

During the early part of this period, the vials contained 15 cc. each, without regard to the potency of the serum, but when more satisfactory methods of potency testing became available, the content was usually 20,000 units of Type I antibody plus a variable amount of Type II antibody, in a volume of not over 15 cc. A small amount of serum has contained too little Type II antibody to be therapeutically useful, and another small amount has contained only Type II antibody. Except on two occasions serum of our manufacture was always available for distribution. These deficiencies were both due to difficulties encountered in processing, not to any lack of crude serum; and were overcome by the purchase and distribution of commercial serum (18 vials in 1932, 108 in 1933).

The number of vials distributed is not an accurate indication of the quantities of crude serum produced because of variations in volume concentration from lot to lot, and because of the amounts lost by unsatisfactory concentration methods. These points will be discussed below.

2. The Production of Diagnostic Serums

No attempt was made to produce agglutinating serums for all of the thirty-two types of pneumococci described by Miss Cooper. Supplies of some of these type serums were obtained from her, while our efforts were devoted to making serums for the types most frequently encountered.*

DIAGNOSTIC SERUMS — CUBIC CENTIMETERS DISTRIBUTED

Year	Horse Serums				Rabbit Serums				
	Type I	II	III	V**	I	II	III	V	VIII
1931	415	290	255	—	—	—	—	—	—
1932	1015	975	1080	325	—	—	—	—	—
1933	1270	1205	1325	300	57	57	57	—	—
1934	550	535	620	10	172	146	159	20	10
1935	565	590	620	—	240	220	194	49	56

** Serum obtained in bulk from New York City Department of Health. All other serum produced here.

The types chosen for manufacture are those of importance from the therapeutic standpoint (Types I and II), from the historical aspect (Type III), or from their close relationship to other types (Types V and VIII are closely related to Types II and III respectively). The introduction and general acceptance of the Neufeld Quellung reaction method of typing necessitated the production of typing serums in rabbits because the serums derived from horses are not suitable for use in this method.

3. The Investigation and Improvement of Methods for Producing Therapeutic Serums

Immunization of Horses: The production of satisfactory therapeutic serums is dependent first of all upon crude serums of high potency. These in turn are obtainable only if the immunity of the horses is developed to a high degree, so our first efforts were directed toward a study of immunization procedures. The details of this investigation, which dealt with the types of vaccine to inject and the number and interval of doses to give, have been published (10). Briefly, the results obtained led us to discontinue the use of vaccines killed by formalin in favor of those killed by heat, to continue the three-week schedule of injections, and to take routine bleedings nine days after the last dose in a course of injections.

Comparisons of the antigenic effect in mice of vaccines made from different strains of pneumococci were carried out, but gave such uncertain results that this work was discontinued. The test depends

---

* Diagnostic serums for Types I, II, III, V, VII and VIII are now or will soon be available, as it is planned to distribute therapeutic serums for all of these types except III.

upon the production of an active immunity which may be partly cellular, whereas in the immunization of horses the presence of antibodies in the serum is the important consideration. Antigenicity tests may be conducted in rabbits and the serum assayed for antibody content, but the expense involved makes this procedure seem impracticable.

The possibility of using vaccines containing a minimum amount of free capsular material has been considered. A small group of horses was injected for over a year with vaccines washed relatively free from excess SSS. It was thought that such a procedure might result in higher titered serums and in a prolongation of the life of the horses. Although the quality of serums from these horses was good and there were no unusual untoward reactions from the vaccines, the lack of striking results and the extra labor involved led us to discontinue this experiment.

Another series of experiments dealt with the relative stability of pneumococcus vaccines prepared in different ways. It was found that organisms killed at 100°C. undergo essentially no autolysis during a period of over four months, while vaccines heated at 56°C. and those killed by the addition of formalin disintegrate very rapidly. It is hoped that the use of more stable vaccines will not only reduce the amount of labor but may also decrease the death rate of horses. Experience so far has fully justified this change in technic.

A certain number of horses were rested for about three months during the summers of 1934 and 1935 to determine whether an increase in serum potency and span of life would result. The numbers of horses rested, and those used as controls were too small to permit satisfactory statistical analyses.

The death rate in horses undergoing immunization is the cause of so much expense and annoyance that measures to lessen the death rate have been tried. These consisted in the general use of smaller doses of vaccine and in the injection of a quite small dose on the day preceding the regular courses of injections. By these means we delayed the death of our horses to the extent that the fifteen horses on hand at the end of the study had been under immunization an average of over nineteen months, or an average increase of not less than four months.

No definite statement can be made of the increase in potency of the crude serums obtained from our horses because of changes in methods of testing. There is, however, no doubt that there has been an increase.

Methods of Concentrating Serum: During the early part of the study the methods of potency testing were not sufficiently accurate to make a study of concentration methods particularly worth-while. We therefore followed the suggestions made by Doctor L. D. Felton, although a few lots were made by methods more or less our own. More recently we undertook an investigation of our own, which is still in progress, prompted by the apparently greater losses involved in the concentration of Type II antibody than in Type I. At present we are using Felton's alcohol method, and studying the effect of alcohol and of acid upon the antibodies. A method of separating antibody by dialysis is also under investigation.

The Testing of Serums for Potency and Safety: As was suggested earlier, adequate methods of potency testing are of fundamental importance. The method of choice would be simple, accurate, inexpensive, rapid, and preferably should not require the use of animals. After comparative trials of various *in vitro* methods, we found (17) that a relatively simple precipitin test yielded results of reasonable accuracy and with less effort than did agglutination tests or the more complicated precipitin tests proposed by Smith, Heidelberger, Felton and others. The *in vitro* methods, however, do not always give satisfactory results with concentrated serums.

Biological methods of testing have, in the minds of some, a more tangible quality than do test-tube reactions. For this reason, biological methods are usually considered a court of last resort although an increasing amount of evidence suggests that in many instances the result of a biological test may be largely fortuitous, and dependent upon the heredity and the numbers of the particular animals used. Be that as it may, biological methods are relied upon for the official assay of antipneumococcic serum. Researches by Parish, Trevan, Felton and Goodner provide adequate basis for explaining the difficulties encountered in testing antipneumococcic serum by the method now in use; and when one compares the present method with those in use at the beginning of the Pneumonia Study, the difficulties we encountered then are easily understandable. The method now in use, which has had the approval of the National Institute of Health since January, 1934, requires the use of ten mice on each of three doses of a standard serum and the same number of mice on each of three doses of serum under test, all mice being injected with a constant amount of virulent pneumococcus culture. The test is repeated until comparable results are obtained. This method differs from those used earlier in one or more of those respects (the inclusion of a standard serum, the use of more than one dose of serum, and the number of mice per dose of serum) which tend to increase accuracy. Previous to the adoption of this method by the National Institute of Health it was impossible to compare the products of various laboratories except by direct test or even to compare the products of the same laboratory if prepared at different times. Consequently there was no satisfactory method of determining the proper dosages for therapeutic use.

Besides the methods employing mice, trial was made of a rabbit method devised by Goodner. Although theoretically interesting and important, it proved to be impracticable because consistent results were unobtainable.

In this connection mention might be made of our attempt at mouse breeding, because the importance of the idea behind it is becoming widely accepted. The advantages of an inbred strain of mice in eliminating at least some of the inaccuracies and discrepancies of the mouse method of testing seemed quite apparent because of work done by Irwin on the relative immunity of different races of rats to infection and by Hartley on the uniform susceptibility of an inbred strain of guinea pigs to diphtheria toxin. We therefore undertook to propagate an inbred strain of white mice for the pneumonia work. Although our effort was not successful, largely because of the impossibility of obtaining suitable personnel, yet the soundness of the idea is gaining general recognition as a result of Webster's extensive experiments with similar inbred strains.

Besides an adequate antibody content, therapeutic serums must also be as free as possible from chill-producing activity. Although apparently any antipneumococcic serum may give rise to a so-called chill reaction when injected into certain individuals, yet there is a good deal of difference in this respect in different batches of serum. Since these reactions may be extremely severe and perhaps fatal, a method of identifying such exceptional serums is necessary. At various times one or another chemical constituent of the serum has been suggested as the cause of these reactions, but at present such ideas are not accepted as correct. Much attention has been directed to this problem and a method (5, 13) of testing the serums in monkeys has been worked out and employed for about three years. This does not solve the problem entirely, for we are still in the dark as to why certain lots produce very few chills whereas other lots, made by the same methods, are so chill-productive as to be useless.

4. Investigation of Other Problems.

A number of other investigations were made of problems bearing on or growing out of our main purpose of producing a more satisfactory therapeutic serum. These will be mentioned briefly.

For the purpose of providing more satisfactory antigens for horse immunization, studies (11) were made of the lethal effect of sodium oleate and ricinoleate on pneumococci, and of methods for maintaining the virulence of pneumococci. Some effort was also expended in an attempt to maintain so-called S and R forms by cultural methods and to convert R forms to S.

Recently an apparent conversion of a Type V pneumococcus to a Type II has been under observation and the occurrence of this conversion confirmed (18). A relationship between these two types has long been known but we believe this is the first time a spontaneous conversion of one type into the other has been recognized.

The fermentative action of pneumococci of various types on glycogen of mammalian and invertebrate origin was compared (9). No differences were observed.

A strain of *Escherichia coli* was obtained which agglutinated with Type I antipneumococcic serum obtained from horses but not with that derived from rabbits. This serological curiosity was of interest because it had been isolated in a routine examination of sputum for pneumococci (16).

A number of batches of soluble specific substance (SSS) were made from various types of pneumococci. We hoped to be able to immunize horses and rabbits with these preparations or with the SSS chemically attached to proteins but extensive trials led to no striking results. There has been a good deal of use for these preparations in performing precipitin tests on our serums; and the experience gained in making SSS preparations may prove of value later.

Pneumococcus endotoxin was also prepared and attempts made to produce an antiserum against it, but without success.

5. Skin Tests in Horses and Rabbits

A study was started in May, 1935 of the reactions resulting from injections of various products of the pneumococcus into the skin of horses. The object of these experiments was to determine whether those horses likely to suffer severe reactions or to die abruptly following regular injections could be detected and preventive measures instituted. Several anomalous results were obtained and the study was continued in rabbits. Although the work is as yet incomplete it appears that there are several factors involved in the elicitation of skin reactions. The skin reaction in rabbits and horses to SSS appears to be the result of local antigen-antibody fixation, at least in part. This point is being studied further in connection with the production of rabbit serums for Neufeld diagnostic work. Since rabbits vary greatly in their antibody response, it may be possible to select, by this method, those animals which will be most valuable. Other applications may develop as the study progresses.

6. Pneumococcus Bibliography and Monograph

The literature on pneumococcus was thoroughly reviewed and reference cards and abstracts made for all articles of any importance. These are now being incorporated in a monograph on pneumococcus.

7. Plans for Continuation of Study

The results obtained in the Pneumonia Study justify the continuation of a large part of the program and funds have been made available to carry on much of the Antitoxin and Vaccine Laboratory work on pneumonia.

The production of therapeutic serum is to be continued. Serum will be made for Types I and II and preliminary work is being undertaken on Type V serum. The choice of Type V is made because it is met with reasonably often, and is related to Type II. It is likely that a monovalent Type I serum will be made and also a bivalent serum containing Types II and V antibody, for this appears to be a more economical arrangement than the present one of making a bivalent Type I and II serum.*

The production of diagnostic serum will be limited to those types for which therapeutic serums are available or which tend to show cross-reactions with those types.

The investigative work will be continued on much the same lines as in the past few years, in accordance with the laboratory's policy of endeavoring to improve products whenever opportunity offers. For this purpose the personnel engaged in the pneumonia work was transferred to the regular staff of the laboratory, and provision made in the regular budget for the necessary supplies.

---

* During 1936 these plans were so revised that the present intention is to produce therapeutic serums for Types I, II, V, VII, and VIII; and diagnostic serums for all of these and also Type III. The therapeutic serums will be a monovalent Type I, a bivalent Type II and V, and a bivalent Type VII and VIII.

PUBLICATIONS OF THE PNEUMONIA STUDY

(1) BIGELOW, G. H. The Serum Treatment of Pneumonia, New England J. Med. 205:242, July 30, 1931.
(2) Masachusetts Department of Public Health. Lobar Pneumonia. The Commonhealth, Vol. 18, No. 3, July-August-September, 1931.
Foreword, Bigelow, G. H.
Epidemiology, Rosenau, M. J.
Diagnosis, Lord, F. T.
Prophylaxis and Treatment, Locke, E. A.
Serum Therapy, Type I, Sutliff, W. D.
Pneumococcus Typing, Beckler, E. A.
Antipneumococcic Serum, White, B.
Nursing Care, Peterson, W.
Massachusetts Pneumonia Program, Heffron, R.
(3) HEFFRON, R. A Study of Lobar Pneumonia in Massachusetts: Preliminary Report. New England J. Med. 207:153, July 28, 1932.
(4) HEFFRON, R. and VARLEY, F. M. A Study of Lobar Pneumonia in Massachusetts: Methods and Results of Pneumococcus Type Determination, 1931-1932. Am. J. Pub. Health, 22:1230, December, 1932.
(5) BARNES, L. A. and KRAMER, S. D. A Test for Reaction-Producing Substances in Concentrated Antipneumococcic Serum: Preliminary Report. Am. J. Pub. Health, 23:616, June, 1933.
(6) HEFFRON R. and ANDERSON, G. W. Two Years' Study of Lobar Pneumonia in Massachusetts. J. A. M. A. 101:1286, October 21, 1933.
(7) SMILLIE, W. G. Epidemiology of Lobar Pneumonia. A Study of the Prevalence of Specific Strains of Pneumococci in the Nasopharynx of Immediate Family Contacts. J. A. M. A. 101:1281, October 21, 1933.
(8) SMILLIE, W. G. and LEEDER, F. S. Epidemiology of Lobar Pneumonia. Am. J. Pub. Health, 24:129, February, 1934.
(9) BARNES, L. A. and WHITE, B. The Fermentation of Glycogen by Pneumococci. Abstracted in J. Bact. 27:106, January, 1934.
(10) BARNES, L. A. and WHITE, B. The Antibody Response of Rabbits During Prolonged Immunization with Type I Pneumococcus Vaccines. Am. J. Hyg. 21:35, January, 1935.
(11) BARNES, L. A. and CLARKE, C. The Pneumococcidal Powers of Sodium Oleate and Sodium Ricinoleate. Abstracted in J. Bact. 27:107, January, 1934.
(12) BECKLER, E. and MACLEOD, P. The Neufeld Method of Pneumococcus Type Determination as Carried Out in a Public Health Laboratory: A Study of 760 Typings. J. Clin. Investigation, 13:901, November 1934.
(13) BARNES, L. A. and ROBINSON, E. S. Monkey Test for Chill-Producing Activity of Concentrated Antipneumococcic Serum. Am. J. Pub. Health, 26:51, January 1936.
(14) ANDERSON G. W. and HEFFRON R. Present Status of Pneumonia Problem. Public Health Nursing, 27:633, December 1935.
(15) LORD, F. T. and HEFFRON, R. Lobar Pneumonia and Serum Therapy With Special Reference to the Massachusetts Pneumonia Study. New York: The Commonwealth Fund, 1936.
(16) BARNES, L. A. and WIGHT, E. C. Serological Relationship Between Pneumococcus Type I and an Encapsulated Strain of *Escherichia Coli.* J. Exper. Med. 62:281, August 1935.
(17) BARNES, L. A., CLARKE, C. M., and WIGHT, E. C. Comparisons of Various Methods for the Routine Titration of Types I and II Antipneumococcic Horse Serums. J. Immunol. 30:127, February 1936.

(18) BARNES, L. A. and WIGHT, E. C. The Spontaneous Transformation of Pneumococcus Type V to Type II. J. Bact. 32:557, November 1936.

APPENDIX

Collaborators

A list of the physicians who acted as pneumonia collaborators during the Massachusetts Pneumonia Study is given below. Eighty-two collaborators are listed in areas outside of Boston and nine in Boston. In several instances physicians are listed who either died or moved elsewhere during the course of the Study.

Area outside of Boston	Collaborator
Ayer	E. Lilly, Shirley
	A. J. McLean, Ayer
	H. B. Priest, Ayer
Beverly	D. L. Buck, Danvers
	R. P. Hallett, Gloucester
	A. E. Parkhurst, Beverly
Brockton	A. M. Champ, Brockton
	W. G. Walker, Brockton
Chelsea	Lt. Commdr. R. C. Satterlee, U. S. Naval Hospital
	Lt. Commdr. D. Ferguson, U. S. Naval Hospital
Clinton	C. R. Abbott, Clinton
	G. L. Chase, Clinton
	E. F. Mitchell, Clinton
Fall River	B. W. Garneau, Fall River
	H. Lubjnsky, Fall River
	W. F. MacKnight, Fall River
	J. C. McAdams, Fall River
	E. M. Morris, Fall River
	J. F. O'Brien, Fall River
Great Barrington	J. E. Canby, Great Barrington
	C. S. Chapin, Great Barrington
	F. S. Leeder, Great Barrington
	H. W. Stevens, Great Barrington
Haverhill	E. S. Bagnall, Groveland
	A. M. Hubbell, Haverhill
	R. C. Hurd, Newburyport
	A. Servetnick, Haverhill
	F. W. Snow, Newburyport
	J. Sproull, Haverhill
	C. F. Warren, Amesbury
Lawrence	L. B. Ainsworth, Lawrence
	R. B. Baketel, Methuen
	H. Coulson, Lawrence
	H. A. Fenton, Lawrence
	V. A. Reed, Lawrence
	A. F. Shea, Lawrence
	W. D. Walker, Andover

Lowell	D. J. Ellison, Lowell
	M. H. Hyman, Lowell
	H. W. Jewett, Lowell
	F. P. Murphy, Lowell
	J. Y. Rodger, Lowell
	W. F. Ryan, Lowell
	A. G. Scoborio, Chelmsford Centre
	E. O. Tabor, Lowell
	W. L. Twarog, Lowell
Malden	W. H. Flanders, Melrose
	H. J. Keaney, Everett
	R. W. McAllester, Everett
	L. W. McGuire, Malden
New Bedford	F. M. Howes, New Bedford
	J. Salles, New Bedford
	P. Wilde, New Bedford
	R. Wood, New Bedford
Newton	S. C. Dalrymple, Newton
	E. E. Kattwinkel, Newton
	D. O'Hara, Waltham
	J. E. Vance, Natick
Pittsfield	M. Criscitiello, Jr., Pittsfield
	A. C. England, Pittsfield
	B. Paddock, Pittsfield
Salem	S. N. Gardner, Salem
	R. H. Shaughnessy, Salem
Springfield	L. Chapin, Springfield
	J. Comins, Springfield
	S. E. Fletcher, Chicopee
	R. Klein, Springfield
	J. Z. Naurison, Springfield
	J. H. Quinn, Springfield
	H. L. Smith, Springfield
	G. L. Steele, Springfield
	E. J. Sweeney, Springfield
	J. Tracy, Springfield
Worcester	A. W. Atwood, Worcester
	R. Cutler, Worcester
	J. J. Dumphy, Worcester
	R. Ellis, Worcester
	M. B. Fox, Worcester
	E. C. Miller, Worcester
	R. Schofield, Worcester
	O. H. Stansfield, Worcester
	R. J. Ward, Worcester
Boston collaborators	E. S. Calderwood
	E. J. Demming
	M. Finland
	D. King
	R. I. Lee
	E. A. Locke
	F. T. Lord
	J. Pratt
	W. D. Sutliff

Laboratories for Typing and Serum Distribution

Facilities are widely available in Massachusetts for carrying out pneumococcus typing and for distributing concentrated Type I and II antipneumococcic serum for the treatment of patients with Type I or II pneumonia who have not been ill longer than four days. Such a service is offered by the State Bacteriologic Laboratory, 527 State House, Boston, as well as by the laboratories of the following sixty-seven hospitals and departments of health.

City or Town	Hospital or Department of Health
Attleboro	Sturdy Memorial Hospital
Ayer	Ayer Community Memorial Hospital
Beverly	Beverly Hospital
Boston	Boston City Hospital
Boston	Faulkner Hospital
Boston	Evans Department of Massachusetts Memorial Hospitals
Boston	New England Deaconess Hospital
Boston	St. Elizabeth's Hospital*
Brockton	Board of Health Laboratory
Brockton	Brockton Hospital
Cambridge	Cambridge Hospital
Cambridge	Cambridge City Hospital
Chelsea	Chelsea Memorial Hospital
Clinton	Clinton Hospital
Everett	Whidden Memorial Hospital
Fall River	Fall River General Hospital
Fall River	St. Ann's Hospital
Fall River	Truesdale Hospital
Fall River	Union Hospital
Fitchburg	Burbank Hospital
Framingham	Framingham Union Hospital
Gardner	Henry Heywood Memorial Hospital
Gloucester	Addison Gilbert Hospital
Great Barrington	Fairview Hospital
Greenfield	Franklin County Hospital
Haverhill	Gale Hospital
Holyoke	Holyoke Hospital
Holyoke	Providence Hospital
Hyannis	Cape Cod Hospital
Lawrence	Lawrence General Hospital
Leominster	Leominster Hospital
Lowell	Lowell General Hospital
Lowell	St. John's Hospital
Lowell	St. Joseph's Hospital
Lynn	Lynn Hospital
Malden	Malden Hospital
Marlboro	Marlboro Hospital
Milford	Milford Hospital
Natick	Leonard Morse Hospital
New Bedford	St. Luke's Hospital
Newburyport	Anna Jaques Hospital
Newton	Newton Hospital
North Adams	North Adams Hospital
Northampton	Cooley Dickinson Hospital
Norwood	Norwood Hospital
Oak Bluffs	Martha's Vineyard Hospital*

City or Town	Hospital or Department of Health
Palmer	Wing Memorial Hospital
Peabody	J. B. Thomas Hospital
Pittsfield	House of Mercy Hospital
Pittsfield	St. Luke's Hospital
Plymouth	Jordan Hospital
Pocasset	Barnstable County Sanatorium
Quincy	Quincy City Hospital
Salem	Salem Hospital
Somerville	Somerville Hospital*
Southbridge	Harrington Memorial Hospital
Springfield	Springfield Hospital
Springfield	Mercy Hospital
Springfield	Wesson Hospital
Taunton	Morton Hospital
Ware	Mary Lane Hospital*
Webster	Webster Hospital*
Westfield	Noble Hospital
Worcester	St. Vincent's Hospital
Worcester	Worcester City Hospital
Worcester	Worcester Hahnemann Hospital
Worcester	Worcester Memorial Hospital

* Added to the list subsequent to the termination of the Pneumonia Study in 1935.

In addition to the sixty-eight places mentioned above, a similar typing and serum distribution service, though limited to patients within the institution, is offered by four other hospitals in Boston.

REPORT OF DIVISION OF FOOD AND DRUGS

During the months of October, November and December 1936, samples were collected in 227 cities and towns.

There were 1,032 samples of milk examined, of which 85 were below standard, from 11 samples the cream had been in part removed, and 3 samples contained added water. There were 1,512 bacteriological examinations made of milk, 1,413 of which complied with the requirements. There were 327 bacteriological examinations made of ice cream, 25 of which did not comply with the requirements; 3 bacteriological examinations of cream, 1 of which did not comply with the requirements; 9 bacteriological examinations of pasteurized cream, 1 of which did not comply with the requirements; 5 bacteriological examinations of chocolate milk, 2 of which did not comply with the requirements; 8 bacteriological examinations of empty bottles, 5 of which did not comply with the requirements; 1 bacteriological examination of egg powder, 1 bacteriological examination of sherbet, and 5 bacteriological examinations of mattress fillings, all of which complied with the requirements.

There were 890 samples of food examined, 121 of which were adulterated or misbranded. These consisted of 7 samples of butter, 6 of which were low in fat, and 1 sample was rancid; 4 samples of eggs, 1 of which was cold storage not marked, 2 were decomposed, and 1 sample of stale eggs sold as fresh eggs; 39 samples of hamburg steak, 18 samples of which were decomposed, 6 samples contained sodium sulphite in excess of one tenth of one per cent, and 15 samples contained a compound of sulphur dioxide not properly labeled, 1 of which was also decomposed; 1 sample of pork scraps which was decomposed; 13 samples of sausage, 6 samples of which were decomposed, 5 samples contained a compound of sulphur dioxide not properly labeled, 1 sample contained starch in excess of two per cent, and 1 sample contained brown leaves; 13 samples of orangeade, 8 samples of which were colored to conceal inferiority, 1 sample of which also contained benzoate not marked, 4 samples were misbranded, 3 of which were also colored to conceal inferiority, and 1 sample contained benzoate not marked; 1 sample of orange drink which contained benzoate not marked; 14 samples of soft drink wash water which were deficient in caustic alkali; 1 sample of candy which contained worms; 5 samples of dried fruits which contained sulphur dioxide and were not properly labeled; 2 samples of olive oil, 1 sample of which contained teaseed oil, and 1 sample contained cottonseed oil; 1 sample of maple syrup which contained cane sugar; 1 sample of vinegar which was low in acid; and 19 samples of mattress fillings, 17 samples of which contained secondhand material, 1 sample contained a mixture of secondhand and new material, and 1 sample was varicolored.

There were 144 samples of drugs examined, of which 15 were adulterated. These consisted of 5 samples of camphorated oil, 8 samples of spirit of nitrous ether, all of which did not conform to the requirements of the U. S. Pharmacopoeia, and 2 samples of argyrol which did not correspond to the professed standard under which they were sold.

The police departments submitted 137 samples of liquor for examination. The police departments also submitted 34 samples to be analyzed for poisons or drugs, of which 3 samples contained opium, 8 samples contained heroin, 4 samples contained cannabis, 1 sample contained codein, 1 sample contained chlorate hydrate, 1 sample contained alkaloids and Epinephrin, 1 sample was found to contain no tobacco, no cannabis or no narcotic drugs, 2 samples contained no alkaloids and no ergot, and 13 samples contained no alkaloids.

There were inspected 398 plants operated for the pasteurization of milk; 32 ice cream plants; 5 cheese plants; 422 bakeries; 62 soft drink plants; 242 mattress establishments; 703 establishments relative to the enforcement of licenses pertaining to wood alcohol and preparations containing over 3% of same; and 51 inspections were made relative to narcotic licenses.

There were 90 hearings held pertaining to violations of the laws.

There were 80 convictions for violations of the law. $2,445 in fines being imposed.

Henry Fee Company, Ideal Grill, Incorporated, Harry Small, Emmanuel Coulouris, and Christos Mirazios, all of Boston; Donald Kirchner, 3 cases, of Pittsfield; Max Miller of Roxbury; and George Zervas of Ipswich, were all convicted for violations of the milk laws. Max Miller of Roxbury appealed his case.

Wellworth Market, Incorporated, Bessie Racoff, Morris Epstein, Abraham Freedman, Morris Bernstine, Joseph Waldman, and Abraham Lamkin, 2 cases, all of Roxbury; Phillip Rosenburg, Glickman's Market, Maurice Kline, and Sunkist Market, Incorporated, all of Dorchester; Harry Berkovitz of Boston; Pasquale Psecione, Anthony Balletto, and Anthony Giovino, of Cambridge; David Stuart of Framingham; Morris Spector, and Waltham Provision Company, 4 cases, of Waltham; North Main Market, Incorporated, Alex's Market, Incorporated, and Consumer's Provision Stores, Incorporated, of Worcester; United Food Stores of Webster, Incorporated, of Webster; Gloria Chain Stores, Incorporated, of Leominster; The Great Atlantic & Pacific Tea Company of Springfield; William Callahan, Louis Shaker, and Sherman's Markets, Incorporated, 2 cases, of North Adams; Main Public Market, Incorporated, Peoples Public Market, Incorporated, and Louis Flink of Fall River; and Nathan Cohen, Samuel Gordon, and Phillip Kaller, 2 cases, of New Bedford, were all convicted for violations of the food laws. Wellworth Market, Incorporated, Abraham Freedman, and Joseph Waldman of Roxbury; Sunkist Market, Incorporated, of Dorchester; Morris Spector, and Waltham Provision Company, 4 cases, of Waltham; Consumer's Provision Stores, Incorporated, of Worcester; Sherman's Markets, Incorporated, 1 case, of North Adams; Louis Flink of Fall River; Phillip Kaller, 2 cases, Samuel Gordon, and Nathan Cohen of New Bedford, all appealed their cases.

Julius Liberman of Boston was convicted for violation of the drug law.

Puritan Ice Cream Company, Incorporated, of Roslindale; and John Campbell, Angelina Lathus, and Sarantos Karampalas of Haverhill, were all convicted for violations of the frozen dessert law and regulations. John Campbell and Sarantos Karampalas of Haverhill appealed their cases.

James Panesis of Hyannis; Snow Crest Beverages, Incorporated of Salem; F. W. Woolworth Company of Boston; Julius Lepovsky, 2 cases, (4 counts) and General Beverage Company, 2 counts, of Springfield; and Alexander Starzec of Webster, were all convicted for violations of the law and regulations relative to the manufacture and bottling of carbonated non-alcoholic beverages.

Arabelle Cummings of Swansea; and Mrs. Angelina Lathus of Haverhill, were convicted for violations of the sanitary food law.

Bay State Mattress Company of Roxbury; Edward Milstone of Lawrence; Louis A. Hirshberg of Cambridge; National Mattress Company, 2 cases, and Sunset Bedding Company, Incorporated, of Boston; George Cohen, Jack Lanes, Hyman Lanes, Harry Miller, Morris Miller, and Israel Weiner, all of Lynn; William Spunt of Hyde Park; and Abraham Moretsky of Chelsea, were all convicted for violations of the mattress laws. National Mattress Company of Boston appealed 1 case.

Albert Waterman of Rehoboth was convicted for violation of the slaughtering law.

Louis Lerner of Dorchester was convicted for assault and battery. He appealed his case.

Louis Lerner of Dorchester was convicted for larceny. He appealed his case.

In accordance with Section 25, Chapter 111 of the General Laws, the following is the list of articles of adulterated food collected in original packages from manufacturers, wholesalers, or producers:

Butter which was low in fat was obtained as follows:

Two samples from Chapin & Adams Company of Boston; and 1 sample each, from M. Winer Company and Smith Brothers of Boston, and Leshner & Sons, Incorporated, of Dorchester.

One sample of butter which was rancid was obtained from Racoff's Market of Roxbury.

One sample of maple syrup which contained cane sugar was obtained from John George Parker of Webster.

One sample of olive oil which contained tea-seed oil was obtained from DeLuca Olive Oil Corporation of New York.

One sample of olive oil which contained cottonseed oil was obtained from Veista Gagono Company.

One sample of vinegar which was low in acid was obtained from Patrick Innella of Lynnfield.

One sample of orange juice which contained benzoate not marked was obtained from Venetian Dairy, Incorporated, of North Adams.

One sample of orangeade which contained benzoate not marked was obtained from Andreson & Patterson of Worcester.

One sample of orangeade which contained benzoate not marked and was also colored to conceal inferiority was obtained from Metropolitan Bottling Company of Roxbury.

Orangeade which was colored to conceal inferiority was obtained as follows:

One sample each, from Bieber Polar Company and Washington Beverage Company, Incorporated, of Worcester; F. W. Fickert & Sons of Middleboro; Coleman & Keating of Boston; American Dry Ginger Ale

Company of Roxbury; Meola Brothers of West Boylston; and Excel Bottling Company, Incorporated, of Malden.

Orangeade which was colored to conceal inferiority and was also misbranded was obtained as follows:

One sample each, from Bieber Polar Company, Kenmore Beverage Company, and American Products Company, all of Worcester.

Hamburg steak which was decomposed was obtained as follows:

Two samples each, from World Market (William Israel) of Fall River; and Charles Dubrow of Lynn; one sample each, from Henry Abrams of South Boston; Samuel Rotenberg of Chelsea; Joseph Waldman, Washington Public Market, and Virginia Market of Roxbury; Sunkist Market, Incorporated, of Dorchester; United Food Stores, Incorporated of Webster; Consumers Provision Company of Worcester; Morris Provision and Waltham Provision of Waltham; Ganem's Market and Arthur Carey of Lawrence; and Central Beef Market of Haverhill.

One sample of hamburg steak which was decomposed and also contained a compound of sulphur dioxide not properly labeled was obtained from G. & G. Market of Dorchester.

Hamburg steak which contained a compound of sulphur dioxide not properly labeled was obtained as follows:

One sample each, from Morris Provision Company, Sam's Market, Glickman's Market, and Maurice Kline of Roxbury; David Stuart of Framingham; Lynn Public Market of Lynn; Squire Provision Company and American Beef Company, Incorporated, of Boston; Henry & Victor Shafrau of Brookline; Hiram Mendelbaum of Chelsea; Atlantic & Pacific Tea Company, and Sherman Market, Incorporated, of North Adams.

Hamburg steak which contained sodium sulphite in excess of one tenth of one per cent was obtained as follows:

One sample each, from Mucci & Pescione, and Pasqueali Pescione of Cambridge; Albert Freedman and Morris Bernstein of Roxbury; P. W. Rounsevell, Incorporated, of Boston; and Jack Shaveitsky of Revere.

Sausage which was decomposed was obtained as follows:

One sample each, from Lynn Public Market of Lynn; Sherman Market, Incorporated, and Shakers Market, of North Adams; Alex Goldstein and Barney Kaizer of Worcester; and Virginia Market of Roxbury.

Sausage which contained a compound of sulphur dioxide not properly labeled was obtained as follows:

One sample each, from P. P. Antonellis and Antonio Cugini of Newton; and Ferrera Brothers and Anthony Giovino of Cambridge.

One sample of sausage which contained starch in excess of 2 per cent was obtained from Colin Barrett of New Bedford.

There were seven confiscations, consisting of 130 pounds of decomposed poultry, 4 pounds of decomposed meat loaf, 9 pounds of decomposed sausage, 15 pounds of decomposed sauce, 30 pounds of decomposed hamburg steak, 25 pounds of decomposed meat scraps, and 675 pounds of Bonita fillets.

The licensed cold storage warehouses reported the following amounts of food placed in storage during September, 1936:—408,750 dozens of case eggs; 904,259 pounds of broken out eggs; 1,000,590 pounds of butter; 1,874,915 pounds of poultry; 2,884,242 pounds of fresh meat and fresh meat products; and 11,192,265 pounds of fresh food fish.

There was on hand October 1, 1936 :—5,396,100 dozens of case eggs; 2,367,713 pounds of broken out eggs; 4,666,766 pounds of butter; 4,419,508 pounds of poultry; 4,201,403 pounds of fresh meat and fresh meat products; and 37,863,951 pounds of fresh food fish.

The licensed cold storage warehouses reported the following amounts of food placed in storage during October, 1936:—941,280 dozens of case eggs; 838,765 pounds of broken out eggs; 803,260 pounds of butter; 2,072,525 pounds of poultry; 2,698,870 pounds of fresh meat and fresh meat products; and 11,255,878 pounds of fresh food fish.

There was on hand November 1, 1936:—4,132,230 dozens of case eggs; 2,157,328 pounds of broken out eggs; 4,200,304 pounds of butter; 5,435,624 pounds of poultry; 4,680,194 pounds of fresh meat and fresh meat products; and 37,633,637 pounds of fresh food fish.

The licensed cold storage warehouses reported the following amounts of food placed in storage during November, 1936:—84,540 dozens of case eggs; 691,329 pounds of broken out eggs; 311,426 pounds of butter; 3,218,172 pounds of poultry; 3,660,477 pounds of fresh meat and fresh meat products; and 9,654,327 pounds of fresh food fish.

There was on hand December 1, 1936:—1,770,420 dozens of case eggs; 1,844,795 pounds of broken out eggs; 3,387,601 pounds of butter; 7,473,093 pounds of poultry; 5,921,526 pounds of fresh meat and fresh meat products; and 38,441,761 pounds of fresh food fish.

MASSACHUSETTS DEPARTMENT OF PUBLIC HEALTH

Commissioner of Public Health, HENRY D. CHADWICK, M.D.

Public Health Council

HENRY D. CHADWICK, M.D., *Chairman*

GORDON HUTCHINS.   RICHARD M. SMITH, M.D.
FRANCIS H. LALLY, M.D.   RICHARD P. STRONG, M.D.
SYLVESTER E. RYAN, M.D.   JAMES L. TIGHE.

Secretary, FLORENCE L. WALL

Division of Administration . . Under direction of Commissioner.
Division of Sanitary Engineering . Director and Chief Engineer,
  ARTHUR D. WESTON, C.E.
Division of Communicable Diseases Director,
  GAYLORD W. ANDERSON, M.D.
Division of Biologic Laboratories . Director and Pathologist,
  ELLIOTT S. ROBINSON, M.D.
Division of Food and Drugs . . Director and Analyst,
  HERMANN C. LYTHGOE, S.B.
Division of Child Hygiene . . Director, M. LUISE DIEZ, M. D.
Division of Tuberculosis . . . Director, ALTON S. POPE, M.D.
Division of Adult Hygiene . . Director,
  HERBERT L. LOMBARD, M.D.

State District Health Officers

The Southeastern District . . RICHARD P. MACKNIGHT, M.D., New Bedford.
The South Metropolitan District . HENRY M. DE WOLFE, M.D., Quincy.
The North Metropolitan District . .
The Northeastern District . . ROBERT E. ARCHIBALD, M.D., Lynn.
The Worcester County District . OSCAR A. DUDLEY, M.D., Worcester.
The Connecticut Valley District . JOHN J. POUTAS, M.D., Springfield.
The Franklin County District . . WALTER W. LEE, M.D., No. Adams.
The Berkshire County District . HAROLD W. STEVENS, M.D., Great Barrington.

PUBLICATION OF THIS DOCUMENT APPROVED BY THE COMMISSION ON ADMINISTRATION AND FINANCE
7M-3-'37. Order 9955.

THE COMMONHEALTH

Volume 24　　　Apr.-May-June
No. 2　　　　　1937

Diabetes

MASSACHUSETTS
DEPARTMENT OF PUBLIC HEALTH

THE COMMONHEALTH

QUARTERLY BULLETIN OF THE MASSACHUSETTS DEPARTMENT OF
PUBLIC HEALTH

Sent Free to any Citizen of the State

Entered as second class matter at Boston Postoffice.

M. LUISE DIEZ, M.D., DIRECTOR OF DIVISION OF CHILD HYGIENE, EDITOR.
1 Beacon Street, Boston, Mass.

CONTENTS

	PAGE
Diabetes and Its Treatment, by Elliott P. Joslin, M.D.	81
The Historical Trend of Diabetes, by Eleanor J. Macdonald, A.B.	87
Insulin and Protamine Insulin, by Alexander Marble, M.D.	96
Instruction of Diabetic Patients, by M. Bernice Moore, R.N.	104
Diabetic Coma, by Alexander Marble, M.D.	112
Gangrene and Surgery in Diabetes, by Howard F. Root, M.D.	116
Diabetes in Massachusetts, by Herbert L. Lombard, M.D., and Sally J. Miner	123
Cardiovascular Disease and Diabetes, by Howard F. Root, M.D.	133
Inheritance of Diabetes, by Priscilla White, M.D.	135
The Prevention of Diabetes and the Prognosis of the Disease, by Elliott P. Joslin, M.D.	137
Pregnancy in Diabetes, by Priscilla White, M.D.	138
Tuberculosis in Diabetics, by Alton S. Pope, M.D.	142
Diabetes in Childhood, by Priscilla White, M.D.	145
Diabetic Camps, by Priscilla White, M.D.	152
The Laboratory in the Treatment of Diabetes, by Hazel Hunt, A.B., and Alexander Marble, M.D.	155
Diabetic Costs, by Allen P. Joslin, M.D.	157
Correction	158
Report of Division of Food and Drugs, January, February and March, 1937	159

DIABETES AND ITS TREATMENT
ELLIOTT P. JOSLIN, M.D.
Boston, Mass.

Three years did not mean much in the diabetic story or to the diabetic years ago, but in the period since the last diabetic issue of The Commonhealth was published in 1934, the number of my patients with onset of the disease in childhood, who have lived fifteen years or more, has grown from fifteen to seventy-five. This is wonderful in itself and all the more so because in children diabetes is so severe that prior to 1922 few children survived the disease twelve months. In 1934 it was only twelve years since the discovery of insulin; in 1937 it is fifteen years and that fact accounts for the many more living diabetic children today because the truly miraculous improvement in the treatment of diabetes is due to insulin.

Lack of insulin is responsible for the disease diabetes. It is insulin in the normal individual which enables the sugar and starch (carbohydrate) of the diet to be stored and utilized. When it is deficient, the sugar and the starch which are eaten are no longer, in whole or in part, of benefit to the body and escape as sugar through the urine. In the severest form of diabetes about a half of the protein (meat, fish, eggs and cheese) and one-tenth of the fat follow the same course. The discovery of insulin changed all this and now by administering it to a diabetic, his disease can be controlled.

The disease diabetes is characterized by the appearance of sugar in the urine and an increase of sugar in the blood. It is caused by a failure of the pancreas to produce insulin. The pancreas is a gland deep in the upper abdomen and is often called the sweet bread. The pancreas is also closely related to other glands with internal secretions, the thyroid, pituitary and the adrenals and likewise to the liver which along with the muscles is the great storehouse of carbohydrate in the body. Diabetes, therefore, is a rather complicated disease and much work remains to be done to explain all its symptoms.

The chief symptoms of diabetes depend upon the inability of the body to get the full benefit of the carbohydrate in the diet and the appearance of sugar in the urine. To excrete the sugar, it must go into solution and this necessitates the passage of large quantities, even at times as much as ten quarts of urine, and this in turn produces extreme thirst. One young girl, before treatment began, counted the glasses of liquid she drank in twenty-four hours and they amounted to thirty-two. It was this thirst which took her to the doctor. Besides thirst (polydipsia) and much urine (polyuria), the diabetic, if a severe case, has an abnormal appetite (polyphagia) and must eat an extra amount of food to make up for the sugar lost in the urine. I reckoned that the patient above mentioned voided one pound of sugar in the twenty-four hours. It is not long before weakness and loss of weight appear and the debility may be so extreme that the patient becomes terribly emaciated. The weight of my severest case in 1922 had fallen from 155 pounds to 69 pounds. Today with insulin and the new protamine insulin her weight is normal. In consequence of the lowered resistance and emaciation the patient becomes a prey to infections which a robust individual might withstand and he becomes liable especially to tuberculosis. Untreated, the wear and tear upon the diabetic accelerates the approach of old age with its hardening of the arteries and perhaps this complication today is the most serious of all. At one time sixty per cent of the patients succumbed to acid poisoning (diabetic coma), but although it is a constant menace, it can always be avoided by an intelligent patient, and the mortality from it is now greatly reduced. In another place in this number of The Commonhealth this is described.

The treatment of diabetes depended almost exclusively upon diet until the discovery of insulin in 1922. It was known that exercise helped in certain instances, but its exact place in treatment was not understood until quite recently. The dietetic treatment of diabetes went through a great many stages and out of them all some definite facts were learned. Most important of all was the demonstration that just as overfeeding with its resulting obesity favored the onset of diabetes in the hereditarily predisposed, overfeeding a diabetic patient made him worse. If the patient is not overfed, various combinations of diets can be utilized, but I think it is fair to state today that a diet which is moderately reduced in carbohydrate and not excessive in fat can be considered the one most generally employed in the United States. The diet today is far less rigorous than formerly and this is because with insulin, which can be injected once or more daily, the carbohydrate can be utilized and if one does not need to reduce the carbohydrate to the extreme then there is not the necessity to raise the fat to high amounts. This is very fortunate, because an excess of fat helps to bring on acid poisoning—diabetic coma.

An average diabetic diet today might be said to consist of a slice of bread and an orange at each meal, vegetables containing 5 per cent carbohydrates, 4 portions, cereal one portion, a mixture of milk and cream one-half pint. In addition one egg and perhaps two strips of bacon would be allowed for breakfast and for the other meals a moderate portion of meat or fish and butter in very moderate quantity.

The details of the above diet are readily calculated from the accompanying Tables 1, 2 and 3. In the latter table various combinations of diets are suggested for those who require more or less of the different components.

The estimation of the values of carbohydrate in the diabetic diet is simple. Thus bread, one slice, weighs usually and can be made to weigh exactly one ounce or 30 grams. In Table 2 it will be seen that this quantity of bread contains 18 grams carbohydrate.

Bread, one ounce, 30 grams = carbohydrate 18 grams x 3 = 54 grams
Orange, one medium, 150 grams = " 15 " x 3 = 45 grams
*5% vegetables, 4 portions, each 150 grams = 20 "
Oatmeal, one large portion, 30 grams dry weight = 20 "
Milk, 4 oz. — 120 cc. — 6 grams ⎫
Cream, 4 oz. — 120 cc. — 4 grams ⎭ = 10

149

* By 5% vegetables is understood a mixture of vegetable containing between 2% to 6%.

As a rule protein in the form of meat, eggs, fish and cheese is regulated according to the age and weight of the patient. For a young child one allows 3 grams of protein per kilogram, 2.2 pounds, and for an old man 1 gram or even less. In Table 2 it is seen that meat, cooked, one ounce, 30 grams, contains protein 8 grams. Fat meat would contain slightly less and very lean meat slightly more protein. Fish contains slightly less protein than meat, and cheese about the same as meat. Bacon varies much in protein according to whether it contains much fat and also according to the way it is served.

Fat as a rule must be lowered as the carbohydrate is raised. As a rule butter 30 grams, containing 25 grams fat, is permitted and the balance of the fat comes from the other food already cited. If the fat is so low that it forms but a small percentage of the diet, carbohydrate may be utilized better and some doctors therefore give as little as 40 grams fat.

A diabetic diet for a man weighing 60 kilograms, 132 pounds, would be sufficient if it contained carbohydrate 150 grams, protein 80 grams, fat 100 grams. Once having learned to make up a diet of this type it is easy to adjust it in any direction by the accompanying Tables 1, 2, 3.

If a patient with a recently discovered diabetes should come to my office I should urge him (1) to go at once to the hospital; (2) place him upon a diet containing about 20 calories per kilogram body weight with carbohydrate at 100 to 130 grams, protein 50 to 60 grams and fat between 60 and 80 grams; (3) give him insulin 5 units before each meal; (4) collect the urine four times a day, morning, afternoon, evening, night, to determine the effect of the diet and insulin; (5) limit exercise to an amount consistent with his diet; and (6) start him upon his diabetic education. The diets usually employed are those outlined in Table 3 and the computations of the diets can be made from the food values in Tables 1 and 2. If the sugar in the urine (glycosuria) did not decrease materially and daily, I should raise the insulin daily until this was accomplished even if the dose of insulin reached 20 — 15 — 20 — 5 units or more. Most patients become sugar free with as little as 10 — 10 — 10 units, few require 15 — 10 — 15 — 3 units.

The above treatment is standard treatment with regular insulin, but today I should prefer to use protamine insulin — 10 units the first day, 20 the second, 30 the third and 40 the fourth.

When the adult patient is sugar free or shows only a few tenths per cent of sugar in the urine and is receiving a nearly maintenance diet, which ordinarily is about 30 calories per kilogram body weight, he can be sent home. It is always well to discharge a patient on somewhat too low a ration than too high a ration, but usually it is safer to increase the diet upon discharge by 5 or 10 grams of carbohydrate, protein and fat to guard against insulin reactions and such increases can generally be made without giving the patient too much food.

The dosage of insulin may change from day to day in the hospital but in order to avoid reactions it is well to lower it upon discharge. Most desirable is it to lessen the number of injections per day. Almost always one can get along with two injections, but if a third is required, that is most conveniently administered upon retiring. The retiring dose is small 2, 3, 4 and almost never as much as 10 units. It is usually given without food and is prescribed so that the patient in the eight hours or more at night will be protected so that he can wake up sugar free. If a patient is sugar free on rising it implies he has glycogen stored in his liver and under such conditions the day is sure to progress more favorably than if the reverse is true.

If a patient does not become sugar free with 30 units of insulin during twenty-four hours, seek (1) for errors in diet, (2) infections of any sort, whether general or local, (3) acidosis, (4) hyperthyroidism, (5) hemochromatosis. The last named condition is not nearly as rare as has been thought and the skin may show little of the typical brown pigmentation.

Exercise is of great help to the diabetic and especially of value when combined with insulin and a proper diet. Patients in bed are aided with exercise and the lack of it always raises difficulties in the management of diabetes. The patient crippled with rheumatism requires large doses of insulin and if his joints can be limbered and he can move about, the insulin can be lowered. A game of golf, Case 632 often told me, was the equal of 5 units.

Exercise is such a distinct aid in the treatment of diabetes that it should be recognized in the cost of the care of the patient. In hospitals patients are taught to exercise for their own good and outside of the hospital there is no reason why patients should not work and thus lessen the cost of their care. The whole scheme of caring for chronic patients and older invalids sooner or later must involve work on their part or else the expense will be overwhelming; and particularly should diabetic patients work if it is possible for them to do so because it is therapeutically advisable.

The advantages of exercise for diabetics are shown most plainly in the diabetic camps. We have found that our treatment of children goes far more smoothly in diabetic camps than it does in the hospital and to a considerable extent this is due to the introduction of exercise according to the need of the individual.

If a diabetic does not do well, there is a reason, and one must not blame the treatment but seek for the explanation.

Week-end treatment for diabetics is quite satisfactory. In these times, when it is difficult to secure or hold a job, repeatedly patients have entered the hospital for a week-end treatment, coming in on a Friday afternoon and being discharged Sunday afternoon or early Monday morning. Most of the patients who have jobs are clever enough to gain a great deal of information in this short period. One day in a hospital spent in contact with other diabetics, seeing patients with gangrene, a patient with a carbuncle, perhaps another with diabetic coma or in hypoglycemia, will do more to instill a knowledge of diabetes than any amount of textbook teaching. Patients may not be able to read and write but they can see and hear and what they learn from observation and from interviews with other patients in the course of two days is astonishing.

The costs of medical care are likewise reduced during a hospital stay, because while being treated for and learning about diabetes all sorts of conditions which affect the diabetes adversely can be rectified. The teeth can be cleaned and if necessary extracted, bad tonsils can be removed, hyperthyroidism can be corrected. In children, the appendix should be removed, if there is a distinct history of an attack, because of the confusion which always ensues when a child has diabetic coma and at the same time has discomfort in the abdomen. A few patients are discovered with gallstones. The eyes should be examined. Finally, every diabetic entering a hospital should have an x-ray of the chest because of the possibility of latent tuberculosis.

Insulin has done so much for diabetics that they hardly could expect anything better for many years, but wonderful to relate a new revolution in the treatment of diabetes has taken place and now we have protamine insulin. There are many advantages to protamine insulin: first of all, because patients require an injection but once a day, but, second and very likely of more importance, instead of the disease being controlled for a portion of the day, with protamine insulin it is controlled all day long and this must lessen complications. A full description of the regular insulin and protamine insulin will be found in another article in this number.

Table 1. Foods Arranged Approximately According to Content of Carbohydrate

Water, clear broths, coffee, tea, cocoa shells and cracked cocoa can be taken without allowance for food content.

Foods Arranged Approximately According to Content of Carbohydrate

VEGETABLES, fresh or canned		FRUITS, fresh or canned (water packed)		
Reckon average carbohydrate in 5% veg. as 3%; in 10% veg. as 6%		Approximate Carbohydrate Substitution Values		
5 per cent		Food	Carbohydrate	
1-3 per cent	**3-5 per cent**		**10 Gm.**	**15 Gm.**
Lettuce	Tomatoes			
Cucumbers	Water Cress	Grapefruit Pulp	150	225
Spinach	Sea Kale	Strawberries	150	225
Asparagus	Cauliflower	Watermelon	150	225
Rhubarb	Egg Plant	Cantaloupe	150	225
Endive	Cabbage	Blackberries	120	180
Marrow	Radishes	**Orange Pulp**	**100**	**150**
Sorrel	Leeks	Pears	90	135
Sauerkraut	Str. Beans, young	Peaches	90	135
Beet Greens	Broccoli	Apricots	80	120
Dandelions	French Artichoke	Raspberries	80	120
Swiss Chard	Green Peppers	Plums	80	120
Celery	Summer Squash	Pineapple	70	105
Mushrooms	Kohl-Rabi	Apple	70	105
		Honeydew Melon	70	105
10 per cent	**15 per cent**	Blueberries	70	105
String Beans	Green Peas	Cherries	60	90
Brussels Sprouts	Jer. Artichokes	Banana	50	75
Pumpkin	Parsnips	Prunes (cooked)	50	75
Turnip	Lima Beans, young	Ice Cream	50	75
Squash				
Okra	**20 per cent**	1 gram carbohydrate, 4 calories		
Beets	Potatoes	1 " protein 4 calories		
Carrots	Shell Beans	1 " fat 9 calories		
Onions	Baked Beans	6.25 " protein contain 1 g. nitrogen.		
Green Peas, very young	Lima Beans	1 kilogram = 2.2 pounds		
	Green Corn	30 grams (g.) or cubic centimeters (cc.) = 1 ounce		
	Boiled Rice			
	Boiled Macaroni	A patient "at rest" requires 25 calories per kilogram.		

Table 2. Food Values Important in the Treatment of Diabetes

30 grams 1 oz. Contain Approximately	Carbohydrates G.	Protein G.	Fat G.	Calories
Vegetables 5%	1	0.5	0	6
Vegetables 10%	2	0.5	0	10
Potato	6	1	0	28
Bread	18	3	0	84
Uneeda Biscuits, 2	10	1	1	53
Oatmeal, dry wgt.	20	5	2	118
Shredded Wheat, 1	23	3	0	104
Milk	1.5	1	1	19
Meat (cooked, lean)	0	8	5	77
Fish, fat free	0	6	0	24
Chicken (cooked lean)	0	8	3	59
Egg (one)	0	6	6	78
Cheese	0	8	11	131
Bacon	0	5	15	155
Cream, 20%	1	1	6	62
Cream 40%	1	1	12	116
Butter	0	0	25	225
Oil	0	0	30	270

TABLE 3
Diabetic Diets

Diets	Total Diet				Carbohydrate (C)						Protein and Fat (PF)				
	Carbo-Hydrate	Pro-tein	Fat	Calo-ries	5% Vege-tables	Orange	Oat Meal	Potato	Bread	Milk	Egg	Meat	Bacon	20% Cream	But-ter
C1 PF1	100	47	61	1137	300	400	15	60	30	120	1	75	...	120	15
C2 PF2	127	59	79	1455	300	400	15	120	45	240	1	90	...	120	30
C3 PF3	151	74	92	1728	300	400	15	150	75	240	1	120	15	120	30
C4 PF4	175	88	104	1988	300	400	15	180	105	240	1	150	30	120	30
C5 PF5	200	100	123	2307	300	400	30	210	120	240	1	180	30	120	45
Acute Illness	152	50	52	1276	...	400	15	...	90	960	1	...	...	...	15

Approximate equivalents. 1 small orange (160 gms) = ½ banana (50 gms) = ⅛ saucer oatmeal (15 gms dry or 120 gms cooked) = 2 large saucers (300 gms) 5% vegetables = 1 large saucer (150 gms) 10% vegetables = potato size of egg = ½ slice (15 gms) bread.

THE HISTORICAL TREND OF DIABETES

ELEANOR J. MACDONALD, A.B.

Statistician, Division of Adult Hygiene,
Massachusetts Department of Public Health

The dependence of advance on exact information derived from scientific and sound investigation is no more evident in any disease than in diabetes mellitus. Most unsupported statements, even if true, are disregarded by scientists today and this attitude toward unproved things is a common heritage with the past. It will be necessary to omit many investigators in the history of diabetes because their discoveries had no direct effect on the future of the disease.

In studying the records of the ancient writers, it is remarkable to find clinical descriptions of disease similar to those of today, but when one reads on, it becomes apparent that the description was the limit of information, for science was in a groping state and when it came upon problems that needed our present knowledge of anatomy, physiology, chemistry, and pathology to solve, these writers usually left the field of certain knowledge for that of conjecture, and the errors made in this natural way by respected and conscientious men left their mark on diabetes by retarding its eventual solution. The remarkable feature in the history of diabetes is the enormous number of serious men who have worked on it and the two thousand years of patient study it represents.

"Diabetes mellitus is a disease of metabolism based on defect in the body's power to store and oxidize carbohydrates due to a decrease in the internal secretion of the pancreas, and marked by an abnormal amount of sugar in the blood and by the passage of an excessive amount of urine containing an excessive amount of sugar." The evolution of this definition is the story of diabetes.

Celsus defined the disease about 50 A.D. and advised treatment and a diet. He introduced one idea which has persisted—that the urine excreted exceeded the amount of liquid intake in the diet. Aretaeus of Cappadocia, writing in the first century, described diabetes among other diseases in the first part of his work, and suggested treatment for it in the second section. Aretaeus is the one who gave diabetes its name which, translated roughly from the Greek, means "to run through a siphon,' and suggests clearly the picture of the disease in his mind. Osler quotes the translation of the description of diabetes given by Aretaeus as "melting down the flesh and bones into urine." Galen (131-201) had two patients with diabetes and from his experience described the disease as a weakness of the kidneys and introduced the idea that urine was unchanged drink. He called the disease "urinous diarrhea." In 200 A.D. a description of the disease was given in China by one of her greatest physicians, Tchang Tchong-king, who called it the "disease of thirst." Aëtius, about 550 A.D., introduced into therapy three measures that were in use for a long period thereafter—bleeding, emetics, and narcotics. Sweetness of diabetic urine was first mentioned in the Ayur Veda of Susruta in India in the sixth century B. C. It was called "Madhumeha" or "honey urine." This discovery of the outstanding symptom of diabetes was not generally known for another two thousand years, however, so, except for academic interest, it had no effect on the development of the disease.

The whole story of medical history was changed by the disruptive influence of the fall of Rome. This event has been explained frequently in its effect on religion, art and literature. It had its special effect also on medical development. Up until the sixth century, each rising civilization assimilated the salient features of the declining one, until Rome came to be a blend of all the former civilizations. With her destruction by a new and barbarous people, all this accumulated culture was submerged and did not again appear until the Italian Renaissance.

The Benedictine monks at Monte Cassino, Italy, as early as the sixth century, had many medical manuscripts in their possession and studied them. It was the successors of this group of Benedictines who recognized the advantages of Salerno and established not only a monastery there but also a medical school. This school of Salerno, which was well established by the eleventh century, has handed down the records of its organization and of some of its great teachers. The founder of modern surgery, Roger of Parma, was one of its teachers. From Salerno, this awakened medical consciousness advanced first in Italy to the Universities of Bologna and Padua and then in France to Paris and Montpellier. The influence exerted by these schools was felt in all parts of Europe and many of the sciences later to be allied under the term medicine began to appear. Leonardo da Vinci with his paintings of the human body, Vesalius with his anatomy, Francis Bacon with his inductive reasoning, Harvey with his physiology, Malphighi with his anatomy, and Morgagni with his pathology—are all the results of this renaissance in medicine.

Thomas Willis (1621-1675), an Englishman, is the one who has been credited with the discovery that the urine of diabetics had the taste of honey or sugar. He did not think that it was sugar, but held to the idea that diabetes was a disease of the blood. He believed that the acid reaction of fermented wine was probably a cause of diabetes. Poor hygiene, worry, and nervous diseases were advanced by him also as causes of the disease. His suggestion for limitation of diet to "thicken the blood and supply salts" introduced the first undernutrition diet. Lime water was the alkali that he used for diabetics and marked the introduction of drugs in treatment of this disease. Though many times in earlier history the sweetish quality of diabetic urine was noted, it was not until Willis's introduction of the idea that it began to be used to its fullest extent in diagnosis. Until then polyuria, or any of a number of symptoms, were thought to have been diabetes, and only after the establishment of Willis's idea was the subsequent dietary regime possible.

It was just a century after Willis that Matthew Dobson, in 1776, finished the experiment by showing that sugar was present in the urine of diabetic patients and in addition, that the blood serum of diabetics had a sweet taste. Twelve years later (1788), Thomas Cawley, in the "London Medical Journal," wrote of his discovery of an atrophied pancreas, with calculi in its secretory ducts, in an autopsy on a diabetic. He, however, thought that the disease was one of the kidneys. After Cawley, Bright, Lloyd, and Elliotson noted pancreatic lesions in autopsies, but none of these men established the relationship between these lesions and diabetes.

In 1796, John Rollo, a surgeon in the English army, treated his first case of diabetes in a radically original way. He began by bleeding the patient and by careful confinement and rest at home. Then followed a strict diet, composed principally of rancid meat, intended to prevent the formation of sugar in the stomach.

One of the interesting features in the history of diabetes is that the first step toward the discovery of insulin was taken by one of the contemporaries of Willis. Conrad von Brunner, in 1683, removed the pancreas of a dog and observed the symptoms that followed. His detailed description of the condition of the depancreatized dog was a typical description of diabetes mellitus. From this period, toward the end of the seventeenth century, progress in diabetes developed along two distinct lines—experimentation with various types of diet and an inevitable trend toward the discovery of insulin through experimentation on animals and growing accuracy in laboratory research. There was not a distinct cleavage between the two lines of research, however, and many of the men experimenting on dogs applied their knowledge clinically and made contributions to the several theories of diet.

The theories on diagnosis and treatment, up to the era referred to by Elliott P. Joslin of Boston as the "Naunyn era," are worthy of mention for each of them had a temporary influence and doubtless, by trial and error, each had an integral part in the development of our present knowledge. Thomas Willis had suggested the first under-nutrition diet; Richard Morton observed the hereditary character of the disease and suggested a milk diet; Richard Mead felt that diabetes was a disease of the liver and supported his contention by a supposed necropsy; Matthew Dobson completed the study of Willis, discovered that not only the urine but the blood serum had a sweetish taste, and introduced the error that the diabetic must eat in excess to make up for the loss of nutritive material; Thomas Cawley made the first diagnosis of diabetes by the demonstration of sugar alone, and also demonstrated a pancreatic lesion in a diabetic necropsy; William Cullen added mellitus to the name of the disease, and felt that diabetes was a disease of the nervous system; John Brown added the idea of exercise as a form of treatment; Johann Peter Frank made a definite distinction between diabetes insipidus and diabetes mellitus; and Francis Home thought diabetes might be cured by a strictly meat diet, although he abandoned this idea before he had experimented with it enough to prove or disprove it.

The additions to diabetic knowledge through chemistry were necessary for later development, but need only be mentioned in this account. In 1857, Petters discovered acetone in diabetic urine. This was followed in a few years by the work of Kussmaul on acetonemia, of Stadelman, Külz, Minkowski, and Magnus-Levy on B-Oxybutyric acid in relation to diabetic coma.

Bernhard Naunyn, who was born in 1839, has given his name to an era in the development of diabetes, not because of any outstanding discovery, but because of his sound judgment, his application of existing knowledge, his outstanding pupils, and because of the discovery at his famous Strassburg school of the pancreatic gland as the seat of diabetic disease. The carbohydrate-free diet was rapidly becoming the accepted method of treatment in practically every country except Germany. Germany, as a whole, was opposed to the carbohydrate-free diet, but Naunyn supported this idea at first scientifically without taking into consideration the fact that any treatment which is too great a sacrifice to follow will be avoided by the average sick person, and later with modifications based on the individual sugar tolerance, and dietary needs. Notable among his pupils was Weintraud who disproved the theory advanced by Dobson that the caloric intake of a diabetic must be abnormal.

Naunyn's school held that diabetes was an inherited tendency, and that it was a functional disorder. The word acidosis was introduced by Naunyn. He judged the severity of cases by the degree of acidosis present. His diet consisted in the gradual withdrawal of carbohydrates. When the glycosuria cleared up, the patient was put on a diet with a gradual replacement of the carbohydrate until the minimum amount tolerated was restored. Naunyn's views on exercise agreed with those of some of his predecessors and consisted of walking, or mild exercise, if the patient were able, or complete rest if he were not. If the sugar did not clear up under this procedure, an undernutrition diet might be temporarily employed. When coma threatened, Naunyn advised giving up trying to get rid of the glycosuria and increased the carbohydrates. Naunyn agreed with some of his contemporaries and predecessors that fat was a main article of diet for diabetics, and as much as could be assimilated without causing indigestion should be used.

In 1902, von Noorden introduced the idea that a diet of oatmeal gruel caused the disappearance of glycosuria. This "oat cure" aroused comment and interest among the medical profession in which it had many followers. The real explanation seemed to be overlooked by most of the physicians—that it was probably the low caloric and protein value in the gruel that bettered the patient's condition.

Naunyn was skeptical of this cure, as he was of all the carbohydrate cures. From Rollo in 1796 down to his time, absence or presence of carbohydrates had been the basis of nearly every cure for diabetes. He held the theory that it was more likely undernutrition than any specific article of diet that caused the improved condition among diabetics. Von Noorden disagreed with the Naunyn school on the cause of acidosis and considered it something more than carbohydrate deficiency, but he agreed with Naunyn on the belief in the potency of fat in the diet. Both also agreed on the good results of an occasional fast day. Of the various men who advanced definite treatments for diabetes Naunyn, until 1914, probably had a larger following than any other.

The "Allen era," which extended from 1914 until 1922, was named for Frederick M. Allen. He and Joslin were discussing a case of Joslin's in which the diabetic patient had contracted tuberculosis. Joslin remarked that as the patient failed in strength from the tuberculosis, the diabetes improved. This case stimulated the experiment from which evolved the Allen fasting treatment. Allen produced a condition in animals which simulated human diabetes by partial pancreanectomy. He varied the disease from mild to severe, according to diet. His dogs died when fed liberally. When they were starved until glycosuria disappeared and then placed on a low diet, they felt better and there was no reappearance of the glycosuria. When this finding was applied to human beings, Allen drew the logical conclusion that no particular type of food was good or bad for a diabetic, but rather that a diabetic must always be limited in amount of diet.

In the light of recent events, this rationalization of Allen's experiment may not seem to be extraordinary, but when it is considered in view of the experience of Joslin who has had so large a clinical experience in the treatment of diabetes, it is a service the importance of which cannot be overestimated. To quote Joslin in speaking of the period following the onset of the Allen era, "During the next eight years the duration of life of my average diabetic increased one-fourth or the equivalent of slightly over one year. As the number of diabetics or pre-diabetics in the country was approximately 500,000, the establishment of this simple but far-reaching principle probably added half a million years, to the lives of American diabetics."

The general adoption of the Allen treatment was largely due to Joslin. One outstanding difference in this diet from that of Naunyn is that fat was at first the only food withdrawn. The theory underlying the Allen fasting treatment was that diabetes is not only a disorder of carbohydrate assimilation, but of the whole metabolism generally. An increase in diet or in weight would, accordingly, constitute too great a strain on the disordered pancreas and, therefore, if the whole diet is lightened, more general improvement would be noted.

In the history of insulin following the observation by von Brunner, in 1683, that the removal of the pancreas in a dog caused typical diabetes, it was over a century before this connection was actually seen. In 1788, Cawley, an English physician, suggested a relationship between diabetes and the pancreas as a result of an observation he made that the pancreas of a person who had died of diabetes had atrophied and had calculi in its secretory ducts.

In 1845 Bouchardat formulated the theory that there exists a diabetes due to a disturbance of the pancreas. With attention thus being focused on the relationship of the pancreas to disease, numerous experiments were tried to see if the removal or ligation of the pancreas would cause diabetes.

Claude Bernard, in a series of papers published between 1849 and 1877, explained the metabolic changes of carbohydrates and announced his discovery of the glycogenic function of the liver. This knowledge had a definite bearing on the discovery of the cause of diabetes.

Although innumerable scientists were working on the subject, it was not until 1889 when Minkowski and von Mering carefully and completely extirpated the whole pancreas of the famous Strässburg dog that mankind was certain of the cause of diabetes. From this experiment it was learned that carbohydrate is formed out of protein in a fairly definite ratio; that levulose is the one type of carbohydrate which, when administered to a depancreatized dog, increases the glycogen in the liver; and that with only a fragment of the pancreas remaining, diabetes does not develop.

Histology was keeping pace with other advance and Paul Langerhans, in 1869, had discovered the division of the pancreas, since called the islands of Langerhans. The other type of cell contained in the acinous section of the pancreas was also known. Between 1889 and 1891, Giulio Vassale showed that there was a functional independence of the islands of Langerhans and the acinous cells of the pancreas. In 1893, Laguesse suspected that the islands of Langerhans produced an internal secretion. In 1899, Diamare and Laguesse, from studies of comparative anatomy, felt that the internal secretion from the islands of Langerhans effected metabolic changes of the carbohydrates, and showed that the islands were ductless glands like the thyroid or adrenals. Opie, in 1901, and Ssobolew, in 1902, from a study of several autopsies, stated that where diabetes was the result of a lesion of the pancreas, this lesion affected the islands of Langerhans, and where diabetes was not present, even though there were pancreatic lesions, these lesions were limited to the acinous portion of the pancreas. Ssobolew suggested that the pancreas of a new-born calf might be a fruitful source of the solution of the gland. All of these demonstrations proving that the islands of Langerhans are ductless glands and secrete something into the blood without which diabetes mellitus would develop, led to the suggestion by Sir Sharpey Schafer, in 1916, that this anti-diabetic hormone, as yet only an hypothetical secrétion, should be named "insulin."

The development of insulin from this point was an attempt through chemical methods to find a substance, the presence of which was hypothetical, and the function of which had been negatively proved through experiments on the islands of Langerhans. One of the first experiments was that of Rennie and Fraser who used as a working basis the glands of certain fish which had been shown anatomically to be the same as the islands of Langerhans, and which were free from the secretions of the cells of the acinous section of the pancreas. They administered by mouth the extracts obtained and lost the benefit of them by the destructive reaction of the digestive juices, for it has since been proved that insulin is abundantly present in the glands with which they worked. One boy received some of the solution which they extracted subcutaneously and he derived benefit from it. Their other findings did not substantiate their original thesis, however, and their experiment was abandoned.

In 1908 there was a near discovery of insulin when Zeulzer extracted the pancreas with alcohol, thus saving it from destruction by digestive juices. Through experimentation, Zeulzer finally obtained an insulin extract which he injected in diabetic patients intravenously. Apparently, in view of our later knowledge, the peculiar symptoms which his diabetics developed were due to overdoses of the extract. However, his experiments were discontinued because of the reaction of patients to them.

Frederick G. Banting, assisted by C. H. Best, a medical student, began a series of experiments in the laboratory of J. J. R. MacLeod of the Medical School of the University of Toronto. Banting was familiar with the experiments in which the ligation of the pancreatic ducts was followed by atrophy of the secretory digestive ducts, leaving the cells of the islands of Langerhans intact, and conceived the idea of using extracts of the atrophied glands. This investigator had an advantage the other earlier scientists did not have—"accurate micro-chemical methods of estimation of the percentage of sugar in the blood, an increase of which, ... is the cardinal symptom of diabetes."

The ducts connecting the pancreas and intestines of a dog were ligated, and a period of time long enough for the atrophy of the gland elapsed before Banting attempted to make solutions from the gland. When extracts from these glandular solutions were injected into diabetic dogs intravenously, there was an immediate approach to normal of the blood sugar of these dogs. This experiment was repeated several times with the same result before the conclusions were considered sound. Naturally, the number of atrophied glands would be limited and, therefore, unless some other method of obtaining insulin could be devised, the thing would be impractical.

Ssobolew had suggested that the pancreas of a new-born calf should be productive of large quantities of this substance, for the digestive processes do not begin until birth. Working on this knowledge, Banting and Best decided to try the pancreas of an unborn calf. This was done and various methods were used to purify the extract to remove all the irritants. The work of this chemical purification was accomplished by J. B. Collip.

It would seem that the greatest part of the work were accomplished at this stage, but there still remained the perfection of a system whereby insulin could be obtained from the pancreas of full grown cattle, and the perfection of a system whereby insulin could be produced on a large and commercial scale. For some time, although the original preparation of the extract was carried out seemingly to perfection, the quantity product was not the efficacious product of the early experiments. The laboratory of the Eli Lilly Company worked with the other experimenters for several months before it was discovered that the cause of the trouble was insufficient control of the degree of acidity at various stages of the extraction process. This acidity was eventually controlled by using isoelectric precipitation to purify—a process which is still in use in the preparation of regular insulin.

The general adoption of insulin therapy caused a dramatic drop in deaths from diabetes. Its manifest action in lowering the blood sugar and promoting the utilization of carbohydrates has restored health to innumerable individuals with beginning or advanced disease. Regular insulin has to be injected two, three, and even four times a day in order to control adequately most cases of the disease, because it is absorbed so rapidly that its effect is temporary.

Dr. H. C. Hagedorn of Copenhagen and his associates carried on, over several years, experiments on the production of an insulin compound which would be slowly soluble in tissue fluid. By using a basic protein substance, instead of the definitely acid regular insulin hydrochloride, he produced protamine insulin. Joslin considers this step of such vital importance in the advance of diabetic therapy that he has named this the Hagedorn era, in honor of its discoverer.

Hagedorn, in seeking a suitable substance for his purpose, used the protamines first described by Miescher in 1868, and used first as protein precipitants by Kossel in 1890. An hitherto undescribed monoprotamine obtained from the sperm of the rainbow trout, the Salmo iridius, proved to be the most efficient. This, in itself, was not sufficient to delay absorption, but when the reaction of the protamine insulin solution was adjusted to a hydrogenous concentration similar to that of the body fluids, a precipitate of the protamine insulin took place which required a breakdown of the compound before absorption. This suspension was of such a practically constant insulin concentration that when it was deposited in the subcutaneous tissues of the body, there was a steady and prolonged absorption of the insulin liberated from the solid particles.

The addition of a trace of a heavy metal, such as zinc, was found to lengthen materially the period of activity of the insulin. The market preparation now available is protamine zinc insulin.

Throughout the world, the experiments of Hagedorn with protamine insulin are being duplicated with similar findings. In the words of Niels B. Krarup, associate of Hagedorn, "All the patients treated with protamine insulinate have been successfully relieved of symptoms due to hyperglycemia and acidosis without the administration of more than two injections a day. Protamine insulinate has proved to be less likely to produce hypoglycemic shocks than is ordinary insulin.

"The present investigation shows that the effect of protamine insulinate is more uniform and of longer duration than that of ordinary insulin and that this action can be advantageously used to lessen the fluctuations in the blood sugar and the consequent indisposition, the glycosuria, and the tendency to acidosis, without necessitating an increase in the number of the injections."

The importance of international medical advance, sponsored by the League of Nations, is perfectly apparent in communicable diseases. It has its place in the treatment of diabetes, too. The Committee on the Standardization of Toxins, Drugs, etc., of the League of Nations, has defined a unit of insulin as one third of that amount of insulin which will lower the blood sugar to an average of 0.045 per cent within five hours of its injection. Thus, a person with diabetes mellitus can obtain accurate and uniform doses of insulin all over the world. Too great lowering of the blood sugar such as would follow the administration of too much insulin would cause excessive discomfort and, in some cases, convulsions. This is one of the reasons why diabetic patients educated in the care of their disease carry one or two lumps of sugar about with them to have on hand in case they feel weakness from too little sugar in their blood.

The history of insulin in relation to diabetes has one of its most humane chapters in the benefit it has been to children. In most cases, diabetes has been a disease largely occurring in the degenerative period after forty years. In many cases, however, it has appeared in children. With them it has been, as a rule, a simple uncomplicated disease with a rapidly fatal termination. Insulin has restored these children not only to life, but to an active normal life. From the point of view of research, its value cannot be estimated. Before the Banting era, it was nearly impossible to study a case of pure, uncomplicated diabetes for any length of time, because these cases occurred only in young children, and most young children with the disease died in a year or two. Now they live and though they may always have to take insulin, a study of their health will clear up many of the points of the disease now in doubt, and make possible an improvement in the methods of treatment for both children and adults.

Bibliography

ALLEN, FREDERICK M.; STILLMAN, EDGAR; and FITZ, REGINALD: "Total Dietary Regulation in the Treatment of Diabetes." The Rockefeller Institute for Medical Research, New York, 1919.

DORLAND, W. A. NEWMAN: "The American Illustrated Medical Dictionary." W. B. Saunders Company, Philadelphia and London, 1932.
GARRISON, FIELDING H.: "History of Medicine." W. B. Saunders Company, Philadelphia and London, 1929.
HAGEDORN, H. C.; JENSEN, B. NORMAN; KRARUP, N. B.; and WODSTRUP, I.: "Protamine Insulinate." The Journal of the American Medical Association, Vol. 106, No. 3, January 18, 1936.
JOSLIN, ELLIOTT P.: "Diabetes. Its Control by the Individual and by the State." Harvard University Press, Cambridge, 1931.
JOSLIN, ELLIOTT P.: "The Treatment of Diabetes Mellitus." Lea & Febiger, Philadelphia, 1937.
JOSLIN, ELLIOTT P.; ROOT, HOWARD F.; MARBLE, ALEXANDER; WHITE, PRISCILLA; JOSLIN, ALLEN P.; and LYNCH, GEORGE W.: "Protamine Insulin." The New England Journal of Medicine, Vol. 214, No. 22, May 28, 1936.
KRARUP, NIELS B.: "Clinical Investigations into the Action of Protamine Insulinate." G. E. C. Gad, Copenhagen, 1935.
LÉPINE, R.: "LeDiabète Sucré." Felix Alcan, Ancienne Librarie Germer Baillière Et Cie, Paris, 1909.
MACLEOD, J. J. R.: "Insulin to the Rescue of the Diabetic." Chemistry In Medicine, The Chemical Foundation, Inc., New York, 1928.
MCCRADIE, ANDREW ROSS: "The Discoveries in the Field of Diabetes Mellitus and Their Investigators." Medical Life, Issue 45, June, 1924, American Society of Medical History, New York.
OSLER, SIR WILLIAM: "Principles and Practice of Medicine." 1913 edition.
WOODYATT, ROLLIN T.: "Diabetes Mellitus." Cecil's Text-Book of Medicine, W. B. Saunders Company, Philadelphia and London, 1933.

INSULIN AND PROTAMINE INSULIN
ALEXANDER MARBLE, M.D.
Boston, Mass.

A. Regular (Unmodified) Insulin

On May 16, 1921, Frederick G. Banting, a young surgeon fresh from war service and Charles H. Best, a second-year medical student, set to work in the Laboratories of Physiology at the University of Toronto with the express purpose of isolating from the pancreas a substance which upon injection into another animal would lower the blood sugar. The production of such a hormone by the islands of Langerhans of the pancreas had been postulated by Laguesse and others some thirty years before but all attempts at its extraction had been unsuccessful. Banting worked on the assumption that the active principle—now known as insulin—was destroyed by the protein-splitting enzymes secreted by the acinar cells of the pancreas. Consequently he tied off the external ducts of the pancreas in dogs, allowed the acinar tissue to degenerate for ten weeks, removed the pancreas from the animal as soon as possible after death and prepared a simple extract of the gland. This extract was found to be potent when injected in 5 cc. dosage into a diabetic dog, reducing its blood sugar in two hours from 0.20 to 0.11 per cent. Since the amounts of material available from such ligature of the pancreatic ducts in dogs or from the use of the pancreases of foetal calves were too small for practical use, soon a method for preparation from adult beef pancreas was worked out. In the elaboration of the method and in the purification of the extract Dr. J. B. Collip played a prominent part and in the researches designed to elucidate the action of insulin, Professor J. J. R. Macleod exerted a guiding influence.

The first dose of insulin ever given to a human diabetic patient was injected on January 12, 1922, in the Toronto General Hospital into a boy of fourteen years by one of the house physicians. Insulin was first administered at the New England Deaconess Hospital here in Boston on August 7, 1922, to a woman (Case 1542), then aged thirty-seven years, who at that time had had diabetes for five years. Insulin transformed her, as it has thousands of diabetics treated subsequently, from an emaciated semi-invalid into an essentially normal person.

Before 1922 the average diabetic lived only 6.1 years after the onset of his disease and died at the age of 46.7 years. By 1935 he was living 11.0 years after onset and his age at death had increased to 62.8 years! Without insulin the life of the diabetic child was measured in days, weeks and months. The diagnosis of diabetes in a child was equivalent to a death sentence and it was a rare child who lived for two years after the onset of his disease. Without insulin, patients with all except the milder grades of diabetes were compelled to so restrict their diet that proper weight and strength could rarely be maintained. Statistics from one clinic show that before 1922 from 40 to 60 of every 100 diabetics died in coma; today only 6 per cent so succumb and we have justifiable hopes that even this figure may be reduced.

Despite all that is known of insulin and its life-giving effect, far too little use of it is made in the country at large. Few, indeed, are the diabetic patients who will not benefit by its use. One's approach to the problem should be not that of avoiding insulin if possible, but rather of demanding a good reason for not using it.

Insulin by Mouth

Insulin is a protein and as such is broken down by the digestive juices of the stomach and intestine. When this happens, potency is lost; consequently insulin by mouth is not effective. Preparations on the market claiming to control diabetes when taken orally are, by and large, quack medicines and advertisements of such products are barred from reputable medical journals. To date insulin is the only agent available which affords treatment specific for diabetes.

Action in the Body

When a suitable dose of regular (unmodified) insulin is injected subcutaneously into a diabetic patient and food withheld, the blood sugar falls progressively, reaches a low point in three to four hours and then gradually returns to the starting level. The whole effect lasts five or six hours. If the dose has been large enough to cause the blood sugar to fall to subnormal levels, symptoms of a more or less distressing nature may be produced and immediate treatment with carbohydrate be necessary for relief. If physical exercise is taken after the insulin has been given, the blood sugar falls more quickly and sharply than if the patient is at rest. Great advantage of this beneficial effect of exercise should be taken in the practical treatment of patients.

The fall in blood sugar and the accompanying decrease or disappearance of sugar in the urine are the easily demonstrable effects of the injection of insulin. Other and more important events occur in the body, however. Only scant information is available as to the action of insulin in the tissues, but we do know that with its use glycogen once more accumulates in a normal fashion in the liver and muscles, and sugar is utilized for the production of heat and energy in a manner approaching the normal. The diabetic person gains in weight and strength and becomes an essentially normal being.

Size of Dose

Using regular (unmodified) insulin, injections are made at 30 to 45 minutes before one, two or three of the day's meals in dosage varying from 4 or 5 units up to 20, 30 or 40 units, depending upon the severity of the diabetes, the age of the patient, the diet employed, the amount of physical activity, and the presence or absence of complications, as infections. Patients with mild diabetes may require only one small dose a day, usually given before breakfast. Patients with severe diabetes may require insulin not only before each meal but also in small amounts, 2 to 6 units, at bedtime or midnight. The average patient requires insulin twice daily, before breakfast and before supper in total daily dosage of 30 to 40 units. The adjustment of the dosage for a given patient is an individual matter and usually demands hospitalization for five to ten days at the outset.

Dosage in Complications

Often in the treatment of diabetic patients during complications such as coma, acidosis, infections and following operations, it is desirable to give insulin in graduated amounts at frequent intervals according to the needs of the moment. For such occasions it is helpful to leave an order with the nurse such as that below.

Secure a single specimen of urine every three hours (the interval may be from 1 to 6 hours), test for sugar with Benedict's solution and give insulin according to the color of the test, as follows:

Red or Orange	Yellow	Yellow-green	Green or Blue
20	15	10	0

The actual number of units as expressed in the fraction must be suited to the individual patient and the above is used simply as an illustration.

Technique of Administration

With almost all patients insulin containing 40 units per cubic centimeter is desirable although with those receiving very large amounts the use of U80 strength is preferable in order to reduce the quantity of fluid injected. Occasional patients taking small amounts may use U20 insulin; rarely, if ever, is the U10 strength indicated.

The syringe and needle should be boiled in water for five minutes just prior to the injection or kept completely and continuously immersed in 70 per cent alcohol. Before withdrawing insulin, the cap of the vial should be cleansed with alcohol as should also the site of injection. We prefer a syringe of simple design, of 1 cc. capacity with ten equal divisions. A needle ½ inch long and of 26 gauge is satisfactory.

Insulin may be injected subcutaneously anywhere over the body. The best areas are over the thighs, buttocks, lower back, upper arms and abdominal wall. By varying the site, no one spot should receive insulin oftener than once in three or four weeks, thereby lessening the possibility of "insulin lumps" or of atrophy of the subcutaneous fat. It is important to remember that insulin is less well absorbed from indurated, scarred areas.

Insulin may be given intravenously as in diabetic coma when the condition is critical and absorption poor from beneath the skin, but ordinarily this is not an advantage nor is it economical since a large part of the insulin so given is promptly excreted in the urine.

Insulin (Hypoglycemic) Reactions

Insulin "shock" or an insulin "reaction" is caused by an overdose of insulin, by too little food or by exercise of severity unusual for the individual concerned. The usual symptoms are nervousness, sweating, tremor, faintness, numbness and tingling especially of the lips, rapid heart action, hunger, headache, double vision, and uncommonly nausea and vomiting. One or more of these symptoms may be present; rarely the hypoglycemia may be so profound as to cause unconsciousness with or without convulsions.

Treatment consists of supplying at once readily available carbohydrate as orange juice, ginger ale, sugar and syrup. Complete relief occurs usually within five to ten minutes. In an unconscious patient adrenaline in dosage of 0.5 cc. may be given subcutaneously or 20 cc. of 50 per cent glucose injected intravenously.

Repeated reactions naturally demand reduction in the appropriate dose of insulin. Ordinarily decreases in the order of 2 or 4 units are adequate. Prior to periods of unusual or strenuous exercise it is well for the patient to take 10 or 15 grams of carbohydrate (in addition to the regular diet) to avoid a possible reaction. It is desirable that such carbohydrate be in the form of food which requires digestion so that gradual absorption of sugar into the blood may occur.

Diabetic patients taking insulin should carry with them at all times an identification card stating that fact together with their name and address, the name and address of their doctor and a query worded as follows: "Diabetic coma or insulin shock—which?"

Sensitivity to Insulin

Many patients experience varying degrees of swelling, redness, itching and pain at the site of injection of insulin because of their sensitiveness to the protein concerned. Such local responses usually come on a few days after treatment is begun and are noted for several days. They are rarely marked enough to be distressing and almost always disappear with continued use of insulin.

Resistance to Insulin

Relative "resistance" or insensitiveness to insulin is seen most commonly in the presence of infections particularly with fever. Patients soon learn to expect this and realize that at such times an increase in the dosage may be necessary. This greater need for insulin is encountered also at times when diabetes is complicated by hemochromatosis, cancer of the pancreas, acute pancreatitis, hyperthyroidism, cirrhosis and chronic passive congestion of the liver and conditions in which the muscles are poorly developed or little used. Very rarely a patient may require enormous doses—300 to 600 units daily—without demonstrable cause.

B. Protamine Insulin

Soon after insulin was introduced into the treatment of diabetes there was sensed the need for a modification which would provide a slower and more prolonged action. In the early days of insulin the duration of action was stated to be eight hours but with better methods of preparation and purification of the product, the length of action was reduced to five or six hours. This short-lived action is of disadvantage in the treatment of severe juvenile cases for, despite a bedtime dose of insulin, there occurs characteristically a rise in the blood sugar after midnight with the production of a high fasting value and marked glycosuria by 6 or 7 A.M.

Various unsuccessful attempts were made to modify this action. Insulin was mixed with gum arabic, oils, protein substances, lecithin, pituitrin, adrenalin, etc. but none of the combinations proved to be entirely satisfactory. Finally Hagedorn working in Copenhagen combined insulin with a basic protein, a protamine derived from the ripe sperm of the rainbow trout. A suspension was produced which when adjusted to pH 7.3, similar to that of body fluids, was very slowly absorbed from the subcutaneous tissues. From such a depot under the skin active insulin is thus slowly released and a gradual, prolonged effect upon the blood sugar secured. The contrast between the effect of a single dose of regular insulin and of protamine insulin is shown well in Figure 1.

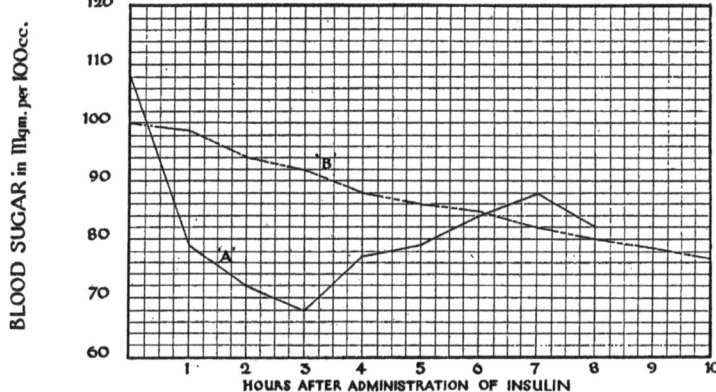

Fig. 1. — Miss M. G., 25 years of age, normal, nurse-dietitian. Curve A, October 23, shows the effect of 8 units of regular insulin (Lilly) given subcutaneously. Curve B, October 25, shows the effect of an equivalent dose of protamine insulinate (Danish). Note the gradual, steady fall in blood sugar in the latter curve. In each case the insulin was given immediately after the first blood sample was taken.

Hagedorn's discovery marked the beginning of a still brighter era for diabetics. News of his work spread to America and confirmation of the results was soon reported from various centers. Laboratories in the United States and Canada cooperated with Hagedorn in the further development of the product. It was found that the addition of a trace of a heavy metal such as zinc materially lengthened the period of activity. Accordingly when the preparation was finally released for sale, it was as protamine zinc insulin (1 mgm. zinc per 500 units of insulin). This exerts an effect over a period of 24 to 30 hours after injection under the skin. One is thus able to accomplish an amazing thing: to regulate tomorrow morning's fasting blood sugar by a dose of insulin given this morning.

Time and Number of Injections

Protamine zinc insulin is given only once daily and usually before breakfast in the morning. (Possibly further clinical trial may show that its use, once daily, at some other time, as at bedtime, may be advantageous.) The dosage selected is that which will allow a normal (or satisfactory) blood sugar and a sugar free urine on the following morning before food is taken. With most patients this one dose of protamine insulin alone suffices to control the diabetes but a certain number will need an accompanying dose of regular (unmodified) insulin given at the same time in the morning before breakfast. This dose of regular insulin helps care for the hyperglycemia and glycosuria which in these patients comes during the forenoon. When both types of insulin are taken, the regular insulin is injected first into one spot and that of protamine insulin into a separate area. If the doses of regular and of protamine insulin are mixed in the syringe and given as one injection, the excess of protamine present will bind part of the regular insulin and this must be allowed for. Occasionally for short periods, as during infections, it may be necessary to supplement the above injections by additional small doses of regular insulin just before lunch and supper, adjusting the amount according to urine tests taken at those times.

Preliminary Adjustment

In shifting a patient from regular insulin two, three or four times a day to the new regime, a hospital stay of from five to ten days is highly desirable and in many cases imperative. At the start, one may give an amount of regular insulin equal to or almost equal to that ordinarily taken by the patient before breakfast. As the simultaneous dose of protamine insulin, one may give from one to one and a half times the total dosage ordinarily taken during the remainder of the day. In making the subsequent changes in dosage which are necessary every day or two until proper adjustment is secured, tests of two specimens of urine are especially important: the specimen just before the noon meal which reflects the dosage of *regular* insulin and the rising specimen which reflects the dosage of *protamine* insulin. Increases or decreases as indicated by the character of these two tests may be made in amounts of two to six or more units. Determinations of the blood sugar upon arising, before lunch and at 4 and 9 P.M. are helpful although not indispensable. Glycosuria after the evening meal usually clears up within a few days until negligible amounts of sugar are wasted at this time.

In beginning protamine insulin with a patient who has never had insulin before, the initial dose (before breakfast) may be 10 or 20 units unaccompanied by regular insulin. In succeeding days, the dosage may be increased gradually to 30 or 40 or more units if necessary. Intermediate dosages may of course be indicated in any individual case. In the average case, a dose of 40 units or less will produce a normal fasting blood sugar. Hypoglycemia in the early morning hours precludes further increases in dosage. If this happens and yet significant hyperglycemia and glycosuria occur in the forenoon, then a small dose of regular insulin, say 10 units, may be given simultaneously with the protamine insulin. From this stage on, finer adjustment of dosage is carried out as outlined in the preceding paragraph.

Sufficient time must be allowed for stabilization with protamine insulin. Especially at the beginning of treatment, best results are secured when changes are made gradually. Patient and physician alike must not become discouraged if diabetic control cannot be brought about in as short a space of time as with regular insulin. Furthermore, experience with the occasional case which, even after a prolonged period, seems to defy attempts at proper balance, should not cause the doctor to withhold protamine insulin from the majority of patients who will readily become adjusted to it and secure its benefit.

Diet

The diet of patients receiving protamine insulin is similar to that on the old regime except that because of the slow, gradual action of the insulin it is helpful to allow somewhat less total carbohydrate and to spread the food out over the waking part of the day rather than to concentrate it all at three main meals. Consequently, without increasing and perhaps even decreasing the total carbohydrate in the diet, lunches of from 10 to 20 grams of carbohydrate may to advantage be given in the mid-morning, mid-afternoon and at bedtime. Incidentally, such lunches lessen the possibility of hypoglycemic reactions.

Hypoglycemic Attacks

"Reactions" due to protamine insulin do not differ from those caused by ordinary insulin except that they may come on more gradually and may recur after having once been relieved by carbohydrate. Headache, particularly occipital headache, occurs more commonly than under the old regime. Uncommonly nausea and vomiting are seen as symptoms of a reaction due to protamine insulin.

Results

Protamine insulin in one form or another has been used in the United States since August, 1935, and has been on sale since February, 1937. That it affords a great advance in treatment is evident. Even apart from the benefits originally claimed for it, namely, a lessened incidence of hypoglycemic reactions and a saving in number of units of insulin required, there are two distinct advantages of outstanding importance: (1) *Convenience of treatment*. With the number of injection periods per day reduced from 2, 3 or 4 to 1, the diabetic is freed from another restraint which has prevented him from leading a normal life. (2) *Better control of diabetes*. With protamine insulin, contr 'l of diabetes to a degree hitherto impossible now can be achieved. Formerly with severe diabetes control at best extended over only 18 of the 24 hours. Now control over practically the entire day can be secured. There is every reason to hope that because of this the diabetic so treated will escape the complications which in the past have beset him, chiefly coma and premature arteriosclerosis. Furthermore, the way has been opened for still further progress in both practice and research.

INSTRUCTION OF DIABETIC PATIENTS

M. BERNICE MOORE, R. N.

*Teaching Diabetic Nurse, N. E. Deaconess Hospital,
Boston, Mass.*

The work of the Teaching Diabetic Nurse in the Hospital is two-fold: the instruction of the postgraduate and student nurses in the fundamentals of diabetic nursing care, and the instruction of diabetic patients in the art of controlling their disease by the use of diet, exercise and insulin.

Many teaching problems arise because of the age and race of the patient, the wide variation in the intelligence and education and the necessity of teaching by means of an interpreter whenever the patient does not understand English. If it is impossible to instruct the patient, arrangements are made to have some member of the family attend the daily classes and to receive individual instruction in the care of the diabetic relative.

The teaching nurse must be certain that the patient or his family understand the following: the Benedict's test for sugar in the urine, the frequency of testing specimens, the technique of the administration of insulin, the causes, symptoms and treatment of insulin reactions, the prevention of coma as well as its causes, symptoms and treatment, the prevention of complications, the care of the feet, the classification of foods and the method of calculating and substituting in the prescribed diet.

Individual problems are many—the necessity of changing the diet instructions into ounces or household measurements, the planning of lunches to carry to school or work and meals to be eaten in restaurants or while traveling. Often special diets are necessary because of the presence of complications such as peptic ulcer, colitis, etc. Frequently, the time and type of meals must be changed to comply with irregular or unusual working hours and varying activity of the patient.

Before discharge all patients should be able to answer the following questions:

1. What organ of the body is at fault in diabetes?
   Answer: The pancreas.
2. What are the common symptoms?
   Answer: Excessive hunger, thirst and urination, loss of weight and strength, and itching, local or general.
3. How is the disease controlled?
   Answer: By diet, exercise and insulin.
4. How is the urine tested for sugar?
   Answer: Put four drops of urine in a test tube and add ½ teaspoonful Benedict's solution. Shake tube well and place it in boiling water for five minutes. Colors after boiling. Blue means no sugar, green shows the presence of a small amount of sugar, yellow a moderate amount, and orange and red a large amount of sugar.

5. How often should the urine be tested?

    Answer: One to four times a day, preferably before meals or at bedtime.

6. Why is insulin given in the treatment of diabetes?

    Answer: Insulin is given in amounts sufficient to make up the patient's deficiency so that he may have enough food to maintain normal weight and energy.

7. What are the chief differences between regular and protamine insulin?

    Answer: Regular insulin lowers the blood sugar rapidly and its effect lasts for a period of six to eight hours. Protamine insulin lowers the blood sugar slowly and its effect lasts for a period of twenty hours to thirty hours.

8. How long before the meal should insulin be taken?

    Answer: About fifteen minutes before the meal.

9. How are the needles and syringe sterilized before an injection?

    Answer: By boiling for five minutes or by keeping them in 70% alcohol constantly.

10. How do you measure your insulin dosage in a 1 c. c. syringe which is divided into tenths?

    Answer: The strength of insulin equals the number of units in 1 c.c. If the syringe is divided into tenths, each space equals one-tenth the strength. For example, each space equals four units if using U-40 insulin.

11. Why is it essential that the site of injection be changed daily?

    Answer: To prevent poor absorption, abscesses, and insulin atrophy.

12. What would you do if a needle breaks during injection?

    Answer: Circle the spot where the needle was inserted with ink or mercurochrome, draw an arrow showing which way the needle was pointed, then report to your doctor.

13. What causes an insulin reaction?

    Answer: A low blood sugar due to too much insulin, from increased tolerance or mistake in measuring, too little food, strenuous or unusual exercise, too long interval between insulin and meal, or if food is unabsorbed because of stasis, vomiting or diarrhea.

14. What are the typical symptoms?

    Answer: Hunger, perspiration, tremor, pallor, double or blurred vision, weakness, faintness, headache, and tingling sensations of the lips or extremities.

15. What would you take to treat a reaction?

    Answer: One lump or 1 teaspoonful of sugar, one-half orange or 1 teaspoonful of any kind of syrup.

16. What could you do to avoid a repetition of the reaction the following day?

    Answer: Reduce the dose of insulin by two units unless reaction is due to unusual exercise or other obvious cause.

17. How can a reaction due to excessive exercise be prevented?
    Answer: By taking ten grams carbohydrate (small orange or 2 uneedas) just before strenuous exercise.

18. What time of day are reactions most likely to occur with regular insulin? with protamine insulin?
    Answer: Three to four hours after injection.
    Answer: May occur at any time but usually more than twelve hours after the injection.

19. What are the six rules for the prevention of coma?
    Answer: In case of illness and fever,
    1. Call the doctor
    2. Go to bed
    3. Keep warm
    4. Have a hot drink hourly
    5. Take an enema
    6. Get someone to nurse you

20. What causes coma?
    Answer: The causes of coma are breaking of diet, too little or no insulin and infections.

21. What are the typical symptoms?
    Answer: Gradual onset of weakness, fatigue, nausea and vomiting, pain in abdomen, deep and difficult breathing, and increasing drowsiness leading to unconsciousness.

22. How would you regulate the dose of insulin on a day of illness?
    Answer: Under your doctor's direction, test a specimen of urine every three or four hours and take graduated doses of regular insulin according to test.
    If you are taking protamine insulin, it is usually wise not to take more than one dose of this a day. At times of illness, continue same dose of protamine and for supplementary doses, use regular insulin.

23. What foods served on your diet contain carbohydrate?
    Answer: Bread, crackers, potato, rice, macaroni, all kinds of vegetables, cereals, milk, ice cream and fruit.

24. What foods served on your diet contain protein?
    Answer: Meat, fish, fowl, eggs, bacon, cheese and milk.

25. What foods on your diet contain fat?
    Answer: Butter, cream, oil, bacon, cheese, meat, fish, fowl, eggs and milk.

26. What foods are considered to have no food value?
    Answer: Tea, coffee, cocoa shells, clear broths, diabetic mayonnaise, mineral oil and distilled vinegar.

27. Why is it important that you do not increase or decrease your diet without permission from the doctor?
    Answer: If the diet is increased, the blood sugar will rise, and sugar will appear in the urine. If the diet is decreased, the patient will not have enough food to maintain normal weight and strength.

28. What type of diet would you use on a day of illness?
    Answer: Soft or liquid diet. For example, one quart milk, three slices of bread, one and a half pats of butter, one egg, one half cup cooked cereal, and two glasses of orange juice.

29. What are the important facts to remember about the care of the feet? What antiseptics are safe to use?
Answer: See directions under "Treatment of Feet."
30. How can you avoid complications of the disease?
Answer: By controlling the disease with correct diet, adequate exercise and sufficient insulin.
A monthly visit to the physician is advisable.

SPECIAL INSTRUCTIONS FOR DIABETIC PATIENTS

The special instructions listed below are designed to help in preventing and distinguishing between diabetic coma and an insulin reaction. Remember that coma comes on gradually in days or hours, but an insulin reaction usually in less than an hour or in a few minutes. Coma comes from too much food and too little insulin: a reaction from too little food and too much insulin. In coma the urine contains sugar, but in a reaction although the first specimen may show sugar, a second specimen invariably will be sugar free or almost sugar free. The respiration in coma is heavy and deep, but in insulin reaction is normal or in severe cases may be feeble.

I. To Prevent Diabetic Coma

A. Never omit insulin unless the urine is sugar free. Keep to your diet and in case of an infection take more insulin if necessary to keep sugar free. It is imperative to test the urine frequently during an acute illness.

B. If you feel sick and especially if you have FEVER, NAUSEA and VOMITING or severe pains in the abdomen: 1. Call a doctor. 2. Go to bed. 3. Take a cup of coffee, tea, cocoa shells or broth every hour and live upon acute illness diet (Oranges 3, Oatmeal, small portion, Bread, 3 slices, Milk, one quart, 1 egg, little butter). If the urine contains sugar, take regular insulin every hour under your doctor's direction. 4. You need the entire time of a nurse or friend to care for you until you are well. 5. Move the bowels with an enema.

II. To Recognize and Treat an Insulin Reaction

A. CAUSES OF AN INSULIN REACTION.
1. Too much insulin.
2. Too little food or too long a period between insulin and food.
3. Food given has been unabsorbed because of indigestion, vomiting or diarrhea.
4. Unusual exercise.

B. SYMPTOMS (may occur 1 to 8 hours after taking regular insulin; considerably later after protamine insulin).
1. Trembling, nervousness, faintness, weakness, pallor, sweating, hunger, double vision, headache.
2. Unconsciousness may occur if the reaction is severe.

C. TREATMENT.
1. When the patient is conscious: Take the juice of an orange,

one or more lumps of sugar, or one or more teaspoonfuls of corn syrup.
2. In unconsciousness: If necessary give 0.5 c.c. adrenalin chloride 1:100 solution hypodermically and repeat in 15 minutes. With return to consciousness as soon as possible give the juice of an orange by mouth. Ten per cent glucose solution may be given by rectum, under the skin or intravenously if the doctor so directs.

III. The best insurance a diabetic patient can have is to see his physician once a month. Take him this paper and a specimen of urine. Always carry this sheet with you or wear an identification tag with your Name, Address and the words—Diabetic Coma or Insulin Shock. Which?

Patients Taking Insulin Should Always Carry Two Lumps of Sugar

Directions for Diet and Insulin for Diabetic Patients

NAME _____ ADDRESS _____ DATE _____

BREAKFAST	Mid A.M.	DINNER	Mid P.M.	SUPPER	Bed Time	TOTAL DAILY DIET	
Reg. Insulin — Units Prot. Insulin — Units		Reg. Insulin — Units Prot. Insulin — Units		Reg. Insulin — Units Prot. Insulin — Units		C. P. F.	Cal.
Grams Portions	Grams Portions	Grams Portions	Grams Portions	Grams Portions	Grams Portions		Grams
Eggs		Eggs		Eggs		Eggs	
Meat, Cooked		Meat, Cooked		Meat, Cooked		Meat, Cooked	
Bacon		Bacon		Bacon		Bacon	
5% Veg.		5% Veg.		5% Veg.		5% Veg.	
10% Veg.		10% Veg.		10% Veg.		10% Veg.	
Oat., Dry		Oat., Dry		Oat., Dry		Oat., Dry	
Oat., Cooked		Oat., Cooked		Oat., Cooked		Oat., Cooked	
Uneedas		Uneedas		Uneedas		Uneedas	
Butter		Butter		Butter		Butter	
Cream, 20%		Cream, 20%		Cream, 20%		Cream, 20%	
Milk		Milk		Milk		Milk	
Orange		Orange		Orange		Orange	
Grapefruit		Grapefruit		Grapefruit		Grapefruit	
Cheese		Cheese		Cheese		Cheese	
Potato		Potato		Potato		Potato	
Bread		Bread		Bread		Bread	

Instructions for Diabetic Patients for Care of the Mouth and Teeth

1. Use a small toothbrush with tufts well separated. Have two brushes and alternate each time you brush your teeth, replacing brush if bristles are soft.
2. A mixture of equal quantities of bicarbonate of soda and table salt is a satisfactory tooth powder.
3. Brush your teeth at least twice daily, morning and night, spending two minutes each time. Be sure that you do this properly. Ask the dental hygienist to show you if you are not sure.
4. After brushing the teeth, massage the gums with your fingers working fingers toward the teeth in a rotary motion. This is particularly important for diabetics.
5. Have your teeth cleaned by a dentist or dental hygienist every three months and the teeth examined for cavities. Keep all cavities filled.

Instructions for Diabetic Patients for Care and Treatment of the Feet

Hygiene of the Feet:

1. Wash feet daily with soap and water. Dry thoroughly, especially between toes, using pressure rather than vigorous rubbing.
2. When thoroughly dry, rub with lanolin as often as necessary to keep skin soft and free from scales and dryness, but never render the feet tender. If the feet become too soft, rub once a day with alcohol.
3. If nails are brittle and dry, soften by soaking in warm water one-half hour each night and apply lanolin generously under and about nails and bandage loosely. Clean nails with orange-wood sticks. Cut the nails only in a good light and after a bath, when the feet are very clean. Cut the nails straight across to avoid injury to the toes. If you go to a chiropodist, tell him you have diabetes.
4. All patients with overlapping toes or toes that are close together should separate them by lamb's wool. Patients with large joints or cramped-up toes should wear shoes without box toes and only vici kid leather.
5. All patients over 60 should have daily rest periods and remove their shoes. Every Sunday morning ask someone to examine your feet.
6. Do not wear bedroom slippers when you ought to wear shoes. Slippers do not give proper support. Do not step on floor with bare feet.
7. Wear shoes of soft leather which fit and are not tight (neither narrow nor short). Wear new shoes ½ hour only on the first day, increasing 1 hour daily.
8. Use bed socks instead of hot water bottles, bags or electric heaters.
9. After 50 years one hears less well, sees less well, and the sense of feeling is diminished. Remember this and be cautious about the feet.

Treatment of Corns and Callosities
1. Wear shoes which fit and cause no pressure.
2. Soak foot in warm, not hot, soapy water. Rub off with gauze or file off dead skin in or about callus or corn. Do not tear it off. Do not cut corns or callosities. Do not try to remove corns or calluses with patent or other medicines.
3. Prevent calluses under ball of foot.
    (a) by exercises such as curling and stretching toes 20 times a day.
    (b) by finishing each step on the toes and not on the ball of the foot.

Aids in Treatment of Imperfect Circulation: — Cold Feet:
1. Exercises. Bend the foot down and up as far as it will go 6 times. Describe a circle to the left with the foot six times and then to the right. Repeat morning, noon and night.
2. Massage with lanolin or cocoa butter.
3. Do not wear circular garters or sit with knees crossed.
4. If you have had gangrene or been threatened with it, keep off your feet 5 or more minutes each hour of the day and if an amputation, 15 or more minutes.

Treatment of Abrasions of the Skin:
1. Proper first-aid treatment is of the utmost importance even in apparently minor injuries. Consult your physician immediately.
2. Avoid strong irritating antiseptics, such as sulpho-napthol and iodine.
3. At once after injury some surgeons recommend applications of sterile gauze saturated with medicated alcohol or hexylresorcinol (S.T. 37). Keep wet for not more than 30 minutes by adding more of the antiseptic solution. Sterile gauze in sealed packets may be purchased at drug stores.
4. Elevate and, as much as possible until recovery, avoid using the foot.
5. Consult your doctor for pain, redness, swelling, or any inflammation.

DIABETIC COMA
ALEXANDER MARBLE, M.D.
Boston, Mass.

That *diabetic coma is preventable* and that *deaths from diabetic coma are needless* have been stated repeatedly during the last decade. The truth of these statements is borne out by the decreasing mortality from diabetic coma as shown in the accompanying chart. This has been brought about by better and better treatment of diabetes and largely through the use of insulin since 1922. However, even today, in many parts of the country the actual treatment of diabetes lags several years behind that indicated by the available scientific facts regarding it.

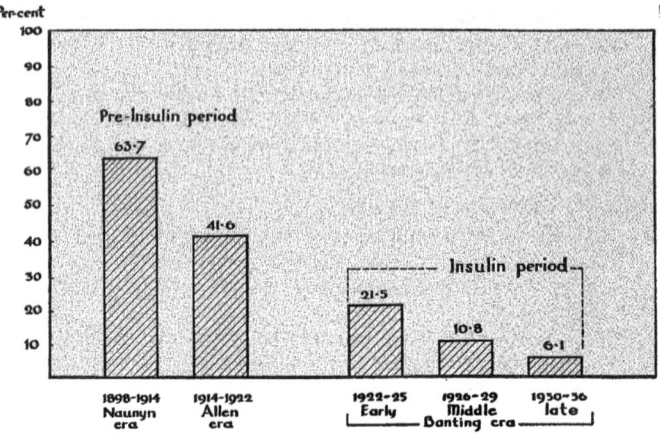

COMA AS A CAUSE OF DEATH
Percentage of all deaths due to Diabetic Coma
Patients of all ages
Experience of Elliott P. Joslin, M.D. and associates, Boston.
(Prepared by the Statistical Bureau of the Metropolitan
Life Insurance Co.)

It is evident from the above that before the introduction of the treatment of diabetes by undernutrition as suggested by Dr. F. M. Allen in 1914, over 60 per cent of all diabetics died in diabetic coma. In the period of the Allen method of treatment (1914-1922), 42 per cent of diabetics died in coma. Insulin revolutionized treatment and mortality statistics alike and in the latest group of patients studied (1930-1936) only 6.1 per cent of diabetic deaths were in coma. Despite this lowered mortality, both doctor and patient must realize that diabetic coma is an antagonist worthy of great respect and that success in its control depends on prompt recognition and aggressive treatment. With insulin the treatment of diabetes is much easier but disastrous results follow when careful regulation is neglected.

Diabetic coma represents the end-result of uncontrolled diabetes.

It is a condition of "acid-poisoning" in which the body is flooded with the incompletely oxidized products of the breakdown of fats. This in turn is due to the inability of the body of the diabetic to utilize carbohydrate in a normal fashion. Large quantities of sugar and "acetone bodies" accumulate in the blood and body tissues and are excreted in the urine. The great loss of fluid from the body leads to marked dehydration.

Precipitating Factors

We teach patients that coma occurs because of (1) too much food, (2) too little insulin, or (3) infections. Too much food may mean deliberate breaking of diet or simply the innocent overeating of the person with undiagnosed diabetes. Too little insulin often means no insulin and here again the omission may not be a willful one. The influence of infections is real. Patients may be progressing serenely with diet, insulin and exercise well balanced when with the development of a carbuncle, pneumonia, upper respiratory infection or other acute febrile illness, acidosis may be precipitated. In the occasional patient in whom acute hyperthyroidism ("thyroid storm") precipitates diabetic coma, a grave and striking clinical picture is produced.

Patients may be instructed as follows: "If you feel sick, (1) call a doctor, (2) go to bed, (3) get someone to nurse you, (4) keep warm, (5) have a hot drink hourly, (6) take an enema and (7) take insulin according to your doctor's orders."

Symptoms

There are no symptoms which are invariably found but usually the onset of definite acidosis is attended by weakness, malaise, nausea, vomiting and abdominal pain. If proper treatment is not instituted, the vomiting and abdominal pain continue and the breathing becomes labored. Respirations are of the long, deep, rapid Kussmaul ("air hunger") type, unless the condition is far advanced in which case the respirations may be simply those of the preterminal breathing of the moribund.

The saturation of the body with the "acetone bodies" is reflected in the fruity odor of the breath which sometimes is so marked that the peculiar smell in the sick room is apparent to those entering. Drowsiness comes, proceeds to stupor and passes finally into coma.

Signs

When first seen, the patient in full-blown diabetic coma presents a distressing picture. He lies in bed, unconscious, or semiconscious, often moaning as with pain, with a dry, cold skin, flushed drawn face, and obviously dehydrated tissues. The eyeballs are soft, the mouth and tongue are dry and present a dirty coating. At intervals the patient vomits dark brown material, obviously changed blood. On being turned or examined, cries as of pain may be occasioned. The abdominal findings may closely simulate those of acute appendicitis. The extremities are cold and the body temperature, in the absence of accompanying infection, is often below normal. The pulse is rapid and weak and the blood pressure low.

Laboratory Findings

The urine usually contains large but not extremely large amounts of sugar. A deep wine color is obtained with the addition of ferric chloride indicating the presence of large amounts of diacetic acid and acetone. The urinary sediment contains "showers" of granular casts. The blood sugar is high, although not always extraordinarily so. Values from 300 to 600 milligrams per cent are common: in one case the initial determination showed 1600 milligrams per cent. The carbon dioxide combining power of the blood plasma shows a marked reduction although there is no absolute parallelism between clinical and laboratory findings in this respect. Severe cases may have values of 10 volumes per cent or lower, and values so low as not to permit accurate reading on the Van Slyke instrument are occasionally obtained. In the pre-insulin days it was noted that cases had almost always a bad prognosis if the carbon dioxide combining power of the plasma was 20 volumes per cent or below. The blood chloride is often appreciably lowered, due presumably to the persistent vomiting. The non-protein nitrogen of the blood may be increased. The white blood count is usually elevated, ranging often from 10,000 to 30,000 and in one child was 81,400 per cu. m.m.

Treatment

Specific treatment is provided with insulin. This must not be given in a half-hearted fashion. On admission a specimen of urine is obtained, by catheter if necessary, to test for sugar and diacetic acid. A large dose of insulin varying usually from 20 to 100 units should be given depending on the degree of acidosis. Occasionally a child with recent onset of diabetes and of coma requires less. Examination of the urine is repeated at half-hourly or hourly intervals during the first several hours and doses of insulin given according to the amount of sugar found. The unconscious patient may require 200 units within the first two hours and the total amount during the first twenty-four hours may be rarely as large as 1,000 units. On admission a determination of the blood sugar and of the carbon dioxide combining power of the blood plasma are made and these tests are repeated one or more times during the first hours of treatment in order at first to make the diagnosis and later to gauge progress of treatment. Access to a chemical laboratory in which analyses of urine and blood can be made promptly day or night is essential for best results and lowest mortality.

Protamine insulin acts too slowly to be used alone in the treatment of diabetic coma of significant grade. A single large dose may be given at the beginning of treatment, however, to supplement the usual doses of unmodified insulin.

The patient in diabetic coma is a patient in shock. The body temperature is subnormal, the extremities cold, the pulse weak and rapid and the blood pressure low. Accordingly, due regard must be given to this phase of the condition. Immediately on admission to the hospital, the patient must be placed in a bed previously warmed. Warm blankets and bed clothing must be used and the patient surrounded by hot water bottles so placed that there is no danger of burning the skin. Fluid in large amount must be provided but not more than 100 cc. an hour should be allowed by mouth; hot liquids are preferable to cold. Often at first, however, because of vomiting, no fluids can be given by mouth. Almost invariably physiological salt solution with or without added glucose, 5 or 10 per cent, must be given subcutaneously or intravenously in quantities which may amount to 5 or 6 liters in twenty-four hours. If the blood pressure is extremely low, ephedrine sulphate may be given subcutaneously or intravenously, hourly if necessary, in doses of 25 to 50 mgm. As an emergency measure one or more doses of adrenalin hydrochloride (1-1000 solution), given subcutaneously in amounts of 0.5 to 1.0 c.c. or in smaller amounts intravenously, may be necessary. Caffeine sodium benzoate may be administered subcutaneously in repeated doses of 0.45 gm. (7½ grains). In appropriate cases transfusion of whole blood should be considered to combat shock as in a non-diabetic emergency.

Gastric lavage should be carried out routinely. It accomplishes two results: first, nausea and vomiting are stopped and the way prepared for subsequent oral feeding and medication; and second, the frequent marked distention of the stomach with resulting pressure on the heart and other viscera is relieved. An enema should be given to clear out the lower bowel.

A most serious symptom is that of oliguria or anuria. To combat this the slow intravenous injection of warm 50 per cent glucose solution in amounts of 20 to 30 c.c. may be helpful. In cases in which there has been persistent vomiting with a resulting low blood plasma chloride, the intravenous injection once or twice of 50 c.c. of a 10 per cent solution of sodium chloride may stimulate the secretion of urine in a remarkable fashion.

Differential Diagnosis

An unconscious patient always presents a problem in diagnosis. When the patient is a known diabetic the possibility of diabetic coma comes quickly to mind. One should not, however, forget that diabetic coma may be the first striking evidence of diabetes and the patient may be brought to the physician without any knowledge on the part of the family that diabetes is present. The past history and events leading up to the present illness are, nevertheless, of great value in calling attention to the correct diagnosis. In differential diagnosis one must consider the following: severe hypoglycemia, cerebral hemorrhage, uremia, meningitis, poisoning as by barbital, and toxicity from overwhelming infections. History, physical findings, examination of the urine, and determination of the blood sugar will allow ready diagnosis in almost every instance. In patients receiving insulin the differentiation between diabetic coma and an insulin reaction (hypoglycemia) may at times be confusing to the family of the patient and even to the doctor. It should be remembered that an insulin reaction occurs because of an excess of insulin and is accompanied by a low blood sugar and a sugar free urine. Whereas diabetic coma comes on gradually over a period of hours or days an insulin reaction is manifested in a matter of minutes. The symptoms of the usual insulin reaction are characteristic; nervousness, sweating, faintness, headache, hunger, and double vision. Only rarely does the condition progress to unconsciousness with or without convulsions. Although at the time of an insulin reaction the first specimen of urine may contain sugar, a second specimen obtained 15 or 20 minutes later will invariably be sugar free. Treatment, which consists in supplying readily available carbohydrate by mouth, under the skin, or by vein, gives prompt relief.

Prognosis

Among the three hundred and thirty-eight cases of diabetic coma in our series treated with insulin between May, 1923, and September, 1936, there were forty-one deaths, a mortality of 12.1 per cent. The danger of coma increases steadily with age. Only three of the total of forty-one deaths were in patients under twenty years of age and there were no deaths under ten years of age. The tremendous insult to the body produced by the acidosis is often too much for the individual with arteriosclerosis and a heart that is none too good. Nevertheless, the situation with the older patients is far from hopeless. A woman of seventy-six years has been known to weather successfully an attack of diabetic coma. The longer a patient has been unconscious before treatment is begun, the worse is the outlook. After eight to twelve hours of unconsciousness without treatment, the prognosis must be regarded as grave. A low blood pressure, particularly one which does not rise or even falls despite treatment, is a bad prognostic sign. Accompanying heart or kidney disease, and particularly oliguria or anuria, indicate a poorer outlook. Other complications as severe infections, particularly in individuals past middle life, make for a worse prognosis. Marked acidosis as indicated by values for the carbon dioxide combining power of the blood plasma below 10 volumes per cent indicate, of course, a serious condition. A consideration of these various guides to prognosis leads to one conclusion, that to obtain the lowest mortality one must prevent diabetic coma by careful, day-by-day treatment of the diabetic condition, but that if coma does develop, it must be recognized early and treated promptly and energetically.

GANGRENE AND SURGERY IN DIABETES
HOWARD F. ROOT, M.D.
Boston, Mass.

The development of complications frequently brings the diabetic to the physician. The diabetes may have been mild, producing few or no uncomfortable symptoms until a slight injury to a toe or a finger fails to heal or a painful boil develops. Then the careful physician who applies the rule—that the urine must always be tested—discovers the sugar.

Gangrene

Gangrene develops chiefly on an arteriosclerotic background, but it may occur in the young with little arteriosclerosis if the infection be severe enough. It seldom occurs without trauma such as pricking a blister, cutting a corn, a frost bite or burn. Even then it is usually accelerated by infection which could have been prevented had the hand or foot been carefully cleaned before it was touched.

Prevention of Gangrene

Mrs. S., age 65 years, with known diabetes for five years, developed an infection of a corn in June 1935. Three of her six children urged her return to the hospital but the other three persuaded her to try other methods. The foot was massaged, plunged in hot and cold water, till in October the gangrene involved the entire sole and lymphangitis extended to the knee. Fortunately she recovered after amputation, but consider how unnecessary and preventable were the pain and final operation. Nearly all such amputations could be avoided if every diabetic and his family understood the danger of delaying proper treatment of slight lesions. Teach every patient that a lesion unhealed in two weeks may mean osteomyelitis and an amputation. Teach every diabetic to keep his feet as clean as his face. Urge the sons and daughters to examine their aged parents' feet once a week and report lesions promptly to a physician.

Diagnosis of Impending Gangrene

Mere calcification of the wall of the arteries of the legs as shown by x-ray is of little significance. The important question is whether occlusion of the arterial lumen or partial reduction of the lumina of many arterial branches has lowered the blood supply to the extremity involved.

The following table summarizes the more important points in diagnosis.

Symptoms and Signs	Deficient Blood Supply	Normal Blood Supply
Intermittent claudication or cramps in calves on walking	+	0
Foot appears blanched or cadaveric on elevation and red or cyanotic when dependent	+	0
Pulsation in dorsalis pedis artery	0 or feeble	+
One foot is cooler than the other below a certain level	+	0

Osteomyelitis and Indolent Ulcers Versus Gangrene

Any infection with purulent discharge on a toe or especially in close relationship to a joint or bone will almost certainly extend into and involve the joint or bone if it remains unhealed over two weeks. Therefore, it is of major importance to treat energetically any such lesion as soon as it begins. Lesions of diabetic feet cannot be treated expectantly or by ambulatory methods unless they are very superficial or entirely free from infection. In such cases they will heal within ten days.

When infection in a callus, corn, or following some trauma has extended into a joint or bone causing osteomyelitis, whether or not the x-ray shows the lesion, it seldom will heal. Amputation of the toe as soon as the diagnosis is clearly established is then indicated. When the blood supply is good such cases of osteomyelitis may remain stationary for many weeks and the patient is loath to accept advice. The result is a long period of procrastination with suffering and expense ultimately leading sometimes to an extension of infection and loss of the entire foot. The decision as to the necessity of amputation must be arrived at early. Procrastination is the great enemy in treating diabetic feet.

Gangrene means the death of tissue usually with resulting black color. Superficial areas of gangrene may sometimes heal without an amputation. When gangrene of a toe or foot is associated with redness and swelling of the nearby tissues, and red streaks of lymphangitis extending up the leg, then delay in amputating the foot may cost a life. It is usually not difficult to convince the patient of the need for amputation, because he or she suffers the pain.

Amputations through the thigh are done so quickly and with so little shock that almost any patient can withstand the operation. Postoperative deaths are almost always due to the fact that the long delay before operation has allowed the infection to extend by way of the lymphatics, blood stream or tendon sheaths above the level of amputation. It is the infection which kills and diabetes itself should never be the cause of death.

Fractures in Elderly Diabetics

In addition to five cases of crushing of the vertebrae with little or no antecedent trauma in elderly diabetics with generalized osteoporosis, 79 fractures have occurred in patients at the George F. Baker Clinic. These cases illustrate the ease with which fractures may occur in elderly diabetics and point the way toward their possible avoidance.

Mrs. A. L., Case No. 1916, aged 65 years, with diabetes of almost twenty years' duration, developed necrosis of one toe on the right foot in June, 1932. In the absence of sufficient blood supply to the foot, amputation of the leg was advised and refused. She then spent three months in another hospital, following which she returned home. From that time until February, 1934, she was confined to bed, the necrosis gradually advancing. On February 27, 1934, she re-entered the Deaconess Hospital with gangrene, fever, ascending infection, and underwent amputation of the right leg. The left leg showed atrophy and some edema. Convalescense was uneventful and she was driven home in her son's auto on April 8, 1934. When almost at the end of the drive, a truck struck the auto and she suffered a fracture of the shaft of the left femur. No one else in the car was injured and apparently the trauma to the thigh as she lay in the back seat was only slight. The atrophy and decalcification of the bone as shown by roentgenogram was extreme.

Mrs. B. P., Case No. 12575, aged 58 years, with diabetes of nine years' duration, while convalescing at home from "grippe," got out of bed, and fell in the bathroom striking her right leg. Roentgenograms showed a fracture of the right hip (comminuted intertrochanteric fracture with impaction).

Crushed Vertebrae

When crushed vertebrae are first discovered in an elderly diabetic, suspicion is naturally directed toward carcinoma. This diagnosis was first made in Case 4966, male, age 64 years. An x-ray of his cervical spine showed destruction and crushing of the upper portion of the sixth cervical vertebra with partial subluxation, causing severe pain and rigidity. To our surprise, nine years later, the patient was in good condition having entirely recovered from pain and disability of that lesion.

Case 4982, housewife, age 64 years in January, 1936, with diabetes of eleven years' duration. She entered the hospital with crushed fractures of the seventh, tenth and twelfth dorsal vertebrae. She also had empyema which had developed following being placed in a plaster cast. Her empyema was drained and her diabetes kept under excellent control with the use of protamine insulin. From February 6, until March 1, 1936, she had protamine insulin twice a day, averaging 24 units morning and night.

Mrs. R. P., Case No. 6360, age 62 years, with diabetes of fourteen years' duration, in April, 1931, had a large colloid adenomatous goitre removed. When first seen in September, 1927, she had partial paralysis of the bladder. The residual urine measured 900 c.c. Under treatment with constant drainage, followed later by frequent repeated catheterizations, the bladder condition improved. However, at times the residual urine measured as much as 2000 c.c. Roentgenogram of the spine in October, 1927, was normal except for arthritis and atrophy of bone. In January, 1934, she complained of a pain in the back and x-ray examination showed two areas of crushing at the first and second lumbar vertebrae. Other bones showed only rarefaction. No primary focus of carcinoma could be found. With rest in bed all pain became less and she has continued to be fairly comfortable except for cystitis since.

Diagnosis of Osteoporosis

The subject of osteoporosis of the bone and the fractures associated with it, requires careful study and diagnosis. Since the description by Doctor Harvey Cushing of tumors of the pituitary of the basophilic type it has become clear that when osteoporosis of the bone is associated with diabetes, one must search for tumors of the pituitary or the adrenal. This syndrome was presented by Case 13999, housewife, age 54 years, with diabetes of at least one year's duration. Her blood pressure was 204/100, she had the typical thin legs but obesity about the waist and shoulders, acne, severe headaches, and marked osteoporosis of the spine with a peculiar osteoporosis of the skull, strongly suggesting multiple myeloma. However, in the eighteen months which have passed since its recognition no advance has taken place in the lesions of the bone and no Bence-Jones protein has been found in the urine. In general, her condition has improved, whether because of irradiation of the pituitary or not, is difficulty to say. Another cause of fracture in the diabetic is Paget's disease. Case 10699, age 66 years, with diabetes of twelve years' duration has had well established Paget's disease for a number of years. In March, 1936, while recovering from a small cerebral hemorrhage, he took a single step and felt a sudden snap in his leg. A spontaneous fracture of the leg had occurred through one of the areas of rarefaction.

As mentioned elsewhere*, factors which may influence calcium and phosphorus metabolism in diabetic patients are: (1) age of the patient, (2) activity of the patient, (3) amount of lime salts in the diet, (4) great excess in the diet of calcium over phosphorus, and vice versa, (5) achlorhydria or hypochlorhydria and diminished or lacking pancreatic lipolytic ferment, (6) prolonged diarrhea, (7) prolonged acidosis, (8) excessive fat in the diet, particularly if unabsorbed, (9) deficient or excessive supply of vitamin D substances.

* Root, H. F., White, P. and Marble, A.: Abnormalities of Calcium Deposition in Diabetes Mellitus—Archives of Internal Medicine 53: 46, January, 1934.

None of the patients described had had recent acidosis, or diarrhea. None had, in so far as known, excessive fat in the diet. The significant facts would seem to be: All are past middle life with ages ranging from fifty-eight to sixty-seven years; all have been obese in the past; all have in late years had little physical exercise and their lack of muscle tone is noticeable. In Case No. 1916 a confinement to bed of twenty months with consequent atrophy of bone and muscle may be held directly responsible for the osteoporosis and fragility of the bones. It is difficult to estimate with any degree of accuracy the amount of calcium, phosphorus, and vitamin D substances received by these patients in the past several years but our impression is that the supply has been inadequate.

Treatment of Fractures

In addition to appropriate measures as regards the fractures, the diets have been so arranged as to include sufficient calcium (at least 0.7 gm. daily) and vitamin D substances. Each patient has received daily from 360 to 600 c.c. of milk and 90 to 300 c. c. of 20 per cent cream. Two patients have received respectively 30 to 60 grams of cheese daily. The amount of calcium from these foods thus averages from 0.53 to 0.82 gm. daily which is in addition to the calcium contained in the rest of the diet (approximately 0.4 gm. daily). Furthermore, we have given by mouth daily suitable doses of calcium gluconate and haliver oil or viosterol.

The diets of all patients should be checked at intervals to insure that they contain an adequate amount of the lime salts and vitamin-containing foods. Physical activity within the ability of the patient should be encouraged and prolonged periods in bed avoided if at all possible. If long-continued bed rest is necessary, appropriate exercises or massage should be provided for. The diabetic condition should be kept under good control.

Surgery

There is almost no group of patients to whom the surgeon is so good a friend. Further, diabetics are good patients. In 2052 consecutive operations the mortality was only 6.0 per cent. Diabetics acquire infections of the skin or extremities easily and these require drainage; their bones are easily fractured; appendicitis and gallstones occur frequently. Retained pus is a grave menace to the diabetic because he develops septicemia so easily. Hence the treatment of every abscess and carbuncle should be considered surgical. Poultices, x-ray treatment and other measures are possibilities or makeshifts which sometimes serve a useful purpose, but the lesion should always be under surgical observation. When good surgical judgment indicates the need for operation, no delay should be permitted. It is delay and procrastination which are responsible for the many deaths from carbuncles.

Appendicitis is even more treacherous in the diabetic than the non-diabetic. The differential diagnosis between appendicitis and beginning diabetic coma is difficult. The urine will contain sugar and diacetic acid in coma, but both may also be present in appendicitis. The board-like spasm of the abdomen in coma may simulate peritonitis due to rupture. Remember the danger of giving a cathartic to any patient with pain in the abdomen until the possibility of acute appendicitis is ruled out.

Differential Diagnosis of Diabetic Coma and Appendicitis

	Coma	Appendicitis
Abdominal pain	General	Localized first in epigastrium, later in lower right side
Tenderness and spasm	General; may be slight or extreme in degree	Localized over the appendix
Leucocytosis	Often exceeds 25,000	Present, usually less than 25,000
Respiration	Air hunger	Normal
Skin and tongue	Dry	Not dry, although tongue may be coated
Rectal examination	Normal	Tenderness below pelvic brim sometimes present
Bowel movements	Obstipation	Constipation, sometimes diarrhea

Preparation of the diabetic for surgery requires (1) careful examination of the patient with special regard for the evidences of cardiovascular disease; (2) complete examination of urine, including sugar, diacetic acid, albumin and the sediment and an analysis of the blood for sugar and, if possible, for non-protein nitrogen; (3) diet including at least 100 grams carbohydrate during the twenty-four hours before operation; (4) care of the water metabolism so that sufficient liquids are given by hypodermoclysis or intravenous route to prevent dehydration; (5) the use of insulin if the urine contains sugar and the blood sugar is above normal.

Insulin

Protamine insulin acts slowly for 24 hours. Its advantage at the time of an operation lies in the fact that it can be injected before operation without the necessity of giving food or glucose. Its action during operation will be slow so that there is almost no danger of an hypoglycemic reaction during the anesthesia, which might not be recognized. After the operation, additional doses of regular insulin can be given at intervals of two to four hours if glycosuria is present.

For the patient who has been taking regular insulin, the dose may be increased by 25 per cent or more if glycosuria is marked. On the morning of operation, nothing is given by mouth if 100-150 grams carbohydrate have been retained during the preceding twenty-four hours. Insulin may be given in small amounts before operation, unless the urine is sugar free. After operation, orders for insulin should be contingent upon urinalysis. Thus a typical order is "Test the urine every four hours; if the Benedict test is red give 15 units insulin; if it is yellow give 10 units; if it is green give 5 units; if no sugar is present give no insulin." Thus the changing condition of the patient automatically is treated by insulin in doses suited to the glycosuria. Food after operation must be simple, such as oatmeal gruel (C.5%) orange juice (C.10%), ginger ale (C.10%), and skimmed milk (C.5%) with a total of 75 - 100 grams carbohydrate. Within forty-eight hours additions of egg, cream or toast may be made so that within a few days the usual diet may be resumed.

If glucose solution is administered intravenously insulin must not be given without a urine test or blood sugar analysis at the time. Hypoglycemia develops easily following glucose administration, as if the patients' pancreas were thereby stimulated to produce extra insulin. When such hypoglycemia develops postoperatively the symptoms may be atypical. Sudden mania, delirium, or mere stupor may occur without the usual premonitory hunger, sweating, trembling and weakness. The use of glucose solution intravenously is an absolute necessity in many cases and of great value in others. Rules adopted at one Boston hospital follow:

"During the twenty-four hours following an intravenous injection of glucose-containing solution, no insulin is to be given without a urine test showing the presence of sugar or a blood analysis. If it is not considered wise to catheterize for a urine specimen, the blood sugar should be determined by micro method if it is desired to save the veins. If the presence of glycosuria or acidosis indicates the need of administering insulin at the same time that the glucose solution is given, the dose given should be moderate, usually from 10 to 20 units. Later doses should be at four-hour intervals, the amount to be given depending upon the degree of glycosuria or hyperglycemia."

Spinal anesthesia gives great satisfaction for operations upon the extremities and lower abdomen. The absence of vomiting is valuable. Although the blood pressure may fall, recovery is usually prompt when the head is lowered. For upper abdominal surgery novocaine infiltration, followed by nitrous oxide and ether, is satisfactory.

Intravenous administration of anesthetics is increasing. Already evipal and pentothal have been useful in operations upon the hand, and for a prostatic resection. These anesthetics can be given repeatedly so that operations can be prolonged as far as is desired.

An inhalation anesthetic of increasing value is cyclopropane.

DIABETES IN MASSACHUSETTS

HERBERT L. LOMBARD, M.D., and SALLY JOAN MINER
*Division of Adult Hygiene,
Massachusetts Department of Public Health*

Knowledge of the epidemiology of diabetes is essential in any concerted attempt at control. Pertinent facts regarding the disease were obtained in the Massachusetts Chronic Disease Survey which included death records, hospital records, and house-to-house visits in fifty-one cities and towns of the Commonwealth. Information was secured from approximately 75,000 individuals in 1929, 1930, and 1931. In 1929, the data covered every member of each family visited. In 1930 and 1931, the survey was limited to those over the age of forty. The presence of chronic disease was ascertained and information regarding care and treatment was obtained. Both sick and well were questioned regarding their habits of living in order to acquire some information on etiology. One tenth of the total population and one forth of the population over forty had some form of chronic disease. Among the individuals interviewed, 9 out of every 1000 of those over forty and about 3 out of every 1000 of those of all ages had diabetes. In all cases, the opinion of the individual questioned was accepted as a diagnosis, but over 97 per cent of those with diabetes admitted they had been told by a physician that they had the disease.

At any one time there are approximately 15,000 individuals in Massachusetts suffering with diabetes. While diabetes may occur at practically all ages, the highest rates are found in late adult life.

The death rates adjusted to age and sex to compensate for the changing age of the population indicate that diabetes has been increasing for many years. (Table I) The female rate has increased faster than the male. In both sexes, the adjusted rates showed the increase to be less than the crude rates. The rates by individual years since 1900 showed a remission in the rise in 1918 and 1919, and another one beginning in 1923. Among males, the subsequent increase following the drop in 1923 did not reach the 1922 level in the adjusted rates until 1934, while among females the 1922 rate was surpassed in 1932. An initial drop later followed by an increase in rate would be expected in a disease in which treatment prolongs life, but does not cure.

As the Manual of Joint Causes of Death gives diabetes precedence over most other diseases, the recorded deaths for diabetes include nearly all of the deaths of individuals who have had the disease, regardless of the immediate cause of death. In 1928, 1930, and 1932, 3,552 individuals died in Massachusetts who had had diabetes. Of this number, 88.6 per cent were certified as dying of diabetes, and the remaining 11.4 per cent of other conditions. Two fifths of this latter group were certified as dying of cancer, one fourth of tuberculosis, and the rest of a few miscellaneous conditions—the most frequent being accidents and appendicitis. Realizing that once a person is diagnosed as a diabetic and in about nine times out of ten he will be certified as dying of this disease, the death rate cannot be expected to drop as long as the disease itself increases.

TABLE I

Mortality Rates, by Sex, for Diabetes in Massachusetts 1860-1936

Rate per 100,000

Year	Males		Females	
	Age, Sex Adjusted Rate*	Crude Rate	Age, Sex Adjusted Rate*	Crude Rate
1860	4.0	3.7	2.6	2.5
1870	5.1	5.0	2.7	2.7
1880	4.3	4.4	4.9	4.9
1890	7.4	7.6	8.9	9.0
1900	12.9	12.9	10.8	10.8
1901	9.6	9.6	12.7	12.7
1902	11.0	11.1	14.8	14.9
1903	12.3	12.4	15.1	15.2
1904	12.4	12.5	15.1	15.2
1905	11.7	11.7	15.7	15.9
1906	11.7	11.8	14.9	15.1
1907	12.4	12.5	17.2	17.4
1908	11.7	11.9	15.6	15.8
1909	12.4	12.4	18.1	18.4
1910	14.4	14.5	19.2	19.6
1911	16.7	16.9	19.6	20.0
1912	14.0	14.3	18.8	19.4
1913	15.4	15.8	19.7	19.5
1914	14.9	15.4	19.2	19.9
1915	15.6	16.3	20.0	20.9
1916	16.9	17.8	23.6	24.9
1917	17.6	18.4	22.1	23.4
1918	15.6	16.5	18.5	19.7
1919	13.6	14.4	17.6	18.8
1920	16.4	17.5	22.1	23.8
1921	14.0	15.2	22.7	24.6
1922	16.9	18.5	26.8	29.5
1923	14.3	16.1	23.7	26.7
1924	12.3	14.2	21.3	24.1
1925	13.7	15.9	20.5	23.8
1926	14.2	16.7	20.6	24.0
1927	12.1	14.3	22.2	26.3
1928	13.6	16.4	23.4	28.0
1929	13.2	16.1	25.4	30.9
1930	13.4	16.3	25.5	31.4
1931	14.5	18.2	24.9	31.2
1932	16.3	21.0	26.9	34.5
1933	15.1	19.6	28.9	37.2
1934	17.3	22.8	28.9	38.1
1935	15.5	20.7	29.4	39.2
1936	17.0	23.1	29.8	40.5

* Adjusted to Massachusetts 1900 population.

The efforts which have been expended to control the disease lie largely in treatment rather than prevention, and the results of treatment which may prolong life for many years will not be well portrayed in death charts. If treatment is sufficiently good as to cause individuals who would formerly have died in a lower age group to die in a higher, there will be improvement shown in these lower groups, but the higher cannot be lessened with the disease itself on the increase. Charts I and II show that just this situation has occurred in diabetes during the Banting era. Under the age of fifty there have been marked declines in the rates in both sexes, between fifty and sixty the rates have not altered greatly, but above sixty an upward trend is observed.

A much better estimate of the value of insulin can be obtained through studies on the duration of the disease and the average age at time of death. Joslin, in his private cases, found between the years 1922 and 1926 that the average duration was 7.6 years, while from 1926 to 1930 it was 8.4, and from Jan. 1, 1930 to Mar. 13, 1935, it was 11.0 years. From the Massachusetts death records a similar increase has been obtained, although both at the beginning and end of the periods studied the duration figures were lower than those furnished by Joslin. It is believed that Joslin's figures more nearly approach the correct duration than the Massachusetts death figures, as the duration obtained from the survey was greater by nearly a year than that furnished by the Massachusetts death records and, in addition, all these individuals were alive at the time of questioning.

The average age at time of death tells a similar story. (Table II) This figure gradually increased in the Naunyn era, continued to increase in the Allen era, and has again increased in the Banting era. The average age for males jumped over four years between 1922 and 1923. Between 1920 and 1935, the average age increased 18.8 per cent among males and 14.7 per cent among females. In the same period, the average age at time of death of individuals with cancer increased 0.3 per cent for males and 2.7 per cent for females; apoplexy 0.1 per cent for males and 0.4 per cent for females; heart disease 2.7 per cent for males and 4.6 per cent for females; nephritis 3.0 per cent for males and 3.3 per cent for females; and pulmonary tuberculosis 8.8 per cent for males and 5.1 per cent for females. This far greater increase in the average age of diabetics, combined with information on duration, seems adequate proof of what insulin is doing.

The diabetic rate in the survey showed no appreciable change in the various economic groups. This contrasted greatly with total chronic disease which had a far greater prevalence among the poor.

The diabetic death rate was greater in the city than in the country, but morbidity appeared about the same in both types of communities.

Of the individuals with diabetes, 5.5 per cent were found completely disabled and 29.0 per cent partially disabled. If these percentages were applied to the estimated cases of diabetes in Massachusetts, complete disability would be found in 850 individuals and partial disability in 4,300.

Diabetes was positively associated with heart disease and arteriosclerosis in both morbidity and mortality data. The mortality data also showed association with nephritis, apoplexy, tuberculosis, and cancer.

At the time of the survey, 77.8 per cent of the diabetics were under the case of physicians, as compared with 44.4 per cent of the total sick individuals found in the survey. Five per cent of those with diabetes

TABLE II

Average Age at Time of Death of Individuals with Diabetes
Massachusetts 1850-1936

Year	Males	Females
1850	35.2	24.1
1860	45.9	29.0
1870	53.9	33.8
1880	48.9	40.3
1890	47.2	50.0
1900	52.8	51.4
1905	52.4	55.2
1910	49.8	56.4
1911	51.9	56.4
1912	52.6	57.1
1913	50.8	54.4
1914	54.8	55.9
1915	52.1	55.6
1916	54.4	57.2
1917	53.8	57.3
1918	53.4	55.6
1919	52.6	58.0
1920	54.3	57.5
1921	53.8	57.3
1922	54.5	58.6
1923	59.1	60.6
1924	59.0	59.8
1925	59.2	61.5
1926	61.5	61.8
1927	61.3	62.1
1928	61.3	62.2
1929	61.7	63.1
1930	62.7	63.6
1931	61.6	63.7
1932	64.0	65.2
1933	63.7	64.9
1934	63.5	65.1
1935	63.8	65.7
1936	64.5	66.0

were following the diet prescribed, in most cases, by physicians several years ago; only 1.0 per cent were receiving care in hospitals; 0.7 per cent employed Christian Science practitioners; 8.6 per cent were treating themselves; and 6.9 per cent were receiving no treatment. Females employed physicians slightly more than did males. Individuals with diabetes were receiving medical attention to a greater extent in the country than in the city.

Individuals who did not have a physician were questioned as to the reason. About one tenth of the group said they were too poor to employ a physician; over one third felt that the physcian could not help them; and almost half of the group felt that their condition was not serious. The failure to recognize the need for medical attention by so large a part of this group indicates a need for further medical education.

During the year preceding the survey 4.8 per cent of those with diabetes employed nurses, and an additional 1.7 per cent needed nurses but could not obtain them because of economic reasons. Less than one half of the nurses employed remained for more than three months.

About 7 per cent of the diabetics were hospitalized during the year preceding the survey. At the time of the survey, 98.5 per cent of the diabetics were being cared for at home. Of these, 12.8 per cent were living in homes unsuitable for their care.

On September 1, 1929, a census of the hospital population with this disease was taken by questionnaire. Replies were obtained from hospitals representing 79 per cent of all hospital beds in the State. In the hospitals that reported, there were 253 cases of diabetes—166 of these being in general hospitals. By assuming that the hospitals of various types not heard from had a number proportionate to those heard from, a theoretical number of cases for each type of hospital has been obtained. This gave 317 cases of diabetes in total hospitals, of which 206 were in general hospitals. The average stay in hospitals was 2.8 weeks for those admitted with diabetes and a similar duration for those admitted in which diabetes was found as additional pathology. Of all beds in these hospitals, 0.72 per cent were occupied by individuals admitted for diabetes, and 0.34 per cent by those in whom diabetes was a contributory factor. The disease was the primary cause for admission in 68.5 per cent of those with diabetes.

Questionnaires were sent to 435 nursing homes in Massachusetts, and replies were received from 35.4 per cent of these homes. The number of diabetic cases reported was 55, with a median stay of 3.8 months. Individuals with diabetes occupied 1.2 per cent of beds in these homes.

Among the wage earners over forty in the survey sick with diabetes, 10.8 per cent were completely disabled economically and 7.5 per cent were partially disabled. Another measure of economic disability is the time lost from work during the year preceding the survey by wage earners. Over one fourth of the diabetic wage earners lost an average of 6.2 months from their work during this period. Applying this figure to the total wage earners in the survey gives 0.09 per cent of the total working time lost by individuals with diabetes during the year, which for Massachusetts as a whole is approximately 677 years of work lost per year. The yearly money loss is over $800,000. These figures do not include time lost by wage earners under forty or time lost by non-wage earners. Neither does this estimate include expenditures for care and treatment.

The Massachusetts death records showed that 14 per cent of the diabetics who were Massachusetts residents died in cities or towns other than their usual residence. Of the individuals from other states who died in Massachusetts, 2.4 per cent were diabetics.

Adjusted mortality rates for diabetes for the thirty-four Registration States showed that the highest rates were in the northern part of the country.

In the Chronic Disease Survey, questions on heredity and environment were asked individuals over the age of forty in order to determine which of these factors, if any, were associated with chronic disease. The mere association does not necessarily signify causation, as two variables may be associated with one another simply because they are both associated with a third. However, such information as has been obtained is of some value in pointing toward possible etiological factors.

In 1930, histories were collected on 134 diabetics; in 1931, on 158. There have been matched five series of controls to each of these series of diabetics. The controls were identical with diabetics in respect to age and sex. The rates for the various factors studied have been computed in the diabetic series and in the controls. Information for some of the variables was obtained only in one year—in these series we have only one diabetic group and five controls. The differences between the rates of the diabetic cases and the controls have been computed with the standard deviations, and significance measured by the table of "t" of R. A. Fisher. (Table III).

Overweight showed the highest degree of significance of any of the variables studied. Many writers have mentioned this relationship, but some have questioned whether the overweight was the cause of the diabetes or whether the same syndromes which cause the diabetes also produce the obesity. Joslin feels overweight is of importance only in those with an hereditary history of diabetes.

Nervous temperament was highly associated with the disease. It is stated in Cecil's "Text-Book of Medicine" that "Depressive emotions, anxieties, fears, unhappiness arising from various causes—such as domestic infelicities, financial losses, etc., are notoriously capable of provoking the onset." Joslin considers exceptionally brilliant children to be good subjects for observation as they often come into the diabetic class. It is probable that the temperament of such children would, in most cases, be classified as nervous, and while our figures deal with adults they point to more diabetes among the nervous than the phlegmatic.

Infections have frequently been mentioned as predisposing to the disease. Individuals who have had bad tonsils, malaria, frequent sore throats, and diphtheria all showed significantly more diabetes than their controls. The group that has had varying combinations of malaria, frequent sore throats, diphtheria, scarlet fever, frequent colds, typhoid fever, and rheumatic fever also showed significance. It is rather surprising to find bad tonsils strongly significant and bad teeth not significant, as infections from pus roots might be expected to have as great a connection with diabetes as tonsils.

Heredity showed a strong relationship. The heredity history was limited to parents, but it is sufficiently strong to warrant the belief that heredity is a real causal factor of diabetes. This view has been substantiated by many investigators. Joslin says, "Diabetes is hereditary. . . . I suspect if we knew all the facts it would be shown that every diabetic had a diabetic relative." Apparently diabetes is more prevalent among the native born of native parents and native grandparents than the foreign born. The literature mentions higher rates among the Jews, but not among the native born of native ancestry. Nativity studies have largely been based on mortality rates. When such rates are studied in Massachusetts, the native born of native parents have significantly lower rates than the foreign born or the native born of foreign and mixed parents and the native born of foreign and mixed parents have higher rates than

TABLE III — *Factors on Heredity and Environment in Diabetes*
Massachusetts Chronic Disease Survey   Rate per 100

Variables with Ten Controls	Diabetes	Controls	t	Probability of Event Happening by Chance Alone	
				If t is:	Probability is:
Twenty per cent and more overweight	48.40 ± 4.26	17.40 ± 1.42	6.90		
Nervous temperament	55.90 ± 3.76	32.13 ± 1.25	6.00		
Heredity	9.71 ± 1.57	2.10 ± 0.52	4.61		
Indigestion	30.45 ± 4.04	16.97 ± 1.35	3.16	3.169	.01
Malaria	8.92 ± 1.60	3.67 ± 0.53	3.11		
Previous illness	44.95 ± 4.86	30.78 ± 1.62	2.77	2.764	.02
Frequent sore throats	8.61 ± 2.23	2.34 ± 0.74	2.67		
Little exercise	17.55 ± 3.74	7.11 ± 1.25	2.65		
Diphtheria	9.25 ± 1.23	5.96 ± 0.41	2.55	2.228	.05
Regular use of laxatives	42.90 ± 7.27	26.84 ± 2.42	20		
Scarlet fever	20.95 ± 4.22	13.94 ± 14.1	48		
Frequent colds	9.48 ± 2.43	5.65 ± 0.81	50		
Native born	67.40 ± 8.24	54.80 ± 2.75	45		
Poor	13.45 ± 4.00	10.20 ± 1.33	07	Not significant	
Typhoid fever	9.08 ± 2.94	6.76 ± 0.98	05		
Damp housing	7.9 + 3.42	5.31 ± 1.14	63		
Bad teeth	37.60 ± 9.62	31.48 ± 3.21	60		
Rheumatic fever	3.64 ± 2.23	2.38 ± 0.74	64		
No regular dentistry	77.50 + 6.59	73.90 ± 2.20	62		
Variables with Five Controls					
Bad tonsils	17.20 ± 1.83	3.69 + 0.92	5.90	4.604	.01
Three and four native grandparents	40.20 ± 2.91	26.36 ±1.46	3.80	3.747	.02
Native parents	46.60 ±.06	31.80 ± 2.03	2.92	2.776	.05
Non-protective foods	44.60 ± 6.11	43.26 ± 3.06	0.18	Not significant	
Dusty trade	3.73 ± 3.05	4.63 ± 1.53	-0.24		

the foreign born. The discrepancy between morbidity and mortality rates by nativity is explainable by higher case fatality and earlier incidence among the foreign race stock groups. In the 1930 survey, the median duration for diabetes was 7 years 4.8 months for the native born of native parents; 5 years 3.6 months for the native born of foreign and mixed parents; and 7 years 9.6 months for the foreign born. The duration, as furnished by the death records for Massachusetts 1930, for diabetes was 4 years 2.0 months for the native born of native parents; 3 years 4.0 months for the native born of foreign and mixed parents; and 3 years 3.6 months for the foreign born. The median present age of the survey group with this disease was 62.7 years for the native born of native parents; 57.1 years for the native born of foreign and mixed parents; and 61.8 years for the foreign born. The median age at time of death for the 1930 mortality records was 68.9 years for the native born of native parents; 63.3 years for the native born of foreign and mixed parents; and 65.8 years for the foreign born. The nativity study indicates lower morbidity rates, higher case fatality, and earlier incidence among the foreign race stocks.

Lack of exercise was slightly associated with diabetes. Significance is not strong and the results obtained might indicate a definite connection with diabetes or an association with some of the other variables. The overweight person would probably exercise less than one of normal weight.

Indigestion showed a fairly strong association with diabetes. On the other hand, over 80 per cent of the diabetic individuals having this condition had, in addition, either nervous temperament, obesity, or an hereditary history of diabetes. It is possible that long-continued indigestion may be a factor in this disease, but the results are by no means conclusive.

Either overweight, nervous temperament, or heredity were present in 78 per cent of the diabetic group. Inasmuch as heredity was measured by the history of father and mother only, it is probable that this figure would have been greater if other ancestors had been included. The control group had only 42 per cent in this category, making the significance very strong.

From the standpoint of prevention of diabetes, excessive overweight should be avoided, a more placid attitude toward living should be adopted, and all infections should receive prompt treatment. These measures are of added importance if an heredity history of the disease is present.

Chart I
MALE AGE SPECIFIC MORTALITY RATES FOR DIABETES
Massachusetts Deaths 1906-1936

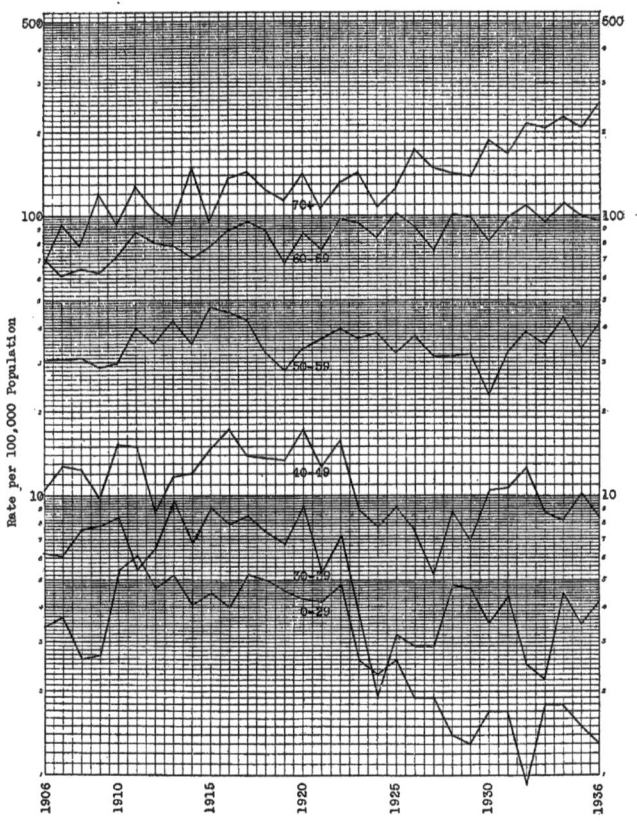

Chart II
FEMALE AGE SPECIFIC MORTALITY RATES FOR DIABETES
Massachusetts Deaths 1906-1936

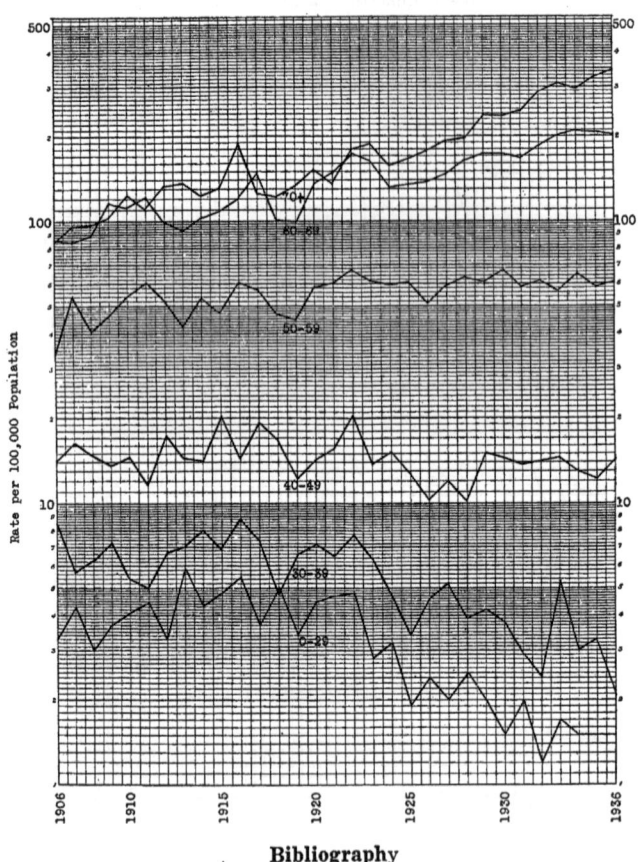

Bibliography

BIGELOW, GEORGE H., and LOMBARD, HERBERT L.: *Cancer and Other Chronic Diseases in Massachusetts*. Houghton Mifflin Company, Boston and New York, 1933

FISHER, R. A.: *Statistical Methods for Research Workers*. Oliver and Boyd, Edinburgh and London, 1925

JOSLIN, ELLIOTT P.: *The Treatment of Diabetes Mellitus*. Lea & Febiger, Philadelphia, 1928

JOSLIN, ELLIOTT P.: *Fat and the Diabetic*. New England Journal of Medicine, Vol. 209, No. 11, September 14, 1933

JOSLIN, ELLIOTT P.: *A Diabetic Manual*. Lea & Febiger, Philadelphia, 1934

JOSLIN, ELLIOTT P., DUBLIN, LOUIS I,. and MARKS, HERBERT H.: *Studies in Diabetes Mellitus. II. Its Incidence and the Factors Underlying Its Variations.* American Journal of the Medical Sciences, No. 4, Vol. 187, April, 1934

WOODYATT, ROLLIN T.: *Diabetes Mellitus.* Cecil's Text-Book of Medicine, W. B. Saunders Company, Philadelphia and London, 1933.

CARDIOVASCULAR DISEASE AND DIABETES

HOWARD F. ROOT, M.D.

Boston, Mass.

Although cardiovascular disease has become "the captain of men of death" among diabetic patients, this fact is not discouraging. Prior to 1922 the average age at death of diabetic patients was under 45 years, whereas now, in the later Banting era ending in 1935, it has reached 62.8 years. When patients have ceased to die of coma, they live long enough to die of arteriosclerosis. Although nearly 56 per cent of all diabetic deaths between 1930 and 1935 were due to arteriosclerotic causes either in the heart, the kidneys, the brain or leg, 30 per cent were due to cardiac causes, so that heart disease now takes first place among diabetic causes of death. Yet even this cause is yielding as shown by the facts brought out by an analysis by Mr. Herbert H. Marks for Dr. E. P. Joslin showing that the average age of death of patients dying with heart disease and gangrene for the last five years has been postponed by two years.

The frequency of cardiac disease in diabetes is dependent almost entirely upon arteriosclerosis of the coronary vessels. Its excessive development in diabetes of long duration, and particularly in those not subjected to careful treatment, may give important clues to the cause of arteriosclerosis in general. The cause of arteriosclerosis is inevitably concerned with the process of aging and degeneration since it develops so much more frequently in later than in earlier adult life. Although much is known about the morphological changes in the vessels and their peculiar localization in diabetes, much remains to be learned about the influence of chemical, physiological, and nutritional causes. Undoubtedly, factors such as the sympathetic nervous system, variation in blood pressure, and heredity are important. It is known that the characteristic atheromatous change can be found in mammals other than man as well as in birds. So far, the only method by which atheromatous changes closely resembling those of the human being have been produced with any great regularity have been by dietary experiment. For many years it has been known that atheromatous lesions can be produced by the feeding of cholesterol and the important relationship of cholesterol metabolism to arteriosclerosis in the diabetic is supported by the well-known fact that diabetic patients not under as good diabetic control or under good insulin treatment tend to have an increase in the cholesterol of the blood plasma. Other chemical changes dependent upon the altered diabetic metabolism, such as dehydration, the glycogen metabolism in arterial musculature, acidosis or disturbed endocrine balance are also to be considered.

One contributory cause appears of prime importance, hypertension. The frequency of coronary arteriosclerosis and vascular disease in the legs is more than twice as great among diabetic patients with hypertension as in those with normal blood pressure. On the other hand, in diabetic patients, hypertension frequently develops after the diabetes rather than before and it is certainly true that the frequency of both coronary disease and of gangrene is greater in diabetic patients even without hypertension than it is in non-diabetic patients. Hypertension is not the only cause of arteriosclerosis in diabetes. In contrast with hypertension, other causes of cardiac disease such as rheumatic fever and syphilis, are extremely rare.

The diabetic heart at autopsy is always found to have more glycogen than the non-diabetic in spite of the fact that we are constantly fearful of reducing the glycogen content in the diabetic heart. Actually, it is extremely difficult to reduce the glycogen content of the normal heart. It has been shown that, even in the presence of hypoglycemia, when further insulin is given, an increase in the amount of glycogen deposited in the muscle occurs. The action of insulin, therefore, on the heart is almost always, even under most adverse circumstances, to increase the amount of glycogen stored. If hypoglycemia is so prolonged and so severe that there remains no sugar which can be withdrawn from the blood, then the respiratory quotient falls indicating that non-carbohydrate sources of energy are used. Other physiological and pathologic observations indicate that insulin rarely if ever can harm the heart directly. The possibility does exist, however, that because insulin, when hypoglycemia occurs, brings about an outpouring of adrenalin that adrenalin might affect the heart injured by coronary disease and even produce attacks of angina pectoris.

Angina Pectoris and Coronary Thrombosis

Coronary arteriosclerosis with angina pectoris is the most frequent type of cardiac disease. It develops gradually with rather mild attacks of pain and may go on to a fatal coronary occlusion after a relatively few minor attacks, or angina pectoris may be mild and continue for years. In one physician attacks occurred for seventeen years before final coronary occlusion. Coronary thrombosis has occurred in young diabetics. At least five cases are known in which coronary thrombosis occurred before the age of thirty-five years.

Deaths from coronary disease may be puzzling. When infarction of the heart occurs it may bring on accidosis and during coma the occurrence of coronary occlusion may be masked by the abdominal pain of coma. Especially in patients in whom painless coronary thrombosis occurs the dyspnea may be deceptive in that it suggests diabetic coma. The pain from coronary disease and the pain due to gallstones must be differentiated.

Multiple infarctions of the heart occur. In one case at autopsy eight separate, distinct areas of healed infarction were found.

The danger of hypoglycemia producing coronary occlusion is easily exaggerated. Actually, but a few cases exist in which definite records show that hypoglycemia actually occurred at about the same time that coronary thrombosis was induced. In one case admitted to the Deaconess Hospital for hypoglycemia, at her death three days later the age of the infarction of the heart was judged by the pathologist to be about the same as the time of the hypoglycemia. Myocardial failure with congestion seems rather less frequent in diabetic patients than one might expect considering the extent of myocardial damage. Cardiac drugs, therefore, are of limited value, although nitroglycerine, aminophylline, etc., have their place. If the severity of the pain is not great enough to justify surgical methods of treatment, a low calorie diet with reduction in weight and careful control of the diabetes by means of insulin is indicated. The danger of the use of insulin in case of coronary thrombosis is greatly exaggerated. If the diabetes is not under control then the judicious use of insulin is indicated.

INHERITANCE OF DIABETES

PRISCILLA WHITE, M.D.

Boston, Mass.

The newer research in the fundamental etiology of diabetes indicates to us that all cases of diabetes are hereditary.* The actual proof of the hereditary nature of diabetes belongs to recent years, for the duration of life of the diabetic was so short prior to insulin therapy that the data of family histories could never be complete. Since there is a certain amount of disagreement concerning it, I wish to review briefly our own investigation of this problem.

The actual evidence in favor of the theory that the potentiality for developing diabetes is inherited rests primarily upon four facts: first, the almost simultaneous occurrence of diabetes in similar twin mates; second, the greater incidence of diabetes in the members of a diabetic than in control families; third, the demonstration of Mendelian recessive ratios in a large series of cases selected at random; and, fourth, in presumably latent cases.

(1) Of similar twins, the most valuable material for the student of human genetics, we have a relatively large series, sixteen pairs. A comparative analysis of similar and dissimilar twins in our own series gives striking evidence in favor of the genetic origin of diabetes. Thus, in 70 per cent of our similar twins both twin mates have contracted diabetes compared with only 10 per cent of our dissimilar twin mates.

(2) Diabetes was found to occur nearly seven times more often in the parents and siblings of diabetics than in the relatives of our non-diabetic patients, and this is a statistically significant difference.

(3) All of this suggests, but does not prove, the hereditary nature of diabetes. To be convinced, we must know even more. We must find and demonstrate the mode of transmission. Here it is that students of diabetes disagree, some finding no pattern, others simple dominance, double dominance, or alternating dominance and recessiveness, or simple recessiveness. For a moment let us review the Mendelian hypothesis. It presupposes that inherited traits occur in pairs and in opposites, in our problem—diabetics and non-diabetics. Second, that the traits of parents with unlike inheritable characteristics generally do not blend, but one tends to recur in the offspring and is dominant, and the other tends to

disappear and is recessive. Third, and the most important in a problem such as ours, is the fact that the traits of offspring of parents possessing unlike inheritable traits can be predicted according to certain ratios. In a series of consecutive cases we believe that we were able to demonstrate Mendelian recessive ratios. According to this pattern, in a cross between two diabetics we expect 100 per cent of the offspring to become diabetic; in the cross between a diabetic and an hereditary carrier, 50 per cent; and in a cross between hereditary carriers, 25 per cent.

Certain factors, however, alter our expectations. First, the mode of selection of these families will do so, for it is true that they were chosen because there was a known diabetic. This is the only method of determining carriers in the study of human heredity. A known mathematical correction is permitted for this, and it lowers our expectations to 100 per cent, 40 per cent, and 16 per cent in the three crosses, respectively.

The age behaviour of diabetes lowers the expection of fulfilled ratios further. It is known that the onset of diabetes occurs anywhere from 0 to 90 years of age, with a peak of incidence at 50. Third, the ordinary chances of death from extra-diabetic causes, such as tuberculosis, typhoid fever, or automobile accidents, will actually destroy 50 per cent of predestined cases prior to any possible identification of the disease. Thus, it is improbable that the relatives of diabetic patients can attain that age, 90 years, which would completely fulfill our simple Mendelian expectation of 100 per cent, 40 per cent, and 16 per cent in the three crosses respectively, and at any given moment of study we will find only a fraction of fulfillment.

What fraction did we find? We found that 24 per cent of the offspring of our diabetic-diabetic cross have developed diabetes. We expected 100 per cent, so this was almost exactly one fourth. We found that 10 per cent of the offspring of our diabetic-carrier cross had contracted diabetes. We expected 40 per cent; again this was one fourth. We found 4 per cent in our offspring of carrier-carrier cross. We expected 16 per cent, so here again we have identified one fourth. But the expected and identified ratios were almost identical, for 16, 40 and 100 are the ratio of $1:2.5:6.1$ and 4, 10 and 40 in the ratio of $1:2.4:5.7$.

(4) Even this analysis is subject to criticism because it is based upon the case histories, so that we actually tested 294 individuals, 169 close relatives of diabetics and 125 controls by sugar tolerance tests and random blood sugars. Supernormal blood sugars, statistically supernormal, were found in 25 per cent of the diabetic relatives and in 2 per cent of the relatives of our control population. Significantly abnormal blood sugars were found to occur in nearly true simple Mendelian recessive ratios of $1:2:4$.* What does this mean? It means that the eugenic control of diabetes is possible.

If a diabetic marries a diabetic, all of the surviving children eventually will develop the disease. If a diabetic marries a carrier, one half of the children will become diabetic. If two carriers marry, one

— Excerpts from "Recent Progress in Severe Diabetes" by Priscilla White, M.D., published in The Canadian Medical Association Journal. 35: 153-161, 1936. Used with permission of the Canadian Medical Association Journal.

quarter may be diabetic, but if a diabetic marries a true non-diabetic, none of the children should develop the disease.

This lesson must be carried to the children of diabetics for they represent true carriers of the disease. Mass sterilization has been advocated for diabetics but control of the spread of the disease would be impossible without sterilization of carriers. Calculating backward from the incidence of diabetes in the general population we estimate that 25 per cent of the entire population are hereditary carriers of the disease.

THE PREVENTION OF DIABETES
and the
PROGNOSIS OF THE DISEASE
ELLIOTT P. JOSLIN, M.D.

Boston, Mass.

The prevention of diabetes depends upon controlling one's heredity. Obviously that cannot be done, but there are certain rules which should be followed by any individual in whose family diabetes exists or who has the disease. These are described in the article on heredity on another page.

The chief inciting cause of diabetes in the hereditarily predisposed is obesity. Between the ages of fifty-one and sixty, one will not find among a thousand patients more than one who has been constantly underweight. The influence of overweight in bringing on diabetes applies especially to middle age because in the young, overweight is not a great factor. Two thirds of all diabetics acquire their disease after the age of forty and, knowing this, any relative of a diabetic should be cautious and under no circumstances allow his or her weight to go above normal. This is such a simple way of postponing or possibly preventing the onset of diabetes that it should be followed far more widely. I know that doctors realize this and today you see far, far less doctors who are much overweight than one did a generation ago.

The outlook for the diabetic today has improved enormously, but the careless patient will not live as long as the careful patient. Common sense counts and knowledge of the disease counts, too. Proof of this is afforded by the fact that doctors who acquire diabetes under the age of forty have a mortality less than one fourth that of all diabetics. This applies to my own series of patients and the information was furnished me through the courtesy of the Statistical Department of the Metropolitan Life Insurance Company. Therefore, if a diabetic wishes to live long, he should learn all he is able to about his disease.

The prognosis of diabetes is improving steadily. Just what it is today one cannot tell because data which are collected are based solely on fatal cases. One compilation prepared by the Statistical Bureau of the Metropolitan Life Insurance Company is shown in Table I.

Table 1. *Average Duration of Life Subsequent to Onset of Diabetes Among Deceased Ex-Patients in Each of the Important Eras of Treatment. By Age Groups at Onset. (Experience of Elliott P. Joslin, M.D., 1898-1935.)* *

Age periods of onset	Naunyn period before June, 1914		Allen period June, 1914 to Mar. 16, 1922		Early Banting period Aug. 7, 1922 to Dec. 31, 1925		Middle Banting period Jan. 1, 1926 to Dec. 31, 1929		Later Banting period Jan. 1, 1930†	
	No. of cases	Duration yrs.	No. of cases	Duration yrs.	No. of cases	Duration yrs.	No. of cases	Duration yrs.	No. of cases	Duration yrs.
All ages	331	4.8	597	6.0	514	7.6	897	8.4	981	11.0
0-9	25	1.2	47	2.7	14	2.6	9	3.1	15	7.4
10-19	39	2.9	69	3.3	30	3.6	22	4.0	29	6.5
20-39	80	3.9	162	5.3	92	7.3	101	10.5	117	16.7
40-59	137	6.9	216	8.1	262	9.4	515	9.6	516	12.3
60-89	50	4.5	103	6.1	116	5.2	250	5.7	304	7.1

* Prepared by the Statistical Bureau of the Metropolitan Life Insurance Company.
† Deaths recorded up to March 13, 1935.

As a matter of fact, the younger the age when diabetes is acquired the longer the patient should live. So far as children are concerned, prognosis is improving by leaps and bounds.

PREGNANCY IN DIABETES

PRISCILLA WHITE, M.D.

Boston, Mass.

Introduction

Nearly all physiological processes progress normally in controlled diabetes, notably the growth and development of the juvenile patient. If failure occurs one should find the cause and remedy the defect. One physiological process still baffles us with failure—that is the viability of the fetus of the diabetic mother. Although progress has been made and the failures reduced 50 per cent among patients who are under close observation, they still occur far more frequently in the diabetic than in the normal woman.

The four questions which are of greatest interest in the study of diabetes and pregnancy are: (1) is the patient truly diabetic? (2) is pregnancy ever a cause of the disease? (3) does pregnancy alter the course of diabetes? and (4) why does the fetus die?

(1) Is the patient truly diabetic? Glycosuria in pregnancy

Glycosuria apparently benign in nature occurs so commonly in pregnancy that some writers go so far as to say that if enough specimens of urine of the pregnant patient are examined one or more will be found to contain sugar in amounts varying from traces to several per cent, and yet the blood sugar remains normal. The incidences reported vary from 35 per cent (Williams) to 65 per cent (R. Richardson) and 100 per cent (L. Chase). Generally this sugar is glucose. The theoretical factors which may produce this are first, lowered renal threshold, which would not predispose to diabetes mellitus; second, hyperactivity of the posterior lobe of the pituitary gland which possesses the "diabetogenic factor." Third is hyperactivity of the thyroid. The latter two conditions are associated not only with glycosuria but also with hyperglycemia, and the hyperglycemia may disappear when hyperactivity of the gland ceases. Richardson goes so far as to report benign hyperglycemia in pregnancy. This is consistent with the endocrine background. Being conservatively trained, we would not dismiss the hyperglycemia or even the glycosuria lightly but would keep such patients under supervision. The fourth possible cause of glycosuria is damage to the liver incident to pregnancy. Glucose and lactose may be differentiated by fermentation; the former ferments and the latter does not.

(2) Is pregnancy a cause of diabetes?

Opposed to the view that pregnancy activates diabetes is the course found in some former juvenile diabetics, atypical cases, not requiring insulin. These patients have gone through pregnancies without development of the clinical signs of the disease. Furthermore, if pregnancy were found a factor one would suppose there would be a rise in the incidence of diabetes in women from twenty to forty years of age. Actually, more men than women develop diabetes prior to forty years of age in contrast to the predominance of women in later decades of onset. The evidence of fact outweighs the probabilities of theory.

THE ONSET OF DIABETES BY DECADES

Decades	Males	Females
1	5.0	4.4
2	7.5	6.1
3	9.3	6.5
4	14.7	11.2
5	23.1	24.1

(3) Does pregnancy alter the course of diabetes?

This brings us to the next problem of the course and treatment of diabetes during pregnancy. The question whether or not pregnancy alters the course of diabetes is still debatable. We must consider this in two phases—first, tolerance for carbohydrate; and second, predisposition to premature degenerative changes.

In the literature one finds reports of gains in tolerance for carbohydrate and an equal number of reports indicating losses in tolerance for carbohydrate. The fairly general consensus of opinion is that a loss occurs in the first trimester, a status which is stationary in the second, and either a gain or loss in the third. In the pregnant diabetic dog Carlson and Drennan were able to demonstrate a great gain in tolerance during pregnancy. That insulin circulates through the placenta of the mother is shown by the experiments of Pack and Barber. Insulin injected into the fetuses of a goat was followed by hypoglycemia in the mother. Some few patients in our series, notably one after coma, were able to give up insulin entirely in the last trimester. A crude analysis of our cases shows that half of the number with suitable records had milder diabetes during pregnancy than at any time before or since the pregnancy, but others have been more severe. Furthermore, we observed one patient for some weeks after the death of the fetus and her insulin requirement did not alter.

Pregnancy may injure the blood vessels of the eye, damage the heart, the liver or the kidneys. If the disease diabetes has just started this need not be expected, but we shall soon have to deal with a new problem—young diabetic women who at thirty may have had the disease for fifteen or even twenty years. Dr. Joslin has often remarked that for the true age of a diabetic one should add the duration of the disease, so at thirty such a pregnant woman might be forty-five or fifty years old so far as her heart and blood vessels are concerned. Of course, this paints the picture rather black. We know this is not the case if the patient has controlled diabetes. Unfortunately controlled diabetes in the young patient occurs too infrequently. In pregnancy the cholesterol is high. This is something we strive to avoid in diabetes.

The direct complications of diabetes, coma and hypoglycemia, are to be feared during pregnancy. The plasma combining power of the blood drops in pregnancy. And in the diabetic with her faulty carbohydrate metabolism it is easy indeed for it to fall even to the low level of coma, 20 volumes per cent.

Hypoglycemia can result easily from the failure of the physician to take the lowered renal threshold into consideration, and in consequence lower the blood sugar excessively during the attempted desugarization.

The management of the disease diabetes during pregnancy is simplified by means of small divided meals, divided dosages of insulin, and a diet high in carbohydrate. Not only must one allow for the storage of glycogen in the mother, but also for that in the fetus. The glucose stored in the liver and muscles of the newborn infant is 35 gms. Besides this, glucose or glycogen is stored in the brain, the skin, and is present in the blood so that a crude estimate of the total amount of carbohydrate stored would be 50 gms. We must provide for this in the daily diet of the mother as an extra for the nutrition of her child. The patient must be kept under close observation by weekly visits to the clinic, and early hospitalization. Every effort should be made to control the weight of the mother thereby controlling the size of the baby. Patients with glycosuria which is apparently benign must be followed for three months after delivery.

(4) **Maternal and Fetal Mortality**

The maternal mortality exceeds that of the child-bearing population at large. It is 3.8 per cent among diabetics of the insulin era compared with 0.6 per cent for the normal child-bearing population. The majority of these deaths, however, were preventable. Survival of the child occurs in only half of the cases. Among 202 diabetic women there have been 306 pregnancies with 154 living children. Of these pregnancies, 130 occurred before the use of insulin (1922) and 176 have occurred since that time. These cases have been scattered throughout the country and thus are not under the supervision of any one group. Of the pregnancies which occurred prior to 1922, 53 per cent ended in live births, 21 per cent in stillbirths, 21 per cent in miscarriages, and 5 per cent in therapeutic abortions. In the insulin era living births have risen to 60 per cent, neo-natal deaths to 5 per cent, and therapeutic abortions to twelve. Stillbirths and miscarriages fell to 14 and 8 per cent respectively. Seven patients died undelivered prior to insulin, and the outcome was unknown in twelve.

The factors which may be responsible for fetal deaths are (1) mechanical, (2) chemical, (3) structural, (4) hormonal.

Both living and dead babies were large, 70 per cent weighing more than 8 pounds. This increased size of the babies of diabetic mothers is so striking that some obstetricians call attention to the fact that it may indicate diabetes in the mother, and any mother who produces these large babies must be investigated for diabetes. One author has reported the condition as gigantism and observed changes in the fetal hypophysis.

Hydramnios occurs in diabetes, thus endangering the life of the child. Acidosis has been considered the cause of fetal death, but against this theory is the fact that of the five patients who had coma, four later had living children. It is presumptuous to suppose that diabetic acidosis occurred more frequently in the pre-insulin era, yet the outcome of the two eras was essentially the same. Supervised treatment helps, however, for in our own cases, the child mortality has been reduced to 17 per cent.

The precipitating cause of diabetes is not the factor, for if it were, the patients with onset in pregnancy would have a worse outcome. The reverse is the case, for the longer the duration of the diabetes, the worse the prognosis for successful termination of pregnancy.

Age of the mother appears to be a factor, because the young and the old do worse than the intermediate group.

Age	Successful Outcome
Under 20	35 per cent
20 — 30	85 per cent
30 — 40	60 per cent
40 +	50 per cent

From 1932 to 1937 our patients have been followed with increasing care. Weekly examinations have been made after the sixth month and since then the course of those patients whose outcome was stillbirth has been observed to be as follows: The pregnancy appears to be progressing in normal manner until the beginning of the sixth month when any time after that a significant albuminuria occurs followed by edema and an abrupt rise of the blood pressure. Within a few days of the onset of the elevation of the blood pressure the fetus has died. The signs of toxemia disappear with the death of the fetus.

This toxemia appears to be related to an abnormal relationship of placental hormones—prolan and estrin. Smith and Smith at the Free Hospital for Women in Boston have shown that prior to this accident serum prolan rises and estrin falls. The practical application of this is either endocrine therapy, with estrin or progesterone, or premature delivery as soon as the signs of toxemia occur.

The first day of life of the infant of the diabetic mother is complicated by congenital defects, hypoglycemia, which may arise from overproduction of the fetal islets of Langerhans or an overdose of maternal exogenous insulin. Parenteral glucose is a wise precautionary measure.

Asphyxia has occurred in 60 per cent of the cases and the mortality in this group is 30 per cent. The cause is undetermined. Possibly it is related to disturbed acid base balance. The alkali reserve of infants of diabetic mothers is low. Such infants require aspiration, respiratory stimulants, oxygen and carbon dioxide and, at the suggestion of and under the supervision of Dr. F. G. Benedict, our infants are placed in an oxygen helium chamber (25 per cent oxygen and 75 per cent helium).

TUBERCULOSIS IN DIABETICS

ALTON S. POPE, M.D.

Director, Division of Tuberculosis
Massachusetts Department of Public Health

It is small comfort to the diabetic patient to tell him that he is two or three times as likely to develop tuberculosis as the normal individual of his age, but it is essential to his safety that his physician recognize that simple fact. Forty years ago a diagnosis of tuberculosis carried with it practically no hope for the individual, but today it is recognized that early discovery is the first step in the successful treatment and prevention of that disease. Since the advent of insulin, even greater strides have been made in the control of diabetes and the successful treatment of tuberculosis in diabetics, as in non-diabetics, depends chiefly upon its early recognition.

In their extensive studies Dr. Elliott Joslin and his group have found active pulmonary tuberculosis in 2.8 per cent of their patients x-rayed. By means of questionnaires Dr. Joslin recently found that in the state and county tuberculosis sanatoria of Massachusetts one patient in every seventy-five has diabetes, as compared with one in three hundred of the general population. Females are more likely to develop tuberculosis in the teens, but after the age of twenty years males outnumber the females two to one. Even in late life tuberculosis is frequent if the diabetes is not controlled. Forty-seven of Dr. Joslin's cases developed tuberculosis after the age of sixty years. In diabetic children under fifteen tuberculosis proved to be thirteen times as common as in children of the same age examined in the Chadwick Clinics. Studies by Dr. Howard Root also indicate that as a rule tuberculosis is a complication of diabetes, rather than the reverse, for in 85 per cent of his cases the diabetes had preceded the tuberculosis.

The importance of diabetes as a predisposing cause of tuberculosis is obvious. For the past seventy-five years the death rate from tuberculosis in Massachusetts has been falling steadily. Since 1900 it has fallen over 75 per cent, while the mortality rate for diabetes in the Registration Area of the United States is now approximately three times as high as at the beginning of the century. In part, these changes can be explained by an increase in the average age of the population, but during the same period there has been a steady increase of deaths from diabetes among the tuberculous. In 1933 the diabetes mortality in one state and in thirty cities equalled or exceeded that from tuberculosis and in Brookline there have been as many or more deaths from diabetes for the past five years. In 1930 Dr. Dublin ventured the prophecy that in ten years the death rate from diabetes would exceed that from tuberculosis. The following diagram of the trends of these two diseases in Massachusetts would seem to justify such a statement:

TREND OF DEATH RATES FROM PULMONARY TUBERCULOSIS
MASSACHUSETTS

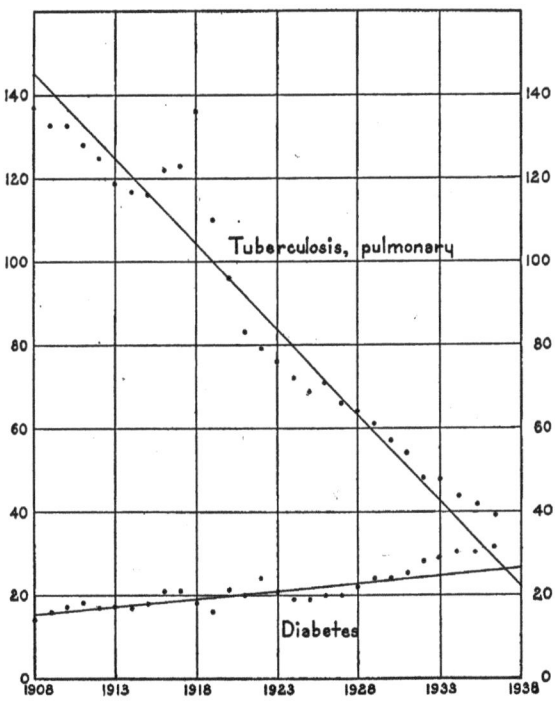

The outlook for the diabetic patient who has tuberculosis has changed completely in the past ten years. With insulin it is now possible to apply modern methods of tuberculosis treatment, including collapse therapy, with results approximating those obtained in the non-diabetic. Control of the diabetes is essential to successful treatment of the tuberculosis, and this is somewhat more difficult than in the average diabetic patient. Nutrition must be maintained while exercise, one of the cardinal factors in the control of diabetes, must be suspended during the active stage of the pulmonary disease. Sanatorium experience has shown that diabetics often respond well to treatment and, if the tuberculosis is found at a reasonably early stage, a substantial number of patients secure an arrest of the disease. Dr. Root says that sanatorium treatment is a necessity and that their cases who have healed tuberculosis cavities have done so in sanatoria. Pneumothorax or thoracoplasty have been performed in many diabetics with increasingly favorable results.

The outlook for the diabetic individual who has tuberculosis depends chiefly upon the stage of his tuberculosis at the time it is discovered. Among patients with tuberculosis alone, the survival rate is about five times as high in those treated when their tuberculosis is in a minimal instead of an advanced stage. Unfortunately, among diabetics, tuberculosis is rarely found in an early stage. The symptoms are as insidious in diabetics as in non-diabetics, and early cases have rarely been discovered in diabetic patients because the x-ray was used too late. Incipient cases do well. Among ten such cases discovered at the Deaconess Hospital all but three have improved or remained stationary. Insulin has doubled the average length of life after the recognition of diabetes, but by prolonging the life of diabetics has made it possible for more of them to contract tuberculosis. On the other hand, the patient whose diabetes is well-controlled is much less likely to develop tuberculosis than the diabetic with occasional acidosis and coma.

The prevention of tuberculosis in diabetics is essentially the same as the prevention of the disease in the general population. Of first importance is avoidance of infection through contact with open cases. X-ray examinations of all family contacts as well as the patient should be a routine procedure when the diagnosis of diabetes is established. In diabetic children tuberculosis must be sought for first by the skin test and second by x-ray. The Mantoux test was positive in 47 per cent of diabetic children both in Boston and Vienna. All such children should have an x-ray of the lungs, which should be repeated at the ages of 14 and 18 years. If they are in contact with an open case of tuberculosis in the family, at work, or at school, such contact must be broken by removal of the child. Such contact must always be sought diligently, because each source case discovered and isolated may save many other infections.

Good hygiene, including adequate diet, sufficient rest and regulated exercise are of special importance in maintaining the patient's resistance. Control of the diabetes by means of diet and insulin is essential. The risk of advanced tuberculosis can be greatly reduced by routine x-ray examination of the chest. Especially should we look for tuberculosis among the cases who have had coma or severe acidosis. One out of twelve may develop tuberculosis within three years. The coma cases must be followed for life with x-ray examinations once a year. In both diabetes and tuberculosis the patient must learn from his physician how to live successfully with his disease, for it is only by such individual effort that these two diseases can be further brought under control.

DIABETES IN CHILDHOOD

PRISCILLA WHITE, M.D.

Boston, Mass.

Of all the phases of diabetes, the study of the juvenile patient is the most interesting, because the living diabetic child is in reality a new individual. Before the use of insulin in 1922, diabetic children when carefully treated lived on the average two years. Now they live indefinitely. The importance of the study of juvenile diabetes rests not in its frequency, since only one child in 8,000 develops the disease, but in its complexity and the fact that here alone we have pure diabetes. Consequently the child will reflect more clearly the true physiology, pathology and etiology of the disease than will the adult.

The chief problems in the management of juvenile diabetics are: (1) the differential diagnosis, (2) the treatment of the uncomplicated case, (3) the prevention and treatment of the complications of diabetes which, in childhood, are largely seven in type: (a) the acute crisis of diabetic coma, (b) infections—tuberculosis, urinary tract infections and infections of the skin, (c) deficiency disease, (d) degenerative changes, (e) metabolic disturbances of the skin, (f) dwarfism, (g) enlargement of the liver.

(1) The Differential Diagnosis

The differential diagnosis of diabetes is obviously the first problem. This is important, because not every patient with sugar in the urine proves to be diabetic. Ordinarily our juvenile patients present no difficulties in diagnosis, since diabetes in childhood is a virulent disease with an acute or gradual onset instead of a slow onset as in the adult and the classical symptoms of polyuria, polyphagia, polydipsia, pruritus, loss of strength, weight and diminished vision are the same whether the patient is two or ninety. In infancy the disease is so virulent and the handicap from the lack of history so great that nearly every case is recognized only in coma. Rarely the parent observes stiffness or stickiness of the linen and if there is diabetes in the family suspects diabetes as a cause.

Illustrative of the patient who comes for diagnosis is Robert D., Case No. 12410 in whose urine a trace of sugar was found when the careful family physician did a complete routine urinary analysis because of *petit mal*. If this patient were diabetic it would be important to start treatment early and keep the case mild; if non-diabetic it would be unfortunate or even harmful to place him on a diabetic regimen.

The routine blood sugar taken three quarters of an hour p. c. was normal so a tolerance test was indicated. A glucose tolerance test is preferably given fasting or at least five hours after a meal. Under fifteen years of age the amount of glucose given is 1.8 grams per kilogram of body weight. The blood sugars are taken fasting one-half hour, one hour and two hours after the administration of the sugar. The interpretation of the curve is unfortunately not standard all over the world. Some clinics base the diagnosis on the rise, some on the fall, others on the entire curve. We rely upon the diagnosis at the peak of the curve plus glycosuria. If the venous blood is 170 mgs. or the capillary blood

200 mgs. the diagnosis of diabetes is made. In this particular instance the blood sugars were normal and he was called an unclassified glycosuric, but was advised to keep under observation for a year. Had the blood sugar been normal and the urine never sugar free the diagnosis would have been that of a renal glycosuria, a benign condition requiring no treatment. Besides true glycosuria when the blood sugars are normal levulosuria and pentosuria must be excluded. These conditions are likewise benign and require no treatment.

(2) Treatment

Many forms of treatment of juvenile diabetes have arisen, but the fundamental principles and aims are the same: first, to promote the normal rate of growth and development; second, to render the urine practically free from sugar and maintain the blood sugar at normal levels; third, to control fat metabolism; and, fourth, to prevent acidosis.

The end-results with a severe and youthful type of diabetes have not been entirely satisfactory, and as a consequence many different forms of dietary treatment have been used. *These concern the partition of the diet into its component parts, carbohydrate, protein and fat, rather than the total calories. Today it is generally agreed by students of diabetes that the average adult over 50 will maintain a normal weight, providing he receives 30 calories per kilogram of body weight, and the child will grow at a normal rate if he receives 100 calories per kilogram during infancy, gradually decreasing to 45 calories per kilogram during adolescence and 35 per kilogram through active early adult life. Every possible variation of carbohydrate, protein and fat has been advocated for the youthful and severe diabetic. There are advocates of low-carbohydrate and high-fat ratios; moderate carbohydrate and moderate-protein and moderate-fat; high-carbohydrate and low-fat; high-protein and low-protein.*

The real defeatists are proponents of the free or normal diet. For our own part, we have had the happiest end-results when the carbohydrate has varied from 150 to 200 grams, using 2:1 or 3:1 carbohydrate fat ratios.

*Desugarization of the child is facilitated by the collection of specimens at nearly two-hour intervals. Qualitative tests are done upon nearly all of these specimens, but only the pre-meal and retiring tests are of value in treatment. We test one day to determine the adjustment of insulin for the following day. If the 11:30 test is poor one day, then the morning dose of insulin is increased the following day. Besides these qualitative tests, quantitative determinations are made upon the twenty-four hour amount and blood sugars are done at weekly intervals. Preferably all these analyses are made on a single day so that we have a picture of the patient's sugar metabolism for an entire twenty-four hours.

Insulin

So far as insulin therapy is concerned, we are in a transitional stage. The problem of the amount of insulin for a new patient can unfortunately not be solved by mathematical precision.*

Our rule with regular insulin has been to give small doses of insulin in childhood. *Under 5 years, we start with 3 units, three times daily; between 5 and 10, 5 units, three times a day; and between 10 and 15, 10 units, three times daily. This is changed each day by the method of trial and error, and at discharge administered twice daily.*

Protamine insulin has revolutionized therapy and the young diabetic profits most for after three years of the disease, all youthful cases show an elevated fasting blood sugar, well over 300 milligrams. *From the third year of duration on, the blood sugar becomes stabilized. There is no tendency for increasing severity of diabetes indicated by increasing fasting hyperglycemia. To counteract this most students of diabetes have prescribed either a dose of insulin between 10 o'clock and midnight, or one at 5 o'clock in the morning. The first method of treatment has resulted in an abrupt fall of the blood sugar at hypoglycemic levels followed by a spontaneous rise, so that even with this extra dose of insulin the fasting blood sugar was relatively high. Insulin given at 5 o'clock in the morning or earlier controls night hyperglycemia, but is inconvenient.* Protamine insulin, in a single dose, flattens this type of blood sugar curve and a single time technique can be adopted regardless of the severity of the case.

New cases require protamine alone. With cases of long standing, small doses of regular insulin are given, in addition to the protamine, at the same time and as a separate injection, fifteen minutes before breakfast.

(3) Complications

Treated, the life and tissues of the young patients are like those of the non-diabetic, but when the disease is chemically uncontrolled, he is liable to the development of (a) coma which even today occurs in one in ten of our diabetic children.

Diabetic coma has primarily but a single cause, overeating. This, however, can be brought about in a variety of ways: (1) diet breaking, (2) omission of insulin, (3) infection, (4) starvation (the body overeating itself), (5) disease of the glycogen storage organs (liver, skin, muscles).

The cardinal signs and symptoms of coma are invariably present but differential diagnosis may be difficult for the nausea, vomiting, abdominal pain and leukocytosis simulate an acute surgical abdomen; the hyperpnoea, pneumonia, the traces of albumin and showers of coarse granular casts, nephritis. The diagnosis depends upon the level of the plasma combining power of the blood. In our clinic the diagnosis of coma is made when the combining power is 20 volumes per cent or below. This is an arbitrary figure selected because few patients whose plasma combining power fell to this level recovered prior to the use of insulin.

The treatment of coma in a child differs little from the treatment of coma in the adult: insulin early and in repeated doses, the amount depending upon the size and age of the patient and the duration of the diabetes as well as the clinical severity of the coma. From 5 to 40 units are given every fifteen minutes for two hours, then hourly until clinical improvement is evident. Actually from 30 to over 600 units have been given. Fluid is used to combat dehydration, from 500 to 6000 c. c. of normal salt solution by hyperdermoclysis in the first twenty-four hours. Gastric lavage and enemata are employed to combat lack of gastro-intestinal tone. Adrenalin may be used to combat circulatory failure which, however, seldom occurs in childhood. Glucose 50% or saline 10 to 20% may be resorted to to avert renal block, and carbohydrate given up to 100 grams by mouth in the first twenty-four hours.

Coma must be differentiated from pneumonia, acute appendicitis, diphtheria and insulin shock.

The Differential Diagnosis of Diabetic Coma and Insulin Shock

Diabetic Coma	Insulin Shock
Cause	
Increase of diet	Reduction of diet
Omission of insulin	Increase of insulin
Infection	Increase of exercise
	Failure of absorption of food
History	
Gradual loss of consciousness preceded by	Rapid loss of consciousness sometimes followed by vomiting
Vomiting	Convulsions
No convulsions	
Physical examination	
Skin dry and flushed	Moist and pale
Breathing hyperpnoeic	Shallow
Pulse feeble	Full and bounding
Blood pressure low	High
Laboratory	
Blood sugar high	Low
CO_2 under 20 volumes per cent	Normal or elevated
Urine sugar + + +	+ or — (2nd specimen 0)
Diacetic acid + + +	0

Elaborate laboratory methods, however, may not be available, then one simple method differentiates the two conditions. The second of two urinary specimens in shock should be sugar free, and in coma not. The first specimen tested may be residual urine secreted by the kidneys before the drop in blood sugar occurred. The second specimen represents the true state of carbohydrate metabolism.

Mild shock is common. Besides the usual symptoms, nervousness, tremor, paraesthesias, diplopia, headache and sweating, the quiet child or the child in a tantrum must be considered hypoglycemic until proved otherwise. The treatment is self-evident: Replacement of carbohydrate by mouth if the patient is conscious, by vein or under the skin if the patient is unconscious. To the unconscious patient we prefer to give a 50 per cent solution of glucose intravenously for this not only tends to replace the needed carbohydrate quickly, but also to combat the cerebral edema which occurs in severe cases of insulin shock.

Prevention of these complications is the up-to-date attitude and for this reason almost any degree of abnormal health in the juvenile patient must be considered an emergency. Slight deviations from normal precipitate acidosis and coma even in a fairly well controlled case in as short an interval as twelve or twenty-four hours. Therefore parents and patients besides being taught to notify the family physician immediately in case of illness must be taught simple rules for the management of such days. These are the same as our own rules for pre- and postoperative treatment—insulin every two, four or six hours depending upon the degree of reduction with the Benedict test: For the child of fifteen years of age, 15 units if red or orange, 10 if yellow, 5 if yellow-green; to the child of ten years of age, 10 units if red or orange, 5 if yellow or yellow-green; to the child of five years of age, 5 units if red or orange, 3 if yellow. The diet should be reduced to carbohydrate 100 to 150 grams and a negligible amount of protein and fat. Such a diet could be one and one-half or two and a half quarts of milk in twenty-four hours.

b. Infection has always played a tragic role in diabetes. Prior to 1922 the infections precipitated coma with fatal outcome. Today they precipitate coma, not with fatal outcome, but a vicious circle is established, for infection precipitates coma and coma in turn predisposes the patient to tuberculosis and urinary tract infections.

c. Deficiency disease in childhood is of one type only, neuritis which has occurred in 1 per cent of the cases. Prevention is sought by control of diabetes. The lesion is treated by a high vitamin diet especially Vitamin C.

d. Degenerative changes. In our juvenile series we find that a total of 75, 6 per cent of our entire number, have survived 15 or more years of the disease. Of this number 70 are living and 5 have died. Twelve have had coma; nine arteriosclerosis; 24 retarded growth and development; 5 infections; 1 tuberculosis; 5 cataracts; and 1 neuritis. Of all the children, 5 per cent are known to have arteriosclerosis. This brief summary shows that failure of growth and development and degenerative complications have occurred too frequently. Uncontrolled diabetes is characteristic of the long-duration cases as well as other youthful cases who have developed such degenerative lesions. Prior to 1922 young diabetics did not live long enough to develop such changes. Coma destroyed childhood cases; tuberculosis destroyed young adults. Uncontrolled diabetes is measured chemically in two ways, either by hyperglycemia and glycosuria or by excess of lipids in the blood, and by ketone bodies in the blood or urine. We have tried to evaluate these various factors, and our own conclusion is that an excess of fat is the precursor and, we believe, the cause of degenerative changes.

e. Metabolic disturbances of the skin are of three types: one, benign,—namely, xanthosis, a yellow discoloration of the palms of the hands, soles of the feet, naso-labial fold and two malignant types, namely, xanthoma diabeticorum and necrobiosis lipoidica diabetica. The former is characterized by the appearance of yellow papules on a rose base and is related to hypercholesterolemia, the latter, undetermined in cause, appears first as papules which tend to atrophy and ulcerate.

f. *Dwarfism. Failure of growth in stature amounting to dwarfism, though an infrequent complication, has been one of our greatest concerns. Whereas 95 per cent of our diabetic children have actually grown and developed normally, 5 per cent have failed to do so. Thus, in our series of 1,126 children there are 61 who have at some time in their diabetic lives been from 4 to 13 inches below the standard average height for their ages. Dwarfism in our experience has not preceded diabetes; although we do not have the height at onset of diabetes in all, many not coming to us until several years after onset, we have sufficient data to know that the stature was normal or even above height prior to the recognition of this disease. Consequently, we have thought that although the primary fault was undoubtedly functional hypoactivity of the pituitary with lack of growth hormone it was to be related to undernutrition. Houssay, however, has reported a similar case in which there were, at autopsy, scars in the pituitary, and he has pointed out to us that it is quite possible that defective pituitary secretion may be responsible for coincident conditions—lack of pancreatropic hormone producing diabetes, and lack of growth hormone producing dwarfism.

Various methods of treatment have been employed, but largely three: high-caloric and high-protein diet; high-caloric, high-protein diet, with the addition of thyroid and pituitary gland extract; high-caloric and high-protein diet with growth hormone. The over-nutrition diet alone stimulated growth somewhat, but those patients treated with thyroid extract had a better rate of growth. We cannot report upon the results of growth hormone, because this work was started only in July, 1935, but in this short period of time the average rate of growth in four months has been one inch compared with one-half an inch for the normal child, and many of these children have been growing at the rate of less than one-half an inch a year. Some of them have grown almost two inches in this period of time. One of the commercial preparations seems to have a beneficial effect on blood sugar, the other no effect. We were hesitant about using these preparations at first because they are not pure; among other impurities, a diabetogenic factor is supposed to be found with the growth hormone, and it might increase the tendency toward glycosuria, hyperglycemia, and acidosis. However, none of these children have presented any harmful effects. Then, too, the newer work on the anti-hormone suggests that the prolonged use of such a substance as growth hormone may in the end retard growth, but with six months' continuous use no harmful end-results have occurred.

g. Enlargement of the liver. Another interesting complication is enlargement of the liver, which has been described only recently. This has been observed in 60 of our juvenile cases. This is not an insignificant enlargement, but actually the liver can be felt at the level of the iliac crest, and these patients often present themselves with a protuberant abdomen, due to the tremendously elongated and infiltrated liver. Such patients present serious problems in treatment because they are very unstable and are liable to frequent attacks both of insulin reactions and of diabetic acidosis. The cause of this enlargement has not been clear. Theoretically it may be due either to an excess of fat or to an excess of glycogen deposited in abnormal fashion. Several post-mortem examinations done in more or less complicated cases have shown that the enlargement has been due to fatty infiltration.

Diabetic dogs have been reported by Soskin, Best and Hershey, and Chaikoff with enlarged livers, infiltrated with fat. The problem with the experimental animal, however, is not quite the same, because, after all, they have been deprived of the external secretion of the pancreas, but in line with this is the possibility that these diabetic children may have had a congenitally small pancreas with a deficient external factor. Four autopsies have been done in this group, and they do not show small amounts of pancreatic tissue. The pancreatic ferments have been studied also, and a deficiency of lipolytic ferments has been found.

Liver function tests reveal little. However, the ratio of free cholesterol to cholesterol ester has been reported to be low in the experimental animal, indicating that this function of fat metabolism of the liver is defective. The total fat, however, may not be abnormal. As far as therapy is concerned, we have to treat these cases as if all were due to infiltration of fat. Best and Hershey have reported excellent results with the use of cholin, lecithin, or whole pancreas. We have been administering betaine hydrochloride, a choline-like substance. There is an immediate change on physical examination. The liver, which has been thick and readily palpated, can no longer be well-defined. There is no change by x-ray in four months. Untreated, these lesions can be of very long duration. We have observed certain cases for a period of five years. It is interesting here to note that excellent results have also been reported by Hanssen with protamine insulin. Whether this alters fat metabolism, or perhaps the storage rate of glycogen progresses in a slower and more normal fashion, one does not know.*

Failures in the treatment of the young diabetic of today are not due to the type of treatment employed, but to the lack of treatment or uncontrolled disease. This we consider hopeful because it can be remedied, yet control of diabetes depends upon the patient—an unfortunate situation in childhood since the child lacks wisdom. Therefore, infinite tact, patience and understanding must be applied to the individual child and his problems, and in addition to a therapy which includes diet, exercise, insulin and education, he requires protection. This has been sought by the establishment of summer camps and winter boarding schools for diabetic children.

— Excerpts from ' Recent Progress in Severe Diabetes" by Priscilla White, M.D, published in The Canadian Medical Association Journal. 35: 153-161, 1936. Used with permission of the Canadian Medical Association Journal.

DIABETIC CAMPS

PRISCILLA WHITE, M.D.

Boston, Mass.

The first diabetic camp in the world was started by the late Dr. Wendt in Michigan in 1924. The original diabetic camp in New England was started by a New England Deaconess Hospital nurse and was entirely a private enterprise. The work had its origin in 1925 when this nurse, Mrs. E. B. Devine, took one child to her home for the summer. The result in this case was so successful and the child had such a good time that Doctor Joslin sent five children to her the next summer. With this beginning a thoroughly adequate but not elaborate organization was created. The camp building consisted of a single unit having two dormitories with lavatories and showers, a dining-room, kitchen and small laboratory. This camp was entirely recreational. There was no organized program. The activities of the day were planned on the spur of the moment and this worked out very well for the younger children. The camp was located ideally on one of the lovely Ogunquit sand dunes. Thirty children were cared for at a time. Unfortunately, this unit was discontinued because of the ill health of the nurse in charge.

In several regulation camps diabetic units have been established—notably two—Camp Teela Wooket for girls in Roxbury, Vermont, and Camp Idlewild for boys in Lakeport, New Hampshire. Here ten or more children are cared for by New England Deaconess Hospital nurses. The diabetic children have participated in all activities, Teela Wooket featuring horseback riding, and Idlewild aqua-planing. They have done so well that they have won prizes for ability and also sportsmanship. These camps are especially suitable for the adolescent period and tend to weaken the child's belief that his life differs materially from the non-diabetic for, save that laboratory tests are done daily, diet charts kept and the diet weighed, their life had no departures from regular camp routine.

Differing from these, the Clara Barton and Prendergast Camps supplement hospital treatment and are more appropriate for our most difficult cases. The Clara Barton Camp at North Oxford, Massachusetts, is a free camp so far as the Universalist Church is concerned, but in a few instances children have paid a small fee. The camp accommodates about thirty-two children at a time or one hundred sixty during the summer. The unit consists of the five dormitories, a scrub parlor, the large remodelled barn which provides a playroom and dining-room and a small but very modern laboratory where all emergency tests required in a general hospital can be performed for the children of the camp and nearby community. These tests are also demonstrated to any visitor who is medically trained and who wishes to acquire technique. The personnel consists of a head nurse with her two assistants, a house mother, a dietitian, laboratory technician, counsellor and cook—all under the efficient supervision of a Camp Director.

The Clara Barton Camp for Diabetic Children had its origin in 1932 when the searching minds of the Universalist Women's Missionary Society and the Young People's Religious Union read an article in the

Boston Transcript. This article described the work being carried on at summer camps for diabetic children—so-called "islands of safety" and carried with it a plea for the creation of similar units. Rightly these minds comprehended this as something very new and worth-while—new because the living diabetic child is an entity of the recent decade and a half. Before the discovery of insulin ten years ago, in this country alone, 1,000 children died yearly of the disease. Today a thousand children contract the disease yearly but instead of dying in days, weeks, or months they are living indefinitely. Students of the disease know that in childhood there are many pitfalls for the patient and therefore the plea which appeared in the Transcript.

The Clara Barton Camp had been carrying on worth-while work as a nutrition center for the underprivileged child but here was an even more vital problem—service for the handicapped child and perhaps a more appropriate memorial for the woman, Clara Barton, who was so medically minded that she had founded the American Red Cross.

An innovation at the homestead was started and the Spring of 1932 saw a corps of workers turning the homestead into a recreational hospital unit.

For this camp a definite health program must be planned before the season starts and the following questions asked:

1. Is this child's disease controlled as much as it should be? If the blood sugar and blood fat are high, the answer is no and the diet and insulin must be corrected to give the desired balance.

2. Are the growth and development normal? Unless the height is ideal for age, the weight for height and age, the answer is no. The diet must be corrected to increase the rate of growth.

3. Are there other defects—anemias, faulty posture, poor muscular development? Is the mental attitude right or is the child depressed or tending toward introspection?

All of these problems must be considered and the appropriate program planned.

An interesting change occurred in our statistics after the establishment of the Clara Barton Camp. Coma began to disappear among girls but continue among boys, so we thought a unit for boys must be established. At this time Dr. J. B. Hawes invited a group of physicians interested in chronic disease to visit Prendergast and pointed out its possible use for chronic diseases other than tuberculosis. We grasped at this opportunity, for it was just what we needed for diabetic boys. Now at the Prendergast Preventorium 30 children are cared for at a time. The Unitarian church contributes generously toward the support of this unit.

The chief functions of the summer camp units are: (1) the provision of a happy and safe vacation for the juvenile diabetic, (2) a release for the parents, (3) better diabetic training and education for the children, (4) the test of the adequacy of our own treatment, (5) the teaching of the important phases of the treatment and course of juvenile diabetes, (6) investigation of long problems, and (7) economy.

One hundred per cent successes in happiness are inconsistent with human nature but the majority of the children had a very pleasant experience. It is a compliment to the personnel that two or three months before the opening of camp, the former children campers write to ask if they may be included this year. This is a compliment, because the majority of children have been brought up with excitement of movies, auto rides, beaches, all of which are missing in these units. Provisions for vacations for the mothers and fathers of diabetic children are as important as those for the children. Vacations, therefore, are provided not only for the 200 children who are in these camps but for the 400 parents. A diabetic child can never be out of the minds of parents unless he or she is protected against emergencies. Only in the hospital, the camp, or home is he safe.

The third function has been improvement in the instruction of the young patient as well as the building of morale. Economic reasons have necessitated a reduction in the period of hospitalization to its present minimum of five or at most ten days and consequently the child has received instruction when his mental processes have been comparatively sluggish due to undernutrition or even acidosis. His diabetic education has thus often been incomplete. The camp can be utilized as a *supplementary* course in instruction. The nurses have very happily created a game attitude toward this and now every camp child can measure and administer his own insulin hypodermically and enjoys doing so, calculate and trade his diet, perform and interpret the Benedict test for sugar, recognize insulin reactions and treat them, and knows the signs and symptoms of coma. At the same time every effort is made to keep diabetes in the background and normal living conditions are stressed, for the children have crafts, fresh water swimming, picnics, hikes, etc.

The success of this venture cannot be measured at the close of the camp season but is known in the next twelve months for, if successful, not one of the children, except in the presence of a severe infection, should have coma. In two years only one Clara Barton camper was treated at the New England Deaconess Hospital for coma!

Morale is strengthened by camp life. It is a relatively easy matter for the diabetic child to be obedient for a year. After this, the routine palls. He begins to visualize years of weighed diets, hypodermic injections, disagreeable reactions, limitation of activities. The recognition of a handicap grows on the child and discouragement ensues. When a group of these young children are brought together each one helps the other to rebuild courage.

In its fourth function, the investigation and critical analysis of our own methods of treatment, the camp has been an invaluable scientific experiment giving us more knowledge of the food requirements necessary for the growth of the diabetic child than we had ever known before. In our first three-week period in 1932 our children lost on the average of two pounds. We were not surprised at this for as a group they were well nourished. In the second group an even greater loss occurred in a week and it was evident that our diets were inadequate for activity. By the method of trial and error we found that a 15 per cent increase in food was necessary. Last year this was done immediately and the average gain was normal, one half pound a month, and now these diets are prescribed for our patients when they leave the hospital.

Three research problems have been carried on at these units.

The children who have failed to grow and develop properly have been treated with Growth Hormone supplied by the E. R. Squibb and Sons Company and the Parke Davis Company. The results justified the treatment.

Children with large livers were observed for long periods of time. Reduction in the size of the liver occurred when choline-like substances were used and protamine insulin administered.

The various preparations of protamine and the methods of administering it were studied. Because of these units 200 children were adjusted to protamine insulin in the first twelve months of protamine therapy. Many could not have afforded hospital care.

The camp project for children stimulated other possibilities such as vacations for the adolescent or even for the adult diabetic. As conditions exist today such patients often plan to spend their vacations in the hospital as they actually do derive benefit not only from medical supervision, but also from the opportunity to relax their vigilance over their disease, which requires perpetual remembrance. Furthermore, it stimulated us to consider the foundation of a diabetic school where our young patients may be cared for and receive suitable vocational or professional training. The winter unit at Prendergast was started in 1935 with this very purpose in mind. In spite of the general optimism in the diabetic state today none of us can deny or fail to appreciate what this handicap means in the formative years.

THE LABORATORY IN THE TREATMENT OF DIABETES

HAZEL HUNT, A.B.

Director, Chemical Laboratory,
New England Deaconess Hospital

and

ALEXANDER MARBLE, M.D.

Boston, Mass.

The chemical laboratory plays a vital part in the successful treatment of diabetes. Proper diagnosis and therapy are almost impossible without it. Unfortunately it can be and often is a factor of considerable expense largely because it is not used to the greatest advantage. It is only by doing tests in large numbers that the cost per determination can be reduced. The chief factor of expense is the time required of a trained technician. He or she, however, can frequently do ten tests almost as quickly as one, and if ten are done the cost per test can often be reduced 75 to 90 per cent. If a single blood sugar is determined once a week the actual cost of that single test may be almost prohibitive. If, however, blood sugar tests are done by the dozens, the cost of each becomes nominal.

If chemical laboratories equipped to do diabetic work are functioning at strategic points or at "diabetic islands of safety" and are actually kept busy by the doctors in the community, there is no reason why diabetic laboratory work should be costly. The average price charged for a blood sugar test in the average laboratory is five to ten dollars. Because of the few tests done, that price is necessary. On the other hand, in a laboratory which serves a diabetic clinic the cost is one dollar or less per test.

The apparatus (excepting a microscope but including a microcolorimeter) needed to equip the laboratory of a small hospital or doctor's office may be purchased for slightly less than two hundred dollars. This apparatus will permit the carrying out of all the tests commonly made with blood and urine including the determination of blood sugar, non-protein nitrogen and plasma bicarbonate.

The services of a trained laboratory technician should be available to doctors everywhere day or night, Sundays and holidays. The successful treatment of the diabetic patient in coma, in profound hypoglycemia or during infections or other complications requires easy access of the physician to a good laboratory. Never hesitate to take advantage of all the aid which the laboratory can give.

Certain procedures are of special help in the treatment of diabetes. These are discussed briefly below:

1. Capillary blood sugar

Methods are available for the accurate determination of the blood sugar on a few drops of blood obtained by puncture of an ear lobe or finger. Such methods have been used extensively in European clinics for years but as yet are all too seldom employed in this country. They permit frequent estimations of the blood sugar with a minimum of inconvenience to the patient and are of particular value with children, elderly or nervous individuals, patients in diabetic coma and patients undergoing special tests requiring serial determinations. The results obtained are comparable to values obtained with venous blood taken simultaneously except that following the ingestion of sugar or food the capillary values are normally 20 to 50 mgm. per 100 cc. higher. This capillary-venous difference is less in patients with uncontrolled diabetes.

2. Quantitative estimation of sugar in urine

The standard method of Benedict for the determination of the percentage of sugar in urine requires too much time if many tests are to be done daily. For years we have used successfully the micro modification of this test devised by Millard Smith. This simple determination with a special pipette requires in trained hands less than two minutes and is thoroughly dependable. Furthermore the saving in chemicals is appreciable. More recently, Sheftel has introduced another method (requiring special though simple apparatus) which is really an adaptation of the Benedict qualitative procedure. This method is also reliable, can be quickly carried out and can be performed readily by patients.

3. Fractional tests for sugar in urine

Although the most accurate idea of the control of the diabetic condition is obtained by testing a specimen of the total twenty-four hour collection of urine, often the testing of specimens at more frequent intervals gives information which is extremely helpful in the adjustment of diet and insulin dosage. Three such procedures are as follows:

a. *Four period test.* This is particularly valuable for use with patients using regular (unmodified) insulin. Collect all the urine voided for twenty-four hours in four bottles as follows:

I. Urine between breakfast and dinner —M orning
II Urine from dinner to supper —A fternoon
III Urine from supper till bedtime —E vening
IV Urine voided during night and including specimen passed upon rising in the morning —N ight

Test urine in each bottle separately.

b. *Two-hourly tests.* With hospitalized patients becoming adjusted to protamine insulin it is helpful to collect single specimens upon arising and at 7:30, 9:30 and 11:30 A.M., and at 2:30, 4:30, 7:30 and 9:30 P.M.

c. *The two specimen test.* The diagnosis of an insulin reaction may be confused by sugar in the urine due to the retention by the bladder of urine secreted by the kidneys some hours earlier. Therefore, in questionable cases, secure a second specimen of urine fifteen or twenty minutes after the bladder has been emptied. A negative test for sugar in this specimen will be consistent with a low blood sugar.

DIABETIC COSTS
ALLEN P. JOSLIN, M.D.
Boston, Mass.

Diabetic costs cover the lifetime of the patient. Hospitalization at the onset of the disease is not only for the regulation and control of diabetes but for diabetic education and is a prime factor in reducing future expenses. Within a period of four to five days, as compared with two or more weeks formerly, a mild diabetic can be taught the pitfalls of the disease so that a coma which costs at least a hundred dollars, or an infected toe which may cost upwards of one hundred and fifty dollars can be avoided. Tuberculosis is not an infrequent complication of a diabetic and if one can escape it through accurate medical study not only life may be saved but years of confining treatment. By learning the fundamentals of the disease at the beginning, the diabetic protects himself and practices preventive medicine.

To keep well is pleasanter and less expensive for the patients because the treatment of diabetes and the treatment of its complications are very different. The patient should be willing to have his doctor at regular intervals so that no complications may arise. This prevents emergencies, gives the patient a chance to keep up with improving treatments and protects the patient's family from losing a possible source of income.

Organized daily lectures by the doctors, twice daily visits to the patient's bedside, individual instruction and contacts with other diabetic patients show them the results of good attention, or carelessness with their disease. It is almost impossible to have a patient do well year in and year out without the advantages of hospitalization. A diabetic's happiness depends upon his ability to realize the pitfalls of his disease and to recognize the fact that he must have a physician and cooperate with him in health as well as illness. Failure to realize this means continual trouble, often perhaps not coming at the onset of his disease but generally at a time when it is least suspected. Hospitalization is intensive training in diabetic methods. (The Training Camp for Diabetics.)

Today, with liberal carbohydrate diets and with almost every kind of food available at reasonable prices, a diabetic diet should not be more than a few cents above any regular menu. Diet lectures bring this point out. Sameness of food should never be a reason for breaking diet; there is too great a variety available.

Insulin is one of the chief costs in a diabetic patient's life. By taking advantage of the principles of treatment, diet, exercise and insulin, careful study often shows where a patient may reduce the insulin dosage ten to twenty or more units daily. If insulin costs one-quarter cent a unit, just a little more care in treatment would save from nine to eighteen dollars a year or the equivalent of two pairs of shoes or a suit. However, in the case of a mild diabetic who should take insulin, spending as little as two and a half to five cents a day frequently saves a limb or perhaps wards off total blindness in later years. Thus we see that by spending a little money in time the diabetic insures himself against future hazards.

First —for hospitalization at onset to insure complete instruction and reduce careless mishaps.

Second—for regular check-ups with his family physician which protect him from impending troubles.

Third —for immediate care of seemingly unimportant developments which, neglected, would prove costly.

A "cent" in time saves nine.

CORRECTION

The editor wishes to correct the name of the author of the article entitled "What Mothers Want to Know about Child Nutrition" which appeared in the October-November-December 1936 issue of The Commonhealth. The authorship belongs to Miss Dorothy Frank, Nutritionist, Massachusetts Department of Public Health.

REPORT OF THE DIVISION OF FOOD AND DRUGS
(As required by General Laws, Chapter 111, Section 25.)

During the months of January, February and March 1937, samples were collected in 196 cities and towns. There were 1,647 samples of milk examined, of which 132 were below standard, from 5 samples the cream had been in part removed, and 5 samples contained added water. There were 2,239 bacteriological examinations made of milk, 1,900 of which complied with the requirements. There were 16 bacteriological examinations made of pasteurized cream, 1 of which did not comply with the requirements; 212 bacteriological examinations of ice cream, 17 of which did not comply with the requirements; 3 bacteriological examinations of chocolate cookies, all of which complied with the requirements; 23 bacteriological examinations of meats, 7 of which did not comply with the requirements; 6 bacteriological examinations of empty bottles, all of which did not comply with the requirements; and 8 bacteriological examinations of mattress fillings, 2 of which did not comply with the requirements.

There were 829 samples of food examined, 133 of which were adulterated. These consisted of 4 samples of butter which were rancid; 1 sample of cereal which contained many moths; 2 samples of cream, 1 sample which was submitted contained dirt, 1 sample of heavy cream was below the legal standard in fat, and 1 sample was misbranded with the words "Government Inspected Bottling"; 5 samples of eggs which were decomposed; 1 sample of pickles which contained sodium benzoate not marked; 2 samples of chocolate covered cherries which contained benzoate not so labeled; 3 samples of olive oil, 1 sample of which contained cotton seed oil; 1 sample contained tea-seed oil, and 1 sample contained mineral oil; 32 samples of hamburg steak, 20 of which were decomposed, 8 contained a compound of sulphur dioxide not properly labeled 2 of which were also decomposed, 3 contained sodium sulphite in excess of one tenth of one per cent 2 of which were also decomposed, and 1 sample contained a compound of sulphur dioxide not properly labeled, contained added water, and was also decomposed; 32 samples of sausage, 16 of which were decomposed, 10 samples contained a compound of sulphur dioxide not properly labeled 2 of which were also decomposed, 4 samples contained sodium sulphite in excess of one tenth of one per cent, and 2 samples contained starch in excess of 2 per cent; 1 sample of pieces of beef which contained a compound of sulphur dioxide not so labeled and was also decomposed; 2 samples of ground beef, 2 samples of frankfort mix, and 1 sample of lamb patties, all of which were decomposed; 1 sample of orangeade which was misbranded, and 16 samples of orangeade which were colored to conceal inferiority and were also misbranded; 14 samples of soft drink wash water which were deficient in caustic alkali; and 14 samples of mattress fillings, 11 of which contained secondhand material one of which also contained starch, 2 samples were mislabeled, and 1 sample was labeled "Down" and contained 76% of feathers.

There were 136 samples of drugs examined, of which 19 were

adulterated. These consisted of 8 samples of argyrol which did not correspond to the professed standard under which they were sold, 1 sample of lime water and 9 samples of spirit of nitrous ether, all of which did not conform to the requirements of the U. S. Pharmacopoeia, and 1 sample of Fowler's Solution with no antidote marked on the label.

The police departments submitted 186 samples of liquor for examination. The police departments also submitted 10 samples to be analyzed for poisons or drugs, of which 3 samples contained cannabis, 3 samples contained heroin, 2 samples contained heroin hydrochloride, and 2 samples contained no alkaloids. The Fish and Game Division also submitted 1 sample which contained no cyanide or strychnine.

There were inspected 349 plants operated for the pasteurization of milk; 19 ice cream plants; 516 bakeries, 118 soft drink plants; 303 mattress establishments; 300 establishments relative to the enforcement of licenses pertaining to wood alcohol and preparations containing over 3% of same; and 2 inspections were made relative to narcotic licenses.

There were 147 hearings held pertaining to violations of the laws.

There were 80 convictions for violations of the law, $1,630 in fines being imposed.

Joseph Chamberlain of Wenham; John Joacquin, 2 cases, of Fall River; The Miller Drug Company, Incorporated, of Roxbury; Albert E. Clayton of Framingham; and Constantine Trearchis of Woburn, were all convicted for violations of the milk laws. John Joacquin of Fall River appealed his two cases.

Mary Joacquin, 2 cases, of Fall River; Leopold Schiavi, 2 cases, of Framingham; John Campbell of Haverhill; Francis Grout of Sherborn; and Frank La Croix of Hingham, were all convicted for violations of the pasteurization law and regulations.

John Kardolski of Salem; and Ralph A. Merrifield of Athol, were convicted for violations of the milk grading regulations.

Robert T. Holden of Bennington, Vermont, was convicted for misbranding milk.

Coleman Andelman, 2 cases, of Arlington; Arthur Corey, 2 cases of Lawrence; Liberty Market, Incorporated, of Newburyport; Great Scott Food Market, Incorporated, of Brockton; P. W. Rounsevell, Incorporated, D. Pettrini Company, Incorporated, and South Cash Market, Incorporated, all of Boston; Camillo Buonaugurio, 3 cases, Pasquale Piscione, 2 cases, Rose De Luca, Fred Razzaboni, Frank Fiorentino, John F. Ruggieri, Benjamin Gross, and John Macera, all of Somerville; George Martin and Joseph Salvick of Springfield; John Moskal and Rose Weiss of Ware; Barney Gorodetzer, 2 cases, of Dorchester; Samuel Rotenberg of Chelsea; Harry Shafran of Brookline; Jack Shavetsky of Revere; Benny Stolzberg and Wilfred Maloney of Haverhill; Abraham Rich of Lynn; The Oscar Spitzler Company, 2 cases, of Holyoke; Main Public Market, Incorporated, of Fall River; Max Bernstein of Gardner; and Cudahy Packing Company of Worcester, were all convicted for violations of the food laws. South Cash Market, Incorporated, of Boston, and Wilfred Maloney of Haverhill, appealed their cases.

Ernest Delmolino of Springfield was convicted for violation of the cold storage law.

Boston Baking Company and Sadie Nagle of Roxbury were convicted for using decomposed eggs in the manufacture of food products.

Adamo Drug Company, Incorporated, of Boston was convicted for violation of the drug law.

Herman Bergmann, Jacob Bergmann, and William J. Kessler of Easthampton; Betty Alden, Incorporated, Max Ostrov, and Jacob Weisbaum of Boston; Morris Eicoff, Joseph Massell, and Sadie Nagle of Roxbury; and Max Silver of Springfield; were all convicted for violations of the bakery law and regulations. On the bakery case against the Ward Baking Company of Cambridge the Judge accepted a plea of "nolo contendere" and dismissed the case on payment of $20.00 as costs.

Frank Kuczarski of Easthampton; Hyman Perlstein of Shirley; Stanislaus Rapulus of Ludlow; Louis Bechard of Lowell; and Frank Francus of Gill, were all convicted for violations of the law and regulations relative to the manufacture and bottling of carbonated non-alcoholic beverages.

Regis Products Company, Incorporated, of Cambridge, was convicted for violation of the frozen dessert law. This company appealed their case.

Jules L. Du Bois of Braintree; Max Kaplan of New Bedford; Joseph Douglas of Lynn; General Mattress Company of Fall River; and Springfield Upholstery Works, Incorporated, of Springfield, were all convicted for violations of the mattress laws.

Harry Bialsky of Dorchester was convicted for obstruction of an inspector. He appealed his case.

In accordance with Section 25, Chapter 111 of the General Laws, the following is the list of articles of adulterated food collected in original packages from manufacturers, wholesalers, or producers:

Butter which was rancid was obtained as follows:

Two samples from Nathan Winer of Springfield; and 1 sample each, from Fenway Market of Boston, and L. W. English of Woodstock, Vermont.

One sample of heavy cream which was low in fat for this grade was obtained from Charles Brown of Feeding Hills.

One sample of extra heavy cream which was misbranded with the words "Government Inspected Bottling" was obtained from S. S. Pierce Company of Boston.

One sample of cereal which contained many moths was obtained from Economy Grocery Company of Roxbury.

One sample of olive oil which contained cottonseed oil was obtained from Cantania Importing Company, Incorporated, of Boston.

One sample of olive oil which contained tea-seed oil was obtained from Steve Girdis of Boston.

One sample of sweet mix which contained sodium benzoate and was not properly labeled was obtained from George Kerkorian of Newburyport.

One sample of "pieces of beef" which contained a compound of sulphur dioxide not so labeled and was also decomposed was obtained from Carl Andelman and Sam Hefferon of Arlington.

One sample of lamb patties which was decomposed was obtained from Stop & Shop of Milford.

Two samples of ground beef which were decomposed were obtained from Omaha Packing Company of Lowell.

Two samples of frankfort mix which were decomposed were obtained from Omaha Packing Company of Lowell.

Hamburg steak which was decomposed was obtained as follows:

One sample each from Colonial Market of Haverhill; Comet Market, Incorporated, of Brockton; Blair's Market of Roxbury; South Cash Market, Incorporated, of Boston; People's Public Market and Main Public Market of Fall River; Charles Dubrow of Lynn; Brockelman's Market of Lawrence; Frank Sigda and George Sigda of Holyoke; White Star Foods, Incorporated, and Woburn Provision Company, Incorporated, of Everett; New Bedford Public Market and Nathan Cohen of New Bedford; Camillo Buonauguiro, Rose De Luca, and Fred Razzaboni of Somerville; Rose Tuvman of Indian Orchard; Liberty Market, Incorporated, of Newburyport; Rose Weiss of Ware; and Solin's Market, Incorporated, of Chicopee.

Hamburg steak which contained a compound of sulphur dioxide not properly labeled was obtained as follows:

One sample each, from Sam Gordon of New Bedford; Pasquale Pesconi of Somerville; Aram Yagjion of Arlington; Norwood Market, Incorporated, of Everett; Morris Provision Company of Waltham; and Jacob Hurovitz of Boston.

Hamburg steak which contained a compound of sulphur dioxide not properly labeled and was also decomposed was obtained as follows:

One sample each, from Norwood Market, Incorporated, of Everett; and Carl Anderson & Sam Hefferon of Arlington.

One sample of hamburg steak which contained sodium sulphite in excess of one tenth of one per cent was obtained from Camillo Buonaugurio of Somerville.

Two samples of hamburg steak which contained sodium sulphite in excess of one tenth of one per cent and were also decomposed were obtained from Pow-Wow River Market, Incorporated, of Amesbury.

One sample of hamburg steak which contained a compound of sulphur dioxide not properly labeled, contained added water, and which was also decomposed, was obtained from Waltham Provision Company, Incorporated, of Waltham.

Sausage which was decomposed was obtained as follows:

One sample each, from Arthur Corey of Lawrence; Frank Fiorentino and Benjamin Gross of Somerville; City Public Market of Gardner; Charles Kisiel & August Kisiel of Ware; Globe Market, Frank Sigda & George Sigda, and John Moskal of Holyoke, The Great Atlantic & Pacific Tea Company of Framingham; Weir Cash Market of Taunton; White Star Market and White Star Foods, Incorporated, of Waltham; Henry Beach of North Attleboro; George F. Bond of Marlboro; and 2 samples from Great Scott Food Market, Incorporated, of Brockton.

Sausage which contained a compound of sulphur dioxide not properly labeled was obtained as follows:

One sample each, from Pasquale Pesconi and John Macera of Somerville; John Moskal of Ware; Self Service Market of Springfield; Thomas Manguso of Milford; K. and M. Market of Hudson; and Marlboro Food Stores of Marlboro.

Sausage which contained sodium sulphite in excess of one tenth of one per cent was obtained as follows:

Two samples from D. Pettrini Company, Incorporated, of Boston; and 1 sample each, from Camillo Buonaugurio and John F. Ruggieri of Somerville.

Sausage which contained a compound of sulphur dioxide not properly labeled and was also decomposed was obtained as follows:

One sample each, from Nellie Komatski of Springfield; and Popular Food Market, Incorporated, of Holyoke.

Sausage which contained starch in excess of 2 per cent was obtained as follows:

One sample each, from Cudahy Packing Company and United Fruit Stores of Worcester.

One sample of orangeade which was misbranded was obtained from Charles L. Woodland of Watertown.

Orangeade which was misbranded and colored to conceal inferiority was obtained as follows:

Three samples from Mayflower Beverage Company, Incorporated of Jamaica Plain; 1 sample each, from Canadian Imperial Dry, Incorporated, of Allston; Red Star Beverage Company of East Boston; Parkdale Bottling Company and Patent Mineral Bottling Company of Boston; White Eagle Bottling Company of Everett; Empire Bottling Company of Malden; and Lowell Soda & Spring Water Company of Lowell.

There were eight confiscations, consisting of 50 pounds of decomposed beef, 2 pounds of decomposed veal chops, 36 pounds of decomposed hamburg steak, 60 pounds of decomposed pork sausage, 27 pounds of decomposed chicken, 602 pounds of decomposed turkeys, 189 pounds of decomposed poultry, 160 pounds of decomposed ptarmigan.

The licensed cold storage warehouses reported the following amounts of food placed in storage during December, 1936:—203,460 dozens of case eggs; 693,561 pounds of broken out eggs; 390,483 pounds of butter; 4,878,793 pounds of poultry; 8,872,276 pounds of fresh meat and fresh meat products; and 7,044,965 pounds of fresh food fish.

There was on hand January 1, 1937:—414,210 dozens of case eggs; 1,581,936 pounds of broken out eggs; 1,911,992 pounds of butter; 10,898,651 pounds of poultry; 13,086,246 pounds of fresh meat and fresh meat products; and 37,372,437 pounds of fresh food fish.

The licensed cold storage warehouses reported the following amounts of food placed in storage during January, 1937:—544,950 dozens of case eggs; 554,930 pounds of broken out eggs; 519,910 pounds of butter; 2,671,146 pounds of poultry; 4,668,755 pounds of fresh meat and fresh meat products; and 4,240,935 pounds of fresh food fish.

There was on hand February 1, 1937:—657,240 dozens of case eggs; 1,278,865 pounds of broken out eggs; 1,537,344 pounds of butter; 11,220,183 pounds of poultry; 15,225,694 pounds of fresh meat and fresh meat products; and 30,930,016 pounds of fresh food fish.

The licensed cold storage warehouses reported the following amounts of food placed in storage during February, 1937:— 792,030 dozens of case eggs; 595,080 pounds of broken out eggs; 328,660 pounds of butter; 2,065,259 pounds of poultry; 1,897,776 pounds of fresh meat and fresh meat products; and 3,484,888 pounds of fresh food fish.

There was on hand March 1, 1937:—1,339,710 dozens of case eggs, 1,029,011 pounds of broken out eggs; 706,262 pounds of butter; 10,377,314 pounds of poultry; 14,099,533 pounds of fresh meat and fresh meat products; and 24,453,844 pounds of fresh food fish.

MASSACHUSETTS DEPARTMENT OF PUBLIC HEALTH

Commissioner of Public Health, HENRY D. CHADWICK, M.D.

Public Health Council

HENRY D. CHADWICK, M.D., *Chairman*

GORDON HUTCHINS.
FRANCIS H. LALLY, M.D.
CHARLES F. LYNCH, M.D.

RICHARD M. SMITH, M.D.
RICHARD P. STRONG, M.D.
JAMES L. TIGHE.

Secretary, FLORENCE L. WALL

Division of Administration	Under direction of Commissioner.
Division of Sanitary Engineering	Director and Chief Engineer, ARTHUR D. WESTON, C.E.
Division of Communicable Diseases	Director, GAYLORD W. ANDERSON, M.D.
Division of Biologic Laboratories	Director and Pathologist, ELLIOTT S. ROBINSON, M.D.
Division of Food and Drugs	Director and Analyst, HERMANN C. LYTHGOE, S.B.
Division of Child Hygiene	Director, M. LUISE DIEZ, M.D.
Division of Tuberculosis	Director, ALTON S. POPE, M.D.
Division of Adult Hygiene	Director, HERBERT L. LOMBARD, M.D.

State District Health Officers

The Southeastern District	RICHARD P. MACKNIGHT, M.D., New Bedford.
The South Metropolitan District	HENRY M. DE WOLFE, M.D., Quincy.
The North Metropolitan District	CHARLES E. GILL, M.D., Boston
The Northeastern District	ROBERT E. ARCHIBALD, M.D., Lynn.
The Worcester County District	OSCAR A. DUDLEY, M.D., Worcester.
The Connecticut Valley District	JOHN J. POUTAS, M.D., Springfield.
The Franklin County District	WALTER W. LEE, M.D., No. Adams.
The Berkshire County Health District	HAROLD W. STEVENS, M.D., Great Barrington.

PUBLICATION OF THIS DOCUMENT APPROVED BY THE COMMISSION ON ADMINISTRATION AND FINANCE
9 M. 6-'37. Order 978,

THE COMMONHEALTH

Volume 24
No. 3

July-Aug.-Sept.
1937

Health Education

**MASSACHUSETTS
DEPARTMENT OF PUBLIC HEALTH**

THE COMMONHEALTH

QUARTERLY BULLETIN OF THE MASSACHUSETTS DEPARTMENT OF
PUBLIC HEALTH

Sent Free to any Citizen of the State

Entered as second class matter at Boston Postoffice.

M. LUISE DIEZ, M.D., DIRECTOR OF DIVISION OF CHILD HYGIENE, EDITOR.
1 Beacon Street, Boston, Mass.

CONTENTS

	PAGE
Changes in Departmental Personnel	169
What Methods Will Promote Health Education, by Jean V. Latimer	170
Health Education in Maternity and Infancy, by Florence L. McKay, M. D.	172
Health Education for the Secondary Schools, by A. Russell Mack	175
The Teaching Unit on "Teeth and Their Care" as Developed in the South Egremont Rural School, by Florence B. Hopkins, M.D., D.M.D. and Jean V. Latimer, B.S., A.M.	177
How May School Health Education Be Improved? by Jean V. Latimer	181
The Keystone Ophthalmic Telebinocular, by Mariam Forster	184
Exhibits and Materials for Health Teaching, by Albertine P. McKellar and John H. McCarthy	189
Health Education for the Community, by H. D. Chope, M. D.	194
Nutrition Facts for Teachers, by Mary Spalding	199
Health Education in the Field of Dentistry, by Florence B. Hopkins, M.D., D.M.D.	208
Health Education in the Field of Tuberculosis, by Arthur Strawson	214
Public Health Nurses as Teachers of Health, by Ann W. Dinegan, R.N.	218
Training of Personnel under the Social Security Act	220
Announcement — American Medical Association	222
Mississippi Valley Medical Society Award	223
Report of Division of Food and Drugs, April, May and June, 1937	226

CHANGES IN DEPARTMENT PERSONNEL

Several important changes in the personnel of the Department have taken place in recent months.

His Excellency, Governor Hurley, made two new appointments to the Public Health Council to replace members whose terms had expired. Dr. Sylvester E. Ryan, of Springfield, who had served continuously since 1920, declined reappointment because of ill health and was succeeded by Dr. Charles F. Lynch, of Springfield. Dr. George D. Dalton, of Wollaston, takes the place of Mr. Gordon Hutchings, of Concord, who had been a member of the Council since 1926.

Both of the retiring members throughout their long periods of service devoted much time and thought to the problems relating to the health of the people of the Commonwealth that came before the Department for consideration. Their counsel was valued highly.

Dr. Gaylord W. Anderson resigned September 1 to accept the professorship of public health at the University of Minnesota. Dr. Anderson came to the Department as Epidemiologist in the Division of Communicable Diseases in August 1929. The following June he was appointed Assistant Director of that Division, and in May 1931 he was made Director and Deputy Commissioner of Public Health. In whatever capacity he was placed his work was outstanding. The service furnished by the Department through its laboratories, and in the field through the District Health Officers, under his direction has been extended and brought to a high degree of excellence.

Several important epidemiological studies have been initiated and carried on by him during his term as Director. One of these was the study of typhoid carriers in relation to reported cases. Another, the value of immunization with scarlet fever toxoid in the control of scarlet fever. He also took a very active interest in the pneumonia program and its development.

A few months after the Massachusetts Health Commission was organized Dr. Anderson was chosen Secretary and did invaluable work with the committees during the year and a half that the study was carried on. The Commission is greatly indebted to him for the painstaking editing that he did on the reports of the subcommittees and in compiling the final report.

Marked success attended his efforts as a public health administrator and his friends in the Department are confident that because of his distinct flair for teaching he has before him a distinguished career in the educational field.

In the reorganization that was made necessary by Dr. Anderson's resignation, Dr. Alton S. Pope, Director of the Division of Tuberculosis since 1930, was appointed Deputy Commissioner in addition to his other duties; and Dr. Roy F. Feemster, who has been with the Department since 1931, first as Epidemiologist, then Assistant Director in the Division of Communicable Diseases, and more recently Assistant Director of the Antitoxin and Vaccine Laboratory, was appointed Director of the Division of Communicable Diseases.

The Department is exceedingly fortunate to have among its

staff such well-qualified physicians to promote to these responsible positions.

WHAT METHODS WILL PROMOTE HEALTH EDUCATION?

JEAN V. LATIMER

Coordinator of Health Education
Massachusetts Department of Public Health

A past president of the American Medical Association once said, "If doctors could apply all they know to all the people, not only would life be prolonged and human happiness increased, but the whole aspect and order of life would be altered." We have seen federal, state and local governments steadily increase their activities in the way of health service, but whether or not such services are effective will depend in no small measure on the health education of the people, both individually and in mass—including the health education of adults and the health education of children in school. Especially in a democratic society is it necessary for public health officials to win the support of not only the organized community but to reach into every home—familiarize the people with the functions of the health department and explain activities that are being carried on.

To open the way—to translate knowledge into action, is definitely the task of education. But health education must be thought of both from the point of view of motivating the individual as to modes of healthful living and educating the mass population to more enlightened standards of thought and action in regard to physical well being.

First, mass education must be carried on. Sociologists have pointed out that, although public opinion is of course made up of individual opinions, it is on a higher average standard than any of the individual opinions which compose it. The advances in public health are constantly calling for new patterns, new ways of social action. Therefore, health education cannot be undertaken solely on any merely individualistic plane such as the adoption of a personal regime of health habits, but must be thought of as a mode of social behavior based on intelligent self-directed action.

In health education we cannot think of the individual outside of his social relationships and contacts. Training in specific health habits has an important place in the health program but it is not the center. The heart of the problem would seem to be to teach the individual to cooperate intelligently and effectively with the professions and social institutions—the medical profession, the dentists, the nurses, the public health departments, etc.—which exist for the conservation and upbuilding of health. Therefore, would it not seem that in the future in looking at our methods of health education we must make more of a study of the organized community and its modes of action?

Thus, health education reaches out into the community and becomes a part of its social organization. Health education requires the cooperative support and the action of the entire community. Home, school and community must be coordinated. Public health officials and teachers alone cannot bring about the health education of any community. All organized groups—citizens, parents, social workers, recreational supervisors, etc., must become acquainted with the objectives of health education.

One of the tasks of the health educator is to analyze for himself the large aims of the health education program which he is trying to accomplish in terms of specific objectives and to make the community conscious of these same goals.

Such a procedure requires careful planning. In a sound educational program concerning any phase of public health the specific objectives must be formulated, the desired audience to be reached must be determined, definite methods to be used must be decided upon and some measurement of results must be attempted. Otherwise, we are shooting in the air without aim or direction.

Community health studies are needed. Too often we have attempted to accomplish specific objectives in localities concerning which we knew too little. What are the racial and other traditions which may facilitate or handicap the health objectives sought? What are the special local problems of disease, of physical handicaps, of relief, of poor housing? Some of such information is available in the files of state and local health departments. The undertaking of additional community studies—using the tools of the statistician and the sociologist should be stimulated as a part of the general program of health education. Such significant studies as those now being carried on in New York City in connection with the Committees on Neighborhood Development and the official health department are advances in this direction.

Second, analysis must be made of the local resources for providing an attack on such problems and an educational campaign launched to provide those which do not already exist. In some communities health agencies are duplicating each other and in other communities we would seem to find neglect on the part of all agencies.

Finally, and possibly the most difficult task in health education, is to motivate the individual so that desirable changed behavior may occur. The problem now becomes one of educational psychology. All public health workers engaged in any type of community health education are primarily teachers, and in order to teach effectively they must understand the principles and methods of teaching. There are many aspects to the learning process, all of which cannot be considered here, but two of the most important are:

(1) Learning is going on all the time—even our most casual contacts in public health are educational or otherwise. Learning takes place through activity and through the constant inter-action of the individual and his environment. Our aim should be to make the thing we wish to teach a part of the life of the person to be taught.

(2) True education aims at self-direction. How far an individual can go in this direction depends upon his native ability and his circumstances. But it is the aim towards which health education should move.

A public health nurse, in bringing to the mother a decision regarding whether or not she should have her child immunized against diphtheria, goes through all of the steps of the learning process. The moment the mother stops to consider what she should do, learning takes place. For instance, an analysis of the steps may be as follows: helping the mother to face the situation—taking into account the factors involved—weighing the value of the factors—deciding what to do—acting upon it—then accepting the consequences. Not everyone will make the same decision because each mother will act in terms of the values she holds. These values are acquired through experience and inter-action with environment. The public health nurse as a teacher can help the learner with the first three steps—she can present the challenge—she can help the mother take into account all the factors and she can guide her in weighing the values. The last three points the learner must make for herself or she is not learning.

A mother may be forced or indoctrinated to have her child immunized but until the nurse has helped that mother realize the importance of immunization, so that she decides it should be done, it will be necessary to impose the same order for all succeeding children. The immediate objective may be accomplished, but in the meantime the mother may have learned to dislike the public health authority which seemingly forces her to act against her apparent needs and values. In order to teach effectively, the health educator must respect other personalities and learn to understand and respect the learner's needs and views, even though they differ from his own. In the end such procedures, though slow and requiring much patience, are the only means of securing permanent results.

However effective an adult health education program may become, it will never be complete without school health education. Adults at their best are slow to receive new ideas; their habits and customs have become more or less fixed; prejudices have been established and old habits are thus changed with some difficulty. It is heartening, though, to look forward to the day when the health education training which pupils are now receiving in schools will begin to have telling effects. Then adults will have a more adequate background of social and scientific insight regarding the health phases of their lives—something which cannot be so successfully conveyed to them in a moment and which is the process of gradual enlightenment.

On the other hand, it should be borne in mind that school education will never take the place of mass adult health education. As scientific medical advancement goes forward, there will constantly be need for the application of new knowledge into practice and need for accepting new modes of social cooperation for the betterment of the health of the public.

HEALTH EDUCATION IN MATERNITY AND INFANCY
Florence L. McKay, M.D.
Assistant Director, Division of Child Hygiene
Massachusetts Department of Public Health

Objectives

There was a time when it was a general belief that having a child endowed the mother with the knowledge and ability to care adequately for herself and her baby. If the mother died in childbirth, as often happened, someone else similarly endowed by motherhood took over the raising of the baby. That was a time when the infant mortality rate was more than three times as high as it is at present.

While many factors have had to do with the reduction of the infant mortality rate we feel sure that the better preparation for parenthood has had a decided influence. We are now making a determined effort to teach prenatal and infant hygiene before the time when parents are called upon to put it into practice. We know that a good start in earliest life toward good health is even more important for a child than for plants and other growing things. Proper prenatal and infant care are the foundations of good health for the growing child. Thus, through what is known as a phase of health education, we are trying to prepare parents to become informed, intelligent and cooperative in the care of expectant mothers and their infants. By this means we hope to give the child the best possible chance for normal growth and development.

Groups to be reached

There are two important groups to be reached for health education in prenatal and infant care—the pre-parental and the parental groups.

Pre-parental group.—As our objective is to reach the potential parents, one of the best groups for contact is the late adolescent.

Parental group.—Parents who have not had opportunity in their early training for education in prenatal and infant care should have this opportunity at least as early as they know that they are to become parents. It is obviously important that the mother be given this opportunity of learning but it is almost equally important that the prospective father should have a similar opportunity.

Methods of meeting this problem in Massachusetts

For the *pre-parental group*, that is, the late adolescents, units are now being introduced into schools, particularly in the junior and senior high schools, on child care and development. A few colleges are doing something in this line. In many schools the courses in general science, home economics, hygiene and physiology contain material correlated in their curriculum which bears upon the subject of prenatal and infant care. Some of the organizations for young people give some instruction in this field.

In the *parental group*, while mothers are given material by their private physicians and nurses, many who do not have this opportunity are gathered together in groups for mothers' clubs, for study groups for studying the problems of prenatal and infant care. These are sometimes made up of prospective mothers although more often the group includes other mothers and sometimes even grandmothers. There should also be groups of fathers.

Some hospitals give in-patient instruction to mothers in the physical care of their babies and also in habit training. At least one hospital extends this in-patient instruction to the fathers as well. In connection with prenatal clinics, instruction is given individually to the mother and the mothers are often given group instruction by the clinic physician or nurse or the public health nurse. Infant care is taught through the private physician and through infant clinics and well child conferences by a physician, nurse, nutritionist and dentist or dental hygienist. In the larger cities there are probably now opportunities for most mothers to have some type of instruction in prenatal and infant care. It is the mother in the rural area who has least opportunity unless the rural area has good public health nursing service.

Physicians, both in cities and rural communities, are giving more and more adequate instruction to their private cases. It is the mother who does not come in contact with her own physician until near the time of delivery, or the mother who is not delivered by a physician, who is least likely to have opportunities for health instruction, particularly in rural areas.

Fourteen cities in Massachusetts have prenatal clinics. Most of those outside of Boston are connected with hospitals and serve only the mothers who are to be delivered in that hospital. Instruction of the mother is an integral part of good prenatal care. Thus in cities which have prenatal clinics there are probably many mothers who fail to have adequate instruction unless their own physician furnishes it or they are found by the public health nurse who makes maternity home visits.

The Division of Child Hygiene of the State Department of Public Health conducts a prenatal and postnatal letter service open to all mothers in the State who request it. One of the prenatal letters is for the father. These letters are sent out once a month during pregnancy and continue every month until the child is two years old.

Content of instruction

There is not space here to give a detailed outline of the content of instruction. However, the material given to the pre-parental and parental groups should include the detailed physical, mental and dental hygiene of pregnancy, stressing the importance of early examination and constant supervision by a physician, and the preparation for breast feeding. There is a new tendency now to include in the content material on hereditary influences and on mental attitudes in the home toward the pregnancy and the coming child. The content of infant care should include the physical, mental and dental hygiene of infancy, stressing the importance of successful breast feeding. Newer outlines now contain more in habit training, in the types of toys proper for the various age levels, in parental attitudes toward the child and his establishment in the home, and in the care of the premature infant.

The Division of Child Hygiene of the Massachusetts Department of Public Health furnishes outlines for local nurses who conduct mothers' health study groups. These outlines contain detailed content of such material as is enumerated above. These are quite widely used in the State and are at present undergoing revision. Several private organizations such as the Parent-Teacher Association and the American Association of University Women furnish study outlines.

Prenatal and infant printed material is available from the State Department of Public Health as well as from the Children's Bureau upon which such instruction may be based by either physician or nurse. There are in addition many good books on this subject available in libraries and book stores. There is probably more reading on this subject by mothers at present than there has ever been. Booklists are published in booklets of the State Department of Public Health and the Children's Bureau.

Instructors in maternal and infant health

While most of the instruction in maternal and infant health is given by physicians and public health nurses and teachers of science, we see from the foregoing account that dentists and dental hygienists, nutritionists, psychiatrists and psychologists, eugenists, physiologists and biologists all have their contributions to make.

There is no doubt that progress is being made in this field of health education for parents but there is also no doubt that there are still many groups of parents in many parts of the State who have not sufficient opportunity for such instruction. Let each community take stock of its opportunities for health education in maternity and infancy and try to make them available to all parents and potential parents.

HEALTH EDUCATION FOR THE SECONDARY SCHOOLS

A. RUSSELL MACK

Supervisor of Secondary Education
Massachusetts Department of Education

When a high school principal discusses health or listens in on a health lecture, he finds himself thinking along two widely different lines. In the first place, he realizes that health is the first of the seven cardinal objectives of secondary education, and it seems to him that he has not stressed it nearly as much as he should have. He is conscious of the fact that there are comparatively few high schools in this state where there are adequate systems of physical education. He wishes that he had done more.

On the other hand, and it is my belief, a high school principal may well congratulate himself upon the success of his health program. An indirect approach to a subject often gets better results than the direct approach. That is, if the teacher were to say to her pupils, "Today we are going to take up character education," or "Today we are going to take up health education," such a procedure repeated day after day would antagonize pupils. They would feel that what was coming would be of a "goody, goody" nature. Whereas, if the work is done indirectly, in connection with civics, science, biology, etc., the results obtained would be far more lasting.

There are 160 of the 257 high schools in the state which offer courses in physical education. Physical education is the subject which comes nearest to a direct teaching of health education. There are 133 high schools that have gymnasiums. It should be realized, however, that a gymnasium is not absolutely necessary for a physical education program. As a matter of fact, when the weather is favorable the work should be done out of doors. Also the increased realization of the value of games in physical education as opposed to the mere flapping of arms and legs, obviates the need of elaborate apparatus.

In the 233 junior high schools of the state there are 150 which definitely require a certain amount of time each week in the gymnasium or playgrounds. This takes various forms including the traditional setting-up exercises, and also a range of activities involving games and intra-mural sports of all sorts.

All high schools today have a regular examination at least once a year by the doctor or school nurse. In addition to this, if there is an epidemic, an examination program is set up immediately. Actually, pupils are safer in school than out of school. For example, wonderful advances have been made in medical science and no one need ever have smallpox or diphtheria. The Chadwick Clinic is examining those boys and girls who have tuberculosis, and offering constructive programs to them.

Certain subjects in the curriculum lend themselves directly toward better health habits on the part of the boys and girls. Some of the subjects are required and others elective. 233 of the 257 high schools offer biology. It is difficult to conceive of pupils taking a subject such as biology without a distinct improvement in their personal health. 182 high schools in the state offer general science. Textbooks in Massachusetts are selected by the local authorities, yet, there are certain to be chapters on air, water, food, etc., which indirectly give the child an added incentive to better living. 131 high schools offer community civics and such problems as improved community services, including health, are taken up.

There are 172 high schools which offer home economics programs. 29 of them include courses in home economics for boys as well as for girls. It should be stated also that certain other subjects as English, History, Chemistry and others which might be named, lend themselves in certain phases of the work to an increased knowledge of health on the part of the pupil.

164 high schools of the state have lunch rooms, and while these vary from very modern to very poor, the large number indicates the realization of the importance of adequate nutrition. The median net length of the school day is five hours and ten minutes, but there are high schools with a gross length of seven hours and ten minutes. The tendency has been in recent years to increase the length of the school day, which means that there is a responsibility to provide food for the boys and girls. Here again is a definite realization of the necessity for health.

There have been, of course, certain periods when there was increased activities in school building programs. The following table shows the amount of building over five year periods. Easily half of the high school buldings in the state have been put up since 1915, or else have been added to. Surely, such buildings are reasonably modern.

MASSACHUSETTS HIGH SCHOOL BUILDINGS

Total Number of Schools Built:

Years	Number of Schools	Additions
Before 1890	29	9
Before 1900	2	0
1890 to 1894	11	6
1895 to 1899	16	5
1900 to 1904	22	4
1905 to 1909	28	4
1910 to 1914	21	5
1915 to 1919	19	7
1920 to 1924	25	5
1925 to 1929	47	2
1930 to 1934	23	2
1935 to 1939	14	1
Totals	257	50

My point in mentioning the above is that the presence of a modern building in a locality shows a desire for the best interests of the pupils including health.

Lighting, heating and ventilation are coming into their own in schoolhouse construction as well as in homes and public buildings. Lighting, especially, is of importance. The present legal requirement of 5 foot candles is too low. Ten and fifteen are recommended by some authorities. More and more, people are conscious of this need, however, which is a hopeful sign.

Anyone who has children in the upper grades or in the high school knows the extremely busy life they lead. There are constant demands upon their health and energy. They have the regular school work involving home study (and I am a firm believer in some home study). They may take music lessons, and there must be time allotted for lessons. They are almost sure to belong to some club or organization. And the wonder of it sometimes is how they do find time to determine "what it is all about." There are many people who feel that in this busy existence of ours there is an over organization, true for boys and girls as well as for adults. This, however, in the case of high school boys and girls may be more of a blessing in disguise than we think, for, "Satan finds work for idle hands to do," and for our boys and girls to be busy within reason makes for better health, mentally, physically, and morally.

It is my very strong belief that the average boy or girl in our schools today is a happy, contented, healthy individual. Every high school principal knows that he can get the whole-hearted support of 95% of his student body for any worth-while project. We have plenty of reason to congratulate ourselves upon the success of the educational offering as well as the health offering in Massachusetts. We cannot, we must not sit by supinely, for we must realize that the price of success in these objectives is eternal vigilance. We must constantly endeavor to improve in every way.

THE TEACHING UNIT ON "TEETH AND THEIR CARE" AS DEVELOPED IN THE SOUTH EGREMONT RURAL SCHOOL

FLORENCE B. HOPKINS, M.D., D.M.D.

JEAN V. LATIMER, B.S., A.M.

Massachusetts Department of Public Health

One way to attack the problem of dental health in the elementary schools is to approach it from an educational standpoint. While it is sometimes difficult to obtain scientific measurement of results, the effectiveness of school health education is increasingly obvious. Also, scientific studies in the field are beginning to reveal some measurement of the effectiveness of health education on the physical condition of children.

For example, a study* of The Influence of Health Education on Growth and Development of School Children made for the Elizabeth McCormick Memorial Fund by Martha A. Hardy, Ph.D. and Carolyn H.

---

* "Healthy Growth" published by the University of Chicago Press. 1936.

Hoefer, M.A., tells us, "The conclusion seems warranted that specific classroom instruction, supplemented by periodic physical examinations with advice to parents, is an effective method of health education for elementary school children. There is some indication that yearly conferences with a physician will stimulate sufficient interest on the part of the child and his parents to produce an appreciable amount of improvement in some aspects of the child's health. When the examinations are followed by health teaching, there is a progressive increase in the improvement as the instruction continues. In general, health education seemed most likely to induce improvement when instruction at school was combined with other means of stimulating an interest in good health."

In the above study the condition of teeth was a specific condition which revealed significant improvement with health teaching. The records show that a larger per cent of children among the group receiving such classroom instruction had their teeth filled during the course of the health program than was the case among the controlled group. The indication is that the introduction of health teaching was followed by an increase in frequency of visits to the dentist and a reduction in the progress of dental caries.

During the past year a serious cooperative effort has been made to work out for Massachusetts a new and more effective program in dental health. It is hoped that such a program will attract the attention of those not already interested and will, through education, develop in everyone the appreciation of the value of dental care and personal responsibility for his own health, thus inspiring change of habits and attitudes on the basis of the information given.

As a demonstration in rural practice, the Southern Berkshire County area was chosen, since here there is a District Health Unit which has in its personnel a dentist devoting half his time to public health activities and the other half to school clinic work. An effort was made to open up avenues for the educational use of the school dentist in the school health education program. This effort met the cordial support and cooperation of Mr. Charles E. Doherty, Superintendent of the schools of Alford, Egremont, Richmond and West Stockbridge. The ungraded school of South Egremont was chosen for the trying out of experimental material on a unit for dental health. This was largely because of the fact that Superintendent Doherty had already introduced the unit method of teaching into the general curriculum of this school and successful results in its use had already been achieved by the teacher, Miss Alice Doty.

Material prepared by the Division of Child Hygiene of the Massachusetts Department of Public Health for the teacher's use included a bulletin of facts for teachers on teeth and their care; an outline of teaching material in unit form, including specific objectives to be achieved; a list of suggested pupil activities for development in class situations; and a list of reference books, visual aids and films.

Also, an individual scoring sheet in mouth health, termed, "My Achievement Record for A Healthy Mouth" was formulated, on which the actual condition of the teeth of the pupil at the beginning of the unit might be recorded and rechecked at intervals throughout the school year. This individual scoring sheet was used because while there is a growing disfavor of giving prizes or inspiring any group competition, research, studies in the field of human emotions seem to indicate that the child needs some measure of awareness of success in any particular learning to keep him going. Success must be emphasized and the ways of improvement made tangible and within the child's reach, but individual competition is to be stressed—the child being encouraged to make improvement on the basis of his own past record.

Dr. John W. Whitehead, Jr., the dentist associated with the Southern Berkshire Health Unit, not only made the dental examinations at the beginning of the teaching unit but collaborated with the teacher and the pupils in the making of visual material and in speaking before the class and their parents at the close of the unit.

Superintendent Doherty and Miss Doty, the teacher in the unconsolidated rural school in South Egremont, report that approximately three and one-half weeks were used for the development of the unit, making use not only of the time allotted for systematic health teaching but also using other school subjects for integration, such as:

Reading

Daily directed reading to find material pertinent to the unit—to answer questions that arise in relation to the unit—to supplement information and observation in connection with the unit.

Language

Oral

Discuss previous group work so that each pupil may have a definite idea of the assignments to be completed.

Formulate simple rules in connection with teeth and their care.

Make and answer health questionnaires.

Report on topics for which individuals and groups are responsible.

Conduct a radio broadcast at the end of the unit in which each child has a topic to discuss about "Teeth".

Explain to visitors the work done on the unit.

Written

Learn to spell words in connection with the unit. Keep individual booklets.

Report on the activity work done each day.

Write for information about teeth to different sources.

Prepare outlines of the facts learned regarding each problem of the unit.

Write invitations to parents and friends to attend an exhibit to see the results of the activities of the unit when completed.

Write descriptive paragraphs summarizing the facts learned regarding each problem of the unit.

Make outlines of various topics of the unit.

Write to various sources for charts and posters in relation to teeth and their care.

Write a letter to the school dentist or dental hygienist asking for his assistance in developing the unit.

Elementary Science

Make a study of the teeth of different animals. Study more about the cow—her care and the value of milk for the building of teeth.

Social Studies

Find out about the diets of primitive people in relation to the conditions found in their teeth.

Compare the Eskimos' diet with ours and also with the care which they give their teeth.

Study about the various countries from which the materials for a toothbrush are obtained (bristles from Russia, cotton for the celluloid handles from the South, etc.).

Find out the various places from which the fruits and vegetables and other tooth-building foods come. Maps may be made showing such areas and showing how the fruits and vegetables are transported to us.

Arithmetic

The application of number work to the unit may be the ability to count to 32. Also counting the number of baby teeth left and the ones that have come in. More skill in making change with toy money when buying inexpensive dentifrices. Playing store, placing price tags on the foods good for teeth. Ability to use rulers when making simple posters.

A knowledge of the cost of filling, extraction and other work done by the dentist. A knowledge of the money saved by regular dental visits.

Make graphs to show the amount of dental work which each child has had done.

Make graphs to show the age at which the permanent teeth come through the gums.

A knowledge of the costs of various dentifrices.

A knowledge of the cost of foods especially good for the teeth— milk as one of the least expensive foods for the great value returned.

A knowledge of proportion can be learned in figuring out the proportion of teeth on charts and in the making of models, etc.

Skill in the use of linear measure can be developed when making posters.

Art and Handwork

Making of food posters.

Letter blocking for the posters.

Dyeing and shellacking booklets, in which individual reports are kept.

Designs for booklets and posters.

Crayon drawing for booklets and posters.

Paper cut-outs of teeth, animals and foods.

Proper foods for each meal artistically arranged.

Paper cut-outs of dentifrices.

Making of food charts.

Molding—with a mixture of half flour and half salt and a little plaster paris moistened with water, a tooth may be molded by placing this mixture on the form of a tooth which has been previously sketched. When it is dry it will represent the raised form of half a tooth and it may be painted in different colors to show the various structures of the tooth. Models of a set of teeth may also be made out of clay.

Since the unit was developed last spring, towards the close of the school term, it is too early as yet to evaluate results, but the continued progress of the children in dental health as shown by actual mouth conditions will be measured this coming school year.

Special appreciation is due Superintendent Doherty whose progressive attitude and vision in educational methods through the use of the unit system of teaching has made him a splendid ally in this endeavor.

Upon this cooperative experiment and others in health teaching, suggestive teaching units in Dental Health Education for Elementary Schools have been built and are now available for distribution by the Division of Child Hygiene of the Massachusetts Department of Public Health.

HOW MAY SCHOOL HEALTH EDUCATION BE IMPROVED

JEAN V. LATIMER

Coordinator of Health Education
Massachusetts Department of Public Health

It is gratifying to find in the professional literature of today so much emphasis on school health education. The most encouraging sign is that the problem is now receiving much consideration from both the public health official and the school administrator. All seem to sense that something is wrong with our present program of school health in the United States and that improvement is necessary.*

What are some of the weak spots and how may we remedy them? First, there must be more continuity between school health teaching, the physical environment of the school and the type of health service offered for the protection and the promotion of health. Positive health cannot be taught effectively in a school where there is poor lighting, inadequate ventilation and other marked deficiencies in physical environment. The school health examinaton, unless it is of good quality, cannot possibly be used as an educational experience for children or adults. The conservation of health cannot be taught to children in a classroom in which, as the school year progresses, nervous tension increases and physical fatigue becomes cumulative.

Schools recognizing such considerations are today talking about "health in the school program" rather than a school health program. This difference implies that health as a basic phase of daily living is now going to be built into the entire program of the school instead of being fitted "onto" an already functioning school program. This means that the school itself will have to be readjusted or made over into a physical and social environment which is more conducive to a better adjustment in health.

Second, the health teaching at each grade level must become more comprehensive, definite and accurate. Before health education is on a sound basis, it must have a definite and satisfying intellectual contact. All would grant that the promotion of public health depends on enlightenment and yet on the intellectual side the school health program is now inadequate. Progressive workers and writers who deal with the problems of teaching health in our schools have placed much emphasis on forming specific health habits in children. As far as they go, they are

* "What is Wrong with Health Education?" by Spencer. The Health Officer, published by United States Public Health Service, March, 1937.

entirely right. But merely to have pupils learn the various facts about sleep, food, exercise and so forth, is certainly not enough. Before health education is on a sound basis it must be more than a routine drill in health.

Kilpatrick* has called the teaching of the "way" of doing things, without teaching the "why" of it, a sleep-walking kind of teaching. He says, "Health habits are all right .... we need more of them, but we need them knit into understandings and built into the child's very personality, so that he sees, feels, and understands the 'why' of it .... The only way in which you really get health education is by the understanding method .... it is the only way for a person to fit intelligently into the world, particularly into our modern changing world." While all of us admit that the amount of knowledge pertaining to the science of health is not always the strongest impelling factor for living a healthy life, we would, nevertheless, grant that simple basic facts, accompanied by desirable attitudes, may be potent factors in motivating self-directed human behavior. This is one of the basic premises of all education and should, therefore, hold true of health education.

On the other hand, experience and educational research warn us that verbal knowledge transfers most easily into practice. Certainly with the growing distrust of verbal learning in itself carrying over into actual conduct, we do not want a revival of the old-fashioned type of recitation. We do not want health facts taught in and of themselves, but rather an integration of all of the pupils' interests, experiences, and environment in such a way that desirable health outcomes will result.

It is fortunate for us that there is already a movement in the schools for an analysis of the whole process of general education into learning units. This reorganization is taking place because it is recognized that subject matter is not valuable for its own sake, but only as it is serviceable in generating intelligent and useful inclinations and abilities in the pupil. The term "unit" may be applied to a series of intimately inter-related learnings which involve a definite theme or topic. It may be defined as a larger learning situation which draws on all phases of experience, and makes use of all kinds of subject matter. In it, pupil purposing, planning, executing, and judging are important factors. The approach and interpretation are psychological and, therefore, flexible; the teacher, however, must conceive of the unit as a more or less logical procedure, starting with definite objectives, carried on through certain series of mental, physical, and social acts, and resulting in specific worthwhile outcomes. Obviously, unit organization is more than an outline of subject matter, and certainly it is more inclusive than a project. In it the health textbook becomes a source of reference and is used to answer questions rather than as the starting point of information.

It would thus seem that the unit organization of teaching-learning situations offers an opportunity of building with the pupils an appropriate background of health knowledge, insights, skills, wants, ideals and conventions.

In a teaching unit of merit there are the following elements: the main objective on which the unit is focused—the subject matter which is selected as pertinent to the understanding of the objectives—the

---

* Proceedings, Sixth American Child Health Education Conference, Sayville, Long Island, 1930.

approach—the pupil activities through which pupils are led to the attainment of the objectives. In addition, measurement of results, both as to knowledge and practice, should constitute the final step.

Unit organization implies the desirability of direct health teaching. The incidental teaching of health too often becomes the presentation of unrelated chunks of facts. Many modern programs for teaching health are often at fault here. They are avoiding the teaching of health information for its own sake, but they are falling into the more serious error of supposing that the only practical health knowledge is an array of unrelated facts.

There is at present a need of the organization of such teaching-learning units, beginning with the fourth grade and continuing through the senior high school. As this writer has previously pointed out,* it is desirable that the primary child, whose health information must of necessity be desultory anyway, be taught health indirectly as a part of the general daily curriculum. But, beginning with the fourth grade, health should be taught in an organized, direct way, at the same time making use of all subject matter and being integrated into the entire curriculum. The teaching unit on "Teeth and Their Care" as developed in the South Egremont Rural school (of which Mr. Charles Doherty is Superintendent and Miss Alice Doty is teacher), a detailed account of which appears in another part of this bulletin,** is an illustration of how a health topic may be developed in its broadest educational significance.

Health units will vary greatly as to their scope and size, according to the significance of the theme of the unit and the intellectual maturity of the learner. For example, a unit for the fourth grade on "Our Community Helpers for Health" may appear again in senior high school in the spiral educative process as a unit on "The Meaning of Public Health". The pupil does not have to master all aspects of a health topic at the time he has his first teaching experience regarding it. Each health experience needs only to be worked out in the fullness that is valuable to the child at a given age and enlarged as he grows older.

What we need is a balanced position of health subject matter and health activities. In our schools even a more comprehensive program of health activities is desirable, for without activities we cannot even make a proper start, since our aim is to raise the type of health behavior rather than to convey knowledge. But activities carried on purely for their own sake and without any relationship to intellectual background may have an immediate value but they gain educative effect when they are associated with the fundamental health principles of which they are the applications. On the other hand, health subject matter comes to life when it is integrated and grasped as an interpretation of significant situations.

One of the immediate tasks ahead for the public health and educational specialists would thus seem to be that of rendering special

---

* "Suggestions for Integrated Health Teaching in the Primary Grades", Commonhealth, Vol. 23, No. 2.
** The Teaching unit on "Teeth and Their Care" as developed in the South Egremont rural school, by Florence B. Hopkins and Jean V. Latimer, also bulletin now in print entitled "Dental Health in the Elementary Schools" published by the Mass. Department of Public Health.

assistance to school systems in the development of a specific health education curriculum.

THE KEYSTONE OPHTHALMIC TELEBINOCULAR

MIRIAM FORSTER

Research Assistant, Research-Learning Project
Massachusetts Department of Public Health

At the present time interest is especially keen in improved school tests for detecting visual defects that may block the child in his learning. In discussions of this subject one often hears the question asked: "What is the Keystone Ophthalmic Telebinocular and what does it offer of value that the standard school tests with the Snellen Charts do not offer?" This brief article is an effort to answer this question and to offer certain suggestions to those interested in its use. It is presented in the nature of a tentative summary on the basis of one year's experience with the instrument and considerable study and discussion with others as to its practicability and reliability.

The Telebinocular is an instrument which provides binocular tests of visual functions. It consists of an instrument similar to the ordinary hand stereoscope mounted on an easily portable stand and so designed that the eyes can be tested as they function at distances ranging from about 12 inches to the equivalent of distant vision (usually considered as twenty feet). The individual to be examined sits before the instrument at a table and looks into it at a set of slides. These slides, ten in number, are called "The Betts Ready to Read Tests." The child reports on what he sees in answer to standardized questions of the examiner, and his responses are recorded on printed blanks which make the recording speedy, easily intelligible and objective.

It is important to emphasize at the beginning and throughout this discussion that in no sense are these diagnostic tests, as used by educators and other laymen, nor do they in any way take the place of an examination by an eye specialist. They are designed, on the other hand, to supplement or supplant the usual school tests of vision in an attempt to pick out those children who need the attention of an eye specialist. In other words, they aim to accomplish only what the Snellen tests have long tried to do, often with small success—aid teachers and school administrators in finding those children for whom a thorough eye examination seems necessary before they can profit by school experience. E. A. Betts, co-designer of those visual tests and author of the text which accompanies the instrument, reports that when he checked the results of Snellen Test Chart against the Visual Sensation and Perception Tests of the Betts Ready to Read unit, he found that only 5 to 40 per cent of the children were identified who needed the help of an eye specialist. It is his belief and that of others that the chief visual factors contributing to school failures are not identified by the Snellen Charts.* Our own experience thus far with the Telebinocular adds further evidence of this kind. Examining approximately 100 children in the upper six grades, most of whom were retarded readers, we found that among those children

---

* "The Prevention and Correction of Reading Difficulties," E. A. Betts, Row, Peterson and Company, Evanston, Illinois, 1936. P. 150.

referred to an eye specialist and found by him to have serious defects there was none whose record in the Snellen tests indicated a need for such an examination.

The main advantages of the Telebinocular examination over the Snellen Chart procedure are said to be:

(1) It provides opportunity for testing the eyes in their normal working state, i.e., it tests the two eyes when both are open and presumably working together. The Snellen Chart routine of testing each eye separately, as ordinarily followed in the school, is inadequate in this respect. It is quite possible, for instance, for a person to have normal visual acuity in each eye alone, yet not have good two-eyed vision.

(2) In addition to testing visual acuity, the only aspect of vision tested by the Snellen Charts, it provides tests of fusion, muscular imbalance, depth perception, and an additional test to detect errors of focus.

(3) It tests the eyes as they function at ordinary reading distance as well as distant vision. The Snellen tests are all given at a distance of twenty feet. An individual's eyes may well provide normal binocular vision at twenty feet yet evidence quite inadequate coordination at ten to sixteen inches. It is this latter aspect of vision, of course, that is important for most school work which involves reading.

A second set of questions frequently asked are of the following nature. Who in a school system could give these tests? Is special training required to render a person qualified to use them? Can an unqualified person do harm to children's eyes by an indiscriminate use of these tests? The general answer would seem to be that the only qualifcations necessary to the use of the Telebinocular with the Betts Ready to Read Tests are the same qualifications required for giving any individual tests to children: i.e., understanding of the child, ability to quickly and easily establish rapport with him and to elicit his cooperation and responses to test materials, and objectivity in reporting his behavior. No special knowledge of optics or any related field is necessary, since the examiner is required only to record responses to standardized questions, interpret them on the basis of instructions given in the manual of directions (we shall speak later of some of the difficulties involved here) and, on the basis of this interpretation, refer children to an eye specialist. A lay examiner is not required and should not attempt to diagnose what the records may indicate as to kind or extent of ocular defects nor, of course, to prescribe treatment. Provided the person who is to give the tests goes through a short period of instruction in the use of the instrument (an hour often suffices), uses only the material included in the Betts Ready to Read Tests, follows the directions carefully and records as objectively as possible, he or she should obtain satisfactory results. Of course, as with the use of any standardized school tests, the more experienced the examiner, the more consistent will be his records. The worst the examiner can do, however, is to annoy the parents or bother the eye specialist by referring a child for an unneeded examination or, conversely, to fail to detect a condition that needs correction.

Another important point to school people already pressed for time is: do not these tests take so much time that testing an entire school population would be practically impossible without an additional member on the staff? It is true that more time is required for these than for present school eye tests, but it is estimated that only 6-12 minutes is sufficient for the average test period. The younger the child, the more time is required, of course,* and rechecks are desirable as with any such tests, before a child is referred to an eye specialist.

It may be of value here to describe briefly just what is included in that set of tests called "The Betts Ready to Read Tests" which are the only tests, among the many sets designed for use with the Telebinocular, usually distributed to schools. This set includes four parts, of which we have used only parts (3) and (4) thus far. (1) Visual Readiness Tests and (2) Auditory Readiness Tests do not require the use of the Telebinocular. Consisting of tests of discrimination and matching of letters and words, understanding and repetition of spoken sounds and phrases, etc., their material is familiar enough to teachers acquainted with the varied reading readiness tests now on the market. (3) Betts Visual Sensation and Perception Tests is the set of tests with which this article is concerned. It consists of ten tests:

1. Introductory: this test elicits interest of the child and checks immediately whether he is using both eyes.
2. Distant Fusion: tests whether child can fuse the images of his two eyes easily for distant vision.
3. Visual Efficiency: tests visual acuity of both eyes together, then the vision of each eye alone while the other eye is open and seeing.
4. Vertical Imbalance: tests whether or not both eyes function in same horizontal plane or whether one eye tends to deviate upward.
5. Coordination Level: a measure of depth perception.
6. Lateral Imbalance: determines whether visual axes of the two eyes tend to remain parallel for distant vision and to converge normally for near vision, or whether they tend to deviate outward or inward more than is normal.
7. Reading Distance Fusion: tests ability to fuse the two images of the eyes readily for near vision.
8. Sharpness of Image: test to detect errors of focus, the most common of which are nearsightedness, farsightedness, and astigmatism.

There is a fourth part of the Betts Ready to Read Tests to which we should make reference: (4) Tests of Oculomotor and Perception Habits. These are also on slides for use in the Telebinocular and provide opportunity to study habits of word, letter and number perception and the coordination of the two eyes in the actual process of reading lists of words. These tests are especially useful for the classroom teacher or the instructor in remedial reading. They consist of four series, ten tests in all, made up of eight lists of words varying in difficulty from first to third grade level, chosen from standard word lists, and one slide each of isolated letters and number combinations. These cards enable the teacher

---
* We find that these tests are not generally satisfactory for children below the third, possibly second grade level.

to observe the pupil's specific difficulties and word recognition skills under regulated conditions. One may observe reversal tendencies, spatial orientation of words, alternating use of the eyes in the reading process, difficulties in focussing on and fusing certain letters of the alphabet and many other common difficulties. We have found also that since the child is looking into the instrument, it affords the teacher an unusual chance to observe the child at close range without his realization of that scrutiny and so to detect faulty habits of enunciation, vocalization, incorrect methods of initial attack on words, general tenseness of attitude, etc. that may have passed unnoticed.

As has been emphasized above, only that set of slides called the Betts Ready to Read Tests is usually distributed to the schools. There are many other sets of material for use in the Telebinocular—"Eye Comfort Base-In and Base-Out Units," "Stepping Stones Unit," units for treatment of squint and amblyopia, calesthenics units, etc. Usually only the eye specialist has these for use in special cases, but it is possible that occasionally some of this material may somehow come into the hands of laymen who lack the technical training in its use and understanding of problems of vision. It cannot be too strongly emphasized that these sets of slides are not to be used by anyone, at any time, under any conditions except at the recommendation and under the supervision of the eye specialist. All of this eye training material, if rightly used, has probable value, but irreparable harm might be done to a child's eyes by indiscriminate use of any sort of orthoptic material, however appealing, easily intelligible or innocuous that material may appear.

If, then, the Betts Ready to Read Tests for the Telebinocular can be used safely by the layman, are there no attendant difficulties in its use? There *are* difficulties that will probably be experienced by anyone using this examination, mainly those of interpretation of records. We have often found it difficult to know just when a child's record on these ten tests warrants referring him to an eye specialist. Anyone using the tests will find many cases in which test results are checked as "questionable", or when only one or two tests check very slightly below what is supposedly normal. It is probably true that none of these tests is so precise that slight deviations from the "normal" can ever be interpreted with unerring judgment. All one can do in such circumstances is to recheck doubtful cases, follow carefully directions for interpretation given in the manual of directions, and when in any real doubt try to have that child's eyes examined by a specialist. In the matter of referring a child for an examination of his eyesight, errors of commission are to be preferred to those of omission!

There are a few suggestive criticisms often made of the Telebinocular that might well be mentioned here. First of all, the tests of visual acuity (Test 3) are often criticized for their inadequacy, especially for their frequent failure to detect cases of farsightedness. They undoubtedly do much better than the Snellen Chart tests in this respect, but the problem of picking out farsighted children is always a very difficult one on non-technical tests. Only the complete refractive examination of the eye specialist can invariably do this. It is a doubly serious problem because of the fact that farsightedness is so common among young children that it can be called a "normal error" and because it is the condition which makes near work such as reading difficult and undesirable, unless the vision is corrected. Nearsighted children (unless the degree of defect be excessive) seldom have difficulty with near work and their defect can usually be detected either by the Snellen or Telebinocular tests. One can only add a word of warning about such children who may very well pass all available tests of eyesight which the school provides and yet seem to fumble unnecessarily over near work. Especially if such a retarded child be among those described as having "wonderful eyesight—better than normal", should he be referred to an eye specialist. Headaches and other symptoms of eyestrain will often mark these cases out for attention.

Similarly, the tests of fusion (2 and 7) often prove adequate only for picking out the "very normal individual." Results in a majority of our cases examined had to be recorded as "questionable." The tests for muscle balance, likewise, we found often did not pick out cases of low error. The whole subject of muscle imbalance and its significance for good reading habits is one so fraught with discussion and disagreement, that it is difficult to say whether or not the crudity of this test is significant. Certainly, this test aided in detecting some of the worst cases of muscle imbalance—those children most in need of attention.

Most of the current criticisms of the Telebinocular come from eye specialists, and the remarks are probably true from their point of view, for they are able to use tests which are simpler, more accurate and more objective to detect these visual defects. Such professional examinations, however, are unfortunately not yet available as part of routine school examinations. Until they are, all we can do is find the best available non-technical tests and hope by their use to screen out the majority of children whose vision is subnormal. For this purpose the consensus of opinion among those who have used these tests appears to be that tests of vision included in the Betts Ready to Read Tests are a decided improvement over most eye tests available at present for school use.

As a final suggestion we must again emphasize that one must not believe that by the use of this instrument one is screening out *all* cases whose educational difficulties are due to visual anomalies. Undoubtedly, one finds those cases with most serious defects. As with all physical handicaps, however, it is not always the degree of defect that determines the degree of difficulty experienced. A child with an acute visual defect may well stand at the head of his class in reading (as much recent research indicates) while a child with a very small visual error may find reading impossible. The deciding factor is always the degree of counterpoise exercised by the individual for any handicap he possesses: It is important, therefore, that the teacher be on the alert for signs of eyestrain and difficulty in even those children who pass whatever routine school tests are given. One of the important results of the use of the Keystone Telebinocular has been an increased awareness on the part of teachers of the need to understand this visual aspect of their pedagogical problems. As to the tests themselves, it can be said that Keystone Ophthalmic Telebinocular marks a step forward in the attempt to find adequate eye tests that can be used in routine school examinations.

EXHIBITS AND MATERIALS FOR HEALTH TEACHING

ALBERTINE P. MCKELLAR, *Public Health Education Worker*
JOHN H. MCCARTHY, *Chief Supervisor of Health Education*
Massachusetts Department of Public Health

Exhibits

For the second consecutive year the Massachusetts Department of Public Health had an exhibit at practically all the two-day fairs held throughout the State.

This ambitious program, attempted last year and repeated in the fall of 1937, has attracted the attention of many people to some of the activities of the Department and has, we hope—judging from the large number of requests for printed pamphlets—been a real educational device.

Often at the fairs we find the person who would never attend a health meeting or read a health article—but who will stop for a glance, become interested, sign for health pamphlets and sometimes talk over his half-truths, or misconceptions. Frequently we hear, "Does the State really do that?—accomplish that?—give that?—I had no idea!"

Planning the Exhibit

This Fair group is a sample-seeking, moving crowd, not especially interested in things educational—and when the Department exhibits were drab affairs on burlap, little wonder that they were usually passed by. Surrounded by brightly colored, attractive commercial exhibits, the educational display just had to go professional in order to compete with its outstanding neighbors. For two years the exhibit has been professionally built with bright colors and other paraphernalia commensurate to the commercial exhibits. Before they realize just what type of a display it is, people look, admire and become interested. Once we have attracted their attention—made them stop to look, almost always they will then read the captions carefully, listen to what is said, then often take the time necessary to fill in an order blank for health pamphlets. An "attention-attracter" we realize is essential and must be especially considered when planning each exhibit.

A health department offers almost an unlimited number of possible subjects for exhibit purposes—the many activities of the department, the services offered, the accomplishments, as well as the vast amount of general health information for the various age groups. Each year three timely subjects have been chosen for the Fair exhibits, each subject planned for one card table. When the Fairs are over, these exhibits are used throughout the State in schools, libraries and by nursing associations, etc.

Essential in our planning, then, in addition to an "attention-attracter", is the consideration of color, compactness, simplicity, and facility for packing and shipping.

There are two advantages for using the same color scheme in all exhibits year after year; first, it gives a distinction—a trade mark that people learn to recognize and associate with the health department; and second, table covers or other articles may be used in other than their original combinations. For these reasons all of our exhibits for the past two years have been blue and white, the State colors.

Compactness is essential for exhibit material that must be transported. Cases made especially for each exhibit are economical as they protect the exhibit in storage as well as in transportation. Cases the same size as card tables can be carried with ease. The plan for using card table exhibits has worked well. The tables are easily transported and thus do away with the great difficulty of finding the right-sized tables on location. The three card tables will fit attractively into any space from 6' to 15', depending upon their arrangement. As all card tables are nearly the same size and readily obtainable, persons who borrow the exhibits find them simple to set up.

Table covers of dark blue cotton sateen made to fit the card tables have added to the attractiveness of the exhibit and have saved time in setting up—(memories of the years and years when we pinned yards and yards!).

We will describe the six card table exhibits that have been successfully used on the Fairs and are available for general use throughout the State.

The Public Health Nursing Exhibit has a 30" cutout figure of a nurse carrying a bag. The caption at the base reads, "The Public Health Nurse Visits". There are six small standing cards, each naming a service of the nurse. Organizations have borrowed this exhibit, thumbtacked their own sign over the one at the base of the nurse—giving statistics for their year's accomplishments and over the small signs clipped ones giving specific information pertaining to each service. The cut-out nurse has been used with ribbons coming from her bag to miniature set-ups of various kinds of services—the home visit, the school, the office, etc.

The Diphtheria Immunization Exhibit is a large 30" x 30" cutout tinted photograph of a baby and preschool child on a background so that it stands up on the back half of the card table. The caption reads, "Is Your Child Protected Against Diphtheria? More than 2/3 of All Diphtheria Deaths Occur Under School Age." Copies of the pamphlet "I Don't Want Diphtheria" are placed in front of the background. This exhibit has been used by many towns giving publicity to their immunization program and by others to show results. Once it was used with a large chart on the table made of a string of outlined figures with the caption, "In Which Group Is Your Child?". A line of figures represented the preschool population—those in blue—"protected", those in red—"unprotected".

The Two-Lunch Exhibit has a high background on a standard with the caption, "Two Lunches—Equal Cost and Equal Calories. But this one Contains 3 X Proteins, 6 X Minerals and 8 X Vitamins". The lunches are on trays on the table in front of the standard—on one an egg salad sandwich, a bottle of milk and an orange; and on the other a frankfurter in a roll, a bottle of pop and a piece of candy. Blocks of different bright colors in front of each tray represent the amount of calories, proteins, minerals and vitamins in each lunch. This exhibit was popular at the Fairs as it was colorful, the food reproductions attracted people and the ever-present interest in calories evidently stopped many a portly lady. The discussion relative to this exhibit brought up various problems in the whole field of nutrition and material pertaining to specific needs was recommended and ordered.

The Comparative Disease Rates Exhibit is new this year—resulting from a desire to call attention to the gigantic problem of gonorrhea and syphilis. It seemed opportune to follow up at the Fairs our Department program as well as the new general interest in these diseases resulting from the frequent articles in popular magazines. Against a shining white background, a standard the width of the table holds five brightly colored 3" wide sticks representing the number of cases reported from 1932 to 1936 of Pulmonary Tuberculosis, Syphilis, Gonorrhea, Diphtheria and Infantile Paralysis. The Gonorrhea stick is much the highest and next is Syphilis. On the front, slanted area of the standard is this copy, "Average Number of Cases Reported 1932—1936". Eagerly we watched the reaction to this exhibit—some looked and, embarrassed, quickly glanced away while the majority stopped to express amazement and ask for more information. The high school age boy and girl is most concerned and will ask questions freely, especially if both a man and woman are on duty and the man can talk with the boy and the woman with the girl. Older men are much more apt to discuss this problem than older women. The white masinite background is fastened ingeniously with chromium plated rods to a dark blue piece covering the table. The standard holding the brightly colored sticks (green, yellow, blue, orange and red) is white. This exhibit is colorful, simple, easily understood and thought-provoking. The sign, "Massachusetts Department of Public Health," in real English silvered letters on a dark blue scroll is attached by means of a slot arrangement to the top edge of the center exhibit.

The Pasteurized—Raw Milk Exhibit. We attempted here to show, particularly to the rural areas where the exhibits are displayed, the story of pasteurized milk versus raw milk. The exhibit more than lived up to expectations, as it always aroused discussion, not to say argument. On the dark blue background are two maps of the State painted in white with red letters indicating the number of Typhoid deaths in each county in 1876 and the total of 1059, compared to the number in 1936 totaling 10 for the whole State. The copy, "This reduction due to" is followed by three arrows pointing to the table top of white with the copy, "Purification of water, Pasteurization of milk, Sanitation of shellfish, Supervision of carriers" and in the center a space bordered with red and blue holds a micro-counter. Petri dishes containing a sample of raw and one of pasteurized milk can be easily seen and the comparative number of bacteria is plainly visible. A few go away with a set expression, stating that nevertheless they would never drink pasteurized milk, but many others are truly impressed and declare to change immediately to only pasteurized milk. The light shining through the micro-counter attracts attention to this exhibit and the fact that they hope to see "disease bugs" draws the crowds.

The Well Child Conference Exhibit. A row of five poster style heads of children ranging in ages from six months to school age go across the top of the dark blue background with the copy, "Only 5 Children Have no Physical Defects Out of Every 100 Examined in State Well Child Conferences". Then across the bottom are four photographs of the procedure at the well child conference—record taking and weighing and measuring, the health examination, the dental conference and the nutrition conference. The table area is divided into three triangular areas, each used to teach a pertinent point relating to the preschool child. On one third there is an outline of the dental arch with arrows pointing to the six-year molar with copy, "6-year Molars are Second Teeth. Erupt 4-8 years. Replace No First Teeth". On the other back third is this copy, "Bad Habits Reported. Sucking, Bedwetting, Nail Biting, Disobedience, Dependency and Temper Tantrums" and a list of reliable books on habit training for the preschool age child. In the center of the front third is a tray of Vitamin C foods—an orange, apple, potato, cabbage and tomato with the copy, "Daily all children need Vitamin C foods". The brightly colored, not too beautiful, heads of children attract attention and the photographs within chromium frames appeal to those who like to see pictures. The tray of reproduced foods also is conspicuous and arouses curiosity.

Other Exhibits. In addition to those exhibits especially planned for the Fairs are several other exhibits that may be borrowed or with very little trouble duplicated by school nurses or teachers.

Prenatal Photograph Exhibit consists of a background of a beautiful mother and baby picture and on the table a series of four photographs showing the physical and dental examinations, the public health nurse making the home visit and the mother resting. These pictures, together with posters explaining adequate care and a copy of the postnatal letters can readily fill the space allowed by two card tables.

Fit Your Food to Your Figure Exhibit is very popular with the high school girls. It has three cut-out figures, one thin, one medium and one rather plump. Ribbons lead from the girls to a table poster that states the variations necessary to make in average meals. The actual foods showing the average breakfast (or lunch or dinner), the one for the thin girl and the one for the fat girl are sometimes used with the poster and cut-outs.

Food Fad Exhibit includes posters and samples of popular materials with standard for determining whether they are facts or fads! This exhibit is most satisfactorily used when accompanied by a talk given by a nutritionist.

Food Habits for the Young Child has a background picture poster of children eating lunch and on the table are various suggestions for teaching good food habits.

Protect Your Smile was the exhibit used extensively throughout the State as a part of the 4-H Club Health project. Some high school groups have used it since that State-wide campaign. It has a picture of an attractive boy and girl as a background and on the table are articles showing the three phases of dental care—the home care, the tooth building and protecting foods and the dentist's care. Appropriate signs make this a self-explanatory exhibit.

Charm Tools is the exhibit used with the high school girl project and consists of an oil portrait of a lovely teen age girl. On the table in the center is a group of protective foods and in the remaining area, a stiff, easily washed hairbrush, a blunt-toothed comb, two tooth brushes (with five rows of bristles) with the sign, "Your Tooth Brush Should be Twins", a salt shaker of home-made tooth powder (equal parts of salt, soda, borax—flavored with a small amount of commercial tooth powder), an orange stick with a rubber end for pushing down cuticle, a bottle marked deodorant, a soft nail brush for cleansing the face and a jar of cream to protect the skin from make-up.

Special exhibits for special occasions are planned in response to requests.

Other Teaching Materials

Visual aids available from the Department of Public Health other than exhibits include:

Cut-out model of a tooth used to teach structure and dental nutrition.

A new model showing the process of decay. A series of teeth showing the process of a carious pit from a small fissure to a large cavity reaching the pulp chamber.

Measuring stick poster showing the necessary foods for an adequate diet.

5 school lunch posters showing a good home-packed and a good cafeteria lunch.

16 black and white nutrition posters for home economics and other teachers showing food elements, daily food requirements and other nutrition factors.

Sources of health educational materials, listing the sources of various material used for exhibits.

Opportunities for Use

The possibilities for using exhibits for health teaching are numerous—the surface has hardly been scratched! Exhibits such as those described must be made to stand hard usage but with a little time and thought and practically no expenditures, splendid exhibits could be contrived for local use. Surely this is the day of visual aids—we learn more quickly and more accurately with our eyes than with our ears. More and more we will depend upon exhibits for health teaching.

In the schools exhibits planned, prepared and explained by the children have educational value. A health class might be responsible for a series of displays for the benefit of the whole school and have a schedule for members of the class to cover. Groups in Home Economics, Science, Home Hygiene, Child Care, First-Aid, Physical Education and Civics also deal with health data readily usable for exhibit purposes.

The public health nurse has many opportunities for using exhibits—a planned series for a well child conference, for publicity in immunization against diphtheria and other projects, for showing services, activities or accomplishments during the campaign for funds.

The library is another splendid place for the self-explanatory health exhibit and a few have already used them in connection with special events such as Better Homes Week, Child Health Day, Florence Nightingale's birthday, etc. A special exhibit of health books for various age groups, changed from time to time, might easily be arranged by the public health nurse and the librarian.

HEALTH EDUCATION FOR THE COMMUNITY

H. D. CHOPE, M.D.
Director of Public Health, Newton, Mass.

The modern public health movement may be divided into three major fields of activity. Named in order of their appearance in the local health program they are
- (1) Environmental sanitation
- (2) Communicable disease control
- (3) Health education.

Environmental sanitation formed the basis for the first public health activities in the early fifties. Communicable disease control was initiated by the discoveries of Pasteur, Koch, and their contemporaries from 1875 on. Health education as such appeared in the early part of this century, but it has not been until the last decade that real emphasis has been placed on the importance of adequate health instruction.

Within the past ten to fifteen years health education has made tremendous strides. In 1922 the Health Education Section of the American Public Health Association was formed. Following this, state and local health departments began to study health education procedures and develop health education programs. The United States Public Health Service did not establish an office of Public Health Education until April, 1936.

Therefore, it is easy to understand why health education being the newest of our weapons is still a little unweildy and not familiar to all local health workers. Exact techniques have not been worked out, much of the health education carried on is done by the unscientific method of trial and error. There are very few people available who are capable of producing results through the medium of health education and such results are not always obvious. Again spending money on health education has little emotional appeal either to voluntary agencies or to official appropriating bodies. To many an organization it seems better public health practice to spend a hundred or a thousand dollars a year on milk for the undernourished child rather than on the salary of a nutritionist or on literature regarding diet which will prevent multiple *future* cases of malnutrition. Public Health Education is not one of the clearly defined phases of health work; it does not carry with it the thrill of accomplishment which results from a successful toxoid clinic or the discovery of a typhoid carrier. However, in spite of this drawback the popularization of health information is the very heart and soul of all preventive medicine.

Like all Health endeavors the public health education program must be well organized if it is to succeed. A few scattered articles in the local paper can hardly be dignified as a health education program. The local health officer must know the character of his community and know what messages he wishes to put over, to what groups, and through what mediums.

The fact that the health education program should have a definite objective is emphasized by nearly all writers on the subject but is perhaps best expressed by Doctor Harry Mustard in his new book on Rural Health Practice. "A health education program should have a clear cut objective.

If this objective is not simple enough to be comprehensible to workers themselves it is not likely to be understood or acted upon by those on whom it is brought to bear. Vagueness, diffuseness, and multiplicity of purposes inevitably defeat the ends in view. A general message on the necessity for maintaining good health does little good and exhortations that the individual perform simultaneously a number of disease preventing chores fall flat." In Newton the objectives set up for the first six months of the year are, usually, Tuberculosis control in association with the Early Diagnosis Campaign, diphtheria immunization in association with the immunization clinics, and administrative problems of the department in association with the Inter-City Health Conservation Contest and the annual budgetary period. In the summer and fall emphasis is placed on the preschool child, school health service, and dental health service. The Newton Hospital and the District Nursing Association carry on the educational programs associated with prenatal, maternity and infant welfare. Routine instruction in these various fields is continuous the year around, but the work is intensified in these specified periods.

Once the Health Officer has determined the objectives of his health education program he must determine to what groups he will address his efforts. Most communities naturally divide themselves into three groups—professional, laity, and school children.

The Health Officer who fails to enlist the assistance of his local medical profession in the health education program overlooks an important potentiality. To successfully practice medicine the modern physician must provide his patients with sound scientific health information. The sharing of scientific knowledge with the layman is one of the responsibilities of the medical profession. It was not long ago when physicians regarded their knowledge of life and death as their own precious possessions, and rarely talked to the public or to their patients about either curative or preventive methods. The practice of medicine was considered as somewhat of a mysterious art understood only by doctors. Physicians still fail to teach their patients enough about preventive medicine but if the health officer can keep before his medical colleagues helpful information about the local health program, new facts in preventive medicine, short reports of new developments in the field of nutrition, communicable disease, and child hygiene he will soon find that he has acquired multiple collaborating health educators, and a very friendly medical profession.

The laity has recently developed quite a thirst for sound health teaching and it is this group which comes to mind when one speaks of health education for the community. Doctor W. P. Shepard has made an important distinction between health instruction and health education. The primary object of education is to influence conduct. It is one thing to provide a person with facts but quite a different problem to engrain them so deeply that these facts will modify his conduct. It is a relatively easy procedure to bring before an adult audience a finished lecture on methods of communicable disease transmission, but one cannot be so sure that certain individuals in that same audience will not continue to taste the lemonade with the same tablespoon with which they stirred it, or report to the office with the early symptoms of the common cold, or moisten their fingers with saliva when looking up a number in a public telephone directory.

Probably the most essential phase of health education is proper training in the schools because here there is the best opportunity for influencing conduct, because school children are open to suggestion, ideas, and habit formation. The health officer is not expected to assume the burden of designing teaching projects for the school department, but he can be of inestimable value in providing teachers with material for health instruction. After all the health officer is the only person who has firsthand information about the health problems of his own community and this experience should provide the best possible teaching material.

The mediums through which health information may be circulated are numerous and, of course, vary from community to community, but there is no community which does not have more than adequate facilities for the purposes of health education.

An incomplete list of these mediums would include radio, posters, newspapers, exhibits, meetings, pamphlets, church calendars, motion pictures, stereoptican slides, daily correspondence, handbills, health plays, pageants, contests, individual contact. The techniques associated with health education are discussed in textbooks on the subject, but can be roughly classed into three groups—mass education, group education, and individual education.

Mass education utilizes the mediums of the radio, newspaper, exhibits, posters, and billboards. A great mass of material is flung hit-or-miss at an unknown audience in hopes that it will attract the interest of some uninformed person and stimulate curiosity about the subject dealt with. These procedures are in reality health propaganda rather than health education, but are frequently necessary to form a background or foundation for more direct or personalized appeals.

Group education entails the use of the public address, the round-table discussion, symposia, moving pictures, stereoptican slides, strip-films and charts. These are usually used with an assembled interested group such as the local medical club, the parent-teachers association, women's clubs, service clubs, and similar groups. This has many advantages but frequently fails to reach the persons most in need of the information, because persons who attend such meetings are not infrequently informed on the subject.

Individual instruction is the most valuable of all and most frequently leads to modification of conduct because the material discussed is of immediate personal interest to the person taught. This is the technique used by the physician and nurse in the prenatal clinic, the well baby conference, the preschool clinic, the school health examination, and in the home call for communicable disease control. The main advantage of this type of health education is that the person instructed has an immediate problem to face and "the emotional urge to attain the end in view" which leads to the ultimate aim of health education—action. It has the disadvantage that only a very limited number of persons can be reached by the average staff of a health department. However, every person engaged in health work—health officer, school physician, nurse sanitarian, milk inspector, laboratory technician and office clerk—must be constantly aware of his or her opportunity to serve as a health educator in every daily contact.

Community health officers are frequently kept so busy with communicable disease control, vital statistics, annual reports, nuisance abatements and other routine activities that there is little time left to study health education procedures and plan well organized educational programs for the community. But all health administrators come to realize sooner or later that the future progress of the health movement depends upon the backing of a well informed community. Doctor Earl Kleinschmidt says, "Health education is proving to be the strongest weapon which the health officer possesses. It is rapidly becoming recognized in some areas as the warp and woof of the public health program." Consequently, it will pay the health officer rich dividends in the conservation of life to study techniques of health education, set up definite objectives for his educational program and contact the proper groups through the accepted mediums of health instruction.

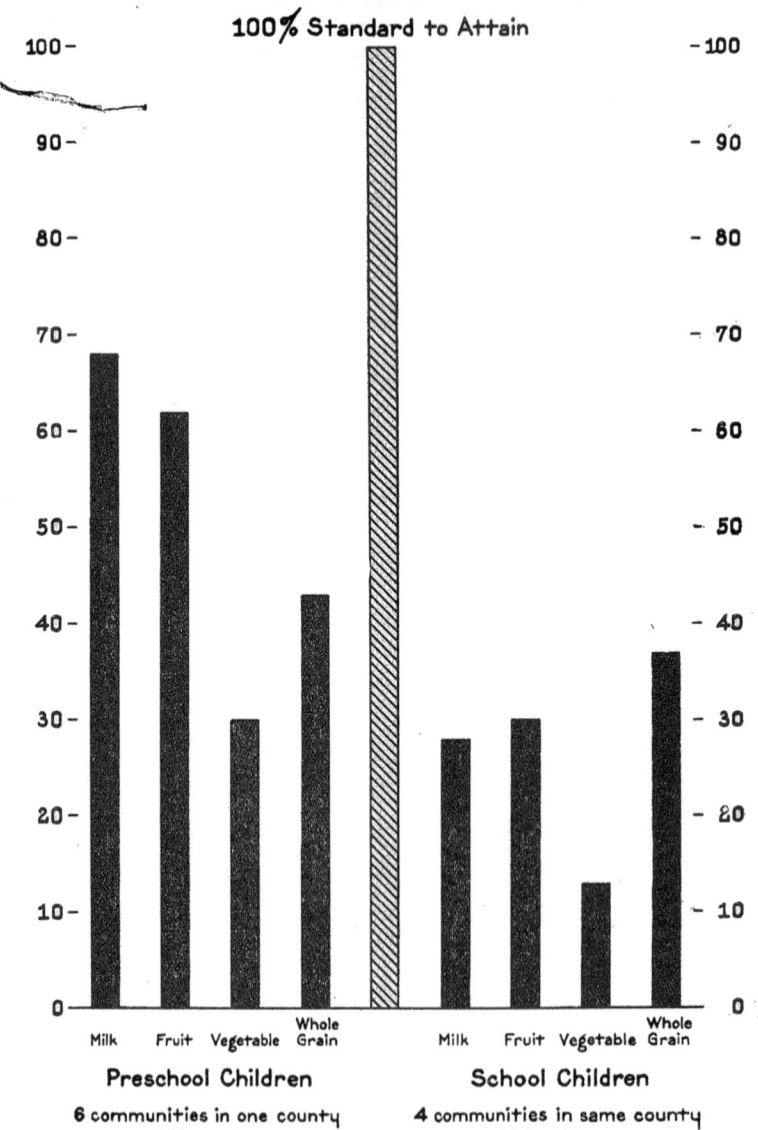

NUTRITION FACTS FOR TEACHERS

MARY SPALDING, AND NUTRITIONISTS

Division of Child Hygiene
Massachusetts Department of Public Health

Surveys of what school children are eating this last year have astounded and awakened certain communities in Massachusetts to the need of help for these children in improving their daily practices. Is this due to a lack of knowledge among these children? Is it because children know—and yet are not inspired to act? Does the school environment provide opportunity for ideal practices, as in a good lunchroom? Are the results of teaching reflected in the homes? Teachers can help more with this subject and help quickly, so that the present generation may benefit. Certain countries at the present time are prescribing food for their children—can we educate our children to choose wisely for themselves?

Nutrition is a growing science. Never before have we known so many helpful practical facts as during these last few years. Vitamin research did not begin until about thirty years ago. Now children may find whether or not they are getting their quota of vitamins A, B, C, and D in their daily meals. We know of what an adequate diet consists. We expect, however, to know more and more each year as to what is the best diet for the family as a whole and for the individuals in the family. A constant challenge to teachers and parents for immediate use comes with these bits of important information pouring in from chemical, biological, physiological, and psychological laboratories and interpretations from social and economic groups. As with any science the student must keep an open mind to new findings. With this science, however, must also come personal action. Dr. Minot, the Nobel Laureate in Medicine, has said that, "Man's future depends very largely on what he decides to eat".

Nutritionists after·years of study, as well as teachers, are finding it hard to keep a balanced point of view and to remember that the present day knowledge of food "must stand foursquare upon full recognition of energy, protein, minerals, and vitamins" and also on the importance of water and the inter-relationships of these substances in the daily meals. Nutrition, too, depends not only on food substances but on factors of sleep and rest, activity, sunshine and fresh air, emotional and mental control, digestion and elimination, correction of defects, heredity and prenatal care, and regularity of living.

Teachers may bring to children daily guidance and inspiration. It is necessary that only true facts in the right perspective be given. The teacher herself and many of her children have been bombarded and sometimes swayed by advertising through radios, papers, and faddists. She must be able to remain firm in this whirlpool of propaganda and emotion and steer her crew as directly as possible towards the goal of better everyday choice of food with the steadfast thought of assisting the children to live efficiently.

As with any subject, the richer the background of knowledge the better the teacher may select and offer her facts. The occasional teacher who does not understand the significance of nutrition may dull children's future interest by skimming off the cream of nutrition knowledge. She must also guard against even giving too much of the rich cream itself for whole milk is most wholesome for a daily food over the long period it is needed. For the above reasons we are submitting a key to primary nutrition facts to teachers who have not yet had the opportunity of a recent course.

Material — Because of the importance of the subject, the Department of Public Health offers free to the teachers of the State the following material as a supplement to texts and reference books. This material may be obtained by writing to the Massachusetts Department of Public Health, 1 Beacon St., Boston.

For elementary schools:

For the individual child (for use at home or at school)

"Keeping Well" (4-6 grades)
A guide by which he may find his needs and may record his attainments.

"Food for the School Child" (6-12 years)
Gives facts on which he may base his activities.
As home and school must work together for the child's nutrition, the teacher may allow the child to take this leaflet home to his parents.

"Brownie Health Rules" (1-2 grades)

"The Measuring Stick for the School Lunch" } Single sheets
"A Measuring Stick for a Family's Meals"

For the elementary teacher:

"Good Eating Habits"
Gives psychological aspect. Prepared especially for the parent and teacher of the little child.

"Your Guide for Buying, Preparing, and Serving Good Meals at Low Cost"—"Food Wise—Money Wise"
Give economic aspect so teacher may understand and help the child get the most food value for his money.

"Food Customs from Abroad"
Gives a social aspect to help the teacher adapt her subject matter to the home environment of the child.

"How To Judge Nutrition of Children"

"Range of Height of Short, Medium, and Tall Children and Their Annual Gain in Mean Weight"

"Cooking for Health"

"Minerals and Vitamins" (Single sheet)

"Vitamin C Foods"

"Aids to Bowel Movement"

"The Nutritional Aspects of Milk Pasteurization" by E. V. McCollum, F.A.P.H.A.—Johns Hopkins—(Reprint from THE COMMONHEALTH)

"Evaporated Milk" (for every milk use)

"Fruit Candies" (a holiday activity)
Physiological aspect—Value of preparation of food

For the secondary grades:

For the students

"Food for the Teens"
The what, how, and why of foods

"Healthful Living"
   A guide for young people
"Food Value Posters" (Being revised)
   Description of an activity to work out food values graphically. Helpful when checked by teacher.
"A Measuring Stick for a Family's meals" ⎫
"Minerals and Vitamins"   ⎬ single sheets—for emphasis
"For Your Teeth and Gums"   ⎭

For the secondary teacher herself or her reference shelf:
   Black and white nutrition posters (may be colored by students)
"Food Customs from Abroad"
   Social aspect
"Bibliography on Food Fads"
   To help give criteria for judging food facts
"Your Guide for Buying, Preparing, and Serving Good Meals at Low Cost"—"Food Wise—Money Wise"
   Economic aspect
"Cooking for Health"
"Vitamin C Foods"
"The Nutritional Aspects of Milk Pasteurization" by E. V. McCollum, F.A.P.H.A.—Johns Hopkins—(Reprint from THE COMMONHEALTH)
"Evaporated Milk" (for every milk use)
"Aids to Bowel Movement"
"Typical School Cafeteria Menus"
   Physiologcal aspect—Value of preparation of food

Other material useful to home economics teachers:
For the students
   "Cooking for Health"
   "Your Guide for Buying, Preparing, and Serving Good Meals at Low Cost"
   "Food Wise—Money Wise"
   "Food Customs from Abroad"

For the home economics teacher:
   "Baby and You"
   "One to Six"
   "Good Eating Habits"
   "How To Judge Nutrition of Children"
      Mimeographed material—"Liver"
                            "Cabbage, Two-Dozen Ways of Using"

Note: We invite constructive criticism of this material so revisions may be improved for your use.

Nutrition Consultant Service — In so far as possible the Department offers the service of its nutritionists to confer with school groups. Here facts may be clarified, references, textbooks, and community facilities discussed, better conditions for children's practices in nutrition planned for the school, solutions for community problems in nutrition advanced, and ways and means suggested of arousing pupil interest. In this way the school group and the nutritionist may become more aware of nutrition problems of the individual child, the school, the home, and the community and work towards meeting them. Where actual conference is not available, correspondence is generally possible with the above nutritionists.

We nutritionists are submitting a few unadorned facts for teachers from authorities; the teacher may have them for ready reference when other texts are not at hand.

What is nutrition?

"Nutrition is the sum of the processes concerned with growth, maintenance, and repair of the living body as a whole, or of its constituents and parts"—Lusk. Good nutrition is the basis for good health.

What are the signs of good and poor nutrition?

General appearance of vitality and vigor	General appearance of fatigue
Eyes bright and clear	Eyes dull
Hair smooth and glossy	Hair coarse and rough
Skeleton strong and straight with well-shaped head and chest	Skeleton malformed with poorly shaped head and chest
Sturdy appearance	Frail appearance
Teeth sound and well-formed	Teeth uneven and decayed
Muscles ready and firm	Muscles flabby and undeveloped
Posture erect	Posture slumping
Good layer of subcutaneous fat	Skin a loose covering for muscles
Clear skin with a healthy glow	Complexion pale
Reddish-pink mucous membrane	Pale and colorless mucous membrane
Good appetite, digestion, and elimination	Poor appetite, digestion, and elimination
Steady nerves	Irritable, over-active and highstrung
Endurance	Tires easily—listless inactivity
Abundance of good spirits	Strained and worried facial expression
Freedom from physical defects	Presence of remedial defects as decayed teeth and poor posture

Are height and weight and age tables a good standard for judging nutrition?

No! They do not consider body build, heredity, and the other points of good nutrition which greatly influence growth.

Of what value is regular weighing and measuring?

Constant gain in weight in relation to height shows growth for the individual child even though the gain may be small. Failure to gain over a period of four to six months may be an indication of nutritional difficulty.

Is an overweight child a well-nourished child?

Not necessarily for he may have poor muscle tone, signs of anemia, and other indications of poor nutrition.

What are the factors which affect nutrition?
  Food, digestion and elimination, sleep and rest, sunshine and fresh air, exercise and posture, regularity of habits, mental and emotional attitude, and physical defects.

What is the part played by food in good nutrition?
  Food furnishes energy, helps the body to run smoothly, builds and renews the tissues of the body, and helps maintain positive health.

What substances must foods contain?
  Foods must contain protein, carbohydrate, fat, calcium, phosphorus, iron, other minerals, vitamins A, B, C, D, and G.

How does protein function? What foods furnish it?
  Protein constructs and repairs or maintains body tissue. It is supplied by milk, eggs, meat, fish, dried beans and peas, and nuts.

What is the function of carbohydrate? What foods supply it?
  Carbohydrate furnishes the body with energy. It is supplied by breads, cereals, sugars, and starches in particular.

What is the function of fat? How is it supplied?
  It is a concentrated form of energy for the body and a carrier for fat soluble vitamin A. Fat is supplied by butter, cream, vegetable oils, lard, and nut oils.

What is the function of calcium? Where is it found?
  It is needed for building teeth and bone and helps to regulate the action of the heart, muscles, and nerves. It is found in milk and cheese, dried beans and peas, broccoli, kale, carrots, and string beans in particular.

Why is phosphorus important? What foods are good sources?
  It is a limiting or determining factor in human nutrition, one of the chief elements in building skeletal structure, aids regulation of osmotic pressure, and is essential in cell structure and that of soft tissues. Eggs, lean beef, wheat, almonds, and dried beans are good sources.

What is the function of iron? What foods supply it?
  It is essential since iron forms part of the red blood corpuscles which act as oxygen carriers in respiration. Liver, eggs, beef, oysters, green vegetables, dried beans and peas, potatoes, dried fruit, dark breads and cereals supply iron.

What other minerals are necessary to the body?
  Iodine, magnesium, sodium, chlorine, sulphur, manganese, zinc, and traces of others.

Is it necessary to plan a diet around the requirements for these last mentioned minerals?
  No! An ordinary mixed diet will usually furnish safe amounts.

What is the function of vitamin A? What foods contain it?
  It aids normal growth and development, helps build strong teeth, lessens the incidence of respiratory infections, skin, ear, and alimentary infections, and prevents xerophthalmia and night blindness. Yellow vegetables such as carrots, eggs, milk, butter, cream, cheese, fish liver oils, and thin green leaves such as beet greens or kale contain it.

What is the function of vitamin B? What foods contain it?
Vitamin B affects growth, promotes appetite, aids the normal motility of the digestive tract, and prevents beri beri. It is found generously in natural foods such as whole grains, vegetables, fruits, milk, eggs, dried peas and beans, liver, and heart.

What is the function of vitamin C? Where is it found?
Vitamin C aids resistance to infection, helps prevent dental defects, and prevents scurvy. It is found in citrus fruits, raw cabbage and onions, apples, bananas, and potatoes.

What is the function of vitamin D? Where is it found?
It prevents and helps to cure rickets, facilitates calcium utilization as in developing bone and normal teeth, and helps protect against dental caries. It is found in sunlight, fish liver oils, egg yolk, whole milk, and foods enriched with vitamin D.

What is the function of vitamin G? Where is it found?
Vitamin G aids growth and normal nutrition, lengthens the prime of life, aids in prevention of digestive disturbances and unhealthy condition of the skin, and prevents pellagra. It is found in green vegetables, liver, kidneys, lean meat, milk, salmon and other fish, beet and turnip tops, eggs, oranges, and bananas.

What more do we hope to find out about vitamins?
We hope to know more about amounts needed by different individuals. The ones now known to exist are being broken down chemically into component parts resulting in the discovery of new vitamins having more exact functions.

What foods which include these properties are necessary every day for optimum growth and health?
The protective foods—milk, vegetables, fruit, and whole grains—with sufficient other foods to provide for the energy needs of the body are necessary each day.

Are the food requirements of the adult and the child the same?
No! During a period of growth the child needs large quantities of body-building material. It is important, therefore, to stress the equivalent of a quart of milk and an optimum amount of other protective foods.

Is milk a perfect food?
No! Although it is the most nearly perfect food it is lacking in some essentials such as vitamin C and iron. It is digested and assimilated more easily than most other foods.

Can milk cheese be considered a substitute for milk?
Cheese can be used in place of some of the daily milk because it is rich in calcium, phosphorus, and protein, but because of difficulty of digestion (concentrated food) it is not practical to use it as a substitute for all the milk in the diet.

Does a high school student require more than a pint of milk a day?
Yes! Generally during the period of rapid adolescent growth it is particularly necessary to have an adequate amount of mineral material, making the equivalent of a quart of milk daily desirable.

Are butter substitutes equivalent to butter?
No! Because they generally lack vitamin A. On families of a low economic level it may be better to buy a substitute, however, and furnish vitamin A through foods such as carrots, yellow turnips, and the like.

How may milk be included in the diet?
As a beverage—plain or flavored, in creamed dishes, in soups, in puddings, and on and in cereals.

Can evaporated milk be considered the equivalent of whole milk?
Yes! It is whole milk with part of the water removed. When that water is replaced, it is again the equivalent of whole milk.

Is it important to use pasteurized milk?
Yes! Because it is safe, clean milk.

Why is raw milk not safe?
Because it may contain bacteria which cause such diseases as tuberculosis, septic sore throat, undulant fever, scarlet fever, and typhoid fever.

Is testing the cows for tuberculosis sufficient guarantee for safe, clean milk?
No. Because the cows may develop the disease between intervals of testing, and the results of this test do not indicate the presence of the bacteria causing other diseases.

Does pasteurization change the food value of milk?
No! It affects only vitamin C of which milk has only a negligible amount, and this may easily be provided by other foods in the diet.

Is ice cream a wholesome food?
Yes! If it is made from clean, pasteurized milk and cream and wholesome ingredients stored only a reasonable period of time and consumed at its proper place in the meal as a dessert.

Why are whole grain breads and cereals important?
They are the most economical source of energy and protein in the diet, and a good source of vitamin B and iron. The bran coatings of grains have a stimulating effect on the intestine.

How often should whole grains be included in the diet?
Whole grain bread or cereal should be served at least once a day.

Is plain bran recommended as a cereal for children?
No! It is apt to be irritating to digestive tissues for children under eight or for people with a sensitive digestive system. Small amounts may be used with other cereals or in muffins.

Why is a whole grain cereal product preferable to a refined product?
It is much superior in minerals and vitamins since by the refining process the bran which contains iron and vitamin B and the embryo which contains the fat, protein, and vitamins have been removed.

What is the value of prepared cereals?
Ready-to-eat cereals may have good food properties and are, like whole grains, a source of energy. Their cost, however, is far greater than corresponding ready-to-cook cereal pound for pound.

Should sugar be used with cereal?
> It is better to serve cereal without sugar so the taste for the delicate cereal flavor will not be destroyed. Too much sugar sometimes produces fermentation.

Can cereals play too important a part in the day's menus?
> Yes! If over one-third of the total number of the day's calories come from cereals, the burden of furnishing the remainder of the minerals and vitamins will fall too heavily on the rest of the diet and the diet will tend to be low in calcium and vitamins A, C, and G.

Why is fruit considered a part of the day's food requirements?
> It is a good appetizer, rich in minerals and vitamins, and acts as a laxative. Citrus fruits are rich sources of vitamin C which is not widely distributed in other foods.

Is cooked fruit as valuable as raw?
> When cooking water is served and eaten, the minerals are conserved but destruction of vitamin B and C through oxidation is probable.

Does canning of fruit destroy vitamin C?
> If it is canned by the cold pack method, vitamin C is not destroyed in any appreciable amount. Commercially canned fruits retain most of their vitamin C.

Does storage of fruit juices destroy vitamin C?
> Yes! The vitamin C content lessens on exposure to the air.

Are fruit jams and jellies good ways of serving fruit?
> If eaten at the first of the meal, they may spoil the appetite for other foods because of their large sugar content. They probably contain little vitamin C. They are useful principally to add interest and color to a meal.

How much fruit is desirable in a day's diet?
> One serving of citrus fruit, such as orange or tomato, and at least one other fruit, raw or cooked.

Are dried fruits desirable to include in the diet?
> Yes! They are an excellent and economical source of vitamin A and iron.

Why is it desirable to serve vegetables daily?
> Vegetables are a good supplementary source of calcium, a good source of iron and vitamins B and G, help maintain the body's alkaline reserve, are mildly laxative, and some are good sources of vitamin A.

What is the usual vegetable requirement of a day's diet?
> One serving of cooked and one of raw besides potato.

What precaution should be used in cooking vegetables?
> The vegetable water should be saved since it contains soluble mineral salts and water soluble vitamins. Cook most vegetables in as little water as possible.

Why should a raw vegetable be included daily?
> Its vitamin and mineral content is well preserved, and it is of value in exercising teeth and gums.

Is it wise to use baking soda to preserve the color of fruits and vegetables when cooking?
> No! Because it aids in the destruction of the vitamins B and C.

What is the place of meat in a day's food plan?
Meat is valuable for its protein, phosphorus, and iron. The organs of animals, such as liver, kidney, and heart, are especially rich in vitamins A and B and iron.

How often should meat be served?
On a moderate income it would seem advisable to serve meat once daily. On a limited income meat substitutes, such as fish, cheese, and dried beans and peas, should be used often.

What is the value of prepared cold meats and frankforts?
Their cost is high, and they are often too highly seasoned to make them a desirable part of the child's diet.

Have eggs a place in the day's meal plan?
Yes! They are an excellent source of protein, phosphorus, vitamin A, and iron.

How often should eggs be included?
An egg per person each day is a desirable standard to set. This may be included in the preparation of other foods or served separately. Three or four a week is the minimum standard for children.

What are suitable sweets for children?
Simple milk or egg desserts, cooked, dried, or raw fruit are good sweets for children. These contain sufficient sugar to meet the child's requirements.

What is the answer to candy claims for a "cheap source of energy?"
Most candies offer little but calories. They are lacking in protein, minerals, and vitamins, so do not give good value for money spent.

Why is it important to keep in good nutrition?
"In our study of undernourished adults we have found that a diet which will preserve a person in nutritive equilibrium is seldom sufficient to bring him back from nutritional failure. Once he gets in this condition he must then have a ration that provides much more food and much larger quantities of the missing factors than would have been originally necessary to keep him in health."—McLester.*

Should weight reduction be brought about by simple reduction of foods?
No! If any large reduction is necessary, the person should first consult his physician. Whenever foods are restricted by an obese person, the essential food substances—protein, minerals and vitamins—must be carefully planned for first, and secondly a fat-carbohydrate balance is necessary.

How may the teacher use the school lunch?
She may use it as a practice test, a committee of children and teachers checking the food chosen.

How may the teacher judge nutrition sources of new information?
Are they reliable?—
    Official health agencies—local, state, or national
    Recognized professional group in medical, public health or nutrition field
    Authoritative books and professional journals

---
* McLester — Milbank Memorial Fund Report.

Less dependable?—
Commercial interests or advertising
Popular books, magazines, and newspapers, unless from recognized authorities
"They say"
Relatives and friends
Dangerous?—
Quacks and faddists—usually making too great claims for simple foods and food constituents

What is the cost of an adequate diet for a family?
This varies with the family. "A low-cost assortment of foods properly selected may give better returns in nutrition and health than a more expensive list chosen at random"—*Stiebeling*. Intelligent food selection and the application of both science and art to the service and preparation of foods help in serving low cost meals that the family will like.

How may lack of sleep influence food intake?
The over-fatigued child loses his appetite. He may not be able to digest his food.

When should rest be taken?
"Before fatigue has developed too much, since it requires two to ten times as long for the body to recuperate after over-fatigue has occurred."—Dr. Charles Manger.

How does exercise affect nutrition?
It stimulates the circulation, improves the appetite, and increases the size and tone of muscles.

Has posture a bearing on nutrition?
Yes! Poor posture may result in poor body mechanics, which in turn may cause digestive disturbances and constipation. It may be the result of poor nutrition or the cause.

How does sunshine aid in food utilization?
The ultra-violet rays from the sun aid the body to produce vitamin D necessary for building calcium and phosphorus into strong bones and teeth.

Is sunshine always a good sourse of vitamin D?
No! In this climate only in summer is it a sufficient source of vitamin D for children.

How does the mental and emotional attitude affect nutrition?
This affects glands and secretions, appetite, and digestion.

What effect have physical defects on nutrition?
With such defects the child may not be able to improve his nutrition.

HEALTH EDUCATION IN THE FIELD OF DENTISTRY

FLORENCE B. HOPKINS, M.D., D.M.D., *Dental Consultant*

Massachusetts Department of Public Health

Probably no phase of public health has increased more in scope and changed more in method during the last few years than that of health education. Continuing interest in prevention of all diseased conditions, whether contagious or not, recognition of the importance of health as a factor in social security resulting in the allotment of Federal funds to promote health education, and the progress of education in general, have all been active factors in bringing about increase and change.

Dentistry as a profession has not lagged behind in its interest in the prevention of disease and the promotion of health education. No one specific phase of health education has increased and changed more than has dental health education in the last two decades.

Many more alterations and improvements are imminent. Federal financial assistance to State Departments of Public Health has enabled them to increase their dental personnel and program. Many states have appointed a dentist on the staff of the Health Department for the first time. Our own Department of Public Health now has also the full time services of a health education expert. Courses in Public Health and in Health Education for dentists have been instituted. The United States Public Health Service, which did not employ dentists before the World War, and where those employed since then were assigned to do routine dental operative work almost entirely, has now assigned some of its dental officers to devote full time to public health administration and health education. Dental health will now, of necessity, be more strongly accented in health programs than ever before.

Since no proven specific cause of dental caries has been found, those working for dental health cannot use a preventive plan as is used in many of the programs so effective in communicable disease control. As in Cancer and Tuberculosis, preventive work can be done through early operative procedures and through much general health education. The changes in our knowledge regarding the factors important to tooth health have caused a constant need for reorganizing and rebuilding dental health education programs.

It will be interesting to briefly outline the work done by a few of the outstanding pioneers of dentistry and see just how their work influenced the progress of dental health education up to the present day.

Just about one hundred years ago the first dental college in the world was started in this country. A few years before, Robertson had said that the dissolution of food particles in the mouth produced acids which in turn decomposed the teeth. Fifty years later W. D. Miller was working on a series of experiments which demonstrated the relation between mouth bacteria and decay of teeth. His views were published in a book in 1890. Out of this grew Dental Hygiene. For the next twenty-five years the dental profession accepted the slogan, "A clean tooth never decays."

In October, 1913, Dr. Alfred C. Fones did something about it. He opened a school to train young women as dental hygienists, teaching them to clean teeth as the dentists did and to teach dental hygiene at the same time. Dr. Fones succeeded in putting these hygienists into the public schools of Bridgeport, Connecticut, for he believed that a dental health education program in the schools could serve to raise the sanitary consciousness of the whole community. Three years later Columbia and Forsyth started their training schools.

These girls were, in fact, the first special teachers of health education. Their field was very limited (a health education specialist today cannot limit herself to one part of the body).

As time went on and new types of investigation brought new ideas to dental hygiene, the truth had to be met that decay occurred sometimes even in a clean tooth or at least in a mouth that had good home care and frequent care by a hygienist. For a time the pendulum of opinion swung far to the other side. The value of so-called "dental prophylaxis" was strongly questioned.

A modern view of such work in public health education is expressed by Dr. Mustard thus:—"The majority of school children have some degree of deposit or discoloration on the teeth. The amount of this depends upon the shape of the jaw, the shape and position of the teeth, perhaps on the mineral content of the saliva, the type of food eaten and the frequency, regularity and thoroughness with which the teeth are brushed. Crooked and irregular teeth receiving the minimum of care will naturally develop a maximum of stains and deposits.

"It is important for the examiner to distinguish between teeth which may be cleaned by the efforts of the child and the mouth which may be put in good condition *only* through the services of a dentist. In the former case, *parents should be stimulated and the child should be stimulated* to give more attention to the use of the toothbrush. Teeth containing calcareous deposits or deep stains may be properly cleaned only by a dentist."

In 1919 Percy Howe in this country, and Wells and Zilva in England, pointed out the importance of Vitamin C in tooth health. Dr. Howe also demonstrated that the teeth of well-fed, nonscorbutic monkeys do not decay and that teeth of scorbutic monkeys are prone to decay.

Hanke made a study of over 400 children at Mooseheart, the resulting figures of which seemed to prove that a supplementary feeding of orange juice added to the average American child's diet would retard caries and generally improve tooth health.

In 1922 Vitamin D was separated from Vitamin A and in 1924 Dr. May Mellanby was investigating the effect of a deficiency of Vitamin D on tooth health. Although her interest was in another vitamin, it did accent the place of nutrition in a dental health program just as did the work of Howe and Hanke.

Many other investigators, such as McCollum, Sherman, Boyd and Drain, all showed us that we could not hope to practice preventive dentistry without teaching proper nutrition even during the prenatal period. Some enthusiasts felt that if we could change the food habits of our nation we could even throw away all toothbrushes.

A study of the dental hygiene programs during 1925-1930 will plainly show a very pronounced accent on nutrition. Many of the school children were taught that a quart of milk and a pint of orange juice would practically assure them perfect teeth. Teachers were told to be careful to rule out all such false propaganda as "A clean tooth *never* decays." Some teachers wondered then and are still wondering whether or not they should teach toothbrushing in their dental health education courses.

Pits and fissures also entered the stage to further confuse the lay teacher. How did these fit into the general scene?

Sir John Tomes, an English dentist who made a minute study between 1873 and 1882 of the bones and teeth and especially of the dentine, concluded that "caries is the effect of external causes in which socalled 'vital' forces play no part, that it is due to the solvent action of acids which have been generated by fermentation going on in the mouth (this much coincides with Miller's Theory but he adds) and when once the disintegration is established in some congenitally defective point, the accumulation of food and secretions in the oral cavity will intensify the mischief by furnishing new supplies of acids."

Fifty years later in 1923 Dr. Thaddeus Hyatt propounded the theory that decay began at points where there were found certain defects in the enamel of the tooth. Whether poor heredity, faulty nutrition or somthing else caused these defects he did not state. When they were discovered, however, there was a chance to prevent further destruction and ultimate loss of teeth by the operation of filling these pits and fissures. Dr. C. F. Bodecker agreed with Dr. Hyatt after making further study. It is now the general consensus of opinion among the majority of dentists particularly interested in preventive dentistry today that it is wise to look well for pits and fissures and to fill them as soon as discovered.

After a debate on "RESOLVED: THAT A CLEAN TOOTH DOES NOT DECAY AND THAT MOUTH CLEANLINESS AFFORDS THE BEST KNOWN PROTECTION AGAINST DENTAL CARIES," between such outstanding dental scholars as Dr. Thaddeus Hyatt, Dr. Alfred Walker, Dr. Maurice Williams and Dr. E. V. McCollum, Dr. Weston A. Price and Dr. Arthur Merritt, "both sides admitted and accepted the soundness of such a premise (normal protective enamel covering is dependent upon proper nutritional diet) and both sides admitted and agreed in substance that a sound tooth, well formed and kept clean, would not decay; and that a defective unsound tooth could not be kept sufficiently clean to avoid decay." Dr. McCollum offered the suggestion that the slogan, "A clean tooth will not decay," might more appropriately be rephrased to read, "A clean tooth with perfection of structure well exercised and well nourished will not decay."

In 1927 the dental hygiene program of the Massachusetts Department of Public Health included among its educational leaflets one on treatment of pits and fissures.

In speaking of this procedure as carried out at the Forsyth Dental Infirmary, Dr. Harold DeWitt Cross said in 1926, "The results following this plan of early attention to the children's teeth given before there are any serious complications, has proved to be of tremendous advantage to the child. So much so, that it is now possible to speak of 'end results' for children 16-18 years of age, in terms of good, vital teeth which have nothing more serious than small 'pit and fissure' fillings, and under ordinary conditions ought to be good for at least forty years, with the possible exception of an occasional renewal of a filling due to recurrent decay.

"End-results in terms of good teeth, i.e., all teeth present with vital pulps and with only small fillings, has not been the usual attainment of dentistry, but that this condition may be obtained, in a very definite manner, and that it is of easy accomplishment, is the natural deduction to be made from the results of the last few years' work in the Forsyth clinics."

Thus, operative procedures were recognized as a part of preventive dentistry.

In 1914 a law was passed in Massachusetts permitting towns to establish dental clinics and by 1920 ninety towns were giving some clinic service to the public school children.

For centuries dentistry had been a reparative procedure. It had dealt with repairing and replacing destroyed teeth of adults. Little or nothing, except extracting or something to relieve severe pain was done for the child with deciduous teeth. With the acceptance of the theory of focal infection the medical profession became more than ever interested in dental care. Then the dependence of general health upon dental health became most apparent. Since children as well as adults are victims of diseases of the heart, joints and kidneys the deciduous teeth were seen to be an important factor in preventive medicine. The pediatrician became especially interested in dental care for his patients and dental schools began courses in dental pediatrics.

This movement had another impetus. Orthodontia became a specialty of dentistry only after the turn of the century. Before this, it had been practiced as a more or less crude attempt to straighten crooked teeth for esthetic reasons. Dr. Norman W. Kinsley wrote the first important book on "Oral Deformities" in 1879. It was thirty years later that Dr. Edward H. Angle, recognizing the occlusion of the teeth as a fundamental biological mechanism and the relation of the arches, one to the other, as more important than the relation of one tooth to the arch, gave orthodontia its most potent inspiration. In his book on orthodontia, in discussing causes of malocclusion, he took up the early loss of deciduous teeth at some length. From his time on orthodontists have been scientifically studying not only mechanical means to correct oral deformities but the causes of, and thereby the prevention of, malocclusions. They were then the chief promoters of dentistry for children. The orthodontists today are our leaders in upholding the standards of dental work on deciduous teeth.

School dental clinics which were frequently intended to be a part of the dental health education program were thus urged to make their major effort toward prevention by accenting care of deciduous teeth. The optimists in the profession felt that if we could do all the dentistry needed in the first three grades of school the dental question would then more or less take care of itself. It is difficult not to become a rank pessimist when the mouths of the high school children are surveyed as a test of this policy.

We know now that we have a most difficult problem to solve in care of teeth during adolescence. During this period children who have had excellent dental care for their deciduous teeth, who have been brought up under the guidance of well qualified pediatricians, whose parents have provided the best known dietaries and who seem to be otherwise in excellent physical condition suddenly show a tragic disintegration of tooth structure. What is the cause? We do not know.

Martha Jones thinks activity of dental caries is not a fixed quality but is rather a fluctuating one, the result of age, state of health, climate, environment, activity and diet. She states that sunshine, cod liver oil, eggs, orange juice, tomatoes and milk do not prevent the rampant disintegration of teeth of children at periods of accelerated bone growth.

Dr. Moore of Philadelphia has made a most interesting study of the incidence of caries at various age levels but she is able to offer no solution to the cause.

Many writers are questioning endocrines as the offenders but none as yet has proven anything.

Although it is evident we must reach the high school group with dental health education to advise them of the danger that they are facing from dental neglect at this time, we cannot give up teaching the value of dental care to all ages. All known factors that can have any influence on tooth health and general health must be included in our instruction.

At the present time there is more controversy about the reasons for tooth decay than there ever has been before. It doesn't mean that we are not progressing in the direction of preventive dentistry, but it does mean that the more we know about the facts involved, the more we are brought face to face with the probable truth that no one cause of dental caries ever will be found, but that all facts influencing general health also influence our dental conditions. In order to arrive near the goal of dental health we must broaden our concept of the interrelation of general health and dental health. This will mean that we must expand our public health dental programs and closely correlate them with all other branches of health education service. And if we are ever prone to feel that dental health education has not accomplished much, just remember that until after 1907 the professions had practically no interest in tooth hygiene, and it was not until after 1917 that active health education programs were established in any material number of localities. It is true we still have many to teach and much to learn, but we have progressed far in twenty years. With all the public health and health education assistance which will be given dentistry from now on, the next twenty years should show remarkable results in the prevention of dental disease.

BIBLIOGRAPHY

ANGLE, EDWARD H.: Malocclusion of the Teeth and Fractures of the Maxillae.

BLACK, ARTHUR D.: Exhibit for Dentistry at a Century of Progress International Exposition. Descriptive booklet.

BODECKER, CHARLES F.: A Microscopic Study of Enamel Fissures with Reference to Their Operative Treatment. Dental Cosmos, October 1924.

BOYD, J. D. and
DRAIN, C. L.: Arrest of Dental Caries in Childhood. Journal of American Medical Association, June 9, 1928.
Endocrine Factors in the Control and arrest of Dental Caries. Journal of American Dietetic Association, March 1935.

BUNTING, R. W.: Report of Successful Control of Dental Caries in Three Public Institutions. Journal of American Dental Association, April 1931.
CROSS, HAROLD DEWITT: Children's Dentistry as Practiced in Institutions and Public School Clinics. The Commonhealth, July 1926.
HANKE, MILTON T.: Role of Diet in the Cause, Prevention and Cure of Dental Diseases. Journal of Nutrition, January 1931.
HOGEBOOM, F. E.: Is Teen Age Caries an Endocrine Problem? Journal of American Dental Association, March 1937.
HYATT, THADDEUS: Prophylactic Odontotomy. Dental Cosmos, March 1923.
KINSLEY, NORMAN W.: Oral Deformities.
KLEIN, JACOB E.: Progress in Nutrition, Journal of American Dental Association, September 1936.
MELLANBY, M. and PATTISON, C. L.: Some Factors Influencing the Spread of Caries in Children. British Dental Journal, October 1926.
MOORE, MARY M.: Observations on the Age Incidence of Dental Caries. Annals of Dentistry, Vol. III, No. 2.
MORSE, JOHN LOVETT: The Attitude of the Medical Profession. Commonhealth, July 1926.
MUSTARD, HARRY S.: Rural Health Practices. Commonwealth Fund, 1937.

The Clean Tooth Debate — Editorial, Dental Cosmos, 1934
Does a Clean Tooth Ever Decay? The Health Officer, April 1937

HEALTH EDUCATION IN THE FIELD OF TUBERCULOSIS

ARTHUR J. STRAWSON, *Executive Secretary,*
Massachusetts Tuberculosis League
Boston, Mass.

One of the chief needs in the field of tuberculosis prevention is that of securing more health education. Our newly completed hospital beds, 160 in Middlesex County Sanitorium and 150 in Westfield State Sanatorium, give Massachusetts a rather adequate supply. Without including these beds and on the basis of the American Medical Association tuberculosis hospital and sanatorium survey of 1935, we have 2.14 beds per death.* Our public health nursing, clinic and laboratory facilities are of the best and "A divine discontent" among our official tuberculosis and health leaders constantly makes for greater perfection in these services.

With these four basic needs being so thoroughly met, it is health education which needs development to bring about their more adequate and proper use. How else, one may ask, can we reverse the percentage of

---
* The United States figure has doubtless somewhat increased since 1935 when Miss Jessamine S. Whitney, statistician of the National Tuberculosis Association, computed it by using the 1934 beds and 1934 tuberculosis deaths.

early and later cases in the institutions? The 1935 American Medical Association study of tuberculosis hospitals of the nation found 13.1 per cent of recorded entrances of patients to be in the early stages. But 29.7 and 57.2 per cent respectively, were in moderately or far advanced stages. Hospitals and physicians, while hoping for a change, can do but little to bring it about. Yet health education here finds a worthy and suitable task. With united effort of all concerned, it well might undertake to reverse the order of patient admissions: to make it read 57.2 per cent incipient, 29.7 per cent moderately advanced and 13.1 per cent far advanced. Here is a goal for tuberculosis workers, all of whom are concerned with health education.

Those with early tuberculosis must be taught to see their physicians before it is too late but if we can go further and induce many to have a periodic physical examination, more tuberculosis and other curable maladies will be found. How few of us as yet have a periodic examination except for our automobiles?

The very minimum to teach in this regard is that anyone who was living with a tuberculosis patient should have proper examinations until his special danger has passed.

Retail and wholesale health education are both necessary. Health education is retailed to their private patients by family physicians, to sanatorium patients by sanatorium workers, to clinic patients and hospital outpatients by their physicians, nurses and medical social workers, while school, health department, industrial and other public health nurses retail health education in the home. This is most effective as it is friendly and personal. It lacks not for understood illustrations. By this method ardent missionaries for health and against tuberculosis are set to work in the community.

In this connection one might quote W. H. Frost, M.D., Professor of Epidemiology, Johns Hopkins University, from his article "How Much Control of Tuberculosis?" published in the American Journal of Public Health, August, 1937:

"Only the relatively small proportion of infections which progress to the stage of open lesion are successful in spreading the infection to others, and it is only these sputum-positive cases that need to be isolated in order to prevent the spread of infection."

But, after retail health education, especially against tuberculosis, has done all it can, it must then be supplemented by wholesale health education. This is necessary to give to every family and to all eventual voters and parents, at least a good "exposure" to the important facts about tuberculosis and the Commonwealth's provision for further treatment and reduction of the disease.

There remains physical resistance building. It is needed by the well who may never be seen in a clinic or hospital. The retail workers cannot reach so many of these people. Some few health workers are obsessed with the great power of disease germs. They forget that proper development of resistance is effective within reasonable limits and is a most valuable aid. For the benefit of these persons one might further quote from Dr. Frost:

"It is probable that one of the most important factors in the decline of tuberculosis has been progressively increasing human resistance, due to the influence of selective mortality and to environmental improvements such as better nutrition and relief from physical stress, tending to raise what may be called non-specific resistance."

Obviously, the securing of this "better nutrition and relief from physical stress" is to be attained chiefly through health education.

Wholesale health education may well be provided for the twelve grades of children in our public and parochial schools, as well as for all college youth. The present generation of Massachusetts school children inherit the precedent of the nationally admired Chadwick Ten Year Plan for childhood tuberculosis. Since the end of those years in July, 1934, the task became a local responsibility. While state, county and city sanatoria, schools and local boards of health and even voluntary health associations and some other agencies are helping, there is work for all to do in making these tuberculin testing efforts more comprehensive and educational. If they are not quite inclusive enough many children who need them most may be neglected. These clinics will complete the job of transforming tuberculosis from a disgrace to a disease. When all that is possible is done by physicians and public health nurses to increase the number of parental consents for these tests, health education is able to further increase the number. One exception to this rule is in certain small towns where the consents are already 100%.

Except for the Metropolis it is hard to find one town of any considerable size in the Commonwealth that is not doing a rather good piece of tuberculin testing of its school children and the service extends to a majority of even the smallest towns.* It is to be hoped that this means of discovering tuberculosis and educating people against it, may be added to the other excellent health services that Boston renders to its school children.

Before leaving this topic, one illustration will be given of the way health education works to increase results in the tuberculin tests. In Newton in 1934 the local responsibility was promptly accepted and work vigorously done in grades 7, 9 and 11. But in 1935 more effort in health education was made and the per cent of those tested in the public schools rose from 53.8 to 64.2. Then in 1936-7, with a splendid effort in health education by the City Health Officer, Dr. Harold A. Chope, the per cent tested was again increased, this time from 64.2 to 78. In 1936-7, enough more were tested by private physicians and in the diagnostic clinic to bring this per cent to 84.7. The corresponding figure for parochial schools was 89.5 per cent.

This is the way it was done: (1) Pupils concerned through the science and hygiene teachers were asked to submit queries on tuberculosis. These were listed with answers as the first part of a ringbinder presented by the Health Officer to each one of these 56 teachers. Also in the ringbinder were seventeen tuberculosis pamphlets provided by the local tuberculosis agency. Among them was the new tuberculosis teach-

---

* In the season of 1935-6, 274 Massachusetts towns and cities with 143,430 pupils in grades 7, 9 and 11, were offered the test. 54% of them or 76,959 were given the tuberculin test.

ing unit prepared by Massachusetts tuberculosis workers and now being nationalized in its use. (2) The Massachusetts Tuberculosis League's sound projector and film "Behind the Shadows", were borrowed and a good talk was given by Dr. Chope before each presentation. At this time a demonstration of testing was usually performed on one of the teachers. (3) Dr. Chope addressed various civic and social clubs where parents of some of these children might be found. (4) Arranged for press notices. (5) Sent pamphlets to 24 ministers. (6) Distributed selectively in all, 14,750 pieces of appropriate printed matter including posters.

Loyalty to our devoted State Health Commissioner, who so well pioneered in work against childhood type tuberculosis, suggests that civic and health minded people of the Bay State may, with advantage, for a few years "put a shoulder to the wheel", accepting the opportunity to make tuberculin testing of school children increasingly effective. It is less expensive than the former system as it takes only the upper grades where more tuberculosis exists and it gives each child three tests if he continues through high school. Many can suggest changes but followers and helpers rather than additional leaders are really needed to make this health-department-approved plan increasingly effective. Its health education value is great. It offers everyone, who will, a chance to help in a sound health measure.

Massachusetts may well boast that the first college in the Union to establish health service for all its pupils was here in the Bay State, at Amherst. Let's get it straight from our leading authority on tuberculosis in colleges, Dr. Lee H. Ferguson, Director of Health Service, Western Reserve University:

"The first suggestion that more than gymnasium programs was needed came from President William A. Sterns, of Amherst, in 1856. Then in 1859, due to the death of two students in the senior class, the trustees of Amherst authorized the construction of a building which was the nucleus and beginning of a department known as Physical Education and Hygiene. The new program then contained:
1. Medical examination of each student.
2. Instruction in the hygienic way of life.
3. Regular prescribed physical exercise throughout the four year course.
4. Treatment of the sick.
5. Annual report of the workings of the plan, and particularly the kind and number of sicknesses from which the students suffered."

But the college health services of Massachusetts are as yet far from complete. Few are satisfied that they have attained the standards set by the Second Five Year Conference on College Hygiene in 1936. The report of this Conference, available through any tuberculosis association, shows that tuberculosis reduction and education along that line are but a small part of the college health service. Incidentally, the attendance from Massachusetts institutions of higher learning at this conference on College Hygiene in Washington, D. C., was most excellent.

Future leaders now being college trained should all have the advantage of some extra health service and health education. Besides reducing tuberculosis deaths, this is a rare opportunity to improve the health services of the State and Nation when such leaders assume responsibility.

Our hope through health education and more intensive use of present facilities for ultimate reduction of tuberculosis, rests on scientific grounds. This also is well stated in the words of Dr. Frost with whose quotation this article closes:

> "We need not assume, then, that tuberculosis is permanently and ineradicably engrafted upon our civilization. On the contrary, the evidence indicates that in this country the balance is already against the survival of the *tubercle bacillus;* and we may reasonably expect that the disease will eventually be eradicated. There can be no certainty of this result, but it is an expectation sufficiently well-grounded to justify shaping our tuberculosis control program toward this definite end."

PUBLIC HEALTH NURSES AS TEACHERS OF HEALTH

ANN W. DINEGAN, R.N.

Consultant in Public Health Nursing Education
Massachusetts Department of Public Health

It is generally accepted today that health teaching by the public health nurse is considered of first importance among her services. A closer analysis reveals that the emphasis has been rightly placed.

First of all, the public health nurse has an entree into every type and quality of home due to the bedside services which she renders continuously. This gives her an opportunity for health teaching such as no other public health worker has. She has a keen appreciation of the needs of the community for guidance and teaching in health matters because of her hospital experience which has brought her in close touch with those problems originating from ignorance of those measures which are for the prevention of disease and the protection of health.

In the early years of public health nursing the nurse was obliged to satisfy this need of the public with a minimum of scientific background. However, as the medical, sanitary and social sciences upon which public health is built have been advancing in knowledge, the public health nurse should realize more and more definitely the necessity for keeping up to date in her education. For only with sound, scientific information in mind can she provide adequate, factual background for her health teaching. She should also realize from her past experience that she must have a knowledge of the psychology of teaching because the possession of factual knowledge on her part without the ability to "put it across" to the individual in need of it is of no benefit.

Public health nurses vary considerably in their ability as teachers of health. However, it is generally true that as their actual knowledge of efficient and adequate measures for promoting and insuring better health enlarges, their interest and effort in this part of their program increases.

Since this is the case, it is in the interest of better health teaching to bring to the attention of public health nurses from time to time, especially to those in isolated nursing units, the newer developments in the field of public health. Let us consider a few suggestions as to how this may be accomplished.

In organizations employing a group of nurses a continuous educational program is generàlly arranged for the staff which serves to provide the needed stimulus to keep pace with the newer knowledge and avoid falling into a rut. It is a much more difficult problem in the case of the nurse working alone, although not a discouraging one.

First of all, the individual nurse herself must be convinced of the need and value of continuous education. She should then endeavor to convince her employing agency of its value in order that this agency will be interested in encouraging her in her efforts to advance her knowledge for the benefit of the community, even though it may necessitate a short leave of absence.

Since the function of the consultant public health nurses in the State Department of Health is to assist local nursing units in the development of their own work, the local nurse may well call upon them for help in developing an educative program to meet her needs.

If the nurse has not had sufficient basic training in public health nursing, it would seem wise for her to consider a course of this nature. This would serve to broaden her vision with regard to the possibilities in health teaching and undoubtedly open up many avenues of interest which she might follow alone later on when she returned to her community.

Even for those who cannot arrange to take a leave of absence there are possibilities of an in-service educative program. A definite time for this professional improvement should be set aside for the nurse each week during her working hours. The plan should be definitely explained to the employing agency as to the increased benefits to the community. Such a program might be planned to take up in turn, the teaching content of each of the services she is rendering, such as maternity, preschool, school, etc. This material may be obtained from reading the current professional journals, literature published by State and Federal authorities and up-to-date books on the particular subjects being considered. Since it is always more interesting to discuss material which one has read with others who are familiar with the same material, it might be possible in many instances for the state consultant nurse to arrange for neighboring nurses to plan a reading program on the same subjects. Plans could then be made for these nurses to meet periodically with the consultant as leader to discuss and pool the information obtained.

The program may be varied by substituting attendance at state and local professional meetings, when they are being held, for the time usually set aside for reading. Occasional group meetings may be arranged with a speaker invited to talk on the special topic being studied with discussion period following.

If a nurse is fortunate enough to be located near a center offering extension courses of interest to her, it would certainly be to her advantage to enroll in one of these courses and to consider this as her plan for continuous education.

We may feel assured that if each public health nurse realizes the importance of her services as a teacher of health and the benefits to be derived from a more adequate knowledge of public health on her part, we may hope for a striking improvement in the health of the community.

TRAINING OF PERSONNEL UNDER THE SOCIAL SECURITY ACT

Several years ago the President appointed a committee to consider ways and means of minimizing social insecurity. This committee was asked specifically to study the problem of insurance as a means of distributing the costs of medical care. The chairman of that committee, the late Dr. Edgar Sydenstricker, insisted that the committee also study the problem of disease prevention through accepted public health procedures. During the deliberations of the committee he succeeded in giving this program precedence over any efforts to distribute costs of sickness.

As a result, the Social Security Act of August 1935 appropriated $8,000,000 a year to assist states, counties, health districts and other political subdivisions in establishing and maintaining adequate public health services including the training of personnel. This fund is distributed among the states according to certain regulations of the Surgeon General of the United States Public Health Service. Generally speaking, these allotted funds are being used in the various states to strengthen state and local public health organizations and to extend the benefits of full time health services to many localities hitherto unable to finance them. In the first year of the Social Security Act, Surgeon General Parran has stated that about one hundred and twenty new health organizations were established. Deficiencies in state health organizations were made up in nineteen states. Thirty-three state health departments strengthened their local health administration. Eleven states added new units or sections for the promotion of industrial hygiene. And so on down the list until as a sort of climax we note that thirty-four states have started special measures for the control of syphilis.

In order to do all this new work it is quite obvious that additional health officers are necessary. In the haste to take advantage of these new opportunities it is necessary, as Dr. Parran says, to guard against two dangers: First is that of permitting partisan influence in appointing health officers and second that of employing untrained personnel.

Public health work is a specialty in medicine no less than in surgery, obstetrics, or pediatrics. All medical specialties are establishing standards so that the public can be assured that the person who alleges to be a specialist really is qualified. Public health specialists should therefore receive adequate training; medical men (or women) without this training are not qualified to be medical officers of health (as health officers are called in England). In the past, during the development of the field of public health from its early comparatively simple problems in environmental sanitation, to its present complexities, most of the work was done by enthusiastic broad-minded medical men, not specially trained for their work except by experience. These men laid the foundations and developed the science of public health. Now, it takes special training to take up the work from the point to which they have brought it.

Accordingly, about ten per cent of the federal allotment to each state is for the training of personnel for state and local public health work. Last year about twelve hundred people received some kind of training under this section of the Act. This includes not only those medical men enrolled for the long courses in public health at the Schools of Public Health of Johns Hopkins and Harvard Universities and at the other universities where graduate instruction in public health work is given throughout the academic year, but it also includes those taking short courses. Engineers, public health nurses, and other public health personnel are also included.

During the last academic year, 4 medical men, 1 engineer, 23 public health nurses, and 8 other public health personnel received training under the provisions of the Social Security Act in Massachusetts, at the Harvard School of Public Health, the Department of Sanitary Engineering of the School of Engineering, Simmons College, and at the Massachusetts Institute of Technology. A subsidy was also granted to the Harvard School of Public Health for training personnel in Child Hygiene. Altogether, the budget for training personnel in Massachusetts was about $30,000.

A similar amount has been allotted for the coming academic year. Three medical men, two engineers, at least five nurses, and four other public health personnel are to receive training at the same institutions to which students were sent last year.

The important change from last year's budget is that instead of subsidizing the Harvard School of Public Health for training in Child Hygiene (this is being provided for by another budget in 1938), the United States Public Health Service has financed the organization of a New England Training Center for the Control of Syphilis and Gonorrhea. This Training Center is being conducted by the Massachusetts Department of Public Health and the Harvard School of Public Health. Two types of training are to be given—the first for medical men who intend to devote their energies toward the development and administration of divisions for the control of syphilis and gonorrhea in the various state departments of public health, and the second for medical men (chiefly practitioners) who desire to take courses of instruction over a period of one or two months only, in order to enable them better to treat their patients. The former course covers the entire academic year.

These new courses are important departures from previous training methods. Instruction in the epidemiology, diagnosis and treatment of syphilis and gonorrhea has been very meager in the medical schools. Schools of public health have not emphasized the subject but have treated these diseases as they have the other communicable diseases. Now that syphilis is receiving public recognition that it is a great menace, and gonorrhea is being dragged along more or less unwillingly (so far as the syphilologists are concerned), it is realized that knowledge of how to cope with these diseases is largely in the hands of a few specialists. Hence the Regional Training Center.

Briefly, this Training Center gives the following instruction: Each morning during the academic year will be spent at a clinic. The syphilis, genito-urinary, and gonorrheal clinics of the Massachusetts General Hospital, Boston Dispensary, Boston City Hospital, and Lowell Board of Health, as well as the neurosyphilis clinic of the Boston Psychopathic Hospital, are the participating institutions. During the afternoons of the first semester, there will be daily lectures and conferences conducted by syphilologists and genito-urinary surgeons. Instruction during the afternoons of the second semester will be at the Wasserman Laboratory, the State Diagnostic Laboratory and in the Division of Genitoinfectious Diseases of the Massachusetts Department of Public Health. Opportunity will be given during this semester to elect certain courses in the Harvard School of Public Health in order that trainees after completion of such a year's work may qualify for a certificate in public health in the Control of Syphilis and Gonorrhea.

The shorter clinical courses are those Graduate Courses offered by the Harvard Medical School, with the addition of other instruction in epidemiology and control measures.

In addition to this training in the diagnosis and treatment of gonorrhea and syphilis there has also been allocated the sum of $4919.00 for the purpose of cooperating with the Massachusetts Medical Society in sending various specialists to the respective District Medical Societies to give lectures to practicing physicians. These lecturers receive small fees for their services to compensate them for the time away from their work.

This public health training is not only giving trained men to the various state and local health organizations, but it is also tending to maintain a high standard among the men selected to fill these responsible positions. The United States Public Health Service in administering the appropriation of $8,000,000 is showing great discernment in allotting ten per cent of the total appropriation to training personnel and in not permitting the deviation of the training personnel budget to other purposes.

ANNOUNCEMENT
To America's Schools — YOUR HEALTH!

Once more, during the coming fall, winter and spring, the Voices of Medicine will salute the people of America, with the toast "YOUR HEALTH". This is the well-known title of the radio program of the American Medical Association and the National Broadcasting Company. The coming season will be the fifth; the first two years were devoted to health talks, and the last two seasons to dramatized health messages. This year, the salutation will be addressed particularly to the teachers and students in the Junior and Senior high schools, in the hope that the program will be helpful in illustrating, amplifying, and enriching the health teaching in those schools. The program will be on the air while schools are in session, so that the program may be utilized directly in the thousands of schools which now have or soon will have radio and public address systems reaching the class-rooms. Programs will be announced in advance in HYGEIA, The Health Magazine. While the program is planned especially for high schools, it will not sacrifice the interest which it has held for listeners in the home. To teachers, students and stay-at-homes, the American Medical Association and the National Broadcasting Company will address their message of health education with the familiar musical theme HALE AND HEARTY, written especially for the program, and the toast, "To America's Schools, YOUR HEALTH!"

AMERICAN MEDICAL ASSOCIATION
Bureau of Health and Public Instruction

MISSISSIPPI VALLEY MEDICAL SOCIETY AWARD

The Mississippi Valley Medical Society offers a cash prize of $100.00, a gold medal and a certificate of award for the best unpublished essay on a subject of interest and practical value to the general practitioner of medicine. Entrants must be ethical licensed physicians, residents of the United States and graduates of approved medical schools. The winner will be invited to present his contribution before the next annual meeting of the Mississippi Valley Medical Society (September 28, 29, 30, 1938), the Society reserving the exclusive right to first publish the essay in its official publication—the Radiologic Review and Mississippi Valley Medical Journal. All contributions shall not exceed 5000 words, be typewritten in English in manuscript form, submitted in five copies, and must be received not later than May 15, 1938. Further details may be secured from

Harold Swanberg, M. D., Secretary,
Mississippi Valley Medical Society,
209-224 W. C. U. Building, Quincy, Ill.

LECTURE SERVICE

Massachusetts Department of Public Health,
546 State House, Boston, Mass.

The Department is glad to supply speakers for organizations or groups of people interested in public health. It does not charge a fee, but reserves the right to ask the local organization to assume travel expense of the speaker.

When requesting a speaker, please give the following information:
Town in which the talk is to be given.
Organization requesting the talk.
Date and hour of meeting. Give choice of dates if possible.
Name and location of place of meeting.
Subject desired, and any special problems you may wish discussed.
Information as to the probable size and character of the audience.

The following list of subjects may serve as a guide to groups desiring speakers.

Organization and Activities of the Department.
Communicable Diseases and Their Control.
Syphilis and Gonorrhea. Program of the Department for Their Control (Chiefly with professional groups).
Tuberculosis Prevention.
Adult Hygiene and Chronic Disease.
Cancer and the Program of the Department for Its Control.
Maternal, Infant, and Preschool Hygiene.
School Hygiene. To parents on the health of the school child; and to teachers, superintendents and school physicians on school health work, including health education.
Public Health Nursing.
Nutrition. Talks to parents, nurses, teachers, welfare workers, school lunch managers and children.
Dental Hygiene.
Health Education.
Publicity for Health Organizations.

MOTION PICTURE FILMS
16 m.m.

The Massachusetts Department of Public Health lends the following films, without charge, for use within the State.
They can be shown in any machine taking 16 m.m. films.
The Department does *not* lend a machine.
Please make reservations as far in advance as is possible, giving a choice of dates on which films could be used.

THE ABC OF FOOD (1 reel). This shows the basic facts of nutrition and their relation to health. For use with adults or high school groups.

FOOD AND GROWTH (1 reel). Shows the food value of milk as compared with tea or coffee by a feeding demonstration with white rats carried on in the classroom. For use with 6th or 7th grades.

A DRINK OF WATER — BREAD AND CEREALS — FRUIT AND VEGETABLES — MILK. These belong to the Good Food series and each are of ½ reel in length. Prepared for use with the first three grades.

FORMING HABITS OF HEALTH (1 reel). This is of value in teaching health habits to junior and senior high school girls. Especially good for 4-H Club groups. Does not appeal to boys.

A HEALTHY CHILD (1 reel). Illustrates all activities in a normal child's life, stressing periodical medical and dental examinations, correct posture, proper food, wholesome exercise, care of the teeth, etc. Valuable in work with junior and senior high schools, 4-H Clubs, Girl Scouts and similar organizations.

ASK YOUR DENTIST (1 reel). An excellent film for children in the 4th grade through the senior high school and of interest to many adults.

CARE OF THE TEETH (1 reel). Shows the parts of the tooth, prophylactic treatment, progress of decay, and rules for home care. For use with grades 5 and up.

HOW TEETH GROW (1 reel). Shows the growth, development and arrangement of the teeth, the different kinds and parts, and their use. For use with grades 6 and up, and at meetings of Parent-Teacher Associations and Mothers' Clubs.

POSTURE (1 reel). Takes in the sitting and standing posture, emphasizing the value of good posture. Prepared for use with grades 5 and up.

FEET (1 reel). Shows the structure of the foot, its use, proper shoes, and common foot defects. Prepared for use with grades 5 and up.

BATHING — CLEAN CLOTHES — CLEAN FACE AND HANDS — KEEPING THE HAIR CLEAN. These are each ½ reel in length, and are part of the Cleanliness series. Intended for use with the first three grades.

HOME NURSING (3 reels). Three reels in this series; one showing the bed bath, and the other two the routine and special procedures for the home care of the sick. For use with home nursing classes or with mothers' clubs.

NURSING (2 reels). This shows the work of the student nurse and the methods used in her professional training, as well as the fields open to her upon graduation.

DIPHTHERIA (1 reel). Shows the nature of diphtheria and methods for its control. Intended for use with grades 6 and up. Can be used with adults.

TUBERCULOSIS AND HOW IT MAY BE AVOIDED (1 reel). Shows tubercle bacilli growing in the laboratory and in the lung tissue of the human body. Daily routine at preventorium is pictured. For high school or adult use.

THE BLOOD (1 reel). Illustrates the separation of plasma from blood cells, protein and salts from plasma, staining cells, counting red blood corpuscles, how white blood cells reach the body tissue, clotting of blood. For high school use.

BREATHING (1 reel). Excellent scenes and animations stress the importance of good lungs and explain the action of the diaphragm, breathing, lung structure and function. For high school classes.

CIRCULATION (1 reel). Animations and photography trace the human circulatory system, compare the human heart with that of a frog, show the cycle of pulmonary circulation. For high school classes.

CIRCULATORY CONTROL (1 reel). Illustrates the pressure of blood in the arteries, methods of measuring blood pressure, the structure and work of the veins, and nature's method of vasomotor control. For high school use.

DIGESTION (1 reel). Covers the complete digestive tract, action of saliva upon food, swallowing, stomach structure, digestion of food, structure and action of both intestines. For high school use.

THE LIVING CELL (1 reel). Pictures the division and growth of single celled organisms; yeast, amoeba, paramecium; many celled organisms; hydra and flatworm, tissue cells; and cell division. For high school classes.

THE SKIN (1 reel). Shows structure and method of growth of human skin and explains sensation of touch, secretion of sweat, growth of hair and nails, and illustrates proper care of the skin. For high school use.

October 1937

REPORT OF DIVISION OF FOOD AND DRUGS

During the months of April, May and June 1937, samples were collected in 248 cities and towns.

There were 2,458 samples of milk examined, of which 384 were below standard, from 19 samples the cream had been in part removed, 11 samples contained added water, and 1 sample was skimmed milk not so labeled. There were 2,097 bacteriological examinations made of milk, 1,551 of which complied with the requirements. There were 21 bacteriological examinations made of pasteurized cream, 9 of which did not comply with the requirements; 179 bacteriological examinations of ice cream, 21 of which did not comply with the requirements; 7 bacteriological examinations of hamburg steak, 6 of which did not comply with the requirements; 4 bacteriological examinations of empty bottles, all of which did not comply with the requirements; 16 bacteriological examinations of meat products, 10 of which did not comply with the requirements; 17 bacteriological examinations of mattress fillings, 4 of which did not comply with the requirements; 2 bacteriological examinations of canned salmon, 2 bacteriological examinations of wash water, 2 bacteriological examinations of chocolate milk, and 1 bacteriological examination of orangeade, all of which complied with the requirements.

There were 632 samples of food examined, 62 of which were adulterated. These consisted of 2 samples of maple syrup which contained cane sugar; 1 sample of orange soda which contained benzoate not so labeled; 2 samples of sweet gherkins, 1 sample of which contained saccharin, and 1 sample contained a compound of benzoic acid not so labeled; 1 sample of olive oil which contained cottonseed oil; 2 samples of butter which were rancid; 1 sample of stale eggs sold as fresh; 12 samples of sausage, 6 of which contained a compound of sulphur dioxide not properly labeled, 5 samples were decomposed, and 1 sample contained sodium sulphite in excess of one tenth of one per cent; 21 samples of hamburg steak, 3 of which contained a compound of sulphur dioxide not properly labeled, 15 samples were decomposed, and 3 samples contained sodium sulphite in excess of one tenth of one per cent; 1 sample of mock chicken legs which was decomposed; 9 samples of wash water which were deficient in caustic alkili; and 8 samples of mattress fillings, 5 of which were labeled "Down" and did not contain the required amount of down, and 3 samples contained second-hand material. The Sharon Board of Health submitted 2 samples of canned salmon, the material in which was not sterile and there was some evidence of decomposition.

There were 55 samples of drugs examined, of which 3 were adulterated. These consisted of 2 samples of spirit of nitrous ether which did not conform to the requirements of the U. S. Pharmacopoeia, and 1 sample of argyrol which did not conform to the professed standard under which it was sold.

The police departments submitted 160 samples of liquor for examination. The police departments also submitted 14 samples to be analyzed for poisons or drugs, of which 9 contained cannabis, 4 contained heroin, and 1 sample contained a derivative of morphine.

There were inspected 437 plants operated for the pasteurization of milk; 24 ice cream plants; 4 bakeries; 133 restaurants; 97 soft drink plants; and 303 mattress establishments.

There were 79 hearings held pertaining to violations of the laws. There were 86 convictions for violations of the law, $1,755. in fines being imposed.

Francis P. McMahon, 2 cases, of Lowell; and David Asadorian of Haverhill, were convicted for violations of the milk laws.

Morris Goldman of Chelsea; Myron Frates of New Bedford; and Joseph A. Jalbert of Southbridge, were convicted for violations of the pasteurization law and regulations.

John B. Campbell and Joseph A. Rogers of Haverhill; William Dufresne of Granby; Hugh Rodden of Salem; and Myron Frates of New Bedford, were all convicted for violations of the milk grading regulations.

Abraham Andelman, 2 cases, Carl's Market, Incorporated, 2 cases, Jacob G. Banks, 2 cases, and Harry Lydeotes, all of Cambridge; Henry Beach of North Attleboro; John F. Ruggieri and Pasquale Pecione of Somerville; George F. Bond and Venanzio D'Aurora of Marlboro; Cudahy Packing Company of Worcester; Adam Sichol of Southbridge; Red Star Beverage Company, 2 cases, of East Boston; Folsom's Market, Incorporated, 2 cases, of Roxbury; Paul Booras and Charles Dubrow of Lynn; Ludwig Routhos, Hyman Bernstein, The Oscar Spitzler Company, Incorporated, Fernando Paradis, W. A. Barsalon, Mohican Market, Incorporated, Frank Sigda, 2 cases, and John Moskal, all of Holyoke; Benjamin Gold of Malden; Nathan Winer of Springfield; Samuel Gordon and New Bedford Public Market, Incorporated, of New Bedford; Jacob Hurovitz, Steve Girdis, and Arthur Podgur of Boston; People's Public Market, Incorporated, of Fall River; Powow River Meat Market, Incorporated, 2 cases, of Amesbury; Morris Spector, Waltham Provision Company, Incorporated, 2 cases, and White Star Foods, Incorporated, 2 cases, of Waltham; and White Star Foods, Incorporated, Jacob Chrusciel and Norwood Market, Incorporated, 2 cases, of Everett, were all convicted for violations of the food laws. Henry Beach of North Attleboro; Nathan Winer of Springfield; Samuel Gordon of New Bedford; Powow River Meat Market, Incorporated, 1 case, of Amesbury; and Norwood Market, Incorporated, 2 cases, of Everett, all appealed their cases.

Joseph Sears of Rockport; Jacob Chruschiel of Everett; Red Star Beverage Company, 2 cases, of East Boston; and Paul Booras of Lynn, were convicted for misbranding.

Sam Janopolis of Provincetown was convicted for false advertising.

Boston Baking Company, 2 cases, and Sadie Nagel of Roxbury; and Samuel Rothblatt, 2 cases, of Salem, were convicted for violations of the bakery law and regulations. Samuel Rothblatt, 2 cases of Salem, appealed his cases.

John Borowicz, 2 cases, of New Bedford; Tip Top Beverage, Incorporated, of Springfield; John Argeros of Peabody; and Samuel Kanter of Beverly, were all convicted for violations of the law and regulations relative to the manufacture and bottling of carbonated non-alcoholic beverages. Samuel Kanter of Beverly appealed his case.

Whitman Dairy, Incorporated, of Pittsfield; and Aniello Coppa of Providence, Rhode Island, were convicted for violations of the frozen dessert law.

Liggett Drug Company, Incorporated, and Joseph Oppenheim of Boston; Liggett Drug Company, Incorporated, of Worcester; and Old Elm Drug, Incorporated, of Roxbury, were all convicted for violations of the drug law.

Emil Bellerose and Joseph P. Power of Southbridge were convicted for violations of the slaughtering law and regulations.

Bay State Upholstering Company, Incorporated, of Hyde Park; Charles J. Ehrlich, Incorporated, of Brockton; and Suffolk Upholstering & Mattress Company of Lynn, were all convicted for violations of the mattress law.

In accordance with Section 25, Chapter 111 of the General Laws, the following is the list of articles of adulterated food collected in original packages from manufacturers, wholesalers, or producers:

Sausage which was decomposed was obtained as follows:

One sample each, from Tilman's Market of Springfield; Jacob G. Banks (Banks Market) and Abraham Andelman (Everybody's Market) of Cambridge; Hyman Arrick of Chelsea; and Mohican Market of Holyoke.

Sausage which contained a compound of sulphur dioxide not properly labeled was obtained as follows:

One sample each, from W. A. Barsalon of Holyoke; Growers Outlet of Springfield; and Solin's Market, Incorporated, of Chicopee.

One sample of sausage which contained sodium sulphite in excess of one tenth of one per cent was obtained from Third Street Market of Leominster.

Hamburg steak which was decomposed was obtained as follows:

One sample each, from Brighton Public Market and Jacob Saievitz of Chelsea; Bernard L. Kolovson, Economy Grocery Stores, Incorporated, and Folsom's Market, Incorporated, of Boston; Pasquale Pescione, John F. Ruggieri, and Abraham House of Somerville; Estate of Felix Klys, and Adam Sichol of Southbridge; Banks Food Centre and Abraham Andelman (Everybody's Market) of Cambridge; Oscar Spitzler, Incorporated (Popular Food Market) and Globe Market (John Moscal) of Holyoke; and Malden Square Market of Malden.

Hamburg steak which contained a compound of sulphur dioxide not properly labeled was obtained as follows:

One sample each, from Fernando Paradis and Hyman Bernstein of Holyoke; and Ralph Mesnick of Chelsea.

Hamburg steak which contained sodium sulphite in excess of one tenth of one per cent was obtained as follows:

One sample each from Abram J. Cohen and Eugene LaJeunesse of New Bedford; and Isadore Waxler of Holyoke.

Two samples of butter which were rancid were obtained from Folsom's Market, Incorporated, of Roxbury.

One sample of maple syrup which contained mostly cane sugar syrup was obtained from Sam Janopolis of Provincetown.

One sample of olive oil which contained cottonseed oil was obtained from Cosmos Food Stores, Incorporated, of Lynn.

One sample of orange soda which contained benzoate was obtained from Cape Ann Fruit Company of Gloucester.

Soft drink wash water which was deficient in caustic alkali was obtained as follows:

One sample each from Lawrence Beverage Company, Incorporated, and Annie Boumila of Methuen.

There were twenty-four confiscations, consisting of 4 pounds of decomposed beef, 55 pounds of decomposed chopped beef; 1 pound of decomposed hamburg; 5½ pounds of decomposed hamburg; 894 pounds of decomposed beef backs; 1000 pounds of decomposed beef rattles; 848 pounds of decomposed beef tongues; 2,827 pounds of decomposed beef rumps and loins; 3,106 pounds of decomposed beef rounds and flanks; 32 pounds of decomposed hamburg steak; 16 pounds of decomposed veal; 25 pounds of decomposed lamb; 1½ pounds of decomposed kidneys; 45 pounds of decomposed sausage meat; 7 pounds of decomposed pork sausage; one pound of decomposed frankforts; 6 pounds of decomposed tomato sausage; 1060 pounds of decomposed lemon sole; 493 pounds of decomposed smoked bloaters; 4200 pounds of decomposed squid; and 14 spoiled oysters in the shell.

The licensed cold storage warehouses reported the following amounts of food placed in storage during March, 1937:—957,570 dozens of case eggs; 1,139,956 pounds of broken out eggs; 317,331 pounds of butter; 2,157,902 pounds of poultry; 2,997,755 pounds of fresh meat and fresh meat products; and 5,674,925 pounds of fresh food fish.

There was on hand April 1, 1937:—2,153,280 dozens of case eggs, 1,231,982 pounds of broken out eggs; 303,239 pounds of butter, 8,355,375 pounds of poultry; 13,081,549 pounds of fresh meat and fresh meat products; and 20,791,567 pounds of fresh food fish.

The licensed cold storage warehouses reported the following amounts of food placed in storage during April, 1937:— 2,257,860 dozens of case eggs; 1,224,397 pounds of broken out eggs; 206,065 pounds of butter, 1,693,255 pounds of poultry; 3,183,826 pounds of fresh meat and fresh meat products; and 4,855,402 pounds of fresh food fish.

There was on hand May 1, 1937:—4,296,180 dozens of case eggs; 1,543,904 pounds of broken out eggs; 209,520 pounds of butter; 6,273,403 pounds of poultry; 12,280,984 pounds of fresh meat and fresh meat products; and 17,466,123 pounds of fresh food fish.

The licensed cold storage warehouses reported the following amounts of food placed in storage during May, 1937:—2,409,060 dozens of case eggs; 2,342,352 pounds of broken out eggs; 853,314 pounds of butter; 2,289,781 pounds of poultry; 3,103,276 pounds of fresh meat and fresh meat products; and 15,329,743 pounds of fresh food fish.

There was on hand June 1, 1937:—4,855,050 dozens of case eggs 2,916,078 pounds of broken out eggs; 854,624 pounds of butter; 5,626,780 pounds of poultry; 9,594,747 pounds of fresh meat and fresh meat products; and 20,204,809 pounds of fresh food fish.

MASSACHUSETTS DEPARTMENT OF PUBLIC HEALTH

Commissioner of Public Health, HENRY D. CHADWICK, M.D.

Public Health Council

HENRY D. CHADWICK, M.D., *Chairman*

GEORGE D. DALTON, M.D.
FRANCIS H. LALLY, M.D.
CHARLES F. LYNCH, M.D.

RICHARD M. SMITH, M.D.
RICHARD P. STRONG, M.D.
JAMES L. TIGHE

Secretary, FLORENCE L. WALL

Division of Administration . . Under direction of Commissioner
Dvision of Sanitary Engineering . Director and Chief Engineer,
    ARTHUR D. WESTON, C.E.
Division of Communicable Diseases Director,
    GAYLORD W. ANDERSON, M.D.
Division of Biologic Laboratories . Director and Pathologist,
    ELLIOTT S. ROBINSON, M.D.
Division of Food and Drugs . . Director and Analyst,
    HERMANN C. LYTHGOE, S.B.
Division of Child Hygiene . . Director, M. LUISE DIEZ, M.D.
Division of Tuberculosis . . . Director, ALTON S. POPE, M.D.
Division of Adult Hygiene . . Director,
    HERBERT L. LOMBARD, M.D.
Division of Genitoinfectious Diseases Director, NELS A. NELSON, M.D.

State District Health Officers

The Southeastern District . . RICHARD P. MACKNIGHT, M.D., New Bedford
The South Metropolitan District . HENRY M. DE WOLFE, M.D., Quincy
The North Metropolitan District . CHARLES E. GILL, M.D., Boston
The Northeastern District . . ROBERT E. ARCHIBALD, M.D., Melrose
The Worcester County District . OSCAR A. DUDLEY, M.D., Worcester
The Connecticut Valley District . JOHN J. POUTAS, M.D., Springfield.
The Franklin County District . . WALTER W. LEE, M.D., No. Adams
The Berkshire County District . HAROLD W. STEVENS, M.D., Great Barrington.

PUBLICATION OF THIS DOCUMENT APPROVED BY THE COMMISSION ON ADMINISTRATION AND FINANCE
11,500. 11-'37. Order 2215.

THE COMMONHEALTH

Volume 24   Oct.-Nov.-Dec.
No. 4   1937

HANDBOOK

FOR

PHYSICIANS

MASSACHUSETTS
DEPARTMENT OF PUBLIC HEALTH

MASSACHUSETTS DEPARTMENT OF PUBLIC HEALTH

Commissioner of Public Health, HENRY D. CHADWICK, M.D.

Public Health Council

HENRY D. CHADWICK, M.D., *Chairman*

GEORGE D. DALTON, M.D.	RICHARD M. SMITH, M.D.
FRANCIS H. LALLY, M.D.	RICHARD P. STRONG, M.D.
CHARLES F. LYNCH, M.D.	JAMES L. TIGHE

Secretary, FLORENCE L. WALL

Division of Administration	Under direction of Commissioner.
Division of Adult Hygiene	Director, HERBERT L. LOMBARD, M.D.
Division of Biologic Laboratories	Director and Pathologist, ELLIOTT S. ROBINSON, M.D.
Division of Child Hygiene	Director, M. LUISE DIEZ, M.D.
Division of Communicable Diseases	Director, ROY F. FEEMSTER, M.D.
Division of Food and Drugs	Director and Analyst, HERMANN C. LYTHGOE, S.B.
Division of Genitoinfectious Diseases	Director, NELS A. NELSON, M.D.
Division of Sanitary Engineering	Director and Chief Engineer, ARTHUR D. WESTON, C.E.
Division of Tuberculosis	Director, ALTON S. POPE, M.D.

State District Health Officers

The Southeastern District	RICHARD P. MACKNIGHT, M.D., New Bedford.
The South Metro District	HENRY M. DEWOLFE, M.D., Braintree.
The North Metropolitan District	CHARLES E. GILL, M.D., Boston.
The Northeastern District	ROBERT E. ARCHIBALD, M.D., Melrose
The Worcester County District	OSCAR A. DUDLEY, M.D., Worcester.
The Connecticut Valley District	JOHN J. POUTAS, M.D., Westfield.
The Franklin County District	WALTER W. LEE, M.D., Greenfield.
The Berkshire County Health District	HAROLD W. STEVENS, M.D., Great Barrington.

THE COMMONHEALTH

QUARTERLY BULLETIN OF THE MASSACHUSETTS DEPARTMENT OF PUBLIC HEALTH

Sent Free to any Citizen of the State

Entered as second class matter at Boston Postoffice.

M. LUISE DIEZ, M.D., DIRECTOR OF DIVISION OF CHILD HYGIENE, EDITOR.
1 Beacon Street, Boston, Mass.

CONTENTS

	PAGE
FOREWORD	232
COMMUNICABLE DISEASES	233
General Information	233
Reporting	233
Quarantine Requirements	234
Diagnostic Laboratories	236
Hospitalization	237
Popular Pamphlets	238
SPECIFIC DISEASES	239
Anterior Poliomyelitis	239
Chicken Pox	242
Diphtheria	242
Dog Bite	244
Dysentery (Amebic)	245
Dysentery (Bacillary)	246
German Measles	247
Gonorrhea	247
Malaria	247
Measles	247
Meningitis (Meningococcus Meningitis)	248
Meningitis (Pfeiffer Bacillus)	250
Mumps	251
Ophthalmia Neonatorum	251
Paratyphoid Fever	252
Pneumonia	252
Rabies	255
Scarlet Fever	255
Septic Sore Throat	256
Smallpox	256
Syphilis	257
Tetanus	257
Tuberculosis	257
Typhoid Fever	266
Typhus Fever	268
Undulant Fever	268
Whooping Cough	268
GONORRHEA AND SYPHILIS	269
Reporting	269
Syphilis	270
Gonorrhea	272
ARTHRITIS	279
BIOLOGICAL PRODUCTS	279
Regulations for Distribution of	280
Sensitivity	281
CANCER	284
Hospitalization	284
Tumor Diagnostic Service	285
Research	285
Clinics	285
Education	287

	PAGE
CHILD HYGIENE	287
Prenatal Letters	287
Postnatal Letters	288
Educational Material	288
Obstetric Package	289
Premature Infant Care	289
Postgraduate Instruction	289
CRIPPLED CHILDREN, SERVICES TO	289
BLIND AND CONSERVATION OF VISION	290
Institutions	291
DEAF AND HARD OF HEARING	291
INDUSTRIAL DISEASES	291
MENTAL DISEASES	292
Diagnosis	292
General Out-Patient Clinics	292
Child Guidance and Adjustment Clinics	292
Habit Clinics	294
Mental and Mental Hygiene Clinics	295
Feeblemindedness Clinics	296
Treatment	296
Insane Persons	296
Epileptics	299
Dipsomaniacs, Inebriates, and Drug Ad'	300
Feeblemin(	301
PUBLIC WEL.	303
Institutions	303
VITAL STATISTICS	304
Births	304
Deaths	305
AMERICAN PHYSICIANS' ART ASSOCIATION ANNOUNCEMENT	307
REPORT OF DIVISION OF FOOD AND DRUGS for July, August, September, 1937	308
INDEX TO "HANDBOOK FOR PHYSICIANS"	311
INDEX TO VOL 24—Nos 1-4, inc.	321

FOREWORD

HENRY D. CHADWICK, M.D.
Commissioner of Public Health

The purpose of this issue of The Commonhealth is to assist the physicians of Massachusetts toward the more effective utilization of certain of the community resources that are at their disposal. So many and so varied are the services that the physician may command to aid him in the proper care of his patient, that it has seemed suitable that the Department should attempt in this way to classify some of these aids and indicate how they may be utilized to the fullest advantage. There have been included in this booklet only those that have a particular bearing upon the public health, purposely omitting many that have but an individual importance.

This handbook was first issued two years ago. To be most useful it must necessarily be revised from time to time. Many changes will be found in this revision, some due to modifications in policy or procedure, others resulting from helpful suggestions by those who have been making use of the information here assembled. Comments, criticisms and suggestions for improvements in future revisions are solicited.

COMMUNICABLE DISEASES
GENERAL INFORMATION

REPORTING: The following diseases are reportable in Massachusetts:

Diseases Declared by the Department of Public Health of Massachusetts to be Dangerous to the Public Health and Reportable Under Provisions of Sections 6, 7, 109, 111 and 112 of Chapter 111 of the General Laws:—

Actinomycosis
Anterior Poliomyelitis
  a. Paralytic
  b. Nonparalytic (preparalytic)
Anthrax
Asiatic Cholera
Chicken Pox
Cholecystitis of Typhoid Origin
Diphtheria
Dog-bite

Dysentery:—
  a. Amebic
  b. Bacillary
Encephalitis Lethargica
German Measles
Glanders
Gonorrhea
Hookworm Disease

Infectious diseases of the eye:—
  a. Ophthalmia Neonatorum
  b. Suppurative Conjunctivitis
  c. Trachoma
Leprosy

Lobar Pneumonia
Malaria
Measles
Meningitis:—
  a. Meningococcus Meningitis
  b. Pfeiffer Bacillus Meningitis

Mumps
Paratyphoid Fever A
Paratyphoid Fever B
Pellagra
Plague
Rabies
Scarlet Fever
Septic Sore Throat
Smallpox
Syphilis
Tetanus
Trichinosis
Tuberculosis (all forms)
Typhoid Fever
Typhus Fever
Undulant Fever
Whooping Cough
Yellow Fever

All reports except of gonorrhea and syphilis should be made to the board of health of the community of residence. Telephone reports should be confirmed in writing. Cards for such reports can be obtained from most boards of health. Gonorrhea and syphilis should be reported directly to the State Department of Public Health, 545 State House, Boston, using special forms obtainable from the Department. (See under these diseases for details of reporting, p. 269.)

ISOLATION AND QUARANTINE

Each city and town determines its own quarantine requirements. In case of doubt inquire of the board of health of the town in which the patient lives. The physican is not entitled to modify these requirements. The requirements recommended by the State Department of Public Health, which are shown in an accompanying table, represent general practice throughout Massachusetts, though minor details may differ in certain communities.

Quarantine Requirements
RECOMMENDED BY THE MASSACHUSETTS DEPARTMENT OF PUBLIC HEALTH

DISEASE	MINIMUM PERIOD OF ISOLATION OF PATIENT	CONTROL OF CONTACTS			PLACARD
		ADULTS	IMMUNE CHILDREN	CHILDREN NOT IMMUNE	
Anterior Poliomyelitis (Infantile Paralysis)	Two weeks from onset of disease, and thereafter until acute symptoms have subsided.	Note 1.	Until two weeks have elapsed from date of last exposure.	Until two weeks have elapsed from date of last exposure.	Yes.
Chicken Pox	One week from appearance of eruption and thereafter until all crusts have disappeared.	No restrictions.	No restrictions.	No restrictions.	No.
Diphtheria	One week from date of onset and thereafter until 2 successive negative cultures, taken at least 24 hours apart, from both nose and throat, have been obtained.	No restrictions save Notes 1 and 2.	If immune as shown by a Schick test or on the basis of a previous attack of the disease, may return to school provided they live away from home, or case is hospitalized, and if two consecutive negative nose and throat cultures taken at an interval of not less than 24 hours have been obtained.	Until one week has elapsed from date of last exposure and until 2 negative nose and throat cultures taken at an interval of not less than 24 hours have been obtained.	Yes.
German Measles	One week from appearance of rash.	No restrictions.	No restrictions.	No restrictions.	No.
Measles	One week from appearance of rash.	No restrictions save non-immune school teachers. These handled as non-immune children.	No restrictions. (Note 3)	Exclusion from school for 16 days from date of last exposure.	No.
Meningococcus Meningitis (Cerebro-Spinal Fever)	Two weeks from onset of disease, and thereafter until all acute symptoms have subsided.	Note 1.	Until ten days from date of last exposure.	Until ten days from date of last exposure.	Yes.
Mumps	One week from onset of disease, and thereafter until all swelling of salivary glands has disappeared.	No restrictions.	No restrictions.	No restrictions.	No.

Recommended Quarantine Requirements—Continued

	Minimum Period of Isolation of Patient	No restrictions save in certain occupations. (Notes 1 and 2)	No restrictions if away from home. (Note 3)
Scarlet Fever	See page 256 for Minimum Period of Isolation of Patient.		Unless child lives away from home one week and continues to live away from home, cannot re-enter school. Yes.
Smallpox	Three weeks from onset of disease and thereafter until all crusts have disappeared and skin has healed.	Note 4.	Note 4. Yes.
Typhoid Fever	One week after subsidence of clinical symptoms and thereafter until three successive negative stool and urine cultures, secured at an interval of at least one week, have been obtained, provided that a person who continues to be a carrier may be released under supervision of and after special permission by the Board of Health.	No restrictions save for food handlers. (Note 5)	No restrictions. No.
Whooping Cough	Three weeks from beginning of spasmodic cough.	No restrictions.	No restrictions. (Note 8) Exclusion from school two weeks from last exposure. No.

NOTES

1. School teachers shall be subject to the same restrictions as school children. Food handlers and others whose occupation brings them in contact with children have no restriction if they live away from home.

2. Food handlers living in a family in which a case of diphtheria or scarlet fever exists shall be subject to the same restrictions as children.

3. A child shall be considered as having had the disease if so shown by the records of the Board of Health or if by a sworn statement from the parent or guardian that the child has had the disease elsewhere.

4. Contacts shall be quarantined until three weeks have elapsed from the date of last exposure unless immunized by a previous attack, by a recent successful vaccination, or showing the immunity reaction.

5. Food handlers living in a family in which a case of typhoid fever exists shall be excluded from their occupation so long as they continue to live in the same house in which the case exists.

DIAGNOSTIC LABORATORIES

Bacteriological Laboratory: The State Department of Public Health maintains a Bacteriological Diagnostic Laboratory at 527 State House, Boston, (Telephone, Capitol 4600; Sundays and holidays, Capitol 4665). Containers for shipment of specimens to the laboratory may be obtained through local board of health. Directions for collecting and shipping the specimens are inside the container and should be followed carefully for best results. Specimens are accepted only from physicians, dentists, hospitals and recognized health agencies. All positive diagnostic diphtheria cultures, positive diagnostic Widals or typhoid cultures, positive pneumonia sputa for which therapeutic serum is available, positive meningococcus reports and positive gonorrheal eye smears are reported by telephone or telegraph at State expense. All other reports are made by mail. No charges are ever made for laboratory examinations. No chemical examinations are made. The following bacteriological examinations are made:

Anthrax cultures
Diphtheria cultures
Dysentery: amebic

Dysentery, bacillary:
  agglutination
  cultures
Gonorrhea smears
Malaria smears

Meningitis — spinal fluid for:
  Meningococci
  Pfeiffer's (influenza) bacillus
  Pneumococci
  Streptococci
  Tubercle bacilli

Pneumonia:
  blood cultures
  typing

Streptococcus cultures

Tuberculosis:
  fluids for guinea pig inoculation
  sputum examination

Typhoid:
  cultures
  Widal reaction

Typhus:
  Weil-Felix reaction

Undulant fever:
  agglutination
  cultures

Vincent's Angina smears

Wassermann Laboratory: This laboratory, located in the Harvard Medical School, 25 Shattuck Street, Boston (Telephone, Longwood 2380), is maintained by the State Department of Public Health. Specimens are accepted only from physicians, dentists, hospitals and recognized health agencies. Special containers for blood samples should be obtained directly from the laboratory or through the local board of health. The following specimens are examined in this laboratory:

Blood for Hinton test
Spinal fluid for Wassermann reaction
Spinal fluid for gold sol test (see page 271)
Blood for gonococcus complement fixation reaction
Animal heads for rabies
Pathological specimens submitted to State Division of Livestock Disease Control

Local Diagnostic Laboratories are maintained by boards of health in some communities. Not all the above examinations are done in each laboratory. When sending specimens to these laboratories, the special outfits furnished by them should be used. Local laboratories are maintained by the following cities and towns:

Arlington	Town Hall
Ayer	Community Hospital
Boston	City Hall
Brockton	City Hall
Brookline	Town Hall
Cambridge	City Hall
Chicopee	City Hall
Clinton	Municipal Building, Church Street
Dedham	Board of Health
Fall River	City Hall
Fitchburg	City Hall
Framingham	Town Hall
Gardner	City Hall (Room 9)
Great Barrington	Fairview Hospital
Haverhill	471 Main Street
Holyoke	City Hall
Lawrence	City Hall (Room 309)
Leominster	Leominster Hospital
Lowell	Clinic Building, Kirk and Paige Streets
Lynn	City Hall
Needham	Town Hall
New Bedford	401 Municipal Building
Newton	City Hall
Pittsfield	City Hall
Somerville	City Hall
Springfield	City Hall
Waltham	781 Main Street
Wellesley	Town Hall
Worcester	City Hall

HOSPITALIZATION

The Board of Health may, if it sees fit, order hospitalization of any case of communicable disease. Before hospitalizing any case the physician should consult with the local board of health, in order to avoid subsequent misunderstandings as to hospital charges. Care of cases of communicable diseases may be obtained in the following hospitals:

Attleboro	Sturdy Memorial Hospital
Boston	Boston City Hospital (South Dept.)
Boston	Children's Hospital
Boston	Massachusetts Memorial Hospitals
Brookline	Board of Health Hospital
Fall River	Fall River General Hospital
Fitchburg	Fitchburg Isolation Hospital
Gardner	David Parker Municipal Hospital
Greenfield	Franklin County Public Hospital
Haverhill	Haverhill Contagious Hospital

Lawrence	Lawrence General Hospital
Lowell	Lowell Isolation Hospital
Lynn	Lynn Health Department Hospital
Malden	Malden Contagious Hospital
New Bedford	New Bedford Isolation Hospital
Northampton	Cooley Dickinson Hospital
Pittsfield	Sampson Memorial Hospital
Plymouth	Jordan Hospital
Pocasset	Barnstable County Infirmary
Salem	Health Department Hospital for Contagious Disease
Somerville	Somerville Contagious Disease Hospital
Springfield	Health Department Hospital
Vineyard Haven	United States Marine Hospital *
Waltham	Waltham Hospital
Worcester	Belmont Hospital

* Principally from the Marine Service, but occasionally local cases have gone there in emergency.

In addition to these hospitals, many general hospitals accept cases of typhoid, infantile paralysis, and meningococcus meningitis.

BIOLOGIC PRODUCTS

Biologic products for aid in the diagnosis, prevention and treatment of communicable diseases are manufactured and distributed free of charge by the State Department of Public Health. (See page 279.)

POPULAR PAMPHLETS

Available through Department of Public Health, 546 State House, Boston
Popular pamphlets are available on the following subjects:

    Diphtheria   Rabies
    Infantile Paralysis   Vaccination
    Measles   Whooping Cough

(See page 288 for list of pamphlets on child hygiene and page 273 for list of pamphlets on gonorrhea and syphilis.)

SPECIFIC DISEASES

ANTERIOR POLIOMYELITIS
(Infantile Paralysis)

DIAGNOSIS

Preparalytic Cases: Based on clinical findings, supplemented by lumbar puncture and spinal fluid examination. Under special circumstances, Department of Public Health will furnish consultant diagnostic service but only upon request of attending physician, where family is unable to afford a private consultant. Requests for such assistance should be made directly to Department, Telephone, Capitol 4600. During July, August and September, night and weekend requests may be made through Kenmore 8100.

Paralytic Cases: Based on clinical findings. Special consultation service is not furnished by Department in such cases.

TREATMENT

Preparalytic Cases: Symptomatic and supportive. (The Department no longer distributes convalescent serum because no good evidence of its usefulness has been obtained. Physicians of this State had almost entirely ceased using it before the distribution was discontinued.)

Paralytic Cases: During acute stages—symptomatic and supportive with special reference to prevention of contractures. Advice in regard to orthopedic treatment to accomplish this end can be obtained through the Services for Crippled Children by applying directly to the Department. In cases of respiratory paralysis, placing patient in a respirator may be of life-saving value. Respirators are located in the following hospitals:

		Number of Respirators
Beverly	Beverly Hospital	2
Boston	Beth Israel Hospital	1
Boston	Boston City Hospital	5
Boston	Children's Hospital	6
Boston	Massachusetts General Hospital	5
Boston	Massachusetts Memorial Hospitals	1
Boston	Peter Bent Brigham Hospital	1
Fall River	Fall River General Hospital	1
Fall River	Union Hospital	1
Holyoke	Carpenter Isolation Hospital	1
Lakeville	Lakeville State Sanatorium	1
New Bedford	St. Luke's Hospital	1
Newton	Newton Hospital	2
Salem	Salem Hospital	1
Springfield	Springfield Health Dept. Hospital	1
Worcester	Belmont Hospital	1
Worcester	Worcester City Hospital	1
Worcester	Worcester Memorial Hospital	1

After acute stage: SPECIAL CLINICS FOR orthopedic care. In addition to the orthopedic clinics in certain hospitals, special clinics for care of paralyzed cases are maintained by or in conjunction with the Harvard Infantile Paralysis Commission as follows:

Arlington Clinic
   Visiting Nurse Assn.
   707 Massachusetts Ave.
   Arlington Centre, Mass.
} Wednesday 1:30 P.M.

Beverly Clinic
   Public Health Dispensary
   84 Cabot Street
   Beverly, Mass.
} Wednesday 9:30 A.M. Alternate weeks

Cambridge Clinic
   Avon Home
   1000 Massachusetts Ave.
   Cambridge, Mass.
} Monday and Wednesday 9:30 A.M.

Dedham Clinic
   Emergency Nursing Association
   School Street
   Dedham, Mass.
} Friday 1:30 P.M.

East Boston Clinic
   Health Unit
   Paris Street
   East Boston, Mass.
} Friday 1:30 P.M.

Haverhill Clinic
   42 Fleet St.
   Haverhill, Mass.
} Wednesday 9:30 A.M.

Lawrence Clinic
   Child Welfare Rooms
   City Hall
   Lawrence, Mass.
} Monday 9:30 A.M.

Lowell Clinic
   Lowell Guild
   17 Dutton Street
   Lowell, Mass.
} Wednesday 9:30 A.M.

Lynn Clinic
   Lynn Hospital, Boston St.
   Lynn, Mass.
} Tuesday 1:30 P.M.

Malden Clinic
   Malden Dispensary
   Malden, Mass.
} Saturday 9 A.M.

Quincy Clinic
   Quincy Dispensary
   High School Ave.
   Quincy, Mass.
} Monday 9:30 A.M.

Somerville Clinic
Old Police Station
Bow Street
Somerville, Mass.
} Thursday 2 P.M.

Waltham Clinic
Waltham Baby Hospital
755 Main Street
Waltham, Mass.
} Tuesday 1:30 P.M.

Hospitals and institutions admitting paralyzed cases for special care are:

City or Town	Name of Institution	Restrictions
Baldwinsville	Hospital Cottages for Children	Under 14 yrs.
Boston	Industrial School for Crippled Children	Day School
Canton	Massachusetts Hospital School for Crippled Children	Between 5 and 15 yrs.
Egypt (Scituate)	Children's Sunlight Hospital	Children 2-6 yrs. Adults 16-35 yrs.
Lakeville	Lakeville State Sanatorium	Over 3 yrs.
Newton Center	New England Peabody Home for Cripped Children	Under 12 yrs.
North Dartmouth	Sol-E-Mar	Under 14 yrs.
Springfield	Shriners' Hospital for Crippled Children	Under 14 yrs.

Applications for admission to these hospitals should be made directly to the Superintendent (Sol-E-Mar admitted through St. Luke's Hospital, New Bedford).

CARE AVAILABLE THROUGH SERVICES FOR CRIPPLED CHILDREN:

Special consultation service is provided by the Department, on the request of the attending physician, for paralyzed cases of poliomyelitis provided the family is unable to pay for the service of an orthopedic surgeon. Applications for this service should be made directly to the Department. If necessary, a consultant will visit the patient, with the attending physician, but if the patient is able to attend a clinic, the facilities of the nearest Clinic for Crippled Children should be utilized. These clinics are described on p. 289.

ISOLATION AND QUARANTINE

(Consult regulations of local board of health. See p. 233.)

Cases: Usually two weeks from onset of disease, and thereafter until acute symptoms have subsided.

Contacts: Usually until two weeks have elapsed from date of last exposure.

PREVENTION

Passive immunization: No method of proven value. Convalescent serum not available for this purpose. Parental whole blood has been tried without proven results.

Active immunization: No safe and proven method yet available.

CHICKEN POX (Varicella)

DIAGNOSIS Based on clinical findings.

TREATMENT Symptomatic and supportive.

ISOLATION AND QUARANTINE
(Consult regulations of local board of health. See p. 233.)
Cases: Usually one week from appearance of eruption and thereafter until all primary crusts have disappeared.
Contacts: Usually no restrictions.

PREVENTION
Passive immunization: Convalescent serum and placental extract have been used for passive immunization.
Active immunization: No practical method of active immunization available.

DIPHTHERIA

DIAGNOSIS
Clinical condition, usually with laboratory confirmation. Nose and throat cultures for diagnosis may be sent to local laboratories (See p. 237), or to the State Bacteriological Laboratory, 527 State House, Boston, outfits obtainable at local board of health. Positive diagnostic reports telephoned or telegraphed prepaid. (See p. 236.)

TREATMENT
Antitoxin furnished free by State through local boards of health. Available in 5,000 and 10,000 unit vials.

Amount of Antitoxin in the Treatment of a Case of Diphtheria

	Mild Cases Units	Mod. and Early Severe Units *	Severe and Malignant Units *
Infants, 10 to 30 lbs. in wgt. under 2 yrs.	5,000-10,000	10,000-15,000	15,000-20,000
Children, 30 to 90 lbs. in wgt. under 15 yrs.	5,000-15,000	15,000-20,000	20,000-40,000
Adults, 90 lbs. and over in wgt.	10,000-20,000	15,000-30,000	20,000-50,000
Method of administration advised	Intramuscular	Intravenous	Intravenous

* When given intramuscularly use the larger amounts indicated.

Cases of laryngeal and naso-pharyngeal diphtheria, moderate cases still active and seen late at the time of the first injection, and moderate cases of diphtheria occurring as a complication of the exanthems should be classified as "severe cases."

In mild and early moderate cases the antitoxin should be injected by means of a sterile hypodermic syringe into a suitable muscle instead of under the skin, because absorption takes place about three times as rapidly from muscles. For intravenous administration, the injection may be made into the vein on the flexor surface of the elbow. Antitoxin for intravenous use should be highly potent and should show no sediment or turbidity. It must be warmed to body temperature and given slowly. For further information see circular accompanying the antitoxin. *All cases should be skin tested for sensitivity before giving serum.* (See p. 281.)

Outfits containing serum properly diluted for this purpose obtainable through local board of health.

ISOLATION AND QUARANTINE

(Consult regulations of local board of health. See p. 233.)

Cases: Usually one week from onset and thereafter until two successive negative cultures from nose and throat taken at least 24 hours apart shall have been obtained.

Contacts: *Immune* contacts (those who have had diphtheria, have been immunized, or have a negative Schick test) usually quarantined until negative cultures obtained; *susceptible* contacts until one week from last exposure has elapsed, and negative cultures obtained.

PREVENTION

Passive immunization: May be obtained through injection of 1,000 units of antitoxin. (See p. 281.) Does not last more than two to four weeks. Not usually recommended if contacts can be kept under observation.

Active immunization: Generally agreed that active immunization is desirable for all children six months or more old, but some disagreement as to best immunizing agent (see below—alum toxoid).

Toxoid: Given in three doses (0.5, 1.0, and 1.0 cc.) three to four weeks apart, recommended for children aged six months to ten or twelve years. Three doses given one week apart or two doses one month apart give high degree of immunity but less than schedule recommended. Best age for immunizing a child is at age of six months. Toxoid contains no horse serum, is more effective and acts more rapidly than does toxin-antitoxin; it produces more severe local and systemic reactions in adults and older children. Toxoid in 1 cc. and 20 cc. vials furnished by State through local boards of health.

Alum toxoid: (Diphtheria toxoid, alum precipitated)—A newer product than ordinary toxoid; its place in public health armamentarium is not clearly established. No evidence that it produces better or more lasting immunity than three doses of ordinary toxoid, properly spaced, and some doubt that it equals latter product. May be given in single injection. Produces high level of immunity. Usually causes a lump in arm that lasts for several weeks with occasional sterile abscess. Not furnished by State at present.

Toxin-antitoxin: Recommended for immunization of adults or children more than twelve years old shown by Schick test to be susceptible to diphtheria. Given in three injections of 1 cc. each at one week intervals. Furnished in 1 cc. and 20 cc. containers by State through local board of health. Not distributed for use in school clinics where children are less than 12 years old.

SUSCEPTIBILITY

May be determined by Schick test. Usually omitted in small children, as a high per cent of this group is usually susceptible. All children above age of 12 should be tested before immunization as many are immune by this age. Schick test useful six months after immunizaton as a check on effectiveness of injections. Material furnished by State through local board of health. Inject 0.1 cc. toxin on right arm, and 0.1 cc. heated toxin for control on left arm, all injections *into but not through the skin.* Observe reactions on fourth day.

DOG BITE

REPORTING

All cases of dog bite, whether or not requiring antirabic treatment must be reported to the local board of health. (See p. 233.)

RECOMMENDED PROCEDURE

The dog: (1) *Do not permit anyone to kill the dog;* if it is killed at once, it may be impossible to determine promptly whether or not it was rabid.

(2) *Keep the dog under observation for two weeks.* When the case is reported to the board of health, the animal inspector will care for this. If the dog is well at the end of two weeks, the possibility of transmission of rabies at the time of biting may be dismissed.

(3) *If the dog becomes sick* have it examined by a veterinarian.

(4) *If the dog dies* have head sent to Wassermann Laboratory, Harvard Medical School, 25 Shattuck Street, Boston, Telephone, Longwood 2380. This is a State Laboratory, examination being made without charge.

The patient: (1) *Cauterize* wound, if possible, with fuming nitric acid. Iodine, mercurochrome, and similar antiseptics do not cauterize, nor are other cauterizing agents effective.

(2) *Antirabic treatment*: Acting under authority of Chapter 375 of the Acts of 1937 (amending Chapter 140, section 145A of the General Laws), the Department of Public Health has adopted the following rules and regulations in accordance with which boards of health are required to furnish antirabic vaccine and treatment. These regulations should not be interpreted as a flat recommendation that all persons so bitten by or exposed to dogs should be given treatment, but rather as those conditions under which boards of health are required to furnish the vaccine and treatment if the clinical circumstances surrounding the case indicate to the physician that the patient is in need of treatment. The board of health is under no obligation to furnish vaccine and treatment regardless of the opinion of the attending physician, unless the case is covered by one of these regulations.

1. Antirabic vaccine and antirabic treatment shall be furnished by the board of health for all persons bitten by or intimately exposed to the saliva of:

    a. A clinically rabid animal.
    b. An animal the head of which was found positive for rabies on laboratory examination.
    c. An animal the head of which was found suspicious for rabies on laboratory examination.
    d. An animal the head of which was in such condition on reaching the laboratory that it could not be examined, and was therefore classified as unsatisfactory for examination.
    e. An animal which could not be restrained for a clinical observation period of fourteen days after the date of biting or exposure.
    f. An animal which was killed without being held for observation and without subsequent laboratory examination of the head.

2. Antirabic vaccine and antirabic treatment shall be furnished by the board of health for all persons bitten on the head. Treatment shall be discontinued at the end of seven days if the dog by which the patient was bitten is

still well and is kept under observation for seven additional days, treatment to be resumed if the dog shows signs of rabies during this second seven-day period.

3. Before antirabic vaccine is furnished to a physician to treat a patient, said physician shall certify in writing to the board of health the name and address of the patient to be treated, the severity of the bite or degree of exposure, the place where the bite or exposure occurred and the identity of the animal responsible for the biting if said is obtainable.

4. If antirabic vaccine and antirabic treatment are given because of a bite or exposure occurring in another community than that in which the patient resides, notice of said facts shall be forwarded by the board of health to board of health and animal inspector of the community where said biting or exposure occurred, and to the county commissioners of the county, other than Suffolk, in which said latter community is located.

5. No charges shall be paid for services other than for the administration of the vaccine.

6. A physician shall be entitled to twenty-one doses of antirabic vaccine for the treatment of head bites or severe multiple lacerations on other parts of the body, and to fourteen doses for the treatment of all other bites or exposures.

7. The board of health may require a statement made under penalty of perjury and signed by the patient to be treated, or, in the case of a minor, by his parent or guardian or person immediately responsible for his supervision, stating the place where said person was bitten or exposed and the identity of the dog if obtained.

Attention: Before beginning antirabic vaccine treatment, obtain vaccine from board of health. Do not purchase vaccine directly as the board of health is not responsible for cost of vaccine which it has not purchased. To avoid possibility of subsequent dispute as to costs of treatment, obtain authorization for this from board of health. The State does not furnish antirabic vaccine.

Antirabic Vaccine: The vaccine at present recommended by the Department of Public Health is that prepared according to the Semple method (phenolized virus). Fourteen injections are usually adequate for simple bites on the trunk and extremities. When the bite is on the head or neck, or there are severe multiples lacerations, twenty-one injections are desirable. All injections are given subcutaneously, preferably in a different site each day to avoid local soreness; the abdominal wall is a frequent site for the injections.

In making decisions in regard to treatment when actual exposure to the virus is doubtful, the slight but very definite danger of paralysis resulting from the use of the vaccine should be taken into consideration.

DYSENTERY (Amebic)

DIAGNOSIS

Clinical findings with laboratory confirmation through examination of fecal specimens.

Vegetative stage of amebae: For best results it is necessary to examine freshly passed specimens, such examination being possible only if patient is hospitalized or sent to laboratory. If local hospital is not equipped for such tests, patient, if ambulatory, may be sent to Department of Tropical Medicine,

Harvard Medical School, a fee being charged for examination. A fixed smear of a freshly passed fecal specimen may be sent to State Bacteriological Laboratory, 527 State House, Boston. Special containers for this purpose are available through local board of health. (See p. 236.) For satisfactory results, directions as to mailing and fixing of smears must be followed carefully. Do not send patient to State Laboratory.

Encysted stage of amebae: Stool specimens may be sent to State Bacteriological Laboratory, 527 State House, Boston. Special containers for this purpose are available through local board of health.

TREATMENT
Numerous specific amebicides available. See New England Journal of Medicine, *209*, 1071, 1933 (November 23).

ISOLATION AND QUARANTINE
(Consult regulations of local board of health. See p. 233.)

Cases: Usually no restrictions during acute stage as vegetative forms are non-infectious. Release from medical supervision should be conditioned by stool examinations for cysts. Carrier should not be employed as food handler.

Contacts: Usually no restrictions.

PREVENTION
No method of immunization available.

DYSENTERY (Bacillary)

DIAGNOSIS
Based on clinical findings with laboratory confirmation. Some strains of dysentery bacilli cause merely a transient diarrhea in healthy adults, or children above twelve years. Stool specimens may be sent to local or State Bacteriological Laboratory, 527 State House, Boston. For best results specimen should be taken early in the disease and from a diarrheal specimen. Agglutinins may often be found in blood after first week of disease. For dysentery agglutination test send at least 5 cc. of blood in sterile test tube to State Bacteriological Laboratory, 527 State House, Boston. (See p. 236.)

TREATMENT
Symptomatic and supportive. In Shiga type (rare in Massachusetts), antitoxin may be of use. Not furnished by State.

ISOLATION AND QUARANTINE
(Consult regulations of local board of health. See p. 233.) Usually same precautions as for typhoid fever.

PREVENTION
No practical method of active and passive immunization available.

GERMAN MEASLES (Rubella)

DIAGNOSIS   Based on clinical findings.

TREATMENT   Symptomatic.

ISOLATION AND QUARANTINE
(Consult regulations of local board of health. See p. 233.)
Cases: Usually one week from appearance of rash.
Contacts: Usually no restrictions.

PREVENTION
No practical method of immunization available. Convalescent serum and placental extract have been used for passive protection.

GONORRHEA

(See Gonorrhea and Syphilis, p. 269.)

MALARIA

DIAGNOSIS
Clinical condition with laboratory confirmation. Smears for diagnosis may be sent to State Bacteriological Laboratory, 527 State House, Boston. Special containers available through local boards of health. (See p. 236.)

TREATMENT Symptomatic and supportive. Specific drugs.

ISOLATION AND QUARANTINE
(Consult regulations of local board of health. See p. 233.) Usually no restrictions except precautions as to screening of patient.

PREVENTION
No practical method of active and passive immunization available.

MEASLES (Rubeola)

DIAGNOSIS   Based on clinical findings.

TREATMENT   Symptomatic and supportive.

ISOLATION AND QUARANTINE
(Consult regulations of local board of health. (See p. 233.)
Cases: Usually one week from date of appearance of rash. Isolation important for patient to reduce incidence of complicating pneumonia.
Contacts: *Immune* contacts, usually no restrictions; *susceptible* contacts, usually kept from school for 16 days from date of last exposure. Some schools permit child to attend school for one week after first exposure, then exclude until 16 days after last exposure.

PREVENTION
Passive immunization and modification: *Passive immunization* (complete protection) is of no permanent value, lasting only two to four weeks, after which the patient is as susceptible as before the injection. It is desirable in hospitals, and for sick, debilitated children, or very young children. The pur-

pose of *modification* is to obtain a mild measles which is usually devoid of complications and usually leaves a permanent protection. All injections are given intramuscularly.

May be obtained through:

(1) CONVALESCENT SERUM—Usually not obtainable except in certain hospitals. For prevention 3 cc. during first four days after exposure*; for modification four to seven days. Inject intramuscularly in buttocks, lateral aspect of thigh, or between scapulae.

(2) ADULT WHOLE BLOOD—Less certain in result. For prevention 30 cc. blood during first four days after exposure*; for modification, four to seven days. Department of Public Health furnishes through local board of health ampoules of 4% sterile sodium citrate solution which may be used in the syringe to prevent coagulation of the blood. (See p. 280.) Preliminary grouping of blood is not necessary as injection is intramuscularly; do not give intravenously without blood grouping. Injections are given in buttocks, lateral aspect of thigh, or between scapulae.

(3) PLACENTAL EXTRACT (Immune Globulins-Human)—For prevention give during first four days after exposure*; for modification four to ten days. Furnished for study purposes by State Department of Public Health directly or through certain local boards of health. Given by intramuscular injection; do not give intravenously.

Active immunization: No practical method available.

* Determination of date of exposure. Measles is communicable three days before the appearance of the rash. Therefore, the date of appearance of the rash in the patient being known, the date of first possible exposure of the contact is three days earlier.

MENINGITIS (Meningococcus Meningitis)

DIAGNOSIS

Clinical findings supplemented by lumbar puncture and spinal fluid examination. If the spinal fluid is cloudy, it is usual practice to treat with antimeningococcic serum until the laboratory rules out this diagnosis. The possibility of the meningitis being due to the Pfeiffer bacillus (see p. 250) should be borne in mind. Specimens of spinal fluids should be examined by direct smear and culture. If local facilities for such examination are not available, spinal fluid may be sent to State Bacteriological Laboratory, 527 State House, Boston. Positive reports telephoned or telegraphed prepaid. (See p. 236.)

TREATMENT

Antimeningococcic serum furnished free by State through hospitals and boards of health listed below. For details of treatment, see circular accompanying serum. Test patient for sensitivity before giving serum (see p. 281). Administration of sulfanilamide, with or without use of serum, appears valuable, at time this is written. If the patient fails to respond to serum, culture of spinal fluid should be sent to Antitoxin and Vaccine Laboratory, 375 South Street, Jamaica Plain, for check against serum. Antimeningococcic serum may be obtained through the following hospitals and boards of health:

City or Town	Hospital or Board of Health
Athol	Board of Health
Attleboro	Sturdy Memorial Hospital
Ayer	Community Memorial Hospital
Beverly	Beverly Hospital
Boston	Boston City Hospital
Boston	Carney Hospital
Boston	Children's Hospital
Boston	Massachusetts General Hospital
Boston	Massachusetts Memorial Hospitals
Brockton	Brockton Hospital
Cambridge	Cambridge Hospital
Chelsea	Chelsea Memorial Hospital
Clinton	Clinton Hospital
Concord	Emerson Hospital
Fall River	Fall River General Hospital
Fitchburg	Board of Health
Framingham	Framingham Union Hospital
Gardner	Henry Heywood Memorial Hospital
Gloucester	Addison Gilbert Hospital
Great Barrington	Fairview Hospital
Greenfield	Franklin County Public Hospital
Haverhill	Hale Hospital
Holyoke	Providence Hospital
Hyannis	Cape Cod Hospital
Ipswich	Cable Memorial Hospital
Lawrence	Lawrence General Hospital
Leominster	Leominster Hospital
Lowell	Lowell Isolation Hospital
Lynn	Lynn Health Department Hospital
Medford	Lawrence Memorial Hospital
Milford	Milford Hospital
Nantucket	Nantucket Cottage Hospital
New Bedford	St. Luke's Hospital
Newburyport	Anna Jaques Hospital
Newton	Newton Hospital
North Adams	North Adams Hospital
Northampton	Cooley Dickinson Hospital
Norwood	Norwood Hospital
Oak Bluffs	Martha's Vineyard Hospital
Pittsfield	Sampson Memorial Hospital
Plymouth	Jordan Hospital
Provincetown	Board of Health
Quincy	Quincy City Hospital
Salem	Salem Health Department Hospital
Southbridge	Harrington Memorial Hospital
Springfield	Springfield Health Department
Taunton	Morton Hospital
Ware	Mary Lane Hospital
Webster	Webster District Hospital
Westfield	Noble Hospital
Woburn	Choate Memorial Hospital
Worcester	Board of Health

ISOLATION AND QUARANTINE

(Consult regulations of local board of health. See p. 233.)

Cases: Usually two weeks from onset of disease and thereafter until all acute symptoms have subsided.

Contacts: Usually until ten days from date of last exposure.

PREVENTION

No practical method of active and passive immunization available.

PFEIFFER BACILLUS (Influenzal) MENINGITIS

DIAGNOSIS

Although the immediate administration of antimeningococcic serum to all cases of meningitis giving a cloudy spinal fluid is the generally accepted rule, the possibility of other organisms being the causative agent must be kept in mind until a bacteriologic diagnosis is made. Therefore, the spinal fluid should be examined by direct smears and by culture by methods which demonstrate the presence not only of meningococci but of Pfeiffer ("Influenza") bacilli, streptococci and pneumococci. If no laboratory facilities are available nearby, specimens should be sent to the Bacteriological Laboratory, State House, Boston. Only in the event that Pfeiffer bacilli are demonstrated should influenzal meningitis antiserum be given.

TREATMENT

Anti-influenza bacillus serum may be obtained from the Antitoxin and Vaccine Laboratory. It is supplied only when cases have been recognized by bacteriological methods. The method of administration is given at length because it differs from that required for other serums. (See also p. 281.)

Because bacteremia is invariably present in cases of Pfeiffer bacillus (influenzal) meningitis, a single dose of 30 to 40 cc. of serum is given intravenously on each of the first two days of treatment. It is unnecessary to add complement to serum that is given intravenously.

Two intrathecal treatments are given daily until several days after the spinal fluid gives negative smears and cultures, at which time the use of serum may be discontinued if the patient appears to be clinically improved and has a normal temperature. At each treatment the cerebrospinal fluid is drained as completely as possible. This is followed by the instillation by gravity of a mixture of 15 cc. anti-influenza bacillus serum and 7 or 8 cc. of complement (see next paragraph). The entire volume of this mixture should be administered only if a large volume of cerebrospinal fluid has been withdrawn. The amount of serum-complement mixture given should always be less than the amount of cerebrospinal fluid withdrawn. The treatments are commonly given by the lumbar route, although the cistern or the lateral ventricles may be used, depending upon special indications. After each treatment by whatever route it is a good plan to elevate the foot of the patient's bed and change his position frequently during the course of the next hour to facilitate the gravitation of serum throughout the intracranial subarachnoid space.

Complement is freshly drawn blood serum. To secure it, about 50 to 60 cc. of blood is withdrawn from a human donor, placed in sterile centrifuge tubes and allowed to clot. (Determination of the donor's blood group is unnecessary.) The clot is separated from the sides of the tubes with a sterile stiff wire and centrifuged down. The serum is aspirated from the clot to fresh sterile containers and is ready for use as complement. Fresh complement should be obtained at least every 48 hours. It should never be used if older than 48 hours and must always be stored in the ice box. Rigid aseptic technique must be observed throughout this procedure.

There is some evidence to suggest that these patients do better if given an adequate fluid intake by constant intravenous drip. A satisfactory fluid for this purpose is a sterile mixture of equal parts of physiological salt solution and either 5 or 10 per cent glucose solution.

Clinical Summaries of Cases treated with this serum are requested and should be sent to the Antitoxin and Vaccine Laboratory.

MUMPS (Epidemic Parotitis)

DIAGNOSIS Based on clinical findings.

TREATMENT Symptomatic and supportive.

ISOLATION AND QUARANTINE
(Consult regulations of local board of health. See p. 233.)

Cases: Usually one week from onset of disease, and thereafter until all swelling of salivary glands has disappeared.

Contacts: Usually no restrictions. Males of age of puberty or older should be protected from exposure because of danger of complicating orchitis.

PREVENTION
No practical method of active or passive immunization available. Convalescent serum has been tried where available.

OPHTHALMIA NEONATORUM

REPORTING
All cases showing inflammation, swelling, redness or abnormal discharge of the eyes within two weeks of birth must be reported to the board of health. ("If either eye of an infant becomes inflamed, swollen and red, or shows an unnatural discharge within two weeks after birth, the nurse, relative or other attendant having charge of such infant shall report in writing, within six hours thereafter, to the board of health of the town where the infant is, the fact that such inflammation, swelling and redness of the eyes or unnatural discharge exists."—(General Laws, Chapter 111, Section 110). Also "if either eye of an infant whom or whose mother a physician, or a hospital medical officer registered under section nine of chapter one hundred and twelve, visits becomes inflamed, swollen and red, or shows an unnatural discharge within two weeks after birth, he shall immediately give written notice thereof, over his own signature, to the board of health of the town. . . ." (General Laws, Chapter 111, Section 111).

DIAGNOSIS
Smears for possible gonococci should be obtained. May be examined in local laboratory or sent to State Bacteriological Laboratory, 527 State House,

Boston. Usual gonorrhea outfits, obtainable through local boards of health, should be used for this purpose. Positive results are telephoned or telegraphed prepaid. (See p. 236.)

TREATMENT

The General Laws of the Commonwealth require that the local board of health upon receipt of a report of a discharging eye as above described "shall take such immediate action as it may deem necessary, including, so far as possible, consultation with an oculist and the employment of a trained nurse, in order that blindness may be prevented."

ISOLATION AND QUARANTINE

Aseptic nursing precautions to prevent spread of possible infection to other eye or to eyes of attendants.

PREVENTION

Silver nitrate solution for instillation in the eye at time of birth is furnished in wax ampoules by State Department of Public Health. Obtainable through hospitals and boards of health. Under authority granted by Section 109A* of Chapter 111 of the General Laws the Department has ruled that only one per cent silver nitrate in individual doses in wax ampoules can be used as a prophylactic in the newborn. (See Gonococcal Ophthalmia Neonatorum, p. 273).

* Added by Chapter 115, Acts of 1936.

PARATYPHOID FEVER

(Same as for Typhoid Fever, p. 266.)

PNEUMONIA

DIAGNOSIS

Clinical, x-ray and laboratory findings: Determination of the type of organism is more important than the distribution of the areas of solidification, since specific serum is available for treating cases due to many types of pneumococci. Ninety-five per cent of lobar pneumonias and about 50% of bronchopneumonias are due to pneumococci. Well over half of all cases of lobar pneumonia and many cases of bronchopneumonia, particularly in adults, are due to types for which therapeutic serum is available. Test for hypersensitivity to horse serum (see p. 281) before injecting serum.

Typing: Specific serum therapy is dependent upon determining type of pneumococcus causing infection and then administering serum of proper type. This should be done as soon after onset of the disease as possible. Type may usually be determined from sputum specimen, but if no sputum is raised, take a throat swab and a blood culture, for these may provide cultures which can be typed. Select specimen of freshly raised sputum; do not be content with saliva as oral cavity may contain pneumococci of type different from that causing the pneumonia. Sputum should be sent to nearest laboratory equipped for typing. Typing service available at all times through State Bacteriological Laboratory, 527 State House, Boston. (See p. 236.) All sputa showing types of pneumococci for which therapeutic serum is available are reported by telephone or telegraph prepaid. Send sputum in special containers available through boards of health, or in any sterile container. Do not use tuberculosis sputum oufits as these contain carbolic acid that destroys pneumococci, making typing impossible. In addition to typing facilities available through State Department of Public Health, pneumococcus sputum typing may be secured through the following hospital laboratories, the charges for the same depending upon the hospital:

LABORATORIES FOR TYPING AND SERUM DISTRIBUTION

City or Town	Hospital or Department of Health
Attleboro	Sturdy Memorial Hospital
Ayer	Ayer Community Memorial Hospital
Beverly	Beverly Hospital
Boston	Beth Israel Hospital
Boston	Boston City Hospital
Boston	Carney Hospital
Boston	Faulkner Hospital
Boston	Massachusetts General Hospital
Boston	Massachusetts Memorial Hospitals
Boston	New England Deaconess Hospital *
Boston	St. Elizabeth's Hospital
Brockton	Board of Health Laboratory *
Brockton	Brockton Hospital
Cambridge	Board of Health Laboratory *
Cambridge	Cambridge City Hospital
Cambridge	Cambridge Hospital
Chelsea	Chelsea Memorial Hospital
Clinton	Clinton Hospital
Everett	Whidden Memorial Hospital
Fall River	Fall River General Hospital
Fall River	St. Ann's Hospital
Fall River	Truesdale Hospital
Fall River	Union Hospital
Fitchburg	Burbank Hospital
Framingham	Framingham Union Hospital
Gardner	Henry Heywood Memorial Hospital
Gloucester	Addison Gilbert Hospital
Great Barrington	Fairview Hospital
Greenfield	Franklin County Hospital
Haverhill	Hale Hospital
Holyoke	Holyoke Hospital
Holyoke	Providence Hospital
Hyannis	Cape Cod Hospital
Lawrence	Lawrence General Hospital
Leominster	Leominster Hospital
Lowell	Lowell General Hospital
Lowell	St. John's Hospital
Lowell	St. Joseph's Hospital
Lynn	Lynn Hospital
Lynn	Union Hospital
Malden	Malden Hospital

City or Town	Hospital or Department of Health
Marlborough	Marlborough Hospital
Middleborough	St. Luke's Hospital
Milford	Milford Hospital
Nantucket	Nantucket Cottage Hospital
Natick	Leonard Morse Hospital
New Bedford	St. Luke's Hospital
Newburyport	Anna Jaques Hospital
Newton	Newton Hospital
North Adams	North Adams Hospital
Northampton	Cooley Dickinson Hospital
Norwood	Norwood Hospital
Oak Bluffs	Martha's Vineyard Hospital
Palmer	Wing Memorial Hospital
Peabody	J. B. Thomas Hospital
Pittsfield	House of Mercy Hospital
Pittsfield	St. Luke's Hospital
Plymouth	Jordan Hospital
Pocasset	Barnstable County Sanatorium
Quincy	Quincy City Hospital
Salem	Salem Hospital
Somerville	Somerville Hospital
Southbridge	Harrington Memorial Hospital
Springfield	Springfield Hospital
Springfield	Mercy Hospital
Springfield	Wesson Memorial Hospital
Taunton	Morton Hospital
Waltham	Waltham Hospital
Ware	Mary Lane Hospital
Webster	Webster District Hospital
Westfield	Noble Hospital
Worcester	St. Vincent's Hospital ·
Worcester	Worcester City Hospital
Worcester	Worcester Hahnemann Hospital
Worcester	Worcester Memorial Hospital

* Therapeutic serum is not available through this laboratory.

Additions to and changes in this list are made from time to time. Due to the high cost of the serum the number of distributing stations is kept as low as possible. At present serum is easily available in all parts of the state. The distribution of pneumococcus antibody solution is restricted to those hospitals, institutions, or agencies equipped to do pneumococcus typing and employing bacteriologists or laboratory technicians who have been approved by the Department of Public Health as to their familiarity with typing procedures.

TREATMENT

See circular accompanying serum for details. The following statement is correct at time of writing but is subject to revision when more information is available.

Antipneumococcic horse serums for types 1, 2, 5, 7 and 8 are or soon will be available, in the form of concentrated monovalent or bivalent serums, through the State Bacteriological Laboratory or through certain of the above listed hospitals, under the following conditions:

1. The type of the infecting pneumococcus must be demonstrated by examination of sputum or other material from the patient.

2. The physician obtaining the serum must agree to furnish a report of its use on the form supplied by the Department.

Although the earlier serum is given the better, the previous restriction limiting the distribution of serum to those patients ill with pneumonia for 96 hours or less has been given up.

The dose of serum given out is the *minimum* required for most cases suffering from an infection of the type demonstrated, and at present is 60,000 units for a type 1 infection, 100,000 for a type 2 or a type 5. This dose should be at least doubled if

1. Treatment is begun after the third day of the disease;
2. The patient is over 40 years old;
3. The patient is pregnant or in the first week of the puerperium;
4. There is involvement of more than one lobe; or
5. Pneumococcic bacteremia is known to be present. Further details are given in the circular accompanying the serum. A blood culture should always be taken before administering the first dose of serum, for it is of the greatest service as an index to further therapy and to prognosis.

Therapeutic serum for some of the higher types of pneumococci are now available through some of the commercial manufacturers. Typing for the higher types is available through the State Bacteriological Laboratory and a few of the above named typing laboratories.

ISOLATION AND QUARANTINE Usually no restrictions.

PREVENTION

No accepted method of active or passive immunization available.

RABIES

(See Dog Bite, p. 244.)

Other animals are occasionally found to be rabid. The possibility of contracting the disease by bites of animals other than dogs should always be considered.

SCARLET FEVER

DIAGNOSIS

Based on clinical findings. Throat cultures of no practical value.

TREATMENT

In most cases along general medical lines. Antitoxin furnished free by State through local board of health. *All cases should be tested for sensitivity before giving serum.* Serum reactions follow scarlet fever antitoxin more frequently than with diphtheria antitoxin. (See p. 281.)

ISOLATION AND QUARANTINE
(Consult regulations of local board of health. See p. 233.)

Uncomplicated Cases: Three weeks from date of appearance of rash. Careful attention should be given to nose and throat to detect existence of discharge or inflammation before considering case as uncomplicated. If upper respiratory tract symptoms appear during month after release from isolation, precautions should be re-established. Nose and throat cultures of little practical value in determining release from isolation.

Complicated Cases: Four weeks and thereafter until abnormal discharges shall have ceased, swollen glands subsided, or three successive cultures of abnormal discharge shall have been found free of hemolytic streptococci. Repeated negative cultures of discharge may warrant earlier release. Nasal discharge especially dangerous and frequently overlooked

Contacts: *Immune* contacts usually not quarantined if living away from patient. *Susceptible* contacts usually quarantined until one week from date of last contact with patient. Nose and throat cultures of no practical value.

PREVENTION

Passive immunization: Use of antitoxin for this purpose not generally recommended owing to frequency of serum reactions.

Active immunization: Dick toxin given in five subcutaneous injections at one week intervals produces high level of protection. Dick toxin is not furnished by State or local health departments.

SUSCEPTIBILITY

May be determined by Dick test. Inject exactly 0.1 cc. into the skin; observe 20-24 hours. Any redness 1 cm. or more in any diameter indicates susceptibility. Dick test material is not furnished by State or local health departments.

SEPTIC SORE THROAT

Is probably not a definite disease entity. Usually includes severe sore throats of streptococcal origin. Abnormal incidence of sore throats in practice of any physician should be reported to local board of health for investigation as to possible spread through milk. Persons with sore throats should not be permitted to work around milk supplies.

SMALLPOX (Variola)

DIAGNOSIS Based on clinical findings.

TREATMENT Symptomatic and supportive.

ISOLATION AND QUARANTINE
(Consult regulations of local board of health. See p. 233.)

Cases: Usually three weeks from onset of disease and thereafter until all crusts have disappeared and skin has healed.

Contacts: Usually quarantined until three weeks have elapsed from the date of last exposure unless immunized by a previous attack, by a recent successful vaccination, or showing the immunity reaction.

PREVENTION

Passive immunization: No satisfactory method available.

Active immunization: Smallpox vaccine virus furnished by State through local boards of health. (See p. 280.) Virus must be kept cold until used (do not carry it in coat pocket). Multiple pressure method advised instead of scarification. (See directions accompanying vaccine). Acetone or alcohol is preferable for cleansing skin; avoid medicated alcohols. *Do not cover site of vaccination with a dressing or shield.*

When to vaccinate: The first year of life is ideal time to perform vaccination, as reactions are least severe and complications at a minimum. Massachusetts law requires that "an unvaccinated child shall not be admitted to a public school except upon presentation of a certificate . . . signed by a registered physician designated by the parent or guardian, that the physician has at the time of giving the certificate personally examined the child and that he is of the opinion that the physical condition of the child is such that his health will be endangered by vaccination." The supreme court has ruled that a school committee may require renewal of such a certificate as often as every two months.

SYPHILIS

(See Gonorrhea and Syphilis, p. 269.)

TETANUS

DIAGNOSIS

Clinical findings with aid of spinal fluid examination. No bacteriological test available.

TREATMENT Antitetanic serum. Not furnished by State.

ISOLATION AND QUARANTINE No restrictions.

PREVENTION

Passive immunization may be obtained through injection of antitetanic serum in certain wound cases. All cases should be tested for sensitivity. (See p. 281.)

Active immunization with tetanus toxoid should be considered for those whose contacts entail an abnormal risk of infection. Not furnished by State.

TUBERCULOSIS

DIAGNOSIS

Diagnosis in early stages based usually on x-ray findings, with or without laboratory data, and upon symptoms or physical signs.

1. **Sputum:** Sputum may be sent to local laboratories or to State Bacteriological Laboratory, 527 State House, Boston. Outfits obtainable through local boards of health. (See p. 236.)

2. **Tuberculin Test:** Old Tuberculin for diagnostic purposes only is furnished in capillary tubes for Von Pirquet test, and in ampoules for making dilutions for Mantoux test by the State through local boards of health. (See p. 280.) Directions for performing tests are included in each package. Saline solution for making dilutions not furnished by the State. Positive tuberculin test indicates tuberculous infection, but gives no indication as to activity of process.

3. **X-ray Service:** Patients unable to afford private x-ray service may be referred to state and county tuberculosis hospitals or to clinics staffed by such hospitals (see 5, below and pp. 262 and 263.) by their family physicians. Reports made only to referring physician.

4. **Diagnostic Out-Patient Departments:** Such departments are maintained at all state and county sanatoria. (See pp. 262 and 263.)

5. **Consultation Clinics:** Consultation clinics to which physicians may refer patients for examination are maintained by state and county hospitals in many communities. Patients accepted only on reference by physician, board of health, or other health agency. Reports made only to referring physician or agency. Consultation clinics are maintained at present as follows:

CONSULTATION CLINICS

City or Town	Location	Time	Auspices
Athol	Memorial Building	4th Wed. 2 P.M.	Rutland State Sanatorium
Ayer	Health Center Building	4th Wed. 2-4 P.M.	Middlesex County Sanatorium
Brockton	Board of Health City Hall	Fridays 4 to 6 P.M. or through Board of Health	Plymouth County Sanatorium
Everett	Whidden Memorial Hospital	Appointments through Board of Health	Middlesex County Sanatorium
Framingham	Framingham Union Hospital	1st and 3rd Tues. and following Thurs. 1-4 P.M.	Middlesex County Sanatorium
Falmouth	Barnstable County Sanatorium	3rd Wed. 2 P.M.	Barnstable County Sanatorium
Gardner	City Hall, Room 9	1st Wed. 2 P.M.	Rutland State Sanatorium
Great Barrington	Fairview Hospital	2nd and 4th Tues. 9 A.M.	Westfield State Sanatorium
Greenfield	Greenfield Hospital	3rd Tues. 9 A.M.	Westfield State Sanatorium
Haverhill	North Reading State Sanatorium	Appointments through Board of Health	North Reading State Sanatorium
Hyannis	Cape Cod Hospital	3rd Tues. 2 P.M.	Barnstable County Sanatorium
Lawrence	North Reading State Sanatorium	Appointments through Board of Health	North Reading State Sanatorium

CONSULTATION CLINICS (Continued)

City or Town	Location	Time	Auspices
Medford	Lawrence Memorial Hospital	1st and 3rd Tues. and following Thurs.	Middlesex County Sanatorium
Milford	Board of Health 129 Main Street	2nd Wed. 2 P.M.	Rutland State Sanatorium
Nantucket	Nantucket Cottage Hospital	Last Thurs. 3 P.M. every 2nd month	Barnstable County Sanatorium
Newton	Newton Hospital	Appointments through Health Department	Middlesex County Sanatorium
North Adams	North Adams Hospital	4th Wed. 9 A.M.	Westfield State Sanatorium
Northampton	Memorial Hall Northampton	Friday 3 to 5 P.M. or through Board of Health	Hampshire County Sanatorium
Provincetown	Town Hall	3rd Fri. 10 A.M.	Barnstable County Sanatorium
Salem	5 St. Peter Street	2nd Mon. 1:30 P.M.	Essex Sanatorium
Southbridge	Town Hall	3rd Wed. 1:30 P.M.	Rutland State Sanatorium
Vineyard Haven	Martha's Vineyard Hospital	Last Fri. 9:30 A.M.	Barnstable County Sanatorium
Worcester	Worcester County Sanatorium	1st Tues. 2 P.M.	Worcester County Sanatorium

6. **Local Clinics:** Tuberculosis diagnostic clinics, independent of state or county sanatoria, are maintained by local boards of health at present as follows:

LOCAL CLINICS

City or Town	Location	Time	Auspices
Adams	Board of Health	Every other Mon., 6-7 P.M.	Adams Board of Health
Arlington	Dr. Pratt's Office 385 Massachusetts Ave.	By appointment	Arlington Board of Health
Attleboro	Sturdy Memorial Hospital	Wed. 4-6 P.M.	Attleboro Board of Health
Beverly	84 Cabot Street	Tues. 3-5 P.M.	Beverly Board of Health
Boston	12 Health Units under supervision of the Boston Health Dept.	....	Boston Health Department
Brookline	Town Hall, Room 23	Tues. 2-4 P.M. Fri. 7-8 P.M.	Brookline Board of Health
Cambridge	1481 Cambridge Street	Tues. and Sat. 9 A.M. Thurs. 3 and 6:30 P.M.	Cambridge Board of Health
Canton	Health Centre 473 Washington St.	3rd Fri. each month 4-6 P.M.	Canton Hospital Nursing Association
Chicopee	City Hall	Wed. 2-4 P.M. Fri. 7-8 P.M.	Chicopee Board of Health

LOCAL CLINICS (Continued)

City or Town	Location	Time	Auspices
Clinton	Municipal Building Church Street	By appointment	Clinton Board of Health
Dedham	378 Washington Street	2nd and last Fri. each month at 5 P.M.	Dedham Board of Health
Everett	379 Ferry Street	Tues. 8 P.M. Fri. 4 P.M.	Everett Board of Health
Fall River	City Hall Annex 66 Third Street	Tues. 6:30 P.M. (adults) Sat. 11 A.M. (children)	Fall River Board of Health
Fitchburg	Burbank Hospital	Wed. 3-4:30 P.M. Fri. 11-12 A.M.	Fitchburg Board of Health
Gardner	City Hall, Room 9	By appointment	Gardner Board of Health
Gloucester	City Hall	Mon. 8:30-9 P.M. Thurs. 4-5 P.M.	Gloucester Board of Health
Haverhill	Board of Health 471 Main Street	Mon. 7-8 P.M. Fri. 4-5 P.M.	Haverhill Health Department
Holyoke	City Hall Annex	Mon. 6-7 P.M. Fri. 4-5 P.M.	Holyoke Board of Health
Lawrence	City Hall	Daily 1-2 P.M. (none on Wed.)	Lawrence Board of Health
Leominster	City Hall, West Street, Room 6	Mon. 3-4 P.M. Mon. 7-8 P.M.	Leominster Board of Health
Lowell	Kirk Street Clinic Rooms	Tues. 4-5 P.M. (children) Thurs. 7-8 P.M. (adults)	Lowell Health Department
Lynn	Lynn Hospital	Mon. 3-5 P.M.	Lynn Department of Health
Malden	351 Main Street	Wed. 7-9 P.M. Fri. 3-5 P.M.	Malden Board of Health
Marlborough	City Hall	Mon. 4-5 P.M. Fri. 6-7 P.M.	Marlborough Board of Health
Methuen	Town Hall	Tues. 6-7 P.M.	Methuen Board of Health
Milton	101 Blue Hill Parkway	1st Wed. of each month at 4 P.M.	Milton Board of Health
New Bedford	Olympia Building Purchase Street	Mon. & Sat. 2-3 P.M. Wed. 5-6 P.M.	New Bedford Board of Health
Newburyport	2 Harris Street	Wed. 9:30-11:45 A.M.	Anti-Tuberculosis Association
North Adams	Municipal Building	Tues. 4-5 P.M. Fri. 4-5 P.M.	North Adams Board of Health
Norwood	Municipal Building Room 11	Thurs. 5:30 P.M.	Norwood Board of Health
Pittsfield	House of Mercy Hospital	Thurs. 10:30-12 A.M.	Pittsfield Board of Health

LOCAL CLINICS (Continued)

City or Town	Location	Time	Auspices
Quincy	32 High School Ave.	Tues. 6-7 P.M. (adults) Sat. 9-11 A.M. (children)	Quincy Board of Health
Revere	453 Broadway	Tues. 7-8 P.M. Fri. 4-5 P.M.	Revere Health Department
Salem	5 St. Peter Street	Sat. 11 A.M.	Salem Association for the Prevention of Tuberculosis
Springfield	Health Department Hospital	Mon. 3:30-7 P.M.	Springfield Health Department
Taunton	City Hall	Every day 11 A.M.-12 M.	Taunton Board of Health
Wakefield	Town Hall	Tues. 4-5 P.M. Fri. 8-9 P.M.	Wakefield Board of Health
Watertown	Middlesex County Sanatorium	Appointment through Board of Health	Watertown Board of Health
Webster	Town Hall, Main St.	Thurs. 5-6:30 P.M.	Webster Board of Health
Westfield	City Hall	Wed. 4-5 P.M.	Westfield Board of Health
Winchester	9 Mt. Vernon St.	Tues. 2-4 P.M. Thurs. 2-4 P.M.	Winchester Board of Health
Woburn	Middlesex County Sanatorium	By appointment through Board of Health	Woburn Board of Health
Worcester	Worcester City Hospital	Mon. 9-12 A.M. Thurs. 9-12 A.M.	Worcester Board of Health
	Belmont Hospital	Wed. and Sat. 9 A.M.	Worcester Board of Health

7. **School Clinics:** Designed to detect tuberculosis in school children. Beginning with the school year 1937-38 examinations will be made in the high school grades, and upon written requests of parents. Procedure is as follows:

1. Tuberculin test (Mantoux) on all high school children whose parents sign request slip.
2. X-ray of all reactors. X-ray service furnished by state, county, or city sanatoria staff.
3. Physical examination of all cases found positive by x-ray. All reports are made to physician designated by parents, and to board of health and school committee.

TREATMENT

Cities and towns are financially responsible for treatment of tuberculosis provided patient is unable to pay for same.

Pulmonary Tuberculosis—Adult: Patients having a legal settlement and unable to pay for care are referable to state, county or city sanatoria. For those able to pay, hospitalization may be found in private sanatoria, at county sanatoria, or at Rutland. (See pp. 262, 263, and 264.)

Tuberculosis—Children: Provision is made for hospitalization of both childhood and adult types at North Reading and Westfield State Sanatoria.

Extra-Pulmonary Tuberculosis: All types of extra-pulmonary tuberculosis (bone, gland, kidney, intestinal, skin, eye, etc.) are acceptable at Lakeville State Sanatorium.

HOSPITALIZATION

The following hospitals and sanatoria are maintained in whole or in part for the care of tuberculosis:

TUBERCULOSIS HOSPITALS AND SANATORIA

FEDERAL HOSPITAL

Name of Institution	Location	Number of Beds	Rates per Week	Superintendent
United States Veterans Hospital	Rutland Heights	472	For Veterans Bureau patients only	Wm. E. Park, M.D.

Application should be made to United States Veterans Bureau, Federal Building, Boston, Massachusetts.

STATE SANATORIA

Name of Institution	Location	Number of Beds	Rates per Week	Superintendent
Rutland State Sanatorium (for adults in early and favorable stage of pulmonary tuberculosis)	Rutland	365	$7.00 to patient. $10.50 to city or town, if not under contract	E. B. Emerson, M.D.
Westfield State Sanatorium (for adults and children)	Westfield	325	Under 21—$7 if paid by pt., or city or town. Over 21—$7 if paid by pt.; $10.50 if paid by city or town	Roy Morgan, M.D.
North Reading State Sanatorium (for children under 17)	North Wilmington	290	$7.00 to patient, or city or town	C. C. MacCorison, M.D.
Lakeville State Sanatorium (for extra-pulmonary forms of tuberculosis)	Middleborough	304	$7.00 for children. $7.00 for adults (if paid by patient). $17.50 for adults (if paid by city or town)	Leon A. Alley, M.D.
State Infirmary (for unsettled cases of tuberculosis)	Tewksbury	280	Free for State cases.	L. K. Kelley, M.D.

Procedure for Admission to State Sanatoria: Application on blank obtainable from local board of health or from Department of Public Health, Room 546, State House, Boston, Massachusetts, should be made out and signed by attending physician, and forwarded to Department at above address. The Department will arrange for approval of local board of health as to financial responsibility for those unable to pay.

Procedure for Admission to State Infirmary: Application on blank obtained from a local board of public welfare or from Department of Public Welfare, Room 30, State House, Boston, Massachusetts, should be filed with the State Department of Public Welfare.

COUNTY SANATORIA

Name of Institution	Location	Number of Beds	Rates per Week	Superintendent
Barnstable County Sanatorium	Pocasset (Bourne)	50	$7.00 to patient $9.10 residents — to town. $28.00 non-residents	J. G. Kelley, M.D.
Bristol County Sanatorium	Attleboro	60	$9.10 residents $28.00 non-residents	G. P. Smith, M.D.
Essex Sanatorium	Middleton	360	$9.10 residents	O. S. Pettingill, M.D.
Hampshire County Sanatorium	Haydenville (Northampton)	100	$12.00 residents $15.00 non-residents	F. E. O'Brien, M.D.
Middlesex County Sanatorium	Waltham	400	$10.50 residents	S. H. Remick, M.D.
Norfolk County Sanatorium	So. Braintree	138	$9.10 residents $28.00 non-residents	N. R. Pillsbury, M.D.
Plymouth County Sanatorium	So Hanson	140	$9.10 residents $28.00 non-residents	B. H. Peirce, M.D.
Worcester County Sanatorium	Worcester (Greendale Station)	125	$10.50 residents $25.00 non-residents	E. W. Glidden, M.D.

Procedure for Admission: Special application blanks obtainable through local boards of health or directly from sanatoria, should be filled out by attending physician and returned to the superintendent of the sanatorium, who will arrange for approval of local board of health.

MUNICIPAL SANATORIA

Name of Institution	Location	Number of Beds	Rates per Week	Superintendent
Boston Sanatorium	249 River St., Mattapan	616	According to ability to pay for residents. $28.00 non-residents	F. L. Bogan, M.D.
Brookline Tuberculosis Hospital	Brookline	30	According to ability to pay for residents. $21.00 non-residents	Miss E. A. McMahon
Cambridge Tuberculosis Hospital	Cambridge	80	According to ability to pay for residents. $21.00 non-residents	Miss M. H. Conlon

MUNICIPAL SANATORIA (Continued)

Name of Institution	Location	Number of Beds	Rates per Week	Superintendent
Fall River Tuberculosis Hospital	Fall River	125	According to ability to pay for residents. $25.00 non-residents	Health Commissioner
Burbank Hospital (Tuberculosis Ward)	Fitchburg	36	$17.50 residents and non-residents	E. R. Lewis, M.D.
Lowell Isolation Hospital	Lowell	54	$15.00 residents $25.00 non-residents	J. J. McNamara, M.D.
Sassaquin Sanatorium	New Bedford	116	$15.50 residents and non-residents	J. F. Brewer, Jr., M.D.
Health Department Hospital (Tuberculosis Wards)	Springfield	50	$15.00 residents $21.00 non-residents	L. J. Smith, M.D.
Belmont Hospital	Worcester	150	$10.00 residents $17.50 non-residents	May S. Holmes, M.D.

Procedure for Admission: Appication blanks obtainable from and returnable to local city health department.

PRIVATE SANATORIA

Name of Institution	Location	Number of Beds	Rates per Week	Superintendent
Channing Home	Boston (198 Pilgrim Road)	27	Sliding scale up to $21.00 a week for patients. $14.00 a week to city or town	Miss Elizabeth Pelton
Central New England Sanatorium	Rutland	75	Sliding scale	....
Jewish Tuberculosis Sanatorium of Massachusetts	Rutland	25	Free	Apply to: Mrs. Rose Eydenberg, 294 Washington St., Boston (Room 440)
Monadnock Sanatorium	Rutland	6	$25.00 per week up	V. J. Alexandrov, M.D., Consultant, J. B. Hawes, 2nd, M.D.
Maple Lodge	Rutland	10	$25.00 per week up	V. J. Alexandrov, M.D., Consultant, J. B. Hawes, 2nd, M.D.
Sharon Sanatorium	Sharon	50	$20.00 for women $15.00 for children	W. A. Griffin, M.D.
Balfour Sanatorium	Sharon	25	Sliding scale $15.00 to $35.00 Average $25.00	Mrs. B. F. Balfour

PRIVATE SANATORIA (Continued)

Name of Institution		Number	Rates per Week	Superintendent
Pittsfield Tuberculosis Hospital	W. Pittsfield	14	$15.00 to patient $12.00 to city or town	Miss E. M. Safford
Frederic S. Coolidge	W. Pittsfield	8	$15.00 to patient $12.00 to city or town	Miss E. M. Safford

Procedure for Admission: Application to be made directly to sanatorium.

ISOLATION AND QUARANTINE

Cases: Special precautions should be observed as to disposal of sputum. Active cases with positive sputum should not be kept in homes where there are children.

Contacts: No special restrictions. Periodic check-up with aid of x-ray is advisable for all family contacts to detect early cases of tuberculosis. If family is unable to pay, this may be obtained through out-patient department or consultation clinic of the tuberculosis sanatorium (see pp. 258 and 262).

PREVENTION

No practical method of immunization available. Separation of contacts (especially children) from open cases of tuberculosis is most effective means of limiting spread.

SUMMER CAMPS AND PREVENTORIA

Camps and preventoria are maintained by certain tuberculosis associations. Are intended for care of children shown to have tuberculosis infection but without evidence of active disease. Preference is given to contacts of known cases of tuberculosis. Admission is on application of family physician to secretary of respective association. The following camps and preventoria are maintained in Massachusetts:

SUMMER CAMPS AND PREVENTORIA

Location	Boys or Girls	Auspices	Apply to
Ashburnham (So. Ashburnham)	Girls	Northern Worcester County Public Health Association, Inc.	Miss Vesta Stone, R.N., 12 Grove St., Fitchburg
Attleboro	Both	Bristol County Public Health Association, Inc.	Mrs. Mary C. Putnam, R.N., Bristol County Court House, Taunton
Bolton	Both	Public Health Association of Southwestern Middlesex County, Inc.	Mr. Franklin D. MacCormick, 214 Concord St., Framingham
Boston (Mattapan)	Both	Boston Tuberculosis Association, Inc.	Miss Bernice W. Billings, R.N., 554 Columbus Ave., Boston
Bourne (Pocasset)	Both	Barnstable County Public Health Association	Mrs. Edna P. Johnson, Pocasset

SUMMER CAMPS AND PREVENTORIA (Continued)

Location	Boys or Girls	Auspices	Apply to
Boxford	Both	Lawrence Tuberculosis League	Miss Kate T. Fuller, 31 Jackson St., Lawrence
Braintree	Both	Norfolk County Public Health Association	Nahum R. Pillsbury, M.D., South Braintree
Cambridge (Shady Hill School)	Girls	Cambridge Tuberculosis and Health Association, Inc.	Mrs. Mabel G. Smith, 689 Massachusetts Ave., Cambridge
Dighton	Both	Fall River Anti-Tuberculosis Society	George C. King, M.D., 150 Purchase St., Fall River
Hanson (South Hanson) Plymouth County Hospital	Both	Plymouth County Health Association, Inc.	B. H. Peirce, M.D., Plymouth County Hospital
Middleton (Essex Sanatorium)	Both	Essex County Health Association, Inc.	Miss Vera Griffin, R.N., 222 Cabot St., Beverly
Northampton (Leeds)	Both	Hampshire County Public Health Association, Inc.	Mrs. G. F. Rockford, R.N., Memorial Hall, Northampton
Pittsfield	Girls	Berkshire County Tuberculosis Association, Inc.	Mrs. Gertrude Brown, R.N., 16 South St., Pittsfield
Salem (Salem Willows)	Both	Salem Association for Prevention of Tuberculosis	Mrs. M. V. Garipay, R.N., 5 St. Peter St., Salem
Sharon (Lake Massapoag)	Both	Southern Middlesex Health Association, Inc.	Miss Margaret Roberts, 661 Massachusetts Ave., Arlington
Sterling (Sterling Junction)	Boys	Southern Worcester County Health Association, Inc.	Mrs. Helen Upham, R.N., 5 Pleasant St., Room 508, Worcester
Westfield (Provin Mountain)	Both	Hampden County Tuberculosis and Public Health Association, Inc.	Mr. Henry P. Coor, 145 State St., Springfield

TYPHOID FEVER

DIAGNOSIS Clinical condition with laboratory confirmation.
   Laboratory tests:
   a. *Blood culture*—Usually positive in the first week; sometimes as late as fifth week in severe cases.
   b. *Widal reaction*—May be positive by the end of first week; usually not until end of second week.
   c. *Stool culture*—Usually not positive until in third week of disease.
   d. *Urine culture*—May be positive in the second week in a small percentage of cases.

All specimens for above tests may be sent to local or State Bacteriological Laboratory, 527 State House, Boston, special outfits obtainable through local boards of health. (See p. 236.) Positive *diagnostic* reports telephoned or telegraphed prepaid.

TREATMENT Symptomatic and supportive.

ISOLATION AND QUARANTINE

(Consult regulations of local board of health. See p. 233.)

Cases: Usually one week after subsidence of clinical symptoms and thereafter until three successive negative stool and urine cultures, secured at an interval of at least one week, have been obtained, provided that a person who continues to be a carrier may be released under supervision of and after special permission of the board of health. Specimens obtained prior to one month after onset of disease should be considered as of diagnostic value only, and not as criteria for release. As three negative cultures are not a guarantee that patient has not become a carrier, it is recommended that a stool culture be obtained once a month for one year after recovery.

Contacts: Food handlers living in a family in which a case of typhoid fever exists are usually excluded from their occupation so long as they continue to live in the same house in which the case exists, and thereafter until usual incubation period has elapsed. Stool and urine cultures should be obtained from these and all other members of the family to find possible carriers. It is recommended that all family contacts with a case of typhoid be immunized against typhoid as soon as the case is recognized.

PREVENTION

Passive immunization: No practical method available.

Active immunization: Vaccine containing killed typhoid and paratyphoid B bacilli supplied by State through local board of health. Three subcutaneous injections (0.5 cc., 1.0 cc., 1.0 cc.) at intervals of seven to ten days. Children in proportion to their weight; those under fifty pounds, one-half the adult dosage. Injection of one cc. each year may be used for those constantly exposed.

Typhoid vaccination is especially indicated for:
1. Family contacts of a typhoid case.
2. Family contacts of a typhoid carrier.
3. Physicians.
4. Nurses.
5. Laboratory workers.
6. Institutional inmates.
7. Campers.
8. Those traveling in areas where they may not be certain as to safety of water, milk, and food supplies.

CARRIERS Two classes of carriers are generally recognized.
1. **Convalescent carriers:** Those shedding typhoid organisms in feces or urine during first year after infection.
2. **Permanent carriers:** Those shedding typhoid organisms in feces or urine one or more years after infection. Certain proven carriers are unaware of previous typhoid, apparently becoming carriers as result of mild unrecognized infection.

RESTRICTION ON CARRIERS
1. All typhoid carriers are reportable to the local board of health, usually as a cholecystitis of typhoid origin.

2. No typhoid carrier may be employed in a food handling capacity.
3. All typhoid carriers are subject to regulations of local board of health.
4. All known typhoid carriers are visited twice annually by representatives of State Department of Public Health.

TYPHUS FEVER

DIAGNOSIS

Clinical findings with aid from laboratory through Weil-Felix reaction. For this test send 5 cc. of blood in sterile test tube to State Bacteriological Laboratory, 527 State House, Boston. (See p. 236.)

TREATMENT Symptomatic and supportive.

ISOLATION AND QUARANTINE Precautions as to vermin.

PREVENTION

No practical method of active and passive immunization available.

UNDULANT FEVER (Brucella Infection)

DIAGNOSIS

Based on clinical findings with support of laboratory findings. For *blood culture* and *agglutination reaction* send 5 cc. of blood in *sterile* test tube to State Bacteriological Laboratory, 527 State House, Boston. (See p. 236.) Special containers for this purpose available through local boards of health (the tubes in the State Wassermann outfit are *not* sterile). *Significance of agglutination reactions—*

1/15—of no significance
1/45—of questionable significance
1/135 and higher—of diagnostic significance

TREATMENT

Symptomatic and supportive. Vaccines of questionable value.

ISOLATION AND QUARANTINE
Usually no restrictions.

PREVENTION

No practical method of active and passive immunization available. Most infections in Massachusetts contracted from raw milk.

WHOOPING COUGH (Pertussis)

DIAGNOSIS

Based on clinical findings. Use of cough plates is valuable in early diagnosis. Requires use of fresh plates and exposure to spasmodic cough. Cough plates are not available through State or board of health laboratories. White blood counts and differential counts are also used as aids to diagnosis. Such tests are not performed in State or board of health laboratories.

TREATMENT: Symptomatic and supportive.

ISOLATION AND QUARANTINE

(Consult regulations of local board of health. See p. 233.)

Cases: Usually three weeks from beginning of spasmodic cough. Some boards of health have permitted earlier release from strict isolation provided the patient is attended by a responsible adult to prevent association with other children.

Contacts: *Immune* contacts, usually no restrictions; *non-immune* contacts, usually exclusion from school two weeks from last exposure.

PREVENTION

Passive immunization: No practical method available.

Active immunization: Favorable results in preventing or reducing severity of subsequent infection have been reported through use of different vaccines. Vaccine prepared according to method of Sauer requires six injections (one in each arm for three successive weeks). Not of proven value.

GONORRHEA AND SYPHILIS

REPORTING

(All of the following reports may be made on the same form.)

1. *All forms and all stages of gonorrhea and syphilis* shall be reported directly (and only) to the State Department of Public Health, 545 State House, Boston, on forms provided by the Department for that purpose. Business reply envelopes are provided for mailing the reports to the Department. *These envelopes are to be used for no other purpose.* Every case is to be reported, whether or not it may have been reported by, or is to be referred for treatment to some other physician, clinic or hospital. The name of the patient is not to be reported except as hereinafter provided (see 3 and 4).

2. If the patient was in consultation previously with another physician over the same infection, the present physician shall notify the other of the patient's change of medical advisor. Otherwise the previous physician will be expected to *report the patient* to the Department as a delinquent in treatment.

3. Patients who discontinue treatment prematurely and who are not known to be under treatment elsewhere, shall be reported by name and address to the Department *within one week* of the missed appointment in case of primary or secondary syphilis, congenital syphilis with active lesions, syphilis in pregnant women, and acute gonorrhea; and within two weeks of the missed appointment in all other cases.

4. Patients with lesions of primary or secondary syphilis on exposed parts of the body or in the mouth, who are employed in any occupation requiring direct contact with other persons (barber, hairdresser, manicurist, waiter, waitress, nursemaid, domestic, etc.) shall be reported by name, address and occupation, to the Department, unless the attending physician will assume the responsibility for seeing that the patient discontinues such occupation until the lesions are healed.

5. The attending physician shall attempt to identify and bring to medical observation all of the patient's contacts, including members of the patient's family, from whom the patient may have acquired and to whom he (or she)

may have transmitted the infection. If any contact, other than a family contact, has not come to medical attention within two weeks of such identification, the contact's name and address shall be reported to the State Department of Public Health. Any patient who refuses to cooperate in the identification of contacts or in arranging for examination of family contacts shall be reported to the Department by name and address as uncooperative.

SYPHILIS

DIAGNOSIS (Literature available from the Department on request.)

1. **Darkfield examination:** The diagnosis of primary syphilis frequently depends upon darkfield examination of serum from the lesion for the spirochete, as blood tests may be negative in the early days of the stage. Most of the clinics in the State and a considerable number of physicians are prepared to make darkfield examinations. A list of the physicians who have indicated that they are "equipped, competent and willing" to make darkfield examinations for syphilis has been sent to every physician in the State, and additional copies of this list are available upon request. The patient must be sent to the examiner's laboratory. Prompt diagnosis of primary syphilis is of paramount importance to the patient and to others. *Seronegative primary syphilis is practically 100% curable.* Seropositive primary syphilis and secondary syphilis are from 80% to 90% curable. Generally speaking, cure is progressively more difficult and prognosis less favorable with lapse of time.

2. **Blood tests:** Serological examinations (Hinton tests) are made at the State Wassermann Laboratory, Harvard Medical School, 25 Shattuck Street, Boston (see p. 236). *There is no charge.* At least 5 cc. of blood should be withdrawn from the patient's vein, into a clean, dry, sterile syringe and transferred to a clean, dry, glass tube. Tubes and mailing containers may be obtained from local boards of health or their authorized distributing stations or directly from the Wassermann Laboratory. The most common cause of unsatisfactory tests is due to transportation. Specimens not transmitted by messenger should be sent by special delivery mail. Physicians using this type of mail service have largely eliminated unsatisfactory reports. Unless all apparatus which comes into contact with the blood is clean and dry, hemolysis or contamination may make the specimen useless.

The blood tests are reported as *positive, negative, doubtful* or *unsatisfactory*, with the following interpretations:

Positive almost always means that the patient has or has had syphilis. However, even if there is clinical evidence of this infection it is well to have the first report checked by a repeat test. In presumably infectious cases, the first treatment may be administered at the time the second sample of blood is submitted for the check test. A positive blood in a syphilitic is not necessarily evidence of infectiousness.

Doubtful suggests syphilis. It is advisable, therefore, to submit three or more specimens and to interpret a persistently or predominately doubtful reaction as presumptive evidence of syphilis.

Negative does not exclude syphilis, despite the high sensitivity of the test used at the State Laboratory. It does, however, make it very unlikely. In treated patients, particularly those whose treatment is begun in the primary and secondary stages, a negative test should not be taken, by itself, as reliable evidence of cure.

Unsatisfactory means that the test was unsuccessful because of the condition of the specimen when received (hemolysis, bacterial contamination, etc.) and is reported "Unsatisfactory".

The Boston Health Department and the Brockton City Laboratory perform Wassermann tests for physicians in those cities. Containers for specimens which are to be sent to those laboratories should be obtained from them.

3. **Spinal fluid examination:** The State Wassermann Laboratory performs the Wassermann tests on spinal fluids. Colloidal gold tests are done only for private physicians. At least 5 c.c. of fluid should be sent to the Wassermann Laboratory for the Wassermann and gold tests. The regular blood specimen outfit may be used, but the tube should first be boiled and a sterile rubber stopper inserted in place of the usual cork stopper.

Chemical analyses are *not* made at the State laboratories, nor are cell counts, which should be done as soon as possible after the fluid is withdrawn.

TREATMENT (Literature available from the Department on request.)

1. **Arsenicals:** The Department provides arsphenamine, neoarsphenamine and sulpharsphenamine free of charge for the treatment of syphilis. Mail requests to the Antitoxin and Vaccine Laboratory, 375 South Street, Jamaica Plain. The Department reserves the right to withhold arsenicals from physicians who neglect to report their cases of syphilis.

Arsphenamine (606) *must be alkalinized with normal sodium hydroxide solution before use.* Detailed directions accompany each package. The sodium hydroxide solution is *not* supplied by the Department.

Neoarsphenamine (914) becomes very toxic after exposure to air for more than 15 or 20 minutes. Should be used at once after opening ampoule.

Sulpharsphenamine is prone to cause arsenical dermatitis if used intravenously, and should be given intramuscularly (in the buttocks).

The arsenicals are supplied by the Department in the following sizes:—

Arsphenamine (For intravenous use only) 0.4 gm., 0.6 gm., 3.0 gm.

Neoarsphenamine (For intravenous use only) 0.3 gm., 0.45 gm., 0.6 gm., 0.9 gm.

Sulpharsphenamine (For intramuscular use) 0.3 gm., 0.6 gm., 3.0 gm.

Double distilled water (*not* supplied by the Department) should be used in making solutions of the arsenicals. Apparatus must be both clean and sterile or avoidable reactions may occur.

2. **Bismuth.** Bismuth subsalicylate is supplied by the Department free of charge for the treatment of syphilis. Mail requests to the Antitoxin and Vaccine Laboratory, 375 South Street, Jamaica Plain. It is supplied in the following sizes:

For physicians:	vials of 12 c.c.
For clinics and institutions and physicians with large numbers of patients under treatment:	vials of 60 c.c.

3. **Tryparsamide** (for the treatment of neurosyphilis) is not supplied by the Department.

4. **Malaria** and other fever therapy is available for the treatment of neurosyphilis at the Boston Psychopathic Hospital and several of the State

Mental Disease Hospitals (see section on Mental Diseases, p. 296). Commitment may be voluntary or by court order. Blanks for either may be obtained from the superintendents of the mental disease hospitals or from the Department of Mental Diseases.

LITERATURE (See p. 273.)

CLINICS (See p. 274.)

CONSULTATION (See p. 276.)

PATIENTS UNABLE TO PAY FOR MEDICAL CARE (See p. 277.)

GONORRHEA

DIAGNOSIS (Literature available from the Department on request.)

1. **Smears:** Smears for organisms resembling the gonococcus may be sent to local board of health laboratories or to the State Bacteriological Laboratory, Room 527, State House, Boston. Outfits, consisting of glass slides, swabs and mailing containers, may be obtained from local boards of health. (See p. 236.) Smears should be taken from the male urethral meatus and, when indicated, of the prostatic secretion. In the adult female, smears should be taken from *Skene's glands (after thorough massage)* and from *within the cervical canal (after thorough cleansing of the cervix with cotton or gauze).* In the female child, smears should be taken in the small cul-de-sac just in front of the hymen. It is advisable to moisten the cotton swab and twist it firmly between the fingers before taking the smear, to prevent loss of the material by absorption into the swab. Smears should be made evenly and about the size of a dime. State Laboratory reports are made as to pus-content of the smears as well as of the presence or absence of organisms resembling the gonococcus. *If organisms resembling the gonococcus are found in smears from the eye, the report is made by the State Laboratory by telephone or telegraph.*

2. **Gonococcus complement fixation** tests are made at the State Wassermann Laboratory, Harvard Medical School, 25 Shattuck Street, Boston. At least 5 c.c. of blood should be withdrawn from the patient's vein, into a clean, dry, sterile syringe and transferred to a clean, dry, glass tube. The regular Hinton test outfit may be used for mailing the specimen to the Laboratory, but *it must be plainly indicated that the test wanted is for gonorrhea.* If both the gonococcus complement fixation and Hinton tests are desired, send at least 10 c.c. of blood and indicate clearly that both tests are desired.

TREATMENT (Literature available from the Department on request.)

The Department does not supply any therapeutic preparation or equipment for the treatment of gonorrhea.

LITERATURE (See p. 273.)

CLINICS (See p. 274.)

CONSULTATION (See p. 276.)

PATIENTS UNABLE TO PAY FOR MEDICAL CARE (See p. 277.)

PROPHYLAXIS OF GONOCOCCAL OPHTHALMIA NEONATORUM

The General Laws, Tercentenary Edition, Chapter 111, Section 109A, requires that: "The physician, or hospital medical officer registered under section nine of chapter one hundred and twelve, if any, personally attending the birth of a child shall treat his eyes within two hours after birth with a prophylactic remedy furnished or approved by the department (of Public Health)." The Department has approved one per cent silver nitrate in individual doses in wax ampoules, and no other prophylactic may be used.

Silver nitrate (1% solution), in individual ampoules, is provided by the Department of Public Health, free of charge. Supplies may be obtained from local boards of health or their authorized distributing stations. There is accumulating evidence that sole dependence upon prophylaxis at birth is dangerous and that gonorrhea should be diagnosed in the mother and so treated that exposure of the baby's eyes will not occur.

LITERATURE

The following literature is available on request for the more detailed information of the physician as to the diagnosis, treatment and control of gonorrhea and syphilis, reactions to treatment, significance of blood tests, etc., and for the information and instruction of the patient.

FOR THE PATIENT

1. Information for the Male with Gonorrhea
2. Information for the Female with Gonorrhea
3. Information for the Male or Female with Syphilis
4. Gonorrhea
5. Gonorrhea and Syphilis in Industry
6. Syphilis
7. Congenital Syphilis

FOR THE PHYSICIAN

1. Minimum Standards for the Diagnosis, Treatment and Control of Syphilis
2. The Management of Syphilis in General Practice
3. Standard Treatment Procedure in Early Syphilis
4. Congenital Syphilis
5. The Economic Aspects of the Management of Syphilis
6. The Epidemiology of Syphilis and Gonorrhea
7. Gonorrhea
8. Minimum Standards for the Diagnosis, Treatment and Control of Gonorrhea
9. Gonococcus Infection in the Male
10. The Laboratory in the Diagnosis of Gonorrhea
11. The Clinical Diagnosis of Gonorrhea in the Male
12. The Clinical Diagnosis of Gonorrhea in the Female
13. The Treatment of Gonorrhea in the Male. General Principles.
14. The Treatment of Gonorrhea in the Male. Details of Procedure.

(See p. 238 for list of pamphlets on communicable diseases and p. 288 for list of pamphlets on child hygiene.)

CLINICS IN MASSACHUSETTS FOR THE TREATMENT OF GONORRHEA AND SYPHILIS

COMPILED BY THE MASSACHUSETTS DEPARTMENT OF PUBLIC HEALTH
Cooperating With
THE UNITED STATES PUBLIC HEALTH SERVICE
* Designated by the Department as Cooperating Clinics.

Beverly

*Beverly Hospital—Herrick and Heather Streets
  Syphilis and Gonorrhea: Men, Women and Children
  Wed., 2 and 6 P. M.

Boston

*Beth Israel Hospital—330 Brookline Avenue
  Syphilis:— Men and Women....... Mon., Wed., Fri., 8:30—10:30 A. M.
  Gonorrhea:—Men and Women....... Tues., Thurs., Sat., 8:30—10:30 A. M.
*Boston City Hospital—818 Harrison Avenue
  Syphilis:— Men and Women....... Tues., Thurs., Sat., 8—10:30 A. M.
  Gonorrhea:—Men .... Daily, 8—10:30 A. M.
          Women .... Tues., Thurs., Sat., 8—10:30 A. M.
*Boston Dispensary—25 Bennet Street
  Syphilis:— Men and Women........ Mon., Wed., Thurs., Sat., 8:45-10:30A.M.
                            Mon., Fri., 5:45—8 P. M.
  Gonorrhea:—Men .... Daily, 8:45—10:30 A. M.
                            Mon., Fri., 5:45—8 P. M.
          Women .... Tues., Fri., 8:45—10:30 A. M.
                            Mon., Fri., 5:45—8 P. M.
Boston Psychopathic Hospital—74 Fenwood Road
  Neurosyphilis:—Men, Women and Children
                            Tues., Sat., 8:30—10 A. M.
*Children's Hospital—300 Longwood Avenue
  Syphilis:— Children .... Monday, 2 P. M.
*Massachusetts General Hospital—Fruit Street
  Syphilis and Gonorrhea: Men, Women and Children
  Daily, 8—10 A. M.
*Massachusetts Memorial Hospitals—88 East Concord Street
  Syphilis:— Men and Women....... Mon., Wed., Fri., 8:30—11 A. M.
                            Tues., 5—7:30 P. M.
  Gonorrhea:—Men and Women....... Mon., Wed., Sat., 8:30—11 A. M.
                            Tues., 5—7 P. M.
N. E. Hospital for Women and Children—Dimock Street (Roxbury)
  Syphilis:— Women and Children... Sat., 9 A. M.
  Gonorrhea:—Women and Children... Tues., 2 P. M.
*Peter Bent Brigham Hospital—721 Huntington Avenue
  Syphilis:— Men and Women....... Mon., Fri., 1:30—3:30 P. M.
                            (Consultation—Wed., 1:30—3:30 P. M.)
  Gonorrhea:—Men .... Daily, 9—11 A. M.
          Women .... (Gyn. Clinic) Mon., Fri., 1:30—3:30 P.M.
        (Daily in Surgical Clinic as emergencies)

Brockton

*Brockton Hospital—680 Centre Street
  Syphilis & Gonorrhea:—Men........ Fri., 4:30—7 P. M.
          Women .... Tues., 4:30—7 P. M.

Cambridge

Cambridge Hospital—(Out-Patient Dept.)—330 Mt. Auburn Street
    Syphilis:— Men and Women....... Thurs., 9—10 A. M.
Cambridge City Hospital—1493 Cambridge Street
    Syphilis:— Men and Women....... Fri., 9—10 A. M.
    Gonorrhea:—Men and Women....... Tues., Sat., 8 A. M.

Fall River

*Board of Health Clinic—City Hall Annex, Third Street
Union Hospital—538 Prospect Street
    Syphilis and Gonorrhea:—Men and Women
    Mon., Wed., Fri., 6:30—8 P. M.
        Children .... Thurs., 8:30—9:30 A. M
    Syphilis:— Men and Women....... Mon., Thurs., 9:30 A. M.
    Gonorrhea:—Women .... Mon., Thurs., 9:30 A. M.

Fitchburg

*Burbank Hospital—Hospital Road
    Syphilis and Gonorrhea:—Men and Women
    Tues., Fri., 6—7 P. M.

Great Barrington

*Fairview Hospital
    Syphilis and Gonorrhea:—Men and Women
    Tues., 5—6 P. M.

Haverhill

*Board of Health Clinic—Gale Bldg., 471 Main Street
    Syphilis:— Men and Women....... Thurs., 12 M.—1 and 7—8 P. M.
    Gonorrhea:—Men and Women....... Tues., 12 M.—1 and 7—8 P. M.

Holyoke

*Holyoke Hospital—Beech Street
    Syphilis and Gonorrhea:—Men....... Mon., 5:30—7 P. M.
        Women .... Thurs., 4:30—6 P. M.

Lawrence

Board of Health Clinic—130 Oak Street
    Syphilis and Gonorrhea:—Men ...... Thurs., 11 A. M.—1 and 8—10 P. M.
        Women .... Mon., 11 A.M.—1 and 8—10 P. M.
                                  And by appointment

Lowell

*Board of Health Clinic—Corner Kirk and Paige Streets
    Syphilis and Gonorrhea:—Men....... Mon., 8:30 A. M. and Fri., 6:30 P. M.
        Women .... Tues., 6:30 P. M. and Thurs., 8:30 A. M.

Lynn

*Lynn Hospital—212 Boston Street
    Syphilis:— Men and Women....... Tues., 6 P. M. and Fri., 8 A. M.
    Gonorrhea:—Men and Women....... Tues., 8 A. M. and Fri., 6 P. M.

New Bedford

*Board of Health Clinic—519 Olympia Building
    Syphilis and Gonorrhea:—Men....... Mon., Fri., 4—5:30 P. M.
        Women .... Tues., 4—5:30 P. M.
                                  Thurs., by appointment
    Gonorrhea:—Women and Children.... Tues., Fri., 10—11 A. M.

Newton

*Newton Hospital—2014 Washington Street (Newton Lower Falls)
Syphilis:— Men and Women....... Wed., 9 A. M.
Gonorrhea:—Women .... Thurs., 9 A. M.

Pittsfield

*House of Mercy Hospital—741 North Street
Syphilis and Gonorrhea:—Men and Women
Tues., 11 A. M.—12 M.
Fri., 5—6 P. M.

Quincy

Board of Health Clinic—Quincy Dispensary, High School Avenue
Syphilis and Gonorrhea:—Men....... Fri., 4—5:15 P. M.
Women .... Thurs., 4—5:15 P. M.

Springfield

*Springfield Hospital—759 Chestnut Street
Syphilis and Gonorrhea:—Men....... Tues., 4:30—6 P. M.
Women and Children ... Thurs., 4:30—6 P. M.

Taunton

Board of Health Clinic—City Hall, Main Street
Syphilis and Gonorrhea:—Men and Women
Fri., 7—8 P. M.

Waltham

*Waltham Hospital—Hope Avenue
Syphilis:— Men and Women....... Fri., 9—11 A. M.

Worcester

*Worcester City Hospital (Out-Patient Dept.)—162 Chandler Street
Syphilis and Gonorrhea:—Men and Women
Wed., 6:30—7:30 P. M.
Mon., Wed., Fri., Sat., 8:30—10:30 A. M.
*Memorial Hospital—119 Belmont Street
Syphilis:— Men and Women....... Mon., 9 A. M.
Gonorrhea:—Men .... Tues., Thurs., Sat., 11 A. M.
Women .... Mon., Wed., Fri., 10 A. M.
Note: See page 277 "Patients Unable to Pay for Medical Care."

CONSULTATION

The Department (Division of Genitoinfectious Diseases) welcomes requests for information concerning any phase of the management of gonorrhea or syphilis. A considerable number of physicians who have had wide experience in this field are always ready to assist the Department in its consultation service. Physicians are urged, also, to make use of the consultation facilities that are available in the various clinics throughout the State.

The Department is prepared to send speakers on the management of gonorrhea and syphilis to any medical society meeting at any time.

CONFIDENTIAL FOLLOW-UP SERVICE

The Department has two trained nurse epidemiologists whose services are available to physicians for the follow-up of patients who have prematurely discontinued treatment and for the follow-up of contacts and sources of infection. The service of these nurses is entirely confidential. Patients and contacts are visited in the names of the physicians for whom the nurses may be working and their relationship to this Department is in no way disclosed to such patients or contacts. The nurses report the results of their investigations directly to the physician concerned, and any further action will be taken only at the direction of the physician. The names and addresses of patients or contacts followed for private physicians are not disclosed to any other person or agency, including the State Department of Public Health, except at the direction of the physician for whom the follow-up work is being done. The services of these nurses may be had upon request.

PATIENTS UNABLE TO PAY FOR MEDICAL CARE

Under the law (General Laws, Tercentenary Edition, Chapter 111, Section 117, as amended by Chapter 391 of the Acts of 1937) the State Department of Public Health is required to provide clinics (which it may do with the cooperation of local agencies) for the treatment of those who have gonorrhea or syphilis and cannot pay for private medical care. The Department is also permitted to otherwise provide treatment for syphilis and gonorrhea.

REGULATIONS REGARDING REIMBURSEMENT OF PRIVATE PHYSICIANS

Under the provisions of this law, the Department has promulgated the following regulations under which clinics, hospitals and physicians may be authorized to treat patients for syphilis and gonorrhea at the expense of the Commonwealth. It is to be noted that no clinic, hospital or physician may contract with a patient for treatment in behalf of the Department without the specific approval of the Department. The following regulations pertain to the reimbursement of private physicians for the treatment of patients with syphilis or gonorrhea: (Application blanks and other forms may be obtained from the Department on request.)

22. Application may be made by any physician licensed to practice medicine within the Commonwealth of Massachusetts, for reimbursement for the treatment of any patient wth gonorrhea or syphilis who cannot pay for private medical care, if, for economic or other reasons acceptable to the Commissioner of Public Health, the patient cannot reasonably attend any one of the Cooperating Clinics.

23. The application shall state the patient's case number (or initials), the city or town of residence, the diagnosis, the reasons for the patient's inability to attend a Cooperating Clinic, and an outline of the proposed plan of treatment.

24. Upon approval of the application by the Commissioner of Public Health the physician shall register the patient with the Department upon forms

which will be provided for that purpose, and shall, thereafter, submit vouchers for every visit made by the patient so long as treatment for gonorrhea or syphilis is continued by said physician.

25. The physician shall notify the Department promptly upon the failure of the patient to continue treatment regularly and shall accept the services of the Department's confidential follow-up service for the follow-up of the uncooperative patient and for such epidemiologic investigation as may be necessary. Failure to accept such service will be grounds for withholding reimbursement.

26. Reimbursement will be made at rates to be fixed by the Department from time to time, for each visit for which a visit voucher has been submitted to and approved by the Department, subject to the following qualification:—If any patient can pay any part of the physician's fee for any visit, he or she shall be required to do so, and reimbursement by the Commonwealth shall then be made for the difference between the fee paid by the patient and the current reimbursement fee, except that if the fee paid by the patient exceeds the current reimbursement fee, there shall be no reimbursement.

27. Bills must be submitted in duplicate promptly at the end of each calendar month on forms provided by the Department for that purpose.

28. The rate of reimbursement is hereby fixed at two dollars ($2) per visit which shall constitute reimbursement in full for all services rendered the patient.

29. Authorized representatives of the Department shall be permitted to check any bill submitted against the patient's record at any reasonable time.

30. Reimbursement will also be made for such sums paid by the physician to patients for necessary transportation to and from the physician's office and which the patient cannot afford to pay; provided that the cheapest form of reasonable transportation be used, unless an acute emergency requires the use of more expensive conveyance. The cost of transportation may be provided, subject to reimbursement, only from the point from which the patient comes directly to the physician's office and to the point to which the patient must go directly from the physician's office, but in no case shall the cost exceed that of transportation to or from the patient's place of residence or employment. Costs of transportation will not be subject to reimbursement by the Commonwealth, except for reasons acceptable in each case to the Commissioner of Public Health, if the cost of treatment and transportation exceeds the cost of transporting a patient to and treating a patient at a Cooperating Clinic.

RECORDS AND REPORTS OF GONORRHEA AND SYPHILIS TO BE CONFIDENTIAL

Section 119, Chapter 111, General Laws—Hospital, dispensary, laboratory and morbidity reports and records pertaining to gonorrhea or syphilis shall not be public records, and the contents thereof shall not be divulged by any person having charge of or access to the same, except upon proper judicial order or to a person whose official duties, in the opinion of the commissioner, entitle him to receive information contained therein. Violations of this section shall for the first offence be punished by a fine of not more than one hundred dollars.

DISCLOSURE OF CERTAIN INFORMATION NOT SLANDER OR LIBEL

Section 12, Chapter 112, General Laws:—Any registered physician or surgeon who knows or has reason to believe that any person is infected with gonorrhea or syphilis may disclose such information to any person from whom the infected person has received a promise of marriage or to the parent or guardian of such person if a minor. Such information given in good faith by a registered physician or surgeon shall not constitute a slander or libel.

ARTHRITIS

Under the provisions of Chapter 393 of the Acts of 1937 arrangements have been made by the Department of Public Health with the Massachusetts General Hospital for the hospitalization of patients with chronic rheumatism for the purpose of diagnosis and treatment of the disease. As the Act provides for the care and treatment of not more than 25 patients at any one time, and further that no person shall be hospitalized for a period exceeding six months, preference will be given in the selection of cases to those patients whose condition requires further study, and to whom some form of therapy can be offered. Preference will also be given to indigent persons, and no patient will be admitted for treatment who has not regularly resided in the Commonwealth at least two out of the preceding three years.

Applications for admission must be made by a licensed physician, upon forms provided by the Department of Public Health, and returned to the Department at Room 546, State House, Boston.

Upon discharge of the patient a written summary of the findings in the case, with diagnosis and recommendations for further care, will be sent to the physician who signed the application for the patient's admission.

BIOLOGIC PRODUCTS

Biologic products are prepared by the Department's Antitoxin and Vaccine Laboratory and distributed without charge, under the regulations given below.

The Antitoxin and Vaccine Laboratory was established in 1894 for the production of diphtheria antitoxin, which at that time was an expensive product and one of which the value was not fully determined. The original laboratory was housed in the Bussey Institution of Harvard University, and the present buildings, erected in 1904-05 and added to in 1927, are on the same grounds adjoining the Arnold Arboretum at Forest Hills.

The successful production of diphtheria antitoxin led to the manufacture of smallpox vaccine, beginning in 1905, and has been followed by the preparation of other products of recognized merit. (See list, p. 280.) The policy of the Department recognizes the desirability of manufacturing and distributing products for which there is a need, from the standpoint of public health, and which can be produced economically and efficiently. Some commonly used products not meeting these criteria, such as tetanus antitoxin and rabies vaccine, and some infrequently needed products, such as botulinus antitoxin, are not manufactured at the Antitoxin and Vaccine Laboratory.

The biologic products prepared by the Commonwealth are distributed without charge through boards of health and their agencies. Physicians should learn from their local board where supplies are kept. As these are perishable products and their cost is borne by the tax levy, it is requested that due care be taken to avoid waste by over-stocking. All out-dated products should be returned to the Antitoxin and Vaccine Laboratory directly or through the local board of health.

The products furnished by the State, directly or through stations, are:

DIAGNOSTIC

Schick Test Solution
Old Tuberculin (undiluted)
Serum Sensitivity Outfits
Pneumococcus Typing Serum

PREVENTIVE

Diphtheria Toxin-Antitoxin
Diphtheria Toxoid
Placental Extract
Silver Nitrate Solution
Smallpox Vaccine
Sodium Citrate Solution
Typhoid-Paratyphoid B Vaccine

THERAPEUTIC

Antimeningococcus Serum
Antipneumococcus Serum (see under pneumonia p. 252)
Diphtheria Antitoxin
Scarlet Fever Streptococcus Antitoxin
Anti-Influenza Bacillus Serum

The drugs for the treatment of syphilis are distributed through the Antitoxin and Vaccine Laboratory for the Division of Genitoinfectious Diseases. (See p. 271.)

REGULATIONS FOR DISTRIBUTION OF BIOLOGIC PRODUCTS

All biologic products are distributed under the following conditions:

1. Distributing stations must supply and use adequate refrigerating facilities for storage of products.

2. The delivery of diphtheria and scarlet fever antitoxin, smallpox vaccine, typhoid-paratyphoid vaccine, Schick test outfits, diphtheria toxin-antitoxin mixture and toxoid, and tuberculin is limited to boards of health, except as noted below.

3. A board of health not equipped to act as a distributing station may designate a hospital or drug store as its agent, but may not designate more than one agency.

4. A board of health may maintain more than one distributing station but products will be delivered by this Department to only one place in each town or city, unless needed for emergency use.

5. Hospitals of over 100 beds may obtain products by sending a messenger to the Antitoxin and Vaccine Laboratory for them.

6. Antimeningococcic serum will be distributed only through hospitals (or stations) selected by the Commissioner. In case of an epidemic other distributing points may be established by the Commissioner.

7. Physicians may obtain prophylactic products and therapeutic products for immediate use by calling at or sending a messenger to the laboratory for them.

8. Delivery of products through channels other than those authorized above may be made if the Director of the Division of Biologic Laboratories considers the exigencies of the situation warrant.

9. District health officers will inspect biologic products on hand at distributing stations at least twice a year and will report their inventory and findings to the Antitoxin and Vaccine Laboratory.

10. These regulations are effective on and after June 1, 1935.

11. These regulations do not apply to State institutions.

For regulations governing antipneumococcic serum and placental extract, see pp. 254 and 248, respectively.

The possibility of reactions following injections of any foreign protein should be kept in mind. The following directions may be followed in avoiding reactions from horse serum (serums and antitoxins):

SENSITIVITY

Whenever giving an injection of any biologic product, epinephrine should be available for treatment of any possible reaction. Although rare, reactions have been encountered even with intracutaneous injections.

PRECAUTIONS ADVISABLE IN THE ADMINISTRATION OF SERUMS AND ANTITOXINS

Reactions of various types may follow the parenteral administration of a foreign protein, such as horse serum, if the person has a natural or acquired hypersensitivity to the protein injected. Therefore, serum therapy should be employed only when definitely indicated and only by those equipped to combat such reactions as may occur.

I. ACUTE ANAPHYLACTIC TYPE OF REACTION

These reactions, although infrequent, are of the utmost importance, because they may prove fatal. They may follow the administration of even minute amounts of serum in extremely hypersensitive persons and may occur following the injection of serum by any route. The symptoms are dyspnea, cyanosis, urticaria, lumbar or abdominal pain, and collapse, any or all of which may begin within a few moments to an hour or more after the injection. Treatment is discussed below in paragraph F.

Such reactions may usually be avoided by observance of the following precautions which are designed to detect hypersensitive persons and lessen the dangers of serum administration.

A. History. Before the injection of serum, patients should be asked whether they have had asthma, hay-fever, eczema, urticaria, or angioneurotic edema. A positive history of these conditions is of importance only in suggesting the need for caution because such individuals probably have an allergic tendency. The method of serum administration described in paragraph C. 4 below is recommended for these patients.

A history of previous serum treatments (diphtheria, tetanus, or other antitoxin, antimeningococcic or antipneumococcic serum, diphtheria toxin-antitoxin mixture, etc.) and their sequelae should also be obtained. One injection of serum sometimes sensitizes to a succeeding injection of serum. If rapid or severe reactions followed earlier administrations of serum, similar reactions may or may not occur again, but preparations should be made to combat them if serum is given.

NOTE: Bacterial vaccines and diphtheria toxoid do not contain horse serum.

B. Tests for Hypersensitivity. Tests are of more importance than history; and at least one such test should be done on each patient who is to receive serum. (Material for testing is available at places supplying other biologic products.) Tests are not infallible but they give us the best information obtainable with our present knowledge. The ophthalmic test, in suitable cases, is probably a more reliable indicator of those individuals who may have severe reactions than is the intradermal test, because the latter apparently is capable of detecting degrees of hypersensitivity below the level of clinical importance. Although occasionally hypersensitive persons may not react to either test, such individuals appear to be rare. Tests should not be done nor any serum administered unless fresh epinephrine solution is at hand, preferably in a syringe.

1. OPHTHALMIC TEST. Observe both eyes carefully for any evidence of inflammation of the conjunctivae. Then put a drop of horse serum diluted 1:10 (if available; if not, use the serum it is planned to inject) in the conjunctival sac of one eye, leaving the other eye as the normal control. A positive reaction is indicated by itching, watering, and a diffuse reddening of the eye within 30 minutes. Severe reactions may be controlled by the installation of a few drops of epinephrine, 1:1000 dilution. The test is of no value in young children, for they may wash out the serum by crying. In adults with marked injection of the conjunctivae it may prove difficult of interpretation.

2. SKIN TEST. If only one syringe is available, first make a control-injection by injecting enough physiological saline solution *into* (not under) the skin of the anterior surface of one fore-arm to give a small elevation. In the corresponding location on the other arm, inject a similar amount of a 1:100 dilution of normal horse serum, having previously ejected some of the diluted serum from the needle to rid it of any water which may have remained from the sterilizing process. (The elevations caused by the injections tend to disappear within a few minutes if the test is negative, but the one produced by the serum may not disappear quite so quickly as the other.)

In hypersensitive patients, the elevation at the site of serum injection rapidly enlarges within 5 to 20 minutes, becomes urticarial in appearance and is surrounded by a zone of erythema. Pseudopodial extensions of the central wheal are considered evidence of the higher and more dangerous degrees of sensitivity. Reactions usually subside within an hour or two.

C. Use of Information Derived from Tests.

1. NEGATIVE TEST. Serum may be administered by any route to persons who do not react to these tests (or to either test, if only one is done). If serum is given intravenously, the first dose should not exceed 5 cc. and should be given very slowly, taking several minutes to administer the first cubic centimeter and at least one minute more for each additional cubic centimeter.

2. POSITIVE EYE TEST.

a. This is so nearly an absolute contra-indication to intravenous serum therapy that no serum should be given by this route except after consultation. Intravenous serum administration probably should not be undertaken at all in these patients, except possibly in a hospital, for severe reactions may be expected.

b. A positive eye test is also a sufficient contra-indication to the administration of serum by any other route to warrant the precautions (consultation and hospitalization) advised in the preceding paragraph.

3. POSITIVE SKIN TEST. The import of positive skin tests is probably less than that of positive eye tests, but the same precautions are advised, particularly if the skin test is strongly positive.

4. DOUBTFUL TESTS. If the tests give doubtful reactions or if the administration of serum is decided upon in spite of positive tests, the subcutaneous injection of a dose of epinephrine (5-15 minims of 1:1000 dilution) given a measured six minutes before the serum, is a procedure which has been used with success and which appears to be rational. Smaller initial doses than usual should be given at a very slow rate.

D. Desensitization. The practice of desensitizing hypersensitive patients by the administration of repeated graduated doses of serum, starting with minute amounts (0.005 cc. more or less) subcutaneously and giving increasing doses at intervals of approximately one-half hour, is no longer recommended.

E. Observation. All patients receiving serum should be kept under close observation for not less than 30 minutes and preferably at least 45 minutes, during which time a physician should be immediately available.

F. Treatment. Fresh epinephrine solution, ready for administration, should be at hand in a syringe whenever serum is administered. The dose is 1 cc. (15 minims) for an adult, correspondingly less for a child. It should be given if the patient complains of lumbar or abdominal pain or shows evidence of urticaria, dyspnea, cyanosis or collapse. The dose may be repeated within a few minutes if necessary, and may be given intravenously. Artificial respiration may be required and measures to combat shock (the application of heat, etc.) instituted if collapse occurs.

II. THERMAL OR "CHILL" REACTIONS

These occur after the intravenous administration of serum and are seen most frequently with antipneumococcic serum, possibly because it is given intravenously more often and in larger doses than other serums. If the patient develops a chill, which when it appears at all usually begins within twenty minutes to one and one-half hours after any dose, the advent of hyperpyrexia should be watched for. Should hyperpyrexia develop, immediate treatment is essential. Epinephrine is of no use at such a time, but procedures advocated for the treatment of heat stroke are indicated, such as the use of ice packs, the application of sheets wrung from ice water, and ice water enemas. Venesection may be of use should pulmonary edema develop.

III. SERUM SICKNESS

This is characterized most often by urticaria, but fever, enlarged glands, and joint pains are other common signs. It may come on any time up to four weeks after serum therapy, most commonly between the fourth and tenth days. Although this complication is disagreeable for the patient, it is not serious. Epinephrine may be given to allay discomfort, but its effect is of short duration.

Cold applications lessen the annoyance of the urticaria. Large doses of salicylate have also been recommended.

IV. ARTHUS PHENOMENON

A local reaction not incited by infection but going on to necrosis, at the site of subcutaneous or intramuscular injections occurs rarely. Serum injected within a period of several days to a few weeks or months after a previous injection is more likely to cause such reactions than is serum given either a few hours or days or some months or years after an injection. Such reactions are said to be most likely to occur if the patient shows signs of serum sickness at the time of injection. The possibility of such reactions should be kept in mind to avoid confusing them with local abscesses.

CANCER

The Cancer Program of the Department of Public Health of Massachusetts was inaugurated in 1926 by legislative enactment, Chapter 391. The program as originally devised, and as still functioning with modifications, contains five major activities: hospitalization, tumor diagnostic service, research, diagnostic clinics, and education.

HOSPITALIZATION

The Pondville Hospital, with a bed capacity of 145, and the Cancer Wing of the Westfield State Sanatorium with 50 beds, cares for any patient with cancer or suspected cancer of all types and stages provided that the patient has lived in Massachusetts for two out of the preceding three years and is certified for admission by a practicing physician.

The charges for individuals able to pay are $10.50 per week. All others are hospitalized at no expense to themselves. Hospital charges to cities and towns for patients unable to pay their own fees are $2.50 per day. No additional charge is made for service or treatment. Diagnostic services are free in the out-patient clinic, while the charge for treatment is $1.50.

Diagnostic, surgical, therapeutic, radium, x-ray (diagnosis and treatment), medical, and nursing services are available. An out-patient clinic for diagnosis and treatment is held at the Pondville Hospital on Thursdays at 1 P.M. and at the Westfield State Sanatorium on Wednesdays at 11 A.M. to 1 P.M.

Application blanks must be filled out by a registered physician and sent to the proper hospital. The applicant will be notified when he may be admitted. Physicians are requested to send letters with their patients when they enter the hospital.

Application blanks may be obtained from the Pondville Hospital, Post Office address Wrentham, Mass., telephone Walpole 386; the Westfield State Sanatorium, Westfield, Mass., telephone Westfield 1700; at 546 State House, Boston; from local overseers of the poor; or local boards of health.

OTHER CANCER SERVICES

Most general hospitals treat a large number of cancer patients. Special services for cancer are available in several of the Boston hospitals: The Collis P. Huntington Memorial, Palmer Memorial, Beth Israel, Massachusetts General, Massachusetts Memorial, Free Hospital for Women, Peter Bent Brigham, and Boston City. Arrangements for admission to these are made directly with the hospital. Patients attending the State-aided cancer clinics may be assisted by the social worker in this matter.

Cases not requiring surgical or other special treatment are accepted at following hospitals, application in each case to be made directly to hospital:

Boston—Long Island Hospital, Long Island (Boston patients only)
Cambridge—Holy Ghost Hospital for Incurables, 1575 Cambridge Street
Fall River—Rose Hawthorne Lathrop Hospital, Bay Street
Tewksbury—The State Infirmary

TUMOR DIAGNOSTIC SERVICE

Tumor specimens for pathological examination may be sent to the Tumor Diagnostic Laboratory, Huntington Memorial Hospital, 695 Huntington Avenue, Boston. The laboratory is maintained jointly by the Department of Public Health and the Harvard Cancer Commission. No charge is made for tumor examination. *Pathological specimens other than suspected tumors should not be sent to this laboratory;* the State makes no provision for such examinations. Containers for shipment of tumor specimens may be obtained from local boards of health or from the State Department of Public Health, 527 State House, Boston.

RESEARCH

The studies have covered the magnitude of the problem; the existing hospital facilities in the State including the availability of radium and x-ray; the medical, social, and economic aspects of the disease; as well as such etiological findings as would be obtained by statistical analysis of death records, hospital records, and home visits to cancer patients. This work is continuing and reports are made on new evidence as it is acquired.

Assistance is also furnished physicians in interpreting the statistical analysis of their papers.

CLINICS

The State-aided cancer clinics are administered by committees appointed by the local medical organizations. These committees have charge of the administrative details connected with their respective clinics but in all cases they must conform with the minimum standards set by the Department. These are:

(a) Group diagnosis: The group must consist of at least three men, preferably surgeon, pathologist, and radiologist. When any of these are not available other physicians may be substituted.

(b) Uniform records: Forms are furnished by the Department for this purpose as is also money for clerical service when needed.

(c) Social service: All cases of cancer and precancerous conditions are referred to social service for follow up. The follow up continues until death in the case of cancer and until removal of the lesion in precancerous conditions. The State either furnishes money to help defray the expenses of the social worker or furnishes the clinic the services of a part-time social worker.

Every physician in the Commonwealth may bring or send his patient to the clinic for free consultative service with the group. If the individual case requires such diagnostic procedure as gastro-intestinal series this must be paid for by the patient if he is able to do so, but if he is not able to do so funds are available for this service.

Each case is returned to the physician who sent him to the clinic, and this physician decides whether or not he desires the assistance of social service in securing treatment for his patient.

The clinics must meet at least twice a month. At intervals determined by the clinic committee, but in no instance less than once a year, some form of teaching for the physician in the community is required. Some clinics perform this service by having consultants come to the clinics at stated intervals; others have adopted the plan of having all the physicians in the community serve on the clinic staff; while still others confine their activities to having an address on cancer by some surgeon from another city.

The clinic itself is furnished the following services by the State: first, advice, information, and literature; second, funds for or services of social worker; third, funds for travel of social worker; fourth, funds for x-ray diagnosis for those unable to pay; fifth, funds for teaching clinics; sixth, funds for clerical assistance in clinics; seventh, funds for postage, telephone, stationery, etc.; eighth, special clinics for the staffs of the clinics; and ninth, reference of cancer cases to Pondville through social service.

The purpose of the clinics is to furnish physicians and the public group consultation service in cancer, as well as to improve the knowledge of cancer among the medical profession and the laity. The group furnishes a diagnosis and outlines a plan of treatment for any person suspected of having cancer, regardless of financial status. Every effort is made to have the family physician either come with his patient to the clinic or send the patient with such information as he cares to furnish. Any individual is admitted to the clinic although it is preferable to have the patients referred by physicians so that any tendency to use the cancer clinic in order to establish a diagnosis of a condition originally not suspected of being cancer may be eliminated.

State aided cancer clinics are conducted in the following hospitals:

Boston	Beth Israel Hospital
Boston	Boston Dispensary
Brockton	Brockton Hospital
Fall River	Union Hospital
Fitchburg	Burbank Hospital
Gardner	Henry Heywood Memorial Hospital
Gloucester	Addison Gilbert Hospital
Greenfield	Franklin County Hospital
Hyannis	Cape Cod Hospital
Lawrence	Lawrence General Hospital
Lowell	Lowell General Hospital
Lynn	Lynn Hospital
New Bedford	St. Luke's Hospital
Newburyport	Anna Jaques Hospital
Norfolk	Pondville Hospital
North Adams	North Adams Hospital
Northampton	Cooley Dickinson Hospital
Pittsfield	St. Luke's Hospital
Springfield	Springfield Hospital
Westfield	Westfield State Sanatorium
Worcester	Memorial Hospital

EDUCATION

The educational program for the dissemination of information concerning cancer consists of the teaching of exact knowledge by an authority in the person of the family physician to the individual as one of a small group. To accomplish this in a State of more than 350 communities, with a population of nearly four and one half million, and over 7,000 physicians, each community in the State has, or is in the process of having, a Cooperative Cancer Control Committee. The individual Cooperative Cancer Control Committees of the several communities in Massachusetts automatically become integral parts of a State-wide Cooperative Cancer Control Committee. More than two-thirds of the communities of the State are organized at this writing. The committees differ from many other educational committees in that they are not selective and consequently restricted to limited groups or classes, but they are rather inclusive in nature, and represent every type of group and individual in the community—religious, political, labor, foreign, social, fraternal, patriotic, and service.

These clubs promise to have at least one meeting a year on cancer. A club does not have to have an impressive membership to become corporate in this plan. The small group of eight or twelve is an ideal size. The group, itself, determines the type of cancer talk it will have. Some groups prefer a formal talk followed by a question period while others prefer the round-table discussion with the physician during which questions are asked. In any case, a question period is desirable.

The local physician is the one who is asked to be the teacher in this program because the decline or increase in early detection of cancer is entirely in his hands, because he will obtain more cooperation from his community if it knows exactly what to do in case of early symptoms and what the early symptoms are, because the local physician knows his community, and because it has always been the natural prerogative of the physician to teach.

CHILD HYGIENE

PRENATAL LETTERS

A series of letters to the expectant mother regarding the hygiene of pregnancy is available through the Department of Public Health. These letters are nine in number, one for each month of pregnancy. The first letter is accompanied by a booklet, "Baby and You", which covers care of infants. The booklet, "Your Premature Baby", is sent with the sixth letter.

A special letter to the "expectant father" goes directly with the first letter, accompanied by the pamphlet, "Congenital Syphilis". All letters are mailed by the Department at regular intervals to all names on the prenatal registry. This registry is strictly confidential and is used for no other purpose. Requests to place names on the registry for prenatal letters are accepted from physicians, clinics, hospitals, nurses, social workers and parents. All requests should be made to the Department of Public Health, Division of Child Hygiene, 1 Beacon Street, Boston, Telephone, Capitol 4600, Extension 273. A sample set of letters and pamphlets will be mailed on request to professional workers.

POSTNATAL LETTERS

A comparable series of twenty-four letters covering child care for the first two years. These letters emphasize the importance of regular medical and dental supervision. Accompanying these letters are the following special letters and pamphlets.

Special Letters:

Cancer in relation to birth injuries
Importance of examination of mother following confinement

Pamphlets:

Vaccination
Diphtheria prevention
"Being a Parent", including list of booklets on habit training, prepared by Massachusetts Department of Mental Diseases
"One to Six", booklet summarizing child care up to time of school entrance
"Cooking for Health", booklet containing useful menus and recipes for home use

Postnatal letters are sent routinely to all names already on the registry for prenatal letters. Requests to have such letters sent directly to patients may be made to Department of Public Health, Division of Child Hygiene, 1 Beacon Street, Boston, Telephone, Capitol 4600, Extension 273. Sample letters and pamphlets are sent on request.

EDUCATIONAL MATERIAL

Popular pamphlets on child hygiene are available as follows, requests to be made through local board of health or directly to Department of Public Health, 1 Beacon Street, Boston:

Aids to Bowel Movement
Attention! Stand Tall
Care of the Child in Cold Weather
Care of the Child in Hot Weather
The Care of the Teeth
Diet from Birth to Two Years
Feeding the Preschool Child
Feeding the School Child
Food for the Teens
Healthful Living for the Teens
How to Judge Nutrition of Children
Gain in Height and Weight by Years for Girls and Boys of School Age
Suggestions for Care During Pregnancy
Supplies Necessary for Confinement
Ten Rules for Healthful Living
Watch Your Step
Baby and You
One to Six
Are You as Attractive as Nature Intended?
A Child Entering School Should Be able To
Cooking for Health
Food Ways to Health
For Your Teeth and Gums
Good Eating Habits
A Health Creed

Keeping Baby Dry
Keeping Well
Minerals and Vitamins
Protecting Two
Sensible Sun Baths
Your Baby's First Teeth
Your Second Teeth
Your Premature Baby

(See p. 238 for list of pamphlets on communicable diseases and p. 273 for list of pamphlets on gonorrhea and syphilis.)

OBSTETRIC PACKAGE

The Division of Child Hygiene furnishes a sample obstetric package with instructions for making and for use so that local women's organizations may copy. These are sterilized at local hospitals and are available to physicians at nominal cost to their patients. Such packages may be procured by physicians from the local organization which prepares them.

PREMATURE INFANT CARE

Section 67, of Chapter 111, as appearing in the General Laws (Ter. Ed.) and amended by Chapter 332 of the Acts of 1937, provides for the reporting as soon as practicable by telephone to the local board of health a premature infant born outside the hospital and confirming this by a written report within twenty-four hours (section 67A). Upon written request of either parent and the attending physician the board of health will provide for transportation to a hospital equipped for the care of premature infants (section 67B). The reasonable charge for the care of these infants of indigent parents in the hospital shall be paid by the local board of welfare without altering the status of the settlement of the parents (section 67C and D).

Hospital centers adequately equipped for the care of premature infants are now being established and physicians will receive notification of such centers in their vicinity.

Instruction of nurses in the care of premature infants will be provided by means of regional institutes.

POSTGRADUATE INSTRUCTION

With the cooperation of the Massachusetts Medical Society, postgraduate courses in Obstetrics and Pediatrics are available for county medical societies. One lecture in this course concerns the care of the newborn and premature infant.

A refresher course for physicians conducting or about to conduct well child conferences is furnished through the Division of Child Hygiene.

SERVICES TO CRIPPLED CHILDREN

Diagnostic Clinics for Crippled Children are conducted as follows:

Brockton	Brockton Hospital
Fall River	Union Hospital
Gardner	Henry Heywood Memorial Hospital
Haverhill	Hale Hospital
Hyannis	Cape Cod Hospital

Lowell	St. John's Hospital
Pittsfield	St. Luke's Hospital
Salem	Salem Hospital
Springfield	Wesson Memorial Hospital
Worcester	Worcester City Hospital

A crippled child is defined, for administrative purposes, as follows:

The term "crippled children" is understood to include those children under twenty-one years of age who are suffering from the residual paralysis of poliomyelitis, bone and joint tuberculosis, congenital defects, arthritis, and such other similar conditions as may lead to, or have produced crippling and which may be treated advantageously. It also includes children who require operations because of burns and accidents, or because of congenital defects such as harelip, cleft palate, and so forth. It is not planned to include children who are the victims of "acute" accidents or who require operations for hernia or for the removal of tonsils and adenoids, nor is it planned to provide custodial care for children of low mentality or for any other children.

Admission of a child to these clinics is secured on application of the family physician. A special committee of each District Medical Society co-operates with the Department. Only those patients whose families are unable to pay for the services of an orthopedic surgeon, hospitalization or necessary apparatus are admitted. Hospitalization or apparatus recommended by the orthopedic consultant in charge of the clinic provided by the Department. The hospital is designated by the orthopedic consultant.

ASSISTANCE TO THE BLIND AND CONSERVATION OF VISION

OPHTHALMIA NEONATORUM
(See p. 251.)

ASSISTANCE TO THE BLIND

The Division of the Blind in the State Department of Education is established to assist those with defective vision. Although reporting of such cases is not compulsory, it is advisable that all persons with a vision of 20/200 or less, and children with 20/70 or less be reported to this Division, 110 Tremont Street, Boston, Telephone Liberty 6006. Assistance offered through this Division not obtainable unless patient is so registered. For those patients so registered, assistance is available through following sources:

1. **Visiting teachers** go into the homes of those becoming blind in adult life, giving home instruction in reading by touch, and in chair caning, sewing and other handwork.

2. **Workshops for the blind:** Six such workshops are maintained, in Cambridge (two, one for men and one for women), Fall River (one), Lowell (one), Pittsfield (one), and Worcester (one). Work carried on here includes caning of chairs, manufacture of brooms, mats, rugs, mops, and fine art fabrics.

3. **The Blind Handicraft Shops,** 73 Newbury Street, Boston, and 39 Eagle Street, Pittsfield,—Maintained for purpose of selling the work of the blind, all money, after deducting cost of materials, going to the producer.

4. **Relief funds:** Limited relief funds are available to certain individuals as supplements to inadequate incomes from other sources.

The Division of the Blind also cooperates with local school departments in establishment of Sight-Saving Classes for those having vision so impaired as to handicap normal school progress. Inquiries about such classes may be made to the Division or to local school department.

INSTITUTIONS

1. **Perkins Institution and Massachusetts School for the Blind,** 175 North Beacon Street, Watertown—Limited to children of normal mentality, 5 to 19 years of age, with vision of 20/200 or less in both eyes. Applications may be made directly through the Division of the Blind, 110 Tremont Street, Boston.

2. **Boston Nursery for Blind Babies,** 147 South Huntington Avenue, Boston—Receives blind children up to 5 years of age. Applications may be made through the Division of the Blind, 110 Tremont Street, Boston.

ASSISTANCE TO THE DEAF AND HARD OF HEARING

FOR THE DEAF

Beverly School for the Deaf, Beverly, Mass. Public, resident.
Boston School for the Deaf, North Main St., Randolph. Public, resident.
Clarke School for the Deaf, 46 Round Hill, Northampton. Public, resident.
Horace Mann School for the Deaf, Kearsarge Avenue, Boston. (A public day school for any Massachusetts child living near enough to attend).

FOR THE HARD OF HEARING

Boston Guild for the Hard of Hearing
Formerly Speech Readers Guild of Boston, 283 Commonwealth Avenue, Boston, a social welfare agency dealing with all phases of deafness. The Guild's *free* consultation service is the focal point to which many agencies, medical centres and physicians of Boston and vicinity refer their problems in regard to those who have deafness. It urges the study of lip reading, the use of hearing aids, and offers social and educational advantages.

INDUSTRIAL DISEASES

The laws of the Commonwealth provide that ". . . every physician treating a patient whom he believes to be suffering from any ailment or disease contracted as a result of the nature, circumstances or conditions of the patient's employment . . ." shall report the same to the State Department of Labor and Industries. Blanks for reporting the same may be obtained from the Division of Industrial Safety, 473 State House, Boston.

MENTAL DISEASES

DIAGNOSIS

General Out-Patient Clinics: Conducted by staffs of State Mental Disease Hospitals. Appointments to be made in advance through respective hospitals. Clinics are held as follows:

GENERAL OUT-PATIENT CLINICS

City or Town	Institution or Other Agency	Time	Auspices
Boston	Boston Psychopathic Hospital	Daily except Sunday and Holidays, 9 A.M.-12 M.	Hospital Staff
Boston	Massachusetts Memorial Hospitals	Tues., 9 A.M. to 4:30 P.M.; Wed. 1-4:30 P.M.	Westborough State Hospital
Danvers	Danvers State Hospital	(By appointment)	Hospital Staff
Fitchburg	City Hall	2nd Wed. of month, 2-4 P.M.	Gardner State Hospital
Foxborough	Foxborough State Hospital	(By appointment)	Hospital Staff
Framingham	Municipal Building	3rd Mon. of month, 6:30 P.M.	Westborough State Hospital
Gardner	Gardner State Hospital	(By appointment)	Hospital Staff
Grafton	Grafton State Hospital	Sat., 9 A.M.-12 M.; other days by appointment	Hospital Staff
Lowell	St. John's Hospital	1st Mon. of month, 6:30 P.M.; Afternoon by appointment	Westborough State Hospital
Monson	Monson State Hospital	(By appointment)	Hospital Staff
Northampton	Northampton State Hospital	Daily 9:30-11 A.M.; 1:30-4:30 P.M.	Hospital Staff
Waltham	Department of Public Welfare, City Hall	2nd and 4th Mon. and 1st Wed., 6:30 P.M.	Westborough State Hospital
Westborough	Westborough State Hospital	Daily except Sat. and Sun., 2-5 P.M.; 1st Sun. in month, 9 A.M.-5 P.M.	Westborough State Hospital
Worcester	Worcester State Hospital		Hospital Staff (By appointment)

Child Guidance and Adjustment Clinics: Conducted in various communities by staffs of State Mental Disease Hospitals. Appointments to be made in advance through respective hospital. Clinics are held as follows:

CHILD GUIDANCE AND ADJUSTMENT CLINICS

City or Town	Institution or Other Agency	Time	Auspices
Athol	Red Cross Rooms	1st Wed. of month, 1-4 P.M., by appointment	Gardner State Hospital
Bedford	Union School	(By appointment)	Grafton State Hospital
Belmont	Junior High School Bldg.	1st and 3rd Mon., 9:30 A.M.-3:30 P.M.	Grafton State Hospital
Bolton	Emerson School	(By appointment)	Grafton State Hospital
Boston	Boston Psychopathic Hospital	Daily except Sun., 9-12 M.	Hospital Staff
Boston	Boston Psychopathic Hospital	Daily except Sat., Sun. and holidays, 9 A.M.-12 M. by appointment	Hospital Staff
Brockton	Brockton Hospital	Wed. 1:30-4 P.M.	Foxborough State Hospital
Carlisle	Highland School	(By appointment)	Grafton State Hospital
Chelmsford	Superintendent of Schools	(By appointment)	Grafton State Hospital
Concord	High School Bldg.	2nd and 4th Mon. of month, 9:30 A.M.-3:30 P.M.	Grafton State Hospital
Fitchburg	Academy Street School	Mon. and Fri., 1-4 P.M.	Gardner State Hospital
Framingham	Framingham Union Hospital	Mon., 1-5 P.M.	Westborough State Hospital
Gardner	High School	Thurs., 1-4 P.M.	Gardner State Hospital
Grafton	Grafton State Hospital	Sat., 9-12 M.	Hospital Staff
Grafton	Superintendent of Schools	(By appointment)	Grafton State Hospital
Groton	High School Bldg.	(By appointment)	Grafton State Hospital
Harvard	Union School	(By appointment)	Grafton State Hospital
Haverhill	High School, Summer Street	Sat., 9-11 A.M.	Danvers State Hospital
Holyoke	Skinner Clinic, Holyoke Hospital	Wed., 1-3:30 P.M.	Northampton State Hospital
Hudson	Superintendent of Schools	(By appointment)	Grafton State Hospital
Lancaster	Superintendent of Schools	(By appointment)	Grafton State Hospital

CHILD GUIDANCE AND ADJUSTMENT CLINICS (Continued)

City or Town	Institution or Other Agency	Time	Auspices
Lawrence	International Institute	1st and 3rd Fri., 9-11 A.M.	Danvers State Hospital
Leominster	Junior High School Bldg.	Fri., 9:30 A.M.-3:30 P.M.	Grafton State Hospital
Lexington	High School Bldg.	Tues., 9:30 A.M.-3:30 P.M.	Grafton State Hospital
Littleton	Superintendent of Schools	(By appointment)	Grafton State Hospital
Lowell	Lowell General Hospital	Wed., 2 P.M.	Div. of Mental Hygiene, Dept. of Mental Diseases
Lynn	Child Welfare House, 15 Church Street	Tues., 9:30-11 A.M.	Danvers State Hospital
Maynard	Roosevelt School	(By appointment)	Grafton State Hospital
Melrose	Calvin Coolidge School Main Street	Thurs., 9:30-11:30 A.M.	Danvers State Hospital
Natick	High School Bldg.	1st and 3rd Thurs., 9:30 A.M.-3:30 P.M.	Grafton State Hospital
Newburyport	Health Centre, Harris Street	2nd and 4th Fri. of month, 2-4 P.M.	Danvers State Hospital
Northampton	People's Institute	Wed., 4-6 P.M.	Northampton State Hospital
Northbridge	Superintendent of Schools	(By appointment)	Grafton State Hospital
Orange	Visiting Nurses' Rooms	1st Wed. of month, 1:30-4 P.M.	Gardner State Hospital
Quincy	Quincy High School, Coddington Street	Thurs., 2:30 P.M.	Medfield State Hospital
Salem	Pinkham Memorial, Hawthorne Blvd.	Mon., 2-4 P.M.	Danvers State Hospital
Springfield	Springfield Hospital	Mon., Wed., and Fri., 2-5 P.M.	Monson State Hospital
Stow	Superintendent of Schools	(By appointment)	Grafton State Hospital
Upton	Superintendent of Schools	(By appointment)	Grafton State Hospital
Waltham	Waltham Hospital, Hope Avenue	Wed., 2-4 P.M.	Metropolitan State Hospital
Worcester	21 Catherine Street	Daily, 9 A.M.-5 P.M.; Sat., 9 A.M.-12 M.	Worcester State Hospital

Habit Clinics: Conducted in several communities by staff of Department of Mental Diseases, Division of Mental Hygiene, 100 Nashua St., Boston, Telephone, Capitol 7320. Appointments to be made in advance through Department or Hospital. Clinics are held as follows:

HABIT CLINICS

City or Town	Institution or Other Agency	Time	Auspices
Beverly	Health Center, Cabot Street	Wed., 9-11 A.M.	Danvers State Hospital
Boston	Boston Dispensary, 25 Bennet Street	Wed. and Thurs., 9:30 A.M.	Division of Mental Hygiene
Boston	Boston Psychopathic Hospital	Daily except Sundays and holidays, 9 A.M.-12 M.	Boston Psychopathic Hospital
Boston	New England Hospital for Women and Children, Dimock Street, Roxbury	Thurs., 9:30 A.M.	Division of Mental Hygiene
Boston	West End Health Unit, 17 Blossom Street	Wed., 2 P.M.	Division of Mental Hygiene
Brockton	Brockton Hospital	Wed., 1:30-4 P.M.	Foxborough State Hospital
Lawrence	Lawrence General Hospital, Garden Street	Tues., 2 P.M.	Division of Mental Hygiene
North Reading	North Reading Sanatorium	1st Tues. of month, 10 A.M.	Division of Mental Hygiene
Norwood	Norwood Hospital, Washington Street	Fri., 9:30 A.M.	Division of Mental Hygiene
Quincy	Woodward Institute, Hancock Street	Thurs., 2:30 P.M.	Division of Mental Hygiene
Reading	Reading High School	Tues., 2 P.M.	Division of Mental Hygiene

Mental and Mental Hygiene Clinics: Conducted in several communities by staff of State Mental Disease Hospitals. Appointments to be made in advance through respective hospital. Clinics are held as follows:

MENTAL AND MENTAL HYGIENE CLINICS

City or Town	Institution or Other Agency	Time	Auspices
Attleboro	Sturdy Memorial Hospital, Park Street	Last Mon. of month, 1:30-4 P.M.	Taunton State Hospital
Boston	Boston Psychopathic Hospital	Daily except Sundays and holidays, 9 A.M.-12 M.	Boston Psychopathic Hospital
Boston	*Boston Psychopathic Hospital	Tues. and Sat., 8:30-10 A.M.	Hospital Staff
Boston	Boston Psychopathic Hospital	Last Mon. of month, 7 P.M.	Foxborough State Hospital
Boston	Massachusetts Memorial Hospitals	Wed., 9 A.M.-12 M.	Westborough State Hospital
Brockton	Brockton Hospital	Wed., 1:30-4 P.M.	Foxborough State Hospital

MENTAL AND MENTAL HYGIENE CLINICS (Continued)

City or Town	Institution or Other Agency	Time	Auspices
Fall River	City Hall Annex, Third Street	Wed., 9:30-11:30 A.M.	Taunton State Hospital
Greenfield	Franklin County Hospital, High Street	3rd Thurs. of month, 1-3 P.M.	Northampton State Hospital
Lawrence	International Institute, 125 Haverhill Street	1st and 3rd Fri., 9-11 A.M.	Danvers State Hospital
Lynn	Lynn Hospital	Wed., 2-4 P.M.	Danvers State Hospital
New Bedford	Olympia Bldg., Purchase and Elm Sts.	Wed., 1:30-4 P.M.	Taunton State Hospital
North Adams	Board of Health, Summer Street	2nd Thurs. of month, 1-3 P.M.	Northampton State Hospital
Pittsfield	House of Mercy Hospital	4th Thurs. of month, 1-3 P.M.	Northampton State Hospital
Springfield	Board of Health Rooms	1st Thurs. of month, 2-4 P.M.	Northampton State Hospital
Taunton	Taunton State Hospital	Thurs., 10 A.M.-12 M.	Hospital Staff

* Neurosyphilitic clinic.

Feeblemindedness Clinics: Conducted at State Schools for the Feebleminded. Appointments to be made in advance through School. Clinics are held as follows:

FEEBLEMINDEDNESS CLINICS

City or Town	Institution	Time	Auspices
Belchertown	Belchertown State School	Wed., by appointment	Hospital Staff
Waltham (Waverley)	Walter E. Fernald State School	Wed., 9 A.M. by appointment	Hospital Staff
Wrentham	Wrentham State School	Wed., 8:30 A.M. by appointment	Hospital Staff

TREATMENT

All hospitalization of mental disease patients is under supervision of Massachusetts Department of Mental Diseases, 100 Nashua Street, Boston, Telephone, Capitol 7320.

Insane Persons:

EMERGENCY HOSPITALIZATION—In emergencies, the superintendent of any institution for the insane (see p. 298) may receive without an order of commitment for a period of not more than five days persons certified by two legally qualified physicians to be dangerously insane. (See p. 297 for definition of "legally qualified physician"). Application blanks for emergency hospitalization obtainable from hospital in question.

VOLUNTARY APPLICATION—Any person whose mental condition is such as to render him competent to make voluntary application may be received by the superintendent of any institution for the insane (see p. 298), and detained as a boarder and patient until after three days' written notice of his intention or desire to leave. Application blanks for voluntary application may be obtained from hospitals for the insane or from Department of Mental Diseases, 100 Nashua Street, Boston.

TEMPORARY CARE—The superintendent of any institution for the insane (see p. 298) may, upon written request of a

(a) Licensed physician
(b) Member of a board of health
(c) Sheriff or deputy sheriff
(d) Selectman of a town
(e) Local or State police officer, or
(f) Agent of Boston Institutions Department

receive and care for a period not exceeding *ten* days any person needing immediate care and treatment because of mental derangement other than delirium tremens or drunkenness. Any such patient found by the superintendent of the institution to be not suitable for such care must be removed from the institution immediately by the person requesting his reception. Application blanks for temporary care may be obtained from hospitals for the insane, or Department of Mental Diseases, 100 Nashua Street, Boston.

TEMPORARY COMMITMENT FOR OBSERVATION—A person may be committed to a State or Federal hospital (see p. 298), or to the McLean Hospital (see p. 299) for a period not exceeding *thirty-five* days in order to observe the person's mental condition. Commitment for observation is through same legal procedure as for regular commitment (see next paragraph). Application blanks may be obtained from hospitals for the insane, from clerks of courts, or from Department of Mental Diseases, 100 Nashua Street, Boston.

COMMITMENT—Except in emergencies, for observation, or temporary care, or on voluntary application, no person may be received at any insane hospital, public or private, except upon an order of commitment from one of the following:

1. Justice of the superior court
2. Judge of probate for Suffolk County
3. Judge of probate for Nantucket County
4. Justice or special justice of a district court (except municipal court of City of Boston)

REQUIREMENTS FOR COMMITMENT

1. Filing with one of above-mentioned judges a certificate signed by two properly qualified physicians certifying as to insanity of said individual. Blank forms for such certificate may be obtained from the clerk of courts, the State Mental Disease Hospitals, or from Department of Mental Diseases, 100 Nashua Street, Boston. Only those physicians are "properly qualified" to sign certificates of insanity who

(a) Are graduates of a legally chartered medical school or college
(b) Have been in actual practice of medicine for three years since graduation

(c) Have been in actual practice of medicine for the three years immediately preceding the signing of said certificate
(d) Are registered in Massachusetts to practice medicine, and
(e) Satisfy the judge as to standing, character and professional knowledge of insanity

2. Issuance of an order signed by one of above-mentioned judges stating that
   (a) Person committed is insane,
   (b) Person committed is a proper subject for treatment in a hospital for the insane.
   (c)-1. Person has been an inhabitant of the Commonwealth for the six months immediately preceding commitment, or
   2. Provision satisfactory to the Department of Mental Diseases has been made for person's maintenance, or
   3. Person would, by reason of insanity, be dangerous if at large.

HOSPITALS ACCEPTING MENTAL PATIENTS
FEDERAL HOSPITALS

City or Town	Institution	Superintendent
Bedford	Veterans' Administration Facility	Winthrop Adams, M.D., Superintendent
Northampton	Veterans' Administration Facility (North Main Street)	F. E. Leslie, M.D., Superintendent

In addition to regular forms of application as above listed, special application must be made to Veterans' Administration, Federal Building, Boston.

STATE HOSPITALS

City or Town	Institution	Superintendent	Post Office Address
Boston	Boston Psychopathic Hospital	Riley H. Guthrie, M.D. Chief Executive Officer	74 Fenwood Rd., Boston
Boston	Boston State Hospital	Harold F. Norton, M.D.	Dorchester Center
Danvers	Danvers State Hospital	Clarence A. Bonner, M.D.	Hathorne, Mass.
Foxborough	Foxborough State Hospital	Roderick B. Dexter, M.D.	Foxborough
Gardner	Gardner State Hospital	Charles E. Thompson, M.D.	East Gardner
Grafton	Grafton State Hospital	Harlan L. Paine, M.D.	North Grafton
Medfield	Medfield State Hospital	Earl K. Holt, M.D.	Harding, Mass.
Northampton	Northampton State Hospital	Arthur N. Ball, M.D.	Northampton
Taunton	Taunton State Hospital	Ralph M. Chambers, M.D.	Taunton
Waltham	Metropolitan State Hospital	Roy D. Halloran, M.D.	Waltham
Westborough	Westborough State Hospital	Walter E. Lang, M.D.	Westborough
Worcester	Worcester State Hospital	William A. Bryan, M.D.	Worcester

PRIVATE HOSPITALS

City or Town	Institution	Superintendent	Post Office Address
Arlington	Ring Sanatorium and Hospital, Inc.	Hosea W. McAdoo, M.D., Med. Supt.	Arlington Heights
Belmont	McLean Hospital	W. Franklin Wood, M.D., Director	Waverley
Boston	Glenside	Mabel D. Ordway, M.D.	6 Parley Vale, Jamaica Plain
Brookline	Bosworth Hospital	George A. Gaunt, M.D.	166 Lancaster Terr., Brookline
Brookline	Bournewood Hospital	George H. Torney, M.D.	300 South St., Brookline
Melrose	Dr. Reeves Sanitarium	Clarence M. Kelley, M.D.	283 Vinton St., Melrose Highlands
Wellesley	Channing Sanitarium	Donald Gregg, M.D.	Wellesley Ave., Wellesley
Wellesley	Wiswall Sanatorium	Edward H. Wiswall, M.D.	203 Grove St., Wellesley
Westwood	Westwood Lodge	William J. Hammond, M.D.	Westwood

Financial responsibility for patients admitted to private hospitals is, in all cases, a personal matter between the patient or his relatives and the hospital. There is no State or local subsidy for such cases.

EPILEPTICS

SANE EPILEPTICS—VOLUNTARY APPLICATION—Any person who is certified to be subject to epilepsy by a properly qualified physician (see p. 297 for definition of "properly qualified physician") and who desires to submit himself to treatment, who makes written application therefor, and whose mental condition is such as to render him competent to make such application (or for whom application is made by parent or guardian) may be received at the Monson State Hospital or a private hospital licensed to receive such patients. (See below.) No such patient may be detained more than three *months* after having given written notice of his intention or desire to leave the hospital. Blanks for voluntary application may be obtained from the hospitals or from the Department of Mental Diseases, 100 Nashua Street, Boston.

INSANE EPILEPTICS—Any insane person who is subject to epilepsy, and is not a criminal, inebriate or violently insane, may be committed to the Monson State Hospital, or to a private hospital licensed to receive such patients. Commitment through same procedure as for insane persons. (See p. 297.) Application blanks obtainable from clerks of courts, hospitals, or Department of Mental Diseases, 100 Nashua Street, Boston.

DANGEROUS EPILEPTICS—Epileptics who are dangerous to themselves or others by reason of epilepsy may be committed to the Monson State Hospital in the same manner as provided for commitment of dipsomaniacs and inebriates (see p. 300). Application blanks obtainable from clerks of courts, hospitals, or Department of Mental Diseases, 100 Nashua Street, Boston.

HOSPITALS RECEIVING EPILEPTICS

STATE HOSPITAL

Town	Institution	Superintendent	Post Office Address
Monson	Monson State Hospital	Morgan B. Hodskins, M.D.	Palmer

PRIVATE HOSPITALS

Financial responsibility for patients admitted to private hospitals is, in all cases, a personal matter between the hospital and the patient or his relatives. There is no State or local subsidy for such cases.

In addition to the private hospitals listed on p. 299, the following are licensed to receive epileptics:

City or Town	Institution	Superintendent	Post Office Address
Newton	Woodlawn Sanitarium	Ewan A. Robertson, M.D.	500 Crafts Street, West Newton

Dipsomaniacs, Inebriates and Drug Addicts:

ADMISSION—VOLUNTARY APPLICATION—The trustees, superintendent or manager of any institution to which a dipsomaniac, an inebriate, or one addicted to the intemperate use of narcotics or stimulants may be committed, may receive and detain therein as a boarder and patient any person who is desirous of submitting himself to treatment and who makes written application therefor and is mentally competent to make the application. No such person may be detained more than three days after having given written notice of his intention or desire to leave the institution. Application blanks obtainable at institution, or Department of Mental Diseases, 100 Nashua Street, Boston.

TEMPORARY CARE—The superintendent or manager of any institution to which a dipsomaniac, an inebriate, or one addicted to the intemperate use of narcotics or stimulants may be committed, may receive and care for in such institution, as a patient for a period not exceeding fifteen days, any person needing immediate care and treatment because he has become so addicted to the intemperate use of narcotics or stimulants that he has lost the power of self control. Application blanks obtainable at institution, or at Department of Mental Diseases, 100 Nashua Street, Boston.

COMMITMENT—Is made in same manner as above under Mental Diseases (see p. 297). In addition to judges there listed as empowered to commit patients, commitments of dipsomaniacs, inebriates, and drug addicts may be made by a judge of the municipal court of Boston. Commitment may be to the State Farm at Bridgewater, to the Massachusetts Reformatory for Women, to the McLean Hospital, or to any private institution licensed by the Department of Mental Diseases for the care of insane, inebriates and drug addicts. Certificate signed by two properly qualified physicians (see p. 297 for definition of "properly qualified physician") must accompany application for commitment. Application blanks obtainable from police departments, clerks of courts, or institution.

HOSPITALS RECEIVING DIPSOMANIACS, INEBRIATES AND DRUG ADDICTS

STATE INSTITUTIONS

City or Town	Institution	Superintendent	Post Office Address
Bridgewater	State Farm	Wm. T. Hanson, M.D., Medical Director	Bridgewater
Framingham	Mass. Reformatory for Women	Miriam VanWaters, Ph.D., Superintendent	Framingham

Financial responsibility for patients admitted to private hospitals is, in all cases, a personal matter between the hospital and the patient or his relatives. There is no State or local subsidy for such cases. In addition to the private hospitals listed on p. 299, the following hospitals are licensed to receive inebriates and drug addicts:

PRIVATE HOSPITALS

City or Town	Institution	Superintendent	Post Office Address
Boston	Private Hospital	Frederick L. Taylor, M.D.	45 Center St., Roxbury
Boston	Washingtonian Home	Hugh B. Gray, M.D.	41 Waltham St., Boston
Boston	Grove Hall Institute	George C. Moore, M.D.	222 Townsend Street, Roxbury

Feebleminded:

Admission to State Schools

VOLUNTARY APPLICATION—Application to be made by parent or guardian of feebleminded person; application to be accompanied by certificate of properly qualified physician (see p. 297 for definition of "properly qualified physician") stating under oath that he has examined said person within five days of signing certificate and that, in his opinion, the person is a fit subject for such school. Application blanks obtainable from superintendent of School for the Feebleminded, or from Department of Mental Diseases, 100 Nashua Street, Boston.

OBSERVATION—Application to be made by parent or guardian. Patient to be detained for observation for a period not exceeding thirty days to determine whether or not feebleminded. Application blanks obtainable from superintendent of School for the Feebleminded, or from Department of Mental Diseases, 100 Nashua Street, Boston.

COURT COMMITMENT—May be made by any judge of probate within his county. Application to be made directly to court, forms obtainable from clerks of courts, superintendent of School for Feebleminded, or from Department of Mental Diseases, 100 Nashua Street, Boston. Application should be accompanied by physician's certificate (see Voluntary Application) certifying as to examination made within *ten* days of signing certificate.

COMMITMENT TO DEPARTMENT OF MENTAL DISEASES—If an alleged feebleminded person is found, upon examination by a properly qualified physician (see p. 297 for definition of "properly qualified physician") to be a proper subject for commitment, the judge of probate for the county in which such person resides or is found may upon application commit him to the custody or supervision of the Department; but no person shall be so committed unless the approval of the Department shall be filed with the application for his commitment. Such patients are not hospitalized but are supervised in the community by the Department of Mental Diseases.

SCHOOLS ACCEPTING FEEBLEMINDED PATIENTS
STATE SCHOOLS

City or Town	School	Superintendent	Post Office Address
Belchertown	Belchertown State School	Geo. E. McPherson, M.D., Med. Supt.	Belchertown
Waltham	Walter E. Fernald State School	Ransom A. Greene, M.D., Med. Supt.	Waverley
Wrentham	Wrentham State School	C. Stanley Raymond, M.D., Med. Supt.	Wrentham

PRIVATE SCHOOLS

Financial responsibility for patients admitted to private schools is, in all cases, a personal matter between the school and the patient or his relatives. There is no State or local subsidy for such cases. In addition to the private hospitals listed on p. 299, the following schools are licensed to receive feebleminded patients:

City or Town	School	Superintendent	Post Office Address
Arlington	The Freer School	Miss Cora E. Morse	31 Park Circle, Arlington Heights
Barre	Elm Hill Private School and Home for the Feebleminded	Geo. A. Brown, M.D.	Barre
Halifax	Standish Manor	Miss Alice M. Myers	Halifax
Lancaster	Perkins School of Adjustment	Franklin H. Perkins, M.D.	Lancaster
Newton	Clarke School	Miss Edith G. Clark	16 Summit St., Newton
Lexington	The Lila Sanatorium: For care of epileptic and feebleminded children under 12 years	Richard C. Eley, M.D.	1557 Massachusetts Ave., Lexington

INSTITUTIONS UNDER DEPARTMENT OF PUBLIC WELFARE

STATE INFIRMARY

The State Infirmary, Tewksbury, maintained by State Department of Public Welfare, 37 State House, Boston.

A general hospital, primarily for care and treatment of poor and indigent persons having no legal settlement, suffering from acute and chronic diseases. Special venereal, tubercular and maternity wards. Minors not admitted without approval of Division of Aid and Relief. Special provision made for any person who has been a resident of the Commonwealth for not less than two years and who is affected with any incurable disease except mental defect or leprosy. Admission subject to regulations established by Department. Insane persons are not admitted.

The Department, through its Division of Aid and Relief, has authority of supervision and discharge of patients; certificates of admission are issued by Boards of Public Welfare, and in Boston by Institutions Department. Persons infected with diseases dangerous to public health are admitted to Infirmary only upon request of Boards of Health and with approval of Division of Aid and Relief. Said approval is generally confined to persons ill with tuberculosis and venereal diseases.

MASSACHUSETTS HOSPITAL SCHOOL

Massachusetts Hospital School, Canton, provides care and schooling for crippled and deformed children of Massachusetts between five and fifteen years of age who are mentally competent to attend public schools; girls taught cooking, sewing, general house work, laundering and a few assigned to office work, telephone desks, typewriting, etc.; older boys taught farming, gardening, care of poultry, work in dairy, baking, engineering, carpentry, painting, shoemaking, automobile driving. Expenses borne by pupils when able, or by those bound by law to maintain them, or by city or town of their settlement whose Boards of Public Welfare request their admission, or by the Commonwealth.

VITAL STATISTICS
REPORTING BIRTHS AND DEATHS

The pertinent facts which the physician needs to know about reporting of births and deaths are outlined here. Increased cooperation in procuring medical, statistical and legal information in regard to births and deaths is much needed. It is hoped that this summary will stimulate interest in these matters.

REPORTING BIRTHS

Birth registration has been compulsory by law since 1840 and it is one of the most valuable personal records used by the individual. Present day conditions have greatly increased the value and use of birth records as a means for the citizen to prove legally the date of his birth for school entrance, the right to vote, and to provide other facts of birth, such as parentage, identity, and so on, as listed below. Birth certificates play an equally important role for statistical purposes in the field of public health, social welfare, and government.

Some of the many reasons why births should be recorded accurate are given below:

To establish identity
To prove nationality
To prove legitimacy
To show when the child has the right to enter school
To show when the child has the right to seek employment under the child labor law
To establish the right of inheritance to property
To establish liability to military duty, as well as exemption therefrom.
To establish age and citizenship in order to vote
To qualify to hold title to, and to buy or sell real estate
To establish the right to hold public office
To prove the age at which the marriage contract may be entered into
To prove age to determine validity of a contract entered into by an alleged minor
To prove age for Old Age Assistance
To prove age for Social Security requirements
To prove age for commercial (railroad, etc.) and public office retirement
To prove age so as to have right to take Civil Service Examinations

A physician is required to make a complete report within fifteen days of every birth of which he has been in charge to the clerk of the city or town in which the birth occurred. If within forty-eight hours after the birth the physician has not already made a complete report, he is then required to render a preliminary notice to the clerk, stating the place and date of birth, the street and number, the ward number (if in a city), and the family name. It is important that every physician be careful, vigilant, and conscientious in this matter, and that he supply all the required facts for record. Blanks for making returns are obtainable from city and town clerks or registrars or from the State Division of Vital Statistics, Room 334, State House.

In the case of an illegitimate birth, the facts concerning the father are not to be returned. Every birth occurring in wedlock must be reported as legitimate regardless of any claim to the contrary.

Birth certificates should be filed in the community where the child is born, but since 1936, births have been allocated by the office of the State Secretary to the place of residence of the parent. This should insure as true a rate as is possible. Previously, municipalities which are large hospital centers, were credited with high birth rates.

The records on file in the Division of Vital Statistics are attested copies of the original returns filed with the local clerk or registrar.

In all cases of stillbirth a birth certificate and a death certificate should be filed. Prior to 1936 much confusion existed, as there was no statute defining a stillbirth. For purposes of vital statistics, the legislature in 1936, (Chapter 100, Acts of 1936) defined it as:

"A stillborn child shall be deemed to be a foetus born after a period of gestation of not less than five months, in which foetus there is no attempt at respiration, no action of heart, and no movements of voluntary muscle."

The statute now clearly defines a stillbirth and precludes any misunderstanding as to what returns should be made.

Further information regarding the reporting of births can be secured from local city and towns clerks or registrars, or by writing to the State Division of Vital Statistics, Office of the Secretary, State House, Boston, Telephone, Capitol 7360.

Laws: General Laws: Chapter 46, Sections 3 and 6.

REPORTING DEATHS

The registration of deaths is essential to the progress of medical and sanitary science in preventing and restricting disease and in devising and applying remedial measures. It serves as evidence in the inheritance of property and in the settlement of life insurance claims. It is useful in preventing crime through the restriction placed upon the disposal of dead bodies, and insures a permanent and uniform record of the death of each individual for innumerable other purposes. In general, mortality statistics are useful in showing the extent and rate of change in population produced by deaths, the average duration of life, the relative frequency with which the several causes produce death. Moreover, this information is vitally important in creating an interest in public health administration and securing support for sanitary measures. By comparing death records with the birth statistics valuable information is obtained regarding the increase or decrease in population.

Certification of death is required as follows:

Attending physicians will certify only to deaths of those persons whom they have attended during their last illness and for a sufficient length of time so as to be able to certify with concrete knowledge as to the cause of death, and to testify that the death is unrelated to any form of injury or violence.

Board of Health physicians will certify only to such deaths as those of persons who, though disabled by recognized disease unrelated to any form of injury, have died without recent medical attention, or whose physician is absent from home when the certificate of death is needed.

Medical examiners are required to investigate and certify to all deaths from injury or supposed injury. These include not only deaths caused directly or indirectly by traumatism (including resulting septicemia) and by the action of chemical (drugs or poisons, including alcohol) gaseous, thermal, or electrical agents, and deaths following abortion, but also deaths from diseases resulting from injury or infection related to occupation, the sudden deaths of persons not disabled by recognized disease, and those of persons found dead who had no recent medical attention. Medical examiners are also required to certify that they have viewed bodies to be cremated, and to make personal inquiry into the cause and manner of death.

The usefulness of mortality statistics depends upon how accurate a picture they give of why people are dying. Those tabulating returns have great difficulty in classifying deaths by the International List of Causes of Death when statements of physicians are vague or when the terms are general instead of specific. Below are listed some of the items which most frequently cause confusion in analysing these returns. Careful observance of the suggestions made result in greatly increasing the reliability of the information obtained from these certificates. Advice and aid will be given by health departments or by the Division of Vital Statistics.

1. Do not use indefinite and non-descriptive terms. Among these are *Cardio-renal Disease, Nervousness, Indigestion, Pleurisy, Rheumatism, Bronchitis, Urinary trouble, Colic,* and many others which arouse conjecture but give no information. Thousands of queries and investigations are made annually requesting more specific statements regarding causes of death. This entails extra work and causes unnecessary expense due to the necessary corrections and changes, as well as dissatisfaction to the people who may be obliged to look at these reports in future years.

2. Do not fail to state if an operation preceded death and name the operation.

3. Record the part of the body affected.

4. Avoid using some remote long-standing illness as a cause of death.

5. Try to state the primary location in all cancer cases.

6. State by what means death occurred by accident; i.e., by fall, fire, drowning, automobile, etc.

7. State if pregnancy or childbirth is associated with any cause of death.

8. Specify if a tumor is benign or malignant.

9. In case of hemorrhage state the location and cause.

Report Blanks.

"Standard Certificate of Death" Form R-301 A. A supply of these is obtainable from your local board of health, City Clerk, or the State Division of Vital Statistics, Office of the Secretary, State House, Boston. The undertaker usually fills in the personal statistical side of the certificate, and the physician verifies the statistical information, fills in and signs the medical side. The undertaker then presents it to the local board of health for a removal or burial permit. Extracts of laws are printed on the reverse side of the report blanks.

Laws: General Laws, Chap. 38, Sect. 6, 7; Chap. 46, Sect. 9; Chap. 114, Sect. 45, 46 as amended.

The Physicians' Pocket Reference to the International List of Causes of Death may be procured by writing or calling the Division of Vital Statistics, Room 334, State House, Boston.

ANNOUNCEMENT

American Physicians' Art Association: This association, a national organization of medical men who have ability in the fine arts, will hold a *first national exhibition* in the San Francisco Museum of Art, San Francisco, California, in June, 1938. (The American Medical Association Convention is June 13-17 in the same city.) The *American Physicians' Art Association* already has an outstanding membership. There are three classifications for membership: active, associate, and contributing. The *first annual exhibition* promises to be of unusual interest with entries to be accepted (after jury selection) in the following classifications: oils, watercolors, sculpture, photography, pastels, etchings, crayon and pen and ink drawings (including cartoons), wood carvings and book bindings. Scientific medical art work will not be accepted. The exhibition is not limited to first showings. All entries close April 1, 1938. Any physician interested should communicate at once with the Secretary of the American Physicians' Art Association, Suite 521-536 Flood Bldg., San Francisco, California

REPORT OF DIVISION OF FOOD AND DRUGS

During the months of July, August and September 1937, samples were collected in 237 cities and towns.

There were 1,885 samples of milk examined, of which 367 were below standard, from 9 samples the cream had been in part removed, and 4 samples contained added water. There were 1,853 bacteriological examinations made of milk, 1,341 of which complied with the requirements. There were 13 bacteriological examinations made of pasteurized heavy cream, 4 of which did not comply with the requirements; 109 bacteriological examinations of ice cream, 19 of which did not comply with the requirements; 11 bacteriological examinations of sherbet, all of which complied with the requirements; 26 bacteriological examinations of crab meat, 12 bacteriological examinations of lobster, and 3 bacteriological examinations of canned shellfish, all of which complied with the requirements; 1 bacteriological examination of an empty bottle which did not comply with the requirements; and 21 bacteriological examinations of mattress fillings, 8 of which did not comply with the requirements.

There were 329 samples of food examined, 47 of which were adulterated, These consisted of 5 samples of butter which were low in milk fat; 1 sample of dirt from an ice cream plant; 19 samples of hamburg steak, 9 of which were decomposed, 8 contained a compound of sulphur dioxide not so labeled and 2 samples contained sodium sulphite in excess of one tenth of one per cent; 6 samples of sausage, 5 of which were decomposed, and 1 sample contained a compound of sulphur dioxide not so labeled; 1 sample of pressed ham which contained maggots and was decomposed; 2 samples of olive oil, 1 of which consisted of mineral oil, and I sample consisted of cottonseed oil; 1 sample of dried fruits, and 1 sample of eggs, both of which were decomposed; 1 sample of orange soda which contained benzoate not marked; 1 sample of fresh fruit orange juice which was adulterated and misbranded; 1 sample of ginger ale sold by a manufacturer who did not possess a permit; 1 sample of soft drink wash water which was deficient in caustic alkali; and 7 samples of mattress fillings; 5 of which contained secondhand material, and 2 samples were labeled "All Wool", but contained a mixture of hair, wool and cotton.

There were 48 samples of drugs examined, of which 9 were adulterated. These consisted of 1 sample of spirit of nitrous ether, 1 sample of olive oil, 6 samples of tincture of iodine, and 1 sample of hydrogen peroxide submitted by the State Purchasing Agent, all of which did not conform to the requirements of the U. S. Pharmacopoeia.

The police departments submitted 126 samples of liquor for examination. The police departments also submitted 6 samples to be analyzed for poisons or drugs, of which 2 contained heroin, 1 contained potassium permanganate, 1 sample of cigarettes which contained cannabis, 1 sample of pills which contained codeine, 2 of these pills also containing morphine sulphate, and 1 sample of meat which contained a large amount of arsenic.

There were inspected 378 plants operated for the pasteurization of milk; 208 soft drink plants; 24 ice cream plants; 64 bakeries; 647 restaurants; and 315 mattress establishments.

There were 96 hearings held pertaining to violations of the laws.

There were 39 convictions for violations of the law, $995 in fines being imposed.

Wilko Mayranen of Westminster, and Joseph C. Souza of Westport, were convicted for violations of the milk laws.

Leonard Anzivino of Cochituate; Howard B. Hiller, 2 cases, of Rochester; Eastland Farms, Incorporated, of Malden; Wallace L. Henshaw of Salem; Herman Kananen of East Bridgewater; and Spittle Brothers Dairy, Incorporated, 2 cases, of Gloucester, were convicted for violations of the pasteurization law and regulations.

Alta Crest Farms, Incorporated, of Spencer, and Arthur E. Law of Methuen, were convicted for violations of the milk grading regulations.

Abram J. Cohen and Eugene Lajeunesse of New Bedford; Solin's Market, Incorporated, of Chicopee; Isaac Tillman of Springfield; Economy Grocery Stores Corporation of Boston; Harry Cohen, 2 cases, of East Boston; David Ginsberg, 2 cases, of Worcester; Israel Nayor, Samuel Simon, Leshner & Sons, Incorporated, and Benjamin Heishon, all of Dorchester; Leshner & Sons, Incorporated, of Roxbury; Main Public Market, Incorporated, of Fall River; and United Food Stores of Webster, Incorporated, of Webster, were all convicted for violations of the food laws. David Ginsberg, 2 cases, of Worcester, and Leshner & Sons, Incorporated, of Roxbury, appealed their cases.

Harry S. Litridis of Pittsfield was convicted for violation of the bakery regulations.

Kohr Brothers, Incorporated, of Wollaston was convicted for violation of the frozen dessert law.

Louis Grigalmas of Athol; Abraham Joffee of Pittsfield; and Washington Beverage Company of Worcester, were all convicted for violations of the law and regulations relative to the manufacture and bottling of carbonated non-alcoholic beverages.

Berkshire Bedding Company of Pittsfield; Edward Milstone of Lawrence; Anthony Marmarale and George Pisiello of East Boston; Sunset Bedding Company, Incorporated, of Boston; and Benjamin London of Malden, were all convicted for violations of the mattress law. Sunset Bedding Company, Incorporated, of Boston, appealed their case.

In accordance with Section 25, Chapter 111 of the General Laws, the following is the list of articles of adulterated food collected in original packages from manufacturers, wholesalers, or producers:

One sample of dried fruits which was decomposed was obtained from Leshner & Sons, Incorporated, of Roxbury.

One sample of orange soda which contained benzoate not marked was obtained from Ochee Spring Water Company of Providence, Rhode Island.

One sample of olive oil which consisted of mineral oil was obtained from Pulcella Olive Oil Company.

One sample of olive oil which consisted of cottonseed oil was obtained from Mrs. Ada Ramboli of Everett.

Hamburg steak which contained a compound of sulphur dioxide not so labeled was obtained as follows:

One sample each, from Andrews & Ollman and Sirloin Stores of Malden; Jacob Shafran & Sons, Alter Brothers, and Babcock Market of Brookline; Samuel Simon of Dorchester; and Harry Cohen of East Boston.

Hamburg steak which contained sodium sulphite in excess of one tenth of one per cent was obtained as follows:

One sample each, from Max Jacobson of Holyoke; and Mayor's Market of Dorchester.

Hamburg steak which was decomposed was obtained as follows:

One sample each, from Farmers Exchange of Chicopee Falls; Puritan Public Market, Incorporated, of Brockton; Brookfield Market (David Ginsburg) of Worcester; Main Public Market, Incorporated, of Fall River; Sam Tillman and Sam Tallent of Springfield; Transfer Meat Market of Dorchester; Mohican Market, Incorporated, of Allston; and Louis Ward of Brookline.

Sausage which was decomposed was obtained as follows:

One sample each, from Harry Cohen of East Boston; Supreme Markets, Incorporated, of South Boston; United Fruit Stores, Incorporated, of Webster; Enterprise Stores, Incorporated, of Everett; and Brookfield Market (David Ginsburg) of Worcester.

One sample of sausage which contained a compound of sulphur dioxide not so labeled was obtained from Woburn Provision Company, Incorporated, of Everett.

Butter which was low in milk fat was obtained as follows:

Two samples from White Creamery Company, Incorporated, of Chelsea; and 1 sample from M. Winer & Company of Worcester.

There were 107 confiscations, consisting of 1664½ pounds of decomposed beef; 3 pounds of decomposed beef kidneys; 15 pounds of decomposed steak; 67 pounds of decomposed hamburg steak; 4 pounds of decomposed lamb chops; 12 pounds of decomposed pork chops; 905 pounds of decomposed pork; 3709 pounds of decomposed hogs' lungs; 215 pounds of decomposed minced and pressed ham; 2 pounds of decomposed ham; 860¼ pounds of decomposed cooked ham; 2 pounds of decomposed veal; 1 pound of mouldy uncooked hash; 113 pounds of mouldy decomposed frankforts; 2 pounds of decomposed sausages; 5 pounds of decomposed livers; 5 pounds of decomposed meat loaf; 6 pounds of decomposed fish; 2 pounds of decomposed lobster; ½ pound of rancid crabmeat; 5 pounds of decomposed soup bone; 40 pounds of wormy prunes; 2 pounds of fermented sauerkraut; 1 quart of rancid tomatoes; 1 pound of rancid tomatoes; 3 pounds of decomposed tomatoes and peppers; 2 quarts of rancid tomato soup; 1 quart of rancid tomato juice; 1 pint of sour beans; ½ bushel of decayed turnips; 1 quart of rancid gravy; and 2 quarts of rancid grease.

The licensed cold storage warehouses reported the following amounts of food placed in storage during June, 1937:—747,450 dozens of case eggs; 2,147,800 pounds of broken out eggs; 4,320,769 pounds of butter; 2,407,062 pounds of poultry; 3,035,006 pounds of fresh meat and fresh meat products; and 14,774,190 pounds of fresh food fish.

There was on hand July 1, 1937:—5,336,070 dozens of case eggs; 3,985,362 pounds of broken out eggs; 4,773,855 pounds of butter; 5,457,622 pounds of poultry; 6,774,374 pounds of fresh meat and fresh meat products; and 26,621,541 pounds of fresh food fish.

The licensed cold storage warehouses reported the following amounts of food placed in storage during July, 1937:—317,070 dozens of case eggs; 1,314,873 pounds of broken out eggs; 3,054,703 pounds of butter; 1,789,186 pounds of poultry; 2,816,728 pounds of fresh meat and fresh meat products; and 10,570,990 pounds of fresh food fish.

There was on hand August 1, 1937:—5,149,350 dozens of case eggs; 4,276,956 pounds of broken out eggs; 7,196,268 pounds of butter; 4,813,073 pounds of poultry; 5,401,956 pounds of fresh meat and fresh meat products; and 28,882,128 pounds of fresh food fish.

The licensed cold storage warehouses reported the following amounts of food placed in storage during August, 1937:—424,410 dozens of case eggs; 1,067,935 pounds of broken out eggs; 1,080,626 pounds of butter; 1,497,443 pounds of poultry; 2,419,472 pounds of fresh meat and fresh meat products; and 7,820,252 pounds of fresh food fish.

There was on hand September 1, 1937:—4,762,200 dozens of case eggs; 4,300,313 pounds of broken out eggs; 7,207,398 pounds of butter; 3,448,309 pounds of poultry; 3,675,239 pounds of fresh meat and fresh meat products; and 25,432,737 pounds of fresh food fish.

INDEX TO HANDBOOK FOR PHYSICIANS

Actinomycosis, reportable 233
Active immunity 243, 256, 257, 267
Addison Gilbert Hospital 249, 253, 286
Adjustment clinics 293
Adrenalin 283
Adult whole blood 248
Alcoholism 300
Alum toxoid, diphtheria 243
Amebic dysentery 233, 245
Anaphylactic reaction 281
Angioneurotic edema 281
Anna Jaques Hospital 249, 254, 286
Anterior poliomyelitis. (See Poliomyelitis, Anterior) . . 233, 239
Anthrax, reportable 233
Anti-influenza bacillus serum 250, 280
Antimeningococcus serum 248, 280
Antipneumococcus serum 254, 280
Antirabic treatment 244
Antirabic vaccine 244, 245
Antitoxin, diphtheria 242, 280
  scarlet fever streptococcus 255, 280
  tetanus 257, 279
Antitoxin and Vaccine Laboratory 279
Arsenicals, syphilis 271
Arsphenamine, syphilis 271
Arthritis 279
Arthus phenomenon 284
Asiatic cholera, reportable 233
Asthma 281
Ayer Community Memorial Hospital 249, 253

Bacillary dysentery 233, 246
Bacteriological Laboratory 236
Balfour Sanatorium 264
Barnstable County Sanatorium 238, 254, 258, 263
Belchertown State School 296, 302
Belmont Hospital, Worcester 238, 239, 261, 264
Benjamin Stickney Cable Memorial Hospital 249
Beth Israel Hospital 239, 253, 274, 284, 286
Beverly Hospital 239, 249, 253, 274
Beverly School for the Deaf 291
Biologic products 238, 279
  Antitoxin and Vaccine Laboratory 279
  diagnostic 280
  preventive 280
  regulations for distribution of 280
  sensitivity 281
  therapeutic 280
Birth, certificate of 304
Bismuth syphilis 271
Blind and conservation of vision 290
  institutions 291
Blood test, syphilis 236, 270, 272
Boston City Hospital 237, 239, 249, 253, 274, 285
Boston Dispensary 274, 286, 295
Boston Guild for the Hard of Hearing 291
Boston Nursery for Blind Babies 291
Boston Private Hospital (mental) 301
Boston Psychopathic Hospital 274, 292, 293, 295, 298
Boston Sanatorium 263
Boston School for the Deaf 291
Boston State Hospital 298
Bosworth Hospital 299
Bournewood Hospital 299
Bridgewater State Farm 301
Bristol County Sanatorium 263

Brockton Hospital	249, 253, 274, 286, 289, 293
Brookline Board of Health Hospital	237
Brookline Tuberculosis Hospital	263
Burbank Hospital	253, 260, 264, 275, 286
Cable, Benjamin Stickney, Memorial Hospital	249
Cambridge City Hospital	253, 275
Cambridge Hospital	249, 253, 275
Cambridge Tuberculosis Hospital	263
Camps, tuberculosis	265
Cancer	284
clinics	285
educational program	287
hospitalization of cases of	284
other cancer services	284
research	285
tumor diagnostic service	285
Cape Cod Hospital	249, 253, 258, 286, 289
Carney Hospital	249, 253
Carpenter Isolation Hospital	239
Carrier, typhoid	267
Central New England Sanatorium	264
Certificate of birth	304
Certificate of death	305
Channing Home, Boston	264
Channing Sanitarium, Wellesley	299
Charles Choate Memorial Hospital	249
Chelsea Memorial Hospital	249, 253
Chicken pox	233, 234, 242
Child guidance clinics	292
Child hygiene	287
educational material	288
obstetric package	289
postgraduate instruction	289
postnatal letters	288
premature infant care	289
prenatal letters	287
Children's Hospital	237, 239, 249, 274
Children's Sunlight Hospital	241
Chill reactions after serum	283
Cholecystitis of typhoid origin	233, 267
Clarke School, Newton	302
Clarke School for the Deaf, Northampton	291
Clinics	
anterior poliomyelitis	240, 289
cancer	286
crippled children	289
gonorrhea and syphilis	274
mental disease	292
tuberculosis	258
Clinton Hospital	249, 253
Collis P. Huntington Memorial Hospital	284
Commitment of mental cases	297, 299, 300, 301
Communicable diseases	233
diagnostic laboratories	236, 237
hospitalization of	237
popular pamphlets re	238
quarantine requirements	233
reporting of	233
Complement	250
Complement fixation test, gonococcus	236, 272
Consultation clinics	
cancer	284
gonorrhea and syphilis	274
orthopedic	289
tuberculosis	258
Contacts, control of	234, 243, 256, 267, 269
Contagious disease hospitals	237
Contagious diseases	233

Contraindications for serum therapy 282
Convalescent serum
    anterior poliomyelitis 241
    measles 248
    whooping cough 268
Cooley Dickinson Hospital 238, 249, 254, 286
Coolidge, Frederic S., Memorial Home 265
Crippled children, services to 241, 289
    admission to clinics 290
    definition of crippled children 290
    diagnostic clinics 289
    services for poliomyelitis 289

Danvers State Hospital 292, 293, 295, 296
Darkfield examination, syphilis 270
David Parker Municipal Hospital 237
Deaf and hard of hearing 291
    institutions for deaf 291
    institutions for hard of hearing 291
Death, certificate of 305
Desensitization 283
Diagnostic laboratories 236
    local 237
    State
        Diagnostic 236
        Tumor 285
        Wassermann 236
Diagnostic products 280
Dick test 256
Diphtheria 233, 234, 242
    diagnosis of 236, 242
    isolation and quarantine 243
    prevention of 243
        alum toxoid for immunization against 243
        antitoxin for passive immunization against . . . 242, 280
        toxin-antitoxin for immunization against . . . 243, 280
        toxoid for immunization against 243, 280
    Shick test 243, 280
    susceptibility to 243
    treatment of 242
Dipsomaniacs 300
Diseases, communicable 233
    industrial 291
    mental 292
    reportable 233
Distributing stations 280
    antimeningococcic serum 280
    antipneumococcic serum 280
Dog bite 233, 244
    antirabic treatment 244
    disposition of dog 244
    laboratory examination of head 244
    regulations re antirabic vaccine 244
    reporting cases of 244
    treatment of patient 244
Drug addicts 300
Drugs, treatment of syphilis 271, 280
Dysentery, amebic 233, 245
    bacillary 233, 246

Eczema 281
Educational material 238, 273, 287, 288
Elm Hill Private School and Home for the Feebleminded . . . 302
Emerson Hospital 249
Encephalitis lethargica, reportable 233
Epileptics 299
Epinephrine 283
Essex Sanatorium 259, 263

Eye, Infectious diseases of	233
ophthalmia neonatorum	233, 252
opthalmia neonatorum (gonococcal)	273
suppurative conjunctivitis	233
trachoma	233
Fairview Hospital	249, 253, 258, 275
Fall River General Hospital	237, 239, 249, 253
Fall River Tuberculosis Hospital	264
Faulkner Hospital	253
Feebleminded	301
Fernald, Walter E., State School	296, 302
Fitchburg Isolation Hospital	237
Food handlers	235
Foxborough State Hospital	292, 293, 295, 298
Framingham-Union Hospital	249, 253, 258, 293
Franklin County Public Hospital	237, 249, 253, 286, 296
Frederic S. Coolidge Memorial Home	265
Free Hospital for Women	284
Freer School	302
Gardner State Hospital	292, 293, 298
German measles	233, 247
Glanders, reportable	233
Glenside Hospital	299
Gold sol test, syphilis	236, 271
Gonocoecal ophthalmia neonatorum, prophylaxis of	252, 273
Gonorrhea	233, 236, 269, 272, 276
clinics	274
confidential follow-up service	277
confidential records and reports	278
consultation	276
diagnosis of	236, 272
disclosure of certain information	279
literature	273
patients unable to pay	277
prophylaxis of gonococcal ophthalmia neonatorum	273
regulations re reimbursement	277
reporting of	269
treatment of	272
Grafton State Hospital	292, 298
Greenfield Hospital	258
Grove Hall Institute	301
Habit clinics	295
Hale Hospital	249, 253, 289
Hampshire County Sanatorium	263
Harrington Memorial Hospital	249, 254
Harvard Cancer Commission	285
Harvard Infantile Paralysis Commission	240
Haverhill Contagious Hospital	237
Hay fever	281
Henry Heywood Memorial Hospital	249, 253, 286, 289
Hinton tests, syphilis	236, 270, 272
Holy Ghost Hospital for Incurables	285
Holyoke Hospital	253, 275, 293
Hookworm disease, reportable	233
Horace Mann School for the Deaf	291
Hospital Cottages for Children, Baldwinsville	241
Hospitalization of communicable diseases	237
Hospitals and sanatoria	
anterior poliomyelitis	239, 241
arthritis	279
blind	290
cancer	284
communicable disease	237
deaf and hard of hearing	291
mental disease	298
premature infant care	289
public welfare	303
tuberculosis hospitals and sanatoria	262

House of Mercy, Pittsfield 254, 260, 276, 296
Huntington, Collis P., Memorial Hospital 284

Industrial diseases 291
   reporting of 291
Industrial School for Crippled Children 241
Inebriates 300
Infantile paralysis (See Poliomyelitis, Anterior) . . . 233, 239
Influenzal meningitis 233, 234, 250
Insane persons 296

J. B. Thomas Hospital 254
Jewish Tuberculosis Sanatorium of Massachusetts 264
Jordan Hospital 238, 249, 254

Laboratories
  biologic 279
  diagnostic 236
    bacteriological 236
    local 237
    pneumococcus typing 253
    tumor 285
    Wassermann 236
Lakeville State Sanatorium 239, 241, 262
Lathrop, Rose Hawthorne, Hospital 285
Lawrence General Hospital 238, 249, 253, 286, 295
Lawrence Memorial Hospital, Medford 249, 259
Leominster Hospital 249, 253
Leonard Morse Hospital 254
Leprosy, reportable 233
Lila Sanatorium 302
Literature
  child hygiene 288
  communicable disease 238
  gonorrhea and syphilis 273
Lobar pneumonia, reportable 233
Long Island Hospital 285
Lowell General Hospital . . . . 253, 286' 294
Lowell Isolation Hospital 238, 249, 264
Lydia E. Pinkham Memorial Hospital 294
Lynn Health Department Hospital 238, 249
Lynn Hospital 253, 260, 275, 286

Malaria 233, 247
Malaria and other fever therapy, syphilis 271
Malden Contagious Hospital 238
Malden Hospital 253
Mantoux test . . . . 258, 261' 280
Maple Lodge 264
Marlborough Hospital 254
Martha's Vineyard Hospital 249, 254, 259
Mary Lane Hospital 249, 254
Massachusetts General Hospital . . . 239, 249, 253, 274, 279, 284
Massachusetts Hospital School for Crippled Children . . 241, 303
Massachusetts Memorial Hospitals . . . 237, 239, 253, 274, 284, 292, 295
Massachusetts Reformatory for Women 301
McLean Hospital 299, 300
Measles 233, 234, 247
  isolation and quarantine 247
  prevention of 247
    adult whole blood 248
      sodium citrate solution 248, 280
    convalescent serum 248
    placental extract 248, 280
Measles, German 233, 234, 247
Medfield State Hospital 294, 298
Meningitis, meningococcic 233, 234, 248
  isolation and quarantine 250

prevention of 250
serum 248
    distribution stations 249
treatment 248
Meningitis, Pfeiffer bacillus (influenzal) 233, 234, 250
    diagnosis of 236, 250
    serum 250, 280
    treatment 250
Mental diseases 292
    clinics 292
    commitment, regulations for 297
    diagnosis of 292
    hospitals 298
        Federal 298
        private 299
        State 298
    schools 301, 302
        State 302
        private 302
    treatment of
        dipsomaniacs, inebriates and drug addicts 300
        epileptics 299
        feebleminded 301
        insane persons 296
Mental hygiene clinics 295
Mercy Hospital, Springfield 254
Metropolitan State Hospital 294, 298
Middlesex County Sanatorium 258, 261, 263
Milford Hospital 249, 254
Monadnock Sanatorium 264
Monson State Hospital 292, 294, 300
Morton Hospital 249, 254
Mumps 233, 234, 251

Nantucket Cottage Hospital 249, 254, 259
Neoarsphenamine, syphilis 271
Neufeld typing 236
New Bedford Isolation Hospital 238
New England Deaconess Hospital 253
New England Hospital for Women and Children . . . 274, 295
New England Peabody Home for Crippled Children . . . 241
Newton Hospital 239, 249, 254, 259, 276
Noble Hospital 249, 254
Norfolk County Sanatorium 263
North Adams Hospital 249, 254, 259, 286
North Reading State Sanatorium 258, 262, 295
Northampton State Hospital 293, 294, 296, 298
Norwood Hospital 249, 254, 295

Ophthalmia neonatorum 233, 251
    diagnosis of 236, 251
    gonococcal ophthalmia 252, 273
    isolation of 252
    prevention of 252
    reporting of 251
    silver nitrate for 280
    treatment of 252
Ophthalmic tests 282
Orthopedic clinics 240, 289

Palmer Memorial Hospital 284
Pamphlets on communicable diseases (See Literature) . . . 238
Paratyphoid fever (A) 233, 252
Paratyphoid fever (B) 233, 252
Parker, David, Memorial Hospital 237
Passive immunity 243, 247, 256, 257
Pellagra, reportable 233
Perkins Institution and Massachusetts School for the Blind . . . 291
Perkins School of Adjustment, Lancaster 302
Peter Bent Brigham Hospital 239, 274, 284

Pfeiffer bacillus meningitis (influenzal) 233, 250
Physically handicapped 241, 303
Pinkham, Lydia E., Memorial Hospital 294
Pittsfield Tuberculosis Hospital 265
Placental extract 248, 280
Plague, reportable 233
Plymouth County Sanatorium 263
Pneumococcus typing serum 252, 280
Pneumonia 252
   diagnosis of 236, 252
   isolation and quarantine 255
   laboratories for typing and serum distribution . . . 253
   lobar, reportable 233
   prevention of 255
   sera for 254
   treatment of 254
   typing of 252
Poliomyelitis, Anterior 233, 234, 239
   diagnosis of 236, 239
   hospitals and institutions for 241
   orthopedic clinics 240, 289
   respirators 239
   services for crippled children 289
   treatment of 239
Pondville Hospital 284, 286
Postgraduate instruction 289
Premature infant care 289
Preventive products 280
Preventoria, tuberculosis 265
Providence Hospital 249, 253
Public Welfare, institutions under Department of 303
   State Infirmary 303
   Massachusetts Hospital School 303

Quarantine requirements for communicable diseases . . . 234
Quincy City Hospital 249, 254

Rabies (See Dog bite) 233, 244, 255
Reeves' Sanitarium 299
Regulations
   antipneumococcic serum 254
   antirabic treatment 244
   biologics 280
   gonorrhea and syphilis 277
   silver nitrate 251, 273
Reporting of
   births and deaths 304, 305
   communicable diseases 233
   gonorrhea and syphilis 269
   industrial diseases 291
   premature births 289
Research — cancer 285
Respirators, hospitals having 239
Rheumatism 279
Ring Sanatorium and Hospital 299
Rose Hawthorne Lathrop Hospital 285
Rutland State Sanatorium 258, 262

St. Ann's Hospital 253
St. Elizabeth'sp Hospital 253
St. John's Hospital 253, 290, 292
St. Joseph's Hospital 253
St. Luke's Hospital, Middleborough 254
St. Luke's Hospital, New Bedford 239, 249, 254, 286
St. Luke's Hospital, Pittsfield 254, 286, 290
St. Vincent's Hospital 254
Salem Health Department Hospital 238, 249
Salem Hospital 239, 254, 290
Sampson Memorial Hospital 238, 249

Sanatoria (See Hospitals and Sanatoria)	262
Sassaquin Sanatorium	264
Scarlet fever	233, 235, 255
Dick test	256
isolation and quarantine	256
prevention of	256
streptococcus antitoxin	255, 280
susceptibility to	256
treatment of	255
Scarlet fever streptococcus antitoxin	255, 280
School, exclusion from	234
School teachers	235
Schools	
For the blind	291
For the deaf and hard of hearing	291
For the feebleminded	302
For the physically handicapped	303
Sensitivity	281
anaphylactic reaction	281
arthus phenomenon	284
serum sickness	283
thermal (chill) reactions	283
Septic sore throat	233, 256
Serum	
anti-influenza bacillus	250, 280
antimeningococcus	248, 280
antipneumococcus	252, 280
convalescent	241, 248, 269
diphtheria antitoxin	242, 280
placental extract	248, 280
scarlet fever antitoxin	255, 280
sensitivity	280, 281
tetanus antitoxin	257, 279
typing, pneumococcus	252, 280
Serum sensitivity outfits	280
Serum sickness	283
Sharon Sanatorium	264
Shick test	243, 280
Shriners' Hospital for Crippled Children	241
Silver nitrate, prophylaxis	252, 273, 280
Smallpox	233, 235, 256
isolation and quarantine	256
prevention of	257
vaccine for	257, 280
when to vaccinate	257
Smallpox vaccine	257, 280
Social service	
cancer	285
crippled children	241, 290
gonorrhea and syphilis	277
tuberculosis	258
Sodium citrate solution	248, 280
Sol-E-Mar Hospital	241
Somerville Contagious Disease Hospital	238
Somerville Hospital	254
Spinal fluid	
anterior poliomyelitis	239
meningococcus meningitis	236, 248
Pfeiffer bacillus meningitis	250
syphilis	236, 271
tetanus	257
Springfield Health Department Hospital	238, 239, 261, 264
Springfield Hospital	254, 276, 286, 294
Sputum	
pneumonia	252
tuberculosis	257
Standish Manor	302
Sturdy Memorial Hospital	237, 249, 253, 259, 295
Sulpharsphenamine, syphilis	271

Suppurative conjunctivitis, reportable	233
Susceptibility	243, 256
Syphilis	233, 269, 270, 276
clinics	274
confidential follow-up service	277
confidential records and reports	278
consultation	276
diagnosis of	236, 270
disclosure of certain information	279
drugs for treatment of	271, 280
literature	273
patients unable to pay	277
regulations re reimbursement	277
reporting of	269
treatment of	271
Taunton State Hospital	295, 298
Tests	
agglutination	236
complement fixation	236, 272
Darkfield examination	270
Dick	256
gold sol	236, 271
Hinton	236, 270, 272
Mantoux	258, 261, 280
Neufeld	236, 252
ophthalmic	282
Shick	243
spinal fluid examination	236, 239, 248, 250, 257, 271
Tuberculin	258, 261, 280
Von Pirquet	258, 280
Wassermann	236, 271
Weil-Felix	236, 268
Widal	236, 266
Tetanus	233, 257
Tewksbury State Infirmary	262, 285, 303
Therapeutic products	280
Thermal (chill) reactions	283
Thomas, J. B., Hospital	254
Toxin antitoxin, diphtheria	243, 280
Toxoid, diphtheria	243, 280
tetanus	257
Trachoma, reportable	233
Trichinosis, reportable	233
Truesdale Hospital	253
Tryparsamide, neurosyphilis	271
Tuberculin	258, 261, 280
Tuberculosis	233, 257
clinics	
consultation	258
local	259
school	261
contacts, examination of	265
diagnosis of	236, 257
hospitals and sanatoria for	262
county	263
Federal	262
municipal	263
private	264
State	262
isolation and quarantine	265
prevention of	265
preventoria	265
summer camps	265
treatment of	261
adult (pulmonary)	261
children	262
extra-pulmonary	262
tuberculin	258, 261, 280

Tumor Diagnostic Laboratory	285
Typhoid fever	233, 235, 266
carriers of	267
cholecystitis of typhoid origin	233, 267
diagnosis of	236, 266
isolation and quarantine	267
prevention	267
vaccine	267, 280
Widal reaction	236, 266
Typhoid-paratyphoid B vaccine	267, 280
Typhus fever	233, 268
Weil-Felix reaction	236, 268
Typing laboratories	253
Typing, pneumonia	252
Undulant fever	233, 268
diagnosis of	236, 268
isolation and quarantine of	268
prevention of	268
Union Hospital, Fall River	239, 253, 275, 286, 289
Union Hospital, Lynn	253
U. S. Marine Hospital	238
U. S. Veterans' Hospital, Bedford	298
U. S. Veterans' Hospital, Northampton	298
U. S. Veterans' Hospital, Rutland	262
Urticaria	281
Vaccination, smallpox	257
Vaccine	
antirabic	244, 245
smallpox	257, 280
typhoid-paratyphoid B	267, 280
Vision, conservation of	290
Vital statistics	304
reporting of births	304
reporting of deaths	305
Von Pirquet test	258, 280
Walter E. Fernald State School	296, 302
Waltham Hospital	238, 254, 276, 294
Washingtonian Home	301
Wassermann Laboratory	236
Wassermann test	236, 271
Webster District Hospital	249, 254
Weil-Felix reaction	236, 268
Wesson Memorial Hospital	254, 290
Westborough State Hospital	292, 293, 295, 298
Westfield State Sanatorium	258, 262, 284, 286
Westwood Lodge	299
Whidden Memorial Hospital	253, 258
Whooping Cough	233, 235, 268
Widal	236, 266
Wing Memorial Hospital	254
Wiswall Sanatorium	299
Woodlawn Sanitarium	300
Woodward Institute (mental)	295
Worcester City Hospital	239, 254, 261, 276, 290
Worcester County Sanatorium	259, 263
Worcester Hahnemann Hospital	254
Worcester Memorial Hospital	239, 254, 276, 286
Worcester State Hospital	292, 294, 298
Wrentham State School	296, 302
X-ray service	
cancer	284
tuberculosis	258
Yellow fever, reportable	233

INDEX TO VOLUME 24.

[See also Index to Physicians Handbook, pages 311-320]

American Medical Association Announcement	222
American Physicians' Art Association Announcement	307
Arthritis	279
Biologic Products	279
Regulations for Distribution of	280
Sensitivity	281
Blind and Conservation of Vision	290
Institutions	291
Cancer	284
Hospitalization	284
Tumor Diagnostic Service	285
Research	285
Clinics	285, 286
Education	287
Chicken Pox	242
Child Hygiene	287
Educational Material	288
Obstetric Package	289
Postgraduate Instruction	289
Premature Infant Care	289
Prenatal and Postnatal Letters	287, 288
Chope, H. D., M.D., Health Education for the Community	194
Clinics:	
Cancer	286
Gonorrhea and Syphilis	274, 275, 276
Infantile Paralysis	240, 241
Mental	292, 293, 294
Tuberculosis	258-261
Communicable Diseases	233
Crippled Children, Services to	289
Deaf and Hard of Hearing	291
Departmental Personnel, Changes in	169
Diabetes:	
Cardiovascular Diseases and Diabetes, by Howard F. Root, M.D.	133
Diabetes and Its Treatment, by Elliott P. Joslin, M.D.	81
Diabetes in Childhood, by Priscilla White, M.D.	145
Diabetes in Massachusetts, by Herbert L. Lombard, M.D. and Sally J. Miner	123
Diabetic Camps, by Priscilla White, M.D.	152
Diabetic Coma, by Alexander Marble, M.D.	112
Diabetic Costs, by Allen P. Joslin, M.D.	157
Gangrene and Surgery in Diabetes, by Howard F. Root, M.D.	116
The Historical Trend of Diabetes, by Eleanor J. Macdonald, A.B.	87
Inheritance of Diabetes, by Priscilla White, M.D.	135
Instruction of Diabetic Patients, by M. Bernice Moore, R.N.	104
Insulin and Protamine Insulin, by Alexander Marble, M.D.	96
The Laboratory in the Treatment of Diabetes, by Hazel Hunt, A.B., and Alexander Marble, M.D.	155
Pregnancy in Diabetes, by Priscilla White, M.D.	138
The Prevention of Diabetes and the Prognosis of the Disease, by Elliott P. Joslin, M.D.	137
Tuberculosis in Diabetics, by Alton S. Pope, M.D.	142
Diagnostic Laboratories	236

Dinegan, Ann W., R. N., Public Health Nurses as Teachers of Health . 218
Diphtheria 242
Dog Bite 244
Dysentery 245, 246
Exhibits and Materials for Health Teaching, by Albertine P. McKellar
    and John H. McCarthy 189
Food and Drugs, Report of Division of:
    October-November-December, 1936 73
    January-February-March, 1937 159
    April-May-June, 1937 226
    July-August-September, 1937 308
Forster, Miriam, The Keystone Ophthalmic Telebinocular 184
German Measles 247
Gonorrhea and Syphilis: 269-278
    Reporting 269-278
Health Education
    for the Community, by H. D. Chope, M.D. 194
    for the Secondary Schools, by A. Russell Mack 175
    in Maternity and Infancy, by Florence L. McKay, M.D. . . . 172
    in the Field of Dentistry, by Florence B. Hopkins, M.D., D.M.D. . 208
    in the Field of Tuberculosis, by Arthur Strawson 214
Heffron, Roderick, M.D., and Elliott S. Robinson, M.D., Final Report of
    the Massachusetts Pneumonia Study and Service, 1931-1935 . 6-70
Hopkins, Florence B., M.D., D.M.D., Health Education in the Field of
    Dentistry 208
  —and Latimer, Jean V., B.S., A.M., Teaching Unit on "Teeth and
    Their Care" as Developed in the South Egremont Rural School 177
Hospitalization
    of Cancer 284
    of Communicable Disease 237, 238
    of Tuberculosis 257-266
How May School Health Education Be Improved? by Jean V. Latimer . 181
Hunt, Hazel, A.B., and Marble, Alexander, M.D., The Laboratory in the
    Treatment of Diabetes 155
Industrial Diseases 291
Joslin, Elliott P., M.D., Diabetes and Its Treatment 81
  —Diabetic Costs 157
  —Prevention of Diabetes and Prognosis of the Disease . . . 137
Keystone Ophthalmic Telebinocular, by Miriam Forster 184
Latimer, Jean V., B.S., A.M., How May School Health Education Be
    Improved? 181
  —What Methods Will Promote Health Education . . . 170
  and Hopkins, Florence B., M.D., D.M.D., Teaching Unit on "Teeth
    and Their Care" as Developed in the South Egremont Rural
    School 177
Lombard, Herbert L., M.D., and Miner, Sally J., Diabetes in Massa-
    chusetts 123
Macdonald, Eleanor J., A.B., The Historical Trend of Diabetes . . . 87
Mack, A. Russell, Health Education for the Secondary Schools . . . 175
Malaria 247
Marble, Alexander, M.D., Diabetic Coma 112
  —Insulin and Protamine Insulin 96
  and Hunt, Hazel, A.B., The Laboratory in the Treatment of Diabetes 155
McCarthy, John H., and McKellar, Albertine P., Exhibits and Materials
    for Health Teaching 189

McKay, Florence L., M.D., Health Education in Maternity and Infancy . 172
McKellar, Albertine P., and McCarthy, John H., Exhibits and Materials
    for Health Teaching 189
Measles 247
    German 247
Meningitis:
    (Meningococcus Meningitis) 248
    Pfeiffer Bacillus (Influenzal) 250
    Pneumococcus 48
Mental Diseases 292-302
Miner, Sally J., and Lombard, Herbert L., M.D., Diabetes in Massachu-
    setts 123
Mississippi Valley Medical Society Award 223
Moore, M. Bernice, R.N., Instruction of Diabetic Patients . . . 104
Mumps 251
Nutrition Facts for Teachers, by Mary Spalding 199
Ophthalmia Neonatorum 251
Pamphlets on Communicable Disease 238
Paratyphoid Fever 252
Pneumonia:
    Final Report of the Massachusetts Pneumonia Study and Service,
        1931-1935, by Roderick Heffron, M.D., and Elliott S. Robinson,
        M.D. 6-70
    Report of Field Director of Study:
        Introduction 6
        General Statement 7
        Outline of Program and of Report 8
        Section
            I. Epidemiological 10
                Respiratory Disease Deaths 10
                Pneumonia in Hospitals 13
                Reporting Current Cases and Deaths 15
                Cases, Contacts, and Carriers 16
                Newer Types of Pneumococci 19
                Home-Treated Cases 22
           II. Educational 25
                Graduate Courses 26
                Pneumonia Meetings in Areas Chosen for Intensive
                    Work 27
                District Medical Society Meetings 28
                Addresses Before State and National Medical Societies 29
           III. Clinical—Pneumonia and Collaborator Areas Organized 31
                Collaborator Areas—Population Served . . . 32
                Training Technicians 34
                Comparison of Typing Methods 36
                Increase in Pneumococcus Typing 38
           IV. Results Obtained in Serum-Treated Cases . . . 39
                Type I and Type II Cases 40
                Lives Saved 47
                Type III and Group IV Cases 47
                Pneumococcus Meningitis 48
                Serum Reactions 48
           V. Result of Plan for Decentralizing Service . . . 50
          VI. Budget and Personnel 53

VII. Summary 53
　　　Conclusions 57
VIII. Recommendations 57
Report of Director, Antitoxin and Vaccine Laboratory:
　　IX. Work Carried on at Antitoxin and Vaccine Laboratory　62
　　　　Production of Therapeutic and Diagnostic Serums 62, 63
　　　　Investigation and Improvement of Methods for Pro-
　　　　　　ducing Therapeutic Serums 63
　　　　Investigation of Other Problems 66
　　　　Skin Tests in Horses and Rabbits 67
　　　　Pneumococcus Bibliography and Monograph . . 67
　　　　Plans for Continuation of Study 67
Bibliography of Articles Emanating from Study 68
Appendix:
　　Pneumonia Collaborators 69
　　Laboratories for Typing and Serum Distribution 71
Poliomyelitis, Anterior. 239
Pope, Alton S., M.D., Tuberculosis in Diabetics 142
Public Health Nurses as Teachers of Health, by Ann W. Dinegan, R.N. 218
Public Welfare, Institutions under 303
Quarantine Requirements for Communicable Disease . . 234, 235
Rabies 255
Reporting of Communicable Disease 233
　　　　of Gonorrhea and Syphilis 269
Robinson, Elliott S., M.D., and Heffron, Roderick, M.D., Final Report of
　　the Massachusetts Pneumonia Study and Service, 1931-1935 . 6-70
Root, Howard F., M.D., Cardiovascular Disease and Diabetes . . . 133
　—Gangrene and Surgery in Diabetes 116
Scarlet Fever 255
Septic Sore Throat 256
Smallpox 256
Spalding, Mary, Nutrition Facts for Teachers 199
Strawson, Arthur, Health Education in the Field of Tuberculosis . . 214
Syphilis:
　　Gonorrhea and Syphilis 269-278
　　　　Reporting 269
Teaching Unit on "Teeth and Their Care" as Developed in the South
　　Egremont Rural School, by Florence B. Hopkins, M.D., D.M.D.
　　and Jean V. Latimer, B.S., A.M. 177
Tetanus 257
Training of Personnel under the Social Security Act 220
Tuberculosis 257-266
Typhoid Fever 266-268
Typhus Fever 268
Undulant Fever 268
Vital Statistics:
　　Births 304
　　Deaths 305
What Methods Will Promote Health Education, by Jean V. Latimer . 170
White, Priscilla, M.D., Diabetes in Childhood 145
　—Diabetic Camps 152
　—Inheritance of Diabetes 135
　—Pregnancy in Diabetes 138
Whooping Cough 268, 269

THE COMMONHEALTH

Volume 25   Jan.-Feb.-Mar.
No. 1   1938

NEW ACTIVITIES
of the
MASSACHUSETTS
DEPARTMENT OF PUBLIC HEALTH

MASSACHUSETTS
DEPARTMENT OF PUBLIC HEALTH

THE COMMONHEALTH
QUARTERLY BULLETIN OF THE MASSACHUSETTS DEPARTMENT OF
PUBLIC HEALTH

Sent Free to any Citizen of the State
Entered as second class matter at Boston Postoffice.

M. LUISE DIEZ, M.D., DIRECTOR OF DIVISION OF CHILD HYGIENE, EDITOR.
1 Beacon Street, Boston, Mass.

CONTENTS

	PAGE
Foreword	3
New Activities of the Division of Adult Hygiene, by Eleanor J. Macdonald, A.B.	4
The Division of Biologic Laboratories, by Elliott S. Robinson, M.D.	8
Progress in the Massachusetts Program of Services for Crippled Children under a Federal Grant from the Children's Bureau, by Edward G. Huber, M.D.	13
The Study of Chronic Rheumatism, by Walter Bauer, M.D.	16
Medical Postgraduate Extension Courses, by Leroy E. Parkins, M.D.	25
New Activities of the Division of Communicable Diseases, by Roy F. Feemster, M.D.	26
The Control of Syphilis and Gonorrhea in Massachusetts, 1894-1937	30
New Work Performed by the Food and Drug Division during the Past Five Years, by Hermann C. Lythgoe, S.B.	39
The Premature Program of Massachusetts, by Florence L. McKay, M.D.	45
Obstetric Package Project, by Florence L. McKay, M.D.	47
The Maternal Mortality Study in Massachusetts, by Raymond S. Titus, M.D.	48
The Health Survey, by Florence L. McKay, M.D. and Sallie H. Saunders, M.D.	50
Course for Well Child Conference Physicians, by Florence L. McKay, M.D.	52
New Activities in the Dental Hygiene Program, by Florence B. Hopkins, M.D., D.M.D.	53
The Research-Learning Project, by Lura Oak, Ph.D.	57
Community Public Health Nurse Demonstration Service, by Helen Chesley Peck, R.N.	61
The Training of Lay Leaders in Parent Education, by Mrs. T. Grafton Abbott	63
Courses for Nurses on "Understanding Human Behavior," by Mrs. T. Grafton Abbott	66
New Materials in Health Education, by Jean V. Latimer, B.S., A.M.	67
Special Courses with Teen Age Girls, by Albertine P. McKellar, B.S.	69
Nutritionists Pioneer in County Health Units, by Mary Spalding, M.A.	72
Massachusetts Advances toward Better School Lunches, by Dorothy Frank, B.S.	76
New Activities of the Division of Tuberculosis, by Alton S. Pope, M.D.	81
New Activities in the Engineering Division, by Arthur D. Weston, C.E.	83
Maternal Deaths in Massachusetts, 1932-1936	86
News Note:	
Study of Positions in Interpretation and Public Relations in Health and Social Agencies	87
Book Note:	
Modern Ways with Babies, by Elizabeth Hurlock, Ph.D.	88
Editorial Comment	88
Report of Division of Food and Drugs, October, November, December, 1937	89

FOREWORD

HENRY D. CHADWICK, M.D.

Commissioner of Public Health
Massachusetts Department of Public Health

This number of "The Commonhealth" is devoted to a discussion of the newer projects and activities of the Department of Public Health. The period when health departments were concerned only with the suppression of nuisances, the control of acute communicable diseases, and the supervision of water supplies has passed. The field has broadened to include practical health education for both children and adults. Tests for hearing by the use of the audiometer and newer methods of eye examinations have revealed many children with defective hearing or vision who had not been suspected of having these handicaps. Furthermore, the state-wide provision for the care of premature infants in well-equipped centers connected with maternity hospitals will save the lives of many babies. A study is being made of chronic rheumatism to attempt to find the causes and most satisfactory form of treatment; cancer clinics and hospitals are maintained to provide facilities for diagnosis and treatment; a pneumonia service that includes typing of sputum and free distribution of five specific serums for treatment is available to physicians; and recently the Department was given the responsibility of providing treatment for all indigents having gonorrhea and syphilis.

The readers of the articles in this number will find much that is interesting and will realize as never before that public health is now a very comprehensive term.

NEW ACTIVITIES OF THE DIVISION OF ADULT HYGIENE

By Eleanor J. Macdonald, A.B.

Epidemiologist, Division of Adult Hygiene
Massachusetts Department of Public Health

During the past eleven years the Massachusetts Department of Public Health has devoted an increasing amount of time and effort to the cancer program. Massachusetts was the first state to initiate such a plan and, consequently, by the experimental method, had to blaze the trail unassisted by precedent. The early years of the program witnessed several transitions in attitude: (1) on the part of the public from resistance to acceptance, (2) on the part of the physician from antagonism to support, and (3) on the part of organized public health from repudiation to general adoption.

In 1934, as a part of the reappraising plan of Dr. Chadwick, a new and improved cancer program evolved. Many of the basic elements of the original program are included in essence in the newer plan, but the improved program is so different in scope, objectives and accomplishments, that in fairness to what it is and has achieved, the new cancer program must be classified as a new activity.

The cancer program in Massachusetts has five main features: (1) a tumor diagnostic service, (2) state hospitals for the treatment of cancer, (3) diagnostic clinics, (4) education of physicians and the laity regarding cancer, and (5) statistical research for the evaluation of the problem.

The Tumor Diagnostic Service is maintained by the Department in conjunction with the Harvard Cancer Commission. Any physician or hospital may have suspected tissue examined to determine the presence or absence of cancer. The tumor diagnostic staff has made many important contributions to medical literature.

The State cancer hospitals, administratively, with all other Department institutions, under the Division of Tuberculosis and Institutions, must be included in any consideration of the cancer program as a whole. At Pondville, a 145-bed institution, and at Westfield, a 50-bed ward are maintained exclusively for cancer by the Commonwealth. Patients with cancer may be admitted to these hospitals after a two-years' residence in the State and certification for admission by a licensed physician.

The diagnostic clinics, as conducted in Massachusetts, have provided a method for improving medical service for cancer patients by augmenting the resources of the individual physician rather than by supplanting the physician himself. The costs of such diagnostic procedures as x-ray, radium, metabolism tests, cardiograms, and certain laboratory procedures are beyond the means of many individuals. By supplying such diagnostic procedures when the need arises, a form of socialized medicine is introduced which is of benefit to both physician and patient.

In the Massachusetts Cancer Program there are twenty-one clinics. Every physician in the Commonwealth may bring or send his patient to one of these clinics for free consultative service. If the patient requires the diagnostic procedures mentioned above and is unable to pay, funds are available for defraying this expense. Every patient is referred to the physician who sent him to the clinic and the physician decides if he needs further assistance in securing treatment for his patient. If he desires it, the State cancer hospitals and the social service staff are at his disposal. These clinics are strategically located so that no individual is more than twenty-five miles from one and they are solely for diagnosis. The clinics are administered by committees appointed by the local medical organizations which have charge of administrative details but in every case certain minimum standards must be conformed with. These are:

1. Group diagnosis — The group must consist of at least three men, preferably surgeon, pathologist, and radiologist. When any of these are not available, other physicians may be substituted.

2. Uniform records — Forms are furnished by the Department for this purpose as is also money for clerical service when needed.

3. Social service — All cases of cancer and precancer are referred to social service for follow-up. The follow-up continues until death in the case of cancer and until removal of the lesion in the case of precancer. The State either furnishes money to help defray the expenses of the social worker or furnishes the clinic the services of a part-time social worker.

The clinics must meet at least twice a month. At intervals, but no less frequently than four times a year, teaching clinics for physicians are conducted. In most cases this is performed by having consultants come to the clinics but, occasionally, members of the regular clinic staff conduct teaching clinics.

The clinic itself is furnished the following services by the State: (1) advice, information, and literature; (2) funds for or services of social workers; (3) funds for travel of social worker; (4) funds for x-ray diagnosis for those unable to pay; (5) funds for teaching clinics; (6) funds for clerical assistance in clinics; (7) funds for postage, telephone, stationery, etc.; (8) special clinics for the staffs of the clinics; and (9) reference of cancer cases to Pondville through social service.

The purpose of these clinics is obvious—to furnish physicians and the public group consultation service in cancer as well as to improve the knowledge of cancer among the medical profession and the laity. The group furnishes the diagnosis and outlines a plan of treatment for every case brought to it regardless of financial status of the individual. Every effort is made to have the family physician either come with his patient to the clinic or to send the information he desires the clinic to have with the patient. By encouraging patients to come through a physician, the tendency to use the diagnostic clinics for conditions other than cancer is discouraged. Since early diagnosis is the basis for cancer control, that phase of the program is stressed in all educational activities directed toward the profession or the public.

The present type of clinic organization is meeting with increased cooperation from the physicians in consideration of the fact that in the first two years of operation 51.4 per cent of all cancer patients coming to the clinics were referred by physicians and in the last two years this figure had increased to 77.3 per cent. The best index of the results of

the work in cancer education and diagnosis is the period that people
delay from the time they have a symptom until they seek medical attention, and the period they delay from the time they are diagnosed until
they put the prescribed treatment into effect. A study of the records
shows that a reduction in both these periods of delay has occurred.
Further analysis makes it evident that the improvement is about 80 per
cent due to the physicians' efforts and 20 per cent to an improved public
consciousness. These facts gave the basis for the new educational
program.

In research the studies cover the volume of the problem; the
existing hospital facilities in the State; the availability of radium and
x-ray; the medical, social, and economic aspects of the disease; as well
as such etiological findings as would be obtained by statistical analysis
of death records, hospital records, and home visits to cancer patients.

The reception of the Cooperative Cancer Control Program in
Massachusetts has proved beyond a question that if a disease and the
present state of knowledge concerning it is explained in a $clear$ way the
public will respond with understanding and intelligence. On the thesis
that if exact knowledge were discussed about cancer and the specific
resources available were made known, the present percentage of cures
would be nearly tripled in this State of more than 350 communities with
a population of nearly 4,500,000 and over 7,000 physicians, each town and
city in the Commonwealth has been or is being organized into a small
Cooperative Cancer Control Committee for the dissemination of this
exact knowledge. Every club or even every small group which meets
regularly is asked to have a meeting on cancer once a year to which
a local physician is invited to be the speaker and to answer questions.
The physician is the pivotal figure. It is he who informs the public
through the medium of these small groups of the relationship of chronic
irritation to cancer, of the percentage of cures of the disease, of the
fallacy of the cancer folk lore, of the need for immediate action when an
abnormality occurs, and of the danger of the cancer quack. All physicians
are participating in this program by giving these talks and answering
questions. By teaching in this way, by receiving regularly the literature
which the Department prepares for this purpose, and by attendance at
regular and teaching clinics, many practitioners are acquiring a better
personal knowledge of the disease.

Another reason for the success of this plan is that it includes
every group in the Commonwealth,—social, fraternal, racial, religious,
military, political, and service. It is the whole population of the State.
The constant and increasing influx of patients to physicians and clinics
since this program started shows that the information is being not
only disseminated but is being acted upon.

This plan retains unimpaired the traditional association of patient and physician which the majority of citizens in this State prefer.
On the other hand, it supplies certain expensive procedures beyond their
means. In this way and for this one disease, the Massachusetts Cancer
Program is meeting the needs of the people as they have never been
met before.

In addition to the regular cancer program, the year 1937 was
celebrated throughout the State in various ways as the tenth anniversary

of the cancer program. During the month of March, His Excellency, Governor Charles F. Hurley, set aside one week as Cancer Week. In his proclamation he expressed gratitude for the tangible results of a cooperating public and medical profession in the control, care, and treatment of cancer.

Among the other new activities of the Division of Adult Hygiene was the preparation of a diabetes number of "The Commonhealth." The Division greatly appreciates the efforts of Dr. Joslin and his associates in helping prepare this journal.

The Director of the Division has been appointed as consultant on cancer to the United States Public Health Service. In connection with the cancer program of the United States Government, epidemiological studies similar to those that have been done in Massachusetts are being contemplated.

With the increasing number of states contemplating special cancer programs, the Director is increasingly sought for consultation because of his long and comprehensive experience as director of the first cancer program. Maine, Connecticut, New York, Georgia, Illinois, and Missouri are among those states which have sought his advice in the last year. On several occasions the Director has been invited to speak outside the State on "A State Cancer Program."

The Director was appointed a member of the Public Health Committee of the Massachusetts Medical Society. This committee in the past year has inaugurated a new series of broadcasts known as the "Green Lights to Health." They are being presented at an evening hour and are being received with much enthusiasm.

The Director has reviewed several books for the New England Journal of Medicine. He also presented a paper entitled "Research Methods in the Epidemiology of Cancer" before the American Epidemiological Association; another at the invitation of the Milbank Foundation entitled "Chronic Disease at the Crossroads"; and collaborated with Dr. Chadwick in the presentation of a paper on "A State Cancer Program" at the annual meeting of the American Public Health Association.

In addition, this Division is conducting a survey by personal interview of all physicians in Massachusetts and a biometrical study based on hospital records, death records, and control records of the arthritis situation. It is continuing its policy of training personnel on a volunteer basis; of rendering epidemiological advice to physicians, staff members, and other research workers; of punching and tabulating data for other Divisions; of periodically appraising the cancer program; of publishing and broadcasting the Health Forum; of planning special broadcasts as needed; and of addressing students in various institutions of higher learning.

THE DIVISION OF BIOLOGIC LABORATORIES

BY ELLIOTT S. ROBINSON, M.D.

Director, Division of Biologic Laboratories
Massachusetts Department of Public Health

I. The Antitoxin and Vaccine Laboratory

Inasmuch as the biologic products prepared are specific in nature, description of the activities of this laboratory is most logically presented in relation to the diseases involved.

1. **Diphtheria.** The production of diphtheria antitoxin was the original purpose of the laboratory and therefore diphtheria has been a major interest for many years. The introduction of the Schick test and of active immunization against diphtheria some twenty years ago produced the need for preparing agents for prevention as well as for treatment of the disease.

The activities of the laboratory in respect to diphtheria have closely followed the development of general knowledge of the subject and at times our own investigations have led to advances accepted elsewhere. Diphtheria antitoxin was originally distributed in the form of an unconcentrated serum and was of such low potency that it would not be employed at all now. Improvements in the production of more potent toxin and in methods of horse-immunization led to steadily higher potency of the antitoxin. About 1907 methods for the separation of the antitoxic pseudoglobulin from the non-antitoxic fractions of the serum were discovered. For some years there was discussion of whether concentrated antitoxins contained all of the therapeutic activities of antidiphtheritic serum, but this dispute has gradually died down and the use of concentrated antitoxins is now universal. The methods of concentration follow in general those for the separation of serum proteins and have improved with increasing knowledge of that subject. It has been believed that antitoxins are proteins with the nature and characteristics of pseudoglobulin and are inseparable from the protein complex. Preparations made by incomplete enzymatic digestion and tested for combining activity in vitro give evidence, however, that antitoxic activity may be retained even when the pseudoglobulin molecule is split, and so give rise to the hope that products with even higher antitoxic activity per gram than those now obtainable may some day be prepared. However, the decreasing need for antitoxin has somewhat lessened the importance of this problem.

The production of diphtheria toxin of high potency has been the object of extensive investigation at the laboratory during the past three years. The researches of Mueller upon the growth requirements of the diphtheria bacillus have been used as the basis for determining the requirements of toxin production. The recognition of the part played by traces of iron in inhibiting or entirely suppressing toxin production has made possible the application of Mueller's findings about growth to our problem. The success of this investigation has been such that the toxin now routinely produced is at least two to three times as strong as that obtained previously. Since the medium now used is of known chemical constitution and contains no nitrogenous material more complex than amino-acids, the preparation of pure toxin from it is relatively easy. The practical applications of this study have not yet been fully worked out, but should be of distinct value in improving all of our diphtheria products.

Active immunization against diphtheria is now established as a routine part of the care of children. The use of toxin-antitoxin mixtures for this purpose was suggested by Theobald Smith, then Director of our laboratory, and applied on a large scale and popularized by Park, of the New York City Department of Health. For some years toxin-antitoxin mixture offered the only means of producing active immunity. Then Ramon, of the Pasteur Institute, introduced the use of "anatoxine," which is a stable, atoxic preparation made by the action of formaldehyde upon toxin at temperatures of 38°—42°C. This product, now usually called "toxoid," was first distributed by the Department in 1932. Until 1937 both toxoid and toxin-antitoxin mixtures were employed for immunization of children, but in the spring of 1937 the Department stopped issuing toxin-antitoxin mixture for use in school clinics. This action was taken because there was no evidence that toxoid was any less efficacious than the mixtures, and considerable evidence that it was probably a better immunizing agent. Moreover, the toxoid, containing no horse-serum, could not possibly give rise to horse-serum sensitivity, whereas toxin-antitoxin mixtures had been accused of doing so.

The substitution of diphtheria toxoid, alum-precipitated, for the crude toxoid has been strongly urged. It has been claimed that a single dose of the alum-precipitated toxoid is sufficient to produce active immunity. Unfortunately, this claim has not been entirely supported by experimental evidence, and the Department is unwilling to substitute the alum-precipitated product for the crude toxoid until further evidence is available. The American Public Health Association is conducting a study to compare the relative value of one and two doses of alum-precipitated toxoid with two or three doses of the crude toxoid. Up to the present, nothing has come of this which would warrant substituting one dose of alum-toxoid for the three doses of crude toxoid, given at intervals of three or four weeks, which the Department now recommends and furnishes.

The Schick test is not as widely used as formerly, for the proportion of younger children who are undergoing immunization is greater than in the early days of diphtheria prevention. Since younger children are quite likely to be Schick-positive, it has become the rule to omit Schick tests before immunization. The use of Schick tests after immunization has been largely given up in public health practice because, with the high proportion rendered Schick-negative by toxoid, it is felt that the benefit to the community is greater when the effort is expended upon immunizing additional children than when it is devoted to testing children previously injected with toxoid. This does not mean that the Schick test is without value or should not be employed, for it still remains the simplest way to determine the result of attempted immunization.

The Department's recommendations about diphtheria immunization are as follows:

1. Children under six months of age should have a Schick test performed and if they are negative they should be retested between six

months and one year of age. If they give a positive reaction they should be immunized with diphtheria toxoid.

2. All children between the ages of six months and twelve years should be immunized with diphtheria toxoid without having the Shick test performed on them. The majority of children of this age group are susceptible and therefore the Schick test is not necessary.

3. All children between twelve and eighteen years of age should have the Schick test performed, and if they give a positive Schick test they should receive three injections of 1 cc. each of diphtheria toxin-antitoxin mixture unless they show a marked combined reaction, when the toxin-antitoxin mixture may be given in divided doses beginning with 0.1 cc., then 0.2—0.5—1.0—1.0 cc. at weekly intervals.

4. All individuals above eighteen years of age who are exposed to diphtheria or may come in contact with it should have the Schick test performed and be immunized with diphtheria toxin-antitoxin mixture with the same provision, however, as stated in the previous paragraph.

5. All persons receiving three doses of diphtheria toxin-antitoxin mixture should be retested with the Schick test six months after the last injection, and if they should still give a positive Schick test they should receive three more injections of diphtheria toxin-antitoxin mixture and be again retested six months after the last injection.

2. **Scarlet Fever.** The production of scarlet fever antitoxin has been carried on routinely since 1925. The discovery that rabbits could be usefully employed in the titration of this antitoxin greatly simplified the labor of producing it and has led to steady improvement in the methods of horse immunization and of concentration, resulting in a product of improved quality. Of great help, too, has been the flocculation test devised by Dr. Leo Rane of this laboratory.

Active immunization against scarlet fever has been studied in cooperation with the Division of Communicable Diseases. Feeling that the usual method of injecting five doses of scarlet fever toxin was not satisfactory, attention has been directed to the employment of three doses of toxoid. The results have not been altogether as satisfactory as is desired, but it is hoped that a method may be evolved which will give a higher percentage of negative reactions to the Dick test than is now obtained with toxoid and will require no more injections and give no greater reactions than does toxoid. From the standpoint of preventing scarlet fever, the toxoid has been definitely of value.

The production of scarlet fever convalescent serum for the prophylaxis of contacts with the disease was undertaken in cooperation with interested boards of health in 1933. The boards of health arranged clinics at which persons who had had scarlet fever within the previous year were bled by members of the Department and the serum was separated and processed at this laboratory. The serum so obtained was returned to the local boards of health. Although several communities took advantage of this opportunity, interest in this use of convalescent serum has died down and the scheme has been abandoned.

3. **Pneumonia.** The distribution of serum for the treatment of pneumonia was undertaken as long ago as 1917. The introduction of concentrated serum made a study of its use desirable, for it offered the possibility of making serum treatment available to patients in their homes

and at earlier stages of the disease than had been previously possible. Therefore, the Department undertook its well-known Pneumonia Study and Service (1931-35), a full report of which will be found in the Commonhealth for January-February-March, 1937.

The Pneumonia Study and Service was so successful that it was incorporated in the routine work of the Department, and production expanded to include serums for types 5, 7 and 8, in addition to those for types 1 and 2. The serums are freely available throughout the State, the only restrictions being that the type of infecting organism must first be demonstrated and that the physician will send the laboratory a brief case report. Neither of these restrictions is burdensome, and the information obtained from the histories is essential to improving the quality of the serums manufactured and of the services rendered by the Department. It is a pleasure to record that physicians and hospitals have been most cooperative in carrying out the details of the program.

4. **Meningitis (Meningococcic)**. Antimeningococcic serum has fallen somewhat into disrepute during the past ten years because it has appeared to be less efficacious than formerly. Whether such an opinion is justified is difficult to tell; but at any rate, every effort has been made to produce more potent serums. The recent introduction of a method of testing serum for its protective activity in mice and of methods for concentrating the serum should be followed by definite increase in its quality.

5. **Meningitis (Influenzal or Pfeiffer Bacillus)**. Studies at the Harvard Medical School and the Children's Hospital with serum produced at this laboratory have shown that it is of value in the treatment of the extremely fatal form of meningitis caused by Hemophilus influenzae (Pfeiffer bacillus, influenza bacillus). Since late in 1936 this serum has been available to physicians having victims of this disease in their care.

6. **Typhoid and Paratyphoid Fever.** Investigations carried out at Harvard by the late Francis B. Grinnell, M. D., and confirmed at the Army Medical School suggested that the strain of E. typhi used in making typhoid vaccine had lost much of its antigenic value, and that a freshly isolated virulent strain would be more efficacious. In conformity with these ideas, a strain furnished by the Army Medical School is now used in making this vaccine.

Considerable attention has been devoted to making the bacterial content of different batches of bacterial vaccine as much alike as possible. This is now accomplished by determination of the nitrogen content and by turbidity readings done with the Gates nephelometer. A high degree of uniformity in the batches is desirable because a moderate increase in bacterial content may give rise to unpleasant local reactions at the site of injection of the vaccine.

The low incidence of paratyphoid fevers in Massachusetts and the elimination of paratyphoid organisms from the vaccine supplied by the Army Medical School led us to omit paratyphoid A and B organisms from our vaccine. Unfortunately an outbreak of paratyphoid B fever occurred shortly after this, and therefore that organism is now again included in the vaccine.

The floods of the past few years have created sudden demands for large quantities of typhoid vaccine. As the supply of vaccine of our own manufacture was insufficient to meet the demand created by the New

England floods of 1936, some was obtained from the Army Medical School to take care of this need. When the floods occurred in the Ohio River Valley in 1937, His Excellency Governor Hurley permitted us to send a large quantity to the stricken area, thus repaying the courtesy previously extended to Massachusetts.

7. **Measles.** Despite its prevalence, measles is a disease about which health departments can do relatively little. Particularly in young children measles may give rise to serious complications. Convalescent serum is of value in preventing the disease but the serum is difficult to obtain, particularly on a large scale. The discovery by Dr. C. F. McKhann of the Children's Hospital that placental extract could be substituted for convalescent serum led to a joint study of the preparation and use of the extract. The preparation of satisfactory extracts has proved difficult and no satisfactory answer has yet been found to all the questions involved, but it has been possible to fill most of the demand for the extract.

8. **Sensitivity to Horse Serum.** The administration of horse serum to persons with a heightened sensitivity to it may be distinctly dangerous. Methods for identifying such individuals rest upon preliminary tests with diluted horse serum. The increasing use of antipneumococcic serum made it desirable that serum already diluted for use be furnished, and therefore packages containing vials of diluted horse serum were placed in distribution in 1937.

9. **Research.** The production of biologic products is inseparably associated with the conduct of investigations of better methods of production and of the failures of current methods. Both the scope and the results of recent and present investigations have been indicated above.

II. The Wasserman Laboratory

The activities of this branch of the Division of Biologic Laboratories are largely serological. During recent years the volume of work has steadily increased.

1. **Serologic Tests for the Detection of Syphilis.** The introduction of flocculation methods necessitated a study of their usefulness in comparison with that of the Wasserman technic routinely employed. Many of the flocculation tests have been tried, particularly the Kahn, but the most satisfactory results have been obtained with the Hinton test which was developed in this laboratory and that of the Boston Dispensary. In 1934 the Hinton test was substituted for the Wasserman for all specimens to which it was applicable, the Wasserman test being reserved for use on spinal fluids and the small proportion of blood specimens which were not suitable for the Hinton test. A microscopic modification of the Hinton test, called the Davies-Hinton, is being studied for its applicability to spinal fluids and to very small amounts of blood serum. Because it is more time-consuming than the Hinton, it will not be employed for the testing of routine blood specimens.

The number of tests performed has risen steadily, the annual increases ranging as high as 25 per cent per year.

2. **Colloidal Gold Tests.** These have been done in small numbers for a good many years.

3. **Gonococcus Complement-Fixation Tests.** Although the complement fixation test is of less value in the diagnosis of gonococcal infection than

is the analogous test for syphilis, yet an increasing number of tests are performed annually.

4. **Examinations for Rabies.** The routine examinations including the necessary animal inoculations, are performed by this laboratory.

5. **Agglutination Tests for Brucella Abortus.** The elimination of infectious abortion from dairy herds is a problem of importance to the public health both because of the possible transmission of undulant fever to man and because of the economic losses entailed by the disease in cattle. The Division of Live Stock Disease Control in the Department of Agriculture is aided in its work of eradicating infectious abortion by agglutination tests done at the Wasserman Laboratory. The number of tests done per year has steadily increased, reaching above 25,000 in 1937.

6. **Other Routine Tests.** Complement-fixation tests for glanders, and miscellaneous pathologic and bacteriologic tests for the Division of Live Stock Disease Control make up a small part of the routine work.

7. **Investigations.** A study of the effect of various intervals between injections of arsphenamine, in rabbits infected with syphilis, and one on cultural methods for detection of gonococcal infections, are under way but not sufficiently advanced to warrant comment.

PROGRESS IN THE MASSACHUSETTS PROGRAM OF SERVICES FOR CRIPPLED CHILDREN UNDER A FEDERAL GRANT FROM THE CHILDREN'S BUREAU

BY EDWARD G. HUBER, M.D.

Director of Orthopedic Unit, Assistant Director of Public Health Administration
Massachusetts Department of Public Health

The first State clinic for crippled children was held at Pittsfield on September 2, 1936. The plan of operation of a statewide service for crippled children, as evolved by the Department of Public Health, had been approved by the Children's Bureau two months before. The intervening time was utilized in making all the necessary preliminary arrangements. The major effort in this preparatory period was directed toward securing the support of the Massachusetts Medical Society and of its constituent district societies. The Council of the Massachusetts Medial Society then unanimously endorsed the plan and approved the methods taken by the Department of Public Health in endeavoring to secure the cooperation of the members of the Society. Many other details were arranged during the summer of 1936, such as the selection of personnel and of hospitals in which to locate clinics, and the consummation of arrangements for statewide hospitalization of patients. By the time the first clinic was held, the major and most of the minor problems of organization had been solved and all that remained was to get the patients and hold the clinics.

After about a year and a half of clinics for crippled children the Department of Public Health feels that the work has been well worth while and that the plan has been fairly successful in its operation. Ten diagnostic clinics, in as many different cities, have been held each month. These clinics are on a regular schedule, which is published weeks in advance. When a child is examined at one of these clinics, and treatment prescribed, that is only the beginning of what is in store for that child. If hospitalization is recommended and the report of one of the medical social workers indicates that the parents of the patient are unable to meet all the necessary expense, nothing stands in the way of immediate admission to a hospital but the consent of the parents. If physiotherapy is prescribed, the field physiotherapist either visits the patient in the home or has groups of patients gather at some specified place, for treatment. If apparatus is recommended, the measurements are taken at the clinic and the order given to a bracemaker.

The program, therefore, includes four distinct features:

Diagnostic clinics   Physiotherapy
Hospitalization   Braces and other apparatus

These four activities involve entirely different services. All of them are essential but there is one feature of the Massachusetts program which is even more important, and that is the constant supervision which the patients receive. Once a child is examined at a diagnostic clinic and the Department is satisfied that the parents need and will accept assistance, that child is under the immediate supervision of a field worker until nothing more can be done for him medically or surgically. This surveillance is not a cursory one. It begins with the diagnostic clinic and is continuous whether the child is hospitalized or not. The members of the field staff not only carry out the instructions of the clinic consultant insofar as physiotherapy and the wearing of apparatus are concerned, but they also guard against any tendency of the patient and the family to neglect their share of the treatment. Besides being frequently seen by the field staff at home or elsewhere, the child revisits the clinic whenever the orthopedic consultant in charge of the clinic wishes to re-examine the patient. A field worker sees to it that the child does attend at the specified time. If the family moves to another part of the State, the field worker of that district is notified, and the follow-up is uninterrupted. If the move is to another state, that information is transmitted to the proper authorities.

During the year and a half since the first clinic was held, about seven hundred children have been admitted to the clinics. These seven hundred children have made about seventeen hundred clinic visits. This is not a large proportion of the crippled children in the State but it is rather surprising that so many children have already been found who are in need of orthopedic treatment. About two hundred children have been operated on, well over two thousand physiotherapy treatments have been given and about one hundred and forty have had apparatus made for them. Massachusetts has taken care of many of its crippled children for years at the Lakeville State Sanatorium and at the Massachusetts Hospital School. Hospital clinics, and clinics conducted by orthopedic surgeons throughout the State, have been giving excellent care to an even larger number for a still longer period. Some of the conservative members of the medical profession, who opposed State clinics for crippled children, insisted that there were no neglected patients of this kind in the State. The fact that so many have already been found shows that there was and is a real need for the clinics. In admitting children to clinics an important prerequisite is that the patient is not, even remotely, under the care of another orthopedist, hospital, or clinic.

Attendance at clinics is very small compared to the reported attendance at clinics for crippled children in some other states. Twenty patients per clinic is the upper efficiency limit; about ten is the average so far, although the trend of attendance per clinic has increased during recent months. More than twenty patients cannot be given careful attention during the clinic period which is generally almost a half day. The Department does not judge the success of the clinic by the number of patients attending but by how thoroughly they are examined.

Almost all the members of the original staff are still with the Orthopedic Unit, which is that section of the Division of Administration of the Department of Public Health which administers the program. One of the original eleven clinics, that at Greenfield, was discontinued. The other ten remain, with the same consultants, with one exception, who first operated the clinics. As the number of children under treatment has increased, additional physiotherapists and clerical help have been employed. At the time of the first clinic, the office and field staff consisted of eight persons. There are now eighteen, including three social workers who divide their time with the Division of Tuberculosis.

There has been an interesting development in the scope of the work. Children requiring plastic operations were included in the original definition of a crippled child, but patients requiring such aid have been more numerous than had been anticipated. In order that the Department might give these children surgical aid comparable to that given by the orthopedic consultants, Dr. Varaztad H. Kazanjian was persuaded to accept an appointment as consultant. Children requiring plastic operations are admitted to the Massachusetts General Hospital where he cares for them.

The original administrative definition of a crippled child included those suffering from cardiac diseases. A few carefully selected children in this classification were accepted as clinic cases last year, but it was soon obvious that we could do nothing for them except to provide domiciliary care. The fundamental principle involved in the selection of children to be recipients of care under Services for Crippled Children is that they must be able to profit by medical and surgical care. Mere custodial or domiciliary care is expressly interdicted. The cardiac cases that presented themselves did not need medical or surgical treatment. There was nothing to do for them except to provide care, and custodial care is excluded under the regulations of the Children's Bureau, so the definition was changed, omitting mention of cardiacs.

The method of admission of crippled children to the clinics is the same, basically, as it was at first. There has been a slight change in the procedure, which is meeting the approval of the members of the Massachusetts Medical Society, particularly the District Medical Societies Committees, which committees were appointed to represent the Massachusetts Medical Society in the selection of patients for clinics. The first requisite for admission to a clinic is the written application of a physician. As soon as possible after receipt of this application a medical social worker, a member of the field staff of the Orthopedic Unit, visits the family and obtains a complete social record of that family, especially concerning the ability of that family to pay for orthopedic treatment. The patient visits the next clinic and is examined and prescribed for by the orthopedic consultant. The chairman of the District Medical Society then is sent the signed application, the diagnosis and prescription of the orthopedic consultant, and the report of the medical social worker. He is asked to approve or disapprove the application. The patient may be able to pay a part of the costs of treatment; if so, he is then asked to pay a certain amount, that amount being determined by the Department of Public Health.

There is one other phase of the problem of the crippled child which, while it does not definitely belong in a medical and surgical program, cannot be ignored. Dr. Parran has given as one of the six points in his program of activity, the restoration of crippled children to lives of usefulness. The Department of Public Health, therefore, does not intend to forget its patients, once it has done all it can to restore them physically and has ceased carrying them as active cases. The field staff, especially the medical social workers, will continue to help them. These workers have become familiar with the respective possibilities and limitations of the patients, during the period of medical and surgical care, and will thus be able to help them find some place where they can be useful. For this purpose the already active relationship with the work carried on by Social Service for Crippled Children of the Department of Public Welfare will be continued to an even greater extent, in order to further the restoration of crippled children to lives of usefulness.

THE STUDY OF CHRONIC RHEUMATISM[*][1]

By Walter Bauer, M.D.

Massachusetts General Hospital
Boston, Massachusetts

Chronic rheumatism is the greatest cause of chronic disease in the State of Massachusetts. As the result of a survey made by the former commissioner of public health, Dr. George H. Bigelow, and Dr. Herbert L. Lombard[2], it was estimated that at any one time there are 140,000 individuals in Massachusetts suffering from rheumatism, 80,000 with heart disease, 56,000 with arteriosclerosis, 31,000 with Bright's disease, 25,000 with active tuberculosis and 10,000 with cancer. Nearly 85% of the 140,000 individuals were over forty years of age. Complete physical disability was present in 4.2% or approximately 6,000 of the cases. Thirty per cent or approximately 42,000 individuals were partially disabled. The same investigators estimated that 46% of the wage earners lost an average period of four and one-half months from work. Applying all of these figures to all wage earners in this state, it is estimated that the total loss of work per year is approximately 6,500 work years. Thus the economic loss caused by chronic rheumatism in Massachusetts approximates $25,000 a day, or $8,000,000 per year. Such figures give one

---

[*] This is publication No. 24 of the Robert W. Lovett Memorial for the study of crippling disease, Harvard Medical School.
[1] From the Medical Clinic of the Massachusetts General Hospital, the Department of Medicine, Harvard Medical School, and the Massachusetts Department of Public Health.
[2] Cancer and other Chronic Diseases in Massachusetts, G. H. Bigelow and H. L. Lombard, Houghton Mifflin Company, Boston, 1932.

a fairly accurate representation of the economic aspect of this most important chronic disease but give one little information concerning the humanitarian or social aspects. Of the estimated 6,000 completely disabled individuals, 600 were living in homes wholly unsuited for proper care and treatment. At the time of the survey, 68% of all cases were either receiving no treatment or were treating themselves. In the poorer group this figure reached a high point of 75%. Thus it will be seen that many of the patients suffering from chronic rheumatism either are unable to seek medical aid or have lost all faith in it because of the little help obtained when it was sought.

It will be extremely difficult to improve this aspect of the problem without providing adequate facilities for the treatment of those patients who are unable to pay. It will further require that all physicians treating patients with chronic rheumatism make full use of the total accumulated knowledge concerning these disabling afflictions. In addition further research will be necessary in order to obtain a more thorough knowledge of the many factors underlying the cause and the cure of these socially and economically important diseases.

These and many other aspects of the chronic rheumatism problem were carefully studied in 1936 by the Committee on Adult Hygiene and Special Diseases before it submitted its final report with general recommendations to the State Department of Public Health of the Commonwealth of Massachusetts[3]. This Committee reported as follows on methods by which better control might be established:

"Since the exact etiology of a large majority of these cases has not been discovered, facilities for research into these causes are of prime importance. The advances in methods of treatment which have been made, especially in the last two decades, are not generally known by the medical profession, or, if known, are not generally applied. Lack of adequate facilities for study and for the carrying out of these methods may be largely responsible for this lack of rational therapy. Be this as it may, it is obvious that postgraduate education is becoming increasingly important. Medical societies are fostering such education by exhibits, addresses and postgraduate extension courses. This is most commendable, but is by no means sufficient. Even if each physician in the Commonwealth should be made conversant with efficient methods looking to the control of these chronic rheumatic diseases, he would rarely possess the personal equipment required for either diagnosis or rational therapy. Both the private and the public facilities which now exist for arriving at sound conclusions as to underlying causes, the administration of immediate appropriate treatment, and the planning of a future regimen are inadequate. While the Commission could wish for nothing better than large private gifts or bequests for the establishment of facilities for the adequate study and care of these crippling diseases under private auspices or in existing institutions, it believes that the Commonwealth should concern itself at the earliest possible moment with improving the facilities for the study and control of chronic rheumatism, and at the same time urges that every effort should be made to obtain such funds from private sources."

[3] Report of the Special Commission to Study and Investigate Public Health Laws and Policies, The Commonwealth of Massachusetts, December 2, 1936.

The Committee further suggested possible methods by which this important problem might be attacked.

"Ideally, every large general hospital should allocate a certain number of its beds for the investigation and treatment of patients with chronic rheumatism. As such an ideal arrangement is probably impossible at the present moment, it is strongly recommended that as an initial move in the attack upon this problem a unit for the study and care of patients with chronic rheumatism be established under state auspices in connection with one of the large general hospitals in the metropolitan area. Such a plan would mean either a state-supported unit in a general hospital, or a small institute, which, if it achieved the success that the Commission believes possible, would serve to point the way for more extensive future developments. The selection of the proper location of such a unit is a problem to which this Commission has given considerable study. Four possibilities suggest themselves:

"1. State support of a limited number of beds in a general hospital.

"2. An institute closely affiliated with or an integral part of a large existing metropolitan hospital.

"3. An institute which may be a part of an existing state institution.

"4. A separate state institute devoted solely to the problem of chronic rheumatism.

"After careful consideration of the relative advantages of the above proposals, including the medical as well as the economic aspects, the Commission believes that from all points of view the first plan, providing for support of approximately twenty-five beds in a general metropolitan hospital, is the most advantageous.

"It cannot be too strongly emphasized that the personnel selected for the conduct of such a unit is of far greater importance than the physical plant. Owing to the ramifications of chronic rheumatism, involving the fields of the many medical specialties, it is essential that there be available adequate personnel skilled in these many diverse branches of the science of medicine. It is further essential for the adequate study of these diseases that there be available the knowledge and skill of the sciences allied to or bearing upon the actual practice of medicine, including the fields of physiology, pathology, bacteriology, chemistry, physics and biology. Only in the larger hospitals can there be found this specialized technical assistance required for the best approach to this problem. It is thus desirable that the closest possible affiliation with a general hospital be established.

"From the economic standpoint there is also sound reason for such affiliation. Any chronic rheumatism research unit, if it is to render efficient service, will require the broadest possible variety of laboratory facilities and x-ray and physiotherapy equipment. Unless it were of far greater size than appears desirable at the outset, it would be economically unsound to invest the necessary funds to obtain these facilities, nor could they be utilized to the fullest degree in a small institution. Affiliation with a large hospital where many of these facilities are already available, or where they might be provided for joint use, would appear to be the most economical procedure at the present time. Such a plan would also reduce the initial cost of construction and the cost of maintenance as compared with the much higher charges for a separate institution.

"In making these recommendations the Commission has in mind a unit to which patients with chronic rheumatism may be referred by the family physician, the patients to be afforded the specialized study needed to indicate the most suitable means of treatment. After these basic facts have been determined and the treatment started, the patient should be referred back to the family physician for further treatment based upon the hospital findings. Specialized treatment, frequently on an out-patient basis or by readmission for periods of a few days, should be continued either through the hospital or through facilities which may be available in communities closer to the patient's place of residence. Such a plan would make possible a fairly rapid turn-over of patients, serving many more than might be inferred from the limited number of beds."

In 1937, the state legislature, on recommendation of the Massachusetts Department of Public Health, passed an act providing for the hospitalization of patients with chronic rheumatism (Chapter 393, acts of 1937). This act reads as follows:

"Chapter one hundred and eleven of the General Laws is hereby amended by inserting after section one hundred and sixteen, as appearing in the Tercentenary Edition, under the title Chronic Rheumatism, the following new section:

"Section 116A. The department, subject to rules and regulations, approved by the commission on administration and finance, may provide for the care and treatment of persons suffering from chronic rheumatism for a period not exceeding six months in case of any one such person, and said department may enter into contracts with one or more existing hospitals within any metropolitan district for the care and treatment of such patients; provided, that not more than twenty-five such patients may be cared for or treated under this section at any one time."

On September 1, 1937, as provided in Chapter 393, acts of 1937, the Department of Public Health of the Commonwealth of Massachusetts entered into a contract with the Massachusetts General Hospital, where since 1930 a group of workers has been engaged in the study of problems relating to chronic rheumatism. These investigations have been supported by the income from the Robert W. Lovett Memorial of the Harvard Medical School and grants from the Rockefeller and the John and Mary R. Markle Foundations. During these seven years, the Massachusetts General Hospital made possible hospitalization of the patients studied and allowed for considerable in the way of laboratory supplies and needs. In addition, some expenses were met by private individuals.

With the added clinical facilities afforded by the Massachusetts Department of Public Health, it was decided to seek additional private funds in order to allow for the continuation of this research work on a broader and more inclusive scale. This search for additional funds was successful. The Commonwealth Fund voted a grant for a three-year period beginning January 1, 1938. From September 1, 1939, this combined care of the patient and clinical research program will be supported by the Robert W. Lovett Memorial, the Massachusetts Department of

Public Health, and the Commonwealth Fund. Such a combination of private and state funds is an ideal one. It should serve a much more useful purpose in the study of the chronic rheumatism problem than if these various funds were spent separately.

With this added financial support and clinical facilities, we shall attempt to develop slowly a research and care of the patient program which will embody many of the important phases of the subject. From the inception of this study, fundamental investigations combined with careful, detailed studies of patients with various types of arthritis have been carried out. The results to date of such interdependent studies indicate that continuation of the broadest possible program for an indefinite period of time is necessary if we are to gain the desired information concerning these socially and economically important diseases.

I shall attempt to present as briefly as possible the scope of these investigations to date and to outline the plans for future work. The list of reprints published to date is appended.

Fundamental Studies Pertaining to Normal Joints

In order to interpret more correctly in terms of the normal, the abnormal findings encountered in various types of arthritis, studies pertaining to the anatomy and physiology of normal joints have been necessary.

An attempt has been made to define as completely as possible the nature and origin of normal synovial fluid. A neighboring slaughter house has been utilized in this work, because the amounts of synovial fluid large enough for detailed chemical analyses along with arterial blood, can thus be obtained at the time of death. Analyses of these data show that synovial fluid is a simple diffusate, with the addition of mucin. The cellular composition of normal synovial fluid has been determined in this species. Other studies pertaining to synovial fluid cytology have included the possible causes of observed cellular variations; the determination of the exact cytology of normal human synovial fluid, and the correlation of cellular variations with the histological appearance of the synovial membrane obtained immediately post mortem from patients without joint disease, dying with or without infection. Such information is necessary before we can interpret properly the cytological changes occurring in joint effusions.

A series of investigations has been done or will be performed in the future in order to determine the factors influencing the drainage of normal joints both through the lymphatic and the vascular systems. True solutions, proteins and other colloids and particulate matter have all been utilized, with attention directed toward the influence of exercise, synovial fluid removal and inflammation. Such information should enable us to devise methods which would allow us to determine why a joint effusion occurs, why it persists, and how it should be treated.

Mucin, the missing link in the complete understanding of normal synovial fluid, has been isolated by Dr. Marian Ropes. She is at present engaged in the laborious task of defining the physical and chemical properties of this substance. Once we possess this information, we shall be in a position to determine more concerning the role of mucin in the fluid exchange of joints and as a lubricant, as well as to establish its origin. Estimation of the amount present in joint effusions may be of diagnostic significance in that it may aid in determining the type of joint changes present. This work should be of much greater physiological significance than that pertaining to joints alone.

Studies have been made of surgically created articular cartilage defects in mature and in growing dogs as well as spontaneous degenerative cartilage lesions probably due to trauma occurring in cattle. These studies reveal that the ability of articular cartilage to repair itself is at best feeble. This inability of articular cartilage to repair itself seems to bear a direct relation to hypertrophic (degenerative) arthritis and has been supplemented by examination of the knee joints of patients from the first to the ninth decades who have never had obvious joint disease. This study revealed that with increasing age, one observed increasing degenerative joint changes indistinguishable from so-called hypertrophic arthritis. It would appear that this type of joint disease represents the wear and tear changes of long continued use, often repeated trauma, and increasing age in a body tissue, articular cartilage, not possessing the same reparative ability found in other body tissues. The results of these studies as well as those designed to determine the changes observed in patellar displacement, unusual use, or trauma, make us question the use of the word "arthritis" in this type of joint disease. We prefer the term degenerative joint disease, because it describes more accurately the pathological changes encountered in such joints.

In addition to the above, many other studies should be undertaken such as the chemistry of cartilage; the factors capable of injuring it; its source of nourishment, etc. Further information concerning the blood, the lymphatic, and the nerve supply of joints is needed. Many of these studies first done on animals must be carried over to human beings in order to have the data necessary to interpret correctly the abnormal states encountered.

Clinical Studies

Detailed clinical studies have been made of all arthritic patients and of individuals presenting unusual diagnostic problems entering the hospital. This has been done in order that we might obtain our own clinical description of the various arthritides. Such an arrangement also makes available an abundance of clinical material for research studies. The most detailed studies have been made on patients suffering from rheumatoid and gonorrheal arthritis.

In case of rheumatoid or atrophic arthritis we have proceeded as though we were dealing with a new disease. It was hoped that this manner of approach would allow us to obtain an unbiased clinical description of the disease. Patients suffering from rheumatoid arthritis have been studied according to a systematic plan. Careful history and examination are made of each along with detailed roentgenological and laboratary studies. These data are entered on a sheet lending itself to statistical study. This group now numbers well over four hundred. Analysis of this group is now being made by Drs. N. R. Abrams and Charles L. Short under the guidance of Professor Edwin B. Wilson and Dr. Herbert L. Lombard. It soon became apparent that the value of this analysis would be greater and the conclusions more convincing if we had similar data on a group of so-called normal individuals, of the same sex, age distribution and social status. Such data do not exist in the medical literature. Therefore, we have been forced to collect it ourselves. Once the analysis of the rheumatoid arthritic and the control groups is completed, we shall be able to give a good cross-section description of the disease and the individuals suffering from it. With this information at hand, we can speak with more certainty concerning the many causative and contributing factors which have been incriminated frequently in the past.

We have adopted no set line of therapy in patients suffering from rheumatoid arthritis. We have prescribed the usual general and dietary treatment, along with removal of obvious foci when indicated. We have enjoyed the full cooperation of the orthopedic service in instituting preventive and corrective measures. We have tried to avoid so-called specific treatment whenever possible in order that we may better evaluate the course of the disease as well as accumulate much needed control data.

In addition, Dr. Coggeshall has made detailed clinical, bacteriological, pathological and roentgenological studies in over two hundred cases of gonorrheal arthritis. Many of these patients have been followed for years. This study will enable us to describe gonorrheal arthritis in detail. It will further allow us to compare the results of non-specific treatment with those obtained with artificial fever and sulfanilamide therapy. Comparison of these data from patients with an infectious arthritis of known origin with similar data obtained from patients with rheumatoid arthritis, a disease of unknown origin, will aid greatly in deducing certain clinical and etiological facts.

On discharge from the hospital, the patients are followed at regular intervals in the out-patient department, and the clinical course of their disease can thus be observed and defined. It is hoped that we can follow most of these patients for years and in many instances complete our studies with a detailed autopsy. If we can follow a sufficiently large group of rheumatoid arthritic patients in this manner, we shall eventually be better able to define the life course of the disease and learn whether the many remissions observed represent therapeutic triumphs or the natural course of the disease. Few detailed autopsies in rheumatoid arthritics have been reported, particularly in younger individuals.

With the additional financial support which we have received, we can now establish a more adequate follow-up system and thereby maintain much better contacts with our patients and their physicians. A better follow-up system will allow for some epidemiological studies and also aid in determining how communities can meet best the many problems relating to rheumatic diseases. We shall attempt to determine whether or not the establishment of a few strategically placed radial arthritic clinics would aid in the care of arthritis patients. If such clinics were established and run by the local physicians, they would aid greatly in the dissemination of knowledge concerning methods of treatment. They might also serve as centers to train men interested in such diseases.

Complete cytological, chemical and bacteriological studies are made on all types of pathological joint effusions. During the past seven years, we have collected data on more than three hundred effusions. Analyses of these findings may reveal that synovial fluid examinations are as useful in a diagnostic and a prognostic sense as is the examination of spinal fluid.

In this seven-year period we have accumulated a very extensive roentgenological collection, in many instances serial in nature, illustrating many features encountered in the various arthritides. Dr. J. W. Zeller has collected data concerning the relationship of rheumatic fever and rheumatoid arthritis. In conjunction with Dr. Stanley Cobb we have made certain preliminary psychiatric studies of patients with rheumatoid arthritis. Dr. Charles L. Short and Dr. A. O. Ludwig have been investigating the neurological manifestations of rheumatoid arthritis. Detailed nutritional histories have been obtained on the rheumatoid arthritics and the control subjects. Analyses of these data will afford information concerning the disease as well as other nutritional facts. We have attempted to evaluate the various tests employed to determine the activity of rheumatoid arthritis. To date, it would appear that the sedimentation rate is the most reliable and accurate. A study has been made of the value of the gonococcal complement fixation reaction as a diagnostic aid in patients with all types of joint disease.

Since the work is carried on in a general hospital, we find many cases with joint signs and symptoms labeled arthritis when some other etiology is present. This has brought out the importance of and frequent difficulties in differential diagnosis. We have found conditions ranging from pulmonary osteoarthropathy to multiple foci of osteomyelitis masquerading under the diagnosis of arthritis. It has likewise taught us that recurrent gout is a relatively common disease which all too often goes unrecognized. Rare diseases exhibiting skeletal or joint manifestations such as periarteritis nodosa, lupus erythematosus disseminata, Boeck's sarcoid, etc., are encountered from time to time.

Pathological Studies

Dr. Granville A. Bennett of the Department of Pathology, Harvard Medical School, has been associated intimately with this work since its inception. This has been a most valuable connection and has made possible many pathological studies which otherwise would not have been undertaken. He has been largely responsible for the various histological and pathological studies previously cited. In addition, he has carried on studies concerning the manner of production of malum coxae senilis; the exact nature of outpouchings about the knee joint; the effect on synovial membrane and synovial fluid cytology of various supposedly innocuous solutions when injected into the joint, and the manner of entrance of pneumococci into the joint and other body cavities.

Through the courtesy of Dr. M. N. Smith-Petersen, we have been allowed to collect valuable pathological material from a variety of joint diseases. Pathological examination of such specimens has added greatly to our understanding of many problems. Rheumatic nodules, muscle biopsies, and joint tissue are obtained from time to time on rheumatoid arthritic patients, thus giving us a more complete picture of the disease. Complete autopsies are obtained whenever possible.

Metabolic Studies

Our activities in this field have been very limited, although we are of the belief that studies along these lines will allow for a better definition of rheumatoid arthritis and the individuals suffering from it. We have done calcium, phosphorus and nitrogen metabolism studies on patients with hypertrophic and rheumatoid arthritis. These will be extended. Preliminary studies on creatinine and acid-base balance studies have been made and will be pursued as time permits. Dr. Beckman and Dr. Coggeshall are studying the acid-base balance on patients receiving sulfanilamide in the hope of obtaining better information concerning the mode of action of this drug.

Bacteriological Studies

To date, we have participated very little in this important aspect of joint disease. This has been due to the fact that no member of our group is trained adequately in this field and our budget has not allowed for such a person. Dr. T. Duckett Jones of the House of the Good Samaritan has made it possible to have all of the important streptococcal immunological tests performed at repeated intervals on a large group of rheumatoid arthritics over a year's period. Analysis of these data will give us information concerning the role of the streptococcus in this disease. We have evaluated the use of autogenous vaccines with negative results. With our increased budget, we have added a part-time bacteriologist and a bacteriological technician in order that the bacteriological aspects of many problems in which we are interested may be adequately studied.

Plans for Future Work

With the added financial support and clinical facilities, we are now in a position to develop slowly a research program embodying the study of many important phases of joint disease. The nature of many of the problems concerning arthritis, particularly of the rheumatoid type, is such that any project aimed at their solution will necessitate continuous work over a period of years. The reason for this becomes obvious if one appreciates that rheumatoid arthritis is a chronic disease of years' duration and that it represents the reaction of the individual's various tissues to the causative agent. The individuals studying the disease must be students of disease and not only students of joints and their reaction to insults.

At the present time we plan to continue our research work along much the same lines as we have in the past, namely, to better define the anatomy and physiology of joints as well as the many clinical aspects of the various arthritides. The present arrangements will allow for a director, several full-time research workers, an associated pathologist and a bacteriologist. It will also allow for a part-time psychiatrist, full-time technicians and secretaries. The addition of a physiotherapist, a nutritionist and a social worker will aid greatly in the care of patients and our follow-up work. It is our aim in so far as is possible to carry out in addition to the clinical studies those bacteriological, pathological, physiological or chemical studies which will aid in promoting our knowledge of the cause and the cure of various types of arthritis.

MEDICAL POSTGRADUATE EXTENSION COURSES

LEROY E. PARKINS, M.D.

Secretary, Executive Committee on Postgraduate Instruction Massachusetts Medical Society

One of the activities of the State Health Department, which should be of great interest and benefit to the public, is the cooperation of the state and federal health agencies with the Massachusetts Medical Society in providing postgraduate extension courses for all the doctors in the Commonwealth of Massachusetts. This makes it possible for the busy doctor to receive the latest advances in scientific medicine without leaving his field of work. A series of clinics and lectures have been arranged by the Massachusetts Medical Society and financed jointly by this organization together with the Massachusetts State Health Department, the United States Public Health Service and the Federal Children's Bureau. This is the first time in this Commonwealth that all of these agencies have joined forces in furthering the advance of medical knowledge among the doctors. This is of importance because it obviates any duplication of effort and insures the highest type of instruction since the courses are carefully selected and approved by the above agencies.

The courses started on January 6, 1938, and are now in active operation in the following places: Taunton, New Bedford, Salem, Melrose, Lowell, Norwood, Quincy, Brockton, Milford, and Fitchburg. This spring similar courses will be given in Hyannis, Pittsfield, Fall River, Greenfield, Springfield, Holyoke, Northampton, and Cambridge.

The courses presented should have an active interest for everyone because of the widespread prevalence of disability as well as fatalities from many of the diseases discussed. Among the subjects offered in the extension courses are pneumonia, rheumatic fever, heart disease, syphilis and gonorrhea. Also, improved methods in obstetrics are taught and a special study of diseases of childhood is being made. These last two courses should improve the maternal and child welfare of many communities.

The doctors who attend these courses receive much benefit which in turn makes it possible for them to render a better service to their patients.

The State Health Department is very happy to make this announcement of the splendid cooperation of the Medical Society with the government health agencies. It is hoped that this good work will continue so that through the medical profession the public will more quickly receive the benefit of discoveries and new advances in medical knowledge.

NEW ACTIVITIES OF THE DIVISION OF COMMUNICABLE DISEASES

BY ROY F. FEEMSTER, M.D.

Director, Division of Communicable Diseases
Massachusetts Department of Public Health

The following is a description of new projects and of present procedures which are departures from activities which have been a part of the program of this Division in previous years.

Pneumonia

This Division has been interested in pneumonia for a number of years and assumed certain responsibilities in carrying out the five-year study. Upon the completion of this study a number of the activities were taken over by the Department. The following is a description of the part which the Division is now taking in the program for handling this disease.

Epidemiologist:

A physician has been employed to take charge of the field aspects of the program, which involves the Division of Biologic Laboratories as well as this Division. It is planned that he should carry on a great part of the work which was handled by the Director of the Field Study. This includes talks before medical groups such as district medical society meetings, hospital staff meetings and other gatherings of physicians. There are also opportunities for him to talk to physicians in their offices when inquiries come to the Division in regard to the use of the pneumonia service.

It is the responsibility of the epidemiologist to analyze the case reports sent in by physicians and to collect material from other sources so that the latest information in regard to the various aspects of the treatment of pneumonia can be made readily available. Wall charts and lantern slides of this material are being made so that it can be used in presenting the subject to medical and lay groups.

He is taking an important part in the plan for approving typing laboratories. Inspection of laboratories and making contacts with the technicians represent an important part of his duties. An attempt is being made to continue the epidemiological investigations formerly carried on by Doctor Smillie. In this work other members of the Division are being used when necessary.

Approval of Laboratories:

Since it is necessary to determine accurately the type of pneumococcus in order to assure results from serum treatment, and because time is an important factor, it has been found necessary to decentralize the laboratory service. This was accomplished during the pneumonia study by approving local laboratories for carrying out these tests. This involved not only the provision of satisfactory equipment and materials but also the services of a qualified technician. The training of these technicians was one of the important contributions of the five-year study. A large number of these individuals have now had good training in pneumococcus typing.

In order to maintain their high standard, however, it was necessary to provide for periodic inspection of laboratories, the training of new technicians who are employed from time to time, and also further training of technicians when new procedures are adopted.

Examination of Blood Cultures:

Many of the approved laboratories have not, in the past, provided for the examination of blood cultures. In the light of recent experience, this type of examination has assumed even greater importance and it has been felt that a great contribution could be made in providing for increased facilities for doing these examinations. Arrangements have been made to have a large number of the approved laboratories undertake to examine blood cultures. This has necessitated additional training of the technicians so that they might satisfactorily perform such examinations.

Training of Technicians:

One of the requirements for an approved laboratory is that it should have a technician who has received training in the State Bacteriological Laboratory. Since there are frequent changes in the personnel of laboratories, a number of new technicians must be trained each year. In addition, it has been felt advisable to have technicians, who have had previous training, return to the State Laboratory every year or two for an additional day. This throws a considerable burden of teaching upon the Bacteriological Laboratory, but the results obtained have fully justified the effort and expenditures.

Although most of the technicians are using typing serum to determine only the types for which the State distributes therapeutic serum (Types I, II, V, VII and VIII), several of the laboratories have supplied themselves with typing serum for the three additional types for which therapeutic horse serum is available commercially (Types IV, VI and XIV), and a few are now equipped to type pneumococci through the 32 types.

Payment for Typing:

Typings done in local laboratories have usually been charged to the patient where he was able to pay, but, in instances where the patient was unable to make payment, many of the laboratories have done the examinations free of charge. It has been felt that the laboratory services might be used much more frequently by physicians caring for indigent patients if this burden upon the local laboratory could be relieved. A fund has therefore been set up to pay for such laboratory tests.

Scarlet Fever Immunization

For several years the Division has been carrying on field work in a study of the usefulness of formalinized scarlet fever toxin in immunizing children against scarlet fever. The study has been carried on in several of the State institutions, in the public schools of several cities and towns and in the parochial schools of three of the large cities. Because of an agreement with the Scarlet Fever Commission, under which it has been impossible to release the material to the medical profession, it has been necessary for the staff of the Division to give all of the inoculations in this study. Over 15,000 children have been Dick-tested, nearly two-thirds of whom were found to be positive and received three immunizing injections of formalinized scarlet fever toxin. Over 50% of these are found one year later to have been rendered Dick-negative. Those who are still positive are given a second series of inoculations and 95% of them are found Dick-negative after the second series. As would be expected, when an agent is being used which does not give complete immunity, a certain number of individuals have contracted scarlet fever after the first series of inoculations. However, a considerable reduction in the number of cases expected has resulted. An attempt is being made to discover a more effective immunizing agent. If this is found, the results should prove even more encouraging.

Health Units

In line with the general trend throughout the country, an attempt has been made to organize local units for administering health activities. This has included the continuation of the health units begun under the Commonwealth Fund. An attempt is being made to organize such a unit in Franklin County, and there is considerable interest in the organization of a similar unit in Hampshire County.

Respiratory Disease Study

In 1933 it was decided that the information gained from the reporting of influenza was not sufficiently valuable to justify the continuation of its reporting. As a substitute for the information so gained, a plan was set up under which a number of industries employing a large number of persons should report absenteeism and, where possible, the incidence of respiratory disease. A number of large public school systems, also, agreed to report absenteeism among school children.

It is felt that these figures will give a warning that the incidence of upper respiratory disease is increasing, and that the information so gained will make it possible to discover when an outbreak of influenza is impending. Since these reports will be coming from all parts of the state, we will have some information as to the distribution of the cases. So far there has not been an outbreak of influenza, so an effective trial of the system has not yet resulted.

Typhoid Fever

Due to the remarkable decrease in the number of cases of typhoid fever, it is now possible to follow up contacts of reported cases much more thoroughly than in the past. With only about 100 cases a year, all of the intimate contacts can be cultured routinely. This has resulted in the finding of several carriers who might otherwise have been missed. The record of finding typhoid carriers has continued to improve since this procedure was instituted.

Because a few typhoid carriers have been discovered among individuals who have been reported as cases of typhoid fever and released by what would appear to be satisfactory release cultures, a study has been undertaken to discover whether or not carriers have been missed by procedures which have been in force in the past. All persons having typhoid fever are now being followed by monthly laboratory specimens for a year where such samples are obtainable. If it should be discovered that there is occasionally a lapse of time before the typhoid bacillus becomes sufficiently established in the gall bladder so that typhoid bacilli begin to be excreted in the bowel, the examination of release specimens early in convalescence would probably fail to indicate that the person would eventually become a typhoid carrier. Whether or not this is the case would be demonstrated by this study.

Assistant Epidemiologists

One of the important phases of public health administration is the discovery of promising young men to fill vacancies which occur in the staff from time to time. In the past, medical students have been employed for summer projects, not only for the purpose of gathering special information but also in an attempt to discover young men who would develop into useful members of the staff. This plan resulted in the discovery of a few excellent workers, but a large number of those so employed eventually went into other fields. A new plan has recently been set up. This involves the creation of a position known as "assistant epidemiologist." Recent medical graduates who have usually had at least one year of internship are employed in this position on a temporary basis for a period of months, usually about a year. During this time they are given an opportunity to see all phases of the work of the Department. This makes it possible for them to discover if public health is the field in which they wish to make their career, and it also makes it possible for the Department to decide whether or not the individual is one who is equipped to become a satisfactory health worker. If so, arrangements are made for him to attend one of the schools of public health for a year of special training, after which he is employed in some permanent position in the Department.

Rabies

Because orders restraining dogs on account of the prevalence of rabies must be passed by each city or town, it has been practically impossible to control the disease by this method, due to the fact that all communities in the area involved would not cooperate by simultaneously passing restraint orders.

This Department has, therefore, turned to inoculation of dogs against rabies as the only hope of affecting the incidence of the disease. Boards of health of many communities have arranged for inoculation clinics where dogs were treated for a small fee or entirely free of charge. Such inoculations have to be repeated annually because of the short duration of the immunity produced.

From the figures which have been accumulated in the communities where such clinics have been held, there is reason to believe that the incidence of rabies has been decreased. The disease was at the lowest level in the history of the state in 1936. Nineteen thirty-seven showed some increase, but this was partially due to the fact that the disease entered into new areas in the state where innoculation of dogs had not yet become common.

THE CONTROL OF SYPHILIS AND GONORRHEA IN MASSACHUSETTS 1894-1937

Legislative History

The first legislative recognition of syphilis and gonorrhea in Massachusetts was the act of 1894 which ordered that no discrimination be made against their treatment in the out-patient department of tax-supported hospitals. In 1895 each city was required to provide treatment for indigents with these diseases. The General Court of 1905 provided that all abnormal discharges or inflammation of the eyes within the first two weeks of life must be reported to the local board of health, which was required to furnish necessary care and treatment. In 1910 the Department of Public Health was directed to furnish a suitable prophylactic against ophthalmia neonatorum.

The State Wassermann Laboratory was opened in 1915, and in 1918 the General Court appropriated $10,000 for arsphenamine. The same year the Department declared syphilis and gonorrhea to be dangerous to the public health, making them subject to the provisions of the general health laws. The control of these diseases was made the function of a subdivision of the Division of Communicable Diseases, with a full-time officer in charge.

In 1934 the General Court amended the law of 1894 so as to prevent any tax-supported hospital from discriminating against the treatment of patients with syphilis and gonorrhea in the wards as well as in the out-patient services. The following year the law of 1895 was changed to require towns as well as cities to provide treatment for indigents. The General Court of 1936 provided that a suitable prophylactic must be used in every baby's eyes at birth.

In 1937 the General Court again amended the law of 1895 to provide that the State Department of Public Health should maintain clinics for the treatment of syphilis and gonorrhea, with or without the cooperation of local agencies, and may otherwise provide treatment, including transportation, for those who have syphilis or gonorrhea and who are not able to pay for private medical care.

Functions of the State Department of Public Health and Local Boards of Health under the Law

The General Laws of the State of Massachusetts provide that:

1. The State Department of Public Health shall define what diseases shall be deemed dangerous to the public health. Gonorrhea and syphilis were declared by the Department to be diseases dangerous to the public health on December 18, 1917.

2. The State Department of Public Health may require the officers of any institution, hospital, dispensary or any board of health or physician to give notice of cases of any disease declared by the Department to be dangerous to the public health.

(a) Special provision is made for the reporting of gonorrhea and syphilis, however, in a law which provides that gonorrhea and syphilis shall be reported to local boards of health either directly or through the State Department of Public Health, in accordance with such rules and regulations as the State Department of Public Health may make "having due regard for the best interest of the public." (Further discussion of the reporting system and the policy behind it will appear below.)

3. Boards of health are authorized to make reasonable regulations which, having been published once in the local newspaper, shall be notice to all persons. Boards of health are required, if a disease dangerous to the public health exists in a city or town, to "use all possible care to prevent the spread of the infection and give public notice of infected places to travelers ..... and by all other means which in their judgment may be most effectual for the common safety."

4. The State Department of Public Health is required to provide clinics, and may otherwise provide treatment, for those who have syphilis or gonorrhea and who are not able to pay for private medical care.

5. Cities are required and towns may upon the request of the State Department of Public Health establish and maintain hospitals for the reception of persons suffering from diseases dangerous to the public health, and cities and towns having such hospitals may accept patients from adjacent cities or towns.

6. Infected persons who cannot properly be isolated or treated at home may be removed by the board of health to a hospital or other suitable place of isolation and such removal may be effected through the issuance of a warrant if necessary.

7. Boards of health are required to destroy, remove or prevent nuisances, sources of filth and *causes of sickness* and make regulations pertaining thereto. The courts have ruled that cases of sickness are in effect causes of sickness within the meaning of this section.

8. The law provides that records pertaining to infection with syphilis or gonorrhea shall not be made public and shall be divulged only on order of the State Commissioner of Public Health to those whose official duties entitle them to the information, and otherwise only upon court order.

9. The law also provides that cities and towns may establish and maintain dental, medical and health clinics and in connection therewith may conduct campaigns of general education relative to matters of public health and various boards of health may unite and cooperate for these purposes.

Further Provisions of the Law:

1. The law provides that a registered physician or surgeon may disclose the infection of a person with gonorrhea or syphilis to any person from whom the infected person has received a promise of marriage or to the parent or guardian of such a person if a minor.

2. The law prohibits the publication of any advertisement which calls attention to a person from whom or an office or place at which information, treatment or advice may be obtained concerning diseases or conditions of the sexual organs, except that the State Department of Public Health may call attention to such places.

It is apparent from the foregoing that, other than to the extent to which the State Department of Public Health may provide certain services, declare which diseases are dangerous to the public health and provide a system of reporting for gonorrhea and syphilis, the actual control of any given case of gonorrhea or syphilis lies with the local board of health. Thus, the direct responsibility for the control of these diseases lies with the 354 city and town boards of health in Massachusetts.

Program of the State Department of Public Health

The program of the State Department of Public Health consists of:

1. The maintenance of a Division of Genitoinfectious Diseases.
2. The provision of treatment for gonorrhea and syphilis for those who are unable to pay for private medical care.
3. The maintenance of a serologic laboratory.
4. The maintenance of a bacteriological laboratory.
5. The distribution of arsenicals and bismuth.
6. The distribution of a prophylactic against ophthalmia neonatorum.
7. The educational program.
8. The follow-up of cases and contacts by local boards of health.
9. The collection and analysis of morbidity data.

1. The Division of Genitoinfectious Diseases:

The control of gonorrhea and syphilis was originally a function of a Subdivision of the Division of Communicable Diseases. This Subdivision was organized in 1918 with a full-time officer in charge. Its budget was enlarged to a considerable extent by funds appropriated by the United States Government under the direction of the Interdepartmental Social Hygiene Board. With the exception of a period of three and one half years, ending in April, 1928, the Subdivision had a full-time officer in charge.

On June 1, 1937, a Division of Genitoinfectious Diseases replaced the Subdivision, and a full-time Director is in charge. The personnel of the Division consists at present of the director, two epidemiologists, one of whom is a physician and the other a registered nurse, two public health nursing supervisors, a part-time public health education worker, a principal clerk who is secretary to the officer in charge, a senior clerk and stenographer, a senior statistical clerk and four junior clerks and stenographers. One of the epidemiologists, both public health nursing supervisors and one junior clerk and stenographer are recent additions to the personnel under Social Security appropriation. The part-time lecturer is employed jointly by the Department and the Massachusetts Society for Social Hygiene, between which agencies she divides her whole time.

The budget for the Division for 1937 was as follows:

Salaries		$14,000
Expenses:		
Arsenicals	$12,500	
Treatment	63,000*	
Educational Material	1,000	
Travel	1,300	
Postage	600	
Furniture, office supplies, telephone and telegraph	600	79,000
Total salaries and expenses		$93,000

* $50,000 for last quarter of fiscal year. This item will be $213,000 in 1938.

Under Social Security appropriation the following additional sums were available beginning July 1, 1936. The figures given are annual appropriations.

Clinic assistance	$25,000.00
Distribution Bismuth	6,000.00
Printing and Supplies	1,762.25
Travel	2,500.00
Salaries	8,280.00
	$43,542.25

Certain reallocations were made in these items before the conclusion of the year because of the Department's inability to secure the full complement of personnel or to expand its program completely on July 1, 1936, so that assistance to the clinics was increased by $8000.

The Wassermann Laboratory is maintained by the Division of Biologic Laboratories and its budget of $22,000 is not included within the budget of the Division of Genitoinfectious Diseases. The expenditure of approximately $1200 for the distribution of silver nitrate is also included in the budget of the Division of Biologic Laboratories and not of this Division.

The budget of the Bacteriological Laboratory is included within that of the Division of Communicable Diseases so that the examination of gonorrhea smears at a cost of approximately $3000 is included in the general budget of that Division rather than of the Division of Genitoinfectious Diseases.

The total budget of the Department for the control of gonorrhea and syphilis is, therefore, approximately $119,200, exclusive of Social Security funds, and this will be increased next year to approximately $270,000. Some $45,000, in addition, were available through Social Security funds.

2. **Provision of Treatment:**

There are approximately thirty clinics in the State which provide treatment for syphilis and gonorrhea to those who are unable to pay for private medical care. Eleven of these have been maintained directly by governmental agencies, such as city hospitals, boards of health and State institutions. The remaining nineteen have been operated by private agencies (usually private hospitals), largely at their own expense.

Prior to August 26, 1937, local boards of health were required to provide treatment for those with syphilis or gonorrhea who were unable to pay for private medical care, just as they are required to provide treatment for persons suffering from other communicable diseases. This delegation of responsibility to the 354 boards of health resulted disastrously to both clinics and patients. Clinics were usually unable to collect more than a very small part of what it cost them to treat the infected, and patients were obliged to identify themselves to their local boards of health in order that their treatment might be paid for. The Special Commission to Study and Investigate Public Health Laws and Policies, in its report to the General Court on December 2, 1936, said:

"The disastrous effects of this decentralized responsibility at once became evident, as follows:

"1. To pay for treatment, the local board of health must know the identity of the patient and establish settlement. Thus although patients are not identified in morbidity reports, inability to pay for treatment results in identification. This is equivalent to requiring that the economically unfortunate be reported by name, an injustice escaped by the economically fortunate.

"2. Identification to the board of health must be followed by investigation of settlement, which usually involves the board of welfare. Payment of the bill involves the municipal treasurer, auditor and their assistants. In some instances a dozen or more persons have thus learned the identities of those who have syphilis or gonorrhea. It is therefore not long before the entire community has the information, to the disgrace and demoralization of the patient, particularly if the community is a small one. This is a double injustice if the infection was innocently acquired.

"3. If settlement is in another community, the entire process must be repeated there, to the further embarrassment of the patient.

"4. If there is no settlement, since the Department of Public Welfare will not reimburse boards of health for the cost of clinic treatment, no official agency will assume responsibility. The end result of all of the disturbance of the patient is the retention of the case by the clinic, at its own expense, or denial of further treatment.

"5. Many patients, fearful of public identification and disgrace, discontinue their treatment.

"It is little wonder that clinics complain at carrying a tremendous burden for which governmental agencies are legally responsible. It is also little wonder that the average patient who is unable to pay the clinic fee cannot be kept under treatment, or be persuaded to permit the examination of other members of the family for purposes of case-finding.

"Adequate treatment is the basis of any program for the control of syphilis and gonorrhea. Experience shows that the present system of local responsibility for these cases operates against the public interest. The Commission therefore recommends that provision for the treatment of the ambulatory patient, who is unable to pay for medical care for syphilis or gonorrhea, be made a state function. As it is obvious that the Department cannot and should not set up and maintain a system of general dispensaries in which to locate clinics for the treatment of syphilis and gonorrhea, it is further recommended that the service be provided by the Department in cooperation, if possible, with those agencies which are now providing the service at their own expense, or which may be willing to establish new services if necessary."

With the passage in 1937 of legislation which amended the old law, the responsibility for providing treatment for gonorrhea and syphilis was placed upon the State Department of Public Health. The Department has designated most of the thirty clinics as Cooperating Clinics upon their application to be so designated. Cooperating Clinics are reimbursed at a rate of seventy-five cents per visit, and this charge may be made for visits by patients or contacts. If the patient pays any part of the fee, the Department reimburses the clinic only for the difference between the amount paid by the patient and seventy-five cents. If the annual cost of maintaining satisfactory clinic service (which must include adequate follow-up service) exceeds the clinic's income from fees, the Department makes up the difference. Furthermore, each Cooperating Clinic is authorized to provide the cost of reasonable transportation for any patient or contact, if necessary, and to seek reimbursement from the Department for such expenditures for transportation as may be made.

Thus the clinics are maintained at the expense of the Department although they are administered by the local agencies, and any patient who is in need of medical care and who is unable to pay for it privately may have treatment without being identified to any board of health.

In those areas where clinic service is not reasonably available, private physicians are authorized, upon the acceptance of their applications, to treat patients who ordinarily would be treated in clinics, and they are reimbursed therefor at a rate not to exceed $2 per visit, plus transportation costs for the patient.

Hospitals are reimbursed for the necessary hospitalization of infected persons who cannot pay for hospital care, the rate of reimbursement not to exceed $3.50 per day. Necessary hospitalization is held to include hospitalization for the purpose of lumbar puncture.

Many of the clinics which heretofore have been unable to secure sufficient funds for adequate follow-up service will now be able to provide that service, and there is no reason why any infected person in the State should not be able, in one way or another, to secure adequate treatment.

The six major Boston clinics found it convenient to pool their field follow-up service. Each of these clinics receives patients from all over the Metropolitan Boston Area including some sixty cities and towns. This entire area, including Boston, has been divided into six districts. Each of the six follow-up workers for the area is assigned to one district and does all of the field follow-up work in that district for all six participating clinics. Each worker spends a sufficient amount of time in each one of the six clinics for which she does follow-up work in her district so that she may become well acquainted with the clinic personnel, with each clinic's procedures and with many of the patients. This cooperative plan has resulted in the saving of a great deal of travel time by concentrating the area in which a given follow-up worker does her work. It also has served to give the six participating clinics a greater sense of being engaged in a community project, and there is no doubt but that the interchange of ideas will favorably affect clinic procedure. A similar cooperative plan is in operation between the two clinics in Worcester.

Several of the Boston hospitals which have prenatal services and syphilis clinics have also combined to employ a full-time follow-up worker for the follow-up of pregnant women with syphilis and of congenital syphilis. This project is intended to provide a clearing house for all syphilis in pregnancy and congenital syphilis in the Boston Metropolitan Area so far as it is handled by the cooperating agencies. It should result in the more adequate treatment of syphilis in pregnancy and in the more adequate study of infants born to women with syphilis. This project is supported financially by the State Department of Public Health.

In conjunction with this treatment service, the Department maintains a confidential follow-up service for private physicians. Its two public health nursing supervisors are loaned to private physicians for follow-up work in syphilis and gonorrhea. These nurses visit the private physician's cases in his name. In fact they are instructed never to permit a person whom they are following to learn that they are employed by any other agency than the physician. Their reports of the results of their investigations are made to the physician, whose responsibility it is thereafter to take such action as may be necessary if the service does not result in the return of the patient to treatment. These workers report to the Department statistically and at no time are they permitted to disclose the identity of any private physician's patient to any person in the Department or to any other person or agency, except as they may be directed to do so by the physician.

3. Serologic Laboratory:

The State Wassermann Laboratory, in operation since 1915 under the Division of Biologic Laboratories, at present examines approximately 200,000 specimens annually. Of these, approximately 5000 are gonococcus fixation tests, 200 are colloidal gold tests, and the balance blood tests for syphilis.

Up to the middle of 1933 the Wassermann test was the official State test, but since that time the Hinton has been substituted for it, although Wassermann tests are still done on special request or if for one reason or another the Hinton test is not satisfactory. Wassermann tests are done also on spinal fluids. These tests are performed for any physician or medical agency in the State, free of charge.

The Boston and Brockton City Health Departments and several of the larger hospitals in the State perform their own serological tests for syphilis, and it is estimated that at least 300,000 blood tests for syphilis are made annually in Massachusetts.

4. Bacteriological Laboratory:

Although many local board of health laboratories and most hospital and clinic laboratories examine smears for the gonococcus, the State Bacteriological Laboratory examines approximately 12,000 specimens annually.

5. The Distribution of Arsenicals and Bismuth:

Arsenicals have been distributed by the Department since 1918. They are distributed free to all physicians and other medical agencies without any charge or other restriction than that the physician or medical agency shall report syphilis. There is no qualification as to the ability of the patient to pay. In 1936, approximately 50,000 grams of arsenicals were distributed at a cost of something over $12,000. Arsphenamine, sulpharsphenamine and neoarsphenamine are the three arsenicals distributed, the distribution of the latter accounting for approximately eighty-five per cent of the total. The distribution to physicians is approximately twenty-five per cent.

Arsenicals have been purchased under five-year contracts from the lowest bidder among those manufacturers licensed to produce arsenicals by the United States Treasury Department.

The distribution of bismuth has just recently been begun under Social Security appropriation. Bismuth subsalicylate in oil is the preparation provided and it is distributed in two-ounce vials for clinics and institutions and in ten cubic centimeter vials for physicians. Insufficient experience has been had with the distribution of this drug to estimate what the annual distribution will be.

6. The Distribution of a Prophylactic Against Ophthalmia Neonatorum:

Since 1910 this Department has furnished one per cent silver nitrate in wax ampoules for the prophylaxis of gonoccocal ophthalmia neonatorum. Distribution has amounted to approximately 60,000 ampoules annually. In 1936 the Legislature required that: "A prophylactic furnished or approved by the Department should be used in every baby's eyes at birth." After a conference with outstanding opthalmologists, obstetricians, bacteriologists, pharmacists and chemists, and upon the recommendation of those consultants, the Department approved only one per cent silver nitrate in wax ampoules for individual use and bearing an expiration date. It is anticipated that since one per cent silver nitrate will replace a great deal of argyrol and other preparations which have been used in many hospitals, the distribution by the Department of its product will materially increase.

7. The Educational Program:

The Director of the Division, the two Epidemiologists, the Public Health Education Worker and the two Public Health Nursing Supervisors are available for talks to public and professional audiences, and although the Massachusetts Society for Social Hygiene maintains a considerable lecture service on the broader subject of social hygiene in general there is a very considerable demand for lectures on syphilis and gonorrhea as problems in communicable disease control. Audiences reached by the staff of the Division include medical societies, medical schools, nurses in training, public health nurses, and other groups of public health workers, women's clubs, service clubs and a considerable variety of miscellaneous groups.

The Department has prepared a considerable literature of its own, both for public and professional distribution, in addition to which it purchases reprints, in large quantities, of noteworthy articles in the current literature. During the last five or six years, it has distributed approximately a million pieces of some fifty or sixty pieces of literature. Pamphlets of information for the patient, for distribution by clinics and physicians, have enjoyed a particularly wide distribution, some three or four hundred thousand copies having been distributed to date.

Although the national broadcasting companies have gained control of the major local stations and have thus effectively prevented further broadcasting on the subject of syphilis and gonorrhea by the Department, the Department was permitted, prior to 1936, to broadcast on seven occasions from local stàtions. Although all of these broadcasts were exceedingly frank in their nature, there was no complaint either on the part of the management of local stations or of the radio audiences against the material thus offered.

Most of the important newspapers in the State and apparently a great majority of the smaller papers are now willing to print the words "syphilis" and "gonorrhea". In fact there has been an increasing tendency on their parts to do so since 1929. The publication of Surgeon General Parran's article in the Reader's Digest for July, 1936, greatly improved the situation so far as newspaper publicity is concerned.

The Public Health Education Worker has been able to lecture on social hygiene, with particular mention of the control of syphilis and gonorrhea, in a considerable number of the public schools in the State.

8. The Follow-Up of Cases and Contacts by Local Boards of Health:

All patients or contacts (including alleged sources of infection) who cannot be followed to a satisfactory conclusion by the clinic follow-up service or by private physicians or their confidential follow-up service are supposed to be reported to the State Department of Public Health by name and address for official investigation. Although most of the persons so reported have been reported by clinics with inadequate follow-up personnel, they have numbered from three to four thousand annually, in the past. It is expected that with the increased follow-up personnel to be employed by most of the clinics, the number of persons who will need to be reported to the Health Department will rapidly decrease.

Upon receipt of such a report, the Department refers the case to the proper local board of health for follow-up. A report is required of the local board of health as to the result of any action taken. The report of the local board of health is confirmed by the State Department of Public Health through communication with the physician or clinic with which the person is said to have resumed treatment or sought medical advice. If the report is confirmed, the agency which originally reported the patient for follow-up is notified of the final result; otherwise the local board of health is asked to repeat the investigation. Thus no case is closed by the Department until some definite action has been taken or until it is obvious that the local board of health will take no action.

Final reports are received from boards of health in more than 95 per cent of the cases. It has been noted, however, that more than 50 per cent of the persons reported to boards of health for investigation cannot be found because of false names or incorrect addresses.

9. The Collection of Morbidity Data:

All morbidity reports of syphilis and gonorrhea are made directly to the State Department of Public Health. The name and address of the patient is not required in the original report, nor thereafter unless treatment is neglected. Report forms are supplied by the Department directly to all potential reporting agencies, including physicians, clinics, hospitals and institutions. Report forms are included with every package of arsenical or bismuth distributed, with every report of a positive blood for syphilis and every report of a positive smear for gonorrhea. Business reply envelopes are provided with the forms so that the reporting agency need not assume the cost of postage.

Upon the receipt of the reports, the information contained in them is transferred to punch cards, from which analytical tables may be prepared at any time.

Complete sets of the various forms used in morbidity reports and the reports of persons by name are available on request to the Department.

NEW WORK PERFORMED BY THE FOOD AND DRUG DIVISION DURING THE PAST FIVE YEARS

BY HERMANN C. LYTHGOE, S.B.

Director, Division of Food and Drugs
Massachusetts Department of Public Health

The Food and Drug Division work is subject to more or less constant changes. Certain types of work have been carried on uniformly and with very little change since the Food and Drug Law went into effect in 1882. Changes in this work are produced by various causes First: New legislation may add to the work. It may change definitions of adulteration or misbranding whereby articles which prior to that change were legal would become illegal subsequent to the change, and, conversely, practices which were illegal have been many times legalized by legislation. Second: New means of adulteration of food and drug products may be developed. Third: Certain types of adulteration may be discontinued after the trade has ascertained the desirability of either ceasing the adulteration in question or by selling the adulterated products in a legal manner. Fourth: New methods of analysis are from time to time developed by means of which adulteration formerly undetectable may be detected and the violators of the law can be successfully prosecuted.

As an example of legislation affecting the work, consider the law pertaining to the use of sodium sulphite in meat. The Department was operating on a regulation based upon that of the United States Department of Agriculture pertaining to the use of sulphur dioxide in food products which regulation required the labeling of the product. In 1933 the Legislature passed an act prohibiting the use of sodium sulphite in meat or meat products. After the law was signed by the Governor and shortly before it went into effect, the newspapers published a story regarding it. As a result of this newspaper publicity a sausage maker in the Western part of Massachusetts introduced another bill which would repeal the law and enact a substitute which provided that sodium sulphite could be used in meat products if the quantity did not exceed one-tenth of one per cent and if each package sold should bear a statement that the sodium sulphite was present to an extent not exceeding one-tenth of one percent. The first law was in effect for two days. It is unfortunate that the first act did not stay on the books as sodium sulphite does not improve meat, has a tendency to make old meat look fresh, has a tendency to deodorize meat, and its preservative action is too little to be of any value. The enforcement of the law, however, is far easier than the enforcement of the regulation. The law fixes a maximum amount of the preservative, and it is not necessary to submit certified copies of the regulation to the courts.

In 1935 new milk grades were established by the Milk Regulation Board consisting at that time of Edgar L. Gillett, Commissioner of Agriculture, Chairman, Joseph E. Warner, Attorney General, and Dr. Henry D. Chadwick, Commissioner of Public Health. These grades were a marked step in advance, and milk was divided into eight grades—milk, raw and pasteurized, Grade A. milk, raw and pasteurized, special milk, raw and pasteurized, and certified milk, raw and pasteurized. Bacterial standards were established for all of these grades, and chemical standards were established for Grade A. milk. As a result of the establishment of these grades the bacterial characteristics of the market milk have been considerably improved. Slightly over 8000 samples of milk were examined bacteriologically by the Division in 1937.

Considerable new legislation has been enacted pertaining to licensing of certain types of business. There had been for some years a law relative to ice cream. In 1934 the industry introduced a very comprehensive act repealing the old law and establishing the new law providing for licensing by local boards of health of manufacturers located within the State and by the Department of Public Health of manufacturers located outside of the State who desired to sell their products in Massachusetts. The license fees vary from $5 to $200 per annum depending upon the quantity of frozen desserts or ice cream mix manufactured. The local fees are paid into the treasury of the city or town where the establishment is located, and the fees from out of state manufacturers are paid into the State Treasury. The act provides for regulations by the Department of Public Health, and, therefore, there is state wide uniformity in the regulations pertaining to the manufacture of these products. Shortly after this law went into effect the Division began an intensive study of the sanitary conditions of the Massachusetts plants, and many prosecutions were made during the first year as the result of unsanitary conditions. This resulted in an immediate improvement in all of these plants, and during the past two years there has been very little evidence of unsanitary conditions. The Department at first accepted reports of inspection of out of state plants made by the state or local officials enforcing the law in the state where the plants were located, but experience showed that this was not always to be relied upon, and it was necessary to revoke a few of the permits which the Department had granted under those conditions. Under this law the fee payable to the Commonwealth is not returnable. If a permit is refused for good and sufficient reasons, which in the past has been for unsanitary conditions, the manufacturer must send another fee with his new application for a permit, and when this fee amounts to $50, a refusal of a permit constitutes a substantial penalty.

For some years there has been on the books a law pertaining to granting of permits to operators of establishments for the manufacturing of carbonated non-alcholic beverages and mineral and spring water. In 1935 at the request of the industry there was a change in this law providing that the permits be issued by the local boards of health as in the former law, but the fee for the permit was increased from a maximum of $10 to a $20 fee, one-half of which was to be paid by the town into the Treasury of the Commonwealth. In addition, the Department was required to issue permits to out of state plants selling carbonated beverages in Massachusetts. The fee for such permit being $20 being paid into the Treasury of the Commonwealth. The regulations under the act are made by the Department and the Department is given the authority to suspend a permit issued either by the Department or by the local board of health for violation of the regulations. An additional inspector was appointed under this act, the fees received being rather more than the salary and expenses of the inspector. Inspections were made equivalent to that of one full-time inspector. Many prosecutions were made during the first year because of unsanitary conditions. One permit issued by a local board of health was revoked. Several permits issued to out of state plants were revoked because of unsanitary conditions found on inspection. A few very long distance plants, one as far as Southern California, have been given permits without inspection, the reports of the state health departments being accepted. Very little of this material is coming into Massachusetts from plants not inspected by this Department.

In 1934 there was a change in the law pertaining to the licensing of dealers in wood alcohol. The law still requires a license from the local board of health with a fee of $1 for each such license to engage in the business of selling, transporting, etc., of this material. The change, however, provided that persons doing a state-wide business could obtain from the Department a license for $10, such license giving them the right to engage in that business throughout the State. A person doing business in ten or more towns could save money by obtaining a State license. In making investigations pertaining to this type of license, it was ascertained that approximately 50% of persons requiring local licenses were engaged in this business without being licensed, and even today that statement is approximately correct, whereas at least 90% of the dealers requiring a state-wide license are so equipped. The boards of health are responsible for some of this violation because in many instances they refuse to grant licenses when such are requested. Many boards of health make no attempt to see that the licenses are renewed after they have expired. In one instance where a man insisted on getting his license from the local board of health, one of the members of the board signed the license under protest. It was necessary to make several prosecutions in one city against persons who had been twice warned by an inspector of the Department to get their local license. The persons in that city requiring state licenses had obtained them.

In 1935 there was an amendment to the Massachusetts narcotic law. The law itself was not materially changed from our former good and satisfactory law. The words *cannabis indica* and *cannabis sativa* were deleted and the word *cannabis* was substituted. This made an improvement in the definition of narcotics because it is for practical purposes impossible by laboratory examination to distinguish between these two types of cannabis. The law, however, provided for licensing by the Department of wholesale dealers in narcotics. All the legitimate wholesale dealers in Massachusetts are now licensed by the Department. The violations of the narcotic law are carried on by the people of the so-called "underworld" and enforcement of this law is a matter of police work pure and simple. The legitimate manufacturers and dealers are complying with the law and are properly labeling the preparations they manufacture and sell.

In 1935 an act was passed providing for the sterilization of feathers, down, and second-hand material intended for use in the manufacture of articles of bedding or of upholstered furniture. Persons doing the sterilization were required to obtain a license from the Department, the fee for such license being $50. Eight licenses are now in existence. Frequently inspectors of the Department obtain samples of the material which these persons have sterilized, and if the material does not show sterilization, an investigation is made. It appears from a recent investigation that one such licensee is not properly sterilizing the material and in all probability a revocation of his license will be necessary.

Considerable research work has been carried on in the laboratory over the past five years. One such piece of research work developed largely by Mr. Racicot pertains to the detection of urea in mattress filling. This method has been used continuously as a means of distinguishing between new and second-hand filling. Another difference between new and second-hand filling is its appearance under ultra violet light, and an ultra violet lamp has been installed in the laboratory of the Department. By means of this lamp mixtures of new and second-hand material can be seen and may be manually separated, and the two portions can then be separately examined for the urea content. An approximate percentage of the mixture of the new and second-hand material can be ascertained by this means.

During 1933 a study was made of the changes in the composition of eggs held in cold storage for various periods of time up to one year. This work was carried on by Mr. Elias B. Boyce, one of the chemists of the Division. The results of the work were very useful in connection with cases involving the sale under a fresh egg label of eggs which were not fresh. This particular type of examination is no longer employed because of a change in the law specifying that the freshness of an egg must be determined by the candling method.

Considerable research work was carried on by Messrs. Ferguson and Racicot pertaining to the use of thickeners in sour cream and in cheese. The results of this work have been published in the Journal of the Official Agricultural Chemists. Investigation of the use of these thickeners in cheese showed that they produced an increase in the moisture content and a cheese could be made with a lower fat content and a higher moisture content which would have the appearance and also the taste of a cheese made without the thickener but containing more cream and less moisture. The use of these thickeners in cheese was legalized by the Legislature in 1937.

During 1935 an intensive campaign was made regarding the sale of olive oil by the Italian and Greek dealers, much of this oil being adulterated with cotton seed oil. During this campaign rumors reached the Department that tea seed oil was being used as an adulterant and the tea seed oil could not be distinguished from olive oil upon analysis. This information was received from reputable olive oil dealers who declined to buy the tea seed oil. Samples of tea seed oil were secured and research work for a considerable length of time was carried on by the chemists of the Division without the development of any successful method for distinguishing between tea seed oil and olive oil. In 1936, however, Mr. Fittleson of the United States Department of Agriculture discovered a test which was specific for tea seed oil. This was given to the Department prior to publication, and an intensive campaign was started. The first case tried at which the test was given was in the United States Court at Concord, N. H., relating to a shipment from Massachusetts to Concord, N. H. Mr. Ferguson of the Food and Drug Division, who examined the oil in question, was used by the United States in this case. He was the first technical witness called and naturally had to stand the brunt of the cross examination. Mr. Howard of the New Hampshire State Board of Health, Dr. Bailey of the New Haven Agricultural Experiment Station, and Mr. Fittleson also testified on the case. The case resulted in a finding in favor of the United States. It is unfortunate that the persons putting this oil on the market did not do so in a legitimate manner by selling it under the name of tea seed oil as a new product rather than by attempting to sell it as olive oil for the purpose of making an excess profit.

During the past year an intensive study was made of the phosphatase method for the detection of improperly pasteurized milk. After about six months of study it was found to be accurate and to be performed easily and quickly. Commercial samples were obtained from those pasteurizing establishments where the inspectors had suspected that the recording thermometer charts were artificially prepared and were not the result of the pasteurization process. These suspected persons were found to be selling milk not pasteurized as was shown by the phosphatase test. The first two cases tried resulted in pleas of not guilty with an admission of finding of guilty. In each case the judge heard the technical evidence and imposed a substantial penalty. It is now fairly well known throughout the trade that this test is being used by the Department and there is less unpasteurized milk sold with a pasteurized label.

In 1934 shortly after the repeal of the prohibition amendment there was an epidemic of sales of rum drops or brandy drops, the vendors being of the opinion that the repeal of the liquor law carried a repeal of the law pertaining to the sale of candy containing alcohol. Such, however, was not the case. Attempts made to trace this material to the manufacturer were in most cases futile. In many instances the manufacturers lived out of the state and the material was often passed through seven or eight different hands before being sold to the ultimate consumer, who in many instances was a school child. The inspectors of the Department obtained much of this material and the retail dealers were prosecuted and convicted. The material was removed from the market in this manner in an unusually short time.

On October 11, 1932 the Department by regulation permitted the sale as pasteurized of milk pasteurized at a temperature of not less than 160° Fahrenheit for a period of not less than 15 seconds. Several pieces of apparatus based upon this type of pasteurization were installed and considerable trouble resulted from such installations, principally because of high bacteria counts and some of the operators of this type of equipment got into difficulties. Studies on the apparatus showed that while in operation there was a steady increase in the bacterial content of the pasteurized milk in comparison with that of the raw milk used during the process. Information was received that small pasteurizers of this type had been devised and salesmen were endeavoring to sell them to Massachusetts milk dealers. The Department, therefore, found it necessary to rescind its former regulation, and the pasteurizers of this type were then replaced by the more satisfactory low temperature pasteurizers.

During the past two years there has been an increase in sanitary inspection in food establishments. Two temporary inspectors were appointed in the early part of 1937 and were used on restaurant inspections. A second inspection showed an improvement in the conditions of the restaurants. Towards the close of the fiscal year both of the inspectors resigned and the positions were discontinued. These positions were paid for out of United States funds.

Due to reports of sickness from eating shellfish, investigations were made of the conditions under which crab meat and lobster meat were prepared. These conditions were far from satisfactory, and there is every opportunity of contaminating the meat because of its being handled and because of the unsanitary conditions of many of these plants where the meat is removed from the shells. There was no trouble from meat obtained from lobster claws and tails since there is but little handling of this meat, but practically all of the trouble resulted from eating crab meat, the meat from the lobster knuckles, and the meat from the lobster legs, all of which are removed from the shells by hand. There also was found a business of salvaging meat from lobster bodies, so called, that is to say, those portions of the lobsters containing the ribs with the legs attached. All of this type of meat is handled and is used in the preparation of lobster salads. For the higher priced salads, the restaurants use the meat from the tails and from the claws of the lobster, but all reports of sickness were traced to the cheaper salads, representing meat from the other portions of the shellfish.

The United States Secretary of Agriculture made a ruling to the effect that the addition of color to orange preparations constituted an adulteration under the act even if the presence of the color was declared upon the label of the package. For practical purposes the enforcement of this ruling was left to the States because interstate shippers of the material did not add the color to the article but sent the color as such in a separate package. The Department attempted to enforce this ruling by prosecuting under the act subsequent to prior warning. All the cases that were tried resulted in dismissals or findings of not guilty. During 1937, however, the United States Department of Agriculture made a seizure in Louisiana which seizure was contested by the owner of the material seized. The case resulted in a finding in favor of the manufacturer and against the Department, and the ruling apparently has no legal value. Subsequent to this decision of the United States Courts no further attempts were made to enforce the ruling.

There has been an increase in the bacterial examinations made by the Division. An additional inspector and technician were added, being paid for out of United States funds. The bulk of the work has been applied to milk, although much additional bacteriological work has been applied to other perishable foods.

In 1937 plans were made for another laboratory to be in Westfield, Massachusetts. The laboratory is to be operated by the transfer of two of the chemists, two of the inspectors and one of the technicians from Boston to Westfield. The furniture and apparatus has been purchased, the laboratory benches have been installed, and provisions are now being made to do the plumbing work, after which the laboratory will be operated.

THE PREMATURE PROGRAM OF MASSACHUSETTS

FLORENCE L. MCKAY, M.D.

Assistant Director, Division of Child Hygiene
Massachusetts Department of Public Health

Why a Premature Program?

The infant mortality rate in Massachusetts over a period of about thirty years has fallen from the neighborhood of 140 per 1,000 live births to 46.6 in 1936. For the past twenty-six years we have had statistics on infant mortality by age groups and we find that during the period from 1910 to 1936 there has been very little fall in the death rate of infants under one month of life, the reduction having been made primarily in the group from one month to one year of age.

On analyzing the mortality under one month, that is, the neonatal mortality, we find that deaths due to prematurity are about 55% to 60% of all these deaths. For instance, in 1936 there were 1810 infant deaths under one month, 1046 or 55% of which were due to prematurity.

In a hospital adequately equipped for the care of premature infants the death rate is about one-half that of the state. We, therefore, feel that in order to further reduce our infant mortality, better care must be given to premature infants. Also, there has been a decided decrease in the number of infants born in Massachusetts. In the past ten years there has been a drop of more than 23,000 births. This makes it even more important for us to preserve the lives of the infants who are born.

Objective

The objectives of our premature program are, therefore, (1) the reduction of deaths of premature infants, (2) the reduction of premature births, (3) the improvement of standards for the care of premature infants.

Organization Plan

Establishment of hospital centers.

In order to improve the care of premature infants, hospital centers for the care of prematures are being established all over the State of Massachusetts in strategic places so that a premature born outside a hospital center will have to travel less than an hour in order to receive adequate care. Thirty-three hospital centers are now established.

The hospitals are chosen not only with a view to their location but also on the basis of their general standards of care and progressiveness. Certain standards are required of these hospitals for the care of premature infants. If the hospital is interested in becoming a center we meet with a hospital group comprising the superintendent of the hospital, the supervisor of the nurseries, a member of the board and such members of the pediatric and obstetric staffs as are interested. The standards are discussed with this group. The maternity, the nurseries and the prenatal activities of the hospital are discussed and viewed. After the hospital decides to become a center and the superintendent feels the hospital is ready, the physicians in that locality are notified.

Prenatal and Obstetric Care

If there is no prenatal clinic at the hospital or in the community this is discussed with the hospital group.

Adequate prenatal care is a very important part of the premature program. In Boston there are eleven prenatal clinics; outside Boston there are nineteen clinics in fifteen other Massachusetts communities. It is well known that prematures of the lower weights have a much higher mortality than those over five pounds. It is also established that the gain in weight in utero increases rapidly in the later weeks of pregnancy so that during the ninth lunar month there is a weekly gain of from eight to twelve ounces per week. It is, therefore, important for the life of the premature if there can be a postponement of delivery, providing that it is not too dangerous for the mother. It sometimes happens that if the mother is kept in bed and carefully watched even though she may have some diseased condition which may threaten premature birth, the premature birth may be postponed or even prevented.

Obstetric care also has its relation to premature births. It has been shown that prematures born by caesarean or breach or after the mother has been given morphine are less likely to live. The question of prenatal and obstetric care should, therefore, be carefully considered in hospital centers.

Premature Law

After the organization for the premature program started a law was passed which facilitates this activity in that it provides that prematures born outside of hospitals adequately equipped for their care may be transported by local boards of health on request of the physician and parent to such hospital. If the patient is indigent the local board of welfare may pay for the hospitalization. Premature births outside of hospitals are to be reported to the local board of health. This law facilitates the program, not only in the transportation of premature infants to centers where they may be adequately cared for, but also in securing information about the number of premature births.

We have no statistics on the number of premature births in Massachusetts. From the hospital records we find that from three to five per cent of the births are premature. From our Well Child Conferences held in various communities in the State we get a percentage of four per cent premature births. As premature births are now to be reported to the boards of health, the boards of health are cooperating with the Department by sending in a report of each birth. We will also be able to get these statistics from hospitals and should know after a year or so how many premature births there are in Massachusetts.

Educational Program

Along with the establishment of hospital centers for the care of prematures is planned an educational program.

a. For physicians. Through the Massachusetts Medical Society postgraduate lecture course in Pediatrics, a lecture is given on the care of the premature infant. When physicians are notified of hospital centers a reprint of an article by Dr. Julius Hess entitled, "The Premature Infant—Its Care and Development," is sent to each physician with the leaflet, "Your Premature Baby," published by this Division for mothers.

b. For nurses. A refresher course for nursery supervisors has been made available in a Boston hospital. Social Security funds pay for the tuition and stipend of each nursery supervisor for a two weeks course and also for the tuition of one of the consultant nurses on our Division staff who will do educational follow-up in the hospital premature wards. We hope at some time to extend some type of nursing education in the care of premature infants to private duty and public health nurses.

c. For mothers. In mothers' groups taught by nurses throughout the state there will be instruction in the care of the premature infant. A leaflet published by this Division is available to mothers and is being sent out constantly at the request of nurses and physicians.

OBSTETRIC PACKAGE PROJECT
By Florence L. McKay, M.D.
Assistant Director, Division of Child Hygiene
Massachusetts Department of Public Health

One of the activities made possible through Social Security Funds was the promotion of an obstetric package for use in rural communities. This package contains gauze and absorbent cotton dressings, cord ties and dressings, towels, leggings, perineal pads, delivery pads and bed protectors, and paper bags for waste. We have kept the cost of these materials as low as possible in order to promote the use of a greater number of packages. (We are, however, glad to have local organizations add sterilized rubber gloves and gowns, if they feel able to add that to the expense.)

Each of the state consultant nurses has a complete package for demonstration purposes. In addition, a miniature package is furnished to each organization making up the package. With the miniature package goes mimeographed instructions for making the package and mimeographed instructions for using the package after it is made.

It is our plan to have these packages introduced to local women's organizations by our consultant nurses and demonstrated by them. The local organizations, if interested, will then make up as many packages as they can afford, or as they deem necessary, for home deliveries in their communities. The packages are to be sterilized at local hospitals and kept at some convenient place that is open twenty-four hours of the day. This means that some are kept at fire departments, police headquarters, drug stores or hospitals.

The packages are to be used by local physicians and nurses in home deliveries. They are to be resterilized after three months if they are not used. Some of the contents of the packages, such as leggings, towels, can be returned to the local organization, washed and resterilized and used in other packages. This, of course, reduces the cost.

Some women's organizations provide these free; others charge amounts varying from seventy-five cents to five dollars for their use.

This project was started in November, 1937, and there are now twelve communities using the package.

THE MATERNAL MORTALITY STUDY IN MASSACHUSETTS

BY RAYMOND S. TITUS, M.D.

Section of Obstetrics and Gynecology
The Massachusetts Medical Society

A study of the maternal mortality in Massachusetts has been started by the Child Hygiene Division of the State Department of Public Health in conjunction with the Section of Obstetrics and Gynecology of the Massachusetts Medical Society. It will include all deaths that occur in the five-year period, 1937-1941, among women whose legal addresses were Massachusetts or who lived outside the state and died in Massachusetts and whose certificates of death could in any way be associated with pregnancy. Similar studies have been carried on in other communities, the Fifteen States Study conducted under the auspices of the Department of Labor in Washington for 1927 and 1928, and the studies carried on by the Obstetrical Societies of New York, Philadelphia, and Boston in their own communities, but no state-wide study has ever been carried on for so long a period or has ever been investigated by men specializing in obstetrics. In these respects this study is unique.

The purpose of this study is to find out all that it is possible to know about the obstetrical situation in Massachusetts. This means much more than the mere compilation of the actual number of deaths in Massachusetts in these years. Of course the actual cause of death in this study will be determined and recorded under the proper classification according to the 1929 revision of the International List Causes of Death, but the study will also show the type of obstetrics being practised in Massachusetts. Many deaths will be found to have been inevitable; others will be found which should have been prevented. Some will have been due to ignorance or negligence on the part of the patient herself; in others the responsibility may be found to lie with the attending physician.

When the Department of Public Health entertained the idea of conducting this mortality study, the officers of the Section of Obstetrics and Gynecology of the Massachusetts Medical Society were consulted. The officers of this section were immediately impressed with the real value of such a study, and approval of the Council of the Massachusetts Medical Society was sought. The Council not only unanimously approved of the Section cooperating with the Department of Public Health in this study but in their vote of approval expressed their hope that the physicians in the state would extend their full cooperation. An editorial to this effect appeared in the New England Journal of Medicine on December 9, 1937.

As it is planned to carry this work through 1941, the Commissioner of Health has appointed a permanent committee of members of the Section of Obstetrics and Gynecology of the Massachusetts Medical Society to assist the Department of Public Health so that continuity and permanence of working personnel will be assured. The Commissioner has also designated a physician in the State Department of Health personally to examine every death certificate on file in the Secretary of State's office for these years and to examine carefully each and every one which has any possible association with pregnancy. It is his duty to send data on all such deaths to the Committee of the Section of Obstetrics and

Gynecology for subsequent investigation. A letter is sent from the State Board of Health to each physician whose name appears on these death certificates apprising him of the fact that a member of the Massachusetts Medical Society will interview him in relation to this death. No physician is interviewed until this letter has been sent.

The men who are investigating these deaths are men specializing in obstetrics. In this regard this study is quite similar to the studies carried out in the cities of Boston, Philadelphia, and New York. It is felt if an investigator be an obstetrician that the opinion of the obstetrical care given each of these patients will be much more valuable.

The information sent from the State House to the Committee and passed on to the investigator is printed on a questionnaire published by the Children's Bureau of the United States Department of Labor (C. B. 122—Revised 6-1937). The questionnaire goes into the prenatal care given, the frequency of prenatal visits, physical examination, Wassermann tests, complications of pregnancy, the type of delivery, the type and classification of hospital, and in detail inquires into the actual cause of death. It is a very comprehensive questionnaire, and when intelligently answered and its contents wisely digested, makes possible an honest opinion of the care given the patient.

The investigators, as it has been said, are men primarily interested in obstetrics. They are all members of the Massachusetts Medical Society. After the letter from the State House has reached the physician whose name appears on the death certificate, the investigator arranges for a personal interview. This is usually done over the telephone, and the interviewer is always willing to meet the physician at a time that the physician himself sets. This interview is held in the physician's office or occasionally at a hospital, and intimate details of the case are thus obtained that in no other way could be obtained. In that way the physician who attended the patient in her last illness is personally interviewed and interviewed by an obstetrician.

It is hoped that this year and the years following the cases may be followed up within two months at most of the patient's death. It has been found that the sooner these interviews are held the clearer is the picture in the attending physician's mind, and in consequence early investigations are much more valuable.

The investigator returns to the Committee of the Massachusetts Medical Society these questionnaires when they are completed. The Committee goes over each and every one. Each case is thoughtfully considered, and an estimate of the care received is made. The blame for the death, if there be any, is placed where it belongs, and the correct diagnosis as to the cause of death is allocated to its proper rubric of the International List Causes of Death. A report of each year's study will be compiled, and the total of the five-year study ultimately tabulated and conclusions drawn. These conclusions will be based on actual facts as brought out by individual investigations. A real evaluation of the sort of obstetrics practised in Massachusetts will be obtained, and based upon these facts improved obstetrics in general will result.

THE HEALTH SURVEY

By Florence L. McKay, M.D.

Assistant Director

and

Sallie H. Saunders, M.D.

*Child Welfare Physician,
Division of Child Hygiene
Massachusetts Department of Public Health*

The addition of Social Security funds to our budget has made it possible to extend the Well Child Conference service to many rural communities where it was heretofore not available.

For some time we have had a demonstration well child conference unit which gives service to communities where there is a local nurse and where there is a possibility of a local well child conference resulting from our demonstration. This meant that only the larger communities in the state could be thus served. We have now added a second well child conference unit, which we call our Health Survey unit, which goes into rural communities of less than 10,000 population and gives this service and follow-up of the children examined in these small rural communities.

Through Social Security additions to our budget we were also able to double the number of district consultant nurses on our Division staff, thereby reducing their territory so that now each nurse has time for more intensive work in her smaller territory. In communities where there is no local nurse our state consultant nurse does the follow-up for this Health Survey.

The consultant nurse is responsible for all of the details of organization for the Health Survey. She plans for it with the Assistant Director of the Division and secures the cooperation of the local board of health, without whose written permission no well child conference is held in any community. She organizes a local well child conference committee, comprising, preferably, representatives from local organizations who would be interested in further well child activities after the demonstration is over. She explains to the committee in detail their responsibilities in the organization and conduct of the conference. She also visits each local physician, dentist and superintendent of schools, explaining to them the nature of the conference and inviting them to attend. If there is a local nurse who is to do the follow-up, the consultant nurse arranges with the nursing committee to have the nurse free, so that she can attend the well child conference and thus at first hand become acquainted with the findings of the conference. During the conduct of the conference she is present to assist in making it run smoothly, and after the conference is over she presents the findings to a group of our Division staff who have to do with this phase of the work in the field, and with them, makes plans for further child health work in the community. She then presents these plans to the local committee with suggestions for their enactment.

The local well child conference committee arranges for a place to hold the well child conference, for publicity preceding and after the conference, makes appointments for the conference, provides for the transportation of children to and from the conference, arranges for a hostess during each session of the conference and for weighing and measuring of the children at the conference and for keeping the children occupied quietly while the mothers are being interviewed. This means that toys of a quiet nature and small chairs and tables are usually supplied also.

Letters are sent from the Department to the local physicians and dentists, the superintendent of schools and other individuals especially interested, inviting them to visit the conference.

The personnel of the Health Survey well child conference unit consists of a pediatrician, a nurse, a dental hygienist and a nutritionist. The contribution of this staff is of an educational, as well as service, nature.

With the unit goes an exhibit, also made possible by Social Security Funds. This exhibit consists of a series of five posters on habit training, the titles of which are

Sleeping   Lessons in Living
Bed Wetting   Helpful Hints on Feeding
Discipline

and a series of posters on toys for this age group, entitled

Toys for the Infant   Toys for Sense Training
Toys for Make-Believe   Toys for Developing the Large
Play Material for Self-   Muscles
  Expression

These posters are to be hung on the wall above three card tables on which is placed the exhibit consisting of approved types of self-help clothing, books for children, books and book lists for parents on the care and training of children, and cut-outs illustrating nutrition facts.

When a child enters the well child conference he is weighed and measured by a local committee member and the history is taken by the nurse, who uses the facts in the history in order to teach the mother the care of the child, as well as the value of prenatal and postnatal care. The child and mother then go to the physician, where a health examination is made with the child stripped. The physician uses the findings of the health examination for teaching the mother the care and training of her child. The child and the mother next go to the dental hygienist, who teaches the care of the mouth and teeth and inspects the mouth of the child. From here the child and mother go to the nutritionist, who bases her instruction to the mother on the findings of the physician and dental hygienist. Our booklet, "One to Six," which describes the care of a child of this age is used as a basis of instruction for the mother and passages especially pertinent to the care of the individual child are marked by each member of the well child conference group as the mother and child visit them. The mother takes this book home with her to read at her leisure. Any member of the staff or of the committee who is free at any time demonstrates the exhibit material to the mother, stressing such points as may be found necessary in the health examination of the child. No other printed material is given to the mother, unless it has some direct bearing upon her problem. In each case the material is brought to the mother's attention and marked for her reading.

The last part of the well child conference day is spent in a conference with the unit staff, the consultant nurse and the local nurse, if there is one, concerning the findings and need of each individual child examined at the conference. The nurse who is to do the follow-up thus does so with the full knowledge of the condition of the child.

This unit started working in the field in April, 1936. Its services were first given to WPA nursery schools, which otherwise had no medical service and at times since then when it has been possible, a similar service, has been given to the nursery schools.

From April 1, 1936, to February 1, 1938, the unit has conducted examinations in 36 nursery schools in 29 towns and has examined 1,010 children. 728 mothers were interviewed and instructed at these examinations. As a result of the examinations,

353 children were referred to their family physician
587 children were referred to their family dentist
214 children were referred to both

The following is a summary of the 4,801 defects found in 991 or 98% of these children:

2,390 or 50% of these defects were major
2,411 or 50% of these defects were minor
423 of the children examined needed habit training
547 of the children examined had some nutritional defect
627 of the children examined needed T.A.T.
878 of the children examined needed vaccination

The services of the unit were also given to 53 towns where 66 well child conferences were conducted and 2,963 children examined. 2,007 mothers were interviewed and instructed at these conferences. As a result of these examinations,

1,011 children were referred to their family physician
1,374 children were referred to their family dentist
542 children were referred to both

The following is a summary of the 12,452 defects found in 2,794 or 94% of these children:

7,203 or 58% of these defects were major
5,249 or 42% of these defects were minor
1,954 of the children examined needed habit training
1,734 of the children examined had some nutritional defect
2,041 of the children examined needed T.A.T.
2,685 of the children examined needed vaccination

COURSE FOR WELL CHILD CONFERENCE PHYSICIANS

BY FLORENCE L. MCKAY, M.D.

Assistant Director, Division of Child Hygiene
Massachusetts Department of Public Health

Among other refresher courses, the Division of Child Hygiene offers a course to well child conference physicians. Physicians who are conducting, or who are planning to conduct, well child conferences in the smaller communities are among the first who are eligible for this course.

The course is given by the Division of Child Hygiene with the assistance of members of the staff of the Harvard School of Public

Health, the Boston Lying-In Hospital, the Children's Hospital, the Boston Habit Clinic and the Ruggles Street Nursery School. It is given on four consecutive Mondays and Tuesdays, beginning at ten o'clock on Mondays and ending at three-thirty on Tuesday afternoon, thus allowing time for travel on both Monday and Tuesday for the physicians who live farthest away and obviating the necessity of their remaining in Boston more than one night. The tuition is paid by the Division of Child Hygiene so that each physician meets only his travel and maintenance expenses for the two days a week.

The course includes the following activities:

Lectures:
 Care of the Newborn and Premature Infant
 Preschool Health Examination
 Dental Examination
 Motor Development
 Body Mechanics
 The Nutrition History
 Nursing Health Services
 Discussion of Pediatric Health Services

Observation at the Well Baby Clinic and the Child Health Conference at the Children's Hospital

Visits to the Boston Habit Clinic and the Ruggles Street Nursery School

Nursing Home Visits

Conferences with members of the staff of the Division of Child Hygiene concerning activities in general and well child conferences, dental, parent education, nutrition and nursing activities, and exhibits in particular.

Those who complete the course satisfactorily are given a certificate signed by the Director of the Division of Child Hygiene. Four physicians attended this course in November and the course is being repeated in March and probably in April.

NEW ACTIVITIES IN THE DENTAL HYGIENE PROGRAM
By FLORENCE B. HOPKINS, M.D., D.M.D.
Division of Child Hygiene
Massachusetts Department of Public Health

The new dental personnel in the Massachusetts Department of Public Health includes:

Physician-Dentist	1 M.D., D.M.D.
Public Health Dental Supervisor	1 D.M.D.
Public Health Dental Hygienist	1 D.H.

The duties of the Physician-Dentist have been outlined by the Director of the Division of Child Hygiene in which the dental program functions as: consultation service to professional groups and organizations, consultation service to communities and lay organizations, consultation service to institutions, promotion and stimulation of adequate dental service to all age groups, participation in health education as it pertains to dental hygiene, supervision of community demonstrations, supervision of professional content of dental hygienist's program, and giving lectures to professional and lay groups.

The duties of the Public Health Dental Supervisor are: assisting in dental program under direction of Physician-Dentist; supervising work of dental hygienist, serving on well child conferences, making community surveys of children, carrying on community and group demonstrations, and giving lectures to lay groups.

The duties of the Public Health Dental Hygienist include: service in well child conferences, participation in community demonstrations, participation in school health program, and participation in health education programs within her field.

Until April 1936 no dentists were employed in the Division of Child Hygiene, the entire dental program being carried on by one dental hygienist under director.

The new dental program is really not a *new* program at all; it is an expansion of dental health work that the Department has been actively engaged in for several years. The State program is entirely educational; no clinical service is supplied and only such examinations and surveys are made as can be useful in the promotion of parent, teacher and child education in dental health.

Through the addition of a dentist and of a physician trained in children's dentistry, the scope of the program has been markedly broadened. It now includes more active participation in medical and dental groups as well as actual teaching in public health to dental and medical school students and hospital staffs. It is hoped, through these contacts, to bring about in the medical fraternity a better understanding of the dentist's point of view and problems and to promote more cooperative effort on the part of these two allied professions in the interest of public health. The establishment of more dental internships in general hospitals is constantly urged.

Active, close cooperation is maintained between the Department and the dental organizations. In the capacity of advisor to agencies working for the correction of dental defects the need for more interest in clinical service by the dental profession is seen. An important part of the work in promotion of dental health for the community is the stimulating of dentists to see the need for professional supervision of clinical facilities. A study of the kind and amount of dental service available to indigent children is being conducted by the Dental Hygiene Council of Massachusetts. One of the dentists in the Division is an officer of the Dental Hygiene Council and is aiding them in this study. It is hoped that a thorough understanding of existing conditions will induce the dentists to work for better standards. This will of necessity bring about professional guidance and supervision of such activities.

Much of the dental program of the Division is devoted to the assistance of dental health teaching in the schools. The dentists give lectures, head discussions and develop materials which provide the teachers with the latest professional information as a background for a sound dental health education program.

A new booklet, "Dental Health in the Elementary Schools," has been issued by the Division of Child Hygiene. It contains the following sections: the dental problem, facts for teachers, educational principles underlying the teaching of dental health in the elementary schools, two suggested teaching units on teeth and their care, a summary of possible integration with subject matter for all elementary grades, references and visual aids. This booklet is available to school administrators and teachers in Massachusetts. In this project, the Physician-Dentist of the Division has worked with the Coordinator of Health Education, the dentist giving the dental knowledge to be adjusted to educational use by the education specialist. It is hoped through this work not only to teach facts about dental health to the school children but to prepare the children so that whatever clinical source is offered to them may be used to its greatest educational advantage.

A definite plan is being worked out for making the best use of school dental examinations to demonstrate the need for dentistry and its value. It is felt that the purpose of the school dental examination should be to provide an educational means of stimulating the child, the parent and the school to be interested in the factors which promote proper growth and health of the teeth, and to develop such habits of daily living as will maintain the optimal health of the child.

Recognizing the trend in progressive education which bases a program of health education on the actual needs of the child, we determine how many children need dental care. The school dental examination should be such that it will make the most of all opportunities, providing education for parent, teacher, nurse and child. Whenever possible, the school dental examination should be done on the same day that the regular school physical examination is conducted. An effort should always be made to have as many parents as possible present at the examination. Time should be allowed so that dental defects found can be demonstrated to the parents and the teacher, in order that this procedure may stimulate interest in their correction. It has been estimated that about five to seven minutes are adequate for such a demonstrtaion of dental defects to the parent. Since in the majority of towns it will be impossible at the present time for the school dentist to conduct this type of dental examination in all grades, it might be well to concentrate in certain grades. The first and third grades, the first year in junior high and the first year in high school are suggested as being the most strategic. In these grades, then, there could be a special emphasis made on specific dental health education. A school survey just for the purpose of finding defects, which we know in at least ninety-five per cent of the cases will be present, would not seem to be an economical use of the school dentist's time.

The idea of using physical examinations as a parent-teaching activity is coming to be very generally accepted by public health authorities throughout the country.

The Virginia State Department of Health in its "Manual for Teachers" states that "in order to secure the best results, it is essential that the parent be present when his child is examined by the physician. A notification of the exact time for the examination and reasons why his presence is desired, are effective means of bringing this about. The parent also should be asked if he will endeavor to attend, and told that if he does not intend to come he should notify the teacher so that the time may be given to another pupil whose parents will attend. Very little is accomplished in examining a small child if the parent is not sufficiently interested to come to the physician."

School health teaching programs are considered possible fields for parent education as well as teacher, nurse and child training. To quote again from the above mentioned Manual, "experience shows that it is not primarily because of lack of money that children do not have dental corrections made, but listed in order of importance the reasons are: (1) ignorance; (2) procrastination; (3) inaccessibility to dentist; (4) fear of dentist; (5) lack of money. Therefore, an educational campaign should precede the services of the dentist."

Well Child Conferences are another means of promoting parent education. The Division now has two units employed in this work. One is a demonstration unit and a dentist serves on this to do the dental examinations. The second is a Health Survey unit which is making a study of the children who have not had conference service. A dental hygienist is doing the dental inspection of these children. The Well Child Conferences are considered the best means available for demonstrating to individual parents and to communities the need for care of deciduous teeth. The promotion of dental care of pre-school children has a big place in the State program.

Among the recommendations of the Special Commission to Investigate Public Health Laws and Policies are the following which have to do with dental health:

"1. That dental examinations in schools and preschool conferences be performed by dentists rather than by dental hygienists or physicians.
2. That greater attention be given to dental education in schools of medicine and of nursing.
3. That community programs of dental hygiene be carried on by specially trained persons who have had also a background of teacher's training.
4. That courses in dental hygiene be included in the curricula of schools of public health.
5. That health and educational agencies develop a cooperative plan for popular instruction in oral hygiene.
6. That where dental clinic facilities are limited these be concentrated upon the care of the younger children.
7. That private philanthropy and government be encouraged to give more support to dental research.
8. That dental internship be further developed."

To summarize then, the Massachusetts Department of Public Health's dental program is:

1. Active participation in medical and dental societies, and contact with or actual teaching in public health, medical and dental schools and hospital staffs and in the promotion of dental internships.
2. Intensive cooperation with health teaching in the schools through preparation of subject matter or content in dental health teaching and the assistance of, or teaching of, teachers in dental material.

3. Parent education through Well Child Conferences, school dental surveys, talks to Parent-Teacher Associations and like groups and the distribution of printed material and the loan of such material as educational films, posters, etc.
4. Developing a definite plan for the best use of school dental examinations to assist in demonstrating the need of dentistry and the value of prevention.
5. Advisory service for school nurses and other agencies carrying on follow-up work for correction of dental defects.

If there are any seeming changes in policy in the new program, although fundamentally there are none, it is only in order that the program may keep abreast of the times. We are trying as much as possible to work in harmony with the Commission's suggestions and in harmony with the latest and most scientific research in the fields of education and dentistry.

THE RESEARCH-LEARNING PROJECT

BY LURA OAK, Ph. D.

Head of Research-Learning Project, Division of Child Hygiene
Massachusetts Department of Public Health

The inclusion of this unit of work in the Division of Child Hygiene is an appropriate departure in keeping with a growing demand for synthesis in the study of related human problems. It represents an effort to attack a complex problem of child development in its many-sided aspects. The purpose of the project is to study school failure among young children from the standpoints of psychology, of neurology, of education, of medicine and of psychiatry and to bring together the varied units in the mosaic of early childhood development as they relate to school adjustment. Such a study should lead to improved diagnostic procedures and to a fuller knowledge of preventable factors. The development of the program provides for the education of personnel and for service to the children included in the field of study. The Advisory Committee of the Division is composed of specialists in medicine, including pediatrics and obstetrics, dentistry, psychiatry, psychology, nursing, public health, child welfare, child development and education.

That a striking proportion of children are failing in school is a fact of great concern to everyone engaged in work with children. Investigations in psychology and education point to a syndrome of contributing pedagogical factors such as premature school entrance or improper teaching. Psychiatry emphasizes emotional disturbances, such as feelings of inferiority and inadequacy, as basic causes of school maladjustment. Pediatrists prescribe tonsillectomy or dietary changes to improve school achievement. All of these efforts represent units of knowledge concerning the problem in mind and occasionally the primary factor is properly treated through one of these means. We frequently see, however, a particularly clear example of the pitfalls of this highly specialized and discreet approach. In a school recently visited it appeared that through their psychological testing service the school had relegated two children to the special classroom at the end of the second grade because of low scores on intelligence tests. These tests required some ability to read. The children give every evidence of high intelligence yet because of a specific reading handicap which is probably curable in the early years, they have spent their school years among defective children acquiring attitudes of frustration, self-depreciation and rebellion at counter purposes with the aims of mental hygiene and of education. In another "special class" we found a boy with a serious visual handicap (macular degeneration) sufficient to prevent normal school work. He had memorized the Snellen chart and so had escaped detection as a case for the doctor. He has now left school, an illiterate, anti-social boy who will soon demand belated care when his vision is entirely gone. Cases in which partial or incorrect diagnoses have done irreparable injustice to children can be cited in large numbers. Inadequate knowledge and a one-sided approach by those responsible have added to the difficulties of the children themselves and have greatly complicated the social problem of the maladjusted individual. There are some instances where a child has avoided reading because of some physical strain. To induce such a child to read without first relieving this strain is to do violence to health and well-being. Yet some educators are drilling poor readers for speed and efficiency without ascertaining the physical limits within which they can safely work.

Students of the specific problems of reading failure are frequently baffled by apparent inconsistencies and by numbers of so-called "exceptional" cases. It sometimes appears that in this mosaic of knowledge units we are seeking to piece together, more parts are missing than are actually at hand. For example, here are some of the facts to conjure with: There is the preponderance of specific reading handicap among boys (the ratio being as high as 4 boys to 1 girl); the acutely handicapped are often children of superior intelligence (we have a case of a boy who can do difficult mental arithmetic and who searches out the numbers in his problems, the words of which he cannot read, and juggles them into several relationships, one of which is usually the solution!); severe vision handicaps are found among some of the most efficient readers; the physically unfit are often successful students and good readers; a higher percentage of children with crossed dominance (left eye, right hand or right eye, left hand) has been found among retarded readers than among unselected groups; some children read easily at the age of three or four.

The work of the Research-Learning staff is of necessity greatly limited in scope. The field staff consists of four persons: an educational psychologist, an ophthalmologist, an educational statistician and a research assistant. The point of emphasis at present is an evaluation of existing diagnostic procedures for detecting factors which interfere with early school achievement. In considering the importance of preventive measures we have concentrated upon a study of certain tests and devices designed to describe the "readiness" state of the younger children for the work of reading. The past year was spent in familiarizing ourselves with the schools in which the studies were to be made, in canvassing centers in Massachusetts where research is being done, in compiling bibiliographical material for study and in working with 100 selected cases of reading failure above the second grade.

The data assembled concerning the cases mentioned above consist of the following: Telebinocular tests (the Betts D.B. series) for screening out vision anomalies and diagnosing certain reading abilities; handedness and eyedness tests; school achievement tests (several, spaced at various intervals); individual intelligence tests (for only a small number); records of physical examinations and Snellen vision tests. While collecting these materials for study, the members of the staff gave a course of lectures to the teachers and nurses in the schools concerned and supervised remedial work undertaken by the classroom teachers. The results of this study will be summarized for publication. At present we are making a comparison of the Telebinocular tests given by the research assistant (twice repeated) and eye examinations given this year by the staff ophthalmologist in approximately 75 of the original 100 selected cases. In order to secure a further evaluation of these screening tests, we are beginning a second group of 100 cases for a similar series. (The Telebinocular tests in this case will be given twice by a nurse or teacher to entire groups without selection on the basis of suspected vision or reading difficulty.) Our further study of vision tests will lead to comparisons of Snellen chart tests with those of the Telebinocular and the findings of our staff ophthalmologist and private doctors to whom many of our subjects have gone for refractive corrections. Also, we have in prospect a vision survey among several groups of preschool children who will soon be enrolled in our study centers. This will be an effort to discover to what extent it is practicable to test the vision of these youngest children before they enter school.

The study of the disability cases referred to above is not an integral part of the major project which is now fairly well under way with groups of first and second grade children in three separate areas in the state. These three school districts, all of which are composed of village or rural schools, present a wide sampling in race and occupational status. We have begun our major project with studies of about 750 first and second grade children, which are designed to continue over a period of from two to three years.

The limits of this paper do not permit a detailed elaboration of the projected study. For each child in the group, which will probably extend to 1,000 cases, there will be a cumulative record covering the two or three years he is included in the survey. The items to be studied number about 100 for each child and include such records as the following: Vision and hearing tests; reading readiness tests; school achievement tests; handedness and eyedness tests; intelligence tests; school marks; physical examination records; family occupational rating; teachers' rating on several separate items; home records; accounts of personal experiences which may affect school progress; attitudes of parents toward school; descriptive records of siblings; accounts of personal guidance and other measures taken to prevent or overcome difficulties. The statistical data are recorded on especially prepared record folders from which the items can be conveniently handled by the punch card system.

Part of the service given to the schools has consisted of the records from our tests and examinations which have been used to advantage by the nurses and teachers. About seventy-five children who have been referred to eye specialists as a result of these tests and examinations by the staff ophthalmologist have already been provided with glasses. The school nurses have been able to secure needed funds from welfare societies, from Rotary and Kiwanis groups, church societies and clubs, and are carrying on an excellent follow-up program in cases where the attention of specialists has been advised. In one instance a welfare group in a small community was responsible for sending a child to a Boston hospital for needed surgery. School physicians and local physicians, generally, have offered generous cooperation and several have visited us when the work of examining was going on.

We have been called upon to examine a few defective children to contribute to the records of the teachers and the school examiners in cases where the proper disposition of a child is a problem. We have made a particular effort to examine some "special class" children for vision defects or special reading handicaps whenever doubt has been expressed as to the child's fitness for the "special class." Besides the case of vision handicap mentioned above, several cases of specific reading disability have been found among special class groups in which the child's intelligence was normal or above.

In one of the centers where our program is being developed the superintendent of schools has freed one of his elementary school teachers for part time, in order that she may work with cases of retarded readers. In each of the two other centers there are plans for the coming year which provide for the service of a teacher, especially trained, to direct diagnostic and remedial work and to further the program as it is being developed. In both instances the plan will provide for a "reading center" for this special work—in one case, within a new wing to be added to a school, and in the other, the work will probably be carried on in a portable building to be set up in a suitable location.

Aside from the major activities mentioned above, members of the staff are called upon for lectures and for consultation service to communities interested in reading problems. It is impossible to meet all of these requests or to examine and help the many individual cases brought to our attention through the office. Whenever the schedule has permitted, we have accepted the invitations of school superintendents to confer with them regarding specific problems in their schools. These are sometimes concerning administrative details such as the most effective procedure for instituting a remedial program or for providing an improved vision testing program. Occasionally a number of children are brought together for examination and recommendations. In the work with individual cases we refer to records from other sources, if they exist, or recommend that complete records be secured. The mental testing service of the Department of Mental Diseases has frequently proved of great value in some of these case studies.

Among the limitations in the work of the project there has been the difficulty of following up some of the referred cases of reading failure to the point of correction, even when we have been reasonably sure there were no physical or other handicaps. The children have needed only intensive drill in reading skills and careful teaching. Many teachers do not have sufficient ability or time to give the individual assistance necessary to make up the deficiencies. Some teachers need to see methods demonstrated and so-called "miracles" performed, in order to appreciate the importance of careful specific methods. Non-learners or slow learners are frequently given up when they do not keep pace with a class. In view of this general need for a demonstration, not only of diagnostic procedures but of skillful individual and group teaching of retarded readers, it is planned to give a summer course with a demonstration school where the staff will work together to illustrate some of the theories and procedures underlying the work of the unit.

COMMUNITY PUBLIC HEALTH NURSE DEMONSTRATION SERVICE

By Helen Chesley Peck, R.N.

Chief Consultant in Public Health Nursing, Division of Child Hygiene Massachusetts Department of Public Health

In response to a growing interest evidenced in various communities throughout the State to secure adequate public health nursing service on a full-time and generalized basis a Community Public Health Nurse Demonstration service was inaugurated in June, 1937, and is in operation in two communities at the present time.

The only nursing service which these communities had had previously was on a part-time basis and limited to the school population. In 1936 the communities had the services of the Well Child Conference Unit of the Division of Child Hygiene for a Health Survey of the children under school age. This service was requested officially by the local Board of Health and sponsored by local committees representing various civic and church organizations. This committee was responsible for a census of the children, for assistance in the conduct of the conference and for planning for future health needs of this age group. After the well child conference the state consultant public health nurse called in the homes of all these children to assist the parents in carrying out the conference suggestions. This demonstration of the benefits of a public health nurse for this age group enthused the townspeople to consider ways and means to secure a full-time service for themselves.

Plan of Administration of this Service

The State Department of Public Health offers the services of a qualified public health nurse for one year, provided the town agrees to assume full responsibility to continue the service at the close of the demonstration. The responsibility is placed with the Board of Health, though the administration may be shared by a joint committee representing Board of Health, School Committee and interested lay people.

The town must provide an office with adequate equipment and assume the expense of travel of the nurse, usually on a mileage basis. The State provides only her salary. At the end of the year the town and the nurse will decide whether she personally will remain, but the service is to be continued.

Massachusetts has legal authority to appropriate funds for this public health nursing service and practically every town has nursing service of some type. Most frequently it is financed by both public and private funds and administered by a joint committee.

"It is the responsibility of a public health nurse to assist in analyzing health problems and related social problems of families and individuals; to help them, with the aid of community resources, to formulate an acceptable plan for the protection and promotion of their own health, and to encourage them to carry out the plan. The public health nurse:

"1. Helps to secure early medical diagnosis and treatment for the sick.
"2. Renders or secures nursing care of the sick, teaches through demonstration and supervises care given by relatives and attendants.
"3. Assists the family to carry out medical, sanitary, and social procedures for the prevention of disease and the promotion of health.
"4. Helps to secure adjustment of social conditions which affect health.
"5. Influences the community to develop public health facilities through participating in appropriate channels of community education for the promotion of a sound, adequate community health program. Shares in community action leading to betterment of health conditions."

All functions of the public health nurse put together form a well rounded public health nursing program.

The community public health nurse is for all the community and approaches her work with the family as the unit. She assists the Board of Health in the control of communicable disease by instruction of family and demonstration of care. She assists not only in the care of the tuberculous patient but in the supervision of all the "contacts" of this patient. She assists the school physician, the superintendent and the teachers in the school health program and acts as interpreter between school and home, between family and teacher. She assists the physicians in the care of the sick, giving care as needed and instructing the family how to care for the patient. She assists the physician in maternity care, beginning with health supervision during pregnancy and continuing through care of the newborn. Since her program includes health supervision of all ages, she is interested in all members of the family. Through these and her many other services she learns to know the entire family and they in turn know her as the community public health nurse who is concerned with health of all the community.

THE TRAINING OF LAY LEADERS IN PARENT EDUCATION
By Mrs. T. Grafton Abbott
Consultant in Parent Education, Division of Child Hygiene
Massachusetts Department of Public Health

One of the great lacks in the field of parent education is adequate leadership. For this purpose a course has been started in the Division of Child Hygiene under the direction of the Consultant in Parent Education which trains lay leaders to work with parents or to give to their communities whatever is indicated as a need in this field. These leaders were selected with the aid of the Consultant Nurses and on a state-wide distribution basis. They are being trained on a purely voluntary basis. They take care of their own travelling and housing expenses during the periods when they are in Boston. The Division has no desire to make these leaders in any sense professional experts. The majority of them are married and are college graduates and have had positions of importance—both lay and professional—in their communities. There were thirty-five selected for this intensive training course over a three-year period. At the end of the period, if their work is satisfactory, this group will be accredited by the Division as lay leaders in the field of parent education and will be given certification accordingly.

The course began in January, 1937, with a week of training at Division headquarters. They met in session from ten to twelve o'clock and two to four o'clock daily for a week's period, following which they took a two-hour examination. The program for the first year included the following topics discussed by specialists:

> Study of Motivation and Interpretation of Behavior
> Inter-familial Relationships. Discussion of Parental Attitudes and Their Effect Upon Children's Behavior
> Habit-Training—Fundamental Principles Underlying Habit Formation. The Making and Breaking of Habits. Temper Tantrums. Fussy Feeding. Enuresis
> Discussion of Feelings of Inferiority and Inadequacy
> Discipline—Theory and Practice. New Techniques
> Community Organization. Group Discussion Techniques. Leadership Qualifications. Materials, Resources, Exhibits, Books, etc.
> Field Trip to Family Information Center, Jordan Marsh Company
> The General Health of the Child
> Nutrition and the Young Child
> Communicable Diseases
> Your Local Dental Program
> Vermont State Program
> Philosophy and Practice of Leadership in the New York State Program

Each lay leader returned to her community and worked out a project for which there was a felt need in her district. These were supervised by the Consultant and monthly reports were required of each leader on her work. The Consultant has personally visited each leader to see her in action in order to criticize and evaluate her leadership.

In addition to the work mentioned, each leader was assigned summer reading from a given list of topics in order that she might become proficient in one general subject on which she would be willing to speak at small meetings as requested. This has proven very effective and the leaders have taken part in each other's group meetings leading discussions on their chosen topics. Such topics have included "Biochemistry of Food," "Music in the Home," "Sex Education," "Safety in the Home," "Children's Fears," "Play Material for Children," "Books for Children," etc.

The projects have been as varied as the types of leaders. They have included such activities as a three-day institute in Berkshire County on parent education—thirty-two cities and towns participating in this community project. A three-year program has been started as an evening course in parent education at the Newtonville High School in cooperation with the Superintendent of Schools, the City of Newton Health Department and the Division of Child Hygiene. Eleven lectures were arranged on successive Monday nights and an average attendance has been maintained varying from 250 to 600. Over 1000 different individual people registered for this course. The requests for further study have been so insistent that plans are being made for the balance of the year. The emphasis this year in Newton has been on the preschool child. Next year they will continue their studies of the school child and the third year, the study of the adolescent—following in substance the type of program for lay leaders in the Division.

Another project has been the training of mother's helpers. Institutes have been held in various parts of the State—varying from one day of lectures to study groups over a year's period. Many of the leaders have conducted small study groups in their communities and have worked with their libraries in assisting them to increase the number of books available for parents. One of the leaders is conducting a course for volunteers for nurses' aids in connection with the Well Baby Clinic in one part of the State, and is giving them much of the material received here in training.

The leaders are encouraged to keep a record of their year's accomplishments in the form of scrapbooks or excerpts which are brought to the May Institute. All press clippings relative to the work in the community by any leader are sent to the office and are filed together with their reports. Any articles or lectures which the lay leaders are asked to give in their communities are submitted beforehand to the Consultant for approval.

The discussion of any local problems in parent education is taken up with the Consultant by the leaders before they are advised to participate actively in it.

A "make-up" group was held in April, 1937, in Worcester for several who had planned to enter the original course but who were unable to do so at the time.

In May a two-day institute was held at Division headquarters at which time all the leaders reported on their work for the year and discussed the possibility of future programs in their communities.

Supplementing the training of the lay leaders, the Consultant has assembled for their use and for use throughout the State material from all over the United States on parent education. Such pamphlets and bulletins are brought to the attention of the leaders as they come in and sometimes suggestions are made to them for purchasing material which might help them to be more efficient.

Any conference or meeting on parent education of which the Consultant is aware is brought to the attention of these leaders and many of them have taken advantage of such meetings. Several attended the Institute of Family Relations at Vermont and fifteen of the leaders attended the two-day session held at the International Institute in Boston. Several, in addition, attended the Regional Conference on parent education which took place in the fall of 1937, at which time parental education and its varying aspects was evaluated by Mr. Ralph Bridgman, Executive Director of the National Council of Parent Education.

The Consultant has obtained permission from various states, where the material in parent education was particularly valuable, to have it restruck for the use of the lay leaders.

Annotated booklists have been worked out for the benefit of the lay leaders and for the people they meet in their communities. This list is a resumé and discussion of the current books and their value, as far as parent education and mental hygiene is concerned.

The second training period started in October, 1937—the emphasis during the week being placed on the problems of the school child. The second-year program includes the following topics discussed by specialists:

Causes of Failure in School Children
Endocrine Aspects of Personality
The Parent's Part in Social Hygiene Education
Meeting Sex Expression in Children
Demonstration Clinic on Behavior and Educational Problems of School Children held at the Judge Baker Guidance Center.
School Lunches
Relationship of Parents to a School Health Program
Health Teaching in the School as a Part of the Community Program
Successful Life Management Through Scientific Money Management

The same procedure was followed as before, and the final week's training period will be held in October, 1938, on the problems of the adolescent.

It is our desire to obtain before the course closes for the first group an appraisal of the leader's work on the part of the community itself in which she has conducted her activities. The work of the leaders, in some instances, has been spectacular and very outstanding—in other cases it has been a slow, steady, definite growth on the part of small groups—all of whom are deeply interested in studying more intelligently the problems of child rearing and their own relationship to their children.

COURSES FOR NURSES ON "UNDERSTANDING HUMAN BEHAVIOR"

By Mrs. T. Grafton Abbott
*Consultant in Parent Education, Division of Child Hygiene
Massachusetts Department of Public Health*

A series of four lectures has been worked out to meet the needs of local nurses in giving them a better understanding of human behavior and family problems in order to make them more efficient in their services in the home.

In some cases, this request has been the outgrowth or by-product of the work of the lay leaders in parent education. Courses have been given consisting of four lectures once a week on the following subjects:

The Understanding of Behavior in General
Family Attitudes as They Affect Children
Feelings of Inadequacy
Principles of Habit Formation
New Techniques in Discipline
Interfamilial Relationships as They Affect Children

Reading lists have been suggested and the nurses have all been requested to take notes of the material given. There has been an opportunity at the end of each lecture for discussion in which the nurses have freely participated. These courses have been held in the following places: Pittsfield, Worcester, Springfield, New Bedford and Dennis, and they are soon to be given in Northampton, Bridgewater, Mansfield, Dighton, Fitchburg and Gardner.

The set-up of the meetings scheduled for next year will be as follows:

A series of four meetings for each district (one day meeting per week: 9:30-12:30; 2:00-4:00), group to be limited to about thirty.

At each meeting five nurses will each present a case for discussion—the other members of the group being auditors. The Consultant will direct the discussion and comment on the case, and what a Public Health Nurse could and should do in each specific instance.

At the last meeting, a presentation of a written case from the Judge Baker Guidance Center to show details of study, analysis, prognosis, and treatment.

The Consultant Nurse will assign each time the nurses who will present the problems to be discussed. The Consultant will also select with the nurses, the problems they will present. The local nurses will have a copy of the types of problems and the outline to guide them in their presentation.

Preparation for Nurses

1. Delinquency (stealing or truanting or persistent lying, etc).
2. a. Behavior Problems (dependency, the aggressive or the shy child, etc).
   b. Emotional Problems (jealousy, fears, etc).
3. Habit-Training Problems (enuresis, temper tantrums, fussy feeding, masturbation, thumb sucking, etc).

4. Parent-Child Relationships (lax discipline, too strict discipline, lack of routine, favoritism, sarcasm, ridicule, etc).

5. Educational Problems (school adjustment, failure in school, etc).

Points of One Case From Each Group and Each Session

The outlines of essentials for each nurse to guide her in her presentation will contain the following points:

1. Statement of the Problem
2. Physical set-up of the home—including conditions of living and economic factors.
3. Physical factors, health and developmental history
   Life of the child and parents, including possible history of mental or communicable diseases.
4. Number of children in the family and parent-child and sibling relationships
5. Estimate of parents' education and qualifications, occupation, mentality, emotional stability, etc.
6. Comments by teachers or nurse through contacts with the patient.
7. Community resources which might be utilized.

NEW MATERIALS IN HEALTH EDUCATION
By JEAN V. LATIMER, B.S., A.M.
Coordinator of Health Education, Division of Child Hygiene
Massachusetts Department of Public Health

To meet the increasing demand in the field and to be of service to local communities in promoting and stimulating new trends in child hygiene, new material has been prepared by the Division of Child Hygiene both in a mimeographed and printed form. Also, material formerly available has been revised and brought up to date. The current list is as follows:

Mimeographed Material

Suggested Reading List on Child Rearing
Educational Methods of Leading Groups
Suggested Reading List on the Preschool Child
Suggested Reading List on the Preschool Child, the School Child, the Adolescent, Family Relationships and Mental Hygiene
Test of Health Consciousness for the High School
An Outline of What Should be the Health Equipment of a High School Graduate
Suggested Teaching Units on Home Nursing and Child Care for High School Girls
Objective Health Knowledge Test to be Used at the Beginning and End of the Teaching Unit on Food and the Body Needs
Teaching Unit on Food and the Body Needs for Grade V
Health Teaching Integration with the Study of Biology and Civics in the Secondary Schools

Health Teaching Integration with the Study of Social Science in the Secondary Schools
A Teaching Unit on a Balanced and Protective Diet for Grade VII and IX
Problems and Pupil Activities for Unit Teaching on Food and the Body Needs for Grades IV, V, and VI
A Teaching Unit on Teeth and Their Care for Grade VIII
Dental Facts for Teachers
What a Dental Certificate Should Mean
The Digest of Health Laws and Policies.
Bulletin No. 2, School Physicians
A Selected Bibliography on School Health Work
Instructions for Use of Children's Bureau Schedule No. 122
List of Sources of Health Education Materials
Description of Improvised Premature Incubator
Directions for Use of Packages for the Obstetrical Attendants
Minimum Requirements for Hospital Care of Premature Infants
Nursing Care of the Premature Infants
Health Survey of the Preschool Child
Instructions for the Well Child Conference Local Committee
Visual Survey Record Sheets
Directions for Audiometer Testing in the Schools
The Faculty-Student Health Council for Junior and Senior High Schools
Patterns for Meals
Evening Meals for Camps
Kitchen Handbook
How Shall I Make a School Lunch Survey
Cookies for Children
Measuring Stick for a Well Chosen Lunch
Fit Your Food to Your Figure
Fruit Candies (recipes)

Printed Material
Your Premature Baby
The Premature Infant (Its Care and Development)
The Premature Law
Dental Health in Elementary Schools
Vitamin C Foods Each Day
Food Wise, Money Wise
Food for the Little Child
No Child Should Ever Have Diphtheria
Prevent Tooth Decay
Baby and You
One to Six
Gain in Height and Weight by Years for Boys and Girls of School Age
Maternal Mortality in Boston for the Years: 1933, 1934, 1935.
How May School Health Education be Improved
Nutrition Facts for Teachers
Suggestions for Integrated Health Teaching in the Primary Grades

SPECIAL COURSES WITH TEEN AGE GIRLS

By ALBERTINE P. MCKELLAR, B.S.

Public Health Education Worker, Division of Child Hygiene
Massachusetts Department of Public Health

Miss Teen Age in the urban or rural high school, in the city settlement house or in the exclusive private school has at least one opinion in common—she invariably says, "One needs so much today—a pleasing personality, an attractive appearance, emotional stability, physical stamina!" Miss Teen Age is avidly concerned with self improvement and wants sincerely to know facts—vital facts pertinent to the everyday problems she faces—facts that help her to understand human behavior (especially her own)—true facts that enable her to evaluate the multitude of suggestions and innuendoes constantly poured out to her from the printed page, from silvery toned radio voices, from the screen and from —"the girl-friend."

And Miss Teen Age in her dilemma naturally turns to the high school as the authentic source for this knowledge, for practical help in the development of these skills. She believes the school should teach her to raise her P.Q. (personality quotient) and her S.Q. (social quotient) as well as her I.Q. Her courses, she complains, often fail to include this type of essential information and consequently shè lends an eager ear to any or every dispenser of knowledge.

There are some high school administrators who are seriously attempting to meet these needs. They realize that the great majority of high school students will have no further formal education, and must be qualified to face life—to take their places as useful members of society. We look to these able educators who have developed courses, who are working on units of study, for valuable and timely contributions.

Other high schools, handicapped by lack of facilities and staff are no less cognizant of the need and have asked for assistance from the State Health Department. Consequently an experimental course, at present called "Understanding and Improving Yourself" is being given to senior high school girls in response to these requests.

The material has been developed over several years with continuous changes. Additions and omissions as suggested by the girls have been incorporated until the present outline has little of the original one. In from four to six sessions, specific understandings in relation to appearance, personality, poise and physical fitness are presented. Briefly, these are the main "understandings":

The process of habit formation (cobwebs today—cables tomorrow)
The far reaching physical and emotional effects of the extreme growth during adolescence
The infallible fact that appearance depends upon daily habits
The component traits of the pleasing personality
Through understanding and care come physical fitness and stamina
Through understanding and control come emotional stability and poise.

Illustrative material, valuable for any health teaching, has been indispensable in this course, as often it is given before large numbers in the assembly hall, the gymnasium, the lunchroom or the town hall. A growth chart (enlarged from page 19, "Psychology of Adolescence") made with a strip of gummed paper tape on a dark green cardboard helps in the explanation and discussion relative to growth. A nutrition poster, "A Measuring Stick for Your Meals" shows vividly and clearly the daily requirements for the protective health diet and a series of food composition charts assist with the presentation of nutrition facts. "Food for the Teens" and "Fit Your Food to Your Figure" are distributed. A wooden cut-out tooth model helps to remind, in an indisputable manner, the fact that teeth are nourished by the blood stream and that their condition depends to a large degree upon tooth building foods. The Good Grooming Tools hold interest and attention while important points having to do with attractiveness are discussed. The "Self-Check on Appearance for Teen Age Girls"—painstakingly filled out by the great majority of girls impresses them with the relation between personal appearance and specific habits of daily living.

A list of helpful books for Teen Age girls is distributed. Frequently real appreciation is expressed for this list, especially by those girls who in their diligent search for information have come upon unfortunate (to say the least) publications. Included with others are such books as:

Healthful Living—Jesse Feiring Williams, Macmillan Co., 60 Fifth Ave., N. Y. $1.56.
Everyday Living for Girls—Adelaide Laura VanDuser, J. B. Lippincott, 227 So. 6th St., Philadelphia, Pa. $2.00.
Eighteen, Carolyn Atkinson Miller, Round Table Press, 354 Fourth Ave., N. Y. $1.50.
Growing Up in the World Today—Emily V. Clapp, Massachusetts Society for Social Hygiene, 1150 Little Building, Boston. No charge in Massachusetts. Outside of Massachusetts, 20c.
How to Develop Your Personality—Sadie Myers Shellow—Harpers Bros. N. Y. $3.
Charm by Choice—Ruth F. Wadsworth—The Womans Press, 600 Lexington Ave., N. Y. $1.
Games for Fun—Fun for All—R. C. Kuehner, Eugene, Oregon. 15c.
Getting Together—Edna Geister, George H. Doran Co., Garden City, N. Y. $1.35.
Ideas for Parties (the Audington Party Book)—Audington Press, N. Y. $1.20.

The Committee of Critics is composed of three leading girls from each class, chosen by the principal for their ability to think and speak clearly. They meet after the course to discuss it. From these dignified, straightforward discussions have come the constant alterations of the material. In fact, very little of the original remains in the present outline. The mature manner and capably expressed opinions of these small groups never fails to impress me.

An encouraging outgrowth of the course with the girls is the meeting of high school mothers held in nearly every town immediately following its completion. The request for this meeting originated with the girls, proved satisfactory, and now is suggested as a definite follow-up procedure. The mothers are given an idea of the material presented, the types of questions asked by the girls and ample opportunity for discussion. Their reactions for the most part are favorable. A few have expressed their approval and appreciation to the school administrators.

A request came from the principals or school nurses in some of the towns for one session with the girls in the junior high school. These girls, they said, were interested in the high school meetings and asked to have one for themselves. This plan has seemed satisfactory and most of the towns arrange for this junior high school meeting.

A Follow-up Questionnaire is the most recent development in an attempt to evaluate the course. Here are the unsigned answers recorded by 219 girls in a high school with a boy and girl population of 425 near Boston:

High School (population of 425)   Questionnaire given to 219.
Year: Freshman .75   Sophomore   59   Junior   47   Senior   38
     Total   219
Did you enjoy this course? Yes   218   No   ("To a certain degree")...
   1 sophomore
Do you think such a course should be given to high school girls? Yes   218   No   ("perhaps")   same sophomore
Have you a suggestion for material that could be included or should be left out? Please explain:
   More on girl and boy problems
   More on vocations for women and the selection of schools
   Less on health—more on personality
   "Include diseases of the blood, as insanity, cancer and tuberculosis"—freshman
Did you receive new information? Yes   202   No   17
Have you attempted to make any definite changes in *your* habits as a result of this course? Explain briefly:

	Some change	Not answered	No change necessary
Seniors	30	7	1
Juniors	40	4	3
Sophomores	42	14	3
Freshmen	50	23	1*

The changes most frequently indicated were as follows:
   getting more sleep   cut down on school night dates
   resting each day   cut out school night dates
   better care and selection of clothes   have gone to dentist
   use less make-up   improving personality

Some interesting notations are quoted:
   (Sr. and Jr.) "As a whole I'm determined to have a finer, cleaner life"—"I've tried hard to get more sleep and I do feel better for it"—"I'm going to be more careful whom I kiss and not so often"—"I've stopped smoking and pet less"—"I've made mother's milk bill larger."
   (Soph. and Fresh.) "I've tried to improve my appearance, to gain poise, personality and self respect"—"I'm forming better living habits"—"I stay home more, drink more milk, get more rest"—"Yes, I've changed a lot, in ways that mean a lot to me and I'm going to keep changed"—"I've stopped having so many dates and begun keeping myself in reserve."

Who do you think should give such a course? Physical education teacher   70
   School nurse   19   Other teacher   1   Person from outside school   115
   (There were two comments here that I think deserve consideration. "The school nurse should not give such a course because it would arouse curiosity among the boys—and they'd make nasty remarks"—junior. "No one in school should give such a course because they know us too well and it would be altogether too personal"—senior.)

Would you approve of mixed classes in a course in Hygiene? Yes   36   No   173
Do you think sufficient time was devoted to this course? Yes   43   No   162
   (48% of freshmen)
Was too much time given to it? Yes   ?   No   214
Have you any suggestions for improvement? Explain briefly:
   More time—allowing for more detail

---

* ("Mother doesn't believe much in this course".)

Separate older from younger
" juniors and seniors from sophomores and freshmen
" according to age and experience (!)—(senior)
" " " mental ability
" " " each year of age
Should be a whole year's course called Hygiene or something more interesting (a freshman)—"Should have a year's course in feminine hygiene" (1)

It was with the groups outside of school that the pioneering was done with the very beginnings of this material. Today leaders of the Y. W. C. A., the Settlement Houses, the Girls League, church groups, the 4-H Clubs and the Girl Scouts are vitally interested. Each of these groups is closely concerned with problems of the teen age girl and many requests for assistance come from them. The less formal, friendly atmosphere—the voluntary attendance—the cordial club or group allegiance—are all significant factors contributing to the general reception that the course, or its ramifications, always receives with these groups.

This endeavor to help Miss Teen Age to understand and improve herself makes no bid for praise. The lamentably few sessions, the single follow-up meeting a year later, the assembly classroom and the omission of the boys are blatant shortcomings. For the present, however, it attempts to meet a definite need. Eventually this exchange and collection of ideas may be helpful to those who will surely develop some similar required course for high school juniors or seniors.

NUTRITIONISTS PIONEER IN COUNTY HEALTH UNITS
By Mary Spalding, M.A.
Consultant in Nutrition, Division of Child Hygiene
Massachusetts Department of Public Health

Massachusetts has an established state nutrition program and with the impetus of Social Security benefits believes it worth-while to demonstrate what nutritionists can do for family health in two district units—one having 26 towns with a population of 134,870 and one with 15 towns and a population of 36,647. This work is pioneer work. The nutritionist with the help of the unit staff has introduced herself and her work to the people in the community. She has acquainted herself with the resources and studied the needs of the community. For this reason the nutritionist beginning such work should have qualifications necessary for opening the way—adaptability with an understanding and liking of people, vision and valor, dependability with initiative, as well as sound practical methods of presenting nutrition subject matter applicable to everyday family living.

In studying the nutritionists' work over a year's period, we see progress as follows: The nutritionist in the district has become better acquainted with the people. People are beginning to know who she is and what she does. They find her more easily when they need her. The longer she stays in a community the more nutrition-conscious people become. Consequently the more they appreciate and ask for her services.

Another point we have found is that although communities may be neighboring, current problems may not be common. Requests for nutrition education from parents, from nurses, from teachers, and from lunchroom managers come in waves. The nutritionist located in a district can better adapt her program to the people's need when felt. It is harder for the nutritionist but more sound educationally for the people. For instance, a food habit survey of school children in a community surprised their teachers by the discovery of food deficiencies. The superintendent and teachers arranged for a series of group meetings to learn more facts about nutrition for teaching purposes. This led to a request for help with nutrition units for different grades in the town. Then the teachers said, "We wish the parents could have similar work." One definite result is shown by the baker's reporting an increase in the sale of dark bread. Children and parents also reported an improvement in habits. A group of nurses in another town requested a series of nutrition conferences on recent facts in nutrition, so they may interpret these facts practically in terms of daily meals to the families they visit. These group meetings were followed by a request for the nutritionist to visit with the nurse certain families with special nutrition problems.

Being in the office with the health officer and the nurse, the nutritionist gets the message from the people sooner than if she were out of the district. Then, too, they help her know where to send news articles and invite her to local organization meetings so as to become acquainted with professional groups.

Examples of work done on a town basis will follow as these give more realistic and vivid pictures.

Town A is a town of three distinct communities. The East section is a partially rural district with a few small stores and no industries. The "Pond" section is a small settlement of English people clustered about an iron foundry. These people were brought into the town by the foundry owner and form a distinct group. The Center is a mill community dependent for livelihood on the fluctuating employment of textile mills and machine works. As the mill business fluctuates, so does the welfare case load.

In Town A a Well Child Conference had been arranged. The county nutritionist served as a member of the Conference staff and had individual conferences about food intake, food habits, budget, and related nutrition facts with each mother who attended. During the same period of time a conference was held with the local welfare agent regarding the food allowance for certain families and with the local W.P.A. commodity distributor with regard to the distribution of surplus foods and their use by the families. During the conferences with mothers the use of the Surplus Commodities was discussed, and new uses discovered by one mother were given as practical suggestions to another. Special nutrition cases were chosen for home visit follow-up with the nurse. For instance, the mother of a four year old child with scurvy welcomed assistance in finding foods containing vitamin C to use in daily meals.

The following is the well child conference summary—

Number Attending—352 children   Number Nutrition Conferences—269 parents

53% showed good nutrition   40% needed more fruit
31% showed slight defect   43% needed more vegetables
14% showed moderate defect   64% needed more whole grains
 2% needed immediate attention   25% needed budget assistance
24% needed more milk

The school nurse and the school superintendent were met at the preschool conference, and this was followed by a call at the school office a few weeks later on school nutrition problems. There is in this town no school lunchroom where consultation could be given.

The health education co-ordinator and the nutritionist then talked over with the superintendent and the high school principal the Faculty Health Council and its effect on health practices of the students.

In this town, then, nutrition service for the families has been introduced through individual parents conferences at well child conferences, case work with the nurse, case work with the welfare agents, group discussion with the school department, and a talk to mothers. The summary of personal contacts is as follows:

1 public health nurse and 2 substitute nurses
1 welfare agent
1 W. P. A. commodity distributor
1 school nurse
1 school superintendent
1 high school principal
12 members of well child conference committee representing local service organizations
269 parents

Summary

Town B—	
Report to physician	1
Well child conferences	61
Summer round-up interviews	30
School clinics for tuberculous children	5
Group meetings with teachers	5
Conference with welfare department	1
School cafeteria visits	4
Conferences with individuals in community	4
School visit to see health posters	1
Health camp home visits	3
Meeting for parents	1

Of 91 reached on conferences
21% needed more milk   76% needed more vegetables
27% needed more fruit   12% needed budget assistance
48% needed more cereal and dark bread

Of 135 children in grades 4, 5, 6 whose day's food habits were surveyed
67% needed more milk   53% needed more whole grains
56% needed more fruit   78% needed more eggs
93% needed more vegetables   32% needed more meat

Town B is a town of four individual communities—one definitely Italian, affected by poverty and racial influences, the others populated by more well-to-do families where psychological rather than budget and racial problems prevail. The canal provides some work for the community. Summer trade and fishing furnish others with livelihood.

After making organization visits, the first nutrition education was done through well child conferences, school lunch surveys, and school clinics. An example of a nutrition problem often met, showing the influence of advertising and fortunately a favorable outcome, was a mother who at the first conference brought a baby with a severe case of malnutrition. At the summer round-up conference when the mother was asked about the baby she said, "He's doing fine! You know, I think a mother knows more about a baby than any doctor does. One of my neighbors gave me a cod liver oil concentrate for him, another calcium tablets, a third a sun nest. I use them all, and he looks so much better that I really don't need to take him to a doctor as was suggested at conference." The conference served as nutrition education to the nurse as well as the individual parent.

The school cafeteria run by an untrained concessionaire presents problems. The arrangement of the counter can well be improved; menus need better balancing; no records are kept; the children's choice needs direction through more education; and too much resale food is sold. Salads and hot dishes are excellent. New menus and recipes were furnished the manager, and suggestions on food selection, buying, and methods of food serving were made. More contacts need to be made before definite accomplishment can be measured. The manager, however, has been to summer school for the week's conference. As a result she has doubled her sale of milk; sandwiches are served in paper bags; the counter arrangement is better; she has sought the help of the home economics teacher in making posters for the lunchroom; the menus are more varied; and she emphasized dark bread in her menus in connection with the nutrition unit.

The home visits were made in connection with summer camp follow-up and accompanied by the summer camp director, so that the visits were both means of nutrition education to the families and a representative of a health agency. Nutrition education for the nurse was carried on through the medium of well child conferences.

With the superintendent's and principal's knowledge and at the teachers' instigation, the nutritionist was enabled to make the food practice survey. This was followed by the presentation of nutrition facts in preparation for units to attempt to improve the child practices and a parents' meeting to present the findings and to ask their cooperation.

The work of these two nutritionists in health units cannot yet be evaluated. The one in the smaller unit has worked for fourteen months; the other in the larger unit for five months (preceded by another nutritionist working four months).

We do know that the nutritionist in this way can be of real use to a group of towns—no one of which could employ her by itself.

That two health officers have generously given a place to her in their programs.

That the nutritionists are finding more work than they can do. The one in the smaller unit has a heavy program and cannot meet all the requests. Therefore, it would seem that local groups begin to recognize a nutritionist as a practical teacher of health.

That a physician on a well baby conference in one town was good enough to say that he now felt he had a perfect set-up with an excellent nursing follow-up and a nutrition service.

That working with each age group—children and parents, as well as families of different income levels, and with professional groups having individual interests—such as physicians, dentists, nurses, welfare workers, teachers, and managers of school lunches—the nutritionist has the advantage of seeing nutrition problems in the community as a whole and of participating more with each group towards their solution.

That most of her work must be on the group habit basis though individual conferences with professional workers are very productive.

Many helpful exchanges occur during well child conferences and school clinics.

That some home visits are necessary for special cases, as budget cases, and for nutritionists to keep a sensitive and practical understanding of home conditions in varying communities.

That the nutritionist must spend more time preparing for group meetings consisting of different types of individuals than if she addressed herself to one type.

That this seems worth-while in considering the breadth of her work.

That she also has to take time to prepare and gather nutrition tools for nurses and others for their daily work with families.

That even in this short time she has been able to bring about changes in family and child practices, so her place on a county health program begins to seem justified.

Our beginning demonstration indicates that a department of health can do much towards solving nutrition problems basic to health by placing nutritionists, having professional calibre, to help practically with problems of families of different income levels, varying degrees of intelligence, and many food customs, and to combat propaganda of unethical advertisers and faddists.

MASSACHUSETTS ADVANCES TOWARD BETTER SCHOOL LUNCHES

By Dorothy Frank, B.S.

Nutritionist, Division of Child Hygiene
Massachusetts Department of Public Health

The Department of Public Health has for a long time been interested in promoting better school lunches. In 1934 it was shown from a survey of 47,000 school lunches, in 305 schools in 87 cities and towns of Massachusetts, made by the schools through principals, school nurses, home economics teachers, and others or by responsible local representatives of the Federation of Women's Clubs, Parent-Teacher Associations, Red Cross, and Extension service, that,

Only 1 out of 4 children had milk
" 1 " " 5 " " fruit and vegetables
" 1 " " 7 " " dark bread
" 1 " " 5 " " as long as 25 minutes for lunch
" 1 " " 9 " was getting a hot dish.

The work was carried on in the recent past by staff nutritionists who participated in the school lunch program but were engaged primarily in other phases of the nutrition in public health field. Much has been accomplished in the past year alone as the following summary shows:

Number of towns visited 56
Number of schools worked in 93
School lunch surveys 7
Number of talks (estimated attendance, 2850) 31
Organization of new lunchrooms' equipment, floor plans, menus 8
More protective foods known to be served 34
Record forms for accounts introduced in making for better food . 6

Conference for lunchroom managers 45
More space secured for seating in lunchrooms 2
Exhibit on lunch at all fairs and meetings.

There is a great need for more work ahead, however. A summary of school lunch surveys in Massachusetts reveals this:

```
Total number in schools ...............       770,651*
Number in schools:—
    having school lunch survey .........      425,114
    taking lunch .......................       78,708
    taking milk ........................       18,332 or 23%
    taking fruit .......................        9,758 or 12%
    taking vegetables ..................       10,975 or 14%
    taking dark bread ..................        9,028 or 11%
    taking hot dish ....................       13,403 or 17%
Total number cities and towns .........          355
Number of cities and towns surveyed to date      169
```

The Department of Public Health now employs in the Division of Child Hygiene under Social Security funds a nutritionist who devotes her time almost solely to service on school lunch matters. No new phases of the work have been attempted. Social Security has made possible an intensifying of those already in progress. The nutritionist goes especially into towns where there are untrained lunchroom managers or teachers serving a hot dish at noon and also to those schools where her services have been requested. She helps them on buying foods, in menu planning, food preparation and service, account keeping, equipment problems, and salesmanship so that the children may have a variety of protective foods in particular at the lowest possible costs and in a form they will eat.

The nutritionist arranges summer conferences for this group and for trained lunchroom managers, and also plans county meetings where they may hear speakers who are actively engaged in the work and have the opportunity for round table discussion of mutual school lunch problems. She interests them in attendance at meetings of national school lunch associations.

Another important part of this nutritionist's work is her help to community leaders making school lunch surveys so that they may know the particular problems in their schools and meet them either by initiating school lunches or sponsoring year in, year out their maintenance at high levels. She presents the problems found to members of the school committee, to the superintendent, to teachers, to community groups and sometimes directly to the school children. To interest the community in the importance of school lunch and the maintenance of a commendable teaching situation, she may talk before local groups, give school lunch food demonstrations, and write articles for lay and professional publications. She also acquaints lunchroom managers with helpful exhibits, printed material, and reference books available and advises on use of such aids. The purpose of these services is to give school pupils an opportunity to procure and to select wisely a good noon meal.

During the state-wide program for betterment of school lunches, more than 169 cities and towns have participated in a survey of their school lunch situations. Pupils, teachers, school administrators, school nurses, lunchroom managers, and parents assist in the surveys which

---
* Pupils enrolled in all public schools in Massachusetts, year ending June 30, 1935.

point the way to progress in the health and happiness of school children and the community.

The nutritionist finds different problems in different localities. In the western part of the state, visiting rural schools, she found the following situation. An English lesson for the eighth grade was in progress. Quietly a sixth grade boy rose from his desk where he had just finished his problems in arithmetic and moved to the small oil stove at the side of the room. It was his turn to prepare the hot drink for the noon lunch. He carefully lighted the stove, measured cocoa and sugar, water and milk into a kettle and it was not long before the characteristic aroma of hot cocoa was sharpening the appetites of all. Lessons over for the morning, the pupils prepared for the noon meal. Much scurrying to wash hands and arrange on the desk contents of lunch boxes brought from home, revealed happy anticipation of this social hour. The children carried their cups to the cook who was now server and received a steaming cupful of cocoa to accompany the assortment of sandwiches, fruit, and desserts taken from their lunch boxes. Suggestions for raising the nutritive quality of the lunches brought from home and practical pointers on hot dish preparation at school were of assistance here. In eastern Massachusetts the nutritionist found some school lunchroom managers having to contend with sidewalk vendors, some needing a system of food and cost control, some wanting to know more about kitchen management.

The problem common to practically all, however, is how to promote better food selection on the part of the pupils. One manager found that when she removed the trays from her counter to a side table, the general appearance of the counter was more attractive. Also, posters suitable to the various holidays as they came along made the room colorful. Providing a pleasant place in which to eat stimulated the pupils to try soups and other hot dishes rather than to hurriedly munch a single sandwich. In another school lunchroom fruit was sold at 2 cents to cut down the sale of 1 cent and 5 cent candy bars. Thus something seasonal and tasty was made available and desirable. Variety and novelty, too, are worthwhile considerations in this problem of promoting better food selection. Many managers say that meat loaf with potato and vegetable is quite a favorite but when hamburgers and cole slaw are on the menu there is a greater demand. The best way to get a child to make the right choices is to serve wholesome, palatable food, attractively displayed.

Much can be done, then, in the lunchroom. The methods are fitted to the individual problem. Teaching is needed, too, in the classroom and in the community. Where junior high school pupils are drinking little milk at noon, for instance, moving pictures shown at school assembly about milk and its value produce good results. If the pupils then study their milk consumption and check to find improvement as they go from junior to senior high, there is more likely to be more milk drinking at school lunch time. Parents' meetings held in the school lunchroom with school lunch foods for refreshments have aided, because such gatherings acquainted the fathers and mothers of the school children with what constituted a good noon lunch and what was available at the school. Co-operation from the home is very necessary if the pupil's knowledge is to be lasting. In the first 3 or 4 grades in some schools, it is suggested that pictures of good lunches with simple printed headings be colored and taken home by the children. In the higher grades letters could be written home by the pupils telling of a good school lunch and what was available at their school; picture books of good school lunch foods could be made to be taken home. Thus parents are given something graphic to let them know what can be put in the school lunch box or bought at school to provide a nutritious noon meal.

Students, parents, teachers, nurse and nutritionist, and local organizations in a community may coordinate their efforts towards the goal of an adequate noonday meal for every school child. The student with the cooperation of the school superintendent and the help of the nurse, a local organization of parents and the nutritionist can make a survey of the school lunch. The home economics and art teachers and the nutritionist may give a school lunch food demonstration and exhibit for the parents and pupils. School physician, school nurse, physical education teacher, nutritionists, and pupils may write articles for the town and school newspapers on healthful foods and school activities. Printing and commercial classes at the school may print and type weekly and daily menus and menus for holidays. The sewing classes may make curtains for the lunchroom and opportunity classes may make table decorations. Proper emphasis is placed on the school lunch as an essential part of the health teaching and health protection in the schools.

The school lunchroom should be used as the vehicle to make the teachings of other departments regarding healthful foods more effective. In science, arithmetic, geography, physical education, art classes, or in practically every subject taught in the schools, there can be thought given to nutritious food and the healthy child. Arithmetic uses quarts of milk for different size families and cans of tomatoes at such and such a price for problems in addition, percentage, discount, etc. Art classes use food subjects for drawings, geography dwells on sources of food supplies. English composition may tell the story of citrus fruits and scurvy. The lunchroom is the proving ground for such teaching in the classrooms. Definite results can be expected from improved lunches—better growth and development, fewer absences from school, increased interest in work, knowledge of choosing good foods at low cost and learning of certain social values.

The State Department of Health has found that the nutritionist can further help those engaged in school lunchroom work by conducting refresher conferences. For the past 3 years such a conference has been held under the joint auspices of the Departments of Health and Education at Fitchburg State Teachers College. Ninety trained and untrained school lunch managers have attended during that time. An interesting contribution of the mangers at the 1937 conference was their material on food costs and selling price. Some reported selling milk, salads, and the main dish with a vegetable at near cost to help meet the needs of the children. Some sell milk, fruit, and vegetables below cost to encourage sales of protective foods. Desserts, candy, potato chips and other resale foods were selling at higher cost to make them less desirable, or were entirely removed from the menu. Some managers said that in their schools candy was being sold by the student government to finance a trip to Washington or to buy new uniforms for the band or new equipment for the football team. Such procedure is undesirable since it attracts money that otherwise might be spent for protective foods such as milk or fruit and also hinders health teaching in the classrooms. The nutritionist has suggested in some instances that the candy be sold only during the last ten minutes of the lunch period and that fruit or wholesome cookies be substituted when possible.

Are these suggestions feasible? How can such a poor practice be eliminated? Those responsible for the noon meal at school have found helpful the "Measuring Stick for a Good School Lunch," "Recipes and Supplement for Quantity Cookery," "Autumn, Winter and Spring Menus," "Food for the School Child," "Suggested Records and Accounts," "Food Quantities for School Lunches," "Kitchen Handbook," "Best Sellers," "Food Cost Work Sheet," "Penny Savers," "Bargain Specials," "Massachusetts Managers Say" and "Typical School Cafeteria Menus" available from the Department of Health. They contain many of the suggestions and methods of those attending these school lunch refresher conferences.

In addition to summer refresher conferences, local meetings in the counties are being planned. Here those in school lunch work will have the additional advantage of discussion with others meeting similar situations in the same locality—food specifications, menu planning in relation to the childs needs, principles of cookery, sales appeal, nutrition education, the use of the lunchroom as a practical problem with home economics classes, etc. Good training is as important as native ability. In the end it is difficult to judge by results which is more important.

Some one with special training such as a home economics teacher should supervise the school lunch wherever possible. Whether the manager be a home economics teacher or not, it is advisable for her to have an advisory committee made up of the principal of the school, a member of the home economics department, a mother and a member of the student government. This results in a more representative and broader point of view on the part of the manager and better understanding and cooperation between the groups represented. The home economics advisor especially has the opportunity here to influence the quality and kind of food served. It is so hard to feed the child adequately without a good noonday meal.

With the impetus given to promotion of better school lunches by this intensifying of the program of the Division of Child Hygiene made possible under Social Security, the Commonwealth is moving steadily forward towards its goal, "For every child in Massachusetts three good meals a day. For every school child the additional assurance of an adequate noonday meal at school or at home."

NEW ACTIVITIES OF THE DIVISION OF TUBERCULOSIS
By Alton S. Pope, M.D.

Director, Division of Tuberculosis
Massachusetts Department of Public Health

Hospitalization of Poliomyelitis at Lakeville State Sanatorium:

Under Chapter 346 of the Acts of 1936 provision has been made for the admission of persons crippled by poliomyelitis to the Lakeville State Sanatorium. This act makes it possible for persons of limited means suffering from the after-effects of poliomyelitis to obtain the type of continued treatment often necessary for the maximum degree of recovery possible from their paralysis. The Act provides that the Department of Public Health may admit to the Lakeville State Sanatorium persons crippled by poliomyelitis; provided, that no person shall be admitted who has not been a resident of the Commonwealth for at least twelve months preceding the date of his application for admission, and that preference shall be given to citizens of the Commonwealth. The charges for those persons able to pay are seven dollars per week. For those persons unable to pay for their care, the charges are met by the local board of public welfare in the city or town where the person has a legal settlement.

At Lakeville adequate facilities are available for care and treatment of poliomyelitis. The medical staff has been augmented by the addition of two visiting orthopedic surgeons. Four physiotherapists have been added to the staff, offering such forms of treatment as baking, massage, muscle training and graduated exercises. Two Hubbard tubs have been added to the equipment, offering the benefit of hydrotherapy in the treatment of poliomyelitis. The brace shop is equipped to make such forms of braces as may be necessary.

Since the time when the first patient with poliomyelitis was admitted on August 3, 1936 to the end of November 1937, there have been eighty cases of poliomyelitis admitted to the Sanatorium. Forty-seven patients have been discharged during the period, and of this number thirty-five showed improvement on discharge, a percentage of 74.5. During the year 1937 there were thirty-eight corrective orthopedic operations performed on these patients:

Conditions for Admission:
1. Patient must have a bona fide residence of at least one year in Massachusetts previous to date of application.
2. Preference is given to citizens of the Commonwealth.
3. All ages accepted.

Procedure for Admission:
Application blanks, obtainable from the local board of health or from the Department of Public Health, 546 State House, Boston, are to be filled out by a licensed physician, and returned to the Department at the above address.

Cancer-Tuberculosis Unit at Westfield:

Under provision of Chapter 337 of the Acts of 1936 the new Cancer-Tuberculosis Unit of the Westfield State Sanatorium was opened for the admission of patients on November 29, 1937. This modern type of hospital building, which provides fifty beds for the treatment of cancer and 144 beds for patients with pulmonary tuberculosis, brings to western Massachusetts the same special facilities for the treatment of those two diseases previously provided in the eastern part of the State.

The Cancer Section includes a complete surgical unit with two operating rooms, a radiological unit with diagnostic and deep therapy apparatus and radium needles, and an out-patient department. Medical service is provided through a combined resident and visiting staff, as at the Pondville Cancer Hospital, with visiting men drawn from the various fields of cancer therapy. The Tuberculosis Section provides all facilities for the diagnosis and modern treatment of that disease, including thoracic surgery, and all operative procedures will be carried out at the sanatorium.

The combination of the treatment of tuberculosis and cancer in the same building embodies a new idea in hospital practice, but one wholly practical with the present type of construction. By the joint use of much of the surgical and x-ray equipment, economies are effected in operating costs, and as tuberculosis continues to decline, and as the demand for hospitalization of cancer increases, the proportion of patients with each condition can be shifted to meet the current needs.

Conditions for Admission to the Cancer Unit:
1. The Massachusetts statutes provide that only persons who have lived two out of the past three years in the State are eligible for admission.
2. Preference is given to persons living in the western part of the State.
3. Patients will be accepted for treatment of any type of malignant tumor, and preference will be given to cases in an operable stage of the disease.

Procedure for Admission to the Cancer Unit:
Patients will be admitted only on signed application by a registered physician, upon a form obtainable from the Hospital, the Department of Public Health, 546 State House, Boston, local boards of public health, or overseers of public welfare. Applications properly filled out should be sent to Westfield State Sanatorium, Dr. Roy Morgan, Superintendent, Westfield, Massachusetts. The charge to the patient will be $10.50 per week to those able to pay, and indigent patients may be admitted at the expense of the board of public welfare of the city or town of legal settlement. Indigent cases without settlement will be accepted at the expense of the Department of Public Health. Patients will be examined in the Cancer Out-Patient Department only upon written request of a licensed physician, and report will be made only to him.

Conditions for Admission to the Tuberculosis Unit:
1. By statute the patient must have resided in the Commonwealth at least six months prior to the date of the application.
2. Adult patients with pulmonary tuberculosis from all cities and towns of Hampden County, except Springfield, will be admitted to Westfield under contract of the County Tuberculosis Hospital District with the State Department of Public Health.

Tuberculosis patients from other towns in western Massachusetts may be admitted with the approval of the local board of health.

Procedure for Admission to the Tuberculosis Unit:

Application on blank obtainable from local board of health, or from the Department of Public Health, 546 State House, Boston, Massachusetts, should be made out and signed by attending physician and forwarded to the Department at the above address. The charge for patients able to pay for their care is $7.00 per week, and the Department will arrange for approval of the local board of health as to financial responsibility for those unable to pay.

Hospitalization of Chronic Rheumatism:

Under the provisions of Chapter 393 of the Acts of 1937 arrangements have been made by the Department of Public Health with the Massachusetts General Hospital for the hospitalization of patients with chronic rheumatism for the purpose of diagnosis and treatment of the disease. As the Act provides for the care and treatment of not more than twenty-five patients at any one time, and further that no person shall be hospitalized for a period exceeding six months, preference will be given in the selection of cases to those patients whose condition requires further study, and to whom some form of therapy can be offered. Preference will also be given to indigent persons, and no patient will be admitted for treatment who has not regularly resided in the Commonwealth at least two out of the preceding three years.

Applications for admission must be made by a licensed physician, upon forms provided by the Department of Public Health, and returned to the Department at Room 546, State House, Boston, Massachusetts.

Upon discharge of the patient a written summary of the findings in the case, with diagnosis and recommendations for further care, will be sent to the physician who signed the application for the patient's admission.

NEW ACTIVITIES IN THE ENGINEERING DIVISION

BY ARTHUR D. WESTON, C.E.

Director, Division of Sanitary Engineering
Massachusetts Department of Public Health

The only new activities which have been assigned to the Engineering Division in the last two years are those relating to the program financed by the Surgeon General's funds under the National Security Act and those in connection with the construction of water works and other sanitary works at State Institutions.

Under our present General Laws the Engineering Division is concerned with a variety of subjects in its work bearing on environmental control which include matters of water supply, sewerage and sewage disposal, investigation of shellfish areas, garbage disposal, swimming pools, special investigations, construction activities at institutions and mosquito control, plumbing regulations, and in addition is frequently called upon to supply data upon inquiry from the officials of other Departments in the State and from other states.

Our new work under the Social Security Act provides for environmental control study in rural districts with particular reference to water supplies and sewage and waste disposal; camp, roadside stand and public water supply examinations and study of cross connections inside hotels, industrial plants and public buildings.

The work in connection with State Institutions includes not only studies with preparation of plans and estimates of cost for providing adequate water supply systems, sewerage and sewage disposal at all State Institutions but also in connection with our own State Institutions a study for fire protection and the installation of fire protection equipment.

Certain of the work carried out at the Lawrence Experiment Station during the past year may be of interest, so a recent news letter follows concerning this work:

Commonwealth of Massachusetts
Department of Public Health
Division of Sanitary Engineering

Summary of experimental work carried on during 1937 at the Lawrence Experiment Station and the Water and Sewage Laboratories of the Department of Public Health, Commonwealth of Massachusetts.

Three samples of rust eradicators examined showed that two consisted chiefly of sodium silicate and the other of a solution containing hydrochloric acid to which had been added an organic inhibitor.

Analyses showed that rubber in several waste products from a rubber factory discharged into a municipal sewerage system resulted in deposits on the stones of the trickling filters.

A series of bacterial experiments made to determine the purifying properties of certain samples of metaphoric rock (reported by the United States Bureau of Agriculture as Amphibolite) indicated that the stones possessed no power to purify water.

A microscopical analysis of a sample of scum collected from the surface of a municipal water filter indicated it to be an algal growth and not deposits of paper pulp as suggested.

Experiments showed that, with the addition of the same amount of copper sulphate in each instance, the amount of copper in solution and in suspension was much less for brackish and salt water than for fresh water.

Experiments with the de-aeration of water by means of a partial vacuum showed that satisfactory de-aeration cannot be obtained by means of a partial vacuum alone but that a partial vacuum with agitation of the water is more efficient in removing dissolved oxygen. It was found that a partial vacuum alone was moderately successful in removing carbonic acid from the water but that a partial vacuum plus agitation of the water was more effective.

Extended experiments are being made to show the effect of galvanic action when dissimilar pipes are brought together. Nine different kinds of service pipe in common use today, using two pipes at a time (making 36 combinations in all) immersed in a ground water before and after corrosive treatment and in a surface water before and after treatment, are being used. The results of this experiment should answer some questions concerning the subject of galvanism through the use of an admixture of metals in the make-up of house plumbing and on other related subjects.

Tests made of the effect of sewages overflowing into the Aberjona River in Woburn showed that the greatest removal of suspended solids and organic matter occurred during the first half hour.

Experiments in treating a newly cleaned water main in a municipality with sodium silicate were not successful. Further work in an attempt to coat the pipe with a deposit of calcium carbonate is still in progress.

Tests on a tannery sludge showed that this sludge alone would not digest with evolution of gas, as is the case with domestic sewage sludge.

Experiments with digester liquors from a bleachery show that after carbonating with flue gas bacterial growth becomes active and that filtration through crushed stone at a rate of one million gallons per acre daily is practicable.

Studies made of the methods of operating sand sewage filters and of the comparative efficiencies of sand filters of different depths showed that intermittent sand filters should be dosed regularly each day rather than to add twice the dose every second day or three times the amount each third day. A depth of three feet of sand seems to be sufficient.

A study of the effect on sewage disposal of very high rates of operation of trickling filters, using two crushed stone filters and one filter of perforated tile, showed that there is a tendency for the stone filters to clog due to failure to unload as a filter operated at a normal rate does. The effluent is very turbid and the purification considerably less than that from filters operated at conventional rates.

Analyses of air from the interior of one of the crushed stone high rate trickling filters showed that during normal operation the air contained about 15 percent oxygen. As soon as clogging became noticeable, the percentage dropped to a few tenths of a per cent but never to zero.

Ferric sulphate in amounts insufficient to cause coagulation was added to the sewage applied to a trickling filter. Passage through the filter caused the iron to coagulate. The results show that the effluent is improved, but there is a tendency for the precipitated iron to clog the filter.

Experiments to determine the effect of the addition of ground garbage to two small house septic tanks and an Imhoff tank in amounts equal to the suspended solids in the sewage, on the dry basis, showed that garbage was successfully disposed of in these tanks without detrimental results.

Filtration of a river water having a B coli index of 6200 per 100 cc of water, turbidity 7 and color 39 showed that alum is the best coagulant, and a pH of around 5.5 is the optimum. The bacterial results of the effluent of a rapid sand filter have averaged better than those from the municipal slow sand filters. The secondary slow sand filters have given little bacterial purification. A circular filter divided into three sectors has been operated as a roughing filter for the river water. Various sizes of sand and pebbles have been used in the different sectors. The results have been disappointing. In order to maintain a high rate, such coarse material had to be used that little purification was obtained.

More detailed information about these studies may be obtained by writing

                        Arthur D. Weston, Chief Engineer
                        Department of Public Health
                        511A State House, Boston, Mass.

MATERNAL DEATHS IN MASSACHUSETTS

Int. List. No.		1932		1933		1934		1935*		1936*	
	Total Maternal Deaths	369		389		317		325		270	
140, 145	Puerperal Septicemia (inc. Abortion with septic conditions)	92	% 26	103	% 26	93	% 29	104	% 32	80	% 30
141, 144	Puerperal hemorrhage and Abortion without mention of septic conditions (including hemorrhages)	67	18	72	19	58	18	57	18	52	19
146, 147	Toxemias of pregnancy (incl. Puerperal albuminuria and eclampsia)	70	19	67	17	59	19	56	17	38	14
148	Puerperal phlegmasia alba dolens, embolus, sudden death (not specified as septic)	64	17	55	14	53	17	47	14	35	13
142, 143, 149, 150	Others	72	20	92	24	54	17	61	19	65	24

MATERNAL AND INFANT MORTALITY RATES

	1932	1933	1934	1935*	1936*
Maternal mortality rate per 1,000 live births	5.4	6.1	5.0	5.2	4.4
Infant mortality rate per 1,000 live births	53.1	51.9	49.2	48.3	46.6

* Allocated to place of residence of deceased.

News Note

From: *Russell Sage Foundation*, Department of Social Work Interpretation, 130 East 22nd St., New York, N. Y.

A steadily mounting interest on the part of health workers in interpretation and health education finds practical expression in the announcement of a study of current positions in interpretation and public relations in health and social agencies in the United States. Undertaken at the request of the Social Work Publicity Council, the study will be carried on by the Department of Social Work Interpretation of the Russell Sage Foundation. Both public and private agencies will be included.

The present study will attempt to learn the number of positions in interpretation and public relations and their distribution geographically and by fields of work; the responsibilities and duties of workers; the preparation required and the salaries paid.

The first step in the survey will be a census of positions. Location of the positions to be studied is already under way through a country-wide census to be made by means of a simple questionnaire, distributed with the cooperation of a group of national agencies whose affiliated membership includes 10,000 local organizations.

An examination of the various positions revealed by this preliminary inquiry will form the second section of the study. This will consist of an intensive analysis of training and experience in relation to salary range, agency program requirements and other factors affecting the status of the individual worker in the particular job.

Other units will be an appraisal of community needs for interpretation and public relations services and an evaluation of available training opportunities in relation to present and future personnel requirements. This final section will include a listing of available courses in schools of public health and schools of social work and in other professional schools by means of which the worker may secure the background knowledge and technical skills necessary to equip him for a high standard of performance.

The study as a whole will be continued throughout 1938, but it is hoped that a preliminary report of the census of positions can be presented in June at the annual business meeting of the Social Work Publicity Council in Seattle.

Book Note

MODERN WAYS WITH BABIES by Elizabeth Hurlock, Ph.D. $2.50. 347 pp. Philadelphia. J. B. Lippincott Company.

This book ought to "add to the pleasure of being a parent," as the author hopes. The physical growth of the baby is outlined briefly, and learning to sleep, eat, walk, and talk, are each given a chapter and gone into in sufficient and interesting detail. Building desirable habits is covered in a clear, concise manner. Excellent suggestions are given as regards undesirable habits such as thumb sucking, enuresis, etc.

A very practical book for the young mother dealing with problems of child development from infancy to three years. These problems are taken up in the order in which they would naturally appear chronologically in the development of the child. The language is simple, direct and explicit. There are sufficient case illustrations to drive the points home.

The young mother will find great help in this book as it is both practical and full of sensible suggestions which are psychologically sound. The correct attitude of the parent toward habit training and the emotional development of the child is made very clear. Many charts, tables, rules, and suggestions are given.

One of the best chapters perhaps is the one on "Baby Emotions" including curiosity which seems to come under this category in infancy. If the ten rules given in this connection were always adhered to, we would see very few nervous and fearful children. The remainder of the book is devoted largely to a discussion of the baby's intellectual growth, his discipline and the development of his personality.

Editorial Comment

The Social Security Grant, through the United States Children's Bureau, has enabled the Division of Child Hygiene to increase its service within the various fields, following closely the former program. This has been accomplished by increase in personnel in all of the specialties.

The new activities have been described in the preceding text. This program covers the fields of maternity, infancy, preschool, school, and adolescent to the age of twenty-one.

REPORT OF DIVISION OF FOOD AND DRUGS

(As required by General Laws, Chapter 111, Section 25.)

During the months of October, November and December 1937, samples were collected in 167 cities and towns.

There were 1,136 samples of milk examined, of which 50 were below standard, from 5 samples the cream had been in part removed, and 4 samples contained added water. There were 1,922 bacteriological examinations made of milk, 1,671 of which complied with the requirements. There were 38 bacteriological examinations made of cream, 4 of which did not comply with the requirements; 86 bacteriological examinations of ice cream, 10 of which did not comply with the requirements; 7 bacteriological examinations of sherbet, all of which complied with the requirements; 1 bacteriological examination of canned crab meat, 1 bacteriological examination of sardines, 2 bacteriological examinations of dog food, all of which complied with the requirements; and 19 bacteriological examinations of mattress fillings, 5 of which did not comply with the requirements.

There were 493 samples of food examined, 72 of which were adulterated. These consisted of 8 samples of butter, 4 of which were rancid, and 4 were below the legal standard in milk fat; 1 sample of olive oil which contained cottonseed oil; 1 sample of infant's food which was rancid; 13 samples of soft drink wash water which were deficient in caustic alkali; 9 samples of hamburg steak, 5 of which were decomposed and 1 sample also contained a compound of sulphur dioxide not so labeled, 2 samples contained sodium sulphite in excess of one tenth of one per cent, and 2 samples contained a compound of sulphur dioxide not so labeled; 8 samples of sausage, 5 of which were decomposed, 2 contained a compound of sulphur dioxide not so labeled, and 1 sample contained starch in excess of 2 per cent; 1 sample of lamb patties which were decomposed; 1 dressed fowl which contained abnormal whitish nodules; 1 sample of dried split peas which contained a filthy material; 5 samples of cider, 4 of which contained sodium benzoate and were not so labeled, and 1 sample was misbranded in that it was not cider; 1 sample of heavy cream which was low in fat for this grade; 3 samples of eggs, all of which were decomposed; 2 samples of apples which contained arsenic spray; 3 samples of sweet relish which contained benzoic acid and were not so labeled; and 15 samples of mattress filling, 12 of which contained secondhand material, 1 was oily mill waste, 1 contained wool, cotton and linen, and 1 sample which was alleged to be wool batting but contained 80.9% wool and 19.1% cellulose fibers.

There were 29 samples of drugs examined, of which 6 were adulterated. These consisted of 5 samples of carbolic acid solution, and 1 sample of ephedrine inhalant, all of which did not conform to the professed standard under which they were sold.

The police departments submitted 81 samples of liquor for examination. The police departments also submitted 2 samples to be analyzed for poisons or drugs, 1 of which contained heroin, and the other sample contained cannabis. There was 1 sample, the stomach of a fox, submitted by the Fish and Game Division of Leominster, for examination, in which sample there was no poison detected.

There were inspected 297 plants operated for the pasteurization of milk; 13 soft drink plants; 158 ice cream plants; 192 bakeries; 442 restaurants; 206 mattress establishments; and 351 establishments visited relative to the issuing of licenses pertaining to wood alcohol and preparations containing over 3% of the same.

There were 65 hearings held pertaining to violations of the laws.

There were 35 convictions for violations of the law, $695 in fines being imposed.

Charles L. Woodland of Watertown; and Parker Gates of Leominster, were convicted for violations of the milk laws.

Louis J. Boucher of Worcester; Ernest Harnisch of Methuen: Abraham Brox, 2 cases, of Dracut; Manuel Arruda of Fall River; John Kydd of Lowell; and Arthur Rabinovitz, 2 cases, and Jennie Schwartz of Chelsea, were convicted for violations of the pasteurization law and regulations.

Thomas Seymour of Lynn was convicted for violations of the milk grading regulations.

Abraham White of Chelsea; The Massachusetts Mohican Company of Allston; Louis Ward of Brookline; Ted Posovsky and Samuel Grossman of Athol; and Ada Ramboli of Everett, were all convicted for violations of the food laws. Louis Ward of Brookline appealed his case.

Patrick Connolly of Boston was convicted for violation of the sanitary food law.

Ada Ramboli of Everett was convicted for misbranding.

Simon Millman of Roxbury was convicted for violation of the law and regulations relative to the manufacture and bottling of carbonated non-alcoholic beverages.

Chester Furniture Company, Benjamin London, and Saul Schlager of Malden; General Mattress Company, Regal Bedding Company, and Harry Tulchin of Fall River; Pioneer Chair Company, Incorporated, Leonard Furniture Company, and Jacob Pollack of Boston; William Goldberg of Roxbury; Samuel Possick of Somerville; Roxbury Mattress Company, Incorporated, and Isaac Schneider of Dorchester; and Samuel Solomon of Medford, were all convicted for violations of the mattress law. Harry Tulchin of Fall River; Pioneer Chair Company, Incorporated, of Boston; and Roxbury Mattress Company, Incorporated, of Dorchester, appealed their cases.

In accordance with Section 25, Chapter 111 of the General Laws, the following is the list of articles of adulterated food collected in original packages from manufacturers, wholesalers, or producers:

One sample of heavy cream which was low in fat for this grade was obtained from Dawn Dairy Products of Athol.

One sample of olive oil which contained cottonseed oil was obtained from Ellen Kavazis of Haverhill.

Hamburg steak which was decomposed was obtained as follows: One sample each, from The Beef Shop of Athol; Jose R. Junior of Lowell; and Abraham Miller of New Bedford.

Hamburg steak which contained a compound of sulphur dioxide not so labeled was obtained as follows:

One sample each, from Colonial Super Market of Waltham; and Farmers Exchange Market of Norwood.

One sample of hamburg steak which contained sodium sulphite in excess of one tenth of one per cent was obtained from Baron's Market of Cambridge.

Sausage which was decomposed was obtained as follows:

One sample each, from Mohican Market, Incorporated and Arthur Corey of Lawrence; Samuel Grossman of Athol; William Karp of Lowell; and August and Charles Kisiel of Ware.

Sausage which contained a compound of sulphur dioxide not so labeled was obtained as follows:

One sample each from Colonial Super Market of Waltham; and Edmund Morini of South Norwood.

One sample of sausage which contained starch in excess of 2 per cent was obtained from Farmers Exchange Market of Norwood.

Cider which contained sodium benzoate and not so labeled was obtained as follows:

One sample each, from H. McCue of Winchester; Ryders Stock Farm, Incorporated, of Lexington; and The Great Atlantic & Pacific Tea Company of Concord.

One sample of cider which was misbranded in that it was not cider was obtained from Harold Keizer of Concord.

One sample of butter which was rancid was obtained from National D Stores Company of Boston.

There were 35 confiscations, consisting of 40 pounds of decomposed butter; 4 pounds of sour milk cheese; 4 pounds of decomposed beef; 2 pounds of decomposed beef; 8 pounds of decomposed beef; 4 pounds of decomposed beef; 2 pounds of decomposed beef; 1 pound of decomposed hamburg steak; ½ pound of decomposed hamburg steak; 55 pounds of decomposed hamburg steak; 40 pounds of sour hamburg steak; 8 pounds of decomposed hamburg steak; 2 pounds of decomposed steak; ¼ pound of decomposed steak; 3 pounds of decomposed steak; ½ pound of decomposed pork; 2 pounds of decomposed pork chops; ½ pound of decomposed ham; 2 pounds of decomposed veal; ½ pound of mouldy frankforts; 2 pounds of mouldy frankforts; 3 pounds of decomposed frankforts; ½ pound of decomposed frankforts; 10 pounds of decomposed sausage meat; 28 pounds of putrid sausage meat; 1 pound of decomposed salami; 52 pounds of rancid poultry; 75 pounds of decomposed turkeys; 1375 pounds of decomposed grey sole; 1800 pounds of decomposed grey sole; 531 pounds of decomposed halibut; 5 pounds of decomposed tomatoes; 4 quarts of decomposed blueberries; ½ dozen of stale doughnuts; and ½ loaf of mouldy bread.

The licensed cold storage warehouses reported the following amounts of food placed in storage during September, 1937:—215,850 dozens of case eggs; 682,099 pounds of broken out eggs; 660,374 pounds of butter; 1,336,233 pounds of poultry; 2,669,188 pounds of fresh meat and fresh meat products; and 11,094,794 pounds of fresh food fish.

There was on hand October 1, 1937:—3,561,060 dozens of case eggs; 4,057,800 pounds of broken out eggs; 6,316,155 pounds of butter; 2,893,739 pounds of poultry; 2,918,081 pounds of fresh meat and fresh meat products; and 25,057,364 pounds of fresh food fish.

The licensed cold storage warehouses reported the following amounts of food placed in storage during October, 1937:—244,320 dozens of case eggs; 406,970 pounds of broken out eggs; 499,816 pounds of butter; 1,768,121 pounds of poultry; 2,710,201 pounds of fresh meat and fresh meat products; and 9,885,914 pounds of fresh food fish.

There was on hand November 1, 1937:—2,142,630 dozens of case eggs; 3,438,006 pounds of broken out eggs; 4,362,285 pounds of butter; 3,098,440 pounds of poultry; 2,521,224 pounds of fresh meat and fresh meat products; and 24,790,718 pounds of fresh food fish.

The licensed cold storage warehouses reported the following amounts of food placed in storage during November, 1937:—327,840 dozens of case eggs; 500,694 pounds of broken out eggs; 452,499 pounds of butter; 3,446,320 pounds of poultry; 2,873,984 pounds of fresh meat and fresh meat products; and 10,106,636 pounds of fresh food fish.

There was on hand December 1, 1937:—1,052,850 dozens of case eggs; 3,016,755 pounds of broken out eggs; 2,589,801 pounds of butter; 5,248,277 pounds of poultry; 2,970,302 pounds of fresh meat and fresh meat products; and 26,221,369 pounds of fresh food fish.

MASSACHUSETTS DEPARTMENT OF PUBLIC HEALTH

Commissioner of Public Health, HENRY D. CHADWICK, M.D.

Public Health Council

HENRY D. CHADWICK, M.D., *Chairman*

GEORGE D. DALTON, M.D. RICHARD M. SMITH, M.D.
FRANCIS H. LALLY, M.D. RICHARD P. STRONG, M.D.
CHARLES F. LYNCH, M.D. JAMES L. TIGHE

Secretary, FLORENCE L. WALL

Division of Administration . . Under direction of Commissioner
Division of Sanitary Engineering . Director and Chief Engineer,
    ARTHUR D. WESTON, C.E.
Division of Communicable Diseases Director, ROY F. FEEMSTER, M.D.
Division of Biologic Laboratories . Director and Pathologist,
    ELLIOTT S. ROBINSON, M.D.
Division of Food and Drugs . . Director and Analyst,
    HERMANN C. LYTHGOE, S.B.
Division of Child Hygiene . . Director, M. LUISE DIEZ, M.D.
Division of Tuberculosis . . . Director, ALTON S. POPE, M.D.
Division of Adult Hygiene . . Director,
    HERBERT L. LOMBARD, M.D.
Division of Genitoinfectious Diseases Director, NELS A. NELSON, M.D.

State District Health Officers

The Southeastern District . . RICHARD P. MACKNIGHT, M.D., New Bedford
The South Metropolitan District . HENRY M. DE WOLFE, M.D., Braintree
The North Metropolitan District . CHARLES E. GILL, M.D., Boston
The Northeastern District . . ROBERT E. ARCHIBALD, M.D., Melrose
The Worcester County District . OSCAR A. DUDLEY, M.D., Worcester
The Connecticut Valley District . JOHN J. POUTAS, M.D., Westfield
The Franklin County District . . WALTER W. LEE, M.D., Greenfield
The Berkshire County District . HAROLD W. STEVENS, M.D., Great Barrington.

PUBLICATION OF THIS DOCUMENT APPROVED BY THE COMMISSION ON ADMINISTRATION AND FINANCE
6M. 4-'38. Order 3594.

THE COMMONHEALTH

Volume 25   Apr.-May-June
No. 2   1938

THE HYGIENE OF HOUSING

MASSACHUSETTS
DEPARTMENT OF PUBLIC HEALTH

THE COMMONHEALTH

QUARTERLY BULLETIN OF THE MASSACHUSETTS DEPARTMENT OF
PUBLIC HEALTH

Sent Free to any Citizen of the State

Entered as second class matter at Boston Postoffice.

M. LUISE DIEZ, M.D., DIRECTOR OF DIVISION OF CHILD HYGIENE, EDITOR.
1 Beacon Street, Boston, Mass.

CONTENTS

	PAGE
Housing and Health, by Murray P. Horwood, Ph.D.	95
Housing, the Individual and the Nation, by Walter C. Voss	102
Health and the New Public Housing Program, by Allan A. Twichell	104
The Home and Tuberculosis, by Gerald G. Garcelon, M. D.	109
Housing Activities, State and Local, by Sidney T. Strickland	111
The Architect's Interest in Housing, by William Stanley Parker	115
The State Program as It Relates to Planning, by Elisabeth M. Herlihy	117
Federal Housing, by Howard P. Vermilya	121
The Development of Government Participation in Low Rental Housing, by Frederick J. Adams	123
Urban Housing, by Calvin H. Yuill	127
Economic Aspects of Housing, by Donald S. Tucker	133
Heating and Ventilation of Homes, by C. P. Yaglou	139
Lighting for Seeing, by M. Luckiesh and Frank K. Moss	143
Healthful Lighting, by William Firth Wells	145
Housing as the Architect Views It, by Eleanor Manning O'Connor	147
Play Places in the House for Children, by Susan M. Coffin, M.D.	150
Low Cost Decorating, by Donald Smith Feeley	152
Garden Minded, by Effie V. Jordan	155
Food Production as Part of the Home Plan, by William R. Cole	156
The Back Yard Improvement Contest in Ward 9, by Dorothy Hayward, R.N.	158
A Settlement Worker Looks at Housing, by S. Max Nelson	161
Home Hazards and Accidents, by Lewis E. MacBrayne	164
Heating, Ventilation, Lighting and Sanitation of Public Buildings, as Required by the State Department of Public Safety, by Eugene M. McSweeney	167
Environmental Sanitation	172
Health in the Economic Brackets, by Joseph W. Mountin, M. D. and Hazel O'Hara	176
Additional Material on Housing	184
Report of Division of Food and Drugs, January, February and March, 1938	184

HOUSING AND HEALTH
MURRAY P. HORWOOD, Ph.D.
*Professor of Bacteriology and Sanitation,
Massachusetts Institute of Technology**

Existence of Housing Problem Recognized

That a housing problem exists in the United States is generally recognized; that it has been a problem of long standing is attested to by the fact that numerous legislative and philanthropic efforts have been made in the past to abolish or ameliorate existing housing evils. The enactment of model housing laws in various cities, the adoption of building codes, the numerous investigations of slum conditions and the construction of model housing units for the poor testify to the existence of housing evils and the recognition of this fact by the socially minded citizens of every community.

Reasons for Development of Housing Evils

The development of housing evils in the United States is due to numerous causes which have been in operation during the rapid development of the country. The amazing increase in population in the United States since 1850 due to successive tidal waves of immigrants when existing housing facilities were woefully inadequate and new construction did not keep pace with the demand, resulted in the development of large and congested urban areas and in a housing situation that grew worse rather than better. Numerous other factors aggravated the problem, such as the lack of cheap and adequate facilities for transporting people to and from their work; the lack of corrective legislation; the lack of city and town planning during the period of most active growth in the United States; and the greed of landlords who transformed one-family houses into three- or four-family dwellings. Furthermore, the herd instinct of the newly arrived immigrant, ignorant of our language and our ways, and hungry for a word of friendship and encouragement contributed to the over-population of slum areas. The poverty of those newly arrived and the desire of those already here to get on financially made it impossible for the poor to afford more desirable housing facilities and stimulated the miserly to skimp on rent and to save money by taking in lodgers. But even where the housing facilities were adequate and satisfactory, the ignorance of the occupants frequently led to gross and serious abuses which transformed desirable facilities into offensive property.

Housing Evils not Limited to Congested Cities

But the development of housing evils was not limited to the congested cities on the Atlantic seaboard. The lack of vision and the rapid expansion of the nation were responsible for the creation of incredible housing conditions on the prairies, on cotton plantations and in the mountains; in mining communities, oil fields, mill towns, farming regions and other places where people congregated and where fresh air, sunshine and space were abundant.

Better Housing, a Problem of National Concern

Since the hectic development of a nation, the United States has come of age. With the advent of the World War, the tidal flow of immigration to the United States ceased and this condition was made permanent by the adoption of legislation restricting further immigration to our shores. The period of assimilation has begun in earnest. With improvement in the standard of living came the realization that a large portion of the population is either inadequately or poorly housed. Socially minded citizens demanded the elimination of slum areas and the occurrence of a serious depression was utilized as an opportunity to provide work for thousands who were

---
* Contribution No. 122 from the Department of Biology and Public Health, Massachusetts Institute of Technology, Cambridge, Mass.

unemployed by erecting new dwellings to replace those in which serious evils prevailed.

Housing has now developed into a problem of national proportions. In 1931, President Hoover assembled a White House Conference on Home Building and Home Ownership in Washington in order to stimulate the construction of new homes, and by so doing to provide work for the unemployed and more satisfactory housing facilities for the people in the low income groups. In 1933, the Roosevelt administration took office and the problem of housing was attacked with increased vigor for the same reasons. The Public Works Administration has made it possible to replace certain slum areas with low rent houses of high quality and decency. The Resettlement Administration has dealt with the development of rural-industrial communities beyond metropolitan limits. The Farm Credit Administration, the Federal Home Loan Bank Board and the Reconstruction Finance Corporation have made loans in order to stimulate the construction of new houses; and the Federal Housing Administration has stimulated private institutions to make loans for the construction of new houses through the partial insurance against losses.

Housing Has Not Been an Important Public Health Activity to Date

The amelioration and elimination of housing evils have not been vital activities in the public health program in this country to date. Sanitary inspectors employed by health departments have often investigated housing evils and have caused certain nuisances and intolerable conditions to be abated, but health departments have not engaged in preventive housing projects as they have in planning campaigns against infant mortality, tuberculosis and diphtheria. The British public health workers have been much more active in promoting good housing and in studying the relationship of housing to health. Governmental interest in housing people in the lower income groups in Europe has antedated the Federal interest in this subject in the United States as is evident from the extensive housing projects initiated in England, Germany, Austria, Czecho-Slovakia, Russia and other European countries. The European appreciation of housing as a public health problem is indicated further by the establishment of a Committee on Housing in the Health Section of the League of Nations.

Recently, however, there has been a growing interest in the United States in housing as a public health problem. The American Public Health Association has appointed a Committee on the Hygiene of Housing under the leadership of Professor C.-E. A. Winslow. At the 1937 convention of the American Public Health Association, held in New York last October, an entire session was devoted to the subject, "The Hygiene of Housing," and numerous excellent papers were presented. The A. P. H. A. Committee on the Hygiene of Housing has enlisted the financial and moral support of the Milbank Fund. At one of the big, general meetings held during the 1937 convention of the American Public Health Association, Dr. Livingston Farrand, President-Emeritus of Cornell University maintained that the two outstanding public health problems in the United States today were housing and nutrition; the former including the elimination of slums and low standard housing areas and their replacement with suitable housing facilities; and the latter dealing with the important problem of providing an adequate and satisfactory diet to every man, woman and child. This change of emphasis in the public health campaign is quite logical for the earlier years were devoted to the elimination and control of communicable diseases and the time is now ripe to emphasize those activities which will help to build up vital resistance and to provide a more definite and positive sense of the joy of living.

Public Health Progress in the United States

Before inquiring into the relationship of housing to health, it is desirable to determine the extent of public health progress which this country has experienced. Since 1880, the death rate has been diminished more than 50 per cent and the average expectancy of life at birth has been extended from 40 years to 61 years. Typhoid fever and diarrhea and enteritis under 2 have diminished almost to the vanishing point; diphtheria has also been greatly reduced; smallpox is under control in all communities where vaccination is practised; infant mortality has been diminished more than 75 per cent; tuberculosis has also been reduced 75 to 80 per cent; hookworm is controlled in the South; yellow fever is now non-existent in this country; and malaria is under better control. This remarkable progress in public health has occurred during a period of increasing congestion and when housing problems increased rather than diminished. Is it any wonder therefore that many experts in the field of public health really doubt whether there is an intimate relationship between housing and health?

The specific progress in saving human life that occurred from 1900 to 1935 is indicated in the following table. It demonstrates also what the mortality would have been among the white population of the United States in 1935 if the death rates of 1900 prevailed in that year.

TABLE I
Actual Deaths in the White Population of the United States in 1935 from all Causes and from Several Prominent Causes, Compared with the Corresponding Deaths that Would Have Occurred in that Year if the Mortality Rates by Age and Sex of 1900 Prevailed.*

Cause of Death	Deaths in 1935 Actual	Deaths in 1935 Expected on basis of mortality in 1900	Lives saved in 1935 by Improvement in Mortality Since 1900	Lives Lost in 1935 by Retrogression in Mortality Since 1900
All causes	1,207,359	1,975,761	768,402	
Tuberculosis, all forms	51,269	224,384	173,115	
Influenza and pneumonia	110,191	232,187	121,996	
Diarrhea and enteritis	17,018	125,448	108,430	
Principal communicable diseases of childhood	13,182	72,127	58,945	
Measles	3,435	12,590	9,155	
Scarlet fever	2,646	9,336	6,690	
Whooping cough	3,673	10,715	7,042	
Diphtheria	3,428	39,486	36,058	
Typhoid and paratyphoid fever	2,386	35,652	33,266	
Nephritis	89,240	115,239	25,999	
Cerebral hemorrhage and softening	85,732	102,535	16,803	
Puerperal state	10,018	14,504	4,486	
Organic heart disease	212,167	153,584		58,583
Cancer	129,124	86,103		43,021
Diabetes	26,606	14,301		12,305
External causes (excluding suicides)	94,851	84,688		10,163
All other causes	365,575	715,009	349,434	

* *Statistical Bulletin*, Metropolitan Life Insurance Company, November 1937, v. 18, No. 11, p. 3.

Relationship Between Housing and Health

The relationship between housing and health is not simple; it is complex. Horwood has demonstrated in his tuberculosis studies of Philadelphia, Boston, Cambridge and Holyoke that there is no correlation between tuberculosis mortality and poor housing. Other factors, particularly racial, are far more significant. The importance of the racial factor in tuberculosis mortality, in the mortality from diabetes and in infant mortality has also been demonstrated in various studies conducted in New York City. In 1927, Annabel M. T. Murray* studied the growth and nutrition of the slum child in relation to housing in Scotland, and by careful statistical methods came

* The Growth and Nutrition of the Slum Child in Relation to Housing. *Journal of Hygiene*, 1927, v. 26, pp. 198-203.

to the conclusion that "no consistent evidence is afforded by the present investigation that the weight and height of children observed under 5 years are related to their inhabiting one or two room houses." On the other hand. "the correlation for weight and height with maternal efficiency shows a closer relationship."

The reason why it is not simple to demonstrate a significant relationship between poor housing and health is because poor housing is often associated with poverty; with ignorance; with inadequate and unsatisfactory food; with scanty or ineffective medical and nursing service; with long hours of toil and hard labor; with hazardous employment; with cold, dampness and exposure; with unhygienic living and with various other factors that have real health significance. It is obviously exceedingly difficult to evaluate the health significance of these factors in order to determine the role of the housing factor per se. Hence any argument in favor of improved housing for those in the lower income groups cannot be made on the basis of lower morbidity and mortality rates. The most that can be said is that poor housing favors over-crowding, lowers the vital resistance, hinders morality and decency and in other indirect ways has an effect on the health of the occupants.

It is obviously impossible, however, to evaluate the significance of housing in terms of morbidity and mortality alone. There are many intangibles associated with the process of living that are recognized as worth while which cannot be evaluated in this way. The house is the environment of every individual from 8 to 24 hours every day. The house is the centre of family life and the family is the basis of organized society. Anything that fosters family life, that tends to make it more healthful, more attractive and more comfortable, gives it more stability; and a stable, contented people makes for a stable, contented society. Hence good housing is desirable from a social as well as a personal point of view.

But there are many factors associated with housing that have definite public health significance. Each house ought to be provided with an adequate and safe supply of running water conveniently located. Preferably, each house should also be provided with hot as well as cold running water. Each dwelling unit should also have a bathroom with indoor toilet facilities and with proper arrangements for sewage disposal. A suitable system for refuse collection and disposal should also be available as well as adequate facilities for storing refuse of all forms between collections. The house should be built on land that is well-drained in order to eliminate mosquito breeding places, as well as hazardous icy ponds in the winter and noisome pools in warmer weather. Damp basements and cellars would thus be avoided. Basement and cellar dwellings should be generally avoided anyway, but especially if they are damp as they undermine resistance and favor disease. Dwellings should be adequately protected against flies, mosquitoes and other insects as well as rodents, and should be free of these pests since they are associated with the transmission of certain diseases. Dark rooms should be avoided because of their undesirable psychological effect on the occupants, and because they favor accidents. Each room should have access to fresh air and sunlight and should be adequately ventilated. Overcrowding should be prohibited since overcrowding interferes with decency and privacy and because it favors the spread of diseases spread by intimate contact. Bedroom overcrowding, including the lodger evil, should likewise be subject to control. Lot overcrowding should also be prohibited, since it interferes with access to light and fresh air and with adequate play space, and because it favors overcrowding. The height of dwellings should be subject to regulation for similar reasons, and dwellings should not be permitted to be too close to each other in residential areas. Unpaved, filthy alleys should be eliminated and adequate attention must be directed to curbing excessive noise and obnoxious gases, odors, and smoke in the atmosphere. By suitable attention to the problem of construction and the building materials employed, much can be done to eliminate noise in apartments, to prevent odors from passing from one apartment to another, to prevent the infestation of the dwelling with crawling insects and rodents and to provide adequate access to fresh air and sunlight. Finally, the house should be as free as possible from fire hazards and from conditions that make for personal injury.

It is obvious, therefore, that while the house itself does not play a very significant role in regulating or controlling morbidity or mortality rates from communicable diseases and that while even a poor dwelling may be transformed into a hygienic environment with intelligence and care, healthful living, insofar as housing is concerned, demands certain sanitary equipment in the home and the immediate environment. However, since healthful living must not be interpreted merely as the absence of disease and the prevention of premature mortality, but must be associated with comfort, decency, morality, convenience and even joy in the daily routine, then housing takes on far reaching public health significance. Poor housing is no longer regarded as the cause of tuberculosis morbidity and mortality, or high infant death rates or high cancer death rates; but poor housing favors delinquency and crime; it fosters slovenliness and lack of civic pride; and it creates an unfavorable psychology which has manifold undesirable community reactions. When housing is associated with dampness, inadequate warmth, darkness, poor ventilation, accidents, vermin and rodent infestation, lack of sanitary conveniences and overcrowding, it does affect the health of the occupants directly both through the transmission of infection and through the debilitating effects of an unfavorable environment.

Housing Problem Aggravated by Serious Shortage

That a real housing shortage exists in the United States has been made evident by numerous surveys. This condition was brought to the attention of the country when on November 29, 1937, President Roosevelt in his address to Congress said:

"Housing construction has not kept pace with either the needs or growth of our population. From 1930 to 1937, inclusive, the average annual number of new dwelling units constructed in the United States was 180,000 as contrasted with an annual average of 800,000 in the seven years prior to 1930. In addition, much of our existing housing has seriously deteriorated, or has been demolished. It is estimated that an average of 600,000 to 800,000 dwelling units ought to be built annually over the next five years to overcome the accumulated shortage and to meet the normal growth in number of families. In other words, we could build over the next five years, 3 or 4 million housing units, which at a moderate estimate of $4,000 per unit, would mean spending from 12 to 16 billion dollars without creating a surplus of housing accommodations and consequently without impairing the value of existing housing that is fit for human occupancy."

Solution of Housing Problem Fundamentally an Economic Issue

There is no dispute, however, concerning the need and desirability of suitable housing facilities for all the people. Doubtless every civic minded individual is in favor of this general thesis. The recent emphasis on slum clearance is further evidence of this general, popular reaction. The real problem is fundamentally an economic one. Who is going to pay for decent housing conditions for the poor? The poor themselves are unable to afford the expense involved. Either they must be aided by government subsidy, as has been done in many European countries, or some means must be found, perhaps through mass production methods, to build houses within the means of the poor. A country that has been able to build and sell automobiles, radios, washing machines, vacuum cleaners and other domestic "necessities" to the extent accomplished here, may yet be able by similar manufacturing methods and by cheaper production costs of essential materials, to solve the problem of decent, satisfactory housing conditions for the poor at a cost within their limited means.

That day, however, is not immediately at hand. According to the U. S. Bureau of Internal Revenue, one-third of the working population earns less than $1,200 per year; one-third earns between $1,200 and $2,000; and one-third earns in excess of $2,000 per year. It is, therefore, impossible for a great many people to burden themselves with a debt of $4,000 to $6,000,—the cost of a single family dwelling for families of moderate circumstances.

In the National Health Inventory conducted by the United States Public Health Service in 1935 in eight American cities, 45 per cent of the families were receiving incomes of less than $1,000 per year; 65 per cent, less than $1,500 per year; and 82 per cent, less than $2,000 per year. This is true in spite of the fact that the standard of living in the United States is superior to that of any other country in the world. Since the annual income must provide not only decent housing, but likewise, adequate nutrition, sufficient clothing and proper medical care, it is obvious that a considerable portion of the population is still unable to provide those fundamental essentials of a satisfactory standard of living. Certainly it would be unwise to spend a disproportionate amount of the family income on shelter, thus curtailing the amount available for adequate nutrition, sufficient clothing and proper medical care. To do so, would jeopardize the public health more than existing housing evils are able to do.

If further evidence is necessary of the inability of large groups in the population either to pay large rentals or to own homes even of modest cost, it will be found in the results of the Real Property Inventory of the Boston City Planning Board conducted in 1934-1935. Of a total of 165,250 rented dwelling units in Boston that were studied, 25 per cent rented for less than $20 per month and 11 per cent for less than $15 per month. In the congested residential districts of the city, the proportion of dwelling units renting for less than $20 per month was much greater. In Charlestown, it was 64.3 per cent; in downtown Boston, 65.5 per cent; in the North End, 57.1 per cent; in East Boston, 48.8 per cent; in South Boston, 43.7 per cent; in the West End, 40.2 per cent; in Roxbury, 35.0 per cent; and in the South End, 31.1 per cent.

The Federal Housing Development in Cambridge, Massachusetts

One of the new housing developments of the Public Works Administration, originated as a slum clearance project, is New Towne Court in Cambridge, Mass. The project is almost ideal from the standpoint of planning, sanitation, convenience and comfort. The apartments are airy, light, sunny, well-ventilated and commodious. Each apartment is equipped with a gas stove and refrigerator, and the rent includes the normal use of gas for cooking and refrigeration, heat and continuous hot water. Special chutes, conveniently located, and leading to an incinerator, are provided for the prompt disposal of garbage and other small combustible refuse. There are community laundries, community ironing boards, indoor facilities for drying clothes, basement storage space, indoor play rooms for children, indoor social rooms for adults, outdoor play space for children, ramps for baby carriages and other conveniences. The apartments contain three, four and five rooms. Each apartment is provided with a bathroom containing a tub, lavatory and flush toilet. New Towne Court will accommodate 294 families. In order that these excellent housing facilities may be used only for families in the low income groups, great care is being exercised in the selection of tenants. Precautions are also being taken to prevent overcrowding, and the number of occupants in each apartment is carefully regulated. The apartments rent for approximately $7 per room per month. It is understood, however, that the cost of construction would normally call for a rental of $15 per room per month if the apartments were rented on a paying basis.

TABLE II
Summary of Some' Salient Economic Data Pertaining to New Towne Court in Cambridge, Mass.

Number of Rooms	Monthly Rent	Maximum Annual Income
3	$23.00	$1380
4	27.00	1620
5	30.80	1848

Some Housing Evils in the United States Today

There is ample evidence that the housing problem existing in the United States today is one of the first magnitude. Not only is there an acute shortage of desirable housing units for people in the low income groups, but the existence of large slum areas is confirmed by the large Federal projects directed as slum clearance. Further evidence has been made available by various recent surveys. The Real Property Inventory conducted by the U. S. Department of Commerce in 1933, included 64 medium and small sized cities and covered every state in the Union. This survey disclosed the lack of elementary sanitary housing facilities in many parts of the country. For example, 17 per cent of the housing units had more than one person per room; 8 per cent, had no running water; 19 per cent, had no inside private toilets; 26 per cent, had no private bathtub or shower; and 6 per cent, did not have electricity or gas for lighting. The situation is even worse under rural conditions as the study made by the Bureau of Home Economics of the U. S. Department of Agriculture in 1933-1934 showed.

Basic Principles of Healthful Housing Already Known

The basic principles of healthful housing have just been enumerated in a preliminary report on the subject by the Committee on the Hygiene of Housing of the American Public Health Association published in the American Journal of Public Health for March 1938. In all, 30 basic principles are enumerated covering the fundamental physiological and psychological needs of the body, as well as protection against contagion and accidents. In each case, the specific requirements are recorded as well as suggested methods of attainment. Since the fundamental requirements of healthful housing have already been broadly outlined earlier in this paper, the more detailed requirements can be ascertained by referring to the preliminary report of Professor Winslow's Committee.

The Solution of the Housing Problem, a Challenge and an Opportunity

Enough is known about the housing problem in the United States to warrant intelligent, public action aiming at its amelioration on a large scale, if not its ultimate solution. The problem is large. Its relationship to the public health is demonstrated even if it is impossible to evaluate it exactly in terms of morbidity, mortality and vital resistance. The requirements for decency, comfort, sanitation and safety are likewise reasonably well established. The importance of educating the population in the proper use of decent housing facilities is also recognized. There remains but the great obstacle of financing the tremendous amount of work required. The enactment of the Wagner-Steagall Bill and the establishment of a Federal Housing Authority will doubtless help. It is expected, too, that private capital assured of a limited return on the investment involved, will eventually make its very significant contribution to the solution of this gigantic social problem. Surely, a country that has conquered typhoid fever, smallpox, diphtheria, infant mortality and scarlet fever; and that has made such excellent progress against tuberculosis, malaria, yellow fever, hookworm and bubonic plague; that has undertaken a nation-wide campaign against the genitoinfectious diseases; that is spending millions of dollars annually in research and in the diagnosis and treatment of cancer; that purifies billions of gallons of water daily; that has improved and safeguarded the milk supply of the country, so that it is no longer a significant factor in the dissemination of disease; that has conquered a continent in the brief span of 100 years and tied every portion of it together with railroads and excellent highways for automobile travel; that has spanned great rivers and harbors; built tunnels through mountains and under rivers; constructed dams and reservoirs, transformed arid areas into fertile valleys; and that has almost limitless wealth as well as great natural resources, important industries and a vigorous, active, socially minded population; surely, such a country must eventually grapple with the housing problem, large and difficult and intricate as it is, and bring some effective measure of solution into it, in order that the great mass of people may have and enjoy that fundamental of decency, happiness and contentment, namely, a satisfactory and healthful home environment. Such at least is part of the American dream, and socially minded men and women are not likely to rest until it is realized to a far greater degree than it is today.

HOUSING, THE INDIVIDUAL AND THE NATION
WALTER C. VOSS
Head, Course of Building Engineering and Construction,
Massachusetts Institute of Technology

There would be no value in Housing of any kind if it did not protect the individual physiologically, psychologically, and from contagion and accident. It would further be a useless adjunct of society, if it did not aim to continuously elevate the social plane of the family. The economic factors in housing seriously affect the national welfare. Many attempts have been directed toward the solution of our housing problem and all of them have been partially or completely wrecked upon the rocks of our present economic practices.

Those who would wish to summarize the physiological needs, the psychological needs, and protection against contagion and accident would do well to read an article in the March issue of the *American Journal of Public Health*, entitled "Basic Principles of Healthful Housing." Work of this kind is being done by many investigators and groups with reasonable success. Minimum requirements are relatively simple to establish. To make them satisfy the individual is another problem. That intangible something which we call "human reaction" invariably steps in to upset our carefully conceived, yet cold, scientific plan.

It is not the province of this paper to discuss such human elements, important though they be, but rather to present those factors which have been given only passing consideration in the whole study of housing. These factors are fundamental to the social and national fabric of America, if not to all mankind. They have to do with land, money, labor, and equity.

The entire housing problem depends upon the economics of actual accomplishment, no matter how successful we may be in building up ideals of health, social influences, and systems of construction. Unless the final scheme can be placed within the reach of most of our people, it will be but a report or a dream. To merely set the goal for better housing under subsidy of one type or another is economically unsound and socially very much more unsound. Patronage, if too greatly extended, will eventually ruin our social fabric.

Perhaps we had better consider each of the vital phases of this part of the housing problem in some detail. The order of discussion is not significant as all phases are acting simultaneously and cannot be segregated in actual operation. One should consider each in the light of all. With this premise may we discuss first what I deem the most important from the standpoint of the preservation of our democratic society.

There are many opponents of the view I will express. It is based upon the healthy ideal which is resident in the pride of individual ownership. Apartments, or rental houses are not the proper answer. The more individual home owners we have in America, the safer our nation. They who desire to avoid all of the social duties that are implied in the ownership of a single house are not our best citizens. People who live in apartments do not have or wish to take the time to keep up a house and its grounds. They are usually commodious in that they wish to indulge their urge to be near all their own desires. They wish to be free to move without any deterring obligations. If we adopt the philosophy of never doing anything which someone else will do for us, we are not only selfish indeed, but a drag on the social advancement of the nation. The truest principles of life are born in the real home and the possibility of their existence in the individually owned home are decidedly favorable.

To bring the individually owned home to the most humble families in our society is the challenge which has confronted the construction industry for a long time. Many have placed the blame for failure entirely or at least mainly on the construction industry. This is distinctly unfair. In the first place some manufacturers of material have indulged in one of the most unsound policies as yet devised for the use of our natural resources. To be sure, it is good business, but it is poor national policy. Here again, may I state my own personal premise. I believe it to be a national error to use exhaustible or irreplaceable materials wherever inexhaustible or replaceable materials will accomplish the desired end. To make the structural frame of a house of steel, when wood will suffice, is a glaring example. We would do much better to use wood, concrete, brick, mortar and the like than to deplete our natural resources of ore which can well be put to much more satisfactory use in places where these other materials cannot be used with safety. Such new schemes for house construction often place a heavy load of cost upon the owner and involve the introduction of untried methods which may prove to be only a passing vogue. The owner lives to pay the bill for such trials. The construction industry is thus involved in trying to make many new materials and methods give satisfactory service at a reasonable price and the obvious result is the elimination of those whose income is in the lower brackets from home ownership.

The exorbitant and unreasonably inflated values of land often imposed upon home ownership are a further deterrent to home ownership. Often they equal the difference between the cost of a house which the workman might own and that which only those who now can afford to pay high prices do own. The writer knows instance after instance where raw land assessed at a value of about $200 per acre has eventually been saddled upon the cost of home ownership at the ridiculous, yet selfish, price of $6000 an acre, merely because plausible values have been trumped up by advertising and the very fact that several poor souls have bought homes in the locality. Why speak about labor rates, schemes of construction, and mass production, when the benefits of all revisions of practice these may offer are nullified for the profit motive of a landowner. Not until such money-mad speculators practice a bit more of golden-rule policy, will housing become a reality.

The question of loans has been considerably improved through the efforts of the government. Previous to this form of government guarantee banks made their exorbitant charges for loans, discounts and other abuses which one can only call terrible. Community governments have also gradually relaxed their taxing orgies, placing an undue share upon real estate, which involved a house. Until security for the home owner can be built into the scheme of home building and ownership and until the bank and the local government realize that they are servants of the public and not dictators of the fiscal policy of the individual, we will, likewise, have no successful home ownership urge.

A further impediment to home ownership by the masses which I will discuss is the relation of the cost of the services in the usual house to the cost of the house itself. The new devices for comfort and convenience are priced far above their proper levels. Manufacturers should realize that by group action in the direction of low unit costs lies the stimulation of purchasing power and that the much touted demand will not materialize until the finished product,—land, mortgage and home—is placed within the reach of those 4,000,000 families which now see nothing but grief in the venture of home ownership. Why not take a leaf out of the book of the motor car industry in this respect?

The final retarding influence on the problem is the labor element. I really believe that it is only an apparent one, however. With a properly organized industry it would be possible to assure the tradesman an annual wage which would be a very much lower hourly rate than the intermittent employment necessitates at present. To be sure labor must bear its share of the blame for the failure of industry to function and labor must make concessions in just as real a sense as the other elements.

To sum up, the writer feels that it is perfectly possible to build a 5 or 6 room house on 10,000 feet of land in almost any community for from $4000 to $5000. To accomplish this desirable end we must have concessions in the public interest from—

(a) land owners
(b) financial institutions
(c) the local taxing power
(d) labor, and
(e) materials manufacturers

With the proper attitude on the part of these elements it would be unnecessary, even now, to wait for a new scheme of construction, to demand subsidy, or to forego all the modern conveniences of living. The whole problem awaits only "the golden rule" and an organizing, public-spirited guidance. The ownership of a home should be the badge of good citizenship instead of the proof of a foolish and costly desire.

HEALTH AND THE NEW PUBLIC HOUSING PROGRAM*

ALLAN A. TWICHELL
*Technical Secretary, Committee on the Hygiene of Housing
American Public Health Association*

Housing is in the headlines. Under the public housing program of the United States Housing Authority, $500,000,000 is being spent for low-

---
* Published by courtesy of The American Public Health Association.

rent municipal housing projects in American cities. It is expected, too, that the new financial aids to home building which are being offered by the Federal Housing Administration will tremendously enlarge the activities of private builders in the middle price ranges.

Much that we read of the public housing program stresses this program as a stimulus to employment in the construction trades. But a good housing program is also a health measure of the greatest importance. Large-scale housing construction is significant for public health not only because it tends to displace slum areas, which are notorious breeding grounds of ill health and social maladjustment, but also because new housing, if properly planned and built, provides and permanently protects the space and light and air and cleanliness which are essential to the positive development of healthful and happy living.

Many competent investigators, both in the United States and in Europe, have analyzed the relation between housing and health. The traditional approach in this field has been to measure the ways in which poor housing damages health. Some of the salient findings of this negative type will be briefly reviewed here. In view of the tremendous housing program now being launched, it is, however, quite as important to consider the means by which proper new housing can enhance the public health. An informed public opinion is necessary to insure that the best technical knowledge will be incorporated in the planning and construction of these new housing facilities, in order that the new housing shall never degenerate to slum status and become in its turn a replica of the thing it was meant to eradicate.

Because of the many complex factors involved, it is difficult to show statistically the extent to which bad housing by itself (aside from low and uncertain incomes, for example) is responsible for the rapid spread of infectious diseases in slum areas, for the prevalence of rickets among groups of tenement children, and the like. But while the role of poor housing cannot be entirely segregated, there is overwhelming evidence that it contributes materially to poor health, both individual and social.

Health Hazards of Bad Housing

Lack of Sanitation

The spread of disease is fostered by inadequate sanitary facilities. These include contaminated water supplies from wells, water polluted within the dwelling by improper plumbing, and insanitary toilets—often shared by several families, so that no one is responsible for their cleanliness. That these problems are not an hallucination of visionary housing reformers is shown by the fact that typhoid fever and serious outbreaks of amoebic dysentery have been traced to faulty plumbing which permits the siphoning of leakage of sewer wastes into water supplies. This condition is by no means restricted to slum dwellings, but must be guarded against by careful design and installation of plumbing systems in all types of dwellings and public buildings.

"Associated with faulty plumbing in congested areas," in the words of Dr. J. M. DallaValle of the United States Public Health Service, "is the lack of sewer connections. An interesting result with regard to the absence of toilet facilities is illustrated by a recent study of two slum areas, in one of which approximately 56 per cent and in the other 92 per cent of the houses were without private toilets. The study revealed, among other things, that the typhoid case rate in the first instance was 39 per 100,000 and in the other 52 per 100,000, an excess of 13 cases per 100,000 in the group having fewer private toilets. . . . As in the case of faulty plumbing, not only do such conditions affect the blighted area where they are found, but also the immediate neighborhood, through the transmission of disease by flies and other insects."

Lack of Light and Sunshine

Lack of sunlight encourages the survival of disease germs and lessens human resistance to certain diseases. "Specifically, it is one of the causes of rickets in children," says Dr. Edith Elmer Wood, an outstanding student of housing problems. "A 5-year study in New York . . . . reported that three out of four babies in the tenement population have rickets from lack of sunshine and/or faulty diet. Autopsies on children in Dresden show that of those born in the fall who die in the spring, 96 per cent have rickets, while of those born in the spring who die in the fall, almost none have. Since there is no reason to suppose infant diet varies with the season, this would tend to assign to deficiency of sunlight the major role." (In this connection it should be remembered that sunlight within the dwelling, when filtered through window-glass, loses its rickets-preventing qualities; but slums frequently do not permit infants and children to receive the needed amounts of outdoor exposure to the sun, through play and sunning in carriages. Tenement areas are usually associated with narrow streets, tall buildings crowded together so as to cut off the sun, and a lack of open playgrounds.)

"In families where there is an advanced case of tuberculosis, the danger of infecting other members of the family is multiplied many times if there are dark rooms or badly lighted rooms, because the bacilli, sprayed about by the coughing of the patient, live—and consequently remain dangerous—so much longer in the dark."

Overcrowding

"Overcrowding," continues Dr. Wood, "is one of the most important factors in the relation between housing and health. The more tightly together people are packed in their homes, above all in their bedrooms and beds, the more surely does disease which is acquired by contact infection, introduced by one member, spread through the family. This applies to a long list of diseases such as common colds, sore throats, bronchitis, influenza, diphtheria, scarlet fever, measles, mumps, chickenpox, whooping cough, cerebrospinal fever, infantile paralysis, pneumonia, and tuberculosis.

"The infant mortality studies of the Children's Bureau afford important statistical evidence of the effect of room congestion on a baby's chance of survival . . . . The figures from eight cities, including Baltimore, were used. In families averaging less than one person per room, the infant mortality rate was 52 per 1,000 live births. Where the density was between one and two, the rate was 95, and for two persons per room and over, it was about 136. After the effect of income and race (earnings of father and race of mother) had been eliminated, it was found that the infant mortality rate in congested homes was still about twice as high as in homes where there was sufficient space.

"It is true that congestion in rooms is a fault of occupancy rather than of structure. It depends on the people, not on the house. But where there is an obvious oversupply of excessively small homes . . . . or where high rents and low incomes force a racial group into overcrowding, as has been the case with Negroes and sometimes with the foreign-born in many of our cities, the matter becomes a part of the general housing problem."

How Bad is Housing Otherwise?

Poor housing affects health in other ways, a few of which can be referred to here. Lack of window-screening or the accumulation of filth and stagnant water in unkempt yards encourages the spread of insect-borne diseases, including malaria in certain regions. Life is endangered by ramshackle buildings of which the porches or stairs cause accidental falls, if in fact the entire dwelling does not collapse, as several have done in recent metropolitan experience. The fire dangers of flimsy construction, too dramatic and well-known to need recital, certainly involve the occupants' chances of survival if not their health in the ordinary sense. Crowding increases family friction and nervous tensions, with probable contributions to nervous disorders which cannot be so readily measured. And finally, educators and psychiatrists agree that the absence of a decent physical environment in the home and the lack of a normal community life, usually associated with substandard housing, are important factors in juvenile maladjustment and delinquency.

There is no space here to review the statistics showing how much poor housing we have in America. But it can be emphatically said that poor housing is not limited to the recognized slum areas. Vast sections of our cities—quite outside the zones of fire-trap tenements or dramatic slums—are so badly planned or so dilapidated that they are substandard from any modern point of view. The phrase which President Roosevelt has made a household word, "One-third of the nation is badly housed," is a conservative statement of the case.

Leaving out of account the conditions prevalent in rural America, where poor housing is almost incredibly widespread, let us examine a single phase of housing deficiency which occurs on a large scale in all American cities, even outside of the sensational slum districts: namely, the matter of insufficient sunlight in the $home$. Rooms (and even whole dwelling-units) which never receive the sun are all too common in our cities, both in apartment houses of a moderately expensive type and in free-standing single-family houses. Over large urban areas, every house or apartment building will be found crowded close to its lot-lines, with neighboring structures only a few feet away and forever cutting off the sun. Add to this the fact that the narrow ends of houses are often oriented toward the street and alley, with front and back porches which effectively shut out the sun, and the result is the sort of cheerless and sunless interior which has been described above as a detriment to health. This type of deficiency, together with certain others, will be cured only when housing in congested areas is built in accordance with a community plan which assures to every dwelling permanent open space and access of the sun. These amenities, and such others as protection of children at play from the hazards of automobile traffic, are cornerstones in the system of community-planned housing which underlies the program of the U. S. Housing Authority and other progressive large-scale housing developers.

Crowding and the Housing Shortage

Overcrowding, referred to above, is a springboard for the government's low-rent housing program. Abnormally low proportions of dwellings are currently vacant in American cities. All competent observers agree that if we do not actually have a housing shortage now, we are on the verge of a serious one. Very little housing has been built during the past eight years, and of that little almost none has been supplied to those groups with moderate and low incomes who need it most. Catherine Bauer, another well-known student of housing, has estimated that over 16 million new dwelling-units will be needed to bring American housing up to a reasonable standard by 1950. This figure includes 5½ million units to replace present substandard dwellings, 6½ million for the expected increase in the number of families, and 4 million to replace those units which will become substandard or obsolescent before 1950. Recent dwelling construction has provided new homes only about one-eighth as fast as they are needed, according to this estimate; for between 1930 and 1937, only about 175,000 dwelling-units were built per year.

The Progressive Character of the Public Housing Program

It is here that the government program of subsidized low-rent housing comes into the picture, in the form of large-scale community housing developments. It will probably surprise many readers to learn that about 50 such projects have been quietly built in recent months by the Housing Division of P.W.A., the fore-runner of the new United States Housing Authority. These projects are scattered through three dozen American cities (Cleveland alone has 3 such developments, completed and occupied). Many of the projects are large, accommodating 700 to 1,000 families each, and some as many as 1,400 or 1,600 families. These housing facilities are so designed that they will afford, not only at the outset but throughout their useful life, those basic elements of light and air and space and cleanliness essential to pleasant and healthful living. And these projects are being so administered that only those who cannot afford to rent good housing at commercial rates may occupy them. In other words, they have been created to rehouse some of those who are now abominably sheltered, and to do this without government competition in the commercial real estate market. The new program of the United States Housing Authority is but an extension of the program of the earlier agency, which had cut its teeth, made many of the inevitable mistakes, and learned its lessons, on a somewhat smaller scale.

How do new housing developments of this type provide health protection? Perhaps the simplest means of indicating this is to review the essentials of healthful housing as presented in a current report of the Committee on the Hygiene of Housing of the American Public Health Association. This report, which has been supplied to all local Housing Authorities as one of the guides for their new programs, analyzes the elements of progressive planning, construction, and housing management which must be provided if the new housing is to be acceptable from the viewpoint of private and public health. These elements, which are given in summary form below, reflect the accepted housing practice of today, and there is every reason to expect that they will be embodied, as a rule, in the projects of the new government program.

(a) *Provision for Physiological Needs*: maintenance of proper heating and ventilation conditions, both through suitable design and equipment; provision of adequate light, both natural and artificial; avoidance of locations or construction which would permit excessive noise to pervade the home, disturbing sleep and causing general irritation; provision of adequate space for exercise and children's play.

(b) *Satisfaction of Psychological Needs*: provision of privacy for individual members of the family; provision of adequate space for normal gatherings of the family and of the community; development of housing facilities on the basis of a neighborhood or community unit so as to encourage natural and desirable community interests and activities; provision of facilities for efficient housekeeping and for cleanliness, both of the person and of the dwelling; provision for reasonable esthetic satisfaction in the home and its surroundings.

(c) *Protection Against Contagion*: provision of a pure water supply; avoidance of water-contamination through faulty plumbing; provision of sanitary toilets and sewage disposal; avoidance of insanitary conditions in the yard or vicinity of the home; use of construction methods which will exclude vermin; provision of adequate refrigeration facilities to protect milk and foods from spoiling.

(d) *Protection Against Accidents*: construction substantial enough to prevent collapse of any part of the dwelling; avoidance of falls and other accident hazards through proper design of stairs, windows, porches, etc.; control of conditions which would cause fires or permit their spread; provision of adequate fire-escapes; protection against gas-poisoning and electrical shocks; protection of children and other pedestrians against automobile accidents while at play or en route to schools, to shops, etc., through proper planning of streets and playgrounds.

If it is difficult to show statistically the past health effects of good housing which has embodied provisions of this sort, it is clearly impossible to predict the effects of future housing which may be built to these standards. Fortunately it is not necessary to justify such standards by resort to statistics, for it is rather generally agreed by all observers of the housing scene that shelter which lacks these basic provisions is substandard and in the long run uneconomic. Long before it is worn out, such inadequate housing suffers from blight, declining rents, increasing vacancies.

The National Association of Housing Officials, which works in close contact and harmony with the United States Housing Authority, and which expresses the viewpoint of the ablest and most experienced housing technicians and housing officials in America, is taking a strong stand for the maintenance of proper health standards in the new public housing program. In this stand it is supported by the American Public Health Association and numerous other professional bodies. There is, therefore, every reason to expect that those who are both nationally and locally responsible for the housing program, while remaining properly critical of unnecessary frills in low-rent housing, will stand firm on a policy of building generously in terms of the basic light and space and cleanliness and safety that spell good housing—and health for the people who live in it.

THE HOME AND TUBERCULOSIS
GERALD G. GARCELON, M.D.
Epidemiologist, Division of Tuberculosis
Massachusetts Department of Public Health

Although tuberculosis arises only from contact with a person who has the disease, or with articles contaminated by him, it differs from most of the other communicable diseases in that it usually requires months or years of intimate exposure to the disease for an individual to acquire the infection. Once the individual becomes infected there is usually a further lapse of several months or years before the disease becomes manifest by the definite signs and symptoms of tuberculosis. In this respect, it is quite evident that a person may be entirely ignorant that he has tuberculosis, and yet that individual may be spreading the disease to members of his family and friends. It is the long, continued, intimate contact with active cases, which is too often unsuspected, that provides the most frequent means of contracting the disease.

As the home affords the best opportunity for intimate contact over long periods of time, tuberculosis is primarily a family disease. It has been shown in many studies by various workers that tuberculous infection takes place earlier and in greater proportion of children in families with an open case of tuberculosis, and also that a much larger proportion of individuals so exposed develop the disease than in the general population.

To evaluate the importance of the home surroundings as a factor in the spread of tuberculosis, it is necessary to account for two factors: First, the home itself, and secondly, the habits of the people. It is difficult to separate poor housing conditions from unhygienic habits of the people themselves as they more often are caused by the same factor, namely, poverty. Low incomes force the very poor into congested areas with unsanitary dwellings and does not permit of their obtaining suitable food and developing good hygienic habits. Tuberculosis itself, affecting the wage earner, lowers further the economic status of the family by reducing or completely eradicating the earning capacity of those affected.

Poor personal hygiene including such factors as improper and inadequate food, insufficient sleep and rest, lack of proper exercise, and dissipation in any form may lead to a lowering of the resistance and thus render the individual more susceptible to the disease. As the source of the germs which cause tuberculosis is, in the vast majority of instances, the sputum of individuals with open cases of pulmonary tuberculosis, the personal hygiene of these individuals assumes an important role in the spread of the disease. Coughing and sneezing with the mouth open and uncovered, failure to properly dispose of the sputum, and the common use of towels, dishes and eating utensils with other members of the family on the part of the consumptive, all tend to disseminate the germs to other members of the household. It has been fully shown that the filtered expired air of consumptives is not infective, so it is quite evident that the consumptive himself is practically harmless except for his sputum and only becomes dangerous through bad habits.

Among the evils of poor housing, overcrowding plays the most important role in regard to the spread of tuberculosis. Overcrowding causes numerous and intimate contacts thereby multiplying the chances of infection if an open case of tuberculosis develops in one of the household. This is particularly true of young children who are readily infected when brought into constant contact with open tuberculosis. A study of disease and mortality rates in Detroit in 1920 indicated that tuberculosis in districts with more than one person per room is from two to three times greater than in districts with an average of 0.6 person per room.

In addition to house overcrowding, other poor housing evils which have a relationship to the spread of tuberculosis include such factors as land overcrowding producing a lack of sunlight, lack of ventilation and heat, and the presence of excessive dampness. Lack of proper ventilation undoubtedly plays a part in the direct transmission of the germ from the open case to the other members of the household. Lack of sunlight, heat and excessive dampness tend to lower the individual's resistance so that once exposed to the disease he more readily becomes infected. The influence of unsanitary dwellings on the death rate of tuberculosis in the experience of Liverpool is interesting. The municipal government tore down large sections of defective buildings and erected sanitary houses in their place. The same people were housed in the reconstructed area who lived in the old homes. In the reconstructed area the death rate from tuberculosis fell from 4 per one thousand to 1.9 per one thousand.

In summary it may be said that tuberculosis is primarily a family affair in that one of the most important methods of its spread is by the intimate contact of members of the household with an unsuspected or careless open case; that those factors of poor housing which tend to increase the intimacy of this contact, such as overcrowding and improper ventilation, and those factors which tend to lower the individual's resistance to the disease, such as lack of sunshine and heat, excessive dampness, improper and inadequate food, insufficient sleep and rest, lack of proper exercise, and dissipation in any form, are conducive to the spread of tuberculosis; and finally, that tuberculosis and poverty, as a rule, go hand in hand inasmuch as poverty is largely the cause of these unfavorable conditions.

HOUSING ACTIVITIES, STATE AND LOCAL
SIDNEY T. STRICKLAND
Member of the State Board of Housing

Generally speaking, most of our commercial and industrial centers of New England have just grown; they were not planned.

Each succeeding step forward, whether it was the railroad, the electric car, or finally in our day the automobile and the aeroplane, has changed materially the character of our cities. For the most part individuals who have been the most successful have tended to leave the inner core of these communities and build without, where there was a greater abundance of light and air.

This process of moving on and out has been fairly rapid, and as the cities spread they left blighted areas near the inner core. Wave after wave of tenants have occupied the houses in these central areas until they have turned from the blighted stage to that of slum.

Today's task is a large one. Planning agencies, social workers, labor groups, and some professional men, have worked for years to develop an understanding of this complex problem. Health officials have been slow to approach this problem. True, there are many aspects to be considered: safety — economy — morality — make this a problem for the master builder — the financier — the sociologist — and education, as well as health, the problem for the health officers.

Have not the public health officials overlooked the value of corrective housing as one of the best preventive measures in their fight against the evils of contagious diseases or improper personal hygiene? Does not housing present a new field in which to establish research; to the end that as a preventive measure better housing may help us to anticipate the problems of the future? Preventive measures will prove to be far less costly than, first, the cost of today's direct attempt to cure, and, second, through ever-increasing public expense for hospitals, penal institutions, etc.

Now, as to the prospects for rebuilding our slums, let us examine what has been accomplished through legislation here in Massachusetts to promote better housing, before we proceed to examine other prospects.

The State of Massachusetts has led the way in housing legislation. In 1913 they voted to establish the Homestead Commission, and the great importance this legislation had upon our present day activities was this: the establishment of the fact that housing was a public concern. A question of constitutionality was solved through the ratification of a Constitutional amendment by vote in 1915. This cleared the way for the appropriation of $50,000 to the Homestead Commission in 1917, to permit the carrying out of its first project. The site selected for this demonstration was in the city of Lowell, and was called the Lowell Homestead; the buildings were completed and occupied in 1919.

No further activity resulted from this piece of Legislation.

In the early summer of 1933, and as a part of the Governmental program to put men to work, $250,000,000 was set aside, under the Secretary of the Interior, for Slum Clearance.

Following closely upon the heels of this announcement, our State Legislature passed Chapter 364 of the Acts of 1933: "An Act establishing in the Department of Public Welfare a State Board of Housing and defines its powers and duties, and relative to certain Limited Dividend Corporations under the control of said Board." This Act was approved July 22, 1933.

The Housing Division, which had been set up under the P.W.A. in Washington, found that the desired results were not to be obtained under the method of Limited Dividend Corporations; first, because it did not actually produce rentals low enough to reach the people with low incomes, one of the primary objects, of course; it also failed in a second way (this of course was in 1934), i.e. private capital could not be induced to participate to the extent of 15% of the value of such a project, even where the Government would furnish 85%.

Desirous of proceeding on a large scale late in 1934, and as it was apparent that locally, throughout the country, there were no proper public corporate bodies capable of administering housing funds, with 45% grants, the Housing Division of the P.W.A. was set up as a central organization to undertake a country-wide housing program, as a demonstration. Fifty-one such projects were undertaken and have been completed at a cost of something over $150,000,000.

Meanwhile, in 1935, additional legislation was enacted by our State Legislature, Chapter 449. This Act permitted the establishment locally of Housing Authorities, to be under the supervision and control of the State Board of Housing. This was approved July 26, 1935.

Under this Act, local authorities have been set up in Boston, Cambridge, Lowell, Chicopee and Holyoke.

During this period the P.W.A. Housing Division undertook two large-scale Housing Projects in this State: One in Cambridge, called New Towne Court, which was a slum clearance project, to house 294 families; the other in South Boston, called Old Harbor Village, to house 1,016 families. This project was developed on vacant land.

Of far-reaching importance, from the point of view of better housing for the people of low incomes, and the elimination of our substandard areas, was the enactment by Congress, in July last, of the United States Housing Act of 1937 (Public Document No. 417—75th Congress; Chapter 896—1st Session).

The Declaration of Policy of this Act is well worth repeating; "It is hereby declared to be the policy of the United States to promote the general welfare of the Nation by employing its funds and credit, to assist the several States and their political subdivisions to alleviate present and recurring unemployment, and to remedy the unsafe and unsanitary housing conditions and the acute shortage of decent, safe, and sanitary dwellings for families of low income, in rural and urban communities, that are injurious to the health, safety, and morals of the citizens of the Nation." This Act was approved September 4, 1937.

Nathan Strauss was appointed by the President as Administrator of the new United States Housing Authority, which has at its disposal $526,000,000.

After formulating the conditions under which these funds were to be administered, it was apparent that we would have to secure amendments to our Act of 1935, as it related to local Authorities.

Stated in its simplest form, the Massachusetts Act of 1935 required under Section 26U: "real estate of a housing authority, together with improvements thereon, shall be subject to taxation at the same rate, and in the same manner as other property in the same city or town."

Resolved into terms of rental, it was found that a project taxed under the above law would be the equivalent of requiring the local authority to pay to the city or town taxes in an amount equal to $3.50 per room per month.

On the other hand, we have an agency of the National Government ready to lend 90% of the entire cost of a project to any local Housing Authority, and in addition they were authorized to pledge, if necessary, an annual grant of 3½% of the entire cost of the project. In other words, the Government, under their law, would help each local project with a sum better than $3.60 per room per month; while the present State law would require the local Authority to establish a rental high enough to cover a tax payable to the city of approximately $3.50 per room per month.

Mr. Strauss interprets the law to read that the rentals should be sufficient to cover the operating costs, amortization requirements, and a fair sum to be paid to the city or town, in lieu of taxes. The latter sum to go toward costs, such as schools, hospitals, police, fire, etc.

House Bill 1706 has been approved by the Committee of Municipal Finance and is now before the Legislature for consideration: so written that it will adjust the Act of 1935 with respect to the tax situation, so that the State can participate under the United States Housing Act of 1937.

Pending the above new legislation, no project from this State can receive Washington approval. On the other hand, the Government Housing Authority has signed leases with both the Cambridge and the Boston Authorities, under the terms of which the direct management of the two completed projects have been turned over to them for local administration.

Provided the legislative requirements will be fulfilled, let us turn our consideration toward other vital problems.

Site selection falls first upon the local Authority, assisted by the State Board. This means the determination of substandard areas: "any area where dwellings predominate, which by reason of dilapidation, overcrowding, faulty arrangement or design, bad ventilation, light or sanitation facilities, or any combination of these factors, are detrimental to safety, health, or morals."

Safety is the most readily understood; all communities have building departments competent to determine these conditions in a given area.

Health is the most difficult to interpret in many ways. While the Board of Health or local social agencies have gathered and maintained statistical information regarding present conditions, these studies have not been tabulated for ready use to the extent that we should like.

Studies which we have made in Boston, Cambridge and Lowell indicate that the highest rates for death, infant mortality, and tuberculosis, are to be found in the densely populated and overcrowded areas.

Overcrowding is difficult to determine because it requires a careful survey to determine its extent. Such a survey in Liverpool, England, indicated that nearly one-sixth of the houses were crowded beyond the limit set by law.

Faulty arrangement, lack of ventilation, light or sanitary facilities: In Cambridge a survey made of the main street area, before it was demolished to make way for the present P.W.A. Housing Project, showed the following:

Of a total of 280 families
5 only had central heat   265 had gas
151 had hot water   151 had baths
250 had electricity   There was one toilet to each family!

The question of sanitary facilities had only recently been improved through the enforcement of improved building law regulations.

This leads to a much more serious consideration, i.e. the lack of accepted standards. Chapter 144 of the Acts of 1913 provided an exemplary Tenement House Act to apply to all cities, except Boston, which accepted it by a vote of the City Council, with the approval of the Mayor. Unfortunately, only a half dozen cities have accepted this law to date. This law establishes a fairly acceptable set of standards for planning proper ventilation; through defining room areas and number of windows required; encourages better planning through the use of proper courts, side and rear yards, etc., which in turn will assist cross drafts and produce proper ventilation.

From the above, it may become apparent how local Boards of Health could be of assistance. In England, for example, the housing program is administered by the Ministry of Health, and local authorities submit their projects to Whitehall. Here, under one head, they have the power to approve local building codes, sanitary ordinances and zoning laws; all of which are most closely related to housing. Under this English system, the local health officer plays an important part in site selection for slum clearance. One great advantage is the fact that local health officers cannot be removed without consent of the central government's ministry.

The State Housing Board has surveyed conditions in over fifteen communities, and the areas requiring attention cover well over 600 acres. A great deal of time will be required to study and analyze these areas, because of the variety of subjects to be considered, from health to city finances, the trend of employment and a study of wage levels, for each city.

We believe that new housing will reduce materially the present per capita cost for hospitals, prisons, police courts, policing and fire protection, for those cities which see their way clear to participate. Studies of a given substandard area in each of five cities, show the following; the relation of the cost to the city for the maintenance of that area, to the income received through taxes, runs from two times, as the case in Springfield, to ten times, as the case of South Boston.

Below are listed some of the factors present with bad housing, with respect to health:
1. Inadequate sanitary facilities:
    (a) Too many families to one toilet.
    (b) Faulty plumbing.
2. Overcrowding:
    (a) As to number of people for each unit.
    (b) As it relates to the land coverage by the buildings.
3. Lack of medical care.
4. Malnutrition.
5. Extraneous influences:
    (a) Dilapidation, leads to rat infestations.
    (b) Poor screening.
    (c) Insufficiency of natural light.
    (d) Improper ventilation.
    (e) Improper heat.

Congested dwellings create a maximum opportunity for the spread of disease.

Bad housing conditions impose a greater burden upon the mother of a family, resulting in less time being given to the preparation of their food.

In Glasgow, Scotland, the Grade School Teachers were asked to report after housing in their district had been improved. The headmaster reported on children 5 to 10 years of age:
   (a) Health improved.
   (b) Intelligence vastly improved (slum children were as a rule 1½ to 2 years backward).
   (c) *Cleanliness greatly* improved.
   (d) Reduction in all charges for medical and other services.

It was stated that the nourishment of families improved, as there is more time for mothers to prepare food, as housekeeping has been simplified.

I believe that good housing is an essential foundation upon which to build a proper health program. Now that we have a national law which states that it is proper to use public funds for slum clearance, we may be able for the first time to improve the living conditions of people in the low income bracket, and with the resultant improvement in their health.

THE ARCHITECT'S INTEREST IN HOUSING
WILLIAM STANLEY PARKER
Fellow of the American Institute of Architects
Member, Massachusetts State Planning Board

While this title was predetermined by others, it is as direct and logical as any for the purpose. Perhaps it might be cynically held that the complete answer to the question it implies would be embraced in the simple statement that the architect's interest in housing is due to its provision of opportunity for the profitable practice of his profession. This simple answer would be equally true and equally incomplete in regard to any other profession and its field of practice. The physician does have an interest in human nature beyond the fees its various ills produce and the architect has many social and intellectual interests in the problem of housing in addition to his normal and legitimate desire to earn a livelihood, in part, by practicing his profession in that section of the construction industry which deals with the homes of our cities, our suburbs and our rural districts.

One of the phases of his interest is to find out just why his practice in this field has in the past been limited to that very small segment of the population that is relatively well-to-do, and whether the impediments to his practice in "low cost" or "low rental" housing, that have existed heretofore, can be overcome and, if so, in what way. His practice in this field has been concerned, in the past, with about 20 per cent of the population, those families having an income of say $3,500 or more. This is what might be called the "upper crust" of the housing pie which is, in truth, a layer cake with increasing social and economic problems as we get into the lower stratifications of income. The "bottom crust" might be said to be the poorhouse which has been a permanently recognized factor in the housing problem.

Perhaps the reason for the condition outlined above has been a reasonably adequate preoccupation of the architect in other fields such as public buildings, commercial and business structures and the rapidly expanding physical requirements of our educational system. Activity in the field of commercial and business buildings responds very quickly to changes in the so-called business cycle and often leaves the architect's office flat on very short notice. The rate of growth of school plants will quite probably be less in the future than in the immediate past. A vast opportunity for the use of the architect's training lies in the most complex field of housing for the relatively low income groups, that 75 per cent of the population that can theoretically pay only $30 or less per month for rent.

The families cover a wide range of conditions and are scattered throughout our rural, suburban and urban communities. No one formula can cover them all. They live in single detached houses, in row-houses, in two-family houses and in apartment or tenement houses. Some of them can find reasonably satisfactory secondhand housing at the rent they can afford to pay due to the fact that they are willing, perforce, to put up with the lack of conveniences or depreciated character of the structures that are reflected in the small rental. Others of still smaller means are forced to live under substandard conditions which is all the private housing market affords for two or three dollars per room per month in a city.

In suburban areas similar families try to solve their housing problem by building shacks, using such material as they can find and doing the work themselves. Light and air are plentiful but plumbing facilities are apt to be unsatisfactory. When these shacks are far enough apart they are isolated problems but too often they gradually accumulate a sufficient density of population to create community problems which can only be adequately solved by total demolition and reconstruction.

What interests architects is the problem of providing such families with decent housing in neighborhoods that are physically respectable and adequately provided with opportunities for recreation. Only part, and the easiest part, of this problem is purely architectural. Most of it is an economic problem. After the architect has devised housing units that take advantage of every reasonable economy available in materials and processes and in their straightforward use, there still remains an economic impasse, as the result is more than many families can afford, the lowest economic rent being beyond their means. Architects as well as all other citizens are interested in how this economic problem can be solved.

Further reductions in cost doubtless will be secured. Perhaps they will be secured by some new process of fabrication or pre-fabrication. Perhaps the houses will be built by four steel workers instead of a dozen carpenters and masons and other mechanics. If this is accomplished, other economic problems will be created through additional technological unemployment among carpenters and masons and plasterers and other crafts. For these craftsmen the housing problem will be intensified even though it may be helped for others. It will be a subtle problem to appraise the net gain.

Houses for these families have in the past been furnished by the so-called speculative builder, in some cities called the operative builder, in either case referring to those who undertake to build houses for sale. There is an inevitable element of speculation, as the price obtainable for the house and the length of time needed to find a purchaser are both matters to be determined generally after the house is built. The element of speculation tends to increase the cost of the money used and the net profit desired, and the probable selling price limit tends to make it expedient for the builder to reduce the cost of construction in every possible way, and frequently some of these possible ways are highly unwise from the point of view of the ultimate purchaser.

In large cities where there is a large-scale demand, there are apt to be some large-scale operators who often perform this function well and provide to some extent a feeling of neighborhood design. The vast majority of such houses are, however, the result of a very large number of small operations consisting of one or two or three houses each. This means that the builder has no single responsibility for the resultant neighborhood which, like Topsy, just grows somehow as the net result of unrelated and largely uncontrolled operations, and almost entirely without benefit of architectural service.

Street after street, thousands of them, have been built in this way. The current vogue of architectural idiosyncracy is inevitably stamped on these rows of houses, so that one can tell that this row was built during the vogue of the Combined-entrance-door-and-Chimney Period, with rubble stones scattered through the brickwork, popular for a brief spell in the 1920's. The so-called garrison type house, with its newly acquired seamface granite facing of the front wall of the first story, will for years proclaim the activity of the middle thirties. For a time in the twenties no intelligent speculative builder would have thought of building a house unless the front door had a gable over it, whether the gable had any intelligent relation to the rest of the design or not.

These houses were readily financed by the loaning agencies. The purchasers in many cases found they had acquired buildings that demanded wholly unexpected expenditures for repairs and replacement of materials and equipment. Their annual rent-equivalent was much more than anticipated. Where the income proved inadequate, the repairs were not made and increasing depreciation reduced property and neighborhood values and the results are sadly visible to the passerby in all our communities.

In the more densely settled areas the development of our building laws has always been one jump behind the development of undesirable conditions of light and air. Tenements sixty feet deep and three feet apart finally caused building law provisions requiring certain minimum side and rear yards and courts. These minimum provisions became the maximum provisions for the average building operation. Again, in tenement house construction, as with small houses, one building after another developed congested districts without any planned neighborhood qualities. Stores and residences undesirably mingled. Playgrounds were inadequate until the city bought and tore down some buildings in order to provide an open space that should have been provided for to begin with and at far less cost.

Here then, in city and suburb alike, is what interests the architect in housing, the problem of how to organize and direct the physical development of our residential sections so as to provide economical, efficient and attractive neighborhoods where young people can have the opportunities for recreation that they need, and where the money invested in the houses will create real and lasting values. The design of these buildings will be simple and unaffected and not dated by some architectural affectation. Every possible economy will be sought, on a long term basis that will mean a minimum of maintenance cost. Housing for the low rental groups will be provided on a rental basis for those, and there are multitudes of them, who cannot afford to run the risks inherent in ownership.

In the lowest rental groups the city, the state, and the nation will cooperate in bearing the costs that the families cannot afford to bear. In doing so they will insist on the total elimination of politics in the management of these properties. On any other basis subsidized housing will do more harm than good. And once more we are back in the corner of the problem where questions become essentially social or economic or political rather than merely architectural and in that corner the architect's interest in housing is that of a citizen, a tax-payer, looking at his city, his state, and his nation and asking himself how to provide homes for all the people that will comport with what we will be glad to show to all comers and say "This is the American Standard of Living."

THE STATE PROGRAM AS IT RELATES TO PLANNING
Elisabeth M. Herlihy, *Chairman*
Massachusetts State Planning Board

Public health is so much a part of planning work that any attempt to analyze the relationship existing between the two leaves one groping for words with which to establish separate entities for functions that are identical in objective and closely correlated in procedure. In no other part of the country, perhaps, is this unity of purpose more definitely understood than in the Commonwealth of Massachusetts. Planning in this Commonwealth owes its birthright to a desire on the part of the General Court to improve living conditions among the laboring classes, together with a realization on the part of the investigating body that the health of the people was a paramount issue.

Planning per se came into existence in this Commonwealth in 1913. Planning in fact, in one form or another, was practiced almost from the settlement of the Massachusetts Bay Colony in 1630. This is particularly true in the case of zoning, long since recognized as one of the essential elements of a planning program, where the law of the land was invoked as early as 1692 to regulate and control the erection of slaughterhouses. At first intended apparently for fire protection, the act was soon broadened to include other noxious trades "or mysteries," and its enforcement placed in the hands of boards of health. Thus, for the first time, the link between zoning and public health was officially recognized and established.

Chapter 607 of the Acts of 1911 provided for the creation of a Homestead Commission which was instructed to formulate a plan "whereby, with the assistance of the Commission, homesteads or small houses and plats of ground may be acquired by mechanics, laborers and others in the suburbs of cities and towns." The work of the Commission was continued under Chapter 714 of the Acts of 1912, with further permission to "recommend such legislation as in its judgment will tend to increase the supply of *wholesome* homes for the people."

As a direct approach to its problem, the Commission elected to study some of the effects of bad home conditions and congestion on child life, having in mind a paper read before the Royal Statistical Society in London, in 1901, by Arthur Newsholme, M.D., in which he declared that

"Infants form a very delicate index of the character and the environment of the individual, and a high infantile mortality may rightly be regarded as indicating unfavorable sanitary or social conditions."

The conclusion finally reached by the Commission was that:

"The problem is one of proper distribution of population. The principal obstacles to its solution are low wages, the high cost of land, difficulty of obtaining funds, inadequate transportation. Yet it is imperative that this problem be solved, not only on account of obligations to humanity, but because the stability of the State is involved.

"The physical condition of the home is so vitally related to morals, *health*, and the general well-being of the family and the individual that the welfare of the State depends upon it."

To quote further from the report—

"All the cities abroad that have made permanent progress in making their communities more healthful and more desirable places in which to live have found planning in advance a necessity.

"Of course to plan the development of a city or town is the only sensible method of procedure. That is the method followed in all other activities. No matter how small the importance of any proposed work it is done according to a preconceived plan. A house, or a fence, or a ditch, all command some forethought and a plan of operation. But cities, the homes of millions, grow by chance, without conscious design, direction, or supervision. A street runs here, of such a width, to such a distance, because it was profitable or convenient to some person to have it so. The general *health*, or welfare, or convenience were not the consideration. Public buildings, parks, and open spaces are scattered here and there with but little forethought, and often as selfish influences dictate. An incalculable waste of effort, efficiency, *health*, and wealth ensues. Narrow, crooked streets, many of them dark, crowded, and impossible to keep in sanitary condition, are lined with buildings in which *health*, mentality, and morality decline. Men and women die before their time, thousands of children perish, and the lives of thousands more are blighted—all because of the lack of study of the resources and possibilities of the locality and some foresight in planning for its needs."

The Commission accordingly urged upon the attention of the Legislature the pressing "need of intelligent planning of the growth of cities and towns, not so much to avoid economic waste and to facilitate and expedite the transaction of business, as to quote the language of the Constitution, for the 'protection and preservation of its subjects' of the Commonwealth and to save the lives of numberless children."

The Commission's conclusions were:

"1. That present conditions are not only unjust to the laboring classes but seem detrimental to the general *health* and may be a contributory cause of unnecessary deaths, breeding disease, poverty, ignorance, vice, and crime, and blighting the lives of thousands who might otherwise have been good and useful citizens.

"2. That these conditions are to some extent the result of the haphazard, unsystematic development of our cities, and the selfish utilization of their natural resources, and the resultant conditions of lack of room, air and sunlight in congested tenement districts undoubtedly tend to increase infantile mortality."

These conclusions impelled the Commission to recommend that Planning Boards be established in each city of the Commonwealth and in each town having a population of more than 10,000; that it should be the duty of such boards to make careful studies of the resources, possibilities and needs of the city or town, "particularly with respect to conditions which may be injurious to the public *health* in connection with rented dwellings, and to make plans for the development of the municipality with special reference to the proper housing of its people."

The recommendation was enacted into law and today there are 144 local planning boards functioning in this Commonwealth, their authority being derived in the first place from a recognized necessity for improving "conditions which may be injurious to the public health."

Strictly speaking, housing work has branched off from the main stem through the creation of the State Board of Housing in 1933, together with Housing Authorities in several of the local communities. This affords opportunity for cooperation with Federal Authorities in the actual development and administration of housing projects. This does not mean that the problem of housing, with all of its implications is taken out of the hands of the planning agencies, for the legislative mandate still stands, strengthened and clarified by the pronouncement of Dr. Thomas Adams of international planning fame, before the President's Conference on Home Building and Home Ownership in 1932, "No one lives in a house nowadays, but in a community." Conditions which may be deemed injurious to the public health in a single house, therefore, are but multiplied, with interest, in a group of houses otherwise known as a community.

Perhaps the most readily recognized attempt at improving health conditions from a planning standpoint is through the development of zoning plans. The four main pillars of the police power, under which zoning is accomplished, are health, safety, morals and the general welfare. The regulation of the size and spacing of buildings promotes healthful provision of light and air, as well as safety from the spread of fires and access for fire fighting apparatus. Public health and safety may be thus promoted by setback building lines as these form part of yard requirements in zoning, as a requirement for plat approval, and as related to future street widenings.

In addition to area restrictions, zoning seeks to promote health through regulating building heights, thus insuring adequate light and air. Through use regulations, zoning plans seek to encourage business and industry in proper locations, while at the same time protecting areas set apart for residential purposes from invasion by other interests. In no other way can the peace and quiet, and privacy of home life be permanently secured.

All of these regulations—height, area and use—must bear a substantial and demonstrable relation to health as to the other attributes of the police power from which they derive their authority. Today 87 communities in the Commonwealth of Massachusetts have adopted zoning plans, which means that 3,165,190 persons, or 73 per cent of our population are living under regulations designed to promote the health, safety, convenience, morals or welfare of their inhabitants. These regulations, carefully drawn and properly enforced, should serve to supplement in a substantial and fundamental way the splendid work of the various health authorities throughout the State.

Nor does the relationship stop there by any means. To quote from a statement of principles issued in 1928 by the American City Planning Institute:

"To improve uneconomic, unattractive, *unhealthy* and socially wasteful conditions, and to prevent their creation, there must be effective control of land subdivision and building development."

This opportunity exists in this Commonwealth today to an extent greater than ever before. The Legislature of 1936 enacted a measure "providing an improved method of municipal planning." One of the outstanding features of this Act is that it confers upon planning boards the authority to receive and pass on plats for subdivisions. This means that the planning board must weigh the evidence submitted in its relation, among other things, to streets and public utilities, parks and playgrounds, light, air and safety, and the use to which the buildings will be put. Wise measures of control can produce types of development in new areas adapted to modern standards of light and air and space, and consciously directed toward developing desirable and healthful community life.

Planning studies of population growth and trends go hand in hand with the more specific social studies of the effect of overcrowding in the homes. Density of business population, particularly when buildings are competing with one another to achieve the greater height, is a serious factor, and every possible means should be taken to minimize the dangers to health and safety surrounding business and industrial workers in many of our large cities.

In the light of Sir Raymond Unwin's statement that "the whole population of the world, at ten families to the acre, would not occupy the State of Kansas," there is little excuse for overcrowding either in buildings or on the land.

The necessity for adequate sewer facilities, and for an abundant supply of fresh water for domestic purposes as well as to meet industrial needs, is so obvious as hardly to require comment. It does require planning, however, in establishing the routes for public utilities in order that the work of public health agencies, in requiring standards of purity and efficiency, may be effective.

Recreation has long been looked upon in the light of playgrounds for children outside of school hours. Recently its economic advantages are being stressed. To say that the expenditures for recreation in this Commonwealth in 1937 reached a total of $200,000,000 is to state an impressive fact. To attempt to estimate the value of recreation from a health standpoint would be as difficult as to attempt to place a unit value upon fresh air, sunshine, ocean breezes, the perfume of flowers or the song of the birds. All these contribute to human health and happiness, and all must be planned for in advance if they are to be brought within the reach of all citizens.

Little more has been attempted in this article than to indicate in a general way a few of the points where the work of health agencies and of planning agencies meet. Each one is strengthened and made more effective by the other. The same is true of workers in other fields of human endeavor. It is only by united effort, by the very finest type of cooperation and good will, that the State Planning Board may hope to accomplish the purpose for which it was created, and develop a plan "which will, in accordance with present and future needs and resources, best promote the *health*, safety, morals, order. convenience, prosperity and welfare of the people of the Commonwealth."

FEDERAL HOUSING

HOWARD P. VERMILYA
Director, Technical Division
Federal Housing Administration

In the three months which have elapsed since the passage of the amendments to the National Housing Act. the Federal Housing Administration has placed on its books business well in excess of $200,000,000. This includes both individual home mortgages selected for appraisal and commitments to insure mortgages on multifamily and group housing projects.

These figures demonstrate the advances which have been made toward the achievement of one of the primary objectives of the National Housing Act . . . the stabilization of the mortgage market by the creation of a nation-wide mortgage insurance system.

The success of the program, especially striking during recent months, should not be allowed to obscure the fact that the Administration has been working slowly and carefully towards the realization of a second objective of the Act, namely, the improvement of housing standards and conditions. Though less spectacular than figures on the volume of business. the results of the standard setting program of the Administration are of wide significance.

The application of property standards and minimum construction requirements developed by the Technical Division to the thousands of houses which are now covered by insured mortgages has exercised a leavening effect upon standards of construction and planning throughout the country. Already, benefits of the program are evidenced concretely by the construction of attractive, well planned and well constructed homes.

It should be remembered that the technical and underwriting activities of the Federal Housing Administration are a basic part of the mortgage insurance activities. The Federal Housing Administration does not regard the home mortgage simply as a financial transaction. Its operations are based upon the conception that the mortgage is a composite of a number of different factors, each of which must be sound if the mortgage is to remain sound.

Stress is laid not only upon the old-fashioned conception of the mortgage instrument but also upon other factors which the FHA considers to be of equal importance. Heretofore these factors have rarely been reckoned in determining the scurity of real estate investment to borrowers and lenders. Lending agencies must prove that they are capable of servicing the loan over a long period of years. The borrower must show that he is undertaking expenditures which are commensurate with his capacity to pay.

Further still, it is necessary that it be demonstrated that the property securing the loan is "substantial and durable in structure, convenient and efficient in arrangement, attractive in appearance" and located in a neighborhood which is "secure from those disintegrating influences which are more certain to destroy property values than deterioration in the buildings themselves."

In the first days of the program, the Federal Housing Administration drew up a set of general property standards which were drafted in the form of recommendations rather than requirements. Experience proved, however, the impracticability of applying any nation-wide set of standards, because of varying climatic conditions and construction methods customary in different parts of the country. Therefore, localized minimum construction requirements and property standards have now been drawn up for nearly all of the offices.

Minimum construction requirements contain specific and detailed provisions as to such matters as lot coverage; dimensions of yards; window area; ventilation for bathrooms, basements, etc.; room arrangement; room sizes; ceiling heights and other such matters.

In general, the requirements set up by the Federal Housing Administration conform to or are slightly more stringent than those set forth in local building codes. In many instances, however, faults in building codes, which are outmoded by modern practice, have necessitated the drafting of construction requirements which differ from local ordinances.

In its requirements for water supply, sewage disposal, heating and wiring installations, the Federal Housing Administration has not attempted to set up standards of its own, but cooperated with local agencies or national boards and departments which have set up applicable standards. In the matter of wiring, for example, the provisions of the "National Electric Code" of the National Board of Fire Underwriters applies in all cases.

In the matter of sewage and water supply systems, the Federal Housing Administration is cooperating with local, state and national public health departments. Where local, county, or state public health departments have drafted sanitary codes which are enforced by local health department inspectors, the Federal Housing Administration requirements are the same as those in effect.

In many communities, public health departments have only advisory jurisdiction. In such cases, the recommendations of the local or state department become a requirement for houses securing insured mortgages. In many communities it has been necessary to adopt the standards of the United States Public Health Service, since neither local, county nor state boards have jurisdiction.

This same condition holds true in the matter of water supply systems for houses. Where local, county or state health boards supervise water supply systems and the installation of wells, the Federal Housing Administration requires compliance with their regulations. If local departments have no authority, the United States Public Health Department recommendations are regulatory.

This method of procedure has done much to improve the sanitary and health conditions in subdivisions in every part of the country. The Federal Housing Administration has been instrumental in establishing in the minds of mortgage lending institutions, real estate dealers and the building trades the necessity for the establishment of healthful conditions in residential neighborhoods. The Federal Housing Administration has, therefore, aided the United States Public Health Service and the local and state department of health in pioneering in this field in hundreds of communities.

The Administration has cooperated with local Planning and Zoning authorities in bringing about better planning of residential neighborhoods, particularly in new subdivisions. While the Federal Housing Administration cannot control the conditions of land subdivision, technically, it has been able, in fact, to influence and strengthen local authorities in the control they exercise.

No single mortgage loan can be accepted for insurance in a new neighborhood until the entire neighborhood has been examined and determined as acceptable for houses secured by insured mortgages. Faults in the subdivision, such as improper platting of the land, poor street arrangement, inadequate provision for health and sanitation, improperly drawn deed restrictions, are noted by the inspectors and suggestions are made to the owners of the subdivisions as to the changes necessary before the neighborhood can be considered to be acceptable.

The Federal Housing Administration insists that subdividers furnish proof that their subdivisions have been examined by the local planning or zoning authority, where a local city plan exists or where a zoning ordinance covers the subdivision. Loans are not insured in subdivisions which do not conform to the existing city plan.

By demanding that adequate deed restrictions be imposed on all property, the Federal Housing Administration is assured that undesirable and unhealthful factors will be excluded from the neighborhood. It is also assured that the original character of the neighborhood will be preserved during the term of the restrictions.

The chief obstacle to the success of any nation-wide program to improve housing standards is the disorganization of the building industry and the multitudinous means and methods employed for the enforcement of existing building and sanitary codes. Inadequate inspection staffs in city, county and state health and sanitary offices and building departments make the enforcement of many of the provisions extremely difficult

The Federal Housing Administration has been able, however, to secure the cooperation of lending institutions and city officials and the joint work of these three groups has been sufficient in many cases to remove many obstacles. Builders and subdividers have cooperated whole-heartedly in most instances.

In many cases, through this means, inadequate local codes have been changed to include adequate provisions; local inspection agencies have been staffed adequately; new codes, new ordinances, and new building departments have been established. Still more important, jurisdictional anomalies have been clarified and means of enforcing existing regulations effectively have been discovered.

While it cannot be said that the accomplishments of the last few years point to an immediate solution of the problems of enforcing nationwide property standards and health provisions, still a start has been made. The means being employed are the only ones available, under present conditions. Until more effective methods of operation are feasible, the Federal Housing Administration will stand squarely behind every constructive effort of local and state authorities to establish sanitary and satisfactory housing conditions.

THE DEVELOPMENT OF GOVERNMENT PARTICIPATION IN LOW RENTAL HOUSING

FREDERICK J. ADAMS
Assistant Professor of City Planning
Massachusetts Institute of Technology

It is truthful to say that the active interest of local and state governments in the problem of providing safe, sanitary, and well-planned homes for families in the lower income groups is closely allied with the public health movement which has made such notable progress in the last century.

We do not need to look far to find the reasons for this interest on the part of governments. The Industrial Revolution of the early eighteen-hundreds brought with it an increased social problem in providing adequate housing for the people who flocked in to the big cities from the country districts in order to find employment in commerce or industry. The problem was further aggravated in the United States by the tremendous flow of immigration that continued with minor interruptions from 1847 to 1929. During the eight years preceding 1855 some 2,500,000 persons from abroad entered the country, settling mostly in the North and West. The total foreign immigration for the three decades ending in 1870 was about 6,300,000. The population of the country as a whole increased by nearly 100 per cent between 1870 and 1900, resulting in a population in the latter year of nearly 80 millions, of which over 10 millions were immigrants. Dr. Thomas Adams has the following to say of conditions during this phase of our country's development:

"The middle period of the century, between 1830 and 1870, was naturally a dormant one in obtaining effective civic improvement, for society was in the throes of a new birth and of the confusion that is the concomitant of revolutionary change. Among other things, the disorder of the industrial period that followed the more controlled order of the Renaissance period did not, at first, bring with it improved living conditions to the mass of the people. Ultimately, however, the negative influences caused by the squalor, overcrowding, and disease in cities during the early decades of the industrial epoch, plus the positive influences of the greater freedom of individuals and the extension of democratic government, forced the legislative action that has brought about the substantial improvements in sanitation and housing since 1870."*

While the problem of foreign immigration was not nearly so serious in European countries as it was in the United States, the development of industrial centers near the sources of raw materials and power, necessarily accessible to large trading areas or transportation routes, resulted in a rural-urban migration which changed radically the social patterns of urban living. This gradual but relentless change is graphically indicated in the following table, which shows the changes in population composition which took place in Germany between 1871 and 1933:

Year	Rural Population %	Town Population %
1871	63.0	36.1
1895	49.8	50.2
1910	40.0	60.0
1919	37.6	62.4
1925	35.6	64.4
1933	33.0	67.0

It is obvious that such population changes were due more to the migration from rural areas to the big cities than from any rise in the ratio of births to deaths. Berlin, for instance, increased from a city of 322,626 in 1840 to a city of over four million inhabitants in 1925.

The problem of providing adequate housing for the industrial workers and their families was one which faced countries like Germany and England first, as it was in these countries that the effects of industrial expansion were first recognized as creating a serious housing problem. In

---
* *Outline of Town and City Planning*, p. 160, Russell Sage Foundation, New York, 1935.

recent years the United States, Russia, and Italy, among other countries, have been forced to give serious consideration to this matter and considerable headway has been made in formulating long term policies by local, state, and federal governments.

It is not possible within the limits of this paper to describe the historical development of a number of European countries, but some idea of their activity may be gained by outlining briefly the events in Great Britain which led to the present program of housing and slum clearance.

A Royal Commission on Health and Housing was appointed in England in 1844, but the first Act of Parliament enabling municipalities to provide houses for the lower income groups was the Housing of the Working Classes Act of 1890. This was followed by the Housing, Town Planning, etc., Act of 1909, and between 1909 and 1915 about 11,000 houses were built by Local Authorities.

The World War brought four years of virtual inactivity in the housing field to Great Britain, but the amount of construction which has been undertaken since that time is considerable, as is indicated in the following table:

Total dwellings built in England and Wales since the War
By municipalities 962,271
By private enterprise with Government aid 424,850
By private enterprise without Government aid 1,971.851

Total ....,......... 3,358,972

England has also attacked the problem of overcrowding of dwellings and a standard has been set up which is enforceable on both landlord and tenant. The standard is a compound one providing for a maximum of persons per dwelling which is further checked by the number per room according to size, and by the age and sex of the occupants.

In a recent lecture to students in the City Planning course at the Massachusetts Institute of Technology, Sir Raymond Unwin, noted authority on housing, made the following comments on present tendencies in the English housing program:

"Considerable freedom is left to Local Authorities to adjust the plans as between the number of rooms and their relative sizes, to suit their local needs. At first all plans were subject to approval by the central government. That is no longer the case, though plans may be called for in any case. In order to stimulate local action, and spread the cost of building new houses for those who could not afford to pay a remunerative rent over the whole country—because very often the greatest need is in the poorest districts—the central government has made grants to the Local Authorities, varying in amount and in detailed terms from time to time but usually taking the form of an annual grant for a period of years which has varied from 60 down to 20. The general subsidy for new houses just to increase the supply has now ceased. The existing grants are tied to special purposes like slum clearance, abatement of overcrowding and for improvement and redevelopment schemes involving the rehousing of displaced occupants. The subsidies at present in operation are not all on the same basis, having been instituted by separate legislation. The Minister of Health, who is responsible for all local Authorities' activities, intends to bring them into accord at the next revision period—for all the subsidies are subject to revision if the circumstances change."

In the United States, individuals and agencies interested in improving social conditions were gradually building up a program for the improvement of health and sanitation which resulted eventually in legislative action.

The first so-called "model tenement" in New York City was designed in 1847 by the Association for Improving the Conditions of the Poor, although never built; but the most important advance in tenement-house planning resulted from a competition sponsored by the Tenement House Committee of the Charity Organization Society at the end of the last century. A study of the plans submitted in this competition formed the basis for the Tenement House Law of 1901, which was applicable to all cities of the first class in the State of New York. The deplorable conditions in which many people are living today is evidenced by the fact that nearly two million New Yorkers are now living in habitations declared unfit for human occupancy by the Law of 1901. The above-mentioned Committee was also largely responsible for the organization of the National Housing Association, which held its first conference in New York City in 1911. One of the most active supporters of the Association was Lawrence Veiller, whose *Model Tenement House Law* and *Handbook on Housing Reform* were published in 1910, followed by the same author's *Model Housing Law* in 1914.

The purpose of this brief historical review is to indicate the extent to which modern industrial conditions have been responsible for the acute housing problem and to show that the present interest in the improvement of housing conditions is the result of the efforts of public-spirited groups of technicians, social workers, and municipal officials who have been giving a great deal of thought to this problem over a long period of years.

The agency largely responsible for the low-rental housing program of the Federal Government until last year was the Housing Division of the Public Works Administration. This Division originally sought to have limited dividend corporations initiate low-rental projects, lending its assistance through building loans. In February, 1934, it discontinued this policy, only seven out of about five hundred loan applications having been granted, and subsequently it has concentrated on the initiation, financing, and construction of public housing projects. By the middle of 1937 the Housing Division had completed, or had under construction, fifty-one projects in thirty-five cities, providing living quarters for some twenty thousand families at a cost of one hundred and thirty-three million dollars. The Housing Division had the choice of leasing these projects to legally constituted local housing authorities or operating them directly through the Federal Government, a choice now exercised by the United States Housing Authority.

According to the Annals of the American Academy of Political and Social Science, entitled, "Current Developments in Housing," published in March, 1937, "the outstanding characteristic of the later stages of development of policy in the Housing Division has been its recognition of the need for decentralized authority. Aware of the criticisms that have been directed against its policy of centralization, it has frankly admitted that eventually decentralization is necessary and that the burden of initiation, maintenance, and partial financing should be placed on the community which stands to benefit. Harold L. Ickes, Administrator of Public Works, at the hearings on the Wagner-Ellenbogen Bill, expressed the opinion, however, that such decentralization cannot be accomplished immediately and that a transitional period will be necessary during which Federal construction of housing projects must continue in those communities not yet prepared to assume full responsibility."

That the provision of living quarters for twenty thousand families is only a very small drop in a very large bucket has been made clear by the results of the first comprehensive survey of housing conditions in America—the Real Property Inventory of sixty-four typical American cities undertaken by the United States Department of Commerce in 1934. One half of the dwellings in the sixty-four typical cities rent for $20 a month or less. Studies made by the Brookings Institute of annual incomes in the boom year of 1929 indicate that two out of five families cannot afford to pay over $25 a month rent and one out of five cannot afford more than $17 a month.

It might be, and has been, argued that families of low income should be content to live in second or third-hand housing, just as they have to be content with second or third-hand automobiles. It is certainly beyond the power and ability of local or federal governments to provide new homes for the millions of families now living in dwellings which by modern standards of health and safety are completely inadequate for decent living. Housing experts recognize that the chief contribution of the government housing program to date has been the provision of employment to building trades workers, and the development of improved methods of design. Such experiments in design may have been expensive, but we learn by our mistakes and the contribution such projects have made to the development of an improved housing technique should not be overlooked.

So much for the housing problem as it exists today. What of the future? Many persons are looking to the Wagner-Steagall Bill, passed by Congress last summer, for the permanent solution of this urgent social problem, although its proponents in the Senate and House never made such a wide claim for it. This Bill, the official title of which is the "United States Housing Act of 1937," provides for annual grants to reduce the rents charged as an alternate to large capital grants toward the costs of construction. This permits control over standards of management and rental policy, as the grants will be withdrawn from any project which does not meet the stringent requirements for maximum rents to be set up by the Federal Housing Board. In this way, competition with private housing of a reasonable standard is avoided, and the dwelling units will be made available only to those in the lowest income groups.

Federal subsidy of housing must not be looked upon as the cure for all our housing ills. It is only a medicine we must take to ameliorate the serious condition into which our urban and rural areas have gotten themselves through faulty digestion of technological improvements. We must use the methods of science and technology to speed our recovery and prevent our being stricken again with the same malady. This means lower costs of financing, lower taxes, lower construction costs, none of which are unattainable if we choose to apply the best brains in the country to this important problem. In addition, we must give more thought to improved methods of city and regional planning, in order that the underlying causes of urban and rural blight shall be removed before they have had a chance to do irreparable damage.

URBAN HOUSING

CALVIN H. YUILL, *Executive Director*
Housing Association of Metropolitan Boston

The Challenge in Housing

"Infant mortality reduced from 10% to 50%." "Marked reduction in the incidence of rickets and complications of measles, whooping cough and pneumonia." "Tuberculosis deaths nearly halved and deaths resulting from infant diarrhea reduced by nearly 70%." "Noticeable improvement in the general aptitude of school children." So read official progress reports of the housing program in English cities.

In the United States we also have reports about housing. Some of them read, "One-quarter of the juvenile delinquents come from a congested district covering only 6% of the city's area." "Infant mortality is double in congested homes in New York City even after applying corrections for the effect of race and income." "Areas of congested housing in Massachusetts cities actually cost from three to ten times more than they pay in taxes." Reports from across the Atlantic give substantial evidence of the value of an aggressive campaign against bad housing. We have innumerable studies indicating the social and economic cost of allowing the continuance of inadequate housing.

In view of the evidence of the benefits derived from substituting good housing for bad, especially in large urban centers, and of our knowledge of the great cost of treating families forced to live in an undesirable environment it is hard to understand why, in a progressive nation such as ours, so little of a constructive nature has been done. Yes, we have given generously of medical service and we have enacted laws that help in correcting severe conditions that are brought to the attention of our authorities. We have built some "model tenements" through which relief has been given to a few.

A Century of Progress

It was in 1838 that Sarah Josepha Hale, then editor of *Godey's Magazine*, first attempted to arouse an indifferent, disinterested and uninformed public to the need for the improvement of urban housing in Massachusetts. Carrying on in similar efforts have been such outstanding personalities as Edward Everett Hale, Robert Treat Paine, Henry Sterling, and Spencer Baldwin. From time to time there have been substantial gains in "the battle against the slum." Investigations have been made by public commissions and private agencies. Building, health, housing and zoning laws have been enacted. "Model housing projects" have been erected by philanthropic groups and individuals.

A century of progress? Yes, but how far we are from ridding our communities of the festering sores that threaten their very life! How tragic that we have waited until today to bring into play the resources of the community against the basic causes of the present unhappy condition of our urban centers! After one hundred years of private and public effort in this field in Massachusetts the proportion of our citizens still living in dwellings that fall below a reasonable standard is inexcusably large.

Some 50,000 homes were either unfit for habitation or were in need of major structural repair in Boston, Cambridge, Newton, Everett, Springfield, Worcester, and Haverhill according to the 1934 Real Property Inventory. These studies also disclosed in these cities 43,000 homes without bathtubs, 7,000 without indoor toilets and 2,300 without even running cold water. A visit to the deteriorated residential sections of almost any city will show alleys and rear yards filled deep with refuse for lack of proper methods of disposal; congested sections with little space for children to play in safety; interior toilets used by several families; roofs and walls so old and neglected that they do not provide protection from the elements; apartments so crowded that adolescents of both sexes must sleep in the same bed, so dark that artificial light must be used all day long; wages and rents so unbalanced that inadequate funds are left for food and other necessities. It is unfortunate that we cannot measure the effect of a continued existence in an oppressive environment on the lives and minds of those forced into intimate contact with the evils of our present day housing. Yes, we have bad housing! And we are just now beginning to realize that something must—not should, but must—be done about it.

The Need for Action

But why such a demand for action when we have managed to exist with bad housing for so many years? Because we have come to recognize the fallacy of spending private and public money to counteract the undermining influences of "slum" living. Because pressure on municipal budgets has become so great that bankruptcy is more than a mere possibility—it is a real danger. And because of the necessity of creating worth-while projects to relieve unemployment.

Past effort has been toward the continued application of palliatives. Public regulation can only relieve—it cannot cure—and the fight to raise legal standards has met with such well organized opposition on the part of minority groups that progress is painfully slow. Philanthropic and private ventures have not had the far-reaching effect hoped for. Health services have produced remarkable results but they cannot be fully successful as long as people continue to live in unsafe and insanitary houses. Juvenile and criminal courts, prisons and reformatories can only lock the door after the horse has gone. If the humanitarian aspects of housing are not sufficient to warrant action, then the dollars and cents analysis of the cost of these services and others that have not been included should convince the taxpayer.

Last year the assessed valuations in Boston dropped by some $70,000,000. Between 1933 and 1938 more dwellings were demolished than were erected. Since the United States Census of 1930, the congested, in-town residential areas have lost nearly a third of their population—and are still congested. This is an alarming picture of what has happened in Boston and of what is happening in many industrial and seaport cities in the East. And the disturbing fact is that costs of municipal services in these areas are not decreasing as the population decreases. Therefore, there is an added tax burden on the entire community which has driven more people and industries away from the city, and we find a vicious circle established with municipal solvency becoming more and more uncertain. The marked increase in the population of suburban towns, co-incident with a rapid decline in birth rates, is evidence of what is happening to the larger cities.

Surprisingly enough, the recent activity of the federal government in public housing was not based on either of these social and economic factors, but on a third—unemployment. The advent of the depression years brought a great increase in the number of unemployed in the country. Architects, engineers, and building tradesmen were affected more seriously than many other groups. It was logical, therefore, that the public works program should include housing projects. The attempt to solve the urban housing program was incidental to the chief purpose of putting men to work.

Unemployment is still serious and there are few indications that it will be relieved in the near future. Surely, a practical program that can contribute toward the solution of both problems—housing and unemployment——is worthy of support.

A Constructive Housing Program

The housing problem will not be solved until each family in the community is housed in a dwelling that provides protection from the weather, with adequate facilities for sanitation, safety, and for the general well-being of the individual members; a dwelling that can be rented or purchased for a sum that will leave sufficient funds for food, clothing, and other necessities; a dwelling located in a neighborhood that is free from influences that tend to undermine character and values.

The accomplishment of this objective will require a comprehensive program of four parts:

(1) the demolition of unfit dwellings;

(2) the satisfactory repair and maintenance of dwellings worth the investment;
(3) the reclamation of depreciated areas; and
(4) the construction of good new dwellings when the existing supply is inadequate.

The elements of this program are inter-related and much harm might result if, for instance, demolitions were to proceed so rapidly that former occupants had to "double-up" with relatives or friends, or if values were depreciated by the construction of a surplus of good dwellings. The program is balanced and must be kept so by those having to do with its administration. It is also important to bear in mind that new or remodeled dwellings must be "good" as defined in the statement of purpose.

Legal Standards

It is not enough for a group of individuals to determine a minimum standard for a dwelling. If that standard is to be enforced, it must be incorporated into laws and ordinances and in such form as to survive the scrutiny of the courts. Here, immediately, are two limiting factors. First, legislators or local officials, as the case may be, must be convinced that the standard suggested is a minimum and that its adoption is necessary. Second, the methods of enforcing the standard must not impose an undue hardship on owners. Both of these obstacles can be overcome if the general public will accept and actively support the proposal.

Law Enforcement

The enforcement of the laws pertaining to the planning, construction, and maintenance of dwellings is probably the best known and oldest method of housing improvement. Every large city today has a zoning law through which certain areas are reserved for industrial, commercial and residential uses and which require specified amounts of open space around the dwelling for light, ventilation, and recreation. So, too, are there building laws designed to insure the continued safety of all types of structures, including provision for the repair or condemnation of buildings that are unsafe. Health laws and sanitary codes require that houses shall be maintained so as not to endanger the health of the occupants and of the public.

That bad housing exists in spite of such laws is due to not one but to many factors. For one thing, they can do little more than prevent the repetition of evils existing at the time of their enactment—they are rarely retroactive. The Building Law of Boston, enacted in 1907, does not require toilets or even a supply of pure running water for each family living in a tenement house built before that year. Tenements erected since then must be equipped with these now accepted essentials for healthful living.

Officials charged with the enforcement of these laws are not always appointed on the basis of ability, training and experience. Too, they are under constant pressure from small, well organized minority groups with vested interests, whereas the people directly affected by lax enforcement policies and practices are either not in a position to protest or are not vocal, and the general public to whom, after all, the official is ultimately responsible is either indifferent or disinterested. And the well-meaning official is all too often handicapped by inadequate funds and staff and by awkward, out-moded, legally established techniques of administration.

Stricter enforcement and more liberal interpretation of existing laws under qualified administrators and staffs is needed in practically all cities. Revisions should be made in most instances to effect improved administrative procedures and to raise inadequate standards. Budgets need to be increased in many instances and officials should be freed from all political interference. If these changes could be realized, housing conditions would be greatly improved. They will not occur, however, until the public, including people living in poor housing as well as all other citizens, become sufficiently aroused to demand them.

Repair and Maintenance

Many older dwellings that have paid off much of their original indebtedness are structurally sound and can be brought up to standard with a small investment. Such buildings, when located in a respectable neighborhood, are potentially good homes and, since the cost of acquisition and repair is usually less than that of a new structure, the rents charged can be comparatively low. In Chicopee Falls, Massachusetts, a group of such houses, sixty years old, were recently acquired by a limited-dividend housing corporation, remodeled, and now rent at a figure that former occupants can afford to pay. Mortgagees have been active in this field, with respect to properties acquired through foreclosures, and many have adopted this practice as the only means of liquidating frozen assets and attracting profitable tenants. Considering the trends affecting blighted areas, it is questionable as to how long the economic life of these properties can be prolonged. However, an extensive modernization program might well stop the spread of blight or even change the character of a neighborhood.

The maintenance of residential property, especially that of a low-rent character, presents a serious management problem. Owners, having suffered severe losses on account of reduced rents and family incomes, must find ways and means of keeping their property in a reasonable state of repair. In most communities this situation has resulted in a less rigid enforcement policy on the part of public officials and in greater distress on the part of tenants. Management of low-rent property is a field that has not developed to any extent in Massachusetts. Where trained housing managers have been utilized elsewhere in the United States and abroad, their success has been marked with lower maintenance costs and improved rent collections. Both owners and tenants have benefited.

Reclamation of Depreciated Areas

As has been pointed out, decentralization of population and industry, encouraged by improved transportation facilities to outlying areas and by high taxes and the discomfort of living in congested centers, has left a heritage of blight in industrial and urban centers. The restriction of immigration and the declining birth rate have hastened the withdrawal of private enterprise from those areas. *We must bring private capital back to the city by providing for the redevelopment of blighted and depreciated areas.* If action is not taken, it is only a question of time before our cities become "abandoned villages."

How can this be accomplished? By thinking and planning in terms of investment rather than speculation. By recognizing that our Massachusetts cities will very shortly stop growing. Deteriorated areas must be replanned and made as attractive as the areas to which families are moving. And these replanned neighborhoods must be protected from the encroachment of undesirable land uses. Nor is it necessary or wise to consider housing as the only use for the site. These areas should be replanned for such use as will best meet the social and economic needs of the community.

Construction of New Dwellings

Building costs, including land, materials, labor, and financing, are such that new dwellings are within the means of a comparative few. Last year the average wage in the industries of this state was but $1200 a year[*] which means that an average family with one wage earner should not

---

[*] *Labor Statistics*, Massachusetts Department of Labor and Statistics (1937)

spend more than $240 a year or $20 a month for rent. In 1929 over one-fifth of the *families* of the United States had incomes under $1000 and 42.4% had under $1500 a year*. The former group should be able to obtain decent housing for $17 and the latter group for $25 a month. On the other hand, new five-room apartments rarely rent for less than $50 a month, even with the advantages of limited-dividend operation. The same size apartment in an old building could be obtained for $25 a month but even then it would hardly meet the definition of a good house.

It is obvious, therefore, that a great many urban families must either live in an undesirable environment or pay too great a proportion of their income for rent. Some do both when their income is very low. It is equally obvious that private enterprise cannot help this group. It follows, then, that unless matters are to go from bad to worse, a subsidy is needed to make up the difference between the cost of a decent dwelling and the amount that the family can pay. The private entrepreneur still has the wide market created by those who can afford to pay a return on money invested.

Types of Subsidy

Although there is general agreement as to the need for a subsidy, there is a difference of opinion as to how that subsidy shall be applied. There are those who advocate a direct relief or family subsidy—giving the family supplementary aid to enable them to pay a rent based on all of the costs of the house. It is claimed that through this method the community is always aware of the amounts spent, the recipients are conscious of receiving aid and strive to improve their economic condition, expenditures for subsidy can easily be checked in the event of a general increase in wages, competition with private business is eliminated, and families living in the least desirable housing can be aided.

Another group holds that the family subsidy places a stigma on the recipient that tends to curb his pride and ambition and that it is difficult and expensve to administer. This group would subsidize the house by tax exemption, interest concessions, direct grants and similar methods. Rents charged under this type of subsidy do not, of course, cover all of the costs of the project. The first group believes that this subsidy introduces competition with private business (although competition of good with bad housing may be justified), creates false standards, is more susceptible to abuse, and tends to kill tenant initiative.

A third group would attempt a combination of the two types, hoping to retain the advantages and eliminate the disadvantages of both.

Certain it is that in the interests of humanity and municipal economy some adequate form of subsidy is needed. Most large cities have had experience with the family subsidy through rent relief allowances of public and private welfare agencies although, unfortunately, in most instances these have been grossly inadequate. Experience with the second type, the house subsidy, is being accumulated under the present public housing program. The better method can only be determined by experience, clear, unbiased thinking, and public understanding of the nature of the problem.

It Can Be Done

A brief paper does not allow for an adequate discussion of all the elements of an urban housing program. It should be clear, however, that these are closely inter-related—that there is no panacea. The attainment of the goal will depend on our ability to accomplish these objejctives:

(1) a review of legal standards and revision of those that are not in accord with the accepted definition of good housing;

---
* *America's Capacity to Consume*. Brookings Institution, Washington, D. C. (1934)

(2) strict enforcement under qualified officials who are free to act in the interest of the public;
(3) stimulating the modernization of sound structures that are worth the investment;
(4) adoption of an intelligent management program for low-rent properties;
(5) evolution of a form of subsidy that will give the greatest benefit with the least cost;
(6) encouragement of private business to provide good homes for those whom they are equipped to serve and to seek methods whereby costs may be reduced without sacrifice of quality; and
(7) creation of an informed, interested—yes, aroused—public opinion that will demand an aggressive housing policy.

Of these, the last is all-important. For without public support the machinery of administration cannot be created or effectively utilized.

ECONOMIC ASPECTS OF HOUSING
DONALD S. TUCKER
Department of Economics and Social Science
Massachusetts Institute of Technology

The moral and health values of good housing are so great that any one who presents the economic aspects of housing must do so with a feeling akin to guilt. We all feel somehow that these higher values should not be measured against money cost, yet money costs may in this instance be so great that they involve losses of other moral and health values. To clarify this situation an effort will be made here to reduce these economic aspects to one general form: "How much of a family's income ought to be spent for housing?"

Better housing is clearly desirable, especially for the poorer sections of our population; but better food, better educational facilities, better medical care, better clothing and more healthful recreation are also needed. To spend all increments of family income for any one of these purposes and to meet other needs inadequately would be obviously foolish. Experience has taught housewives that the family income must be apportioned among various needs. The national income is but the sum of all family incomes. Total family expenditure is limited by the total magnitude of these incomes. The problem of wise expenditure is one of proportion. The experience of multitudes of families gives us certain conclusions.

(1) Annual Expenditure for Housing Alone ought not to Exceed about One-sixth of the Family Income

How much can be spent for home maintenance depends on the number of items included in that term. If furnishings, heat, light and other operating costs are included, American experience indicates that for some families expenditures as high as one-third of the total income may be justified. It is true that justification here must consist only in voluntary repetition; but if a family after spending approximately one-third of its income in this fashion, voluntarily repeats this expenditure, and if this repetition is found to occur in many families, then that repetition may be taken as evidence that this expenditure brought returns at least as great as could be secured by spending that share of the income for other desirable goods. Since we discover, however, that families do not in general voluntarily spend more than this amount, we may assume that expenditures for home-maintenance greater than one-third of the income cause disproportionate sacrifices of other goods.

If furnishings and the minor operating expenses be omitted from this category, American experience indicates that expenditure for housing, heat, hot water and light ought not to exceed about one-fourth of the family income. If heat and light also be excluded from this category, then the share of the income to be spent for housing diminishes to about one-sixth of the income. Precise rules are difficult here. When family incomes are increasing rapidly, the share spent on rent may fall to one-eighth of the income. When family incomes are greatly reduced, rent alone may consume temporarily a share considerably larger than one-sixth; but the tendency of family expenditures to return toward a somewhat stable pattern is good evidence that experience with other distributions leads families to the conclusion that expenditures for housing in excess of about one-sixth of the income are undesirable.

(2) The Average Annual Cost of Occupancy of Single-family Homes Exceeds 10% of the Investment Cost

Most of the costs of home ownership bear a direct relationship to the amount of investment in the house. Difficulty arises because the appropriate ratios of annual burden to investment cost differ for each community and for each type of structure. Taxes in some communities may exceed four per cent of the assessed valuations and assessed valuations may be fully equal to the investment cost. In other communities tax rates and assessments may both be lower. A tax rate of 3% on an assessment equal only to 60% of the cost would give rise to a carrying charge less than 2%. Whether the tax cost will be 2% or 4% or some other figure depends on local conditions.

Depreciation is similarly difficult to compute. Well built structures have lower rates of physical depreciation than do houses flimsily built; but good construction is not necessarily wise. Quite apart from interest and taxes on the additional investment necessary to secure good construction, it is not certain that the well-built house will always last longer under American conditions.

Obsolescence resembles damage by fire. In any one year the normal house owner may expect to escape loss from this cause, but obsolescence is very expensive when it occurs. Its cost must therefore be estimated in some fashion. Five room apartments may become unrentable and it may be necessary to rebuild a house in order to provide smaller apartments. Coal stoves must perhaps be replaced with gas, old-fashioned bathrooms or heating systems may be replaced with new. Sheathing or even air conditioning may perhaps become necessary.

Obsolescence may be a small cost in some communities. Homes without running water are still rentable in many places, but obsolescence as a cost in house ownership is undoubtedly increasing in importance. As family incomes have grown larger, and as tenancy, in place of home ownership, has become more common, the demand for up-to-dateness has grown more insistent. Technical progress also seems to be proceeding at an increasing tempo and this promises to make obsolescence a heavier cost in the future than it has been in the past. Districts also seem to be changing more rapidly and the street suitable for homes of one type may within twenty-five years become suitable only for uses of a different type. Such changes involve occasionally complete obsolescence of structures.

Ordinary repairs, repapering, repainting and the like must also be included in any estimate of maintenance costs. Superior maintenance will of course reduce annual depreciation. Physical depreciation alone may be as little as 2%, but it would be a bold man who would estimate total maintenance, obsolescence and depreciation at much less than about 5% of the cost of the structure or perhaps about 4% of the total investment.

Supersession is an additional cost for home owners, but this cost is substantially nonexistent for tenants. The house appropriate when the family is small, ceases to be appropriate as the family grows up. After children have left the home, the care of a big house may become a burden. Reconstruction of a home to fit such alterations in needs is usually so expensive that families prefer to sell and move, but selling involves costs of its own and usually also losses because costly improvements which made the home attractive to its present owners, may have no value in the market. Since these costs of supersession fall only upon those who buy their homes, they will be omitted from consideration here. Maintenance of garden, though often very expensive for home owners, will also be omitted here for the same reason.

Interest on the investment in a house constitutes normally the largest single element in the annual cost of ownership. Ten years ago first mortgage money in Massachusetts cost about 6%, and second mortgage money could be secured at a net annual cost of 12%, but such low rates could be found only along the Atlantic seaboard. In many western states these costs were far higher. Investigation of title, appraisal, and a return on the owner's equity brought the annual cost of capital up to fully 7% of the investment cost during the nineteen-twenties.

If insurance and the minor items be also included, the total annual cost of occupancy for those who owned single-family homes during the twenties seems to have ranged from 11% to 15% of the price of the house. Costs both above and below this range could of course be found; but if capital losses due to the depression be omitted, the annual cost of home owners of single-family houses seems to have fallen normally within this range. Rented houses seem to have shown rather lower annual costs. For them a common range seems to have been from 10% to 12%. During the nineteen-twenties it became approximately true that houses were worth about one hundred times a month's rent or that rent should be 12% of the value of a house.

Recently interest rates have declined and rates of taxation on houses have been increased. In many communities these two forces have not counterbalanced each other precisely. Substantial equivalence of these opposing tendencies will nevertheless be assumed here because differences between communities and between specific houses are so great that no single figure can be really typical of the annual cost of occupancy. It seems safe, however, to make two generalizations: (1) If depreciation, and obsolescence and maintenance be omitted from calculations, and if interest on the owner's equity be forgotten, it is possible to get very low figures for annual cost of house ownership. (2) If all costs be included, the annual cost of house occupancy will on the average certainly exceed 10%. Some houses in some communities will without doubt show ratios lower than this; but so many houses will be injured by obsolescence that it is impossible to estimate the average cost of occupancy at a figure as low as 10%.

(3) Investment in a Single-family House should not Exceed the Occupant's Income for Twenty Months

If the annual cost of occupying a house were really as low as 10% of the purchase price, and if the occupant were willing to spend as much as 16% of his income for rent, then a purchase price equivalent to sixteen-tenths of the family's annual income would cause the annual cost of occupancy in dollars to equal precisely the rent the family was willing to pay.

During the early years of occupancy depreciation and obsolescence would cause no disbursements. During this period an owner could save annually six and one-half per cent of his income (4% of the investment cost), and purchase bonds. Some of these bonds he must expect to sell later in order to pay for the more expensive occasional costs of modernizing his home. The remainder of this accumulation plus the price of the land would constitute the return of his investment when the house was finally torn down.

Owners of single-family homes would in general find the annual costs of occupancy well above 10% of the investment cost because pride of ownership leads them into excessive maintenance. Such maintenance may nevertheless be well justified. Even if it were necessary for the home owner to dress more shabbily or to sacrifice his vacation trip, it is nevertheless true that, if care of the home and work in the garden gives the owner his recreation, it is proper to spend his vacation budget as well as a normal rent upon his home. Home owners can be criticized for financial unwisdom only if (1) they fail annually to accumulate in bonds, in savings bank deposits or in debt reduction a sum equal to the full amount of the total depreciation, or if (2) they fail to appreciate that such accumulation is mere provision for a deferred expense.

Owners of houses for rent are apparently much less likely to make mistakes. Because their thinking is not confused by a delusive hope that some buyer will some day pay for all improvements put into the house, owners of property for rent are usually more conservative about expenditures for maintenance, improvement and modernization.

A home owner who is willing to keep his total cost down to 12% of the purchase price can buy a house which costs him an amount equal to the income of 20 months and may yet find that home ownership costs but little more than a normal rent. For each $100 of income his investment cost will be $166, his annual occupancy cost would be 12% of $166 or $19.92. This is more than one-sixth of the family income, but immediate disbursements will be rather less. Success in making home ownership cost no more than a normal rent depends on two factors: (1) the ratio of the price of the house to the owner's income, and (2) the ratio of annual cost of occupancy to the investment cost of the house. The latter depends on forces over which a purchaser has relatively little control. It is self-restraint which may deter an owner from excessive expenditure for improvements, but it is the community which determines the magnitude of his taxes and interest charges.

Ratio of purchase price (investment cost) to the owner's income is to be regarded as the most important element in the cost of home ownership because this is the only element really subject to a purchaser's control. Men whose incomes exceed $20,000 a year buy on the average homes whose investment cost is less than a year's income. Men whose incomes exceed $50,000 a year buy apparently homes whose investment cost is on the average far less than a year's income. Two forces contribute to these low ratios: (1) It is possible for these men to buy very comfortable homes for less than a year's income. (2) It is possible also that these income recipients have had more experience in the ownership of property and have therefore become accustomed to calculating depreciation at rather liberal rates. Large homes are becoming a smaller percentage of the total number of homes.

Urban life is also altering our need for housing. A century ago the family lived in its home and found most of its entertainment there. The radio is doing something to restore this condition, but the forces of urbanization are very powerful. Now the family finds its recreation in restaurants, the automobile, the movies, the municipal park, and, if wealthy, at the country club. These tendencies are probably undesirable, but they exist.

Young people can no longer be kept at home merely by additional expenditure on a house. A happy family life is certainly more desirable than an attractive home. The conditions of the former are being altered. Data on ratios of home investment to income are not available for the earlier period; but budgets collected in recent years all indicate that housing has a high but somewhat limited utility.

Purchase of a house which costs more than two years' income makes the purchaser a poor credit risk. Families whose incomes are less than $3000 will, therefore, find usually that ownership of a single family home is undesirable. Multiple-family housing (two- and three-family houses, tenement and apartment houses) offers real economies in construction and operation. Families whose incomes are limited find it wise normally to take advantage of these economies.

(4) Excess Investment in Housing may be Wise if Due to a Deficit of Income Which is only Temporary

If a family's income has been $3000 and if it owns a home valued at $5000, then, if the family income is reduced, the question arises whether continued occupancy of the home is wise. If the reduction of income is both serious and permanent, (because, perhaps, of the failure of some source of income), then continued occupancy of expensive housing may lead to an unwise distribution of the family's expenditure. If, however, this reduction in income is temporary only, then continued occupancy of the more expensive quarters may prove to be wise. Changing a residence costs more than the direct costs of moving. These indirect costs of moving must, together with the direct costs, be balanced against the losses due to maldistribution of the family's expenditures.

Young couples frequently buy homes which cost more than their current incomes can afford, but may succeed, nevertheless, in retaining the home purchased if the husband's income increases rapidly. In a period of general business depression, all incomes are reduced. In such a period some investment in excess of the ratio suggested above is probably warranted. How great such excess may properly become, is more difficult to estimate.

(5) Direct Subsidies, if Given, should in Normal Years Supplement the Income of the Occupant Rather than the Construction of Houses

If a family's income is so low that its members need relief, it will be discovered normally that relief is needed along all lines. The family of five whose income is $10 per week needs more than housing. Provision of adequate housing will leave nearly five-sixths of the family's needs still unmet. Free housing might solve a family's problem if the total relief needed amounts to no more than one-fifth of the family's present income; but a small subsidy toward housing would be totally inadequate for the needs of the families that are really in want. Subsidies to housing can do little toward reducing the cost of relief.

Subsidy of housing for families not on relief must depend on other considerations. Government subsidies for housing families whose incomes are below the average but above the need of relief seem difficult to justify except in-so-far as the government may perform some functions more cheaply or more effectively than can private organizations. Subsidies have had an odious record in American history. To provide free public schools, free roads, free parks and free facilities of many kinds has been found wiser than to subsidize private enterprises in the provision of such services. In some foreign lands the subsidy has been less objectionable than in the United States, but American experience thus far has suggested that the humanitarian activities of government become most effective if rendered free of charge. Specific objections to the subsidy of housing on a large scale appear also in the difficulty of laying down clear standards for the selection of families who should receive partial relief in this form.

Government experimentation in housing construction may indeed be defended on the ground that such experimentation is very costly. There is no private organization within the building construction industry which is large enough to afford the cost of this experimentation. Even if such a private organization did exist, it might find experimentation unprofitable because improvements in this field are in general not patentable. The General Electric Company, the General Motors Corporation and the American Telephone Company can afford to subsidize research only because they are large. It is profitable for them to do so only because the results of research in their fields are frequently patentable.

Government construction of housing in periods of depression may also be defended if the investment is viewed as an expenditure for the relief of the workers employed. Such houses when completed should of course be used. Limitation of tenancy in such houses to families who can afford the least rent means that a minimum amount of income will be diverted from private landlords. Such a policy of partial relief to landlords is defensible when real estate also is depressed but would become more debatable if existing houses were completely occupied. As a form of charity to tenants it is almost certainly wasteful. If certain tenant families need to be helped to the extent of perhaps ten dollars a month, it seems arbitrary to require them to spend all this relief income for rent. Superior housing at rents normal for such tenants does nothing to relieve their other burdens. It is a poor substitute for an adequate diet.

Recently a wave of sentiment in favor of subsidizing housing for the sake of the tenants seems to have arisen. Housing is so conspicuous that its defects are more obvious than defects in diet and recreation. It has seemed desirable therefore to indicate here the nature of the economic objection to this policy and to point out that such a policy would go beyond the present policies of our federal government.

(6) Compulsory Minimum Standards in Housing Should Be Advanced only as Per Capita Income Increases

To set high minimum standards for housing without providing the income necessary to meet the added costs may do great injury to families whose incomes are substandard. Higher standards for housing involve in almost all instances a higher investment cost per family. Higher investment costs entail higher costs of occupancy. To make occupancy expensive without providing the income necessary to meet these costs may reduce the amounts available for more necessary expenditures. Because the capacity of society to subsidize family incomes is definitely limited, any widespread improvement in housing conditions must therefore wait upon normal increases in family income.

Knowledge concerning correct housing practice differs from income available for rent. During recent years there has been a great increase in our knowledge concerning proper housing. The impulse to make correct practices universal is therefore exceptionally strong at this time. For this reason it is unfortunate that recent progress in our knowledge about housing has not been paralleled by an increase in the national income. Because the average family income is now smaller than in 1929, efforts to improve the minimum quality of new homes would at this time have chiefly the effect of restraining the erection of substandard housing; they would not promote the construction of adequate housing. More rigid housing standards in a period of diminished income would do little except to increase family congestion within the houses already built.

The chief economic prerequisite for improved housing is increased family income. The chief economic prerequisite for increased family income in a period of business depression is a revival of general business. The chief economic prerequisite for a revival of general business is an increase in construction activity. Conditions which may stimulate construction activity are therefore important here.

Lower prices for construction materials would help to stimulate construction activity, lower hourly wage rates for construction workers and improved methods of construction would also be useful. Re-examination of building codes to eliminate requirements that were needlessly costly would also help to stimulate construction. At this time, however, any change in building codes which increased the cost of constructing new homes would definitely delay the revival of construction and would thus operate to delay the revival of family incomes and of good housing.

Compulsory standards in housing resemble compulsory standards in consumption of any other kind. They are goods that we can afford only after we acquire the capacity to afford. The child who has learned to eat with knife and fork may very properly be prohibited from using a spoon for his vegetables, but this prohibition should wait upon his acquisition of the capacity to use knife and fork. The community with ample income should of course be required to provide schools and to make school attendance compulsory, but proper schooling for all children would be an impossibility in many Chinese villages. In the United States a century ago per capita income was smaller than at present, and housing standards were therefore necessarily lower. As family income has increased we have become able to afford better and better housing. As we become able to afford the better, we can afford also to discard the worse. The point important here is that we should not discard the worse until we can afford the better.

The nature of housing standards should be dictated by the facts discovered by public health investigators and by other workers in the fields of physical and biological science, but the speed with which this knowledge can be applied is limited by facts of a different order. Actual standards in housing can be improved only as the growth of family incomes permits. Minimum standards should be advanced only after current actual practice has led the way. The chief economic requisite for better housing is an increase in per capita income from production.

HEATING AND VENTILATION OF HOMES

C. P. YAGLOU

Department of Industrial Hygiene
Harvard University School of Public Health

Essential Requirements

The purpose of a heating system is not to warm the occupants, but to control the rate of heat loss from their bodies so as to produce a condition of comfort at the lowest possible air temperature that will alleviate contrasts in passing from a warm room to cold outside air.

Air and Wall Temperatures:

The heating system in itself is only half of the problem. The kind and quality of building materials composing the exposed walls, floor, and ceiling have an important bearing on the comfort, healthfulness, and heating economy of a home. This is because our feeling of warmth depends not only on the temperature of the air, but also on the temperature of the surrounding room surfaces to which the human body loses heat by radiation. Under ordinary conditions during the heating season, each degree drop in the mean room-surface temperature must be counteracted by approximately a degree increase of air temperature to maintain the same feeling of warmth.

In a properly insulated home, the temperature of exposed walls is but a few degrees below air temperature and comfortable conditions may be attained with air temperatures at knee height, between 69°F and 73°F in the coldest weather. Poorly built homes may be uncomfortable at 75°F or even at 80°F in cold weather. Aside from excessive radiation loss from the human body, the cold walls and windows in buildings of this kind chill the air in contact with them and also allow much leakage of cold outside air through cracks and crevices. The cold air falls to the floor and chills the feet, while the warm air is pushed up to the ceiling. The temperature may be as low as 60°F near the floor and as high as 85°F near the ceiling, resulting in stuffiness and dryness in the nose.

Suitable insulation of exposed walls, windows, and doors not only improves demonstrably the comfort of a room, but it permits a reduction in the size of heating equipment if the insulation is planned before the house is built. Insulation also effects a substantial saving of fuel to pay for its cost in the course of years.

Humidity:

The usual variations of humidity in homes during the heating season are relatively unimportant to our comfort, and there is no evidence to show that artificial humidification is necessary for health, except in special cases. In properly built homes in New England, the relative humidity seldom, if ever, drops below 20%, owing to a stabilizing action of hygroscopic materials in the walls, furniture, etc. Condensation of moisture on windows and walls limits the maximum relative humidity that can be artificially maintained in cold weather to between 30% to 40%. Higher humidities may lead to serious trouble from condensation and freezing of moisture inside the exposed walls.

Humidification of air permits a small reduction of temperature, about 2°F for a rise of 20% in the relative humidity. This is the maximum amount of humidification allowable in cold weather. No fuel economy results from such a lowering of temperature because it takes more heat to humidify than to maintain a temperature 2°F higher.

The most satisfactory humidifiers are those forming an integral part of the heating unit. They are well adapted to automatic control and are reasonably provided against overhumidification. Their cost varies from $150 to $350.

Air Cleanliness:

Smoke, dusts and gases in ordinary city air may cause considerable damage to property and vegetation, yet there is no conclusive evidence to show direct damage to health, except under unusual circumstances. Studies now in progress may settle the dispute. It should be pointed out that the best commercial air filters do not remove fine solids, or gaseous impurities, which are capable of penetrating deep into the lungs.

The essential requirements, insofar as we know them today, are, therefore good building construction and means for maintaining a uniform temperature of about 70°F in the living quarters, and between 60° and 65°F in bedrooms during the heating season. Additional heat for babies, aged and ill persons may be provided by the use of one or more portable electric heaters. Overheating should be avoided as much as possible. When these requirements are fulfilled, all secondary factors will be taken care of automatically in the average home.

Heating of Homes

Aside from stoves and open fires for small low-priced homes, three principal methods of heating are commonly used in New England: hot air, steam, and hot water, with coal, oil, or gas for fuel. No general agreement exists as to which of the three systems is the best for health, because of the numerous factors upon which health depends and the difficulties of holding these factors constant in any study of relative healthfulness of various heating systems.

The old disreputed hot-air furnace that leaked coal gas and cinders into the air has recently come back under the reverent name of winter air conditioning. It now includes air filtration, humidification, and forced air circulation, in addition to heating. The chief objections to furnace heating, regardless of epithets, are the difficulty of keeping the fire-pot joints tight, and the scorching of dust and soot in the air passing over the hot surfaces of the furnace which may be at 1,000°F or more. Various hydrocarbons are volatilized from atmospheric impurities and these products irritate the mucous membranes of the nose and throat and make the air feel excessively dry. Other more-or-less serious disadvantages are the transmission of noise, odors, and dust throughout the house, owing to the multiplicity of air ducts and the necessity of recirculating air in the interest of economy. The ducts may be insulated against noise, but the odor problem will remain. In a multiple apartment building, a common central hot-air system is unsuitable for this reason, even when the kitchens are separately ventilated by individual exhaust fans.

An important advantage of forced warm-air heating systems is that they lend themselves easily to summer cooling by addition of cooling equipment, or by circulation of cool night air through the building. In homes of allergic persons, much of the pollen content in the air can be filtered out by the use of suitable filters. Street noise is partially shut off by keeping the windows closed.

With steam heating, the objectionable features are the liability of overheating the building in mild weather, and the scorching of dust and soot by hot radiator surfaces. The ordinary one-pipe system is simple and low in first cost, but it may prove wholly unsatisfactory from the standpoint of temperature control, economy of operation, noise, and odors from air valves, if not properly designed and operated. This system is now obsolete in the better-class homes. Two-pipe steam systems equipped with vacuum air valves cost a little more to install, but they are more economical to operate and not so objectionable from the standpoint of steam circulation, odors, and noise.

Hot-water heating possesses many qualities of an ideal system for homes. It provides an even, mild heat and an extremely flexible temperature regulation, by manual or automatic control of the water-heating unit. It is simple, noiseless, and odorless, and does not scorch dust and soot because the radiator surfaces are kept at a comparatively low temperature. One disadvantage is the large size of radiators and pipes by comparison with steam systems.

Radiators should be placed under the windows in order to compensate for the cooling effect of windows and outer walls, and to produce a more uniform temperature distribution in the room. Each radiator should be provided with a hand control valve, and when the boiler draft, oil, or gas burner are controlled thermostatically, the room temperature may be adequately maintained.

In regard to costs of heating equipment, gravity hot-air heating is the least expensive, excepting stoves and pipeless furnaces. One-pipe steam systems cost about a third more than the gravity hot air; two-pipe steam costs a quarter more than one-pipe, and hot-water systems costs about as much as the two-pipe steam. The extra cost of winter air conditioning (without summer cooling) is about 25% over that of hot-water, or two-pipe steam systems. As a general rule, the cost of the heating system should not exceed 10% of the total building cost. Stoves, or a pipeless furnace, are indicated when this limit is exceeded in low-priced homes.

The selection of fuels and fuel-burning equipment for New England homes is a complex matter to be decided by the owner with the assistance of the contractor or engineer. Careful consideration should be given to the economic status of the owner or tenant, the availability of fuels in a given locality, the construction of the building, initial and maintenance costs of heating equipment, as well as the owner's ideas about comfort, convenience, cleanliness, noise, odors, and general appearances.

Gas, oil, and district steam are the cleanest and most desirable sources of heat for those who can afford the price. In low-priced, rural homes where wood is plentiful, the choice rests mainly between stoves and hot-air furnaces of the pipeless or piped type. Hand-fired coal furnaces or boilers are next in order. Where small-size coal for automatic stokers can be had at a cost lower than that of hand-fired coal, a stoker may save enough fuel by preventing overheating to pay for itself eventually. It does not completely solve the problems, however, of ash removal, dirt, and noise.

Automatic oil and gas-burning equipment entail not only additional initial and maintenance costs, but also additional cost for fuel. Gas is the ideal fuel, but it is also the most expensive, excepting electricity. Its advantages over coal stokers and oil can only be intangibly evaluated in terms of cleanliness, convenience, freedom of noise, and small space requirements. For well-insulated homes in localities where gas is available at nominal rates, the cost of gas-fired system is well within the budget of many moderate-income families.

Oil in New England costs considerably less than gas, and will more than offset the higher initial and running costs of oil-burning equipment. In all cases, and especially when gas or oil is used, it is essential to burn the fuel as completely as possible to guard against overheating and to avoid unnecessary waste of heat through windows, doors, and fireplaces. Proper cleaning and servicing of the equipment by a competent person once a year is an important factor in the life and economic operation of the system.

Ventilation of Homes

Winter Ventilation:

The average detached home has too much air leakage in cold weather to require artificial ventilation. With storm sash and storm doors, the leakage may be reduced to about half an air change per hour and still provide sufficient ventilation when the air space per occupant is 500 cubic feet or more. Kitchens must be ventilated separately to remove cooking odors, excessive heat, and moisture, at the source. The preferred method is by means of a kitchen exhaust fan attached to a wall opening near the ceiling or to the upper half of a window, as near as possible to the kitchen range.

Summer Ventilation and Cooling:

Air cooling and dehumidification in warm weather unquestionably contribute much to our comfort and efficiency, but the cost of artificial refrigeration is still too high for general use. For most homes in New England, good building insulation, including awnings on the sunny sides of the building, and the circulation of cool night air from outside will serve as a substitute for artificial cooling, except in hot spells of long duration. The best arrangement is to install in the attic an exhaust fan having a capacity between fifteen and thirty air changes per hour. The fan should be started after sunset and air should be drawn through the first-story windows in the early evening and through the second-story during the rest of the night. Starting with a cool house in the morning, the insulation will keep the inside temperature below the outside if the windows and blinds are kept shut.

In low-priced homes, where the cost of an attic fan may not be justified, reliance must be placed on structural design with respect to cross ventilation. Natural ventilation of the attic during the day will help in all instances.

It should be kept in mind that the comfortable temperature in the summer varies from 70°F to 85°F, according to the outside temperature, owing to the fact that we become adapted to warm weather and we wear thinner and fewer clothes.

LIGHTING FOR SEEING
M. LUCKIESH AND FRANK K. MOSS
Lighting Research Laboratory: General Electric Company
Nela Park, Cleveland

This is a half-seeing world because the eyes are so often defective, partially disabled by inadequate light and improper lighting and dulled by misuse and the steadily increasing demands of exacting visual work. The enormous increase in the number of newspapers, magazines and books which has taken place in modern civilization is but a single example of the increasing use of the eyes for difficult visual work. On every hand are found other cases of increasing use and abuse of the eyes. Our modern mode of living, although it may be admirably suited to civilized man's desires and ambitions, is not necessarily best nor ideal for his inherited physical being. Certainly the prevalence of defective vision indicates that modern life is not generally ideal for the well-being of the eyes. In this "machine age" the human machine is sometimes neglected. It is in need of a few adjustments to fit it better for its tasks.

Much has been done to save the eyes of infants by means of medical care and of adults by mechanical protection from hazardous industrial operations. These are largely measures of prevention. Of the millions who begin life with normal eyesight, why is it that relatively few reach maturity with perfect eyes? If eye defects could temporarily be changed into comparable degrees of crippled legs, one would be greeted with a heart-rending spectacle! Standing on the street of a city one would see a continuous parade of persons limping along—some slightly, others on crutches, still others in wheel-chairs. Every other person passing by would be perceptibly crippled. Certainly it is worthwhile to prevent or to minimize or even to counteract by other means as much of this defectiveness of vision as possible.

Although the modern age imposes certain abuses upon the eyes, its sciences have developed effective corrective measures if they were widely appreciated and skillfully utilized. The optical and medical professions have made many advances in preventing and correcting defective vision and through lighting development ideal lighting is available to assist the eyes in their arduous tasks.

Seeing is the result of a partnership of lighting and vision. If eyes are defective, proper lenses are available for compensating the defects and for relieving the eyes of some of the strain and fatigue. Eyes without light are sightless. Eyes with inadequate light are inefficient, easily fatigued and defective vision is invited. Ideal lighting is essential if we are to see clearly, quickly and comfortably. Ideal lighting demands an adequate quantity of light and proper lighting free from glare. Since the eyes evolved for use under the abundance of daylight, they are entitled to more than the primitive artificial lighting exhibited in inadequate light and improper lighting so commonly encountered.

The unit of intensity of illumination is easily defined. If a surface is placed one foot from an ordinary candle so that the rays of light fall perpendicularly upon the surface, or nearly so, the intensity of illumination is about one *footcandle*. The intensity of illumination will be the same whether the surface is a white paper, a black cloth, a colored bookcover, or anything else. However, it will be noted that these various surfaces will appear of different brightnesses. The object of light is to produce brightness and the latter depends upon the reflection of the object. On a horizontal surface outdoors the intensity of illumination reaches a maximum of 10,000 footcandles at midday on a clear day in summer. On an overcast day it is often several thousand footcandles; and when in the open the intensity is as low as 1000 footcandles, the day is considered as a dull or dark one. Indoors and at a window the intensity of illumination is commonly as high as 300 footcandles, but at a distance of a few feet from the window it may be only a few footcandles. Almost everywhere in the indoor work-world artificial light is in use and the average intensity of illumination is only a few footcandles—and one footcandle is common. In view of these facts the following recommendations of intensities of illumination are considered as conservative.

100 Footcandles or more—For very severe and prolonged tasks, such as fine needlework, fine engraving, fine penwork, fine assembly, sewing on dark goods and discrimination of fine details of low contrast, as in inspection.

50 to 100 Footcandles—For severe and prolonged tasks, such as proofreading, drafting, difficult reading, watch repairing, fine machine-work, average sewing and other needlework.

20 to 50 Footcandles—For moderately critical and prolonged tasks, such as clerical work, ordinary reading, common benchwork and average sewing and other needlework on light goods.

10 to 20 Footcandles—For moderate and prolonged tasks of office and factory and when not prolonged, ordinary reading and sewing on light goods.

5 to 10 Footcandles—For visually controlled work in which seeing is important, but more or less interrupted or casual and does not involve discrimination of fine details or low contrasts.

0 to 5 Footcandles—The danger zone for severe visual tasks, and for quick and certain seeing. Satisfactory for perceiving larger objects and for casual seeing.

It is a very simple matter to obtain desirable intensities of illumination. In a bridge lamp there is a 60-watt lamp. About one foot from it the photometer or footcandle-meter registers 80 footcandles, and at two feet, about 20 footcandles. On replacing this lamp with a 100-watt lamp more than 150 footcandles are obtained at a distance of one foot and 100 footcandles at a convenient distance for reading, sewing, etc. Before the mirror in the bathroom the intensity of illumination is 40 footcandles from two 60-watt lamps in diffusing shades, one on each side of the mirror at the height of the face. A 500-watt portable lamp in the bathroom provides mild ultraviolet and penetrating infra-red radiation for health purposes. Three feet from it the photometer registers 1000 footcandles! How easily such an intensity of illumination is obtained and how hopelessly low the common intensities of illumination indoors really are. Such comparisons aid materially in demonstrating the value of quantities of light which are natural to us as seeing-machines, because we are still products of outdoor environment.

It is seen that levels of illumination of 100 footcandles and more, obtained easily and inexpensively with artificial light, are still meager compared with common daylight intensities, but they are far above those found almost everywhere in the indoor world. In homes low-wattage lamps are prevalent. It is difficult to find a boudoir lamp for the bedside in which a 100-wat lamp can be inserted. In railway stations, where one passes the time reading, less than a footcandle usually prevails at night. In many of the old stations this is not exceeded much in the daytime. Few schools have more than five footcandles of artificial light. Progressive stores, offices and factories may have five to ten footcandles and, in rare cases, 20 footcandles; but, for the most part, the artificial world is scarcely emerging from the age of candles in the intensities of illumination on visual tasks.

The eyes of children demand all the assistance that science is capable of providing. Young eyes in the formative period are easily injured. In an attempt to compensate for poor lighting, objects to be seen are held too close to the eyes, and the defect of nearsightedness is a common result. Improper lighting causes children and even adults to assume awkward postures in order to see better. Thus habits are formed which place abnormally severe strains upon the ocular muscles. Lighting skillfully employed assists in acquiring correct postures, thereby eliminating useless and detrimental muscular strain. Then there are old eyes to consider. They need more light than average adult eyes. The same is true of imperfect eyes. Still, even normal adult eyes are seldom provided with ideal lighting.

As the eyes of adults grow older, many changes occur which should be considered. The pupils are smaller and more light is necessary. The lens of the eye becomes less flexible with age and a book must be held farther away in order to be in focus. In this case the reading matter is not so easily seen and eyeglasses and better lighting become increasingly helpful. Sciene has proved that good lighting helps those most who need help most.

The eyes are remarkable for their ability to adjust themselves for a variety of conditions. No other piece of apparatus can approach them in their marvelous range of adaptability and sensitivity. They are slow to complain of their need for glasses and for better lighting. Therefore, they are being penalized for their ability to overcome unfavorable and injurious conditions. Even though eyes can see some objects at low levels of illumination and defective eyes can see to some extent without glasses, they should not be sentenced to do so for long periods daily. An automobile may climb a steep hill in low-gear; but no sensible motorist will drive a car for hours in "low." It is built for continuous operation in "high." An automobile has the advantage of complaining in very positive ways against mistreatment. The eyes are penalized because they do not always complain and, when they do, they are likely to complain indirectly and indefinitely. We should be considerate of our eyes because they are so considerate of us—and they are invaluable.

HEALTHFUL LIGHTING

WILLIAM FIRTH WELLS
Instructor in Sanitary Science
Harvard School of Public Health

The recent emphasis upon the apparently mysterious therapeutic and bactericidal effects of light is likely to fix these as the predominant health factors in the public mind. Granting light the role of the great purifier, its important physiological effects and curative properties, as also the claims of irradiated foods, there remains in the field of illumination engineering a major public health factor. The indirect benefits of good lighting on health are out of all proportion to the more spectacular direct applications of light to disease, or even to the recorded injury and death resulting from faulty lighting.

Vision provides the primary channel through which the human being receives impressions from the environment. From birth to death the environment is being constantly explored by sight. Education is largely a process of visual imagery, and our picture of the world about,—whether direct, or through pictures, or the printed word, or even the spoken language, which depends for its effectiveness upon an appeal to visual memory,—is a visual impression. It is not surprising therefore to find that one-half of all the sensory nerve fibers entering the brain are visual, and considering the dependence of life upon the continuous adjustment of the individual to the environment, we must recognize the protection of the eye as a public health problem second only to life itself.

Until community life becomes complex enough to have a public health significance light comes as naturally to us as air, for such simple purposes as may be needed. Concentration of population, however, creates artificial conditions of existence. Life phases formerly separated in time by daylight or darkness depend more and more upon location. Suitable conditions for work, play and sleep are more difficult to secure in the same area, and so industrial, residential and recreational zones are established. Congestion drives buildings upward, further limiting both light and air, and requiring artificial devices to provide the primary requisites of healthy existence. Public health, faced with a study of the consequences, discovers hitherto overlooked health benefits from the scientific control of lighting.

Artificial lighting cannot be passively regarded as merely an expedient in community development. Removal of the limitations of natural lighting gives more complete control of our environment and thus makes more healthful living conditions possible. For fifteen centuries the candle furnished our only independence from sunlight, but the last century has evolved in succession the gas jet, the kerosene lamp, the gas mantle, the arc light, the incandescent lamp and luminous tubes. How much these have affected modern life requires little memory or imagination. The possibilities of improving conditions of healthful living can only be disclosed by further study. Anyone can test the degree to which the illuminating engineer can meet required conditions by witnessing the achievements of the motion picture. Only the specification of the physiologist remains to be elaborated in placing light at the service of public health.

Economic considerations have already brought about fundamental improvements in lighting. Although contented workers, because of more agreeable working conditions, reduced eyestrain, elimination of accidents, together with the intangible psychological effects of cheerfully lighted surroundings, are a distinct asset to their employer—cutting down labor turnover and compensation—there are more direct earnings on an investment in good lighting. Making the dark hours useful and raising the efficiency of the workmen has increased production from ten to twenty-five per cent with no other addition to plant equipment than an up-to-date lighting system costing but one to five per cent of the payroll. This does not include the great improvement in the quality of the work which results from better lighting nor the effective supervision it makes possible. Spoilage due to poor lighting is said to cost American industry more than $28,000,000 annually. Bad lighting was responsible for nearly 25% of the 91,000 accidents in 1910. Better lighting cut this percentage more than a third in the next eight years, still leaving, however, a considerable loss of time. It is estimated that a million dollars in wages are lost annually in Massachusetts.

While these figures do not begin to measure the effect of lighting on health, they serve to indicate the vast importance of the effect. If employers can gain so much in lifting the strain from the worker, the benefit to the worker himself must be evident. The first effect of inadequate lighting is eyestrain, leading to a slowing down of the work. Continuance brings permanent impairment with ultimate reduced visual efficiency. Until this damage eliminates the worker, the employer also shares the loss in efficiency, after which the cost is borne by the worker. It then concerns, the public, and if health may be regarded as a position condition of life, this concern is a problem in public health.

HOUSING AS THE ARCHITECT VIEWS IT

ELEANOR MANNING O'CONNOR

Member, American Institute of Architects

Since architecture is by definition the art of building superlatively, the architect's primary concern is to create shelter which functions; shelter which protects its inmates against cold and heat, against snow and rain. The architect must so design this shelter that it performs these physical functions easily, satisfying the most rigid requirements imposed by climate, situation, use, and price. He must above all add to these physical satisfactions the psychological factors which give aesthetic pleasure. If the shelter is to come under the heading of architecture, the designer must make the structure practical and beautiful. Housing, which is shelter for living, includes in its broad scope the tailor-made house especially designed for the individual to suit luxurious tastes and a corpulent purse, as well as the small suburban house built from stock plans and financed by a loaning agency. It includes the house provided in quantity by the real estate operators who speculate in land and in houses of all prices and of all types from the palatial apartment houses to the wooden three-deckers. In every housing category the fundamental architectural problem is the relation of the house to the land; to plan for living, the architect should first shape his building to make the most out of the site; he should utilize the land so that sun and air, wind and vista, are all considered from the point of view of the persons who are to live in the house. For the large detached house on a spacious plot of ground in Weston where the minimum size of lot is one acre of land, the problem is a simple one of deciding upon size and shape of house and of placing the rooms to take advantage of sun, air, and view. For the smaller detached house which might be built in Wellesley where, by zoning ordinance, one quarter of an acre is the minimum size, there is still possible a goodly amount of sun, perhaps some pleasant vistas, and the correct placing of the rooms within the area of the house for cross draft. In both these sites the house with its long dimension north and south can be kept near the north lot line to get the greatest amount of land space to the south and west for sun and prevailing breeze. Within the house if no cramping of shape is brought about by the pressure of neighboring properties, the use of rooms may determine their position.

Houses built upon land of this sort fall into the class of good housing almost automatically, provided that certain elementary rules of planning are observed. Rooms should have windows for light and doors for ingress and egress; corners are valuable in a climate where hot weather may prevail, because of beneficent cross drafts. Passageways make it practical to maintain privacy within the rooms. Closets and cupboards are essential for good housekeeping; and as much sanitary plumbing as the budget will cover may start with the modicum of one bathroom, which has an outside window, and a kitchen with a combination sink and laundry tray.

Good housing today is heated housing although air-conditioning is feasible only within the higher budget. Electric lighting is likewise a sina qua non.

In the higher categories house-planning can be criticized principally because of failure to develop a pleasant connection with the land. A garden may be planted to furnish a setting for the house; but too often the charm of living on the land is not recognized; if no door leads one from the house to a terrace, the garden fails of a primary purpose. Both the higher- and lower-priced houses of the detached type in this country often fail to realize the delight of privacy upon one's land achieved by boundary walls, fences, or hedges. An extension of living into the open air becomes practical only when one can live upon the land without the sense of exposure which is often facetiously called "living in a gold-fish bowl."

When the problem becomes one of providing good housing for the lower wage earner, the architect's work may be hampered by the method of land subdivision, by the size of the plots. In suburban developments narrow lots are sold for single houses and two unfortunate results eventuate. Too much of the ground is covered by the house which is placed so close to both sides of the lot that light and air in the side rooms become impossible to obtain. The only facades which have light and air and a chance for sun face the street and the back yard. With a small back yard, a narrow street, and narrow side yards the first characteristic of bad housing is evident: an overcrowded lot, too great land coverage to guarantee to the interior the first requirements for health, sun and air.

Probably the best plan of land development, which would give low-priced lots light, air, and privacy within the house, is the narrow lot arrangement with the house built like the English cottage with party walls. This allows what is called the row house to be built in groups or blocks in a fashion not unlike our city houses except that the width should be greater than the depth in order to get adequately lighted rooms. When the area of land within the block is "pooled," that is, thrown into one area, a playground for children is an additional asset. With this type of small-house development it is essential to keep the depth of the house from becoming so great that dark interior rooms are found in the no man's area between the outside front and back rooms. In many of the newer real-estate renting projects this row house idea has proved successful. Some of the larger apartments of the Old Harbor Village project in South Boston are two-story row houses planned in this way and it will be interesting to observe their popularity. It is the recognized cottage plan in England but it has been unfortunately slow to appeal to the individualistic American. The American who buys or even rents a small house would put up in general with side yards practically nonexistent, would put up with lack of privacy, with the noise of neighbors too close for comfort, with a plain view of all their activities, with all the stupidities of planning imposed by a narrow lot of land; provided only that he has no direct physical connection with his neighbor.

Until private enterprise builds the row house in quantity in not too large blocks which may become monotonous, with varying setbacks for landscape and architectural charm, with varying but harmonious architecture to make for community individuality, the lower wage earner will have to take what he can get; and what he can get is in this country usually a makeshift compared with the housing provided by other countries for the same type of family. In Sweden and parts of Germany the modern two-story terraced houses with plenty of glass area in the front and back walls give one answer. In this country the Chatham Village of Pittsburgh with a difficult topography; Mariemont near Cincinnati; Kingsport in Kentucky show different architectural solutions.

Multiple family houses as they have been built by the Federal Government are practical exemplars of good housing. They have set standards of open land development and of the placing of the houses on the land to get sun in the greatest number of rooms; standards which will at least make people think about the advantages of light rooms. In the placing of the apartment buildings on the land they have avoided land overcrowding. Thirty-three families to the acre of land may not compare favorably with England's twelve to sixteen families but it is a vast improvement over the four hundred families crowded on an acre of land in the North end of Boston. The provision of play areas for the little children is a social advantage which is outside the province of this brief survey to dwell upon. But the development of the basements of apartment buildings to give space for locked baby carriage garages, community laundries, play rooms for the children of all ages at different times of day, of social rooms for neighborhood festivities in the evening—these present an architectural solution of a social requirement.

How do the plans of the living quarters within the newer type of apartment differ from the old type? One has only to fly over Boston to see many streets with the wooden three-deckers peculiar to this part of the United States and to compare it with the view one gets of Old Harbor Village, to get one answer to this question. The old-type, three-decker had a narrow front, was long from front to back, and when the long side faced the sun, the five-room apartment was good housing. It had usually a parlor, living room and kitchen on one side with two bedrooms and bath on the other. It was only when the narrow-fronted, long-sided structure was placed on a narrow lot, two, three, or at most four feet between it and its similar neighbor, directly on the street as in East Boston, and little backyard, that it was made automatically into bad housing.

The newer plans are wide in front and shallow, only two rooms from front to back so that the immediate improvement is noted. A cross draft is obtainable in every apartment because of the two exposures; but more than that there is no dark interior room and no room looks directly into a neighbor's rooms across a narrow chasm. The better layout of streets allows wide paths to serve the back cellar entrances; money is now wasted on unnecessary streets. The fact that there are no closed courts guarantees less noise inside the apartments.

The rooms themselves are so organized as to make for flexible use. In low-cost housing the need for sleeping space is obvious and the living room often must serve the combined uses of sleeping room by night and living room by day and evening. In the newer plans the kitchen serves as a passageway to the small hall connecting the bedrooms and bathroom. The need, too, for dining space in the kitchen is recognized and the most efficient arrangement of electric or gas range, working table, sink and laundry tray, and electric refrigerator, saves steps for the busy home-maker. Garbage and waste paper is disposed of in an incinerator on each floor of the apartment houses. Closets for each bedroom and entrance hall and a linen closet and broom closet, make it easy to preserve order.

Steam heat and electric light, domestic hot water, gas or electric range and refrigerators are provided in addition to the standard bathroom, and these amenities unquestionably make housekeeping better because of the simplification.

A standard for amount of window area for a definite cubic contents of room; and also a definite area of room space per person obviates room overcrowding, which is one of the evils of bad housing. Durable materials for the structure, fire resistant and easily cleaned, undoubtedly add to the charm of the new housing and presents a further contrast with the wooden buildings which so quickly become dilapidated.

Fundamentally, however, the appeal to the architect, in the newer low-cost housing, is the sane use of the land, attractively planted with trees and shrubs; the openness of the apartment groups, the inspiring effect of sun and air, and within the structure the pleasant outlook through windows which are large enough to insure light; the light stairways; the lack of dark, waste space inside the buildings. All these make for good housing, for health, mental and physical, in suroundings which one goes home to with pleasure.

PLAY PLACES IN THE HOUSE FOR CHILDREN
Susan M. Coffin, M.D., *Consultant*
Massachusetts Department of Public Health

In planning a home, whether in a house or an apartment, play space indoors and out for the children is an important item. The idea would be, of course, to have a separate bedroom for each child and a large playroom for the use of all the children. But this ideal is beyond the reach of most families today and as so many live in apartments the space available has to be carefully adjusted to the children's needs.

If there is only a baby and one preschool child to be considered they can share one good sized bedroom comfortably but additional play space is necessary for the older child, especially in cold weather.

A playroom, even though it is small, is a great asset with children of all ages. If it is impossible to give up a room, the child's bedroom can be converted into a playroom. A convenient closet with low shelves and hooks, a low chest of drawers for clothing and a small cupboard or chest for playthings, all add to the young child's comfort and aid in his training.

Furniture should be simple, sturdy and easily movable, so that it can be pushed back and a good space arranged in the middle of the room. A low table and chairs are much enjoyed by little children and they help in keeping good posture. Being able to rest the feet firmly on the floor helps children to maintain better posture when sitting at meals, games, or to look at picture books, etc.

In cold or stormy weather it is a good plan to open all the windows wide in the room used for play, have the children put on out-of-doors play clothes and then let them play in the fresh air for an hour or more. Fresh air has a marvelous effect on appetites and dispositions!

A porch or sunroom is a great advantage, especially in upstairs apartments where no yard is available or where it is too far away for the little child to play alone. Here the baby and preschool children can take their naps as well as play in the open air. If there is room, a hammock and a small swing will add much to the children's pleasure and help to keep them contented. With the child who seems never to want to play in the open air, first make sure that he is not suffering from some physical condition that makes him unduly sensitive to cold and heat.

We find the only child who has no neighbors of his own age is sometimes quite opposed to playing out of doors by himself at any time. Keeping some well-liked playthings that are only to be used out of doors helps to interest him in staying out.

Walking and riding with adults can never take the place of active, out-of-doors play with suitable play material.

A portable play pen for the baby or child who is just learning to walk is an excellent safety device as well as a great help to the baby and to his busy mother. A large number of accidents occur in homes and many of them happen to babies and runabouts, so any device such as the play pen, that helps to prevent injuries is of great value.

If there is a room to spare, opening off the dining room or kitchen, as sometimes does happen in apartments, a gate can be hung in the doorway and the child put in this room with his playthings. Mother can easily "keep an eye" on him and give him a word of encouragement in his play as she goes about her work. Teaching children to amuse themselves is a valuable thing in early habit training. Nothing is more pathetic than to see children who are wholly dependent on being amused and it is a habit that is apt to persist for a lifetime.

In some crowded homes, temporarily at least, it is possible to provide only a "play corner" for the children but even this small space means a good deal to the child. The play corner may be in the living room, dining room or bedroom. It is the place where each child can have a box in which to keep his own playthings and where there can be shelves for the children's books. If there is room for table and chairs so much the better. The ordinary "cutting" table does not take up much room and can have the legs shortened to make it a convenient height for younger children. A substantial "bench" or single seats can be made from packing boxes.

Attics are almost unknown nowadays but a basement room is quite often available and if it has good light and ventilation, with sufficient heat in winter, it can be most useful. The small children can use it as a playroom in cold or stormy weather and the older children can enjoy it for games, plays, etc. An inexpensive game table may be made or bought second hand. With a few comfortable chairs and two or three good pictures, or gay hangings, even a basement room can be made home-like and pleasant and the expense of fixing it up will not be too great.

A play yard, however small, is a great possession. Mother and father may have to give up their yearnings for an attractive yard with flowers and shrubs, during the years the children need it so much for play, but they will be amply repaid—and gardening can wait for middle age when the children are grown up!

Of course, every proper yard has a sand pile for "the youngest in the family" to use in warm weather. Simple play apparatus can be constructed or bought without great expense. The Children's Bureau, Washington, D. C., and the Massachusetts Extension Service, Amherst, Mass., have leaflets showing how to build swings, slides, seasaws, etc. Large building blocks or boxes, a big "soft" ball, a wheelbarrow to carry stones and dirt about—these and other things can be added gradually. A small shed in which to store these out-of-doors playthings is quite necessary.

If there is a garage that can be opened wide on the sunny side of the building, it will provide an excellent "windbreak" in cold weather and so make a good place for children to run, play ball, hop scotch, etc., on windy days in late fall and winter.

To sum up briefly: We provide for one of the essential needs of children by planning play space indoors and out. When planning for indoors play we must always bear in mind that fresh air and good lighting are absolutely necessary to the health of the child.

For out-of-doors play we need to think of the value of direct sunlight on the body and to remember that nothing takes the place of active play—walking and riding are not enough.

In both instances it may be necessary for the grown-ups to sacrifice, for a time, a room or garden that might be made much more beautiful if not given over to the children. But who wouldn't rather see children with ample space to play in and benefiting from it in body and spirit, day by day!

LOW COST OF DECORATING

DONALD SMITH FEELEY
Co-Director, Modern School of Applied Art

Interior decoration is no longer recognized as a mere pastime for the unnecessarily rich but as a duty of every homemaker irrespective of their financial resources. Beauty in the home is not dependent upon the expenditure of large sums of money but rather upon the exertion of intelligence. It is not so much what we use that makes our homes attractive and individual but more the way we use things. Beauty is found in cotton as well as silk. It may be a different type of beauty to be sure but nevertheless artistically correct. Home decorating should be the reflection of good taste as against the revelation of one's purse and art in the home can be adjusted to any purse. It is in communities where sordidness reigns over beauty that crime and immorality best thrive. The homemaker's heart must be in and of the home if that home is to reflect the joy of living. I have seen tenements of two or three rooms, erstwhile dirty, slovenly places fit more for the habitation of rats than human beings, turn under the magic wand of good taste into clean, cheerful and attractive homes. I have seen cold, dreary rooms made to reflect warmth and joy by merely applying the right type of paint or paper to the walls. A wealthy client of mine once insisted that his casement windows throughout one of his homes be equipped with draw curtains of unbleached muslin with resultant good taste. On the other hand, I have seen poor people use cheap imitations of damasks about their rooms which did no more than to reveal a false sense of values and ignorance.

The real homemaker knows how to become acquainted with beauty. She knows the public libraries have reliable books on the subject and she goes there and consults them and applies the theories to her home decorating problems. Homes are the reflection of our personalities. An ugly home is a mirror held up to stupidity, ignorance or criminal indifference.

"What is the most important thing in interior decoration?" This is a question frequently asked of a decorator. The only answer to that is that there is no "most important thing." The professional or amateur decorator must give as much thought and attention to the smallest objects he uses as to the more conspicuous appointments. Artistically speaking no one thing is more important than another.

Just as in a fine painting every object the artist portrays lends so much charm and meaning to the finished composition, so in decorating a room every thing used should contribute its bit to the completed interior. Perhaps if the question were asked, "Where is the most effective place to start redecorating a room?" the reply could be more helpful and more definite. The background of a room is really the most important area. By background is meant the ceiling, walls and floor. These features are the functional structure of our rooms. They enclose a room and, therefore, form its most conspicuous part.

In interior decoration, contrary to the usual procedure in life, we begin at the top and work down. The next time you call a painter to consult about one of your rooms notice that the first place to arrest his attention is the ceiling. Although we sometimes see dark ceilings used to fashionable advantage, it is usually advisable to have the ceiling the lightest value in the room. Floors should be the darkest value and walls should range in value between the lightness of the ceiling and the darkness of the floor. People are prone to use papers or paints on their walls that are too dark. Dark colored walls, unless rich in color, can only cast gloomy reflections about a room and make the people in them look like bad cases of liver complaint. Rooms that have little sunlight in them should have warm hues on the walls. Yellow makes a very cheerful room out of a gloomy one. Where there are sunny exposures, cooler colors may be used to advantage such as gray, green blue or blue. In doing over a room one must consider the exposure of the room, its use and the personalities of the individuals to use the room.

As a practical example let us invent a decorative scheme for a bedroom of northern exposure occupied by a boy of ten years. We will paint the ceiling a light butter yellow and the walls a deeper value of the same hue. The woodwork, doors and window frames we will paint to match the walls for it is a small room and we do not wish to call attention to the broken wall spaces. With this treatment we will considerably enlarge the apparent size of the room and experience a sense of greater freedom and breathing space. The floor, which we already know theoretically should embrace the darkest value in a room, we will paint a deep golden brown. A deck paint will withstand the abuse of heavy boots and we must be practical. Incidentally, on the walls we will use a flat paint, knowing the tendency of a glossy surface to take on an institutional look besides reducing the apparent size of the room.

Venetian blinds are too expensive for this particular problem, for what is appropriate for Johnny at ten will not hold true at sixteen. We must think fast for something other than Venetian blinds but as effective. Porch screens in natural straw color are our decision in this respect and we will tie them up with brown cords just to give an added smartness. Silks or satins or such smooth textures would never do in this room for Johnny does not want to be called a "sissy," so the window draperies must be of a more virile stuff. Brown burlap is the answer and along the edges and across the bottoms we will pull woolen threads of a bright tangerine with here and there a blue strand. This treatment gives a rather peasanty effect and so we are right up on fashion, whether it is "spinach" or not. By all means we decide to have the draperies full length and not split. We are sick and tired of skinny curtains and so will use width.

Floor carpets are so expensive for a youngster of this age that we must think of something cheaper yet as effective. Let us try sewing strips of straw matting together until we have achieved a mat nine feet by twelve. We will bind the four outer edges with a tangerine bias binding and if any of us have a yen for borders we can just stencil a simple conventionalized one about six inches deep around the four edges using brown and tangerine colored paints.

Hurrah! The background of our room is complete and now for the furnishings. Let's see! That mission desk and those mission chairs with the torn leather seats are all right from a structural point and, since we advocate using to the best advantage those things we already possess, we will paint them a dark navy blue. The leather seat coverings can be replaced with awning cloth having tangerine and blue stripes. The old brass bedstead is an eyesore, but oh so comfortable. It will look better under a coat of blue paint along with the golden oak bureau. For a bedspread cotton crash is just the thing to withstand careless muddy feet and the resultant frequent washings. We will bind the edges with tangerine and cover loads of pillows with blue denim. This sturdy material thrives on pillow fights. Just for smartness a cord of our cheerful tangerine can be stitched around the edges of each pillow.

The lamp bases would be best in pewter finish and for shades we could make some very effective ones out of oiled wrapping paper. It, however, will be much easier to buy some parchment paper ones and not much more expensive. These we can rebind in passepartout, Chinese red in color. The small accessories about the room such as handkerchief boxes, et cetera, can be painted Chinese red just to give the final seasoning to our color scheme. It is in these smaller items that we can be a bit daring and use stronger color than elsewhere in the room. Perhaps we can paint an old cedar chest or steamer trunk dark blue to match the furniture. Placed under one of the windows, it will provide grand storage space for boxing gloves and footballs. Copies of old sporting prints in Chinese red frames will bring a needed touch to the empty wall spaces. There! That finishes the room. We certainly worked hard to make it a decorative success but what a "swell" feeling of satisfaction overcomes us when we regard the results and realize how little in actual money the metamorphosis has cost.

Now we will simply have to do something about Jenny's room to avoid any feeling of partiality after showering so much attention on her brother. Of course, her room will be quite different because she has naturally a different personality. Then, too, her room faces south and has floods of bright sunlight. We know that exposure and personality must be our first considerations. This sunny exposure gives us the opportunity to use that nice pale blue she adores because it is a cool color. We will paper the walls with that new scrubable wall paper that comes in such a variety of fascinating plain colors. The line includes just the blue we are after. A pale yellow ceiling will make a pleasing contrast. The doors and windows must be painted to match the wallpaper because her room is small too. The floor will take a dark blue very nicely and tie up properly with the general background. Over the floor let us place scatter rugs. We can buy some of those inexpensive machine-made braided ones in rose and tan.

The curtains at the windows can be made to draw across. It is always so dramatic to shut out the gaze of the vulgar public by simply pulling a cord at the side of the window. These curtains can be made of white cotton crepe and along the edge a short bushy fringe of rose will be exciting. For an added surprise several rows of rose rick-rack braid can be stitched inside the fringe. This will make them look much more important and individual. White cotton crepe can serve as the bedspread also, the valance of which can be slightly shirred. At the bottom of the valance, and working up, rows of ruffles can be attached and each edged with the same rose fringe used on the curtains. Jenny, too, will want a sea of pillows on her bed. These will look well covered in rose and white checked crepe. To make them very smart white crepe ruffles should surround each pillow. These must be at least five inches deep and the edges self fringed. This is so easily done by merely pulling threads that the entire family can be put to work on it.

The furniture, which is the customary bedroom variety in stupid golden oak, we will cover beneath coats of yellow paint. Not nondescript ivory but rather a sort of buttercup yellow. The little boudoir chair we plan as a birthday present will be upholstered in blue glazed chintz with a printed floral motif in gay colorings. Next year when she will be fifteen going on sixteen we might arrange a dressing table for her. This will be smart draped in the same pink and white checked cotton crepe we have decided for her pillows. The accessories in this room could be amethyst as far as color is concerned. Her youth, however, and the coarser texture of the materials already used call for a less subtle and delicate color.

A deeper blue than employed elsewhere in the room will be more youthful for the nicknacks. Blue pottery lamp bases with pongee shades, pin trays of deep blue glass, boxes painted blue without and rose within will serve as vehicles to carry this strong color accent about the room. A few floral prints nicely matted and framed will sparkle to advantage when hung against the cool blue walls and add a further spirit of freshness to this naive room. Presto! Once again we have waved the wand of good taste about the room with surprising results and with but the slightest tug on the purse strings.

Thus in almost every room simplicity and good taste will unravel the most baffling decorating problem. Where beauty dwells there also dwells intelligence and a sense of fitness to purpose. Crime and beauty seldom go hand in hand. Children are easily swayed by either. The shiftless homemaker is the country's number one criminal.

GARDEN MINDED
EFFIE V. JORDAN
Boston, Massachusetts

One hundred thousand motorists toured the Nashoba Valley this spring to view the unusually early flowering of apple blossoms out Westford way. Lines of cars miles long wound up to the highest point where the drivers stopped and parked at the side of the road. At their feet as far as the eye could see stretched acre upon acre of foamy, fairylike blossoms. The sight was beautiful, breathtaking, with a touch of the spiritual.

In the very heart of our city, within walking distance of both uptown and downtown business, the Public Gardens showed a magnificent array of gorgeous tulips. They ran through the gamut of color from paper white to purply black and their spacing was an artistic triumph. People from all walks of life strolled up and down the paths drinking in their beauty and one couple found this spot so alluring that time flew on golden wings and the Cunard liner Laconia sailed without them.

Mothers' Day blossoms opened with a bang. Florists decorated the streets in front of their shops with baskets of luscious colored pansies, blue forget-me-nots and golden marigolds. There were pots of geraniums and boxes of English daisies and the sale of these simple glowing blossoms shot far ahead of the usual gardenia and the elegant orchid. Mother likes growing things. She tucks them in the garden and makes them grow all summer.

And the next week the lilacs were at their peak at the Arnold Arboretum and folks journeyed thither, discussing the beautiful purple plumes of the hybrids, wondering how they would grow in a certain spot in their own garden. This early spring blossoming made everyone more flower conscious than ever. And those who are intensely flower minded are always more or less garden minded. If you love all this beauty why not have a garden of your own? It can be done even if the office takes up the greater part of your time.

My neighbor started his garden eight years ago. It has been a constant joy to him ever since. The man fairly oozes happiness when the first warm day of Spring appears. His is an office man's garden, with a background of perennials, where iris gives him bloom in late Spring and June and where his various species of lilies bloom one after the other during the summer months. In front of the perennials he plants those simple but invaluable, no trouble at all, "from June to frost" bloomers like zinnias, marigolds, petunias and snapdragons. He has no time to experiment with seeds or flats—so buys sturdy plants. He catches the 5:15 from the office, eats supper, dons an old straw hat, goes into his garden and pops his plants into the already prepared ground. This done he lights his pipe and loafs comfortably on his old bench—and enjoys the fruits of his labor. He will soon have blossoms and by June his garden will be brilliant with bloom. One evening I met him at his gate and we walked down the garden path together. The air was filled with the most delightful perfume. "What is it?" I asked. "Nicotiana," he said pointing to a huge bed of white swaying flowers. He told me that they are at their best and their perfume the strongest about the time the 5:15 pulls in. Its botanical name may be Nicotiana but we always call it the Office Man's flower.

But—you say—your neighbor lives in the suburbs while we live in the city and have only a back yard. Ah—so you have a back yard! Well, do you know that most of the courtyards in France and Italy lie at the back of the house and are in reality back yards dressed up? Study your back yard a bit. Find out when and where the sun strikes it. Sweeten the soil with lime, give it a little feeding of commercial fertilizer, then tell your nurseryman what you have in the way of sun and shade and he will tell you what to buy. Do not plant seed—buy good growing plants. You will have bloom almost at once and through the whole summer. Again I mention petunias. Get large ones all colors; they cover well and are one of those "June to frost bloomers." Have some shrubs if you like. Their green branches give a sense of coolness. Live in your garden; put some chairs and a table there. It is lots more fun to entertain your friends in the garden in the summertime than in a stuffy living room.

"That's all very well," says another friend, "but what about me? I have no back yard and yet I'm just as garden minded." "How about me?" grieves another, "I'd like a garden but I live in a two-room apartment." Well, even if you live in one room you are sure to have windows and where there are windows there can always be window boxes. Buy metal ones, scatter a layer of pebbles or broken flower pots at the bottom and have the florist fill the box with loam. Leave one inch at the top so the rain will not drive the earth against your window panes. Again let me advise buying sturdy plants. Don't overcrowd. Six plants to a box is enough, for they will need room for spreading. Let them sprawl. A plant is never ungraceful. Try balcony petunias in combinations of colors, try marigolds, try any little plant that is a constant bloomer; let them cascade over the edge of the box and presto you have a miniature "hanging garden of Babylon."

But whatever you do, have a garden——in the suburbs, in the city, on your window ledge have a garden——satisfy that garden consciousness. It's easy, it's sane, it's delightful. It has a future and gives you one. Try it.

FOOD PRODUCTION AS PART OF THE HOME PLAN
William R. Cole
Extension Specialist in Horticultural Manufactures
Massachusetts State College, Amherst, Massachusetts

The home garden can be a source of profit as well as pleasure. Recent studies indicate that vegetables bought at retail cost between $25 and $35 per person for a year's supply. Multiply this figure by the number of members in your family and you can easily see how much the garden can help cut your food budget.

Also scientists tell us that vegetables are rich in minerals and vitamins which promote growth and maintain the health of children and adults. The family with fresh vegetables in the home garden nearly always has a nourishing diet. The family also has the pleasure of getting its vegetables fresh when they are most appetizing and delicious.

Many town people are turning to vegetable gardening for recreation. Women seem to take to gardening naturally and find it an agreeable relief from the tasks of the household.

A well-planned and carefully developed home plan will provide garden space for the growing of vegetables and fruits and also include a storage room in the house for holding a supply for winter use.

It is difficult to describe accurately a plan for the production and storage of vegetables and fruit crops for home use and which will fit all sizes of family and all conditions of economic station, environment and physical setup.

It is possible to lay out such a program for a family of a given size with an arbitrary determination of the factors of economics, environment and physical equipment.

The sometimes suggested average family size is five; two adults and three children. Such a family needs for its adequate dietary program to be eaten fresh from production, from cans, or from a cold room during the winter somewhat over one ton of vegetables, not including potatoes, or one and one-half tons including potatoes.

The fruits used should total about one-quarter ton, but only a small part of this can easily and efficiently be grown in a home garden. Most of this volume will be made up of tree fruits or their juices and it is a difficult problem to successfully grow apples, peaches, etc. in home garden conditions.

The production area needed to supply the needs for fruits and vegetables for a fairly complete year's supply for a family of five is 7500 square feet or somewhat more than one-eighth of an acre. This area is not sufficient to produce the potatoes for the family. They will call for about another one-eighth of an acre. It is best not to try to grow them in home gardens.

The garden area of 7500 square feet includes permanent crops such as asparagus and rhubarb, and raspberries, blackberries and the semi-permanent strawberry plot.

One hundred feet of row each of raspberries and blackberries will give an abundant supply under favorable weather conditions.

One hundred feet of asparagus row will supply the family need for fresh eating and for canning.

The strawberry plot should include 150 feet of row.

Three or four rhubarb plants will give an adequate supply.

The vegetable garden to produce the ton or more of crop necessary to supply the fresh, canned and stored need will be 5000 square feet.

This garden planned for an inclusive list of varieties and quantities will include about every sort of product that grows well in the temperate zone. Such a garden will begin to produce with radishes and continue through lettuce, beets, peas, etc. from May to October. The plan as used may follow the outlines prepared by nutrition or garden specialists or it may be a plan worked out by the homeowner and which uses more or less of some crops depending on the preference of the family. It will, however, if correctly planned include a total volume or tonnage closely approximating a standard set by specialists.

Many of the crops grown are produced under successive plantings. This means that the 5000 square feet of area may be in part used more than once in a season and then the area becomes greater.

Of the total production the vegetables to be eaten fresh amount to about 750 pounds. Canning an adequate supply for winter uses another 750 pounds, while the well-stocked cold room of stored vegetables will contain 500—600 pounds of roots—cabbage, celery, etc.

For a successful garden the plot used should have good soil, be well drained and adequate amounts of fertilizer be used. Many home garden plots do not have the right type of soil for all kinds of vegetables and in such cases adjustments as to varieties grown need to be made.

From the point of view of planning the home the cold room or storage for winter vegetables is of next importance. Providing this storage room is not an expensive or difficult job either when planning and building new or when attempting to complete an already built home. In either case it will probably be a corner of the basement partitioned off and equipped with ventilating flues and bins, shelving, etc., to hold the various crops to be stored.

For a family of five this room needs to be 6 or 8 feet by 10 or 12 feet in floor area. It should have access to outside air and be located as far as possible from the heating plant.

The walls of this room are usually made up of studding set on a sill securely fastened to the floor. Most modern cellars have cement floors and if the cold room is being built into an existing cellar this sill should be spiked down. In planning new cellars the sill can be set in place in the cement.

Partition walls must make good joints with the cellar walls so that the cold room will hold even temperature.

The studding is covered on both sides with paper and matched boards. If some sort of insulation fill is put in between the studs it will help to hold an even temperature in the cold room. Ordinary planer shavings work all right. Other fills will occur to the builder.

The ceiling of this storage room should be papered, sheathed and filled with insulation in order that discomfort in the room above due to the storage room cold, may be avoided. It also keeps upstairs heat out of the storage.

The doorway should be three feet wide and six or six and one-half feet high. A good wide door is easy to get through with a box or basket of vegetables. The door itself must be well made and carefully fitted.

Cooling and ventilating is taken care of by means of a flue attached to an opening in the cellar wall. This flue is so made as to allow for a circulation of air into the lower part of the room and out from the upper levels.

There should be a preserve closet with a total shelf area of about 100-125 square feet to hold the canned vegetables and fruits and any jams, jellies, etc.

Bins for potatoes; racks to hold boxes or crates of beets, carrots, turnips can be built in. There will be adequate space for all the crops necessary to a family supply.

Readers of *The Commonhealth* may obtain bulletins and other helps on gardening, canning, storage from the Massachusetts State College.

THE BACK YARD IMPROVEMENT CONTEST IN WARD 9
DOROTHY HAYWARD, R.N.
Health Education Secretary
Boston Tuberculosis Association

When Dr. Murray Horwood made the Tuberculosis Survey of Boston in 1925 he pointed out to the Boston Tuberculosis Association the amazing and shocking state of affairs concerning the mortality from tuberculosis in Wards 12 and 13, now Ward 9, of Boston. The death rate from tuberculosis in those wards where the Negro population of Boston was concentrated was very nearly as high as that found in any large Southern city. Among his recommendations he urged that an intensive survey of Ward 9 be made, to find out the reasons and to remedy them if possible. A Negro public health nurse familiar with this type of problem was hired, and started her work by getting the cooperation of the medical profession, the clergy and all other groups in the neighborhood.

In 1929 a block in Ward 9 was studied. The block chosen was the one bounded by Tremont Street, Shawmut Avenue, Kendall and Sawyer Streets. The block study showed that bad housing, ignorance of general health and hygiene laws, poor sanitation and inadequate income were some of the outstanding problems, and also that the Negro people did not visit the clinics. A program was planned to meet the needs of the whole community. This included a series of lectures on tuberculosis, demonstrations and lectures on cooking, and Red Cross Home Hygiene classes. All of these projects were popular and valuable and have been continued up to the present time. A Backyard Improvement Contest to stimulate interest in cleaner and more attractive surroundings was inaugurated. The people in the block studied formed a Neighborhood-Get-Together Club. This aroused interest in improving the large back yards and the alleys. The Massachusetts Better Homes Committee cooperated with the Boston Tuberculosis Association in planning a clean yard contest. About five yards entered the contest that first year with pathetic attempts at gardening. When the yards were visited by the judges, who represented the cooperating agencies, the cleanest and neatest yards were awarded prizes. The outstanding result of that first contest was that the yards entered were clean. People came from all parts of the neighborhood to see these clean yards with a few plants in bloom and to enjoy the sight of a clean alley.

In 1930 twenty yards were entered in the contest. These were entered from eight different streets. Loam, which was badly needed, was donated by the Massachusetts Better Homes Committee. Cash prizes given by the Massachusetts Horticultural Society in memory of Mr. Galen S. Stone were made available for contestants. This proved a great stimulus to our gardeners. Other prizes were awarded by the Women's Municipal League and Massachusetts Better Homes Committee. All of the yards entered in the contest showed improvement at the end of the summer and prizes were awarded to four exceptionaly good ones. These prize winning yards were, indeed, a great improvement over the efforts of the preceding year. A large outdoor meeting was held when these prizes were awarded, with an attendance of over 400 people. Lantern slides were shown of prize-winning yards, and representatives of the participating organizations spoke. This meeting gave great impetus to the project.

In 1931 the contest had twenty-five entrants. Eleven of these were awarded prizes at the end of the summer. The need for seeds and plants was met by the Benevolent Fruit and Flower Mission. This was most helpful as it was not possible for the contestants to buy these. At the end of the third contest a marked change in the quality of the improvement was beginning to take place. No longer were the yards just clean. Fences were repaired, whitewash applied and flowers as well as green things were growing. Along with this garden work our health program was continued and a sincere effort made to correlate the two with a better, cleaner, healthier neighborhood the goal. Home Hygiene lessons were being applied in the homes, health given more attention and physical examinations were gradually becoming the fashion.

Early in 1932 the Negro nurse doing this work resigned and the work was taken over by the writer. I found a neighborhood interested in its own problems and anxious to do what was possible with the facilities at hand. When I look back to the contest in 1932 I realize what an excellent foundation had been laid. The people were no longer antagonistic but anxious for help. With very little difficulty 200 people were persuaded to enter their yards in the contest so that they and their children could reap the health benefits of clean attractive yards, and a spotless alley free from garbage and filth. The Benevolent Fruit and Flower Mission met our needs for more and more plants and seeds, and loam was a very welcome gift from the Massachusets Better Homes Committe. The people themselves were not only more interested than formerly, but also the other agencies in Boston. Without the cooperation of these agencies the contest would have been very difficult as our contestants could not possibly purchase anything for their gardens.

The contest in 1932 was such a colossal affair that in 1933 it seemed wiser to organize the neighborhood a little better in the beginning. Sixteen blocks were organized with a chairman in charge of each block. These chairmen met regularly every two weeks at the Association headquarters and in the yards of some of the contestants. The duties of the chairmen were to have the people in their blocks sign the entrance slips, to report any sanitary problems to the local sanitary inspector, to assist and organize groups of children interested in gardening, to plan demonstrations in their blocks which would stimulate the interest of the laggers, to distribute plants, seeds and loam to those entered in the contest whenever they were given to us, and to inspect the yards in her block regularly. The plan was that once a week I would visit each block, inspect and visit the yards with the chairman and help each chairman with the problems in her section. This plan worked extremely well. In fairness I must say that, although some of the chairmen were excellent workers, they were a little tactless with their people and many awkward and sometimes entertaining incidents occurred. Many people having filthy yards were indignant when asked by the chairman if they would clean up their yards and enter the contest. The usual reply was, "No one has to tell me when to clean up my yard." However, the neighbors soon found ways of shaming those who would not do their part. As the contestants knew me better, I found endless opportunity for helping with health problems, sanitary problems, and the many ills that beset a home and family. Many times the example set by a plant not receiving enough sunshine was an excellent means of showing a mother how important and necessary sunshine is for her babies. As the contest continued to grow, contestants were encouraged to use their yards as outdoor living rooms, to serve meals in them and to make them as useful as possible. Up to this time the women and children had done most of the work, but in 1933 the fathers seemed to become more interested. Waste lumber became something to be coveted as inventive minds had found that swings, seesaws, tables, benches and sandboxes could be made right at home. Back yard playgrounds became the style.

The plan worked out in 1933 seemed to be a good one, and since that time the contest has been conducted along the same lines and has continued to grow. Last year the Negro nurse who started the work came back to do it again under the joint auspices of the Massachusetts Better Homes Committee, the Women's Municipal League, and the Boston Tuberculosis Association. At the end of the summer, 300 yards showed improvement.

Some parts of the work are very gratifying. One of the things that I think is particularly nice is that the block chairmen themselves run a party in one of the improved alleys each year to raise money for children's prizes. As a result of this encouragement, the children are some of our best gardeners now and do a great deal to raise the standards of the community. The sum raised is usually about $30. Clubs and organizations in the neighborhood are also starting to donate prizes. It is pleasing to see the people themselves have so much confidence in the idea and do what they can to improve conditions in their own neighborhood. It is discouraging to have people move when they have improved their yards as it sometimes takes a year to educate the newcomers to the ways of the neighborhood, but that is one of the problems that will always be with us and continued effort is the only way we can hope to hold the ground we have gained.

There is no question in my mind about the value of this work. It provides an excellent means of becoming acquainted with the families in the neighborhood, and of teaching them to spend their spare time in the open air during the summer months. Parents and children reap the benefits of fresh air and sunshine as well as having the satisfaction of making things grow where only rubbish flourished formerly, and at the end of the summer they have benefited physically as well as mentally. The neighborhood is cleaner, more attractive, and a happier spirit prevails.

New friends made during the contest in the summer enroll in the Red Cross Home Hygiene and First Aid courses which are conducted at the Association headquarters in the winter. Since the work first started in 1928 approximately 600 girls and women have received certificates for these courses. Anyone who is familiar with the *Red Cross Text Book* knows how valuable the instruction is to these pupils. All those receiving certificates join the Boston Tuberculosis Association Health Guild which meets at 554 Columbus Avenue one evening a month. This Guild has officers and very small dues. The objects are *first*, "to be healthy yourself," *second*, "to preach the gospel of good health in the neighborhood." At each meeting a speaker or motion picture is featured after the business meeting. Money is raised each year to send children needing care, but not meeting the free bed requirements, to the Prendergast Preventorium. Gifts are taken at Christmas time to patients from this neighborhood who are sick at the Boston Sanatorium. The tuberculosis clinics serving this section are now very well attended by the Negro people. Tuberculosis is no longer a word which terrifies. Everyone has been taught that tuberculosis can be cured if found early. By means of these many and varied methods the Boston Tuberculosis Association is endeavoring to do all within its power to reduce the death rate in this section of Boston.

A SETTLEMENT WORKER LOOKS AT HOUSING

S. MAX NELSON
General Director
East Boston Health Unit

Housing, because it stands for shelter, a primitive need, has always been one of the principal concerns of the social settlement. Settlement houses, founded as they have been in "underprivileged" city neighborhoods, are conscious of inadequate housing, socially bad housing, dangerous housing, economically wasteful housing, chiefly because those who work in the settlement and share its neighborhood life realize, through close contact, the relationship of housing lacks to the total picture of social inadequacy which the neighborhood presents.

The effects of poor housing upon the life of a family and of a neighborhood are insiduous rather than dramatic. It becomes accepted by people in all classes of society that conditions in the vicinity of noisy, smelly, ugly industries, railroad yards, marshes, dumps, etc., must be sordid and shabby. Even in old city neighborhoods, formerly fashionable, deterioration and decay, littered streets, grassless parks, corner gangs, drunkenness and general hopelessness have become expected facts for those passing hastily through in a trip across the city,—houses old, neglected, shabby, because rents are low; rents so low because, among other reasons, the houses themselves, though once first-class residences, are now so old, neglected and shabby.

An observer, nonresident in the area, if he gives the social picture in such a district a thought, probably wonders why people live there at all. "Why don't they move to a small town or out into the country where there is room for the kids to play," forgetting the practical aspects of security, even though it be "relief," and the hopeless, oppressive inertia imposed by that collection of inadequacies. the heritage of those living in a depressed area, which combine to keep the "less-privileged" socially inactive when by all signs they should rebel against the manner of their life and seek better conditions elsewhere.

The uneconomic aspect of substandard housing areas from the standpoint of cost of public services has been recognized for years. Inevitably such neighborhoods cost much more to maintain than others in better condition. Poor health, mounting delinquency, greater fire risks, higher accident rates, greater calls upon all types of city services are made. Society as a whole thus pays unnecessarily, through taxes, for destructive waste which might have been avoided, for a social situation which has nothing to recommend it unless it be that society thus provides a place for families of low income to live. *The amount which society pays, through taxes, to support the unnecessary extra cost of occupied substandard housing areas is a subsidy.* This subsidy makes it possible for those of lowest incomes to buy shelter in the "inadequate shelter" market, the substandard area.

As settlement workers well know, unfortunate housing conditions, due to inability to purchase better, do not in individual cases prevent a high degree of real home life. The home in every case is dependent not so much upon the adequacy of the house as upon the adequacy of the mother and other cooperating members of the family who see to it, bravely and well, that the spirit of the home is unbroken. Always, however, inadequate, substandard housing adds a heavy handicap to an already badly handicapped family in the matter of providing an adequate home. The settlement supplements the home in providing rooms for recreation, social clubs, mothers' clubs, summer camps, opportunities to learn useful arts and crafts, home-making classes and demonstrations, a warm and cheery meeting-place where all rate as equals and where there are always friends to help in emergencies.

Because the worker in the social settlement lives in the neighborhood, because he sees the direct relationship between the cause, as presented by bad and improper housing in the mass, and the effect, as shown in actual happenings and in statistics, he becomes at all times a champion of better housing. Many moves for better housing which have resulted in housing projects were inaugurated and have been supported vigorously by settlement workers. Nor are theirs lone voices crying in "the city wilderness." Several years ago an enthusiastic throng of tenement mothers, representative of many hundreds, members of the League of Mothers' Clubs of the United Neighborhood Houses of New York, went en masse to Albany and so impressed the legislators that many important housing reforms were won, over the strong opposition of the owners' lobby. These women knew the facts through actual experience and deprivation. They demanded decency and safety for their families.

But whether housing reform is brought about by such a demonstration "from within" or whether it comes as the result of slum-clearance and housing "projects," the plight of the lowest income families as regards bad housing has not been solved. New housing, subsidized though it is, is not available within the price range of the most needy.

Let it be argued, as it can be with truth, that the poor man cannot afford to live decently in the city, where the high cost of land and high assessments make it imperative for owners to receive rentals out of proportion to the accommodations provided. Can he afford to live in the country? Not unless employment, a demand for his particular skill (if indeed he has one, as so many wage earners of low income have not) exists in the country or smaller town. It is conceivable that industries will increasingly follow the lead of a few and establish themselves neatly and efficiently in country locations, building model houses for their workers, selecting these workers carefully (now more than formerly appraising each man for his special fitness and probable term of effectiveness) establishing benevolent communities which in themselves seem to provide every opportunity for decent, healthy and happy living. Generally speaking, however, it is not the employees or the potential employees of such industries who make up the low income group of the population. The draining-away of the skilled and more effective from the city neighborhood will only serve to lower the general social level of the residuum and increase the volume of city services necessary and imperative in addition to the supplementation possible through neighborhood agencies.

Weighing all the factors now present, and estimating the future on the basis of present trends, one sees the low income group becoming increasingly dependent upon society for the opportunity to live decently. Since privately owned industry cannot absorb the great numbers of unskilled workmen, heads of families, now living in our cities, it is obvious that either they and their families must be supported outright or opportunities afforded them to earn an amount enabling them to maintain their families decently at the minimum living levels. Whether the final responsibility for this falls upon municipal, state or federal government, is administered by one party or another, is not so important as that those in positions of responsibility recognize the principle that public interest in the United States demands that no family be allowed to live under conditions, in houses and in neighborhoods, which are inimical to health, safety and morals. Fundamental in such situations are the living quarters of these families. It is possible to make over old houses of good fundamental construction into acceptable homes. Multiple dwellings, of themselves, are not detrimental to proper living. Overcrowding of neighborhoods, by permitting more than a certain number of individuals per acre, can be prevented. The relation of population to area of parks and playgrounds in any given area is controllable (indeed in many cities if substandard housing were demolished there would be ample available space for playgrounds and parks) but the control over the number of people who shall be allowed to inhabit a given number of rooms, the fitness by location, size, exposure, windows, etc., of these rooms for human habitation is not at present a sharp or vital concern of government. A family buys the housing which it can afford and there is now no low level below which a house-hunter cannot go except as a building is considered structurally unsafe and is therefore barred.

On thorough-going analysis it becomes obvious that the same agencies which recognize the right of a family to food, clothing, fire and shelter cannot afford to stop there. The kind of shelter and the type of use is equally a responsibility of society through government (at whatever level).

Those who oppose the razing of all substandard housing as a matter of public welfare will argue that thereby a housing shortage will be created. Such razing need not be done all at once but over a period of time, beginning with the worst, and gradually working up to those buildings which are acceptable both by design and condition, for human habitation on a safety level. Regulation of the number of persons to the number of rooms is a more difficult problem, but education in health matters, a raising of the weekly wages from the bare subsistence level, as at present, to a decency level will make it possible for families to avoid the deplorable overcrowding in rooms and beds which settlement workers know has been the unavoidable lot of many persons for the past eight years. People do not want to live so. As individuals they are helpless. Erase dangerous and improper housing, provide that fraction more in budget which will enable them to live decently rather than at the bare subsistence level and they will automatically provide for themselves more adequate shelter.

Authorities and those in charge of city finances will argue that neither can we afford to tear down potential (though not reliable) sources of real estate taxes nor increase the "relief" or "work-relief" burden by raising family allotments and wages. Such a suggestion on the part of settlement workers may be dismissed impatiently as impractical. Nevertheless, it is because settlement workers see the results of physical and social inadequacy as manifested in depressed city areas that the situation seems to them to offer no choice of action if a large segment of the population is to be saved.

Those in possession of the facts, armed with real support for their projected measures, must move in on the situation as a whole, displacing many partial and relatively feeble measures with a total plan. Delay only piles up the social disintegration of the people of such districts in menacing volume. Not only is the situation becoming steadily much worse but it is already intolerable.

The residents of settlement neighborhoods are ready to cooperate with helpful agencies to the extent to which and as soon as housing aid is offered. The municipality, state or nation cannot afford to let them wait long for such fundamental help.

A building program, primarily for people in the lowest income group, embracing model housing as well as reconditioning of certain buildings now standing, would be tangible help. This program might be extended over a period of years, keeping pace with the demolition of unfit buildings but with a definite date set beyond which substandard dwellings might not legally be occupied.

Certainly it is evident that with the social vision evident in the United States and in the several states, a total plan to meet a total housing situation will not be long delayed. The people of our depressed city areas want to live decently. Alone and unaided it is not possible for them now to do so.

HOME HAZARDS AND ACCIDENTS

Lewis E. MacBrayne, *General Manager*
Massachusetts Safety Council

There is a theory, more easily advanced than proven, that at certain periods over a term of years the accident trend of the United States moves up or down without much reason, and apparently due to causes not easily discovered. This has been observed especially in motor vehicle accidents on the highway, which from time to time appear to have the same trend across the entire United States, regardless of climatic conditions which are never the same in all 48 states.

States that are endeavoring to reduce accidents at such a time may find their casualty rate under the general trend—this has been true in Massachusetts—but it will still show something of an upward bulge. For the past several months motor vehicle fatalities in large areas of the United States have shown a marked reduction. If this is merely due to one of these periodic "waves," it will not be wise for those of us who are permanently engaged in accident prevention work to cheer too lustily lest we be called upon later to explain why the reduction did not become permanent. If, on the other hand, the national highway safety campaign that has been going on for the past two years is finally bearing results, then we should soon discover that the "safety consciousness" that is being established in the minds of millions of people will not be limited to highway accidents alone.

In theory, at least, if we could train the individual to observe and avoid special hazards that he encounters during a part of the day, we should be giving him equal protection during the balance of his waking hours. The fact remains, however, that in many industries where the safest possible working conditions have been established, and where the worker himself has been trained to be observant of accident hazards, more of these men are being hurt on the highway and in the home, than in the plant itself. There is, however, a reason for this.

In the factory, the men are taught the hazards of dangerous machines, of improperly handling material, and of falling on stairways or slippery floors. This training, however, has not included the measuring of the hazard of an approaching motor vehicle by its speed, rather than by its distance from the pedestrian crossing the highway. Nor does the workman who has kept the aisles of his shop free from objects over which he might stumble, always remember to put up the garden tools when he has finished his home work, or inspect the cellar stairs for a wash pail that may have been left there.

A great deal has been written and spoken in the past three years about the dangers of the home. A favorite slogan for speakers has been the phrase, "There's no place like home—for accidents." It appears to have a problem all of its own. In a research study that the Massachusetts Safety Council is undertaking at the present time, the report of which will be published about June 15, we are seeking to answer the question, "Is home really the most dangerous place?" It is possible that our conclusion may be that the home itself is no more dangerous than any other part of the community, but that the problem is one of the individual. A large number of accidents occur there because of the physical condition of the occupants. We are charging to accidental causes many injuries received because of physical weaknesses due to age.

In the age group over 65, more than twice as many persons are killed each year in home accidents as in motor vehicle accidents, and in the group of children under 5 years of age, five times as many home fatalities occur as motor vehicle deaths among young children. It is quite apparent that age is the primary factor in such injuries; with the added fact that these people spend more time at home than on the highway. Both of these groups should be under constant observation in the home, even after all the visible causes of accidents have been corrected. Nearly one-half of all fatal home accidents are among persons older than 64 years. It is a common experience that an elderly person whose general health is good, and whose mind remains alert, often fails to recognize the slowing down of the physical side of the body.

I saw this well illustrated recently when reaction tests were being given to a number of motorists. Among the persons examined was a man of 70, still active as an executive in business, and with a mind as keen as that of a man under 40. In the test the person is seated at a steering wheel similar to that of an automobile, and is told to watch a set of traffic signals, ready to apply the brake when the red light flashes. A machine records the interval in a second or its fractions in which the brake is applied. It was quite apparent that this elderly man's mind instantly gave the signal to his foot to apply the brake, and yet the best time that he could make was a second and a half. At the conclusion of several tests, he remarked, "For the first time I realize that my body is not keeping up with my mind."

It is because of this condition that so many persons past the age of 64 fall in the home; and falls head the list of home accidents. It does not imply that they are living in a disorderly house, but rather that they have not made a personal study of the conditions under which falls may occur. In the age group of the young children injured, the poor home where there are many children and an overworked mother is more often the scene of an accident than the home where living conditions are more prosperous. Nobody has ever undertaken to compute how many accidents may have been prevented in the home that can afford a "hired girl," but visiting nurses have told me that in the kitchen where they find the washtub full of hot water on the floor, the food cooking in pans with the handles turned outward, within the reach of young children, and sharp knives not yet washed and put away after the previous meal, an injured child is often to be found.

I do not believe that any accident was ever prevented by the use of statistics alone, and yet the accidents that do occur in the home are so frequent as to make this whole problem as formidable statistically, as the menace of disease. We have seen a remarkable reduction in illness from contagious diseases, as people have become familiar with the cause and the methods by which it can be prevented. It has taken long years to win this fight against disabling and fatal germs, and yet a similar knowledge, followed by preventive action, can give us the same reduction in home hazards.

On the average, 106 persons are killed every day in an American home, and every hour of the day 640 persons are more or less seriously injured, giving a total that has been estimated at its peak as high as 38,500 deaths, and 5,620,000 injuries annually. Even when we remember that there are more than 30,000,000 families in the United States, this is a high enough rate to give us serious concern. To be sure, a majority of these injuries are minor in their nature and respond to first aid treatment; and yet a single insurance company—one of many doing business in Massachusetts—has paid more than 36,000 claims for injuries received in home accidents during the past five years. This, of course, was for the entire country. It is interesting to note the breakdown of these claims paid. There were nearly 25,000 for injuries resulting from slips and falls; 6,200 for injuries caused by sharp instruments and broken glass; 2,500 for wounds received when struck by falling objects; 1,750 were injuries caused by burns; and more than 700 for injuries received from explosions.

In managing the modern home, just how are we to prevent these accidents from falls that are of such frequent occurrence? In the group of 25,000 such injuries just referred to, 5,510 occurred on steps or stairs. The first precaution is, of course, to make certain that no toys or cleaning utensils have been left on the stairway. Pails and mops and brushes are too frequently to be found on the cellar stairs, and small objects are abandoned by children elsewhere. We do not always fall on the stairways with which we are familiar. The whole problem comes back to the importance of the individual understanding that the fall is the easiest form of accident to occur, and that we should pay more attention to the trite old remark, "Look where you are going." In the same group studied there were 3,625 falls that occurred on floors or rugs. There are still many homes in which the loose rug is not anchored, but often these falls are caused by haste or by tripping over pieces of furniture left in the way. Falls on the ice, though a seasonable hazard only, injured 1,453 of these persons, and 1,947 tripped while walking on uneven ground.

We are prone to receive with amusement the statement that more people fall in bathtubs and under showers than from chairs and tables, or from ladders. Yet in the above group 1,057 falls occurred in the bathroom, 914 from chairs and tables, and 767 from ladders. Even getting in and out of bed resulted in 410 claims for injury which cost an insurance company more than $45,000.

There are many booklets of recent publication that have listed the hazards that should be corrected in the modern home. The best list contains 50 of them, and the average housewife would probably fail to complete the reading of them as soon as she discovered that a considerable number did not exist in her own home. It is not necessary to tell the average woman today that she should never use gasoline to cleanse clothing inside of the house. The modern mother also knows that for every medicine containing poison there is now one equally good that is nonpoisonous, and these should be the only bottles admitted to the medicine closet; but we do not all understand that the general prevalence of smoking has greatly increased the fire hazard within the home, and that many children lose their lives each year when such fires get beyond control.

What the modern home needs to be as safe as we can make it is, first of all, an understanding of the objects that may cause accidents. This applies especially to very small objects left on the floor that small children may swallow, and that may cause elderly people to stumble and fall. It applies to a proper place for every sharp instrument used in the kitchen, and for the prompt removal of broken glass. It applies to the proper arrangement of furniture, electric light cords, Junior's bicycle, and occasionally the lawnmower, which may be seen in the daytime but may be stumbled over in the dark. Second, the plan for protecting the home should include a frequent inspection of all of the rooms in which accidents are likely to occur if the first rule has not been followed. And last of all, the members of the family, especially those who are impetuous and hasty, should be supervised when they are appearing to become accident prone.

In a survey that the Massachusetts Safety Council made at one time of 100 homes belonging to members of women's clubs, it was found that while the average home had reported no accident within two years, a few had a record as high as seven. In such cases there appeared to be at least one member of the family prone to accidents; and this condition was often chargeable to worry, nervousness, or fatigue. The accidents did not reflect upon the home itself.

I did not intend to argue in writing this article that accidents in the home should be prevented simply because they cost a lot of money. We should seek to avert them because of the human suffering that they involve, and the interruption in our home life. Yet it is interesting to note that the 36,000 accidents to which I have referred, and upon which claims were paid, cost a total of $3,708,000. In relatively few cases is there any insurance protection, so that the home itself must bear the loss; and this annually amounts to a distressingly large sum of money. Perhaps we may add that an important expense item not often included in the house budget, but upon which the mother can make a saving, is this cost of accidents. Careful management of the home and the family may eliminate it entirely.

HEATING, VENTILATION, LIGHTING AND SANITATION OF PUBLIC BUILDINGS, AS REQUIRED BY THE STATE DEPARTMENT OF PUBLIC SAFETY

EUGENE M. MCSWEENEY

Commissioner, Massachusetts Department of Public Safety

The matter of heating, ventilation, lighting, and sanitation of public buildings has been a part of the work of the Building Inspection Division of the Department of Public Safety since the reorganization of the State Departments in 1920. Prior to that time the work was under the Factories and Public Buildings division of the Massachusetts District Police, and has been effectively supervised by the State Building Inspectors since 1888.

It is not the intention of this article to go into the theoretical or scientific arguments in connection with heating and ventilation in public buildings—which include schoolhouses—but simply to direct attention to the methods and systems which, through actual experience, have proven satisfactory.

The Massachusetts Legislature during the year 1887 enacted certain laws relative to ventilation and sanitation in certain public buildings. The following year a law was enacted providing for the enforcement of the laws relating to the ventilation and sanitation of every public building, schoolhouse, or place of assemblage under the jurisdiction of the Inspection Division of the Massachusetts District Police. The enactment of this law added much additional work to the Inspection Division of the District Police, and work which at that time was largely in an experimental stage.

Rufus R. Wade, then Chief of the Massachusetts District Police, commenting on the conditions at that time, had the following in his report for the year 1888: "It would seem that there could be no misapprehension as to the scope of this act nor the exact meanings of its several sections. A public building or schoolhouse may not be in such a filthy and unwholesome condition as to call for the interference of the Board of Health; yet the ventilation may be radically bad, its drains or privies defective and foul, its air laden with vile effluvia injurious to the health of the person therein. That such evils have long existed will not be denied by any one conversant with the facts. Public school teachers have made frequent complaints of defective drainage of schoolhouses, and offensive odors arising from the privies, which are placed in most cases near the building, and in other cases in the basement or cellar. The vile stenches arising therefrom are complained of, but not always is the remedy applied. Some makeshift is relied upon to get rid of the complaint. It would shock and disgust parents to know what crude and defective arrangements for sanitary purposes are maintained in schoolhouses, where the indifference of janitors and others in charge imperil health and life."

It was early determined that the ventilating and sanitary conditions in schoolhouses was the most important matter demanding attention. The first problem undertaken was to try and ascertain when the air in a schoolhouse was exhausted to the point of being injurious to the health of the persons therein. Next, what amount of fresh air should be supplied to, and foul air removed from, any schoolhouse or public building, in order that the air might be kept fit for respiration and not be injurious to health. The enforcement of the law was predicated on a proper settlement of these two important problems.

The purity or impurity of the air was determined by the proportion of carbonic acid gases found present therein. Excessive presence of these gases indicated the presence of other injurious matter. Air was universally agreed to be pure when it was found to contain only four parts of carbonic acid gas in 10,000. In relation to the fresh air supply and the removal of foul air it was found by study in the division that eminent authorities had differences of opinion regarding the amount of air necessary to secure good ventilation. The division found that valuable progress had been made in this matter and it felt justified in accepting as its guide the more modern authorities, among whom were: Quetelet, Dr. Edward Smith, Brown Sequard, Arsonval, Claude Bernard, Dr. Billings, Professor Carpenter, Professor Draper, Dr. Frank Wells, Dr. Parkes, Dr. Briggs, Charmont, Professor Woodbridge, and others.

As a result of investigations, inspections and tests of apparatus for heating and ventilation, the standard for schoolrooms adopted by the Massachusetts Inspection Department was a minimum of 30 cubic feet of fresh air per pupil per minute, and for auditoriums seating a large number of persons, the standard adopted was 2½ cubic feet of fresh air per square foot of floor space or 15 cubic feet of air per seat.

The amount of air supplied and the removal of vitiated air in schoolhouses and public buildings was thought by some critics to be excessive, but it was found after inspection and tests in many well ventilated school buildings in Massachusetts that the systems approved by the division would furnish from 40 to 50 cubic feet of fresh air per minute for each pupil if the system was properly managed.

The matter of humidity was also carefully considered in the experiments, and tests made by the inspectors of the division. It was found that in schoolhouses where an ample quantity of moderately warmed air was supplied, there was seldom complaint of dryness of the air. To feel comfortable and to produce the best results in ventilation, the air should be from 50 to 60% saturated with moisture.

Systems for heating and ventilating of schoolhouses and public buildings were designed which gave satisfactory results. These systems were known as the gravity indirect system, i.e., heating the air by furnaces and steam radiators and controlling the temperature by a mixing damper or other satisfactory device. They also designed and approved systems mechanically operated for large school buildings. These systems were found proficient in every detail.

For the information of the public and especially heating engineers, the department made plans, details and specifications of the various systems. The department also made plans, details and specifications which were exhibited at the Columbian Exposition in Chicago in 1893, the Louisiana Purchase exposition at St. Louis in 1894, the Lewis & Clark Exposition at Portland, Oregon in 1905, and at the Paris Exposition in Paris in 1900. At all these Expositions the department received awards, and at the Paris Exposition, competing against the world, received the Grand Prize.

The success or failure of obtaining satisfactory results for heating and ventilation in schools and public buildings depends on the design of the system, the care with which it is installed, and after installation, the operation of the system by the janitor or engineer in charge. Complaints have frequently been made that the ventilating system was not operating satisfactorily. These complaints after investigation usually have been discovered to be the fault of the engineer or janitor in charge, and not the apparatus in the building. The janitor or engineer who is negligent of his duties can easily give poor results with a properly installed system.

The human element must be considered as an important factor in the operation of any properly installed heating and ventilating system. An incompetent person in charge of such a system may cause serious damage to the apparatus under his charge. The rapidly changing climatic conditions peculiar to this part of the country necessitate the use of good judgment in addition to a thorough knowledge of the apparatus.

The Inspectors of the Department are furnished with modern instruments and the latest equipment for the purpose of testing the heating and ventilating systems in schools and public buildings, and are constantly on the alert to see to it that the laws of the Commonwealth are lived up to. When the impurities of the air given off by the occupants of the schools and public buildings are considered one realizes that large quantities of pure air of the proper temperature must be supplied and diffused throughout the rooms without uncomfortable drafts. In a schoolroom the temperature should not vary more than three degrees Fahrenheit in any part of the room two feet from the outside wall.

It is the opinion of this Department that the present standards for supplying and removing air from schoolhouses and public buildings, which standards have existed since 1888, should not be reduced. The proper operation of a heating and ventilating system installed in any building should have one main result—the health and comfort of the occupants.

For theatres, public and special halls, the auditorium is required to have such means as to insure the removal near the floor levels, through ventiducts with approved regulating dampers, of at least two and one-half (2½) cubic feet of air per minute for each square foot in area of the auditorium and gallery floors, and to supply pure air equal in amount at such height from the floor as to insure proper circulation, with means for the proper heating of such air when necessary, with approved methods for regulating the temperature, and sufficient means for heating to maintain a temperature throughout the auditorium of sixty-five (65) degrees Fahrenheit in zero weather. The velocity of the air entering the ventiducts shall not exceed five hundred (500) feet. and of the air entering the auditorium horizontally shall not exceed three hundred and fifty (350) feet per minute, unless permitted by the Supervisor of Plans. Provision may be made for reversing the above circulation for use when heat is not required. Where circumstances will not permit the installation of the above method of heating and ventilation, an approved plenum chamber system may be used.

Sanitation:

Where suitable water service and sewerage can be obtained, there shall be sufficient toilet rooms for each sex. For the auditorium floor and each gallery, at least one water-closet for every three hundred (300) seats or majority fraction thereof, for women; and at least one water-closet for every six hundred (600) seats, or majority fraction thereof, for men; and a water-closet for each sex, connected with the dressing rooms. All water-closets and urinals shall have approved fixture ventilation, or rear wall vent. Toilet rooms for males, shall be clearly marked MEN'S TOILET, and for females WOMEN'S TOILET. Each toilet room must have an approved number of lavatories.

Lighting:

The foyers, corridors, passageways, stairways, exits, courts and the auditorium and each gallery thereof shall be suitably lighted at all times when occupied. Artificial lighting may be by electricity or gas, or by oil lamps if electricity or gas is not available.

If electricity is used as the principal source of illumination of a building, auxiliary means of illumination of exits, corridors, passages, stairways and the auditorium shall be provided, and such auxiliary lights shall be kept lighted when the building is in use. Where gas is available it shall be used as the auxiliary means of illumination unless the department accepts some other source.

Electricity from a supply main entirely separate from that used as the principal source of illumination, or electricity supplied by a storage battery located in the building, may be accepted in place of gas, at the discretion of the department.

If electricity from a separate supply main or from a storage battery is used, means shall be provided for turning on the auxiliary lights automatically upon failure of the main supply.

Schoolhouse Class and Recitation Room Windows: Lighting:

In buildings hereafter erected, and in existing buildings if so directed, windows shall have not less than one square foot of glass to each five (5) square feet of floor area, and the top of the windows shall be not more than eight inches (8") below the ceiling. For rooms lighted from one side only, the width of room from that side shall be not more than two and one-third times their height.

All rooms, corridors, stairways and egresses, including outside steps, shall be suitably lighted when in use. Artificial lights when used shall provide illumination of an intensity equal to at least the minimum intensities specified hereafter, and may be by electricity or gas, or by oil lamps if electricity or gas is not available.

Minimum Intensities to be Provided:

For stairways, corridors, toilet rooms	1 ft. candle
Auditorium, gymnasium except when used for displaying still or motion pictures	3 ft. candle
Ordinary class, recitation and study rooms, library and physical and chemical laboratories in schoolhouses	5 ft. candle
Rooms used for instruction in manual training and mechanical drawing in schoolhouses	8 ft. candle
On typesetting racks and composing stones in rooms for instruction in printing in school buildings	12 ft. candle

It has been contended by engineers of lighting companies that the foot candle should be increased. The regulations of this division provide for minimum conditions. Each building is a problem in itself for lighting and must be so considered by the Engineers.

Emergency Lights:

A number of lights sufficient to illuminate exits and to clearly define all aisles in an auditorium shall be installed and used when still or motion pictures are shown.

In addition to the electric lights described for illuminating exits and aisles, gas lights shall be installed sufficient in number to provide the illumination specified, if gas service is available. Emergency lights shall be kept burning whenever the rooms are in use and artificial light is required.

The switches controlling exit lights, lights for minimum illumination specified, emergency lights and for the remote controlled switch if one is used, shall be located at a convenient point outside the auditorium or gymnasium, enclosed in a suitable cabinet, unless they are in a room not open to the public. If a storage battery is used to operate emergency lights, a switch shall be provided which will automatically turn on the battery current when principal supply fails.

Sources of Supply for Corridor, Exit and Emergency Lights:

In especially large buildings where required by the department, a separate service shall be brought in from the supply mains and used for these lights. For other buildings the branch circuits shall be supplied by mains which are not used to supply light for any other purpose, and which are connected to the service mains close to the meter and on the load side thereof.

Each branch circuit shall be properly fused, and the fuses protecting this main shall be at least three times the capacity of the largest fuses used to protect a branch circuit.

If gas is not available for auxiliary service, then a storage battery of sufficient capacity to supply the exit and emergency lights or a separate groups of lights giving equivalent illumination, shall be installed, together with suitable devices for automatically keeping the battery charged at all times.

Heating and Ventilation

Operation of Heating and Ventilation System:

Every person or municipality having the responsibility of control of the heating and ventilation in a school shall continuously operate the system according to the provisions of these regulations during such times as the building is occupied.

Approved Materials:

Any source of heat may be used which does not contaminate the air in the building and which does not conflict with any existing health, fire or building ordinance.

Radiation of the several types and other devices commonly found on the market may be installed subject to the rules of the Department.

New apparatus, devices, specialties, unit type ventilators, or their equivalent, etc. shall receive the approval of the department before installation. If required, manufacturers shall, in order to secure approval, submit their apparatus, devices, etc. to designated representatives of the department for test and inspection in such place and manner as the department shall direct.

Fresh Air Inlets to Buildings:

The air supply to schools shall be taken from an uncontaminated source free from dust or other impurities.

Chapter 149, Acts of 1888, the original law, has been amended but it will be noticed that the law is substantially the same except for a change in phraseology and the addition of district health officers who have jurisdiction in the protection of health of pupils in school buildings. Section 42. Chapter 143, General Laws is as follows:

"Every public building as defined in section one, except schoolhouses in which public or private instruction is afforded to less than eleven pupils at one time, shall be kept clean and free from effluvia arising from any drain, privy or nuisance, shall be provided with a sufficient number of proper water closets, earth closets or privies, and shall be ventilated in such a manner that the air shall not become so impure as to be injurious to health. If it appears to an inspector that further or different heating, ventilating or sanitary provisions are required in any such public building, in order to conform to the requirements of this section, and that such requirement can be provided without reasonable expense, he may issue a written order to the proper person or authority, directing such heating, ventilating or sanitary provisions to be provided. A school committee, public officer or person who has charge of, owns or leases any such public building, who neglects for four weeks to comply with the order of such inspector, shall be punished by a fine of not more than 'one hundred dollars. The district health officers or such other officers as the department of public health may from time to time appoint shall make such examinations of school buildings subject to this section as in the opinion of the department the protection of the health of the pupils may require. This section shall not apply to Boston."

Through the enforcement of the laws, rules and regulations relating to Public Buildings, the Building Inspectors of the Department of Public Safety have made an enviable record in contributing to the health and safety of the people of Massachusetts. As the many new devices and systems for heating and ventilation come on the market, much time and study is given by the department to make certain that they will conform to the laws and regulations and do the work which is so vital to the general welware of all the people.

ENVIRONMENTAL SANITATION
Arranged by the Division of Sanitary Engineering
Massachusetts Department of Public Health.

The report of the Special Commission to Study and Investigate Public Health Laws and Policies (Mass. House 1200-1937) states that "The sanitation of the environment is one of the oldest of public health activities. Tremendous progress in disease prevention has been achieved through certain of these programs. Other activities, while not contributing directly to specific disease prevention, have definitely promoted a higher standard of living and thus furthered the general community well-being."

Water Supplies

The General Laws, regarding the establishment and maintenance of public water supplies, grant to the Department of Public Health the authority to advise and approve as to local water systems, and the majority of the special enabling acts under which these supplies were established have given to the Department the power of approval of the sources of supply. The Department, however, has only advisory power relative to some of the older systems which were developed under enabling acts some of which were passed prior to the establishment of the Department. The Department also has authority to require after a public hearing improvements in any existing water treatment works.

Under existing laws the Department may adopt rules and regulations to protect sources of water supply used within the limits of the Commonwealth, but no such power is available to protect local watersheds that serve communities of neighboring states.

Stream Pollution and Sewage Disposal

It is the opinion of some persons that all streams should be kept suitable for recreational purposes, regardless of their industrial value, and that all pollution of streams should be prevented. Others would permit the pollution of all streams, regardless of their location and value for recreation, if they might be used to any advantage for the disposal of sewage or industrial wastes. Between these two extemes there exists a middle ground of common sense and reason.

In Massachusetts, as in other states, certain rivers by usage have become designated as industrial streams. These streams probably could not be used for water supplies or made into trout streams except at considerable expense and their value for certain forms of recreation is nil. They are, however, of great industrial value, and their use for this purpose has contributed to the prosperity of the Commonwealth. While we should not condone willful defilement of any stream, it is believed that the most that can be expected in such cases is that the manufacturers use all practicable means to prevent pollution. Certain other streams are, except for a very few industries, comparatively free from pollution and excellent for all forms of recreation. Such streams should be protected with possible reservations for future use for water supply purposes, and should be protected from further contamination. New industries should not be permitted to pollute them and existing industries should be required to remove present pollution as far as is practicable. Such streams are well adapted for recreation, and their use for such purposes should be encouraged.

While the present Massachusetts laws have assisted in protecting some of the streams and tidal waters of this Commonwealth, they give little or no assistance in preventing pollution of interstate streams. Actually they prevent action by the Department to improve the condition of the Connecticut and Merrimack rivers and a part of the Concord River so that they may better be used for water supply sources. Some who have studied this problem would classify waters and set up laws to keep them under classifications, such as recommended by a committee appointed to facilitate the drafting of a tri-state agreement between New York, Connecticut and New Jersey to protect the tidal waters of these states. It is believed that in this State the Department of Public Health, with limited additional powers, can provide adequate protection. The Department has authority under Chapter 83 of the General Laws to approve the use of land for sewage disposal works and to order improvements in works for the treatment and disposal of sewage.

Watershed Authorities

Recent years have seen the development of so-called "watershed authorities," the function of which is to prevent pollution of streams and to promote their most effective use to the community. Legislation for such "authorities" have been provided for the Merrimack and Blackstone valleys but this legislation does not provide legal power to prevent pollution except through Federal funds. Such watershed authorities could be further developed, but they should act in conjunction with the Department of Public Health to prevent improper use of the various streams. The functions of such watershed authorities might well include flood control measures, the drainage of wet lands for the control of mosquito breeding, and the conservation of streams to improve sanitary conditions and to serve water power and transportation facilities, fisheries, agriculture and forestry.

Plumbing Regulations

At present the plumbing regulations throughout the Commonwealth are not uniform. Such rules, of course, must vary according to local circumstances, but it is possible to draw a minimum code sufficiently flexible to meet local requirements. These minimum requirements should not deprive the local boards of health of the right to adopt such additional regulations as may be deemed necessary. Under Section 8 of Chapter 142 of the Tercentenary Edition of the General Laws, the Department of Public Health has drafted proposed plumbing rules and regulations for adoption.

Cross Connections

The menace of improperly installed cross connections between the public water supplies and fire or industrial supplies which are not suitable for drinking purposes has been frequently demonstrated. Similarly there is ample evidence of the danger of improper plumbing connections whereby sewage or other polluted matter may enter water systems. The Department of Public Health on February 9, 1937, adopted rules and regulations concerning cross connections between fire and industrial supplies and public water supplies and has recommended that plumbing regulations be so drawn as to prevent plumbing connections which will permit back siphonage of polluted matter into drinking water systems.

Nuisances

The control of nuisances is delegated to local boards of health. The provisions of the General Laws covering nuisances are contained in Chapter 111, Sections 122 to 142, inclusive. The present statutes, dating in part from 1692, are adequate in most respects and have been strengthened through a long series of court decisions.

Garbage and Rubbish Collection

Responsibility for supervising the collection of garbage and rubbish is delegated in many communities to the local board of health, even though many believe that such supervision may have only slight public health significance. With the development of present-day methods of disposal, both activities are becoming more and more sanitary engineering problems. Certain communities have transferred these functions to the public works board or a similar bureau which, from its other duties, may be better equipped to handle this problem. The General Laws, Chapter 111, Section 31A, provide that no person shall remove or transport garbage, offal or other offensive substances through the streets without first having obtained a permit from the board of health of the city or town.

Smoke Control

Whether or not excessive smoke pollution of the atmosphere is a real health hazard may be open to question. All would agree, however, that it constitutes a nuisance which may render habitation uncomfortable and seriously depreciate property values. We should not be unmindful of the fact that, while the prosperity of the Commonwealth depends in large part upon proper industrial development, there are many places where needless and troublesome atmospheric pollution caused by smoke and other products of improper combustion occurs. Except as provided under the provisions of Section 132 of Chapter 140 of the General Laws which permits a town to declare a nuisance if dark or dense gray smoke is emitted for more than five minutes continuously or during ninety minutes of any continuous twelve hours, the present laws relative to smoke nuisances do not apply to the entire Commonwealth. Under Chapter 25 of the General Laws provision is made for smoke inspection in connection with the district set-up under Chapter 651 of the Acts of 1910 as amended.

Sanitation and Ventilation of Schools and Other Public Buildings

The Department of Public Safety is at present authorized to adopt and enforce rules and regulations as to the sanitation and ventilation of all public buildings, including schools. When these rules were first promulgated they constituted a very progressive step, especially in the field of ventilation.

It should be recognized that arbitrary standards such as exist today cannot be adopted to cover all situations and no single ventilation standard can be fixed to apply under all conditions, nor is it possible to standardize on methods or apparatus. The air requirements for ventilation of a school building are not constant but may vary within wide limits, depending upon many factors, such as age of the pupils, activity, air space allowed per person, the length of time the room is occupied, effectiveness of air distributors, and methods of air treatment. Each case must therefore be considered on its own merits. All standards of ventilation, lighting and sanitation must be drawn up in terms of conditions to be maintained rather than in terms or methods of achieving these ends.

Under the General Laws, Chapter 111, Section 22, the Department of Public Health must approve plans of station houses, houses of detention and lockups and the provisions for lighting, heating, ventilation and disposal of sewage and the dimensions and form of construction of the cells.

Housing

Although the effect of poor housing conditions upon the public health is not as readily measured as is that of such factors as impure water or milk, it is none the less agreed that the crowding of persons in unsanitary tenemehts exerts a deleterious effect upon their general well being. Various community services have tended to reduce the harm caused by these conditions so that today the health hazards of the congested tenement districts are much less than in former years, and at times these may appear to be no greater than in other sections of the community. However successful may have been our attempts to correct these unhealthy conditions, they should not blind us to the basic fact that in many communities large groups of people are living today under unnecessarily poor sanitary conditions. These include not merely overcrowding, but even lack of certain basic facilities for the maintenance of decent standards of cleanliness. The promotion of proper measures for the improvement of housing conditions is therefore a proper activity for health departments.

Chapters 144 and 145 of the General Laws provide tenement house laws which become effective in any community only if locally adopted. These laws pertain to the construction of all houses or buildings intended for occupancy by two or more families. They include not only certain minimum specifications as to construction, but also provide for proper maintenance. They have been adopted in but nineteen cities and towns, though many communities have standards of their own.

Summer Camps and Overnight Camps

Surveys in recent years have shown some 250 summer camps in Massachusetts providing accommodations for over 16,000 children. For several years the Department of Public Health has made inspections of such camps and recommended desirable changes in both physical equipment and maintenance. While unquestionably such inspection has brought about marked improvements, there is still much need for further supervision. Accordingly, legislation has been introduced to the Massachusetts Legislature for licensing "Summer or Vacation Camps, Overnight Camps and Trailer Camps" by local boards of health. This proposed legislation provides that the source of water supply and the works for the disposition of the sewage must be approved by the Department of Public Health. In many states legislation has been enacted which requires the licensing of all recreational and health camps by the state health department. The same ends can be attained, however, through a system of local licensing.

Shellfish

The revision of the shellfish laws, Chapter 329 of the Acts of 1933, was the result of several years study by legislative committees. It continued the authority of the Department to determine which areas are so badly contaminated that shellfish are not safe for use as food. The taking of shellfish from such areas is prohibited. The authority of issuing shellfish certificates was transferred from the Department to the Supervisor of Marine Fisheries. The law provides that no one shall deal in shellfish commercially without a certificate. These certificates are issued under rules and regulations promulgated by the Supervisor of Marine Fisheries but these rules and regulations are subject to the approval of the Department of Public Health so far as the sanitary requirements are concerned. The law also provides that the Supervisor shall revoke and cancel a shellfish certificate at the request of the Commissioner of Public Health after a hearing but that pending a hearing the certificate shall be deemed to be suspended.

The law also provides for approval by the Department of certificates for shipping shellfish from other states and provinces into Massachusetts and for the operation under rules and regulations promulgated by the Department of plants for the purification of shellfish obtained from moderately polluted areas. There is a special law under which the Department can prevent new sources of pollution in the tidal waters of Barnstable, Dukes and Nantucket counties from which shellfish are taken and it would seem advisable that this special law be enlarged to cover the tidal waters of the other coastal counties.

Noisome and Offensive Trades

Provisions are made under the General Laws, Chapter 111, for boards of health to assign certain places for use for noisome and offensive trades and to prohibit the exercise of any trade or employment which is a nuisance or hurtful to the inhabitants, injurious to their estates, dangerous to the public health, or is attended by noisome and injurious odors. If a place or building so assigned becomes a nuisance by reason of offensive odors or exhalations therefrom, or otherwise hurtful or dangerous to the neighborhood or to travellers, the superior court may, on complaint, revoke such assignment and prohibit the further use of the place or building, and cause the nuisance to be removed or prevented.

Under these laws written consent and permission of the mayor and city council or of the board of selectmen or the board of health of a town is also necessary for a person to occupy or use a building for carrying on the business of slaughtering cattle or other animals or for a melting or rendering establishment or for noxious or offensive trades and occupations.

Under Section 152 of Chapter 111 of the General Laws the Department of Public Health, upon application and after a hearing, may order any person to desist from carrying on an offensive trade or occupation if, in the opinion of the Department, the public health, comfort and convenience so require. These laws also require a license for slaughtering or rendering of animals and license for the use of a building as a stable.

Cemeteries

While the operation of a cemetery may have little or no effect on environmental sanitation, the Massachusetts General Laws provide that permission be obtained from a town or the mayor and aldermen of a city before land can be used for burial purposes unless this land is private land to be used exclusively by the family of the owner of the land. These laws also provide that no land other than that so used on April 10, 1908, shall be used for the purposes of burial if it is so situated "that surface water or ground drainage therefrom may enter any stream, pond, reservoir, well, filter gallery or other water used as a source of public water supply or any tributary of a source so used, or any aqueduct or other works used in connection therewith." until approved by the Department of Public Health. Provision is made in these laws for appeal to the Department of Public Health from the decision of the local board of health in the matter of use of land for cemetery purposes and under the provisions of Chapter 114 of the General Laws, as amended by Chapter 319 of the Acts of 1936, the Department of Public Health has certain jurisdiction in the matter of use of lands and equipment for the cremation of bodies, the reception or disposal of ashes after cremation, the use of buildings for the purpose of cremation and the erection of community mausoleums or crypts.

Bottled Waters and Nonalcoholic Beverages

The manufacture and sale of bottled waters and nonalcoholic beverages are controlled by the boards of health of cities and towns under the provisions of Chapter 94 of the General Laws which provide that a permit must be issued for the purpose and that the Department of Public Health and the local boards of health may make rules and regulations relative thereto. Under the rules and regulations adopted by the Department of Public Health no permit shall be granted for bottling mineral or spring waters unless the source of supply has been approved by the Department of Public Health and all waters used in the manufacture of beverages shall be subject to the approval of the Department of Public Health.

HEALTH IN THE ECONOMIC BRACKETS*

JOSEPH W. MOUNTIN, *Surgeon*
and
HAZEL O'HARA
United States Public Health Service

One errs only on the side of platitude in pointing out that the average American wishes to postpone the unhappy event of his death as long as possible, and that he sets a high value on spending the intervening time in physical comfort. He is oriented to a civilization wherein sanitation throws a cordon of safeguards about him, and medical science stands by to help him resist the onslaughts of accidents and disease. The one he accepts as operating automatically in the background of his life; the other he calls for when some part of his organism signifies that trouble is brewing. Ask a random selection of individuals what in their opinion is the element most necessary to the satisfying life, and the chances are that nine out of ten will answer "good health." It is surely due to no accident that our most frequent salutation is "How are you?"

Despite this high value placed on feeling well, an anomalous situation prevails in the application of the personal services which medical science has to offer. While it is generally accepted that there must be numerous halls of learning to which each generation may turn its steps for the purpose of having the mind put under cultivation, public thinking does not include any comparable scheme for promoting health. Illiteracy has become déclassé, but not sickness and disability.

Without a doubt if health promoting measures were applied on the same broad scale as educational measures are, they would relieve much personal and group misery rampant in the country today and lighten the

---
* From the Division of Public Health Methods, National Institute of Health.

financial burden that illness now lays upon society. A talented Robert Louis Stevenson stricken with tuberculosis may yet meet life so charmingly that the children of his mind survive him as a boon to millions of people. But the day laborer down with the same disease may bequeath his physical children, perhaps also infected, to society for support.

Chief among life's ironies one might point to the spread of sickness among those who are short of the easements of existence. This controverts a certain superficial opinion, now on the wane, that the poor through some mysterious immunity arising from poverty preserve their health, while the rich riotously throw theirs away. The poor may not suffer from diabetes to the same extent as do the rich, but the consensus of a large number of surveys shows that there is much excess of sickness among the poor and relief families from tuberculosis, pneumonia, nephritis, and rheumatism. The rate for disabilities from other important diseases and from accidents is also higher among the poor.

Surveys of health have long indicated that illness rates in general are highest among the poor and decline with increasing income. One study of 9,000 families in 18 states showed that wage earners in families having less than $1,200 annual income lost more than twice as many days per person per year as did gainful workers in families whose income was more than $3,000. The loss of even a day's wages to a laborer's family may spell distress, whereas among those families in the second group it may be of very little moment.

Inquiries made during the past few years have penetrated into the wide strata of relief families, and reveal that the total illness rate of the poor on relief definitely exceeds that of the poor who are not on relief. By using inability to work for seven days or longer as a measure of illness, it was found through a survey of 280,000 persons in 8 large cities that a total illness rate of 156 cases per 1,000 persons prevailed among families having annual incomes of $3,000 or more, as compared with rates of 188 for families with annual incomes of less than $1,000, and 262 for families receiving public relief. These figures indicate a concentration of poverty, sickness, and general misery that most individuals not directly experiencing them would find hard to imagine.

Mortality rates by broad occupational groups also reveal that sickness tends to camp among those who are least able to put up with it. In the United States, for instance, the death rate from pulmonary tuberculosis among skilled laborers is nearly three times what it is among professional workers, and among unskilled laborers it is seven times the rate for professional men. Other occupational groups fall between these extremes. The mortality rate for pneumonia among unskilled workers is three and one-half times the rate among professional workers. The same statement holds true for accidents. Mortality rates from cancer and from heart and kidney diseases, on the increase as the average span of life is lengthened, show an excess of 30 to 50 per cent for laborers as compared with higher salaried people. The death rate from all causes is about 25 per cent higher for skilled laborers than it is for those in intellectual pursuits, and for unskilled laborers is more than 100 per cent higher.

The poorer classes also experience greater loss through infant deaths than do those better off. To mention the findings of a recent study made in Denver, infants in families with an annual income of less than $500 died at a rate of 168 per 1,000 live births, as contrasted with 30 per 1,000 in families having incomes of $3,000 or more. The whole problem of caring for the infant and the mother, of reducing the mortality and morbidity rates of both, demands a confluence of medical, public health, social, and economic measures.

All these measures enter into the whole problem of clearing up the unwholesome conditions of existence; now one and then another slips forward as being at the moment most important. One family may stand in need of actual medical care, while their next door neighbors find their troubles best eased through the help of an experienced social worker. Poor housing, insufficient food and clothing, overfatigue, worry, disease, all enter into the picture. Medicine cannot be offered as a cure-all. It cannot be counted upon to combat successfully diseases directly contingent upon social causes. It can, however, do an enormous amount of good. But there exists between the science of medicine and a large sector of the public an obstacle marked "Ability to Pay." Only a relatively small proportion of those who have no money and are in need of help find their way around it.

Any one who lets himself be aware of the unpleasant side streets of existence is able to cite offhand the sort of personal dramas that take place under this scheme of distribution. A mother who has to exercise financial legerdemain to keep the landlord and grocer in good humor simply cannot get the money together for an adenoid operation for little Stella. The child goes on breathing through her mouth and adding to the several factors which alter the proper contours of her face; thus she is being marked for that particularly piercing humiliation which comes to those who do not conform to the norm in physical appearance. A shop worker whose wages are perpetually attached experiences fever, sweating, and lassitude but puts off going to the doctor with "maybe next month we can spare the money." When he has reached the point of going to a physician, tuberculosis is well advanced and the man has also reached a milestone in his shortened life beyond which he will never earn wages again.

Surveys that have been made express the same facts in a quantitative way. They show that the poor receive less medical care per person and much less per case of illness than do those in more fortunate circumstances. Even among families financed on a modest scale, the percentage of illnesses attended by a doctor increases noticeably with small difference in income. Among the 29,000 persons surveyed in 7 large cities, 59 per cent of the illnesses causing inability to work were attended by a doctor in families with an income of less than $150 per capita per annum, while 71 per cent were attended in those families whose income was $425 or more per capita. The average of calls per case attended for the first group was 4.2 and for the second 6.4.

The same survey shows that the poor fare a little better in hospital care than those who are just a step or so above being poor, presumably because of a fair supply of free hospital beds in large cities where the studies were made. It is the family that has sufficient income to meet the ordinary necessities, but not enough for expensive hospital costs that feels the pinch most when one of its members needs to go to the hospital.

The number of surgical operations, as might be expected, varies with income, especially those which are not necessarily of an emergency character but which should be performed some time. Among the poor a convenient time seldom arrives for surgery that is not absolutely necessary.

In the survey of 9,000 families in 18 states surgical operations of all kinds were recorded. Among families with annual incomes of less than $1,200, the data showed 52 operations per 1,000 persons as compared with 94 in families with $5,000 or more. This excess of 82 per cent carries implications of long chances being taken by many a small wage earner on remaining alive and well.

The rates for tonsillectomies were approximately the same for families with income up to $2,000, but among those whose incomes ran above $2,000 the frequency of this operation increased regularly with their salaries. Rates for appendicitis operations increased less markedly with income, but the rate among those receiving more than $5,000 a year was well above that for those living on $1,200 or less a year. Operations on benign tumors varied largely with income. The rate in the $5,000 and over income group was about six times that among families with incomes under $1,200. Thus poverty is seen to operate directly against one of the chief admonitions to the public in the program for cancer control—at the first sign of a lump or growth in your body, see a physician. The cancer death rate, be it noted, is now considerably higher among those in the lower income brackets than among those in the higher.

A simple emergency operation commonly required by young children is puncturing of the eardrum in cases of infection of the middle ear. If this surgical procedure is not applied, the eardrum usually bursts, after some damage has been done to the ear, but not infrequently the infectious process extends to the mastoid cells or to the meninges in which case life may be endangered. The frequency of this operation, too, shows wide variation with income.

As to those medical services which are preventive rather than remedial, that part of the public within financial reach of medical care, probably does not realize the extent to which many are forced to do without commonly accepted measures of prevention.

Periodic physical examinations might be classed offhand as a luxury of those who have money over and above their needs, and the available data bear this out. The situation among school children as expressed by gross examination rates is somewhat masked because of the volume of service of this type performed in the schools. As age increases between 15 and 45 years, the frequency of physical examination decreases in the low income groups, but tends to increase slightly among those with more means. Particularly large is the variation with income in the examination rate in the older age groups. For the ages 45 years and over, the highest income group had a physical examination rate that was more than 15 times the rate in the lowest income class.

The extent to which the younger age groups are protected by immunization is probably greatly misinterpreted. Since these services are usually performed under the supervision of the health department or the school authorities, it is easy to assume that they are distributed to one and all. Available data, however, show these preventive measures also vary with income. In the school ages, where immunization has become largely a public function, little difference shows up in the frequency of this procedure for the various income groups. In the preschool ages, however, there appears great disparity in the volume of service described as smallpox vaccinations and diphtheria immunizations. Diphtheria immunization is particularly important in the preschool age, for the peak of the death rate from this disease occurs before children enter school. Yet in those early ages immunizations were three times as frequent among children from families with annual incomes of $5,000 or more than they were among children from those families with less than $1,200 income. Approximately the same ratio for smallpox vaccinations prevailed in the preschool ages between these income groups.

As to dental care, its value is so widely recognized that probably little notion of how many must go without it exists among those who allow for it in their budgets. Probably no other form of medical care is so completely denied the individual in the underprivileged classes. The immediately important fact is not that reparative dentistry would improve their appearance, but that it is a vital element in the prevention of tooth loss and several serious diseases. While the filling of cavities in the teeth is not the complete and final answer to the problem of dental caries, the repair of dental decay is the most efficient way now known to arrest that decay and is a service which should not be denied to any person, particularly a growing child to whom it may mean health in later life.

The same study of 9,000 families in 18 states revealed a woeful lack of dental care in the low income brackets. Dental fillings were made at a rate of 141 per 1,000 persons in families with less than $1,200 annual income, as compared with 997 in the income group of $5,000 and over. Reconstructive work was done eight to ten times more frequently in the higher income groups than among the low income families. It is not possible to explain this on the grounds that the well-to-do may need more care. Such data as are available, on the contrary, indicate that the need for care is greatest among the poor. Nor is it reasonable to assume that the poor are not as interested in dental services. In many a modest home it is accepted that as the children get through school and find work they will have their teeth "fixed up." Frequently, however, it is too late for the dentist to do more than stave off the ravages of decay a bit longer.

Health Facilities

The lineup of the opposing forces, diseases and their scientific antagonists, seems a bit illogical, considered from the detached point of view, with medical measures reaching in the least degree those who need them most. The situation, of course, like many another is simply an outgrowth of public thought. The attitude toward public facilities for health has not been conditioned to the same degree of expectation as has the attitude toward institutions for achieving justice or education. A man does not usually rely upon the invisible powers that be to send him justice at law. Nor does he seek his education solely from books. He takes it for granted that judges and teachers are available to him in the proper public buildings and that it is to this end that tax monies are paid into governmental exchequers.

The promotion of health, however, is not generally accepted as a major interest of government. True it is that there exist many more centers of public health activity now than there were at the beginning of this century, but a few indices will show the great inadequacy of what is being done as compared with what is needed.

A health department, the symbol of disease prevention in any community, may be appraised by the scheme of organization and by the amount of funds at its disposal. By these criteria, it is apparent that even the best of departments are not in a position to give reasonable application to what is known regarding the prevention of disease and promotion of health. Of 2,500 predominantly rural counties in the United States, only 738 employed full-time health officers in 1935, and after a year under the Social Security Act the number was only 946 in 1936. The other rural counties depend on local practicing physicians, and in some instances on untrained laymen, for the administration of such rudimentary service as may be provided. With respect to the employment of qualified health officers, the average performance of cities is no better than that of counties.

Most students of public health administration agree that an annual budget equivalent to two dollars per capita is required for the preventive services commonly assigned to the health department. This level of public support is seldom reached. In fact, most county health department budgets fall below fifty cents, and only occasionally is a city reported to have appropriated more than one dollar per capita.

Public health programs are particularly remiss in the field of illness that is unattended or only partialy attended. \Care of the mentally afflicted and the tuberculous is now generally accepted as a function of the government. Otherwise, public medical service is usually 'restricted by the terms of the law to those who are accepted as public charges. Budgetary perhaps more than legal restrictions now serve to confine public medical service, particularly of the home and office type, to a very small fraction of the population who might benefit therefrom.

Aside from the regular avenues of public health activity, there are, it is true, establishments where the poor may receive medical treatment. The actual number of such places is often magnified by those who refer to them with optimistic vagueness and with a dismissing wave of the hand for the whole problem of low income and dependent groups. This rather grand idea of the extent of twentieth century benevolence has given rise to the oft repeated statement that the poor are treated as royally as the rich. The actual facts, however, reveal a rather different picture of the scope of free medical care.

Out-patient departments of hospitals are relatively few in number and for the most part are located in large cities. In all, about 770 hospitals have units that might be classed as true out-patient departments organized to serve the very low income group of the population. While it is true that many other hospitals give some care to their discharged patients and others who seek treatment of an emergency character, such service for ambulatory patients is not to be confused with that rendered in an organized out-patient department.

Hospitalization in general has this decided relationship to economic status—it is available for the most part only to those who can pay for it. This is putting the situation broadly and bluntly, and excludes certain disorders which are accepted as a public responsibility and will be considered separately. Eighty-five per cent of all general and allied special hospitals are nongovernmental, and they depend for about three-fourths of their income upon fees from patients. It stands to reason that individuals of some financial status occupy most of the beds.

The distribution of hospitals gives the people of certain sections an advantage in the securing of institutional care. Generally speaking they are concentrated in the more populous counties. In the South and West where the urbanization is less, the average distance to hospitals is greater than in the North and East. This factor of distance to be covered probably decides on many occasions whether there shall be hospitalization, especially among the poor and the nearly poor.

One striking exception to the direct relationship between hospitalization and the income of the sick is the category of mental disorders. Public care of those who are mentally ill, once a highly controversial subject, is now almost an article of political faith. To the public mind it is fitting and necessary that there be institutions erected and maintained out of tax monies to take care of the mentally incompetent members of society.

Mental hospitals of the United States show a total of some half million beds, of which but 4 per cent are nongovernmental. More than 95 per cent of the beds in the tax-supported hospitals are reported occupied. Many of the government institutions report acceptance of patients beyond their rated capacity for taking care of them.

Specialists in the field of mental disorders, viewing the work at close range and with the critical attitude of the perfectionist for his chosen subject, are impressed with the immense amount of work yet to be done. They are justly disturbed by the overcrowding and the frequent failure to utilize all that medical science has to offer in this field. In a review of the whole general subject of hospitalization, however, that part which has to do with mental disorders stands out in high relief through the substantial way in which the burden of care has been transferred from the family to the institution.

Another exception to the general concentration of hospital treatment among those who have the means to pay for it is in the care of the tuberculous. Society's acceptance of responsibility in the treatment of tuberculosis is largely a growth of the twentieth century. So also is individual willingness to admit his condition and seek the proper place for care. Growing confidence in the curability of this disease, agitation of benevolent citizens that the tuberculous be given adequate care, the passage of laws to this end, and the growth of sanatoria have all combined to mold public opinion to the eminently sane conclusion that a tuberculous person without means should be able to go to a place of cure provided by government and stay there until he is well.

The specialist in this field, too, points to the mountain of need that is still to be scaled. The facts in the case support his contention that many more beds are needed before the forces opposing this disease reach adequate proportions. Tuberculosis still leads as a cause of death among the young adult group, among the poor, and the colored. Despite the importance of prompt treatment, more than 80 per cent of the cases are in a fairly advanced stage at the time of hospitalization. Minimum standards set up for treatment of this disease call for one bed for each annual death, but many of the states have not reached this quota. However far short of perfect adequacy the endeavors fall, they nevertheless have succeeded in hauling tuberculosis down from its high estate as a leader among the causes of death in 1912 to seventh place in the year 1937.

The case against syphilis has also been receiving special pleading before the bar of public opinion. The population at present is in the evolutionary process of becoming really aware of this disease and its social implications. The incidence of syphilis is enough to alarm the body politic. From data gathered by the United States Public Health Service, it is estimated that one out of ten adults in the United States today has or has had syphilis, many of whom will remain a potential treatment problem throughout life. If infected persons actually needing treatment followed it up until they had been rendered noninfectious, and safe against late manifestations of the disease, present facilities would care for only 30 per cent of the present syphilis treatment load.

The problem here is not that of providing institutions, but of inculcating the disposition to seek treatment and to follow it up until cured. It is more nearly allied to general medicine than to the special therapy of those who need to be removed from society temporarily or permanently. It touches upon the institutional problem, however, in that syphilis leads so inevitably in many cases to mental disorders. Provision for and utilization of adequate treatment facilities would, it is believed, eliminate 10 per cent of first admissions to mental institutions now occurring as a result of syphilis.

The presentation of data along these lines could be extended indefinitely, for the field is large and the work just under way. Tuberculosis and syphilis being in the nature of scourges may seem to lead, but the many other problems of lesser magnitude contribute to the total of evil consequences which after all constitute the essence of the situation which needs to be attacked. The force and the effects of the attack will depend very largely upon the answers to these questions: How much responsibility will the social conscience accept? What trends will public thinking follow? Possible changes in public thought on the subject of health are not contemplated in this discussion. It is well, however, to recognize and to frankly admit human health has not attained such a stature that it might be classed among the primary purposes of social organization.

Figure 1. Frequency of illness per annum among members of families in various income brackets.

Figure 2. Annual rate of dental fillings experienced by persons in families having large and small incomes.

Figure 3. Proportion of illnesses causing inability to work for seven days or longer that were attended by a doctor in families of different economic levels.

Figure 4. Proportion of children in families of high and low income groups that were immunized against diphtheria.

Figure 5. Average annual death rate for the eleven most frequent causes in the United States 1930-1935.

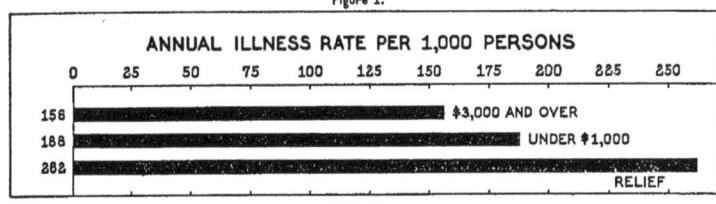

Figure 1.

ANNUAL ILLNESS RATE PER 1,000 PERSONS

- 156 — $3,000 AND OVER
- 188 — UNDER $1,000
- 262 — RELIEF

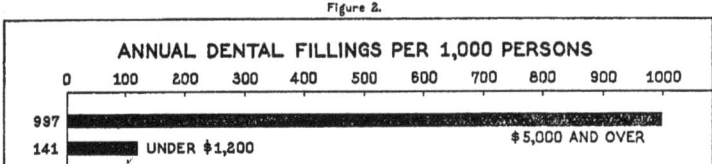

Figure 2.

ANNUAL DENTAL FILLINGS PER 1,000 PERSONS

- 997 — $5,000 AND OVER
- 141 — UNDER $1,200

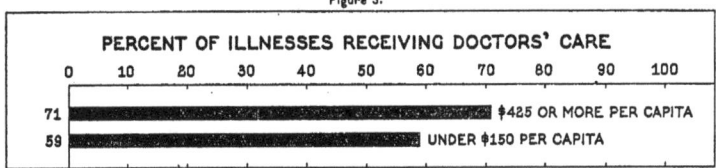

Figure 3.

PERCENT OF ILLNESSES RECEIVING DOCTORS' CARE

- 71 — $425 OR MORE PER CAPITA
- 59 — UNDER $150 PER CAPITA

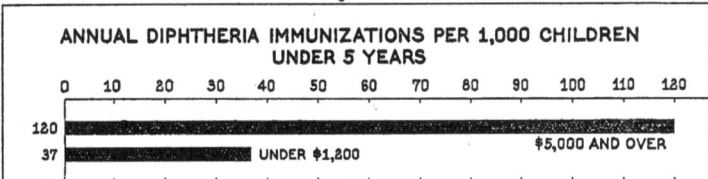

Figure 4.

ANNUAL DIPHTHERIA IMMUNIZATIONS PER 1,000 CHILDREN UNDER 5 YEARS

- 120 — $5,000 AND OVER
- 37 — UNDER $1,200

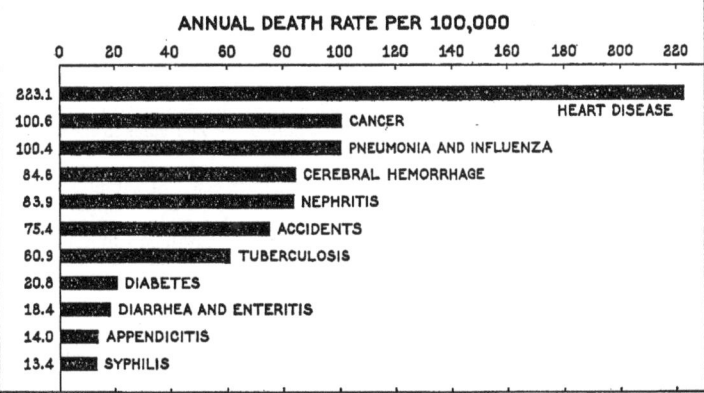

Figure 5.

ANNUAL DEATH RATE PER 100,000

- 223.1 HEART DISEASE
- 100.6 CANCER
- 100.4 PNEUMONIA AND INFLUENZA
- 84.6 CEREBRAL HEMORRHAGE
- 83.9 NEPHRITIS
- 75.4 ACCIDENTS
- 60.9 TUBERCULOSIS
- 20.8 DIABETES
- 18.4 DIARRHEA AND ENTERITIS
- 14.0 APPENDICITIS
- 13.4 SYPHILIS

Additional Material on Housing

Catching Up with Housing by Carol Aronovici, Ph.D., Lecturer on Housing and Urbanization at Columbia University and New York University, and Elizabeth McCalmont, Public Relations Department, Beneficial Management Corporation. $2. 243 pp. Newark, N. J. Beneficial Management Corporation. 1936.

Contains much interesting material, including extracts from the National Housing Act.

"Student Housing Survey" by David T. Loy, M.D., and M. W. Husband, M.D., Student Health Service, Kansas State College, Manhattan, Kans., *The Research Quarterly* 9:100, March, 1938.

Some Factors which Affect the Relationship between Housing and Health by J. M. DallaValle, Passed Assistant Sanitary Engineer, United States Public Health Service. Reprint No. 1840 from the Public Health Reports, Vol. 52, No. 30, July 23, 1937. For sale by the Superintendent of Documents, Washington, D. C. price 5c.

REPORT OF THE DIVISION OF FOOD AND DRUGS

(As required by General Laws, Chapter 111, Section 25.)

During the months of January, February and March 1938, samples were collected in 190 cities and towns.

There were 1,396 samples of milk examined, of which 92 were below standard, from 2 samples the cream had been in part removed, and 20 samples contained added water. There were 2,374 bacteriological examinations made of milk, 2,127 of which complied with the requirements. There were 91 bacteriological examinations made of cream, 23 of which did not comply with the requirements; 44 bacteriological examinations of ice cream, 2 of which did not comply with the requirements; 1 bacteriological examination of sherbet which did not comply with the requirements; 1 bacteriological examination of orange drink, and 1 bacteriological examination of corned beef, both of which complied with the requirements; and 49 bacteriological examinations of mattress fillings, 13 of which did not comply with the requirements. A bacteriological examination was made of cheese, said to have caused sickness, which sample complied with the requirements. There were 8 bacteriological examinations made of bandages to see whether or not they were sterile. There were 2 sterility tests made on absorbent cotton which complied with the requirements. Experiments were made on the Resazurin Tests and most of the results have been compared with the direct bacteriological microscopic counts on the same samples.

There were 768 samples of food examined, 144 of which were adulterated. These consisted of 7 samples of butter, 5 of which were below the legal standard in milk fat, and 2 samples were rancid; 16 samples of cream cheese, all of which did not conform to the legal standard; 2 samples of cider which contained sodium benzoate and were not so labeled; 7 samples of fruits which were too high in spray residue; 1 sample of pasteurized cream which was not properly pasteurized; 4 samples of shrimp which were decomposed; 1 sample of maple syrup which contained cane sugar; 1 sample of cooked chicken meat which was decomposed; 31 samples of hamburg steak, 24 of which were decomposed, 5 contained a compound of sulphur dioxide not so labeled, and 2 samples contained sodium sulphite in excess of one tenth of one per cent; 31 samples of sausage, 16 of which were decomposed, 14 contained a compound of sulphur dioxide not so labeled and 1 sample was also decomposed, and 1 sample contained starch in excess of 2 per cent; 2 samples of dried fruits which contained sulphur dioxide and were not so labeled; 4 samples of sweet relish which contained benzoic acid and were not so labeled; 5 samples of wash water which were deficient in caustic alkali; and 32 samples of mattress fillings, 27 of which contained secondhand material not so labeled, 2 were a mixture of secondhand and new material, and 3 samples contained shredded cloth.

There were 48 samples of drugs examined, of which 4 were adulterated. These consisted of 2 samples of argyrol which did not conform to the professed standard under which it was sold; 1 sample of spirit of nitrous ether and 1 sample of aromatic spirits of ammonia, both of which did not conform to the requirements of the U. S. Pharmacopoeia.

The police departments submitted 104 samples of liquor for examination. The police departments also submitted 18 samples to be analyzed for poisons or drugs, 8 of which contained heroin, 3 contained cannabis, 1 contained morphine derivative, 1 contained ergot and oil of apiol, 1 contained acetphenetidin, and 4 samples were examined for poison with negative results.

There were 336 plants operated for the pasteurization of milk; 22 restaurants; 77 soft drink plants; 34 ice cream plants; 23 bakeries; 447 mattress establishments; 283 establishments visited relative to the enforcement of license pertaining to wood alcohol and preparations containing over 3% of the same; and 1 store visited relative to a narcotic license.

There were 57 hearings held pertaining to violations of the laws.

There were 66 convictions for violations of the law, $1,490 in fines being imposed.

Lyndonville Creamery Association of Watertown; Anthony Rogers of North Andover; John D. Chiesa of Lexington; and Patrick J. Quinn of Amesbury, were convicted for violations of the milk laws.

Lyndonville Creamery Association of Watertown; Cass Dairy Company of Athol; Frank Lanzillo, 2 cases, of Wakefield; Walter Read, 2 cases, and Lincoln Stetson, 2 cases, of Abington; Leopold Schiavi of Framingham; Albin Taavitsainen of Gardner; and Charles Puleo of Salem, were convicted for violations of the pasteurization law and regulations. Walter Read of Abington appealed his two cases.

Abraham Miller of New Bedford; August Kisiel of Ware; Phillip Engelman, 2 cases, of South Norwood; Alex Lodgen, 2 cases, and Public Food Market of Roslindale, Incorporated, of Roslindale; Max Rabinovitz, Morris Levine, and United Markets, Incorporated, of Springfield; Jacob Goldfarb of Worcester; Main Public Market, Incorporated, of Fall River; Frank Bonerbi of Beverly; National Distributing Company of Boston; Paul Baltrusunas of South Boston; John Berkson and Barney Lass of Charlestown; Ermanno Cesati, 2 cases, and George A. Legare of Haverhill; Michael Feldman, Esther Leiben and Washington Public Market, Incorporated, of Roxbury; John Macera, 2 cases, James Mitchell, 2 cases, Samuel Mogul, Benjamin Gross, and Salvatore Mucci of Somerville; M. M. Mades Company, Incorporated, 2 cases of Lowell; Isadore Mazoff, Charles Battaglia, Charles Dubrow, Frank Cataldo and Morris Caswell of Lynn; Fred Tombari and Emil Torrelli of Framingham; Miller Brothers, Incorporated, of Hudson; and James Mancuso of Milford, were all convicted for violations of the food laws. The case of James Mancuso of Milford was filed without a finding. Frank Bonerbi of Beverly; George A. Legare of Haverhill; National Distributing Company of Boston; John Berkson and Barney Lass of Charlestown; M. M. Mades Company, Incorporated, 2 cases, of Lowell, all appealed their cases.

Frank Bonerbi of Beverly; Omaha Packing Company, Incorporated, of Lowell; Reading Preserving Company of Reading; and Angelica Lathas of Haverhill, were convicted for violations of the sanitary food law.

Wingate Chemical Company of Cambridge for a violation of the narcotic law, was held for the Grand Jury.

Louis Young of Brockton; Peter B. Bebchick and Milton E. Hadley of Lowell; and General Mattress Company of Fall River, were convicted for violations of the mattress laws. General Mattress Company of Fall River appealed its case.

James T. Worth of Nantucket was convicted for a violation of the slaughtering law.

In accordance with Section 25, Chapter 111 of the General Laws, the following is the list of articles of adulterated food collected in original packages from manufacturers, wholesalers, or producers.

One sample of butter which was rancid was obtained from Springfield Butter Company, of Springfield.

Butter which was low in fat was obtained as follows: One sample each, from Mayflower Creamery Company and National D. Creamery of Boston; Carl Gold, Meyer Burstein, Mayflower Butter & Cheese Company, and M. Winer Company, all of Springfield.

Dried fruits which contained sulphur dioxide not so labeled was obtained as follows:

One sample each, from Venice Grocery Company, Incorporated of Boston, and Samuel Garmon of Dorchester.

Cider which contained sodium benzoate and was not so labeled was obtained as follows.

One sample each, from Economy Grocery Stores Corporation of Beverly and Boston.

One sample of maple syrup which contained cane sugar was obtained from Keech Kalfa of Westfield.

One sample of relish which contained a compound of benzoic acid not so labeled was obtained from Silver Lane Pickle Company of Silver Lane, Connecticut.

Hamburg steak which was decomposed was obtained as follows:

Two samples, from M. M. Mades Company of Lowell; and one sample each, from Benjamin Gross and Joseph Rodragoas of Lowell; Amedia H. Gingras of Holyoke; Charles Cerullo of Somerville; Barney Lass and John Berkson of Charlestown; Antonio Rosa Beatriz and Edward Morse of New Bedford; Washington Public Market, Incorporated, of Roxbury; United Meats, Incorporated, and Morris Levine of Springfield; Virginia Market (Benjamin Cohen) and Morris Provision Company (Morris Epstein) of Dorchester; Cataldo's Market of Lynn; Main Public Market, Incorporated, and People's Public Market, Incorporated, of Fall River; Comet Market, Incorporated, and Ideal Market (Morris Kenion) of Brockton; Publix Food Market of Roslindale; Hudson Market Incorporated, of Hudson; George A. Legare of Haverhill; and Myer L. Elgart of Woburn.

Hamburg steak which contained a compound of sulphur dioxide not so labeled was obtained as follows:

One sample each, from John Macera of Somerville; Eddie Mason and Meatland Market (Michael Feldman) of Dorchester; and Isadore Mazoff and William Kline of Lynn.

Hamburg steak which contained sodium sulphite in excess of one tenth of one per cent was obtained as follows:

One sample each, from Samuel Mogul of Somerville; and Sam Smokler of Boston.

Sausage which was decomposed was obtained as follows:

One sample each, from Fred Tombari of Framingham; Hub Market of Roxbury; Hanover Market (Morris Caswell), Charles Battaglia, and Charles Dubrow, of Lynn; Thomas Tillman and Levine's R. & W. Markets, Incorporated, of Springfield; Salvatore Mucci and Benjamin Gross of Somerville; Skiddell & Chook and Paul Baltrusunas of Boston; George A. Legare of Haverhill; Ideal Market (Morris Kenion) of Brockton; Gordon Brothers Market of Lowell; James Miller of Hudson; and John Moskal of Northampton.

Sausage which contained a compound of sulphur dioxide not so labeled was obtained as follows:

One sample each, from Eugene Vecchirello, Charles Cerullo, and John Macera of Somerville; Gloria Chain Stores, Incorporated, and James Mancuso of Milford; Venice Grocery Company, Incorporated, of Boston; Morris Abrams of South Boston; Frank Bonerbi and Charles Bucci of Beverly; Central Beef Company of Haverhill; and Stella Chain Stores of Lynn.

One sample of sausage which contained a compound of sulphur dioxide not so labeled and was also decomposed was obtained from Lodgen's Market of Roslindale.

There were 17 confiscations, as follows:—12 pounds of decomposed broilers; 44 pounds of decomposed turkeys; 30 pounds of putrid beef; 10 pounds of putrid beef; 6 pounds of decomposed lamb; 6 pounds of decomposed hamburg steak; 50 pounds of decomposed hamburg steak; 30 pounds of putrid hamburg; 50 pounds of putrid sausage meat; 6 pounds of decomposed sausage meat; 15 pounds of putrid sausage meat; 30 pounds of decomposed sausage meat; 4 pounds of decomposed pork sausage; 10 pounds of decomposed pork sausage; 20 pounds of putrid cod; 20 pounds of putrid haddock; and 10 pounds of putrid smelts.

The licensed cold storage warehouses reported the following amounts of food placed in storage during December, 1937:—90,600 dozens of case eggs; 362,680 pounds of broken out eggs; 443,314 pounds of butter; 2,911,213 pounds of poultry; 2,828,474 pounds of fresh meat and fresh meat products; and 7,568,946 pounds of fresh food fish.

There was on hand January 1, 1938:—318,480 dozens of case eggs; 2,451,488 pounds of broken out eggs; 1,552,159 pounds of butter; 6,400,905 pounds of poultry; 4,094,068 pounds of fresh meat and fresh meat products; and 25,042,553 pounds of fresh food fish.

The licensed cold storage warehouses reported the following amounts of food placed in storage during January, 1938:—92,910 dozens of case eggs; 415,360 pounds of broken out eggs; 340,756 pounds of butter; 1,506,669 pounds of poultry; 4,367,837 pounds of fresh meat and fresh meat products; and 5,618,486 pounds of fresh food fish.

There was on hand February 1, 1938:—139,650 dozens of case eggs; 2,043,888 pounds of broken out eggs; 1,002,372 pounds of butter; 6,186,837 pounds of poultry; 6,439,250 pounds of fresh meat and fresh meat products; and 22,297,557 pounds of fresh food fish.

The licensed cold storage warehouses reported the following amounts of food placed in storage during February, 1938:—98,520 dozens of case eggs; 503,244 pounds of broken out eggs; 236,276 pounds of butter; 943,508 pounds of poultry; 3,268,051 pounds of fresh meat and fresh meat products; and 3,806,478 pounds of fresh food fish.

There was on hand March 1, 1938:—99,870 dozens of case eggs; 1,752,251 pounds of broken out eggs; 530,386 pounds of butter; 4,996,442 pounds of poultry; 6,826,749 pounds of fresh meat and fresh meat products; and 15,381,885 pounds of fresh food fish.

MASSACHUSETTS DEPARTMENT OF PUBLIC HEALTH

Commissioner of Public Health, HENRY D. CHADWICK, M.D.

Public Health Council

HENRY D. CHADWICK, M.D., *Chairman*

GEORGE D. DALTON, M.D.	RICHARD M. SMITH, M.D.
FRANCIS H. LALLY, M.D.	RICHARD P. STRONG, M.D.
CHARLES F. LYNCH, M.D.	JAMES L. TIGHE

Secretary, FLORENCE L. WALL

Division of Administration	Under direction of Commissioner
Division of Sanitary Engineering	Director and Chief Engineer, ARTHUR D. WESTON, C.E.
Division of Communicable Diseases	Director, ROY F. FEEMSTER, M.D.
Division of Biologic Laboratories	Director and Pathologist, ELLIOTT S. ROBINSON, M.D.
Division of Food and Drugs	Director and Analyst, HERMANN C. LYTHGOE, S.B.
Division of Child Hygiene	Director, M. LUISE DIEZ, M.D.
Division of Tuberculosis	Director, ALTON S. POPE, M.D.
Division of Adult Hygiene	Director, HERBERT L. LOMBARD, M.D.
Division of Genitoinfectious Diseases	Director, NELS A. NELSON, M.D.

State District Health Officers

The Southeastern District	RICHARD P. MACKNIGHT, M.D., New Bedford
The South Metropolitan District	HENRY M. DE WOLFE, M.D., Braintree
The North Metropolitan District	CHARLES E. GILL, M.D., Boston
The Northeastern District	ROBERT E. ARCHIBALD, M.D., Melrose
The Worcester County District	OSCAR A. DUDLEY, M.D., Worcester
The Connecticut Valley District	JOHN J. POUTAS, M.D., Westfield
The Franklin County District	WALTER W. LEE, M.D., Greenfield
The Berkshire County District	HAROLD W. STEVENS, M.D., Great Barrington.

PUBLICATION OF THIS DOCUMENT APPROVED BY THE COMMISSION ON ADMINISTRATION AND FINANCE
6600. 6-'38. Order 4338.

THE COMMONHEALTH

Volume 25　　　July-Aug.-Sept.
No. 3　　　　　　1938

CANCER

MASSACHUSETTS
DEPARTMENT OF PUBLIC HEALTH

THE COMMONHEALTH

QUARTERLY BULLETIN OF THE MASSACHUSETTS DEPARTMENT OF
PUBLIC HEALTH

Sent Free to any Citizen of the State
Entered as second class matter at Boston Postoffice.

M. LUISE DIEZ, M.D., DIRECTOR OF DIVISION OF MATERNAL AND CHILD
HEALTH, EDITOR. 1 Beacon Street, Boston, Mass.

CONTENTS

	PAGE
Foreword, by Henry D. Chadwick, M.D.	191
History of the Massachusetts Cancer Program, by Eleanor J. Macdonald, A.B.	192
The State Cancer Hospitals, by Ernest M. Daland, M.D.	202
Epidemiological Aspects of the Massachusetts Cancer Program, by Herbert L. Lombard, M.D.	221
Massachusetts State-Aided Cancer Clinics, by Frederick G. Medinger, M.D.	229
Beth Israel Hospital Cancer Clinic (An Appraisal of the Aid Given the Cancer Clinic), by Harry F. Friedman, M.D., and Ethel Cohen, M.S.	230
Boston Dispensary Cancer Clinic, by William M. Shedden, M.D.	233
Brockton Cancer Clinic, by Frederick F. Weiner, M.D.	237
Cape Cod Cancer Clinic, by Farrar Cobb, M.D.	237
Fall River Cancer Clinic, by Thomas Almy, M.D.	239
Fitchburg Cancer Clinic, by Rudolf F. Bachmann, M.D.	240
Franklin County Cancer Clinic, by William J. Pelletier, M.D.	241
Gardner Cancer Clinic, by Harold C. Arey, M.D.	242
Gloucester Cancer Clinic, by Ezra E. Cleaves, M.D.	243
Lawrence Cancer Clinic, by J. Forrest Burnham, M.D.	244
Lowell Cancer Clinic, by Lowell Cancer Clinic Staff	246
Lynn Cancer Clinic, by William T. Hopkins, M.D.	247
New Bedford Cancer Clinic, by Edwin D. Gardner, M.D.	249
Newburyport Cancer Clinic, by Lincoln C. Peirce, M.D.	250
North Adams Cancer Clinic, by Martin M. Brown, M.D.	251
Northampton Cancer Clinic, by Thomas F. Corriden, M.D.	252
Pittsfield Cancer Clinic, by Pittsfield Cancer Clinic Committee	253
Springfield Cancer Clinic, by John E. Dwyer, M.D.	253
Worcester Cancer Clinic, by Ernest L. Hunt, M.D.	255
Cancer Education in Massachusetts, by Frances A. Macdonald, A.B.	256
The State Tumor Diagnosis Service, by Shields Warren, M.D.	261
Cancer Statistics in Massachusetts, by Bernard E. Bradley	266
Report of the Division of Food and Drugs, April, May and June, 1938	270

FOREWORD

TO THE PHYSICIANS OF MASSACHUSETTS:

At this time, in the third "Cancer Number" of *The Commonhealth* I wish to express my appreciation to the physicians of Massachusetts fo their help in making the Cancer Program the success that it is. Much tim and effort was expended by them in the thousands of cancer talks that wer given last year, and I think we may all be satisfied with the results. It i encouraging to note that cancer among females is on the decline, and th rate for males is practically stationary.

In the second "Cancer Number" of *The Commonhealth* (Oct.-Nov. Dec. 1934) the new cancer policy was outlined and the enthusiastic re sponse, both from physicians and laity, justified the optimism felt at tha time.

This policy is being continued, and the hope is expressed that th present issue of *The Commonhealth* will be of further help to the professio in carrying out the program.

HENRY D. CHADWICK, M.D.,
Commissioner of Public Health

HISTORY OF THE MASSACHUSETTS CANCER PROGRAM

ELEANOR J. MACDONALD, A.B.

Epidemiologist, Division of Cancer and Other Chronic Diseases
Massachusetts Department of Public Health

The Massachusetts Cancer Program, officially launched in 1926, was a logical milestone in the development of organized public health in this State. The first public health regulations originated in the Massachusetts Bay Company. From then on for one hundred years these rules were bounded by the necessity for regulating sanitation and quarantine. An attempt was made in 1721 by Reverend Cotton Mather and Zabdiel Boylston to introduce inoculation as a preventive for smallpox, but the opposition raised was so bitter that the experiment was stopped. Dr. Benjamin Waterhouse reopened the question in 1800 by vaccinating his own family.

The inhabitants of Boston recognized the importance of health measures and in 1799 chose a Board of Health with Paul Revere as chairman. This Board gradually worked out satisfactory arrangements for obtaining a pure water supply, for water analysis, and for the construction of sewers.

In 1850, one of the most important contributions to public health in the United States was presented by Lemuel Shattuck in the form of a Legislative Document, familiarly known as the "1850 Report of the Sanitary Commission." Shattuck sensed the need of a definite health program and outlined a plan of public health administration so comprehensive in nature that it is even now in the process of realization. His report was tabled and not resurrected for active use until the establishment in 1869 of the State Board of Health. This Board functioned until 1914, except during the period 1879-1886 when it was replaced by the Board of Health, Lunacy and Charity.

From the first the practice, which is still in effect, was inaugurated of studying varying conditions, of educating the public to ideas of prevention and reform, and then of sponsoring bills to effect the correction of inadequacies. Housing conditions, ventilation, use of intoxicating liquors, industrial diseases, sale of poison, and vital statistics are some of the many diversified problems that were treated. A special tribute must be given to the work done by the Board in the latter part of the nineteenth century in the purification of water supplies. This was a pioneer achievement and the research carried on at the Lawrence Experiment Station produced methods for sewage disposal which have been copied in many parts of the world.

The need for cancer control was first noted and recorded in Massachusetts in 1896. In the report of the Massachusetts Board of Health of that year the local cancer situation was reviewed from 1856 through 1895. The excellence of this study betokened a growing cancer consciousness comparable to the earlier surge of interest in the need for pure water, sanitary rulings, and communicable disease control. In 1899 the preliminary work was authorized for the famous Whitney Report—a statistical study analyzing the alleged increase of cancer in Massachusetts. This same year Harvard University appointed the Harvard Cancer Commission, a group which has played a part of vital importance in the development of the Massachusetts Cancer Program. The interest in cancer in this State has continued without interruption from this period.

In 1913 Dr. Francis D. Donoghue was sent by Governor Foss as delegate to represent the Commonwealth of Massachusetts at the Third International Cancer Conference held in Brussels. Dr. Donoghue's interest in the use of mesothorium and other methods of treating cancer was well known. He wrote a paper about the conference after his return and appended a bibliography of all the literature together with a recommendation that cancer needed institutional care because the materials necessary for treatment were so costly that no individual could afford the necessary expense. This report was never published and is not available.

On January 23, 1914, Dr. Donoghue introduced a resolve into the House of Representatives in which he recommended that the Governor appoint a committee to study the various methods of cancer therapy, to report the need of further hospitalization, and to devise means of procuring curative agents prohibitive in price to the average person. He advised that the committee make such recommendations for legislation as its investigation warranted. The Transcript for March 9, 1914, gave a lengthy account of the hearing on Dr. Donoghue's bill. According to the report, Dr. Donoghue said that the cause of cancer was the greatest unsolved medical problem in the United States; that there was great value in radium, mesothorium, and other active radio-active substances; and that Massachusetts should have an active board to handle the distribution of radio-active material whenever an "enlightened state government or a national government could provide them." He advised against the duplication of the work of research laboratories which public-spirited citizens had contributed. The State should concern itself with the treatment and care of cases which otherwise might be the cause of great suffering and danger to the community. Many physicians and surgeons had themselves recorded as in favor of this resolve. On March 16th this bill was reported favorably to the Senate. The Ways and Means Committee ruled that it ought not to pass. The House accepted the report and rejected the bill.

It was at this same session of the General Court that the act was passed creating the State Department of Public Health with the authority to exercise all the powers and perform all the functions of the State Board of Health.

John N. Levins introduced a resolve into the House in 1915. He was a member of the Legislature and acted from a desire to help his fellowmen, and not from a knowledge of previous legislation. To quote his own words:

"The first thirty years of my life were spent in the closely populated section of South Boston, and in a section of this kind, constituted of hard-working people who are having a struggle to get along, there is an overwhelming disposition to help one another. Accordingly, people from South Boston, or people from sections such as East Boston, Charlestown, Roxbury, and places of the same kind in any other city, are in close contact with sorrow, trouble, and suffering and are only too willing to offer assistance in any direction to ease the difficulties of others.

"Included in the sufferings of our neighbors and friends in South Boston was the terrible affliction of cancer, and my contact with relatives, neighbors and friends who were thus afflicted, made me gasp in the realization of their sufferings. The tuberculosis hospital at Rutland, which was the result of activities as a State representative and senator on the part of the late Congressman James A. Gallivan, acting on the ideas of his brother, Dr. William J. Gallivan, provided the thought that something similarly beneficial could be worked out in the case of cancer. In other words, if some special attention were afforded unfortunate and hopelessly doomed cancer victims by concentration in one place under the guidance of skilled specialists, it would be possible to ease their sufferings. Such concentration would also seem to afford the means to intensively study the history of cases and determine causes, whether hereditary or otherwise, to develop if possible the prevention of cancer in those not afflicted and the cure of those afflicted incipiently.

"Obviously with such concentration, the history of each case showing environment, home conditions, food, occupation, mental attitude, heredity, etc., would be under the close observation of skilled specialists in the treatment of the afflicted, who would collaborate in their findings and ideas.

"Therefore, as a member of the Legislature in 1915, I presented a bill asking for the establishment of a State Cancer Hospital. I had devoted considerable time with the medical profession to secure data, and any information which would be of help in the passage of the bill through the State Legislature."

Representative Levins filed a bill (House 742) in which it was recommended that a State hospital for cancer under the supervision of the State Department of Public Health be established. This bill was referred to the next annual session, was brought up again the following year, and was finally given leave to withdraw.

The influence of this preliminary work was felt in 1919. Dr. Eugene R. Kelley, Commissioner of Public Health, presented the following resolve which was passed:

"Resolved that the state department of health, for the purpose of gathering information about the prevalence of cancer and for purposes of prevention and control of this disease, is hereby authorized to expend during the year nineteen hundred and nineteen, for salaries and other expenses, a sum not exceeding three thousand dollars."

The appropriation of this money enabled the State Department of Public Health to cooperate with the Harvard Cancer Commission in furnishing diagnostic service to physicians and hospitals. It also made possible a preliminary educational campaign against cancer. This appropriation was continued annually until these activities became absorbed in the present cancer program. Dr. Kelley, with the foresight into public-health needs which characterized his administration, continued to study the cancer problem, and at the 1923 meeting of the American Public Health Association pointed out certain needs connected with the control of cancer. He felt that the five important requirements dealing with the situation were as follows:

"1. The great need of discussion and study by health department administrators to determine just what their proper niche is in the cancer struggle.

"2. The need of better statistical data as to the present facts and the need of additional personnel and funds for health administrators to adequately collect, collate, analyze and diffuse these facts.

"3. The need of more extended facilities for early diagnosis and of stimulating the profession to utilize fully these facilities when established.

"4. The need of better hospital facilities for the inoperable group of cancer victims.

"5. The supreme and pressing need of new and efficient methods of both arousing and retaining public interest in and understanding of the significance of cancer whereby a large degree of success may be reasonably anticipated even with our present faulty weapons for combating the menace of malignancy."

The next independent step in the cancer movement was the presentation by Mr. Brimblecom of Newton, at the request of Wilbur E. Trussell, of the bill to establish a hospital for the care and treatment of persons afflicted with cancer. Mr. Trussell's interest in cancer was the result of a personal experience. His wife's mother had a cancer which was not recognized in its early stages, and which resulted in a four-or five-year period of invalidism. During the period when she was cared for in the Trussell home the fears of the neighbors of contracting cancer by association created the unhappy condition of more or less severe social ostracism for the family. Mr. Trussell eventually was able to have the invalid placed in the House of the Good Samaritan where she remained until her death. Mr. Trussell was a telegraph operator and had eight children. The financial strain of three years of hospitalization was an acute one. Mr. Trussell held no public office, nor was he a legislator, but his interest in his own experiences and those of other people in similar circumstances convinced him that something should be done. He organized a group which called itself "The Massachusetts Society for the Control of Cancer." The society decided to make its opinion felt so that legislative action might be taken to provide adequate treatment for cancer cases. It wished also to go on record with an appeal that the public might be educated in its responsibility toward these people and their relatives. The cost of membership in this society was one dollar. When the bill came up at the hearing the entire society attended. Mrs. Trussell told her experiences, as did many others in the group. This bill was withdrawn but its presentation aroused public interest and as an independent project it had a specific place in the evolution of the cancer program.

A bill was filed at the same time that Mr. Trussell filed his bill, containing a resolve accompanying a petition of Representative Charles H. McGlue for the purchase of radium and the distribution of radium emanations by the State. According to the resolve, no charge was to be made for the use of radium, and physicians were to receive instructions in its use before obtaining it. Representative McGlue was a personal friend of Mr. M. Douglas Flattery, who was the head of the Special Committee on Medical Research for the Boston Conservation Bureau and was also a member of the Harvard Cancer Commission. Mr. Flattery was an enthusiastic advocate of radium treatment and he felt that the people of Massachusetts would insist on having the benefits of this treatment, if it were presented to them properly. In a report on this resolve by the Committee on Public Health, it was recommended that the Department of Public Health should study the situation and consider the advisability of the purchase of radium by the Commonwealth for the reasons given in the last bill mentioned. This bill was referred to the next annual session. Representative McGlue continued to work for this bill. He refiled it and followed its progress until 1926 when it was altered and combined with the cancer hospital bill.

In 1925 and 1926 the bills were filed that were directly responsible for the establishment of the hospital. The background figure in this movement was the Right Reverend Monsignor Ambrose F. Roche, then Pastor of St. Patrick's Church in Watertown. From the time of his ordination he had made a study of medicine in its several aspects. He had been particularly interested in the subject of cancer for many years as it was constantly kept before him on his sick calls. He had been in a parish in an older community and with the aging of the population he had observed an increase of deaths from cancer. He studied existing information on cancer and facilities for caring for the sick. He studied intensively before he considered taking any action. He finally realized that if anything was to be done to assist afflicted persons, it must be done by the State to be effective for all classes. The Holy Ghost Hospital in Cambridge, of which he was Chaplain at the time, was one of the very few hospitals that would admit terminal cancer patients. There was always a longer waiting list than could be accommodated. He was in a position to see the distress which could not be relieved. Early in 1925 Monsignor Roche enlisted the aid of the Honorable Frederick W. Mansfield. Mr. Mansfield drafted a bill to establish a hospital modeled after the bill which established a school for the feeble-minded, with such changes as were necessary to adapt it to this purpose. Mr. Mansfield recommended that the hospital not be called a Cancer Hospital. He sent a copy of the bill to Monsignor Roche for his approval and recommended immediate filing.

Monsignor Roche requested Mr. Mansfield to have his bill presented to the Senate. Mr. Mansfield had the bill filed in the Senate by the Honorable Walter Shuebruk. Mr. Mansfield sent a copy of the bill to Dr. Donoghue and requested him to support it if he approved. Dr. Donoghue agreed to attend the hearing. Mr. Mansfield then contacted Mr. M. Douglas Flattery of the Harvard Cancer Commission and asked him to take up the matter of the bill with the Commission. At the same time he wrote to Dr. Henry P. Walcott, who was chairman of the Harvard Cancer Commission, and asked him to take up the measure with the Commission. Dr. Kelley, State Commissioner of Public Health, was sent a copy of the bill and asked to cooperate if he were in sympathy and to communicate with Mr. Mansfield if he were not. Mr. Flattery said that he felt the bill was well drawn but that Mr. Mansfield had perhaps not considered the difficulties behind such an institution. He still felt that the distribution of radium was of more value than the hospital for cancer and suggested that the bill of Representative McGlue on radium be discussed at the same hearing with the bill for the cancer hospital.

Simultaneously with the request to Mr. Mansfield to draft a cancer bill, a second request was made by Monsignor Roche to Mr. Robert J. White, Assistant District Attorney of Middlesex County and prominent in the American Legion, to sponsor a bill for him in the House. Mr. White complied with this request. For months he spent much time assembling data on the statistics of cancer as well as on its medical aspects. He convinced himself by his study that the State should have a cancer institution. He went even further and stated that he felt the State should have an economic as well as a humanitarian interest in the plan. Bills of both Mr. Mansfield and Mr. White were referred to the next annual session.

At this time, the Honorable Warren C. Daggett introduced a resolve for the investigation of the prevalence of cancer and for facilities for treatment of this disease. He petitioned that the Departments of Public Health and Public Welfare make a joint study of the situation with special attention to inoperable cases and to the number of beds available. This resolve was passed. The two departments reported the joint study in House Document 1200, General Court of 1926.

The study was reported by a committee of four, comprised of Dr. John H. Nichols and Mr. Frank W. Goodhue, appointed by Mr. Richard K. Conant, the Commissioner of Public Welfare; Dr. George H. Bigelow and Dr. Merrill E. Champion, appointed by Dr. Eugene R. Kelley, the Commissioner of Public Health. Dr. Herbert L. Lombard was the field investigator. The resources of the Department of Vital Statistics of the Harvard School of Public Health were placed at the disposal of the committee by Professor E. B. Wilson. Others who contributed were: Dr. Carl R. Doering, Mr. C. G. Gray, Mr. Edgar A. Bowers, Dr. Henry P. Walcott, Dr. Robert B. Greenough, Dr. E. E. Tyzzer, Dr. J. Homer Wright, Mr. M. Douglas Flattery, Dr. Frederick L. Hoffman, Dr. J. W. Schereschewsky, Mr. J. Arthur Burke, and Mrs. Ruth Boretti. The report contained a comprehensive review of the cancer literature, a statistical study of the disease, the existing facilities, an estimate of the bed needs, and the result of interviews with individuals familiar with the cancer situation, regarding the need for State service in cancer.

The committee was unable to agree upon a recommendation for a new State hospital because of a difference of opinion as to the relative importance to be assigned to the facts brought out in the report. It recommended that the Department of Public Health be empowered to direct and stimulate the extension of existing facilities for the care of cancer patients, and the education of the public to the necessity of proper treatment.

In December, 1925, this report was made to the General Court of Massachusetts. The individuals interested in the establishment of this hospital had based this interest on years of study and were not deterred by the divided opinion of the committee regarding hospitalization but continued to exert pressure for the hospital. Monsignor Roche arranged a conference with Representatives William P. Prendergast and John J. McCarthy, and Senator William J. Francis. He explained the cancer situation in detail and traced for them the steps he had taken in attempting to interest men in public affairs in the need of a cancer hospital under the State control. They agreed to have Representative Prendergast file a new petition for a hospital. Representative Prendergast communicated with Mr. Robert J. White, who turned over all the information he had collected on the subject to him. Representative Prendergast then enlisted the aid of the press, and had hundreds of blanks prepared and sent all over the State for the purpose of obtaining signatures from the constituents of the various representatives and senators who were endorsing the bill. In the meantime Monsignor Roche contacted the leaders of the Daughters of Isabella, an organization numbering at that time about ten thousand members and having a circle in nearly every community in the State. He asked these leaders if he could work through the members of their organization to effect a personal education for the needs of adequate care and control of cancer, so that the individual members might work for this worthy purpose in the several communities in the State. The cooperation of the Daughters of Isabella was responsible more than any other one thing in the successful establishment of a cancer program. This organization received through its regents pamphlets and reports of various findings of cancer experts, and conducted through its members, both verbally and in the newspaper, extensive publicity. When the bill came up finally for a hearing, the Daughters of Isabella sent representatives fom all over the State. This gradual awakening of interest in every part of the State resulted in what seemed a simultaneous demand that something be done for people in every profession and every walk of life.

The Committee on Public Health in House Document 1455, combined a report on all the cancer bills. The chairman of this committee, Representative William J. Bell, was one of the most earnest agitators for the cancer hospital. The essentials of all the several bills, except those concerning the purchase of radium, were included in this report.

On February 21, 1926, in the Gardner Auditorium, the hearing was held. It had one of the largest attendances of any hearing of that year. Those who came to speak for the bill included physicians, bankers, overseers of the poor, members of the General Court, representatives of the Daughters of Isabella, and the Swedish Society of the State. Newspapers all over the State carried detailed accounts of the hearing, the most conservative of which showed clearly the State-wide interest the measure had aroused. In anticipation of a possible refusal because of the difficulty of choosing a site for the hospital, Miss Catherine Hagarty of the Daughters of Isabella suggested the use of the Norfolk State Hospital, a group of buildings which had originally been erected for alcoholics and narcotics, later used by the Federal Government as a hospital, and for the last few years unoccupied. The Committee reported favorably on the bill. It recommended that the sum of one and one-half million dollars be provided for the construction of a hospital in Boston. The bill was debated in the House for two days, after which it was passed. The Senate also passed the bill. When the time came for the appropriation of the necessary money, it was found that it had not been included in the budget. Senator McCormack then offered the amendment, suggested by Miss Hagarty at the hearing, that a group of buildings known as the Norfolk State Hospital and located between Wrentham and Walpole and unused, be used for this purpose. The sum of $100,000 was to be used to recondition these buildings and an additional $30,000 was to be appropriated to establish cancer clinics throughout the State. It was in this form that the bill finally passed.

The bill for the cancer hospital was still in jeopardy, however, because simultaneously with its presentation before the Governor two other bills were presented—one for the Sesquicentennial in Philadelphia and the other for the erection of the St. Mihiel Memorial in France. There was only enough money to provide for one of these three recommendations. Governor Fuller decided in favor of the hospital and signed the bill which authorized the use of the Norfolk State Hospital and directed the Department to establish cancer clinics with or without cooperation on the part of municipalities, local physicians, or other agencies and to formulate further plans for the care and treatment of cancer. This bill was signed on May 29, 1926, in the presence of Lieutenant Governor Frank G. Allen, Representative Prendergast, Representative Bell, Representative Walker, and Senator McCormack.

Following the death of Dr. Eugene R. Kelley in the early part of the investigation by the Departments of Public Health and Public Welfare, Dr. George H. Bigelow became Commissioner of Public Health. He served from then on in the double capacity as a member of the study committee and as commissioner of one of the departments with which the decision rested as to the merits of the report. Dr. Bigelow felt as Commissioner of Public Health that the Department should include cancer statistics, educational activities, and clinics for early diagnosis of the disease. He did not believe a health department should include within its scope a cancer hospital which would be largely therapeutic rather than preventive. Prevention, rather than treatment, had been the general policy of the Department of Public Health. However, with the decision of the Legislature that the hospital for cancer should be part of the State health program, Dr. Bigelow gave as much effort to make the whole program a success as if he had felt from the beginning that hospitalization under public health auspices was sound.

An Advisory Committee was immediately appointed by Dr. Bigelow to work out the mechanics of the cancer program. It included the following individuals:

Mr. Edward H. Allen, Medical Director, John Hancock Life Insurance Company.
Mrs. Edith R. Avery, Chairman of Public Health Department of State Federation of Women's Clubs.
Dr. Franklin G. Balch, American Society for the Control of Cancer.
Dr. Walter P. Bowers, Boston Medical and Surgical Journal
Mr. W. J. Bell, House Chairman, Legislative Committee on Public Health.
Dr. Walter L. Burrage, Secretary, Massachusetts Medical Society.

Miss Ida M. Cannon, Social Service Department, Massachusetts General Hospital.
Mr. Richard K. Conant, Commissioner, Massachusetts Department of Public Welfare.
Dr. Francis G. Curtis, Board of Health, Newton.
Dr. William Duane, Research Fellow in Physics, Harvard Cancer Commission.
Dr. Kendall Emerson, Cancer Committee, Massachusetts Medical Society, Worcester.
Dr. Robert B. Greenough, Huntington Memorial Hospital; Director, Harvard Cancer Commission; and Chairman, Cancer Committee, Massachusetts Medical Society.
Mr. James B. Hayes, St. Mary's Infant Asylum.
Mr. Robert W. Kelso, Boston Council of Social Agencies.
Dr. Francis X. Mahoney, Health Commissioner, Boston Health Department.
Dr. G. Forrest Martin, Trustee, Tewksbury State Infirmary, Lowell.
Rev. George P. O'Conor, Catholic Charitable Bureau.
Miss Florence M. Patterson, Director, Community Health Association, Boston.
Miss Gertrude W. Peabody, Massachusetts Association of Directors of Public Health Nursing, Cambridge.
Dr. Henry M. Pollock, Superintendent, Massachusetts Homeopathic Hospital.
Dr. Stephen Rushmore, Dean, Tufts Medical School.
Dr. J. W. Schereschewsky, United States Public Health Service.
Dr. James S. Stone, President, Massachusetts Medical Society.
Dr. William J. Taylor, Massachusetts Homeopathic Hospital.
Dr. E. E. Tyzzer, Harvard Cancer Commission.
Dr. E. P. Truesdale, Cancer Committee, Massachusetts Medical Society, Fall River.
Dr. Shields Warren, Instructor, Department of Pathology, Harvard Medical School, and Chief Pathologist, Palmer Memorial Hospital.
Mr. H. S. Wellman, Massachusetts House of Representatives, Topsfield.
Professor Edwin B. Wilson, Department of Vital Statistics, Harvard School of Public Health.
Dr. J. Homer Wright, Pathologist, Harvard Cancer Commission.

The opinion of this committee as a group, and of Robert B. Greenough as an individual, formulated the outline of the program which is still in operation. In a paper presented at the National Conference of Social Work in Boston in June, 1930, Dr. Bigelow stated, "From the beginning Dr. Robert B. Greenough, now President of the Massachusetts Medical Society, has given more time and thought to this cancer matter than any other member of the medical profession in Massachusetts. Although Sodom and Gomorrah, I believe, would have been saved by two, any state may be saved from the disgrace of complete indifference to the cry of cancer by one such man!" The plan of the committee consisted of five major subdivisions, each of distinct importance but each in a sense necessary to the other.

The first subdivision, the Tumor Diagnosis Service, had been established in anticipation of the more comprehensive plan and was equipped to furnish any physician, at no cost, a pathological report on the nature of specimens suspected of being malignant. The second was the subdivision of biometric research, which was to supply a sound foundation upon which to base the evolving program. This subdivision was to carry on, simultaneously with its work on measurements and evaluations, epidemiological research into the various etiological and therapeutic factors related to the problem. Hospitalization was the third part of the program and was to furnish immediate hospital facilities for all types of cancer cases. The fourth subdivision was to be the establishment of diagnostic clinics. The fifth subdivision was established to disseminate knowledge concerning cancer.

Of these five branches, the Tumor Diagnosis Service had been in effect for several years; the biometric and educational subdivisions began as soon as planned; the first of the twenty-one clinics was opened on December 17, 1926, at Newton; and the cancer hospital, named the Pondville Hospital, opened formally on June 22, 1927, in the presence of Governor Alvan T. Fuller and five hundred guests, and opened for patients the following day, June 23rd. The gradual integration of this five-part plan is now a part of the history of the cancer program as a whole. Subsequent recommendations to the General Court have all tended to augment existent phases of cancer work rather than to inaugurate new departures in the field.

The purchase of radium for use at the Pondville Hospital was authorized by the Legislature of 1927.

In 1927 two bills were introduced to make the reporting of cancer compulsory. These bills were withdrawn. The following year Representative Walker introduced a bill relative to admissions to Pondville Hospital. This bill was passed. It stated that for admission to the hospital a two-years' residence in the Commonwealth was necessary, and gave the Department authority to regulate charges for the support of patients.

In 1929 the General Court appropriated money for an addition to Pondville Hospital. Monsignor Roche's humane interest was not lost after the attainment of the first objective. He studied the situation as it progressed. His anxiety over the delay caused by the long waiting list at Pondville caused him to work again for the establishment of this addition to the Pondville Hospital. The formal opening of the addition, which included new clinic quarters and a hospital unit, was on May 20, 1930. The principal speaker was His Excellency, Governor Allen.

In March, 1930, the Committee on Public Health reported on a petition accompanied by the resolve of Representative Thomas F. Carroll for an investigation by the Department of Public Health relative to the expenditure of additional sums for the purpose of eradicating cancer in adults. The bill was rejected.

In 1934, work was begun on a service and surgical building, and a twenty-five-bed addition at Pondville, which opened the following year.

On August 14, 1935, an act authorizing the establishment and maintenance of a wing at the Westfield State Sanatorium for the care and treatment of persons suffering from cancer was approved. This was another manifestation of the indefatigable zeal of Monsignor Roche. He was acquainted with the often-repeated reaction of individuals from Western Massachusetts that a hospital for cancer should be situated nearer to that area so that invalids and their visiting friends and relatives would not have so far to travel. It was suggested by Dr. Chadwick that inasmuch as tuberculosis was on the decline, it would be wise to build a cancer wing at the Westfield State Sanatorium. In this way the established plant could be used, and eventually as the beds were no longer needed for tuberculosis they could be used by cancer patients. Monsignor Roche agreed with this suggestion and again organized the Daughters of Isabella to work for the new cancer project. They obtained thousands of signatures. The hearing had several hundred in attendance, and an unprecedented degree of enthusiasm was manifested.

Several days after this hearing, Monsignor Roche died. His foresight, energy, and enthusiasm had coordinated the several individual channels of interest in cancer in one broad and forceful stream. Unassumingly he had worked for years for the objective of the relief of the cancer situation in all its phases. This was only one manifestation of his extreme versatility. He was a graduate architect before he entered the priesthood, was an authority on international and constitutional law, was an accomplished composer, vocalist, pianist and organist, a lifelong student of clinical medicine, and a recognized national advocate of the soundest doctrines of improved sociological conditions. He should have first place in the hearts of these citizens of Massachusetts who are grateful for the facilities of the cancer program, because he foresaw its advantages and worked practically unassisted over a long period of years to effect its establishment. Even after the program began, he studied its evolution and worked, again nearly unassisted, for additions to make it more generally available. On April 30, 1938, a public tribute was given to Monsignor Roche at the Westfield Hospital. His portrait was presented to the hospital. State and local officials and over one hundred interested individuals from all over the State attended this first public recognition of the work of one of the three great benefactors to the State in cancer work.

The second man whose work for the promotion of the control of cancer had a momentous influence was the late Dr. George H. Bigelow. When he assumed the Commissionership in 1925, the Department of Public Health was adapting itself to the rapidly increasing growth of administrative and advisory duties which had been granted to it since 1914. The State and country were just emerging from the first post-war economic depression only to be plunged into the second and more lasting depression of the last several years. These external conditions had a very definite bearing on the whole policy of the State, and Dr. Bigelow was acutely conscious of their actual and implied potentialities. He was an able, fearless administrator. If personal effort could have achieved the immediate passage of laws to allow only pasteurized milk or milk from nontuberculous cows to be sold, or the immediate and possible eradication of rabies, to mention only two of the projects for which he fought against overwhelming odds, these things would have been accomplished years ago. He saw the advantages of medical social service and incorporated this addition to the Department. He worked for proper scientific shellfish control. He established health units and a Division of Adult Hygiene, the first of its kind in the United States. He obeyed the legislative mandate concerning cancer control with characteristic enthusiasm, even though at first he questioned its place in the field of preventive medicine. The Department, under his leadership, made notable contributions epidemiologically and otherwise to many fields of research, particularly in cancer and other chronic diseases. The tradition of his predecessors to lead to new heights by personal example was nowhere better demonstrated than in Dr. Bigelow. Cancer work lost an aggressive champion in his death.

The third outstanding contributor of time, interest, example, and personal effort to the cause of cancer was the late Dr. Robert B. Greenough. The loss to cancer work nationally and locally in his death on February 16, 1937, cannot be overestimated. A member of the Cancer Advisory Committee from its inception, Dr. Greenough exerted a decisive influence in the development of the program as it is today. His interest increased and was constant in the Massachusetts Cancer Program as long as he lived. The multiplicity of his obligations as physician, surgeon, leader of innumerable national organizations, so obviously taxed only a part of his tremendous capacity that he was always willing to add more to his responsibilities without giving any external signs of undue pressure or fatigue. The type of administration in effect at the cancer hospital and the constantly improving standards of the diagnostic clinics were real concerns of his, and due in large part to him. Epidemiological research in cancer was another phase of the work in which he took a personal part. The Cooperative Cancer Control Program was of intense interest to him and was presented by him to various professional groups throughout the United States. He repeatedly said that he felt that this thorough and penetrating approach to the problem of cancer education, even though it entailed endless labor and an enthusiastic personnel, must be the ultimate method employed generally if sound results were to be expected in this field of cancer control. The immeasurable loss of Dr. Greenough's friendship and guidance to the members of the Cancer Division increases with the passage of time.

No history could be complete without mentioning the significance of the labors volunteered without stint or remuneration of the twenty-one clinic chiefs and their assistants, and particularly of those physicians who have given of themselves from the beginning. They have become the radiating foci of cancer education and interest in their own communities. To their work, largely unheralded, the story must be added of the seven thousand practitioners participating in cancer education by speaking before small groups in their own communities, of the five thousand individual lay committee members who are working without reward for the control of cancer, and for the more than four million inhabitants of Massachusetts who are adding their support as rapidly as the need for it is explained to them. The Massachusetts Cancer Program is historically an example of what may be accomplished by intelligent cooperation and the recognition of a need.

Bibliography

BIGELOW, GEORGE H., M.D. and LOMBARD, HERBERT L., M.D.: *Cancer and Other Chronic Diseases in Massachusetts*. Houghton Mifflin Company, Boston and New York, 1933.

THE STATE CANCER HOSPITALS
ERNEST M. DALAND, M.D.
Chief of Staff

The Pondville Hospital

History

The first move toward a state cancer hospital was made in 1914 when Dr. Francis D. Donoghue filed a resolve with the Massachusetts House of Representatives calling for an investigation of the need for further hospitalization of cancer patients. This resolve, together with bills calling for a state cancer hospital introduced by Representative John N. Levins in 1915 and 1916, was defeated. In 1923 the Commissioner of Public Health, Dr. Eugene R. Kelley, pointed out "the need of better hospital facilities for the inoperable group of cancer victims."

In 1925, through the efforts of the Right Reverend Monsignor Ambrose F. Roche, bills were filed in both departments of the Legislature calling for a state cancer hospital. More interest was shown than previously, but the bills were defeated. However, a resolve was passed which called for an investigation of the prevalence of cancer and the facilities for treatment. This study was made by a committee of four who reported, among other facts, that but one hundred beds were available in the State for the care of patients with advanced cancer. No recommendation for a hospital was made, but it was suggested that existing facilities be expanded. This did not satisfy Monsignor Roche and the other proponents of a cancer hospital. In 1926 a new bill was introduced and passed by the House and Senate. This bill provided for the construction in Boston of a hospital to cost one and one-half million dollars. However, as this money had not been included in the budget, it was not available.

At this time there was an unused group of buildings at Norfolk, known as the Norfolk State Hospital, built by the Department of Mental Diseases in 1914. At first this had been used as a hospital for alcoholics and narcotics and later as a federal hospital for mental diseases. For several years it had been unoccupied. It was proposed to use this for a cancer hospital. The bill was duly amended and an appropriation of $100,000 was made to recondition the buildings for a state cancer hospital, to be called the Pondville Hospital. In order to obtain the above-mentioned sum of money, it was necessary to abandon a plan to have a Massachusetts building at the Philadelphia Sesquicentennial, as there was not enough money for both projects.

Then followed nearly a year of reconstruction of the old buildings, all of second-class construction. The original arrangement of the hospital consisted of three main central buildings with a group of smaller buildings higher up on the hill used for segregating small groups of patients. Under the new plan this arrangement was reversed. Two of the central buildings were connected by a new wing and the third building was to be used for ambulatory patients. The smaller cottages were altered for use by the physicians, nurses and other employees. This provided ninety beds for patients. All of the rooms that were built in the connecting wing, as well as those added since, were single rooms, as it was felt that some types of patients should not be assembled in larger wards.

A new operating room was built, although it was thought that very little operating could be done on the type of patient such a hospital would draw. Through a special appropriation, one gram of radium was purchased and an emanation plant set up. The latest type of high voltage X-ray machine (200 K.V.) was installed. It was necessary to purchase complete equipment for the wards, rooms and operating rooms with the exception of a few old beds which were on the premises. Some of these were repaired for temporary use, and incidentally are still in use.

Next, it was necessary to organize and employ a complete hospital operating force from the nurses on the wards to the engineers in the power plant and the clerks in the business office. Dr. Lyman Asa Jones was appointed superintendent of the hospital and served for about two and one-half years. On him and Miss Elizabeth Ross, the superintendent of nurses, fell the brunt of organizing this group and purchasing the supplies and equipment.

A medical staff was the next detail to be considered. Dr. Ernest M. Daland was appointed Surgeon and Chief of Staff. The others of the staff were Dr. Isaac Gerber, radiologist; Dr. J. Homer Wright, pathologist; Dr. D. Crosby Greene, laryngologist (due to illness, he never served); Dr. Roger C. Graves, urologist; Dr. Richard Norton, oral surgeon; Mr. J. Cramer Hudson, physicist; Dr. Henry Jackson, Jr., internist; Dr. Joe Vincent Meigs, gynecologist and Dr. Arthur M. Greenwood, dermatologist.

Patients with cancer or suspected cancer were eligible for admission to the hospital, provided they were recommended by a physician licensed to practice in Massachusetts. At first it was required that patients should have lived in the State for two full years, but this was later changed to two out of the last three years. It is to be noted that the thought running through all the legislative discussions was that a hospital was needed for the patients with advanced cancer. Fortunately, no such restrictions were placed on it, and all patients with cancer were to be admitted. The charge for patients was fixed at $10.50 a week. Provision was made that cities or towns should pay a part of the bills of indigent patients.

The Pondville Hospital was formally opened on June 22, 1927 with His |Excellency, Governor Alvan T. Fuller the principal speaker. The first patient, suffering from cancer of the rectum, was admitted on June 23, 1927.

The Superintendents

Dr. Lyman Asa Jones was appointed superintendent before the hospital was opened and did splendid work in organizing and conducting the hospital. He resigned in October, 1929 to enter the employ of another State department, and died in October, 1933.

Dr. George Sullivan was the successor of Dr. Jones. He served from October, 1929 to January, 1934. Dr. Sullivan was a dynamo of enthusiasm and efficiency. He served during the period of greatest growth in the work of the hospital and his services were greatly appreciated by the Department and by the staff.

Dr. George L. Parker has served in this office since February, 1934. He had previously worked under the Department at the Lakeville Hospital, but immediately before his appointment was Assistant Superintendent at the Wrentham State School. Dr. Parker has seen a constant growth in the work of the hospital and a considerable expansion in the buildings. He has been of great service in the way he has conducted his part of the hospital work.

The Visiting Staff

From a small group of ten, the visiting staff has gradually been enlarged to a group of twenty-five. These men are all practicing their specialties in Boston or Worcester and are affiliated with other hospitals in those cities. They bring to Pondville an experience greater than could be developed in our hospital alone. They take back to their other hospitals a vast experience in the study and treatment of cancer.

The Present Staff is as Follows

Ernest M. Daland, M.D., Surgeon and Chief of Staff; Grantley W. Taylor, M.D. and Horatio Rogers, M.D., Surgeons; Richard H. Wallace, M.D. and Thomas Anglem, M.D., Assistant Surgeons; Joe Vincent Meigs, M.D. and Langdon Parsons, M.D., Surgeons in charge of Gynecology; Roger C. Graves, M.D. and Charles J. E. Kickham, M.D., Surgeons in charge of Urology; John S. Hodgson, M.D., Neurological Surgeon; Richard H. Norton, D.M.D., Oral Surgeon; Carl Ernlund, M.D., Laryngologist; Henry Jackson, Jr., M.D. Physician; Dudley Merrill, M.D. and Maxwell Finland, M.D., Assistant Physicians; Arthur W. Greenwood, M.D., Dermatologist; Hugo B. C. Riemer, M.D., Ophthalmologist; Charles E. Dumas, M.D., Roentgenologist; John Turner, M.D., Assistant Roentgenologist; Harry W. Harding, D.M.D., Dentist; James C. Hudson, Ph.D., Physicist; Shields Warren, M.D., Pathologist; Olive Gates, M.D., Assistant Pathologist; Joseph Tartakoff, M.D., Anesthetist; F. H. L. Taylor, Ph.D., Physiological Chemist.

The Staff of Resident Physicians

Two resident surgeons were appointed at the opening of the hospital. At first it was difficult to secure men of the proper qualifications who were willing to stay with us a full year. Each year we have had an increasing number of applications from men well qualified. We require two years of hospital work from a candidate; many men have had three or four years. Year by year additional men have been added as the number of beds has been increased and the amount of work multiplied. In 1938 we have nine resident men on duty. The duties of the Assistant Superintendent are partly administrative, but largely that of chief of the residents. There are four residents in surgery, two in pathology, one in medicine and one in radiology.

The greater amount of the major surgery is performed by the visiting staff. The resident surgeons perform all the minor surgery and transfusions but assist in all the major operations. After their ability has been proven, they are permitted to do some of the major work, under supervision. Each man has charge of a ward of approximately thirty-five patients.

The medical resident is in charge of all pulmonary cases, the lymphomas and the leukemias. He gives special attention to the patients with anemia and deficiency diseases, both common in cancer patients. He is of great aid to us in helping to evaluate the condition of the patient for surgery and in caring for the complications from surgery.

The two residents in pathology perform all the autopsies. In 1937 there were 252 deaths and on 199 patients (79%) post-mortem examinations were performed. All the surgical specimens are examined in this laboratory and all diagnoses are checked with the visiting pathologists. One man is always available for frozen section work in the operating room. Studies of various groups of tumors have been made in conjunction with the visiting staff.

The resident in radiology conducts the visits by the visiting radiologists who outline studies to be made and direct the treatment. All treatments are carried out under his direction. The results of the treatments are viewed and determined by the radiologists, frequently with the surgeon or the internist. With a very efficient house staff and adequate laboratory studies, much of value may be learned about a patient. With trained dietitians the elements lacking in the patient's diet may be supplied and he will gain in weight and strength. Liver and iron, blood transfusions, intravenous saline and glucose may help in the building-up process. On this basis, we have no hesitancy in purposely delaying operation on a patient with cancer of the stomach, rectum or colon, one, two or three weeks. While cancer operations must still be considered urgent, operations must be done when the patient is at the peak of condition.

During the past eleven years we have had a part in training fifty-six residents besides those now at the hospital. Forty-six of these have had residencies in surgery, six in medicine, and eight in pathology. Of the surgical men, twenty-three have been in service one year or more, seven for six months and twelve for shorter periods. Of these graduates of a year or more, six are practicing surgery, eleven are doing general practice and surgery, one general practice, four are working in other institutions, one is doing radiology and is chief of our department and the occupation of another is unknown. Thirty-five of these fifty-six men have located in Massachusetts. Doubtless their training will play a part in reducing the Massachusetts death rate in the next few years. This is another accomplishment in the Massachusetts cancer campaign.

Nursing

The nursing at the Pondville Hospital is carried out by graduate nurses and attendants. No training school for nurses is conducted, although for a time a six-months' training course for attendants was given. Miss Dorothy Silver, a graduate of the Faulkner Hospital, is the Superintendent of Nurses. At the present time, there are thirty-six graduate nurses and forty-eight attendants on duty.

The nursing service has been very good and the esprit de corps of the nurses is excellent. There are many changes in the personnel each year, due chiefly to the distance of the hospital from the cities, the absence of any gathering place for recreation and the inadequate quarters for housing. At one time there was a recreation building equipped with a moving picture machine, where the nurses and other employees congregated for movies, dances and card parties. This building was condemned three years ago and has not been replaced. With the coming of the 48-hour law for all employees, a considerable number of employees was added. Quarters that were already crowded are now badly overcrowded. A new nurses' home is very urgently needed.

Social Service

From a social service department of one we have expanded to a department with three workers and two stenographers. This is one of our most important departments. Workers investigate the needs of applicants for admission, make contacts with home and physician, give much needed help while the patient is in the hospital and arrange for the patient's return home. They carry on the follow-up work and keep the staff informed of the results of the treatments.

Great aid is given the workers at Pondville by the social service departments in other hospitals and in the State-aided cancer clinics. Arrangements are made for patients to be transferred to these clinics and reports are sent us as to the progress of the patients.

Enlargement of the Hospital

With ninety beds at the opening there was genuine doubt as to our ability to keep them full. Patients and visitors could obtain transportation only by buses (Boston to Providence) or by private car. However, within six months the hospital was full. Shortly thereafter there was a waiting list which has existed ever since.

In planning the hospital no provision was made for outpatients. When the need was apparent, two small rooms were put to that use and a Thursday afternoon clinic was started. These rooms proved inadequate and plans were at once drawn to enlarge the hospital. A new connecting wing was built to the isolated building, throwing the whole hospital under one roof and adding twenty-five beds. In the basement of this wing new quarters were built for the X-ray and radium department and seven examining rooms for an outpatient clinic. This building was opened on May 20, 1930 with fitting ceremony, including an address by His Excellency, Governor Frank G. Allen. Further changes were made in the old building with the building of a second operating room and the fitting up of a library and new clinical and pathological laboratories.

In 1936 another addition of about thirty beds was added, bringing the total bed capacity to 150, including three beds in an infirmary for employees. At the same time a new service building was built directly behind the hospital and connected with it by a corridor. In this building were furnished new kitchens, dining rooms, four operating rooms and quarters for the employees of the business office and record rooms. This addition was the most important one made since the opening of the hospital. The building is of first-class construction and contains three stories, while the remainder of the hospital has but two. The suite of operating rooms is as good as any in the State. Additional outpatient examining rooms and new social service rooms were provided. The present needs of the hospital, in addition to the nurses' home, are a new administration building, equipped with an auditorium for medical assemblies and for recreation, business offices and record rooms and new pathological and biological laboratories.

For 1937 the daily average number of officers and employees was 191.8. This includes the visiting staff who are on part-time duty.

The Diagnostic Clinic

On Thursday afternoons from two to four, a diagnostic clinic is held to which physicians may bring or send patients.

Patients admitted to the hospital directly have all been referred by physicians. Those patients who came first to the diagnostic clinic sometimes came without the advice of their physicians. These patients could be admitted on the advice of the clinic physicians. At first many came to the clinic because of newspaper articles or at the suggestion of friends. We have constantly advised patients to see a physician first and we have tried to work through the physicians. In this way we have kept down the number of patients coming to us who did not have cancer. Table I demonstrates the success of our endeavors.

Reports are sent to the physicians with advice as to the treatment to be carried out. Unless the physician has referred the patient for treatment also, no treatment is given. However, the majority of these patients are returned to us to have the treatment carried out.

This same clinic gives us an opportunity for follow-up of patients discharged from the hospital and for carrying out treatments to patients who do not need hospitalization. Follow-up clinics in urology, gynecology and nose and throat are held at other times during the week. In 1937 there were 1073 new patients seen in these clinics and 473 of these subsequently entered the hospital. A total of 5332 clinic visits were made.

Type of Patients Admitted

As has been mentioned, the intent of the Legislature in providing funds for this hospital was to care for the advanced cancer patient with a bad prognosis and this is what the hospital did during its early years. It soon became evident that the diagnoses made before admission were not always correct; the disease was not always cancer; those that did have cancer were not always as hopeless as their physicians thought. Patients began to recover, to return home, and to tell their friends that one with cancer did not always die. Physicians began sending the earlier and more favorable cases to us. Year by year the percentage of patients with cancer early enough to attempt a cure has steadily increased and with it the percentage of cures.

There are still a large number of patients with advanced cancer who are treated. Many of the cases to whom we have been able to give some palliation spend their last days with us. In determining which patients shall be admitted and in which order we make three groups. Class 1 is made up of those cases for whom something positive can be done—operation on the early case, palliative operations to relieve pain or obstruction and cases for irradiation. In Class 2 are those with more advanced disease who have been treated previously in this hospital. In Class 3 are the advanced cases who need nursing or custodial care, patients who have had their earlier treatment in other institutions. Patients in Class 1 are admitted first, usually within a week, those in Class 2 next and finally those in the third group. Some of these have a month's wait and this automatically sends them to other hospitals. Certain of our patients who are beyond active treatment are moved to other institutions for nursing care. The chief institutions of this type are the State Infirmary at Tewksbury, Long Island Hospital, The Holy Ghost Hospital in Cambridge and the Rose Hawthorne Lathrop Hospital in Fall River—a hospital of 100 beds for incurable cancer patients without means.

In 1937, there were 1431 admissions to the hospital. Of these, 442 were readmissions. Patients were received from 182 cities and towns and from sixteen other state institutions. The average length of stay was 35.4 days. There were 252 deaths in the course of the year. (Table II).

Surgery

During the first years there was very little operating. In three years we saw one case of cancer of the rectum that was operable and no stomach cancers that were operable. In 1937 we did twenty-six radical removals of rectal cancers and ten radical resections for cancer of the stomach. In 1937, 529 major operations and 973 minor operations were performed. We list below some of the more important operations and diagnostic procedures.

	CASES		CASES
Esophagoscopy	23	Nephrectomy	3
Gastrostomy	31	Suprapubic cystostomy	29
Subtotal gastric resection	9	Total cystectomy	2
Total gastrectomy	1	Ureteroenterostomy	5
Colostomy	23	Prostatectomy	2
Cecostomy	3	Radical mastectomy	43
Right colectomy	1	Simple mastectomy	14
Resection of sigmoid	4	Alcohol injection	32
Proctoscopy	96	Chordotomy	10
One-stage abdominal—perineal resection	25	Bronchoscopy	14
		Laryngectomy	4
Other types of rectal resections	6	Laryngoscopy	35
Cholecystgastrostomy	5	Amputation of arm or leg	9
Dilatation and curettage	86	Skin graft	33
D & C with radium	49	Groin dissection	10
Vaginal hysterectomy	3	Neck dissection	13
Supravaginal or total hysterectomy	40	Transfusion	215
Cystoscopy	335		

X-ray and Radium

The hospital is equipped with over a gram of radium. Its use is chiefly in the treatment of gynecological cases and mouth cases. More and more X-ray is being used with radium or in place of radium. In 1937 radium treatments were given 393 times.

The X-ray equipment includes two 200 K.V. deep therapy machines, one machine for superficial therapy, two diagnostic and fluoroscopic machines and a portable diagnostic machine. During the past year 6342 X-ray treatments were given and 5584 X-ray plates were taken.

Laboratories

The hospital is equipped with a pathological laboratory in which all the surgical specimens and autopsy material is studied. A new bacteriological laboratory has recently been equipped. All of the laboratories are too small for the work which is done in them. A clinical laboratory for blood chemistry, routine urine examination and blood studies is located in the basement. This department is in charge of two visiting pathologists, one chemist, two resident pathologists and six laboratory technicians. The amount of autopsy material to be studied can be noted from Table II.

Table I.—Reason for Coming to Clinic
Rate per 100*

Reason for Coming to Clinic	1927	1928	1929	1930	1931	1932	1933	1934	1935	1936	1937
Physician	67.0	66.7	69.7	64.5	67.1	67.4	72.3	75.4	78.8	79.4	82.1
Friends or Relatives	9.9	12.4	14.0	16.4	14.2	12.3	10.2	3.7	1.6	3.2	2.4
Past Experience or Former Patient	5.5	7.8	10.6	17.9	20.7	23.4	29.0	29.7	33.5	31.8	32.7
Newspapers	13.2	11.4	2.8	2.1	1.0	0.2	0.3	0.0	0.0	0.0	0.1
Social Worker or Nurse	2.2	1.2	4.1	3.9	2.4	3.3	4.6	8.4	7.5	2.8	1.8
All Others	4.4	5.4	3.9	1.7	1.7	1.5	1.6	1.0	1.1	0.3	0.4

* Does not total to 100%, as some individuals gave more than one reason.

Table II.—House Admissions (by fiscal year)

	Total	New	Readmissions	Deaths	Autopsies
1927*	123	112	11	17	6 (35%)
1928	688	513	175	180	83 (46%)
1929	656	450	206	188	81 (43%)
1930	806	581	225	231	98 (42%)
1931	907	626	281	264	113 (42%)
1932	1013	722	291	253	127 (50%)
1933	1203	852	351	256	154 (60%)
1934	1222	824	398	283	173 (61%)
1935	1186	799	387	210	131 (62%)
1936	1474	964	510	248	166 (67%)
1937	1431	989	442	252	199 (79%)
Total	10709	7432	3277	2382	1331 (56%)
1938**	703	456	247	136	93 (68%)
Total	11412	7888	3524	2518	1424 (57%)

* 1927—from June 30, 1927
** 1938—through the first 6 months

Publications

The following papers have been published from the hospital by members of the staff:

Statistical

Reprint No. 4. *The Pondville Hospital.* Ernest M. Daland, M.D. Surgery, Gynecology & Obstetrics, Feb. 15 (No. 2A), 1931, Vol. LII, 527-528.

This paper tells the story of the founding of the Pondville Hospital and explains its purpose and organization.

Reprint No. 5. *An Analysis of Cases at the Pondville Hospital During its First Two Years.* By The Staff. American Journal of Cancer, Supplement to July, 1931, Vol. XV, No. 3, pp. 2359-2433.

This was a study of 1444 cases seen at the Pondville Hospital or clinic during the two years after the opening of the hospital. All cases have been followed for at least one year. This was not intended as an end-result study but more as an analysis of the material at hand with a report of progress. Eleven members of the staff analyzed groups of cases within their specialty. It is apparent from this study that a large percentage of the patients admitted to the hospital during these two years were cases of advanced cancer referred from various hospitals within the State. There was a comparatively small number of early cases on which cure could be attempted. It was also apparent that a great deal had been accomplished in the palliative care of many of the cases with advanced cancer.

Reprint No. 13. *A Further Report on the Cases Admitted to the Pondville Hospital During its First Two Years.* By The Staff. The American Journal of Cancer, Vol. XXI, No. 3, July, 1934.

This is a secondary report on the cases of the first two years of the hospital with a three-year follow-up of 99.5 per cent. Four cases were lost. In this group three-year end-results have been tabulated. The number of operable, curable cases was small but the three-year results were quite satisfactory. In making this study and the previous study the staff was able to evaluate the type of treatment being used, to discard certain types of therapy entirely and to change to other more promising methods.

Reprint No. 32. *Life Expectancy and Incidence of Malignant Disease—I. Carcinoma of the Breast.* Ira T. Nathanson, M.D. and Claude Welch, M.D. The American Journal of Cancer, Vol. XXVIII, No. 1, September, 1936.

This is the first of a series of studies on the life expectancy of patients with malignant disease. One thousand five hundred and sixty-five cases of carcinoma of the breast are included in this study of life expectancy, the cases being taken from the Huntington Memorial and Pondville Hospitals. The median duration of life in patients with cancer of the breast who were not treated is 2.5 years. The longest length of life in an untreated patient was slightly less than 15 years. The median age in the treated group was 3.5 years. The latter figure is six times less than the normal life expectancy of a woman at this age. The median length of life was less in patients below forty than in an older group.

Reprint No. 40. *Life Expectancy in Malignant Disease—Part II. Carcinoma of Lip, Oral Cavity, Larynx and Antrum.* Claude E. Welch, M.D. and Ira T. Nathanson, M.D. The American Journal of Cancer, Vol. 31, No. 2, October 1937.

Carcinoma of the lip and tongue are more malignant in the young. The median life expectancy of untreated intraoral carcinoma is 10 months, of treated cases 17 months in the males and 21 months in the females. The median life expectancy of patients with treated carcinoma of the lip is 66 months; buccal mucosa 24 months; palate 18 months, upper alveolus 20 months, lower alveolus 18 months, tongue 17 months, floor of the mouth 17 months, tonsil 15 months, pharynx 14 months, antrum 17 months and larynx 18 months.

Reprint No. 43. *Life Expectancy and Incidence of Malignant Disease—III. Carcinoma of the Gastro-Intestinal Tract.* Ira T. Nathanson, M.D. and Claude E. Welch, M.D. The American Journal of Cancer, November, 1937, Vol. XXXI, No. 3.

Without treatment patients with cancer of the esophagus will live, in the median, 7 months; with cancer of the stomach 13 months; and with cancer of the rectum 14 months after the first symptom appears. There is a slightly better prognosis for women than men in all groups when treated.

The treated stomach cases lived but 15 months, in the median case, or but 2 months longer than the untreated case. The patients with cancer of the esophagus lived 3 months longer when gastrostomy was done and 2 months longer than the untreated when radiation alone was used.

Reprint No. 44. *Life Expectancy and Incidence of Malignant Disease—IV. Carcinoma of the Genito-Urinary Tract.* Claude E. Welch, M.D. and Ira T. Nathanson, M.D. The American Journal of Cancer, December, 1937, Vol. XXXI, No. 4.

The median length of life in untreated carcinoma of the cervix is 14 months, bladder 14 months and prostate 12 months. When treated the life span is cervix 27 months, fundus of uterus 40 months, ovary 22 months, penis 75 months, testicle 24 months, prostate 26 months, bladder 27 months and kidney 22 months.

Reprint No. 45. *Life Expectancy and Incidence of Malignant Disease—V. Malignant Lymphoma, Fibrosarcoma, Malignant Melanoma and Osteogenic Sarcoma.* Ira T. Nathanson, M.D. and Claude E. Welch, M.D. The American Journal of Cancer, December, 1937, Vol. XXXI, No. 4.

Patients with Hodgkin's disease live 30 months, with other types of lymphoma 24 months. Treatment prolongs life 6 months. The median length of life of fibrosarcoma patients is 43 months; malignant melanoma 39 months; and osteogenic sarcoma 21 months.

Reprint No. 2. *Gastrostomy as a Palliative Measure.* Ernest M. Daland, M.D. and Alfonso A. Palermo, M.D. New England Journal of Medicine, Vol. 203, No. 7, pp. 317-318, Aug. 14, 1930.

The use of gastrostomy for feeding purposes in patients with advanced cancer is discussed, with particular reference to the Ssbanajew-Franck method. In this type of gastrostomy a portion of the stomach is pulled out through the abdominal wall to act as a funnel for feeding purposes. A group of ten operations, seven of this type, without mortality, is reported.

Reprint No. 3. *Interscapulo-Thoracic Amputation.* Ernest M. Daland, M.D. New England Journal of Medicine, Vol. 203, No. 15, pp. 722-725, Oct. 9, 1930.

The technique of interscapulo-thoracic amputation is described with two case reports. This operation is useful in traumatic and malignant conditions of the arm and shoulder where a lower amputation or simple disarticulation is insufficient. The operation is not difficult and requires about one hour. There is no mortality in the two cases described.

Reprint No. 7. *Plastic Reconstruction of the Lower Lip.* Ernest M. Daland, M.D. New England Journal of Medicine, Vol. 205, No. 24, pp. 1131-1141, Dec. 10, 1931.

A new method of reconstruction of the entire lower lip is described. The lip is constructed from the mucous membrane brought down from the buccal surface and from a flap of skin and fat brought down from the nasolabial fold. Nineteen case histories are cited. There are also many photographs showing the patients before and after operation.

Reprint No. 12. *Cancer of the Mouth in Women.* Grantley W. Taylor, M.D. New England Journal of Medicine, Vol. 210, No. 21, pp. 1102-1105, May 24, 1934.

Cancer of the buccal mucosa is comparatively rare in women but cancer of the upper jaw is more common than in men. Tobacco and bad teeth appear to have some etiological basis for the greater number of cancers of the mouth in men. The grade of malignancy in this group of patients was higher in men than in women. Cancer of the buccal mucosa metastasizes earlier in men. The general prognosis for women with cancer of the mouth is better than for men.

Reprint No. 12A. *Arsenical Keratoses and Carcinomas.* Clifford C. Franseen, M.D. and Grantley W. Taylor, M.D. The American Journal of Cancer, Vol. XXII, No. 2, October, 1934.

This is a review of the literature on the subject with abstracts of nineteen cases. In nine cases the carcinoma was definitely due to arsenic and five where arsenic was probably the causative agent. The other cases showed lesions typical of arsenical keratosis and carcinomas without definite proof that arsenic caused them. Carcinoma may occur as late as forty years after the use of arsenic. Inorganic arsenic, usually in the form of Fowler's solution, is the chief offending agent. Lesions following administration of organic arsenicals are very rare. One third of the carcinomas described were basal cell and the other squamous cell. Metastases to the regional glands have been found in many cases and regional nodes and dissection is advocated.

Reprint No. 22. *The Use of Dilaudid in Treating Patients With Cancer.* Ira T. Nathanson, M.D. and Ernest M. Daland, M.D. New England Journal of Medicine, Vol. 213, No. 16, pp. 741-746, Oct. 17, 1935.

Dilaudid was used in one hundred and fifteen patients with malignancy. Its effect compared with other opiates was studied. It was found that it acts faster than the others and the duration and degree of relief compare favorably with morphine. It has very little hypnotic power and may have to be combined with a barbiturate to obtain sleep at night. It is less likely to produce undesirable side-effects than morphine, but there was more itching and respiratory depression. Small doses at frequent intervals were more satisfactory than larger doses at greater intervals. It is just as habit forming as the other drugs.

Reprint No. 23. *Chronic Cystic Mastitis; Practical Management in a Cancer Clinic.* Horatio Rogers, M.D., F.A.C.S., and Ira T. Nathanson, M.D. New England Journal of Medicine, Vol. 212, No. 13, pp. 551-556, March 28, 1935.

Endocrine therapy in the form of ovarian residue and progynon were used in certain cases of mastitis where there were certain changes in the breast tissue and where there was pain. It was found that many of these patients returned to normal after the administration of these drugs. Those that did not return to normal were considered to have chronic cystic mastitis and it was felt necessary to either observe them carefully or to operate on them. One hundred and seventy-seven cases diagnosed clinically as "chronic cystic mastitis" were analyzed.

Reprint No. 24. *Carcinoma of the Stomach in Identical Twins.* Raymond E. Militzer, M.D. The American Journal of Cancer, Vol. XXV, No. 3, November, 1935.

This paper was a report of twin brothers (identical twins) aged seventy, who were in the hospital at the same time with identical carcinomas of the stomach. These two patients were identical in appearance except for acquired deformities; one having had a fracture of the nose with deviation to the left, the other the same type of injury with deviation to the right. Both had had bilateral inguinal hernias repaired. Their gastric symptoms were similar and X-ray examination showed the lesion to be in a similar position. Post-mortem examination was done on both patients substantiating the location of the cancer.

The literature is reviewed and a total of forty tumors occurring in twenty sets of identical twins is summarized.

Reprint No. 28. *One Hundred Untreated Cancers of the Rectum.* Ernest M. Daland, M.D., Claude E. Welch, M.D. and Ira T. Nathanson, M.D. New England Journal of Medicine, Vol. 214, No. 10, pp. 451-458, Mar. 5, 1936.

In this paper, the writers have attempted to trace the natural course of untreated cancer of the rectum in the same way that one of the writers had previously studied cancer of the breast. It was found that the median duration of life in one hundred cases of untreated cancer of the rectum from onset of symptoms was fourteen months. The longest duration of life was forty-nine months. When plotted in a curve the length of life was compared with that in eighty patients with colostomies only. It was found that the length of life was exactly the same. When compared with forty-two cases treated by radical resection, all these operations being done at other institutions, the length of life of the operative group was much longer than when no treatment was given. The mortality on the group having colostomy was 12.5 per cent, and in those with radical resection 26.2 per cent. The five-year curability was 30 per cent.

Reprint No. 29. *Pathological Fractures Due to Malignant Disease.* Claude E. Welch, M.D. Surgery, Gynecology and Obstetrics, April, 1936, Vol. 62, 735-744.

Sixty-six pathological fractures occurring in carcinoma or osteogenic sarcoma are reported. There was no evidence of healing in 80 per cent; 5 per cent healed with firm union; 9 per cent showed moderate healing and 6 per cent showed slight healing. Of the nine cases that healed either partially or fully, six cases received X-ray therapy to the bone after the fracture. The group is too small to draw the conclusion that X-ray therapy had any part.

Reprint No. 30. *A Precaution in Stab Wound Colostomy.* Grantley W. Taylor, M.D. Surgery, Gynecology and Obstetrics, August, 1936, Vol. 63, 230.

The writer suggests the use of a tubular rubber wicking over a straight Ochsner clamp and over the end of a cut segment of bowel, in order to bring the bowel out through a stab wound without contamination of the wound.

Reprint No. 33. *The Relief of Pain in Cancer Patients.* Ernest M. Daland, M.D. U. S. Public Health Service, Supplement No. 121 to Public Health Reports.

This is a summary of the measures used to combat pain in patients with cancer, with special attention paid to the minimal amounts of drugs necessary to relieve the pain. Distinction should be made between medication for sleep and medication for relief of pain. Nonnarcotic drugs should be tried before opiates are started and later should be combined with the narcotics. The amount of opiates needed by the average cancer patient is extremely small.

Reprint No. 41. *The Rationale of Artificial Menopause in Carcinoma of the Breast.* Grantley W. Taylor, M.D., F.A.C.S. The American Journal of Roentgenology and Radium Therapy.

The mortality from cancer in women who have not reached the menopause is greater than in older women. This appears to be due to the fact that the degree of malignancy is greater in the younger women, with more rapid growth and earlier glandular involvement because of this.

The technique of irradiation of the ovaries to accomplish sterilization is described. Dresser's previous report is mentioned and the statement is made that where recurrent or inoperable cases have been treated there has been some apparent benefit. Sterilization is being advised in the younger women as a prophylactic measure after radical surgery.

Reprint No. 42. *Blood Loss in Cancer Operations.* Weston T. Buddington, M.D. and Grantley W. Taylor, M.D. New England Journal of Medicine, Vol. 218, No. 7, pp. 285-287, Feb. 17, 1938.

The total amount of blood lost at operation was calculated on a group of 74 cancer cases by collecting all the blood from the linen and gauze and comparing the solution obtained with a standard solution previously compared.

The average loss in 11 cases of radical mastectomy was 430 c.c., the lowest 134 c.c.; in 1 total gastrectomy and 3 subtotal gastrectomies the loss was less than 300 c.c. in each case. These studies aid the surgeon in planning for transfusions in certain cases and demonstrate that it is not needed in other types. In radical resections of the rectum (average loss 1050 c.c.) one transfusion does not replace the amount lost.

Reprint No. 46. *"Inflammatory Carcinoma" of the Breast.* Grantley W. Taylor, M.D. and Adolph Meltzer, M.D. The American Journal of Cancer, 32; 33, 1938.

Thirty-eight cases of "inflammatory carcinoma" are presented. The lesion may be primarily "inflammatory" or it may occur secondarily in a scirrhous carcinoma of some standing. It is characterized by an ill-defined, rapidly growing tumor with marked enlargement of the breast, with local heat, edema and redness of the skin, rapid dissemination of the growth throughout the skin lymphatics with early involvement of the lymph nodes.

The results of treatment are poor. Rapid recurrence follows surgery. X-ray treatment gives the best palliation.

Urology

Reprint No. 9. *Cysts of the Prostate.* Roger C. Graves, M.D. and C. J. E. Kickham, M.D. New England Journal of Medicine, Vol. 209, No. 8, pp. 367-368, Aug. 24, 1933.

A case report of a cyst of the prostate removed through the bladder. No malignancy was found.

Reprint No. 11. *Bone Metastases from Carcinoma of the Urinary Bladder.* Roger C. Graves, M.D. and Raymond E. Militzer, M.D. The Journal of Urology, Vol. XXXI, No. 5, pp. 769-789. May, 1934.

Reports of five cases of carcinoma of the bladder with metastases to bone are presented. The pelvic bones, femurs, dorsal vertebrae, ribs and olecranon were involved. Two cases of Paget's disease of the bone simulating bone metastases are also reported.

Reprint No. 15. *Carcinoma of the Prostate with Metastases.* Roger C. Graves, M.D. and Raymond E. Militzer, M.D. The Journal of Urology, March, 1935, Vol. 33, No. 3.

This is a summary of the clinical and X-ray findings in eighty-one cases of carcinoma of the prostate of whom seventy-five showed bone metastases. The pelvis and sacrum were the chief bones involved. High voltage X-ray therapy gives very satisfactory relief of pain in these bone metastases. In a large group of post-mortem examinations numerous metastases were found in lymph nodes, lungs and livers.

Reprint No. 16. *The Treatment of Malignant Diseases of the Penis.* Roger C. Graves, M.D. The Journal of Urology, Vol 32, No. 5, November, 1934.

The technique of operation illustrated by drawings for radical treatment of cancer of the penis is described. The writer mentions the indications and the technique of dissection of the inguinal regions.

Reprint No. 20. *Calcified Hydrocele of the Tunica Vaginalis Testis.* Charles J. E. Kickham, M.D. New England Journal of Medicine, Vol 212, No. 10, p. 419, March 7, 1935.

A case report of an apparently solid tumor of the testis which proved to be a calcified hydrocele.

Reprint No. 21. *Adenocarcinoma of Kidney Recurrent after Twenty Years.* Roger C. Graves, M.D. and Roy E. Mabrey, M.D. New England Journal of Medicine, Vol. 212, No. 10, pp. 416-417, March 7, 1935.

This is a report of a patient, aged fifty-three, who entered the hospital twenty years after a right nephrectomy for hypernephroma. There was a recurrence in the operative scar and in the liver. Biopsy of the recurrent areas showed what was taken to be a renal adenocarcinoma.

Reprint No. 27. *Carcinoma of the Prostate Simulating Primary Rectal Malignancy.* Charles J. E. Kickham, M.D. The Journal of Urology, March, 1936, Vol. 35, No. 3.

The difficulty of making the diagnosis between carcinoma of the prostate and carcinoma of the rectum is mentioned. This is elaborated by four case histories in several of which microscopic examination was the sole answer.

Reprint No. 34. *The Bladder Complications of Carcinoma of the Cervix.* Roger C. Graves, M.D., F.A.C.S., C.J.E. Kickham, M.D., and Ira T Nathanson, M.D. Surgery, Gynecology and Obstetrics, December, 1936, Vol. 63, 785-793.

This is a study of the bladders in 209 cases of carcinoma of the cervix. In this group of carcinomas of the cervix, a routine cystoscopy was done before any other treatment was given. The purpose of this examination was to determine whether there was any definite involvement of the bladder or pressure on the bladder. The ulcerative type of growth in the cervix is of higher malignancy and tends to invade the bladder more than the others.

In the early part of the series studied, radium reactions in the bladder either early or late were quite common. The later cases in this group, when radium seeds were not used, have shown no bladder reactions. There were many autopsy cases in this series.

Reprint No. 35. *The Ureteral and Renal Complications of Carcinoma of the Cervix.* Roger C. Graves, M.D., Charles J. E. Kickham, M.D. and Ira T. Nathanson, M.D. The Journal of Urology, Vol. XXXVI, No. 6, pp. 618-640, December, 1936.

In a series of cancer of the cervix cases studied clinically and at autopsy, obstruction of the ureters was encountered in more than 70 per cent. This means that when a patient with this disease finally succumbs to it the chances are that there will be obstruction of the ureters. It is important that potential obstruction be determined before treatment is given and that actual obstruction be determined as early as it appears. Retrograde pyelograms or intravenous pyelography or both, together with an estimation of the blood N.P.N. and the renal function by the phenolsulphonphthalein test were carried out in the majority of these cases. The use of all of these measures is advocated before irradiation and during the period following irradiation.

Reprint No. 38. *The Urological Complications of Carcinoma of the Cervix.* Roger C. Graves, M.D. and Charles J. E. Kickham, M.D. New Series, Vol. XXXVIII, No. 1, October, 1937, pp. 168-172.

This article contains much of the same material in resumé that appeared in reprints 34 and 35.

Pathology

Reprint No. 8. *Multiple Primary Malignant Tumors. A Survey of the Literature and a Statistical Study.* Shields Warren, M.D., and Olive Gates, M.D. The American Journal of Cancer, Vol. XVI, No. 6, November, 1932.

This is a very thorough study of cases of multiple malignancy collected from the literature. In addition, forty cases of the writers are described. On the basis of all statistics the frequency of multiple malignancy is 1.84 per cent of cancer cases. In the writers' 1078 cancer autopsies the frequency is 3.7 per cent. Multiple malignant tumors occur more frequently than can be explained on the basis of chance. This may be explained by a predisposing or susceptibility to cancer in certain persons or the action of some factor favoring the development of malignancy. The nature of this predisposition is as yet unknown.

Reprint No. 19. *Mucous Gland Tumors of the Female Perineum.* Shields Warren, M.D. and Theodore P. Eberhard, M.D. The American Journal of Cancer, Vol. XXIII, No. 2, February 1935.

This is a report of two cases of an unusual type of tumor of the female perineum, one an adenocarcinoma and the other an adenoma. These were both mucous gland tumors, the first to be reported from this region in the literature.

Reprint No. 31. *Osseous Metastasis of Carcinoma of the Prostate with Special Reference to the Perineural Lymphatics.* Shields Warren, M.D., Paul Harris, M.D. and Roger Graves, M.D. Archives of Pathology, August, 1936, Vol. 22, pp. 139-160.

It has always been a problem as to why patients with cancer of the prostate should have so much pain, even before metastases could be demonstrated in the bones by X-rays. In this study large sections of the prostate and neighboring organs have been sectioned and studied serially. It was found that in all cases extension of the disease was via the perineural lymphatics and through them into the bone. In some of their cases these lymphatics were involved without bone infiltration. In one case of carcinoma of the bladder so studied there was no involvement of the perineural lymphatics.

The dissemination of the tumor through the perineural lymphatics may be either by continuity or through embolism. Direct involvement of the bone occurs as invasion of the marrow spaces through the cortical ostia.

Reprint No. 36. *Cavernous Hemangiomata of Small and Large Bowel.* Lauren V. Ackerman, M.D. The American Journal of Cancer, Vol XXX, No. 4, August, 1937.

This is a report of three cases of hemangioma of the gastrointestinal tract found among 1,200 autopsies over a ten-year period.

Reprint No. 37. *Cutaneous Metastases of Malignant Disease.* Olive Gates, M.D. The American Journal of Cancer, Vol. XXX, No. 4, August, 1937.

The material in this study is taken from 2233 autopsies and 80,000 surgical specimens from the Pondville, Huntington and New England Deaconess Hospitals and from the Pathological Laboratory of Harvard Medical School. In 2298 autopsies on malignant tumors, 2.7 per cent showed metastases to the skin. Carcinomas were the most common type, making up more than one-half the total, but carcinoma metastases were found in only 2 per cent of the whole group of carcinoma autopsies. One-half of the malignant melanoma cases and 23 per cent of the lymphomas showed skin metastases. Frequently skin metastases are the first manifestations of malignancy. They are of limited value in prognosis since the behavior of the skin tumors does not always indicate the rate of growth of the primary tumor.

Medical

Reprint No. 10. *The Calcium, Potassium and Inorganic Phosphate Content of the Serum in Cancer Patients. The Effect of Roentgen Radiation on the Level of These Substances in Blood Serum of Cancer Patients.* Henry Jackson, Jr., M.D., and F. H. L. Taylor, Ph.D. American Journal of Cancer, 19: 379-388, Oct. 1933.

This study was undertaken to prove or disprove the common idea that cancer patients are low in blood calcium. The blood calcium of thirty-one patients with malignancy was studied and was found to be normal or above normal in one-half the cases. It was apparent that the hypocalcemia existing in some of the patients was due to disturbed nutrition and not to cancer per se. No change in the level of the serum potassium or of the inorganic phosphate was found. After intensive irradiation no change was noted in the blood potassium, calcium or phosphorus.

Reprint No. 14. *The Carbohydrate Tolerance in Cancer Patients and the Effect of Roentgen Ray Radiation.* F. H. L. Taylor, Ph.D., and Henry Jackson, Jr., M.D. The American Journal of Cancer, Vol. XXII, No. 3, November, 1934.

Thirty-five cancer patients were studied for their carbohydrate tolerance. A lowered tolerance for glucose is often found in people between fifty-five and seventy years of age, particularly if they are not well nourished. In this series one-third of the patients showed a decreased tolerance prior to the use of roentgen therapy. No consistent effect was found on the sugar tolerance of the cancer patients following roentgen radiation and there was demonstrable relationship between the decreased tolerance and the total serum calcium.

Reprint No. 17. *Mistaken Diagnoses of Cancer.* Dudley Merrill, M.D. New England Journal of Medicine, Vol. 211, No. 18, pp. 801-803, November 1, 1934.

This is a tabulation of the case reports of five patients admitted to the hospital supposedly with malignant conditions. All of these proved to be benign lesions. A lesson from this paper is that all supposed cases of cancer should be restudied for confirmation or denial of the diagnosis. In a cancer hospital one must always be on the lookout for nonmalignant conditions simulating cancer. Many of these are curable.

Reprint No. 25. *Dangers Inherent in the Clinical Diagnosis of Cancer.* Dudley Merrill, M.D. The Yale Journal of Biology and Medicine, Vol. 8, No. 3, January, 1936.

The writer has summarized eight cases sent into the cancer hospital presumably with malignant tumors. Careful study of these cases revealed many other conditions, among them being diverticulitis, aneurysm, lead poisoning, anomaly of the aorta, scurvy, hypochromic anemia, tuberculosis and syphilis. Mention is made of nineteen cases of pernicious anemia most of whom were sent to the hospital with a diagnosis of carcinoma of the stomach. Emphasis is made on re-examining and checking the diagnosis on all patients, even though they are supposed to have advanced stages of cancer.

Radiology

Reprint No. 1. *An Unusual Case of Osteogenic Sarcoma.* Richard Dresser, M.D. and Charles Dumas, M.D. American Journal of Roentgenology and Radium Therapy, Vol. XXIII, No. 1, Jan. 1930.

A man of forty had had a tumor removed from the metatarsophalangeal joint for osteochondroma fourteen years previously. On admission to the hospital he had a recurrence which was proven to be an osteogenic sarcoma of the sclerosing type. This was of interest because of the malignant recurrence of a supposedly benign tumor. A second unusual point was the discovery of a metastasis in the first lumbar vertebra.

Reprint No. 6. *Lymphogranulomatose der Knochen.* Richard Dresser, M.D. Strahlentherapie 41: 401-416, 1931.

The author reports twenty cases of lymphoma with involvement of bones. In a previous series of ninety-five cases four cases of bone involvement had been found. In the present series sixteen cases out of one hundred and forty-nine studied, approximately 10 per cent, showed bone involvement. The bones involved were the skull most commonly, pelvis, sternum and vertebrae. All these cases were treated by X-ray. Many patients received relief from pain with temporary disappearance of the tumor.

Reprint No. 18. *Radium Dosage and Technique in Carcinoma of the Breast.* Grantley W. Taylor, M.D. The American Journal of Roentgenology and Radium Therapy, Vol. XXXII, No. 6, January, 1935.

Forty cases of carcinoma of the breast treated by radium needles are included in this report. Only cases too far advanced for treatment by surgery were treated. In the majority of cases X-ray treatment was also used as well as the radium needles. The technique followed is similar to that described by Keynes except that needles were not used in the intercostal spaces and in most cases not used above the clavicle.

Regression of the local disease was secured in nearly all cases. The response in the axilla and supra-clavicular metastases was not as marked, but a certain amount of regression was obtained. This method of treatment gives a certain amount of palliation in inoperable carcinoma of the breast.

Reprint No. 26. *The Radiological Management of Cancer of the Breast.* Richard Dresser, M.D. and Valmore A. Pelletier, M.D. New England Journal of Medicine, Vol. 214, No. 15, pp. 720-723, Apr. 9, 1936.

In this paper great emphasis is laid on the study of the bony skeleton and lungs before considering surgical measures. In a group of five hundred cases of cancer of the breast in all stages examined roentgeneologically, seventy-three showed metastases to the lungs, only eighty-six had metastases in the bones only and forty-eight showed metastases to both bones and lungs. The type of palliative treatment given to inoperable cases and the method of treating postoperative recurrences is summarized. A study was made of a group of cases who had irradiation sterilization. In 30 per cent of those who had not reached the menopause there was a regression of the bone metastasis lasting from several months to three years. In patients who had reached the menopause there was no bone regeneration in any case.

Gynecology

Reprint No. 39. *Cancer of the Cervix Treated by the Roentgen Ray and Radium.* Joe Vincent Meigs, M.D. and Richard Dresser, M.D. Annals of Surgery, Vol. 106, No. 4, October, 1937.

A report of a new method of treatment for cancer of the cervix in that a complete course of deep X-ray therapy precedes two treatments by radium. The physical measurements of the amount of irradiation actually delivered to the cervix and adnexa by the X-ray and the radium is stated.

The results three and one-half years after treatment are far better than in earlier series and better than the results obtained in other hospitals by the writers using radium only. There have been no irradiation effects in the bladder by this method of treatment.

Cancer Section, Westfield Sanatorium

History

In January 1935, Senator Frank Hurley of Holyoke filed Senate Document No. 308 providing for the establishment and maintenance in the western part of the Commonwealth of a hospital for the treatment of cancer and for the temporary relief and treatment of persons suffering from cancer. Right Reverend Monsignor Ambrose F. Roche, through the cooperative efforts of the Daughters of Isabella, had arranged for the presentation of this bill. The Daughters of Isabella circularized their own individual communities and obtained thousands of signatures of interested citizens. They sent several hundred delegates to the public hearing. Also in attendance were representatives of professional groups in the State. Many representatives and senators recorded themselves publicly at the hearing as in favor of the bill. Several days after this hearing Monsignor Roche died. Senator Daley, as a tribute to Monsignor Roche, who had been his personal friend, carried on the enthusiasm already awakened in this new hospital for cancer.

Then followed a study of the best available location and type of hospital to be built. The possibility of renting an already built hospital or part of it was considered, as was the possibility of a new hospital in a new location. Inasmuch as the Westfield Tuberculosis Sanatorium had already made plans for a new building for adult patients with tuberculosis, it was thought advisable to consolidate the cancer hospital with the tuberculosis hospital. This would cut down on the overhead and reduce the cost of such a hospital greatly. Accordingly, plans were made for a fifty-bed cancer wing in a building providing beds for one hundred and fifty adult tuberculosis patients.

On August 14, 1935, the act authorizing the establishment and maintenance at the Westfield State Sanatorium of a building for the care and treatment of persons suffering from cancer was approved. Attached thereto was the following emergency preamble: "Whereas the deferred operation of this act would tend to defeat its purpose, therefore it is hereby declared to be an emergency law, necessary for the immediate preservation of the public health and convenience."

The construction of a building of two hundred beds and of a nurses' home of one hundred and fifty beds was started soon after. The formal opening of the hospital occurred on December 18, 1937 with His Excellency Governor Charles F. Hurley making an address. The first patient was admitted on December 6, 1937.

The Visiting Staff

The following men were appointed to the visiting staff of the hospital:

Ernest M. Daland, M.D., Medical Director; Frank Baehr, M.D., Eugene Beauchamp, M.D., Archibald Douglas, M.D., and Frederick Hopkins, M.D., Visiting Surgeons (6 months' service); Ladislaw E. Pfeiffer, M.D., Alfonso A. Palermo, M.D., Matthew J. Bachulus, M.D., and John V. Greany, M.D., Assistant Surgeons (3 months' service); John E. Dwyer, M.D., Allen Johnson, M.D., Patrick Moriarty, M.D., and James Quinn, M.D., Visiting

Physicians (3 months' service) ; James A. Seaman, M.D., Winford O. Wilder, M.D., and Ambrose Connelly, M.D., Visiting Urologists (4 months' service).

Consultants from the Pondville staff: Shields Warren, M.D., Pathologist; Joe V. Meigs, M.D., Gynecologist; Roger Graves, M.D., Urologist and John Hodgson, M.D., Neurological Surgeon.

Local consulting staff: Adolph Franz, Sr., M.D. and George Henderson, M.D., Internal Medicine; Harry F. Byrnes, M.D., Laryngologist; Harold Owens, M.D., Ophthalmologist; Richard Rochford, M.D., Gynecologist; Sylvester Ryan, M.D., Proctologist and Charles Furcolo, M.D., Neurological Surgeon. Since the opening of the hospital, Dr. Sylvester Ryan has resigned as a consultant and his place has been taken by Dr. A. H. Riordan. Dr. Arthur Horrigan has been appointed as consulting roentgenologist. Dr. Henry Turner has been appointed full-time roentgenologist, dividing his time with the Pondville Hospital.

Dr. Roy Morgan is Superintendent of the entire institution. Under him is an Assistant Superintendent in charge of the cancer section. There are also two surgical residents. The pathological clinical laboratories are under the direction of a trained pathologist. The assistant superintendent of nurses and several of the head nurses were selected because of their experience in the Pondville Hospital. By selecting a group who had worked together previously, it was possible to start active work with very little confusion, as soon as the hospital was opened.

The cancer wing consists of a three-story building and basement located at one end of the large building. In the basement are the laboratories. The first floor is devoted to an outpatient department and X-ray department. The X-ray department is equipped with the latest type of high voltage X-ray machine and two diagnostic X-ray machines and with 200 mgs. of radium. All of the X-ray work for both parts of the hospital is done in this department. The second and third floors each have twenty-five beds. These are single rooms with the exception of two four-bed wards on the third floor. Lying in the wing between the cancer and the tuberculosis division is the operating suite, the dental department and the library. The operating suite consists of three well equipped operating rooms. All of the operating in both departments of the hospital is done in this suite.

A diagnostic clinic is held on Wednesday mornings between ten and twelve o'clock. No patients are admitted unless referred by a physician. Examinations are made and reports sent back to the physician with recommendations for treatment. Up to July 1, 448 patients with a total of 1419 visits have been made to the clinic. This clinic also serves as a follow-up clinic for patients previously treated in the house and for patients who received treatment as outpatients.

Admission to the house is by application and the requirements for admission are the same as at the Pondville Hospital. Up to July 1 there have been 331 patients in the hospital with an average stay in the hospital of 21.52 days. There have been 112 major and 269 minor operations performed. Thirty-three hundred and sixty-one X-ray treatments and fifty-seven radium treatments have been given.

Two social workers are assigned to the cancer section. In addition to making the usual social service contacts with the patients and their physicians, they are of great aid in connecting up the hospital with the clinics referring the patients. A considerable number of patients in the western part of the State, who have previously been treated at Pondville, have now been transferred to Westfield either for active treatment or for follow-up.

EPIDEMIOLOGICAL ASPECTS OF THE MASSACHUSETTS CANCER PROGRAM

HERBERT L. LOMBARD, M.D.

Director, Division of Cancer and other Chronic Diseases Massachusetts Department of Public Health

Epidemiology and statistics comprise an integral part of the activities of the Division of Adult Hygiene.* Data regarding cancer and other chronic diseases are collected, tabulated, and analyzed. The facilities for care and treatment are studied, the activities of the cancer clinics are appraised, and the effects of educational programs are determined. The various epidemiological aspects of chronic disease are examined inductively in the search for additional information on etiology. Data are obtained from the death, hospital, and clinic records, questionnaires to physicians, and house-to-house visits. This material is transferred to punch cards and tabulated, and later subjected to critical analysis.

Two types of statistics are used: one, the purely descriptive; the other, inductive. Descriptive statistics are necessary to measure such factors as hospitalization, the volume of clinic attendance, and the cancer death rate. Inductive statistics are used when, from the observed data, generalizations are made regarding such subjects as the future needs in cancer control, etiology of cancer and other diseases, appraisal of types of treatment, and other related problems. It is in the field of inductive statistics that the biometric measures devised by Professor Karl Pearson, and later amplified by other investigators, are most frequently applied. The following case history illustrates one type of such research work:

The patient died of cancer of the uterus. Her history shows that she was born in Northern Europe; had an exceedingly nervous temperament; had gonorrhea when she was sixteen years of age; married when she was twenty; received a tear at the birth of her first child which was never repaired; had two other children; and then used contraceptives for the remainder of her childbearing period. Her diet contained no vegetables except potato, and she drank one quart of tea daily. Her teeth had been removed a few months before the cancer was discovered and all of them had pus roots. Her mother died of cancer of the uterus. Her paternal aunt had cancer of the breast. What caused the patient's cancer?

The examination of her record, or that of any other individual, fails to give the answer, save in the mind of some enthusiast with a pet hobby. The physician who believes that uterine tears are the cause of all cancers of the uterus immediately points to the tear and forgets the rest of the history. Another physician who believes diet to be an etiological factor points to the lack of vegetables and thinks his point is proved. The vast majority, however, admit that they do not know the cause. They realize uterine tears, contraceptives, and gonorrhea may at times cause irritation, and chronic irritation is believed to be a precancerous condition. Heredity may be of importance. Foci of infection and dietary habits may so alter the body metabolism that cancer develops. Other variables as yet unthought of may be the cause. They do not know.

It is only by collecting the histories of a large number of individuals—some with cancer, some without—and comparing the records, item by item, that one is able to arrive at results approaching soundness. Even so, it is not an assured fact that a specific person had cancer as the diagnosis in many cases was only clinical. In other cases, the possibility that some individuals without cancer would have developed the disease had they lived

---

* Name changed to Division of Cancer and Other Chronic Diseases.

a few months longer is apparent. If all the individuals with cancer had uterine tears and all the individuals without cancer did not, and if all the other variables were equally distributed between the two groups, conclusions easily could be drawn. This is never the case. An exhaustive analysis is required before even tentative conclusions may be postulated. Such conclusions must be made subject to reservation, with a keen realization of the inadequacy of some of the data. This is epidemiology applied to chronic disease.

The science of epidemiology for many years was limited to the study of epidemics, and only comparatively recently has it been extended to include other diseases and even other conditions not essentially morbid which the full meaning of the word should include. This broader interpretation of the word is justified from its Greek derivation, as well as from the fact that the methods of approach are nearly identical whether studying acute or chronic disease. A study of epidemic disease is easier than a study of chronic disease as the search for the source of infection may be limited to short periods of time. In chronic disease the sources of the disorder may cover a lifetime. This, combined with the element of human fallibility, adds to the difficulty.

The epidemiologist studies the incidence of disease in relation to local environment, personal habits, history, and individual traits. He attempts to gain a better understanding of the nature, source, and means of spread of the disease, and to learn under what conditions it may be checked most effectively. In clinical medicine the unit is the individual. In epidemiology the unit is the group and mass phenomena must be studied.

The practicability of such studies is easily seen. If the evidence warrants the assumption that women with uterine tears are more apt to have cancer of the uterus than others, the repair of such tears becomes a preventive measure. If the unclean mouth is the precursor of oral cancer, frequent visits to the dentist are indicated. If statistics show the reasons for the delay of individuals with suspected cancer in seeking advice, educational methods can be better devised for handling such a problem. If statistics show that two types of treatment are equally effective whereas one is more expensive, budgets may be lowered by the choice of the less expensive method. These are all examples of how statistical and epidemiological methods may be used in programs for the control of disease.

The epidemiologist is endeavoring to shed additional light on chronic disease. He is continually searching for the cause of disease in order to decrease its prevalence. From time immemorial it has been the custom of human beings to reason that because one event followed another event, the first one was the cause.

Sumner, in his *Folkways*, related that in Molamba, Africa, pestilence broke out shortly after the death of a Portuguese there. So certain were the natives that this death caused the pestilence, they took every precaution to prevent any other white man from dying in their country. The historian tells in another instance of some natives of the Nicobar Islands who died shortly after the art of making pottery was introduced. From that time on, pottery making was given up and never again attempted.

One does not need to revert to ancient times and primitive people for examples of this *post hoc, ergo propter hoc* form of reasoning. One is constantly finding specimens of it in all walks of life, and particularly in cancer theorizing. For instance, a little child had cancer. Her grandmother cared for her and later developed cancer. This caused the statement that the grandmother contracted the disease from the child. On another occasion, a mother had cancer and later her daughter developed the disease, which resulted in the claim that heredity was the cause. Three brothers, also, had cancer, and the fourth, who did not, attributed his freedom from the disease to the fact that he drank alcohol while his brothers did not. These and similar theories must be either established or disproved by epidemiological methods.

This is the task of the epidemiologist—to separate the true from the false, to clarify the unknown, and to assist medicine in the conquest of disease.

Certain principles in daily use by biometricians but not well known to individuals in many other fields need some explanation in order that the reader may more readily comprehend the terminology used in papers of this nature. The term "death rate," as ordinarily implied, means the crude death rate, that is, the total number of deaths from a given disease divided by the total population in which the deaths occurred and expressed usually as a rate per 100,000. If all deaths are considered collectively, the unit of expression is usually per 1,000. The indiscriminate use of such rates tends to furnish erroneous opinions. For example, the cancer death rate among bankers would be high due to the average age of these individuals while the cancer death rate among newsboys would be relatively low for the same reason. No comparison on crude rates between bankers and newsboys would express an honest difference between the hazards of the two occupations in respect to cancer. This inconsistent type of study is being made constantly.

Differences in the age distributions of populations makes comparisons between states and countries difficult until refinements are introduced into the computations.

Another error which may frequently befog the issue is the certification by place of death rather than by usual residence. Localities with hospitals that treat individuals from other communities may well show a much higher cancer death rate for this reason. In preparing material for comparison between places, between occupations, and between the same place at different time intervals, it is necessary that the rates be so adjusted as to eliminate differences solely due to such factors as deaths away from home and non-comparable age sex distributions. This is done by the use of a standard population and the elimination of nonresident deaths.

The age specific rate is one in which both the deaths and the population on which the rate is based belong to a small age sex group as, for example, females between forty-five and fifty. By obtaining age specific rates for all age groups and multiplying them to a population that is constant, the most common of which is that of England and Wales of 1901, one obtains a theoretical number of deaths which would represent the number of deaths in the community under consideration, provided this community had the same age sex distribution as did that of the standard population. Dividing this number of deaths by the standard population gives the adjusted rate for that locality. A similar procedure gives a rate for the remainder of the universe to be compared. This process enables the biometrician to compare very dissimilar populations with a reasonable assurance that the results will approximate the truth.

Two methods in studying relationship between different variables are known as association and correlation. One states the relationship; the other gives a mathematical measurement as to the degree of relationship. If two variables are independent, that is, if no connection exists, one would expect the same percentage of variable A, cancer, for example, to occur in a field of variable B, users of tobacco, for example, as occurs in the general population. If a larger percentage of cancers occurs among the users of tobacco, positive association is present. Whether or not such association is of importance must be determined in part by the significance of the association. Here the calculus of probability is used and one tries to determine what the probability is that the occurrence which has been observed could happen as a chance phenomenon. If this probability is exceedingly small, one is justified in feeling that a real association exists. Correlation is a method by which the relationship between two variables is measured and the resultant figure always lies between 0 and +1 for a positive correlation and 0 and —1 for a negative one. Here, again, significance is measured by the calculus of probability. The results of both methods must be tested, however, by the criterion of common sense and efforts made to determine if other variables, associated both with A and B, may not be the determining factor for the association. The association itself does not prove causation even if extremely significant. Added to other items of information, it is a useful indication.

A comprehension of the ordinary statistical paper will be immeasurably increased by an understanding of the significance of these technical terms, although there are many other terms used in biometric research.

A short review of the statistical findings over the eleven and one-half year period of the Massachusetts Cancer Program has been compiled as the result of innumerable requests for this information. These have been reported in part in many different journals, and few are familiar with them in their entirety. The data quoted were applicable as of the date of the papers and subsequent changes have in several cases altered the findings.

The first scientific paper printed discussing the Massachusetts Cancer Program appeared in the *Boston Medical and Surgical Journal*, March 4, 1926. It was a review of House Document 1200—the report to the Legislature on the cancer situation in Massachusetts. The statistical findings at this time showed that:

"1. Cancer is on the increase, but there are indications that the peak of the cancer curve may be nearly reached.

"2. Massachusetts has the highest death rate of any state in the Union.

"3. The proportionate mortality for cancer among inmates of almshouses and insane institutions is lower than among the general population of the same age distribution.

"4. The cancer rate increases with density up to a population of about 4000 per square mile. From there it remains nearly stationary.

"5. The cancer rate increases from west to east in Massachusetts.

"6. The average duration of life for operated cancer cases which die of cancer is 22.8 months and for non-operated cases 20.0 months.

"7. The average duration from onset to operation is 10.3 months.

"8. The average patient comes to a doctor eight months after first noticing symptoms."

House Document No. 400, which appeared in 1927, reported a survey conducted at the behest of the Legislature. It showed that the average length of stay in hospital of cases that leave the hospitals alive was 17.7 days and of those that die in hospitals 33.6 days. The rural communities had fewer cancer deaths in hospitals than the larger communities. As the size of the community increases, the ratio of hospital admissions to deaths increases.

In the October 1927 issue of the *Proceedings of the National Academy of Sciences* an explanation was presented to account for the density phenomenon previously noted. This paper showed that the greater part of the difference of the cancer rates in Massachusetts was due to different nativity distributions, the foreign born and their children having much higher cancer rates than the native born.

On May 10, 1928, in the *New England Journal of Medicine* and in September, 1928, in the *American Journal of Public Health*, the Department reported the results of two morbidity surveys—one in Shelburne-Buckland and the other in Winchester. These two surveys attempted to measure the general sickness rate in two communities in Massachusetts. Approximately one-third of the group surveyed reported illness for the year preceding the survey—an average of 1.2 times. Females had a higher morbidity rate than males but a lower mortality rate. These studies advised further studies for comparison and since that time a number of somewhat similar studies have been conducted by various groups, the largest of which was done by the United States Public Health Service.

On April 26, 1928, in the *New England Journal of Medicine*, a method was outlined for dealing with habits of cancer patients and their controls. This was one of the earliest attempts made to handle this type of data and while the results were admitted to be incomplete for significant conclusions, this paper has stimulated other workers to adopt a similar method and the Division is now (1938) analyzing the records of a survey far more extensive in character, based on somewhat similar lines.

Following the special cancer week in Massachusetts, April 23-27, 1928, known as the "Massachusetts Cancer Campaign," a study reported in the *New England Journal of Medicine* of August 30th of that year showed that during the week, and the one following it, clinic attendance doubled but rapidly subsided to normal. In the same period, the physicians of the State reported that for every patient that went to the clinic twenty-two went to the private office. Physicians in clinic cities had a larger percentage of patients come to the offices than did those living in other communities. The fact that the cancer campaigns failed to arouse continuous interest in the subject has been used in the effort to make cancer the activity of the whole year rather than that of a week or a month. In 1938, Congress designated April as Cancer Month. Massachusetts cooperated in this nation-wide movement by publicizing its regular program to which it added one or two broadcasts. This program is so much more basic and comprehensive than those in operation elsewhere that each new presentation to the public creates renewed and almost sensational interest. On the basis of experience, the special featuring of a limited period as a focus for cancer interest is felt to be an unsound procedure, more spectacular than effective. The gradual unpublicized approach to every physician and individual has proved to be the only method that produces tangible results.

On May 23, 1929, in the *New England Journal of Medicine*, the Department reported on a study made at the request of the hospital committee of the town of Wayland. A thorough study of the individuals in that community who attended hospitals, as well as those who were sick and unhospitalized, resulted in a recommendation that even though at the time of the survey the people of Wayland were receiving adequate hospitalization and did not need additional accommodations, in view of the fact that money was available and hospital facilities could be bettered, a ten-bed wing be added to an existing hospital.

In Volume 16, No. 4, 1929, of *The Commonhealth* a report on the increase in chronic disease was made. It was shown that:

"1. The population of Massachusetts has been gradually growing older.

"2. The crude death rate has decreased, but for age groups over fifty there has been an increase.

"3. Infections; tuberculosis; old age, ill-defined, and unknown; epilepsy, convulsions, and sudden death in individuals over fifty have a downward trend.

"4. Cancer, diabetes, heart disease, appendicitis, nephritis, and a group composed of leukemia, biliary calculi, diseases of the prostate, benign tumors of the uterus, and accidental gas have an upward trend which apparently is caused by factors other than errors in diagnosis and certification, public health activities, and changes in the people and their environments.

"5. All other diseases show an initial increase followed by a decrease. This trend gives the impression that it is caused by changes in the composition of the people and their living conditions."

In the same issue of *The Commonhealth* a report was made on the reasons for the delay of individuals with cancer:

"1. The median delay between first symptom and first consultation with a physician for individuals with cancer coming to the State-aided cancer clinics in Massachusetts is 6.5 months.

"2. Males delay longer than females except for skin cancers.

"3. The greatest delay is in cases of cancer of the skin and the shortest delay is among those patients having cancer of the uterus.

"4. Thinking the condition was a minor malady is the largest single cause of delay. Among the males, this reason is considerably greater than among the females.

"5. The greatest single cause of delay between consultation with physician and treatment was because of poor advice on the part of the attending physician.

"6. Forty-five per cent of the cancer patients had a median delay of six months after consulting a physician while 55 per cent received treatment within a short time following diagnosis.

"7. The median interval of delay is increasing each year since our first figures in 1927. This is profoundly disappointing in view of the intensive medical and lay education carried on. Possibly it is in part due to the fact that the percentage of individuals with skin cancers attending the clinics has increased, as this group delays much longer than any other. Our current figures, however, indicate that the delay in skin cancers is increasing, while other types remain about the same."

In *The Journal of Preventive Medicine*, September, 1929, a further study on the nativity problem in relation to cancer was made. The conclusions drawn were as follows:

"1. A sufficiently close correlation exists between the Social Classes in England and the nativity groups in Massachusetts in respect to the cancer death rate, to warrant the opinion that economic social conditions are a factor in the causation of cancer.

"2. The foreign born have much higher rates than the native born of native parents in cancers of the buccal cavity and the stomach.

"3. Cancer of the stomach is abnormally high among both males and females for all foreign-born groups, and cancer of the buccal cavity among the Irish, English, and Teutons.

"4. Cancer of the lower intestinal tract in females is high among the Irish and English, while it is low among the Italians.

"5. The Canadians have a high rate for cancer of the uterus, and the Russians a low rate.

"6. Both the Italians and the Russians have low rates for cancer of the breast.

"7. The Irish and the Italians show higher rates in Boston than in their native countries.

"8. The sex ratio (females per male) is much higher for the native born of native parents than for any of the foreign nativity groups which have been studied in Boston and Europe.

"9. The Irish have slightly poorer diagnostic facilities than the other foreign groups, but the foreign born taken as a whole have sufficiently good diagnosis to eliminate the factor of diagnosis in discussing the high cancer death rate of the foreign born."

Beginning in 1929 and for the four years following, the Division studied, by the survey method, the chronic disease problem in Massachusetts. Preliminary reports were made in the journal, *Hospital Social Service* in November, 1930, and May, 1933, and in the *Courier of the International Catholic Federation of Nurses* in November, 1931. The final report was incorporated in a book published in 1933 by Houghton Mifflin Company under the title of *Cancer and Other Chronic Diseases in Massachusetts*. This book, with 172 pages of text and 147 pages of tables, covers the results of the chronic disease survey in Massachusetts, together with an account of the earlier part of the Massachusetts Cancer Program.

Outstanding among the findings in the book was the presentation of the amount of chronic disease in the State. About one-third of the population over forty was found to be afflicted with either early chronic disease or its more advanced form. Between the ages of forty and fifty, about one-fifth of the population was thus afflicted. There was no geographic distribution. Both city and country shared equally. Poverty was the most important factor, the disease rate among the poor being about twice as great as among the well-to-do. About 5 per cent of the individuals were completely disabled. If the survey figures are an indication of Massachusetts as a whole, which seems extremely probable, due to the slight variations in the different geographic areas surveyed, over twenty thousand individuals in the State are completely disabled with one or more of the chronic diseases. Many individuals had multiple diseases, the average being 1.3. Poor hygiene was associated with chronic disease, and there were far greater numbers in the sick group who failed to eat the proper foods, took too little exercise, were overweight, and had poor dental hygiene than in the well group. Heredity seemed of some importance, as did also nervous constitution.

The most prevalent single disease was chronic rheumatism, with an estimated number of approximately 140,000 cases in the State. The cardiovascular renal group, if combined, exceeded the rheumatism group, but when treated separately heart disease was second to rheumatism, arteriosclerosis was third, and nephritis was sixth.

About one-third of the sick individuals had received no medical treatment during the year preceding the survey. The percentage varied in different diseases. Approximately 90 per cent of the individuals with diabetes had been under treatment, and about one-half of those with rheumatism. The principal reasons for not having a physician in attendance were a feeling that the condition was not serious and that the disease was of such a nature that the physician could not help them. Economic reasons were given only in about one-eighth of the cases.

In 1931 a survey was made of the practicing physicians in four clinic cities and one nonclinic city, and reported in the *New England Journal of Medicine* of November 12th of that year. The study was made to determine the reaction of the physicians to the State Cancer Program and to obtain advice from them. This study, later followed by other similar studies and by several questionnaires to the entire profession, has molded the program.

A second sample of cases in which the relationship between the environment and cancer was discussed was reported in *Public Health Nursing* of November, 1931. This paper again emphasized the need for further work along this line.

In 1932 two important papers were published on March 24th and December 1st in the *New England Journal of Medicine*. In the one on hospitalization of cancer in Massachusetts, a review was made of hospital admissions which appeared between 1928 and 1930 for comparison with five years earlier. This study showed that more individuals were entering hospitals and the methods of handling them were better. The economics of the Massachusetts Cancer Program discussed the program in relation to its costs and made comparisons with various types of business. It appeared that the so-called profits of the Massachusetts Cancer Program exceeded those of any of the businesses discussed.

On March 8, 1934, a change in the Massachusetts cancer trend was reported in the *New England Journal of Medicine*. It was shown that "the trend of cancer mortality in Massachusetts is changing with the curve flattening out and a slight decrease noted among females. The rate for the foreign-born females is decreasing faster than for the other groups. While the death rates indicate that cancer of the digestive tract in females has the greatest improvement, it is believed that erroneous classification in the earlier years is responsible and that the decrease is really in breast and uterine cancer. It is the opinion of the authors that the improvement in the cancer death rate is caused by the concerted drive against cancer, by changes in the composition of the foreign population, and by the possibility of a saturation point in cancer being reached. The relative significance of each of these factors must be determined in the future, if at all."

In the same year, in June, the *Bulletin of the Boston Health League* published information on cancer facilities in Boston.

In February, 1936, in the *Radcliffe Quarterly*, appeared a review of epidemiological methods used in making studies.

In the same year, in the August 13th issue of the *New England Journal of Medicine*, was published a statement of the cancer clinic statistics coupled with information about the revised program.

Similar papers discussing the revised program have appeared in the *Journal of the Connecticut State Medical Society*, August, 1937, and the *American Journal of Public Health*, January, 1938.

On April 28, 1938, in the *New England Journal of Medicine*, a paper on the familial aspects of cancer was published which showed that of one hundred families in which one of the parents had cancer, approximately 10 per cent of the children had cancer, while in a similar number of families in which neither parent had cancer, approximately 8 per cent of the children had cancer. This indicates a slight familial tendency toward cancer.

In 1938, an important contribution on the accuracy of the cancer death records was published in the July issue of the *American Journal of Public Health*. This paper showed that the death records portray the incidence of cancer as a whole in 95 per cent of the cases. They are only about 75 per cent accurate as far as location of cancer is concerned.

At the present time there are several studies in the process of completion, the most important one dealing with the possible association of cancer with certain environmental factors. This is an improved and enlarged piece of work somewhat similar to the two studies previously reported. In this research, some eighty variables were chosen for study. Work has been progressing along these lines for several years and is now nearing completion.

This review of the epidemiological aspects of the cancer program clearly demonstrates that the knowledge of cancer is being advanced—gradually, perhaps, but nevertheless on a firm foundation. It remains for some research worker of the future to correlate the existing information with new material and obtain a completed whole.

MASSACHUSETTS STATE-AIDED CANCER CLINICS

FREDERICK G. MEDINGER, M.D.

Assistant Director, Division of Cancer and Other Chronic Diseases Massachusetts Department of Public Health

The Massachusetts State-aided cancer clinics are administered by committees appointed by the local medical organizations. These committees have charge of the administrative details connected with their respective clinics but in all cases they must conform with the minimum standards set by the Department. These are:

(a) *Group diagnosis.* The group must consist of at least three men, preferably surgeon, pathologist, and radiologist. When any of these are not available, other physicians may be substituted.

(b) *Uniform records.* Forms are furnished by the Department for this purpose as is also money for clerical service when needed.

(c) *Social Service.* All cases of cancer and precancer are referred to social service for follow-up. The follow-up continues until death in the case of cancer and until removal of the lesion in the case of precancer. The State either furnishes money to help defray the expenses of the social worker or furnishes the clinic the services of a part-time social worker.

Every physician in the Commonwealth may bring or send his patient to the clinic for free consultative service with the group. If the individual case requires such diagnostic procedure as gastrointestinal series this must be paid for by the patient if he is able to do so, but if he is not able to do so funds are available for this service.

Each case is returned to the physician who sent him to the clinic, and this physician decides whether or not he desires the assistance of social service in securing treatment for his patient.

The clinics must meet at least twice a month. At intervals determined by the clinic committee, but in no instance less than once a year, some form of teaching for the physician in the community is required. Some clinics perform this service by having consultants come to the clinics at stated intervals; others have adopted the plan of having all the physicians in the community serve on the clinic staff; while still others confine their activities to having an address on cancer by some surgeon from another city.

The clinic itself is furnished the following services by the State: first, advice, information, and literature; second, funds for or services of social worker; third, funds for travel of social worker; fourth, funds for X-ray diagnosis for those unable to pay; fifth, funds for teaching clinics; sixth, funds for clerical assistance in clinics; seventh, funds for postage, telephone, stationery, etc.; eighth, special clinics for the staffs of the clinics; and ninth, reference of cancer cases to hospital through social service.

The purpose of the clinics is to furnish physicians and the public, group consultation service in cancer, as well as to improve the knowledge of cancer among the medical profession and the laity. The group furnishes a diagnosis and outlines a plan of treatment for any person suspected of having cancer, regardless of financial status. Every effort is made to have the family physician either come with his patient to the clinic or send the patient with such information as he cares to furnish. Any individual is admitted to the clinic although it is preferred to have the patients referred by physicians so that any tendency to use the cancer clinic in order to establish a diagnosis of a condition originally not suspected of being cancer may be eliminated.

AN APPRAISAL OF THE AID GIVEN THE CANCER CLINIC BY THE USE OF STATE FUNDS

HARRY F. FRIEDMAN, M.D., F.A.C.R.
Director, Cancer Clinic, Beth Israel Hospital
and
ETHEL COHEN, M.S.
Director, Social Service Department, Beth Israel Hospital
Boston, Massachusetts

The problem of the recognition or diagnosis of early cancer and its treatment has not yet been solved. McCarty defines an early cancer as one that measures 2.5 cm. in diameter, because a lesion of this size is much smaller than the average operable cancer ordinarily seen. In a series of 7,750 surgically removed cancers he found the average diameters were for the breast 3.2 cm., the stomach 6.1 cm., the rectum, rectosigmoid, and sigmoid 5.7 cm., and the rest of the large intestine 6.9 cm. The average size of the lesions seen in McCarty's series is undoubtedly much smaller than that seen by the general practitioner and general surgeon, for we must acknowledge the fact that only fifty per cent of all breast cancers are operable when first seen by the physician. The percentages of operability of cancer in other parts of the body when first seen by the physician are as follows:

   Stomach .... 25 per cent
   Large intestine .... 58 "   "
   Body of the uterus .... 65 "   "
   Lip .... 75 "   "

These figures would seem to indicate that as a rule the disease is not in an early stage when discovered by the medical profession. It can also be said that for the most part we are not diagnosing cancer early enough. When we can predict that from 100,000 to 150,000 individuals in the United States will die next year from cancer, we admit our inability to cope with this problem to any great degree. What are we to do about the group of individuals who, unknowingly, are to die from cancer five, ten, or fifteen years hence? The life history of cancer is not one of a few months' duration or of a year; it is a disease that takes several years to run its course, and, in many instances, several years to manifest itself.

At present we are interested in the really early cancer, the lesion no larger than a ten-cent piece. We are interested in removing or destroying cancer before we can make the clinical diagnosis of the disease. How are we to accomplish this?

In 1926 the Massachusetts Cancer Program was instituted under the auspices of the State Department of Public Health. This Program is now in its twelfth year, and the mortality records of Massachusetts for 1935 show a decrease in the number of cancer deaths for the first time in the twentieth century. Grateful acknowledgement of this encouraging fact should be included in any appraisal of the aid given the cancer clinic, the medical fraternity, and through them the people of the State.

The function of a cancer clinic is manifold. Its main purpose is to give to the suspected cancer case the benefit of the most modern accepted methods for diagnosis and treatment. There is also the need for preventive measures and an educational program which includes not only the laity but the medical profession as well. This broad scope necessitates a large medical personnel properly trained to meet the needs of the complex methods for diagnosis and treatment, as well as a trained social service group which performs a very important and necessary function in a properly conducted cancer clinic.

A cancer clinic is an indispensable part of a large general hospital. It must attract to its staff physicians trained in oncology. To accomplish this, every facility for the care of the cancer patient must be available. Most hospitals are run at too great a deficit to undertake the additional financial responsibilities entailed by a properly operated cancer clinic. The cost of operating an active cancer clinic is much above the cost of any other clinic in the hospital, and for this reason the aid given by the State is of inestimable value.

The State-aided cancer clinics are administered by committees appointed by the hospital or by local medical organizations. In the large general hospital the clinic is administered by a director, responsible to the Cancer Committee appointed by the Medical Board. The two major standards established by the State are:

1. *Group Consultation Diagnosis*: Every physician in the Commonwealth may bring or send his patients to the clinic for free consultation service with the group. Each member of the clinic has the opportunity of studying the history and examining the patient. The most important factor, however, is the interchanging of ideas and the free discussion in the group relative to the case at hand. Thus, we no longer have one individual making the diagnosis and advising treatment, but, on the other hand, a group opinion based on many past experiences and a conscious knowledge of the accepted medical literature on the subject. No longer is the disposition of a case decided by the opinion of only a surgeon or a radiologist, but by a decision of an entire group. This one factor alone would justify all the effort and money spent in the operation of the clinic.

2. *Uniform Records*: Forms are furnished by the State Department of Public Health for this purpose as is money for clerical service. This enables the clinic to employ a full-time clerk and clinic executive.

In the Beth Israel Hospital Clinic every facility for the diagnosis and treatment of cancer is available, including beds for surgical patients. The clinic also has sufficient radium and high voltage X-ray apparatus to meet the needs of the cancer patient. In the clinic associated with a large hospital the patient will be accepted for treatment if the referring physician so desires.

The purpose of the cancer clinic is to provide group consultation service in cancer for the laity and physicians. However, a very important function of the clinic is to furnish additional knowledge of cancer to the medical profession, and for this purpose cancer conferences by the clinic staff in conjunction with the regular staff of the Hospital are held frequently, and teaching cancer clinics for members of the profession are held at stated intervals. These teaching cancer clinics give to the attending physicians an opportunity to examine the patient, learn the accepted methods of treatment, and become more familiar with the statistics of cancer therapy.

Educational campaigns have greatly increased public information on the subject of cancer but wide-spread fear and prejudice regarding it

still exists in all economic levels of society. In order to make an effective contribution to the care of the patient the social worker for the cancer clinic must have both knowledge of the disease and understanding of the different types of treatment recommended. Of equal importance with this knowledge is a sensitivity to the implications of the disease for the patient and his family in the practical and material as well as in the emotional aspects. Described in broad terms the function of the social worker is twofold, administrative and case work. In her administrative role she has the following responsibilities:
1. Nonmedical direction of the clinic.
2. Preparation of special records and reports required by the State Cancer Program which includes an annual living cancer report to the State Department of Public Health.
3. Medical follow-up for:
   (a) Return of patients with lapsed clinic appointments for study or treatment.
   (b) Appointments for admission to the hospital wards
   (c) Special clinic educational demonstrations.
4. Transportation when the patient is unable to provide it himself for clinic supervision and surgical and X-ray therapy.

In her role as case worker the social worker has an interview with every patient with questioned or definite diagnosis of malignancy, in order to become acquainted with each individual and to ascertain whether there exists any obstacle to carrying out clinic recommendations either in the material conditions of the patient's life or in his emotional reactions to medical care. In the course of this social review, there is often the need or the desire for further interpretation, to the patient or his family, of the clinic and of the doctor's recommendations, in supplementation of what the physicians have already given.

These social inquiries reveal many kinds of difficulties, which require concrete readjustments in the patient's environment, either to make it possible for the patient to be studied for diagnostic purposes or for alleviation and treatment of his illness. In some instances, only advice and guidance from the social worker is necessary. This may be in the form of information as to resources in the community previously unknown to the patient, or of suggestions for rearrangements in home or work, which he or his family are perfectly capable of carrying out themselves. Many of these patients return to the social worker repeatedly as conditions change for more suggestions, for reassurance and encouragement, but continue in their ability to carry on themselves. Many other patients, however, are incapable of such complete self-maintenance for a great variety of reasons. Some of these are due to limited intelligence, emotional instability in varying degrees, economic inadequacy, heavy family responsibilities, lack of normal family relationships, and severe physical or emotional disability. For these patients the social worker, by individual case work treatment, attempts to meet their particular needs. This may involve financial assistance for the family from community agencies or relatives; assistance in vocational rehabilitation or occupational therapy; placement of children, aged or handicapped dependents through community agencies or friends, arrangements in the home or in institutions for chronic or terminal care of the patient.

Aside from the need often to provide special appliances, such as colostomy outfits, artificial breasts, etc., the worker must appreciate the possible reactions of patients to these deviations from the normal. Some individuals are able to accept these compromises, some even with gratitude that science has provided substitutions which make possible continued activity and independence both financial and personal. Other patients see in such appliances only defeat and frustration, loss of status, whether of their womanhood, or their comfortable functioning as a member of their particular social group.

An important contribution of the social worker to patients ill with cancer is her understanding and acceptance of the patient with all his fears, anxieties and deep emotional problems. The relationship between patient and worker has been frequently a source of real strength to the patient, because here he has found someone who accepts him with disfigurement and disturbed function without fear or disgust, who will listen with patience and sympathy to oft-repeated recitals of symptoms and of anxieties, and who is prepared with practical advice and suggestions when necessary.

Physicians look to the clinic social worker for close collaboration in everything but the strictly medical aspects of the patient's care. There is continuous interchange of data and counsel concerning the patient's problem. The medical and social services are so interwoven that each service assists the other at whatever point in the handling of the case that particular support is required. This is especially true in dealing with extreme fear and apprehension with which many patients receive the recommendation for hospital study for a lump in the breast or bleeding from the cervix. Doctors believe that the explanation by the social worker as to the importance of exact diagnosis and early treatment of the condition must be added to their own interpretation in order to avoid delaying opportunities for the alleviation or cure of the disease.

Physicians also value as a contribution of the social worker her preparation of the patient for the reaction that follows certain types of treatment. For example, a patient, who was to receive X-ray therapy for cancer of the larynx, knew that his severe throat pain was the expected result of that treatment, not a manifestation of his disease. This reassurance was a real aid in the future handling of this patient. Limited space prevents the inclusion of other examples of this aspect of clinic work.

The services offered by the cancer clinic, diagnostic, therapeutic, consultative, educational and social case work should constitute the main components of every clinic dealing with this disease. The well-formulated program of the Massachusetts Department of Public Health in establishing subsidized clinics throughout the State has advanced greatly progress in the attack on cancer.

BOSTON DISPENSARY CANCER CLINIC

WILLIAM M. SHEDDEN, M.D.
Chief of Clinic

It is our belief that the progress of each cancer clinic is directly determined by its underlying philosophy. We believe further that the destiny of each clinic is dependent on all the others in the State. One cannot separate for discussion one group without immediately realizing the interlocking interdependence. Our course in the New England Medical Center has been charted in accordance with what we believe to be sound trends in policy throughout the State. A short discussion of these trends will not be out of place.

During the past decade there has come a gradual alteration in the conception as to what constitutes the most effective attack on one of the world's most efficient killers—cancer. At the outset, it was obviously necessary to develop a group of men whose primary interest should be the study of the weaknesses and strengths of this disease. These pioneers were developed. As a corollary, and to widen the scope of the foray, there were constructed secondary lines of offense—the diagnostic cancer clinics. Their function was to receive and sort out from the mass of material presented those cases suitable for treatment and to present them to the specialist for treatment. This work has been and is being accomplished well.

However, we have moved into a second phase of the war on cancer. The original group of pioneers has developed into a small army. We can no longer concentrate treatment in a few camps. The attack must be carried out on a more extensive front. The "cancer hospitals" are carrying a capacity number of admissions. Obviously treatment will be administered in many areas as soon as adequate equipment and personnel is developed. We emphasize "adequate." No one would wish to contemplate any change that would weaken the original structure.

In our opinion the most efficient setup of the future will be a continuance of the State Cancer Advisory Committee whose membership is derived from the State Department of Public Health and the Cancer Committee of the Massachusetts Medical Society.

All participants in the attack—the research laboratories, the medical schools and the large body of Massachusetts physicians—must be properly allocated where their work is most effective. In some quarters there is material as yet untouched. In others it is being strained to its utmost.

This situation calls for constructive criticism on the part of all of us. Differing opinions are best adjusted through a central clearing house.

In 1929, one hundred and thirty-three years after the founding of the Dispensary, there was joined to that institution the Floating Hospital and the Tufts College Medical School, the three forming the New England Medical Center.

In 1932 the New England Medical Center reorganized its cancer clinic to conform with the standards set by the American College of Surgeons. It already possessed an efficient roentgen therapy machine with a peak strength of 200,000 volts, which is the standard for most therapeutic X-ray machines in the United States today. One hundred milligrams of radium element were purchased in the form of ten milligram needles, nineteen millimeters long, with a screening of 0.5 millimeter of platinum-iridium. This group of one hundred milligrams is quite flexible. The entire amount can be used interchangeably in the uterus, mouth or skin or individual needles can be inserted into or around malignant tissue.

The cancer clinic staff was expanded. It now was administered by a surgeon-in-chief with three assistant surgeons, two junior assistants, a roentgenologist, a dermatologist and a pathologist. The last three with at least two surgeons administer each clinic, since it has been found that such an organization is distinctly more efficient than one in which the pathologist, the roentgenologist or the dermatologist is merely called in for consultation.

Special types of malignancy, gynecological, urological, otolaryngological, etc., are administered by members of a permanent consulting staff and are seen on special days. These special types of malignancy, however, appear also in the cancer clinic at stated intervals for observation and check up. In this way a more efficient coordination of the whole field of malignancy is obtained.

The New England Medical Center Cancer Clinic cares for all indigent patients who apply. The complete facilities of the clinic are tendered to all patients regardless of their fiancial status.

The year 1937 showed a marked increase in the number of patients entering the clinic. The visits totaled 2156, an increase of eighteen per cent over 1936. The first four months of 1938 showed a forty-eight per cent increase in X-ray and radium treatments over the similar period in 1937.

Abundant material is available for efficient teaching. A pathologist is constantly present during the clinic and is prepared to demonstrate the patient's biopsy or other pathological material. The teaching is enhanced by a view of the histological slide projected on the screen by a projectoscope and a study of the case is pursued with the pathologist, roentgenologist, surgeon and dermatologist.

The teaching clinics are carried on as follows: The patient first is booked by the clinical clerk and after an interview with the social worker enters one of the examining booths where the history is obtained by a medical student. In the conference room, equipped with a blackboard, the case is discussed with the whole group as soon as complete data are assembled. The roentgenologist exhibits X-ray films and gives his opinion as to therapy. The histological slide is placed on a projectoscope and the enlarged projection is thrown on the wall in full color. If it is a dermatological problem, the dermatologist makes his comment. There is then a full discussion and the surgeon in charge describes the management of the particular case under advisement. Patients representing a wide variety of malignant conditions are demonstrated during the clinic. Both the usual and the unusual are encountered in the same morning.

While the teaching is going on, other members of the staff attend to those cases which have not any particular teaching value. The teaching groups are small enough to allow firsthand experience and a certain amount of individual instruction. Emphasis is placed on early diagnosis of lesions which may be met by the practitioner in his office.

This form of instruction is believed to have a very definite place both with graduates and undergraduates. It is plastic and can be altered as diagnosis and therapy advance.

At the request of the Massachusetts Department of Public Health, members of the cancer clinic staff of the New England Medical Center have been invited to conduct special teaching clinics for larger groups of Massachusetts physicians. The last teaching clinic held at the New England Medical Center was on April 29, 1938. Fifty-nine physicians were present. Short demonstrations on the following subjects were given:

CANCER OF THE TONGUE, Roy E. Mabrey, M.D.
Surgeon, Tumor Clinic Staff.
CANCER OF THE NOSE AND THROAT, Philip E. Meltzer, M.D.
Consultant in Otolaryngology, Tumor Clinic Staff.
CANCER OF THE BREAST, Grantley W. Taylor, M.D.
Surgeon, Pondville Hospital Staff.
CANCER OF THE STOMACH, Irving Walker, M.D.
Boston City Hospital Staff.
CANCER OF THE GENITOURINARY TRACT, Roger Graves, M.D.
Consultant in Urology, Tumor Clinic Staff.
CANCER OF THE UTERUS, Louis Phaneuf, M.D.
Consultant in Gynecology, Tumor Clinic Staff.
CANCER OF THE RECTUM, William M. Shedden, M.D.
Surgeon-in-Chief, Tumor Clinic Staff.

In addition, a moving picture—a thousand feet of reel on the surgical treatment of cancer of the rectum—was made for us. The film presents one of our staff operating to show the technique of the one-stage abdominoperineal resection (Miles). This film was shown to groups of physicians at Hyannis, Lynn, Webster, Chelsea, Brockton and at Waterville, Maine. It was shown also at the New England Hospital for Women and Children, the Cambridge Hospital and at the Scientific Exhibit of the Massachusetts Medical Society.

Physicians are welcome as visitors to the cancer clinic of the New England Medical Center and may bring patients with them for aid in diagnosis. Hospital beds are available for more complete study of the doubtful or obscure cases.

The following diagram is a floor plan of the Tumor Clinic:

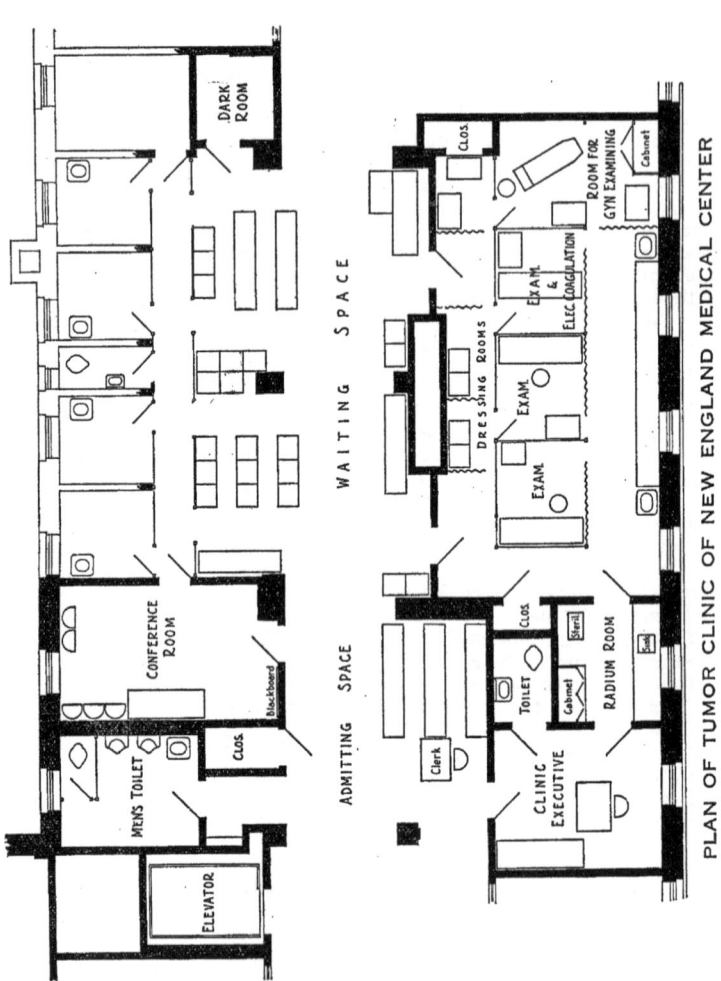

BROCKTON CANCER CLINIC

FREDERICK F. WEINER, M.D.
Chairman, Brockton Cancer Committee

The Brockton Cancer Clinic was started in June, 1930, following the appointment of a committee from the Plymouth District Medical Society whose function was to organize and supervise the clinic activities. Up to June, 1938, 2478 patients have been examined by the clinic of which 425 have been diagnosed as cancer.

The clinic as it functions today is still supervised by a committee of doctors from the Plymouth District Medical Society and consists of seven men from Brockton and surrounding towns. This committee meets several times during the year to consider the problems that arise in connection with the clinic. Under its direction several teaching clinics are held each year.

In April, 1938, the clinic participated in the State program for cancer week with an exceptionally well-attended teaching clinic at which were presented cancer cases that had been cured for five years or longer. At this time, seventy-five "cured" clinic cases were reported and in part demonstrated by a Boston consultant.

The active staff attending the clinic consists of nine regular men and four alternates who substitute during the enforced absence on the part of the regular attending physicians. Three doctors are present at every clinic and include a surgical, medical and X-ray consultant. It has been the policy of the cancer committee to appoint on the active attending staff men from surrounding towns as well as Brockton and have found that this has resulted in a wider and greater interest in the work done by the clinic. All patients are examined and, in so far as possible, diagnoses made but no treatment is given in the clinic, the patient being referred back, with a report to his own physician for treatment or proper treatment arranged for if the patient and his physician request that it be done. This policy is never deviated from and I believe is one of the main causes for the success of the clinic; and the fact that of all patients admitted during the last year there was a material increase of those referred by their physicians.

The social service and clerical departments have rendered great aid in the follow-up and management of the clinic affairs and in providing transportation for patients to the clinic, Pondville and other hospitals.

At the present time the Brockton Cancer Clinic has on its rolls 260 living cancer cases which it is following. These cases come from twenty-six different towns in the Brockton district.

CAPE COD CANCER CLINIC

FARRAR COBB, M.D.
Chief of Clinic

Cape Cod Cancer Clinics have been held at the Cape Cod Hospital in Hyannis, which has the largest population of any community on the Cape, although it is itself in the Town of Barnstable. This Hospital is the only one on Cape Cod. The first cancer clinic was held September 22, 1936. This was a teaching clinic. The late Dr. Robert B. Greenough was the special consultant at this clinic, and there was a fairly representative number of physicians of the Cape present. At this meeting the purpose of the cancer clinics was explained and the cooperation of the medical profession was urged.

The conditions governing the maintenance of a cancer clinic on the Cape are somewhat different from the conditions in other parts of the State because of the large number of widely separated towns and scattered communities from Provincetown to Falmouth; the campaign of education has to be spread throughout all these diversified settlements. The population of Cape Cod, not including the transient summer population, is in the neighborhood of 35,000. There are fifteen townships, each one of which is made up of several smaller towns and villages. The hospital and cancer clinic serve the residents of forty different communities from Provincetown to Falmouth. The population and the doctors of these communities have had to be reached insofar as possible in the educational campaign about cancer. From some of the communities the interest and response of the people and of some of the physicians has been indifferent and discouraging, but within the first six months of 1938 it has been evident that there is an increasing knowledge and appreciation of the value of the clinic. Perhaps no class of persons in the State of Massachusetts are as reticent on the whole to accept new facts as the natives of Cape Cod. New methods and doctrines are accepted only after deliberate and oftentimes grudging consideration. Some of the physicians have expressed themselves as seeing no advantage in the cancer clinics. It has been found that there is a widespread feeling among the population of Cape Cod, including even a few physicians, that cancer can be cured by injections of serum, diet and medicines. One of the most important parts of the work of the clinic has been the combatting of this pernicious idea. It is alarming that so many of the population have had this regrettable belief instilled into them and that some cases of cancer have been deprived of a fair chance of cure by radical surgery or radiation because of taking this serum treatment. Clinics should be continued because of the necessity for continued education and because there has been an encouraging increase in the interest in the last year.

Since September, 1936, regular clinics have been held on the second and fourth Tuesdays of every month and special teaching clinics once in three months. The total number of new patients seen at the clinic has been sixty-eight, of which number thirty-six were found to have cancer. The towns referring cases were:

Barnstable and West Barnstable	3	Hyannis	7
Bourne	1	Marstons Mills	3
Brewster	3	Onset	1
Centerville	3	Orleans	10
Chatham	3	Osterville	1
Cotuit	2	Provincetown	7
Dennisport	2	Sandwich	3
Eastham	3	Wellfleet	1
Falmouth	12	Yarmouth	2
Harwich	1		

The site of malignant disease was as follows:

Cancer of abdomen	1
" " back	1
" " breast	4
" " cervix	4
" face	10
" " lip	6
" " liver	1
" " rectum	1
" " sigmoid flexure	2
" " stomach, inoperable	2
" " transverse colon	1

Sarcoma of head 1
Hodgkin's disease 2

There were eight cases operated upon, seventeen were treated by radium or X-ray, eleven were too far advanced for anything but observation and terminal care; fifteen cases were sent to Pondville for treatment, six cases to other institutions in this State, five were operated upon in the Cape Cod Hospital; eleven of the cases have died. The number without symptoms June, 1938, was fourteen. There were thirty-four clinics from September, 1936, to June, 1938, total attendance, one hundred, average clinic attendance, three. There were six teaching clinics, at which the consultants were the late Dr. Robert B. Greenough, Dr. Shields Warren, Dr. George A. Leland, Jr., and Dr. William M. Shedden. The average attendance of patients at the teaching clinics was six, total of thirty-eight; average number of doctors attending the teaching clinics, nineteen; number of doctors referring cases for diagnosis and treatment, sixteen.

In common with the other cancer clinics throughout the State, a teaching clinic to report on and show cured cancer cases was held at the hospital on April 26, 1938. The cases, representing private patients of Cape Cod physicians, were:

Cancer of the breast, alive and free from recurrence from 5 to
  20 years 4
Cancer of the breast, free from recurrence over 3 years and
  under 5 2
Cancer of the cervix (radical Wertheim operations free from
  recurrence from 10 to 30 years) 3
Cancer of the cervix alive over six years after radium treatment 1
Cancer of the cervix treated by radium and high voltage
  X-rays, free from recurrence from 1½ to 2½ years 4
Number of five-year cures 8
Survivals 3½ to 5 years 3
Total surviving from 1½ to 20 years 13

FALL RIVER CANCER CLINIC

THOMAS ALMY, M.D.
Chairman, Fall River Cancer Committee

The Fall River Cancer Clinic became State supervised January 19, 1937. Before this date a cancer clinic had run as a part of the outpatient department of the Union Hospital for about ten years. With the increase of personnel it has been possible to give closer follow-up and improve our records. The teaching clinics have drawn a good attendance of physicians and have done much to make us all more cancer conscious. The Union Hospital is giving splendid service especially in admitting without delay cancer patients for study or treatment. The following figures summarize the work since January 19, 1937:

Total number of patients 236
Total number of new admissions 148
Total visits of cancer patients 90
Total number of new admissions for cancer 57
Operation 47
Radiation 37
Observation or terminal care 5
Pondville 27
Local Hospital 53

Other Institutions 4
Without symptoms 50
Dead 20
Disease active 20

It will be noted that about one-third of the cases seen were recommended to Pondville Hospital for treatment.

The present staff of the clinic is Dr. Thomas Almy and Dr. Henry C. Lawson, Gynecology; Dr. Richard Butler and Dr. Roger Buck, Surgery; Dr. Walter S. Lyon, Medical; Dr. Samuel Sandler, Genitourinary Surgery; Dr. James H. Walsh, Pathology and Dr. Matthew N. Tennis, X-ray.

The teaching cancer clinics held every three months have been generally very successful. Outstanding for interest was the April, 1938, Achievement Clinic at which were presented a select group of cured cancer cases as a nucleus for a seminar on the clinical problems of cancer control. At each teaching clinic, the group entertains a Boston consultant, expert in the field of cancer.

FITCHBURG CANCER CLINIC

RUDOLF F. BACHMANN, M.D.
Chairman, Fitchburg Cancer Clinic Committee

The Fitchburg Cancer Clinic originated in 1928 as the Worcester North Cancer Clinic under the subsidy of the Commonwealth and included the towns of Fitchburg, Leominster and Gardner. At that time under the supervision of the State Department of Public Health a clinic was held every two weeks successively in the three towns. The Worcester North Cancer Clinic was regulated locally by the Worcester North District Cancer Committee whose members were elected from and by the Worcester North District Medical Society. The clinic functioned regularly and successfully during these early years and much appreciation is due Dr. Frederick H. Thompson, Sr., the original chairman, who although considerably incapacitated by his advanced years, is still an interested member of the committee and to Dr. Walter F. Sawyer, Secretary-Treasurer, active until May, 1938, both of whom have given much of their time and energy in forwarding this pioneer movement in public health.

In 1936, Dr. Thompson, Sr., resigned the clinic chairmanship and Dr. Rudolf Bachmann was elected to succeed him. Just previous to this Leominster withdrew its participation and Gardner voted to function as a separate clinic. Consequently, upon due authority, the Fitchburg Cancer Clinic now functions as a separate unit supervised by members of the Fitchburg Cancer Clinic Committee. The Committee has determined the following policy for clinics, all of which are held at the Burbank Hospital. Each first Tuesday of the month the clinic is conducted by a nonresident consultant, expert in cancer work, and each second clinic by the active medical and surgical staffs on duty at the Burbank Hospital. The teaching consultant, rotating for each month of the year, is chosen by the clinic committee. The committee feels that the services of the consultants are valuable from every point of view because experience has shown that the interest and attendance of both patients and physicians has been greatly stimulated. Although it is the purpose of the clinic to be self-reliant, in accordance with the policy of the State Department of Public Health, the present situation in this locality makes for the need of frequent consultation teaching clinics.

In the past, some of the local physicians labored under the misconception that the cancer clinic meant State medicine rather than an aid to public health but, as time passes, these physicians appreciate that the cancer clinic is helpful rather than detrimental to their private practice.

At the regular clinics the local physicians establish all clear-cut diagnoses and make the necessary recommendations to the referring physician for immediate treatment. If the diagnosis of cancer is doubtful the teaching clinic with its expert consultation service gives both the patients and the physicians the advantage of another opinion.

In the early days, clinic meetings were advertised in the local papers and this procedure brought a large attendance of patients who saw a chance to receive free medical advice. This resulted in the cluttering of the clinic with many not even cancer suspects. During the past few years this has been overcome by the policy of no advertising and of accepting mainly those referred by physicians or recognized public health agencies. The policy of making each clinic a consultation service and of referring each patient back to the family physician with letters of findings and recommendations has been a definite aid in arousing the interest of the doctors in the cancer clinic.

Another service which has proved of great value to the physicians of Fitchburg and surrounding towns has been the provision for free diagnostic tests to the so-called medically indigent patient.

As a result of the present policies and setup of the Fitchburg Cancer Clinic, many more early malignant and premalignant lesions are being seen and, with the weeding out of the former conglomeration of nonmalignant conditions, the clinic staff obtain valuable information concerning cancer at each clinic attended.

The present cancer committee consists of: Doctors E. R. Pickwick, H. B. Pitcher, Secretary-Treasurer pro tem; G. P. Keaveny, L. M. DeCicco, D. E. Bennett, Frederick H. Thompson, Sr. (inactive), W. P. Sawyer (Secretary-Treasurer inactive because of illness), and R. F. Bachmann as Chairman. This committee meets regularly four times a year and whenever it is thought necessary to plan any special activity. The cancer committee believe that the present policy has brought gratifying results and has stimulated a great deal more local interest in the problems of cancer. It hopes for even greater interest in the future in order that the clinic continue to function as a successful aid in protecting the health of this community against the great scourge of cancer.

FRANKLIN COUNTY CANCER CLINIC

WILLIAM J. PELLETIER, M.D.

Chairman, Franklin County Cancer Clinic

In 1927 under the direction of the State Department of Public Health, the Franklin County Cancer Clinic was first organized. The clinic was inaugurated with an enthusiastic publicity campaign directed particularly to the laity with little attention being paid to the medical profession. For the following few months this clinic flourished with a large attendance of patients. A consultant was present at each clinic held monthly and rotating alternately between the Franklin County Hospital in Greenfield and the Farren Memorial Hospital in Montague City. A staff of four local physicians rotating for three months' service, was appointed by the Cancer Committee of the District Medical Society. Because it became apparent that the patients were attending the clinic solely to have the services of the same out-of-town consultant, local physicians soon became discouraged. In addition, the patients, for the most part not referred by their family physicians, were coming to the clinic for all sorts of conditions unrelated to cancer, resulting in a great loss of time and interest.

This setup became more unfavorable and finally it was impossible to enlist the cooperation of any of the local medical men and resulted in a free private clinic conducted by the Boston consultant. When the Department of Public Health abandoned clinic publicity in 1934 the activities and attendance of patients decreased so sharply that the continuance of the clinic was not warranted.

Under a reorganization plan the clinic was resumed in 1935 with the understanding that there was to be no publicity to the laity. An active cancer committee was organized from the ranks of the local district medical society. This committee selected the Franklin County Hospital as the logical geographic location for meetings to be held the first and third Fridays of each month at ten A.M. Patients are restricted as much as possible to those referred by their family physician for a suspected cancer or advice concerning treatment. Instead of having a regular consultant at each clinic there are now special teaching clinics conducted by outstanding men experienced in the diagnosis and treatment of cancer. The teaching consultants assist in the conduct of the clinic and discuss with members of the local profession special problems in cancer control or other questions in order.

In addition, under the reorganization, the cancer committee has corralled all physicians interested in cancer work and from this group five men are detailed for two-month periods to conduct the clinic. In this group of five, one member of the cancer committee is always included to act as senior member. Under these conditions the clinic has remained very successful, not measured entirely by the patient attendance because the locality is small, but because of the great interest evidenced by the physicians and the benefits derived by them from the experience gained.

At each clinic, it is fair to estimate an average attendance of between eight and ten very interesting cases. The staff attend very well and at a teaching clinic it is not uncommon to have nearly half of the available medical men in our district attending.

The Franklin County Cancer Committee would like to take this opportunity to express their appreciation to the State Department of Public Health and its personnel in charge of cancer clinic activities, for the help they have given us, which is, in no small measure, responsible for our success.

GARDNER CANCER DIAGNOSTIC CLINIC

HAROLD C. AREY, M.D.
Chief of Clinic Staff

From 1928 up until October, 1935 a cancer clinic associated with the Fitchburg and Leominster clinics was conducted in Gardner at the Henry Heywood Memorial Hospital. Conducted under this joint arrangement, it was very difficult to maintain the interest of the local physicians and but few of the physicians in the surrounding towns realized that such a clinic could serve them. During the late summer of 1935 all the physicians in Gardner, Athol, Orange, Winchendon, Ashburnham and Templeton were contacted to determine whether they wished to serve as members of a rotating examining staff of a newly organized cancer diagnostic clinic of Gardner functioning as an independent unit under the supervision and support of the State Department of Public Health. At a monthly staff meeting in September, a committee of physicians read an organization plan with clinic rules and regulations submitted by the Department of Public Health. Representative officials from the Department present were very helpful in explaining the value of the clinics to the physicians. Emphasis was placed upon the rule that the clinic was to be reorganized as a diagnostic clinic and that no treatment could be given. It was impressed upon the Hospital staff physicians that, in voting to accept State funds for the support of such a clinic, the members must be willing to serve as the clinic diagnostic staff.

About ninety per cent of the Gardner physicians and twenty-five per cent of the physicians from the outlying towns have responded in this way. We have seen a clinic that was seldom admitting a patient now changed to an active organization. In the past two and one-half years since reorganization the largest attendance of patients present at any clinic has been sixteen and the largest attendance of physicians, twenty, from a group of fifty doctors in the district served by the clinic. One of the most helpful items that holds the interest of the physicians is the quarterly teaching clinics conducted by physicians from Boston, specialists in cancer work.

The Hospital has liberally furnished the clinic with nursing service and whatever equipment is needed for the examination of patients. Our clinics are held on the second and fourth Fridays at nine A.M., when the consulting roentgenologist is present. The hospital pathologist is obliged to attend all clinics. Physicians specializing in genitourinary, eye, ear, nose and throat diseases are always ready to respond to the demands of the clinic.

During the past year the clinic has recorded a total attendance of ninety-eight patients, fifty-four new admissions and forty-four follow-up cases. It is very evident that the physicians are making more and more use of the cancer clinic for diagnostic consultation and are finding much value in its services.

GLOUCESTER CANCER CLINIC

EZRA E. CLEAVES, M.D.
Chairman, Gloucester Cancer Committee

The Gloucester Cancer Clinic was organized in November, 1935. It is held at the Addison Gilbert Hospital, Gloucester, Massachusetts, a well-equipped, modern hospital of one hundred beds, with excellent laboratory and X-ray service. The facilities of the hospital are freely placed at the disposal of the clinic by the Board of Trustees, and the cooperation shown by all departments of the hospital is most commendable.

The cancer clinic has a limited territory from which to draw its patients. The area comprises the City of Gloucester and Towns of Rockport and Essex, with a combined population of about 30,000. Consequently, our clinic is a relatively small one.

The Chairman-Treasurer of the Clinic is appointed by the Medical Staff of the Hospital at its annual meeting. He is given full authority to appoint the committees for clinic administration and for group diagnostic service. The former committee consists of five members and the latter of six members, four serving permanently and two additional members acting in a rotary service of three months each. Thus all members of the medical staff of the hospital who desire are given an opportunity to participate in the diagnostic service of the clinic and to acquire experience in the diagnosis of diseases which come to the clinic, whether malignant or otherwise.

The clinic is held on the first and third Wednesdays of each month at ten A.M. At least four teaching clinics, conducted by eminent authorities on the subject, are held each year. These are of especial interest and value to the physicians of whom a considerable number are usually in attendance.

The method of conducting the clinic is as follows: The chairman assigns one of the patients to a member of the Diagnostic Committee who is furnished with a history of the case taken by the clinic social worker. A nurse, provided by the hospital, is present at the examination. The patient is examined by the physician assigned to the case and other members of the committee present participate in the examination. If further examination is required such as X-ray, biopsy, or laboratory procedure, this is carried out and the case is thoroughly discussed by the committee. A diagnosis is made and appropriate treatment advised the patient's physician.

The conclusions reached by the committee are dictated to the clinic stenographer who later types them and the case history is added to the clinic files. Other cases are assigned to other physicians in turn and the procedure is repeated. This feature of the clinic has a decided educational value to the physicians who take part in this work.

Since the opening of the clinic two and one-half years ago, one hundred and twenty-five patients with suspected cancer have been referred to and examined at the clinic. Of this number seventy-one were noncancer and fifty-four were cancer, the disease being located in various organs of the body, such as: skin, breast, ovaries, stomach, etc. Of the fifty-four cancer patients, four were treated at Pondville Hospital and thirty-five in Boston institutions such as the Huntington Memorial and Palmer Memorial Hospitals. The remaining number were treated at the local hospital. Seventeen patients in whom the diagnosis of advanced cancer was made died; six cases, diagnosed as cancer, are living with the disease still active. Of the fifty-four cases where a diagnosis of cancer was made thirty-one patients are living and without symptoms of the disease at the present time. This represents fifty-seven per cent with arrested disease.

It is our belief that the favorable results thus far obtained demonstrate the fact that the Gloucester Cancer Clinic fulfills a very important public health service in the community of Cape Ann.

THE LAWRENCE CANCER CLINIC

J. FORREST BURNHAM, M.D.
Chairman, Lawrence Cancer Committee

This clinic was established April 24, 1928, at the Lawrence General Hospital, Lawrence, Massachusetts, upon invitation of the Massachusetts Department of Public Health and has functioned semimonthly without intermission since that date. It has proved valuable to the cancer patients, to the physicians of the north half of Essex County, including those holding positions upon the Medical Staff of the hospital, to those others who have referred cases to the clinic and to those who have attended the teaching clinics now held five times annually. Before opening the clinic, the Lawrence Cancer Committee made a thorough study of the matter in its various relations to patient and physician, and finally came to a decision that the plan was worth while. This judgment has been verified by experience. For eight years the clinic covered the whole district encompassing the territory included in the Essex North District Medical Society, a district society of the Massachusetts Medical Society, but two years ago Newburyport instituted a cancer clinic of its own, under the supervision of the State Department of Public Health, at the Anna Jaques Hospital, located in Newburyport.

The growth in value of the clinic has been steady, and has been accompanied by the increasing confidence and respect of the physicians located in the vicinity of the clinic, as is demonstrated by the larger percentages of the cases which are referred to it by these physicians.

The publicity which the teaching clinics receive consists of a reading notice descriptive of the coming clinic and giving date and hour, in the preceding issue of the *New England Journal of Medicine*, and a first-class mail printed notice sent to the address of every physician in the district served by the clinic. A supply of large cards, six inches by ten inches, announcing the days and hours upon which the clinic is held, has been distributed to such physicians as wished to hang them on the wall of office or reception room. Smaller cards, three by five inches, giving similar information have been furnished to every physician in the district for handy desk reference.

The first regular teaching clinic was held in 1929 and they have continued without interruption. The teaching clinics are operated on a time schedule, beginning on the scheduled hour, with our consultant always prompt. The cases are presented in an orderly succession, the table, or reclining ones, being reserved for the last section. Many times certain cases are used as examples of a class which can be discussed in general terms, bearing on such divisions of the subject as breast, lip, etc. The attendance of physicians and cases has kept up well during the life of the clinic and is an indication of the continued value of the work.

The clinics are manned by the senior surgeon on duty in the hospital, associated with the senior medical man on duty, the roentgenologist, the pathologist, representatives of the various specialties as needed, and a member of the Junior Staff in turn.

The Lawrence General Hospital and its complete organization has been cooperative and helpful to the fullest degree in the work of the clinic, as indeed it has in all forward movements relating to every branch of medicine. Without this hearty interest, it is probable that the work of the clinic would not have reached its present standard.

The Medical Staff of the Lawrence General Hospital has afforded 100 per cent of its services during the past ten years and is a vital unit, by its assistance to the clinic, in supplying its scientific medical and surgical needs.

The clinic has cooperated with the State Department of Public Health in all its special occasions and anniversaries, and the Department has been loyal to the Lawrence Cancer Clinic at all times. The columns of the *New England Journal of Medicine*, the official organ of the Massachusetts Medical Society, under its present title, and the *Boston Medical and Surgical Journal*, its former name, have been ever open to aid our clinic through publication of our notices. For this assistance the clinic is appreciative.

Among the interesting features of the clinic has been the number of grateful patients who have been willing and able to appear as examples of cured cancer cases or ameliorated ones, who by the prompt action of the family physician working with the clinic, the hospitals and other allied instrumentalities have been placed on the road to complete or partially complete health. Since 1928, 1174 new patients have attended the Lawrence Cancer Clinic. Of this total, 394 have been new admissions diagnosed cancer. Thus, one of every three new admissions is a cancer patient. In April, 1938, at the time of our achievement celebration, sixty-nine cancer cases of five-year or longer survival with no recurrence were reported. These latter achievements have been gradually replacing the gloomy outlook which has for many years accompanied a diagnosis of malignant disease. Thus is the cancer problem on its way to a better solution.

LOWELL CANCER CLINIC

LOWELL CANCER CLINIC STAFF
Chairman, John H. Lambert, M.D.

The Lowell Cancer Clinic was organized under the auspices of the State Department of Public Health in 1927, with a cancer committee made up of physicians appointed by the Middlesex North District Medical Society as its representatives. Since there are three class A hospitals of nearly the same size in Lowell, these hospitals were all represented in this original committee. In the formation of the clinic staff two surgeons and a medical man are appointed from each hospital and the services so arranged that each group serves for two months. Each group includes one older man who has had the most experience and two younger men who have had less experience in the cancer clinic. In this way the group idea of examination is carried out and at the same time a larger and younger group of men are being interested in the work and trained to carry it on in the years to come. The so-called chief of clinic, who is chairman of the cancer clinic staff, attends each clinic and works with each group in turn for a part of the time in order to coordinate the methods throughout the various services. The clinic has the privilege of consulting with specialists in most of the major fields; that is, eye, ear, nose and throat, genitourinary, roentgenology, radiology, pathology and dentistry. The staff holds conferences at irregular intervals to consider and discuss various problems arising at the clinic.

By arrangement with the hospital authorities the clinic is held at the Outpatient Department of the Lowell General Hospital each week on Friday morning. The clinic is completely equipped with an adequate number of examining rooms and all facilities for special examinations.

The clinic has found great value in maintaining a uniform routine at all its meetings. First, the patient's history is taken, usually by the social worker, and the patient is made ready in one of the examining rooms by the nurse. The history is then read by one of the group of examining physicians and further details obtained if necessary. The patient is examined by the entire group with a graduate nurse in attendance. The case is then discussed in a separate room and each examining physician gives his opinion independently. The discussion is carried on until an agreement is reached as to the diagnosis and the form of treatment advised. This is then dictated to the regular clerk of the clinic in the presence of the clinic social worker so that if there are any obscure points she may get them cleared up immediately. The patient is then turned over to the social worker who carries out, so far as possible, the directions of the examining group. Any case requiring further investigation by a specialist is referred at once to one of the consulting specialists. The pathologist, radiologist and roentgenologist are usually in the hospital and easily called in if it is considered advisable. If necessary, the patient is admitted to the hospital for biopsy or other methods of diagnosis before his treatment is recommended.

The disposition of the patient is made according to his financial situation, personal wishes, and the equipment of the institution to which he desires to go. All patients referred by physicians are referred back with diagnosis and recommendation as to treatment. Cases not referred by a physician are sent to whatever hospital or physician may be desired. The social worker cares for all special arrangements for admission to the hospital and for treatment with the physician.

Excluding the Pondville clinic, the Lowell clinic has had the greatest total volume of clinic admissions. Through December, 1937, there were 3744 total new admissions and 584 new admissions for cancer. In April, 1938, the clinic, at a special teaching demonstration, reported seventy-five cases of cancer living with no recurrence for five years or longer.

In accordance with the policy of the State Department of Public Health, teaching clinics with consultants from Boston and New York, are now conducted by the Lowell Cancer Clinic. These have been attended by the majority of interested physicians of Lowell. They have proved to be of considerable value to those who attend them.

LYNN CANCER CLINIC

WILLIAM T. HOPKINS, M.D.

Chairman, Lynn Cancer Clinic Committee

The Lynn Cancer Clinic is one of the Massachusetts State-aided diagnostic cancer clinics, approved by the American College of Surgeons.

In cooperation with the State Department of Public Health, the clinic is conducted under the management of the Lynn Cancer Committee which consists of five members of the Lynn Medical Fraternity appointed by the president of that society which includes in its membership one hundred physicians resident in Greater Lynn. The personnel of this committee remained unchanged during the first ten years of operation of the clinic.

The clinic meets each Friday at Lynn Hospital which furnishes quarters, equipment for examination and a nurse, as a contribution to the project.

For the first eight years of its activity the staff was composed of the three chiefs of surgical service of Lynn Hospital, serving singly for four months each, with a consultant from Boston in attendance once a month during the first three years. For the past eight years a consultant has conducted a teaching demonstration clinic three or four times each year.

Staff conferences are held four times a year.

To both of these exercises all members of the profession are welcome.

In its early days the Lynn Cancer Committee appointed a subcommittee called the educational committee which was composed largely of laymen. This group still functions as the Lynn Cancer Clinic Association.

Educational efforts have chiefly consisted of providing doctors to address small or large groups of people upon the subject of cancer whenever opportunity offered or could be induced, such as the occasion of the annual Y. M. C. A. health week and at meetings of social, religious or labor organizations and service clubs. An occasional public luncheon has been conducted with an address by some speaker of note and a report of progress by the clinic committee.

Publicity has been generously offered by the newspapers and has been freely used until three years ago when the policy was changed and no advertisement of the clinic has since been made in articles furnished the newspapers.

This change of policy has been followed by a great falling off of patients coming as a result of newspaper publicity and a notable increase in patients with cancer coming upon the recommendation of physicians. The net result has been a smaller total of new patients but still an increase in the number of patients coming with cancer. This might be regarded as a desirable outcome and such may prove to be the case. Unfortunately, however, a good many of these new cases coming from physicians are well advanced in the course of the disease, which is no reflection upon the doctor, since he sends them promptly, but leads one to wonder if the former newspaper publicity might have brought some of these patients to the clinic in an earlier and more hopeful stage. As a result of this speculation and of their own initiative the Lynn Cancer Committee proposes to resume local newspaper publicity.

On March 1, 1935, the staff of the clinic was enlarged and since that date three surgeons, a gynecologist, an internist and a pathologist are assigned to each clinic. Under the present arrangement two surgeons act as chiefs of service in periods of two months each. Before a diagnosis of cancer is recorded at least three of the staff must concur in this opinion.

From the beginning of the clinic it has been required that the diagnosis of cancer must be supported by confirmatory pathological report for the final record.

Patients acknowledging no family physician are assisted by the social worker in securing prompt adequate treatment. Anyone, of course, is at liberty privately to consult a doctor of his own selection but such arrangements may not be made at the clinic or through the agency of the clinic.

No charge has ever been made to a patient for consultation at this clinic. Patients who are financially able are expected to pay for X-ray service. If unable they receive the service free. The same is true of rapid frozen section diagnosis and the Aschheim-Zondek test.

Most of the cases requiring surgical treatment only can be cared for locally, but of the 109 cancers new to the clinic seen in 1937 it was necessary to send sixty to other hospitals for treatment by radiation.

In addition to the funds supplied by the State Department of Public Health a small contribution is usually made annually by the Community Fund Association of Greater Lynn which finances wholly, or in part, the twenty-five affiliated private philanthropies of our community. Appreciative patients or friends also give their mite.

These contributions are of financial importance but are especially welcome because of the implied endorsement of the usefulness of the clinic to the community.

The achievement of the clinic can, perhaps, best be indicated by the following figures:

Total number of new patients, April 22, 1927, to July 1, 1938 .. 3,648
Total number of cancer patients, same period 874
Total number of cancer patients, April 22, 1927, to January 1, 1933 363
Five-year survivals after treatment, as of January 1, 1938 159

The five-year survivals of cancer patients seen prior to the beginning of the five-year period ending January 1, 1938, is thus equivalent to 43.8 per cent.

The number of certified deaths from cancer in Lynn in 1937 was 111
The number of new cases of cancer seen by the clinic in 1937 was 109

These figures may be used as a basis of estimate of the service to the community by the clinic.

The Lynn Cancer Clinic Association is conducting a campaign to raise, by public subscription, a radiation fund for the purchase of radium and a high voltage X-ray machine with which to treat cancer patients in Lynn. About twenty per cent of the estimated amount necessary is in sight.

A member of the clinic staff has been designated to receive intensive instruction in the science and technique of radiation and has been acquiring this knowledge for more than a year already. It is expected that when the equipment becomes available the clinic will be prepared to furnish to patients whatever treatment may be required.

The needs of the community with respect to cancer are an awakening to a livelier realization of the importance of the subject, a more accurate knowledge of facts and a more correct appreciation of the possibilities of cure, on the part of both the general public and the medical profession.

Correct information upon cancer might well be included in a required course on hygiene in the junior high schools in an attempt to forestall the implantation of the traditional false views now generally held.

The needs of the clinic are radium and a high voltage X-ray machine with which to treat cancer in Lynn.

The foregoing figures are sufficiently impressive to demonstrate the possibilities of benefit of treatment and the usefulness of the clinic to the community. It would seem that the community which is the beneficiary of the activities of the clinic would be willing to provide the necessary equipment for still greater service.

The prospect is good. The rate of speed only is in question.

NEW BEDFORD CANCER CLINIC

EDWIN D. GARDNER, M.D.
Chairman, New Bedford Cancer Clinic

The State-aided Cancer Clinic in New Bedford has now been in existence for ten years. Since the purpose of this article is to state the methods by which this clinic is conducted, I do not feel that a discussion of clinic statistics would be of any great value. However, I feel that it would not be out of place to state that during these ten years we have seen 2844 new patients and of this number, there have been 600 new admissions with cancer. In our experience the site of cancer most frequently seen is the skin, with the breast a close second, and female genital organs third.

All of the cases who definitely have cancer are followed until the patient is lost or dead. Precancerous lesions are followed in our clinic until there is a definite cure. The interval between visits in this follow-up naturally varies according to the nature and site of the lesion.

This clinic is purely a diagnostic and follow-up clinic. It is true that the staff recommends the nature of treatments to be given but do not institute treatments unless the case be a private patient of one of the clinic staff or is admitted to the wards of St. Luke's Hospital while one of the clinic staff is on hospital service.

Until the present it has been found impractical to maintain a cancer ward in the Hospital. The staff of St. Luke's Hospital has been advised that the cancer clinic staff are glad at any time to see any cancer patient who may be in the Hospital. We do not feel that we are in a position to do more than that under existing circumstances.

Every physician who refers a patient to the cancer clinic is sent a written report of the staff's opinion as to the diagnosis and suggestions for treatment and care is taken not to exceed this limit. All physicians are always welcome to visit the clinic and join in the diagnostic consultation. However, of this privilege small advantage has been taken.

The routine through which a patient goes when he comes to our clinic is as follows: The social status and history of complaints from a lay point of view is carefully elicited by our social service worker. Following this, a medical history is taken by a hospital interne. The patient is then dispatched to a private clinic room and is prepared for examination by the nurse. There is a preliminary examination of the patient by one member of our staff. Unless the diagnosis is very evidently not cancer, three or four members of this staff examine the patient, thereby making the diagnosis and suggestions for treatment as certain as possible. There is this individual conference after the examination of each patient and after all patients have been seen a final conference, including all members of the staff, is held to discuss and evaluate any special problems. After the consultation for each patient one member of the staff dictates to the stenographer all the findings and suggestions and the letter to be sent to the referring physician. For every case carefully typewritten records of the initial visit, special diagnostic measures and follow-up notes are prepared and filed by the social worker.

The clinic organization is as follows: On the active staff, which includes only those who attend the clinic regularly, are two surgeons, an internist and a radiologist. In addition to these there is a social service worker, a stenographer, one or more internes as necessary, and a graduate nurse who is in charge of the Hospital Outpatient Department. When necessary the supervising nurse has available the services of several other nurses. The hospital pathologist is actively consulted by the clinic staff and is always available for consultation. In addition to the above-mentioned the staff have the services of physicians representing various specialties who have agreed to see cases in consultation at any time.

The staff present in the clinic always feel free to give an opinion either as to diagnosis or treatment and it is our feeling that the conferences contribute in large measure to the teaching value of this clinic. If any physician at any time has any constructive criticism we welcome it inasmuch as our desire is to improve the clinic as much as possible.

NEWBURYPORT CANCER CLINIC

LINCOLN C. PEIRCE, M.D.
Chairman, Newburyport Cancer Clinic Committee

The Newburyport Cancer Clinic, serving an area comprising the cities and towns bordering the Merrimack River from Haverhill to the sea and down the shore to Rowley and Ipswich, has completed the first two and one-half years of its existence. As evidenced by the attendance of patients, there is a real need for such a clinic in this northeast corner of the State. The Anna Jaques Hospital, where the clinics are held the first and third Tuesdays of each month, serves as a very satisfactory point for this service.

The personnel of this clinic is comprised of an active committee of three, and an advisory committee of physicians representing the various cities and towns in the district. There is a part-time social worker and secretary. For the first two years there was an active rotating staff of three doctors for each clinic, including most of the physicians of the district. Beginning in 1938 a permanent staff has been serving, these members having been selected from those who have shown the most active interest in the clinic. During the first two years, the cancer committee chose to have the services six to eight times a year of one consultant, Dr. Grantley W. Taylor, of Boston, the value of whose counsel was well borne out by the good attendance at these consultation clinics. This was an excellent arrangement because it gave our local clinic staff a more conversant knowledge of cancer in general. With the advent of 1938, it was decided to rotate our consultants in order that added stimulus might be obtained from the opinions and advice of a group specializing in cancer work.

The attendance at clinic of patients and doctors is somewhat increasing at present and it is felt that the clinic will continue to fill its need in this part of the State. This need would seem to be actual, notwithstanding the fact that Newburyport is favored with excellent consultants in all branches of medicine and surgery. Naturally a good many cases of cancer are handled privately through these channels. The clinic has, nevertheless, seen about three new cases at each of its meetings and has a good attendance of follow-up patients each clinic day.

In July, 1938, the clinic staff are anticipating a visit from Dr. Harry Friedman, consultant from Boston whose X-ray work in the field of cancer is well-known, and whose visit to us should be of special interest because the medical group in this part of the State is at present considering the feasibility of adding new X-ray therapy apparatus to the Anna Jaques Hospital equipment.

In the conduct of the clinic, there are attendant difficulties, chiefly in securing punctual attendance of the staff physicians. Clinic attendance imposes obvious impingements on one's duty to his private practice. The doctors are interested in the success of the cancer clinic but the demands of one's private practice can not always be circumvented in any way without considerable personal sacrifice. We have overcome this difficulty somewhat by the appointment of staff alternates. Another great difficulty is that the staff necessarily is made up largely of general practitioners who are not supposed to know any more about cancer than their colleagues referring patients to the clinic. This for a moment is a deterrent to its progress but with the appointment of a permanent staff it is hoped that the knowledge gained by constant attendance at these clinics will augment the authoritative prestige of such a permanent staff. Until such a status exists, the staff are making frequent use of the services of a consultant and thus elevate the value of the clinic in the estimation of all local doctors.

In the Newburyport Clinic the proportion of cancer to noncancer cases is about one to every four patients. As yet we have not been in existence long enough to show a group of cured cancers but we feel, of course, that a great many of our cancer cases already treated will fall into the cured group five years hence.

The clinic to date attended by 162 new patients has met fifty-eight times. This would seem to justify the existence of the clinic; the staff looks to the future with considerable hope.

NORTH ADAMS CANCER CLINIC

MARTIN M. BROWN, M.D.
Chief of Clinic

The North Adams Diagnostic Clinic sponsored by the Massachusetts Department of Public Health is under the local management of a special committee chosen from members of the Northern Berkshire Medical Society. The present committee is Dr. J. W. Bunce, Secretary-Treasurer; Dr. R. J. Carpenter, Dr. N. B. McWilliams, Dr. Byron Howe and Dr. Martin M. Brown, Chairman and Chief of Staff.

The North Adams Cancer Committee submit the following brief report of clinic activities: The North Adams Cancer Clinic, approved by the American College of Surgeons, meets the second and fourth Thursdays of each month at 4:00 P.M. The North Adams Cancer Clinic was originally a part of the Berkshire County Cancer Clinic which began in 1928. In 1934, under clinic re-organization, the North Adams Clinic became a separate entity and has continued so until the present time. The estimated total attendance of new patients at the clinic for this period has been 235. The total attendance of new patients with cancer is fifty-four. The clinic has shown a slow but progressive growth especially during the past two years. Since January, 1937, a total of ninety-three patients have been examined and referred back to their attending physicians; or if special treatment were required, arrangements for admittance to the State cancer hospitals or other institutions were made through the assistance of our social worker. Of this group of ninety-three, twenty were diagnosed and proven cancer. All cancer patients are receiving periodic follow-up. During the same period seven have received irradiation, four have been relieved by surgical operations and two improved by palliative measures. The remaining seventy-three proved noncancerous have been aided by the reassurance which the clinic consultation offers.

The clinic staff is pleased to note the increase of a large number of apparently cured cases that have gone five years or more after receiving correct treatment. On April 27, 1938, a special cured cancer clinic with presentation of thirteen clinic cases and a number of private cancer cases was held at the North Adams Hospital. This proved valuable not only from the point of view of demonstrating clinic activities and accomplishments of the past few years but also for publicizing the work of cancer control for which the clinic is a nucleus.

The staff of the North Adams Cancer Clinic believes the public at large and the profession as a whole are realizing the importance of an early diagnosis and curative treatment and that every possible means should be utilized to broaden the scope of our diagnostic clinics.

NORTHAMPTON CANCER CLINIC

THOMAS F. CORRIDEN, M.D.
Chairman, Northampton Cancer Committee

The Northampton Cancer Clinic was established at the Cooley Dickinson Hospital on September 5, 1935. It was endorsed by the Committee on Postgraduate Instruction of the Massachusetts Medical Society and supported by the Department of Public Health of the Commonwealth of Massachusetts.

Clinics are held the first and third Thursdays of each month at ten A.M. and teaching clinics are held four times a year. To date, there has been a total of one hundred and sixty-two patients receiving the benefits of this clinic.

The purpose of the clinic is to furnish physicians and the public the services of group consultation in cancer and to improve the knowledge of cancer among both physicians and laity. The group furnishes a diagnosis and outlines treatment for any person suspected of having cancer irrespective of financial rating.

While any individual is admitted to the clinic, every effort is made to have the family physician either come with the patient to the clinic or send the patient with such information as may be available. All patients are referred back to their family physicians.

From September, 1935, through 1936, fifty-six patients attended the clinic, while during the year 1937 sixty-one patients attended. Of this total number of patients, sixteen were Northampton residents, fifty-seven were State Mental Hospital patients, and forty-four cases were from outlying towns.

Fifty-nine of these cases were treated at the Cooley Dickinson Hospital, twenty at Pondville and four at other hospitals. There were thirty-four cases who refused treatment or required none.

In April, 1938, a "cured cancer clinic" was held at the hospital with Dr. Channing C. Simmons of Boston as the guest speaker. At this clinic, attended by thirty-eight local physicians, there were eleven cases presented which can be considered as "cures."

PITTSFIELD CANCER CLINIC
PITTSFIELD CANCER CLINIC COMMITTEE

The activities of the Pittsfield Cancer Clinic consist mainly of regular clinics held twice a month, conducted by a staff of three to six local doctors, and occasional special teaching clinics conducted by visiting doctors who are well-known authorities on the diagnosis and treatment of cancer.

Our special teaching clinics are very interesting, helpful and well attended. Consultants have been Dr. Dean Lewis, Dr. Shields Warren, Dr. Leland McKittrick, and Dr. Ernest M. Daland. The average number of doctors attending these special clinics is thirty-eight and the average number of patients eighteen. The clinics conducted by visiting consultants are definitely stimulating.

As an aid to attendance, clinic notices are mailed to the physicians and dentists of Pittsfield and Southern Berkshire a few days before the first clinic of each month. Patients are also notified when they should return for check up.

For the first six months of 1938 forty-two patients have been seen at the local clinic; fourteen of these were new admissions, twenty-four were follow-up and four were nonclinic cases; i.e., private patients demonstrated to the doctors attending one of the teaching clinics.

Cases requiring treatment with radium or deep X-ray therapy are sent to the Cancer Section of the Westfield State Sanatorium. Westfield, only fifty-five miles from Pittsfield, makes cancer therapy easily accessible when needed.

In conducting both our teaching clinics and regular clinics, St. Luke's Hospital has supplied ample room equipment and efficient hospital service so the patients are cared for readily and without too much intermingling of patients with unpleasant conditions.

When arranging for the Achievement Clinic held on April 26, the clinic staff were impressed with the helpfulness of these cancer clinics since there were a large variety of "cured" or arrested cases to present.

SPRINGFIELD CANCER CLINIC
JOHN E. DWYER, M.D.
Chief of Cancer Clinic Staff

The cancer clinics in Springfield were established on March 4, 1927 under the sponsorship of the Massachusetts Department of Public Health. The three Springfield hospitals were represented by doctors selected from each staff and the clinics were held in rotation in the respective hospitals on Friday afternoons until May, 1935. At that time it was decided that for all concerned it would be much more advantageous to have the clinic at one hospital and the members of the cancer groups representing the Wesson Memorial Hospital, the Mercy Hospital, and the Springfield Hospital met and selected the Springfield Hospital as a place where the cancer clinics would be held in the future. The same method of rotating groups from the three hospitals is still in use.

In the beginning a group of lay persons selected from officers of the Visiting Nurse Association, the Anti-Tuberculosis Association, the Springfield Federation of Women's Clubs, as well as groups from various industries, formed a committee to publicize the cancer clinics. This publicity has been discontinued for several years.

From the beginning a graduate nurse has been in charge at the clinics, at first only part time but as the volume of work increased she has been made a full time worker. The staff representing each hospital consists of a surgeon, an assistant surgeon and a pathologist and any others who might wish to volunteer. One physician from each staff assumes the responsibility for the conduct of his clinic and the selection of the staff. The scope of the work consists in diagnosis and recommendation for treatment, and where patients are referred by physicians, reports are sent to them stating the result of examination and the suggested methods of treatment. Patients who have not been referred by physicians and have no regular attending physicians are referred to local hospitals in the event that they are able to pay their expenses and if not, they are referred to the Pondville Hospital. Since the opening of the Cancer Section of the Westfield State Sanatorium, however, these patients are referred there.

The responsibility of seeing that the clinic recommendations are carried out rests primarily with the clinic nurse or the social worker. The social service includes follow-up of all cancer and precancer cases and continues until removal of the lesion in case of precancer or until death in the case of cancer. At the present time there are 175 cancer patients on the follow-up list. The attendance at these clinics has averaged about 332 patients a year for the past five years:

1933	266 patients examined	38 cancers		
1934	415	"	"	45 "
1935	359	"	"	54 "
1936	289	"	"	35 "
1937	326	"	"	43 "

The average number of cases diagnosed as cancer was forty-three per year during the past five years. During this time numerous biopsies have been performed and where there has been a qeustion of gastrointestinal lesion, complete X-ray series have been taken. The value of this service is unquestionable and it has a very definite use in this community. It is noticeable that more patients are being sent in by physicians for confirmation or diagnosis of suspicious lesions, and it is encouraging to the cancer group that more physicians are taking advantage of the clinic yearly.

For the past three years there have been teaching clinics held with recognized workers in the cancer field presiding. This year on April first, the clinic was conducted by Dr. Ashley W. Oughterson, Assistant Professor of Surgery, and Dr. Hugh Wilson from the X-ray Department, both of Yale University Medical School. Five year or longer "cured" cancer patients were discussed. A list of forty patients who have shown cures from five to ten years are now on our records; of these, twelve were brought to the clinic and presented and their cases discussed. Seventy-five doctors attended this clinic representing twelve cities and towns in Hampden County. Dr. Oughterson and Dr. Wilson made a very impressive and instructive team and their discussion was highly appreciated by those in attendance. On April seventh another teaching clinic was held at the Springfield Academy of Medicine where Dr. Clarence C. Little of the Roscoe B. Jackson Memorial

Laboratory of Bar Harbor, Maine, gave a most interesting and informative talk on recent advances in cancer research based on his experiments with mice during the past twenty-five years and the more recent knowledge of mouse cancer with reference to heredity and type. About one hundred physicians from the cities and towns in Hampden County were in attendance.

It is planned to have several more of these teaching clinics for the fall months.

WORCESTER CANCER CLINIC

ERNEST L. HUNT, M.D.

Chairman, Worcester Cancer Clinic Committee

The activities of the Worcester Cancer Clinic, which has been in operation for eleven years, may be divided into two periods.

During the earlier period each of five hospitals held one or more clinics per week conducted by its own staff. With this arrangement the local cancer committee and the social worker served as coordinating agencies and the clinics covered diagnostic, consultative and treatment phases. During this period, the educational effort aimed to reach the public was largely through the public press.

In the later period our clinical activities were reduced to a diagnostic-consultative service, leaving treatment in the hands of the referring doctor, hospital or other agency. In 1935 the clinic was concentrated at Memorial Hospital where excellent office and examining facilities were put at our disposal by the hospital authorities. The policy relative to educational work was also changed to utilize the physicians as the chief medium through which, by means of informal talks to small groups, the public might be informed.

Our experience for the entire period of eleven years, 1927 to 1937 inclusive, is in summary as follows: 2788 cases have been examined of which 869 were diagnosed as cancer, 789 new patients and 80 patients first seen postoperatively. Of these, 441 have died and 428 are living. Of the living, 166 of a total 408 patients seen prior to January, 1933, have survived five or more years. Four of these are known to have recurrences, leaving 162, or 39.6 per cent as our score for five-year cures and 40.6 per cent for five-year survivals.

The total clinic expenditures, appropriated by the Commonwealth of Massachusetts, have been $17,334.44. Our chief items of expense have been the salaries of our social worker and her clerk, office incidentals, and transportation of patients. This does not include funds raised by the local Junior League to pay part of the social worker's salary and to transport patients during the first two years of the clinic. Except for halls in which to hold public meetings the clinic committee have never had to pay rentals because the hospitals have generously furnished accomodations for the clinics both routine and teaching. Since 1935, Memorial Hospital has furnished a comfortable and convenient office with clinical facilities in the Outpatient building where all routine clinics are conducted. Worcester City, St. Vincent's, Hahnemann, Milford and Clinton Hospitals, as well as Memorial, have cooperated splendidly as hosts for our teaching clinics.

All doctors serving the clinic, except those coming from other cities to conduct the special teaching clinics, have served without remuneration. Each patient is seen on the average by three doctors, all experts in some phase of cancer work. Had they received the customary minimal fee of five dollars each, the cost would have been approximately doubled. Thus it may be said that the clinic staff has furnished gratuitous service amounting to $13,940.

While the crude cancer death rate of Worcester has risen during the period in which the clinic has been operating, when the aging of the population has been considered the rise is extremely slight and so much less than the New York experience as to warrant an optimistic conclusion.

It is difficult to make a just appraisal of the value of the work of the clinic. During our achievement week we derived some satisfaction from the fact that we could list 162 five-year or longer verified cancer cures. They, at least, are tangible evidence of service rendered. There are, however, many less tangible services to the credit of the clinic. Among these intangibles perhaps the greatest is the comfort to the minds of those persons examined and found *not* to have cancer. These total 1919 persons since 1927. Next I would place the mitigation of hardship and suffering of those having incurable cancer through the ministrations of our social worker so splendidly seconded by the district nursing associations. Again there is the constant effort to educate both the physician and the population to the importance of early discovery, prompt diagnosis, prompt and appropriate treatment. At present, the plan of utilizing the local physicians to instruct lay groups in their own communities has seemed to be excellent and of increasing promise in our educational campaign. The large number of lay groups who have heard these talks and the lay committees cooperating with the State Department of Public Health merit and receive our sincere thanks.

Unspectacular and often baffling as is the effort to cheat cancer of its victims, one has but to reflect that each case which comes to a fatal termination has had to undergo six to eighteen months or more of invalidism, often associated with much pain, always distressing in its onward march to inevitable death, nearly always a heavy economic burden both in loss of productivity and in cost of care, to realize that prevention, mitigation and cure of cancer is an outstanding humane imperative upon science and upon the State to whom the health and well-being of its citizens is a trust.

CANCER EDUCATION IN MASSACHUSETTS

FRANCES A. MACDONALD, A.B.
*Junior Epidemiologist, Division of Cancer and Other Chronic Diseases
Massachusetts Department of Public Health*

The educational plan of the Massachusetts Cancer Program as it operates today is a highly decentralized type of organization conceived as the result of studies evaluating the first eight years of the whole program. These studies indicated that the local physicians, when once consulted by cancer patients, had reduced appreciably the average delay of these patients in obtaining treatment whereas no reduction in the average delay in consulting physicians on the part of cancer patients was noted over this period.

Because the physicians, broadly speaking, were educating their cancer patients to the extent that they followed the treatment advised, promptly, and because the local physician rather than the cancer specialist is the first to see incipient cancer, the program calling for the organization of a Cooperative Cancer Control Committee in each community in Massachusetts was devised with the local physician as the pivotal figure.

Prior to this change in policy, the educational objectives had been to disseminate sound information on cancer, with emphasis on the curability of early cancer, and its symptoms, and to publicize the cancer clinics in and around those communities in which they were held.

Newspaper releases, the use of radio, lectures by specialists on the various aspects of cancer, and the distribution of pamphlets were the methods employed.

Local associate committees were formed in each of the clinic centers, whose members were appointed by the medical cancer committee. These associate committees were made up of representatives of the various social agencies and other civic-minded persons, usually nonmedical. They encouraged local organizations to accept speakers on cancer, provided either by the Department or by their clinic staffs, distributed pamphlets, carried on local newspaper publicity for the clinics, and were of assistance to the clinics in other exigencies.

In order to provide for the educational work in communities not represented on the associate committees Department staff members asked the cooperation of individuals in a number of these communities, in some cases the president of the Visiting Nurse Association, or the public health chairman of a women's club, in giving out information regarding the State Cancer Program, distributing literature and placing speakers.

Under the former policy State-wide campaigns were held at various intervals. In 1928 the first of these was conducted during five days in April under the joint direction of the Massachusetts Medical Society, the Massachusetts Branch of the American Society for the Control of Cancer, and the State Department of Public Health.

The plans outlined by the Campaign Committee included the following:

1. A mass meeting in each city in which there was a State-aided clinic.
2. A request addressed to each of the eighteen District Medical Societies that a special meeting to consider cancer control be held during that week.
3. Special clinics for physicians to be conducted in connection with the regularly established cancer clinics.
4. The cooperation of the larger industrial, mercantile, and public service concerns by the distribution of pay envelope slips and bill enclosures; by publishing in their house organs an article on cancer control from material to be supplied by the committee; and by arranging for speakers to address their employees.
5. Extension of the scope of the speakers' bureau through an enlarged staff of speakers which included a number of eminent medical men from outside the State.
6. An information booth centrally located where literature and information would be available.
7. Extensive use of the press and the radio.

In 1932 an "Achievement Week" was conducted. The Cancer Committee of the Massachusetts Medical Society in cooperation with the Massachusetts Branch of the American Society for the Control of Cancer and State Department of Public Health asked the Boston Dispensary, the Free Hospital for Women, the Collis P. Huntington Memorial Hospital, the Massachusetts General Hospital, the Palmer Memorial Hospital and the Pondville Hospital to cooperate in offering "cured" cancer clinics. Selected cases demonstrating palliation were shown in addition to the "cured" cases. Sections of these "cured" cases were reviewed by a committee of pathologists to confirm the initial presence of cancer.

A series of meetings was held with lectures comprising a course on cancer, to which all physicians and dentists were invited. Special clinics were held for dentists at the Harvard University and Tufts College Dental Schools.

Meetings for the cancer education of the laity were held in Boston and the other clinic cities. The local medical cancer committees arranged for the public meetings in their respective localities.

This educational work served to change the public attitude toward hearing about cancer from one of reluctance and often fear encountered early in the program to one of agreeable acceptance after several years of gradually improved manner of presentation of cancer information. This change of attitude was prerequisite to the introduction of a new method of education.

The new type of educational program begun in 1934 was devised to include in active participation all physicians and all adult lay persons in individual communities, by means of a cooperative organization with communty responsibility its basis for eventual success in controlling cancer. The major defects of the methods of education previously employed had to be overcome.

The opportunity to learn about cancer had to be made as uniform as possible in every community in the State. Consistent and far-reaching presentation of cancer information throughout the year had to be tried because concentrated publicity in limited areas at varying intervals had shown no lasting effectiveness. The public educational meetings during cancer campaigns at which as many as two hundred to one thousand persons might be present, were not conducive to questions or general discussions, which are essential to the clarifying of misconceptions concerning cancer.

The Cooperative Cancer Control Committee program has as its objective the dissemination of cancer information by continuous and consistent teaching of individuals as members of small groups. The local physicians whose efforts were bringing about the only tangible improvement noted during the first eight years of the program are the teachers in this new plan of education.

Preliminary to the organization of a Cooperative Cancer Control Committee the community is studied by the Department to ascertain its type, whether residential, agricultural, industrial, etc.; its population structure, its age, sex and nationality distribution and language difficulties; its organizations—religious, fraternal, social, labor, foreign, political, patriotic and service; the number of physicians serving it and other pertinent information that may be obtained from census reports or directories. A representative of the Department then calls on the local board of health to enlist its cooperation and to obtain supplementary information.

The physicians in the community are then contacted. In some of the larger communities the cooperation of the physicians has been obtained by presentation of the program before the local medical society, in other cases by letter, but in most of the communities the physicians have been personally contacted.

As the object of the program is to have each adult person know enough about cancer to act promptly in the event of any abnormalities, the logical approach, both from the point of view of reaching the greatest number of persons with an almost individual type of teaching, and of answering the problem of meeting places for these persons, is through the various types of groups, mentioned above, which are already organized. The head of each organization is interviewed and asked to delegate a member of his group to be present at an organization meeting where representatives of every group will gather, to hear the program and the disease cancer discussed, and to elect a permanent Central Committee.

At this organization meeting the Chairman of the local Board of Health, or someone delegated or suggested by him, usually presides. Staff members of the State Department speak on the cancer program and cancer, the disease. The five major activities of the cancer program are described, namely; hospitalization, tumor diagnostic service, research, diagnostic clinics, and education. The educational plan whereby small groups are asked to invite a local physician to speak to them on cancer once a year is described. The importance of having a local physician speak is emphasized because he is the one who first sees the cancer case and he is the one who can educate the local individuals to cooperate in its early detection, because he knows better than anyone else the particular fears and misinformation which may be hindering individuals in the community from giving early attention to any abnormalities. The advantage of a group small enough so that its members will feel free to ask any questions in a round-table type of discussion with the physician is stressed over the large group in which diffidence on the part of some individuals and the unwieldly size of the audience may inhibit discussion so that the phobias and false ideas which may be carried to the meeting are retained without any satisfactory answer.

A medical member of the staff of the State Department speaks on the disease cancer at this organization meeting, and answers any questions at the end of his talk. By this procedure the representatives of the organizations present hear the sort of talk that their organizations may expect to hear and are enabled to inform their groups that nothing objectionable to individual sensibilities may be expected.

The presiding officer selects a nominating committee, its number ranging generally from three to six depending on the size of the community. This committee retires to an adjoining room and selects from two to twenty members to a Central Committee, depending on the number of organizations in the community and the number of major divisions of groups which must be represented. In a small town with ten or twelve organizations, a chairman and secretary are usually enough; whereas in a large city with two to four hundred organizations as many as twenty members may be required in order to have each broad group—foreign, labor, fraternal, etc.—represented on the Central Committee by one member. After the slate is approved by the whole group present, the members of the newly elected committee are asked to remain after the adjournment of the meeting to arrange to meet in the very near future to allot the work to be done among its several members. A representative of the Department in many cases attends the first meeting of this Central Committee in order to answer questions which may arise. Pamphlets on the State Cancer Program and cancer, the disease, are available at the organization meeting for those who desire them.

Each representative of a cooperating organization is considered a member of the Cooperative Cancer Control Committee. The Central Committee is elected to aid organizations desiring assistance in making arrangements for a local physician to speak, to remind organizations of the program at intervals if they have not had a cancer talk, to see that the cancer talks held are reported to the State Department of Public Health, and to serve as a contact with the Department not only in the event of some special problem in relation to the local program but also when the local progress is followed from time to time by visits from a Department representative.

There are some adult individuals in almost every community who are not members of any organized group. The committees are attempting to reach these individuals in various ways. Individual clubs in some instances hold open meetings, inviting the public when a cancer talk is to be heard. A group of women not affiliated with any club has met in a private home with a physician to discuss cancer. When Cooperative Cancer Control Committees are organized in all the communities in the State a more uniform effort to reach these unorganized groups will be made.

With two hundred and seventy-two communities already cooperating in the fourth year of this program, it is possible to evaluate its influence now to a greater degree than was anticipated at its inception. In a program having five phases the influence of one cannot be separated completely from the others as each activity hinges to some degree on the other. The effectiveness of this type of education over the former type has been manifest from an early period in the Cooperative Cancer Control Committee organization program and has persistently increased. The median delay in months of patients with cancer in the State-aided clinics between first symptoms and visit to a physician, which had not been shortened during the first eight years of the program, was shortened by a month in 1936 and this improvement continued through 1937. The percentage of cancer patients being referred to the clinics by physicians has increased at a greater rate since the inauguration of this program. That this education is acquainting more physicians as well as lay persons with the facilities offered by the State Cancer Program is evidenced by a much larger increase in the percentage of physicians sending pathological specimens to the tumor diagnostic service, maintained by the Department in conjunction with the Harvard Cancer Commission, from communities having Cooperative Cancer Control Committees than from the communities without these committees.

The cooperation of the medical profession in agreeing to speak on cancer has been practically universal. In those instances where a physician has been uwilling to speak, bad health or some other substantial reason has usually prevented it. Their agreement with the aims and method of this educational program has been almost one hundred per cent. Many physicians have requested to receive the cancer bulletins sent out each month by the Department and many have made use of sample talks on cancer which are furnished on request. Several of the physicians who can speak in foreign languages have, in addition to speaking to foreign groups locally, given of their time to travel to other communities to speak before foreign groups when there was no local physician who could speak in the given language.

The laity has an appreciation of the simplicity of operation of this plan and the way in which it is adaptable to all types of organizations. The prompt cooperation of so many organizations in having cancer talks indicates the need many of their members have felt for the intelligent discussion of the problem which the authorized local practitioner can present.

In 1938 in order to cooperate in the nation-wide observance of April as "Cancer Month", in addition to "cured" cancer clinics conducted by each State-aided Clinic, and special radio addresses on cancer, local committees at the request of follow-up workers from the Department encouraged individual groups to hold cancer talks during that month. There were approximately one thousand meetings in April held in the communities organized at that time with an approximate attendance of thirty thousand.

At this writing (July, 1938,) two hundred and seventy-two communities have Cooperative Cancer Control Committees, with eight thousand cooperating organizations. The progress of organization has necessarily been slower than is considered desirable from the standpoint of the population covered because of the small staff which is available for this work. As the result of experience in the communities organized earlier in this program, the organization work has evolved into such a thorough and efficient system that there is reason to expect little need of reorganization among the communities more recently organized.

Follow-up visits to committee members in organized communities have been less frequent than is considered the optimum but have proved to be most beneficial in precipitating action on plans for cancer talks which have been in the minds of cooperating groups but needed only to be brought before their attention again by the Central Committee.

Eighty-three communities including all of Boston with the exception of Hyde Park remain to be organized. Preliminary work is being done in Boston at present. Although there is a large percentage of the population of Massachusetts in Boston and the communities surrounding it, it is felt that these communities have been in a position to suffer less by being organized last than the communities which were never or rarely reached by the cancer program before 1935.

THE STATE TUMOR DIAGNOSIS SERVICE
SHIELDS WARREN, M.D., *Director*

The function of the State Tumor Diagnosis Service is to provide pathologic diagnosis on all material obtained by biopsy or complete removal of lesions known or suspected to be neoplastic. Recognizing that pathological service was not available in many parts of the State, yet such service was absolutely essential to the adequate treatment of both benign and malignant tumors, the Tumor Diagnosis Service was established in 1919 with the main purpose of providing pathological diagnostic facilities for those doctors and hospitals without established pathological services of their own.

In order to afford the best possible diagnostic facilities, the laboratory was established at the Huntington Hospital with the cooperation of the Harvard Cancer Commission. At this time the Huntington Hospital was the only special hospital for cancer in New England. Moreover, the director of the Tumor Diagnosis Service during the early years was Dr. James Homer Wright, pathologist to the Massachusetts General Hospital and to the Huntington Hospital, who had unusual skill in the diagnosis of malignant conditions. Doctor Wright continued as director of the laboratory until shortly before his death in 1928.

During this period the steady growth in the number of specimens submitted to the laboratory attested to its value to the practitioners of Massachusetts. During the first year 1,005 specimens were received. Two years later 1828 specimens were received; in 1924, 2253 specimens; in 1925, 3080; in 1927, 3338; in 1929, 3397. During these earlier years the interest in cancer was steadily growing throughout the State as is attested by the rapid growth in the number of specimens received. In general, however, the work in cancer had not become sufficiently refined to demand detailed pathologic diagnosis. During most of these earlier years the three diagnoses which appeared most frequently in the files were "carcinoma," "sarcoma," and "no malignancy." During this period there was one scientific article which appeared from the laboratory, "Concerning the Nature of Protozoan-like Cells in Certain Lesions of Infancy," by Drs. Ernest W. Goodpasture and Fritz B. Talbot, published in the *American Journal of the Diseases of Children*.

In 1928 Dr. Shields Warren became director of the laboratory and for the first few years it served as the laboratory for the newly established

Pondville Hospital for Cancer. The large number of specimens received from this new hospital accounts for the sharp increase in number of specimens from 1927 on through 1931 when a pathological laboratory was established at the Pondville Hospital.

With increasing interest in cancer and with more adequate means of therapy available, it is natural that more detailed diagnoses of the material submitted were required. A more exact specification of the material diagnosed was attempted combined with histologic grading of the degree of malignancy of many types. There has been a determined effort not only to make the diagnoses as accurately as possible, but to return them to the physicians sending the specimens as promptly as possible. In the case of a number of the smaller specimens, diagnoses can be sent out within twenty-four hours after the receipt of the material. With larger specimens forty-eight hours are required, and in particularly puzzling cases requiring more detailed histologic investigation an even longer time.

An interesting feature is that many of the hospitals using the facilities of the Tumor Diagnosis Service have found pathologic diagnosis so valuable that they have established laboratory services of their own, and thus their material no longer comes to the Tumor Diagnosis Service and that of new users takes its place. It is of interest to note that during the past year, specimens were received for diagnosis from 654 doctors and 115 hospitals.

As more and more pathological material accumulated and more doctors turned to the laboratory for diagnostic help, two other functions than mere diagnosis were of necessity developed. The first of these was a study of groups of cases to determine the response of tumors to different types of therapy so that the Tumor Diagnosis Service might be able not only to provide a pathologic diagnosis, but to recommend in the case of a given lesion the therapy found most satisfactory for it, if the doctor in charge of the case desired such information. In order to have such information available, much of which cannot be found in the literature even at the present time, it became necessary to obtain information as to the ultimate outcome of some of the borderline and more obscure cases.

A second function was the development of pathological research, primarily focused on the problems of malignant disease. The first publication in this series appeared in 1928, "A Study of a Malignant Tumor Simulating Bone Marrow," which originated in the renal pelvis and became widely diffused throughout the body with ultimate death of the patient.

In the course of study of the specimens received, it was noted that fibroid tumors of the cervix uteri more frequently showed evidence of malignancy than similar tumors occurring in the body of the uterus. This was made the basis of a study in 1930 by Dr. William H. Lewis, Jr., then resident in the laboratory, who found that the cervical tumors were nearly ten times as likely to be malignant as the fibroids occurring in the uterine body. Interestingly enough, in several of the reported cases the sarcoma arose in the cervical stump after supracervical hysterectomy.

The following year several groups of cases were reported upon. The director, together with Dr. Howard M. Clute, published in the *American Journal of Cancer*, "A Study of Cancer of the Thyroid Gland," in which a combined histologic and clinical classification of thyroid malignancy was presented, calling attention to the importance of accurate histologic diagnosis in both determining therapy and in establishing group prognosis. In general, it was found that the adenomas with blood vessel invasion showed the least malignancy and the relatively undifferentiated giant cell carcinoma and the diffuse small cell carcinoma showed the highest degree of malignancy.

An unusual case of pulmonary embolus due to intravenous growth of a chondrosarcoma of the ilium was reported by the director in the *American Journal of Pathology*. Together with Dr. R. L. Mason the director reported in the same journal an unusual case of metastatic carcinoma of the breast, metastasizing to the parathyroid gland and simulating hyperparathyroidism.

Carcinoma of the cervix uteri is one of the tumors most commonly seen in this laboratory, and on the basis of an autopsy group of fatal cases of carcinoma of the cervix, the importance of the histologic grade was further established. Grade I tumors very rarely metastasized and when they did seldom extended beyond the regional nodes. The Grade II tumors showed a high percentage of lymph node metastasis and one-third metastasized to various of the viscera. In Grade III, the highest malignancy, two-thirds of the cases metastasized widely, involving the viscera.

A second study of thyroid tumors attempted to evaluate the significance of blood vessel invasion in adenomas of thyroid gland. The basis of study was 1100 adenomas, three per cent of which showed blood vessel invasion and six per cent of these died with widespread metastasis.

The following year a study of multiple malignant tumors was undertaken with Dr. Olive Gates, the assistant director. This was published in the *American Journal of Cancer* and presented a study of the literature up to that time, together with an addition of forty new cases of multiple malignancy. On the basis of this study, it was clearly established that multiple malignant tumors occur more frequently than can be explained on the basis of chance alone and probably represent a definite predisposition or susceptibility to cancer in certain persons. The incidence was 3.7 per cent. In this study it became necessary to establish criteria for the selection of cases of multiple malignancy, which have become generally accepted by cancer investigators.

In the course of the study of post-mortem cancer material, it became apparent that the immediate causes of death varied a good deal in cancers of various sites and consequently a study of the immediate causes of death in 500 autopsied fatal cases was undertaken. Thus in carcinoma of the cervix, by far the commonest cause of death was renal insufficiency from impairment of bladder or ureteral function. In carcinomas of the upper respiratory tract and of the buccal mucosa, pneumonia and lung abscess were most striking. In carcinoma of the breast cachexia and pulmonary insufficiency were the outstanding causes.

Because of the importance of metastasis in malignant disease, a long range study of various features of this process was undertaken. This study is still being carried on at the present time. The first stage was an evaluation of the distribution of metastases in various types of the more common forms of malignant tumors. First, those in carcinoma of the cervix uteri were studied. There was close parallelism between the degree of malignancy and the total number of sites of metastasis of the tumors of a given grade. Thus, the highly malignant epidermoid carcinomas averaged over three different sites of metastasis apiece, whereas those of low malignancy showed no metastases or only one. Of those cases in which metastasis appeared after treatment 80 per cent occurred within a year. In a group of 162 autopsied cases of cancer of the breast no relationship was found between the distribution or extent of metastases and the histological appearance of the primary tumor. Metastases are usually widespread in the case of breast carcinoma, averaging over five different sites per case, and practically every organ or tissue of the body was noted as a site of metastasis in one or another of the cases.

In contrast to the breast, the histologic grade of malignancy is of marked importance in carcinoma of the large bowel, there being a very close parallelism between the higher degree of malignancy and the greater frequency of metastasis. In fact, in the least malignant group, malignant adenoma, metastasis is comparatively rare, whereas it occurred in 60 per cent of those of high malignancy. In a study of 69 cases of carcinoma of the stomach, the distribution of metastases was found to be relatively limited. Of particular importance was the finding that if the regional lymph nodes, peritoneum, and the liver are free from metastasis, the presence of metastasis elsewhere in the body is extremely unlikely.

There has been much interest in the assumed immunity of the spleen to metastasis from malignant tumors, and several theoretical explanations have been offered, particularly emphasizing the protective role of the lymphocyte. However, in the course of this study it was found that an appreciable number of the cases had metastasized and indeed the spleen had fully as many metastatic nodules as did the kidney. Such infrequency of metastasis as does occur is apparently readily explained by the very slight lymphatic supply and to some extent the motility of the organ.

In a study with Dr. W. B. Macomber, 41 cases of metastasis to the ovary were analyzed, and they were found to be disproportionately frequent in the ovaries of women still of childbearing age. In addition while tumors of the gastrointestinal tract metastasize frequently to the ovary (Krunkenberg tumor), carcinomas of the breast metastasize to them just as frequently.

In line with these clinical observations on metastasis, Doctor Gates and the director have been carrying on some experimental work. They have devised a means of utilizing the ascitic fluid from animals with carcinomatosis peritonei, so that uninjured tumor cells may be implanted in any site desired and their subsequent fate studied. This has provided a useful tool for experimental study of metastasis.

With Dr. Myrtelle M. Canavan of the Department of Mental Diseases the director studied the incidence of cancer in the insane hospitals of the Commonwealth. A great deal of uncertainty exists in the literature as to the frequency of malignant disease in the insane population. On the basis of this study, which was not entirely adequate, there did appear to be a definitely less frequency of malignant disease in the population of the insane hospitals than in the population as a whole.

With Doctor Gates the frequency of various grades of histologic malignancy was studied among 5052 cases of epidermoid carcinoma, and it was found that there was a fair correlation between the clinical malignancy and the histologic malignancy. The histologic malignancy was independent of both age and sex. Metastases tended to be of the same grade as that of the primary tumor from which they arose. The histologic malignancy was no greater in those cases of multiple malignancy than of single cancer. A rare case of multiple malignancy with a metastasizing carcinoma of the ileum and associated miliary tuberculosis was reported.

With Dr. T. P. Eberhard an apparently new type of tumor of the mucous glands of the female perineum was reported, one benign and one malignant example being found.

A pathologic study of the tumors of the parathyroid gland was carried out with the help of Dr. J. R. E. Morgan, in the course of which evidence was brought forward that all forms of the parathyroid cells are apparently capable of producing parathyroid hormone. In addition several criteria for the diagnosis of adenoma of the parathyroid gland were presented.

A number of fibrosarcomas have been received at the Tumor Diagnosis Service, and it became obvious as various of these cases were followed that certain ones showed an appreciably higher degree of malignancy than others. With the help of Dr. George N. J. Sommer, Jr., 163 cases were analyzed. Contrary to general opinion fibrosarcoma is not a disease of young persons, the average age at onset being about fifty years. In practically all these cases radiation therapy has been disappointing. The best results have been obtained with operation. From the histologic standpoint, the most important detail to check is the presence or absence of tumor giant cells. If these are present the mortality is definitely higher and the duration of the disease shorter than in the cases where they are absent. Recurrence is quite frequent, occurring in over one-third the cases and has a grave prognostic significance. It usually occurs early and is rare after the first year.

The significance of detailed histologic grading of basal cell cancer was undertaken with the help of Doctor Gates and Dr. Paul W. Butterfield. It was found that the degree of differentiation is a helpful index of malignancy in this group. Thus, the somewhat specialized skin appendage tumors have a definitely lower malignancy than the less differentiated basal cell tumors. The importance of biopsy for satisfactory treatment of all carcinomas was brought out very definitely by the results of the study.

The recent increase in importance of radiation therapy in malignant disease has made imperative a better understanding of the effects of radiation on tumor cells and on normal cells. Consequently, there has been undertaken with the aid of Drs. Lloyd C. Fogg, Alfred Marshak, and John Ungar, Jr., a series of studies leading toward a closer analysis of the radiation effect on the cell. We are of the opinion that the chief effect of radiation is upon the nucleus, that the cell is most sensitive to radiation at the time of the early prophase of mitosis, that the cytoplasmic elements are of relatively slight importance in the radiation reaction although fairly marked changes may be produced in the Golgi apparatus. The mitochondria show virtually no change until actual cellular degeneration begins.

A study by Doctor Gates of the cutaneous metastases of malignant disease was based on 93 cases obtained from some 2233 autopsies and 80,000 surgical specimens of all types. The frequency of skin metastasis in cancer apparently lies between two and three per cent. It is not infrequently the first evidence of the existence of malignancy. Sometimes skin metastases may precede death by months or even years. Since the behavior of the skin metastases does not necessarily follow that of the primary tumor, observations of their growth are of limited prognostic value.

I cannot close this discussion of the Tumor Diagnosis Service without a word regarding biopsy. In general, it may be said that wherever possible one should not cut through tumor tissue, but remove the nodule under suspicion by cutting through surrounding healthy tissue. If this is done, probably a wait of even a few days is not dangerous and certainly preferable to going ahead without knowing the exact nature of the tumor. While ideally diagnosis would be established by immediate frozen section, this is impractical in the vast majority of cases, and the slower procedure apparently does not cause harm. In general, adequate incisional biopsies are definitely preferable to punch or aspiration biopsies, owing to the greater adequacy of the material and the more satisfactory means by which it could be studied.

Finally, the director wishes to thank all those physicians of the State who have given their time and help in aiding him to learn more about the behavior of tumors, malignant and benign.

CANCER STATISTICS IN MASSACHUSETTS

BERNARD E. BRADLEY, *Epidemiologist,*
Division of Cancer and Other Chronic Diseases
Massachusetts Department of Public Health

Table I. The number of cancer deaths has been increasing with minor fluctuations since the first records were published in Massachusetts. There is no question but that a part of this increase is due to an increase in the population of the State. Between 1900 and 1937 the crude rate, which makes allowance for increases in population, slightly more than doubled, 2.2, whereas the actual number of deaths increased 3.4 times. Another factor responsible for the increase is the changing age composition of the people. Massachusetts is gradually growing older and as cancer is a disease largely of late adult life more deaths would therefore occur. The adjusted rates take this into consideration. These rates rose steadily for both sexes up to 1921. The rates for males have increased since then, but for females have remained practically stationary and the last three years indicate a slight drop.

Table II. The percentage of cancer deaths among total deaths in the various age sex groups is shown in this table. While cancer is largely a disease of late adult life, it is interesting to note that approximately one-eighth of the deaths in women between the ages of thirty and thirty-nine are from this disease and nearly one-fourth between forty and forty-nine.

Table III. The digestive tract comprises about one-half of all cancer deaths; uterus and breast about 10 per cent each; while deaths from cancer of the skin are exceedingly low. The deaths from cancer of the skin do not begin to measure the incidence of this disease as the number of cures is very large.

Table IV. The percentage distribution of cancer by age and sex is given in this table. The greatest percentage of deaths occurs between the ages of sixty and sixty-nine.

Table V. The average age at time of death from cancer varies with the organ affected. Deaths from cancer of the uterus and breast occur earlier; deaths from cancer of the skin later.

Table VI. The median duration of delay between first symptoms and first physician consulted varied very little between 1927 and 1935. Since that time there has been a decided drop. This figure is a better one to use for this measurement than the average, as it represents the middle point of the distribution. The delay before first visit to cancer clinic has dropped about four months. Both of these delays should be further reduced.

Table VII. This table shows the State-aided cancer clinic cities which had much-lower increases in cancer deaths between 1927 and 1937 than did the State as a whole. All of these clinics have been operating through the major part of the cancer program.

TABLE I.—CANCER DEATHS IN MASSACHUSETTS
1900 — 1937

YEAR	Cancer Deaths			Crude Rate per 100,000 Population			Age, Sex Adjusted Rate* per 100,000 Population		
	Male	Female	Total	Male	Female	Total	Male	Female	Total
1900	684	1314	1998	50.2	91.6	71.5	50.2	91.6	71.5
1901	704	1376	2080	50.6	94.1	72.9	50.6	93.7	72.7
1902	686	1455	2141	48.1	97.5	73.4	47.9	97.0	73.0
1903	741	1502	2243	51.0	98.8	75.4	50.9	97.8	75.0
1904	808	1613	2421	54.5	104.3	79.9	54.2	102.9	79.2
1905	843	1658	2501	55.8	105.3	81.0	55.5	103.7	80.3
1906	977	1626	2603	63.4	101.5	82.8	63.1	99.5	81.8
1907	932	1812	2744	59.4	111.2	85.8	58.9	108.7	84.4
1908	966	1848	2814	60.5	111.6	86.5	59.9	108.7	84.9
1909	991	1880	2871	60.9	111.6	86.7	60.3	108.5	85.0
1910	1065	1963	3028	64.3	114.7	89.9	63.7	111.3	88.1
1911	1177	2022	3199	70.1	116.5	93.7	68.8	112.1	91.0
1912	1115	2167	3282	65.5	123.0	94.8	63.5	117.6	91.3
1913	1282	2244	3526	74.3	125.6	100.4	71.5	119.7	96.2
1914	1295	2291	3586	74.0	126.5	100.7	70.9	119.6	95.9
1915	1374	2334	3708	77.5	127.1	102.7	73.7	119.5	97.2
1916	1474	2516	3990	82.1	135.1	109.1	77.1	126.5	102.5
1917	1483	2574	4057	81.5	136.4	109.5	76.2	127.0	102.3
1918	1558	2540	4098	84.5	132.8	109.1	78.6	123.2	101.5
1919	1574	2538	4112	84.3	131.0	108.1	77.9	120.5	99.7
1920	1741	2753	4494	92.1	140.3	116.7	84.5	128.6	107.1
1921	1814	2831	4645	95.1	142.7	119.3	85.9	129.4	108.2
1922	1806	2844	4650	93.8	141.8	118.3	83.5	126.9	105.8
1923	1890	2885	4775	97.2	142.3	120.2	85.4	125.8	106.1
1924	2087	2987	5074	106.3	145.8	126.5	92.2	127.5	110.3
1925	2078	3118	5196	104.9	150.6	128.3	89.6	130.0	110.4
1926	2230	3111	5341	111.6	148.7	130.6	94.3	127.5	111.4
1927	2234	3220	5454	110.7	152.4	132.0	92.5	128.9	111.1
1928	2330	3281	5611	114.5	153.7	134.6	94.3	128.8	112.0
1929	2362	3310	5672	115.0	153.5	134.7	93.3	127.4	110.8
1930	2488	3325	5813	120.1	152.7	136.8	96.8	125.4	111.5
1931	2459	3400	5859	118.1	155.4	137.3	93.5	126.2	110.3
1932	2590	3563	6153	123.8	162.0	143.4	96.7	129.2	113.4
1933	2779	3603	6382	132.3	163.1	148.1	101.5	128.7	115.5
1934	2995	3680	6675	141.9	165.8	154.1	107.2	129.4	118.6
1935	2836	3647	6483	133.7	163.6	149.0	99.2	125.2	112.5
1936	3077	3700	6777	144.4	165.2	155.0	105.9	124.9	115.7
1937	3063	3768	6831	143.1	167.4	155.6	102.8	124.5	114.0

* Adjusted to Massachusetts 1900 Population

TABLE II.—PERCENTAGE OF CANCER DEATHS TO TOTAL DEATHS,
BY AGE AND SEX
Deaths in Massachusetts, 1937

Age Group	Male			Female			Total		
	Cancer Deaths	Total Deaths	Per Cent	Cancer Deaths	Total Deaths	Per Cent	Cancer Deaths	Total Deaths	Per Cent
-10	11	2,158	0.5	4	1,652	0.2	15	3,810	0.4
10-19	15	582	2.6	7	367	1.9	22	949	2.3
20-29	23	792	2.9	32	769	4.2	55	1,561	3.5
30-39	49	1,271	3.9	128	1,042	12.3	177	2,313	7.7
40-49	248	2,731	9.1	432	1,935	22.3	680	4,666	14.6
50-59	607	4,514	13.4	794	3,113	25.5	1,401	7,627	18.4
60-69	1,001	6,317	15.8	1,092	5,374	20.3	2,093	11,691	17.9
70-79	862	5,983	14.4	902	6,172	14.6	1,764	12,155	14.5
80 +	247	3,047	8.1	377	4,468	8.4	624	7,515	8.3
Total	3,063	27,395	11.2	3,768	24,892	15.1	6,831	52,287	13.1

TABLE III.—PERCENTAGE DISTRIBUTION, BY LOCATION OF CANCER

Cancer Deaths in Massachusetts, 1937

Location of Cancer	Deaths	Percentage Distribution
Buccal Cavity	275	4.03
Digestive Tract	3354	49.10
Respiratory System	372	5.45
Uterus	624	9.13
Other Female Genital Organs	222	3.25
Breast	729	10.67
Male Genitourinary Organs	602	8.81
Skin	90	1.32
Other or Unspecified Organs	563	8.24
Total	6831	100.00

TABLE IV.—PERCENTAGE DISTRIBUTION, BY AGE AND SEX

Cancer Deaths in Massachusetts, 1937

Age Group	Male		Female		Total	
	Deaths	Percentage Distribution	Deaths	Percentage Distribution	Deaths	Percentage Distribution
-10	11	.16	4	.06	15	.22
10-19	15	.22	7	.10	22	.32
20-29	23	.34	32	.47	55	.81
30-39	49	.72	128	1.87	177	2.59
40-49	248	3.63	432	6.32	680	9.95
50-59	607	8.89	794	11.62	1401	20.51
60-69	1001	14.65	1092	15.99	2093	30.64
70-79	862	12.62	902	13.20	1764	25.82
80 +	247	3.62	377	5.52	624	9.14
Total	3063	44.84	3768	55.16	6831	100.00

TABLE V.—AVERAGE AGE AT TIME OF DEATH, BY LOCATION OF CANCER

Cancer Deaths in Massachusetts, 1937

Location of Cancer	Average Age
Buccal Cavity	69.4
Digestive Tract	65.8
Respiratory System	60.2
Uterus	59.6
Other Female Genital Organs	59.8
Breast	61.6
Male Genitourinary Organs	68.0
Skin	73.1
Other or Unspecified Organs	58.4
Total	64.1

TABLE VI.—MEDIAN DURATION IN MONTHS OF PATIENTS WITH CANCER BETWEEN FIRST SYMPTOM AND FIRST VISIT TO PHYSICIAN; BETWEEN FIRST SYMPTOM AND FIRST VISIT TO CLINIC
Massachusetts State-Aided Cancer Clinics

Year	Duration Before First Visit to Physician	Duration Before First Visit to Clinic
1927	6.0	12.8
1928	6.0	12.5
1929	6.3	12.8
1930	6.6	12.2
1931	6.5	11.5
1932	6.1	9.4
1933	6.1	9.2
1934	6.2	9.0
1935	6.1	9.1
1936	5.0	8.6
1937	5.0	8.9

TABLE VII.—PERCENTAGE INCREASE IN CANCER DEATHS BETWEEN 1927 AND 1937

Cancer Clinic City	Percentage Increase
Fitchburg	5.5
Lawrence	0.0
Lowell	4.0
Lynn	8.4
New Bedford	5.9
Springfield	7.7
Worcester	10.3
State	25.2

REPORT OF DIVISION OF FOOD AND DRUGS

(As required by General Laws, Chapter 111, Section 25.)

During the months of April, May and June 1938, samples were collected in 278 cities and towns.

There were 1,903 samples of milk examined, of which 262 were below standard, from 10 samples the cream had been in part removed, 11 samples contained added water, and 1 sample of skimmed milk marked was below the legal standard. There were 2,646 bacteriological examinations made of milk, 2,070 of which complied with the requirements. There were 84 bacteriological examinations made of cream, 30 of which did not comply with the requirements; 186 bacteriological examinations of ice cream, 12 of which did not comply with the requirements; 3 bacteriological examinations of sherbet, all of which complied with the requirements; 8 bacteriological examinations of chocolate and coffee drinks, 4 of which did not comply with the requirements; 24 bacteriological examinations of candy, 4 of which did not comply with the requirements; 1 bacteriological examination of an empty bottle which did not comply with the requirements; and 11 bacteriological examinations of mattress fillings, 9 of which complied with the requirements.

There were 569 samples of food examined, 76 of which were adulterated. These consisted of 2 samples of butter, both of which were rancid; 1 sample of eggs which was decomposed; 3 samples of heavy cream which were low in fat for this grade; 2 samples of maple syrup which contained cane sugar; 1 sample of relish which contained sodium benzoate and was not so labeled; 3 samples of clams which contained added water; 1 sample of hydrogen peroxide which did not conform to the requirements of the U. S. Pharmacopoeia; 1 sample of lamb patties which was decomposed; 1 sample of pieces of beef which contained a compound of sulphur dioxide and was not so labeled; 1 sample of fish which was decomposed; 17 samples of hamburg steak, 9 of which were decomposed and 1 sample also contained sodium sulphite in excess of one tenth of one per cent, 5 samples contained a compound of sulphur dioxide not so labeled and 1 sample was also decomposed, and 3 samples contained sodium sulphite in excess of one tenth of one per cent; 15 samples of sausage, 10 of which were decomposed, 3 samples contained a compound of sulphur dioxide and were not so labeled, and 2 samples contained starch in excess of 2 per cent; 17 samples of wash water, all of which were deficient in caustic alkali; 1 sample of orangeade which was misbranded; and 10 samples of mattress filling, 5 of which contained secondhand material, 1 contained partly secondhand material, 2 contained a mixture of new and secondhand material, 1 sample labeled as containing hair, sisal and lamb's wool contained horse hair and sisal, but no lamb's wool, and 1 sample was a feather pillow which contained goose, duck and hen feathers, but no down.

There were 28 samples of drugs examined, of which 5 were adulterated. These consisted of 5 samples of spirit of nitrous ether which did not conform to the U. S. P. requirements.

The police departments submitted 92 samples of liquor for examination. The police departments also submitted 21 samples to be analyzed for poisons or drugs, 12 of which contained heroin, 2 contained opium, 4 contained morphine, 2 were examined for cannabis with negative results, and 1 sample was examined for poison with negative results.

There were inspected 418 plants operated for the pasteurization of milk; 9 restaurants; 251 soft drink plants; 197 ice cream plants; 24 bakeries; 316 mattress establishments; and 2 stores visited relative to a narcotic license.

There were 83 hearings held pertaining to violations of the laws.

There were 47 convictions pertaining to violations of the law, $1,180 in fines being imposed.

Frank Bento of North Tiverton, Rhode Island; Emo Nelson of Seekonk; James Reid, Jr., of Raynham; Hampden Creamery Company, 2 cases, of Everett; and John Saunders of Westfield, were all convicted for violations of the milk laws.

Clarence Archambault, 2 cases, of Haverhill; Samuel Bookless of Pittsfield; Farmers Cooperative Milk Exchange of Westfield; Harold L. Tyler, 2 cases of Lexington; John V. Veloza of Somerset; Alfred J. Wright of Attleboro; Joshua W. Zwicker of Danvers; Alfred Governo of Fall River; Walter H. Lee of Worcester; and Charles Schauer of Holyoke, were convicted for violations of the pasteurization law and regulations. Clarence Archambault of Haverhill appealed his two cases.

Hudson Market, Incorporated, of Hudson; Edward Morse, Antoni Rosa and Modern Market, Incorporated, of New Bedford; Edward Simons, Hyman Racoff, and Barney Less of Roxbury; Benjamin Chook of South Boston; Benjamin Gordon and Benjamin Gross of Lowell; John Moskal of Northampton; Anthony Maietta, 2 cases, of Cambridge; Genoa Packing Company of Boston; Abraham Yoken, Benjamin Yoken, World Foods Incorporated, Fall River Trading & Finance Company, and People's Public Market, Incorporated, of Fall River; and Frank Filosa and James E. Till of Milford, were all convicted for violations of the food laws. Fall River Trading and Finance Company and People's Public Market, Incorporated, of Fall River, appealed their cases.

Dave Glucksman, 2 cases, of New Bedford; and Ward Baking Company of Cambridge, were convicted for violations of the bakery laws and regulations.

A. Warren Cox of Waltham was convicted for violation of the soft drink laws.

Suffolk Upholstering & Mattress Company of Lynn; Turin-Blank Upholstering Company, 2 cases, of Roxbury; and Young Brothers Mattress Company, Incorporated, of Providence, Rhode Island, were convicted for violations of the mattress laws.

In accordance with Section 25, Chapter 111 of the General Laws, the following is the list of articles of adulterated food collected in original packages from manufacturers, wholesalers, or producers.

Two samples of butter which were rancid were obtained from Hyman Racoff of Roxbury.

One sample of orangeade which was misbranded was obtained from L. R. Smith of Greenfield.

Maple syrup which contained cane sugar was obtained as follows:

One sample each, from Biltmore Cafeteria, Incorporated, of Taunton, and Paul Psomos of Boston.

Cream which was low in fat for the specified grade was obtained as follows:

One sample each, from H. P. Hood & Sons, Incorporated, of Hyannis; John J. McGrath of West Newbury; and Oliver Rondeau of Palmer.

Clams which contained added water were obtained as follows:

One sample each, from Carl Savage of Rowley; J. B. Wright of Gloucester; and Merrimac Shellfish Company of Newburyport.

One sample of lamb patties which was decomposed was obtained from Atlas Food Mart of Quincy.

Hamburg steak which was decomposed was obtained as follows:

Two samples from Philip S. Mogul of Somerville; and 1 sample each, from Sam De Luca of Somerville; Edward Bloom of Newburyport, World's Food, Incorporated, of Fall River; Barney Less of Roxbury; Modern Market, Incorporated, of New Bedford; and Anthony Maietta of Cambridge.

Hamburg steak which contained sodium sulphite in excess of one-tenth of one per cent was obtained as follows:

Two samples from Pasquale Piscione of Somerville; and William Waldman of Roxbury.

Hamburg steak which contained a compound of sulphur dioxide not so labeled was obtained as follows:

One sample each, from Morris Shore of Taunton; Paul Psomos of Boston; and Harry Tesler of Attleboro.

One sample of hamburg steak which contained sodium sulphite in excess of one-tenth of one per cent and was also decomposed was obtained from Hub Market (Esther Leiben) of Boston.

One sample of hamburg steak which contained a compound of sulphur dioxide not so labeled and was also decomposed was obtained from Philip Engleman of South Norwood.

Sausage which was decomposed was obtained as follows:

One sample each, from B. Sherman of Allston; Economy Grocery Stores, Incorporated, of Dorchester; Arthur Minsk of Lynn; Colonial Super Market of Waltham; Abraham Yoken & Son and People's Public Market, Incorporated, of Fall River; Economy Grocery Stores, Incorporated, of Milford; Anthony Maietta of Cambridge; Puritan Stores, Incorporated, of New Bedford; and David Ginsberg of Worcester.

Sausage which contained starch in excess of 2 per cent was obtained as follows:

One sample each, from Penn Public Market of Lynn; and Hub Market (Esther Leiben) of Boston.

Sausage which contained a compound of sulphur dioxide not so labeled was obtained as follows:

One sample each, from Atlas Food Market and Leo Feinstein of Quincy; and Vincent Siravo of Taunton.

There were 102 confiscations, consisting of 27 pounds of decomposed chickens; 89½ pounds of decomposed fowl; 13 pounds of decomposed geese; 90 pounds of decomposed beef; 153 pounds of decomposed corned beef; 9 pounds of decomposed beef flank; 7 pounds of decomposed beef kidneys; 4 pounds of decomposed beef liver; 26 pounds of decomposed beef steak; 120 pounds of decomposed hamburg steak; 7 pounds of decomposed calves' liver; 60 pounds of decomposed hogs' liver; 11 pounds of decomposed lamb; 25 pounds of decomposed lamb chops; 5 pounds of decomposed lamb forequarter; 80 pounds of decomposed lamb legs; 8 pounds of decomposed lamb loin; 4 pounds of decomposed tongue; 72 pounds of decomposed ham; 1 pound of decomposed Scotch ham; 10 pounds of decomposed pig's head; 15 pounds of decomposed pig's kidney; 2 pounds of decomposed spare ribs; 12 pounds of decomposed shoulder; 164½ pounds of decomposed corned shoulder; 106 pounds of decomposed smoked shoulder; 53 pounds of decomposed veal; 14 pounds of decomposed veal legs; 5 pounds of decomposed veal scraps; 10 pounds of decomposed veal roll; 78 pounds of decomposed sausage meat; 16 pounds of decomposed butter; 59 pounds of decomposed pork; 6 pounds of decomposed spare ribs; 19 pounds of decomposed pickled pork; 17 pounds of decomposed frankforts; 7 pounds of decomposed bacon; 40 pounds of decomposed suet; 10 pounds of decomposed tripe; 3 pounds of decomposed haddock; 264 pounds of decomposed pickles; and 2 pounds of decomposed mushrooms.

The licensed cold storage warehouses reported the following amounts of food placed in storage during March, 1938:—357,150 dozens of case eggs; 577,161 pounds of broken out eggs; 209,895 pounds of butter; 1,081,988 pounds of poultry, 2,178,950 pounds of fresh meat and fresh meat products; and 6,885,831 pounds of fresh food fish.

There was on hand April 1, 1938:—348,030 dozens of case eggs; 1,496,065 pounds of broken out eggs; 339,673 pounds of butter; 3,929,546 pounds of poultry; 5,954,633 pounds of fresh meat and fresh meat products; and 13,369,738 pounds of fresh food fish.

The licensed cold storage warehouses reported the following amounts of food placed in storage during April, 1938:—1,806,960 dozens of case eggs; 1,026,735 pounds of broken out eggs; 676,909 pounds of butter; 1,023,903 pounds of poultry; 2,152,238 pounds of fresh meat and fresh meat products; and 9,680,738 pounds of fresh food fish.

There was on hand May 1, 1938:—2,095,770 dozens of case eggs; 1,667,676 pounds of broken out eggs; 641,863 pounds of butter; 2,978,574 pounds of poultry; 5,293,571 pounds of fresh meat and fresh meat products; and 17,157,775 pounds of fresh food fish.

The licensed cold storage warehouses reported the following amounts of food placed in storage during May, 1938:—1,506,240 dozens of case eggs; 1,325,260 pounds of broken out eggs; 1,406,243 pounds of butter; 1,130,866 pounds of poultry; 1,984,767 pounds of fresh meat and fresh meat products; and 11,335,281 pounds of fresh food fish.

There was on hand June 1, 1938:—350,631 dozens of case eggs; 2,094,617 pounds of broken out eggs; 1,563,743 pounds of butter; 2,575,702 pounds of poultry; 4,652,074 pounds of fresh meat and fresh meat products; and 21,595,896 pounds of fresh food fish.

MASSACHUSETTS DEPARTMENT OF PUBLIC HEALTH

Commissioner of Public Health, HENRY D. CHADWICK, M.D.

Public Health Council

HENRY D. CHADWICK, M.D., *Chairman*

GEORGE D. DALTON, M.D.
FRANCIS H. LALLY, M.D.
CHARLES F. LYNCH, M.D.

RICHARD M. SMITH, M.D.
RICHARD P. STRONG, M.D.
JAMES L. TIGHE

Secretary, FLORENCE L. WALL

Division of Administration . . Under direction of Commissioner
Division of Sanitary Engineering . Director and Chief Engineer,
    ARTHUR D. WESTON, C.E.
Division of Communicable Diseases Director, ROY F. FEEMSTER, M.D.
Division of Biologic Laboratories . Director and Pathologist,
    ELLIOTT S. ROBINSON, M.D.
Division of Food and Drugs . . Director and Analyst,
    HERMANN C. LYTHGOE, S.B.
Division of Maternal and Child
  Health . . . . . Director, M. LUISE DIEZ, M.D.
Division of Tuberculosis . . . Director, ALTON S. POPE, M.D.
Division of Cancer and Other Director,
  Chronic Diseases . . .   HERBERT L. LOMBARD, M.D.
Division of Genitoinfectious Diseases Director, NELS A. NELSON, M.D.

State District Health Officers

The Southeastern District . . RICHARD P. MACKNIGHT, M.D., New Bedford
The South Metropolitan District . HENRY M. DE WOLFE, M.D., Braintree
The North Metropolitan District . CHARLES E. GILL, M.D., Boston
The Northeastern District . . ROBERT E. ARCHIBALD, M.D., Melrose
The Worcester District . . OSCAR A. DUDLEY, M.D., Worcester
South Connecticut Valley District . JOHN J. POUTAS, M.D., Westfield
North Connecticut Valley District . WALTER W. LEE, M.D., Greenfield
The Berkshire District . . HAROLD W. STEVENS, M.D., Great Barrington.

PUBLICATION OF THIS DOCUMENT APPROVED BY THE COMMISSION ON ADMINISTRATION AND FINANCE
14,500. 8-'38. Order 4797.

THE COMMONHEALTH

Volume 25   Oct.- Nov.- Dec.
No. 4   1938

MILK

MASSACHUSETTS
DEPARTMENT OF PUBLIC HEALTH

THE COMMONHEALTH

QUARTERLY BULLETIN OF THE MASSACHUSETTS DEPARTMENT OF
PUBLIC HEALTH

Sent Free to any Citizen of the State
Entered as second class matter at Boston Post Office

M. LUISE DIEZ, M.D., DIRECTOR OF DIVISION OF CHILD HYGIENE, EDITOR.
1 Beacon Street, Boston, Mass.

CONTENTS

	PAGE
Public Health Aspects of the Dairy Industry, by J. H. Frandsen	277
Milk in Massachusetts, by C. J. Fawcett	281
Production of Quality Milk, by Harley A. Leland	283
Milk-Borne Diseases, by A. Daniel Rubenstein, M.D.	289
Bang Abortion Disease, by Charles F. Riordan	293
Bovine Tuberculosis, by Harrie W. Peirce, M.D.V.	296
Tuberculosis and Milk, by Alton S. Pope, M.D.	305
The Progress of Milk Regulation, by Vlado A. Getting, M.D.	308
The Grading of Milk, by Hermann C. Lythgoe, S.B.	311
The Pasteurization of Milk, by Hermann C. Lythgoe, S.B.	315
Pasteurized Milk is Safe Milk, by Francis B. Carroll, M.D.	320
The Care of Milk in the Home, by Frederica L. Beinert, B.S.	321
Milk for the Whole Family, by Mary Spalding, M.A.	323
Milk Consumption among Children of Massachusetts, by Dorothy Adolph, B.S.	330
Milk in Relation to Sound Teeth, by Florence B. Hopkins, M.D., D.M.D.	332
Facts and Fancies Concerning Milk, by Dorothea Nicoll, B.S.	335
Teaching People to Drink Milk, by Jean V. Latimer, B.S., A.M.	338
The Cold Storage of Food in Massachusetts, by Hermann C. Lythgoe, S.B.	341
Book Notes:	
Pneumonia and Serum Therapy, by Frederick T. Lord, M.D., and Roderick Heffron, M.D.	357
Syphilis, Gonorrhea, and the Public Health, by Nels A. Nelson, M.D., and Gladys L. Crain, R.N.	357
The Traffic in Health, by Charles Solomon, M.D.	358
Report of Division of Food and Drugs, July, August, September, 1938	359
Index to Volume 25	365

PUBLIC HEALTH ASPECTS OF THE DAIRY INDUSTRY*

J. H. FRANDSEN

Department of Dairy Industry
Massachusetts State College

Commissioner Chadwick and Fellow Health Workers: It seems very much like "carrying coals to Newcastle" for me, a dairyman, to talk to you about the health aspects of the dairy industry. However, I am a great believer in the conference way of studying our mutual problems. Perhaps by gathering around the table we may arrive at a more sympathetic and, hopefully, a more constructive plan for safeguarding our milk supply. True, milk is sometimes the cause of epidemics, but it is equally true that milk is sometimes blamed for epidemics that can be traced to other sources. I hope that you sanitarians will give our best food, milk, at least an even break.

Importance of the Dairy Industry

In dollars and cents the farm value of milk produced on American farms last year exceeds the value of all the gold dollars manufactured in the United States since 1886, and the value of milk on the farm was greater than the combined value of the entire cotton, wheat and potato crops in 1937. Dairy products even exceed in value the entire motor industry, or the steel industry.

The value of all the buildings erected in the cities of the United States in 1928 was barely equal to the value of dairy products on the farm.

Back of the industry are 4,500,000 farmers and families, nearly one-fifth of the population of this country, and these people care for 30,000,000 cows.

However, with all this great value, the dairy industry is lacking in efficiency. When we realize that the average gross income from each cow last year was only $100 per cow we can see how inefficient we really are. To increase the production of dairying is a long time job; that is, a program of breeding, feeding, and weeding. It is not more cows we need, but better cows. It is not more milk we need, but better and safer milk. With more attention to quality and sanitation of milk and other dairy products will come increased consumption and better profits to farmers and distributors.

Transmission of Disease by Milk

For milk to be an asset to one's existence, it must be of good quality and must be safe from a health point of view. The consumer wants to be certain that, in addition to containing all the natural properties of health, the milk he buys is free from disease and possible infection.

There are two principal ways in which milk may become infected:

(1) Bovine disease directly transmissible to man through milk.
(2) Human disease directly or indirectly transmissible to man through milk.

---

* Address delivered at Twelfth Annual Health Conference of Connecticut Valley, Franklin and Berkshire Districts.

Bovine Diseases

With the continued development of modern dairy science we are able to almost completely safeguard ourselves against bovine diseases. The first attempt was made against bovine tuberculosis. The infection of man with the bovine germ has been the subject of exhaustive studies for many years and is now quite generally understood. In a relatively small proportion of cases, milk becomes infected with bovine tubercle bacilli, due to udder tuberculosis. More frequently, however, the method of infection is by passage of the bacilli through the intestinal tract, the organisms being excreted in the feces of some tuberculous cows. Under ordinary dairy conditions, it is very easy for more or less manure from such cows to be introduced into the milk during the milking, thus infecting it with the bovine organism.

Protection against human tuberculosis of bovine origin has come about in this country through the operation of two factors: (1) the tuberculin test of dairy cattle and (2) the pasteurization of the ordinary market milk supplies in the centers of population. If the bovine type of infection in man continues to occur in the United States, it is likely to be a rural problem. It is largely associated with families or small communities which are using milk from untested herds and using it raw.

The basic solution for the prevention of bovine tuberculosis infection in man naturally rests in the eradication of the bovine disease. This is coming about rapidly through the operation of the national cooperative eradication program engaged in by the state and federal governments since 1917.

Pasteurization has played a big part in decreasing tuberculosis in man, but, in a fundamental sense, it has served only as a substitute for a better means. The idea is becoming increasingly prevalent that any process such as pasteurization should not replace standards of health for dairy herds and dairy employees and standards of sanitation for dairy methods.

Some people are inclined to question the efficiency of the tuberculin test of dairy cattle. Progressive dairymen are not concerned so much about the relatively small number of so-called non-lesion reactors removed from the herds as they are about the possibility of the occasional cow that may be actually infected and yet fail to react. Federal results over a number of years, however, have shown that this possibility is 1 in 262. It indicates an efficiency of the tuberculin test which compares very satisfactorily with other known diagnostic tests.

Another disease of cattle which has attracted considerable attention is Brucella abortus infection, the germ of infectious abortion. In 1924, it was discovered that Brucella abortus produced an infection in man that is very closely related to Malta fever. It has been called "undulant fever" because the temperature rises and falls like waves. According to statistics, it is apparently increasing in man, although this perhaps can be explained in part by present-day better methods of diagnosis.

There is no typical set of symptoms for this disease. Early symptoms are much like tuberculosis, the person feeling generally tired and run down. Certain symptoms which might be picked out are: Chill, followed by profuse sweating; then a definite weakness; then the person affected feels pretty well but soon the cycle starts over again. The disease is somewhat like malaria except that the time between attacks is longer and there is a rheumatic pain in the joints which is absent in the case of malaria. There is a loss of appetite, loss of weight, and a general physical letdown.

As far as I know, there is no specific biological serum to use for undulant fever. The infected must, so to speak, "groan and grunt" it out over a period of approximately three months to a year. The mortality rate is low—being only about 3%—but it may frequently incapacitate an individual completely.

The disease is extremely widespread in the cattle of the United States, especially in eastern dairy cattle. There is some spread now among range cattle. In many dairy sections 20% to 50% have been found to be infected.

In our section of the country there has been a very definite increase in the incidence of undulant fever. Prior to 1925 only 128 cases were reported in the country; in 1932, 3000 cases were reported. Recently there have been 40 to 50 cases reported each year in Massachusetts although, except in communities where they occur, we don't hear much about them.

Forty-five per cent of the cases in the nation occur in cities; the other 55% occur outside. City dwellers may get the disease from drinking raw milk, either from their regular milk supply or through carelessness of using raw milk while on vacation. Outside the city, undulant fever can be considered as an industrial disease because persons can also become infected by coming in contact with the viscera of the animal—hog, cow, or goat. Many slaughterhouse employees contract the disease.

The disease can be controlled by making use of the following steps:
1. Prompt reporting—Undulant fever is now a reportable disease in Massachusetts.
2. Correct diagnosis.
3. Segregation and eradication of infected animals.
4. Pasteurization of milk.

There is little that can be done at present for the infected cow other than isolation and hygienic treatment. It is possible, however, for all dairy herds to be made free of abortion by eliminating from the herd all reactors, and using care in not bringing in infected animals—male or female.

Human Diseases

So far we have been considering bovine diseases transmissible to man. As regards human disease transmissible through milk, we find two types of spread.
1. The milk may become infected directly from the human source, as in typhoid fever.
2. The milk may become infected indirectly by the establishment of a focus in the udder, as in septic sore throat and scarlet fever.

In the case of typhoid fever, the human carrier is the element which must be eliminated. This is recognized in all well organized supervisory systems that control milk supplies, whether raw or pasteurized. It is essential that all milk handlers should be examined by suitable tests and every effort made to exclude the possible carrier. Milk has no bactericidal action against typhoid bacilli. Not even pasteurization can be depended upon as an absolute safety factor if the carrier has access to the milk following the heat treatment. This was illustrated in San Francisco when the work of efficient pasteurization was nullified by a typhoid carrier, who operated a bottling machine. In Montreal an epidemic was caused in 1927 by a carrier in charge of the pasteurizing apparatus.

Septic sore throat and scarlet fever are of special interest in milk because they present two possibilities in relation to milk infection.
1. The infection may be direct from a milker or other dairy employee.
2. The infection may be indirect as through the infection of a cow's udder by a human carrier.

Extensive infection of milk supplies with human types of streptococci can occur through the medium of the udder of the cow as a secondary host. This has been the case in a number of milk-borne epidemics of septic sore throat in which *streptococcus epidemicus* has been introduced into one or more quarters of an udder by an infected milker. The same occurrence has been noted in cases of streptococcus scarlatinae. The subsequent multiplication of these streptococci in the udder tissues may result in millions of these pathogens being discharged into the milk produced by the infected cow, and thus infecting the product of the herd.

Milk is an almost perfect food for bacteria. The germs of diphtheria, typhoid fever, and septic sore throat thrive in raw milk and have been responsible for epidemics of milk-borne diseases of appalling magnitude. A few years ago a milk-borne outbreak in Montreal caused over 5100 persons to be stricken with typhoid fever and killed over 500 of them. The U. S. Public Health Service receives reports each year of 30 to 50 outbreaks in this country. It is estimated that 5,000 children die every year in the U. S. from tuberculosis caused by drinking milk containing the tubercle bacillus. Septic sore throat epidemics can be very serious. In Portland, Oregon, several years ago a milker infected a cow's udder and 487 persons became ill and many died of septic sore throat. In 1929 in a community of 4000 population in Massachusetts, many people were infected. Nearly 1000 cases occurred and 40 persons died within two weeks, with 7 of these dying on July 4. This epidemic, according to the Commissioner of Public Health, was traced to a cow infected by a sick human milker. Hemolytic streptococci were found in the cow's milk, udder; throat of milker's child; blood, throat, and ears of patients.

Preventive Measures

These facts are of tremendous significance. These diseases are caused by drinking raw milk infected with germs from the cow, the milker, or the dairy worker. These diseases can be entirely prevented by pasteurizing or boiling the milk. Boiling the milk is an effective preventive measure, but many people do not like the taste of boiled milk. The best method of destroying bacteria and preserving the taste of milk is pasteurization.

Health authorities today, with but few exceptions, recommend pasteurization of milk. The most common method, the only legal method in

Massachusetts, is to heat it to at least 142°F. and hold it at that temperature for 30 minutes and then rapidly chill it. This treatment kills disease germs which might be transmitted through milk. Pasteurizing milk does not materially lessen its food value.

From this, the necessity for intelligent and effective supervision of milk supplies is evident. This supervision must primarily insure adequate protection for the public health; and, secondarily, improve the quality of milk and its many products at their source.

MILK IN MASSACHUSETTS

C. J. FAWCETT

Extension Animal Husbandman
Massachusetts State College

No other item in the human diet can compare with milk in its ability to supply all the nutrients necessary for sustaining life and promoting growth of the body, yet people do not use enough milk for maximum health and economy or for the prosperity of those engaged in its production and distribution.

One reason for this may be because it is such a universal product that there is little to take it out of the commonplace, and its use becomes too monotonous to be especially interesting. Should the supply be cut off for even a day, however, its importance would be immediately realized.

Another reason for not using as much milk as we should: it is a perishable product and may very easily become unpalatable. It is only in recent years that the methods of producing and handling milk have developed to a point where it is difficult to find any considerable quantity of milk, at least in Massachusetts, which is not perfectly wholesome and safe to use.

The Producer's Difficulties

This is a rather happy situation as it affects the consumer, but it is doubtful if he fully appreciates it or realizes just how it has been accomplished.

There is not enough profit in milk to permit of extensive advertising. Much space is used and many dollars are spent in telling how certain beverages are blended or aged in the wood and how tobaccos are processed and toasted to make the best cigarette in the world. Sales and profits of these luxuries evidently justify all this expense.

In producing and merchandizing milk the process has been almost exactly opposite. Boards of health, federal, state and local, have insisted on regulations which would make the milk supply safe for the public. In some instances little regard was given by enforcing officers as to whether the rules laid down could be put into effect by the producer without a prohibitive expenditure of money for new equipment or alterations. County and State Extension Services have been ready to step in at this point and try to bring about a solution of the problem which would insure a safe milk supply and at the same time allow producers to remain in business.

Profit Not the First Consideration

To further show how little the profit motive has entered into these efforts to *produce* a valuable food rather than to *sell* a product of questionable merit, it might be well to list some of the things which are being done.

At least one county agricultural school has spent several hundreds of dollars to equip a laboratory in which samples of milk can be tested for bacterial content and other qualifications which are essential to a good quality of milk and yet which must be continually checked due to variations in weather, in feed supply, and in the health of the herd. Some 1000 samples are examined yearly at actual cost to the producer. In another county thousands of samples are checked at a laboratory set up by the extension service. If a dealer complains of the quality of milk sent in by any producer, this laboratory affords an opportunity to check the sample against the complaint and clear up the trouble in the shortest time possible.

All the county extension services are ready to assist producers and distributors in their efforts to make and sell the kind of product which the public has a right to demand, because milk must be safe even if the expense of making it so is not properly offset by the price for which it sells.

Consumers Are Not Informed

The average milk consumer cannot know how many factors are involved in the production of an adequate and safe supply of milk for every day in the year. Eternal vigilance is the price of safety. Stated simply, good milk must come from healthy cows kept in clean surroundings, fed wholesome feed and cared for by healthy persons who appreciate the necessity for cleanliness and sanitation in the barn and milk room. From this point on, the milk must be handled in a strictly sanitary manner by persons who are healthy and who are absolutely cleanly in their habits. As a still further safeguard most milk sold in towns and cities is heated to about 142°F. and kept at this temperature for 30 minutes, then rapidly cooled and bottled. Pasteurizing milk in this manner takes away very little of its food value and when properly done has little effect on its flavor. It does, however, kill practically all harmful bacteria and causes the milk to remain sweet for a longer period. So-called raw or natural milk can be purchased in most markets, but it should be produced under carefully supervised conditions. Certified is the safest kind of raw milk and it brings a higher price.

While the conditions necessary for a safe milk supply can be easily and quickly stated, the process of bringing these conditions to pass is anything but simple.

A successful dairyman must have not only healthy cows but they must be good producers. Less than half the cows being milked in Massachusetts today produce enough milk to be profitable. Some of these low producers may get by because their owners are able to provide home grown feed at a comparatively low cost. It is seldom, however, that good feeding methods are found on the same farm with poor cows.

In every county of the State, herd owners have come together into groups for the purpose of keeping accurate records of production and of feed costs. They are assisted in this by county and state extension services with the result that better cows are being purchased and raised on the farm, better feed and larger crops are being grown, and a closer check is being made on the health of the cattle and on the quality of the milk produced.

One of the most discouraging things for a dairyman to tackle is the problem of "off flavor" in his milk. Any one of half a dozen things may be responsible for this condition and it may or may not be due to carelessness on the part of the operator. It is important to find the trouble at once since such milk will not be accepted at the plant. Often a representative of the State College will go to a farm and carefully check every operation, hopeful that he can locate the trouble promptly. It would be a fine thing for all concerned if such a trained "trouble shooter" could be available whenever needed.

New Uses for Milk

There is no question as to the food value, the safe and adequate supply and the many uses to which milk can be adapted. If more people could know about these things it is safe to say that one-third more milk would be used. This would just about take care of any surplus at the present time, and would insure a better return to the industry.

Any well-equipped soda fountain or milk bar now features a wide variety of milk drinks. The Extension Service at the Massachusetts State College has just issued a folder on "New Ideas in Milk Drinks." This is Extension Leaflet 177 and features 22 different combinations, all of which can be prepared at home. This folder can be obtained by writing directly to the State College at Amherst, Mass.

Consumers of milk, and that means just about everybody, would do well to realize that milk is one of the best and most economical foods that can be purchased and that the people of the world who make the most liberal use of milk also are the healthiest and the most efficient.

PRODUCTION OF QUALITY MILK

HARLEY A. LELAND

Assistant State Club Leader
Massachusetts State College

The production of quality milk has been an important subject for older club members enrolled in our 4-H dairy project. Local and state dairy inspectors have given the members a great deal of information concerning the health aspect of quality milk production, and exhibits of quality milk utensils and equipment have been featured at local and county gatherings.

So great has been the interest in this topic that more than half of our 4-H demonstration teams have chosen this for their topic. The boys and girls of these teams have demonstrated before their local meetings and at state gatherings. For two years demonstration teams from Massachusetts demonstrated this subject at the National Dairy Show and both times won the National contest. In 1931, a team composed of Joseph and Helen Sena of Easthampton took first place with twenty other states competing and received gold watches and medals. When asked if they put into practice at home what they were demonstrating they said, "Yes, twice a day for 365 days in the year and have been doing it for several years." Now Joe is in partnership with his father retailing several hundred quarts of quality milk in four towns in western Massachusetts. They have built a new model dairy barn and the milk house with all the necessary up-to-date equipment for the production of a quality product.

In 1937 Paul Lehtola and Philip Bamberg, two boys from Norfolk county, demonstrated this topic at the National Dairy Show at Columbus, Ohio. They won the National contest with 37 other states competing. Each boy received a $400 scholarship for higher education at an agricultural college.

A great many club members in the state are working with their parents on the home farm where quality milk is produced. Mildred Sanford of Ludlow, 16 years old, owns over 15 purebred Ayrshires in partnership with her father, and they produce certified milk for a large concern in Springfield.

Massachusetts State College

United States Department of Agriculture and County
Extension Services in Agriculture and Home Economics Cooperating

DEMONSTRATION—THE PRODUCING OF QUALITY MILK

Prepared by Paul Lehtola and Philip Bamberg in
cooperation with C. Hilton Boynton, County Club Agent
Distributed by Harley A. Leland, Assistant State Club Leader

Foreword

This demonstration was given by Paul and Philip at the National Dairy Show, Columbus, Ohio, in 1937. The demonstration won first prize in the New England division and was finally awarded first place in the National Contest over divisional winners from the other three sections of the United States.

Demonstration

PAUL:

We are the Norfolk County 4-H Dairy Demonstration Team. I am Paul Lehtola of South Weymouth and my team mate is Philip Bamberg of Walpole. Both Phil and I have been 4-H Club members for five years. We have chosen for the subject of our demonstration "The Producing of Quality Milk." We feel that this subject is very appropriate because both Phil and I are dairymen. Phil produces milk from his two cows and retails it to his neighbors, while on my home farm my father and I produce and retail 125 quarts of raw milk daily. Consequently, we feel that the production of quality milk is a vital subject to us.

Phil will now perform the first step in producing a quart of quality milk, namely, the milking of the cow. First he will brush the cow, second, wipe the udder, third, make use of the teat cup. Now we will let Phil go on with his milking.

The average consumer is interested in milk only to the extent that it is white and pours out of a bottle. Now I wish to point out to you consumers what you should look for in buying a quart of milk.

First, Food Value

Milk has often been called nature's most nearly perfect food; it contains so many of the nutrients which our bodies need and supplies them in such easily available forms! For example, it contains proteins, carbohydrates, fats, which furnish food energy for supporting the demands of the body for both work and play. It is rich in calcium and phosphorus from which our bones and teeth are formed. It is also one of the best sources of vitamins A and G, and a good source of vitamin B. From an actual food value standpoint one quart of milk is equal to 9 eggs, 6½ oranges or ¾ of a pound of steak.

Second, Cleanliness

Clean milk is a product of uniformly low bacteria count and free from dirt. It is produced from healthy cows free from tuberculosis and other diseases, and it is handled by healthy employees using sanitary methods and clean and sterile equipment and utensils.

Third, The Consumer Is Interested In the Keeping Qualities of Milk Because It Affects the Pocketbook

Milk which retains its sweetness is usable over a longer period of time. When milk is properly produced the organism bacillus lactis, which causes souring, is greatly reduced. This type of bacteria in itself, is harmless, but it is often associated with more harmful types.

Fourth, Healthfulness

No longer need the consumer feel that milk is a dangerous source of contagion. Public health departments are supervising more strictly the production of milk. Cows are state and federal tested for tuberculosis. They may also be tested for abortion. Officials inspect annually the barn, milk room and premises for cleanliness and general sanitation. This assures a more healthful product for the consumer.

Fifth, Flavor and Odor

One day a housewife complained to me of her milk having a fishy taste. When she was questioned it was found that she had placed the bottle of milk uncapped next to some fresh fish in the refrigerator. Very often the milkman is blamed for situations similar to this one, which in many cases is due to carelessness on the part of the consumer. Milk is a product which readily absorbs foreign flavors and odors from materials such as fish, onions and bananas. Undesirable flavors and odors are a distinct disadvantage from a commercial standpoint. A good producer avoids using feeds which cause objectionable odors and off flavors.

To sum up what has aleady been said, quality milk is a food that is produced under clean, sanitary conditions, that comes from a healthy cow and is free from any off flavors and odors.

I have just pointed out to you consumers the reasons why you should be interested in buying quality milk. Now I wish to raise the question "Why should the producer be interested in producing quality milk?"

First, the Health of the Consumer

It is our responsibility as producers to be concerned about the health of the consumer. The animals in both Phil's and my herd are tuberculin tested and have met state and federal requirements for an accredited herd. In all herds all infected cows are eliminated as soon as such conditions are found. Cattle which abort are also removed, and cows infected with mastitis are isolated from the herd. The health of the handler is also a very important consideration. All attendants should be in the best of health. Some very serious epidemics have been traced through the milk to milkers affected by a disease.

Second, Better Price for Product

The producer has an eye for profit also. The dairyman, who has the reputation for producing a quality product, can command a higher price. A good example of this is the price range between grade A milk and family milk in our country. Family milk sells for thirteen cents a quart while grade A milk brings sixteen cents a quart. In addition to this, quality milk also increases the sales.

Third, Less Bacteria

Quality milk contains a limited number of bacteria. Raw milk which is produced according to the Massachusetts standards shall show a bacterial count of not more than one hundred thousand colonies per cubic centimeter when delivered to the consumer. We are producing milk of seventy-five hundred on our home farm. Milk containing a large amount of dirt and sediment is naturally high in bacteria.

Fourth, Keeping Qualities

There is a close relationship between the number of bacteria in a quart of milk and its keeping qualities. A large number of bacteria, particularly of the lactic type, decreases the length of time the milk remains sweet. There are certain types of bacteria which cause souring that are frequently found in milk not properly handled.

These are the primary reasons why the producer should be interested in producing quality milk.

Now I wonder what Phil has for us.

You will notice that he has been using a small top milk pail. This space limits the space through which dirt may fall. He is also a dryhand milker. Show them your hands, Phil.

We recently had a rather interesting experience on our home farm. My father hired a man to assist with the milking. The first morning that he milked he asked for the lard, to our surprise. There are several methods used to simplify the process of milking such as greasing the hands with lard, as this man was in the habit of doing. Any practices such as this are very undesirable because they increase the possibility of getting more bacteria into the milk.

Phil will now continue with the demonstration while I proceed to take samples of milk and prepare them for testing.

PHILIP:

This chart lists the five important factors in the production of quality milk.

First, A Clean Barn

The dairy barn should be of durable but simple construction so it can easily be cleaned. It is best to have the floors of concrete. Walls and ceilings should be of smooth material painted cream or white or even whitewashed, with no protruding beams to collect dirt and dust. Plenty of window space properly arranged will provide ample light and natural ventilation. Sunlight, we all know, plays an important part in retarding bacterial growth.

Second, Health of Cow and Milker

Paul has already told you considerable about the health of the cow and the milker. I merely emphasize again that milk from a healthy cow, handled by a clean milker, helps decidedly in assuring the customer a clean product.

Third, Sterilization of Utensils

In the first place, utensils should be seamless and always carefully washed and sterilized every time they are used. There are two methods of sterilization: by chemicals and by steam or boiling water. (Some dairy farms are equipped with a steam boiler and can employ both of these methods.) There are several good commercial chemicals on the market, most of which contain a chlorine base.

Fourth, Clean Milk Free from Dirt

Most of the dirt found in milk accumulates in the dairy barn so this should be the place in which to correct conditions. Cow's flanks and udder should be clipped in order to prevent dirt and dust from clinging to the hair and falling into the milk. At each milking the cow should be thoroughly brushed, the flank and udder wiped off with a damp cloth. Also the small top milk pails prevent dirt from falling into the milk.

Fifth, Cooling the Milk as Soon as It is Drawn Checks Bacterial Growth

The milk should be reduced to a temperature between forty and fifty degrees F. within thirty minutes after milking. The two methods of cooling are by aeration and in a tank. The aerating method is more efficient as the milk can be brought to the required temperature in a shorter time. You will notice we are using a cone-cooler of the aerating type. When the milk is sufficiently cooled, it should be held at that temperature until it is bottled—preferably until it is used. Some distributors refrigerate their product while it is in transit to the consumer.

These five points are essential in the production of quality.

A strainer is employed to eliminate all loose hair, dirt and dust before the milk is bottled. Essentially, the strainer should be of simple construction and seamless. This is a seamless strainer composed of only three parts: bowl, a wire ring, and a perforated disc. A new cotton disc is used and the old one destroyed after each straining of forty quarts.

Now that we have strained the milk, there may be a question in your mind—why cool milk? When milk is properly cooled and reduced to the temperature stated before, bacteria, which thrive in warm conditions, cannot grow. To be a little clearer, let me state that bacteria are present but they fail to multiply.

Now to prove the points which we have discussed, we would like to run two simple tests to substantiate the statements that we have made. These two are the Sediment and Methylene Blue Tests.

Sediment Tests

The presence of sediment in milk is evidence that such milk has not been handled properly. It shows that at some point in its production someone has neglected, or carelessly carried out, some important step which is essential for the production of clean and safe milk. The sediment in itself may not be dangerous, but, on the other hand, it may be a real source of infection.

The proper use of the sediment test may be of great assistance in improving the milk supply. This is one test which brings before the producer, in a concrete and convincing manner, the cleanliness of his product.

There are three types of sediment testers—The Wizard, which is the oldest and the least used; the Wisconsin, which is the most expensive and not as good as the Vacuum type that we are going to use. This tester is composed of two parts—the cylinder and the plunger. A filter disc is held in place by this wire clip, the plunger is then inserted and a pint of milk poured into the cylinder. The plunger is slowly withdrawn creating a vacuum which draws the milk through the disc. We have several samples of discs which we have taken from some producers in our own district. You will notice how favorably our sample compares with these.

The Methylene Blue Reduction Test

This test depends upon the reduction of color by bacterial action in milk. One cc. of a solution of methylene blue is added to 10 cc. of milk giving it a blue color. This solution will decolorize according to the number of bacteria present in the milk. Excessive numbers of bacteria decolorize the milk rapidly. Milk which remains blue six hours or more is rated as desirable. Practically all bacteria reduce the intensity of methylene blue; and those of the lactic type reduce it much more quickly than other bacteria commonly found in milk.

The equipment used for this test is a 1 cc. pipette, a 10 cc. pipette, a test tube, a hot water bath and a methylene blue solution. This solution is made by dissolving one of these tablets in 200 cc. of water. Or in other words, one of these tablets will make about 200 tests.

Ten cc. of milk is placed into this test tube. One cc. of methylene blue solution is added to the milk giving it a blue color. Due to the limited amount of time we have prepared several samples. This test tube has remained in the hot water bath for five hours and not lost its color. This test has been in the hot water bath only two hours and it is white, thus, the latter sample has a considerably greater number of bacteria than the former sample.

This concludes our demonstration.

MILK-BORNE DISEASES

A. DANIEL RUBENSTEIN, M.D.

*Epidemiologist, Division of Communicable Diseases
Massachusetts Department of Public Health*

That bacteria are the cause of many common human diseases is now axiomatic. The methods by which they are transferred are coming to be well known. Some are conveyed by touching either the ill person or articles which he has used; some by breathing the germs expelled into the surrounding air by coughing or sneezing; some by food or water which has been contaminated by material from the sick; some by insects which bite first the sick and then the well; a few are diseases of animals which may be transmitted to man. The problem of avoiding disease is made more complex by the "carrier" who harbors disease germs without being ill.

Milk as a Carrier of Disease

Of the foodstuffs which transmit disease, milk has in the past been most frequently incriminated. There are several reasons for this. In the first place, bacteria grow well in milk and thus a small number of disease-producing organisms accidentally introduced into milk may produce widespread and serious results. Secondly, of all of our foodstuffs, milk is the most difficult to handle and distribute in a satisfactory condition, and finally it is one of the few of our foods obtained from animal sources which is still being consumed in the raw state by large numbers of individuals.

Milk-borne disease may be considered under two headings. On the one hand there is the spectacular epidemic form where many individuals suddenly come down with a single disease almost simultaneously. The most common diseases in this category are scarlet fever, septic sore throat, typhoid fever, and diphtheria. On the other hand, milk may convey other diseases less dramatically because, instead of many individuals becoming ill simultaneously, they take to bed one by one over a longer period of time. Undulant fever, tuberculosis of bovine origin, bacillary dysentery, foot-and-mouth disease, and some of the diarrheal infections of children are included under this latter grouping. With the advent of an ever increasing amount of pasteurized milk, the dysenteries and infantile diarrheas are becoming less important as milk-borne disease.

Bovine Tuberculosis

Bovine tuberculosis is that form of the disease which is contracted by ingestion of raw milk or milk products infected with tubercle bacilli or the germs of tuberculosis. It is rarely if ever the cause cf the usual adult form of the disease which involves primarily the lungs. On the other hand, it is a very important factor in other forms. "Scrofula" or tuberculosis involving the glands of the neck and causing unsightly swellings, suppurative at times, was at one time a fairly common disease in children. Similarly, the marked deformities produced by bovine tuberculosis of the spine, hip, and other bones present an ever decreasing incidence. In general, it has been shown that all forms of bovine tuberculosis including those of skin, abdomen, bones, and glands have become much less common in recent years.

Undulant Fever

Undulant fever is a disease primarily of livestock and secondarily of man. It is a general infection with Brucella organism which is also known as Bang's bacillus. Undulant fever is remarkable for its low mortality, repeated attacks, and long drawn out course. It is characterized by profuse sweats, constipation, frequent lapses accompanied by pain of rheumatic or neuralgic origin. The mode of transfer to man is usually through raw milk and sometimes through dairy products, such as, butter, cheese or cream: It may be conveyed by direct contact with infected animals or their tissues. In Massachusetts, practically all cases are associated with consumption of raw milk. In a few instances, infection was acquired by direct contact with animals. An increasing number of cases is being reported to the Massachusetts Department of Public Health. This increased incidence may be, however, more apparent than real. Physicians are displaying a greater interest in this disease and are diagnosing and reporting more cases. (See Table I).

Table I

INCIDENCE OF UNDULANT FEVER IN MASSACHUSETTS.

Year	No. Cases	Case Rate	No. Deaths
1930	6	.1	0
1931	15	.4	0
1932	15	.4	0
1933	11	.3	0
1934	15	.3	0
1935	42	1.0	1
1936	53	1.3	4
1937	43	1.0	2
1938 (6 mos.)	17	.8	1

Milk-Borne Epidemics

Turning our attention to those milk-borne diseases which occur in epidemic form, one notes several characteristics which are common to the entire group. Milk-borne epidemics sometimes have an explosive onset, rise to a peak, and decline gradually. Many outbreaks show a greater incidence of the disease among women and children, who are usually credited with drinking more milk than men. There is apt to be a short incubation period; however, the disease may be mild or virulent. Multiple cases may occur simultaneously in the same household. As a rule, milk outbreaks last a comparatively short time and extend over a circumscribed area, as the disease follows the milk wagon. At first the disease occurs almost exclusively among users of the infected milk. Later secondary cases may occur among contacts.

Milk-borne outbreaks of disease are almost always due to raw milk; often milk of good quality. It is interesting to note that sometimes only one person of a number living in the same house is attacked, and such a one is the only person who drinks the milk raw. There is no record of a milk-borne outbreak attributable to milk properly pasteurized and properly distributed.

Scarlet Fever

At the present time scarlet fever is the most common milk-borne disease occurring in epidemic form. The rash, high fever, sore throat, and characteristic strawberry tongue are familiar findings of this disease. In epidemic form, scarlet fever is sometimes extensive and serious. Very often, multiple cases occur in a single family. Some of these may fail to show the typical rash, although all other findings are characteristic. At times, evidence of acute mastitis can be found in the herd which is the source of the infected milk supply. In Massachusetts, twenty-nine outbreaks of milk-borne scarlet have been reported, the last outbreak having occurred in 1933.

Septic Sore Throat

Epidemics of septic sore throat are probably always milk-borne. The disease may be quite severe and result in death. It is not readily communicable from person to person. The inflammation and swelling of the tonsils and lymph nodes of the neck may become quite marked. The course may be prolonged and complications, such as abscesses, glandular enlargement, arthritis, and kidney damage, may result.

The infection usually gets into milk from human sources. The streptococcus which produces septic sore throat is found in both cases and carried in man and in cows. It may become seeded in the udder of the cow. Once the germ has entered, it may remain six weeks or longer. This explains why milk-borne outbreaks of septic sore throat are sometimes long drawn out. In Massachusetts, records of twenty-five outbreaks of septic sore throat with more than 5,000 cases have been collected, the last having occurred in 1932.

Typhoid Fever

Typhoid fever was formerly responsible for more milk-borne epidemics than any other disease. Today this disease with its severe symptoms and serious complications has become quite rare. The greater incidence of this disease during August and September naturally affords potential foci for the infection of milk. Moreover, once the infection of milk has occurred, the greater difficulty of maintaining milk at a low temperature in the hot weather permits a more ready multiplication of the initial contamination. The typhoid carrier is the most important single source of infection for milk, although outbreaks may be caused by convalescent or missed cases. The incubation period is usually short. In this state, 135 instances involving over 2,000 cases have been reported in which the cause was traced to milk. The last outbreak of milk-borne typhoid occured in 1932.

Diphtheria

Milk-borne diphtheria is becoming a rare disease. The disease is characterized by sore throat, high fever, marked prostration, and membrane formations usually in the throat and nose. Diphtheria germs in milk practically always come from human sources, either cases or carriers. In a few rare instances, ulcers upon the teat of the cow have become infected with diphtheria and the germs then transferred to milk. The usual route is, however, direct contamination from human sources.

Fourteen outbreaks of milk-borne diphtheria have occurred in Massachusetts, the last in 1925.

In addition to the more common forms of milk-borne disease, other conditions may occur in epidemic form. Meningococcic meningitis and infantile paralysis have been known to produce milk-borne outbreaks. Bacillary dysentery and summer diarrhea of infants are other diseases which may assume this form of spread. The one factor common to all such epidemics is raw milk.

Milk-Borne Epidemics in Massachusetts

The Massachusetts Department of Public Health has for many years recorded and analyzed milk-borne epidemics. Table II is a chronological record of milk-borne outbreaks in Massachusetts from 1881 to the present. It will be noted that 188 reported outbreaks have been recorded. Analysis of these epidemics reveals a gradual but definite diminution in milk-borne outbreaks. It has been pointed out that the sharp decline noted in Massachusetts is much less marked in the country as a whole. This is explained partly by the irregularity in reporting of milk-borne outbreaks and partly by a higher percentage of raw milk sold in other states.

Table II

Years	Outbreaks	Years	Outbreaks
1886-1890	3	1916-1920	32
1891-1895	4	1921-1925	17
1896-1900	15	1926-1930	12
1901-1905	20	1931-1935	9
1906-1910	28	1936	0
1911-1915	45	1937	0

The occurrence of communicable disease on farms and dairies may precipitate milk-borne outbreaks. The presence of such cases on any farm or dairy producing milk products should be reported at once by the physician to the local health authorities. If no physician is in attendance, it becomes the legal responsibility of the owner or person in charge to notify boards of health. Milk handlers must be impressed with the fact that disease may be transmitted by milk. The presence of illness among employees or their families should be called to the attention of owners or of the health authorities by workers. Such symptoms and signs as sore throat, rash, diarrhea, and unexplained fever are particularly suspicious.

The prevention of milk-borne disease can only be accomplished by several factors operating simultaneously. Methods of milk sanitation must be maintained at a high level. A stricter adherence to sanitary codes and milk laws must be practiced. The success or failure in the proper handling of milk can only be properly evaluated by suitable laboratory tests. An ever larger proportion of communities are requiring bacteriological examinations of milk supplies. Tuberculin testing and subsequent disposal of positive reactors has been an important factor in lowering the incidence of bovine tuberculosis. The single major method in the prevention of milk-borne disease is pasteurization. It is the most important defense against the spread of disease by means of milk. Prevention without pasteurization is practically impossible.

BANG ABORTION DISEASE

CHARLES F. RIORDAN

Director, Division of Livestock Disease Control
Massachusetts Department of Agriculture

It was once said, quoting in part from a speaker on the subject of public health, that a public health program cannot be considered adequate or complete unless all agencies capable of contributing to such a program are utilized in carrying it forward for the benefit of the entire citizenship of a community. With that thought in mind, Bang Abortion disease, although wholly a disease of animals, is not, I believe, out of place in this issue of *The Commonhealth*.

Close association and the relationship that exists between man and domestic animals has tended to create a certain hazard, as has been evidenced by the many diseases common to both, such as, tuberculosis, rabies, trichinosis, etc. Of the many such diseases directly transmissible to man, it is only comparatively recently that Bang Abortion disease, a disease common in cattle and for many years named and referred to as "Contagious Abortion," has been recognized as being of importance from the standpoint of public health and now agreed to be a common cause of the condition in man diagnosed as Undulant Fever.

Its importance from a public health view, however, is not to be compared with that of bovine tuberculosis and possibly of other diseases of animal origin, many of them fatal, but it is of the greatest importance to the livestock industry from an economic viewpoint and from which viewpoint this article is written.

Prior to what is now referred to as the practical eradication of bovine tuberculosis, the annual financial loss caused by tuberculosis through its effect on the general health of cattle and through the condemnation of diseased carcasses as unfit for food was estimated well up in the millions of dollars. With that menace to animal health practically under control, attention has been turned to Bang Abortion disease and the losses from that disease through the premature birth of calves with a resultant loss of milk production, by the breaking down of the natural resistance to other disease processes, as a predisposing cause of mastitis and as the active cause of sterility, all of which tend to a monetary loss estimated at even a higher figure than that of bovine tuberculosis.

Prevalent in all countries, Bang Abortion disease has unquestionably existed for centuries, records showing that its occurrence in this country was referred to in agricultural publications dating back more than a hundred years. In the year 1884 the General Court of Massachusetts passed a law (Chapter 232) requiring the then Cattle Commissioners to make inquiries and gather facts and statistics in relation to the prevalence among the neat stock of the State of the disease known as abortion in cattle and its effect on the healthfulness of milk as an article of food, etc. Little good, if any, was accomplished by this early effort to determine the cause and effect of the disease.

The discovery of the causative agent of tuberculosis by Professor Koch focused attention on bovine tuberculosis and so occupied the attention of those interested in livestock disease prevention that it acted practically as a smoke screen as pertaining to other animal disease problems. Now with the tuberculosis problem out of the way, attention is again directed to this other menace to the health of animals, Bang Abortion disease.

With the discovery of the organism which causes this disease by Professor Bang, a Danish investigator, and which organism he called Bacillus Abortus, much of the mystery which had surrounded the disease was cleared up and later the disease itself was given the name of Bang Abortion Disease.

Rarely found to occur in unbred heifers, it may be classed as a disease of adult animals and, although diagnosed at times in nonpregnant adult animals, it can also be considered a disease of pregnancy. Again, although known as abortion disease, premature birth is of rather infrequent occurrence as compared with the number of animals which are shown by test to harbor the disease. When such act does occur, it is, however, the most readily observed and about the only definite symptom of the disease shown. Abortion may, however, occur from causes other than Bang Abortion disease. In abortions due to the bacillus abortus, the placenta together with the discharges which follow and which continue for varying periods of time from the genital tracts become the source of the spread of the infection through contamination of bedding, litter, floors, cleansing utensils, etc. From this, it being now practically universally conceded that the digestive tract is the channel through which the disease is most commonly contracted, it is evident that careful attention is necessary and must be given to sanitation. Separate calving pens should be provided; all afterbirths, whether from premature or full time births, and contaminated litter should be burned or buried; prompt, thorough cleansing and disinfection of pens, floors and utensils should be done; and, where possible, separate attendants from those that have contact with the main herd should be employed.

Although for many years, attempts had been made by individual owners of dairy herds, and in the year 1917 the United States Bureau of Animal Industry started definite research work on vaccination against the disease, attention was not in general called to the alarming extent to which the disease was occurring until in the year 1934 the government conceived and adopted the so-called elimination plan for the purpose of reducing the oversupply of cattle then existing. Under this plan compensation up to a stated amount was made available for payment for cattle that were declared by veterinarians in the Federal employ to be diseased and were tagged, branded and slaughtered. Under this plan owners of cattle were and are now required to sign certain agreements relative to the purchase of replacements, disposition of reactors, etc., somewhat similar to regulations that had been adopted 20 years before in connection with the tuberculosis program. Under this plan 47 of the 48 States in the Union are now operating, although only eleven of these States are as yet themselves paying additional State indemnity.

In the examination of animals for the detection of Bang Abortion disease, no diagnostic physical test, such as tuberculin, has as yet been developed as is solely relied upon in the test for tuberculosis, diagnosis depending wholly upon results obtained by the blood agglutination test, which test is now universally accepted and adopted by all authorities and investigators interested in this problem. Antigen used and interpretation of readings of the test have been standardized so that the variance in results that at first were so frequently reported are now practically eliminated.

The interpretation of low titre readings is still a subject of discussion but it is now generally conceded that positive results to titres of 1-100 and higher indicate the animal from which blood is drawn to be diseased, while positive results to lower titres are rated as doubtful or suspicious, to be handled as decided upon by the authority to whom such case is reported.

Referring again to reimbursement or compensation, lack of legislation providing for additional payment for condemned animals in States other than the eleven mentioned is having a decidedly deterring effect on the part of those interested in the dairy industry who otherwise would undoubtedly welcome an opportunity on a cooperative basis to rid their herds of infected animals. Congress was itself apparently of the opinion that the present method of handling the elimination program was too one-sided, as this year an act was passed whereby payment of indemnity on and after May 1, 1939 will only be approved in States where Federal compensation is at least matched by State indemnity. Referring to the question of indemnity, it must not be overlooked that the eradication method by blood testing and slaughter is not by any means universally accepted as the best method of handling the problem, which fact in itself has considerable bearing on State legislation. An ever increasing number of experiments with vaccine, conducted by government and private individuals, although it is too early now to arrive at a definite conclusion, would indicate that by the inoculation of calves between the ages of four and eight months an immunity or protection can be established. This may possibly, if properly conducted, ultimately end in the elimination of the disease or at least get it under as near control as could ever be done by the test and slaughter method and at a greatly reduced expenditure of capital.

Today in our State, Massachusetts, Bang Abortion disease is not handled as are other contagious diseases of animals. It is not required that affected animals be either reported or quarantined, nor is it required that known reactors to the blood test be branded or reported and neither is their movement or disposition restricted in any manner.

It is not, however, intended to imply that no action whatever has been taken, as regulations were put into effect at the time the government elimination plan became effective, by which the transportation of known blood test reactors and of so-called abortors into the State was forbidden. Provision had also already been made for the furnishing of laboratory service for examination of blood samples and the furnishing of vials for obtaining samples, both of which, service and vials, are provided without charge.

In the year 1930 a plan referred to as the Massachusetts plan for the establishment of Bang Disease-Free Accredited Herds was also put into operation, under which many of the outstanding herds of the State have been freed of the disease through the efforts of their owners and are now rated as accredited herds.

The present year a definite step was taken by the passage of a law requiring that cattle intended for dairy purposes transported in any manner into the State must be accompanied by a certificate of health bearing the signature of the proper livestock official of the State of origin, indicating that said cattle were negative to a blood agglutination test made within 30 days of date of entry.

Although the State is not yet taking an active part in either an eradication or a control program, this law prevents the State from becoming a dumping ground for infected animals from other States.

Other legislation passed this year, and now law gives the State authority, through the Division of Livestock Disease Control, to vaccinate calves between the ages of four and eight months of age for such owners as may request that type of service.

Whether or not it is feasible for the State to attempt, or assist in, eradication of Bang Abortion disease by test and slaughter, and at the same time attempt to build up an immunity by vaccination, is a question. However, in the interest of those bent on eradication, it would appear that in order that such persons should be able to avail themselves of Federal indemnity the State should cooperate with the government by seeking legislation whereby State compensation would be available.

BOVINE TUBERCULOSIS

HARRIE W. PEIRCE, M.D.V.

Chief Veterinary Health Officer
Division of Livestock Disease Control
Massachusetts Department of Agriculture

Foreword:

In complying with a request for an article for publication in the quarterly bulletin *The Commonhealth* on the history of the eradication of tuberculosis from the dairy herds of Massachusetts, I feel that it would not be out of place to submit the following paper prepared for and presented by me in connection with the "Achievement Day" exercises held at Boston on October 31, 1935, in recognition of the Commonwealth of Massachusetts as a "Modified Accredited Tuberculosis-Free Area" under the title of

A Tabloid Review of the History Pertaining to Bovine Tuberculosis in the Commonwealth of Massachusetts

In preparing this contribution to the Achievement Day program I have endeavored to tabulate in a more or less chronological sequence and as briefly as possible such facts, statements or incidents as appeared to be appropriate to a condensed story of bovine tuberculosis and its near eradication in this Commonwealth.

The data as to the early history of this disease is taken from annual reports of the different livestock officials who held office in the period from 1880 to 1910, and from a paper on the subject prepared and read by Dr. Austin Peters at the International Congress on Tuberculosis held in Washington, D. C., September 21 to October 12, 1908.

Credit for the first attempt to call attention of Massachusetts farmers to the nature, importance and seriousness of bovine tuberculosis should be given to one Noah Cressy, who, in addition to holding a degree of V. S., also had the degrees M. D. and Ph.D. and who had held the chair of Professor of Veterinary Science at the Massachusetts Agricultural College.

According to his own statement, he had severed his connection with the college on account of differences of opinion between himself and some of the members of the faculty on the question of tuberculosis.

As a speaker at several farmers' institutes held in the western part of the State during the winter of 1879 and 1880, Dr. Cressy called attention to the prevalence and danger of tuberculosis. His addresses excited comment at the time and were given considerable newspaper publicity. *The Springfield Republican* on January 30, 1880, printed an article under the heading "A Rural Sensation" and referred to a farmers' institute held the previous day in the town of Warren where Dr. Cressy had read a paper on "The Diseases of Farm Animals," in which he included mention of tuberculosis in cattle. He had stated among other things that the herd of cattle maintained at the Massachusetts Agricultural College was badly affected with tuberculosis and that the trustees were allowing cattle from the herd to be sold to farmers throughout the State for the purpose of improving their stock and were in this way spreading the disease. He believed that the disease could be conveyed to humans and as proof of his contention he caused quite a sensation by introducing a Mr. Paige of Hardwick, who was brought onto the platform in a wheelchair. Mr. Paige informed the audience that in the spring of 1877 he had purchased three Ayrshire heifers of the Agricultural College, that in November, 1879, one of the heifers upon being slaughtered was found badly diseased, and that his paralysis and also a sickness from which his children were suffering were attributed to the use of milk from these heifers.

Immediate exception was taken to this article in the *Republican* and to the statements of Dr. Cressy, by Professor Levi Stockbridge who had been connected with the State department having control of contagious diseases of animals since the year 1869 and who for thirteen years up to that time had also been connected with the Massachusetts Agricultural College. Professor Stockbridge replied in the next issue of the *Republican*, January 31, 1880, that the college had never bred an animal that had tuberculosis there or that had developed it within two years of the time it was sold; that "the disease is only consumption and may attack any breed of cattle in any part of the country"; that "the milk is healthy until the animal's constitutional vigor is utterly reduced"; and that "Mr. Paige's statement that the milk gave him paralysis is preposterous," adding that Dr. Cressy's statement that he left the college because of a disagreement regarding tuberculosis was "an unmitigated and outrageous falsehood."

This controversy attracted a great deal of attention and at an institute held in Brookfield on February 5, 1880, which was very largely attended, Professor Stockbridge took the platform early in the proceedings and read from the January 30th issue of the *Republican*, paragraph by paragraph, asking Dr. Cressy at the end of each paragraph if such a statement was made by him. As each question was asked, Dr. Cressy, who evidently lacked the courage to maintain his position, shook his head.

On February 12, 1880, at a farmers' institute held at Northampton, Professor Stockbridge presided and the following resolution was endorsed: "Resolved: We believe the reports on the disease tuberculosis exaggerated and the attempt to connect the college with it unjust."

Dr. Austin Peters evidently was of the opinion that Dr. Cressy had been right as in his paper he stated. "Dr. Cressy's statements regarding the condition of the college herd and the danger to other herds by the introduction of cattle from it were correct. At that time a cat could not be kept in the cattle barn at the college without developing a cough, becoming emaciated and pining away in a few months."

Apparently the first reference by the Board of Cattle Commissioners to tuberculosis as a specific disease appears in a report by them to the legislature under the date of January 7, 1881, which reads, "The question of the contagiousness and virulence of tuberculosis is still under consideration and further research is necessary to elucidate and establish certain important points in connection with it. We have, therefore, declined to consider it within the intent of the law which describes our duties and obligations." This appears to be the first official recognition or refusal of recognition of such a disease and quite evidently was indirectly the result of the agitation caused by Dr. Cressy the previous winter.

Although this was the first mention of tuberculosis as a disease, it is quite evident by reading the reports regarding contagious pleuropneumonia during the period between 1860, the year in which the first livestock commission was appointed, and 1866, the year in which the disease was declared eradicated, that animals destroyed for contagious pleuropneumonia were extensively diseased with tuberculosis but little attention was paid to it as it was not known to be contagious.

In the report of January 10, 1882, the reference is made that "Inflammation of the lungs, or tuberculosis, may be engendered in the stock on any farm by undue exposure, want of ventilation or confinement in damp and filthy enclosures."

The bacillus of tuberculosis was discovered by Koch in that year, 1882, but little attention was given to it by the commissioners. Records show that in December, 1885, Dr. Frank S. Billings, a Boston veterinarian, prepared a paper on "Tuberculosis in Cattle" which was presented at a winter meeting of the State Board of Agriculture at Framingham, but as he did not personally present the paper there was little discussion of the same.

On November 29, 1886, at a special meeting of the State Board of Agriculture called by request of the Cattle Commissioners at Barre, Dr. J. F. Winchester of Lawrence, who had been appointed to the Commission the preceding year and who is referred to as a "young veterinarian and graduate of the Massachusetts Agricultural College," called attention to the "presence of bovine tuberculosis in the State, its hereditary nature, transmissibility and insidiousness, the difficulty of diagnosis, and the inability of the Board to assist owners of affected herds under the existing laws." He was followed on the program by Professor Stockbridge who evidently was still skeptical of the dangers of tuberculosis and who stated that the Board had long known of the existence of the disease but that the veterinary colleges had never agreed upon the question as to whether or not it was contagious, and that "There had been a long and acrimonious dispute in relation to it and the consequence has been that the Cattle Commission have never recognized it as a contagious disease."

In January, 1887, the report states, "Notwithstanding all that is certainly known of the disease and the great losses it entails, it is surrounded with such obscurity and uncertainty and presents such apparently unsurmountable obstacles to its eradication that we have made no direct attempts to combat it."

In the annual reports of the Board of Cattle Commissioners for 1889 and 1890 there appear the following:

1889. — "Should the disease materially increase in those sections of the State where milk is produced for town or city markets, as a measure to guard the public health it may become the duty of the Commissioners or Local Boards of Health to cause inspection of herds producing market milk and the removal therefrom of all animals exhibiting the slightest symptoms of this disease."

1890. — "Careful observation during the past years fails to convince us that this disease is becoming more prevalent; but the published experiments of sundry investigators, the zeal of veterinarians for the public welfare or their own personal interests, have pointed out the methods by which it is propagated, and newspaper reporters have aroused public attention to the matter by sensational or erroneous reports of a very few special cases. The disease has been here ever since white men or cattle occupied the land."

Primarily, with the exception of the attempt of Dr. Cressy, the honor of bringing to public attention the prevalence of bovine tuberculosis and the danger of the same to man and beast belongs to an organization known at that time as the Massachusetts Society for Promoting Agriculture. There is no question but that to it at least belongs the credit for the first legislative action taken pertaining to the disease.

In the spring of 1887 this organization, in cooperation with the State department, rented a farm in Mattapan to be used as an experimental station for the purpose of determining if there were any danger from the use of milk from tubercular cows, and a herd of cows believed to be tubercular was kept there for three years. The work was conducted under the supervision of Dr. Harold C. Ernst, professor of bacteriology at Harvard Medical School, Dr. Henry Jackson, Dr. Langdon Frothingham and Dr. Austin Peters. The experiment demonstrated the fact that milk from tubercular cows could and did contain tubercle bacilli, and tuberculosis was produced in calves and pigs fed upon the milk from this herd.

In a report made by Dr. Ernst appears the definite conclusion that:

1. While the transmission of tuberculosis by milk is probably not the most important means by which the disease is propagated it is something to be guarded against carefully.

2. The possibility of milk from tuberculous udders containing the infectious element is undeniable.

3. It is equally undeniable that milk from diseased cows with no appreciable lesion of the udder may, and frequently does contain the bacilli of tuberculosis.

This report was presented to the legislature of 1891 with a petition that the legislature procure an inspection of all cattle in Massachusetts. After considerable delay the legislature made an appropriation of $2,500 to be used by the State Board of Agriculture to investigate and ascertain the best methods to be adopted in order to protect the citizens of the Commonwealth from the presence of tuberculosis in food products of cattle. This appropriation was much less than had been asked for and the Board deemed it inadequate for the purpose and so reported, at the same time calling attention not only to the dangers to human health and life from tubercular animals but also to the danger of the spread to other animals. Recommendation was made, among other things, that the law be passed providing for the inspection by the State of all cattle sold at Brighton and Watertown markets, also that the Commission be given authority to condemn and slaughter without appraisal or payment all animals found to be affected with tuberculosis.

Evidently reports regarding the controversy in Massachusetts over tuberculosis had reached the ears of the livestock authorities of other states, as the report of 1891 in one place exhibits considerable ire against the State of Maine, which state apparently had issued an order prohibiting the shipment to Maine of neat cattle from Massachusetts because of the apparent prevalence of bovine tuberculosis. This action was regarded by the Massachusetts Board as unconstitutional.

Many of the recommendations of the Board referred to above were incorporated in the law by the legislature of 1892. In that year, ten years after the discovery of the tubercle bacillus by Koch, tuberculosis was declared in the law to be one of the contagious diseases of animals. In this year, 1892, two veterinarians, Drs. Charles P. Lyman, Dean of the Harvard Veterinary School, and Maurice O'Connell of Holyoke, were appointed to the Board and during their first year in office the legislature provided for payment for condemned cattle (one-half value based on their food and milk value).

In June, 1894, another veterinarian, Dr. F. H. Osgood, was added to the Board, making a membership of five,—Stockbridge, Herrick, Lyman, O'Connell and Osgood. In October Levi Stockbridge resigned after twenty-seven years of service and C. A. Dennen took his place.

On September 20, 1894, Drs. Lyman and Osgood made a report of the results of an extended experiment conducted by them on the use of tuberculin. This report resulted in the adoption of the following plan: to

1. Test all suspected animals.
2. Regulate the importation of cattle.
3. Quarantine and test all imported cattle.
4. Establish quarantine stations at which all imported cattle shall be delivered.
5. Forbid importation except to quarantine stations.

6. Brand all cattle that pass and are clean.
7. Systematically examine by tuberculin testing all cattle in the Commonwealth.

On November 21, 1894, tuberculin testing was started at the quarantine stations at Watertown and Brighton.

A general order was also issued quarantining all cattle in the counties of Barnstable, Dukes and Nantucket. As a result of this order the movement of cattle into these counties was forbidden unless the cattle were properly branded by the Commission as free from tuberculosis.

A crew of eight men in charge of Commissioner Dennen tuberculin tested all cattle in Nantucket, 665 head, and found six reactors. From there they went to Dukes County and tested 1,300 head between December 29th and February 22nd, with three reactors. On March 4th they started in Barnstable County and tested in eight towns 1,556 head, with six reactors. In addition to the work in these counties other herds scattered throughout the State were also being tested, with the result that the appropriation was exhausted and testing was stopped.

The avowed intention of the Board to test all cattle in the State aroused a great deal of opposition among the cattle owners. The Board was having its troubles also at the quarantine stations at Brighton and Watertown where, after testing from November 21, 1894, to April 30, 1895, "with the drovers fighting, objecting and placing every obstacle in the path of the Commission that they possibly could, the work was temporarily abandoned and cattle were allowed in on test charts." In localities where there were no veterinarians tests were accepted made by the laity who were practical cattlemen, castrators, and the like. "This method soon became a farce and fraud upon the public as much of the work was done dishonestly to please the cattle dealers, particularly cattle drovers attending the weekly market at Brighton."

Cattle condemned as reactors were at this time declared unfit for food, which resulted in the rendering of many carcasses that might have been passed for food.

In 1895 payment for reactors was allowed for full appraised value not exceeding $60.

In 1896 Dr. Lyman was succeeded by Dr. John M. Parker and in November Dr. Osgood resigned and was replaced by Dr. Austin Peters.

As a result of the growing objection to compulsory testing a law was passed in April, 1896, limiting the use of tuberculin. Many farmers had no interest in the attempt to eradicate the disease, but had the test made at their own expense as a matter of speculation with the idea of selling cattle of little value for more than they were worth. It is reported this resulted practically in a raid on the appropriation and as a consequence the legislature of 1897 appointed a committee to investigate the work of the Commission. This committee consisted of Dr. Harold C. Ernst, Dr. Theobold Smith, Dr. N. Kinnell of Pittsfield, Dr. Frank Billings of Grafton and Dr. Charles R. Wood of Lowell. Their report resulted in the passing of a law limiting compensation to cattle tested by authorized agents of the Board.

In 1898 the House voted to abolish the Commission. The Senate refused to concur and the Governor wrote the legislature recommending a further appropriation. The House again voted to abolish the Commission and the Senate again refused to concur. Without any provision for an appropriation the Commission decided to continue without official authority during the remainder of the year, which they did. However, the legislature of 1899 passed a deficiency appropriation bill sufficient to pay the members of the Commission the arrears in their salary. The legislature also recodified the laws relating to contagious diseases of animals, reduced the Commission to three members, Peters, Herrick and Dennen, and reduced payment for reactors from $60 to $40.

In 1902 the Board was abolished and a Cattle Bureau of the State Board of Agriculture was established with Dr. Peters as chief of the Bureau. During the eight years that he served the State in this capacity little progress was made as far as eradication or even control of the spread of tuberculosis was concerned. Such cattle as showed clinical symptoms of the disease were condemned and destroyed. Cattle moved into the State unless accompanied by test charts were held and tested either at the quarantine station or outside. That Dr. Peters was not at all satisfied with the method of conducting this branch of the work of his bureau, but which he was practically forced to adopt according to the law, is shown by statements which are made in the annual reports of the Bureau during that period.

In the report of 1904 we find, "Owing to the difficulty of having all the tests outside of the State made honestly and carefully it would be more satisfactory to test all animals after arrival," and further on, "If the money now expended in paying for bad cases of tuberculosis could be used for testing and cleaning up entire herds, more permanent headway might be made toward diminishing its frequency. The testing could be commenced in cattle raising districts in the western part of the State and as these localities were cleaned up work could be undertaken on the same plan in the eastern part. If such measures were adopted the State ought to disinfect the stables where cattle were killed and the owner should be required to sign a binding agreement to buy only tested cattle in the future."

In the year 1908 Dr. Peters is quoted as saying, "It is doubtful if the work as present being carried on against bovine tuberculosis in Massachusetts accomplishes much in the direction of decreasing the percentage of tuberculosis among the herds in the State as a fresh crop of badly diseased cattle, mostly cows, is harvested year after year."

The fact that the carcasses of reactor cattle were at this time, under certain conditions, allowed to be used for food purposes was called to the attention of the public by a Boston newspaper in connection with a shipment of reactors from Martha's Vineyard which were consigned to a slaughtering establishment in Somerville and there killed. The sale for food purposes caused widespread controversy and was undoubtedly the direct cause of Dr. Peters' failing to be reappointed as chief of the Bureau.

Dr. Peters was succeeded in office by Fred Freeland Walker of Burlington, farmer by occupation, but who also bred, raised and dealt more or less in purebred Holstein cattle. His term extended from October 5, 1910, to January 2, 1915, during which period the Cattle Bureau of the Department of Agriculture, by act of legislature, was abolished and a

Department of Animal Industry created. Little other than an attempt to improve the sanitary condition of buildings used for the housing of cattle was done as far as tuberculosis was concerned during this period. Foot-and-mouth disease broke out in the fall of 1914 and all work in regard to tuberculosis was stopped.

On January 2, 1915, Dr. Lester H. Howard, a Boston veterinarian, was appointed to succeed Mr. Walker. Foot-and-mouth disease shortly afterward was declared eradicated. The importation and tuberculin testing of cattle and the condemnation of clinical cases was continued along the same lines as had been followed the previous eighteen or twenty years.

Conditions similar to those in the Commonwealth of Massachusetts apparently existed in other parts of the United States. Tuberculosis, bovine, porcine, avian and even certain types of human tuberculosis, was apparently on the increase, as is shown by Government reports of condemnation of livestock at time of slaughter and reports of investigation of tuberculosis in children. Other than the testing of the cattle in the District of Columbia, the Federal government had taken little action.

On May 1, 1917, the United States Bureau of Animal Industry established a Tuberculosis Eradication Division and in the appropriation for the Bureau for the year beginning July 1 $75,000 was allotted for "investigating the disease of tuberculosis of animals for its control and eradication."

Aroused by the necessity for action to combat the ravages of the disease the government started, in cooperation with the owner, to conduct tuberculin testing in purebred herds. This resulted in the adoption of the so-called Accredited Herd Plan by the United States Sanitary Live stock Association at Chicago in the fall of the year 1917 in cooperation with the United States Department of Agriculture, Bureau of Animal Industry. Originally intended to apply only to purebred herds, it soon became necessary to include both purebreds and grades.

As information regarding the workings of this method of combating tuberculosis, and reports of the accrediting of herds and the issuing of certificates of accreditation were spread by farm publications, government reports, etc., interest in the plan began to be shown by many livestock owners of our own State.

Testing under Government supervision had already been done in a few of the purebred herds of the State but it was not until the year 1920 that any definite attempt was made for legislation through which the cattle owners of the Commonwealth could avail themselves of the benefit of the cooperative testing plan. A commission appointed by the legislature of that year to study the situation reported in 1921 in favor of the cooperative plan and recommended legislation, which, however, did not meet with success.

In the month of June, 1921, in conjunction with officials of the U. S. Bureau of Animal Industry and the livestock officials of the other New England states, a two-day tuberculosis eradication conference, financed by the members of the Massachusetts Veterinary Association, and attended by a large number of livestock owners, health officials, veterinarians, etc., was held at Boston.

Opposition, similar in type to that shown when eradication was attempted in the years 1894 and 1895, was finally overcome and the General Court of 1922 enacted legislation providing for the payment of compensation for reactors to tuberculin tests, etc. Credit for the passage of this legislation was, I believe, largely due to the efforts of the Hampden County Improvement League, which organization chartered a special car for the trip from Springfield to Boston in which a large delegation arrived for the hearing before the legislative committees. This law went into effect on August 1, 1922, with an original appropriation of $15,000, which proved inadequate and, therefore, an additional appropriation of $10,000 was granted for the period ending November 30th, the end of that fiscal year.

As the work of testing progressed the appropriations increased proportionately, reaching a peak in 1931, in which year $800,000 was appropriated. The peak for indemnity payments was in 1932 when 23,156 reactors were paid for, amounting to $793,244.32.

After passage of the Acts of 1922, laws were passed and rules and regulations prescribed to further assist in the ultimate eradication of tuberculosis. October 15, 1923, all cattle handled in the dairy section at Brighton were required to have recently passed a tuberculin test. In 1924 the sale of reactors except for immediate slaughter was forbidden, as was also the removal of reactor tags from ears of reactor animals.

In 1925 the Federal allotment for compensation gave out, causing a slowing down of new test work from November, 1925, to July, 1926. In 1926 all testing was discontinued from August 17 to October 11, pending the investigation of the so-called "cattle frauds."

On October 5, 1926, Dr. Howard resigned as Director and on November 6, 1926, Frank B. Cummings of Newton was appointed. He held office until June 1, 1928, when he resigned and Evan F. Richardson of Millis, a farmer and cattle owner, assumed office.

During the term of Mr. Cummings, in 1927, the first area test bill was passed giving authority to test all cattle in a town if eighty-five per cent of the cattle in the town were already tested. In 1929 legislation was passed declaring Barnstable County a Modified Accredited Area and authorizing the Director to make rules and regulations relating to the movement of cattle into said county.

In 1930 there was an increasing demand for the test due to pressure which was brought to bear by local boards of health, and to regulations in effect requiring milk from tuberculin tested cows. The area test law was also revised giving authority to conduct area work on the petition of seventy-five per cent of the owners, or the owners of eighty-five per cent of the cattle in any given town.

In 1931 the towns of Gloucester, Rockport, Douglas, and Heath were declared Modified Accredited Areas. The larger milk concerns were refusing milk except from tested herds. County agents were active in obtaining signatures to petitions for area work in towns in their respective counties.

In 1932 area work had been completed in 157 towns of which 42 were declared Modified Accredited Areas. Franklin County was declared a Modified Accredited Area.

In 1933 testing was practically restricted to area work alone.

In 1934 the law was amended giving authority to declare the entire Commonwealth a quarantine area when eighty-five per cent of all cattle permanently kept in the State were under test. On July 2nd the State was so declared. Under the cooperative plan of testing, the Federal government assigned veterinarians in federal employ to assist in the work of testing, the number of such men usually equalling the number of State salaried men. Up to 1934 the number of Federal men in Massachusetts varied at times from three to five, which number was increased by the assignment of four additional men in that year. On November 30, 1934, the end of the fiscal year of the Division, the entire State was once tested.

The percentage of reactors had dropped from 38.7 per cent of the total first tests to 3.28 per cent at time of entire State last test on that date.

On January 28, 1934, Evan F. Richardson was succeeded by Edgar L. Gillett of Westfield, who held office up to December 28, 1934, when he was succeeded by the present Director, Charles F. Riordan, upon whom descended the honor of accepting the coveted title of "MODIFIED ACCREDITED AREA" for the good old Commonwealth of Massachusetts.

To each of the five men under whose directorship this goal has finally been reached belongs a part of the credit for same:

Dr. Lester H. Howard, under whose regime the work actually started; Frank B. Cummings, who successfully guided the Division through a period of biased criticism; Evan F. Richardson, through whose undaunted courage, strength of conviction and aggressiveness this celebration in the year 1935 instead of 1940, as was generally predicted, was made possible; Edgar L. Gillett, who furthered the work to a marked degree; and Charles F. Riordan, under whose guidance the work was successfully completed, but whose work in reality has only begun, as to him is given the responsibility of maintaining the Commonwealth as a "TUBERCULOSIS-FREE ACCREDITED STATE."

TUBERCULOSIS AND MILK

ALTON S. POPE, M.D.

Director, Division of Tuberculosis
Massachusetts Department of Public Health

Tuberculosis is one of the few diseases that is equally at home in man and in his domestic cattle. Streptococcus infection, either septic sore throat or scarlet fever in man, may originate from infection in the udder of the cow but is not common as a spontaneous disease in cattle. Undulant fever, on the other hand, is primarily a disease of cattle which is only occasionally transmitted to man, while milk-borne infection of such diseases as diphtheria and typhoid fever is chargeable to contamination of the milk from human sources.

For a number of years the tuberculosis of cattle was considered identical with the human disease but in 1901 Robert Koch announced that the danger of the transfer of the tuberculosis of cattle to man is negli-

---
Note: The percentages of infection as shown by results of the tuberculin test for the past three years were:
1935 — .18%;   1936 — .12%;   1937 — .08%.
Cattle population, November 1937 — 210,201.

gible. Further studies, however, soon showed that this sweeping statement was unwarranted. It is true that the bovine tubercle bacillus differs slightly from the human organism and that it only occasionally gives rise to pulmonary tuberculosis, but the idea of its harmlessness to man has been thoroughly disproved. In a recent study of the situation in England and Scotland Griffith found that 35 per cent of the cases of nonpulmonary tuberculosis were due to the bovine type of bacillus, while in children under five 54 per cent were ascribable to bovine infection. Even in pulmonary tuberculosis the importance of bovine infection cannot be ignored as 2.3 percent of over a thousand cases studied yielded bovine bacilli. Griffith estimates that infection from tuberculous cattle is responsible for at least 2,000 deaths per year in England and Scotland, chiefly in children. In short, the tuberculosis of cattle can give rise to all forms of tuberculosis in man and has a virulence for man as great as that of the human strain.

Infection of human beings with bovine tuberculosis is almost always due to the drinking of raw milk from infected cows. Contamination of the milk may be due to tuberculosis of the udder but in the majority of instances is probably due to dust and hairs which become contaminated with the organisms from the lungs of diseased cattle and fall into the milk at the time of milking. Milk may also be contaminated with human tubercle bacilli by a careless milker who has open tuberculosis but there is no evidence that this often occurs.

The danger of human infection with bovine tuberculosis depends obviously upon the prevalence of tuberculosis in dairy herds. In England and in Holland this is believed to reach a figure of 10-20 percent. Samples of the milk shipped into London in 1935 indicated that 12.6 percent was infected with tubercle bacilli, and in 1936 the percentage was 9.3. In 1909 Hess found 16 percent of the samples of market milk examined in New York City contained tubercle bacilli and in 1910 Tonney reported 10.5 per cent of the samples examined in Chicago so infected. The cooperative tuberculosis eradication campaigns of the Federal and State Departments of Agriculture have in the past twenty years made tremendous progress in the control of tuberculosis in cattle in this country. At the present time there are only two states not on the modified accredited herd list, indicating that not over 0.5 percent of the cattle tested react to the tuberculin test. In Massachusetts the last county areas were accredited as practically free from bovine tuberculosis in October, 1935.

In spite of this gratifying reduction of tuberculosis in the dairy cattle of Massachusetts the problem of bovine tuberculosis is not yet solved. The eradication campaign as conducted here is so expensive that no other large country has been able to undertake it and, successful as it has been, authorities doubt whether it can ever exterminate tuberculosis in cattle. At present between one and two thousand Massachusetts cows are condemned annually as reactors to the tuberculin test.

As previously indicated, infection with bovine tuberculosis results largely in the nonpulmonary forms of the disease in man. Tuberculosis of the glands, skin, bones and joints and tuberculous meningitis are the most frequent results of bovine infection. So far as the incidence of extrapulmonary tuberculosis can be taken as an index of bovine infection the decline of death rates in Massachusetts is encouraging. While the death rate from pulmonary tuberculosis has fallen 66 percent since 1916, the rate from extrapulmonary tuberculosis has dropped 89 percent, and is now less than 7 percent of all tuberculosis, while in Great Britain extrapulmonary forms are responsible for approximately a quarter of all tuberculosis deaths.

To measure the seriousness of this problem in Massachusetts a study was made at the Lakeville State Sanatorium in 1935 of 200 cases from which culture material could be obtained. Here Chang found that 27.5 percent of the patients studied were infected with the bovine type of bacillus. The age distribution of these cases was striking. Under 5 years 71 percent of the children showed bovine infection while over 16 only 11 percent yielded bovine organisms. Evidently the milk of tuberculous cattle is still an important source of extrapulmonary tuberculosis in children.

Why intelligent people continue to run the risk, even though it is a diminishing one, of exposing their children to possible infection with tuberculosis through the milk they drink, is one of the enigmas of public health. For more than 20 years it has been well established that proper pasteurization affords complete protection against tuberculosis as well as against other milk-borne diseases. At one time it was claimed that pasteurization destroyed the vitamin content of milk and seriously reduced its growth-producing properties. That this is not the case was conclusively shown by investigators of the United States Public Health Service who found that among several thousand children studied, children who are fed the average supplementary diet in addition to milk, grow as rapidly and thrive as well on pasteurized as on raw milk and contract such diseases as tuberculosis, diphtheria, scarlet fever and dysentery less frequently.

At the present time approximately 85 percent of the milk sold in Massachusetts is pasteurized. Forty-four cities or towns have ordinances requiring that all milk sold in the community be pasteurized or be produced under medical certification. In spite of the progress that has been made raw milk which is not certified is being sold in over half the towns in the state. From time to time as milk-borne outbreaks of undulant fever or other communicable diseases occur additional towns adopt pasteurization or certification ordinances. Infection with tuberculosis through milk is more frequent but less spectacular so that official action to prevent it seldom results. No communicable disease can be more simply or more completely controlled than milk-borne tuberculosis. How long it will continue as a crippling disease of childhood rests wholly with public opinion.

THE PROGRESS OF MILK REGULATION

VLADO A. GETTING, M.D.

Assistant Epidemiologist, Division of Communicable Diseases Massachusetts Department of Public Health

Clean Milk

Early in the twentieth century pure food laws were passed in order to insure the public wholesome unadulaterated foods. Milk was included as one of these foods, the watering and adulteration of milk was forbidden. Milk preservatives were outlawed, and an effort was made to give the public its money's worth of a wholesome clean milk. The federal, state and local authorities began to pass regulations for the standardization of milk production. Barns were inspected, cows were examined and tuberculin tested, and milk handlers were required to be healthy and free from known disease. Almost simultaneously, standards were established for the quality of milk. Laws were passed establishing minimum standards for butter fat and total solids, the maximum bacteria count in the different grades were likewise prescribed. In this way, the public was assured of a clean and wholesome milk, yet this did not stop the spread of disease. Bovine tuberculosis, undulant fever, and milk-borne epidemics of typhoid, scarlet fever, diphtheria, and septic sore throat still occurred.

Tuberculin Testing of Cows

It is not so long ago that surgeons received their earliest operative training on tuberculous glands of the neck of little children. Orthopedic surgeons spent a large proportion of their time treating children with tuberculous hips and spines. Hunchbacks were much more common thirty years ago than today. They were, in the vast majority of cases, the tragic results of tuberculous infections of the spine. Practically all these forms of extrapulmonary tuberculosis are caused by bovine tuberculosis, tuberculosis spread by milk from infected cattle. In 1926, over one-third of the cattle in Massachusetts were infected with tuberculosis. Three years later, Dr. Bigelow, then Commissioner of Public Health, remarked that Massachusetts had the highest proportion of tuberculous cattle of any state in the Union. Through the combined action of the Departments of Public Health and Agriculture, a state-wide program to eliminate tuberculous cattle was undertaken. Cattle were tuberculin tested, the positive reactors were destroyed, the farmer was compensated for his loss and thus the state record was gradually improved. By 1935, Massachusetts became an accredited state. This means that less than one-half of one per cent of the cattle in Massachusetts are reactors to the tuberculin tests.

Safe Milk—Pasteurization

Gradually the public became aware that a clean and wholesome milk was not necessarily safe. Campaigns for safe milk were conducted in all the large cities. People began to demand safe milk and pasteurizing plants were installed by all the large dairies. Pasteurization was soon established in many communities and the public was more and more demanding safe milk. By 1927, the health authorities were given power to license all pasteurizing establishments. This licensing power stimulated the demand for pasteurized milk so that in 1928 the amount of milk which was pasteurized was more than double that of ten years before. The proportions of milk pasteurized in the communities of various sizes are shown in Table I. It at once becomes obvious that the smaller the community, the smaller the per cent of pasteurized milk.

Table I
PER CENT OF MILK PASTEURIZED BY SIZE OF COMMUNITY

Group	Population	1919	1923	1926	1928	1931
I	50,000 and over	—	82.3	91.3	93.0	96.1
II	25,000—50,000	—	65.1	63.9	84.5	89.5
III	15,000—25,000	—	43.4	35.6	61.2	80.0
IV	10,000—15,000	—	10.8	34.1	62.1	59.8
V	5,000—10,000	—	—	—	51.8	55.3
	Weighted Average	34	74	83.0	85.7	89.7

Not long after the health authorities were empowered to license pasteurization plants, communities began to pass regulations for the standardization of clean, wholesome and safe milk. At first these regulations required that all milk that was pasteurized be processed as prescribed by law. Later the cities and towns passed regulations requiring that all milk which was not pasteurized be from tuberculosis-free herds.

Thus although pasteurization made milk safe, there was still a supply of raw milk, which although from tuberculin-tested herds still contained high bacteria counts and was a potential source of epidemics.

Certified and Pasteurized Milk

Although pasteurized milk properly handled is safe milk, some people still hold the mistaken idea that raw milk is healthier than pasteurized milk. Such individuals feel that they should be able to obtain raw milk. To provide for this group, in 1928, Boston was the first community in Massachusetts to pass a regulation requiring that all milk which was not pasteurized be certified. Certified milk is as safe as milk can be reasonably made without pasteurization. It is produced from tuberculosis-free herds, is handled in an approved manner, and the maximum bacteria count is set at a low level by law. In this way those demanding raw milk are furnished with a supply that is as safe as can be provided.

Since Boston's regulation went into effect in 1928, forty-five other communities in the state, representing approximately sixty-five per cent of its population, have passed regulations requiring that all milk which was not pasteurized be certified. In Table II are listed these communities requiring pasteurization or certification of milk, together with dates and populations.

Table II

Date Effective	Community	Population 1930
December 31, 1928	Boston	781,188
September 1, 1929	Chelsea	45,816
October 18, 1929	Winchester	12,719
January 1, 1930	Salem	43,353
April 1, 1930	Waltham	39,247
July 1, 1930	Fall River	115,274

Date Effective	Community	Population 1930
August 1, 1930	Newton	65,276
October 1, 1930	Ayer	3,060
November 17, 1930	Winthrop	16,852
January 1, 1931	Watertown	34,913
April 15, 1931	Dedham	15,136
December 23, 1931	Brookline	47,490
May 28, 1932	Swampscott	10,346
May 2, 1933	Lexington	9,467
September 1, 1934	Framingham	22,210
October 1, 1934	Cambridge	113,643
January 1, 1935	Stoneham	10,060
April 1, 1935	Milton	16,434
June 1, 1935	Everett	48,424
August 1, 1935	Natick	13,539
August 1, 1935	Wellesley	11,439
September 1, 1935	Revere	35,680
January 1, 1936	Lowell	100,234
March 21, 1936	Beverly	25,086
April 1, 1936	Quincy	71,983
July 1, 1936	Woburn	19,434
May 1, 1936	New Bedford	112,597
July 15, 1936	Somerville	103,908
September 1, 1936	Braintree	15,712
November 1, 1936	Weston	3,332
January 1, 1937	Pittsfield	49,677
February 1, 1937	Springfield	149,900
June 15, 1937	Haverhill	48,710
June 30, 1937	Lynn	102,320
October 1, 1937	Worcester	195,331
December 8, 1937	Greenfield	15,500
January 1, 1938	Chicopee	43,930
January 1, 1938	Malden	58,036
January 1, 1938	Medford	59,714
January 1, 1938	Needham	10,845
February 1, 1938	Fitchburg	40,692
March 7, 1938	Melrose	23,170
April 1, 1938	Concord	7,477
June 1, 1938	Belmont	24,831
June 2, 1938	Hull	3,039
July 1, 1938	Holyoke	56,139
Totals	46	2,853,163

THE GRADING OF MILK
HERMANN C. LYTHGOE, S.B.

Director, Division of Food and Drugs
Massachusetts Department of Public Health

The early attempts at milk grading were based purely on sanitary conditions—namely upon the cleanliness of the stable and the bacterial content of the milk, and in some grades tuberculin testing of the cattle was required. Perhaps the earliest attempt at a system of this sort was that put into effect in New York City prior to 1915. That system of grading prohibited the sale of raw milk except Grade A raw milk, which, in order to conform with the regulation, must have been of a quality resembling Certified milk. Tuberculin testing of cattle was essential for that grade of milk, and in those days tested and nonreacting cattle were more of a curiosity than they are at present.

The Grade A milk was obtained from cows housed in better stables than was required for housing cattle furnishing the other grades of milk, and, furthermore, the milk was required to have a lower bacteria count both before and after pasteurization.

The Grade B milk represented the bulk of the milk sold and was obtained from cows housed in stables not conforming to the rigid requirements of the Grade A dairies, and the maximum bacteria counts prior and subsequent to pasteurization were higher than such requirements for Grade A milk.

The Grade C milk was an inferior pasteurized milk and was sold only for cooking purposes.

Many other cities and towns in New York State and elsewhere operated on the principles of this system. It should be noted that there were no chemical standards involved in this grading system, and if a person asked the health commissioner if the Grade B milk was any less safe than the Grade A milk, the commissioner was obliged to reply that they were equally safe.

A few years prior to the passage of the Massachusetts Grade A milk law, one of the milk dealers put out milk which he called Grade A milk and specified on the bottle cap that the bacterial count did not exceed 10,000 and the fat content was at least 4%. At that time the market milk had an average fat content of about 3.7%, and since this so-called Grade A milk contained 10% more cream than the market milk, the purchaser could naturally taste the difference.

In 1924 there was a bill before the Massachusetts Legislature of such a character that it was felt that a standard for Grade A milk could be reported under that bill. The late Dr. Gilbert, the then Commissioner of Agriculture, consulted with the late Dr. Kelly the then Commissioner of Public Health, regarding the advisability of establishing a standard for Grade A milk. As a result of this conference a bill was drafted, Dr. Gilbert presented it to the committee, the bill was supported by the Department of Agriculture, by the Department of Public Health, and became law. This law required the Department of Public Health to make standards for Grade A milk including fat standards and bacterial standards, the standards so made after a public hearing to be submitted to the

Governor and Council for approval. In preparing these standards, the Department consulted both the industry and the local boards of health. Several conferences were held both with the boards of health and with the dealers. Committees were selected from each group to work on the regulations, and the final committee represented both the local boards of health and the dealers. There was but one difference of opinion between the boards of health and the dealers—namely the bacteria count of the milk. The draft with the difference of opinion was submitted to the Food and Drug Committee of the Public Health Council of the Department of Public Health. The committee gave a hearing to interested parties and split the difference between the two bacteria counts submitted by both groups. The Department then gave the public hearing required by statutes, the regulations were duly adopted, and were approved by the Governor and Council.

In drafting these regulations, it was felt by the Department that if Grade A milk was to be "put over" on the public, it must be done in such a way that the purchaser knew that he was obtaining a superior product, and although a few dealers and a few boards of health objected to this suggestion, the bulk of the representatives of the trade and of the boards of health favored a fat content of 4%. The customer could taste the extra food value far easier than he could taste the absence of bacteria. This 4% fat requirement, furthermore, has a public health significance since the pediatricians prefer milk with a 4% fat for infant feeding.

A few years ago during a visit to Pennsylvania, a representative of the State Board of Health stated that a certain milk dealer succeeded in marketing Grade A milk in a certain city. It had been tried many times, and it would not sell. In that state the grade was based entirely at that time on the bacteria count. The dealer who succeeded in marketing Grade A milk put out a milk containing nearly 5% fat, and it apparently was the 5% fat which sold the milk rather than the Grade A requirements of the regulations.

The Massachusetts standards for Grade A milk were fairly successful, and, on the whole, were complied with by the milk dealers.

In 1933 it was deemed advisable to amend the milk grading law to include the establishment of grades other than Grade A milk. Such a law was passed, the grades being established by the Milk Regulation Board, consisting of the Commissioner of Agriculture, the Commissioner of Public Health, and the Attorney General. The grades established were subject to the approval of the Governor and Council. After considerable study, many informal hearings and two formal hearings, the following grades were established: Milk Raw, Milk Pasteurized, Grade A Milk Raw, Grade A Milk Pasteurized, Special Milk Raw, Special Milk Pasteurized, Certified Milk Raw, and Certified Milk Pasteurized. Of these grades, Raw Milk had been on the market for years subject to local boards' of health regulations; Pasteurized Milk had been on the market for years subject to regulations by local boards and the State Department of Public Health; Grade A Milk Raw was on the market as Grade A Massachusetts Milk; Grade A Milk Pasteurized had been on the market for nearly ten years; Certified Milk Raw had been on the market for years subject to regulations of the American Association of Medical Milk Commissions and the Department of Public Health; Certified Milk Pasteurized was a newer grade of milk put on the market by the certified milk dealers with the approval of the Medical Milk Commissions because of the increased demand for pasteurized milk. There was a demand on the part of certain milk producers to establish a grade of special milk which was to be between Grade A and Certified Milk, and for the benefit of persons having herds of cattle which would not give milk with a 4% fat content, it was decided that this special milk need conform only to the statutory requirements of milk solids and milk fat as applied to all market milk.

The statute under which these grades were made provides that it shall not interfere with the rights given to boards of health to make milk regulations, and consequently, if a board of health by regulation provided that Certified Milk shall be the only raw milk sold under its jurisdiction, the presence of two other grades of raw milk cannot interfere with the operation of such a regulation.

The Milk Regulation Board has the power to set standards for fat and solids in Grade A Milk and bacterial standards for all grades. In preparing these standards, the following assumption was made—namely that the process of pasteurization if properly carried out will reduce the bacterial count of raw milk by at least 90%, and consequently the maximum count for the raw milk prior to pasteurization must, therefore, be ten times the maximum count set for the same grade of milk subsequent to pasteurization. It was conceded that milk which was too high in bacteria to be sold to the consumer was also too high in bacteria to be pasteurized, and, therefore, in all these grades the count of the raw milk sold as such was made equal to the count of the raw milk intended for pasteurization. In studying the question of the bacterial count to be set for these various grades, the data of such counts made by the Department of Public Health, aided to some extent by those of local boards of health, were studied extensively. The season of the year also was taken into consideration. Experiences show a liability that raw milk going to pasteurizing plants would have a higher bacteria count during April and September than other parts of the year, the reason probably being the saving of ice by the producer.

The Department of Health officials felt that too rigid a standard should not be set up, but the old Grade A standard was felt to be too liberal. The old Grade A milk standard provided a maximum count of 25,000. This was reduced to 10,000, therefore, making the Grade A raw milk standard a maximum of 100,000. The standards made by the Department of Public Health under the milk pasteurization law were 750,000 prior to pasteurization and 50,000 after pasteurization. This was reduced to 40,000 after pasteurization, making the count 400,000 prior to pasteurization or if sold raw for consumption.

A different attitude was taken regarding Certified Pasteurized milk which was based upon repeated examinations of this product. This milk was required to be pasteurized on the premises where produced, and under such conditions was handled by persons who were very familiar with the art of preventing bacterial infection of milk. The milk naturally was not so old prior to pasteurization as the milk of the other grades, and, therefore, a count of 500 was established for pasteurized Certified milk which is 5% of the maximum count of Certified milk permitted to be sold raw. This figure, however, is altogether too high based upon market conditions. It is unusual for Certified Pasteurized milk to have a count above 100, and the average count over a period of years is about 25.

The legal grades with their standards are as follows:

	Maximum Bacterial Count of Raw Milk When Sold Or When Pasteurized	Maximum Bacterial Count When Sold After Pasteurization
Milk Raw	400,000	
Milk Pasteurized	400,000	40,000
Grade A. Milk Raw[1]	100,000	
Grade A Milk Pasteurized[1]	100,000	10,000
Special Milk Raw	50,000	
Special Milk Pasteurized	50,000	5,000
Certified Milk Raw[2]	10,000	
Certified Milk Pasteurized[2]	10,000	500

[1] Fat not less than 4%, milk solids not less than 12.20%.
[2] Fat content to average 4% as per regulations of American Association of Medical Milk Commissions.

In addition to the above requirements regarding bacterial count and chemical standards, there are other requirements pertaining to the physical condition of the dairy farm, tuberculin testing of cows in the case of certain grades, the age of the milk when sold or when pasteurized, special caps on milk bottles for all but the first two grades, testing of employees to see whether or not they have had typhoid fever in the case of special milk and general medical inspection of employees on certified milk farms. It may be interesting to know how these grades work out, and the following figures are taken from the 1937 report of the Department:

	Total Samples	Number Complying	Lowest Count	Average Count
Certified	74	70	150	
Pasteurized Certified	63	56	10*	15
Grade A Pasteurized	370	258	100*	5,400
Grade A Raw	88	73	1,000	
Pasteurized Milk	2,249	1,643	200	19,000
Raw Sold As Such	581	494	2,000	43,000
Raw to be Pasteurized	4,588	3,737	1,000*	77,000
Special Pasteurized	28	19	500	
Special Raw	6	6	7,600	

* Less than.

While the number of samples not complying with the regulations may seem high, it should be understood that a warning must be sent after the first high sample, and then within a period of from seven days to two months, an additional collection of three samples must be made, and if two of the three samples show bacteria counts higher than the regulations permit, it is then deemed to be a violation. As a rule the second sets of samples are in compliance with the law. In 1937 there were ten prosecutions for violation of the milk grades, all of which resulted in conviction. Of these cases, eight were for selling milk with a high bacteria count and two were for selling Grade A milk with a low fat content.

THE PASTEURIZATION OF MILK

HERMANN C. LYTHGOE, S.B.

Director, Division of Food and Drugs
Massachusetts Department of Public Health

The pasteurization of milk, which is now considered a public health measure, was first performed as a purely commercial proposition carried on for the sole purpose of arresting decomposition and reducing loss of milk as well as reducing complaints from the dealers' customers. When this product first appeared on the market, it was opposed by boards of health, by physicians, and by the general public, but because the dealer could sell better milk, even by such inefficient pasteurization as he performed, he continued to do so in spite of opposition.

This type of milk naturally appeared first in those portions of the state where the population was the most congested. After a few years of operation of pasteurization of this character, it began to be observed that certain infectious diseases were decreasing in those localities where most of this pasteurized milk was sold. When this was ascertained, the public health aspects of the process began to be apparent.

The process was fairly common in 1912, and in order to give the public some assurance that it was properly carried on, the Department in 1917 recommended to the legislature the establishment of a standard, and the legislature that year passed an act providing a penalty for representing as pasteurized any milk not pasteurized by heating to a temperature of not less than 140° nor more than 145° Fahrenheit, and kept at such temperature for a period not less than thirty minutes.

This outlawed the so-called flash pasteurization method which was extensively employed by many milk dealers operating comparatively small milk routes, if they represented the milk to be pasteurized. This flash method at that time consisted in permitting the milk to flow over a heated surface of such area that the milk would reach a temperature of 160° Fahrenheit, and then it would immediately flow over the cooler. This method of treatment would materially reduce the total bacteria count, and consequently would retard the souring of the milk, but it would not kill the bacteria of tuberculosis as well as a few other heat resisting pathogenic bacteria.

The demand for pasteurized milk increased, and milk dealers were obliged for commercial reasons to represent or to advertise the milk they were selling as being pasteurized, consequently the flash system of pasteurization gradually stopped, and the dealers changed to the holding system defined by the statutes. This definition remained on the books for fifteen years, and then it was felt that a change was desirable, which in part resulted from a material improvement in the so-called flash process of pasteurization.

In 1932, as a result of certain legislation intended to legalize the flash method of pasteurization, the legislature changed the law to read in part, "at not less than 142° Fahrenheit for not less than thirty minutes or at such higher temperature for such shorter time as the Department of Public Health may from time to time determine."

During the ten years preceding this change much scientific work had been done on this commercial process. A temperature of 142° for thirty minutes gave a wider margin of safety than the former legal temperature for the same holding time. There has been considerable improvement in the mechanics of the flash process, and it was believed that the temperature of the milk could be more accurately controlled, and if followed by fifteen seconds holding at 160° Fahrenheit, it had been shown by both laboratory and plant experiments that the tubercle bacillus as well as other heat resisting pathogenic bacteria were actually killed.

Subsequent to the passage of the act the Department legalized this new flash method of pasteurization, but within a comparatively short time was forced to revoke this action. A few pieces of apparatus for high temperature, short time pasteurization were installed, and then it was ascertained that they were not functioning as well as was expected, for the bacteria counts on the product were frequently high. While the efficiency of the apparatus was what would be expected at the beginning of each day's run, this efficiency decreased during the run to a considerable extent, resulting in many instances of the dealer selling milk with a higher bacteria count than was permitted by the regulations. Many dealers who never were troubled with high bacteria counts on the milk which they were selling began to be unable to explain the high counts of the market milk pasteurized by this flash method until the Department made efficiency tests at the plants and found that it was the fault, not of the operator, but of the apparatus.

About twelve years ago it was assumed that if milk was pasteurized, or was said to be pasteurized, it was perfectly safe for use and no further inquiry need be made. The inspectors of the Department, however, reported increasing unsanitary conditions in many of the smaller pasteurization establishments, and the Department deemed it advisable to place this industry under license. In 1927 the Department requested legislation to that effect, and that year the legislature passed the present law substantially as it was recommended by the Department. This law provides that each pasteurization establishment shall annually obtain from their local board of health a license to operate the plant, the fee for the license being $10. The plant is to be equipped and operated in accordance with the regulations made by the Department, and if not so equipped or operated, the board granting the license or the Department may close the plant, or unless the necessary corrections are made within a reasonable time, may suspend the license.

At the time this act was passed there were approximately five hundred pasteurization establishments in the State, of which at least twenty-three were equipped with the so-called Park holders. These were continuously operating holders and consisted of two cylinders. The heated milk flowed on a baffle plate upon the top of a cylinder. The speed of the milk was such that it took fifteen minutes to fill this cylinder. From the bottom of this cylinder by means of an inverted siphon, the milk then flowed to the top of another similar cylinder, taking fifteen minutes to fill this cylinder, and then the milk flowed by means of another inverted siphon to the top of a cooler. Apparently it took thirty minutes for the milk to pass through this apparatus. It was felt, however, that there might be convection currents inside of the cylinders, and there was no means of ascertaining the character of these currents.

The bacteriologist then suggested testing the apparatus using water and seeding the incoming water with a specific bacteria which could be easily identified. Samples of water were then removed from the outlet at about five minute intervals and examined for the specific bacteria. This test indicated that some of the bacteria came through the apparatus in less than thirty minutes. There were certain objections made to this because the test was performed cold, and then the chemist suggested putting a dye stuff in the milk or water and performing the test hot. As a result of this test with the dye stuffs, it was shown that while the average flow was thirty minutes or more some of the material passed through the holder in seventeen minutes, and some stayed in the holder for nearly forty-five minutes.

The new act went into effect ninety days after it was signed by the Governor, and when the act became law, only five of the twenty-three Park holders were left, and these were shortly replaced by apparatus in conformance with the regulations. This was a fairly expensive piece of business for these dealers, and they made the change with only one complaint, and that man installed new apparatus when he was informed that it was advisable to do so.

There are several types of pasteurizers in this State of which the vat type is the commonest in use. In this type the milk is dumped or pumped into a vat, it is agitated and then heated to the pasteurization temperature by suitable means, and when that temperature is reached, an adjustment of the heating is made, and the milk is kept at the pasteurization temperature for the necessary thirty minutes, after which it is pumped or flows from the vat over the cooler. If the dealer has a very large output, he may have a series of four such vats. Under these conditions the milk is preheated to the pasteurization temperature. It flows into the vat, and when this vat is full, it flows into the second vat. The speed of flow is so adjusted that when the third vat is filled, the milk in the first vat had been held at the pasteurizing temperature for thirty minutes, and the first vat is then emptied while the fourth vat is being filled. From this point on the process becomes a continuous one.

Another type of apparatus is the pocket type which, as its name implies, consists of a series of pockets into which the milk flows. When one pocket is filled, the milk automatically flows to the next pocket, etc. This is a continuous process, but there are only a few of this type in the State.

A third type is the so-called continuous flow holder which is somewhat different from the old Park holder. The pre-heated milk flows through a large pipe, it strikes a plate at the end of the pipe and is shunted back through another pipe and is repeatedly allowed to flow down hill, back and forth through the holder.

The same trouble can occur in this apparatus but to a lesser extent than in the Park apparatus—namely, an increase of speed in the flow of milk in the central portion of the pipe. Efficiency tests, however, show only a slight gain in time, and, therefore, apparatus of this type is usually timed for forty minutes in order to be assured that no milk gets through the holder in thirty minutes. This type of apparatus can be easily timed by the inspector if he arrives at the plant when pasteurization is going on. There are recording thermometers at the entrances and the exits of the holder. If the inspector will subtract the elapsed time shown on the recording thermometer at the outlet from the elapsed time shown on the recording thermometer at the inlet, the difference represents the holding period.

Another method of pasteurization is that of pasteurizing in the final container. There are but few of these pasteurizers in the State. The milk is put into the bottle, is sealed with a crown cap, and is heated by means of hot water and then cooled. Recent experiments on this process indicate that the heating of the milk in different parts of the apparatus is not always the same, and it has been found that a very long holding time is necessary in order to be positive that all the milk in all the bottles has been legally pasteurized.

There are many technical requirements in order to insure proper pasteurization. For example, leak escape valves, by means of which any milk passing through the valve when closed will flow through an outlet and be wasted, are required on the inlet and the outlet of pasteurizers in order that no raw milk can pass into the vat during the holding and emptying period, and no incompletely pasteurized milk can flow into the outlet pipes during the filling and holding periods.

Mercury and recording thermometers are required for each vat, the mercury thermometer being used as an index of temperature during pasteurization, and the recording thermometer is used to give the owner of the plant a record of his operations.

If during the process of pasteurization milk is heated for too long a time or at too high a temperature, the fat will get into such a physical condition that the cream will not completely rise, and although the cream is all there, the customer believes that he is getting a shortage. This is one reason why many of the operators of the smaller plants violate the law by bottling incompletely pasteurized milk as pasteurized. If the plant is overworked, there is a tendency to reduce the holding period. If an irresponsible boy is permitted to do the pasteurizing, he may apparently properly pasteurize the milk, but he may be able to gain an extra twenty-five minutes in which to play baseball by cutting down the holding time. This process consists in heating the milk to 142° during which period 80% of the total bacteria, but few, if any, of the highly heat resisting bacteria, will be killed. He then rotates the recording thermometer chart to show thirty minutes elapsed time. The milk is then passed over the cooler and bottled.

Catching a violation of this character can be done only by arriving at the plant at the psychological moment, and, furthermore, knowing how to proceed. There are slightly more than seven hundred plants in the State, and yet in 1935 the two inspectors assigned to this work were able to apprehend fourteen persons because of this violation and secured thirteen convictions.

There have been several chemical methods published to differentiate between raw and pasteurized milk. These methods have been studied by the Department and found not to be sufficiently reliable for adoption. In the early part of 1937 the Department studied for a period of six months the so-called phosphatase test and ascertained that, while the absence of the phosphatase did not conclusively prove that the milk was legally pasteurized, the presence of phosphatase was 100% accurate in showing that the milk was not pasteurized as defined by law, or it was constituted of a mixture of raw and pasteurized milk. The Department then proceeded to collect samples from persons long suspected of manipulating the recording thermometer. These persons were caught, were prosecuted, and convicted. Prior to prosecution, however, an efficiency test was made on the apparatus, and in all instances it was found that when the apparatus was properly operated the pasteurized milk did not give a test for raw milk, although generally the milk pasteurized on the prior day showed incomplete pasteurization by this same test. Many of these people were given hearings, and they were unable to explain why it was that on two days they sold improperly pasteurized milk as pasteurized, but on the third day when the milk was pasteurized in the presence of an inspector of the Department, the tests showed that the milk was pasteurized. We were, however, able to obtain a very few confessions. One man put pasteurized caps on raw milk because one or two of his customers wanted pasteurized milk. One milk dealer living in a town where the board of health regulations required raw milk sold to be certified milk solicited the business of one of the departmental employees, telling him that he would furnish him raw milk but with a pasteurized cap. In a few instances the boss left the work to the tender mercies of the hired man, name and present address unknown, who was fired by the boss the day after the samples were obtained and a few days before the efficiency test was carried on.

There have been many samples of cream obtained which showed improper pasteurization. Confessions have been secured in a few instances to the effect that pasteurized heavy cream was purchased which was diluted with raw skimmed milk in order to reduce it to the minimum fat percentages of the various grades of cream.

The annual report for 1938 will show a much larger number of prosecutions and convictions for representing as pasteurized, milk not pasteurized than has the previous year's report. As a rule one prosecution will stop this type of violation on the part of the individual prosecuted. The work has been directed mainly towards persons whom we have reason to suspect were violating and were escaping, although occasionally other persons were caught in the net. The persons carrying on improper pasteurization are largely confined to the relatively small dealers, and it is safe to say that only a very little of the entire supply of pasteurized milk is improperly pasteurized.

PASTEURIZED MILK IS SAFE MILK

FRANCIS B. CARROLL, M.D.

*District Health Officer, The Berkshire District
Massachusetts Department of Public Health*

Milk is our most *important* food. The exceptional value of milk is due to the fact that it contains the most essentials of a well-balanced diet; the quality of its protein is especially good, its fat favors growth, and it has a high calcium content in readily usable form. Milk is palatable, readily digestible, and is the chief ingredient of a large variety of nutritive dishes. Even at present prices, it is one of the least expensive of the standard articles of diet and the most economical source of protein. Milk is a protective food in that it guards against certain deficiency diseases when used in combination with other foodstuffs of either animal or vegetable origin.

While safe milk has done more than any other single food to obtain and maintain health, unprotected milk was formerly responsible for more sickness and deaths than perhaps all other foods combined. There are several reasons for this:—(1) Milk conveys a greater variety of infections than any other food. Bacteria grow well in milk, therefore a very slight infection may produce widespread and serious results; (2) Of all foodstuffs, milk is the most difficult to collect, handle, transport, and deliver in a clean, fresh, and satisfactory condition; (3) It is the most readily decomposable of all our foods; (4) Finally, milk is the only standard article of diet obtained from animal sources regularly consumed in its raw state.

Milk is the only single substance which in nature approaches being a complete food. It is a perfect food for the suckling of the same species. The milk of one mammal does not fit all the needs of the nursling of another kind: cow's milk is best for the calf, lion's milk for the whelp, bear's milk for the cub, and mother's milk for the baby. After weaning, cow's milk is the best single food to promote growth and nutrition in children. Children should drink about a quart of milk daily and adults should have about a pint daily in their diet.

In view of the many advantages and few drawbacks, sanitarians unanimously encourage the production and use of pure milk and discourage the distribution and use of unprotected milk.

Because of the fact that milk is apt to convey the germs of a number of diseases harmful to man, it is essential that milk be subjected to some process which will prevent this hazard. The simplest, cheapest, least objectionable, and most trustworthy method of rendering milk safe is by pasteurization.

Pasteurization consists in heating milk to a temperature below that of boiling, holding it at that temperature for a definite time, and then chilling it rapidly. The time and temperature of pasteurization are designed to be sufficient to kill the harmful microorganisms with the least possible effect on the milk itself. An excess of heat is not necessary and is not desirable because it destroys the cream line, alters the taste, and otherwise changes the milk.

The Vitamins A, B, and D which are present in milk are quite stable and are not destroyed or affected by pasteurization. The amount of Vitamin C, which prevents scurvy, found in milk depends upon the quantity contained in the feed of the cow. Stall-fed cows in winter furnish a milk which contains practically no Vitamin C. Experiments have shown that the temperatures of pasteurization recommended decrease this property in milk somewhat. In any case, cow's milk cannot be depended upon to protect children against scurvy and they should, therefore, receive articles rich in Vitamin C, such as oranges or tomatoes, whether the milk is raw or pasteurized. Pasteurization does not alter the digestibility of milk, in fact pasteurization tends to make the curds smaller and consequently easier to digest. There can be no more objection to the heating of milk in pasteurization than there is to the cooking of meat.

Pasteurization is not proposed as a substitute for, but as an adjunct to, clean production. Proper inspection of production assures us cleaner and fresher milk but does not necessarily give us safe milk. Pasteurization destroys the dangers inspection cannot see. The combination of clean production and pasteurization corresponds in all respects to the modern principles of furnishing a safe water supply to a large city. The watershed, through inspection, is kept as clean as practicable, but the water is purified to protect the consumer.

Nature has no danger signal for infected milk. Milk may be teeming with typhoid bacilli and other disease-producing germs without any noticeable change in its taste, odor, or appearance.

The only object of pasteurization is to destroy the disease germs which may from time to time be found in milk and which may cause infection in man. The following diseases are known to be milk-borne: tuberculosis, undulant fever, typhoid fever, scarlet fever, diphtheria. septic sore throat, infantile paralysis, milk sickness, foot-and-mouth disease, dysentery, and other gastrointestinal troubles, especially in infants.

The only milk which we know to be safe is properly pasteurized milk. Even those who use certified milk, because its production is surrounded by every known safeguard, are demanding that it be pasteurized as a final measure of safety.

THE CARE OF MILK IN THE HOME
FREDERICA L. BEINERT, B.S., *Nutritionist*
Massachusetts Department of Public Health

The milk that arrives on the doorstep of the consumer's home each morning has been, in most instances, handled with extreme care. The rules of cleanliness in milk production and transportation are community made and community regulated, but the responsibility becomes that of the consumer when the milk is taken into the home. The same care and cleanliness is essential in this environment.

The use of covered containers and maintenance of a consistently low temperature are essential to safe handling of milk. Too often milk is allowed to remain outside in the warm sun for several hours. This, of course, encourages bacterial growth and spoilage. When the milk is taken in from the doorstep, the top of the bottle (the lip), and the cap should be carefully and well wiped off with a clean damp cloth. It should then be placed in a clean refrigerator which is maintained at a temperature of 50° F.

Pasteurized milk is safe, clean milk, but pasteurization will not make dirty milk clean nor stale milk fresh. The pasteurized milk which comes into the home must meet a certain standard of cleanliness and bacterial count before pasteurization. This is, then, a consumer's guarantee of a worthy product.

Should pasteurized milk not be available to the consumer, the milk coming into the home can be made safe in several ways. The following "Home Pasteurization" method was worked out by Dr. Lloyd Arnold of the Illinois State Health Department:

Equipment needed is a quart size thermos bottle (smaller sizes do not hold the heat well), a rubber stopper, a sauce pan, a thermometer and a rubber tip to put over the mercury.

The thermos bottle is thoroughly cleaned, and filled with HOT water. The stopper is boiled. Heat the milk in a saucepan to 145° F., using the rubber tipped thermometer for stirring. Empty the hot water from the thermos bottle, pour in the milk, and insert stopper (touch only the outside of the top). Allow to stand for one hour (no longer). Pour out the milk into a jar which has been sterilized, cap, and cool as rapidly as possible. The milk should be kept cool until used.

It is important to follow instructions in detail, as milk which has been similarly treated at a lower temperature is not pasteurized. Lower temperatures merely incubate and do not kill the germs. Be sure that the thermos bottle is clean and warm; that the milk is heated to 145° F.; that it is kept for only one hour in the bottle; and that it is cooled rapidly and kept cool.

Another method of home pasteurization is an adaptation of the Freeman's pasteurizer. This method is of especial value where formulæ must be prepared for the infant.

Place the milk or prepared formula in sterilized nursing bottles, each bottle containing the amount the child consumes at one feeding. A whole day's supply may be pasteurized at once. Place the nursing bottles, lightly stoppered with sterilized stoppers, into a large saucepan, together with another bottle containing water and a thermometer. The cold water in the saucepan should reach to just above the level of the milk or formula in the bottles. Place the saucepan on the stove, heat until the thermometer registers 145° F. Continue to heat for one-half hour, keeping the temperature 145°-150° F. Then press the stoppers in tightly. Cool at once and store in refrigerator until used.

When pasteurization at home is advisable and equipment limited, either of the following methods of making milk safe may be used:
From *League of Nations Quarterly Bulletin* for June 1937:

Pour fresh milk into a saucepan of adequate size and bring to a rapid boil over direct heat. Boil actively for 5 minutes. Pour the milk into clean, sterilized jars which have been set in a pan of warm water. Cool quickly by letting cold running water circulate around the bottles. Store in a cool place until ready to use.

From Children's Bureau Publication No. 8, *Infant Care*:

Pour fresh milk into the top of a double boiler. Fill the lower part of the utensil with cold water, so that the water outside and the milk inside are at the same level. Cover tightly. Place the double boiler on the stove. When the water boils, note the time and allow the milk to cook for 20 minutes. At the end of that time pour into clean sterilized jars as in the above directions. Be sure that the water is boiling rapidly during the 20-minute cooking.

Unpasteurized milk may also be made safe by using it in cooked foods made from milk such as chowders, soups, puddings, and creamed dishes.

"Keep safe, clean milk safe and clean for all the family" is the byword of the wise housewife.

MILK FOR THE WHOLE FAMILY

MARY SPALDING, M.A.

Consultant in Nutrition
Massachusetts Department of Public Health

The homemaker may well feel that she has contributed to the health of her family by providing her table with milk and milk dishes. If she offers milk in varying forms attractive and suitable for both the children and adults who sit around that table, she will not only serve this important food but find it eaten with satisfaction. Milk is the foundation of meal planning for all ages and fortunately for assorted purses as well. From studies of the effect of milk supplements for young and old we are continually learning of results in better growth, vitality, and longevity.

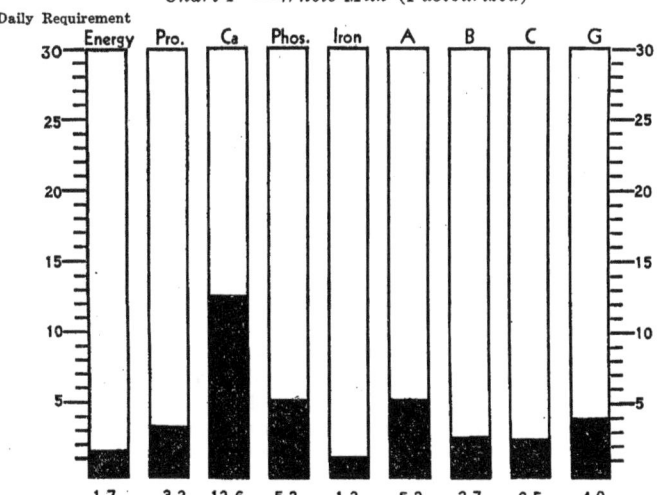

Chart I* — Whole Milk (Pasteurized)

We feel we understand its value. Chart I, however, reminds us graphically what one glass of milk gives toward the daily human require-

---

* Chart printed by courtesy of Frances Livingston Hoag, The Philadelphia Dairy Council.

ment of food substances. When we consider the article on "Milk Consumption among Children in Massachusetts," such a striking picture strengthens our purpose in increasing its use. Where else can we get calcium for promoting the building and upkeep of bones and teeth, for helping to regulate the beating of the heart, and to maintain the nervous system? This chart shows that the glass of milk gives over one-fourth of the day's requirement of one gram of calcium. To get a similar amount we should have to munch two cups of carrots or cabbage or kale. Unless we have a real allergy for milk, it is easier to get our calcium from it.

Milk for Adults

Admiral Byrd undertook the transportation of three cows, among them the Deerfoot Farm Maid of Massachusetts, as well as ten thousand cans of evaporated milk, to provide milk for the use of his men in the Antarctic Expédition. It is much easier to build well-balanced meals with milk even for men. Observation at restaurants shows they are really choosing it more. Dr. Sherman at the meeting of the Massachusetts Dental Association said that experiments he is carrying on in enriching the diet lead him to believe that fathers may possibly invest in extra calcium for a longer life, while mothers invest in extra calcium for better children.

Evidence of its use for mothers keeps coming from public health officials and scientific workers. Our former Commissioner of Public Health, Dr. Bigelow, said, "A quart of milk for each girl until she has weaned her last baby." Dr. McGonigle of Great Britain finds that a calcium addition lessens the pain and discomfort of pregnancy and childbirth. Lady Rhys Williams in South Wales compared the death rate among 7,000 pregnant women whose diets were increased in regard to milk, protein, and vitamin B with 14,000 others without this increase in diet. She found only a small fraction of the death rate among the 7,000 with the milk-improved diet as compared with the death rate of the 14,000 women with the unimproved diet. Physicians in general prescribe milk for the pregnant and nursing mother as a good source of building material for the baby.

Students also need more milk. Dr. Jeghers finds poor adaptation to dark and other signs of vitamin A deficiency in epithelial cells, such as dry skin, even among a large number of medical students and nurses. These symptoms were tied up closely with the skipping of meals, low food allowances, and poor choice of food rich in vitamin A as is milk. Such eye defects are considered of real danger in night driving. Dr. Chaney found from 2,859 records kept for five years of girls at Connecticut College that those who drank two glasses of milk daily and ate two or more servings of fruits and vegetables daily showed less frequency of colds, less fatigue, fewer headaches, and less menstrual disturbances. Corry Mann in the study of a case of a sedentary worker believes that a large proportion of the protein of milk may be of more value than the protein of meat in preventing a feeling of weariness and giving a feeling of well-being. Three cups or twenty-one ounces brought about the latter condition.

Ease of digestion of this bland food allows it to be used by the aged and the convalescent. Dr. McLester says many a patient with nephritis or hypertension was probably saved in the old days because of being allowed milk. At that time milk was not considered a protein food, as is known now.

For reasons such as these the Massachusetts Department of Public Health recommends in its leaflets—

For each adult—1 pint of milk in some form—at least 1½ cups

For each expectant and nursing mother—generally 1 quart of milk

For the young person—3 to 4 cups of milk.

Such amounts would provide for the maintenance of normal tissue function in the mature person, so would help increase general health and working efficiency.

Milk for Children

Milk does help the rate of growth and the state of buoyant health in children. Probably the most significant experiment was that of Corry Mann (1926) carried for a period of four years in one English institution for boys between six and eleven years of age. These boys lived in nineteen houses, so their diet could not only be controlled but also varied easily. Various foods were added to the "original diet chosen with every regard for the welfare of the children." The group that received the milk addition of one pint daily showed the largest gains of all in height and in weight. The control group gained 3.85 lbs. and 1.84 inches each, while the milk group gained 6.90 lbs. and 2.63 inches. "The boys of the house receiving this extra ration of milk were obviously more fit. In addition they became more high spirited and irresponsible and though it is not possible to measure the change in their mentality by statistical methods, yet the change was unmistakable."

The protein of milk is an unusually good supplement for the protein of cereals. Deficiencies in the amino acid of cereals are made good by the amino acid of milk. The homemaker may well consider this in planning meals at low cost for children, using cereal with milk instead of with syrup.

Dr. Hopkins' article on "The Value of Milk for Dental Health" describes its calcium and phosphorus value so necessary for bones and teeth. Young children should have about 3,000 International Units of vitamin A. A quart of milk—depending on the breed of cows, their feed, and the season—furnishes much of this vitamin, at any rate more than a thousand units. Butter, cream, and green and yellow vegetables make up the rest of the day's requirement. Milk is also relatively good in vitamin B. This vitamin helps the body utilize other foodstuffs. Vitamin D milks furnish some of the units of vitamin D needed to deposit calcium and phosphorus in bones and teeth. Milk furnishes some vitamin C, but children need in addition an excellent source each day, such as citrus fruits. For adolescent boys and girls during spurts of growth milk is very necessary as building material.

"Food for the School Child" and "Food for the Teens" recommend—

For children—3 to 4 cups of milk or at least 1 pint

For the 'teen age—3 to 4 cups of milk or at the very least 1 pint

Such amounts would give valuable protein, calcium, phosphorus, vitamins A, B, and G.

Food Value for Money

"You're penny wise and pint foolish if you let your family's milk quota fall below a full quart a day for each child and at least a pint for each adult." — Dr. E. V. McCollum

When its food value is considered, milk is a most economical food both for families with low incomes as well as for those with higher incomes. A family with six children needs an equal amount for each child as does a family with three children. In a study, however, of the milk consumption of 9,728 families, those with six children and those with three children bought about the same amount of milk, so the children in the larger families had only one-half as much apiece. The income of the family seems to govern the amount eaten. People want more milk as shown by increase in amounts consumed with increase in income.

In order to help families on low incomes get the most milk or milk products for their money, Table A presents a few ways and means—

Table A

Cost of Different Grades and Types of Milk and Milk Products Equal in Food Value to One Quart of Whole Milk in a Massachusetts Town in August, 1938

Certified (pasteurized)	20-22c. a quart	Delivered to the home
Certified with 155 International Units D (pasteurized)	20-22c a quart	Delivered to the home
Grade A (pasteurized)	16-17c. a quart	Delivered to the home
Irradiated (ultra-violet ray with 155 International Units D (pasteurized)	17c a quart	Delivered to the home
Family milk (pasteurized)	12c a quart (only grade available)	Bought at store
	13c. a quart (1 quart plus 1 tablespoon cod liver oil = 1 quart irradiated plus extra vitamin A—costs 13¼c.)	Delivered to the home
Liquid skim milk (pasteurized)	35c an 8 quart can (1 quart plus 1½ ounces butter = 1 quart whole milk—costs 7½c.)	Available at central milk distributing stations
Chocolate milk (pasteurized)	14-16c. a quart "Chocolate Drink" is usually made with skim milk only	
Evaporated milk (unsweetened)	14½ ounce can (3 for 25c.) (17 ounces = 1 quart whole milk—costs 9.8c.)	Independent grocer
	14½ ounce can (4 for 23c.) (17 ounces = 1 quart whole milk—costs 6.7c.)	Chain store

Irradiated evaporated milk	14½ ounce can (9c.) (17 ounces = 1 quart irradiated whole milk—costs 10.6c.)	Independent grocer
	14½ ounce can (2 for 15c.) (17 ounces = 1 quart irradiated whole milk—costs 8.8c.)	Chain store
Dried milk	Klim—67c. per lb. (2½ lb. can costs $1.63)	Drug store
	Dryco—59c. per lb.	Drug store
Dried skim milk	$5.35 per 100 lbs. (can be bought for 6c. per lb. in grain store) (1 lb. plus ½ lb. butter equals 5 quarts of whole milk—1 quart costs approximately 4½c.)	Grain store
Buttermilk (pasteurized)	10c. a quart (1 quart plus 2 oz. butter = 1 quart whole milk—costs 14c.)	
Cottage cheese	15c. a lb. (Although much of the food substances are lost in production, 5 ounces of cottage cheese will equal approximately the amount of protein of 1 quart of whole milk) 5 ounces cottage cheese costs approximately 5c.	
American cheese	25c. a lb. (5 ounces equals 1 quart whole milk—costs 8c.)	
Butter	30-34c. a lb.	

For instance, a family of five (2 adults and 3 children) might need 4 quarts of milk daily or 28 quarts a week. They could buy—

14 cans evaporated milk $ .938
14 quarts family milk   1.680   or 28 quarts certified milk $5.60
                         ―――――   ―――――
                         $2.618 $5.60

Both types of milk would give good food value. Skim milk as shown by Chart II is a valuable food except for vitamin A and calories.

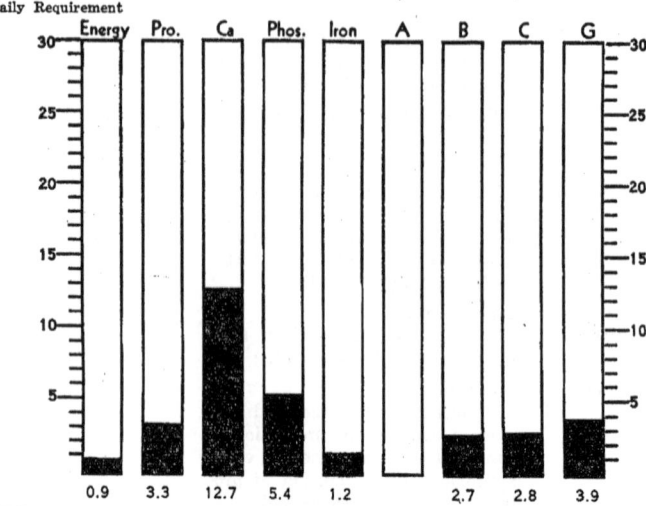

Chart II* — Skim Milk (Pasteurized)

* Chart printed by courtesy of Frances Livingston Hoag, The Philadelphia Dairy Council.

Professor Nourse of Brookings Institute spoke on the "new economics" by which foods are produced in larger quantities to sell at lower prices to greater numbers of people, "differing from the old promotional economics." Milk producers are providing pasteurized milk in varying grades, evaporated milk, dried milk, and inexpensive cheeses in a safe form. As milk is a basic food for all income groups, these producers may well consider greater production and consumption if prices can be kept within the pocketbook of the large number of families.

The homemaker may contribute to her milk fund by buying her own milk from the store and saving her penny a quart for delivery cost. She may also assist in keeping down the general price of milk by seeing that no milk bottles are carelessly used or broken. Some families on relief in Boston this year learned this lesson by not getting their free milk quota unless the bottles were returned each day. Some cities are using pasteboard bottles, but like paper towels these may or may not be an economy.

Varying Milk Dishes for Many Tastes

"For Breakfast and Supper, Milk, Milk-Pottage, Water-Gruel, Flummery, and twenty other Things, that we are wont to make in England, are very fit for Children; only, in all these, let Care be taken that they be plain, and without much Mixture, and very sparingly season'd with Sugar, or rather none at all; especially all Spice, and other Things that may heat the Blood, are carefully to be avoided."

—SOME THOUGHTS CONCERNING EDUCATION
by Mr. John Locke
Printed for a Society of Stationers, and Sold by F. Baker at the Black Boy in Pater-Noster-Row. 1710.

The family may buy and serve the right amount of milk for all its boys and girls but the wise housekeeper tries to offer it in forms acceptable to the tastes of the football son and the young woman tired from her work in the office. She does not generally need to use the sweetened and flavored powders that are on the market any more than Mr. Locke suggested in A.D. 1710. These added to milk are supposed to increase the appetite or put one to sleep. They may have a psychological value. Many may be oversweetened so they sate the appetite quickly. As a result a valuable vegetable may not be eaten. Milk is a bland food. Small children like it unless their appetites or tastes have been spoiled by sweet-flavored additions made by adults with milk idiosyncracies. The flavor, texture, and appearance of milk dishes should be considered as in any other dish served. For dessert on a hot day the obese member of the family may get her meal's quota of calcium from a glass of cool buttermilk and a thin molasses cookie. Junkets, custards, floating islands, and milk puddings of various kinds are well liked by many families. Plain milk as a beverage food will always take care of the largest supply for the family. In all of our school lunch material we say, "for each child at noon, a glass of milk or two milk dishes."

Here are samples of beverages, soups, protein dishes, and desserts that may be used to make up the day's supply of cooked milk dishes—

Cream of Rice and Onion Soup

Milk .... 1 qt. in double boiler   Seasonings salt, celery salt, paprika
Rice (washed) .... 2 tbsps.   Butter .... 1-2 tbsps.
Onion (sliced) .... 1 large
    (2 tbsps. chopped parsley or celery cut fine may be used)

Put in rice, onion; stir; simmer three hours. Add butter just before serving the hot soup. Good for a cool evening.

Cream of Potato Soup

Potatoes   6 medium   Dry milk powder .... 1¾ cups
Onion ....   3 large slices   Celery salt .... ¼ tsp.
Salt .... 2 tsps.   Dash of pepper and paprika
Boiling water . . .... 5 cups   Parsley (chopped) .... 3 sprigs
Cold water .. . . 2 cups   Butter .... 4 tbsps.

Pare and slice potatoes. Place in a saucepan; add onion, salt, and boiling water, and cook until tender. To the dry milk powder slowly add the cold water, stirring vigorously until smooth. Then add this to the potatoes and stock, and reheat. Add seasonings and butter. If a smooth-textured soup is preferred to one with potato slices, potatoes may be mashed. Serve very hot. Serves 5 or 6.

Orange Nog

Water .. .. 1 cup   Orange juice .... 1 cup
Evaporated milk . ... 1 cup   (or other fruit juice)
Sugar .... 1 tbsp.   Grated orange rind . . .. 2 tsps.
                              Chipped ice

Measure water, milk and sugar into shaker or fruit jar. Shake well (with ice). Add orange juice and rind and shake vigorously. If orange juice is very sour, more sugar may be needed. Yield: 4 servings (1½ pints).

Scalloped Cheese

Bread (stale)	5-6 slices	Milk (hot)	1½ cups
Butter	2 tbsps. (or less)	Eggs	1-2
Cheese	1 cup	Salt	½ tsp.

(grated or cut up in fine pieces)

Butter bread; cut in quarters and triangles. Put layer in oiled baking dish. Sprinkle with cheese; repeat until bread and cheese are used. Beat eggs slightly; add milk and salt. Cover bread with mixture. Bake in a slow oven (325°F.) for 20-30 minutes.

Baked Indian Pudding

Milk	1¼ qts.	Cinnamon	¾ tsp.
Molasses (dark Porto Rican)	2/3 cup	Nutmeg	⅜ tsp.
Sugar (granulated)	1/3 cup	Salt	1 tsp.
Cornmeal (yellow)	½ cup	Butter	4 tbsps.

Heat four-fifths of the milk and add molasses, sugar, cornmeal, salt, spice, and butter to it. Cook 20 minutes or until mixture thickens. Pour into baking dish; add remaining cold milk. Do not stir. Put into slow oven (300°F.) and bake for three hours without stirring. Serve warm with cream or hard sauce or ice cream.

Fish Chowder

Haddock or cod	2 lbs.	Hot milk	4 cups
or		(fresh or evaporated)	
Salmon (pink)	1 tall can	Salt pork	2-inch cube
Onion	¼	Water	6 cups
Potatoes	4	Salt and pepper to taste	

Put head, skin, and bones in kettle with cold water. Simmer ½ hour. Strain off water from this, saving it. Put it into a kettle. (If canned fish is used, this first step would be omitted.)

Cut fish in 1-inch pieces. Add to kettle. Fry the onions in fat until brown. Strain fat into the kettle. Add potatoes which have been pared and cut in cubes. Cook until potatoes are soft. Add the hot milk and seasonings. Serve with crackers. Serves 6.

Milk Sherbert

Milk	1 qt.	Lemon juice	1/3 to ½ cup
Sugar	1¼ cups	(Orange juice, if desired)	1 cup

Heat ½ cup of milk; add sugar. Stir until dissolved. Cool the mixture; add the remaining cold milk. Chill. Stir in fruit juice and freeze. Freeze in cubes in cooling unit if desired.

MILK CONSUMPTION AMONG CHILDREN OF MASSACHUSETTS

A Collection of Figures, Interpreted

DOROTHY ADOLPH, B.S., *Nutritionist*
Massachusetts Department of Public Health

Are there many Massachusetts children not having an adequate amount of milk each day? We have no means of knowing the exact number. However, Well Child Conferences, school clinics, and school lunch surveys reveal the following facts:

Small children under school age to whom milk is very important for growth, good tooth and bone development, and general well-being are not getting enough of this valuable food because (1) the family's food money is low, (2) what money there is for food is spent more often for expensive meats, prepared foods, or sweets, and (3) children have not always been taught to like milk in various forms.

A four-year Well Child Conference study of 1932-1935 shows a small steady increase in the number of recommendations for greater milk intake. Improvement, however, is seen in the amounts of fruits and vegetables used. In 1938 out of 760 children seen by a nutritionist from January through June, almost one-third needed more milk. The nutrition condition of the child was judged by a physician, and suggestions for increased intake of *milk* and advice on the food budget and eating habits were given by the nutritionist.

Even the *older children* whom we would expect to drink less milk since they are "growing up" have a surprisingly small amount. From a study by nutritionists of 500 high school pupils with histories of tuberculosis or tuberculous contacts it has been found that—

203 or 41% had daily 4 cups of milk or 3 cups and a milk dish
96 or 19% had daily 3 cups of milk or 2 cups and a milk dish
107 or 21% had daily 2 cups of milk or 1 cup and a milk dish
55 or 11% had daily 1 cup as a beverage or in a food
37 or 7% had daily less than .1 cup
2 or 1% had none.

In one town where various age groups were studied over a period of two years, a survey during the first year showed that—

52% had no milk at all each day
31% had very little
17% had nearly adequate amounts—but none had adequate amounts.

After some nutrition education, the survey during the second year yielded the following results—

There were no children having no milk at all each day
73% had very little
23% had nearly adequate amounts
4% had adequate amounts.

In *one county* 386 school children out of a group of 596 were not getting enough milk each day.

At *a school lunch counter* serving 1,200, less than one-half selected milk to drink or a dish made with milk.

At other schools:

Where 65 children brought their lunch from home only 23 had milk to drink
Where 40 children brought their lunch from home only 14 had milk to drink
Where 15 children brought their lunch from home none had milk to drink
Where 30 children brought their lunch from home none had milk to drink
Where 135 children brought their lunch from home only 40 had milk to drink.

Not only are we trying to teach parents how to help their children to enjoy drinking milk but also how to provide adequate amounts of milk each day by incorporating it in other foods.

The school lunch manager has an opportunity to encourage

greater milk consumption in the school lunchroom by making it more attractive, perhaps through offering it on a plate lunch at a bargain price or serving it in a variety of puddings, soups, creamed dishes, or frozen desserts.

Teachers may help by suggesting to the children ways in which milk can be brought in the box lunch from home. Physicians, dentists, and nurses may further the use of milk in contacts with the individual members of the family.

A guide to the most for money in food value is available from the Massachusetts Department of Public Health. It gives the hows and whys of adequate daily food on a small income.

Statistics are convincing that it is necessary to stress the value of milk for children, show how to provide it on a low budget, build up a liking for it, and teach ways to serve it either as a beverage or in combination with other foods.

MILK IN RELATION TO SOUND TEETH
FLORENCE B. HOPKINS, M.D., D.M.D.
Division of Child Hygiene
Massachusetts Department of Public Health

The place of nutrition in dental health is a subject much studied and much discussed. A well-known authority in nutrition says, "Although the relation of nutrition to the teeth is far from being wholly understood, it is now recognized that an unbalanced diet plays a major role in the development of abnormalities in teeth and jaws. . . There is far from universal agreement, however, as to the major dietary factors concerned and their mode of action. A few points are, however, generally agreed upon and it is these that will be briefly reviewed here.

"It is agreed by all that during the developmental period nutrition is of paramount importance in building well-formed teeth and jaws and likewise their supporting tissues. It is obvious that the mineral salts, especially calcium and phosphorus, of which both jaws and teeth are so largely composed, must be supplied during this period in ample amounts together with abundance of the calcifying factor, Vitamin D. There is evidence, moreover, that both Vitamins A and C play specific roles in dental conditions either in determining the structure of the teeth themselves or in maintaining the integrity of the gum tissues. It is probable, moreover, that although certain factors are particularly important in tooth development, optimum conditions are obtained only when a diet adequate in all dietary essentials is provided. Since the development of teeth is proceeding from early in the prenatal period until the last teeth are erupted at eighteen or twenty years, it is evident that during this entire period a failure to have all the required building material as well as other environmental requisites could result in improperly developed teeth and jaw bones. . . The fact that all these defects are highly prevalent during childhood is evidence that the average American dietary is far from optimum from the standpoint of tooth development and preservation."[1]

To understand how nutrition may affect the health of teeth one must know something of the embryology, anatomy and physiology.

The ameloblasts, the cells which form the enamel, are derived from the outer embryonic layer, so enamel may be considered as a highly specialized epithelial tissue.

The odontoblasts, or cells from which dentine is formed, are the cells forming the outer layer of the dental papillae which is of mesodermic origin, and can therefore be said to be more analogous to bone.

Both structures attain their ultimate special hardness through the deposit of lime salts in the cells, the difference being that in the case of the enamel, the ameloblasts are so perfectly calcified that there is practically no cell protoplasm left and when calcification is completed the activity of this group of cells is finished, while with the dentine, the odontoblastic layer lying next to the pulp, remains active during the life of the tooth and new or so-called secondary dentine may be laid down at any time when the need arises.

It can be seen then why many dentists feel that little or nothing can be done for the adult enamel through calcium metabolism, but none can deny that there is such a thing as secondary dentine which may become much harder than the primary structure. Many workers express it thus: "There is no natural repair possible to injured or diseased enamel but there can be repair to dentine,' or "adult enamel is not affected from within by dietary changes but there may be such a change wrought in the hardness of dentine."

No dental worker should deny that nutrition is a big factor in the healthy development of the teeth.

It is well known that diseases coming during the formative period of life may leave more permanent marks than those occurring in later years. This is obvious in rickets in the resulting changes in the skeleton, and as true but less recognized in the damage done by rickets to nerve and brain cells. "If the anomaly of metabolism which is manifest in tetany is allowed to persist for a considerable time during the period when the pyramidal cells and other constituents of the brain are forming and developing, it may result in permanent mental defects."[2] Poor nutrition during the growing period leaves its mark on all tissues of the body.

It has been an accepted fact for some time that xerophthalmia resulting in blindness is a result of Vitamin A deficiency, and that severe infections such as pneumonia, bronchitis, pyelitis, and so forth are prevalent in cases lacking sufficient Vitamin A in the diet.

The best and most complete study of the effects of Vitamin A deficiency have been done by Dr. Percy Howe and Dr. S. Burt Wolbach at Harvard University Medical School. They have found keratinization of epithelial tissues, which in their normal state are highly specialized, everywhere in the body and also found atrophy of certain organs constant. Cysts produced in salivary glands were frequently noted. In advanced cases of avitaminosis slight, but demonstrable, atrophy of the hair follicles was found. In the growing tooth, enamel formation ceased. The enamel-forming cells in advanced stages were either shrunken and atrophic or replaced by a narrow layer of stratified epithelium. (A report of this study was published in the Journal of Medical Research).

Dr. E. Mellanby observed in his first experiments on puppies that a Vitamin A and D deficiency produced abnormal structure of the teeth.[3]

While the studies of Drs. Howe and Wolbach were for the most part on white rats and the experiments of E. Mellanby on puppies, a fatal human case of avitaminosis coming to autopsy during the first mentioned study showed conditions definitely corroborating the pathology found in experimental animals. Dr. E. Mellanby's study on the effects of diet on children in certain institutions in England bore out her husband's findings in the case of experimental dogs.

In 1930 Guttorm and Kirsten Toverud (Norsk Tandlaegetidende) reported on a study on calcium metabolism in pregnant women and they further studied the effect of diet on pregnant dogs. They were able to show, as did Mellanby, that prenatal diet has a marked influence on formation of teeth of the offspring.

Hundreds of prenatal nutrition histories, along with the examination of deciduous teeth done at Forsyth Dental Infirmary and at Well Child Conferences conducted by the Division of Child Hygiene of the Massachusetts Department of Public Health, show a very definite correlation between prenatal nutrition and the health of deciduous teeth. The lack of milk in the mother's diet almost certainly goes hand in hand with an early breaking down of the first set of teeth in the offspring.

In stressing the influence of nutrition on the deciduous teeth we must never forget that some teeth are in the process of forming during a long period of life. Contrary to our former belief the crowns of the first permanent molars do not begin to calcify until shortly after birth.[4] From this time on until the roots of the third permanent molars (wisdom teeth) are completed there are teeth constantly growing and calcifying. The development of the gingivae and alveolar processes is simultaneous with the growth of the teeth, the alveola bone growing with the growth of the roots of the teeth and disappearing with the loss of the teeth. This means progressive and continuous calcification and decalcification of bony structures as well as tooth structure from birth to the age of eighteen years or over. Calcium metabolism, therefore, must be an important factor in the building of healthy teeth.

We know that abnormal mineral metabolism may be due to lack of lime salts supplied in the diet or to failure of the body to properly absorb and utilize the minerals. We know that faulty metabolism may result in varying degrees of malnutrition in spite of an excellent diet. We must admit. however, that perfect metabolic function cannot properly nourish a body if the lime salts and necessary vitamins are not supplied.

Since whole milk and milk products, such as cream, butter, cheese, etc., are the best sources of calcium, phosphorus and Vitamin A in our American dietary, it is safe to conclude that milk is one of the most important items in a diet which is valuable in providing and promoting the health of the teeth.

Bibliography

[1] ROBERTS, LYDIA J.: *Nutrition Work with Children*. University of Chicago Press.

[2] BLOCK, C. E., M.D.: *Effects of Deficiency in Vitamins in Infancy*, American Journal of Diseases of Children 27:139-184, 1924.

[3] MELLANBY, E.: *Experimental Rickets*, Medical Research Council Special Report Series No. 61, London, His Majesty's Stationery Office.

[4] Chart, *Periods of Calcification and Eruption of the Deciduous Teeth*,

adapted from Logan and Kronfeld, by Charles F. Bodecker, Columbia Dental and X-ray Corp., 181 E. 23rd St., New York.

FACTS AND FANCIES CONCERNING MILK

DOROTHEA NICOLL, B.S., *Nutritionist*
Massachusetts Department of Public Health

In discussing any food facts and fancies it is necessary to remember that, at times, it is very difficult to draw a definite line between the true and the false.

I. **Some statements while apparently true give only a one-sided picture.**

For example:

"Milk is fattening"

One pint of milk has 360 calories. These should form the basis of the total for the day. About 2,200 to 3,000 calories are needed for energy by the average woman and man in one day. Extra calories from any source—whether milk or other foods—will be stored as fat. Sweets at meals and nibbles between meals are more apt to give the extra calories. For instance—1 glass of milk gives 180 calories, 1 doughnut—200-300,— 1 serving lemon meringue pie—350-450, 1 ice cream sundae—450-600. One glass of skim milk with only ½ the calories of whole milk has most of the protein and minerals and vitamins, except vitamin A.

"Milk is constipating"

Milk or cheese *alone* may be constipating because they are so completely digested and lack bulk or roughage. However, a general mixed diet, consisting of fresh and cooked foods would nullify this effect.

"Milk builds strong teeth"

Milk is an important factor in building strong teeth because of its excellent supply of calcium and vitamin A. But it is also necessary to have an adequate supply of phosphorous and vitamin D before the calcium can be utilized for tooth structure.

"Milk causes anemia in children"

A child getting only milk, or having so much milk that he will not eat other foods rich in iron and vitamin C (which are found only in small amounts in milk) will naturally have an unbalanced diet and may have a tendency to anemia. A child needs a good variety of foods as well as three to four cups of milk as beverage and in other ways. Milk, however, should not crowd out other valuable foods.

II. **Occasionally statements distort the truth by overemphasis, as in this instance:**

"Milk is a perfect food"

Milk is *not* a perfect food for its contains very little iron, copper, or vitamin C. Nevertheless it is one of our most nutritious foods—since it is an excellent source of most other nutrients.

"Pasteurized milk has lost all its food value"
(*Dr. Hay claims it is a "dead" food because it is cooked*)

Pasteurization of milk, when properly done, does not change the food value of milk with the exception of vitamin C—which is sensitive to heat. However, even raw milk is not relied upon as source of vitamin C since the amount of this vitamin in milk is small and varies considerably with the feed of the cow. Use pasteurized milk for safety and raw fruits and vegetables for vitamin C.

*"Feeding milk too long to children will cause them
to be over-fed with protein" (Dr. Hay)*

Growing children need plenty of good quality animal protein for growth, building and repair of muscles and body tissue. Milk and milk products such as cheese, meat, fish and eggs are all excellent sources. The necessary amount for any individual may be supplied from one or from several of the above foods, depending on the quantity taken.

*"Adults do not need milk because
they are no longer growing"*

Milk supplies not only protein for repair as well as growth of tissue but also calcium which aids in normal heart action, contraction and relaxation of muscles, digestion and circulation. It is also a good source of Vitamins A, B, and G. Irradiated milk will add vitamin D. Dr. Henry Sherman says—"It is difficult to get good results with any one at any age without milk."

III. **"I can't drink milk—it doesn't agree with me" is a common statement.**

It is undoubtedly true that "one man's meat is another's poison," and that not all individuals can be required to conform to a certain hard and fast rule in regard to foods.

"Milk is indigestible"

Pure fresh pasteurized milk taken unhurriedly with a meal is seldom the cause of indigestion in the average individual. Any food eaten at a time of great emotional strain, extreme fatigue or gulped in a hurry may cause distress.

"Milk causes hives"

Milk, like many other protein foods, may cause an allergic reaction in individuals who have a hypersensitivity to certain proteins. For the few so affected some substitutes for the milk must be found.

"Eating milk and fruit together is harmful"

Acid fruits and milk, taken separately, or mixed in the same meal are not harmful as long as both are in good condition. The acid of the fruit juices sometimes does "curdle" or separate the milk. This is, however, one process in digestion and will be accomplished by the gastric juices in the stomach anyway. The curd produced by the fruit acid is soft and easily digested. Lemon milk sherbet is a wholesome dessert for children.

*"Milk and fish in the same meal (such as
lobsters and ice cream) are poisonous"*

Fish and milk combine very well as in fish chowder, scalloped fish, clam chowder, and lobster stew. Difficulty following such combinations is more apt to be due to overeating, eating in extreme excitement or hurry, or because some part of the meal was not fresh and in good condition when it was eaten.

IV. **The experiences and advice of one person are sometimes applied indiscriminately to a group. This may be merely conversation** between neighbors, but occasionally it spreads and is commercialized into a diet fad.

"Milk diet aids in menopause disorders"
If added to a poorly balanced diet it might be of assistance in improving general nutrition and health but would have no specific action.

"Milk causes lead and arsenic poisoning"
There is little or no danger that milk will absorb lead or arsenic from modern utensils used in pasteurization. In case lead is already in the body Rosenau says—"Milk taken frequently and in generous amounts has long been known to be preventive of lead poisoning. It was formerly believed that milk acted by keeping down the acidity of the gastric juice, but it now appears that milk is preventive because it is rich in calcium which keeps the lead safely stored in the bones."

V. **Statements may be based on incomplete scientific information or misconstrued facts.**

"Milk causes cancer"
The actual cause of cancer is not yet known. Much research is still being done. "As yet no element of diet has been convicted of a guilty relationship with cancer"—Dr. Clarence Little.

"Milk causes cataracts"
Experiments have been carried on with rats by Dr. Helen Mitchell of the State College at Amherst, Massachusetts, showing the influence of large amounts of galactose (milk sugar) in the production of one type of cataracts. These studies are still in the experimental stage and under no condition can the present results be applied to human beings.

"Milk coats the lining of the throat and 'cuts off the wind' of athletes so they should not use it on the day of a game"
There is no sound physiological basis for this statement. Wind comes to and from the larynx and the trachea in breathing through the nose. The only part of the passage milk would touch would be the post-pharyngeal wall, which is a surface part of the air tract and digestive tract.

"Raw milk cures syphilis"
This statement has absolutely no foundation in facts. Syphilis is caused by a germ.

The best method of checking on either new or old statements in regard to foods is to go to an authority.

In the nutrition field, books by Dr. Henry C. Sherman, Dr. E. V. McCollum and Dr. Mary Swartz Rose are always dependable. Individual inquiries on food and nutrition problems may be answered by the local nutritionist, or by the nutritionists of the Massachusetts Department of Public Health, Division of Child Hygiene, 1 Beacon Street, Boston.

In the public health field, questions on pasteurization of milk, food inspection, food handling problems, etc. should be referred to the local health officer or city board of health.

References:
SHERMAN, HENRY C., *Food and Health*, New York: Macmillan, 1935.
Chemistry of Food and Nutrition, New York: Macmillan, 1937
ROSE, MARY SWARTZ, *Foundations of Nutrition*, New York, Macmillan, 1938
ROSENAU, MILTON J., *Preventive Medicine and Public Health*, New York, Appleton.

TEACHING PEOPLE TO DRINK MILK

JEAN V. LATIMER, B.S., A.M.

Coordinator of Health Education
Massachusetts Department of Public Health

Considering the importance of milk in the diet, certainly we drink too little. The problem, therefore, of the health educator would seem to be that of having knowledge actually function in practice.

For some years past, this writer has been making observations of the food habits of people eating in public places, such as cafeterias, drug store counters, etc. Certainly the so-called "man on the street" in gratifyingly large numbers is drinking milk. In our own generation we have seen a remarkable increase in the consumption of milk, but from community and school surveys and other authentic sources, as well as our own observation, the home consumption of milk is still too low.

We owe much to the milk producers and dealers, in that they have helped to publicize it for us. Community milk campaigns, if conducted in an educational way, may be of real help, for "people need not only to be told, but reminded." To have this done, not solely through printed matter, but through posters and exhibits, is effective.

"How can I make my child drink milk?" is one of the most common questions asked our doctors and nutritionists in the Well Child Conferences. While there is no one answer which can be given as a panacea, we do know that one of the most important health habits of the preschool child pertains to milk drinking and that the laws of habit formation as applied to any aspect of the child's life are equally as applicable in the teaching of a child to like and to drink milk.

Little children are inclined to do the routine thing—the expected thing. Eternal vigilance on the part of the mother is important in seeing that each day the young child doesn't get by without drinking the expected amount of milk at each meal. Serving the milk in attractive glasses and conditioning the child to associate pleasure with his meals are ways of developing favorable attitudes toward milk drinking. The child's attention may be called to the fact that his favorite animals, too, like milk Certainly an early favorable conditioning is equally important as stressing the routine of milk drinking.

A young four-year-old boy, with his family in a summer hotel dining room, where a great variety of food was being served at the table was heard to exclaim, when there was some delay on the part of the waitress, "I want my milk!" This same child, at this same meal, asked for prunes for dessert, although pies and parfaits were being served to the adult members of his party. This is an illustration of how effective early food conditioning may be.

Even little children are tremendously interested in the process of growing up. The following story is a rather humorous illustration of how strong this growth interest is and of how teaching in regard to milk drinking may even become of exaggerated importance in the child's mind. There is a story of a little boy who, one night at his evening meal, continued to drink and drink milk. Finally, when asked the reason, he replied, "I want to drink enough tonight so that when I wake up in the morning my legs will be long enough to drive daddy's car."

Not only drinking milk, but encouraging its use in various forms in the home is desirable. The use of milk in soups, desserts, etc., are all to be cultivated.

But sugar-coating by serving chocolate milk in schools would seem to be negative teaching. There is a story of a first-grade child who, always accustomed to the drinking of milk, exclaimed when chocolate milk was served to her class, "I like my milk white!" Then there are cases of children who, having learned to drink chocolate milk in school have refused to drink milk served "as is" in the home.

The health educator, if successful in influencing the food practices of any family must, of necessity, be influenced by the amount of money which is available for the food budget.

All of us realize how difficult it is for many families, especially where there are a large number of children, to provide what the nutritionists tell us is an adequate amount of milk each day for every child.

Teaching "first things first" when making up a food budget will, of necessity, show the importance of milk and may help to divert the amount spent on less essential foods. Teaching the homemaker the possibilities of using milk in its less expensive forms, such as evaporated, will help.

The sanitary care of milk and the great health risk involved in using milk which has been carelessly handled also must be taught.

Certainly the school, from the time the child enters the first grade through high school, may do much in assisting the home for cultivating milk drinking as one of the most important of our health practices.

In the primary school, where all the health teaching is most informal, the teaching regarding milk will, of course, be emphasized. In the first grade where the general activities are centered around the central ideas of home and school life, health teaching may be tied up with things in which children are already interested. In developing the activity, "Cooking and Serving Meals," as a part of the unit concerned with household activities, the best food for a child's breakfast, dinner and supper may be considered. Pictures illustrating desirable foods may be drawn or cut from magazines. Play setting the table and serving breakfast, dinner and supper.

In the second or third grade where study is given to farm life, interest may be aroused in learning more about milk. That the enlargement of the background of the city child is needed along this line is illustrated by the story of a second-grade child who said, when her class visited a farm, "I am glad I saw a cow. Before, I thought milk always came from a bottle."

The natural tendency, especially of the primary grade child, to regard all experiences as a part of a total experience makes it pertinent to integrate health teaching with the large learning situations which, in turn, are integrated and unified round wholesome living.

It is desirable to emphasize the combination of essential foods rather than overemphasize any one food. An illustration of how such teaching may be violated is found in a recent health education curriculum of a city school system in a distant state. This course of study states that milk is to be taken up in the first grade as a separate unit for a time allotment of six weeks; again in the second grade there is to be a separate unit on milk for another six weeks, and in the third grade a unit on milk, teeth and bones for six weeks. Even seven weeks is to be given to the topic in the fourth grade. Such procedures, if continued throughout the grades, would lead to the pertinency of a recent remark of a boy who, on entering high school, was heard to say to his principal, "There are two things I hope we don't have to hear about in high school—George Washington and milk." Overteaching is never good teaching.

However, from the experimental school studies which the Division of Child Hygiene has been conducting the past few years, we are convinced that a small amount of specific unit teaching on nutrition should begin in the fourth grade and continue through the high school and that definite pupil activities regarding milk should, as a part of the nutritional units, receive emphasis.

In the fourth grade, to emphasize milk as a food especially needed for growth, pupils are taught through such activities as a rat feeding demonstration or through showing of films which emphasize milk as a food for both children and animals. In the fifth grade, where food is taken up for the first time in relationship to such body needs as growth, repair, energy and for keeping the body in good working order, milk is again emphasized in a natural setting.

To supplement such direct procedures, the children study the food habits of children of other lands which, of course, will include milk.

In the sixth grade, pupil activities such as visiting a dairy where milk is being pasteurized, having class discussions as to the sanitary ways of keeping milk in the home, finding out why milk should be protected against flies, comparing food values of various forms of milk, finding the cost of a quart of different kinds of milk sold in your neighborhood, making a poster telling of the ways of keeping milk from bacteria, are illustrations of pupil activities which may enlarge its significance.

Special emphasis on milk is needed at the close of the elementary school, for it is at this age that many children fall off in regular milk drinking. Mothers do not watch the practices of older children as closely. Many boys and girls grow to think milk is just a baby food for small "kids" and that they do not need to drink it any longer. Not long ago, this observer, while conducting a class in health education for teachers, had one teacher after another raise her hand and say, "What can I do to make older children continue to drink milk?" Practically all of these teachers were from the sixth or the junior high school grades. There is necessity, not only for mere repetition, but also for a different approach and an enlargement in our teaching regarding milk.

Even junior high school pupils should be made conscious of the fact that they are still growing and that milk is needed for their growth and protection. The health education specialist going into a junior high school asked a group of pupils the following questions: "How old are you now?"—"How many more years before you are grown?"—"How many years have you left to grow and how can you afford to stop drinking your usual amount of milk?"

Young girls in the junior high schools especially need to be encouraged to regard milk as nonfattening and encouraged to leave off some of the desserts and other foods which are less essential.

Boys and girls in the senior high schools today receive nutrition teaching as a regular and important part of their general health education curriculum. While the home economics department contributes much, it is not enough and also as a rule does not reach the boys.

Science teaching offers many possibilities for enlarging and making more interesting the teaching regarding food. Taking milk apart and seeing the various food elements which it contains is an experiment which is today being carried on in general science classes.

Somewhere in the high school, there should be a gathering together of all the factors of nutrition with such a unit as "A Balanced and Protective Diet." The study to include such problems as, "How Is the Necessary Amount of Daily Food Measured?", "What Are the So-Called Protective Foods?", "What is the Meaning of a Balanced Diet?" and for the last problem, "The School Lunch—What Does It Mean to You?"

Since we are always more interested in practice than in theory, the high school cafeteria should actually serve milk in an attractive way so that pupils may be encouraged to drink it. Just recently, in one of the poorer financial sections of the state, through a community and school educational campaign, we were able to raise the consumption of milk 20%.

To repeat again the quotation used in the first part of this article, "People need to be reminded as well as told." Therefore, our endeavors in health education for milk drinking, as well as for all other health needs, can never end.

THE COLD STORAGE OF FOOD IN MASSACHUSETTS*

HERMANN C. LYTHGOE, S.B.

Director, Division of Food and Drugs
Massachusetts Department of Public Health

The commercial cold storage of food is a business operated for the purpose of making a profit. The fundamental economic principle involved is the preservation of surplus perishable foods, produced in quantities too large for immediate consumption, to be released for consumption when there is a scarcity of the food so stored.

There is nothing particularly new in the cold storage business, and it is not entirely confined to highly civilized people. Certain of the Eskimo tribes catch wild birds in the spring, place the carcasses in caves of perpetual ice and eat the carcasses in the winter months when fresh meat is scarce. It is also a practice in some farming communities to slaughter a steer in the winter, to cut up the meat, allow it to freeze and keep it frozen in a shed for consumption from time to time during the winter season.

Cold storage of food produces an equalization of wholesale prices, and also stimulates an increased production. If we did not demand eggs during November when the production of eggs is curtailed, there would be no incentive to raise a surplus of eggs in the spring months, but if there were no means to store the surplus eggs produced in the spring, it

* A summary of this paper was presented before the Tenth International Congress of Chemistry, Rome, Italy, May 16, 1938.

would for practical purposes be impossible to consume them all before they spoiled.

The popular opposition to cold storage food has been decreasing, and while even today there are many people who will not voluntarily buy and eat such food, there is much cold storage food sold to the public as such.

The Massachusetts law pertaining to the cold storage of food was enacted in 1912. This law was passed as the result of repeated public criticism regarding the sale of cold storage food as fresh food and also because of many false statements relative to the character of such food. The law itself, however, was a result of a very careful study by a recess legislative committee appointed in 1911. The report of that committee, House Bill 1733, filed under date of January 10, 1912, is a remarkably complete document upon the business of keeping food in cold storage. The report deals in part with the economic aspects of the subject and discusses retail and wholesale prices over a period of several years. It contains an appendix covering the cold storage legislation in existence at that time in the United States and Canada. The cold storage legislation in the United States is now much more elaborate and more nearly uniform than it was in 1912.

Another document of 909 pages, the hearings before the Committee on Agriculture of the Sixty-sixth Congress relative to cold storage legislation, published in 1919, contains many facts and considerable demagogy relating to cold storage. No legislation of a national character resulted.

The Massachusetts Law has been amended several times, and as it now stands, it provides for the licensing as cold storage warehouses of all places artificially cooled where food is stored at a temperature at or below 45° Fahrenheit for thirty days or more. The license fee is $10 per annum. Each warehouse must be properly equipped to carry on the business of cold storage, and must be kept in a sanitary condition subject to the penalty of revocation of the license in whole or in part.

Food is defined in this act to include fresh meats, fresh meat products (except in the process of manufacture), fresh food fish, poultry, eggs and butter. No food may be placed in cold storage or may remain in cold storage if deemed by the Department of Public Health to be diseased, tainted or otherwise unwholesome. Cold storage food once placed on the market for sale at retail cannot be returned to cold storage, although cold storage food may be transferred from one warehouse to another if such transfer is not for the purpose of evading the provisions of the act.

No articles of food may be held in cold storage for more than one year except with the consent of the Department. The date of storage must be marked upon each container, or, if the food is stored in bulk, on or in connection with the article. If the food was originally stored elsewhere than in Massachusetts, it must be labeled with the date of original storage. Because of the impossibility of obtaining this date under certain circumstances, the Department adopted the following regulation:

"When articles of food have been kept in cold storage for twelve calendar months, report of such fact shall be made to the Department of Public Health by the person having custody of such articles, and such articles shall not be removed from cold storage by the owners until they have been inspected by the agents of the Department of Public Health, and released by order of the Department. Articles of food which have been in cold storage without this Commonwealth, the date of original storage of which cannot be ascertained, may be placed temporarily in cold storage, and the depositor thereof shall immediately notify the Department of Public Health, and shall request permission to keep such articles for a definite period less than twelve calendar months. On receipt of this request, the articles will be examined and if found to be in satisfactory condition, permission to retain such articles in storage may be granted. Cold storage warehouses receiving articles of food which appear to have been previously in cold storage and not bearing any date of original storage may temporarily place such articles in cold storage and shall immediately notify the Department of Public Health of such action."

The Department usually requires the depositor of food frozen elsewhere than in the State to file an affidavit relating to the date the food was frozen. Upon one occasion an obviously erroneous affidavit was furnished, which the Department refused to accept, and the material was ordered out of storage. News of actions of this character travels through the trade with great rapidity, and since that time apparently no affidavits giving false dates of freezing have been submitted to the Department.

An exception is made regarding the dating of frozen fish. If packed in containers, the date of freezing must be stated on the package, but otherwise the articles need not be dated. The warehouse, however, is required to keep a record of the storage dates of the various lots, and the length of time of storage is limited as in the case of other articles of food. There is, however, one exception pertaining to undated frozen fish frozen without the Commonwealth: such fish may remain in storage in Massachusetts for a period of only six months subject, however, to extension of time by the Department as in the case of other articles of food.

Persons selling cold storage food must display a sign, "Cold Storage Goods Sold Here." and the statutes provide a penalty for selling as fresh, any articles of food which have been held in cold storage.

Each licensed cold storage warehouse is required to submit to the Department of Public Health a monthly report of the amounts of food placed in storage and the amount of food on hand in storage. The Massachusetts Department of Agriculture is required to obtain statistics relative to the holdings of various articles of food whether or not in cold storage. Most of the large warehouses in the country make voluntary reports of holdings to the Bureau of Agricultural Economics of the United States Department of Agriculture which are compiled and published.

In order to relieve the warehouse of too much multiplicity of details in collecting and reporting these statistics, the Department of Public Health and the Department of Agriculture of the State have agreed upon a joint form of report which corresponds very closely with the report form submitted to the United States Bureau of Agricultural Economics. The report is made in duplicate to the Department of Public Health, which Department sends one copy to the Massachusetts Department of Agriculture, and compiles only that portion of the reports pertaining to the statutory definition of articles of food. The following two tables show a recent compilation of a month's report of holdings of butter, eggs, poultry, meat and of fish.

Report of Massachusetts Department of Public Health on Fish Placed in Cold Storage Between March 15 and April 15

	1937	1938
Bluefish, pounds	1,774	1,414
Butterfish, pounds	2,643	1,379
Catfish, pounds	62,964	29,422
Ciscoes, pounds		
Cod, hake, pollock, haddock, pounds	637,187	1,142,069
Flounders, pounds	38,800	37,639
Haddock fillets, pounds	3,213,445	3,548,916
Halibut, pounds	45,306	96,146
Herring, pounds	34,080	2,850
Herring, cured, pounds	301,540	266,965
Mackerel, pounds	47,874	34,731
Salmon, fall and silver, pounds	13,876	24,583
Salmon, mild-cured, pounds	4,400	
Salmon, all others, pounds	2,500	23,200
Shad and shad roe, pounds	394	517
Smelts, eulachon, pounds	24,310	41,990
Squid, pounds	4,080	18,250
Whitefish, pounds		11,174
Whiting, pounds	471,737	467,107
Miscellaneous frozen fish, pounds	768,015	1,137,479
Totals	5,674,925	6,885,831

Fish on Hand in Storage on the Fifteenth Day of April

	1937	1938
Bluefish, pounds	8,481	9,981
Butterfish, pounds	6,700	65,556
Catfish, pounds	100,533	31,445
Ciscoes, pounds	686	1,870
Cod, hake, pollock, haddock, pounds	5,483,890	3,437,396
Flounders, pounds	39,850	162,611
Haddock fillets, pounds	3,195,320	3,597,935
Halibut, pounds	90,238	77,192
Herring, pounds	25,442	127,671
Herring, cured, pounds	1,057,016	1,216,203
Mackerel, pounds	420,180	389,313
Salmon, fall and silver, pounds	18,306	58,500
Salmon, mild-cured, pounds	49,273	52,191
Salmon, all others, pounds	17,772	33,292
Shad and shad roe, pounds	56,894	7,959
Smelts, eulachon, pounds	424,813	425,703
Squid, pounds	36,920	365,949
Whitefish, pounds	1,142	7,084
Whiting, pounds	6,705,714	470,676
Miscellaneous frozen fish, pounds	3,052,397	2,831,211
Totals	20,791,567	13,369,738

Report of Massachusetts Department of Public Health on Articles Other Than Fish Placed in Cold Storage During March

	1937	1938
Butter, pounds	317,331	209,895
Eggs, case, dozens	957,570	357,150
Eggs, frozen, pounds	1,139,956	577,161
Broilers, pounds	194,272	101,184
Roasters, pounds	264,839	170,631
Fowls, pounds	301,666	204,879
Turkeys, pounds	1,079,924	492,570
Ducks, pounds	27,973	23,075
Miscellaneous poultry, pounds	289,228	89,649
Frozen beef, pounds	963,064	621,013
Frozen pork, pounds	1,321,384	604,066
Frozen lamb and mutton, pounds	97,765	65,358
Miscellaneous meats, pounds	615,542	888,513
*Totals	7,570,514	4,405,144

Articles Other Than Fish on Hand in Cold Storage on the First Day of April

	1937	1938
Butter, pounds	303,239	339,673
Eggs, case, dozens	2,153,280	348,030
Eggs, frozen, pounds	1,231,982	1,496,065
Broilers, pounds	1,338,720	315,962
Roasters, pounds	2,106,268	1,121,912
Fowls, pounds	808,919	324,913
Turkeys, pounds	3,194,910	1,809,604
Ducks, pounds	50,700	32,217
Miscellaneous poultry, pounds	855,858	324,938
Frozen beef, pounds	2,678,943	1,296,796
Frozen pork, pounds	8,154,651	2,983,030
Frozen lamb and mutton, pounds	408,968	309,864
Miscellaneous meats, pounds	1,838,987	1,364,943
*Totals	25,125,425	12,067,947

The Department is given authority to extend the time of storage of food beyond twelve months. Many of these requests for extensions are due to unforeseen business conditions. If a mill shuts down for a long period its employees are liable to leave the city and go back to the farm. In the meantime the baker who has contracted for a considerable quantity of frozen broken out eggs finds he cannot use them until the mill starts up again, and consequently will ask for an extension of storage time. Considerable fish is stored with the intention of its being consumed during Lent. If, however. the anticipated stormy season does not arrive, and there is plenty of fresh fish received every day, the depositors of this storage fish find a surplus on hand, and are obliged to ask for extensions of time or take a total loss.

The amount of food upon which extensions of time are granted is not large. During 1937 the total amount of food placed in cold storage was 198,210,185 pounds and the total amount of food upon which extensions were granted was 1,124,198 pounds, representing only 0.56% of the total weight of food placed in storage subject to extension.

* Inasmuch as the contents of one dozen eggs weigh one pound, the dozens are added as pounds.

Massachusetts is not a food producing state—it is a manufacturing state, and while there is considerable food produced in Massachusetts, there is much more food imported from other states. Massachusetts, however, is a fish producing state and produces fish not only for its own use, but also for export to other states.

Chart I on arithmetic-logarithmic scales shows the cold storage holdings of eggs as dozens and of butter as pounds during the past five years. These figures are comparable since the contents of one dozen eggs weigh approximately one pound. Most of the storage of butter and eggs is in the public storage warehouses, but there are a few private warehouses storing these articles which do not accept such material from the public. The butter and egg holdings show the usual seasonal variation of production.

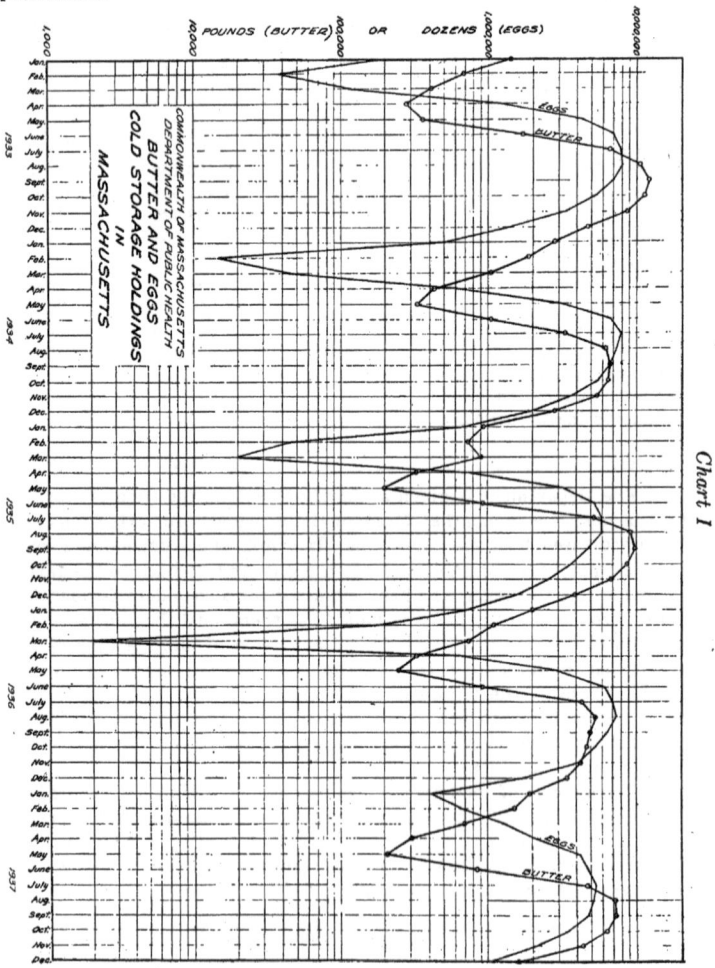

Chart I

The low point in the egg holdings is in February, and it is the custom in the warehouses not to begin any egg storage in the rooms where eggs have been previously stored until the room is thoroughly cleaned and whitewashed, and whereas the combined reports always show some eggs in cold storage, each place where eggs in the shell are stored is emptied before the spring surplus production is stored.

A curious variance from the usual low figure of egg holdings is shown in January, 1937. This was due to an unusually early spring, and surplus eggs came upon the market very early.

There is considerable storage of broken out eggs such as egg whites, egg yolks, and whole eggs known as "mixed eggs." Upon freezing the yolks will coagulate, and upon thawing the yolks and mixed eggs will be "scrambled" but, the whites will be liquid. Sugar is sometimes added to the yolks and to the mixed eggs prior to freezing and the material so treated will thaw out liquid. Preparations of this character are used by bakers in the manufacture of bakery products when liquid eggs are necessary and sugar is also an ingredient. Recently, and for the first time, a request was made for an extension of time in storage of salted egg yolks. An investigation was made regarding the intended use of the mixture as it was surmised that the material was "tanners' yolks," more or less decomposed, to which salt had been added to prevent coagulation, in which case there was no time limit of storage. This, however, was not the case as the material was intended for use in the manufacture of mayonnaise. The salt content was approximately five percent.

The surplus production of butter is in June, which is also the time of the maximum milk production. Milk production decreases during the summer and autumn and reaches a minimum in February. There is always a spring surplus of milk, and there is generally a shortage of milk during the warm days in September, and this time of shortage naturally reduces the production of butter. There is no great incentive to kill hens for food purposes while they are laying eggs, but when the hen has reached the age that her egg production is not equal to the cost of her feed, it is far cheaper to kill the hen and place the carcass in cold storage until such time as there is a demand for fowl, which demand, due to the peculiarity of the human animal who "wants what he wants when he wants it," frequently occurs at the time when hens are busily engaged in producing eggs.

Chart II, showing the poultry holdings, gives the seasonal variation in the storage of different types of birds. The first birds going into storage are the fowl, the storage beginning about June or July when egg production begins to drop. These birds reach the high point in storage during September and October. Next the broilers are stored, the storage beginning in July and August, the high point of holdings being in November, December and January. The roasting birds go into storage during October and November and the high point of holdings of this type of poultry is in February and March.

Turkeys produced in the United States are mainly for the Thanksgiving and Christmas holidays. The surplus Thanksgiving turkeys are stored in the latter part of November and the first of December, and the surplus Christmas turkeys are stored in the last of December and early January. These holdings reach the high point about the first of February.

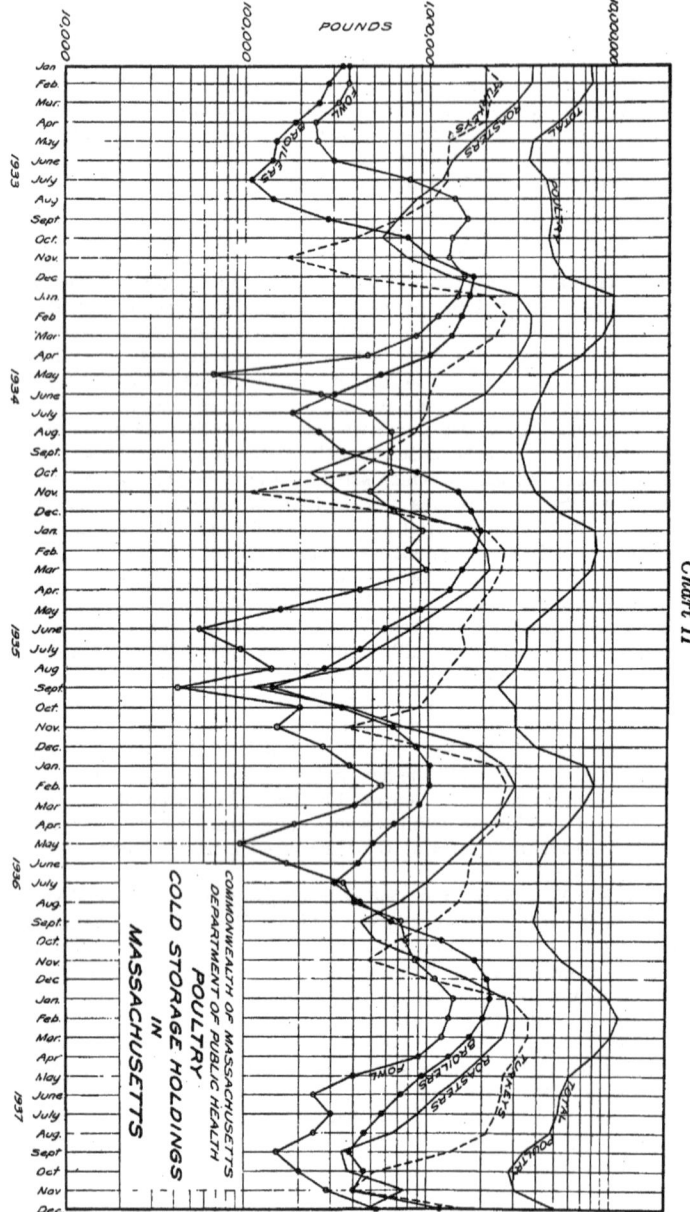

Chart II

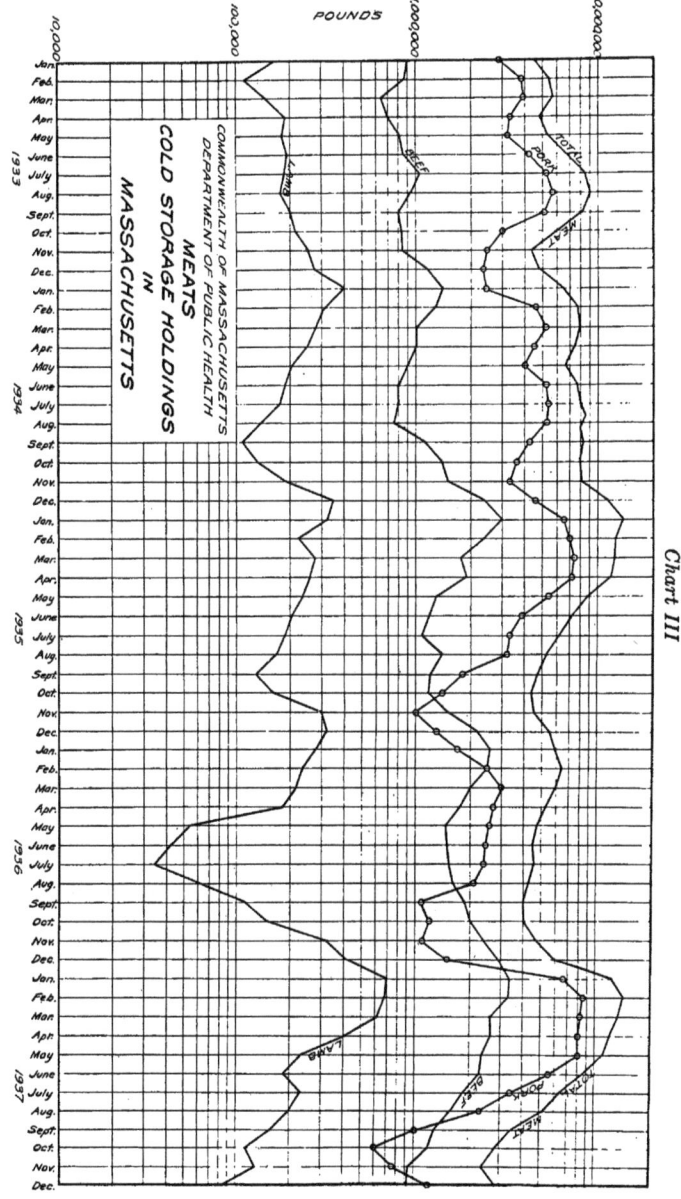

Chart III

Some cold storage poultry is sold direct to the consumer for household use, but most of this material is used by the hotel and restaurant trade when there is a demand for out-of-season poultry.

Chart III shows the holdings of beef, pork, and lamb as well as of total meats. The statistics of beef, pork and lamb holdings covering the whole United States and published by the United States Department of Agriculture show a seasonal variance. These figures for Massachusetts, while they to some extent parallel the United States figures, are not so seasonally significant particularly as to beef and lamb. Most of this material is first stored in the west where the animals are slaughtered and is shipped to Massachusetts as may be demanded for consumption and occasionally for export to foreign countries. The beef holdings usually show a low point in the spring and a high point in January.

The pork holdings as a rule parallel those reported by the United States, with the high point in February, March, and April and the low point in December and January. This was not the case in 1933 and 1934, due to pork shortage in the United States during those years. Many hogs are raised in Massachusetts and many are slaughtered here. Much of this surplus pork finds its way into Massachusetts cold storage warehouses.

The freezing of pork has a public health significance. Any trichinae present are killed by thirty days of commercial cold storage at a temperature of 12° F. It is unfortunate that this practice is not made compulsory by legislation.

The holdings of lamb and mutton are of little significance when compared with the population. At the most it rarely exceeds one pound per capita in recent years. In 1920, however, 10,000,000 pounds of New Zealand frozen lamb was stored in Massachusetts for five months and was subsequently shipped to England for which country it was originally intended. Only a little of the first shipment was consumed in this country, but its mere presence in cold storage reduced the retail price of lamb by 10c. per pound.

The cold storage holdings vary from year to year. This is particularly true of meat. For example, in 1921 and 1922 the beef holdings in Massachusetts varied from 2,600,000 pounds to 5,300,000 pounds, and the pork holdings from 8,700,000 pounds to 18,000,000 pounds, much higher than during the past five years.

Chart IV on arithmetic scales gives the poultry and beef holdings in 1927 and 1937. There is but little difference between the poultry holdings of these years, whereas there is a great difference in the beef holdings, particularly in the latter part of 1937 when the beef holdings were the lowest on record. There is but little opportunity of making a profit on a high market, particularly if there are possibilities of its becoming a falling market; consequently storage is curtailed under such circumstances.

There has been considerable change in the character and quantity of fish placed in storage in Massachusetts during the past ten years, a notable difference being a material reduction in the amount of squid so stored and a great increase in the amount of cod, haddock, pollock and hake. One reason for this increase has been the marketing of fish fillets. much of which is made from this type of fish. The fillets removed from the fish are placed in small containers, and then are frozen. The con-

Chart IV

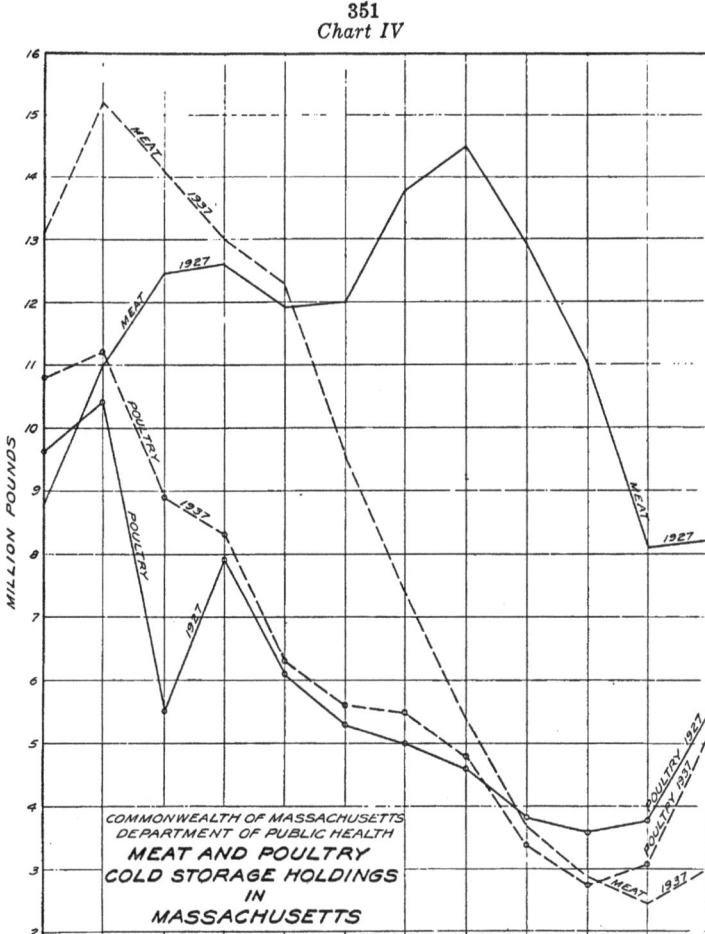

COMMONWEALTH OF MASSACHUSETTS
DEPARTMENT OF PUBLIC HEALTH
MEAT AND POULTRY
COLD STORAGE HOLDINGS
IN
MASSACHUSETTS

tainers are of such character that they may be then packed in a freight refrigerator car and shipped to the central portion of the United States where salt water fish is not particularly plentiful.

Since 1932 the warehouses have been reporting cod fillets as a separate item. This resulted in a slight drop in the reported holdings of cod, but the combined holdings of cod and cod fillets show a substantial increase in the freezing of this type of fish. The storage of the other types of fish depend a lot upon the catch, but there is otherwise not much variance.

The marketing of whiting, otherwise known as shiny hake, has been materially changed during recent years. It was formerly the practice to place these fish in pans, to freeze them, and then during the winter months to ship the frozen blocks of fish in wooden boxes to the midwest. This fish is not a commercial article in retail stores in New England. It can be marketed successfully only in a frozen condition. It is a low-fat, high-moisture fish and consequently is very easily decomposed.

During the past four or five years the practice has developed and is now increasing of removing the heads and evicerating these fish either before or after freezing, placing the cleaned fish in small containers, freezing them in the containers, and then shipping them in refrigerator cars earlier in the season than was formerly the case. This practice has resulted in an increase in the sales of whiting as well as an increase in the quantity stored because the fish when so packed occupies much less volume than under former conditions. There is also a substantial saving in freight charges.

The total amount of fish placed in storage each year in Massachusetts is above 100,000,000 pounds. There are seven warehouses in Massachusetts devoted almost exclusively to fish storage. Six of these are private warehouses, but there are a few public warehouses where any person may deliver fresh fish and have it frozen and stored. The bulk of the fish is placed in storage during the summer months. The private fish freezers are, as a rule, empty in the latter part of February and the rooms are given a thorough cleaning prior to beginning the season's business.

Chart V shows the total annual storage of certan fish over a period of thirteen years.

Cold storage is now being used for articles of food other than those enumerated in the statute. The Massachusetts Department of Public Health has no statistics covering the amount of such material placed in storage. It is, however, increasing. The "Birds Eye" process of quick freezing has been responsible for freezing in small packages fruits and vegetables such as peas, beans, corn, strawberries, cherries, etc. Portable freezers are taken to the fields, the fresh peas are gathered, placed in the small containers, are immediately frozen and are then transferred to the storage warehouses for holding. One such portable freezer is reported to have travelled 6,000 miles during twelve months, to have been operated more than 200 days during that period and to have quick frozen more than 750,000 pounds of food. The small frozen packages are transferred to retail stores and held in refrigerated compartments, are sold frozen to the consumer, who then places the contents of the package still frozen into boiling water, and in a comparatively short time the vegetables may be placed on the table for consumption.

The United States Bureau of Agricultural Economics is now gathering and publishing statistics of the storage of this variety of food and the reports show an increasing business. The holdings for the entire United States of frozen fruits consisting in part of strawberries, blueberries, cherries, etc., during 1937 were 70,622,000 pounds on January 1; 63,610,000 pounds on February 1; 55,825,000 pounds on March 1; and 48,289,000 pounds on April 1. Similar figures for 1938 were 124,660,000 pounds on January 1; 117,804,000 on February 1; 110,807,000 pounds on March 1; and 98,833,000 pounds on April 1. The holding of frozen vegetables consisting in part of peas, beans, corn, spinach, etc., also show a

Chart V

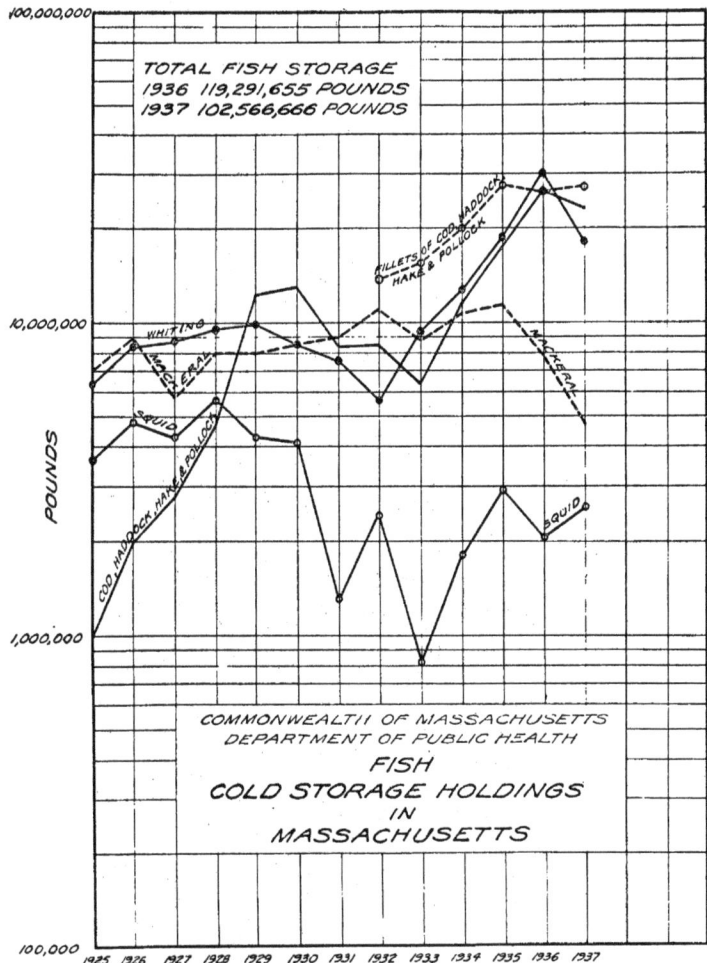

marked increase during 1938 as compared with those of the prior year. The figures for the first four months of 1937 averaged 9,726,000 pounds and for 1938 averaged 26,825,000 pounds.

The quick freezing process is also used in the preparation of meat, poultry, and fish, the consumer removes the frozen article, already prepared for cooking, and places it in the cooking utensil and proceeds in the usual manner.

The retail price of this material may be slightly but not much higher than is that of the unfrozen material in season, yet for very small families or for persons living alone and doing their own cooking, there is considerable saving of what otherwise might be wasted because of the ability to buy the food in substantially small quantities.

One item of value of this process of quick freezing is the reduction of time in cooling the food through the zone of maximum crystal formation resulting in an improvement in the quality of the product as compared to that produced by the slow freezing process. For a resumé of the literature pertaining to the scientific, engineering, and economic aspects of the subject, see published articles of Poole and Zarotschenzeff*.

There has been for several years in Massachusetts an increase in the storage of cranberries for manufacture into cranberry sauce. These berries are frozen in individual packages, and each day a sufficient number of packages are removed from the freezer to furnish sufficient work for the factory workers engaged in the manufacture of canned cranberry sauce. By utilization of cold storage, the factory can be kept continuously operating throughout a somewhat long period, thereby giving a more steady employment to persons engaged in this type of work, otherwise there would be a rush of work in the early winter months and no work the balance of the year. The shipment of canned cranberry sauce throughout the United States has produced an opportunity for the increased production of these berries.

In dealing with the requests for extensions of time in storage, the Department may grant such extensions only if the material is satisfactory for further storage.

Fortunately there are but few chemical changes taking place in frozen food, although under certain circumstances changes may take place.

Eggs in the shell are not frozen, and consequently there is a constant deterioration of this class of food in storage. The Department has never received a request for an extension of time on shell eggs. A person storing eggs in the shell who fails to sell them all by the second week in January invariably loses money on the balance.

Frozen eggs apparently do not change in storage as shown by chemical examination of such eggs stored by the Department for a period of six years, examinations being made from time to time during that period.

Meat and poultry sometimes show considerable shrinkage due to evaporation of moisture. The holding chambers are naturally moisture free, and if the material stays too long in such chambers and at the same time is exposed to air currents, sufficient evaporation may take place on long storage to cause reduction in the market value of the material. Whenever too much "drying out" is observed, extensions are granted only for a comparatively short period of time.

Butter occasionally develops a rancidity on long storage. The odor of the butter is a good index as to whether this rancidity has started, but a chemical examination is preferable and is frequently performed.

On requests for extensions of time for butter storage a sample is collected and the acid number of the fat is determined. Experience has shown that if the acidity of the fat is equal or greater than 10 cubic centimeters of 1/10 normal acid per 100 grams of fat, the butter is rancid.

---

* Ice and Refrigeration, September, October and November, 1936.

If the acidity of the fat begins to approach this figure, the extensions are refused except for very short periods of time.

Sometimes fish fat will develop a rancidity in storage, although the figure for acidity of the fat is not that used in the case of butter.

The inspectors of the Department have the authority without court procedure to confiscate food which is decomposed. Occasionally such food finds its way into cold storage, and it is generally found by one of the inspectors before the storage period expires. Under these circumstances the owner of the food is informed of the findings of the inspector and is requested to sign an order on the warehouse transferring the material to the Department of Public Health. The owner is also informed that if he questions the judgment of the inspector, samples will be taken for analysis, and he is given an opportunity to be present when such samples are taken.

Chemical examinations are made first for rancidity of the fat and second for decomposition of the proteins if the material is poultry, meat, or fish. If the material is butter the acidity of the fat is determined. If the material is broken out eggs the fat and ammonia are determined, but in the case of egg whites a titration for acidity or alkalinity is made. If the material is meat, fish, or poultry the ammonia, total nitrogen and sometimes the acidity of the fat are determined.

The figures representing the limiting factors used for determining decomposition have been determined by the laboratory workers of the Department. The figure for the acidity of butter fat represents the analyses of 408 samples of cold storage butter. The use of this figure for this purpose was first suggested by C. A. Browne.*

Egg whites are normally alkaline to phenolphthalein and as decomposition develops they become acid. There is no evidence of the development of ammonia by decomposing egg whites. The decomposing yolks, however, develop ammonia, and the fat will become acid. In the examination of egg yolks or mixed eggs the fat and ammonia are determined and the ammonia is calculated on a 10% fat basis, that being the average fat content of the average egg. Sometimes frozen eggs may consist of a mixture of good and bad eggs resulting in a low ammonia content of the mixture. The odor is of value under these circumstances. Newly laid eggs will have an ammonia content varying from 0.75 to 1.25 milligrams per 100 grams. Commercial eggs which have not been in storage, and which are edible but which cannot be sold as fresh by reason of age will have an ammonia content varying from 2.0 to 3.5 milligrams per 100 grams. Cold storage eggs when placed on the market for sale at retail will have an ammonia content within the same limits. This variance in the cold storage eggs depends upon the character of the eggs when placed in cold storage and the length of time stored. Eggs stored in April and sold in September are liable to have a lower ammonia content than non-storage eggs a month old. When the ammonia content reaches 4.0 milligrams per 100 grams, the egg is definitely decomposed.

In examining the meats and fish the ammonia and the nitrogen are determined, and the ratio between these two figures is calculated. This method of computation eliminates the fat and the moisture, both of which will reduce the ammonia content by dilution. Normal meat and fish

---

* Jour. Am. Chem. Soc. 1899, p. 975.

will show a ratio of nitrogen to ammonia of from 0.35 to 0.40 as **percent.** In many instances decomposition occurs when this ratio exceeds 0.40% but in all cases it is very evident when it is 0.50% or more.* The ammonia content as an index of decomposition is of little value when applied to cooked food because the cooking process affects the amount of ammonia in meats, fish, and eggs.

The Department uses the well-known aerometric method of the late Otto Folin** for the determination of ammonia in these products, using Nessler solution as the reagent. Twenty-five years of experience have proven its simplicity and accuracy.

There are at present but few violations of the cold storage law. The owners of the warehouses comply with the act practically 100%. A depositor may occasionally violate the law to a minor extent, but this is very unusual. Wholesale dealers in foods do not violate the law in dealing with their customers. A very few retail dealers violate in respect to the sale of cold storage eggs without the required label, but the great majority of such dealers sell cold storage eggs in cartons so labeled. Persons operating upon the cold storage laws of Massachusetts are apparently of the opinion that laws are not made to be enforced but to be complied with.

---

* Report of Analyst, Massachusetts State Board of Health, Annual Report for 1913.
** Jour. Biol. Chem. 11:532 (1912)

Book Notes

PNEUMONIA AND SERUM THERAPY by Frederick T. Lord, M.D. and Roderick Heffron, M.D. $1. 156 pp. New York. The Commonwealth Fund. 1938.

The appearance of this volume, a revision of the author's *Lobar Pneumonia and Serum Therapy*, emphasizes the rapid advances taking place in this field, for it is only two years since the publication of the earlier volume. Increasing knowledge has necessitated numerous changes, beginning with the title. The omission of the adjective "Lobar" from the title acknowledges the current belief that the etiology rather than the anatomical distribution is the important characteristic of pneumonia.

The authors have assembled in brief readable form the essentials of the serum therapy of pneumonia. In addition to the details involved in the treatment of individual patients, there is included material relating to pneumonia control programs, laboratory diagnosis, and serum production. Whereas the earlier volume considered in detail treatment for cases due only to Type I or II pneumococci, the present edition includes the available information on treatment of other types, as well as a consideration of rabbit serum.

Thanks to the close contact between workers in this field, the authors have been able to include much very recent and some still unpublished material, thus making available up-to-the-minute opinions and figures.

Like other Commonwealth Fund publications, this too shows care in the selection of paper, type and binding as well as in proofreading and indexing. The book is highly recommended to every physician interested or employing serum therapy for the treatment of pneumonia.

—Elliott S. Robinson, M. D., Director,
Division of Biologic Laboratories.

SYPHILIS, GONORRHEA, AND THE PUBLIC HEALTH by Nels A. Nelson, M.D., and Gladys L. Crain, R.N. $3. 367 pp. New York. Macmillan. 1938.

Syphilis, Gonorrhea, and the Public Health, by Nels A. Nelson, Director of the Division of Genitoinfectious Diseases of the Massachusetts Department of Public Health, and Gladys L. Crain, Epidemiologist of the Division of Genitoinfectious Diseases of the Massachusetts Department of Public Health, (Macmillan Company, 1938), makes its bow in a comparatively new field of literature, the diagnosis and treatment of Syphilis and Gonorrhea combined with the preservation of the rights of the uninfected. This combination of treatment of the individual with public health aspects of these disease entities is admirably presented in keeping with the still limited essential contributions from the research point of view for Gonorrhea and the more adequate situation for Syphilis. Evidently the authors do not intend that this publication shall be considered adequate to replace more detailed treatment of these subjects in larger publications which already exist. By careful selection from the material available, adequate information for general use in practice is presented for both diseases.

Although the genitoinfectious diseases were well recognized in antiquity, intensive statistical study for effective control is comparatively new, as yet not well standardized in the various states of the Union, and the variable data available is difficult to make use of. The authors have wisely utilized material from the Massachusetts program which is familiar to them and representative of the best efforts so far produced among the more progressive states. The problems encountered are, of course, common to all, and the usefulness of the book is by no means limited by state boundaries.

At this stage of the effort to control Syphilis and Gonorrhea, particularly with reference to recent widespread publicity about these diseases, the chapters on the peculiarity of the problem, and the educational efforts directed toward physicians, health officers, public health nurses, medical social workers, medical students, the future physicians, and social hygiene aspects. are timely. Even the taxpayers might read with interest the chapter on costs to the community.

This book is adequate for diagnosis and treatment of genitoinfectious diseases. It does not, however, attempt to supplant texts which are primarily aimed at treatment. It is excellent in presentation of epidemiology and setting forth the principles for coordination of effort of all workers in the field of treatment of infected cases, control of cases under treatment, and case finding. In this strength lies its greatest value to the medical profession whose training in many instances has been in diagnosis and treatment to the neglect of public health aspects about which they have received little instruction and consequently have little interest.

Physicians, public health officers, medical social workers, public health nurses, and students will find in this publication a point of view concerning their relation as individuals to the problem of control of Syphilis and Gonorrhea which has not previously been available.

—E. Granville Crabtree, M.D.,
Boston, Mass.

THE TRAFFIC IN HEALTH by Charles Solomon, M.D. $2.75. 393 pp. New York. Navarre Publishing Company.

The Traffic in Health by Charles Solomon, M.D., is a lively discussion of patent medicines and cosmetics. In addition to presenting the problems of the sale of patent medicine, it digresses somewhat from its theme in that it goes into the history of disease and its treatment in some detail. However, such a publication may be timely in light of the growing desire of the public for education in matters of personal hygiene and preventive medicine.

REPORT OF THE DIVISION OF FOOD AND DRUGS
(As required by General Laws, Chapter 111, Section 25)

During the months of July, August and September 1938, samples were collected in 299 cities and towns.

There were 1,429 samples of milk examined, of which 132 were below standard, from 7 samples the cream had been in part removed, and 8 samples contained added water. There were 1,609 bacteriological examinations made of milk, 1,201 of which complied with the requirements. There were 115 bacteriological examinations made of cream, 46 of which did not comply with the requirements; 75 bacteriological examinations of ice cream, 5 of which did not comply with the requirements; 9 bacteriological examinations of chocolate and coffee drinks, 1 of which did not comply with the requirements; 1 bacteriological examination of an empty bottle which did not comply with the requirements; 1 bacteriological examination of a "sterile" bottle which was not sterile; 18 bacteriological examinations of crab meat, 14 of which did not comply with the requirements; 10 bacteriological examinations of lobster meat, all of which did not comply with the requirements; 5 bacteriological examinations of fruit cocktail, all of which were sterile; 5 bacteriological examinations of Dextrose Solutions, all of which were sterile; 5 bacteriological examinations of miscellaneous milk; 1 bacteriological examination of sour cream; and 9 bacteriological examinations of mattress filling, all of which complied with the requirements.

There were 432 samples of food examined, 118 of which were adulterated. These consisted of 3 samples of butter, all of which were rancid; 3 samples of cream, all of which were low in fat for the specified grade; 2 samples of stale eggs which were sold as fresh eggs; 73 samples of clams and 1 sample of oysters, all of which contained added water; 1 sample of cookies and 9 samples of candy, all of which were wormy; 2 samples of dried fruits which contained sulphur dioxide and were not so labeled; 1 sample of olive oil which contained cottonseed oil; 2 samples of fish, 1 sample of stew meat, 1 sample of lamb patties, and 2 samples of sausage, all of which were decomposed; 1 sample of pork which had a rancid odor; 7 samples of hamburg steak, 6 of which were decomposed, and 1 sample contained sodium sulphite in excess of one-tenth of one per cent; and 9 samples of mattress filling, 2 of which contained second-hand material, and 7 samples were labeled as containing a certain percentage of different kinds of down and feathers. which samples did not contain the materials as specified.

There were 37 samples of drugs examined, of which 4 were adulterated. These consisted of 1 sample of argyrol which was not up to the professed standard under which it was sold; 1 sample of aromatic spirits of ammonia, 1 sample of sulphuric acid dilute, and 1 sample of spirit of nitrous ether, all of which did not conform to the U. S. P. requirements.

The police departments submitted 100 samples of liquor for examination. The police departments also submitted 21 samples to be analyzed for poisons or drugs, 8 of which contained heroin, 3 contained opium, 1 contained morphine, 2 contained cannabis, 1 sample was examined for cannabis with negative results, and 6 samples showed negative results.

There were inspected 437 plants operated for the pasteurization of milk; 135 restaurants; 41 soft drink plants; 46 ice cream plants; 27 bakeries; and 297 mattress establishments.

There were 101 hearings held pertaining to violations of the laws.

There were 72 convictions pertaining to violations of the law, $1,875 in fines being imposed.

William Coury and William Daly of Springfield; and James Daly of Pittsfield, were convicted for violations of the milk laws.

Gosselin Dairy, Incorporated, of Chicopee; Harland R. White, 2 cases of Holbrook; Sam Perlmutter and James Daly of Pittsfield; Konstanty Niezgoda, 2 counts, of Holyoke; Ernest Jefferson of Palmer; Henry K. Davis of Southbridge; Charles A. Bean of Sherborn; Fairfield Farms, Incorporated, of Lynn; Agnes Hornstra of Hingham; Alfred Governo of Fall River; George A. Sampson of Marlboro; Dutchland Farms, Incorporated, of Brockton; Cyrill Lambert of Methuen; and Carl Hirsch of Pelham, N. H., were all convicted for violations of the pasteurization law and regulations. Harland R. White of Holbrook appealed his two cases.

W. E. Reid of Abington; Simon Pelczar of Dracut; and Warren Fuller of Ludlow, were convicted for violations of the milk grading regulations.

Philip S. Mogul, 2 cases, and Sam DeLuca of Somerville; Esther Lieben, 3 cases, Folsom's Market, Incorporated, and William Waldman of Roxbury; Morris Shore and Vincent Siravo of Taunton; Leo Feinstein of Quincy; Lional Masse and Peter Pappas of Springfield; James Danas, 2 cases, George Danas, and Mark Bogdonoff, of Lowell; Philip Engelman, 2 cases, of Norwood; Main Public Market, Incorporated, 2 cases, of Fall River; Josephine Viola and Angelina Valvo of Boston; Harold Arrington and William J. Taylor of Lynn; Arthur Houde of Essex; John E. Hutcheson, Jr. of Lawrence; Isadore W. Stavis of Chelsea; Nestor Thurlow and George Welch of Newburyport; John B. Wright of Gloucester; Federico Tombari of Framingham; and Eva M. Hawksley of Riverside, R. I., were all convicted for violations of the food laws. Mark Bogdonoff of Lowell; Philip Engelman, 2 cases, of Norwood; Nestor Thurlow and George Welch of Newburyport; and John B. Wright of Gloucester, all appealed their cases.

Rich's Diner, Incorporated, 2 counts, of Newburyport; and G. Capaldi & Son, Incorporated, of Watertown, were convicted for violations of the sanitary food law. They appealed their cases.

Andrew Mavros of Lynn; and Colgate Caterers, Incorporated, and Edward J. Bertozzi, 2 cases, of Pawtucket, R. I., were convicted for violations of the frozen dessert law and regulations. Andrew Mavros of Lynn, and Colgate Caterers, Incorporated, of Pawtucket, R. I., appealed their cases.

Carl Freedman, 2 cases, and Sadie Nagel, 2 cases, of Roxbury; Tillie Robbins, of Pittsfield, 3 counts; Robert Buttimer of Newton; and Green Freedman Baking Company, Incorporated, of Boston, were all convicted for violations of the bakery laws. Carl Freedman, and Sadie Nagel, of Roxbury, appealed their cases.

Mechanics Upholstering Company, Incorporated, of Worcester; Max Haflich of Roxbury; Morris Rothman of Boston; and Moe Fink, 2 counts, of Providence, R. I., were all convicted for violations of the mattress laws. Max Haflich of Roxbury, and Morris Rothman of Boston, appealed their cases.

In accordance with Section 25, Chapter 111 of the General Laws, the following is the list of articles of adulterated food collected in original packages from manufacturers, wholesalers, or producers:

One sample of butter which was rancid was obtained from Chamberlain & Company of Boston.

One sample of candy which contained worms was obtained from Sarah Grasso of Belmont.

One sample of cookies which contained worms was obtained from Sarah Grasso of Belmont.

One sample of olive oil which contained cottonseed oil was obtained from Michael Valvo of Boston.

Cream which was low in fat for the grade specified was obtained as follows:

One sample each, from H. P. Hood & Sons, Incorporated, of Auburn; Deerfoot Farms, Incorporated, of Southboro; and Whiting Milk Company of Edgartown.

Hamburg steak which was decomposed was obtained as follows:

One sample each, from United Markets, Incorporated, Haymarket Provision, and Folsom's Market, Incorporated, of Boston; Cambridge Provision Company, Incorporated, of Cambridge; and Mark Bogdonoff of Lowell.

One sample of hamburg steak which contained a compound of sulphur dioxide not so labeled was obtained from National Meat Stores (Sarah Snider) of Boston.

One sample of hamburg steak which contained sodium sulphite in excess of one-tenth of one per cent was obtained from William Waldman of Boston.

One sample of stew meat which was decomposed was obtained from Main Public Market, Incorporated, of Fall River.

One sample of lamb patties which was decomposed was obtained from Main Public Market, Incorporated, of Fall River.

One sample of pork which had a rancid odor was obtained from Vincent Rando of Concord.

Sausage which was decomposed was obtained as follows:

One sample each, from Brockelman Brothers, Incorporated, of Marlboro; and Moro Meat Market of Framingham.

One sample of oysters which contained added water was obtained from Economy Grocery Company, Incorporated, of North Weymouth.

Clams which contained added water were obtained as follows:

Eight samples each, from Newburyport Shellfish Company of Newburyport, and Soffron Brothers, Incorporated, of Ipswich; 5 samples from Rowley Shellfish Company of Rowley; 4 samples from F. H. Snow Canning Company of Pine Point, Maine; 3 samples each, from Harold Arrington of Lynn, and James Hook of Boston; 2 samples each, from Ralph Garabedian of Worcester, Arthur Houde of Essex, William Stopford Company, Incorporated of Salem, I. W. Stavis of Chelsea, and E. M. Hawksley of Riverside, R. I.; and 1 sample each, from Merrimac Shellfish Company and Carl Savage of Rowley; Fred H. Christopherson of Haverhill; Bill's Fish Market of Waltham; Samuel Cahoon of Falmouth; Arthur Harris of Buzzards Bay; Schroeder & Besse of Onset; Economy Grocery Stores of Lawrence; and J. W. Anderson of Quincy.

There were 264 confiscations, consisting of 45½ pounds of decomposed chicken; 140 pounds of decomposed fowl; 9 pounds of decomposed turkey; 67 pounds of decomposed beef; 125 pounds of decomposed corned beef; 2½ pounds of decomposed dried beef; 12 pounds of decomposed pigs' kidneys; 38 pounds of decomposed calves' livers; 100 pounds of decomposed lamb chops; 249 pounds of decomposed lamb; 36 pounds of decomposed pork; 50 pounds of decomposed salt pork; 3 pounds of decomposed pork chops; 44 pounds of decomposed smoked shoulder; 25 pounds of decomposed ham; 25 pounds of decomposed pressed ham; 19 pounds of decomposed corned shoulder; 3 pounds of decomposed spare ribs; 15 pounds of decomposed tongue; 14 pounds of decomposed veal; 3 pounds of decomposed veal chops; 119½ pounds of decomposed mixed meats; 61 pounds of decomposed bacon; 50 pounds of decomposed frankforts; 10 pounds of decomposed pork sausages; 67 pounds of decomposed sausage meat; 35 pounds of decomposed hamburg steak; 1 gallon of decomposed shucked clams; 25 pounds of decomposed haddock; 60 cans of decomposed sardines; ½ gallon of decomposed scallops; 48 boxes of wormy chocolates; 2 boxes of wormy peppermints; 14 packages of putrid fruit packs; 4 pounds of decomposed assorted candies; 12 cans of raspberries the cans being swollen; and 2,750 pounds of decomposed frozen lemon sole.

The following articles were all confiscated because they had been under flood water:—

71 pounds of butter; 72 pounds of oleomargarine; 74 dozen eggs; 25 pounds of ducks and turkeys; 25 pounds of poultry; 430 pounds of beef; 118 pounds of corned beef; 8 pounds of kidneys; 16 pounds of liver; 23 pounds of lard; 35 pounds of salt; 18 pounds of pork; 2 pounds of pork chops; 16 pounds of veal; 1,865 pounds of mixed meats; 113 pounds of frankforts; 16¼ pounds of pork sausages; 66 pounds of sausage meat; 2 pounds of blood sausage; 66 pounds of hamburg steak; 75 pounds of cheese; 11 pounds of head cheese; 400 pounds of potatoes; 20 pounds of Lekner; 15 pounds of suet; 12,593 pounds of flour; ½ barrel of flour; ¼ barrel of doughnut flour; ½ barrel of rye meal; 77 pounds of lard; 8 pounds and 6 jars of peanut butter; 90 jars of apple jelly; 25 pounds of sugar; 36 five-cent bars of candy; 10 bars of cooking chocolate; 10 pounds of molasses kisses; 36 boxes of chocolates; 8 pounds of cocoa; 27 cans of marshmallow fluff; 20 pounds of marshmallow fluff; 14 packages of cream cheese; 27 gallons of ice cream; 7 quarts of buttermilk; 17 cases of tonic; 1 bottle of malted milk; 80 quarts of maple syrup; 1 bottle of cod liver oil; 2 bottles of Mellen's food; 2 bottles of emulsion; 1 quart and 2 jars of molasses; 48 bottles of tomato juice; 25 cases of tomato soup; 40 packages of tea; 100 bags of tea; 30 pounds of coffee; ½ barrel of salt; 30 packages of pepper: 12 packages of cream of tartar; 20 packages of dry mustard; 18 bottles of catsup; 45 dozen lemons; 51 dozen oranges; 20 pounds of prunes; 40 packages of rice; 15 packages of vegetables; 25 packages of cooked food; 75 packages of York State beans;

25 packages of yellow eye beans; 10 packages and 2 gallons of pickles; 6 quarts of vinegar; 19 packages of cloves; 6 packages of potato chips; 287 pounds of cookies; 84 packages of Uneeda biscuits; 96 packages of pudding; 10 pounds of chop suey; 6 bottles of syrup of figs; 1 bushel and 8 gallons of clams; 25 pounds of fish; 9 pounds of haddock; 50 pounds of pickled herring; 1 quart of scallops; 2 gallons and 2 pints of oysters; 150 cigars; 24 packages of wax paper; 50 rolls of toilet tissue; 50 packages of scouring powder; 12 tooth brushes; and 24 Seidlitz powders.

In addition to these articles, 3 large truckloads of foods which had been under flood waters were dumped. The Department did not confiscate any hermetically sealed cans or bottles.

The licensed cold storage warehouses reported the following amounts of food placed in storage during June, 1938:—800,760 dozens of case eggs; 1,362,760 pounds of broken out eggs; 4,242,127 pounds of butter; 1,700,118 pounds of poultry; 1,990,400 pounds of fresh meat and fresh meat products; and 14,149,471 pounds of fresh food fish.

There was on hand July 1, 1938:—4,115,100 dozens of case eggs; 2,434,022 pounds of broken out eggs; 4,963,987 pounds of butter; 3,062,941 pounds of poultry; 4,179,253 pounds of fresh meat and fresh meat products; and 27,979,897 pounds of fresh food fish.

The licensed cold storage warehouses reported the following amounts of food placed in storage during July, 1938; 308,040 dozens of case eggs; 1,121,560 pounds of broken out eggs; 2,139,031 pounds of butter; 1,256,420 pounds of poultry; 1,959,868 pounds of fresh meat and fresh meat products; and 11,169,649 pounds of fresh food fish.

There was on hand August 1, 1938: 3,982,620 dozens of case eggs; 2,687,631 pounds of broken out eggs; 6,387,240 pounds of butter; 2,893,291 pounds of poultry; 3,247,831 pounds of fresh meat and fresh meat products; and 30,263,835 pounds of fresh food fish.

The licensed cold storage warehouses reported the following amounts of food placed in storage during August, 1938:—184,770 dozens of case eggs; 925,136 pounds of broken out eggs; 697,165 pounds of butter; 1,360,691 pounds of poultry; 2,440,464 pounds of fresh meat and fresh meat products; and 12,120,401 pounds of fresh food fish.

There was on hand September 1, 1938:—3,515,190 dozens of case eggs; 2,613,031 pounds of broken out eggs; 5,363,756 pounds of butter; 2,783,108 pounds of poultry; 2,733,683 pounds of fresh meat and fresh meat products; and 32,504,186 pounds of fresh food fish.

MASSACHUSETTS DEPARTMENT OF PUBLIC HEALTH

Commissioner of Public Health, ——————— ———————

Public Health Council
——————— ——————— Chairman

GEORGE D. DALTON, M.D. RICHARD M. SMITH, M.D.
FRANCIS H. LALLY, M.D. RICHARD P. STRONG, M.D.
CHARLES F. LYNCH, M.D. JAMES L. TIGHE

Secretary, FLORENCE L. WALL

Division of Administration . . Under direction of Commissioner
Division of Sanitary Engineering . Director and Chief Engineer,
  ARTHUR D. WESTON, C.E.
Division of Communicable Diseases Director, ROY F. FEEMSTER, M.D.
Division of Biologic Laboratories . Director and Pathologist,
  ELLIOTT S. ROBINSON, M.D.
Division of Food and Drugs . . Director and Analyst,
  HERMANN C. LYTHGOE, S.B.
Division of Child Hygiene . . Director, M. LUISE DIEZ, M.D.
Division of Tuberculosis . . Director, ALTON S. POPE, M.D.
Division of Adult Hygiene . . Director,
  HERBERT L. LOMBARD, M.D.
Division of Genitoinfectious Diseases Director, NELS A. NELSON, M.D.

State District Health Officers

The Southeastern District . . HAROLD W. STEVENS, M.D., Middleboro
The South Metropolitan District . HENRY M. DE WOLFE, M.D., Braintree
The North Metropolitan District . ———————
The Northeastern District . . ROBERT E. ARCHIBALD, M.D., Melrose
The Worcester District . . OSCAR A. DUDLEY, M.D., Worcester
South Connecticut Valley District . CHARLES E. GILL, M.D., Westfield
North Connecticut Valley District . WALTER W. LEE, M.D., Greenfield
The Berkshire District . . FRANCIS B. CARROLL, M.D., Great Barrington.

INDEX

Abbott, Mrs. T. Grafton, Courses for nurses on "Understanding Human Behavior" 66
Training of lay leaders in parent education 63
Accidents, Home hazards and, by Lewis E. MacBrayne . . . 164
Adams, Frederick J., The development of government participation in low rental housing 123
Adolph, Dorothy, B.S., Milk consumption among children of Massachusetts 330
Adult Hygiene, New activities of the Division of, by Eleanor J. Macdonald, A.B. 4
Almy, Thomas, M.D., Fall River Cancer Clinic 239
Architect's interest in housing, by William Stanley Parker . . 115
Arey, Harold C., M.D., Gardner Cancer Clinic . . . 242
Back yard improvement contest in Ward 9, by Dorothy Hayward, R.N. . 158
Backmann, Rudolf F., M.D., Fitchburg Cancer Clinic . . . 240
Bang abortion disease, by Charles F. Riordan . . . 293
Bauer, Walter, M.D., Study of chronic rheumatism . . . 16
Beinert, Frederica L., B.S., The care of milk in the home . . 321
Beth Israel Hospital Cancer Clinic (An appraisal of the aid given by the cancer clinic), by Harry F. Friedman, M.D., and Ethel Cohen, M.S. 230
Biologic Laboratories, Division of, by Elliott S. Robinson, M.D. . . 8
Book Notes:
    Modern ways with babies, by Elizabeth Hurlock, Ph.D. 88
    Pneumonia and serum therapy, by Frederick T. Lord, M.D., and Roderick Heffron, M.D. 357
    Syphilis, gonorrhea, and the public health, by Nels A. Nelson, M.D., and Gladys L. Crain, R.N. 357
    The traffic in health, by Charles Solomon, M.D. . . . 358
Boston Dispensary Cancer Clinic, by William M. Shedden, M.D. . 233
Bovine tuberculosis, by Harrie W. Peirce, M.D.V. . . . 296
Bradley, Bernard E., Cancer statistics in Massachusetts . . . 266
Brockton Cancer Clinic, by Frederick F. Weiner, M.D. . . 237
Brown, Martin M., M.D., North Adams Cancer Clinic . . 251
Buildings, public, heating, ventilation, lighting and sanitation of, as required by the State Department of Public Safety, by Eugene M. McSweeney 167
Burnham, J. Forrest, M.D., Lawrence Cancer Clinic . . . 244
Cancer clinics 230
Cancer education in Massachusetts, by Frances A. Macdonald, A.B. 256
Cancer program, history of the Massachusetts, by Eleanor J. Macdonald, A.B. 192
Cancer statistics in Massachusetts, by Bernard E. Bradley . . 266
Cape Cod Cancer Clinic, by Farrar Cobb, M.D. . . . 237
Care of milk in the home, by Frederica L. Beinert, B.S. . . 321
Carroll, Francis B., M.D., Pasteurized milk is safe milk . . 320
Cleaves, Ezra E., M.D., Gloucester Cancer Clinic . . . 243
Cobb, Farrar, M.D., Cape Cod Cancer Clinic . . . 237
Coffin, Susan M., M.D., Play places in the house for children . . 150
Cohen, Ethel, M.S., and Friedman, Harry F., M.D., Beth Israel Hospital Cancer Clinic (An appraisal of the aid given the cancer clinic) . 230
Cold storage of food in Massachusetts, by Hermann C. Lythgoe, S.B. . 341
Cole, William R., Food production as part of the home plan . . 156
Communicable Diseases, New activities of the Division of, by Roy F. Feemster, M.D. 26
Community public health nurse demonstration service, by Helen Chesley Peck, R.N. 61

Control of syphilis and gonorrhea in Massachusetts, 1894-1937 . . 30
Corriden, Thomas F., M.D., Northampton Cancer Clinic . . . 252
Courses for nurses on "Understanding Human Behavior," by Mrs. T.
   Grafton Abbott 66
Course for well child conference physicians, by Florence L. McKay, M.D. 52
Crippled children, Progress in the Massachusetts program for, by Edward
   G. Huber, M.D. 13
Dairy industry, Public health aspects of the, by J. H. Fransden . . 277
Daland, Ernest M., M.D., The state cancer hospitals 202
Decorating, Low cost, by Donald Smith Feeley 152
Dental hygiene program, New activities in, by Florence B. Hopkins, M.D.,
   D.M.D. 53
Development of government participation in low rental housing, by
   Frederick J. Adams 123
Disease, Bang abortion, by Charles F. Riordan 293
Diseases, Milk-borne, by A. Daniel Rubenstein, M.D. 289
Division of Biologic Laboratories, by Elliott S. Robinson, M.D. . . 8
Dwyer, John E., M.D., Springfield Cancer Clinic 253
Economic aspects of housing, by Donald S. Tucker . . . 133
Engineering Division, New activities in the, by Arthur D. Weston, C.E. . 83
Environmental sanitation 172
Epidemiological aspects of the Massachusetts cancer program, by Herbert
   L. Lombard, M.D. 221
Facts and fancies concerning milk by Dorothea Nicoll, B.S. . . . 335
Fall River Cancer Clinic, by Thomas Almy, M.D. 239
Fawcett, C. J., Milk in Massachusetts 281
Federal housing, by Howard P. Vermilya 121
Feeley, Donald Smith, Low cost decorating 152
Feemster, Roy F., M.D., New activities of the Division of Communicable
   Diseases 26
Fitchburg Cancer Clinic, by Rudolf F. Backmann, M.D. . . . 240
Frandsen, J. H., Public health aspects of the dairy industry . . 277
Frank, Dorothy, B.S., Massachusetts advances toward better school
   lunches 76
Franklin County Cancer Clinic, by William J. Pelletier, M.D. . . 241
Friedman, Harry F., M.D., and Cohen, Ethel, M.S., Beth Israel Hospital
   Cancer Clinic (an appraisal of the aid given the cancer clinic) . 230
Food and Drugs Division, New work performed by the, during the past
   five years, by Hermann C. Lythgoe, S.B. 39
Food and Drugs, Report of the Division of:
   October, November, December, 1937 89
   January, February, March, 1938 184
   April, May, June, 1938 270
   July, August, September, 1938 359
Food, The cold storage of, in Massachusetts, by Hermann C. Lythgoe, S.B. 341
Food production as part of the home plan, by William R. Cole . . 156
Foreword, (Cancer Number), by Henry D. Chadwick, M.D. . . 191
Garcelon, Gerald G., M.D., The home and tuberculosis . . . 109
Garden minded, by Effie V. Jordan 155
Gardner Cancer Clinic, by Harold C. Arey, M.D. 242
Gardner, Edwin D., M.D, New Bedford Cancer Clinic . . . 249
Getting, Vlado A., M.D., The progress of milk regulation . . 308
Gloucester Cancer Clinic, by Ezra E. Cleaves, M.D. 243
Gonorrhea and syphilis in Massachusetts, the control of . . . 30
Grading of milk, by Hermann C. Lythgoe, S.B. 311

Hayward, Dorothy, R.N., Back yard improvement contest in Ward 9 . 158
Health and social agencies, Study of positions in interpretation and public
 relations in, (news note) 87
Health and the new public housing program, by Allan A. Twitchell . 104
Health education, new materials in, by Jean V. Latimer, B.S., A.M. . 67
Health, Housing and, by Murray P. Horwood, Ph.D. . 95
Health in the economic brackets, by Joseph W. Mountin, M.D., and Hazel
 O'Hara . . 176
Health survey, by Florence L. McKay, M.D., and Sallie H. Saunders, M.D. 50
Healthful lighting, by William Firth Wells . . 145
Heating and ventilation of homes, by C. P. Yaglou 139
Heating, ventilation, lighting and sanitation of public buildings, as re-
 quired by the State Department of Public Safety, by Eugene M.
 McSweeney 167
Herlihy, Elisabeth M., The state program as it relates to planning . 117
History of the Massachusetts cancer program, by Eleanor J. Macdonald,
 A.B. 192
Home and tuberculosis, by Gerald G. Garcelon, M.D. 109
Home hazards and accidents, by Lewis E. MacBrayne . . . 164
Hopkins, Florence B , M.D., D.M.D., Milk in relation to sound teeth . 332
Hopkins, William T., M.D., Lynn Cancer Clinic . . . 247
Horwood, Murray P., Ph.D., Housing and Health 95
Hospitals, the state cancer, Ernest M. Daland, M.D. . . . 202
Housing activities, state and local, by Sidney T. Strickland . . 111
Housing, Additional material on 184
Housing and health, by Murray P. Horwood, Ph.D. . . 95
Housing, The architect's interest in, by William Stanley Parker . . 115
Housing as the architect views it, by Eleanor Manning O'Connor . . 147
Housing, Economic aspects of, by Donald S. Tucker . . . 133
Housing, Federal, by Howard P. Vermilya 121
Housing, low rental, The development of government participation in, by
 Frederick J. Adams 123
Housing, the individual and the nation, by Walter C. Voss . . . 102
Housing, A settlement worker looks at, by S. Max Nelson . . . 161
Housing, the new public program, health and, by Allan A. Twichell . . 104
Housing, Urban, by Calvin H. Yuill . . . 127
Huber, Edward G., M.D., Progress in the Massachusetts program of ser-
 vices for crippled children 13
Hunt, Ernest L., M.D., Worcester Cancer Clinic . . . 255
Improvement contest in Ward 9, Back yard, by Dorothy Hayward, R.N. . 158
Jordan, Effie V., Garden minded 155
Latimer, Jean V., B.S., A.M., New materials in health education . . 67
 Teaching people to drink milk 338
Lawrence Cancer Clinic, by J. Forrest Burnham, M.D. . . . 244
Leland, Harley A., Production of quality milk . . . 283
Lighting for seeing, by M. Luckiesh and Frank K. Moss . . 143
Lighting, Healthful, by William Firth Wells . . . 145
Lighting, heating, ventilation and sanitation of public buildings, as re-
 quired by the State Department of Public Safety, by Eugene M.
 McSweeney 167
Lombard, Herbert L., M.D., Epidemiological aspects of the Massachusetts
 cancer program 221
Low cost decorating, by Donald Smith Feeley . . . 152
Lowell Cancer Clinic, by Lowell Cancer Clinic Staff . . . 246
Luckiesh, M., and Moss, Frank K., Lighting for seeing . . 143
Lynn Cancer Clinic, by William T. Hopkins, M.D. . . . 247

Lythgoe, Hermann C., S.B., The cold storage of food in Massachusetts . 341
    The grading of milk 311
    New work performed by the Food and Drugs Division during the
        past five years 39
    The pasteurization of milk 315
MacBrayne, Lewis E., Home hazards and accidents 164
Macdonald, Eleanor J., A.B., History of the Massachusetts cancer program 192
    New activities of the Division of Adult Hygiene . . . 4
Macdonald, Frances A., A.B., Cancer education in Massachusetts . . 256
Massachusetts advances toward better school lunches, by Dorothy Frank,
    B.S. 76
Massachusetts cancer program, epidemiological aspects of the, by Herbert
    L. Lombard, M.D. 221
Massachusetts cancer statistics, by Bernard E. Bradley 266
Massachusetts state-aided cancer clinics, by Frederick G. Medinger, M.D. 229
Maternal deaths in Massachusetts, 1932-1936 86
Maternal mortality study in Massachusetts, by Raymond S. Titus, M.D. . 48
Medical postgraduate extension courses, by Leroy E. Parkins, M.D. . 25
Medinger, Frederick G., M.D., Massachusetts state-aided cancer clinics . 229
Milk-borne diseases, by A. Daniel Rubenstein, M.D. 289
Milk, The care of in the home, by Frederica L. Beinert, B.S. . . 321
Milk consumption among children of Massachusetts, by Dorothy Adolph,
    B.S. 330
Milk, Facts and fancies concerning, by Dorothea Nicoll, B.S. . . 335
Milk for the whole family, by Mary Spalding, M.A. 323
Milk, The grading of, by Hermann C. Lythgoe, S.B. . . . 311
Milk in relation to sound teeth, by Florence B. Hopkins, M.D., D.M.D. . 332
Milk in Massachusetts, by C. J. Fawcett 281
Milk, The pasteurization of, by Hermann C. Lythgoe, S.B. . . 315
Milk, Pasteurized, is safe milk, by Francis B. Carroll, M.D. . . 320
Milk, Production of quality, by Harley A. Leland 283
Milk regulation, The progress of, by Vlado A. Getting, M.D. . . 308
Milk, Teaching people to drink, by Jean V. Latimer, B.S., A.M. . . 338
Milk, Tuberculosis and, by Alton S. Pope, M.D. 305
Moss, Frank K., and Luckiesh, M., Lighting for seeing . . . 143
Mountin, Joseph W., M.D., and O'Hara, Hazel, Health in the economic
    brackets 176
McKay, Florence L., M.D., Course for well child conference physicians . 52
    Obstetric package project 47
    The premature program of Massachusetts 45
    and Saunders, Sallie H., M.D., The health survey . . . 50
McKellar, Albertine P., Special courses with 'teen age girls . . 69
McSweeney, Eugene M., Heating, ventilation, lighting and sanitation of
    public buildings, as required by the State Department of Public
    Safety 167
Nelson, S. Max, A settlement worker looks at housing . . . 161
New activities in the dental hygiene program, by Florence B. Hopkins,
    M.D., D.M.D. 53
New activities in the Engineering Division, by Arthur D. Weston, C.E. . 83
New activities of the Division of Adult Hygiene, by Eleanor J. Macdonald,
    A.B. 4
New activities of the Division of Communicable Diseases, by Roy F.
    Feemster, M.D. 26
New activities of the Division of Tuberculosis, by Alton S. Pope, M.D. . 81
New Bedford Cancer Clinic, by Edwin D. Gardner, M.D. . . 249
New materials in health education, by Jean V. Latimer, B.S., A.M. . 67

New work performed by the Food and Drugs Division during the past five
    years, by Herman C. Lythgoe, S.B. 8
Newburyport Cancer Clinic, by Lincoln C. Peirce, M.D. . . . 25
News Note:
    Study of positions in interpretation and public relations in health
      and social agencies 8
Nicoll, Dorothea, B.S., Facts and fancies concerning milk . . 39
North Adams Cancer Clinic, by Martin M. Brown, M.D. . . . 25
Northampton Cancer Clinic, by Thomas F. Corriden, M D . . 25
Nutritionists pioneer in county health units, by Mary Spalding, M.A. . 7
Oak, Lura, Ph.D., The research-learning project 5
Obstetric package project, by Florence L. McKay, M.D. . . . 4
O'Connor, Eleanor Manning, Housing as the architect views it . . 14
O'Hara Hazel, and Mountin, Joseph W., M.D., Health in the economic
    brackets 17
Parent education, the training of lay leaders in, by Mrs. T. Grafton Abbott 6
Parker, William Stanley, The architect's interest in housing . . 11
Parkins, Leroy E., M.D., Medical postgraduate extension courses . . 2
Pasteurization of milk, by Hermann C. Lythgoe, S.B. . . . 31
Pasteurized milk is safe milk, by Francis B. Carroll, M.D. . . . 32
Peck, Helen Chesley, R. N., Community public health nurse demonstra-
    tion service 6
Peirce, Harrie W., M.D.V., Bovine tuberculosis 29
Peirce, Lincoln C., M.D., Newburyport Cancer Clinic . . . 25
Pelletier, William J., M.D., Franklin County Cancer Clinic . . 24
Pittsfield Cancer Clinic, by Pittsfield Cancer Clinic Committee . . 25
Planning, The state program as it relates to, by Elisabeth M. Herlihy . 11
Play places in the house for children, by Susan M. Coffin, M.D. . . 15
Pneumonia and serum therapy, by Frederick T. Lord, M.D., and Roderick
    Heffron, M.D. (book note) 35
Pope, Alton S., M.D., New activities of the Division of Tuberculosis . 8
    Tuberculosis and milk 30
Postgraduate extension courses, Medical, by Leroy E. Parkins, M.D. 2
Premature program of Massachusetts, The, by Florence L. McKay, M.D. 4
Production of quality milk, by Harley A. Leland 28
Progress in the Massachusetts program of services for crippled children,
    by Edward G. Huber, M.D. 1
Progress of milk regulation, by Vlado A. Getting, M.D. . . . 30
Public health aspects of the dairy industry, by J. H. Frandsen . 27
Report of Division of Food and Drugs, October, November, December, 1937 8
Report of Division of Food and Drugs, January, February, March, 1938 . 18
Report of Division of Food and Drugs, April, May, June, 1938 . . 27
Report of Division of Food and Drugs, July, August, September, 1938 . 35
Research-learning project, by Lura Oak, Ph.D. . . . 5
Rheumatism, chronic, Study of, by Walter Bauer, M.D. . . . 1
Riordan, Charles F., Bang abortion disease 29
Robinson, Elliott S., M.D., Division of Biologic Laboratories . .
Rubenstein, A. Daniel, M.D., Milk-borne diseases 28
Sanitation, environmental 17
Sanitation, heating, ventilation and lighting of public buildings, as re-
    quired by the State Department of Public Safety, by Eugene M.
    McSweeney 16
Saunders, Sallie H., M.D., and McKay, Florence L., M.D , The health
    survey 5
School lunches, Massachusetts advances toward better, by Dorothy Frank,
    B.S. 7

Settlement worker looks at housing, by S. Max Nelson . . . 161
Shedden, William M., M.D., Boston Dispensary Cancer Clinic . . . 233
Spalding, Mary, M.A., Milk for the whole family 323
    Nutritionists pioneer in county health units 72
Special courses with 'teen age girls, by Albertine P. McKellar, B.S. . 69
Springfield Cancer Clinic, by John E. Dwyer, M.D. 253
State cancer hospitals, The, by Ernest M. Daland, M.D. . . . 202
State program as it relates to planning, by Elisabeth M. Herlihy . . 117
State tumor diagnosis service, The, by Shields Warren, M.D. . . 261
Strickland, Sidney T., Housing activities, state and local . . . 111
Study of chronic rheumatism, by Walter Bauer, M.D. 16
Syphilis and gonorrhea in Massachusetts, the control of, 1894-1937 . . 30
Syphilis, gonorrhea, and the public health, by Nels A. Nelson, M.D., and
    Gladys L. Crain, R.N., (book note) 357
Teaching people to drink milk, by Jean V. Latimer, B.S., A.M. . . 338
Teeth, Milk in relation to sound, by Florence B. Hopkins, M.D., D.M.D. . 332
Titus, Raymond S., M.D., The maternal mortality study in Massachusetts 48
Traffic in health, The, by Charles Solomon, M.D. (book note) . . . 358
Training of lay leaders in parent education, by Mrs. T. Grafton Abbott 63
Tuberculosis and milk, by Alton S. Pope, M.D. 305
Tuberculosis, Bovine, by Harrie W. Peirce, M.D. 296
Tuberculosis, new activities of the Division of, by Alton S. Pope, M.D. . 81
Tuberculosis, The home and, by Gerald G. Garcelon, M D . . . 109
Tucker, Donald S., Economic aspects of housing 133
Twichell, Allan A., Health and the new public housing program . . 104
"Understanding Human Behavior," courses for nurses on, by Mrs. T.
    Grafton Abbott 66
Urban housing, by Calvin H. Yuill 127
Ventilation of homes, heating, and, by C. P. Yaglou 139
Ventilation, heating, lighting and sanitation of public buildings, as re-
    quired by the State Department of Public Safety, by Eugene M.
    McSweeney 167
Vermilya, Howard P., Federal housing 121
Voss, Walter C., Housing, the individual and the nation . . . 102
Warren, Shields, M.D., The state tumor diagnosis service . . . 261
Weiner, Frederick F., M.D., Brockton Cancer Clinic 237
Well child conference physicians, course for, Florence L. McKay, M.D. . 52
Wells, William Firth, Healthful lighting 145
Weston, Arthur D., C.E., New activities in the Engineering Division . 83
Worcester Cancer Clinic, by Ernest L. Hunt, M.D. 255
Yaglou, C. P., Heating and ventilation of homes 139
Yuill, Calvin H., Urban housing 127

THE COMMONHEALTH

Volume 26   Jan.-Feb.-Mar.
No. 1   1939

COMMUNICABLE DISEASES

MASSACHUSETTS
DEPARTMENT OF PUBLIC HEALTH

THE COMMONHEALTH

QUARTERLY BULLETIN OF THE MASSACHUSETTS DEPARTMENT OF
PUBLIC HEALTH

Sent Free to any Citizen of the State

Entered as second class matter at Boston Post Office

M. LUISE DIEZ, M.D., DIRECTOR OF DIVISION OF CHILD HYGIENE, EDITOR.
1 Beacon Street, Boston, Mass.

CONTENTS

	PAGE
Foreword	3
Control of Communicable Diseases, by Roy F. Feemster, M.D.	4
Don't Say "Serum" When You Mean "Vaccine," by Laura A. Thorpe	8
Chicken Pox, by Olive S. Feemster, M.D.	10
Diphtheria, by Edwin H. Place, M.D.	14
Dysentery, Bacillary, by Walter W. Lee, M.D.	11
Gonorrhea, by Ernest B. Howard, M.D.	18
Infantile Paralysis, by Ralph W. Daffinee, M.D.	20
Measles, by Charles F. McKhann, M.D.	23
Meningitis, by LeRoy D. Fothergill, M.D.	26
Mumps, by Harold L. Higgins, M.D.	29
Paratyphoid Fever, by B. Barrett Gilman, M.D.	31
Pneumonia, by F. Randolf Philbrook, M.D.	32
Rabies, by B. Barrett Gilman, M.D.	42
Scarlet Fever, by John E. Gordon, M.D.	46
Smallpox, by Roy F. Feemster, M.D.	50
Syphilis, by Ernest B. Howard, M.D.	54
Trichinosis, A Preventable Disease, by Donald Augustine, Sc.D.	56
Tuberculosis, by Alton S. Pope, M.D.	60
Typhoid Fever, by Charles E. Gill, M.D.	64
Undulant Fever, by A. Daniel Rubenstein, M.D.	68
Whooping Cough, by Conrad Wesselhoeft, M.D.	70
Reportable Diseases Rare in Massachusetts, by Roy F. Feemster, M.D.	74
Regulations Relative to Diseases Dangerous to the Public Health	79
Regulations Governing the Control of Gonorrhea and Syphilis	85
Regulations Relative to the Conveyance of Bodies Dead of Any Disease Dangerous to the Public Health	88
Funeral Regulations	89
Maternal Deaths in Massachusetts, 1933-1937	90
Report of Division of Food and Drugs, October and November, 1938	91

FOREWORD

PAUL J. JAKMAUH, M.D.
Commissioner of Public Health
Massachusetts Department of Public Health

There is a wide interest among the citizens of this State in the subject of communicable diseases, and many inquiries come to the Department for information in regard to them. Through the cooperation of a number of prominent medical men of the State, up-to-date information has been compiled in regard to the more important communicable diseases and is presented in this number of *The Commonhealth*. If it is found that the issue meets a need, plans will be made to revise the material periodically and reprint it as often as the accumulation of new information will justify.

CONTROL OF COMMUNICABLE DISEASES

By Roy F. Feemster, M.D.
*Director, Division of Communicable Diseases
Massachusetts Department of Public Health*

One of the first requirements in any plan for the control of communicable diseases is to know where cases are occurring. To accomplish this, health laws provide that physicians shall report all cases of such diseases to local boards of health who in turn send the information to state departments of public health. At weekly intervals, state health officers report to Washington by telegraph the number of cases of certain important diseases. These are tabulated and reports for the country as a whole are sent back to each state so that all are informed as to the general prevalence of these diseases.

In some communities, machinery for reporting communicable diseases breaks down. It may be that the physician fails to report, or the local board of health neglects to send the information to the state. By law, householders are required to report these diseases when no physician is in attendance, but reports practically never come from this source. The better the reporting becomes, the more efficiently will health workers be able to plan their work.

The health officer's task begins when the report of a communicable disease reaches him. The first step is to investigate in order to detect the source of the infection, discover other possible cases, prevent further spread, and to insure that those ill are receiving proper treatment.

The next step is to see that the patient is properly isolated in order to prevent members of the family and others from acquiring the disease. In consultation with the attending physician, it is determined whether the patient must be cared for in the home or sent to a hospital.

In some diseases it is necessary to quarantine those who have been in contact with the patient. The decision as to which are to be quarantined and for what period depends upon the disease, the speed with which it causes the patient to become ill, and the manner by which it spreads. These periods of isolation and quarantine are given in the regulations printed at the end of this issue of *The Commonhealth*.

The control of the spread of human diseases is a complicated affair because of the differences in the diseases themselves and the many ways by which they are transferred from person to person.

Causes of Disease

One of the important differences between diseases is the variety of agents responsible. Some of the main classes of causative organisms are:

(1) *Bacteria*. Small living plant cells of varying shapes, called cocci, bacilli, and vibrios.
(2) *Yeasts*. Larger vegetable cells similar to the familiar variety used in making bread.
(3) *Molds*. More complicated vegetable structures similar to the household molds.
(4) *Viruses*. Ultramicroscopic living agents.
(5) *Spirochetes*. Spiral organisms, usually classified as small plants.

(6) *Protozoa.* Small unicellular animals.
(7) *Helminths.* Members of worm family, such as hookworms and tapeworms.

Incubation Period

Varying lengths of time elapse between exposure and the onset of the first symptoms of disease. The time depends upon how rapidly the germs multiply in the body. In some only a few hours to a day or two are necessary, as in paratyphoid fever, diphtheria and scarlet fever. In others, a week or two usually passes. In still others, the period may be several weeks, as in delayed cases of rabies and tetanus. The length of the incubation period determines the period of quarantine of contacts.

Period of Infectivity

Diseases vary greatly in the length of time during which the germs continue to be given off by the patient. In yellow fever, the virus cannot be obtained from the patient after the third day. In others, the period lasts for a week or two. In the case of "carriers" the person may carry the germs for the rest of his life. The length of isolation is determined by the period of infectivity.

Modes of Spread

(1) *Diseases spread by inanimate objects.* In this case, the organism causing the disease must be able to survive in the environment long enough to be transferred to another individual. Diseases of the alimentary tract, such as typhoid fever, paratyphoid fever, dysentery, and cholera belong to this group, though scarlet fever and several other diseases must be included. Dishes, linens, and other objects coming directly from the sick room, as well as foods and milk which have been handled by ill persons or carriers, and water supplies contaminated by material from such persons, are the most important ways by which such diseases are carried.

(2) *Diseases transferred by contact.* Most of the diseases in this group are acquired by breathing the organism into the nose and throat, or into the lung. Some are very highly contagious, such as, smallpox, measles, influenza, and chicken pox. Others spread less readily, such as diphtheria, scarlet fever, and pneumonia. Some are apparently so difficult to spread by direct contact, such as infantile paralysis and encephalitis, that there is reason to believe that other means, such as the bite of insects, may play a part. Other diseases in this group are communicable mainly by direct personal contact, such as syphilis and gonorrhea.

(3) *Diseases in which prolonged contact is necessary.* Tuberculosis is rarely transferred except after living in a household with an infected person for a considerable length of time. The same is true of leprosy and trachoma.

(4) *Diseases transmitted by insects.* Malaria is carried by mosquitoes, Rocky Mountain spotted fever by ticks, typhus fever by body lice and other insects, and bubonic plague by fleas. Typhoid fever and certain other diseases may sometimes be carried by houseflies, in this case, however, on the feet and wings and not by the bite.

(5) *Diseases acquired from animals.* Rabies, trichinosis, psittacosis, and tularemia are diseases which man acquires directly from the

infected animal. Undulant fever and bovine tuberculosis likewise come from animals, but in most cases through drinking infected milk.

From this survey of the modes of spread, it will be seen that a measure which would be effective in preventing the spread of one disease might be entirely ineffective in controlling the spread of another. The method of attack must be individualized for each group and also, in many instances, for each disease.

Methods of Control

There are three points in the spread of disease at which the problem can be attacked: (1) Eliminate the sources of infection; (2) Break the chain of spread; (3) Protect the susceptible. In certain diseases one method of attack is by far the most profitable. For example, diphtheria toxoid inoculations are very effective in protecting the susceptible against the disease. However, health workers are not content to depend entirely upon a single method. We also supervise the sources of infection and break every chain of spread possible. In the following discussion, it will be noted that the plan of attack on each disease often combines all three methods.

Historically, the first measure instituted which proved widely successful was that of breaking the chain of spread in the environment. Long before the discovery of disease-producing germs, it had been demonstrated by physicians that diseases could be spread by water. William Budd showed that typhoid fever could be spread in this way, and John Snow proved that cholera had been spread by water. A movement to provide pure water supplies was well under way by the time bacteria were discovered, and that discovery redoubled the interest in providing safe water. Likewise, sanitary disposal of sewage became an important public health measure. The work done by sanitarians along these two lines has produced a remarkable fall in diseases of the alimentary tract, such as typhoid fever and dysentery. Other advances along sanitary lines have been made. Foods have been guarded more and more against the introduction of disease-producing bacteria. Pasteurization of milk is becoming almost universal in some areas, particularly in Massachusetts. Great strides have been made, therefore, in controlling diseases in which the organism can survive outside of the human body.

Progress is much more difficult when we consider diseases which are transferred by direct contact. A clean environment has practically no influence upon the spread of highly communicable diseases, like smallpox, influenza, and measles. The method of attack must, therefore, be entirely different. The surest means of cutting down the incidence of such diseases is to find a way of protecting susceptible individuals. Such a means has been discovered for the control of smallpox. Vaccination will not only keep an individual from acquiring the disease but will entirely eliminate it from any community where vaccination is universal. This is illustrated by the fact that Massachusetts has not had a single case of smallpox in the last six years. A similar method of attack has resulted in a remarkable decrease in diphtheria because we now have means of increasing the immunity of individuals to such a point that no child should ever have the disease. Certain other diseases can be prevented by this method of specific immunization and it is the hope of health workers that many others will be added to the list eventually. Since gonorrhea and syphilis are spread mainly by direct contact, environmental measures cannot be depended upon to reduce the prevalence. There seems to be little hope that a means of specific immunization will be found. In these two diseases, therefore, control measures are limited to the discovery and elimination of the sources of infection.

Insect-borne diseases constitute a special problem. Some insects capable of carrying disease are present in large numbers in some of our communities. The wood tick has found favorable living conditions on Cape Cod and Martha's Vineyard. It is known to carry Rocky Mountain spotted fever and may, perhaps, carry other diseases. As long as these ticks remain free of the infection, they constitute no menace to us. The only ways by which they may become infected are for ill persons to go into the area or for infected ticks to be imported on dogs and other animals.

Mosquitoes abound in most of our communities and are a special plague near salt marshes. The special varieties which carry malaria are not numerous, which probably accounts for the fact that this disease, very prevalent in colonial days, has practically disappeared. Recently a very fatal type of encephalitis due to a virus from the horse has been suspected of being carried by certain mosquitoes. Fortunately the life of the mosquito is usually short and, if the sources of the virus do not become too numerous, the spread of this disease may be prevented.

The cost of eliminating these two insects would be very great, so it is hoped that other means of controlling the diseases spread by them will prove effective.

Diseases of animals also constitute special problems. Fortunately, tuberculosis of cattle is an economic problem of sufficient magnitude that the disease is being eliminated from dairy herds by the cattle owners with the assistance of the government. Any accidental remaining sources of bovine tuberculosis can be rendered harmless by pasteurization of milk. Undulant fever can also be eliminated by pasteurization of all milk. The most hopeful method of controlling rabies is to encourage the universal immunization of dogs with antirabic vaccine. Psittacosis is being kept out of the state by rather stringent regulations regarding the shipment of parrots and parakeets. Trichinosis can be prevented by thorough cooking of pork and pork products. Anthrax is an occasional hazard which can be controlled by the proper handling of hides, furs, wool and bristles and by eliminating the disease from animals in our own state.

While much can be done to prevent the spread of disease, none of the measures are perfect and many persons become ill in spite of every precaution. In this case we still have one last line of defense to prevent deaths from occurring. . Serums for the treatment of diphtheria, scarlet fever, meningitis, and pneumonia save many lives every year and medical science will eventually add other serums to the list.

Because of the importance of specific immunization for the prevention of disease and of serums in the treatment of disease, the Massachusetts Department of Public Health maintains a well-equipped biologic laboratory where these valuable agents are manufactured. This is not a new venture. It was begun in 1894 with the manufacture of diphtheria antitoxin and year by year, as new products have been found of proven value, they have been added to the list. These are all available free of charge to the citizens of the Commonwealth.

DON'T SAY "SERUM" WHEN YOU MEAN "VACCINE"!
By Laura A. Thorpe
Massachusetts Department of Public Health

In these days when the words "serum" and "vaccine" are used almost as commonly as "pneumonia" and "smallpox," it becomes increasingly important that these terms be interpreted and used correctly. "Serum" and "vaccine" are so often mistakenly interchanged or used synonymously even by those who are quite well informed that it is not surprising that the terms are a source of constant confusion to the layman.

Serum and vaccine are NOT the same. They are used for different purposes, and although either serum or vaccine may be used for the same disease under proper circumstances, they are used for diverse reasons and accomplish different results.

Active vs. Passive Immunity

Perhaps it would clarify a confusing situation a bit to say that vaccine is a material which produces active immunity, its primary purpose being to protect a person against disease. Serum, on the other hand, is a material which produces passive immunity, its primary purpose being to cure a person already ill.

Active immunity is produced within the human body itself, through the introduction of an outside medium called "vaccine." This immunity results from complex chemical action that takes place within the body tissues and the blood stream in building up resistance to the vaccine.

The word "serum" refers to the fluid part of the blood left when the blood clot is removed. In this serum is found the protective substances that develop when vaccine has been injected into a healthy animal. These protective substances formed in the animal's serum may be given to a human suffering with the same disease for which the animal was vaccinated. This serum is used to convey passive immunity, so-called because the human body does not build up this immunity, but receives it passively from the outside source.

Briefly, the difference between active immunity and passive immunity is that in the former the patient develops the protective substances in his own body in response to vaccination, while in the latter he receives the protective substances after they have been developed in another animal by the injection of serum.

Vaccines Produce Active Immunity

Vaccines are divided into three classes: those made from living organisms; those made from bacteria which have been killed; and those made from the toxin or other bacterial products thrown off during the growth of bacteria.

The "living virus" vaccine is used for the prevention of smallpox, and was one of the first accepted vaccines. Smallpox virus from mild cases was once used, but severe cases of smallpox sometimes resulted, so today cowpox virus, closely related but much less virulent, is employed. Cowpox, also known as vaccinia, has the advantage of producing only mild symptoms but is very effective in creating immunity against smallpox. When cowpox virus is scratched onto the skin and the vaccination "takes," a powerful resistance to the smallpox virus is developed.

The second class, vaccine from killed organisms, is used for a number of diseases. Typhoid fever, whooping cough, rabies, undulant fever, and tularemia (rabbit fever) are most commonly prevented by such vaccines. To a lesser degree, they are used as a safeguard against dysentery, cholera, plague, and pneumococcus, meningococcus, streptococcus, staphlococcus and gonococcus. When the vaccine is injected under the skin, the dead bacteria are gradually absorbed into the blood stream and the body promptly begins building up the immunity to the disease which is the goal of successful vaccination.

Still a third class of vaccination is that secured when toxin from bacteria, usually modified in various ways, is injected subcutaneously. Toxin-antitoxin and toxoid of this group prevent diphtheria; tetanus is prevented by toxoid; and scarlet fever by toxin. In vaccination of this type, the antitoxin produced in the human body against the toxin of the injected vaccine gives immunity.

So much for vaccines, protectors and life guards to hundreds of thousands of people.

Serums Confer Passive Immunity

Serums are divided into two classes—antibacterial serums, and antitoxins. Technical as it may sound, the story of serums is a simple one.

Antibacterial serums work directly against the bacteria invading the blood stream. Pneumonia and meningitis (meningococcus and influenza bacillus) are most commonly robbed of their high fatality rate by these serums. Undulant fever, anthrax, tularemia, cholera, plague and gonorrhea are to a much lesser degree coming under the control of the antibacterial serums.

Antitoxins are those serums which work against the toxins spread throughout the body by the bacteria, rather than against the bacteria. Persons ill of diphtheria, scarlet fever, erysipelas, tetanus, gas gangrene, or botulism (canned food poisoning) are benefited by the proper antitoxins.

With such outstanding differences between them, don't say serum when you mean vaccine! Remember: Vaccines prevent; serums cure.

CHICKEN POX

By OLIVE S. FEEMSTER, M.D.
Brookline, Mass.

Chicken pox, otherwise known as varicella, is one of the most contagious and least dangerous of all the acute infectious diseases and sooner or later it attacks a large percentage of children. The few who do escape it in childhood often have it in a more severe form later in life. In most instances one attack protects for life.

It seldom causes serious illness or death except in the case of very young and delicate children or when it occurs during convalescence from some other disease, such as scarlet fever, diphtheria or pneumonia. It is most common between the ages of one to eight years and is exceedingly rare during the first few months of life. This is probably due to the fact that an immunity is conferred by the mother upon the newborn babe. This immunity gradually decreases and by the end of the first year an infant is fully susceptible to the disease.

We have no record of the earliest appearance of chicken pox because it was first thought to be the same disease as smallpox. The two were differentiated in 1553. While the causative organism has not been thoroughly studied it is known to be due to a filtrable virus which can be obtained from the vesicles. The rabbit is the only animal other than man in which the virus can survive for any length of time.

The disease is contracted by exposure to another case, rarely through the medium of a third person or inanimate objects such as books or playthings. The virus is believed to enter through the respiratory tract, being breathed in from the air surrounding the person who is ill. The lesions on the moist surfaces of the mouth and throat break easily and the infectious material is spread to the air each time the patient coughs or sneezes.

The time that elapses between exposure and the development of the first symptoms is usually from fourteen to sixteen days, but the range may be considerably wider than this. During this period there are, as a rule, no evidences of disturbed health. In children the first sign of the disease is apt to be the appearance of the eruption though close observation often reveals a slight rise in temperature, vague pains and chilliness a few hours before the rash is noted. In adults the symptoms preceding the eruption may be even more marked. The mucous membrane lesions often appear earlier than those on the skin and the disease becomes infectious before it can be recognized.

The eruption appears first upon the back, then spreads to the face and the rest of the body, being well marked on the scalp. As a rule, the palms of the hands and soles of the feet escape completely, the eruption preferring the covered surfaces. The papules come in crops, new ones continuing to appear for three or four days upon the same part of the body. The earlier ones begin to dry up before the later ones emerge so that all stages of the eruption may be present in one region at the same time, this being one of the most distinguishing features of the disease. Some of the papules disappear but many of them become blisters or vesicles, which soon become pustular, and these in turn dry up to form crusts or scabs which fall off in from five to twenty days depending upon the depth of the skin involvement. When the vesicles become infected deeper ulceration may occur and the scabs may remain for weeks. Pock marks, or pitting, seldom occurs when the lesions do not become infected. The distribution of the eruption may be influenced by irritation of the skin prior to eruption.

The temperature is highest when the lesions begin to appear but it seldom reaches more than 99°-100° F. and disappears in one or two days, except in very severe cases.

The recognition of chicken pox is usually easy, important points in the diagnosis being the history of exposure and the slow appearance of the eruption which comes out in crops so that papules, vesicles, pustules and crusts may be seen in the same area simultaneously. The disease with which it is most apt to be confused is a mild case of smallpox. In fact, sometimes the first intimation of the presence of smallpox is to have several cases of chicken pox in adults reported from one small area. Since adults seldom have chicken pox such an incident immediately arouses suspicion of a wrong diagnosis.

Due to the mildness of the disease little treatment is usually necessary. Serums or vaccines specific for the disease have not been discovered. Quarantine in schools and institutions is seldom successful and in the home is usually unnecessary unless there are other children in delicate condition. It probably remains contagious as long as there are scabs on the body. When there is a temperature the child should be kept in bed and given a bland diet. The skin should be kept clean, and scratching, especially in infants, should be prevented, so that complications such as secondary infections of the skin will not occur. Local applications may be used to allay severe itching.

BACILLARY DYSENTERY

By Walter W. Lee, M.D.

District Health Officer
North Connecticut Valley District
Massachusetts Department of Public Health

Every year and everywhere people suffer singly and in groups from attacks of vomiting and diarrhea of varying degrees of severity. Usually, however, though acute and painful while it lasts, the attack is short in duration and soon forgotten. The diagnosis is usually simple, a physician rarely being called, and the sufferer announces, "I guess it was something I ate." In the summer, the disturbance is often attributed to "green apples" or other unripe fruit or vegetables. Unfortunately, acute attacks of vomiting and diarrhea are not always as harmless as the public is prone to believe. Whenever groups of individuals are attacked the Board of Health should be informed so that an investigation of the sources and cause can be made. Many outbreaks are due to infections of the paratyphoid or dysentery groups of organisms. Either of these groups of organisms may produce fatal disease, and some of those who recover usually become permanent carriers.

Carriers of these diseases are persons who have recovered from the disease and still harbor the organisms somewhere in the gastro-intestinal tract, such as in the gall bladder in the case of typhoid carriers. Unknown to themselves or to their contacts, they continually or intermittently give off to their environment living, virulent organisms which may get into the food they are handling and in this way initiate another outbreak of the disease.

From the standpoint of public health, the danger of producing carriers of these diseases is of much more importance than is the danger from mortality, which fortunately is low. Under certain conditions it may cause considerable mortality; for example, when it runs riot in the wards of institutions for the insane, or among infants, or the debilitated.

The determination of the causative organism responsible for acute outbreaks of diarrhea is largely a laboratory diagnosis and depends upon finding the specific organism in the stools.

The onset of the infection varies anywhere from one day to a week after consuming the polluted food or drink. The symptoms vary with the individuals involved; a few may show mild discomfort that is noticed only when seen in relation to the other infected members of the family; some may have a few cramps with little diarrhea; a larger number may be nauseated and may have violent vomiting, with or without intestinal disturbance; some will show only mild diarrhea with a few loose movements; and others almost continuous bowel movements, often accompanied by severe abdominal cramps. Stools of severe cases contain much mucus and are often bloody. Cases exhibit fever from 99 to 105 during the acute stages. Where vomiting or diarrhea has been severe, the patient will show evidence of dehydration. Muscular pain is also quite a regular symptom, probably due to the general toxemia present in all but the milder cases.

When patients are found presenting such symptoms, a report should be made to the local Board of Health. The patient and nurse should be immediately isolated and if the symptoms do not subside within a few hours blood and stool specimens should be forwarded at once to a competent laboratory for identification of the causative organism. The local Board of Health should investigate immediately to find the source of infection. The trail of a dysentery epidemic quickly grows cold and unless promptly investigated the chances of success in finding the source of infection rapidly diminish.

Every case or outbreak of dysentery is produced by infection from an acute case or a convalescent carrier. The infection is carried into the body of the new case through the medium of food or drink. It is taken into the stomach and intestines where the organisms establish themselves, produce damage and invade the body of the patient. The wall of the large intestine is attacked, the inflamed membrane secretes large quantities of mucus, and small areas of ulceration occur with consequent small hemorrhages. This accounts for the blood-streaked mucus in the stools. Due to the inflammation of the bowels their musculature becomes irritable, and peristalsis is markedly increased, which accounts for the violent cramps and frequent bowel movements.

Food may be contaminated if the cook is a carrier. If the contaminated food is cooked thoroughly between the time when it is contaminated by the carrier and eaten by the consumer, there will probably be no case of disease. However, if the carrier prepares food to be eaten raw, such as salads or green vegetables, such food becomes an excellent medium for the spread of the disease. For example, suppose chicken salad is prepared by a carrier a day or so before it is to be eaten and is stored in the meantime in large containers in the ice box. The organisms have opportunity to multiply so that when the salad is eaten it has become a rich culture of virulent organisms. In such an instance, the large number of dysentery bacilli cause the symptoms to come on rapidly.

Private well water supplies may be, and often are, intermittently polluted by a privy or septic tank which is too close to the well. This may cause little or no trouble until a case or carrier visits the home, when the privy or septic tank becomes seeded with virulent organisms, and the well water promptly becomes polluted with disease-producing bacteria. Such water, used in preparing uncooked food or for drinking, may produce an outbreak of dysentery. Raw milk supplies may thus be easily polluted and become a source of an epidemic.

Attacks of dysentery are not infrequent in rural areas where inadequately constructed dug wells are so frequently polluted by the family privy which has been constructed and placed with a view to convenience rather than sanitation. When such an epidemic occurs in a household, it is prone to involve the entire family group, being passed from person to person. If the family includes infants or old people, deaths may occur.

When dysentery occurs on a dairy farm, the same precautions must be taken as in a case of typhoid fever. Anyone in contact with the case in any way must not work in a dairy. When the presence of this disease is known and proper precautions taken, there is very little danger of spread by milk, but sometimes the harm is already done before the disease is recognized. In such a case pasteurization offers a reasonable safeguard. Pasteurization temperature of 142° F. for thirty minutes is more than adequate to destroy any dysentery organisms in the milk. Though we know this to be true we are not justified in allowing the sale of milk, even to be pasteurized, which has been handled by persons who have been in contact with a known case of dysentery.

When a case of dysentery occurs in a home, and the case is not removed to the hospital, the patient should be rigidly isolated from the rest of the family and the nurse should take strict precautions. Frequently, however, the mother is the nurse and at the same time cooks for the family. In this way the entire susceptible membership of the family may become infected.

In the care of the case special precautions must be taken with the excretions of the patient. First, they must be disinfected with a creosote preparation or chlorinated lime, and then buried at least 100 feet from a water supply. In homes with flush toilets connected with municipal sewage systems, the excretions may be disposed of down the sewer without the necessity of disinfection. The nurse, after disposing of these discharges or otherwise handling the patient, should rigidly disinfect her hands and the vessels used with a good disinfectant. All dishes used by the patient should be thoroughly washed and boiled, and all food handled by the patient adequately disposed of.

The patient should not be released from isolation until one week after subsidence of clinical symptoms. Thereafter, by special permission of the local Board of Health, he may be released under their supervision, which will continue until three successive negative stool and urine cultures, secured at weekly intervals, have been obtained.

DIPHTHERIA

By Edwin H. Place, M.D.

Physician-in-Chief, South Department, Boston City Hospital; Clinical Professor of Pediatrics, Tufts Medical School.

Among the common contagious diseases diphtheria is one of the most ancient lineage. Descriptions by the Cappadocian physician, Aretaeus, of "Egyptian sore throat" about 100 A.D. are characteristic of diphtheria. Epidemics of diphtheria were frequent in the middle ages and the American Colonies early suffered from the disease in epidemic form.

Its history is also notable for the fact that it was the first disease in which a soluble poison or toxin was discovered by Roux and Yersin in 1888 as well as the first for which an antitoxin was discovered by von Behring in 1890.

The name "diphtheria" was first given the disease by the great French physician, Bretonneau, and modified to the present equivalent French form by Trousseau who is known for his work on tracheotomy and the invention of the trachea tube which is still used in essentially the same form.

A method, including special ingenious tubes for relieving the suffocation which is so dramatic a feature of this disease, was devised by the New York physician, Dr. Joseph O'Dwyer, in 1880-1885. So painstakingly and skillfully were these tubes worked out that, in spite of the great advances in this mechanical age, no important change has been made in them to this time. They are used almost universally and, in the prevention of suffocation, have largely displaced tracheotomy (a procedure which creates an artificial air passage between the windpipe and neck).

In 1913, Dr. Bela Schick, of Vienna, now of New York, devised the method of testing for the presence of antitoxin in the blood. This Schick test has replaced the older, more expensive, and slower method with guinea pigs in a laboratory and has given physicians everywhere a simple, easy means of telling when a person is immune, and whether immunization has been successfully accomplished.

The characteristics of diphtheria are: (1) the formation of a somewhat tough, whitish, false membrane at the site of the infection, (2) paralysis of various muscles due to the poison acting on the nerve trunks, (3) serious heart damage, and (4) the tendency to strangulation from the formation of the membrane in the respiratory passages.

The local inflammation may occur in many places but is most common in the nose, throat and upper trachea. It may occur in the eye, ear or in wounds. It is usually sufficiently characteristic that the nature of the disease can be made out, but this is not always so. The diphtheria bacillus is readily found and fairly easily identified, and by taking cultures the physician is greatly aided in recognizing the disease.

The symptoms felt by the patient, however, are not distinctive. Usually he does not feel very ill, and this may lead him to neglect prompt attention, as many people unfortunately think that so serious a disease must produce alarming symptoms. Cases in which the larynx is involved usually show a croupy cough, some change or loss of voice and, if at all marked, a peculiar sound in breathing called "stridor." Infection of the throat varies from a mild tonsillitis to a severe swelling, closing the throat. There may be a small patch of membrane in mild cases, or at the beginning of severe cases; or membrane may form over large areas of the throat and extend out into the mouth. There is often a peculiar odor or fetor that is at times sufficiently typical to indicate the nature of the disease. So great is the variation in the severity of the infection that any sore throat should be considered suspicious enough for cultures to be taken unless the characteristics are so clear as to make some other diagnosis certain.

Swelling of the throat in diphtheria always indicates severity. It may extend out to the neck on one or both sides, or from ear to ear. Such cases are apt to be very serious unless treated at the very outset. The soreness of the throat may not seem great. Well-marked diphtheria has been found in children who denied feeling at all sick.

Nose infection, one of the least serious forms, is most likely to be a source of spread. Symptoms are mild and often only the nose causes trouble. There is obstruction, a thin discharge of yellowish secretion and crusting or excoriation about the nostril and upper lip. The cases must be distinguished from colds, sinus disease, etc., chiefly by cultures.

Diphtheria usually progresses from day to day, but very rapid advance may occur so that great swelling of the throat and neck, causing "croup," may cause suffocation in 24 to 48 hours.

Diphtheritic paralysis occurs in 1 to 4 weeks after the onset of the sore throat, often after the acute illness has gone. It increases slowly over a period of time from a day to weeks, and may last for 3 to 4 months. It varies from very slight weakness to a state of practically complete helplessness. The most serious form involves the muscles of breathing, and these patients may have to be put in the respirator or "iron lung." The most common paralysis is of the throat, producing a peculiar "nasal voice." All diphtheritic paralysis finally disappears in from one to twenty weeks and leaves no damage. Rarely, after diphtheria, another form of paralysis due to brain damage may occur which may be permanent.

Heart damage occurs during early convalescence, usually 1 to 3 weeks after onset. It is quite different from most other heart diseases. The symptoms appear suddenly and resemble "shock" with pallor, listlessness, restlessness, pain in the abdomen, and vomiting. The blood pressure falls. About half the cases will die in 2 to 3 days; in those that recover, improvement begins within 7 to 10 days, and recovery is practically always complete although sometimes only after a prolonged convalescence.

Strangulation is produced usually by the false membrane which clogs the breathing passages, although swelling of the throat or the larynx alone may cause this. This is so dramatic a feature of diphtheria that novelists of the 19th century have several times mentioned it in their works. The effects are usually gradual, causing increasing difficulty in breathing, but at times a detached false membrane may suddenly choke the patient so that hospitals for the care of such cases have elaborate emergency systems that call the staff at a moment's notice, day or night, like the fire department. The instruments are always laid out ready for immediate use. It is interesting that the dramatic relief of strangulation secured by O'Dwyer tubes, and in other ways by laryngoscopy, was largely the result of work by American physicians.

The disease is most common in children, especially in the early runabout age, but may occur at any age. It is extremely serious in the cases which attack the larynx. In the days before antitoxin was available for treatment, nine out of ten died of the laryngeal form, whereas four out of ten died of the pharyngeal form. The younger the child, the

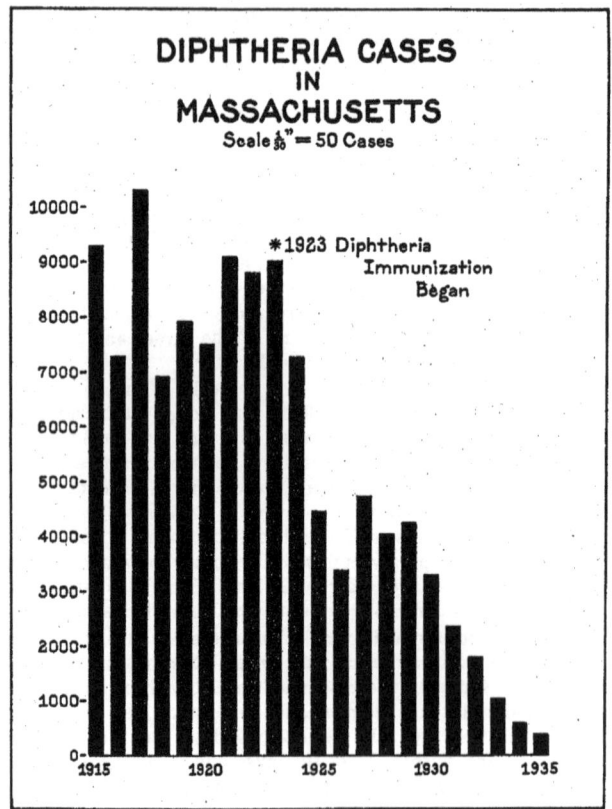

greater the fatality. It was once the most fatal of the common contagious diseases.

After the use of antitoxin, in 1895, the death rate, although extraordinarily reduced, still kept at a level only slightly under 10%. If given early enough, antitoxin invariably prevents the complications and saves the patients' lives. However, a fatal poisoning in the disease may be reached in severe cases within 24 to 48 hours, and as the symptoms in such cases are not particularly alarming to persons without special knowledge of the disease, many cases are not given antitoxin in time.

In 1913, von Behring published results of active immunization. This had been suggested as scientifically possible by our famous Dr. Theobald Smith of the Harvard Medical School four years earlier. Active immunizing was taken up by Dr. W. H. Park of New York, and with his assistant, Zingher, he demonstrated on a large scale the great value of the procedure. The methods have been improved, and now the majority of children in this country are protected. The procedure is simple—two or three injections of a preparation of modified diphtheria toxin are used. Little reaction is observed, and no ill effects are produced. It is best used at six months to one year of age.

The results of active immunization have been remarkable (See Graph). Diphtheria as a cause of death has dropped below whooping cough, measles and scarlet fever. At its high point in Boston, in 1881, diphtheria caused the deaths of 217 persons in every 100,000 population, while in 1937 the death rate was only one in 200,000 population.

The conquering of this disease is well shown by the figures from the Massachusetts Department of Public Health, and the Boston Health Department over ten-year periods.

Average Yearly Deaths per 100,000 Population

Years	Massachusetts	Boston
1856—1865	86.1	110.7
1866—1875	58.4	134.3
1876—1885	127.2	164.3
1886—1895	73.7	119.1
1896—1905	38.4	57.9
1906—1915	19.4	23.8
1916—1925	15.2	22.2
1926—1935	3.8	4.6
1936	0.6	0.9
1937	0.4	0.5

One must clearly appreciate that the efforts that have produced this marvelous and desirable result must not cease. Diphtheria has not been eliminated nor become relatively harmless. It is not beyond possibility that some change in the disease may occur in time from long-continued high immunity of people, but it is now just as potent as ever. We cannot relax our vigilance to the slightest degree. Cases have been reduced by making children immune, but the diphtheria bacillus has not disappeared. It is constantly present in all larger cities and appears periodically even in the smaller communities. Every child should be immunized by the end of its first year, or as soon afterwards as possible.

GONORRHEA

By Ernest B. Howard, M.D.

*Epidemiologist, Division of Genitoinfectious Diseases
Massachusetts Department of Public Health*

It has been said that by the sheer weight of the misery it produces throughout the world, gonorrhea should force itself upon public notice. It is only recently, however, that the people have become aware of its importance as a public health problem.

The disease is an old one in history. Moses may be said to have been the first health officer to make sanitary measures for its control. Scientific knowledge has increased slowly; in fact, it was not until the latter half of the 19th century that gonorrhea was accepted as a communicable disease. For many years it was thought to be a form of syphilis until Philippe Ricord in 1832 definitely proved that gonorrhea and syphilis were entirely different diseases. (Even today many people do not realize this fact.) In 1789, Neisser discovered the germ (gonococcus) that causes gonorrhea and laid the groundwork for the modern understanding of the disease. Since the time of Neisser the most important advance has been the development of a new drug, sulfanilamide, for the treatment of gonorrhea. This drug seems to have a very powerful healing effect. It is too early to pass a final opinion as to its worth, but it definitely shows promise. It should never be used except under the direction of a physician because, otherwise, it may be very dangerous.

The disease is spread almost entirely by sexual intercourse. Gonorrhea of the eyes and many cases of the disease in children are exceptions. Fortunately the gonococcus, like the spirochete of syphilis, dies rapidly outside the body. For these reasons, persons infected with the disease are not dangerous in ordinary social contact, nor in industry. It is unfair and unnecessary to discharge infected persons from food-handling jobs since the disease cannot be spread through food or utensils. Mothers may spread the infection to the eyes of the baby at the time of birth by way of the birth canal if special care is not taken. Nowadays this rarely happens because a special solution which kills the germs before any damage is done is used to wash out the baby's eyes at birth. Up to a few years ago gonorrhea was one of the commonest causes of blindness in infants and children.

The disease affects the reproductive system although it may involve other parts of the body. In the male, two to seven days after exposure, the urethra (water-passage) becomes inflamed and a discharge of pus occurs. Often there is a burning sensation and the passage of urine is painful. After a few days the discharge disappears and the patient often thinks he is cured. Usually, however, the germs spread up the urinary passage and lodge in a gland (the prostate gland) near the bladder. The patient may now have frequent, painful urination, backache, and fever. Gradually, the inflammation in the prostate gland becomes less, the patient's discomfort disappears, and he again believes he is cured. However, the germs may be present in the gland for months even when there are no symptoms. If the patient's conduct is poor, particularly with regard to drinking of alcoholic beverages and sex conduct, the disease may become more serious. It may spread to a part of the reproductive system, the testicle, and cause a very painful, acute inflammation that often results in sterility. Sometimes the germs enter the blood and involve the joints, skin, heart, or other organs. If the patient has good treatment and follows the doctor's advice regarding alcoholic drinks and any type of sex excitement, he can be cured and the serious complications can be avoided. In no disease is the patient's cooperation more important.

Gonorrhea in women is often missed at the beginning because it usually causes so little pain or discomfort. Occasionally the urinary passage is affected enough to cause painful urination. Usually, however, the only early sign of infection is a discharge from the vagina. Many women infected in marriage believe the discharge is a normal result of marital sex relations. The further course of the disease depends a great deal upon the conduct of the patient. Within a few weeks the germs spread into the reproductive organs—the womb, tubes, and ovaries. This is accompanied by a change in the character of the monthly period, usually an increased flow. The reproductive organs may be seriously impaired and permanent sterility may follow. Collections of pus may develop in the tubes and spread to the tissues in the pelvis, causing peritonitis. The patient suffers from pain and discomfort, may have an early change of life, and often has to undergo major operations on the reproductive organs. Gonorrhea in women can be cured, but cure requires the cooperation of the patient and the control of her conduct, just as in the case of male patients.

Gonorrhea also occurs commonly among girls under the age of 14. In fact, over 10 per cent of the female gonorrhea reported in Massachusetts is in this young age group. The course of the disease is different than in adults in that it does not usually spread to the womb. There is usually a copious discharge of pus from the reproductive passage accompanied by burning and itching of the private parts. Occasionally other parts of the body, particularly the eyes, joints, and rectum may be affected. Gonorrhea in young girls may be acquired by other than sexual contact, although the latter is probably a frequent method of infection.

Of all communicable diseases, gonorrhea is one of the most common. The U. S. Public Health Service has estimated that over a million new infections occur every year, and this estimate does not include as many more who never seek medical care. Apparently no communicable diseases except measles, chicken pox, and the common cold are more common than gonorrhea. It is furthermore a disease of youth. Over half of the patients are between 18 and 25 years old. Many of the infected acquire the disease innocently, through no fault of their own. This is true of the infections acquired after marriage from husbands who believed themselves cured. The children under 14 who acquire gonorrhea are, of course, often as innocent of any conscious wrongdoing as are infants born with infected eyes.

The control of gonorrhea depends upon the same factors as does syphilis. Patients must seek treatment early and remain under treatment until the physician pronounces them cured; good facilities for treatment of all patients including those who cannot afford to pay must be provided, just as is being done in Massachusetts; and a continuous program of public education must be maintained. Progress will be slow, but if each gain is held and enough interest can be aroused, there is every reason to expect the same degree of success in the control of gonorrhea as in the control of syphilis.

. . . . . .

Due to the fact that gonorrhea and syphilis have many problems in common, information on certain important matters is purposely omitted here because they are covered in the article on syphilis.

INFANTILE PARALYSIS
By Ralph W. Daffinee, M.D.
Poliomyelitis Consultant
Massachusetts Department of Public Health

Infantile paralysis, known in medicine as anterior poliomyelitis, is the contagious disease most dreaded by parents. The popular belief is that it strikes a community with mysterious suddenness, which accounts for the wave of uncontrolled terror similar to that which followed the great plagues of earlier centuries. Poliomyelitis, however, is no unexplainable disease. It is spread from person to person just as measles and smallpox; the virus or germ has been isolated, and it is believed that many people have the disease in an unrecognized form and recover entirely from it, thereafter having complete immunity.

Infantile paralysis is primarily a disease of temperate climates, although scattered outbreaks have occurred in arctic and tropical regions. Most of the cases are reported in the late summer, but there are cases the year round. The age of greatest susceptibility is, like measles and many other contagious diseases, the preschool and school group, although any nonimmune person may contract it at any age. It strikes even the healthiest children in the better neighborhoods.

The germ is a filtrable virus, so small as not to be seen by the microscope. By injecting the virus into monkeys, the progress of the disease can be studied at various stages. The virus has been found in the noses of healthy contacts as well as patients sick with the disease; it has been recovered from the feces of patients. By preference it attacks the central nervous system, particularly the spinal cord, although the brain is very frequently involved.

When the virus gains access into the body of a susceptible person, there is first an incubation period of 6 to 15 days, when nothing untoward happens. Then the patient is seized with a vague illness, characterized by fever, vomiting and general malaise. Sometimes diarrhea, grippy aches and pains, or sore throat may be present. This is the stage of general invasion, and cannot be distinguished in any way from any of the numerous febrile upsets which plague the human race. After a short while—1 to 7 days—this phase passes, and the patient may even feel well enough to return to school. Evidence all seems to point to the fact that for most of us this is as far as the disease progresses, and that our immunity is received in this mild, nonparalytic attack.

If, however, the virus attacks the central nervous system, the picture rapidly changes. Fever returns, vomiting and headache become persistent, and the identifying sign of stiffness of the neck and back appears. This sign is found in all cases, if carefully searched for, but it varies from the obvious stiffness which the mother can see to a barely perceptible stiffness which only a trained observer will note. I remember a toe dancer with poliomyelitis who could touch her forehead to the floor between her feet while sitting on the floor. Although this is more than most of us can do, it represented stiffness in her case, because normally she could get her chin to the floor. The temperature is rarely over 101.5° but the patient is drowsy and hates to be disturbed. Constipation is usually present. The reflexes are increased, and a coarse tremor of the hands may appear.

In a suspected case, lumbar puncture will prove the diagnosis. Under aseptic precautions a small quantity of fluid is drawn from the spine, and this fluid tested with chemicals and examined under the microscope. This procedure, if properly performed, is harmless and practically painless. It has been done on five-year-old children with no general anesthesia and no restraint.

The symptoms will vary somewhat depending on the portion of the central nervous system which is involved. If the brain is affected, the clinical picture is exactly like other forms of encephalitis. If the upper part of the spinal cord or the medulla is involved, little or no evidence of nervous system damage will appear, even the spinal fluid may appear normal to all tests. This particular form of the disease is almost impossible to diagnose before the onset of the paralysis, and many such cases are labeled pneumonia or typhoid fever or grippe until the telltale paralysis appears.

In the usual case, paralysis, if it is to appear, comes on within 3 or 4 days after the stiff neck. This paralysis is not always permanent. In fact with care a great deal of it will disappear. The nerve fibers which are compressed by the swelling in the cord will recover if they are not compressed too long, and the paralysis then clears up.

Treatment consists mainly of keeping the patient at rest, and protecting any weakened muscles. No medicine seems to be effective, no serum has been found which will cure paralysis or prevent its spread. When it was first discovered that blood serum from recently recovered monkeys or humans had the power of rendering the virus incapable of producing the disease, hope was aroused that it might be of value in active cases. Hundreds of former victims of the disease volunteered their blood to help those who were attacked by infantile paralysis. However, this has proven to be a false hope. Once the disease process has entered the nervous system, no amount of serum seems to halt its progress. Vitamins and endocrine products have been tried, all with no definite result.

Active immunization has been attempted, but the products available so far have not been satisfactory. When living virus is used in vaccination, there is always the danger that even the small amounts used may be too much for a susceptible individual. On the other hand, when the virus is killed it appears to be entirely inert.

Recently the use of antiseptic sprays has been advocated, and has even reached dramatic heights in the movies. Since we believe the portal of entry to be the nose and throat, it would seem that by increasing the local resistance in these areas, we might prevent the virus from getting a foothold. Three substances have been found to be of use in protecting monkeys: alum, picric acid, and zinc sulfate. Although of value theoretically, they have been found of little use from a practical standpoint. The strong chemicals may be harmful to the mucous surfaces. Moreover, they must be administered by a trained physician, since home spraying is probably worthless because the chemical fails to reach the vulnerable areas deep in the nasal passages. To keep a community protected would require the services of more physicians than most communities possess. This line of research, however, should not yet be abandoned, but should be considered in the experimental stage. We may yet find an innocuous substance which may be applied by any atomizer.

Treatment of the severely paralyzed cases may be carried out by use of hypertonic solutions injected intravenously. This is done to combat the edema which is present in the affected areas of the cord.

In the main our treatment must lie in the protection of muscles already paralyzed, and in the reeducation of muscles which have some function remaining. Deformity must be prevented by the use of mechanical apparatus under skilled orthopedic supervision as soon as the muscle soreness has disappeared. In cases where the chest muscles are involved, the use of a respirator often keeps a patient breathing artificially until muscle power returns. Massage, tonic lamp treatments, electrical stimulation of muscles, and underwater exercises are all of value in the aftercare. Later on, surgical transplantation of muscles will provide substitutes for completely paralyzed muscles. Braces, of course, are of invaluable aid in protection and support.

It is obvious that in the control of such a disease, our methods must depend on the particular epidemic. Since poliomyelitis is a contagious disease, we employ the same measures that are used in the case of measles, diphtheria, and scarlet fever. Early recognition of cases and immediate isolation of them will help to prevent further spread.

During an epidemic the question often comes up whether or not schools should be closed. Unless children can be kept out of centers of gathering, and their contacts limited sharply to their own immediate neighborhoods, they are much safer in schoolrooms under the eye of teachers and nurses who are trained to watch for the earliest signs of the disease. We gain nothing by closing the schools and leaving the movie houses open.

There appears to be some natural immunity in most of us which helps to overcome the infection in its earliest stages. It is estimated that of every 1,000 population, less than 10 will develop poliomyelitis in the paralytic form at any time in their lives. Furthermore, of those developing the disease, between 40% and 80% will survive and many will recover almost complete function of their muscles. It is obvious that several other diseases should be feared much more than poliomyelitis. Whooping cough and measles are greater killers, rheumatic fever cripples larger numbers. The public does not yield to blind hysteria on the approach of these diseases; we should not do so when poliomyelitis appears.

Further research will help us in our battle. We must find a test as simple as the Schick test to identify susceptibles; we must unearth a method of immunizing these susceptibles—a method which has no harmful results or dangerous complications. Until such research is accomplished, we must base our attack on the early recognition and isolation of the sick.

MEASLES

BY CHARLES F. McKHANN, M.D.

*Visiting Physician, Infants' and Children's Hospitals;
Associate Professor of Pediatrics and Communicable Diseases,
Harvard Medical School and School of Public Health.*

Measles is an acute, highly contagious disease which few persons escape. It is among the most common of the acute infectious diseases and is endemic throughout the year in larger communities, but during the winter and spring months becomes epidemic at intervals of two to four years. The period is longer between epidemics in small communities than it is in cities. After almost all susceptible individuals have suffered from the disease, the epidemic subsides to reappear a few years later when a new generation of susceptibles has developed.

Adults who have not experienced measles are usually not immune to the disease but have failed to have contact with it. When measles breaks out in populations from which the disease has long been absent or in groups which have never encountered the disease before, the epidemics become extremely severe and individuals of all ages are attacked. During the World War measles was a major health problem in army camps.

No age, race or sex is immune to measles; the possible exception to this is the newborn baby, who is immune for a few months if his mother has had the disease. Otherwise he, too, is susceptible.

Measles is one of the most communicable of human ailments. The extreme susceptibility of individuals and the permanent immunity conferred by one attack serve to account for measles being primarily a disease of childhood.

The importance of measles is illustrated by the incidence of the disease. In Massachusetts over 40,000 cases have been reported in two of the past ten years, and in no year within that period has the number of cases fallen below 13,000. When it is borne in mind that many cases of measles are not seen by a physician and are thus not reported to the health department, it is apparent that these figures might have to be almost doubled to indicate the actual incidence of the disorder. In spite of this high incidence, the number of deaths from measles has steadily declined and is at present quite small (See Graph). The decline in the deaths from measles is probably due not to diminished severity of measles but to a better understanding of the dangers of the disease by parents, teachers and lay health workers as well as by physicians. It has been forcefully brought to the attention of all of these groups that the dangers of measles reside in the severe complications rather than in the disease itself. Secondarily invading microorganisms such as the streptococcus, the influenza bacillus or the pneumococcus give rise to infections in the lungs, ears, mastoids, sinuses, bronchi and intestines. Tuberculosis is particularly apt to be activated by an attack of measles. Undernourished, debilitated children have frequently fallen victims to the complications of the disease.

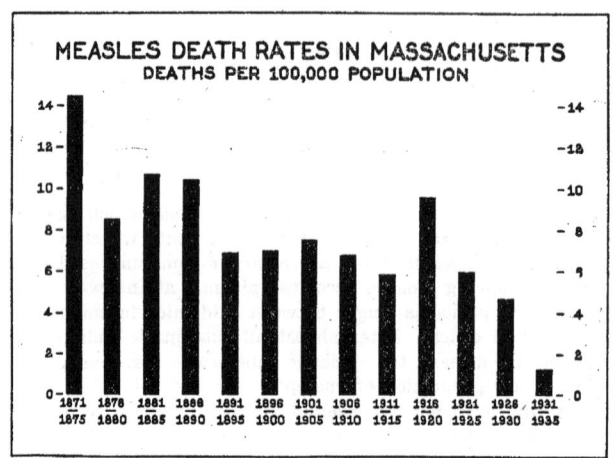

The isolation of measles patients from one another has undoubtedly diminished the incidence of complications, particularly of secondary pulmonary infections. In years past it was customary in hospitals to segregate children with measles in large wards on group isolation, on the basis that they could not transmit the disease to one another. However, the interchange of pharyngeal organisms resulted in so many secondary infections that most institutions have placed measles patients on individual isolation protection.

The improvement of nutrition among children and the disappearance of deficiency diseases have served to reduce the number of chronically ill, debilitated children among the general population, children in whom measles was especially dangerous.

The extreme susceptibility of individuals to measles and the great ease of communicability of the disease together with the fact that patients are infective in the early stages before the nature of the disorder is recognized account for the failure of public health measures to control outbreaks. While isolation of recognized cases, reporting of cases, placarding of homes and closing of schools have had some influence upon the incidence of the disease, they have not been successful in controlling epidemics. Measles is thus a disease in which a method of active immunization is urgently needed. However, no satisfactory method of active immunization has been developed. Experimental work in this direction has been going on for many years in this country and abroad, but the problem remains unsolved.

The clinical picture of measles after the appearance of the eruption is surprisingly uniform and leads to an ease of diagnosis which is sometimes misleading. Two other diseases in particular are apt to be confused with measles (1) a disease seen almost only in infants—roseola infantum, and (2) German measles—occurring in older children. Both of these diseases have rashes which resemble measles. They are, however, diseases of less serious import than is measles. In recent years certain drugs have come into rather wide use which may produce rashes in patients who have taken them for a period of time. These eruptions may be very similar to measles, and have led to confusion even by experienced observers.

The fact that almost 100 per cent of the population sooner or later acquire measles, and the fact that many of the cases are comparatively mild have led to an attitude of indifference on the part of parents to this disease. Although measles cannot be prevented and although there is no specific treatment for the disease once it has appeared, it is nevertheless a disorder in which medical attention is demanded, particularly so that complications may, if possible, be avoided.

The treatment of measles must be directed toward the relief of symptoms. Care of the eyes, applications to the nose and throat to counteract the severe rhinitis, laryngitis and bronchitis which accompany the disease, constitute the major therapeutic indications.

The only method for the control of measles at present available is the use, now well-established, of human immune serum for the passive immunization of exposed patients. Convalescent serum, adult immune serum, or placental immune globulin may be used for this purpose. Injection of any of these substances in proper dosage as long as four days after exposure leads to an immunity in upward of 95 per cent of the cases. This immunity, passive in character, lasts but a few weeks and suffices only to cover the immediate exposure. Because the protection is of short duration and only postpones the time at which the patient will have measles, complete protection of the patient would not be desirable except in the case of acutely or chronically ill, debilitated or malnourished children or infants between six months and two years of age. In other children, particularly normal, healthy children exposed to measles, modification of the disease should be sought by administration of the serum at a little later time in the incubation period. In the modified type of the disease, the incubation period is often prolonged, the severity of the disease is reduced, the complications and sequelae are minimized, and the attenuated attack usually results in a permanent immunity. In hospitals or convalescent homes modification is seldom desirable; rather a complete eradication of the disease should be sought inasmuch as the attenuated form or modified form is still readily communicable and does not eliminate the necessary periods of quarantine. Furthermore, there are many patients in hospitals who are sufficiently ill that they should not be permitted to have even a mild form of measles.

Of the three substances for use in the prevention or modification of measles, convalescent serum and placental immune globulin are most effective. These materials are apparently of almost equal potency. Placental globulin can be made available on a large scale and is now furnished to physicians of Massachusetts by the Massachusetts Antitoxin and Vaccine Laboratory.

Adult immune serum, although less effective than convalescent serum or placental globulin, is also readily available. The physician need not type the blood of the donor. Of course only blood of donors who have once suffered from measles is effective. Such blood taken in quantity of 30 cc. citrated, may be injected intramuscularly into the susceptible patient. This dosage, in contrast to the 4 cc. of convalescent serum or 2 to 4 cc. of placental globulin, is usually effective in producing modification of the disorder.

While it is recognized that measles remains a disease in which further advance must be sought, particularly in the way of active immunization, pending such developments, the utilization of the present means of passive immunization in selected cases should not be neglected.

MENINGITIS

By LeRoy D. Fothergill, M.D.
Assistant Professor of Bacteriology and Immunology
Harvard University Medical School

Meningitis is an acute inflammatory process involving the meninges or enclosing membranes of the brain and spinal cord. The disease may be due to any one of a number of pathogenic bacteria; the more common causative agents being the tubercle bacillus, the meningococcus, the influenza bacillus, the hemolytic streptococcus, and the pneumococcus. Other organisms such as the colon bacillus and the staphylococcus are occasional causes of the disease. The following table describes the relative frequency of the different bacterial types of meningitis as observed at the Children's Hospital, Boston, over a period of 16 years. There was no epidemic increase of any one type during this period. The figures would have been quite different had there been an epidemic. Moreover, these figures represent the incidence in children which is different from that in adults. One of these bacterial types rarely occurs in adults.

Causative Organism	Number of Cases
Tubercle bacillus	321
Meningococcus	187
H. influenzae	129
Hemolytic streptococcus	105
Pneumococcus	107
All others	77
Total	926

It must be emphasized that, with rare exceptions, the bacteriological type of meningitis cannot be recognized by the clinical features alone. It is true that certain findings may be observed more commonly in one type than in another. For example, some patients with meningococcus meningitis may exhibit characteristic petechial skin lesions, for which reason the disease was at one time spoken of as "spotted fever." However, an absence of such skin lesions does not negative a diagnosis of meningococcic meningitis.

The diagnosis of the bacterial type of meningitis depends entirely upon a careful and proper bacteriological examination of cerebrospinal fluid obtained by lumbar puncture. For the purpose of this examination, as well as others of great clinical importance, an adequately equipped laboratory in charge of a competent bacteriologist is necessary. The use of valuable specific treatment is often delayed unnecessarily or is administered in a type of meningitis for which it has no value because of incompetent laboratory assistance in diagnosis. There are few diseases in which the mortality is influenced so much by prompt diagnosis and institution of proper treatment as in meningitis.

Meningitis occurs much more commonly during infancy and early childhood than during any other period of life, although it may occur at any age. Indeed, one type, namely, that caused by the influenza bacillus, occurs almost exclusively during early childhood. It practically never occurs during adult life. On the other hand, meningococcus meningitis often occurs in epidemic outbreaks and during such episodes individuals of adult ages are often victims of the disease.

Meningococcus meningitis has received more attention than any of the other types, largely because it does occur as an epidemic disease. In untreated cases the mortality is high, i.e., about 80 per cent. Moreover, many of those who recover without treatment are left with serious and permanent damage to their central nervous system such as deafness, blindness, spastic paralysis, impaired mentality, hydrocephalus, etc.

This type of meningitis is undoubtedly spread from person to person by droplet infection. The organism may be carried from either an active case or a healthy carrier to a susceptible individual. It is harbored in the nasopharynx. Methods are available for detecting such carriers. However, the utility of the procedure has been greatly exaggerated in the past. The bacteriological procedures required for the isolation of the meningococcus from the nasopharynx and its identification are both difficult and time-consuming. Such examinations, to be reliable, should be done only by those who have had considerable experience with the technique.

The usefulness of carrier examinations is limited for the following additional reasons. We do not have a simple susceptibility test, applicable to the examination of large numbers of people, such as in the case of diphtheria. Therefore, it is impossible to pick out those persons liable to develop the disease if adequately exposed. It is possible to appraise an individual's resistance by determining the bactericidal power of his blood for the meningococcus. Such tests are difficult and so far have been used for special study purposes only. Such studies as have been done have shown that a considerable percentage of adults possess a naturally acquired immunity against the disease which agrees with the low incidence of cases even during the course of an epidemic. Again, the volume of carrier studies is limited by the fact that we have no simple method for the determination of the virulence of strains isolated from the nasopharynx. By means of certain very elaborate procedures, not at all practical for large-scale field studies, it is possible to compare the relative virulence of different strains of meningococci. Studies of this character have shown that many strains isolated from the nasopharynx are avirulent and would be unlikely to produce disease in a susceptible person.

In our opinion it is useless to embark upon a search for meningococcus carriers when an epidemic occurs. When such studies are done, carrier rates of such magnitude may be found as to render isolation and quarantine out of the question. In most individuals the carrier state is transitory while others may harbor the organism continuously. There is no effective method of treatment to cure an individual of the carrier state.

The control of epidemics of this disease involves such commonsense procedures as: Elimination of crowding, particularly in institutions and barracks; good ventilation and adequate spacing of beds in sleeping quarters -(i.e., in army barracks, institutional wards, etc.); avoidance of excessive fatigue, undue exposure, etc.; and guarding against such contacts as may be factors in the spread of the common infections of the upper respiratory tract.

For many years effective serum for the treatment of meningococcus meningitis has been available. The proper use of this therapeutic agent has unquestionably saved many lives. There are two factors of paramount importance in the successful use of serum. The first is early and accurate diagnosis of the disease followed by prompt administration of serum. Each day's delay reduces the patient's chances of a complete recovery. Serious complications are more common in those patients treated late. Another factor of great importance is the use of a potent serum effective for the organism infecting the individual patient. There are certain practical laboratory procedures of aid in such a selection of serum.

Recently, a drug, sulfanilamide, has been shown to be very effective in the treatment of meningococcus meningitis and is likely to supplant the use of serum. In some clinics the drug has been used alone with great success whereas in others it has been used together with serum.

As we have already indicated, meningitis caused by the influenza bacillus is almost exclusively a disease of early childhood. In fact, about 85 per cent of cases occur during the first three years of life. The age distribution of this disease depends upon the gradual acquisition of active immunity by individuals of older ages. It should be emphasized that there is no relationship between this disease and epidemic influenza. The latter is caused by an infectious agent belonging in that general class known as filtrable viruses.

A serum has been developed for the treatment of influenza bacillus meningitis that is of some, though not very striking, value. Its use in a large series of cases has reduced the mortality from about 99 per cent to 84 per cent. While this result is not striking, it is of such value as to encourage further efforts toward improving the serum.

The pneumococcus and hemolytic streptococcus more frequently cause meningitis secondary to some other infection, particularly of neighboring anatomical structures, such as mastoiditis, lateral sinus thrombosis, sinusitis, etc. Formerly the mortality in these two types was very high. It has been shown during the past few years, however, that sulfanilamide is very effective in the treatment of hemolytic streptococcal meningitis. Recently, the successful treatment of pneumococcal meningitis has been reported following the combined use of this drug and immune serum.

Tuberculous meningitis is essentially a 100 per cent fatal disease. It is always secondary to some other tuberculous lesion such as pulmonary tuberculosis. It is nearly always an accompaniment of that dreaded syndrome known as miliary tuberculosis, which is actually a generalized seeding of the entire body with tubercle bacilli. There is no known method of value for the treatment of tuberculous meningitis. It is, however, an entirely preventable disease. Its prevention depends upon the prevention of tuberculosis in general.

MUMPS

BY HAROLD L. HIGGINS, M.D.

Chief, Children's Medical Service, Massachusetts General Hospital
Assistant Professor, Pediatrics, Harvard Medical School

Mumps is a contagious disease occurring usually in epidemics. The cause of mumps is a virus, an ultramicroscopic organism. Mumps may affect various organs of the body, as the salivary glands, the parotid, the submaxillary, and the sublingual in that order of frequency, the mammary glands, the pancreas, the testes, and the brain and spinal cord. In most cases, however, the involvement is only of the parotid glands, and only in rare cases do the parotids escape involvement entirely.

Mumps is also called "epidemic parotitis." Parotitis is inflammation of the parotid gland. There are two parotid glands, one on each side of the face, in front of and below the ear. The glands produce saliva which flows through the parotid duct to enter the mouth on the inside of the cheek opposite the upper bicuspid teeth. The submaxillary salivary glands are located under the corner of the jaws, and the sublingual salivary glands under the tongue. The sign of involvement of the salivary glands is swelling.

The first symptom of mumps is a fullness of the face in front of and under the ears, with pain on eating. Sometimes both sides are involved, and sometimes only one. This swelling is more easily recognized by one of the family than by a stranger who does not know the normal contour of the patient's face. The swelling varies from a hardly perceptible fullness to the size of a tangerine. The fullness is seen rather than felt, being soft, jelly-like, and without clearly outlined edges. If the flow of saliva has been interfered with there is a feeling of tenseness in the gland. There is a common belief that if only one parotid gland is involved the patient may in a later epidemic develop mumps in the other parotid gland; this belief is probably incorrect.

The "old family test" for mumps is to feed the patient something sour as lemon juice or a pickle; the test is positive if pain follows. This test is not infallible. One will get pain in the jaw if the swelling of the parotid gland prevents the flow of saliva into the mouth. This means that with the taking of the sour food, more saliva is formed than can be eliminated and, therefore, causes further swelling and pain. But in not every case of mumps is there blockage of the flow of saliva, and on the other hand, the parotid duct may be blocked from some other cause, as infection or tumor.

Other glands of the body that may show inflammation are the mammary glands and the pancreas. Pain and swelling in the breasts occasionally occur in mumps in older girls and in women; this is only temporary and annoying. When the pancreas is involved, there is pain in the upper abdomen, accompanied by indigestion; fortunately this is usually rare and but temporary.

Much more disturbing is the inflammation of the testes (orchitis) of the male. This may precede, or occur simultaneously with the parotitis, but usually follows it by a few days. It is marked by swelling and tenderness. It occurs only after puberty and appears in approximately 20 per cent of men having mumps. Ultimately atrophy and failure to function of the testes may occur. For this reason, mumps alone of the common contagious diseases is more serious for the adult than for the child. Women may have a similar involvement of the ovary (oophoritis) but this is not common or serious.

Much more rarely, the nervous system and its covering (the meninges) are involved in mumps. Mumps encephalitis and meningitis are characterized by headache, stiff neck and back, pain on motion, drowsiness and often vomiting, delirium, and high fever. The occurrence of parotitis aids in its being differentiated from other types of meningitis. Fortunately cure is usually spontaneous and complete within a few days.

Several conditions have to be considered before a diagnosis of mumps is definitely made. They are (1) tumor of the parotid gland, (2) abscess of the gland, (3) stone in the parotid duct with blockage of the flow of saliva, and (4) inflammation of the duct. This latter condition usually occurs with an upper respiratory infection; the swelling of the duct prevents the flow of saliva and the gland becomes swollen; on pressure of the gland, a cloudy saliva may be seen entering the mouth through the duct; this condition tends to recur; thus recurrent parotitis is probably not mumps.

Mumps is a self-limited disease and not serious except for the concurrent orchitis or encephalitis. The patient should stay in bed so long as there is any fever and remain quietly at home so long as swelling of the glands is present. A hot water bottle or ice bag may be applied locally for relief of pain. Aspirin is frequently advised to relieve headache or general discomfort. An adult male should remain in bed for at least one week to avoid involvement of the testicles. The use of a suspensory bandage is advisable in orchitis.

The virus of mumps is transmitted from person to person probably through the saliva, by droplets from the mouth of one person entering the nose or mouth of another. Mumps, also, can be transmitted by use of a common drinking cup or dishes. Certain domestic animals—as the cat, dog, and goat—are susceptible to mumps and may transmit the disease to man. There is practically no evidence that mumps is transmitted from one person to another through a third who does not have the disease; thus a teacher whose own children are at home with mumps will not transmit the disease to the children in his class at school.

Mumps is not so "catching" as many of the other contagious diseases; close contact is necessary for one to contract the disease. This is in large part due to the fact that coughing is not a symptom of mumps. If a patient has a respiratory infection, or measles, or whooping cough, in addition to mumps, he becomes a potent spreader of the disease.

Patients with mumps are contagious for at least one week. Quarantine regulations usually read "the quarantine of the patient with mumps shall be at least one week, and until the swelling of the salivary glands has receded." Contacts are usually not held in quarantine. It is definitely advised, if in a family there are adult males who have not had the disease, that they avoid contact so far as possible with the mumps patient. Occasionally the question arises in a hospital or a boys' or girls' camp, "Is there any way to protect the other children after a case of mumps has appeared?" It is probable that protection could be given for a short period to those who have been exposed, by intramuscular injection of 10-20 cc. of blood from a person who has had mumps.

The symptoms of the disease appear about two and one-half weeks after the patient is exposed. This period between the exposure and the coming down with the disease is known as the "incubation period." An individual is ordinarily not contagious while incubating mumps.

PARATYPHOID FEVER

By B. Barrett Gilman, M.D.

Assistant Director, Division of Communicable Diseases
Massachusetts Department of Public Health

Paratyphoid fever is an acute communicable disease caused by an organism closely resembling the typhoid bacillus. Although it may affect large numbers and sometimes cause death, it is generally milder than typhoid fever and may be looked upon as a close relative of that disease. Massachusetts had been relatively free of paratyphoid fever up to 1937, but in the past two years we have seen a marked increase in the number of cases.

After the causative organism enters the body, if symptoms are to appear at all, they may begin within a few hours or may be delayed four to ten days. Nausea, vomiting, diarrhea, fever, and prostration may occur, but in some cases only one of these symptoms may appear. The severe case may resemble typhoid fever very closely, with bowel hemorrhage, delirium, and even pneumonia. Such a case can be distinguished from typhoid fever only by laboratory procedures.

As with typhoid fever and dysentery, the causative organism must be carried from the infected person to the alimentary tract of a susceptible individual. Outbreaks have occurred after ingestion of water, raw milk, pastry, chicken salad, and other foodstuffs which have been contaminated with the causative organism from a case or carrier of the infection.

Very mild cases of the disease are frequently seen. In fact, a person may harbor the organism without ever having had a suspicious illness in the past. Persons so infected, with little or no symptoms, may continue to carry the organism just as long as one who is seriously ill, and in ignorance of their infection they are likely to spread the infection through the community.

As with typhoid fever, the control measures of pasteurized milk, safe water supplies, and control of carriers contribute much toward the prevention of large outbreaks; but, as with dysentery, the frequency of the mild or missed case makes the problem of control more difficult. Every case of this disease in Massachusetts is thoroughly investigated, and cultures are taken from all contacts who may have been the source of the infection or who may have become infected, with or without obvious symptoms. This is, at best, slow and painstaking work. The citizen can do his part in the control of this and similar diseases by making sure that his hands are thoroughly washed with soap and water after the use of the toilet. He should realize that every diarrhea is of potential danger to the members of his household. The organism which gives a mild infection in one person may cause death in another.

Those persons who are most likely to come in contact with this disease, either because of occupation or travel, may increase their resistance to this infection by taking vaccine inoculations. The vaccine which is supplied free of charge by the Massachusetts Department of Public Health contains material which will raise a person's resistance against both typhoid and paratyphoid fever. Because of the relatively low incidence of these diseases in Massachusetts, and because of the excellent state of sanitation within our borders, universal use of this material is not advised for the citizens of the Commonwealth so long as they plan to remain within the State.

PNEUMONIA

By F. RANDOLF PHILBROOK, M.D.
Epidemiologist, Division of Communicable Diseases
Massachusetts Department of Public Health

I. What Pneumonia Is.

In the Commonwealth of Massachusetts pneumonia is exceeded only by heart disease and cancer as a principal cause of death. It is the most frequent cause among communicable diseases. About 4,000 die annually in the State. This disease is a germ-caused inflammation of the lungs which attacks infants, adults in the prime of life and the aged. No age group or race is exempt.

Sometimes the inflamed areas in the lungs are scattered in small patches. This distribution of inflammation is referred to as "bronchopneumonia." More typically, however, an entire large section or lobe of a lung is inflamed. When this occurs the patient has "lobar pneumonia." One or more of the three right or two left lobes of the lungs may be involved. When the inflammation occurs in parts of both lungs at the same time the layman may be told that the patient has "double pneumonia."

WHAT PNEUMONIA IS

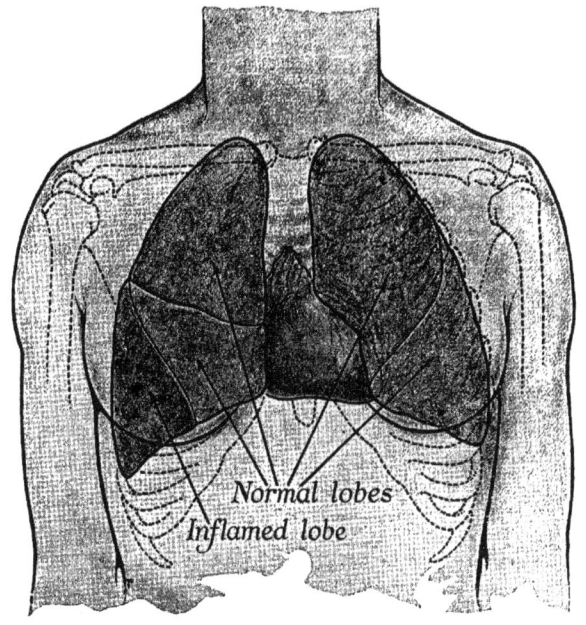

Normal lobes
Inflamed lobe

PNEUMONIA IS INFLAMMATION OF THE LUNGS

LOBAR PNEUMONIA — *Inflammation of One or More Lobes.*

BRONCHOPNEUMONIA — *Patches of Inflammation.*

II. What Causes Pneumonia?

Most cases of pneumonia are caused by a family of germs called "pneumococci." There are more than thirty kinds or "Types" of these organisms. Instead of a name each is given a number, accordingly the members of this family are referred to as Type I or Type II or Type III pneumococci, and so on. Since serums are available for the treatment of pneumonia caused by certain of these types it is more important to determine which type of germ is causing the disease than it is to determine whether the pneumonia is the broncho- or the lobar variety. Under the microscope the pneumococci all look like small dots usually occurring in pairs. Each is covered with a translucent envelope called a "capsule."

WHAT CAUSES PNEUMONIA

Pneumococci

MOST CASES OF PNEUMONIA ARE CAUSED BY GERMS CALLED "PNEUMOCOCCI"

There are more than Thirty Kinds or "Types" of Pneumococci.

III. When to Suspect Pneumonia.

Frequently pneumonia patients do not have the great benefit of early treatment with serum because they do not call the doctor until the disease is well advanced. They do not realize that they have pneu-

WHEN TO SUSPECT PNEUMONIA

USUAL FIRST SYMPTOMS OF PNEUMONIA ARE—

1— *Bad Cold with Fever.*
2— *A Chill.*
3— *Pain in Chest or Side.*
4— *Reddish or Bloody Sputum.*

monia. Accordingly everyone should learn to recognize the usual first symptoms of the disease. These are, briefly,

(1) Bad cold with fever or chill.
(2) Pain in side or chest.
(3) Reddish or bloody sputum.
(4) Difficult rapid breathing.

Such symptoms as these demand immediate action! Call a doctor! Nowadays, pneumonia is as much an emergency as appendicitis.

HOW PNEUMONIA IS RECOGNIZED

DOCTOR DIAGNOSES PNEUMONIA BY—

1—*Story of the usual first symptoms.*
2—*Examination, particularly of the chest.*
3—*Sometimes by X-ray.*

IV. How Pneumonia Is Recognized.

The doctor diagnoses pneumonia on the basis of a careful history and physical examination. He considers the story of the usual first symptoms which leads him to suspect pneumonia. He acquires other verbal information and then carefully examines the patient. With the stethoscope he listens to the breath sounds in the chest and by tapping the chest-wall with his fingers he acquires important evidence. Sometimes the X-ray is valuable but most usually the diagnosis can be made without its aid.

HOW SERUM FOR TREATMENT IS SELECTED

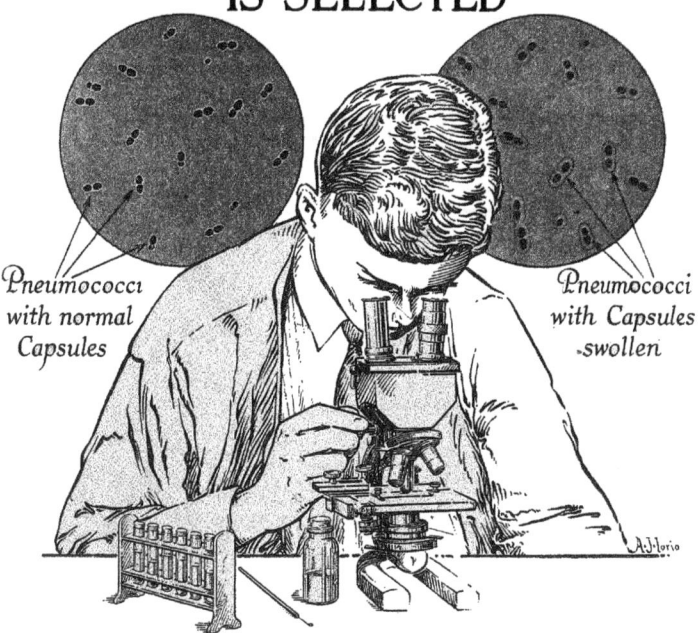

Pneumococci with normal Capsules

Pneumococci with Capsules swollen

Patient's sputum (containing pneumonia germs) is sent immediately to laboratory. Sputum is mixed with several types of pneumonia serums.

The serum causing swelling of capsules of pneumonia germs is proper type for treatment.

V. **How Serum For Treatment Is Selected.**

Serums are available which may be used to treat pneumonias caused by several of the types of pneumococci. Since a Type I serum must be used for the treatment of patients infected by Type I pneumococci and since a Type II pneumonia case is desperately in need of Type II serum, it is very important to learn immediately which serum to give.

A specimen of the patient's sputum, which contains the pneumonia germs coughed up from the lung, is rushed to a laboratory where a procedure called "typing" is carried out. There the sputum is divided into several small samples, each mixed with a different type of serum and examined under the microscope. That type of serum which causes a swelling of the capsules of the pneumococci is the proper type to use for treatment of the patient from whom the sputum specimen was obtained. For instance, if the capsules of the pneumonia germs in the sputum swell when mixed with Type I serum, the significance is that they are Type I pneumococci and that the patient must be given Type I pneumonia serum to combat that specific member of the germ-family.

WHERE SERUM IS OBTAINED

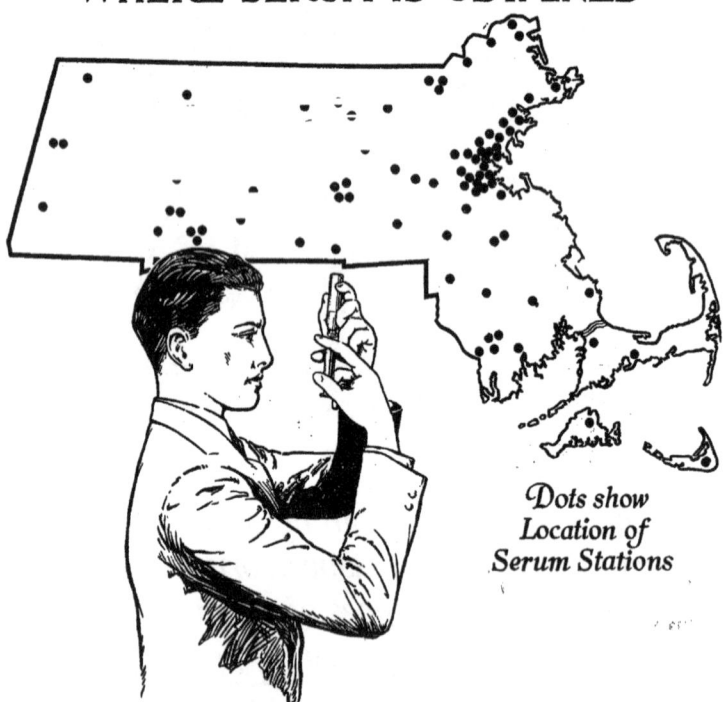

Dots show Location of Serum Stations

Serums for Common Types are available free. They are kept in many Hospital Laboratories. Serums for Infrequent Types may be purchased.

VI. Where Serum Is Obtained.

In an effort to provide a means for rapid distribution of pneumonia serum to all doctors in the State a network of serum depots has been established throughout the Commonwealth by the Department of Public Health. These depots are hospital laboratories convenient for the doctors, where "typing" can be done and from which the proper serum can be issued immediately. Few, if any, doctors are more than twenty miles from the nearest supply of serum. There are more than seventy such storage places. Most of these laboratories have only the most frequently needed Type I serum but about twenty laboratories carry Type I, Type II and Type V serum and from time to time when the supply is sufficient they have Types VII and VIII. There are more than eighty laboratories approved by this Department where "typing" is done.

Serums against the commoner types of pneumococci are available to physicians at these stations after the sputum has been examined. Though very costly, these serums are issued free by the Department of

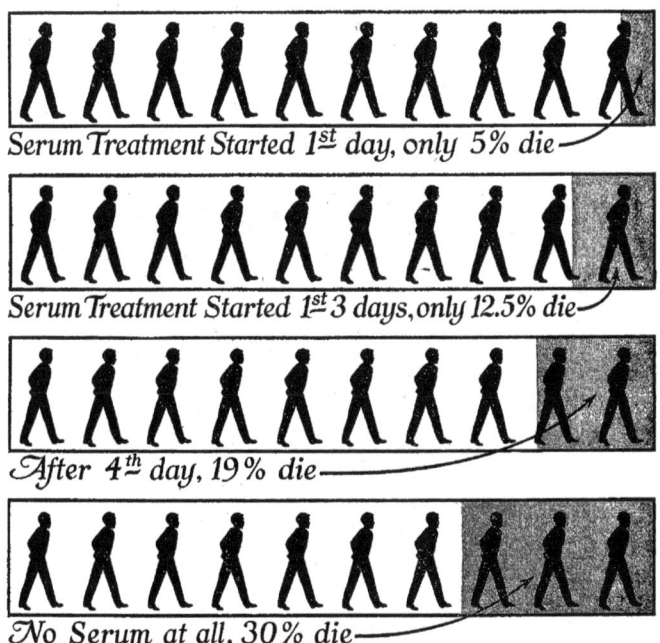

CALL THE DOCTOR AT FIRST SYMPTOMS

Serum Treatment Started 1st day, only 5% die

Serum Treatment Started 1st 3 days, only 12.5% die

After 4th day, 19% die

No Serum at all, 30% die

The earlier pneumonia serum is given the more lives are saved.

CALL THE DOCTOR EARLY

Public Health. Unfortunately there are not serums for all types of pneumonia, but those which are available can be used to treat about 65% of cases and other serums will probably be added as time goes on. Certain of the rarer types of serum are obtainable commercially at present. Most but not all cases of pneumonia may be treated with serum. The doctor must decide.

VII. Call the Doctor at First Symptoms.

The chances for complete and rapid recovery from pneumonia are much greater among those patients who receive an adequate amount of serum early in the disease than among those who are treated later.

HOW TO PREVENT PNEUMONIA

PREVENT PNEUMONIA

1- *If you have a Bad Cold, Go to Bed.*
2- *Call Doctor Immediately if Chills or Fever develop.*
3- *Stay away from people with Colds.*
4- *Avoid crowds, Particularly in "Pneumonia Season."*
5- *Live and Work in Well-Ventilated rooms.*
6- *Remember Pneumonia is Contagious.*

Hours count. Pneumonia is an emergency. In fact, early adequate serum treatment can save at least half of those who would otherwise die. If all pneumonia patients could be treated on the first day of the disease a tremendous saving of lives would result. These facts drive to the conclusion that the layman must learn what the early symptoms of pneumonia are and that the doctor must be called as soon as pneumonia is even suspected. No one but a doctor can administer serum.

VIII. How to Prevent Pneumonia

The prevention of pneumonia affords a very difficult problem. As yet, there is no vaccine which is proven to be of practical value but recently great strides have been made toward the development of such a product. Certain general measures may be of value in cutting the incidence of this disease. Many factors which predispose persons to infection by pneumococci are to be avoided. These factors are somehow associated with a lowering of bodily resistance to the pneumonia germs and enable these organisms to gain a foothold in the lungs and to cause inflammation there.

Among the more important are chilling, exhaustion, dissipation and exposure. Certain common infections of the upper respiratory tract are also predisposing factors. If for some reason there has been overexposure to cold or wet or some other excess, or if one is overfatigued, the time-honored measures of good food, hot bath and bed-rest are well advised and may result in regaining bodily resistance and in prevention of pneumonia.

Recent studies have shown that certain common virus infections, especially the common cold and grippe or influenza, may actually cause specific inflammatory changes in the lung tissue, as well as in the upper respiratory tract, and may prepare the lung tissue for invasion by pneumococci.

Many physicians believe that to avoid or properly care for the common cold is to remove the most important single predisposing factor of pneumonia. The majority of pneumonia patients tell the doctor that it started with a cold. Anyone with a bad cold should go to bed. If chills or fever develop a doctor should be called immediately. Overcrowding of living, sleeping or working quarters greatly favors the spread of the causative agents of colds and of pneumococci. Avoid crowds, particularly in the months of November through April, a period which has been aptly called the "Pneumonia Season."

Pneumonia, though not as contagious as scarlet fever or measles, is definitely communicable. Many cases of contact infection have been observed. Special precautions must be taken to avoid unnecessary exposure to patients or to recently recovered cases who may still harbor the pneumococci in their throats. Each person caring for a case of pneumonia should avoid contact with sputum, nasal secretions or breath droplets from the patient as these contain the germs. It is by getting these into the nose or mouth that the disease may be contracted or spread.

Sometimes certain types of pneumonia occur in epidemics. Remember, pneumonia is contagious!

RABIES

BY B. BARRETT GILMAN, M.D.

*Assistant Director, Division of Communicable Diseases
Massachusetts Department of Public Health*

Rabies, sometimes called "hydrophobia," is a fatal disease in man. Once the symptoms of this disease develop, death is certain to result. Although the disease may attack all mammals, the dog is most frequently afflicted, and this animal is almost always responsible for the infection of man.

It is essential that the layman be informed about this disease because it is highly probable that some time in his life a member of his family or a neighbor will be bitten by a dog, and the possibility of rabies will then automatically arise. Furthermore, the well-informed layman who owns a dog can do much to protect his valuable pet against the disease.

Cause and Method of Spread

Rabies is caused by an organism so small that it will pass through the finest of filters and therefore is called a filtrable virus. A few other diseases which are produced by a filtrable virus are measles, influenza, and infantile paralysis. The virus of rabies can be found in the brain, several organs of the body, and, most important of all, in the salivary secretions of an animal which has the disease. Animals and man contract rabies through the salivary secretions of a rabid animal. Generally the portal of entry is the wound resulting from a bite. But it is important to know that a cut, scratch, or other break in the skin, if contaminated with the saliva of a rabid animal, may produce the disease. The virus may be found in the saliva of animals several days before any symptoms of rabies actually appear. When introduced into the body, the virus travels through the nerves to the brain. Symptoms of the disease usually develop about six weeks after exposure to rabies. This incubation period varies a good deal. Symptoms may appear in ten days to six months or longer. The closer the portal of entry is to the brain and the more severe the lacerations, the shorter is the time before symptoms develop. If early and adequate treatment is instituted, there is practically no chance that rabies will occur.

Symptoms of Rabies in the Dog

The dog owner should familiarize himself with the symptoms of this disease in the dog. When most people speak of a rabid dog, they picture an animal running madly through the streets and biting all in his path; but probably no more than half the rabid dogs behave in this manner. There are two types of canine rabies, the dumb and the furious. The symptoms in the dog may be divided into three stages.

In both the furious and dumb forms, the initial stage is frequently overlooked because the symptoms may be extremely mild. Sharp observation will generally show that the animal is somewhat irritable, restless, and gloomy. The dog's eyes, however, seem unusually alert, and occasionally the dark pupil is larger in one eye than in the other. The animal often snaps at imaginary objects, slinks into out-of-the-way places in the home, and may at times show unusual affection by licking the shoes, hands or face of members of the household. This stage lasts for about one day.

In the second stage of the dumb form, the animal has a peculiar howl, shows difficulty in swallowing; paralysis attacks the jaw so that the mouth hangs open, and he drools a ropy saliva. Usually at this stage the owner imagines that a bone or some other object is caught in the animal's throat, and the owner will frequently reach into the animal's throat to remove the suspected object; it is during such a procedure that his hands become thoroughly covered with saliva, which contains the rabies virus. Infection may well follow such a procedure if there are cuts, scratches or abrasions on the hands.

The second stage of the furious form is quite different. Here there is no difficulty in swallowing, although the animal generally refuses its food. He howls continually, is markedly restless, and chews all manner of objects including shoes and furniture. He begins to snap at people and animals, and as the disease progresses he strives to leave the house. If he succeeds, he is apt to wander for miles, biting indiscriminately all moving objects, be they man or animal. It is during such a run that a number of animals and people become inoculated with the rabies virus. This second stage lasts for about three to four days.

The final stage is the same in both types. The animal becomes dull; the eyes become lusterless; the mouth hangs open, a dry tongue and ropy saliva becoming more apparent; progressive paralysis follows, as evidenced by inability to swallow, staggering, and convulsions.

If any of these symptoms appear, a veterinarian should be called so that the disease may be diagnosed before the infection is spread to people or animals. It is important to remember that in both the dumb and furious forms the virus of rabies is exactly the same. The prophylactic treatment of the person exposed is the same no matter which form of rabies is displayed in the animal.

The Control and Prevention of Rabies

If we could prevent the infected animals from spreading the disease to the noninfected, we would control rabies. England has managed to accomplish this feat because the island is geographically isolated, and measures of isolation and quarantine of all dogs brought into England have prevented the introduction of infected animals to the island. With the government setup in this State it is impossible to administer area control effectively. An enlightened community, which requires muzzling or restraint of dogs and combines with this an effective program of removing stray dogs, can do much toward preventing bites and the possibility of rabies. However, if its neighboring community has not embarked on such a program, much of its good work is spoiled. The dog owner and other members of the community can do much toward the furtherance of such control measures by their sympathy and support of such regulations when they are put into effect.

Muzzling and restraint orders are at best only temporary expedients, and the dog owner must face the fact that his animal may at some time be exposed to rabies. There are measures which can be taken to increase the resistance of the dog to rabies so that possibility of this disease is markedly reduced. Dog owners can have their dogs inoculated with a single dose of vaccine each year. Such a yearly inoculation would not only protect a valuable pet but would do a great deal toward preventing the spread of this disease to humans and animals alike. The occasional failure of such inoculation is usually encountered where the animal has been severely bitten, particularly about the head or neck. Some communities in Massachusetts provide clinics where, at a nominal fee, the dog owner may have his animal inoculated against rabies.

The final method of preventing this disease is the protective immunization of persons known to have been exposed to a rabid or suspected rabid animal. It was Louis Pasteur who, toward the close of the last century, discovered a method of preventing this disease. He found that there was enough time between exposure to rabies and the appearance of symptoms to allow for the administration of an efficient vaccine for prevention. Even today the injections are frequently referred to as "Pasteur treatments." The heavy toll of life taken by this disease before Pasteur's discovery has now been markedly reduced.

Since the disease in man is fatal, and since the number of persons bitten by dogs which had or may have had rabies is so large, a great number of persons annually receive the antirabic vaccine. In 1937, Massachusetts had well over ten thousand persons bitten by dogs, and treatment had to be recommended to over one thousand such persons. To insure that the exposed individual can readily obtain antirabic vaccine, a legislative act was passed in 1934 which made it incumbent upon the local boards of health to provide antirabic vaccine treatment when indicated. Generally the board of health is reimbursed for such treatment from the dog fund administered by the county commissioners.

What to Do in Case of Dog Bite

It is important for the citizen to know what to do in the event that he is bitten by a dog. Such information will lead him to take steps which frequently will obviate the necessity of receiving antirabic inoculations. Intelligent action upon his part will prevent any possibility of his contracting this disease. The following is the procedure recommended by the Massachusetts Department of Public Health:

(1) Do not kill the dog. If you are the owner, tie it up until your local animal inspector has pronounced it safe to release. He will keep it under observation for two weeks to make sure that it is not developing rabies. If the dog is owned by someone else, obtain the name of the owner and notify the local board of health. They will notify the animal inspector, who will keep the dog under observation. If the dog is a stray and its owner is unknown, notify the local board of health, giving as complete a description of the animal as possible so that they may take steps to find it.

(2) After learning the identity of the dog, go at once to your family physician. He will cauterize the wound to help prevent the development of rabies in case the dog proves to be rabid. Cauterization helps but it cannot be relied upon. Mercurochrome or iodine does not cauterize.

(3) If you have been bitten about the face, head or neck, or have received many severe lacerations, you should begin antirabic treatment immediately. It is with such bites that rabies is most likely to occur in a comparatively short time, and the earliest possible treatment is therefore indicated.

(4) If it is impossible to locate the dog which did the biting, you will never know whether or not it was rabid. In this case the only safe course to follow is to take antirabic treatment.

(5) If the dog is located, it must be kept under observation. Should it become sick, the animal inspector will arrange to have its head examined in the State Laboratory. It is possible to tell by such examination whether or not the dog had rabies, but if the dog was killed immediately, such examination often shows nothing, for the disease may not have progressed far enough to be detected under the microscope, even though the saliva may contain the virus.

(6) If it is necessary to shoot an animal for the protection of others, it should not be shot through the head, since this may interfere with the laboratory examination of the brain.

(7) If the biting animal has been killed without being held for observation and without subsequent laboratory examination of the head, you will never know whether or not the animal had rabies, and the safest procedure is to take the preventive inoculations.

(8) If laboratory examination shows the dog was rabid, you will be notified by the State Department of Public Health. With this notification, you and other persons bitten or intimately exposed to this animal will be urged to take the antirabic vaccine. It does not pay to take a chance, for if rabies develops, there is no treatment for it.

These statements should not be interpreted as a flat recommendation that all persons so bitten or exposed to dogs should be given treatment, but rather as those conditions under which treatment is recommended if the circumstances surrounding the case indicate to the attending physician that the patient is in need of treatment.

REMEMBER:

(1) Don't kill or permit another to kill a dog that has bitten someone; keep it under observation.
(2) Always consult your physician at once.
(3) Report all dog bites to your board of health.
(4) If the dog is rabid, antirabic treatment should be begun at once.
(5) Bites on the face, head or neck, or multiple severe lacerations usually require immediate antirabic treatment.
(6) Bites by stray dogs or those which cannot be located should be treated as though the dog were known to be rabid.
(7) If the dog is pronounced rabid by a veterinarian, don't wait for the laboratory report; begin treatment at once.

SCARLET FEVER

By J. E. Gordon, Ph.D., M.D.
*Professor of Epidemiology and Preventive Medicine
Harvard Medical School, Boston*

For many years scarlet fever has been a well-recognized member of that group of acute infectious diseases characterized by an eruption of the skin. Scarlet fever still conforms to the descriptions of early medical men, but gradually it has become apparent that there is more to scarlet fever than the ordinarily accepted form; that many mild indefinite infections occur; that scarlet fever may be scarlet fever and yet lack even its most distinctive feature, the rash. The problem medically and as it affects the public health, is not as simple as once supposed.

Classical scarlet fever is a well-defined entity. If the disease is to develop following exposure to the infectious agent, the first symptoms usually appear within an interval of three or four days. The first manifestations are a feeling of indisposition, lassitude, a sense of tiredness, perhaps some fever. With children, attacks of vomiting are not uncommon. These initial disturbances are not essentially different from those of many other acute infectious diseases. Rather quickly comes the first indication that the disease may be scarlet fever. The patient develops a sore throat. This is a relatively severe sore throat in comparison with the sore throat of a similar infectious disease, diphtheria. A generalized eruption of the skin, the most characteristic feature of scarlet fever, develops two or three days after the first indication of illness. First noticed on the chest and body, it extends rapidly to include most of the skin surfaces, except that the face is largely spared. This is a truly red rash, so red that the name "scarlet fever" is well taken. There are really two parts to this rash; a well-defined, generalized flush, and superimposed on it, innumerable bumpy spots which give a distinct roughness to the skin. The eruption lasts for three or four days, then begins to fade and usually has disappeared by the end of a week. The last stage of the disease, desquamation of the skin, comes some time later, as a rule in the third week of illness. The outer layers of the skin peel off, usually in fine, bran-like scales, but sometimes in fairly large pieces. The extent of desquamation conforms in general to the severity of the rash; the more extensive and well-defined the rash, the greater is the amount of desquamation. Desquamation occurs because of injury to the skin caused by toxin or poison formed by the infectious agent, a hemolytic streptococcus. The patient has usually made a complete recovery after two weeks, although desquamation may continue for another week or more. Barring intervening complications, which unfortunately are all too frequent, scarlet fever has now run its course.

Complications may develop at any time during the illness, but are most common in the second or third week. They represent a wide variety of medical conditions, but can be divided into four general groups. The first includes conditions resulting from extension of the local infection in the throat to neighboring parts of the body. Thus, enlargement of the glands of the neck, involvement of the nasal sinuses, or infection of the ear and the nearby mastoid process, are of fairly common occurrence.

The second group of complications includes those related to generalized dissemination of the poisonous substances elaborated by the infectious agent. The kidneys and the heart are affected. This group of complications is much less common in the United States than formerly, chiefly because scarlet fever these days is so much milder than it used to be.

The infectious agent that causes scarlet fever usually remains localized in the throat. Sometimes it escapes into the circulating blood and can then give rise to the most diverse complications in remote parts of the body, causing blood poisoning, meningitis, or the production of pus in the chest. Fortunately these serious manifestations are uncommon.

Finally, as is true of many infectious diseases, the lowered general resistance that follows an attack of scarlet fever may permit successful invasion by a second infectious agent. Children convalescing from scarlet fever occasionally develop pneumonia.

Scarlet fever in the typical form described serves as its own warning. Unfortunately the manifestations are not always so definite. The rash may last for only a few hours and there may be no subsequent peeling of the skin. In other circumstances, no eruption is observed and the infection is first recognized as scarlet fever by low grade desquamation. These indefinite forms of scarlet fever may have equally severe complications, without the valuable warning to obtain good medical care that is furnished by the fiery red eruption of the classical disease.

Finally, scarlet fever infection can occur in so mild a form that there is only sore throat, or no more than a slight fever. There is good evidence that the infection may extend still further into hazy indefiniteness, so that signs may be completely lacking even to the eye of the expert physician; and yet the existence of scarlet fever infection can be demonstrated by appropriate laboratory tests and, more important, by the fact that the affected individual thereafter remains immune.

A tendency exists to discount these mild, atypical and indefinite forms of scarlet fever. This is unfortunate; unfortunate from the standpoint of the person affected because with neglect there is increased liability to complications; unfortunate from the standpoint of the community, because these mildly infected persons can spread the infection to others just as well as a person with all the features of scarlet fever, perhaps even more so because contact is not limited by proper isolation. Mild, indefinite and unrecognized scarlet fever infections are common. Much progress in prevention will result if sore throats of children are given more consideration and have the adequate medical attention which they so well warrant.

Year by year scarlet fever has become a milder disease in the United States. The proportionate number of deaths is at present less than it was twenty years ago and, compared to conditions fifty or sixty years ago, the death rates indicate almost another kind of disease (see Graph). While the number of deaths per unit of population has decreased, the infection is nevertheless just about as prevalent now as it ever was. Stated differently, the number of deaths from scarlet fever has decreased remarkably, whereas the number of cases remains about the same. There are now relatively few deaths from the acute infection itself, and those that occur are almost wholly due to complications.

Not all people contract scarlet fever in the course of a lifetime. This is in contrast to measles, a disease that relatively few escape. The reason for this is that many persons become immune through inconsequential,

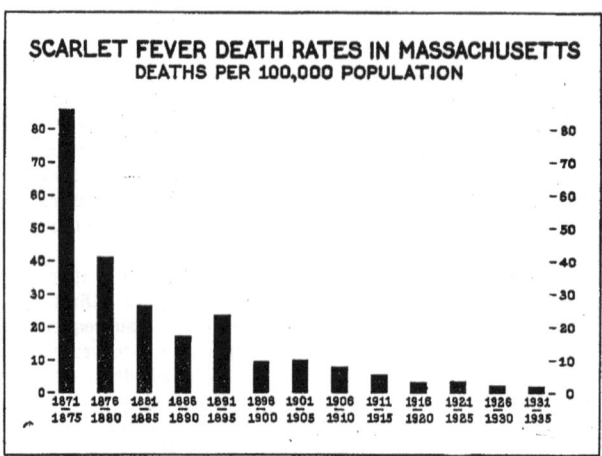

ill-defined infection, and thus are protected against the normal attack. Infection thus appears to be well-nigh universal, but the disease in its recognized form is not. That such mild infections can engender protection, naturally suggests the practicability of artificially induced resistance through immunization procedures.

Preventive measures against scarlet fever have the objective of decreasing both number of deaths and number of cases. Quite apparently three groups of people are concerned. The first includes patients who have contracted scarlet fever; the second, persons who have been directly exposed to infection through contact with the patient; and the third, members of the general community.

With scarlet fever as mild as it currently is in the United States, the ordinary infection responds well to rest in bed and the well-ordered regimen which a physician may prescribe for any acute infection. A hemolytic streptococcus antitoxin has been developed and its use is advisable in the more severe infections. It exerts a beneficial effect on the acute symptoms and few complications occur during convalescence. This serum is derived from immunized horses. Serum prepared from the blood of people recently recovered from scarlet fever can be substituted to good end, if horse serum is not well tolerated. The curative effect is essentially the same. In the uncommon but severe form of the disease known as septic scarlet fever, the best results follow transfusion of whole blood from another person in early convalescence. Under all circumstances, a prolonged and carefully ordered convalescence is essential. Scarlet fever more than most infections requires the advice of a competent physician, because there can be so many and such unexpected events.

Common public health practice prescribes strict isolation of a patient with scarlet fever until recovery. The benefits of this procedure to the general health of the community have probably been overrated. Not so many years ago, all patients with scarlet fever were isolated for six weeks. Today, three weeks' isolation is the usual recommendation, and in a number of cities adults with scarlet fever are isolated for no more than two weeks. Distinction should be made between isolation for the protection of the public and isolation for the protection of the patient. From the standpoint of the public, all that can be expected from isolation will likely be attained by restriction for three weeks. Strictly medical reasons may demand further limitation of the patient's activities. Given sanitary home conditions and the guarantee that adequate medical care and isolation can be provided, it is advisable that most patients with scarlet fever remain at their homes. Hospitalization is indicated when an infection is unusually severe, because of a serious complication, or because of inability to provide adequate home isolation.

What of the members of the family and others who have been exposed to infection? Most public health regulations require that persons in intimate contact be confined to the premises until one week after the last contact with the patient, and this means a relatively long quarantine period if the patient remains at home. Young children are best removed at once to the home of relatives or friends. They can then resume their usual activities of school or play after one week. In general, the current tendency is toward more liberal regulations in respect to employed adult members of the family. With reasonable precautions, it appears safe for the head of the household to continue with his usual employment, unless it has to do with food preparation. The economic loss from quarantine procedures is material and liberalization within limits of safety should be encouraged.

Like most infectious diseases, scarlet fever is particularly dangerous for young children. For individuals of this age and for all children not in good health, brief protection can be afforded by administration of human convalescent serum, the same product used in the treatment of severe cases. This will protect about 85 per cent of susceptible contacts for three weeks.

There remains the consideration of control measures as they affect the community at large. One of the first essentials is that every case of scarlet fever, no matter how mild, be reported to the recognized health authority. This is a legal obligation not only of physicians and of nurses, but of the householder as well. Reporting should be considered as something more than a legal requirement. It is a moral obligation of every member of a community. Only through knowledge of where scarlet fever exists can the extent of an outbreak be determined and appropriate control measures applied.

The same attention should be given to sore throats, as to any other form of scarlet fever among family contacts.

Much progress has been made in the control of diphtheria since a reliable method of artificial immunization was developed. Immunity to this disease can be produced before the age at which danger to the infection commonly occurs. This would be the desirable measure for protection of the community against scarlet fever. Unfortunately a satisfactory method has not as yet been developed. By injecting a small amount of streptococcus toxin into the skin, it is possible to determine whether or not a person is resistant to the disease. It is likewise possible to inject larger quantities of the toxin and artificially produce resistance. This immunity certainly acts against a part of the symptoms of scarlet fever, the rash, the toxemia and certain of the complications. It cannot be assured that infection without these symptoms does not occur. The use of this method involves a series of five treatments and the reactions are generally too frequent, and sometimes as severe as the disease itself. The procedure is recommended for those whose occupation brings them into repeated contact with scarlet fever infections, such as nurses and hospital attendants. It is worth-while in countries where the acute manifestations of scarlet fever are unusually severe. Clear-cut evidence that it will appreciably limit the spread of scarlet fever in a general population is still lacking. It is a worth-while measure for selected individuals and under particular circumstances, but as yet has not been developed to the point where it can be recommended as a general public health measure.

SMALLPOX

By Roy F. Feemster, M.D.
Director, Division of Communicable Diseases
Massachusetts Department of Public Health

The story of smallpox is a fascinating one. Its beginning dates back to earliest antiquity. All of the most ancient medical writers mention the disease, but their descriptions show that it had not been separated from other acute diseases characterized by a skin rash. In fact, it was not until modern times that measles, scarlet fever, and chicken pox were recognized as being different from each other and from smallpox.

It is difficult for us in the present age to realize that until less than 150 years ago medical men were helpless to stop the epidemics of smallpox which periodically invaded every continent and every community, laying low every person who had not previously had the disease, slaying outright one-quarter of those who became ill, and leaving the features of most of the survivors disfigured with deep blemishes. Even the royalty in the capitals of the nations could not escape, though artists were sometimes kind and failed to reproduce all of the pock marks when painting their portraits. The disease was so highly contagious that when it gained access to a population which had been free from it for a few years, it spread like wildfire in spite of every effort of medical men of the day.

The first attempt to control the disease in the western world began in 1716 when Lady Mary Montague wrote from Constantinople to friends in England about how people in that part of the world inoculated themselves with material from a mild case of smallpox and acquired a mild form of the disease instead of waiting to get the severe form when the next epidemic came along. The practice, called inoculation, soon spread throughout Europe and was popular until vaccination was introduced.

Inoculation was not a perfect solution of smallpox prevention. Some of those inoculated really died of the resulting smallpox, but the chances of surviving were much greater, only about one case in 100 proving fatal, instead of 25 out of 100. The inoculated disease was just as contagious as the natural disease, and severe cases were contracted from individuals who were only mildly ill.

It remained for an observation made by farm folk to start an investigation which produced a more perfect solution. Farmers in England had observed that those who milked cows infected with cowpox and acquired the disease on their hands, failed thereafter to catch smallpox. Edward Jenner, a country physician, in 1796 heard a dairymaid say, "I am not afraid of smallpox because I have had cowpox." He went to see John Hunter in London, who had been his former instructor, and asked him what he thought about the idea. To this question Hunter made his famous reply, "Don't think. Try it." So Jenner went back and began transferring material from cowpox lesions to individuals who had not had smallpox. When these individuals were later exposed to smallpox, they failed to contract the disease. Jenner published his observations in 1798 in a book entitled "An Inquiry Into the Causes and Effects of Cowpox." In such a simple manner a discovery was made which was to rid the world of a disease which had caused more suffering, more permanent disfigurement, and more deaths than any other single disease.

It will be interesting at this point to see how quickly these new ideas reached the American shores. Early in Colonial days smallpox had become firmly established on this continent. It is usually agreed that it was absent from the New World until brought over from Europe by early explorers. For instance, a negro slave who had the disease was with the expedition of Cortez in 1520 and started an epidemic in Mexico which spread from tribe to tribe and eventually caused the death of more than three and a half million Indians. It was imported by ship to these shores time and again, and is supposed to have been the disease which killed a large number of Indians in New England just before the landing of the Pilgrims, which aided that small group to maintain its foothold on these shores. The disease, therefore, became as serious a scourge on this continent as it had been in the Old World for many centuries.

In 1718, two letters, which had received very little attention when published in the *Transactions of the Royal Society of London*, were brought to Massachusetts. These letters, one a communication from a physician in Constantinople, and the other from Venice, described the practice of inoculation which later Lady Mary Montague was to make popular in England. These two letters were read by Cotton Mather, the famous Boston preacher who, with Doctor Zabdiel Boylston, began to favor the practice. Despite the opposition of a large number of the influential people of the Colony, Doctor Boylston continued to inoculate those who applied to him, and by the end of ten years many of those who had been the greatest opponents of inoculation had been convinced that it was better to have the mild disease than to have it in the severe form. Thereafter, inoculation was practiced widely throughout the Colonies.

In 1799, Doctor Benjamin Waterhouse, of Cambridge, received a copy of Jenner's book. He began immediately to try to obtain cowpox material from England. He eventually received a supply and on July 8, 1800 vaccinated his son, Daniel, aged 5. Four other individuals were likewise vaccinated and two months later these individuals were sent to a smallpox hospital where they were inoculated with material taken from a smallpox patient. Not one of them contracted smallpox. The same kind of experiment was repeated two years later, this time with nineteen children who had been vaccinated, with the same result.

After these clear-cut demonstrations of the efficacy of vaccination with cowpox, the practice became quite popular throughout the States. In 1809, Massachusetts passed a law which made it compulsory for towns to choose committees to have charge of the vaccination of the inhabitants. The number of deaths from smallpox began to drop immediately, but by 1837 a population had grown up which did not know at firsthand the horrors of smallpox, and the law was changed so that the formation of such committees was voluntary. During the years 1837 to 1855, vaccination fell into disuse, and smallpox again became an important cause of illness and death. A great increase in cases in 1854 and 1855 finally led to the passage of a law which required parents and guardians to vaccinate all children at two years of age, and unvaccinated children were to be excluded from schools. These laws were poorly enforced, however, and the number of unvaccinated individuals continued to increase.

In 1872, a widespread epidemic swept through Boston and other communities, and special efforts were made to see that the laws passed in 1855 were satisfactorily enforced. Due to the agitation and better cooperation of local boards of health, a larger proportion of the population were vaccinated but not enough to eliminate the disease. In fact it took the epidemic of 1901 and 1902 in Boston and other Massachusetts communities to spur boards of health and school committees to bring the proportion of persons vaccinated up to a satisfactory level. The results of these efforts are shown by the fact that there has not been a single case of smallpox in Massachusetts since February, 1932.

While Massachusetts and certain other States are entirely free of smallpox, other States in the Union have a higher rate of infection than in most of the rest of the world. These high rates are in States where vaccination is neglected. In fact, there is a direct relationship between the laws of the States and the number of cases of the disease. During the last five years, those States which have compulsory vaccination laws had less than one case per 100,000 population each year. Those in which there is local option had six times as many cases, and those without any compulsory vaccination laws had twenty-three times as many cases (see Graph.)

Two varieties of smallpox are now found. The milder variety, which probably originated somewhere in the tropics, has spread to many parts of the world including the United States. While this variety does not produce as severe illness or as many deaths, it is still a loathsome and prostrating disease and much more to be feared than the mild reaction of vaccinia which results from vaccination. The severe form is still found in many parts of the world and continues to be as dreaded a disease as it has been in former centuries. From time to time an individual from one of these areas imports the severe type into our country, and in areas where vaccination is not practiced many deaths sometimes occur.

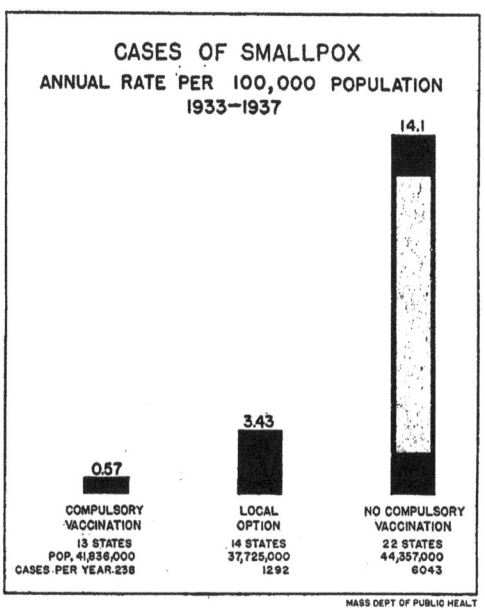

The first symptoms of the disease usually appear about ten to fourteen days after exposure. It is ushered in with a chill, high temperature, vomiting, and severe aches and pains. Occasionally a rash appears at this stage. The characteristic eruption appears with remarkable regularity on the third day of the illness. It usually appears first upon the forehead and near the edge of the hair, then spreads rapidly to the rest of the face, wrists, trunk and extremities. The eruption continues to multiply for two or three days before its definite limit is reached. It begins as small red spots which gradually increase in size and number. Within 24 hours they become elevated and are called papules. About the fourth or fifth day, these papules become vesicles, and when the fluid within the vesicles becomes pus the lesions are called pustules. Each pustule consists of many pockets so that the contents can not be completely evacuated by a single puncture. At the height of the eruption the patient presents a horrible spectacle with a very offensive odor. As the pustules begin to dry, they form scabs or crusts and other symptoms disappear gradually, while itching becomes almost unbearable, and scratching increases the liability of infection. As the crusts are shed, scarring or "pockmarks" often remain, their extent depending upon the depth to which the skin has been involved.

We can expect that sooner or later our good record of no cases of smallpox for over six years may be spoiled by having a person exposed to the disease enter the Commonwealth and become ill after arrival. While it may be impossible to keep smallpox entirely out of our State without vaccination of every citizen, as long as we continue the good work of recent years we need have no fear of a large outbreak because so many will be protected that there would be little chance of spread.

SYPHILIS

By ERNEST B. HOWARD, M.D.

Epidemiologist, Division of Genitoinfectious Diseases
Massachusetts Department of Public Health

Syphilis is a dangerous communicable disease caused by a germ (*Spirocheta pallida* or *Treponema pallidum*), and usually spread by intimate sexual contact. It was first recognized in Europe in the last few years of the 15th century when it became epidemic. The disease had no definite name until Fracastor, in 1530, wrote his famous poem, *Syphilis, Sive Morbus Gallicus* (Syphilis, or the French Disease) from which time it has been known as syphilis. Clinical knowledge of the disease increased rapidly but it was not until 1905 that Schaudinn and Hoffman saw a corkscrew-like germ under the miscroscope which they correctly recognized as the cause of syphilis. In 1907 Wassermann developed his famous blood test, and, in 1910, Ehrlich, after long and patient research, produced arsphenamine (606) for the treatment of the disease. With these three great discoveries the modern period in our knowledge and control of syphilis began.

The disease is usually acquired through sexual intercourse when the germ passes through the delicate mucous membranes and skin of the genitals and in less than 24 hours into the blood. A sore (chancre) develops, at the spot where the germs entered, about 10 days to eight weeks later. The chancre is usually painless and may look like a harmless pimple or cold sore.

It is very important to recognize this first sore of syphilis, because treatment started in this early stage gives the best results. Even without treatment, the chancre will soon disappear, but in a few weeks there may be many other signs of the disease. Usually a rash appears on the body and in the mouth, and there may be swollen glands, a sore throat, falling hair on the head and eyebrows, and vague pains in the muscles and joints. The rash and other symptoms may be so mild that the patient does not even notice them. This is called the secondary stage, and, as in the chancre stage, all the symptoms and the rash usually disappear even without treatment and most patients believe they are cured. Usually a long period of anywhere from three to 30 years elapses before the next, or tertiary, stage. In this last stage the serious, crippling complications of syphilis may occur. The most serious of these are syphilis of the brain and spinal cord causing insanity and locomotor ataxia, and syphilis of the heart, causing a very severe type of heart disease. A few fortunate patients never have any of these serious complications.

A pregnant woman with the disease can pass it on to the unborn child (so-called congenital syphilis). This may result in miscarriage, stillbirth, or early death of the infant born alive. Those babies who live often later develop serious eye trouble which may lead to blindness. A few develop insanity. On the other hand, some infants grow up normally and never have any trouble from the disease. Those born with syphilis cannot pass the disease on to their own children.

Syphilis is not spread by doorknobs, car straps, and toilet seats. The spirochete is so delicate that it quickly dies outside the body. Most patients are infected through intimate sexual contact, a very few through kissing, and very rarely a nurse or physician may be accidentally infected during the performance of some professional duty. The communicability of the disease grows less with time, the most infectious periods being the early, chancre stage and the secondary stage. In the chancre the germs are very numerous, and in the secondary stage the sores in the mouth and on warm, moist parts of the body may be highly infectious. After the secondary period has passed, usually less than a year after the onset of the infection, the disease can rarely be spread except by sexual intercourse, and after three to five years even this close contact will not often cause infection. Children born with the disease may have a discharge from the nose or sores on the body which are infectious, but these rarely occur after the age of six months. When these children are older they are not a source of danger to others, and when they marry they do not spread the disease in any contact.

With treatment, communicability in any ordinary social contact disappears in a matter of days and does not return unless treatment is irregular or insufficient.

Syphilis can be cured. Doctors now have efficient drugs which, if used regularly over a prolonged period, will stop the progress of the disease in almost all cases and also prevent its spread to the unborn infant. Treatment requires regular weekly injections for at least one and one-half to two years because serious relapse is liable to occur if treatment is irregular or is stopped too soon. Pregnant women with syphilis who are treated starting before the fourth month of pregnancy can be practically assured of a normal, healthy baby. Even if treatment is started later in pregnancy, the chances of bearing a normal baby are appreciably increased. Infected women should be treated throughout every pregnancy since treatment during one pregnancy does not insure normal offspring in later pregnancies. When the course of the disease is explained to patients, and when physicians, nurses, and social workers who manage their care have the proper sympathy and tact, it is found that most patients continue their treatment faithfully until cured.

Blood tests for syphilis become positive within two to four weeks after the chancre appears and usually remain positive for the patient's lifetime in the absence of treatment. During the two weeks before the blood test shows the disease, the diagnosis is made by obtaining fluid from the chancre and finding the spirochetes by examination under the microscope. A positive blood test, supported by signs and symptoms of the disease, means infection with syphilis but it does not tell if the disease is in a communicable stage nor does it indicate the future course of the disease. It does not show whether the disease was acquired in infancy or in adult life. The blood test does very little more than help the physician to detect the disease.

Syphilis is not a new public health program. Massachusetts, unlike most other states, has had an active program for the control of syphilis and its mate, gonorrhea, for many years. As early as 1894 the General Court passed an act which ordered that no discrimination be made against their treatment in the outpatient department of tax-supported hospitals, and a year later each city was required to provide treatment for patients who could not afford to pay. In 1918, Massachusetts became the first state to supply arsphenamine (606) free to physicians, clinics, and institutions treating syphilis. Since then other arsphenamine products and bismuth have been made available, and the Wassermann Laboratory and Bacteriological Laboratory have increased their services to the medical profession. The Department has maintained an active educational program including lectures to lay and professional groups, radio broadcasts, the distribution of over a million pieces of literature in the past few years, and, in cooperation with the Massachusetts Medical Society, a series of postgraduate medical lectures to the medical profession. In 1937, the legislature passed an act making it possible for the Department to provide clinic and other medical care for all patients with syphilis or gonorrhea who could not pay. This service has been provided in cooperation with local agencies.

The first national program to control syphilis, based on a sound idea of its prevalence and its manner of spread in society, was started by Surgeon General Parran in 1936. He publicized many facts that forced the public to recognize the problem and demand its solution. He pointed out that over a half million new infections occur every year, that at least 60,000 babies are born with syphilis every year through no fault of their own, and that 50 per cent of syphilis in women is innocently acquired after marriage through sexual contact with their husbands.

Much remains to be explained concerning the nature of the disease and the problems connected with its control, but it is probably safe to say that the stage is set for its control within our generation. To attain our goal we must maintain a healthy attitude toward the problem; we must realize the enormous number of innocent victims of the disease and also that it is necessary to cure all the infected, whether innocent or not.

TRICHINOSIS, A PREVENTABLE DISEASE

By DONALD AUGUSTINE, SC.D.

Department of Comparative Pathology and Tropical Medicine, Schools of Medicine and Public Health, Harvard University

Perhaps there is no other parasitic disease which has caused greater widespread interest of late in the United States than that commonly known as trichinosis. This disease occurs in almost every country, but, unlike most other parasitic diseases, is encountered most frequently in the Northern Hemisphere and rarely in the tropics. Recent studies carried on in Boston, Rochester, N. Y., Washington, D. C., New Orleans, Minneapolis, San Francisco and elsewhere show an extraordinary prevalence of trichinosis in the United States. In all probability it constitutes a greater health problem here than in any other country in the world.

Trichinosis is caused by very small parasitic worms known to science as *Trichinella spiralis*. They are commonly called "trichinae." The adult male and female worms live in the intestines of various mammals. After copulation the gravid female worm burrows deeply into the wall of the intestine where she deposits her progeny, hundreds of small, larval worms, directly into the lymph spaces. With the flow of lymph they are eventually carried into the blood stream and by the blood stream they are carried through the lungs to every part of the body. Only those larvae live which reach and successfully enter the fibers of the skeletal muscles. All others are destroyed and disposed of within a short time by the white cells of the blood within the tissues to which they were carried by the circulating blood. The larvae, safe within the muscle fibers, first grow somewhat in length. Each small worm then assumes a spiral form and a capsule is formed around it. These capsules are so small that they usually cannot be detected with the unaided eye, and the worm within the capsule can never be identified except by microscopic examination. It is now known as an encapsulated or encysted larva and is the infective stage of the parasite.

The life span of the adult worms in the intestine is limited to about four or five weeks. After the reproductive period is over they die and are then discharged from the intestine with the feces. The encapsulated larvae, however, may remain alive, but dormant, for years within the skeletal muscles. It is only when such parasitized (*trichinous*) meat is eaten by another susceptible individual that the infection can be transmitted. When this occurs, the capsules are digested away by the action of the gastric juices of the new host and the liberated worms pass into the small intestine. Here they rapidly grow into adult male and female worms. Reproduction and the dissemination and encystment of a new crop of larvae again take place. Human beings, swine and rats are highly susceptible to this infection.

Trichinosis in man is almost invariably due to the ingestion of raw or undercooked infected pork or to the ingestion of inadequately cooked or cured meat products containing infected pork muscle. Of late, a few severe and fatal cases of trichinosis developed in California from eating infected bear meat. Trichinosis in swine is usually the direct result of their ingesting raw trichinous pork, either in garbage or the offal at the time of slaughter. Trichinosis is seldom encountered in swine raised on pasture lands, grain or root vegetables. Swine fed upon cooked garbage and cooked offal are also free of trichinosis, provided the garbage and offal were adequately cooked.

The incidence of trichinosis among rats is usually very high. The source of rat trichinosis is, like that for swine, raw infected pork scraps in garbage collected for swine, or in raw infected pork scraps that may be picked up in market districts or at slaughter establishments. Because of the high incidence of trichinosis in rats many authorities long held that rats were important reservoirs of infection for swine trichinosis. Swine are known to eat dead rats readily when such are thrown to them, but they are seldom known to kill and eat rats, even when rats are numerous in hog pens or around garbage-feeding establishments. It is now generally accepted that rats are not a reservoir of trichinosis for swine, that trichinosis in swine is chiefly of porcine origin (raw or inadequately cooked pork scraps and offal) and that the infection in rats is also of porcine origin and further transmitted from rat to rat through their cannibalistic habits, but that the infection in the rat is rarely transmitted to swine.

The severity of trichinosis largely depends upon the number of encapsulated parasities ingested, the tissues invaded by the larval forms and the physical condition of the individual. Gastrointestinal symptoms, nausea, vomiting, diarrhea and abdominal pain, are frequently noted within a few days after eating the infective meat, which are followed by muscular pain and tenderness, fever and chills, cough, edema of the eyes, a skin rash and prostration. Complete recovery is slow. Vague rheumatic pains, experienced particularly upon rising, may persist for about a year. Death occurs most frequently during the third to the sixth week and seldom before the end of the second week or after the eighth.

Trichinosis manifests such a variable symptomatology that the diagnosis is often obscured when the patient is first seen by the physician. This is particularly true in mild and isolated cases. The disease is frequently confused with typhoid, colitis, influenza, bronchitis, sinusitis, pneumonia, scarlet fever, undulant fever, neuritis, heart diseases, encephalitis and meningitis. It is difficult, in the majority of cases, to demonstrate the actual presence of the parasite at any stage of the disease. The demonstration of the parasites in the meat responsible for the disease is most helpful in establishing the diagnosis and is not a difficult procedure with the present laboratory methods, if a sufficiently large piece is obtainable. Unfortunately, however, in many instances, the meat has been entirely consumed before the symptoms appear and the physician is consulted. The recognition and correct diagnosis in most cases must therefore depend on a careful history of the patient's illness, a complete physical examination, repeated blood examinations and serologic tests.

Every year outbreaks of trichinosis involving from a few to hundreds of persons are reported in the press from various parts of the United States. The outbreak is frequently due to swine raised privately and fed on garbage collected from a near-by town. At the time of slaughter the meat is widely distributed among relatives and friends. A good portion of the meat is made up into sausages which are allowed to dry somewhat and are then eaten after very little cooking. Early in 1935 an outbreak of this type occurred in Portland, Maine, which involved seventy-two persons with two deaths. Trichinae were found in the pork used in the manufacture of the sausage.

Again, early in December, 1936, a somewhat similar outbreak occurred in Flathead County, Montana. A father of eighteen children prepared sausages with pork from hogs slaughtered on his farm. Some of these sausages were eaten by his immediate family, and some were generously distributed to his married sons and daughters who, in turn, divided their portions with neighbors and friends. Most of the recipients ate their sausages without cooking or only after slight cooking. Thirty-four of these persons became ill with trichinosis, one of them died. One of the daughters ate some of the sausage only after it was well-cooked. She, alone, escaped infection. Samples of the sausage were sent to the laboratory of the Montana Livestock Sanitary Board for examination. They were found heavily infected with trichinae.

More recently an outbreak of trichinosis occurred in Rochester, New York. A large picnic was held by a social organization at which pork sausages, hurriedly cooked, were served. Eighty-five persons became ill with trichinosis and one died.

Trichinosis is always shocking when it thus occurs in epidemic form and many persons are involved. However, without question, the actual number of sporadic and isolated cases far exceeds the number involved in reported outbreaks. Such cases constitute a serious phase of the trichinosis problem. They are often but mildly ill, they fail to come under the care of a physician, or they may present such variable symptoms that, without laboratory facilities, they pass unrecognized.

Unfortunately, pork infected with trichinae has all the outward appearance of uninfected pork. The dealer who has had the misfortune of selling trichinous pork which may have caused human suffering was no more aware that that particular roast, shoulder or chop contained trichinae than was the customer who made the purchase. We have no reliable means to guarantee fresh pork safe and free from trichinae. Microscopic inspection for trichinae is highly imperfect and is not included in the system of meat inspection in this country. The government stamp "United States Inspected and Passed" on pork does not mean that the meat is trichinae free and can be eaten safely without sufficient cooking. It may be infected with living trichinae, but, when adequately cooked, is absolutely safe, and is as wholesome and as nutritious as non-infected pork. In fact, all the human suffering from trichinosis could have been easily avoided, if only the pork had been adequately cooked. Pork should not be omitted from the diet because "it may be infected and therefore dangerous." Thorough cooking always renders it absolutely safe. The process of cooking it is merely another safeguard to human health comparable to the chlorination of drinking water and the pasteurization of milk.

A logical step in the prevention of human trichinosis would be the elimination of the source of the infection to swine. This would call for marked improvements in our present methods of hog raising, particularly, the abandonment of feeding raw or undercooked meat scraps. The cooking of garbage prior to feeding is possible. It is done successfully in a few places. In Canada, the feeding of swine upon garbage or swill, meat scraps and offal obtained elsewhere than on the premises where fed is prohibited under the Animal Contagious Disease Act. The measure is definitely a step in the right direction but, for obvious reasons, would fail to bring the problem under control.

For the present, our one and only reliable means of preventing trichinosis is the thorough cooking of all pork before it is eaten. In other words, the control of trichinosis rests within the household and with the housekeeper.

TUBERCULOSIS

By ALTON S. POPE, M.D.
Director, Division of Tuberculosis
Massachusetts Department of Public Health

From the standpoint of annual number of deaths and financial and social costs, tuberculosis still maintains its position as the most serious of the communicable diseases in the Commonwealth. In spite of a decline of 75 per cent in the death rate since 1900 (See Graph), tuberculosis last year took a toll of slightly over 1,900 lives, a total between four and five times as great as all of the recorded deaths from all other acute communicable diseases excepting influenza and the pneumonias. When to this is added the fact that the average duration of a case of tuberculosis is between three and four years and the cost of hospitalization per patient is approximately $1,000, some idea can be obtained of the burden of tuberculosis. Since the peak of tuberculosis comes between the ages twenty to forty years, the wage earner is frequently involved and in a large proportion of cases the care of the remainder of the family becomes the responsibility of the community, thus adding materially to both the financial and social costs of the disease.

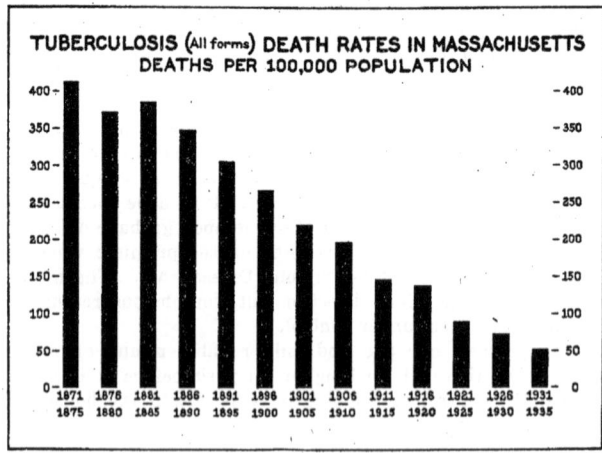

The steady decline of tuberculosis over the past seventy-five years should lead not to complacency but rather to a revaluation of the whole problem of control and a search for further factors which contribute to the continuation of tuberculosis, and especially to the development of more effective preventive measures.

Because of the long duration of the individual case of tuberculosis, the high case fatality, the long incubation period, and the social implications of the disease, control measures must differ widely from those with which we are familiar in such diseases as scarlet fever or diphtheria. On account of a duration of years instead of weeks, isolation of the patient and quarantine of the contacts is obviously not feasible, nor is it necessary. Infection with tuberculosis takes place, as a rule, not from single exposure, as in smallpox, but rather from continued contact with the patient with positive sputum, usually in the home or under similar conditions of close and continued contact. For the control of tuberculosis, we have available neither a specific immunization, which has reduced the deaths from diphtheria some 95 per cent in the past few years, nor any type of environmental regulation similar to that which has resulted in the practical disappearance of typhoid fever in Massachusetts.

Lacking these more direct means of control, we must attack tuberculosis with weapons suited to the nature of the disease. One of the most effective measures in the prevention of infection is the sanatorium treatment of the patient. In addition to hastening recovery, successful treatment renders the individual's sputum negative or noninfectious, thus making it possible for him to return safely to his family and community. Furthermore, the isolation of the patient in a sanatorium automatically separates him from others whom he might infect, and so removes the source of infection. Obviously, the earlier the disease can be recognized so that effective treatment can be started, the less is the danger of continued spread from sick to well individuals.

To insure prompt hospitalization of all active cases of tuberculosis as soon as the diagnosis is made, it is necessary to have both a sufficient number of sanatorium beds and provision for the financial support of patients unable to pay for their own care. It has been estimated that at least two sanatorium beds are necessary for each annual death from tuberculosis in a community. Taking into consideration state, county, municipal and federal sanatoria Massachusetts now has approximately 2½ beds for each annual death from the disease. To make these beds freely available to all who need them, the statutes provide that the city or town of legal settlement shall be financially responsible for the sanatorium care of tuberculosis patients who are unable to assume the burden themselves. Thus, modern sanatorium facilities are now freely available to all citizens in need of them.

One of the greatest obstacles to the prevention and the successful treatment of tuberculosis is the fact that the disease rarely gives rise to symptoms or signs until moderately or far advanced. This means that other members of the patient's family are often infected before he goes to the sanatorium and that his own prospect of recovery is much less favorable than if his disease had been recognized earlier. Since patients with early tuberculosis are unlikely to apply to their doctors or to clinics for examination, it has been necessary to reorganize our system of diagnostic dispensaries, and in Massachusetts this has been done chiefly around the sanatoria. All state and county sanatoria are authorized to maintain diagnostic outpatient departments and, upon request of cities and towns, to furnish this diagnostic service, including X-ray examination, in the surrounding communities. As a result, some twenty-two consultation clinics are now being operated by state and county sanatoria, both in the outpatient departments and in the outpatient departments of local general hospitals where X-ray facilities are available. In certain cases where arrangements with general hospitals cannot be made, clinics are being held with the use of portable X-ray units. Persons suspected of having tuberculosis may be referred to such clinics by their physicians or by local boards of health, and reports are made only to persons referring them.

Probably the most important change in preventive and control measures in tuberculosis has been the shift in emphasis from treatment to prevention. Although prevention and treatment are inseparably connected in tuberculosis, the difference in point of view is very significant. Too often the clinician has looked upon tuberculosis as an individual problem and has lost sight of its broader public health aspects. To be sure, the tubercle bacillus has been recognized as the cause of tuberculosis for over fifty years, but only within the past ten or fifteen years have we attempted to deal with tuberculosis primarily as a communicable disease. Hospitalization of the tuberculous individual has, it is true, reduced the individual foci of infection, but too often we have lost sight of the fact that this infection had been acquired from a previous case and and that other persons may have been infected from the same source. This means that if control measures are to be truly effective they must do the thing that is already being accomplished with such a disease as typhoid fever—determine the original source of infection, separate the infectious case from susceptible contacts, render him noninfectious, and be certain that further spread of the disease has not already taken place.

In tuberculosis this means examination with X-ray not only of the patient but of all members of his family and other persons with whom he may have come in intimate and continued contact. Only in this way can we be sure that a given source of spread has been eliminated. To do this, then, arrangements must be provided by which X-ray examination of the indigent cases and suspected cases, and all members of their families, may be available upon the same basis on which laboratory examination for sputum is now furnished. This requires in the first place a sufficient understanding of the nature of tuberculosis and the manner of spread so that the average person is willing to submit to such examinations. Such education is the function of the voluntary tuberculosis agency. Next, provision must be made for such examinations through the sanatoria as outlined above, or in the large cities through the local boards of health. Last and perhaps most important of all, the practicing physician must be sufficiently interested in the problem of tuberculosis control so that he routinely requires not only the X-ray checking of the individual case but the radiograph checking of each case and X-ray examination of family contacts who may provide the source of infection or the results of further family spread. The remarkable reductions of the acute communicable diseases have all resulted from the intelligent application of preventive measures, and in the long run the reduction of mortality depends far more upon prevention than upon treatment. In tuberculosis, this is equally true. The principal difference is the chronic nature of the disease which, to a peculiar extent, calls for individualization and concentration upon the individual as the source of infection.

What is the future in tuberculosis? Can we look forward to a situation comparable to that in typhoid fever or in diphtheria? As already pointed out, the problem in tuberculosis is more difficult than in either of those diseases, yet the general principles are the same. If the present trend in tuberculosis mortality can be continued for another twenty years, the disease will no longer be one of our major public health problems. Students of tuberculosis have reached the point where they are willing to say that the disease can be controlled. The case was recently well stated by the late Dr. W. H. Frost:

"It is a fair inference that in this country as a whole we have already reached the stage at which the biological balance is against the survival of the tubercle bacillus. . . . Eradication is an expectation sufficiently well grounded to justify shaping our tuberculosis program toward this definite end."

In Massachusetts such optimism seems justified. In the last fifteen years the percentage of reactors to the tuberculin test among school children has decreased approximately one-half. With further decrease of the incidence of infection in the general population, concentration of attention upon known cases and their contacts becomes relatively more effective. As case finding becomes more complete and routine X-ray examination assures the elimination of foci of infection, the proportion of unrecognized spreaders in the community will be further reduced. In addition to this, certain other techniques of case finding must be considered: first, routine X-ray examination of those groups known to have the highest incidence of tuberculosis. Association of tuberculosis and poverty is well known. In New York City it is found that among persons on the welfare rolls approximately 2½ per cent are suffering from tuberculosis.

Because tuberculosis occurs with the greatest frequency in the young adult age groups, persons employed in industry offer a fertile field for case finding. Misunderstandings on the part of workers and lack of appreciation of employers have seriously delayed work in this field, but routine pre-employment examination and subsequent re-examination of workers in industry, especially in trades known to be hazardous, offer one of the most promising fields for tuberculosis control.

An even more productive project would be routine X-ray examination of all patients admitted to general hospitals. Examinations in certain institutions have shown that approximately 1½ to 3 per cent of such persons have unrecognized tuberculosis. Here the cost of examination would not be prohibitive and the technical facilities are already available.

In Massachusetts some 700,000 school children have been tuberculin tested and the reactors X-rayed for the discovery of early tuberculosis in a group where the prognosis is otherwise poor. Although the incidence in this group is relatively low, in the high schools it is only by routine examination that cases can be found in a hopeful stage. Emphasis is now being placed upon the examination of high school rather than grade school students. As the majority of cases of tuberculosis are found through routine examination of family contacts, it should be possible in the future to omit the general examination of school children.

At the present time, services exist in Massachusetts for doing a complete job on the examination of contacts of all known cases of tuberculosis. The crying need is for more complete utilization of these facilities. This means the cooperation of patients, doctors, boards of health and nurses. The future course of tuberculosis in the Commonwealth depends upon the effectiveness of this cooperation.

TYPHOID FEVER

By Charles E. Gill, M.D.
District Health Officer, South Connecticut Valley District
Massachusetts Department of Public Health

The amazing decline in the number of cases and deaths due to typhoid fever during the last half century is one of the outstanding accomplishments of the public health agencies. The decline in the disease began as early as 1880 in Massachusetts (see Graph) and has continued without interruption since 1913 (Table I). During the years 1933-1937, less than three persons in each 100,000 population contracted the disease each year as against a figure of fifty-four during 1913-1917. At present, the chances of contracting typhoid fever in Massachusetts are one-fourth as great as in the United States as a whole. Among nine important diseases, typhoid fever ranked last (Table II) both as the cause of sickness and of death in the year 1937.

Certain outstanding features of the disease under present conditions are: typhoid fever is a year-round illness but still shows a tendency to be a "vacation" disease; the proportion of fatal cases is as large as when the disease was more prevalent; all age groups are about equally liable to contract the illness under proper conditions; and further reductions in mortality from this cause must depend upon preventive measures directed toward reducing the number of human cases and carriers from whom the infection may be spread.

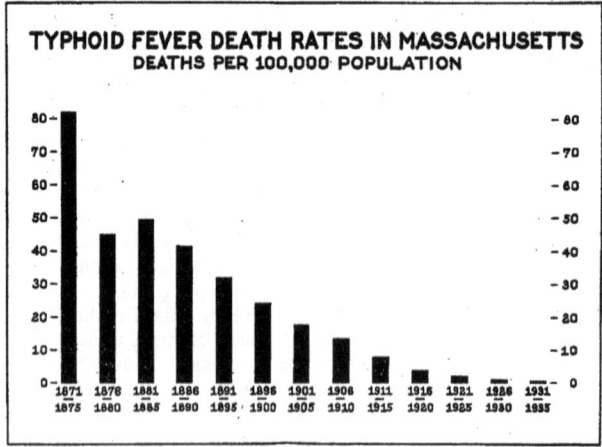

Table I.—Typhoid Fever in Massachusetts
1913-1937

5-year periods	Reported cases	Deaths	Percentages fatal cases
1913-1917	9996	1144	11%
1918-1922	4550	567	12%
1923-1927	2793	316	11%
1928-1932	1399	171	12%
1933-1937	657	68	10%

Table II.—Reported Cases and Deaths from Certain
Communicable Diseases in Massachusetts during 1937

Disease	Cases	Deaths	Percentage fatal cases
Tuberculosis (all forms)	3,897	1,887	
Lobar pneumonia	5,322	1,846	35%
Whooping Cough	13,333	95	
Meningicoccus meningitis	166	72	43%
Scarlet fever	8,480	38	
Measles	21,136	28	
Poliomyelitis	351	22	6%
Diphtheria	175	18	10%
Typhoid fever	114	13	11%

For the present generation with little firsthand acquaintance with this illness, a brief description is warranted. Typhoid fever is an acute communicable disease, of varying degree of severity, leading to death in 10% of cases, with a prolonged course of several weeks of bed-confining disability. The period from infection to onset is around two weeks, but variable from a few days to as long as a month, depending upon the number and manner of entrance of the typhoid bacilli into the body and the resistance of the person affected. The onset is gradual, featured by headache, fever, and loss of appetite; the height of the illness is reached in another week or so with continued high fever, skin eruption, delirium, restlessness, and loss of strength and weight. Convalescence is slow and full recovery may require several weeks or months. The principal sites of damage in the body are in the small intestine, bile passages, liver, and spleen. This damage may be of such severity as to lead to the serious complications of this illness, bleeding from and perforation of the intestinal tract. The cause of the disease is the typhoid bacillus taken into the body through the mouth with infected food or drink or other contaminated objects. The sick patient throws off the germs in the stools and urine during his illness, and a small percentage (2%-5%) of recovered patients become chronic "carriers" of the infecting germs. The treatment of such a severe and prolonged illness calls for the best medical and nursing care, not only to assure recovery of the patient but to prevent spread of the infection to well persons. There is no specific treatment in the form of drugs, vaccines, or serums, such as we possess for diseases like pneumonia and diphtheria. Most patients require and are given the advantages of hospital care during the acute stage of their illness. The detection of this now uncommon disease calls for laboratory studies of the blood, stools, and urine. This service is available through hospital and health department laboratories.

Knowledge of the means by which the typhoid germ reaches and enters the human body from another human "source" in dosage sufficient to produce typhoid fever is necessary for the understanding and application of effective preventive methods. A review of our experience during the last five years offers many helpful leads. During the period, 1933-1937, 657 cases have been reported and carefully investigated. Of this number only eighty-one cases could be related to outbreaks, the remaining cases occurring singly or in very small groups with little in common with other cases. Two of the outbreaks, causing ten cases and one death, were suspected of being due to private water supplies which were subject to pollution. Public water supplies in Massachusetts are surrounded by every safeguard, but private supplies in factories and homes in rare cases may be polluted by human sewage or accidental admixture with infected water not intended for drinking purposes. The remaining seven outbreaks, some merely multiple cases in a family, causing seventy-one cases and four deaths, were attributed to the contamination of food by typhoid "carriers" helping in the preparation or serving of the food. In each outbreak the "carrier" was found as a result of routine stool cultures obtained from the various persons engaged in preparing and serving the suspected food. Investigation of possible sources of infection in the larger group of cases not related to outbreaks led most often to the "carrier" as the source. Occasionally other members of the household or attendants of the sick patient contract typhoid fever, but these secondary cases are fewer each year, since hospital care has become so common and household contacts and nursing personnel are promptly and routinely protected by typhoid inoculations and careful antisepsis. Water-borne and milk-borne epidemics, even of small proportions, have fallen to very low levels with the availability and increasing use of safe public and private water supplies, effective methods of sewage disposal, and pasteurized milk. The principal source of infection under present conditions is the healthy "carrier" of the infecting organism. Among the sources of infection discovered in the investigation of cases, the "carrier" stands at the top of the list.

No domestic or wild animals have been found to harbor the germ. The disease must, therefore, be acquired from some human source, usually a healthy person giving a history of typhoid fever at some time in the past. Often, however, no illness recognizable as typhoid fever is remembered by the patient. The Widal test on the blood serum is positive or suspicious in over 90 per cent of such persons, and repeated cultures of the bile and stools yield the typhoid bacillus in abundance. This "carrier" through careless personal habits may readily contaminate, with infected fecal material, food and drink intended for himself as well as others. Such food or drink, unless the germs are killed by cooking, will produce typhoid fever when taken into the intestinal tract through the mouth in sufficient dosage by a susceptible person. During the last twenty years, 213 "carriers" have been discovered and their names placed on a confidential follow-up list for semiannual visiting by the district health officers. Of these, 165 were found in the course of investigating current typhoid cases by routine stool cultures on all available contacts of the reported case. The remaining "carriers" were found when routine release cultures obtained during the first year after onset of known typhoid fever showed the presence of typhoid bacilli throughout the whole year. At present, the list of known persons carrying the infecting germ numbers 135, while the estimated number of undiscovered "carriers" is probably nearer one thousand. As the result, we believe, of the semiannual visits emphasizing hand hygiene and periodic inoculation with typhoid vaccine of the household contacts, the known "carrier" seldom is responsible for additional cases. For the occasional "carrier" whose livelihood calls for public food handling, treatment of the condition by removal of the gall bladder is recommended. Such candidates for surgery are thoroughly studied before and after operation by cultural methods to assure accurate diagnosis and complete recovery from the "carrier" condition. To date, forty-two "carriers" have undergone gall bladder removal, nineteen at state expense, and none have failed to be cured eventually as shown by repeated stool and bile cultures obtained during the year following operation, although three who recently underwent operation have not as yet ceased to excrete organisms. Every such patient had demonstrable gall bladder disease, many with stone-formation, and not one had died at operation or during convalescence. With the continuing decline in the yearly toll of typhoid cases, the number of "carriers" produced and discovered each year will be outnumbered by those "carriers" dying of natural causes or submitting to surgical cure, thereby bringing about a net decline in the number of potential sources of infection.

It must be apparent that preventive measures depend upon steps taken to interrupt the "short circuit" between the infected intestinal excreta of the sick person or "carrier" and the food and drink of the susceptible population. Thus, the prevention of water-borne and milk-borne epidemics has largely materialized through the wider use of safe public water supplies, public sewage disposal systems, and pasteurized milk supplies. This approach is not always practicable on a large scale in other than urban areas. However, individual water and milk supplies, as well as sewage disposal methods, can be made safe at small cost and these measures have been more widely applied in recent years in certain areas under Federal aid. Typhoid vaccine is of real value in protecting certain groups, such as the armed defense forces, household contacts of typhoid cases and "carriers," hospital personnel, and other groups exposed to sewage-pollution hazards. The doses must be repeated periodically to maintain a satisfactory level of immunity, and only relative protection can be expected. Effective hygienic precautions in the care of the typhoid case and the same precautions exercised by the known "carrier" will prevent many needless secondary cases. The menace of the "carrier" becomes less when diligent search for them is made on every occasion when one or more cases of typhoid fever develop. Every available contact during the month preceding illness should be sought out for stool culture. With a satisfactory Widal technique, the search is more rapid and less costly. In addition, the recovered cases should be followed for three months or longer with repeated stool cultures to rule out a "carrier" condition. "Carrier" supervision is an effective step and gall bladder removal may be used in selected cases to effect a large percentage of permanent cures.

UNDULANT FEVER

By A. Daniel Rubenstein, M.D.
Epidemiologist, Division of Communicable Diseases
Massachusetts Department of Public Health

History.

The discovery of the cause of undulant fever, a disease transmitted from animal to man, the identity of its cause with those of Malta fever of goats and Bang's disease of cattle are landmarks in the history of medicine. Hippocrates described a condition in man characterized by long continued fever with a tendency to relapse. This may have been the first account of undulant fever. In 1886, Sir David Bruce, a British army surgeon, investigating human cases of Malta fever which were quite numerous in the region of the Mediterranean Basin, and particularly on the Island of Malta, discovered the germ and named it "micrococcus melitensis." The first accurate knowledge, linking the disease with goats, appeared in 1905. It was shown that on the Island of Malta, goats' milk was the usual source of infection; ten per cent of the goats were found to be discharging the germs in their milk.

Contagious abortion in cattle, now known as Bang's disease, likewise has a record of great antiquity. The disease in Europe has been known for centuries. Its infectiousness in cattle was described by Moscall in 1567 and by Lawrence in 1805. Bang, a Danish veterinarian, in 1896 discovered the germ involved in contagious abortion and called it "bacillus abortus." In 1918, Dr. Alice Evans, of the United States Public Health Service, demonstrated the close identity of the germs which produce disease in hogs as well as in goats and cattle, indicating that all of these were members of a single family group of organisms. It has since been proved that undulant fever in humans can be caused by any of these germs.

Prevalence.

Contagious abortion in cattle is the most serious economic disease, next to tuberculosis, with which the animal industry has to deal. In the United States, it exists everywhere and attacks swine, goats, and sheep, in addition to cattle. The disease in man has been found in all sections of the country. In 1929, for example, it was reported from every state in the union. In 1930 undulant fever was declared a disease dangerous to the public health by the Massachusetts Department of Public Health and, as such, is reportable to boards of health. Table I indicates the extent to which it has been reported by physicians of the State. The gradual increase in the number of cases is more apparent than real, and is explained by a growing interest on the part of the medical profession in undulant fever, which is illustrated by the increasing number of agglutination tests done by the State Bacteriological Laboratory on specimens sent in by physicians.

Table I.—*Undulant Fever*

Year	Cases Reported	for Diagnosis Laboratory tests
1930	6	267
1931	15	368
1932	15	339
1933	11	374
1934	15	457
1935	42	742
1936	55	1105
1937	43	1393

Modes of Transmission.

Undulant fever usually is contracted by drinking raw milk, or by contact with infected animals. The fact that ingestion of raw milk produced the disease was first shown on the Island of Malta. The usual source of milk in Malta is the goat. The germ of Malta fever was demonstrated in the milk of infected animals. Measures instituted to reduce the infection in goats brought a decrease of the disease among humans. Investigation of cases of undulant fever reported in Massachusetts indicates that the usual mode of infection is through the medium of raw cow's milk.

Furthermore, it is generally accepted that infection can be acquired by direct contact with animals. From experimental evidence, it appears that the infection may enter in wounds or breaks in the skin, and perhaps even through the intact skin. Butchers, slaughter house employees, animal inspectors, cattle handlers, and veterinarians are particularly prone to this form of infection which is, however, more common in the Western States than in Massachusetts. Laboratory technicians working with the germ of undulant fever are frequently infected.

The Disease in Man.

In general, it may be said that the severity of undulant fever depends a great deal upon the type of germ concerned. By certain laboratory tests, three types of the organism are differentiated: (1) the Caprine, which causes the disease in goats; (2) the Porcine, found in hogs; and (3) the Bovine, or Abortus type, found in cattle. The goat and hog varieties tend to be more serious when transmitted to humans than the bovine. However, any one case of undulant fever cannot be labeled as one or the other type on the basis of symptoms alone. Actually, there is a great variation in symptoms. Very often the diagnosis is difficult to establish. The onset may be insidious, with fever and pain in the back and limbs. Long continued fever, with relapse and recurrence, is a characteristic of the disease. Indigestion, insomnia, constipation, or diarrhea may be pronounced in individual cases. The spleen may become enlarged; hip, shoulder, ankle, or knee joints frequently become painful and swollen. Perspiration may be profuse. In many cases a fever of long duration with afternoon elevation is the only manifestation. The prolonged course may sometimes cause the disease to be confused with tuberculosis until a careful study of the case is made. The incubation period—that is, the interval of time between infection and beginning of symptoms—varies from six to thirty days, or longer.

Various laboratory tests are available to physicians to aid in the diagnosis of undulant fever. One of the most important of these is the so-called "agglutination test" which depends upon the development of antibodies in the blood of persons who have been infected with undulant fever. This test is performed free by the State Bacteriological Laboratory on blood specimens submitted by physicians. By means of this and other tests the diagnosis is established.

Prevention.

Our knowledge of the cause and modes of transmission of undulant fever makes the prevention of this disease in man a comparatively simple problem. To eradicate the disease from domestic herds is, however, no easy task. Tests for contagious abortion performed on cattle from various sections of the State reveal that a large number of animals are infected. To eliminate all infected animals from herds is exceedingly expensive because it necessitates the slaughter of such animals. Actually this procedure is not necessary in order to prevent humans from acquiring the disease through milk. It is well known that pasteurization will kill the germs of undulant fever. Thus, whether or not the infection is present in the milk, pasteurization will prevent the disease and is, therefore, our best safeguard. Fortunately, over 85% of the milk supplied in Massachusetts is pasteurized. Hence, only a relatively small percentage of the population is exposed to undulant fever through the medium of raw milk. Undulant fever is very often acquired by persons on vacation while using raw milk for varying intervals of time. It is, therefore, well for travelers and vacationists to inquire into the source of their milk supply to determine whether or not it has been pasteurized. By this simple procedure, undulant fever will be prevented while on vacation. Boiled milk, as ordinarily used in infants' formulas, renders it safe for use.

The problem of contact infection, except among those who handle animals, is of minor significance because very few cases which occur in this State are acquired in this way. Cattle dealers and others handling live or dead animals must exercise common-sense measures as regards hand-washing and general cleanliness in order to avoid infection.

Since vaccines have not proven effective in preventing the disease the only effective barrier against the spread of the disease among humans is pasteurization of milk.

WHOOPING COUGH

BY CONRAD WESSELHOEFT, M.D.

Physician-in-Chief, Haynes Memorial Hospital;
Associate in Communicable Diseases, Harvard Medical School and
Harvard School of Public Health

Whooping cough or pertussis is an acute infectious disease which most individuals get through with in early childhood, one attack usually affording an immunity which lasts for life. The disease is caused by a specific bacterium known as the Bordet-Gengou bacillus which bears the names of the discoverers. It is spread from one human being to another largely by droplet infection; that is to say, a patient with whooping cough in the act of coughing and sneezing throws out a spray of fine droplets which contain these bacilli. Usually within seven to ten days after inhaling these infected droplets a susceptible individual will begin to show signs of an ordinary cold in the head with sneezing, running of the nose, and a bronchial type of cough which is apt to be worse at night. A positive culture which establishes the diagnosis can be obtained at this time by holding a plate containing a special culture medium in front of the patient's mouth while he is coughing. The eyes are often watery as they are in a severe common cold. At this stage the symptoms are not unlike those of the earliest signs of measles, a disease which also begins with a cold and a persistent hacking cough that is apt to be worse at night. But in measles there are the Koplik spots seen on the inside of the cheeks by which one is able to make the diagnosis before the rash appears.

These symptoms of a cold continue through the first week. Gradually the nose ceases to run, but there may be paroxysms of sneezing. In rare instances these attacks of sneezing persist throughout and are more prominent than the cough. This curious type of the disease is more often seen in babies than in older children. In the usual type the cough becomes more and more persistent and finally paroxysmal in character. With a stethoscope the trained ear can sometimes detect a tympanitic quality to the breath sounds before any definite bronchitis is established.

During the so-called catarrhal stage, changes in the blood count begin to take place. The white blood corpuscles are increased, and among these the lymphocytes preponderate, giving rise to what is known as a lymphocytosis. This blood picture is another aid to forming an early diagnosis. However, with all these early signs the physician will be apt to lean most heavily on the circumstantial evidence of a known or suspected contact with another case of whooping cough, or the knowledge that the disease exists in the neighborhood, in the kindergarten, in the school, or—not to be forgotten—the Sunday school. Taking plate cultures is not generally done because the method of identifying the bacillus is more elaborate than that of identifying the diphtheria bacillus and is less reliable for diagnosis if negative. In whooping cough positive cultures are generally obtained in 80 per cent of the cases during the first week in the catarrhal stage, in 60 per cent during the second week when the paroxysms begin, and in only about 20 per cent during the third week.

Somewhere between one and two weeks after the onset of the cold symptoms the cough becomes definitely paroxysmal and staccato. Finally, after one of these paroxysms of coughing in which the child has expelled more air from the lungs than usual, the air is sucked in with a characteristic whoop, which clinches the diagnosis beyond all doubt. In very rare instances other conditions may give rise to a whoop. I well remember a baby who had swallowed a small safety pin which produced sudden paroxysms of coughing with a definite whoop. The use of the tongue depressor to look into the throat caused a particularly violent cough which brought up the safety pin, whereupon the cough stopped immediately. In whooping cough laughing, crying, or eating a cracker may start up a prolonged attack of coughing. If several children with whooping cough are together, a paroxysm in one child is apt to start all the rest of them coughing.

The severe paroxysm is a distressing sight to witness. The cough comes as rapidly as a machine gun, followed by the whoop of inspiration. The child loses his breath, the eyes water and bulge, and the face becomes blue. A glairy, transparent, stringy mucus is coughed up which often gags and induces vomiting. Then the child whimpers and sinks back exhausted. Sometimes the coughing so tires the abdominal muscles that the child complains of pain in this region. Other children seem to take these paroxysms with stoicism, and after the attack is over begin to play with their toys, smile, or continue eating the meal even though they have just vomited. The attitude of the parent or nurse is of importance here, because if those about the patient appear frightened this will be reflected in the child's attitude. A cheerful note of encouragement after the attack is over is helpful.

Whooping cough is far more dangerous to babies than to older children. The deaths are largely confined to the first two years of life. In Massachusetts 80 per cent of all the deaths from this disease occur in the first year, and 96 per cent of the deaths occur in the first two years. This striking fact emphasizes the importance of protecting babies from this infection. The newborn appear to lack that relative immunity which they have for measles, mumps, scarlet fever, and diphtheria. Therefore, every effort should be made to protect them from exposure. The number of cases of whooping cough continues at a high level, but the number of deaths has been materially reduced during recent years, as can be noted in the accompanying chart.

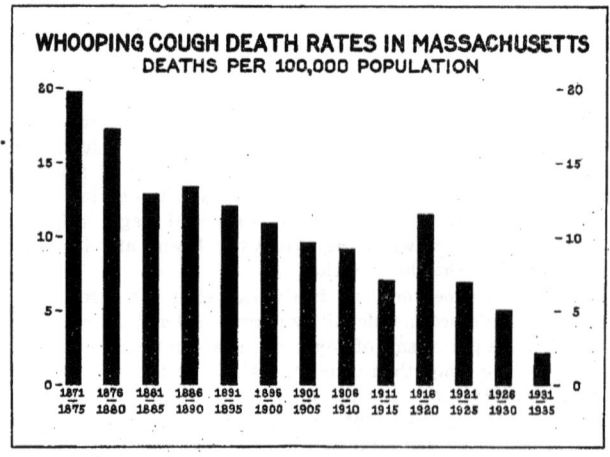

Another very important factor is the great danger of mixed infection. Influenza is the worst offender, because this disease superimposed on whooping cough reaps a high toll of deaths. Measles with whooping cough is also very dangerous; consequently every means should be applied to avoid this combination. Bronchopneumonia may be a straight complication of whooping cough, but more often it is due to a mixed infection, especially with a strain of streptococcus which changes the blood picture from a lymphocytosis to a polymorphonuclear leukocytosis. The more violent the cough the higher the white count. The highest we have found at the Haynes Memorial Hospital is 167,000. A persistent small area of bronchopneumonia is the commonest cause of a protracted cough over many weeks and also of relapses with renewed paroxysms and whooping after periods of improvement. Another common cause of protracted cough is the persistence of enlarged bronchial lymph glands which can be seen in X-ray pictures.

Convulsions are apt to occur with bronchopneumonia, but in babies they may occur in conjunction with very severe paroxysms. For a long time it was thought that the mechanical factor of the violent paroxysms was responsible for the many and varied derangements of the central nervous system which in some cases lead to mental impairment. While these may be due in part to strain put on the blood vessels in the brain, it is probable that mixed infections play an important part in bringing about these serious complications.

Nosebleeds are not uncommon, and infants that have cut their lower incisors may develop a small ulcer under the tongue from holding the tongue out during the cough. Malnutrition often becomes a very serious problem especially in infants. In young children it is better to give them their supper two hours before they are due to go to sleep, because they are apt to wake up with a sudden paroxysm when they first fall asleep and lose the contents of the stomach. If they get their supper at 4 p.m. it is more apt to be retained.

From what has been said so far, it will be seen that this disease is not to be looked upon merely as one of those childhood diseases that all of us have had and survived. The point is that many do not survive, and the large majority of these are babies. Whooping cough in this country claims more lives than diphtheria, measles, and scarlet fever. It is highly infectious during the catarrhal stage before the whoop is established. The degree of infectivity diminishes with each week. Carriers, which are so important in typhoid fever and diphtheria, appear to play only an insignificant role in the spread of whooping cough. The two greatest difficulties in the control of the disease are that the early stage is so very infectious and that mild cases without a whoop go unrecognized. The disease continues in Massachusetts throughout the year, but owing to the lessening of other infections in summer, whooping cough is safest in these warmer months.

The treatment of whooping cough is still in that unsatisfactory stage where no specific method is established on scientific grounds. I have made a collection of the names of no less than 104 different medicines—not including patent medicines—that have been recommended for this malady. Of these ipecac, belladonna, and antipyrin are most frequently used, but they should be prescribed only by a physician. Fresh clean air is always desirable, and a change of air especially into the country away from city dust is often advantageous. Unless there is fever, patients should be allowed to go out, but they should be kept from spreading the disease to other children. The food should be simple and given at frequent intervals. An abdominal binder is sometimes of comfort.

The prevention of whooping cough is best obtained by careful isolation through the infective stage. The hands of the mother or other attendant can carry the bacteria from one child to another unless carefully washed with ordinary soap and water.

The whole question of immunization with the vaccine of this specific bacillus is too complex to discuss here. That some definite progress is being made is now fairly well established, but it must be clearly understood that the value of these preparations in preventing whooping cough is not to be compared with the value of vaccination against smallpox or immunization against diphtheria and typhoid fever. Only by accepting a very much lower standard of efficacy can one consider the prophylactic value of even the newer whooping cough preparations.

REPORTABLE DISEASES RARE IN MASSACHUSETTS

By Roy F. Feemster, M.D.

Director, Division of Communicable Diseases
Massachusetts Department of Public Health

Actinomycosis

This is a disease of cattle which is sometimes transferred to man. It is rare in animals in Massachusetts, and rarer still in humans. The condition best known to the public is that of "lumpy jaw" in cattle, in which the bone of the jaw is affected, causing a large swelling, but the disease may attack various parts of the body, particularly the lung and certain locations in the alimentary tract.

The disease is caused by an organism intermediate between bacteria and molds. It usually enters through small wounds and abrasions, particularly those produced by the sharp points of grasses and grains. Prevention is largely through the avoidance of chewing sharp straws, grains, or grasses, and by the destruction of the carcasses of animals which are found to be infected.

Anthrax

This is another disease of animals which is sometimes transferred to man. Those most exposed to the infection are workers with animals and those who handle hair and hides of animals.

The disease is an important one in the history of bacteriology because of the fact that it was the first disease proven to be due to bacteria. It is difficult to control due to the fact that the spores of the bacteria are very resistant and may lie dormant in the soil for many years where an infected animal has been buried.

The disease is of such importance that the United States Department of Agriculture requires that all hides shipped into this country shall be treated with antiseptics, to kill the bacteria and spores of anthrax.

Cholera

Most people think of cholera as a disease of faraway lands. This is true in the present day, but in the past, the disease has invaded even this country, and at one time advanced up the Mississippi Valley as far as Pittsburgh on the Ohio River. It is only the constant vigilance of the physicians of the United States Public Health Service that keeps this disease out of our country.

The disease is caused by an organism which affects mainly the alimentary tract, producing a severe inflammation of the intestine and, because of the violent purging, rapid dehydration results, usually leading to death. It is transferred in much the same way as typhoid fever and consequently preventive measures used in that disease are effective against cholera.

Infectious Encephalitis

Encephalitis is a medical term which refers to any inflammation of the brain. There are, of course, a number of different causes of such inflammation. It has been known for a long time that encephalitis occasionally occurs as a complication of other acute infectious diseases such as measles and whooping cough. In such cases, the disease very seldom produces any permanent damage to the brain, and most cases recover almost completely.

Another variety known as "encephalitis lethargica" is popularly called "sleeping sickness." This is a disease which most frequently affects adults and, in a large per cent of cases, the individual goes into coma which may persist for days or weeks. Permanent damage to the brain is frequent. The causative organism of this disease has not as yet been identified.

In 1935, an epidemic of encephalitis occurred in areas near St. Louis. This disease was likewise most prevalent among adults. A very intensive study of the cases was made and much information in regard to the disease was accumulated. A filtrable virus was isolated from some of the cases, and it is believed that most of those ill were affected by this virus. Because of the concentration of cases in and around St. Louis, the causative organism is now called the "St. Louis virus." A similar disease, but due to a different virus, has been described in Japan.

During the summer of 1938, a number of cases of encephalitis occurred in southeastern Massachusetts where horses were dying of a disease called "encephalomyelitis." Most of the human cases were in small children, although a few adults were attacked. More than half of those affected died. A filtrable virus was recovered from the brain tissue of eight fatal cases, and it has been proven that this virus is identical with that which was causing the disease among horses. It is suspected that the horse disease is transmitted from animal to animal by the bite of mosquitoes, so it is reasonable to believe that the human disease may be transmitted by the mosquito or by some other biting insect. Preventive measures will probably be largely directed towards the reduction in the number of mosquitoes and any other insects which may eventually be discovered to be carriers of the disease. Since the horse is the only important reservoir of the virus known at the present time, inoculation of horses with the specific vaccine is recommended.

Leprosy

Cases of this disease are discovered very rarely in the State, and then usually in individuals who have acquired it in other countries. It is regarded by the public with a fear and loathing entirely out of proportion to its danger largely because of the external changes which it produces, particularly the mutilation of the face and extremities. Leprosy is caused by a germ similar to the bacillus of tuberculosis, and contrary to the popular idea, it is very difficult to transmit from one person to another. In fact, the disease is acquired only by long and intimate contact, such as living in the same household for a period of years.

Massachusetts once had an institution for caring for lepers. It was situated on Penikese Island off the southern coast of the State. When the United States Public Health Service established a hospital for such cases at Carville, Louisiana, the institution on Penikese Island was closed and all patients sent to the Federal institution. The disease can be cured with chaulmoogra oil and other modern drugs, and some of those sent to Carville are eventually able to return home.

Malaria

This disease was quite prevalent in Massachusetts in Colonial times. Graphic descriptions of persons going through an attack of "ague" can be found in the literature of those days. At the present time, the disease is practically unknown in New England except for a few imported cases.

Malaria is due to an animal parasite belonging to the family of protozoa which attacks and lives in the red blood cells. Since the disease is transmitted only by the bite of a particular kind of mosquito, the disappearance of the disease can be largely attributed to the great decrease in the prevalence of these particular mosquitoes. Changes resulting from the increase in population have rendered New England an unsatisfactory place for the breeding of these mosquitoes. They still occur in small numbers but very seldom become numerous even in localized areas.

Plague

This is another disease which the vigilance of the United States Public Health Service keeps out of our country. It is primarily a disease of rats transferred from animal to animal by the rat flea, and when there is a severe epidemic among these animals, the fleas leave the dead rats and go to humans who in turn acquire the disease from the bites of the fleas. On the Pacific coast the disease has become established in scattered areas because ground squirrels and other small rodents have become infected, but there is no reason to believe that such small animals have acquired the disease along the Atlantic coast.

Bubonic plague is caused by a small bacterium which produces a very fatal disease in human beings. One of the signs of the disease is a great swelling of the lymph glands in various parts of the body which gives the disease its name of "bubonic plague." In some epidemics in the Orient where pneumonia is caused by the germ, it can be spread through the upper respiratory tract, in which case the disease is known as "pneumonic plague." This form is practically always fatal.

Psittacosis

This is a disease of the parrot family, although other birds have been known to be infected. It is caused by an ultramicroscopic virus and is readily passed from birds to humans, in whom a very fatal malady is produced. The problem has become sufficiently important that some

States will not allow members of the parrot family to be imported for any purpose except for scientific research, and then under the strictest of regulations.

Rocky Mountain Spotted Fever

Until recently it was thought that this disease was limited to certain small areas in the Rocky Mountain states, where some valleys have been practically depopulated due to the fact that the disease in a very fatal form was prevalent. The story of the conquering of this disease by vaccines and serums is a dramatic one. It is caused by small parasites called "rickettsia" which have not yet been satisfactorily classified among the causes of human disease. It is transmitted by the bites of insects, ticks being one of the most important carriers. Within the last few years, cases of the disease have been discovered along the Atlantic coast, and it has been shown that the common tick found on bushes and upon dogs and other animals can transmit the disease. Two or three isolated cases have been discovered in which it is suspected that the disease may have been acquired in Massachusetts. While it appears that the ticks of this State have not yet become infected with the germ of this disease, those who go into areas where ticks are numerous should take proper precautions so that if an infected tick should be encountered the disease will not be acquired. A booklet describing these precautions can be obtained from this Department.

Septic Sore Throat

This is a very severe form of sore throat occurring almost entirely in epidemics spread by milk, which has become infected with a germ known as the "streptococcus." The source of the disease is usually a cow whose udder has become infected from a milker with sore throat. The germs grow profusely in the udder and large numbers are contained in the milk. Of course, milk from such a cow should never be sold, but careless dairymen sometimes use milk from such cows. Fortunately this disease has reached a very low prevalence in Massachusetts due to the fact that over 85 per cent of our milk is pasteurized, as this treatment is quite effective in killing the streptococcus.

Tetanus

This disease, popularly known as "lockjaw," is not communicable in the usual sense of the term. It is caused by a germ which does not grow in the presence of oxygen. It is, therefore, most dangerous in wounds into which foreign material has gained access, such as puncture wounds, or in severe lacerations where the blood supply has been greatly interfered with. The germ grows readily in the intestinal tract of most warm-blooded animals, including man. Spores are formed which can lie dormant for long periods of time in the outside world so that when wounds are contaminated with dirt from the street, barnyard, or fertilized field, the spores may gain access to the wound. A deadly toxin is formed which attacks the central nervous system and causes the symptoms.

Those who may be particularly exposed to the disease can have their resistance greatly increased by the inoculation of tetanus toxoid. Individuals who have received puncture wounds or severe lacerations should be given a dose of tetanus antitoxin.

Tularemia

This is a disease of animals, particularly of rabbits, which resembles bubonic plague in some respects, particularly in the causative organism which was once confused with the germ of bubonic plague. Up to the present time, only a few cases of this disease have occurred in Massachusetts, and in practically every instance it is likely that the disease was acquired outside of the State. However, with present-day methods of rapid transportation, the disease may eventually obtain a foothold in this State. The importation of infected animals is the most likely way by which it may gain access. Those most exposed to the infection are individuals who handle rabbits, particularly those engaged in dressing these animals.

The problem of infected rabbits is of sufficient importance that this Department has ruled that no carcasses of such animals killed outside the State may be sold in the Commonwealth unless they had been held in cold storage at a temperature of less than 30 degrees Fahrenheit for a period of at least thirty days.

Typhus Fever

This is another disease caused by "rickettsia," closely related to the causative organism of Rocky Mountain Spotted Fever. The Old World type of typhus fever which is transmitted by body lice is rarely found in this country. The form most frequently seen is the so-called New World type, and is transferred by other insects such as fleas from field mice and other small rodents. Unrecognized cases of this disease have undoubtedly been occurring in Massachusetts for many years. Recently these cases have been found largely through the interest and cooperation of Doctor Hans Zinsser of the Harvard Medical School, who has developed a serum for the treatment of the disease and a vaccine to increase resistance against it.

Yellow Fever

This disease occurs largely in tropical areas, but has at times in the past invaded the United States. Cases have been found as far north as New York and Boston. The disease is caused by an ultramicroscopic virus, and is transmitted by a variety of mosquito different from that which transmits malaria. In order to become infected, the mosquito must bite the patient during the first three days of his illness and thereafter must live for a period of several days before it can transmit the disease to another individual. Fortunately, none of the mosquitoes which transmit the disease are found regularly in Massachusetts. A few from time to time may be imported on vessels coming from the tropics, but they do not survive in this climate for many weeks. For this reason, it is very unlikely that yellow fever will be a problem of any consequence in New England.

RULES AND REGULATIONS

RULES AND REGULATIONS OF THE DEPARTMENT OF PUBLIC HEALTH RELATIVE TO DISEASES DANGEROUS TO THE PUBLIC HEALTH, MADE UNDER THE PROVISIONS OF SECTION 6, CHAPTER 111, OF THE GENERAL LAWS, AS AMENDED BY CHAPTER 265 OF THE ACTS OF 1938

Regulation 1. Reporting cases of diseases dangerous to the public health on dairy farms. When a case of typhoid fever, paratyphoid fever, diphtheria, scarlet fever, epidemic or septic sore throat, poliomyelitis (acute anterior), amebic or bacillary dysentery, or Asiatic cholera occurs on any farm or dairy producing milk, cream, butter or other dairy products for sale, it shall be the duty of the physician in attendance to report immediately to the local board of health the existence on such farm or dairy of such case. If no physician is in attendance it shall be the duty of the owner or person in charge of such farm or dairy to report forthwith to the local board of health the name and address of any person, who is affected with a disease presumably dangerous to the public health, and who is employed or resides on or in such farm or dairy or who comes in contact in any way therewith or with its products.

It shall be the duty of the local board of health to report immediately to the state district health officer by telephone or telegram the existence on such farm or dairy of a case of disease mentioned in this regulation, together with all facts as to the isolation of such case, and to give the names of the cities and towns to which such dairy products are delivered.

Regulation 2. Reporting of illness suspected of being due to consumption of food. Every physician and every superintendent or other person in charge of any school, hospital, institution, dispensary, laboratory, labor camp or other camp, who shall have knowledge of the occurrence of a number or group of cases of illness believed to have been due to the consumption of food, shall report the same immediately, by telephone or telegram, to the local board of health.

Regulation 3. Notification of outbreaks of food poisoning, diarrhea, jaundice, epidemic influenza, glandular fever, sore throat and undiagnosed febrile disease. Whenever there shall occur in any municipality an outbreak of suspected food poisoning or an unusual prevalence of diarrhea, gastroenteritis, enteritis, colitis, enterocolitis, cholera nostras, cholera infantum or other disease in which diarrhea is a prominent symptom, or whenever jaundice, epidemic influenza, glandular fever, sore throat or any undiagnosed febrile disease is unusually prevalent, it shall be the duty of the health officer to report immediately the existence of such an outbreak to the Department of Public Health by telephone or telegram.

Regulation 4. Control of carriers. No person found to be harboring typhoid, paratyphoid, dysentery or other pathogenic intestinal organisms may engage in a food-handling capacity until it is demonstrated to the satisfaction of the Department of Public Health that the said person no longer harbors the organism.

Regulation 5. Carrier, contact, isolation, placard and quarantine are defined as follows:

a. *Carrier.* A person who, without symptoms of a disease dangerous to the public health, harbors and may disseminate the specific micro-organisms of that disease.

b. *Contact.* Any person known to have been sufficiently near an infected person or animal to have been presumably exposed to transfer of infectious material directly, or by articles freshly soiled with such material.

c. *Isolation.* The separation of persons suffering from any disease dangerous to the public health, or carriers of the infecting micro-organism, from other persons, in such places and under such conditions as will prevent the direct or indirect conveyance of the infectious agent to susceptible persons.

d. *Placard.* An official notice, written or printed, posted as a warning of the presence of a disease dangerous to the public health on the premises or in the apartment or room so placarded.

e. *Quarantine.* The restriction to the premises, house or apartment of materials and persons that presumably have been exposed to a disease dangerous to the public health.

Regulation 6. Isolation and quarantine requirements. The following shall be the minimum requirements for isolation and quarantine of diseases dangerous to the public health:

Isolation and Quarantine Requirements by the Massachusetts Department of Public Health

Disease	Minimum Period of Isolation of Patient	Minimum Period of Quarantine of Contacts Adults	Immune Children	Children not Immune	Placard
Actinomycosis	No restrictions	No restrictions	No restrictions	No restrictions	No
Anterior poliomyelitis (infantile paralysis)	Two weeks from onset of disease, and thereafter until acute symptoms have subsided.	Notes 1 and 2	Until two weeks have elapsed from date of last exposure.	Until two weeks have elapsed from date of last exposure.	Yes
Anthrax	Until lesions are healed	No restrictions	No restrictions	No restrictions	No
Asiatic cholera	Same as typhoid fever	Seven days from last exposure, and until a negative stool is obtained. Note 3.	Same as adult	Same as adult	Yes
Chickenpox	One week from appearance of eruption and thereafter until all crusts have disappeared.	No restrictions	No restrictions	No restrictions	No
Cholecystitis of typhoid origin (typhoid carrier). See Regulation 4.	Supervision by local board of health until released from the carrier list by the Department of Public Health.	Food handlers living in a household with a typhoid carrier shall be excluded from their occupations unless they have been inoculated with typhoid vaccine within two years and agree to observe precautions prescribed by the board of health.	No restrictions	No restrictions	No
Diphtheria	One week from date of onset and thereafter until two successive negative cultures, taken at least twenty-four hours apart, from both nose and throat, have been obtained.	Food handlers and persons, whose occupation brings them into contact with children living in a family in which a case exists, shall be subject to the same restrictions as children only in so far as it applies to their occupation.	If immune as shown by Schick test or on the basis of a previous attack of the disease, no restrictions provided they live away from home or the case is hospitalized, and if two consecutive negative nose and throat cultures taken at an interval of not less than twenty-four hours have been obtained.	Until child lives away from home one week and until two negative nose and throat cultures taken at an interval of not less than twenty-four hours have been obtained. No restrictions thereafter if child continues to live away from home.	Yes

Isolation and Quarantine Requirements by the Massachusetts Department of Public Health—(Continued)

Disease	Minimum Period of Isolation of Patient	Minimum Period of Quarantine of Contacts Adults	Minimum Period of Quarantine of Contacts Immune Children	Children not Immune	Placard
Dog bite	No restrictions	No restrictions	No restrictions	No restrictions	No
Dysentery, amebic	Same as typhoid fever	Note 3	No restrictions	No restrictions	No
Dysentery, bacillary	Same as typhoid fever	Note 3	No restrictions	No restrictions	No
German measles	Four days from appearance of rash	No restrictions	No restrictions	No restrictions	No
Glanders	Until lesions are healed	No restrictions	No restrictions	No restrictions	No
Gonorrhea	See "Regulations Governing the Control of Gonorrhea and Syphilis."				
Hookworm disease	No restrictions	No restrictions	No restrictions	No restrictions	No
Infections encephalitis	One week after onset in insect-free room	No restrictions	No restrictions	No restrictions	No
Leprosy	Until disease is arrested	No restrictions	No restrictions	No restrictions	No
Lobar pneumonia	Until recovery	No restrictions	No restrictions	No restrictions	No
Malaria	No restrictions	No restrictions	No restrictions	No restrictions	No
Measles	One week from appearance of rash	Note 1	No restrictions. Note 4.	Exclusion from school for fourteen days from date of last exposure. Note 7.	No
Meningococcus meningitis	Two weeks from onset of disease, and thereafter until all acute symptoms have subsided.	Notes 1 and 2	Until ten days from date of last exposure	Until ten days from date of last exposure.	Yes
Mumps	One week from onset of disease, and thereafter until all swelling of salivary glands has disappeared.	No restrictions	No restrictions	No restrictions	No
Ophthalmia neonatorum	One week after subsidence of symptoms and until two successive cultures from each eye at an interval of not less than forty-eight hours are negative for gonococci.	No restrictions	No restrictions	No restrictions	No

Disease				
Paratyphoid fever, A and B	Same as typhoid fever	Note 8	No restrictions	No
Pellagra	No restrictions	No restrictions	No restrictions	No
Pfeiffer-bacillus meningitis	No restrictions	No restrictions	No restrictions	No
Plague	One week after subsidence of all symptoms	In pneumonic cases, until seven days, and no restrictions thereafter provided patients are hospitalized or they live away from home.	Same as adults	Yes
Psittacosis	Until recovery	No restrictions	No restrictions	No
Rabies	During course of disease	No restrictions	No restrictions	No
Scarlet fever	Uncomplicated Cases: three weeks from date of appearance of rash. Careful attention should be given to nose and throat to detect existence of discharge or inflammation before considering case as uncomplicated. (If upper respiratory tract symptoms appear during month after release from isolation, precautions should be re-established.) Complicated Cases: four weeks and thereafter until abnormal discharges shall have ceased, swollen glands subsided, or three successive cultures of abnormal discharge shall have been found free of hemolytic streptococci.	Food handlers and persons, whose occupation brings them into contact with children, living in a family in which a case exists, shall be subject to the same restrictions as children only in so far as it applies to their occupation.	If immune as shown by Dick test or on the basis of a previous attack of the disease, no restrictions, provided they live away from home, or cases are hospitalized.	Until child lives away from home one week, no restrictions thereafter, if child continues to live away from home.
Rocky Mountain spotted fever	No restrictions	No restrictions	No restrictions	No
Septic sore throat	Until one week after onset and until recovery, except milk handlers, who shall be excluded from their occupation until satisfactory evidence is obtained that the danger of conveying the disease has passed.	No restrictions except for milk handlers	Same as for adults	No
Smallpox	Three weeks from onset of disease and thereafter until all crusts have disappeared and skin has healed.	Note 5	Note 5	Yes

Isolation and Quarantine Requirements by the Massachusetts Department of Public Health—(Continued)

Disease	Minimum Period of Isolation of Patient	Minimum Period of Quarantine of Contacts — Adults	Quarantine of Contacts Immune Children	Children Not Immune	Placard Immune
Suppurative conjunctivitis (acute epidemic conjunctivitis, pink eye)	Exclusion from school and public gatherings until recovery	No restrictions unless suspected of being infected.	Same as for adults	Same as for adults	No
Syphilis	See "Regulations Governing the Control of Gonorrhea and Syphilis."				
Tetanus	No restrictions	No restrictions	No restrictions	No restrictions	No
Trachoma	Exclusion from general school classes during acute stage	No restrictions	No restrictions	No restrictions	No
Trichinosis	No restrictions	No restrictions	No restrictions	No restrictions	No
Tuberculosis (all forms)	Note 6	No restrictions	No restrictions	No restrictions	No
Tularemia	During acute stage	No restrictions	No restrictions	No restrictions	No
Typhoid fever (Typhoid carrier: see "Cholecystitis of typhoid origin.")	One week after subsidence of clinical symptoms. Thereafter may be released on special permission of and under the supervision of the local board of health, supervision to continue until three successive negative stool and urine cultures, secured at intervals of at least one week apart, have been obtained.	Note 3			
Typhus fever	In vermin-free room until recovery	In presence of lice, until fourteen days after last exposure	Same as for adults	Same as for adults	No
Undulant fever	No restrictions	No restrictions	No restrictions	No restrictions	No
Whooping cough	Three weeks from beginning of spasmodic cough	Note 1	No restrictions. Note 4.	Until two weeks from last exposure	No
Yellow fever	In mosquito-proof room first four days of fever	No restrictions	No restrictions	No restrictions	No

Isolation and Quarantine Requirements by the Massachusetts Department of Public Health
(Concluded)

NOTES

1. Schoolteachers, only as it applies to their school activities, shall be subject to the same restrictions as children.
2. Food handlers and persons whose occupation brings them in contact with children have no restrictions if they live away from home.
3. Food handlers living in a family where a case of typhoid, cholera, amebic or bacillary dysentery or paratyphoid A or B exists shall be excluded from their occupation so long as they continue to live in the same house in which the case exists, and thereafter until freedom from infection, as judged by clinical and laboratory evidence, has been demonstrated to the satisfaction of the Department of Public Health.
4. A child shall be considered as having had the disease if so shown by the record of the local board of health or by a sworn statement from the parent or guardian that the child has had the disease elsewhere.
5. Contacts shall be quarantined until three weeks have elapsed from the date of last exposure unless immunized by a previous attack, by a recent successful vaccination, or showing the immune reaction.
6. Patients with open tuberculosis should in most cases receive sanatorium treatment. Those who remain in their homes shall observe all precautions necessary to prevent infection of the members of their families and of others with whom they may come in contact. This shall include approved methods of collection and disposal of the sputum, the sterilization of any articles of clothing and of toilet articles which may become contaminated by the sputum, the use of separate dishes and eating utensils and proper sterilization of the same. The patient should sleep in a separate room and must in any case occupy a separate bed. For further details concerning precautions in home care see *Home Care of Tuberculosis Patients*, a pamphlet of the Department of Public Health.

No person who has tubercle bacilli in the sputum or other bodily discharges shall be allowed to engage in the preparation or serving of food or be employed on a dairy farm or in a dairy plant in any capacity which may bring him in contact with milk or milk products.

7. In communities with good school inspection children exposed to measles may be permitted to attend school seven days after the first exposure, thereafter to be excluded from the seventh to fourteenth days.

—Approved by the Massachusetts Department of Public Health, August 9, 1938.

REGULATIONS OF THE DEPARTMENT OF PUBLIC HEALTH RELATIVE TO THE CONTROL OF GONORRHEA AND SYPHILIS, MADE UNDER THE PROVISIONS OF SECTION 6, CHAPTER 111, OF THE GENERAL LAWS, AS AMENDED BY CHAPTER 265 OF THE ACTS OF 1938

REPORTING

1. Whenever a physician has reason to believe that a person whom he has examined is suffering from gonorrhea or syphilis in any form or stage, he shall:

    a. Report immediately to the Department of Public Health, on forms provided by the department for that purpose, stating the name of the disease and its form or stage, the age, sex, marital status and community of residence of said patient and whether or not said patient has been under treatment elsewhere for the same infection, but not the patient's name or street address except as hereinafter provided.

    b. Report the change in medical adviser to the physician, if any, who last treated said patient for the infection.

    c. Report to the department any failure on the part of said patient to return for observation or treatment, unless said physician has satisfactory evidence that said patient is under the care of another physician for the infection, or has received adequate treatment for the infection, stating the name, address, age, sex and marital status of said patient, the name and stage or form of the disease, the date of the last visit to said physician, and, in case of gonorrhea, or syphilis of less than two years' duration, the approximate date of infection. Said report shall be made to the department not more than one week after the date of the missed appointment in case of syphilis of less than two years' duration (whether acquired or congenital), syphilis in a pregnant woman and gonorrhea in any form or stage; and not more than two weeks after the date of the missed appointment in all other forms or stages of syphilis, provided that any physician who has available and uses the services of a competent epidemiologist within the time limits herebefore prescribed, may defer reporting said patient's failure to return for observation or treatment for two weeks from the date of the missed appointment where one week is herebefore prescribed and for four weeks where two weeks are herebefore prescribed.

    d. Report to the department the name, address, sex, age, marital status and occupation of the patient who, having syphilis, has open lesions of the disease in the mouth or upon exposed portions of the body unless said physician is satisfied that said patient has discontinued his occupation, or is so employed that no other person is likely to be exposed to said patient's infection.

    e. Report to the department the patient who fails to co-operate with said physician in his attempt to bring to medical observation those persons, including members of the patient's family, from whom said patient may have acquired, or to whom said patient may have transmitted, his infection, stating the name, address, age, sex and marital status of said patient and the reason for the report.

    f. Report to the department the name, address, age, sex and marital status, or as complete identification as can be obtained, of any person, other than the patient's husband or wife, from whom a patient who has gonorrhea, or syphilis of less than two years' duration, may have acquired, or to whom he may have transmitted, his infection; provided that if said physician is satisfied that such person cannot be identified by said patient or, within two weeks of identification to said physician has been brought under medical observation, such report need not be made.

    2. The department may forward to any board of health of any city or town a report stating the name, address or place frequented by or place of employment of, age, sex and marital status of any person reported

to the department by name under Regulation 1, together with the reason for the report. Immediately upon the conclusion of such action as said board of health may take following receipt of such report, the said board of health shall report the result of such action to the department, provided that if said person cannot be found, the said board shall so report to the department.

CONTROL

3. Whenever a board of health shall receive a report from the department stating the name and address of, or place frequented by, a person who resides, or may be found, in the community in which said board has jurisdiction, and who is alleged to have been exposed to infection with gonorrhea or syphilis, the said board shall immediately advise said person to obtain medical attention. Not less than five days or more than one week after so advising said person, the said board shall determine whether, and by whom, such examination has been made. If, within two weeks of the date when first so advised, said person has not satisfied said board that he is under medical care or is free from infection with gonorrhea or syphilis, the said board shall isolate said person until said board is satisfied that said person is not infected with gonorrhea or syphilis.

4. Whenever a board of health shall receive a report from the department stating the name and address of, or place frequented by, a person who resides, or may be found, in the community in which said board has jurisdiction, and who has prematurely discontinued treatment for gonorrhea or syphilis, the said board shall immediately request said person to return to medical care. Not less than five days or more than one week after such request, the said board shall determine whether, and with whom, medical attention has been resumed. If, within two weeks of the date of said request, the said person has not resumed medical attention, the said board shall isolate said person until it has been satisfied that said person's infection with gonorrhea or syphilis is no longer communicable, or that said person will immediately return to medical care for said infection.

5. Whenever a board of health shall receive a report from the department stating the name and address or place frequented by, a person who resides, or may be found, in the community in which said board has jurisdiction, and who has open lesions of syphilis in the mouth or upon exposed portions of the body and who is employed at any occupation requiring contact with other persons, the said board shall request said person to discontinue such occupation until the said board is satisfied that the lesions are healed and that the said person will remain under medical care for the infection. If the said person fails to discontinue such occupation immediately, the said board shall remove said person to his home or to a hospital where he shall be isolated until said board is satisfied that the lesions are healed and that said person will remain under medical care for the infection.

6. Whenever a board of health shall receive a report from the department stating the name and address or place frequented by a patient suffering from gonorrhea, or syphilis of less than two years' duration, who resides or may be found in the community in which said board has jurisdiction, and who is said to have failed to co-operate with his physi-

clan in said physician's attempt to bring to medical observation any person from whom said patient may have acquired, or to whom he may have transmitted, said infection, said board shall immediately isolate said patient and shall retain him in isolation until he will so co-operate, or until his infection is no longer communicable.

—Approved by the Massachusetts Department of Public Health, August 9, 1938.

REGULATIONS OF THE DEPARTMENT OF PUBLIC HEALTH RELATIVE TO THE CONVEYANCE OF BODIES DEAD OF ANY DISEASE DANGEROUS TO THE PUBLIC HEALTH, MADE UNDER THE PROVISIONS OF SECTION 107, CHAPTER 111, OF THE GENERAL LAWS, AS AMENDED BY CHAPTER 265 OF THE ACTS OF 1938

The following terms hereinafter used are defined as follows:

"To transport" shall mean to convey or remove a dead human body from the place of death.

"To ship" shall mean to convey a dead human body by train, boat or airplane.

"Diseases dangerous to the public health" are those which have been so declared by the Department (reportable diseases).

"Deaths due to diseases dangerous to the public health" for the purposes of these regulations shall be interpreted as those of persons dying during the stage of the disease when it can be communicated to other persons.

Rule 1. No bodies dead of any disease dangerous to the public health may be transported or shipped, except as provided by Rules 3 and 4, without having been prepared for burial by thorough embalming and disinfecting.

Rule 2. Bodies dead of anthrax, glanders, leprosy, plague, smallpox or tularemia, which may produce dangerous surface lesions, and if such lesions occur on such bodies, may not be transported unless further prepared by being enveloped in a sheet saturated with bichloride of mercury, 1:500, and securely pinned; provided that if such lesions do not occur on head, neck or hands such parts may not necessarily be enveloped. When in doubt as to the preparation of such bodies for transportation, consult with the representative of the local board of health.

Rule 3. Bodies dead of diseases dangerous to the public health but without dangerous surface lesions may be transported to the morgue of a funeral director without arterial and cavity embalming provided that such bodies have been prepared before transportation by thorough surface washing and disinfecting and by stopping and disinfecting of orifices and by enveloping in a sheet saturated with 1:500 bichloride of mercury and securely pinning the same. Before removal from such morgue the body must be thoroughly embalmed and disinfected.

Rule 4. Bodies dead of any disease dangerous to the public health may be transported directly to the place of burial within twenty-four hours of death, or within a reasonable period of time after death if the body is kept under adequate refrigeration in a place especially provided for such purpose, without arterial and cavity embalming, provided such bodies are prepared before transportation by disinfecting and by the stopping of orifices and by enveloping in a sheet saturated with 1:500

bichloride of mercury and securely pinning the same. Such unembalmed bodies are to be placed in sealed caskets or cases not to be reopened, and may be shown only under sealed glass panels. If such unembalmed bodies are to be shipped, they must be placed in hermetically sealed cases.

Rule 5. Bodies dead of any disease dangerous to the public health shall not be accompanied by articles which have been exposed to the infection of the disease, unless such articles have been properly disinfected.

Rule 6. No disinterment of the bodies of any persons who have died of any disease dangerous to the public health shall be allowed within six months from date of death, except by special permission of the representative of the local board of health.

—Approved by the Massachusetts Department of Public Health, August 9, 1938.

REGULATIONS OF THE DEPARTMENT OF PUBLIC HEALTH RELATIVE TO FUNERALS OF PERSONS DEAD OF ANY DISEASE DANGEROUS TO THE PUBLIC HEALTH, MADE UNDER THE PROVISIONS OF SECTION 107, CHAPTER 111, OF THE GENERAL LAWS, AS AMENDED BY CHAPTER 265 OF THE ACTS OF 1938

Rule 1. Funerals of those dead of anterior poliomyelitis, Asiatic cholera, diphtheria, encephalitis lethargica, leprosy, meningococcus meningitis, plague, psittacosis, scarlet fever, smallpox, streptococcus sore throat or typhus fever, when conducted on the premises where such deceased persons died, shall be attended only by members of the immediate household, clergymen, undertaker and undertaker's assistants; when held from a place other than where such persons died, the representative of the local board of health may permit a public funeral if the bodies, in his opinion, have been prepared or enclosed according to the regulations of the Department of Public Health and provided such persons as are probable carriers of the infection, by reason of conduct, shall be forbidden to attend such funeral.

Rule 2. Bodies dead of anthrax, glanders, leprosy, plague, smallpox or tularemia, which may produce dangerous surface lesions, and if such lesions occur on such bodies, after preparation for transportation as regulated by the department, must be placed before the funeral in a sealed casket, not to be reopened, and the funeral may be either public or private. Such bodies may be shown only under a sealed glass-paneled burial case.

—Approved by the Massachusetts Department of Public Health, August 9, 1938.

MATERNAL DEATHS IN MASSACHUSETTS

Int. List No.		1933		1934		1935*		1936*		1937*	
	Total Maternal Deaths	389		317		325		270		252	
140, 145	Puerperal septicemia (inc. abortion with septic conditions)	103	% 26	93	% 29	104	% 32	80	% 30	67	% 27
141, 144	Puerperal hemorrhage and abortion without mention of septic conditions (including hemorrhages)	72	19	58	18	57	18	52	19	49	19
146, 147	Toxemias of pregnancy (inc. puerperal albuminuria and eclampsia)	67	17	59	19	56	17	38	14	50	20
148	Puerperal phlegmasia alba dolens, embolus, sudden death (not specified as septic)	55	14	53	17	47	14	35	13	27	11
142, 143, 149, 150	Others	92	24	54	17	61	19	65	24	59	23

MATERNAL AND INFANT MORTALITY RATES
Per 1,000 live births

	1933	1934	1935*	1936*	1937*
Maternal mortality rate	6.1	5.0	5.2	4.4	4.1
Infant mortality rate	51.9	49.2	48.3	46.6	43.8

*Allocated to place of residence of deceased.

REPORT OF DIVISION OF FOOD AND DRUGS
(As required by General Laws, Chapter 111, Section 25)

During the months of October and November 1938, samples were collected in 136 cities and towns.

There were 799 samples of milk examined, of which 49 were below standard, from 1 sample the cream had been in part removed, and 4 samples contained added water. There were 984 bacteriological examinations made of milk, 855 of which complied with the requirements. There were 70 bacteriological examinations made of cream, 18 of which did not comply with the requirements; 23 bacteriological examinations of miscellaneous food, 8 of which did not comply with the requirements, consisting of 1 sample of pork seasoning, 1 sample of candy, and 1 sample of filled doughnut, 2 samples of flour, and 3 samples of vegetables; 177 bacteriological examinations of scallops, 75 samples of which did not comply with the requirements; and 1 bacteriological examination of an empty bottle which did not comply with the requirements.

There were 403 samples of food examined, 134 of which were adulterated. These consisted of 4 samples of cream which were low in fat for the grade specified; 9 samples of clams which contained added water; 1 sample of cider which contained benzoic acid and was not so labeled; 1 sample of candy which was worm-eaten; 1 sample of dried pop corn which contained worm-eaten and mouse-eaten kernels; 2 samples of split peas which contained worms and worm leavings; 1 sample of dried peas which contained rat excrete; 1 sample of dried beans which was moldy; 94 samples of scallops, all of which were decomposed; 2 samples of hamburg steak, 1 of which was decomposed, and 1 sample contained a compound of sulphur dioxide not so labeled; 1 sample of sausage, 1 sample of meat pattie, and 1 sample of broken out eggs, all of which were decomposed; and 15 samples of mattress filling, 12 samples of which were labeled as containing a certain percentage of different kinds of feathers and down, which samples did not contain the materials as specified, 1 sample contained secondhand material, and 2 samples were mislabeled.

There were 48 samples of drugs examined, of which 4 were adulterated. These consisted of 1 sample of aromatic spirits of ammonia, 1 sample of milk of magnesia, 1 sample of dilute sulphuric acid, all of which did not conform to the requirements of the U. S. Pharmacopoeia, and 1 sample of argyrol which did not conform to the professed standard under which it was sold.

The police departments submitted 45 samples of liquor for examination. The police departments also submitted 11 samples to be analyzed for poisons or drugs, 4 of which contained heroin, 1 contained cannabis, 1 sample of brown seeds contained strychnine, 1 sample of white powder contained 96.9% of sodium fluoride, 1 sample of brown paste was opium, and 3 samples were examined for narcotics with negative results.

There were inspected 293 plants operated for the pasteurization of milk, 16 restaurants; 18 soft drink plants; 4 ice cream plants; 17 bakeries; 1 candy factory; 8 roadside stands; and 180 mattress establishments.

There were 24 hearings held pertaining to violations of the laws.

There were 24 convictions pertaining to violations of the law, $330 in fines being imposed.

J. F. McAdams & Brothers of Lynn, and Vito Vidonas of Andover, were convicted for violations of the milk laws.

John Teehan, 2 cases, of Springfield; James Herlihy, 2 counts, of Westfield; and George A. Sampson of Marlborough, were convicted for violations of the pasteurization law and regulations.

Nellie Lachut of Dracut was convicted for violation of the milk grading regulations.

Miran Barsorian and William Karp of Lowell; Salvatore Grasso of Belmont; John W. Anderson of Quincy; James Hook, 2 cases, of Boston; The Massachusetts Mohican Company of Waltham; Arthur C. Parent of Haverhill; Soffron Brothers, Incorporated, 2 cases, George Soffron and Stephen Soffron of Ipswich; Brockelman Brothers, Incorporated, of Marlborough; Cambridge Provision Company, Incorporated, of Cambridge; and Abram Holland of New Bedford, were all convicted for violations of the food laws. John W. Anderson of Quincy, James Hook, 2 cases, of Boston, and The Massachusetts Mohican Company of Waltham, appealed their cases.

Puritan Ice Cream Company of Boston, Incorporated, of Roslindale, were convicted for violation of the frozen dessert law.

New Bedford Dry Goods Company, New Bedford was convicted for violation of the mattress laws.

In accordance with Section 25, Chapter 111 of the General Laws, the following is the list of articles of adulterated food collected in original packages from manufacturers, wholesalers, or producers:

One sample of candy which was worm-eaten was obtained from Sandler's Department Store, Incorporated, of Lawrence.

One sample of dried beans which were moldy was obtained from Sandler's Department Store, Incorporated, of Lawrence.

One sample of dried peas which contained rat excrete was obtained from Sandler's Department Store, Incorporated, of Lawrence.

One sample of dried pop corn which contained worm-eaten and mouse-eaten kernels was obtained from Sandler's Department Store, Incorporated, of Lawrence.

One sample of cider which contained a compound of benzoic acid and was not so labeled was obtained from J. A. Thompson & Son, of Melrose, Connecticut.

One sample of split peas which contained worms was obtained from M. Winer Company of Dorchester.

One sample of split peas which contained worm leavings was obtained from Elm Farm Foods, Incorporated, of West Roxbury.

One sample of hamburg steak which contained a compound of sulphur dioxide and was not so labeled was obtained from Samuel Gordon of New Bedford.

One sample of hamburg steak which was decomposed was obtained from Samuel & Louis Peldes of New Bedford.

One sample of meat patties which was decomposed was obtained from Matthew Gula of Northampton.

One sample of sausage which was decomposed was obtained from People's Super Market of New Bedford.

Cream which was low in fat for the grade specified was obtained as follows:

One sample each, from Fillmore's Creamery of Hudson; and Herlihy Brothers of Somerville.

Four samples of clams which contained water were obtained from Soffron Brothers, Incorporated, of Ipswich.

There were 63 confiscations, consisting of the following items that had been under flood water: 335 pounds of butter; 700 pounds of lard; 17 pounds of lamb tongues; 300 pounds of pigs' feet; 50 pounds of mixed dried fruits; 29 pounds of cream cheese; 490 pounds of flour; 525 tons of tapioca flour; 16 pounds of tea; 10 dozen bottles of food; 108 quarts of tonics; 50 pints of tonics; and 25 cases of tonics.

The following items had been under flood water and were confiscated in the field: 1 acre of cabbage; 2 acres of celery; 1¾ acres of spinach; 2 acres of parsnips and carrots; 5 acres of horse radish; and 9½ acres of assorted vegetables.

The following articles were confiscated because they were decomposed: 41½ pounds of fowl; 27 pounds of beef; 41 pounds of corned beef; 1 pound of tenderloin steak; 5 pounds of lamb chops; 3 pounds of lamb patties; 6½ pounds of pork chops; 10 pounds of link pork sausage; 30 pounds of pork sausage; 8 pounds of shoulder; 80 pounds of sausage meat; 198 pounds of mixed meats; 34½ pounds of hamburg steak; 5 pounds of frankforts; ¼ pound of cheese; ½ gallon of clams; 1 gallon of oysters; 22,504 pounds of sea scallops; and 370 gallons of sea scallops.

The licensed cold storage warehouses reported the following amounts of food placed in storage during September, 1938: 340,410 dozens of case eggs; 751,103 pounds of broken out eggs; 412,194 pounds of butter; 1,112,108 pounds of poultry; 1,810,810 pounds of fresh meat and fresh meat products; and 5,857,406 pounds of fresh food fish.

There was on hand October 1, 1938: 2,415,030 dozens of case eggs; 2,355,180 pounds of broken out eggs; 4,264,096 pounds of butter; 2,829,585 pounds of poultry; 2,288,247 pounds of fresh meat and fresh meat products; and 27,627,540 pounds of fresh food fish.

The licensed cold storage warehouses reported the following amounts of food placed in storage during October 1938: 240,180 dozens of case eggs; 810,200 pounds of broken out eggs; 2,456,661 pounds of butter; 1,774,684 pounds of poultry; 1,976,701 pounds of fresh meat and fresh meat products; and 8,035,190 pounds of fresh food fish.

There was on hand November 1, 1938: 1,198,740 dozens of case eggs; 1,985,451 pounds of broken out eggs; 5,452,134 pounds of butter; 3,713,427 pounds of poultry; 2,397,273 pounds of fresh meat and fresh meat products; and 26,778,351 pounds of fresh food fish.

MASSACHUSETTS DEPARTMENT OF PUBLIC HEALTH
Commissioner of Public Health, PAUL J. JAKMAUH, M.D.

Public Health Council
PAUL J. JAKMAUH, M.D., *Chairman*

GEORGE D. DALTON, M.D.	RICHARD M. SMITH, M.D.
FRANCIS H. LALLY, M.D.	RICHARD P. STRONG, M.D.
CHARLES F. LYNCH M.D.	JAMES L. TIGHE

Secretary, FLORENCE L. WALL

Division of Administration	Under direction of Commissioner
Division of Sanitary Engineering	Director and Chief Engineer, ARTHUR D. WESTON, C.E.
Division of Communicable Diseases	Director, ROY F. FEEMSTER, M.D.
Division of Biologic Laboratories	Director and Pathologist, ELLIOTT S. ROBINSON, M.D.
Division of Food and Drugs	Director and Analyst, HERMANN C. LYTHGOE, S.B.
Division of Child Hygiene	Director, M. LUISE DIEZ, M.D.
Division of Tuberculosis	Director, ALTON S. POPE, M.D.
Division of Adult Hygiene	Director, HERBERT L. LOMBARD, M.D.
Division of Genitoinfectious Diseases	Director, NELS A. NELSON, M.D.

State District Health Officers

The Southeastern District	HAROLD W. STEVENS, M.D., Middleboro
The South Metropolitan District	HENRY M. DE WOLFE, M.D., Braintree
The North Metropolitan District	————
The Northeastern District	ROBERT E. ARCHIBALD, M.D., Melrose
The Worcester District	OSCAR A. DUDLEY, M.D., Worcester
South Connecticut Valley District	CHARLES E. GILL, M.D., Westfield
North Connecticut Valley District	WALTER W. LEE, M.D., Greenfield
The Berkshire District	FRANCIS B. CARROLL, M.D., Great Barrington.

PUBLICATION OF THIS DOCUMENT APPROVED BY THE COMMISSION ON ADMINISTRATION AND FINANCE
8,500. 1-'39. Order 6462.

THE COMMONHEALTH

Volume 26   April-May-June
No. 2   1939

DENTAL HEALTH

MASSACHUSETTS
DEPARTMENT OF PUBLIC HEALTH

THE COMMONHEALTH

QUARTERLY BULLETIN OF THE MASSACHUSETTS DEPARTMENT OF
PUBLIC HEALTH

Sent Free to any Citizen of the State
Entered as second class matter at Boston Post Office

M. LUISE DIEZ, M.D., DIRECTOR OF DIVISION OF CHILD HYGIENE, EDITOR.
1 Beacon Street, Boston, Mass.

CONTENTS

	PAGE
A Diploma in Her Hand and Twenty-One Cavities in Her Teeth	97
Oral Hygiene, Report of the Special Commission to Study and Investigate Public Health Laws and Policies	98
A Pediatrist Looks at Children's Teeth, by Merritt B. Low, M.D.	104
The Iowa Plan for Dental Health Education, by John C. Brauer, D.D.S., M.Sc., F.A.C.D.	106
Dental Extractions, by Frank W. Rounds, A.B., D.D.S.	108
Is Sugar the Lone Factor in Producing Dental Caries? by Mary Spalding, M.A.	111
The Promotion of Dental Internships in General Hospitals, by Richard H. Norton, D.D.S., D.M.D.	114
Extension of Dental Facilities, by William Hayes Hoyt, D.D.S.	117
Developments in Dental Education, by Howard M. Marjerison, D.M.D.	119
New Jersey State Dental Society Program—Dental Health Education, by J. M. Wisan, D.D.S.	121
Recent Studies Point the Way to Better Dental Health, by F. C. Cady, D.D.S., C.P.H.	123
The Preparation and Training of Dental Hygienists, by Evelyn B. Morse	126
Prenatal Dental Service, by Susan M. Coffin, M.D.	131
Progress in School Dental Health, by Jean V. Latimer, B.S., A.M.	133
Public Health Nursing and Its Relation to Dental Hygiene, by Ann W. Dinegan, B.S., R.N.	135
Dental Needs and the Suppy of Dentists, by Fred W. Morse, Jr., M.D.	136
The Importance of an Adequate Dental Program, by Arthur E. Westwell, D.M.D.	138
Structural and Nervous Effects of Thumb-Sucking, by Earl W. Swinehart, D.D.S.	141
The Teeth in Congenital Syphilis, by Florence B. Hopkins, M.D., D.M.D.	145
Dental Health Exhibits, by Albertine P. McKellar, B.S.	148
Book Note:	
Maternity Care in a Rural Community, by Maxwell E. Lapham, M.D.	152
News Note:	
Vocational-Placement Service to Public Health Nurses	153
Report of Division of Food and Drugs, December, 1938, January and February, 1939	153

A DIPLOMA IN HER HAND
AND TWENTY-ONE CAVITIES IN HER TEETH

"Yes, Doctor, it's a fact; 'Mary Dunn' graduated from high school with a diploma under her arm and twenty-one cavities in her teeth," was the emphatic remark of John S. Morrell, the superintendent of city schools, Beloit, Kansas, a city of 3500. He was discussing the need for health education in schools with Doctor Leon R. Kramer, Director, Division of Dental Hygiene, Kansas State Board of Health.* "It takes a shock like this," he continued, "to awaken one to the fact that the schools have other important tasks to perform than simply to teach the subject matter enclosed between the two covers of a textbook. Not until I learned of "Mary's" case did I think of the importance of health teaching to the extent that I felt I should do something about it."

One year later, in Beloit, a banquet was given in celebration of a new dental health program carried out successfully, and all the groups associated with the project were invited to attend. At the conclusion of the banquet, the case of "Mary Dunn" came up for discussion. Superintendent Morrell told about her diploma and her neglected dental education. To him "Mary Dunn" represented a grave deficiency in the educational system of his schools. Her case showed him what was in store for hundreds of other children now in school—the prospect of being handicapped perhaps for life because their dental education had been neglected. Mr. Morrell told the guests that when he heard about "Mary Dunn" he realized that something must be done at once. His first step was to cooperate, during the next school session, in securing dental examinations for the 850 children in his school.

"Only 15 per cent," he said "had mouths that would pass inspection. More than 2500 cavities and other diseased conditions were found. The inspection gave us the needed data on which to base our corrective program. By submitting our analysis to relief offices we found that 34 per cent of the students could not afford to pay for dental care. One-third were paid for by the county, one-third, by the Red Cross, and one-third received free dental service at the Community Hospital. Actual costs were approximately $250.00 for the county, $175 for the Red Cross, and 85 students were taken to the Community Hospital.

"Because of the cooperation of the teachers, various agencies, and dentists, the dental program was successfully completed for the year with all corrections having been taken care of."

After explaining the dental health program the superintendent then called upon others at the banquet for comments. To a public school teacher who spoke briefly, the case of "Mary Dunn" meant countless instances of children she has observed day after day in her classes; children whose minds are being trained but whose health and appearance are so affected by dental disease that they haven't a normal chance for happiness or success.

To the county commissioner who spoke next, preventing the devel-

---

* Kramer, L. R : A One Man Dental Health Program. Oral Hygiene 25:1508 (November) 1935. The Dental Chronicles of the Indigent, Oral Hygiene 27:1319 (October) 1937.

opment of dental caries in "Mary Dunn's" teeth meant a sound investment in community health. "My business experience," he said, "has taught me that money spent for prevention of destruction, or the early repair of conditions that lead to destruction of valuable assets is good business and money well spent."

A representative of the Red Cross considered the case of "Mary Dunn" from the point of view of unnecessary pain and suffering:

"Too often," he said, "we associate pain and suffering with catastrophies, such as wind storms and floods and fail to realize the amount of pain and suffering resulting from ignorance, neglect, and poverty . . . I am told that toothache is the source of more pain to children than all other sources combined."

A man from the local welfare office thought that "Mary Dunn's" twenty-one cavities were mainly important, because they had stirred the school and other groups to develop a practical dental health program that would serve as a guide for other communities in their efforts to preserve the health of the community.

For the dentists, "Mary Dunn's" case spotlighted the need for and importance of preventive dentistry, which is the constant objective of the dental profession. Doctor C. S. Spain, co-chairman of the dental program in Mitchell County, represented the dentists. "The ideals of the dental profession," he said, "are more completely embodied in the preventive phases of dentistry than in any other of its activities. There are more young people disqualified for jobs in certain fields of activity on account of dental defects than from any other cause. We were glad to make concessions in Beloit so that the underprivileged child may not suffer this experience when applying for a job a few years hence. We hope to expand this program so that eventually every school child in the county will be included in the dental program."

At the conclusion of the evening, Doctor Kramer was introduced as the man who has been responsible for "the various oral health programs over the state of Kansas." He congratulated the Beloit group on their excellent dental health program, saying it was the first time to his knowledge that dental corrections had been made for the children of an entire school system. He was also glad to note that the service was given to children in dental offices rather than in clinics.

ORAL HYGIENE

Report of the Special Commission to Study and Investigate
Public Health Laws and Policies
December 2, 1936

Oral hygiene is a relatively new addition to the field of organized public health endeavor, and will, in all probability, assume greater importance in the future. In former years dentistry was confined very largely to mechanical reparative measures, and was interested in the perfection of mechanical treatment. This was a concession to expediency. Teeth decayed and became painful, requiring removal and frequently replacement. Thus mechanical procedures developed rapidly. More recently there has been increasing recognition of the fact that the tooth is an integral part of the human body, subject to general influences that may affect the entire human mechanism, and that therefore the hygiene of the teeth and the mouth are also integral parts of preventive medicine and public health.

Importance of Oral Hygiene

The importance of prevention, early recognition of defects, and wise corrective measures is nowhere more apparent than in the field of dentistry. The development of the teeth in the embryo is at least partly dependent upon the proper diet of the expectant mother. The formation of sound, strong teeth in the child, especially the permanent teeth, is conditioned by the elements of the diet as well as by the attention given to the first teeth. The maintenance of proper masticating surfaces is also not without its preventive aspects, as proper chewing of the food is of importance as a preliminary to digestion. In adult life the correction of oral defects, notably the elimination of diseased teeth, is of prophylactic value in the prevention of certain systemic diseases.

It is thus obvious that oral hygiene is an essential part of any program that has as its aim the maintenance of health. It is an important part of the program of maternal hygiene, of all phases of child hygiene, and of adult hygiene. With the inevitable future advances in scientific knowledge, particularly as to the relation between diet and teeth, oral hygiene promises to become of even greater importance, and to hold far greater possibilities for development than in the past.

Present Programs

The present programs, either under official or private auspices, are aimed very largely at the prevention and correction of incipient defects in children's teeth. Unfortunately the greater part of this work is limited to the group of school age, a limitation in scope as illogical and uneconomic as is the limitation of child hygiene to this same age group. The preliminary examinations have been made by dentists, dental hygienists or by school physicians. This program in Massachusetts provides for the periodic examination of children's teeth, with the aim of referring for dental care all those in need of attention. Children whose parents are able to afford dental care are referred to the family dentist, and clinic facilities have frequently been provided locally for those otherwise unable to afford such attention.

Dental Hygienists

In such programs in recent years there has been a growing tendency to utilize the services of dental hygienists for examination of children's teeth to discover defects. These hygienists have been trained essentially as dentists' helpers. They have been compelled to crowd into a single year too great a variety of subjects to qualify them for independent public health activities. The training of the dental hygienist was honestly conceived and sincerely planned, but her education is based on empirical methods. Undoubtedly she has a place, but her present training is too rudimentary for public health service.

On the other hand, there is a place in the public health program for well-trained workers in dental hygiene. There is actually a great need for them, but it would appear to the Commission that this service could be rendered better by public health nurses or other workers trained in the basic sciences, who have been given special training in oral hygiene and nutrition. Their greater training and experience would better fit them for the broader aspects of public health service. If to these qualifications could be added that of training or experience in teaching, the worker would be ideally equipped to carry on an effective program of dental health education. The Commission therefore recommends that more attention to oral hygiene be given in public health courses, and that, so far as possible, the dental hygiene work outside of the clinics be carried on by those who, in addition to special training in dental subjects, have a basic pedagogical background.

Dental Examinations

It has been pointed out above that the dental examinations in the schools have been made by dentists, dental hygienists or by physicians. The inadequate training of the hygienists, and therefore their unsuitability for this work, has also been stressed. The training of the physician at the present time usually gives too little consideration to the teeth to equip him with the necessary knowledge or experience to make satisfactory dental inspections, It is the belief of the Commission that these examinations are essentially dental procedures which should be carried out by trained dentists so far as possible, just as the general physical examination is made by physicians.

Dental Clinics

Children's clinics are usually maintained by boards of health or by private philanthropic groups. In theory they aim to provide dental care to children, not simply as a service to the indigent, but also as an educational measure. In too many instances, however, the educational aspect has been either omitted or made so secondary to the reparative program that the clinic has developed into merely a welfare endeavor. While this may serve a useful social need, it does not leave with the child any basic appreciation of the value of oral hygiene, so that this subject is often neglected by the child after he outgrows the age for which clinic service is available.

Many of the dental clinics, and especially the traveling dental clinics in small communities, are measured purely by the volume of operations. There is often no check on the value of their work. False standards may thus be created in the minds of both sponsors and the public. The Commission believes that the dental clinics can render more real service to the community if they aim to do worth-while work on a limited number of children rather than attempting to do something for so large a number that none can be properly served. This means that severe restrictions must be placed upon the volume and type of service rendered in these clinics.

In the selection of the age group to be served by any dental clinic service it would appear to the Commission that the community will derive the greatest returns from a given expenditure of money and effort if attention is concentrated upon the younger children. Meager as may be our knowledge of all the factors influencing dental disease, we do know that in this as in other fields correction of minor defects early in life is one of the best means of limiting the development of more extensive serious defects in later years. Thus a given amount of service in the preschool group may yield more permanent results than the same service in adolescence. With each year of age there is a diminishing return on dental corrective service. It is therefore recommended that where facilities are limited these be concentrated upon the care of the younger children. This does not mean that dental work in the adolescent or adult is not important, nor that it is devoid of preventive possibilities. There are both opportunities and needs in these groups, but the needs are so great that were any serious attempt made to meet them with present dental budgets it would mean complete neglect of the more important child group.

Adult's Clinics.—The need for more dental service for indigent adults is well recognized and has been given serious attention by many different groups. In few branches of the healing arts are the needs greater and the facilities fewer. Although this is a matter beyond the scope of the Commission, it should be pointed out that frequently facilities exist in connection with the children's clinics which might be used on certain occasions for older groups.

Dental Certificates

The present dental hygiene program as carried on in the public schools of Massachusetts is built around the issuance of an annual certificate to those children who have had all existing dental defects corrected. It has thus introduced a spirit of reward as well as competition. The exact influence of this certificate program is hard to measure. That it has brought about the correction of many dental defects in children is unquestioned, as in a single year over 117,000 children have received certificates stating that all necessary dental work has been completed. In over 42,000 of these cases the work had been performed by the family dentist. An additional 20,000 children received certificates as needing no corrective work at the time of the examination. To this extent it has been a real success. To what extent any program that is based upon rewards and which introduces the spirit of competition accomplishes a lasting educational effect is hard to determine. If the effect of the program is merely to correct defects year after year for no other purpose than that the child may receive a reward, and without inculcating an understanding of the reasons for such work, there is then serious doubt as to its permanent value.

Dental Health Education

Education is the keystone in any public health program. Dental health education is, however, in need of further study and evaluation in order to bring forth the best and the most practical methods. It should have some strong appeal to the public in order that full and intelligent cooperation may be given. Educational, health and other agencies must approach this problem with a flexible program suited to the varying local needs.

Public Education.—There can be no popular acceptance of a program for better oral hygiene without an understanding of the gravity of dental disease, its underlying causes, and the sequelae of neglect. Such a program should stress the value of adequate and proper nutrition, the importance of early and regular care of the teeth beginning in the preschool age, and the necessity of mouth cleanliness. Attention should also be given to the education of adults, and particularly of parents who are responsible for the care of children. Special stress should be laid upon child education, to the end that proper habits of dental care may be developed during the formative years. It is therefore recommended that health and educational agencies unite in a coordinated plan for public education in dental health. The Commission has already pointed out the desirable type of training for those who are to carry on this work in the community.

Professional Education.—Education of the public in oral hygiene is of no avail unless the dental and public health professions are equipped to meet the demands so created. Dental education should therefore stress the preventive approach to the problems of disease of the mouth and teeth, and increasing attention should be given to the relationship of the teeth to the general health of the human body. Dental hygiene should be given its proper place in the curricula of schools of public health. Public health officers should have an appreciation of the need of dental health, and dentists engaged in this work should be sufficiently acquainted with other phases of public health, so that they may see the proper relation of their special field to the work of their associates. It is therefore recommended that a course in dental hygiene be incorporated in the curricula of the schools of public health, and that such courses be a part of the training of those engaged in public health dental programs. The Department of Public Health can do much to promote the postgraduate education of dentists in newer developments in the preventive aspects of their profession.

Need for Research

Further progress in oral hygiene is dependent upon research. It is no criticism of our present knowledge of oral hygiene and dental physiology to say that progress in these fields has been slower than in other medical fields. This lack of progress has been due in large part to lack of research facilities. Foundations have been generous to the medical and social sciences, and the results have been gratifying. Until lately they have not been generous to dentistry. It is now apparent to both social and professional groups that the methods and knowledge of dentistry are inadequate. The social significance of the prevention of dental disease has emphasized the need of better understanding of social and biologic causes. It is absolutely necessary in a purely social sense that the problem be attacked intelligently. The public is entitled to the best services that can be given, not only in medicine and nursing, but also in dentistry. Health service must be brought within the reach of those with modest incomes. This cannot be accomplished in dentistry at the present time. A generous public which has been taught to give freely to medical and social research must now be taught to give as freely for dental research in order that simpler and more effective methods of prevention and control may be found. It is also imperative that governmental agencies should be equipped to pursue research studies in this field.

Dentistry as a Specialty of Medicine

At the present time dentistry is too often considered as a profession in itself rather than as a specialized branch of the broad field of medicine. The care and treatment of diseases of no other part of the human body have been so separated from consideration in relation to other parts of the human mechanism. Whether or not this separation may have been wise in the past, when dentistry was more largely a mechanical art, it is apparent that the time has now arrived when dentistry should be treated as a medical specialty just as is ophthalmology or otology. It is therefore essential that comparable professional standards should be observed. To a large degree many of the dental schools have already so adapted their admission requirements as to equal those of the schools of medicine. There is a need, however, for greater opportunities for postgraduate instruction and training through the provision of dental internships comparable to those in medicine. Very few such internships or residencies exist at the present time, far too few in Massachusetts to offer such training to more than a small fraction of the graduates of the dental schools in the Commonwealth. The Commission recommends that such facilities be established on a basis similar to the medical or surgical internships in general hospitals.

Dental Advertising

Protection of the individual against fraudulent exploitation is well recognized as a governmental responsibility. It is recognized in many statutes, including those for the licensing of certain professions. Although the public usually looks askance upon medical advertising, it fails to show comparable discrimination in other professional fields, including dentistry. The Commission believes that the best interests of the public would be served if greater restrictions were placed upon advertising of dental services.

Recommendations

1. That dental examinations in schools and preschool conferences be performed by dentists rather than by dental hygienists or by physicians.

2. That greater attention be given to dental education in schools of medicine and of nursing.

3. That community programs of dental hygiene be carried on by specially trained persons who have had also a background of teachers' training.

4. That courses in dental hygiene be included in the curricula of schools of public health.

5. That health and educational agencies develop a cooperative plan for popular instruction in oral hygiene.

6. That where dental clinic facilities are limited these be concentrated upon the care of the younger children.

7. That private philanthrophy and government be encouraged to give more support to dental research.

8. That dental internships be further developed.

A PEDIATRIST LOOKS AT CHILDREN'S TEETH

MERRITT B. LOW, M.D.

Pediatrician, Eaglebrook School
Deerfield, Massachusetts

The modern pediatrist looks at the "whole" child. Because it is often difficult to evaluate the history in a child's case, and because the subjective story is unobtainable or inaccurate in dealing with small children, the "child specialist" must be one keenly trained in observation. Because the teeth are (most always!) easily seen in children, the pediatrician's eye is naturally cast upon them in their relation to the body as a whole. Thus has come his interest in teeth in a broad sense, as he, a general practitioner working in a special age group, is interested in normal child development and preventive and curative medicine. In an apologetic, somewhat presumptive, but at the same time very interested mood, do I therefore launch myself on some very general comments and observations about a subject of which I know very little in any detailed sense.

A little over a year ago (and similar occurrences have happened before and since) a mother walked into my office with a five-year-old child who just "wouldn't eat," who looked pale (and a neighbor had said this was probably due to heart trouble), and who had occasional spells of abdominal pain (which caused the mother to worry about appendicitis). The child was brought in to have heart trouble and appendicitis ruled out. The mother was quite concerned over these two possibilities. Physical examination was not especially remarkable, except that there were four badly carious "two-year molar" teeth. The child had never been to a dentist (though I regret to say some similar children *have* been to the dentist). It seemed interesting psychologically that here was an intelligent mother, genuinely interested in her child's health, focussing on questionable hidden possibilities, while staring her in the face were four badly diseased teeth. I wondered why this phenomenon seemed to exist. I tried to explain the situation to her, referred her to a good dentist, and had the pleasure of seeing the child gain rapidly in the next few months after the teeth had been attended to. The symptoms, furthermore, disappeared.

Certainly one thing we need is a clarification for lay people of dentists' viewpoints as to the proper procedures involved in caring for children's teeth in a preventive way. Differences of opinion are interpreted by parents as meaning confusion in the ranks of dentists, and where there is confusion and lack of realistic clarification it is altogether too easy to adopt an ultraconservative do-nothing-until-things-are-straightened-out policy. We cannot be too dogmatic and yet we must have a set of rules to which to adhere, a working formula to guide us and to present to intelligent parents. The difficulty in handling small children in the dentist's chair is another reason which holds back progress, although this difficulty is by no means insurmountable. Perhaps there should be "children's dentists," men who by personal inclination and training have the time, patience, and desire to handle children's special preventive and corrective problems.

It seems that certain children have bad teeth no matter what care is given. There is some inherent, possibly hereditary, factor which seems to cause "soft" teeth. All our modern knowledge of preventive dentistry applied in prenatal and postnatal supervision appears to fail in these instances. Adequate calcium and Vitamin D intake, prenatally and postnatally, is certainly not the whole solution, as so many of us know. Further researches in biochemistry and metabolism must give us the answer, if indeed there is one. Fortunately this type of circumstance is relatively rare. The other condition is much more common, i. e., bad teeth caused by improper handling of an individual situation. We can further subdivide this second group into (a) bad teeth the result of poor or inadequate nutrition and (b) bad teeth the cause of poor nutrition. Sometimes it is difficult to tell to which subgroup a given child belongs. In some cases the situation is directly attributable to special inadequacies of diet, especially as regards calcium and Vitamin D intake. Applied scientific dietetics help us here. In this connection it may be said that some children seem to have more "reserve" than others; they are in astonishingly good condition (teeth included) despite apparently gross dietary inadequacies. In other instances there is a "secondary malnutrition," and the child becomes malnourished and cannot chew and digest his food because his teeth are so poor. A vicious circle is instituted. Sometimes there are other less obvious reasons for poor teeth. The parents are inadequate and cannot follow through on simple, inexpensive, routine procedures advised for home practice. They grow to expect a benevolent, paternalistic "government" or social agency or other outside force to carry them along.

Education is thus here again a cornerstone of progress, although agreement among dentists as to fundamental concepts must come first. In education we need not overstress the importance of the teeth as "foci of infection" in children. That has already been stressed. And I already see about me, in dealing with children, too much fear psychology. We should not, even though we can, frighten people into caring for their children's teeth.

What then does the pediatrist ask of the dental profession as regards children's teeth? The facts are well known. In Franklin County alone, of over five hundred preschool children examined in summer Well Child Conferences, it is conservatively estimated that more than one hundred and fifty were in marked need of dental care. Certainly the idea that the temporary or deciduous teeth are not worth bothering about must be relegated to the limbo of long outworn dicta. Certainly the fact that abscessed teeth should be removed must be made a matter of common knowledge. Certainly some recommended system of periodic examination and preventive work must be developed. Certainly parents must be educated to know that something must be done to decayed teeth besides "nothing." Certainly the gauntlet is being laid down to those who are interested in preserving the American method of treating dental and medical health in an individualized, personalized way.

The needs for clarification and unification of standards, for education, and for improvement and organization of treatment are obvious to an "outsider" who is interested in child health and optimum growth, who likes to think he is looking at the forest *and* the trees. The principles of routine home care for the baby's and preschool child's teeth must be outlined, dietary factors and rules must be re-emphasized, periodic examinations in individual or group form must be planned for and recommended, and there must be unification, elucidation, and dissemination of knowledge concerning established procedures for the care of defects in children's teeth when they appear.

THE IOWA PLAN FOR DENTAL HEALTH EDUCATION
JOHN C. BRAUER, D.D.S., M.Sc., F.A.C.D.
Director of the Bureau of Dental Hygiene, State University of Iowa;
Department of Preventive Dentistry, State University of Iowa,
College of Dentistry, Iowa City, Iowa

For fifteen years the children of Iowa have been under the influence of some dental health educational program. The tremendous effect it has had on the minds and bodies of the present young adults and growing generation can well be exemplified by the attitude and opinions expressed. The child, the young adult, the parent, and the educator, who has come in contact with this program and utilized it, feel that dentistry and its service is a necessity. Dental examinations and corrections become a yearly routine and are for the major part conducted in the dental office.

Education, through its leaders in their various capacities, is of one accord when it feels that it is the duty of the schools to teach the art of living in its broadest sense. This, then, includes how to keep the body, and with it the mind, physically fit. Dental health can no longer be separated from general health problems, for the two are synonymous. The following account will present the working principles of the Bureau of Dental Hygiene.

The first activities in dental hygiene in the State of Iowa began in 1924 under the provisions of the Sheppard-Towner Act. It was an integral part of the division of maternity and infant hygiene of the Extension Division of the University of Iowa. Prior to 1927 all efforts were directed to the preschool child (Sheppard-Towner); however, since the latter date the Iowa Dental Health Plan has had as its principle objective the teaching of the elementary school child.

The Bureau of Dental Hygiene is not associated with the Extension Division of the University of Iowa, nor is it a part of the State Department of Health. It is a separate bureau sponsored and financed by the State University of Iowa, and is housed in the College of Dentistry at Iowa City. There is a very close relationship and correlation between the Bureau and the State Department of Health, as well as the Extension Division of the University.

The Bureau staff consists of a Director who is also the Head of Preventive Dentistry and Professor of Pedodontics, a field worker who is a trained public health nurse, a full-time secretary, and a part-time educational consultant.

The "Iowa Plan" for dental health education embodies three main objectives: namely, education, prevention, and correction. EDUCATION—The development and presentation of material educationally sound in the classroom is a very vital factor in stimulating the child. Teachers have an unusual opportunity to instill and develop positive health habits in the child which often become lifelong routine. PREVENTION—Prevention must start at home through the routine program of mouth hygiene and dietary habits. Literature and personal contact is the medium employed in presenting the material to the parent. CORRECTION—Systematic and regular dental inspection within the dental office, as well as completing the necessary corrections is of major importance. The point is stressed that inspection should be made primarily in the dental office in order that the dentist may properly proceed to make a more adequate and more thorough diagnosis.

Purposes of the Plan

(1) To arouse mouth health consciousness
(2) To present sound principles in nutrition so that pupils may better build and maintain stronger and healthier teeth
(3) To create an appreciation for regular and early dental attention and to establish early the daily habit of home care of the mouth.
(4) To impress upon pupils the close relation between mouth health and general physical well-being.

Literature

The literature available from the Bureau includes a Handbook of Dental Health Education for the Elementary School Teacher, Parent Bulletins, and general dental educational leaflets for teachers and children, the latter two being prepared from time to time.

Progress in the Program

There has been a gradual increase in activities and results from the beginning of the Plan. In 1928 there were rural schools of 11 counties and 58 towns participating in the program. In the year 1937-1938 rural schools of 83 counties and 450 towns, consolidated, and parochial school systems, were active. Over 450,000 pieces of literature were distributed from this office during 1937-1938.

The county health programs are under the direction of the county superintendent of schools who has supervision of a hundred or more rural teachers. In counties where public health nurses are employed, valuable assistance is offered by them. The actual teaching, however, of dental health education becomes the duty of the classroom teacher.

The following table presents a summary of the number of children reached in active towns and rural schools in Iowa and the per capita cost.

NUMBER OF CHILDREN REACHED IN TOWN AND RURAL SCHOOLS PARTICIPATING IN THE IOWA DENTAL HEALTH EDUCATION PLAN

SUMMARY OF COST

1927-1928	1928-1929	1929-1930	1930-1931	1931-1932	1932-1933
?	46,000	113,000	180,000	176,000	150,000
1933-1934	1934-1935	1935-1936	1936-1937	1937-1938	
251,146	255,022	287,099	235,070	250,000	

SUMMARY

Total Number of Children Served	1927-1938	1,943,337
Cost of Service	1927-1938	$97,862.86
Cost Per Capita over Period	1927-1938	$ .05
Cost Per Capita for Year	1937-1938	.027

DENTAL EXTRACTIONS

FRANK W. ROUNDS, A.B., D.D.S.
President, Massachusetts Dental Society

The meaning of this title is obvious. It refers of course to the removal of teeth. According to dentistry's nomenclature this phase of practice is termed "Exodontia" and the person who performs these operations is an "Exodontist." These two designations were inaugurated in 1913 by Winter of St. Louis, who at that time published the first comprehensive textbook on the subject. Hence, this specialty has just passed its twenty-fifth birthday. Prior to that date there was no distinctive term used to describe this department of dental practice nor was there any standardized guide for operative technique. Undoubtedly the oldest of surgical procedures, very little change had been made in methods during all the years which we generally understand as "modern times."

The standards of present day Exodontia are not those of the last century or even those of the first decade of the present one. The earlier day criterion was mainly to get the aching tooth out wholly or in part and to relieve discomfort. The science of anesthesia was in its infancy. Dentistry to its credit had contributed to medical knowledge in discovering nitrous oxide and ether as anesthetic agents but none of the refinements in anesthetic administration nor the safeguards now uniformly employed were in use. The value of premedication for psychic or physical reasons was undreamed of and the virtue of basal anesthetics had yet to be recognized.

In 1910 Hunter of England caustically criticised American dental practice chiefly because of filthy mouth conditions caused by ill-fitting crowns and bridges. In response to his diatribes our profession analyzed its methods and began to realize that whereas its work had been properly catalogued with that of tradesmen and artisans it now had in addition a health function to perform. Fortunately the X-ray was coming into general use and the diagnostic findings thereby brought to light greatly enlarged our vision. Educational requirements for the dental degree became immeasurably broadened. Research in pathology and bacteriology was inaugurated and stimulated in many institutions. The results of these developments established the fact that dentistry has a definite duty to perform in the control of public health. Today that opinion has been confirmed in the minds of all who are connected with health work.

Mayo publicly stated that a large proportion of human ills obtain ingress through the oral cavity and Osler long ago insisted that unhygienic mouths and infected teeth were prolific sources of various phases of constitutional disease.

All of this indicates that the specialty of Exodontia has a big part to play in the maintenance of healthy mouths and an even larger part in helping answer some of the medical problems. There has been made, therefore, a great deal of progress in the average dental office relating to the conduct of this specialty. Unsanitary paraphernalia has been generally replaced by attractive, hygienic and efficient equipment. Rational methods of procedure have been instituted looking to a full consideration of the patients' physical welfare and mental comfort. The efficient operator is warranted in assuring his patient relative freedom from discomfort during surgical interference and he has developed a diagnostic ability in interpreting unhealthy mouth conditions which, combined with a constantly increasing operative skill, has largely eliminated empiricism. An intelligent psychological approach, expertness in the interpretation of subjective and objective symptoms, safe and clean surgery, and a "golden rule" attitude is embodied in the modern Exodontist's make-up. Such a conception of professional responsibility makes it a far cry from the day when the dentist was a mere "tooth puller." The laity are demanding expert services for, through the educational influences of health campaigns as promulgated by the press, radio and other sources, they are making an increasing demand for the highest qualifications from their dental consultants.

The X-ray is not an infallible guide in diagnosis but is a necessary supplement to the clinical story. If radiographs are properly angulated and processed they furnish information quite proportionate to the operator's ability to interpret them. Poorly produced radiographs can be and often are misleading. With opportunities at our hand to obtain correct radiographs it is a shortsighted policy to be satisfied with less than the best. If the dentist correctly radiographs every tooth he is to remove he goes far in eliminating uncertainty and by the preoperative knowledge to be attained minimizes much trauma. Trauma is wound and is a necessary sequence to any surgical interference. Much unnecessary trauma, however, can be eliminated by having all the evidence at hand before operation and the patient benefits because of a minimization of unfavorable postoperative results. Immediate postoperative radiographic checkups are quite universally made and are very illuminating.

The preliminary radiographic routine is of course supplemented by careful clinical examination which includes not only the area to be operated but also the mouth as a whole. The presence of active pathological manifestations greatly influences the dentist in his care of the case. As a general rule he avoids surgery in the presence of acute reactions and attempts by local medication and general treatment to bring the tissues back to as near a normal condition as possible. There are times though when immediate interference is indicated. As an example of this conservatism it is very rare when it is wise to interfere surgically in the presence of an acute Vincent's infection.

While complete physical examinations are not in the province of the dentist and are not often essential yet a general understanding of the patient's mental make-up and the presence of general constitutional diseases are contributing factors in outlining procedure. A casual conversation with the patient, a few simple preliminary tests and keen powers of observation often bring to light important data. One of the chief benefits of such precaution is its bearing on the choice of the anesthetic to be employed and the technique of administering it. As examples; nervous and wrought-up patients are usually more amenable and less unhappy if a narcosis is advised. However, if they prefer local anesthesia or if it is advocated by the dentist there is usually an indication for premedication to obviate psychic shock and reduce the high tension which they are undergoing. In my experience the end results of extractions for children are better if nitrous oxide is employed. Paleness of lips and skin combined with puffiness under the eyes suggest anemia. These signs tell us that liberal oxygenation must be used if nitrous oxide is the agent selected. The hard and engorged vessels of the arteriosclerotic and the noisy, wheezing of the asthmatic are guideposts for the alert operator. It is quite usual for the cardiac or the specific case or the hemophiliac, the tubercular and the diabetic to voluntarily disclose something of their history. If a general anesthetic in the office is contemplated a careful examination is made to be sure that airways are unobstructed. Many points could be cited to illustrate the means by which valuable diagnostic information may be obtained without unneccessarily alarming the patient.

There are various accepted anesthetic agents available to the Exodontist. Among these are ethyl chloride by inhalation, nitrous oxide and oxygen and local anesthesia. These are the favored office anesthetics; ethyl chloride being used only for transitory operations for children. For hospitalized cases we have evipal, vinethene, avertin and ether. Unless emergencies necessitate, these agents should not be employed in office practice.

In the earlier days the dentists in general felt their obligation was fulfilled when the tooth or teeth were removed but today the dentist realizes that his duty is to follow his case through to complete recovery, hence adequate postoperative care is a routine. This involves attention to such postoperative complications as prolonged or recurrent hemorrhage, the so-called dry socket, postoperative pain and maintenance of adequate drainage in acute infections.

Space does not permit an extended discussion of technical procedures, the purpose of this brief sketch mainly being to impress upon the mind of the reader that Exodontists today are fulfilling their function intelligently and in the interests of the patients' welfare and comfort and further that dentistry realizes fully its obligations in the field of oral and general health.

IS SUGAR THE LONE FACTOR IN PRODUCING DENTAL CARIES?

MARY SPALDING, M.A.

Supervisor of Nutrition
Massachusetts Department of Public Health

Dr. Nina Simmonds of the University of California College of Dentistry gives us the following summary based on many careful studies—

"1. If an individual is susceptible to tooth decay, he should reduce his intake of all sweet foods to a minimum. In this way he will keep the flora of his mouth low in those organisms known to be acid formers. Starches and fats should be his main energy foods.

"2. In addition to keeping the intake of sweet foods low, each person should plan his diet so that all factors, including vitamin D, are present in abundance.

"The disadvantages of these suggestions is that no one can do these tasks for us. Each individual must accept the responsibility for taking a highly satisfactory diet and also for lowering his own intake of sweets. Parents must assume the responsibility for children."

Dr. George Minot also points this out insofar as general health is concerned. As he states it, "The future of mankind depends to a great extent on what he chooses to eat." We could not improve tooth health without the information coming in to us from scientists, physicians, dentists, and others. The great question then is how we may interest the four and one-half million men, women and children in Massachusetts to follow these teachings.

The amount of sugar consumed in the United States per capita in 1932 was 112 pounds. The only country in the world to exceed this amount is Australia. Since that time it has increased tremendously. Massachusetts is one of the greatest candy eating states. Visit many of our lunchrooms and watch the young people with just ten cents to spend, using five cents of it for candy or frosted cakes to appease healthy noonday appetites, so not paying heed to Dr. Simmonds' proposition for getting all food factors in their diet. Candy tempts them in all kinds of delectable packets with appealing names. Some schools are still displaying these as the children begin their line at the counter.

Nutrition Notes for February, 1939, tells us that a large candy concern "announces that they are now adding a cod liver oil concentrate to the lollypops they make, each to contain the vitamin equivalent of a half-tablespoon of standard cod liver oil. Many parents (the wise ones) will not welcome this announcement. Children may think they now have an indisputable reason for obtaining the penny that will buy one of these candies, and mothers and fathers will now have one more argument to combat when refusing their children this popular sweet. For despite the vitamins, candy eaten between meals will still tend to spoil the appetite for bland foods."

A study made at the University of Witwatersrand, Johannesburg, showed that refined white sugar produced decalcification in healthy teeth incubated in this media, while brown cane juices caused very few to decalcify. Whole wheat caused some teeth to decalcify, but highly refined white flour attacked a significantly greater proportion of teeth. For reasons such as these we suggest molasses and more dried fruits as sources of sweets. (See "Fruit Candies" published by the Massachusetts Department of Public Health.) Psychologists tell us we are more successful in getting individuals to act if we do not drastically try to take away a common food.

Moreover, dark bread may well consist of some hard bread, such as hard rye, rather than all soft bread. In the German Research Committee Study two groups of children, twenty in each, from 4 to 12 years, were observed. There were three times as much caries in the soft bread group as in the hard bread group after the two years of the experiment with only this difference in diet. As Leonard says, "A dietary of easily masticated foods leads to hurried eating, resulting in under-development and insufficient functioning of the periodontal tissues which are an easy prey to bacterial invasion. It also leads to unclean teeth through deficient detergent action and insufficient salivary stimulation." Hard dark breads as well as muscle meats, and vegetables such as raw carrot strips and celery are then good sources of both food value and an opportunity for vigorous mastication.

Dr. E. H. Schiotz, who was instrumental in getting the famous Oslo breakfast for school children, made a careful study of two hundred children in the national schools, the 0.21%, the only ones who possessed healthy teeth. He investigated the character of feeding from birth, the dietaries of the mothers during pregnancy, economic status of the parents, and the present height and weight of the children. He also studied the dietaries and teeth of the children in the twenty-three homes where accurate data were kept. He found that the social and economic status of the family plays an important part; well-to-do children having 13.5 times as good a chance to possess healthy teeth as children from poor homes. The healthiness of the teeth he felt appeared to be proportional to Dr. Simmonds' second point on the regular supply of protective foods. He found no correlation established between the consumption of sugar and the health of teeth in different institutions whereas the regular supply of cod liver oil in winter seemed to play a beneficial part. We wonder if he had an opportunity to study the kinds and amounts of sweets used in the past.

Efficiency of vitamin D leads in our winter darkened state to a necessity for following Dr. Bion R. East's findings, showing that the more remote the season is from summer, the greater the caries, the three winter months producing the greatest number. If enough Vitamin D, 400 International Units, was given, improvement in tooth health was noted. Again remembering Dr. Simmonds' point, partial vitamin D deficiency causes some degeneration of intercellular substance and periodontal tissue as well as in other tissues, enamel, dentine, and jaw bone.

Again improvement is brought about when the vitamin C requirement is met. Fortunately most people like daily an excellent source of vitamin C (noted in the Department's "Vitamin C Foods Each Day") or at least can afford two good sources as suggested there.

It goes without saying that milk is the best source of calcium and phosphorus, especially in consideration of the other valuable food substances it contains. Now the problem is how are we going to interest expectant mothers, high school students, and others to take their daily quota. A very interesting psychological study of milk drinking habits has been made by Dr. Lazarsfeld of the University of Newark, where 5,227 boys and girls between 11 and 18 years of age in three Newark schools were asked about their likes and dislikes. Interviews were held with the 415 children who reported they disliked milk as well as with 217 of their mothers. Money seemed to have something to do with the problem, for more children drank milk with lunch at home than at school. It was interesting to find that early troubles at the time of weaning accounted for a quarter of the difficulties, and that one-third of the difficulties were caused by unpleasant incidents at school. Those who liked milk but did not drink it gave as a reason that they did not wish to gain weight or wished to be more grown up.

Summary: The dentist is in a strategic position to influence the nutrition of his patient. No one wants to suffer from poor teeth. People like to have good-looking teeth, especially young people. Mothers want good teeth for their children. In the short time the dentist has for talking with patients he may emphasize an obvious difficulty to overcome, such as too many sweets. He may wish to give "Does Your Family's Food Measure Up?" to a mother in order to indicate to her what a balanced diet is, or some such booklet as "Your Guide for Buying, Preparing, and Serving Good Meals at Low Cost" to the family on a low income. As the League of Nations Health Organisation advises, he may well improve diets in terms of everyday meals by suitable combinations of ordinary foods in most cases rather than correct deficiencies by means of pure vitamins, minerals, or yeast.

If some such expedients are not sufficient, he may wish to call on the nutritionist to study the family's foods, as well as their purchase, preparation, eating habits of the family, and other possibilities for which he may not have the time or the training, for education in nutrition is a long time job even with the knowledge we now have at hand. Miss Ruth L. White of the Nutrition Department, Forsyth Dental Infirmary, has well demonstrated this service.

Well-balanced meals, together with a will to do and knowledge to practice, and not "sugar as a lone factor" help prevent dental caries.
Material available from the Massachusetts Department of Public Health, Division of Child Hygiene, 1 Beacon St., Boston, Mass.

    Vitamin C Foods Each Day
    Vitamins and Minerals
    Does Your Family's Food Measure Up? (a measuring stick for a family's meals)
    A Measuring Stick for a Well-Chosen Lunch
    Your Guide for Buying, Preparing, and Serving Good Meals at Low Cost
    Fruit Candies

Bibliography

SIMMONDS, NINA, "Present Status of Dental Caries in Relation to Nutrition"—*Am. J. of Pub. Health* 28: 1381-1387, December, 1938.

OSBORN, T. W. B., NORISKIN, J. N., and STAZ, J., "Comparison of Crude and Refined Sugar and Cereals in Their Ability to Produce in Vitro Decalcification of Teeth"—*J. Dent. Research* 16: 156-171, June, 1937.

HABER, GUSTAV G., "Influence of Bread Nutrition in Germany and Switzerland upon Development of Caries, Calculus, and Film due to Certain Methods of Feeding"—German Research Committee.

KOEHNE, MARTHA J., "Relation of Diet to Oral Health,"—*J. Am. Dent. A.* 25: 1767-1780, November, 1938.

LEONARD, H. J., "Dietary Factors in Periodontal Disturbances"— *J. Am. Dent. A.* 25: 102-114, January, 1938.

EAST, BION R., "Nutrition and Dental Caries,"—*Am. J. Pub. Health.* 28: 72-76, January, 1938.

SCHIOTZ, E. H., "Dental Caries and Nutrition"—*Nord. Hyg. Tideskr*, V. 19: 242-308, 1938.

LAZARSFELD, P. F., "Milk Drinking Habits among Young People"— Milk Research Council, Inc., and University of Newark Research Centre, 1938.

"*Nutrition Notes*"—February, 1939.

THE PROMOTION OF DENTAL INTERNSHIPS IN GENERAL HOSPITALS

RICHARD H. NORTON, D.D.S., D.M.D.

*Professor of Oral Surgery and Anesthesia,
Director of Interns, Tufts College
Dental School*

To give us a clearer understanding of this subject, it might be of interest to historically review internships in general. Although there is a definite date when medical and surgical interns were officially appointed, it is the consensus of opinion that these appointments originated at the time general hospitals were recognized by organized medicine.

In 1765, the Pennsylvania Hospital in Philadelphia was established it being the first general hospital founded in this country. Shortly after this the New York Hospital was incorporated, and in 1820, the Massachusetts General Hospital was opened in Boston. These institutions had an intern service represented by medical students and young graduates. At the Massachusetts General Hospital the undergraduate interns were called house pupils and have continued under that name to the present time.

Before general hospitals were introduced there were buildings where people were segregated and isolated, and rightly named, pesthouses. They were seldom supervised by medical men, and treatment and care was given by volunteer laymen who had had smallpox or similar contagious diseases. Obviously these volunteer workers had to live in the pesthouses, and they might well be considered a forerunner of the early hospital intern. They did receive some advice from a few interested and philanthropic medical men, and so again might be likened to our modern intern as they were a go-between for the medical profession and the patient.

As previously stated, the early intern was a senior medical student or young graduate and was on continuous service. He lived at the hospital, receiving his room and board and sometimes his laundry. This situation filled a longfelt need in medical education as it gave the young practitioner an opportunity to study and treat cases. This was particularly beneficial as these interns were supervised by experienced doctors. The student automatically became the liaison officer between the private practitioner and the patient. These appointments rapidly became popular, and at the present time all general hospitals have efficient interns and house officers on their staffs. It is the requirement of medical education that a graduate must serve at least one year in a recognized hospital.

It is an interesting fact that one of the larger hospitals of New England which opened in 1871 with five beds, soon required sixteen beds to meet their demands, and immediately felt the need of a resident doctor. The medical staff appointed a young physician at once who was given his room and board for this service. One year later a second intern was appointed, and in March, 1873, the first student internship was given. This latter assignment marked a definite change and improvement in the education of the medical school associated with the hospital, for it stimulated a desire on the part of other students to seek internships. These appointments gave the young men an excellent opportunity for correlation and then demonstration of theory obtained during their student days. It also made it possible for the staff at the hospital to keep in close contact with their patients and to keep proper records while following their cases.

As dental education has advanced during the past decade and has closely approximated medical education, general hospitals, through their staffs, have increasingly felt the need of a dental service. Soon after the close of the late war, externs and outpatient dental clinics were established in recognized hospitals. In 1926, two graduates were appointed from the Tufts College Dental School to a hospital in Syracuse, New York, and one to the Presbyterian Hospital in New York. They were appointed as dental house officers and were on service for a period of one year. They were immediately and wholeheartedly accepted by the medical staff and their fellow medical interns, and filled a much needed gap in medical care. With that beginning, and as a result of the service rendered, and demand created, there are in the East at least one hundred hospitals available for dental interns, ranging from one to six appointments. This represents hospitals approved by the American Medical Association's Board on Medical Internships.

In 1938 there were approximately two hundred dental graduates appointed to internships in the above-mentioned hospitals. The Tufts College Dental School, one of forty class A institutions, has assigned one hundred and seventy-three graduates to general hospitals since 1926. Although for the past eight years, one-fifth of the senior class have been appointed to dental internships, this year there seems to be a very definite increase in the demand. This means that for the year 1939 and

40 the number of graduates receiving dental internships will definitely raise the percentage.

Very encouraging reports have come from a large percentage of the institutions with dental interns, and they have all stated that the service is now an absolute necessity. The medical staffs are very happily surprised to find that the dental men are obtaining a very liberal medical education and a clear understanding of medical problems, and this is particularly true as they refer to dental and oral complications. Following their service, the dental interns have expressed great enthusiasm for the post-graduate work that they have received, not only because of the chance to correlate their undergraduate studies in making a diagnosis, but also the excellent opportunity to work with the medical graduate, which of course broadens his point of view.

It is equally true that the medical and surgical interns are receiving a liberal dental education. Very recently after speaking to a group of medical interns, I was delighted to note their expressions of enthusiasm for the dental service and the opportunity that they were given to understand the many problems in that field. It is most unfortunate that the medical student is not given a more liberal dental education. Perhaps the interest stimulated by the dental interns may awaken our medical educators to this need. It is evident that a dental internship should only be given in institutions where medical interns are on service for it is a proven fact that it is a mutual benefit to all concerned. Many patients are expressing their enthusiasm concerning the dental care that it is possible to receive while they are confined.

It may be of interest to briefly mention some of the types of service that the dental interns are rendering at the present time. Oral cavities are put in a healthy condition preparatory to the administration of general anesthetics, definitely minimizing the hazards of postoperative pneumonias. Potential foci of infection are being eliminated, raising the resistance of the patient and many times removing the specific cause for a given disease, and many vague oral complications are being diagnosed by the dental intern following the request for a consultation by the medical staff.

In many institutions the dental intern is also serving in the outpatient dental department, and as his service here is enhanced by early graduates and volunteer externs from the senior classes of the dental schools, it is felt that this is a big step forward in solving the dental problem for indigent patients. With this dual role being played by the dental resident, cases that must be hospitalized are promptly placed in the house and intelligently and correctly cared for by the dental service. There is also the added advantage of having an efficient medical service that can be called upon to cooperate when there are systemic disturbances.

At the present time the dental profession is divided into several specialties, and perhaps the most outstanding one is the field of oral surgery. A dental internship in a general hospital gives the dentist an excellent opportunity to do postgraduate work in this field, and it is hoped that in the near future any dentists who may choose to specialize in the field of oral surgery, will be required to serve an internship in a recognized hospital.

EXTENSION OF DENTAL FACILITIES
WILLIAM HAYES HOYT, D.D.S.
Professor of Prosthetics, Tufts College Dental School
Chairman of Public Relations Committee, Massachusetts Dental Society

No matter what opinions one may have about Government medical care or supervision, the fact remains that one of the outstanding needs today in medical social service is facilities for dental care. No matter what our opinions may be about the conditions which brought about this need or the effects on the future practice of dentistry, the need still exists. It is useless to argue that social experimentation will result in permanent practices because we well know that every institution established by man has always been undergoing modification and in some cases extinction.

The call for dental services has increased to such an extent in the last year, that social agencies are seeking names of practitioners to whom they may refer patients who do not want institutional services and who expect, and want, to pay for personal attention—necessarily at lower fees than the traditional fees commonly accredited to the dental profession. It is expected that the profession will voluntarily supply this want. Just what the effects of such action will be upon the future practice of dentistry no one dare venture.

Regardless of our political or social affiliations, in candid moments we must admit what is so evident, the need of a wider spread of dental services for a wider range of people. This can only be given either by complete reorganization of the systems of dentistry or discovery of simpler methods of treatment—the first is the only method possible today since the second is not yet discovered.

The profession knows how inadequately it is equipped to render a widespread social service. It knows, only too well, how little is its knowledge of the causes of dental disease, but since it has always to act with the knowledge it has, it becomes at once apparent that something must be done. Done—even if we do not know what to do or how to do it; for the fact that we are willing to experiment might eventually aid in a happy solution.

Cities and towns have had the problem of administration and of care of their aged poor for many years. The load has been increased recently because of world-wide economic conditions. To be sure, most local governments have received aid through Federal or State grants, mostly for work programs, but as the conditions have continued, those who found precarious labor under those grants, could not care for unexpected medical needs. Local governments have had an outlet for those needing medical care through county and local hospitals, but no outlets for those who need dental services. Wherever possible, some authorities have arranged with local practitioners to care for the needy cases at fees worked out jointly by the welfare officials and the practitioners. This arrangement, far from satisfactory, has at least served the needs of the local officers. Now comes the need for more extensive attention, for rehabilitation of personalities and for reasons of health among those who are sick. These needs are growing and local boards are finding it increasingly difficult not only to finance such services, but also to find men to do them. They may admit the need, but are faced with the facts that they first have to keep their recipients housed and fed to subsistance levels. There is no immediate prospect of relief, but there is a possibility of Federal Funds for health measures.

However, there promises a method of local autonomy whereby municipalities may control their dental problem. Most cities and towns of any size already have school dental clinics under Board of Health control with civil service operators—extension of the services of these clinics to local inhabitants and under local control would acquaint the whole neighborhood with the seriousness of the dental problem and the expense of operation. The objection will be that they are not equipped for the adult services for extraction and prosthesis. This can be solved very simply by having the operators selected to render these services, bring their own instruments. Prosthetic services, when necessary in the opinion of the Welfare Boards, could be cared for by these operators up to the point of laboratory services, then the local board could select one or two local commercial dental laboratories to complete the prescription of the dental operator—adjustments of cases, of course, would have to be done by the dentist. Such a setup would place the responsibility squarely on local shoulders, and there is no happier situation than such a responsibility, anywhere.

Until such time as the State Commission of Health has widely increased powers, the Commission could act as advisor in the setup and conduct of these clinics. The difficulty of no responsible state head of dental services is not serious, in fact it is propitious, for without state control, the local governments would, perforce, have to act upon their own responsibility—a wise American system—seeking the advice of the local practitioners who quite naturally will act for their own protection as well as the needs of their local public.

All traveling clinics, such as are sent to rural localities, should be immediately placed under the control of the Health Commission, both as to the extent of the services to be rendered and fees to be charged. Better still—have the local community bear all the expense of the operations of the clinic while within its jurisdiction for services to its indigent, the operator to be a State health officer under the State Health Board and responsible for the type and extent of service to the Commission. While this may seem a contradiction of local autonomy—it is the only solution whereby the quality, not quantity, of service could be guaranteed when towns purchased for their people this type of attention—and here again the local practitioners would fit into the picture as consultants.

Those of the profession who are familiar with the usual School-Health Board dental clinics are disturbed at the inadequacy and inefficiency, in many cases, of their operation. Such plans as outlined would acquaint the responsible laymen of the communities involved with the problem—because it means money—and would awaken the community to the need of honest, efficient and adequate medical and dental care for those of their neighbors who, though less effective, are none the less human—particularly the children.

It is about time that Massachusetts did a little unorthodox experimentation in social welfare, and if need be, to seek the aid of the General Court to modify laws temporarily to permit experimentation. For we must admit that man has arrived at his present state only by experimentation and adventure in social living. It is certain that should the plans for local volunteers among the dentists to aid those self-respecting Americans who want to pay but can't pay much, and the responsibility of local governments for their own people fail, the people through their representatives will try social experimentation themselves.

If the biology of our profession was understood we would probably find that the greatest stimulus to our advance lies in the lack of knowledge of our problems and the challenge of a need which we cannot meet.

The doctors are ready and willing. They have already given. It is the people who sleep.

DEVELOPMENTS IN DENTAL EDUCATION
HOWARD M. MARJERISON, D.M.D.
Dean, Tufts College Dental School

Society at large is the ultimate victim for good or evil of the product of dental education.

The quality of teaching which is provided by institutions which are charged with the responsibility of training men for any phase of health service touches the individual more closely than any other field of education. For this reason dental schools, in common with other professional schools, are in reality public service corporations. The public, therefore, is entitled to know the facts concerning their administration and development. Hence we welcome this opportunity to explain the nature of some of the developments in the field of dentistry during the past few years.

Prior to the World War a recruit to the field of dentistry had two avenues by which he could enter the profession: (1) by successfully passing an examination given by a state board of registration which legally entitled him to practice dentistry irrespective of his educational background—the majority who chose this avenue usually acquired the rudiments of the profession by becoming apprenticed to a dentist; (2) by taking a formal course in a dental school consisting of three years' professional training with a high school diploma or its equivalent as an entrance requirement. At the successful completion of this course he received a degree in dentistry and was then required to pass the state board examination to receive his legal right to practice.

It is interesting to note in passing that in 1901 about 40% of the dentists then practicing in this country had never attended a dental school, but had entered the profession by passing examinations given by various state boards following an apprenticeship in a dental office. From 1900 on, however, the majority of dentists have received a degree from a dental school, and from 1917 to the present time a dental degree has been a prerequisite for the practice of dentistry.

Since the World War sweeping changes have been made in the standards, aims, and objectives of dental education culminating in the present curriculum which requires that candidates for a degree in dentistry must spend at least two years in a college of liberal arts, the so-called predental course, and four years' professional training in a dental school, a total of six years' intensive study, before he can qualify for a degree in dentistry. Having received his degree he must then pass an examination which is given by the state board of registration before he can legally practice his profession. Thus it may be seen that dentistry has increased its educational requirements one hundred per cent, in a relatively short time, and if we include the noncollege trained group, the percentage is higher.

In addition to these major developments in the field of undergraduate teaching, opportunities have also been provided for the graduate dentist to continue his education. In 1915 the Forsyth Dental Infirmary for Children was established in Boston, the first institution of its kind in the world to give free dental service to children. This magnificent institution was built and endowed by the Forsyth brothers and treats thousands of children annually. The Forsyth Dental Infirmary was followed by similar institutions elsewhere, notably the Eastman Clinic in Rochester, and the Guggenheim Dental Clinic in New York. These clinics in addition to rendering a service to the community also aid in furthering educational development by offering internships to graduate dentists.

The last twenty years has also witnessed a great increase in the number of dental clinics in hospitals. Many hospitals now have full-time resident dental interns, and the number is increasing from year to year.

Another important advance during the last ten years has been the establishment of three centers for graduate study in dentistry at Yale, the University of Rochester, and the University of Chicago for the primary purpose of training research scientists and teachers in the field of dentistry.

What has been the propelling motive behind all these great changes? How can they be justified? In the first place, advancing knowledge forced recognition of the fact that the teeth and jaws belong to the rest of the body and that diseases common to the oral cavity were in many instances symptoms of abnormal conditions elsewhere in the body. It brought into the open the fallacy of considering the teeth and jaws as separate entities. It emphasized the fact that the role which the structures of the mouth play in health and disease is just as serious and important to the health of the individual as the eye, ear, nose, or any other organ of the body. Hence, it became evident that if dentistry was to assume its position in the field of medical science where it belonged, if it was to keep pace with advancing knowledge, if it was to meet its responsibility to the public, it should train its practitioners on the same fundamental basis as any other specialty of medicine. In the second place, dentistry faced the fact that its traditional educational approach (three years' training) was inadequate to meet the implications of this new viewpoint. In spite of the developments in technical methods of treatment which this system of training emphasized and with which American dentistry has gained a world-wide reputation, the cause of caries, pyorrhea, and abnormalities of the jaws still remains an unsolved mystery. As a result the methods of treatment which dentistry now has at its disposal are of necessity preventive and empirical; moreover, they are too complicated and expensive to meet the public health needs of society. The widespread prevalence of dental disease which exists in all civilized countries and the inability of present methods of dental treatment to cope with the situation bears witness to the necessity for a deeper, more fundamental approach to the study of dental problems.

From the foregoing analysis it is clear that the changes in the educational status of dentistry have been made not to satisfy an academic whim or theory, but for the practical purpose of rendering a greater service to society through a clearer understanding of the real nature of its problem. To accomplish this purpose, there appears to be no other course to pursue but that dental education should be just as scientific, just as severe and testing as the education which is demanded of any other branch of medicine. The advances which have been made thus far, however, constitute only a step in the direction of attaining the goal toward which dentistry is striving. It will be no easy task to raise the status of dental education from that of a vocational system to that of a university discipline. Not only must dentistry train practitioners on a broad biological foundation, but it must also provide facilities for the development of research workers and teachers. Science today does not have the answer to its problems. Dentistry must therefore delve into the field of the unknown. It may take years to achieve its objectives, but whatever the cost in time, money and men, the establishment of dental education on a real university basis in which search for truth is the major consideration offers the greatest promise of yielding a solution to the riddle of dental disease, and it is only by being in possession of such knowledge that dentistry will be in a position to meet its major objectives—the development of superior methods of treatment and control which will enable it to extend its services to more people.

NEW JERSEY STATE DENTAL SOCIETY PROGRAM DENTAL HEALTH EDUCATION

J. M. WISAN, D.D.S.

Chairman, Council on Mouth Hygiene
New Jersey State Dental Society

New Jersey's Council on Mouth Hygiene considers its paramount objective to be the dissemination of authentic dental health information. Being a committee of the State Dental Society, it obtains its funds from that organization and in turn has placed it—The New Jersey State Dental Society—in a position of leadership in state-wide dental health education.

The program of the Council is well diversified, including a number of activities. In this article it is the purpose of the author to outline briefly the objectives, to list the activities of the Council and, lastly, to explain in detail one project now being promulgated.

Objectives of the New Jersey Council on Mouth Hygiene

Among the objectives of the Council may be mentioned:
(1) Cooperating with official agencies
   (a) State Board of Health
   (b) Department of Public Instruction
   (c) Department of Institute and Agencies
(2) Assisting oral hygiene committees of component dental societies
(3) Cooperating with voluntary health and welfare agencies
(4) Assisting individuals (dentists, nurses, etc.) in furthering dental health education
(5) Coordinating the efforts of educators, public health authorities and dentists for the improvement of dental health contions

Activities

How the objectives are achieved may be explained by listing the activities of the council:
(1) Participating in state, county and local health conferences: e.g., three members of the Council will speak before the Institute for Public Health Nurses arranged by the Bureau of Maternal and Child Health
(2) Collaborating with the Medical Society of New Jersey in a thirteen-week radio broadcast over the Mutual Network
(3) Presenting an accredited dental hygiene course in Extension Division of the New Jersey State Teachers College at Newark. This course is taken by teachers and nurses
(4) Cooperating with component dental societies in arranging local oral hygiene programs
(5) Preparing and disseminating authentic dental health material
   (a) Utilizing the New Jersey State Dental Journal
   (b) Preparing annual dental health bibliography
   (c) Cooperating with official departments: e.g., "Useful Baby Molars" with State Board of Health
   (d) Publishing material aimed at specific problems
      (1) Poster-Leaflet Project

Poster-Leaflet Project Explained

The poster-leaflet project may be considered under the heading of activities 5D1—"Publishing material aimed at specific problems." The posters show the wording:
"What is Preventive Dentistry?—Ask Your Dentist"

The four leaflets attempt to answer the question, "What is Preventive Dentistry?" for the expectant mother, preschool children, school children and high school students. Thus the posters and leaflets are concomitant items in a state-wide dental health education program.

The Poster

The aim of the poster is to encourage nurses, teachers, pupils and dentists to give more consideration to preventive dentistry. Moreover, it is hoped that individuals challenged by the question, "What is Preventive Dentistry?" will be guided by the suggestion—"Ask Your Dentist" to seek dental health information from competent dentists and not through commercial propaganda.

The wording is a departure from the dogmatic, dictatorial messages usually displayed on posters. Instead of telling the reader what to do, it encourages original creative thought. The individual is stimulated to obtain an understanding of his dental needs.

Through local oral hygiene committees the posters are being displayed in schools, health centers, Y. M. C. A.'s and libraries. In schools the posters are finding their greatest usefulness. Teachers use them to initiate class discussion and teaching units. Amazing, indeed, are the many ingenious devices invented by classroom teachers. One alert health supervisor used the picture on the poster to discuss the question: "Why did the child leaving the dental office show friendliness to the dental nurse?" Another teacher used the words "preventive" and "dentistry" as vocabulary study.

The Leaflets*

The contents of the four leaflets deal with the four age periods particularly suited for preventive dentistry—prenatal period, preschool age, school age and adolescence. While the first two were written for adult reading, the school age leaflet was prepared for both adults and older school children. The high school leaflet was addressed to the pupils so that junior and senior high school instructors might utilize them as a basis for their dental health discussions and instruction.

Approximately 50,000 leaflets are being disseminated by private dental practitioners. At present a second edition is being printed for distribution through schools, health departments, Parent-Teacher Associations, health centers and other health agencies.

RECENT STUDIES POINT THE WAY TO BETTER DENTAL HEALTH

F. C. CADY, D.D.S., C.P.H.

Dental Surgeon
U. S. Public Health Service

Until research has provided a means to prevent dental caries the road to better dental health is indicated by a number of recent studies. These studies point definitely to the high incidence of dental caries in the child population and have provided considerable information on the variations in prevalence for different localities and in different age groups.

Studies[1] made by the Public Health Service on approximately 5,000 elementary school children, 6 to 15 years of age, in a representative American community, are very illuminating respecting the amount of treatment required and received by these children and the amount of time the dentists devote to this work. The following is a pertinent quotation from a report of those studies, "From the findings, it is immedi-

---

* Single copies will be sent upon request if accompanied by a self-addressed stamped envelope. Address: Dr. J. M. Wisan, Chairman, Council on Mouth Hygiene, 1143 E. Jersey Street, Elizabeth, New Jersey.

[1] Klein, H., Palmer, C. E., Knutson, J. W.; Dental Status and Dental Needs of Elementary School Children. Public Health Report 53: 751-765 (1938).

ately apparent that the filling of permanent tooth surfaces for this group of children is being accomplished at a rate which is about one-sixth of the rate at which the defects are accruing. Identification of this disparity between the rate of development of defects and the rate of placement of fillings largely explains, quantitatively, the existence of the present accumulated dental needs of the children and leads to the conclusion that if such an accumulation of untreated defects in the permanent teeth is to be avoided in the future, some provision should be made to give elementary school children (in the form of fillings alone) approximately six times the service they now receive."

This study points out that 30 per cent of the time of the 32 practicing dentists of this community during one full year would be required to furnish the present elementary school population with complete dental treatment in the form of fillings for the permanent teeth, provided the amount of dental caries found in this group, plus the expected annual increment of new caries, is used as a basis.

These investigators also estimate that only 10 per cent of the dentists' time would be required to care for the initial and annual increment of new dental caries in the permanent teeth of children entering school each year. These calculations are, of course, based upon arbitrary estimates of professional time requirement.

It is of interest to know that, upon the basis of these estimates, the dentists of this community have been devoting only 2 per cent of their professional time to the elementary school children.

Since it is known that the proper placement of fillings greatly retards tooth loss, periodic tooth mortality rates may be used as an index of the adequacy of a dental care program in a community.[2]

It was demonstrated also that the lower first permanent molars contribute 75 per cent of the total permanent tooth loss in this group of almost 5,000 school children and that the distribution was bilaterally equal. Under these circumstances a periodic check of one of these teeth would serve as an index.

Further studies on this group show a lack of any sex differential in susceptibility to dental caries.

Many surveys of comparable small communities and at different periods in the same communities have demonstrated the value of early and periodic treatment to prevent tooth loss. The method of evaluation has varied, some using a complete examination of the mouth, others using a count of correction certificates returned by the dentist.

Some interesting findings[3] on the amount and type of dental treatment obtained by a representative group of people in a large city are revealed in the recent study made by the Public Health Service in Detroit, Michigan, as a part of the National Health Survey. This house to house inventory of over 66,000 persons of all ages and economic status showed that only 22 per cent of them visited a dentist for any reparative dental service during the study year. Of this 22 per cent, the percentage of persons in the age group 15 to 24 years who visited the

---

[2] Knutson, J. W., Klein, H.: Tooth Mortality in Elementary School Children. Public Health Report 53: 1021-1032 (1938).
[3] Britten, R. H.: A Study of Dental Care in Detroit, Michigan. Public Health Report 53: 446-459 (1938).

dentist was *three* times as great as the percentage of those in the caries susceptible age group 3 to 11 years. This shows that the great majority of people are not even visiting a dentist at an age when an effective control service can be rendered.

The studies referred to and others clearly illustrate the magnitude of the problem and how ineffectively it is being met. As previously shown, we are confronted with tooth morbidity in 90 out of 100 children under sixteen years of age and with dental defects accumulating six times as fast as they are being corrected.

These findings truly point to the need for a concerted effort on the part of all responsible groups for more effective health instruction and professional service.

Headed by the nation-wide dental survey of school children made in 1933-34 by the United States Public Health Service in cooperation with the American Dental Association there has been reported scores of studies on the prevalence of dental disease, all pointing in the same direction.[4]

As Dr. Hugh Cabot remarked at the National Health Conference, surveys started in 1492 and the drift of them has been the same. It is now time to get over this survey business and get on with the war.

The objective of a dental health program is for the moment singularly clear-cut and universally agreed upon—The Technical Committee of the President's Interdepartmental Committee to Promote Health and Welfare, the American Dental Association, the Association of Public Health Dentists, to quote only a few of the organizations concerned, have gone on record as recommending the early and periodic control of dental disease.

A large part of the responsibility for attaining this objective will fall upon the local health administrator. The health officer of today must concern himself with projects other than environmental sanitation and communicable disease control, since the great killers and cripplers of the people today are not amenable to traditional public health methods and practice. Dental disease with its unprecedented prevalence offers a challenge to the health administrator that requires serious consideration.

Surgeon General Thomas Parran says, "Whenever any disease is so widespread in the population, so serious in its effects, so costly in its treatment that the individual unaided cannot deal with it himself, it becomes a public health problem."

Dental disease, with an incidence higher than all others, is serious, disabling, and costly when neglected, and unquestionably qualifies under this definition. It is time to take positive action on a very broad front.

---
[4] Public Health Bulletin No. 226.

THE PREPARATION AND TRAINING OF DENTAL HYGIENISTS

EVELYN B. MORSE

Dental Hygienist
Division of Child Hygiene
Massachusetts Department of Public Health

When we speak about the preparation and training of dental hygienists, it seems necessary to divide the profession into two distinct groups. In the first group is the hygienist who is employed by a dentist and whose duties are confined to a private practice. In the second group is the hygienist who is engaged in some phase of public health work. This group includes those hygienists employed by schools, institutions, local boards of health and state health departments.

By dividing the profession into these two groups we do not intend to imply that the hygienist engaged in private practice does not have the opportunity to offer some contribution to public health. Indeed, she is in a strategic position to make her patients public health conscious. In this case her problem is concerned with the individual situation teaching, and not necessarily with education of the group.

The dental hygienist in private practice has the advantage of personal contact with the individual. She sees this person for a period of time and has the opportunity of seeing the same individual year after year. She meets him in childhood and she will continue to come in contact with him for years to come. She becomes more of a personality and friend to this patient. This type of hygienist is continually confronted with opportunities to teach public health, and she must have the knowledge and training as well as the ability to take advantage of these situations.

The problem of the dental hygienist in public health work is an entirely different one. This hygienist has to deal with mass teaching. The individual is subordinate to the group. She does not have the same advantage of personal contact—therefore, her technique has to be entirely different from that of the hygienist in private practice. Because of this it seems only feasible that her training vary from that of the other type of hygienist. Her talks, demonstrations or studies must be directed toward the group rather than the individual.

The hygienist who plans to enter a dentist's office after her training would probably choose a school which offers a one-year course. In general, the entrance requirements to these schools is primarily the same; namely, that the candidate must be a graduate of a high school and upon completion of the dental hygiene course must have reached the age specified by the board of registration in the state in which she desires to practice. This age varies in the different states, but is generally eighteen to twenty years of age. The candidate must be in good health, have an attractive personality, a professional attitude and be adapted to her work. Some schools require a personal interview before the candidate is accepted.

In general, the curriculum in these one-year institutions includes the following subjects:

Gross anatomy and physiology
Dental anatomy, lecture
Dental anatomy, laboratory
Dental histology and embryology
Elementary and dental bacteriology
Elementary and dental chemistry
Dental assisting
Public speaking
Essay writing
Dental hygiene and prophylaxis
Dental prophylaxis and assisting

Nutrition and hygiene
Child hygiene
Community dental hygiene
Laboratory assisting
First aid and nursing ethics
Dental pathology
Dental pharmacology
Child psychology
Dental radiology
Surgical assisting and anesthesia

During the school year the student's time is largely consumed in learning how to clean teeth. While many subjects are listed, such as those mentioned above, the courses are of the briefest duration and can in no way give a really good foundation in these sciences.

After completion of this one-year course the dental hygienist must pass a state board examination required by states permitting them to practice. Following is a list of the states in which state board examinations are given for dental hygienists:

Alabama
Arkansas
California
Colorado
Connecticut
Delaware*
Florida
Georgia
Iowa
Louisiana
Maine
Massachusetts
Michigan
Minnesota†
Mississippi
Montana
New Hampshire
New York
North Carolina
Ohio†
Oklahoma
Pennsylvania*
Rhode Island
South Carolina
Tennessee
Vermont
Washington
West Virginia
Wisconsin
Wyoming
District of Columbia

* Requires 1 year of interneship.
† Two-year course.

The schools in the United States offering a one-year course in Dental Hygiene are the following:

Columbia University, New York, N. Y.
Forsyth Dental Infirmary, Boston, Mass.
Howard University, Washington, D. C.
Marquette University, Milwaukee, Wis.
Meharry Medical College, Nashville, Tenn.
Murry and Leonie Guggenheim Dental Clinic, New York, N. Y.
North Pacific College of Oregon, Portland, Oregon
Rochester Dental Dispensary, Rochester, N. Y.
Temple University, Philadelphia, Pa.
University of Pennsylvania, Philadelphia, Pa.

There is another group of professional women known as dental assistants, which is becoming more and more popular. These assistants work in dental offices. They are usually graduates of a Dental Assistants' School, and are well versed in secretarial subjects as well as being capable of doing all types of laboratory work. A state license is not required of this assistant; therefore, she is not allowed to do any prophylaxis work. She is trained, however, to assist the dentist in the operating room. Many dentists depend on them almost entirely for their laboratory work, in which they are usually very well trained. Because of her secretarial knowledge, the dental assistant is often more valuable to the dentist than is the dental hygienist. The dentist who prefers to do his own prophylaxis work finds the dental assistant more economical, because of her varied training, and just as valuable to his practice as a dental hygienist.

The dental assistant's course usually covers one year and sometimes a second term is offered for additional technical training. Preferably, all candidates are graduates of a high school or its equivalent. In general, the subjects given are as follows:

Language of the dental office
Elementary anatomy and description of the teeth
Elementary physiology of the teeth
Instruments—types, uses, sterilization
Preparation before, and care of patient after, surgical operation
Anesthesia—assistance, preparation
Study of the more common diseases of the mouth
Use of microscope
Study and care of dental operating room
Equipment
Materia Medica
Operating room assistance
Assistance during chair work: mixing of fillings, root canal work, extraction
First aid
Laboratory work
X-ray work
Secretarial duties

The dental hygienist desiring to enter the field of public health should have more education than the hygienist engaged in private practice. Some states make a definite requirement that a dental hygienist present a degree from a liberal arts college or a teacher's certificate from a teachers' training school in order to be employed by boards of education to participate in school programs. Hygienists engaged in school work need this additional training because of the nature of their work. In many instances they participate in classroom teaching as well as prophylactic work and in order to qualify for this type of position they need more than the four years of high school training in addition to their dental hygienist degree.

The requirements of the various states for hygienists engaged in public schools vary; however, it is generally conceded that a two-year course in dental hygiene should be required. Some states require a college degree in addition to this two-year course, or one year of normal school training. Pennsylvania and Delaware require a period of internship before granting certificates.

The requirements to become a dental hygiene teacher in New York State are that a dental hygienist must have a provisional or a permanent teacher's certificate for school service. To obtain a provisional certificate a candidate must be a high school graduate, must have completed a curriculum offered by a recognized school of dental hygiene and in addition, six semester hours in approved professional courses:

Courses	Semester Hours (Min.)	(Max.)
An orientation course in education	2	2
Child psychology	2	2

This certificate is valid five years from the date of issuance. A holder of a provisional certificate is eligible for a permanent certificate after the completion of twelve semester hours in approved professional courses in addition to the minimum preparation required for the provisional certificate.

Courses	Semester Hours (Min.)	(Max.)
Nutrition	2	4
Bacteriology	2	4
Family case work or sociology*	2	4
Health service in public schools	2	4

During each successive two-year period from the date this provisional certificate is issued the holder must complete six semester hours in approved courses or the equivalent in approved and appropriate professional activities.

The minimum qualifications of dental hygienists employed by the Connecticut State Department of Health are graduation from high school supplemented by college training preferably, and at least a one-year course and graduation from a Class A school of dental hygiene.

Several schools are offering a two-year course to dental hygienists instead of the former one-year course, due to the general trends in professional education. The University of Michigan School of Dentistry has increased its course to two years. The University of California has increased its course to four years and gives the degree of Bacheler of Science in Dental Hygiene. Marquette University offers a five-year course upon the completion of which the candidate receives a Bachelor's degree in addition to the one in Dental Hygiene.

Schools offering the two-year course of study are:
University of Tennessee, Memphis, Tenn.
Northwestern University, Chicago, Ill.
University of So. California, Los Angeles, Calif.
University of Minnesota, Minneapolis, Minn.
University of Michigan, Ann Arbor, Mich.

There is a training school in Hawaii which offers a four-year

---

* Including community relationships, social welfare, racial problems, delinquency, the family and the home.

course. In order to qualify for the licensing requirements in the Territory of Hawaii, students take the same course in normal school as required of student teachers, except that they specialize in dental or oral hygiene instead of a teaching subject.

Such courses would include the following subjects:

First Year

Anatomy and physiology
Dental anatomy
English and composition
Histology
Drawing
Materia Medica
Oral Hygiene
Prophylaxis
Bacteriology

Elementary inorganic chemistry
Elements of prosthetics and
  laboratory techniques
Ceramics
Anatomical demonstrations
General pathology
Public speaking
Radiography

Second Year

Anesthesia and surgical assisting
Child psychology
Dental assisting
Dental pathology
Economics
Dental health education
Ethics and jurisprudence
First aid
Food and nutrition
Health and care of the family

Elementary orthodonture
Principles and practice of
  prophylaxis
Sociology and public health
Dental literature
Fundamentals and general nursing
Habit formations of early childhood
Principles of teaching
Parliamentary law

Positions in public health departments, state health departments and school clinics are usually competitive and a Civil Service examination is required. Their requirements may not state in writing that a college degree is necessary. It is only to be expected that a dental hygienist with this additional training or degree is given preference. This profession as well as other professions is advancing and more and more requirements are placed on its graduates.

Bibliography:
Bulletins from all dental colleges listed.
Career as a Dental Hygienist published by the Institute for Research, Chicago, Illinois. 1938.
Dental Hygiene published by the Institute of Women's Professional Relations, Research Headquarters, Connecticut College, New London, Conn. 1936.

PRENATAL DENTAL SERVICE

SUSAN M. COFFIN, M.D.

Division of Child Hygiene
Massachusetts Department of Public Health

Good dental care should, of course, be a routine part of adequate prenatal care, but unfortunately it is often neglected.

It is truly appalling the number of mothers with diseased teeth whom we see each year at our Well Child Conferences. Many tell us that their teeth "began to go" during pregnancy. It is our belief that this is one of the causes of the all-too-common complaint of impaired health following childbirth.

Many mothers never go to the dentist during pregnancy except for relief of toothache too severe to be borne. Far too many women still feel that dental trouble is to be expected during pregnancy—the old notion of "For every child a tooth" dies hard! A mother remarked recently that she always "lost two teeth with each baby." As she had two children and was expecting a third, dental care was imperative and she was urged to go to the dentist at once.

Some mothers think that it is "bad for the baby" to have dental work done and fear that it may cause abortion. In fact, it is obvious that both private and prenatal clinic patients needs much more teaching and reassurance in regard to their dental needs. Lack of money does not appear to be the only cause of neglect, by any means. We know that correct diet, daily home care and regular visits to a competent dentist are necessary to dental health and that at no time are they more essential than during pregnancy.

Responsibility for dental care lies with five persons—mother and father, physician, dentist, and public health nurse. We feel that there is a lack in teaching all along the line. Medical, and even dental students doubtless are not sufficiently impressed with the importance of a clean mouth in maintaining health. A normal mouth with a set of well cared for teeth is an essential item in disease prevention at all ages.

The doctor usually says to his maternal patients, "You should see your dentist" but he may neglect to explain why dental attention is always an important part of good prenatal care. Also, some physicians do not seem to realize that a physician is not trained to make a thorough dental examination and that teeth that "look all right" often have enough wrong with them to make trouble before pregnancy is over. Dentists do not always emphasize the need of more frequent visits during pregnancy. Often the mother does not tell her dentist of her condition, which is the wise thing to do.

The mother herself often delays going to the dentist though she knows perfectly well she should go. Frequently the young mother also puts off going to her physician or to the prenatal clinic because she dreads the examination and blood test. Many mothers tell us this is why they "didn't go early." Also mothers of several children often delay because they "always get along all right" and they go only in time to secure a bed in the hospital. With these groups of mothers who get no instruction on diet and dental care until late in pregnancy, dental caries frequently gets a big start and it really is too late to do a large amount of dental correction by the time they get to the physician's office or to the prenatal clinic. We must still urge increasing education of parents in the need of early prenatal care.

The public health nurse, who sees the mother first more often than not, may forget to urge dental care unless the mother complains of pain or sore mouth. Young mothers, especially, can be appealed to on the score of appearance. No woman wants her looks ruined by bad teeth and many consider dentures a sure sign of old age! The nurse can also remind her patients that mothers find it more difficult to take time to visit the dentist after the arrival of the baby than during pregnancy. If mothers do not get necessary dental work done before confinement it is most apt to be neglected later and more serious trouble develops which means much greater expense. Also, mothers, more than most people, need undisturbed rest—and aching teeth are great robbers of sleep!

Busy physicians, dentists and nurses can use good printed material on caring for the teeth at no expense to themselves or their patients. Readable material is useful with a large number of patients and can be obtained from your State Department of Public Health and from various private publishers.

Approximately 75% of the mothers in Massachusetts are delivered in hospitals and as a large number of these mothers attend prenatal clinics, here lies one of our biggest opportunities to attack this problem of dental neglect during pregnancy. But a serious obstacle is encountered and one which seems to merit the attention of all who are interested in decreasing maternal mortality and morbidity. This obstacle is the great lack of dental service in connection with our prenatal clinics.

Without a doubt a considerable number of mothers can and do go to their private dentists even from the prenatal clinics. But a large number cannot afford this service at ordinary fees and so get no care except in cases of acute dental conditions. Extraction in cases of actual suffering, from abscessed or extremely carious teeth, is often provided for through welfare departments or in the hospital outpatient departments, but at present no provision is made for routine dental examination and care at all prenatal clinics. A notable exception is seen in one large prenatal clinic in Massachusetts where all mothers are referred at once to a dental clinic conducted by a private organization which has special prenatal service. This is of course an ideal arrangement. Also, in some hospitals there is a dental intern and in one of these, at least, prenatal patients are referred to him.

Various methods are possible for obtaining dental service and it is hoped that one or another of them may prove practical for every prenatal clinic in Massachusetts in the near future. The following suggestions are offered:

A dental clinic may be conducted by any private organization, or group of organizations, which has interest in such activities and the funds for it. It would be well worth while to arouse the interest of local organizations along this line. The expense need not be a prohibitive factor. Such an arrangement does exist in one city, as mentioned before, and has proved valuable.

When there is a dental clinic already established in the outpatient department of a hospital holding prenatal clinics a plan could be developed to furnish dental service for all prenatal clinic patients. It is, of course, necessary that every mother attending the prenatal clinic have an early appointment for dental examination. Only the dentist can find first evidences of dental disease and he alone can decide whether treatment is necessary during pregnancy to save the teeth. Obstetricians can help by referring each mother, at her first visit, for dental examination.

The question of hospital dental internships is also worthy of careful consideration. Such a service may be practical in solving the problem of adequate dental care. It provides dentists with valuable experience and an opportunity for special study as well as helping to supply the hospital's need. Several hospitals in Massachusetts now have dental internships.

As we realize, more keenly each year, what a tremendous lack of prenatal dental care exists, we feel that any method that promises a fair amount of success in providing such care is worth trying out. Dental care is only one item in maternal care but it is of major importance. Without it we cannot claim that mothers are receiving adequate care in any type of prenatal service.

PROGRESS IN SCHOOL DENTAL HEALTH

JEAN V. LATIMER, B.S., A.M.

Coordinator of Health Education
Division of Child Hygiene
Massachusetts Department of Public Health

While there is still much to be done in the schools, there has been evidence this year that the dental health program is receiving increasing attention, not only from the medical, dental and nursing, but also from teaching professions. From the first grade through the junior high school, teachers now are beginning to include in their health education program more emphasis on dental health.

We have evidence that teachers, while as yet not many are using the unit method of instruction in its entirety, many are nevertheless carrying on worth-while activities in regard to dental health.

Not long ago I visited a primary teacher who had aroused quite a lot of interest in her first grade by having the children get better acquainted with their own teeth and their care of them. Special emphasis was placed on the new six-year molar as the first of the permanent teeth. The children had made a big cutout tooth to represent this tooth, and had colored it. They were also discussing what kinds of teeth their pet animals had and how they were similar to their own. The class dramatized "My Mother Takes Me to the Dentist."

The splendid new health education texts now available are being considered as supplementary readers in the first three grades. In these we see the topic of dental health coming to the front. Recently while visiting a classroom I listened to a second grade child read on the topic of teeth. Even in these readers the problem method is used, in that questions are raised and answered. This little girl read some of these questions on dental health and asked various members of the class to answer them.

This Division, believing that dental service in the schools should be linked to the teaching program, has been offering during the past two years dental health surveys, in order that the children and the teachers themselves may realize the actual conditions of the children's mouths. We have been gratified in some instances to have the findings of this survey form the basis of the actual health teaching in the classroom— both the children and the teacher keeping records of the actual conditions of the teeth as found by this survey. Following this we have encouraged individual improvement by the use of such records as "My Achievement Record for a Healthy Mouth" rather than the group or class competition with the use of banners, et cetera, for 100% dental corrections. In the future we hope to see even more link-up between the general remedial work offered to children in dental health clinics and the teaching program.

In the middle grades there is evidence that the teachers are awake to the realization that this is the time to begin to build more of a factual background regarding dental health, as well as to stimulate activities which interest children in their teeth. It is in these grades that children may begin to really know more about the true nature of dental decay and some of the reasons necessitating regular and periodic treatment by the dentist.

The visual material loaned by this Division to schools has been of real assistance to the teachers throughout the State. Especially is this true of the three-dimension model of a tooth which can be taken apart to show the inside structure of a tooth. One boy, on seeing this, was heard to exclaim, "Gee, I never knew before from those flat pictures in the textbooks why I ought to go to the dentist before my tooth hurt— but now I know something about the nature of dental decay."

The charts and posters published by the American Dental Association and on loan from this Division, are being increasingly used. Especially have such films as "Care of the Teeth," "Ask Your Dentist," "How Teeth Grow," and "A Healthy Child" (also on loan from this Division) been of value in making the teaching of dental health more concrete.

We are especially gratified to report that a specific unit on dental health prepared by this Division is being incorporated in the course of study in health education for junior high schools which is now in the process of being printed by the Massachusetts Department of Education.

While we believe that teaching in regard to dental health should even be extended through the senior high school, we have yet to formulate teaching plans for this age level. Possibly the biology and science teachers will assist us here in showing how such teaching may be incorporated in their subjects.

PUBLIC HEALTH NURSING AND ITS RELATION TO DENTAL HYGIENE

ANN W. DINEGAN, B.S., R.N.

Supervising Instructor in Public Health Nursing Education
Massachusetts Department of Public Health

Dental Hygiene is now considered as one of the functions of the public health nurse to be included in all of her various services.

Beginning with the maternity service the public health nurse supplements the teaching and advice of the physician with regard to visiting the dentist early in pregnancy. She follows up the visit to the dentist with instruction regarding the kind of diet necessary to preserve the mother's teeth, and to build sound teeth for her baby, which she explains to the mother are formed before he is born. She also makes sure that the expectant mother understands and practices the proper mouth hygiene for this period.

In the infant and preschool service, the public health nurse, in her home and well child conference visits, teaches the mother regarding the development of the teeth and the reasons for establishing good dental hygiene at the time the back teeth appear. She advises the mother to take the baby to the dentist as soon as he has all twenty baby teeth, explaining the reasons for this early examination. The public health nurse records on the health record the advice given by the dentist to the mother, which she uses as a basis for her dental hygiene teaching. In her health supervision visits she inspects the teeth of the infant and preschool child, follows up the instructions of the dentist regarding daily cleaning and proper diet for teeth building, and encourages the mother to return to the dentist at the time he suggests for the next examination. Any special problems which the dentist discovers, such as thumbsucking, are handled by the public health nurse according to his instructions.

In the school health program the role of the public health nurse in dental hygiene is mainly one of providing the teachers with proper source materials on dental hygiene which they may use in their general classroom health teaching. The public health nurse aims to promote, through the teacher, regular dental examinations, cleaning and repair work including the care of deciduous teeth and the six-year molars; mouth hygiene, including the discriminate choice and use of the toothbrush; a wise choice of foods; sufficient rest, sunshine and fresh air, which come under general hygiene teaching but have their relationship to tooth decay. It is the function of the public health nurse to promote community dental resources for the care of children who cannot afford a private dentist. As time goes on and more educational work is done among the prenatal, infant and preschool groups, the problem of dental correction for school children should diminish markedly.

The public health nurse working among adult groups in industry and in the homes does a great deal to promote better dental hygiene as a part of her program of teaching for healthful living.

In the tuberculosis service, the public health nurse makes every effort to provide dental care for patients being cared for at home, with the permission of the attending physician. This service is now recognized as an important part of the care of such patients in sanatoria, and also in the home wherever it is possible to provide for it.

The public health nurse is encouraged to write to the Division of Child Hygiene, State Department of Public Health, for advice regarding possible means of providing necessary dental care to patients in any of her services who cannot afford a private dentist and where clinic facilities are not available.

DENTAL NEEDS AND THE SUPPLY OF DENTISTS

FRED W. MORSE, JR., M.D.
*Assistant Professor of Oral Medicine
Harvard University Dental School*

Dental disease is the most prevalent of human ailments. Dental disease affects more persons at any time of life after the age of two than the common cold. Moreover, dental disease never repairs itself, and, in the words of Alfred Walker, D.D.S., "Seldom if ever ceases to increase without operative intervention by the dentist."

Surveys made here in Boston some years ago by Dr. Percy Howe, Director of the Forsyth Infirmary, showed that about 95 per cent of school children of this region had some dental decay. This general statement can be elaborated a little by information given by Dr. John Oppie McCall of New York in his annual report of the Murry and Leonie Guggenheim Dental Clinic, for 1934. His records show that even in children at the age of two years, 47 per cent had cavities, and 13 per cent had seven or more cavities. At three years those with cavities had increased to 79 per cent, and 37 per cent had seven or more cavities; while at the age of five, 96 per cent had cavities and 60 per cent had more than six cavities. And, as Dr. McCall points out, "It has been found that preschool children with seven or more cavities have an average of at least one tooth requiring extraction." In other words, uncared for dental decay results in deep-seated infection, which in turn means an infected tooth, an abscess, and the loss of the tooth.

In the reports of the White House Conference on Child Health and Protection, data was presented showing that 95 per cent of American children had dental defects, while only 10 per cent had received any dental attention.

Thus far, we see that dental disease is well-nigh universal among children. Since the destruction wrought by dental disease never repairs itself, we can assume that practically 100 per cent of the adult population is affected by some form of oral disease.

From the reports of the Committee on the Costs of Medical Care it has been shown that not more than 25 per cent of the population receives systematic dental care, with a per capita expenditure of $8.90 per year. Seventy-five per cent of the population receives little dental care, or at the most only enough to relieve unbearable pain. This is evidenced by the fact that not more than $2.00 per capita is expended on dental service by at least 75 per cent of the population. We can estimate that 3,000,000 of the 4,000,000 people in Massachusetts are going around with mouths which contain decayed teeth, broken teeth, loose teeth, and diseased gums, although perhaps most of them are not having a severe toothache at the moment.

The problem of the dental needs of our local community, of our State, or of the United States is vast. And as we observe the mouths of people in other nations, we realize that their dental problems are even greater than ours. Will the number of dentists now in practice in the United States supply the needs for dental service which have just been outlined?

In Massachusetts, the list of licensed dentists for 1937 was approximately 3,000, or one to every 1,300 people in the State. In Boston there was one dentist for somewhat fewer than 700 people. If we were to have the same proportion of dentists in the United States as in Massachusetts, it would require 100,000 dentists. Today we cannot count more than 77,000 for the entire country. But these are practicing dentists trying to earn a living. Dentistry is still looked on by a great many people as a luxury. Hence the figures of one for every 1,300, or one for every 700 are not indicative of the service one dentist can give. Only about 25 per cent of the population are really getting anything like adequate protective service and hence not over 1,000,000 people in Massachusetts are getting this grade of dental care. This would be in proportion of one dentist for 333 people. This is about the right ratio for effective dental service. In order, then, to give adequate service for the good health of the people in Massachusetts, we need 12,000 dentists instead of 3,000 to 3,500. But if the preservation of health by dentistry is a luxury, more than half of these 12,000 dentists would be unable to make a living in Massachusetts.

From another angle, let us look at the proposals brought before the Department of Health in New York City and the Committee on Community Dental Service of the New York Tuberculosis and Health Association. These proposals are for the care of the school children of New York City. It was estimated that 840 dental hygienists working full time and 2,500 dentists working full time would be required. This would cost a little over $8.00 per child per year. Nearly half the total number of dentists practicing in New York would be needed to take care of the school children. Since adults need more dental work than children, under present conditions, it seems definite that many more dentists than are at present available would be needed, or perhaps some 20,000 for New York City alone.

But we must note this: After a very few years of complete service for school children such as is proposed above, the number of dentists required to do the work could be reduced by one-half, because early dentistry makes less dentistry necessary. If 1,250 dentists were required to take care of the 1,250,000 children, or about one dentist to every 1,000 children, it would seem that perhaps the remaining 5,000,000 people could be taken care of by from 8,000 to 10,000 dentists instead of the 20,000 estimated above.

From the public health viewpoint, early and continuous dentistry on all children would be an economical and healthful method of maintaining mouth health. From the practical standpoint it would seem that for the next twenty years there will be a distinct shortage of dentists. Any seeming surplus will be due to unsatisfactory distribution, which has always been a problem.

Lastly, is there danger of shortage or of a surplus in the dental profession? Two years ago, 1,722 men and 17 women graduated from dental schools in the United States. Three years ago two less men and but 16 women entered the profession. Only 2,165 students entered the 39 dental schools in the United States in 1936, and even fewer in the years preceding. At this rate it would take forty or more years to replenish the present supply of dentists. So the number of practicing dentists is diminishing and the shortage of dentists will continue.

THE IMPORTANCE OF AN ADEQUATE DENTAL PROGRAM*
Arthur E. Westwell, D.M.D.
Resident Dentist
Belchertown State School, Belchertown, Mass.

This Association with a fine record of contributions to the care and training of the Mental Defective, may well pause to direct the attention of its members to that important phase of health, the adequate dental program. This paper will deal with no spectacular elevations in I. Q. which have allegedly come as a direct result of the removal of certain diseased teeth. Instead, an attempt will be made to emphasize a basic truth agreed upon by all, in theory, but disregarded by many, in practice. It will further outline a plan of action for those desiring a definite program. The basic truth upon which all agree is this: A comprehensive health program should precede any attempts at mental training. The mere realization that Defectives suffering actual dental pain cannot give their limited concentration to attempted mental training is not sufficient. Nor is the alleviation of pain and subsequent repair of teeth the final goal of the dental program. Failure on the part of the institution to supply a well-balanced diet, leaves the dentist in the position of a man attempting to fight a three-alarm fire with a medicine dropper.

With our institutions headed almost one hundred per cent by physicians, it is difficult to understand why these fundamentals of health remain so sadly neglected in some quarters. We are forced to conclude that the answer lies in the budget. Ten years ago it was the speaker's privilege to offer a paper on recreation to this Association. In connection with its preparation, a survey of all listed state institutions in this country and Canada revealed that while recreation was praised to the high heavens as an important part of institutional life, relatively few real programs were offered, and the reason given was lack of funds. Fortunately for both the Defectives and the institutions, times have changed. Whether there is more money or not, both the quantity and quality of institutional recreation have improved. It is to be earnestly hoped that the plea for better dental service, which descends upon the Association from three different directions this year, will result in some

---
* Read before the Sixty-second Annual Meeting of the American Association on Mental Deficiency held at Richmond, Virginia. April 20-23, 1938. Reprinted from the Proceedings of the American Association on Mental Deficiency Vol. 43: 207-210, 1938.

very definite action. Let us pause once more in the busy fields of mental training long enough to repeat the motto of the Training School at Vineland: "Happiness first. All else follows." Or for emphasis with no change in meaning: "Health and happiness first. All else follows."

1. A Program of Dental Care in an Institution

Such a program may be divided into two equally important parts:
A. Services rendered by the dentist.
   1. Periodic examination, cleansing, repair and restoration
B. Services rendered by the institution.
   1. The assurance of a balanced diet.
   2. Supervised care of the teeth daily.
   3. Organization for the care of incapables.

Since the purpose of this paper is to spread the gospel of better dental care, and since this is not a dental group, a detailed discussion of professional procedure is hardly of special interest. Such procedure may be left where it belongs, with the Dentist, as we approach the problem from an institution standpoint. Institutional responsibility for the first part of the program consists of engaging the services of the dentist, supplying suitable equipment, cooperation, and adequate remuneration. The dentist, in turn, must realize that the dental program is not a thing apart, but one of many programs which must be coordinated within the complicated structure of institutional routine. As his knowledge of, and acquaintance with the various types of patient grows, so will his opportunities for greater service increase.

With the subject of diet already stressed, we now turn to the important subject of daily care. This care will depend for its success upon the application of that golden rule of the Mental Defective, supervision. Supervision not only of patients, but also of employees to whom the responsibility of that care must be delegated. If the selection of employees is wise, the battle is half won. Every institution can boast, (but usually does not), of employees who have dedicated their lives to the sympathetic care of the Defective. While to the Statistician the Defective must needs appear as a serial number with an M.A., an I.Q. and an obscure place in some percentage or other, to these employees he is a real person with a capacity for joy and sorrow, and for behavior good and bad. Just as we are dependent upon the Statistician for future progress, so must we rely upon these employees for present happiness.

With the proper employees chosen, the following must be supplied: a plainly marked toothbrush for each patient; suitable racks to hold brushes; a safe tooth powder or paste and dispensers for it. At least twice daily the brushes should be passed out to those capable of self care. After this, selected patients may be organized for the care of incapables. After use, each brush should be rinsed under the water tap, replaced in the rack and except in freezing weather exposed to air and sunlight until dry. We might qualify as supreme optimists were we to believe that lengthy discourses on mouth care really amount to very much. Such success as we note will come as a direct result of the clocklike routine, carefully supervised. Let no one try to place the final responsibility on the patient. Commitment to the institution is sufficient indication that he rates no such confidence. Let him try out his wings if you will, but keep a close check on the results. The teeth are too valuable for experimentation.

2. Methods of Care for Varying Mental Levels

While the Dentist will soon learn what sort of behavior may be reasonably expected from patients of various levels, the problem remains an individual one. That the approach should be sympathetic, goes without saying. The exercise of patience will pay big dividends especially as the confidence of younger children is gained. Experience teaches that no great secrecy need be maintained as dental work is being done. If care and the judicial use of the local anesthetic is employed, the patient in the chair will do much to dispel the fears of those who wait. Procedure with high grades differs little from that in ordinary practice. Artificial dentures may be supplied in many cases but a knowledge of the physical and mental handicaps of the individual is essential. Some Spastics for instance, handle a plate fairly well, but in spite of rugged construction, breakage tends to be high. As he attempts to replace the plate in the mouth, he is inclined to throw it over his shoulder. This is but one example of the need for the study of the individual.

The very low grade presents many difficulties. He can not cooperate; he is incapable of dislodging food particles from between the teeth, and he responds to treatment by biting at everything that comes within range, be it instrument, toothbrush, or an unfortunate finger. Such natural means of cleansing as come to the normal individual by the action of the tongue in conversation and exploration, are denied him as he sits for hours with tongue and jaw motionless. Into such a fertile field for infection, he will introduce everything upon which he can lay hands. If no system of daily care is in operation, you will find fragments from day before yesterday's meals, packed away between teeth and cheeks. With many of these cases we expect to, and do find extensive decay. Radical as it may seem, the well-being of these people is often best served by the removal of all teeth. Cases should be carefully selected and specially prepared diets assured. But from any standpoint, the smooth relatively clean surfaces of the edentulous mouth are more to be desired than the diseased foul, food trap.

3. Coordination of the Dental Program With Institution Routine

While prompt relief is the first consideration, routine dental operations may be carried on in a manner which will not seriously interfere with departments of service and training. Patients should be taken from these departments on such days and at such hours as they can best be spared. This requires the cooperation of department heads, and a general familiarity with individual assignments. No set rules can be laid down, but as an illustration: Certain days in the laundry may be busier than others, and while the changing of the day of the appointment will mean little to the Dentist, it may aid the laundry a great deal. The same would be true of certain patients employed on the farm, and in the various services dealing with food, heat and light. While this matter may not seem important at first glance, those in charge of such departments will readily testify as to its worth.

4. Suggestions for those Interested in the Installation
of a Dental Program

Institutions of any size are beginning to look with favor upon the idea of a Resident Dentist. Aside from the great advantage of having his services available at all times for the emergency, he also becomes more closely interested in the aims and objects of the institution in which he makes his home. The dental problem should not await his coming. If circumstances will not permit a Resident Dentist at this time, a temporary solution may be found by taking your problem to the following:

1. The local or nearby Dentist.
2. The county, state or American Dental Association.
3. Your nearest Dental School, where, by some arrangement, upper class men might be able to complete some of their required operative work at the institution under competent instruction.

The installation of the daily program, however, awaits only a brush for each patient, racks, powder or paste, instructions in brushing, and last but not least, that eternal supervision.

In conclusion, these are the fundamentals of an adequate dental program. It is not presented as the only program, nor the ideal program, but results seem to indicate that it may be regarded as a step in the right direction.

STRUCTURAL AND NERVOUS EFFECTS OF THUMB-SUCKING*

EARL W. SWINEHART, D.D.S.
Baltimore, Md.

Because of the great prevalence of the strikingly abnormal habit of thumb-sucking and finger-sucking and the possibility of damage to children, a voluminous literature has grown up around the subject. In large measure, it has been concerned with the etiology of the habit and has ranged through the philosophic and biologic discussions of such men as James, Dearborn, Freud and Levy to the unscientific writings of laymen. Despite this, there seems to be no lessening in the number of new cases, and millions of American children continue to practice the habits for varying lengths of time. As dentists have appropriated the mouth as their special field of work, and thumb-sucking is a mouth habit, it should be of especial concern to them to know whether it is harmful, and if so, to what extent.

At present, there is much difference of opinion as to the effects. From time to time, various authors have called attention to certain associated structural abnormalities and have cited these habits as causes. In the main, thought has been focused on the probable effects on occlusion of the anterior teeth. Much credit is due Samuel J. Lewis for producing the first accurate evidence on several controversial points through his systematic study of a group of young thumb-sucking children in Detroit. Among other important things, he found that, in those cases, the habits

---

* Extracts from paper read before the Section on Children's Dentistry and Oral Hygiene at the Seventy-Ninth Annual Session of the American Dental Association, Atlantic City, N. J., July 13, 1937.
Journal of the American Dental Ass'n. & Dental Cosmos, Vol. 25, May 1938. Reprinted by courtesy of the Journal.

were all formed before 1 year of age; that malocclusion was invariably present in the deciduous teeth while the habits were in force, and that there usually was a tendency toward self-correction of the irregularity of the incisor teeth if the habits were broken before the children were 5 years old. Nevertheless, many still believe that the structural effects are negligible and transitory and do not justify widespread methods of prevention and cure. Certain physicians even encourage practice of the habits and advise that the immediate pacifying effect is beneficial to children.

In the hope of adding something of value to the fund of information concerning the subject, I wish to present some results of a study of thirty-eight such cases. The group was composed of fifteen boys and twenty-three girls, whose ages ranged from 2½ to 15 years. All of them were actively practicing the habits and all were cured. They were treated during the years from 1931 to 1935 inclusive, so that from one to five years have been available for observation. Adequate records of the group have been kept.

Malocclusion

Tabulation and analysis of these data have yielded surprising facts, indicating that in considering these habits as simple practices of childhood the effects, if any, of which are slight and transitory, we have been making a serious error. Typical anterior malocclusion was found in more than 90 per cent of the cases, but was of minor importance as compared with other structural and nervous consequences noted. The other structural effects were frequently seen as a general malocclusion that was not amenable to self-correction and a malgrowth of the bone of the internal face that was beyond correction by either medical or dental means.

The records corroborate the findings of Lewis in that all of these habits were found to have been in existence during the first year of life, most of them in the early part of it. In three of the group, the habit was noted before the mothers left the hospitals. The fact of the very early and continued practice of the habits is of prime importance in weighing the potentiality of the habits as factors in the structural malformations that will be shown. Two things must be remembered: 1. In infancy, the bones are very plastic and can be molded easily by mechanical force. 2. Growth to maturity is a "fluid process." The bones reach their typal form and size only when there is continued equilibrium of the prescribed natural forces that have been set up to govern their growth. Any abnormal force continually applied may be sufficient to inhibit bone growth or to distort its form.

Study of the abnormal forces of the individual habits and malocclusion showed that the method, time and intensity of the habits were determining factors in the character and degree of the malocclusion. Whenever the abnormal forces were exerted in line with the natural courses of growth, there was overdevelopment. If they were in opposition to them, lack of growth and distortion were seen.

Nasal Deformity

An investigation is now in progress to determine whether the effects of thumb-sucking extend beyond the mouth to the structures of the nose. This appears a logical assumption. The vault of the palate and the floor of the nose are formed by the same plate of bone. Its distortion upward would necessarily lessen the height of the nasal space.

Nervousness

The close association of abnormal nervous and psychologic phenomena with thumb-sucking is so apparent that scientists and laymen alike call attention to it. The child in which the persistent types are seen is often termed a high-strung or even a problem child. This close association has naturally led to the frequently proclaimed belief that whatever may be the exciting causes, the habits are really expressions of constitutional nervousness. Apparently, the failure to evaluate more correctly the relationship between the conditions has been due to lack of opportunity for accurate observation. Such cases have usually been studied individually and collectively only while the habits were in force and while treatment to cure them was being carried on in the home in the usual haphazard manner. As a rule, this home treatment has been a long and trying ordeal for parents and child. Often, it has extended over several years, while one method after another has been tried. Some of these methods have cruelly interfered with sleep and the normal activity of childhood. Other children have been continually harassed by shaming, scolding and punishment. The effects of these measures often increase the nervous symptoms and encourage deceit and resentment and tend toward an inferiority complex. When finally the habits have been abandoned, victory has seemed sufficient unto itself and the cases have been considered closed. The former abnormal physical and mental phenomena have been regarded as natural conditions of childhood.

Fortunately, the study to be presented has been made under more favorable circumstances. In all of the thirty-eight cases under discussion, mechanical appliances were used which immediately prevented and permanently stopped the habits. This immediate stoppage of the habits has provided unusual opportunity to study in sharp contrast the nervous and psychologic phenomena of these cases during practice of the habits and after they had been suddenly prevented. It is unfortunate that the observations were not made by a competent psychologist, who doubtless would have greatly enhanced the value of the findings.

Conclusions

1. There are three main abnormal forces exerted in thumb-sucking: (a) the passive force of the digit held between the arches; (b) abnormal contraction of the cheeks against the sides of the arches, and (c) abnormal muscular pressure of the digit against the palate. These forces begin in the plastic age of infancy and are often continued through the formative period of childhood.

2. In this group of children, the effects of these forces on the teeth were seen as high percentages of certain types of regional and of general malocclusion. Force "a" caused maxillary incisor protrusion, mandibular incisor retrusion and open bite of the incisors. Force "b" was found closely associated with narrow maxillary arches. The close association of force "c" with unilateral mesiocclusion of the maxillary arch indicated that it is a cause of that type of general malocclusion. The cause for this

condition has been unknown. The above-mentioned cases of high percentage malocclusion were all found fully established as early as 3 years of age. In most of the cases, the malocclusion was of such character that complete self-correction seemed extremely unlikely if the habits had ceased even at that early age. Taken together, these types of malocclusion caused by the habit in this group comprise a large proportion of cases of adult malocclusion. It appears, therefore, that this habit is one of the most important causes of malocclusion.

3. The malocclusion of the incisor teeth caused by thumb-sucking encourages abnormal habits of the lips and tongue, and mouth-breathing. All of these secondary habits tend to persist throughout life and maintain or exaggerate the malocclusion. Mouth-breathing often seriously affects the general health.

4. The abnormal forces of the habit distort the form of the structures of the internal face. In these cases, whenever the forces were exerted in the same direction as the inherent course of growth, there was overdevelopment. If they were in opposition to the normal process, underdevelopment in that direction was seen. They apparently inhibited lateral growth in the maxillary bone and positively prevented downward growth of the palate. These inhibitions of growth were found associated with less than normal width and height of the nasal space, deflection of the nasal septum and the consequent pathologic manifestations of such abnormal conditions. There remain, I believe, only the questions of extent of deformity and the percentage of cases. Such nasal malformation often is incurable. It is common and is the source of much ill health. If thumb-sucking is a cause of these conditions, it is time that, as an important health measure, a more serious attitude be taken toward the habit.

5. Thumb-sucking causes definite and often serious nervous disturbances. The evidence of this was so common and so clear among these children that there can be no doubt of the fact. When practice of the habit was positively stopped by the use of mechanical appliances, the nervousness attending the habit was reduced or cleared up. If the habit was resumed, the same abnormal symptoms reappeared. Through nervousness, the habit exerts its influence on the general physical and mental processes. Its physical results may be such conditions as muscular tics, retarded growth, deficient weight or disordered bodily functions. Some of its principal nervous and psychologic consequences are unsound sleep, deficient appetite, abnormal restlessness, excessive crying, tantrums, lack of power to concentrate and unfavorable social behavior. There may be one outstanding symptom or a number of them in a given case. In this group, they were as apparent among the youngest children as among the oldest ones. The severity of the abnormal nervous phenomena was definitely related to the method, time and intensity of the habit. The nervous effects on the physical and mental well-being and personality were, in some cases, far more important than the structural ones.

6. The findings of this investigation can be verified in any dental practice. It seems, therefore, that dentistry, as guardian of the structures of the mouth and of the general health, should assume its special responsibility in preventing or curing these pernicious habits.

THE TEETH IN CONGENITAL SYPHILIS

FLORENCE B. HOPKINS, M.D., D.M.D.

Division of Child Hygiene
Massachusetts Department of Public Health

Have you ever advised a patient to have a Wassermann Test just because of the teeth? Were you justified in doing this?

The incidence of syphilis is hard to establish. Probably half the number of people who acquire the disease never seek treatment. Some cases practically defy a diagnosis. Many cases are not properly diagnosed and more are not reported. Therefore, our estimates are apt to run below rather than over the true figures.

We are told that 186,000 women in the United States suffer from active syphilis. It is not surprising, therefore, to hear that 60,000 syphilitic infants are born yearly.* Diagnosis of congenital syphilis in the newborn is extremely difficult. Many of the infected infants go untreated. Congenital syphilis produces late manifestations of the disease in over one-half the syphilitic children who survive infancy.

Fifty-two per cent of all patients seeking treatment because of congenital syphilis have or have had interstitial keratitis. This comes on usually between the ages of five and sixteen years or even much later, and constitutes four to six per cent of all eye cases treated in large clinics. It does actual serious damage to forty per cent of the patients, leaving only sixty per cent with recovery of useful vision.

Ten to fifteen per cent of congenital syphilis cases have inner ear involvement which frequently results in total loss of hearing. The onset of this manifestation is usually at puberty.

At least thirty-two per cent of the children infected with syphilis prenatally have definitely characteristic teeth, while another thirty per cent will probably have teeth which may be termed suggestive.

The lack of accurate knowledge and understanding about the teeth of congenital syphilis is most amazing. Both medical and dental students seem quite untaught regarding the matter. Yet it is adequately described in medical literature.

Dr. Stokes shows a splendid picture of syphilitic upper central incisors in his volume, *Modern Clinical Syphilology*. Under the photograph he prints, "This patient had had interstitial keratitis, undiagnosed for years; had become almost totally deaf, and had suffered a collapse of the nasal septum, before syphilis was sufficiently suspected to lead to a blood Wassermann test and treatment."

I am acquainted with the case of a girl who was under treatment at a dental clinic for many months, who entered the orthopedic service of a large hospital for treatment of a spastic paralysis with contractures, and was operated on without thought of a test for syphilis. She had both incisors and molars that warranted a diagnosis of congenital syphilis but neither the dentists nor the orthopedic specialists noted them. A positive Wassermann corroborated this. Both parents were found to be positive

---

* Whipple, Dorothy V., and Dunham, Ethel C., Congenital Syphilis. Part II, Prevention and Treatment. J. Pediat. 13: 101-119, July, 1938.

also. The father, who was listed as a "shell shock" victim had evidently not been tested for lues before.

Another case referred for Wassermann and treatment because of the typical Hutchinsonian teeth was found to have had this past history: attended medical clinic for chronic coryza at very early age, referred to nose and throat clinic where examination did not show need for treatment. Returned to clinic a few months later because condition persisted and was recorded as having "tonsils large but not infected." However, tonsilectomy was advised as a means of correcting of chronic sniffles. To be sure, this occurred before the second incisors had erupted. Nevertheless, sniffles is a major landmark of a tardive heredosyphilis and an X-ray of the unerupted incisors would have shown the characteristic teeth. These two symptoms would have almost demanded the taking of a Wassermann of the child and her family.

Dr. Stokes also shows in his book a picture demonstrating "unerupted Hutchinsonian teeth by the X-ray ... in a case of a five-year-old child who had lost her first dentition incisors and whose delayed second dentition incisors had not yet erupted."

Dr. George Morgan had an example of unerupted teeth deformed by syphilis and shown by X-ray among the many excellent lantern slides which accompanied his lecture at the American Dental Association Convention in St. Louis last year.

While examining a group of school children not long ago I found two pupils with both Hutchinsonian incisors and mulberry molars. I reported these to a public health physician saying that these children had teeth pathognomonic of congenital syphilis. I was asked if I knew the definition of "pathognomonic," and was also told that no "authority" would presume to make the diagnosis of syphilis on teeth alone. The physician didn't think it was a symptom which would even warrant our asking for a Wassermann. He referred me to Stokes's *Modern Clinical Syphilology* for study. From this I quote. "Should a diagnosis be based on teeth alone? The classical Hutchinsonian tooth can be regarded as practically pathognomonic, and I have never known the finding to remain unconfirmed by history or course." My own experience has agreed absolutely with this.

To be sure, we must be very careful not to confuse hypoplastic molars and anteriors with mulberry molars and syphilitic incisors. We must keep in mind that there are many nonsyphilitic dental dystrophies. It has even been necessary to point out to the medical profession that perfectly normal newly erupted second incisors often have noticeably serrated edges. There are teeth that can justify only our suspicion of lues if accompanied by other suspicious signs.

The dentist and the physician who examines children and young adults should make himself familiar with those teeth that do call for further investigation.

"We know enough about syphilis, its prevention and control and its treatment, to limit it enormously, provided the knowledge and the facilities at hand were utilized wisely and to the fullest extent."* The

---
* "The Preventive Aspects of Venereal Diseases" by Alfred T. Osgood, Preventive Medicine, January, 1939.

complications of interstitial keratitis and deafness can be prevented. This can only be done by early diagnosis and persistent and prolonged treatment.

The diagnosis of congenital syphilis has a significance beyond the treatment of the one case discovered. It is a sign for the examination of parents and other children in the family.

Medical and dental schools turn their students out with inadequate knowledge of dental dystrophies and their significance. Thus a small but important step in the prevention of the dire results of syphilis is completely ignored.

Dr. R. A. Vonderlehr, Assistant Surgeon General, United States Public Health Service, concludes a paper on "The Role of the Dentist in the Control of Syphilis" with these sentences:

"The dentist's contribution to the problem of case finding may contribute to the syphilis-control campaign.

"The control of both acquired and prenatal syphilis may be materially aided by the wary dentist who arranges for the administration of proper treatment of his patients by a physician."

At a recent meeting of the Association of American Medical Colleges, Dr. J. E. Moore of Johns Hopkins told the members, "If syphilis is to be wiped out of this country, medical students must be given more comprehensive training in the subject. The medical student must be prepared to think of syphilis when he sees patients with any of its symptoms."

Both dentists and physicians should take time to improve their knowledge and understanding of the importance of malformed teeth in the diagnosis of prenatal syphilis with all its implications and importance in preventive medicine. Medical and dental schools should see that their students do not graduate ignorant of this diagnostic measure.

We are justified in asking for further diagnostic aids if we recognize teeth that are typical of congenital syphilis.

Bibliography

ANDERSON, BERT G. "Dental Defects in Congenital Syphilis." *American Journal of Diseases of Children.* 57: 52-57, January, 1939.

WHIPPLE, DOROTHY V., and DUNHAM, ETHEL C. "Congenital Syphilis. Part II. Prevention and Treatment." *J. Pediat.* 13:101-119, July, 1938.

HOWARD, P. J., M.D. "Congenital Syphilis, A Ten-Year Study of Forty-Five Children." *Am. J. of Pediat*, 14: 220-233, February, 1939.

MERRITT, H. HOUSTON and MOORE, MERRILL. "The Problem of Syphilis on the Wards of a Large General Hospital." *New England Journal of Medicine*, November 24, 1938: 219: 834-835.

STOKES, JOHN H. *"Modern Clinical Syphilology."* Saunders, Philadelphia, 1934.

UGART, F. "Dentition and Fontanels. A New Sign of Congenital Syphilis," Review of Current Dental Literature. *Dental Cosmos*, 78: 555, May, 1936.

VONDERLEHR, R. A. "The Role of the Dentist in the Control of Syphilis." *Journal of American Dental Association and Dental Cosmos*, 24: 1935-1940, December, 1937.

"Abstracts Reviewed in Compilation of Venereal Disease Information on File in The Division of Venereal Diseases, January 1924." Issued by the U. S. Public Health Service for use in its Cooperative Work with State Health Department. VM 613.

DENTAL HEALTH EXHIBITS
ALBERTINE P. MCKELLAR, B.S.
*Public Health Education Worker
Division of Child Hygiene
Massachusetts Department of Public Health*

The exhibit is becoming more and more popular as a method for health education. It has far more teaching value than the poster and offers unlimited opportunity for the portrayal of health material.

Interest and Appeal

Exhibits on dental health are perhaps the most popular and offer more possibilities than those on any other health subject.

First, dental health has an interest for all age groups and involves so much of the complete health story—nutrition, adequate home care, regular care by the dentist, etc. Secondly, dental health exhibits have a definite appeal to attractiveness, beauty, popularity, economy, prevention of pain, and even duty—all strong motivations—and the basis for valuable advertising slogans.

Opportunities

Dental exhibits are essential as a part of the school health program—used in formal health teaching and in the informal teaching at the dental clinic.

The dentist's office offers one of the very best opportunities for the display of dental health educational material. Some industrial nurses have successfully used health exhibits in the visiting room of the first aid office. A carefully planned simple exhibit set up in the dentist's office would interest the patient, take up his time while he waited for the dentist and doubtless be more enjoyable than the 1928 publications.

Other opportunities for dental health exhibits would include all those for general public health exhibits, such as: settlement houses, Y. W.'s and Y.M.'s, annual meetings of various organizations and associations, the fairs, libraries, rest rooms in various industries or office buildings, recreation centers, etc.

Exhibit Principles

A review of the fundamental exhibit principles described in other articles in *The Commonhealth* seems to be a necessary part of this paper. (Other *Commonhealth* articles on exhibits are "Exhibits and Materials for Health Teaching" by Albertine P. McKellar and John H. McCarthy, published in the "Health Education" number, Volume 24, No. 3, 1937; and "The Nutritionist Says It with Exhibits" by Dorothea Nicoll, published in the number entitled "Nutrition in the Community," Volume 23,

No. 1, 1936.) *Who* and *What* are the first big decisions to be made by the exhibitor—for whom is the exhibit planned and exactly what do you wish to teach? Where a mixed age group will see the exhibit (such as in a dentist's office) a feasible idea would be to plan for one specific group at a time and emphasize its most significant problem.

For instance, Dr. Hopkins decided that she wished to teach parents the fact that at six years of age a child has in his mouth—all at the same time—baby teeth with disappearing roots very close to developing permanent teeth and an erupted six-year molar. That was our problem and throughout this paper I'll refer to this exhibit and show how we developed it for the general lay public.

Where will the exhibit be displayed? There is a great advantage in having a definite stationary location for exhibits. In visiting rooms, clinics, etc., this is possible and helpful. The same background, table and cover could be used and persons would soon be familiar with its location and learn to look for it. When the exhibit must be moved from place to place the best plan, we believe, is to have a department or organization "type" of exhibit as well as the same ("trademark") color scheme. These help to label your exhibit and even before the sign is visible your exhibit is recognized.

If possible, choose the best location by experimentation. Come into the room and observe where your attention is drawn. Try to have the exhibit well lighted and not in front of a window. Watch out for nearby competing interests, and try to avoid or cover them. Plenty of space prevents the sensation of crowding and haste, so if possible provide spacious and ample room for chairs.

With Dr. Hopkins' problem we had no choice as to colors. Blue and white have been established as the State Health Department color scheme. The size of the exhibit is also standardized—to that of a regulation card table—with a 30" background. This rigid policy of card table exhibits is more economical, as the packing cases and tailored sateen table covers can all be the same size. This idea also offers flexibility. We plan as many "units" (separate card table exhibits) for any given space as the specific subject and the area will accommodate attractively. *How* to portray the desired information in an attractive, interesting and easily understandable way?

Attention attractors must be planned—something to call attention to your exhibit—bring people over and then, once there, the interest aroused by the educational material should be in the proper doses for immediate consumption! Pictures—of lovely ladies, beautiful babies, happy family groups, etc.—are valuable for attracting attention. They should be well mounted, with backgrounds that emphasize them. Color and light (especially changing light) and motion are used successfully to attract attention, and clever slogans or captions will often do the trick.

The "meat" or educational material should be simple and brief and shown as interestingly as possible. Life-sized articles, maps, micro counters, photographs, foods, models, graphs and the printed word have all been used. Usually the simpler and fewer the words the better! Try to avoid crowding and confusion.

Individual participation has been proven valuable and many of the newer exhibits depend upon the "onlooker" to take part by turning cranks, pulling levers or, as with our Question Box Exhibit, indicate answers to public health questions by pushing buttons.

Source of further information should always be considered—one exhibit can't possibly tell the whole story. When the exhibit is covered (a person in attendance) many individual interests can be ascertained and specific material recommended. The order blank method for securing pamphlets saves the pamphlets and gives more value to the material—having to stop and fill in an order makes the whole thing seem much more important than stuffing some "free booklets" into a pocket or bag. In a dentist's office, however, doubtless a pile of dental health pamphlets would not be wasted.

In developing our problem of showing the temporary and permanent teeth in the mouth of a six-year-old, we decided to use light as the attention attractor, together with the picture of an attractive child and a clever (we hope!) caption.

The exhibit will be a lighting box, 30" in width to fit the table top and table back, and built on a 45° angle—making the horizontal line on the table 24" and the vertical line of the back 24". On the 6" of the back which is extended above this box will be this caption IF YOU HAD X-RAY EYES —in blue and white. On the 6" table top extending beyond the front edge of the box, in blue and white, will be the words JAW OF A SIX-YEAR-OLD. The material used in construction will be one-quarter-inch Masonite.

On the front slanted surface of the box will be an enlarged head of a six-year-old child, painted in colors (profile view). Within a rectangular panel enclosing the section of the face from the bottom of the upper lip to within a half inch of the bottom of the jaw, the cheek will be removed, showing the teeth in the lower jaw and the gums below.

A double lighting arrangement is set up inside the box, whose interior is painted a brilliant white enamel to give good diffusion of light. Under the gums the roots of the first teeth are cut out and also the roots of the six-year molar and the developing second teeth. Thus, with the double lighting arrangement, when the lights are on, the roots of the first teeth are silhouetted on the gums (X-ray style) in a pinkish white and the roots of the six-year molar and the developing second teeth are shown in a whiter tint. This clearly shows the six-year molar as a second tooth although it is already in the jaw with the first teeth. When the lights are off the roots do not show—only the red surface of the gums.

A small trap door in the back of the box will permit the bulb to be changed when it is necessary. The box is one complete unit with a slot at the top to receive the 6" x 30" piece of background containing the caption. Likewise a slot is in the lower front edge to receive the 6" x 30" piece of table top with the second caption. A carrying case of fibre made to fit this 45° angle lighting box will contain both the box and the two 6" x 30" pieces which complete the exhibit.

Some Suggestions for Exhibits as given (with a few minor changes) by the student hygienists at Forsyth in our course in Health Education Materials are as follows:

(1) Caption: BEAUTIFUL TEETH OF THE FUTURE
DEPEND ON
MOTHER OF TODAY
Poster background—picture of mother and baby

Table top: Diagram of baby's jaw
HIS TEETH GROW BEFORE BIRTH
Picture of necessary vitamin foods
MOTHER NEEDS MORE TOOTH BUILDING FOODS
Picture of woman in dentist's chair
THE DENTIST AND DOCTOR HELP TO PROTECT TWO
Pamphlets on table, too.
—Esther Wilkins

(2) Caption: BE AN UP TO "DATE" TEEN
Poster background—picture of boy and girl dating

Table top: Food
Care—brushes, etc.
SEE DENTIST TWICE A YEAR
—Gertrude Robertson

(3) Caption: HIS TEETH ARE STRONG—ARE YOURS?
Poster background—picture of boy drinking milk

Sign along back of table—NECESSARY FOODS FOR STRONG TEETH
A pile of foods attractively arranged on table top
Very simple exhibit
—Eunice Nelson

(4) Caption: DO *YOUR* TEETH LOOK LIKE THIS?
Poster background—picture of young girl with lovely teeth

Table top: Large model molar and toothbrush with sign, GOOD TEETH ARE PRICELESS ASSETS
HOW YOU CAN DO YOUR PART
3 pamphlets—Brush
Diet
Dentist
—Rita Snow

(5) Caption: HEALTH FOR HAPPY SCHOOL DAYS
Poster background—colorful high school group

Table top: Lunch box with adequate lunch
2 pictures on dental care:
boy brushing teeth
girl going to dentist
Pamphlets: "Healthful Living"
"Self-Check on Personal Appearance"
—Shirley Hartford

(6) (a poster exhibit)
　　Slogan: ITS SMART TO BE HEALTHY
　　　　3 pictures on background:
　　　　　playing a game
　　　　　eating nutritious food
　　　　　sleeping
　　　Table top used for carefully selected pamphlets
　　　　　　　　　　　　　　　　　　　　—Olive Nelson

(7) Caption: YOURS TO BE LIKE THIS?
　　　　with a very appealing baby picture
　　On table top: Sign DOCTOR with 4 small pictures showing adequate prenatal care
　　　　Sign DENTIST with 4 small pictures showing dental care and information regarding formation of teeth during pregnancy
　　　　Sign NUTRITION with picture of necessary food (or real food)
　　　　A small picture showing rest and one showing exercise on each side of the nutrition picture.
　　　　　　　　　　　　　　　　　　　　—Constance Viner

Book Note

MATERNITY CARE IN A RURAL COMMUNITY — Pike County, Mississippi, 1931-1936, by Maxwell E. Lapham, M.D. $0.25. New York, The Commonwealth Fund, 1938. 65 pp.

　　This is a report of a study in Pike County, Mississippi, for the years 1931-1936. Pike County has a population of 32,000, less than one-third of which is urban. The foreword is written by Dr. Frank Walker of the Commonwealth Fund.

　　The objective of the study was to take stock of conditions and facilities in Pike County and to find ways of further improving maternal care. The study contains interesting findings, charted and otherwise, not only of mortality rates but of medical and nursing services and midwife practices. The chart showing the rapid increase in antepartum and postpartum visits, medical and nursing, is worthy of special note. A detailed study of one hundred current cases reveals certain needs and an estimate of twenty-five maternal deaths, eighty-five stillbirths and seventy-five neonatal deaths that might be prevented. To meet these demands and to prevent mortality the last chapter entitled " A Suggested Maternity Program" outlines activities that would improve maternal care not only in Pike County but in numerous other counties in the United States.

News Note

Vocational-Placement Service to Public Health Nurses
From: Nursing Bureau of Manhattan and Bronx, Inc., 205 East 42nd St., New York, N. Y.

The Nursing Bureau of Manhattan and Bronx, Inc., New York, New York, opens a vocational-placement service to public health nurses and the field on May 1, 1939. The service has the tentative approval of the Committee on Vocational Counseling of NOPHN. Full approval is dependent upon analysis of the service in action.

Letha Allen, R.N., formerly Director of the Public Health Nursing Organization of East Chester, Tuckahoe, New York, has been appointed Secretary of Public Health Placements. The Nursing Bureau of Manhattan and Bronx, Inc., has been conducting a placement-vocational service for private practice and institutional nurses since 1933. The service to public health nurses and nursing organizations is now added because a need for it in New York City was created when the Public Health Nursing Service rendered by Joint Vocational Service in New York City was transferred last July to the Nurse Placement Service in Chicago.

All level positions will be handled, the service will cover the entire United States.

REPORT OF DIVISION OF FOOD AND DRUGS

(As required by General Laws, Chapter 111, Section 25)

During the months of December, 1938, January and February, 1939, samples were collected in 228 cities and towns.

There were 1,577 samples of milk examined, of which 164 were below standard, from 22 samples the cream had been in part removed, and 2 samples contained added water. There were 2,080 bacteriological examinations made of milk, 1,857 of which complied with the requirements. There were 112 bacteriological examinations made of cream, 14 of which did not comply with the requirements. There were 153 bacteriological examinations made of scallops; 1 bacteriological examination of canned soup; 3 bacteriological examinations of tonic; 1 bacteriological examination of chocolate milk, all of which complied with the requirements; 1 bateriological examination of an empty bottle which did not comply with the requirements; and 24 bacteriological examinations of mattress fillings, 4 of which did not comply with the requirements.

There were 849 samples of food examined, 330 of which were adulterated. These consisted of 1 sample of butter which was rancid; 30 samples of clams, 29 of which contained added water, and 1 sample was decomposed; 3 samples of oysters to which water had been added; 116 samples of scallops, all of which were decomposed; 1 sample of shrimp which was decomposed; 24 samples of fish which contained formaldehyde; 3 sample of eggs, 2 of which were decomposed, and 1 sample of cold storage eggs sold as fresh eggs; 1 sample of egg whites which were decomposed; 4 samples of pickles and sweet relish containing sodium benzoate not so labeled; 2 samples of split peas which contained worm-eaten peas and worm excrete; 4 samples of soft drinks which contained sodium benzoate not so labeled; 7 samples of wash water which were deficient in caustic alkali; 22 samples of cream cheese not conforming to the legal standard; 1 sample of peppermint leaves which contained considerable stem dirt, woody matter, an oat, leg from an insect, and a cocoon; 2 samples of buttermilk in which the solids not fat were below 8.5% and 1 sample also contained added gelatine; 12 samples of cranberries which were moldy; 16 samples of hamburg steak, 10 of which were decomposed and 1 sample also contained sodium sulphite in excess of one-tenth of one per cent, 1 sample contained pork, and 5 samples contained a compound of sulphur dioxide not so labeled; 39 samples of sausage, 32 of which were decomposed and 1 sample also contained added water, 6 contained a compound of sulphur dioxide not so labeled, and 1 sample contained sodium sulphite in excess of one-tenth of one per cent; 1 sample of meat for hamburg, 1 sample of cooked meat loaf, and 5 samples of lamb patties, all of which were decomposed; and 35 samples of mattress fillings, 33 of which were labeled as containing a certain percentage of different kinds of feathers and down, which samples did not contain the materials as specified, and 2 samples contained a mixture of new and secondhand material.

There were 65 samples of drugs examined, of which 8 were adulterated. These consisted of 3 samples of boric acid ointment, 1 miscellaneous drug, and 4 samples of mercurochrome, all of which did not conform to the requirements of the U. S. Pharmacopoeïa.

The police departments submitted 94 samples of liquor for examination. The police departments also submitted 27 samples to be analyzed for poisons or drugs, 14 of which contained heroin, 1 contained cannabis, 2 contained quinine, 1 sample proved to be powdered sugar, 1 sample was identified as lysol, 1 sample was a solution of soap, formaldehyde, and an essential oil for perfuming purposes, and 7 samples were examined for narcotics with negative results.

There were inspected 371 plants operated for the pasteurization of milk, 30 restaurants; 114 soft drink plants; 48 ice cream plants; 281 bakeries; and 353 mattress establishments.

There were 87 hearings held pertaining to violations of the laws.

There were 45 convictions pertaining to violations of the law, $1,235 in fines being imposed.

Malcolm D. Ferguson of Canton; Stuart C. Whitman of Pittsfield; John Michonski of Easthampton; and George A. Sampson of Marlboro, were convicted for violations of the pasteurization law and regulations.

Howard I. Bray of North Hanover was convicted for violation of the milk-laws.

Ernest Roy of Salem; Ignatius Aggelis and Economy Grocery Stores, Incorporated, of Roxbury; P. Efstration and Publix Food Markets, Incorporated, of Somerville; The Great Atlantic & Pacific Tea Company, Joseph Greenstein, and Abraham Miller of New Bedford; Charles Samios of Boston; The Great Atlantic & Pacific Tea Company of Rockland; H. W. Fanger of West Roxbury; M. Winer Company of Dorchester; Napoleon Desauliers of Southbridge; John Moskal of Holyoke; Louis Pappas, 2 cases, of Amherst; Frank Rainor of Adams; Louis

Rudnick of North Adams; Joseph Syper of Palmer; Victor Wells of Revere; Max Common of Cambridge; Sydney Nataubsky and North Main Market, Incorporated, of Worcester; Philip Leader, 2 cases, Herman Busansky, Oscar Spitzler, Incorporated, Philip Tillman, Economy Grocery Stores, Incorporated, and Theodore Tillman, all of Springfield; Sam Gritton and Simon Jegelewicz of Westfield; and Stanley Pereksli and John West of Athol, were all convicted for violations of the food laws.

Harry Haletky of Dorchester was convicted for violation of the soft drink regulations.

Louis Ferris of Pittsfield was convicted for violation of the cold storage laws.

Myer N. Bernstein of Worcester; M. Maisel Company and The L. Buchman Company, Incorporated, of Brooklyn, New York; and Comfort Pillow & Feather Company of Somerville, were convicted for violations of the mattress laws.

In accordance with Section 25, Chapter 111 of the General Laws, the following is the list of articles of adulterated food collected in original packages from manufacturers, wholesalers, or producers:

One sample of butter which was rancid was obtained from Wilson & Company, Incorporated, of Boston.

One sample of peppermint leaves which contained considerable stem dirt, woody matter, an oat, leg from an insect, and a cocoon, was obtained from Nature Food Centre, Incorporated, of Boston.

Cream cheese not conforming to the legal standard was obtained as follows:

Eighteen samples were obtained from East Smithfield Farms, Incorporated, of Philadelphia, Pa.; and 3 samples were obtained from Abbott's Dairy, Incorporated, of Philadelphia, Pa.

Three samples of relish which contained sodium benzoate not so labeled were obtained from Hi Hat Food Products Company of Providence, R. I.

One sample of eggs which was decomposed was obtained from Bernard Fish of Greenfield.

One sample of cold storage eggs sold as fresh eggs was obtained from Louis Ferris of Pittsfield.

Split peas which contained worm-eaten peas and worm excrete were obtained as follows:

One sample each, from The Great Atlantic & Pacific Tea Company of Rockland; and Economy Grocery Stores, Incorporated, of Roxbury.

Soft drinks which contained benzoate not so labeled were obtained as follows:

Two samples from Crystal Soda Company of Holyoke; and one sample each, from Herman Braun of Pittsfield; and Albert & Charles Singer of Adams.

One sample of clams which was decomposed was obtained from Abraham Glass of Worcester.

Clams to which water was added were obtained as follows:

Five samples were obtained from Ipswich Shellfish Company of Ipswich; 3 samples were obtained from I. W. Stavis of Chelsea, and 1 sample from I. W. Stavis of Seabrook, N. H.; and 1 sample each, from

Essex Street Fish Market, and Brockelman's Market, Incorporated of Lawrence; Quality Fish Market of Worcester; First National Stores, Incorporated, of Salem; Victor Wells of Revere; George Welch of Newburyport; and Fred Snow of Pine Point, Maine.

Oysters to which water had been added were obtained as follows:
Two samples from Auditorium Market, Incorporated of Pittsfield; and one sample from Berkshire Fish Company of Pittsfield.

One sample of meat loaf which was decomposed was obtained from Louis Pappas of Amherst.

One sample of meat to be used for hamburg steak which was decomposed was obtained from Blackstone Supply Company of Boston.

One sample of hamburg steak which contained pork was obtained from The Great Atlantic & Pacific Tea Company of Holyoke.

One sample of hamburg steak which was decomposed and also contained sodium sulphite in excess of one tenth of one per cent was obtained from Harry Gillis of Boston.

Hamburg steak which contained a compound of sulphur dioxide and was not so labeled was obtained as follows:
One sample each, from Harry Krivitsky, Frank Astuti, and Arnold Scheu of Boston.

Hamburg steak which was decomposed was obtained as follows: One sample each, from The Great Atlantic & Pacific Tea Company of New Bedford; P. Efstration of Somerville; Blair's Market of Roxbury; Economy Grocery Stores, Incorporated, of Lawrence; Chicopee Falls Super Market of Chicopee Falls; Rood & Woodbury, Incorporated, of Springfield; and Simon Jegelwicz of Westfield.

Lamb patties which were decomposed were obtained as follows: One sample each, from Anna Klys of Springfield; Antonia Klys of Palmer; Stanley Pereksli of Athol; Frank Rainor of Adams; and Louis Rudnick of North Adams.

One sample of sausage which was decomposed and also contained added water was obtained from Joseph MacLean of Greenfield.

One sample of sausage which contained sodium sulphite in excess of one tenth of one per cent was obtained from Benjamin Shuffain of Boston.

Sausage which contained a compound of sulphur dioxide and was not so labeled was obtained as follows:
Two samples from Frank Astuti of Boston; and 1 sample each, from Jack Saletsky and Diamond Beef Company of Boston; Economy Grocery Stores, Incorporated, of Cambridge; and Publix Food Market, Incorporated, of Somerville.

Sausage which was decomposed was obtained as follows: Two samples each, from Philip Leader of Springfield; and Northampton Public Market of Northampton; and 1 sample each, from John West of Athol; Tremont Market and Sydney Nataubsky of Worcester; Max Common of Cambridge; Abraham Miller and Joseph Greenstein of New Bedford; Moran's Market of Waltham; Antoni Fratoni and The Great Atlantic & Pacific Tea Company of Attleboro; Henry Beech of North Attleboro; Louis Pappas of Amherst; John Moskal of Holyoke; Napolean Desaulniers and Central Meat & Grocery, Incorporated, of Southbridge;

Sam Gritton of Westfield; C. F. Pease of Warren; Louis Zionts of Pittsfield; Harris Tillman, Bernard Roberts, and Peter Fertig of West Springfield; Oscar Spitzler, Incorporated, Philip Tillman, Herman Busansky, Elizabeth Morrad, Theodore Tillman, Anna Klys, and Harold Dumais, of Springfield.

There were 33 confiscations, consisting of 19 pounds of rancid butter; 3½ pounds of decomposed fowl; 70 pounds of decomposed beef; 100 pounds of old hamburg steak, unfit for consumption; 6 pounds of decomposed pork; 3 pounds of decomposed pork chops; 25 pounds of decomposed pigs' feet; 15 pounds of decomposed pickled meats; 324 pounds of wormy green split peas; 516 pounds of decomposed Cape scallops; 31,910 pounds of decomposed sea scallops; and 180 pounds of decomposed shrimp.

The licensed cold storage warehouses reported the following amounts of food placed in storage during November, 1938: 187,740 dozens of case eggs; 861,981 pounds of broken out eggs; 918,650 pounds of butter; 4,019,975 pounds of poultry; 3,049,757 pounds of fresh meat and fresh meat products; and 7,285,136 pounds of fresh food fish.

There was on hand December 1, 1938: 371,310 dozens of case eggs; 1,761,618 pounds of broken out eggs; 4,310,929 pounds of butter; 6,470,733 pounds of poultry; 3,302,060 pounds of fresh meat and fresh meat products; and 26,211,813 pounds of fresh food fish.

The licensed cold storage warehouses reported the following amounts of food placed in storage during December, 1938: 92,730 dozens of case eggs; 714,685 pounds of broken out eggs; 311,463 pounds of butter; 3,206,038 pounds of poultry; 3,374,216 pounds of fresh meat and fresh meat products; and 3,476,963 pounds of fresh food fish.

There was on hand January 1, 1939: 83,910 dozens of case eggs; 1,514,676 pounds of broken out eggs; 3,304,671 pounds of butter; 7,396,410 pounds of poultry; 5,103,169 pounds of fresh meat and fresh meat products; and 21,612,505 pounds of fresh food fish.

The licensed cold storage warehouses reported the following amounts of food placed in storage during January, 1939: 61,620 dozens of case eggs; 605,795 pounds of broken out eggs; 262,753 pounds of butter; 1,867,814 pounds of poultry; 3,174,694 pounds of fresh meat and fresh meat products; and 4,307,425 pounds of fresh food fish.

There was on hand February 1, 1939: 41,790 dozens of case eggs; 1,280,739 pounds of broken out eggs; 2,708,266 pounds of butter; 7,282,725 pounds of poultry; 6,127,543 pounds of fresh meat and fresh meat products; and 16,445,072 pounds of fresh food fish.

MASSACHUSETTS DEPARTMENT OF PUBLIC HEALTH

Commissioner of Public Health, PAUL J. JAKMAUH, M.D.

Public Health Council

PAUL J. JAKMAUH, M.D., *Chairman*

GEORGE D. DALTON, M.D.
FRANCIS H. LALLY, M.D.
CHARLES F. LYNCH, M.D.
RICHARD M. SMITH, M.D.
RICHARD P. STRONG, M.D.
JAMES L. TIGHE

Secretary, FLORENCE L. WALL

Division of Administration	Under direction of Commissioner
Division of Sanitary Engineering	Director and Chief Engineer, ARTHUR D. WESTON, C.E.
Division of Communicable Diseases	Director, ROY F. FEEMSTER, M.D.
Division of Biologic Laboratories	Director and Pathologist, ELLIOTT S. ROBINSON, M.D.
Division of Food and Drugs	Director and Analyst, HERMANN C. LYTHGOE, S.B.
Division of Child Hygiene	Director, M. LUISE DIEZ, M.D.
Division of Tuberculosis	Director, ALTON S. POPE, M.D.
Division of Adult Hygiene	Director, HERBERT L. LOMBARD, M.D.
Division of Genitoinfectious Diseases	Director, NELS A. NELSON, M.D.

State District Health Officers

The Southeastern District	HAROLD W. STEVENS, M.D., Middleborough
The South Metropolitan District	HENRY M. DE WOLFE, M.D., Braintree
The North Metropolitan District	
The Northeastern District	ROBERT E. ARCHIBALD, M.D., Melrose
The Worcester District	OSCAR A. DUDLEY, M.D., Worcester
South Connecticut Valley District	CHARLES E. GILL, M.D., Westfield
North Connecticut Valley District	WALTER W. LEE, M.D., Greenfield
The Berkshire District	FRANK B. CARROLL, M.D., Great Barrington.

PUBLICATION OF THIS DOCUMENT APPROVED BY THE COMMISSION ON ADMINISTRATION AND FINANCE
10,500. 5-'39. Order 7225.

THE COMMONHEALTH

Volume 26   July-Aug.-Sept.
No. 3   1939

RADIO NUMBER

MASSACHUSETTS
DEPARTMENT OF PUBLIC HEALTH

THE COMMONHEALTH

QUARTERLY BULLETIN OF THE MASSACHUSETTS DEPARTMENT OF
PUBLIC HEALTH

Sent Free to any Citizen of the State
Entered as second class matter at Boston Post Office

M. LUISE DIEZ, M.D., DIRECTOR OF DIVISION OF CHILD HYGIENE, EDITOR.
1 Beacon Street, Boston, Mass.

CONTENTS

	PAGE
The Adaptation of Public Health Education to the Radio, by Lila Owen Burbank, M.D.	161
Samples of Radio Health Forum:	
Massachusetts Saves Prematurely Born Babies, by Florence L. McKay, M.D.	165
The Prematurely Born Baby Needs Specialized Nursing Care, by Madelen P. Pollock, R.N.	166
Control of Typhoid, by Gaylord W. Anderson, M.D.	167
Trichinosis, by John J. Poutas, M.D.	169
Just a Little Routine, by Hermann C. Lythgoe, S.B.	170
Overnight Camp Sanitation, by William H. Doggett, M.S.	172
Pulmonary Tuberculosis—How It Spreads in the Home and Family, by David Zacks, M.D.	173
Pulmonary Tuberculosis—How Its Spread in the Family Can be Prevented, by David Zacks, M.D.	175
Sample of Health Review:	
The Humanitarian Movement, by Eleanor J. Macdonald, A.B.	176
Samples of Green Lights to Health:	
The Laboratory Fights Pneumonia, by Elliott S. A. Robinson, M.D.	179
Clinics for Crippled Children, by Arthur Wakefield, M.D.	183
Endocrine Glands, by James H. Means, M.D.	187
Arthritis, by Francis C. Hall, M.D.	190
What to Eat and Why, by Sara M. Jordan, M.D.	193
Nervous Fatigue, by Vernon P. Williams, M.D.	197
Samples of Special Broadcasts:	
The Massachusetts Cancer Program, by Herbert L. Lombard, M.D.	201
Gonorrhea and Syphilis—Notions versus Facts, by N. A. Nelson, M.D.	209
Book Notes:	
Teaching Procedures in Health Education, by Howard L. Conrad and Joseph F. Meister	213
How to Conquer Constipation, by J. F. Montague, M.D.	213
Report of Division of Food and Drugs, March, April and May, 1939	215

THE ADAPTATION OF PUBLIC HEALTH EDUCATION TO THE RADIO

LILA OWEN BURBANK, M.D.

*Public Health Education Worker in Charge of Radio
Massachusetts Department of Public Health*

The attitude of the leaders of the public health movement in Massachusetts has been from the first one of enthusiasm and interest in ways and means of presenting preventive medicine to the individual members of the Commonwealth in the most personal and adaptable manner. It was to be expected when the medium of radio emerged in 1922 as an untried influence on the daily life of the State that the Commissioner of Public Health, Dr. Eugene R. Kelley, should acknowledge its place in health education and sense its potentialities long before the general public.

This appreciation of the power of this instrument in health education was recognized simultaneously by the Director of the Westinghouse Electric Company at Springfield, Massachusetts, who requested Dr. Harold E. Miner, the District Health Officer of the State Health Department for the Connecticut Valley, to take over the Wednesday evening broadcasts and tell the listeners of the work of the State Department of Public Health in its several aspects. All those presenting papers traveled to Springfield for the occasion and enjoyed the newness of the experience. Broadcasting facilities were just being developed and the casualness of being able to request the unseen audience to "stand by for ten minutes" due to some unforeseen occurrence, probably gives as graphic a picture of the change that has come over the conduct of this industry as it is possible to convey.

In June, 1922, this series was begun. Following the presentation of Departmental activities, a group of individuals was asked to prepare papers on general health subjects with the intention of measuring the value of radio. In the Annual Report for 1922, Dr. Kelley stated, "The importance of this educational activity is clearly apparent, and its far-reaching effect is only limited by the number of people who own radio receiving outfits. Not of the least importance is the fact that by this arrangement only sound public health medical knowledge is disseminated and the propaganda for the spread of unsound movements may be eliminated. . . . Constant use of this privilege has been made by the Department ever since with the assurance that an audience was being reached of a size not obtainable in any other way."

Aside from the papers on the activities of the Department, such subjects as the following were presented: "The Perfect 32" by Miss Maria Schmidt; "What Are You Good For?" by Dr. Merrill Champion; "The Importance of Perfect Posture as a Basis of Health" by Dr. Joel Goldthwait; "Adult Chronic Disease" by Dr. Lila O. Burbank.

From 1923 until 1929 the Department had no established policy in regard to radio broadcasting. The radio stations contacted the Department when events of special interest were anticipated, and members of the Department on these occasions prepared and broadcast pertinent articles. In 1924 a number of talks was prepared for broadcasting in Worcester in cooperation with the local Visiting Nurse Association of that city. In 1925 a large number of special talks on personal health and particular subjects such as the May Day celebration was presented. State-wide interest was being aroused in Massachusetts because of the inauguration of the Massachusetts Cancer Program, the first of its kind in existence, and the broadcasting stations requested papers on the subject from 1925 on. In fact, in 1926, during State Cancer Week in April, six special radio broadcasts were requested on the subject.

In May, 1929, the Division of Adult Hygiene requested WEEI to allot time for a series of talks in the interest of cancer education. These six broadcasts prepared and presented by Dr. Lila Owen Burbank were entitled, "Cancer Not a Hopeless Disease," "Cause of Cancer and Who Is Likely to Have It," "Pain and Fear in Relation to Cancer," "Woman's Responsibility in the Control of Cancer," "Cures of Cancer," "What to Do to Be as Safe as Possible about Cancer." These broadcasts aroused so much enthusiasm that the studio requested the time allotment be continued indefinitely for all phases of public health education.

The response to this request resulted in the inauguration of the series known as the "Health Messages." These were broadcast weekly by well known physicians, and the names and affiliations of the participants were announced at that time, a practice which was later discontinued. In October, 1930, WBZ allotted ten minutes each week to the Department, and was granted the "Health Messages" after arrangement with WEEI, because it reached a much larger area. WEEI began to broadcast the "Radio Health Forum." This feature was also carried by forty-eight newspapers throughout the State. Dr. George H. Bigelow, then Commissioner of Public Health, stated concerning it in his Annual Report, "This fall we have started a weekly Health Forum which is run by 48 newspapers, and broadcast. . . . As has been said, we hope to keep this from the menace of a beauty column. It is run as questions and answers (preceded by a foreword on one subject). So far the questioners seem largely interested in a correspondence school diagnosis and treatment, but, of course, we are fighting shy of this and are attempting to raise it to the higher and more impersonal and less financially pertinent plane of prevention. Our experience will be interesting. . . . This gives an admirable media for our adult hygiene education."

For four years the Division of Adult Hygiene was responsible for the preparation and broadcasting of the "Radio Health Forum." Many fine and some touching letters from listeners attested to its importance in their lives. In 1934 it was deemed necessary to discontinue the question and answer period, which was resolving to a personal rather than a broadly general educational project. Two articles on medical subjects were prepared by the several divisions and broadcast as the "Health Forum" by the Director of the Division or his appointee. This is the current practice and has been enthusiastically received and favorably commented upon from its inception.

In January, 1931, a series of broadcasts known as the "State House Broadcasts" was established to give the public information of the various activities carried on in the separate divisions of the Department.

The talks were given weekly by the Directors or their appointees, in turn. For convenience a microphone was installed by WEEI in the State House, but was later removed because the room containing the microphone was required by the Legislature. Broadcasts continued thereafter from the studio of WEEI itself until December, 1933, inclusive.

Station WEEI, which has been one of our staunchest friends and advisors from the start, particularly in the person of Mr. Arthur F. Edes, whose interest and encouragement has never been solicited without immediate response, requested the Department's cooperation in a series of broadcasts on cancer or any other subject it wished to cover. Beginning in October, 1931, sixteen weekly broadcasts were given. The subjects covered were various phases of the cancer problem and the "Findings of the White House Conference on Child Health and Protection." Some of these broadcasts were given in dialogue and others in a round-table discussion. Several famous American specialists were secured for this series.

Late in 1933 the Division of Adult Hygiene was asked to take a regular fifteen minute period weekly to broadcast a series on any chosen subject. From January, 1934, for forty-six weeks, exclusive of the summer months, a program entitled the "Health Review" was prepared and broadcast by Miss Eleanor J. Macdonald, Statistician and Historian of the Division of Adult Hygiene. This series started to cover by important historical steps the development of the history of public health from the days of the ancient Hebrew, down through the Greek and Roman periods, through the different sociological evolutions with their attendant changing problems, to the present time. The series as outlined was planned for a six-year period, and was discontinued with sincere regret by both WEEI and by the Department because the pressure of work made it impossible for the author to give it the time required to maintain its exceptional excellence.

Station WBZ was for many years a very cooperative supporter of the dissemination of State programs through its facilities. Mr. W. Gordon Swan devoted much time to discussion and assistance in an attempt to adapt scientific material to the limitation of radio presentation. In November, 1930, in addition to the time already referred to above, WBZ added five minutes to the time alloted for the "Health Messages." A series called the "Question Box" was initiated to fill this time. The broadcasts were similar to the "Radio Health Forum" series when it was presented in question and answer form except that the foreword was omitted. When the questions and answers were eliminated from the "Radio Health Forum" it was decided to discontinue the "Question Box" entirely.

In March, 1931, the "Health Messages" acquired the additional sponsorship of the Massachusetts Medical Society, with the approval of every paper by the Public Education Committee a routine procedure. At that moment and by this committee it was decided to omit from announcements at the microphone the names, affiliations, and qualifications of physicians presenting these papers. The Studio agreed to the ethical provisos, but insisted upon the use of the name of the physician broadcasting. This was allowed.

A series of thirteen dramas was presented over WBZ through the Department beginning in January, 1933. The plays were secured from the Detroit Department of Public Health, author Rex White. The WBZ players were the actors, and Commissioner of Health, Dr. George H. Bigelow, introduced each play.

In 1935 WBZ stopped the "Health Messages" broadcasts in April, although the station had agreed to carry on until June. The station had become part of a large chain and obviously the continuance of the local programs was no longer completely in the hands of those with whom the Department had had a continuous association since 1929. Station WAAB, the Colonial Network, took over the remaining talks of the series, very courteously adapting their schedule to this purpose. Mr. Roy L. Harlow gave hours of his own time, attending committee meetings and planning with the Medical Society on concrete ways of improving the broadcasts. Their presentation in dialogue form has been unprecedentedly successful. The hour allotted has been advantageous, and the volume of requests for reprints of the talks increases with each broadcast. The Department is grateful to Mr. Harlow for the large part he played in the excellence of this series. While WBZ would have been willing to take the new series in 1938, the Medical Society felt that it was better to continue with Station WAAB, since that station had cooperated in their production so willingly. In 1936 the name of this series was changed to "Green Lights to Health."

There would not be time nor space to enumerate the large number of special broadcasts which have been given to emphasize certain days or weeks. Examples are "Achievement Week" in March, 1932, "Child Health Day" each year, "Gonorrhea and Syphilis" during the past few years, and the 1938 Thanksgiving Day broadcast of the Massachusetts Cancer Program in panel discussion over Station WORL which was repeated in February, 1939, over Station WNAC, by request under the sponsorship of the Massachusetts Federation of Women's Clubs. Practically every station in and around greater Boston has offered its facilities to the Department. Insofar as has been possible, these facilities have been used, and at this moment the Department expresses its grateful appreciation for the friendliness and cooperation inherent in these associations.

The Department has always attempted to measure the results of its several activities. Inasmuch as a number of individuals have questioned the value of health information through the means of the radio, a survey was conducted in 1933 and reported in "The Commonhealth" in the Jan.-Feb.-March issue of 1934. At that time it was estimated that at least twelve thousand individuals were regularly listening to one or more of the Department broadcasts. A comparison of the letters received at the present time with those received in 1933 indicates that the radio audience is now much larger than this. Any health activity which reaches from twelve to thirty thousand individuals each week is a dynamic influence in a public health program.

MASSACHUSETTS SAVES PREMATURELY BORN BABIES

FLORENCE L. MCKAY, M.D.

Assistant Director, Division of Child Hygiene
Massachusetts Department of Public Health

In Massachusetts a premature baby is defined by law as one that weighs five pounds or less, regardless of its time of birth. These babies are small and feeble but they can catch up to normal if given a good chance. Do you not know, as I do, several adults now living useful lives who were prematurely born?

Premature babies are born before they are ready to live. Their equipment for meeting the struggle of life is not complete. They need a type of care that is far more specialized than that given to normal full-term infants. For instance, their thermostatic or temperature control is incomplete so they have to live in an air-conditioned room or bed (an incubator) that will do their temperature regulating for them. Many are not able to nurse and must be fed through a tube. It is of greatest importance that they have mother's milk. Babies born at full-term get from their mothers in the few weeks preceding birth protective substances which help them to resist infection. Premature babies by their very prematurity are cheated out of such protection and are, therefore, unusually subject to infections. Only the most scrupulous cleanliness and complete isolation will prevent them from acquiring infections. Then, too, their breathing apparatus is far from efficient, and frequently spells of breathlessness or blueness require the prompt administration of oxygen or stimulants or blood transfusions to prevent sudden death.

From this it may be plainly seen that the best place for the care of premature babies is the hospital which is adequately equipped with air-conditioned nurseries or incubators, with nurses and physicians to give specialized care and to meet emergencies, with oxygen, operating facilities and other necessities always immediately available.

By law, local boards of health are required to furnish transportation of premature infants born in homes to hospitals equipped for their care, and local boards of public welfare can pay for hospitalization of the baby if the parents are unable to do so.

The Massachusetts Department of Public Health, through the Division of Child Hygiene, has established forty-eight hospital centers adequately equipped for the care of premature infants. These centers are strategically located so that any premature infant born at home would have a comparatively short journey to a center. Baskets fitted to keep prematures warm on the journey are available to all communities. Physicians, public health nurses and boards of health and welfare know the location of hospital centers and carrying baskets.

The nursery supervisors of the hospital centers have had special training at the Boston Lying-In Hospital, where very few prematures die. The public health nurses are having opportunities to attend institutes on the "Care of the Premature Infant." Through the Massachusetts Medical Society, courses are offered to physicians to refresh their memories as to methods of premature care and good prenatal care, which is an important factor in preventing premature births and deaths. Printed material relative to this subject has been sent to each physician by the Massachusetts Department of Public Health.

Public health nurses give mothers prenatal nursing supervision and teach them the care of the premature. A leaflet for mothers called "Your Premature Baby" is distributed by the Massachusetts Department of Public Health with prenatal letters, as well as by physicians, nurses and hospitals.

Thus, with mothers, physicians, public health nurses and hospital nurses, and boards of health and welfare, conscious of methods of meeting special needs of premature infants and with a sufficient number of hospitals equipped to care for them, it is hoped that all prematures born in Massachusetts will have a good chance to grow up to be useful citizens.

THE PREMATURELY BORN BABY NEEDS SPECIALIZED NURSING CARE

MADELEN P. POLLOCK, R. N.

Public Health Nursing Supervisor
Division of Child Hygiene
Massachusetts Department of Public Health

Any newborn infant is utterly dependent upon those to whom his care is entrusted. He does, however, arrive equipped by nature to withstand the vigors of this life. His body functions normally and if his care or treatment is not to his complete satisfaction he can readily, thanks to fully expanded lungs, makes his predicament known to his listening audience.

Arriving unexpectedly, the premature infant frequently finds that no provision has been made for him. His hosts are usually amazed and a little terrified at his sudden appearance and need a great deal of help in making an adequate home for this unexpected guest.

Unquestionably, a hospital adequately equipped to care for prematures is the safest place for his birth. He needs to arrive into a prewarmed atmosphere so that his body temperature can be maintained from the moment of birth. Perhaps no other single factor is as important as this one of providing adequate heat for the premature infant.

His initial cry is not long enough nor strong enough to fully expand his lungs. For this reason the premature baby is subject to frequent cyanotic attacks or so-called "blue spells."

During one of these spells which occur frequently with no warning the baby will recover easiest and quickest if pure oxygen or a mixture of carbon dioxide and oxygen is administered immediately.

The baby must be handled as little as possible and at no time be exposed to chilling.

He does, however, have to be fed. The very best food for this infant is breast milk. Vitamins C and D and iron are frequently added early.

Feeding these infants takes skill and patience. The food must be given to the baby with the least possible exertion on his part. The very small premature is frequently tube fed, that is, nutriment is literally poured into the baby through a small rubber tube. This has the advantage of causing him no effort, but requires a person skilled in the procedure. A medicine dropper is another popular method of feeding. When the baby is strong enough to suck he can be fed from a small bottle with a small, freely running nipple. Feeding the premature, no matter what the method, requires patience and skill, for these infants truly "eat to live," they never "live to eat," since by the time a premature develops an appetite he is usually well out of the realm of danger.

Babies arriving prematurely have less equipment to withstand even the slightest infection. For this reason they must be kept in as isolated and sterile an atmosphere as possible. Everything that comes in contact with them must be scrupulously clean. Doctors and nurses caring for the premature should wear sterilized gowns and have their nose and mouth covered with a gauze mask. The hair, too, should be completely covered with a sterilized cap. The baby cannot protect himself and is utterly dependent upon those who come in contact with him. If he does pick up an infection it is of necessity one brought to him by an outside source. Even the mildest infection is often too much for the small premature to combat successfully.

If these principles of care can be provided, that is:

If body temperature can be maintained from the moment of birth

If breast milk can be provided

If the premature can be guarded against even the slightest invasion of infection

If skilled medical and nursing care can be provided throughout his first few weeks of life

the hazards that accompany the arrival of an infant before he is expected will be greatly reduced.

CONTROL OF TYPHOID

GAYLORD W. ANDERSON, M.D.

Nestled among the Berkshire hills lies a community, where for a number of years there continued to be more typhoid fever than would have been expected in a town of this size. The water supply was above suspicion. There was no evidence that milk was causing any of the cases, and yet they continued to occur, not a great many, yet every so often there would be another case and then another. Careful investigation yielded no clue as to their source. These people didn't know each other, hadn't been the same places, in fact the only thing they had in common was that they all developed typhoid, and any of them would gladly have foregone that experience. One day someone discovered a lead. Up in the hills on a nearby farm lived a farmer who had had typhoid a number of years ago. He was selling butter in the city and of course in making it brought his hands in contact with it. Some of those that were sick had purchased butter that he delivered in the city. Careful study of this farmer showed that he was in fact a typhoid carrier, one who though perfectly well himself was carrying within his body and giving off the germs of typhoid fever. Not realizing his condition, he had unquestionably infected some of his butter, and some of those who ate it developed typhoid. The story would not be complete were we to leave this farmer at this point. As a matter of fact, he came to the city, where a surgeon removed his gall bladder to cure him of being a typhoid carrier. In the five years before this there had been 44 cases of typhoid in this city; in the next five years there were but 5. Let us hope that this farmer reads this statement, that few of us ever are able to make such a contribution to the health of our fellow beings as was this man who underwent surgery to be cured of a condition which made him a menace to others.

For a number of years the city of T—— had been virtually free of typhoid. One, or at most, two cases a year were all that had occurred for the preceding five years. And then for no reason whatsoever in a single year 10 cases appeared between March and December, about one a month. As before, these had apparently nothing in common. They did not know each other, nor had they been the same places so far as they knew. And yet, they all had typhoid in a city that had been remarkably free from it. Eventually, a boy of eighteen who came down with typhoid told the story of working in a small restaurant run by a woman who said she could sympathize with him because she, too, had typhoid a number of years before. Examination of this woman showed her to be a typhoid carrier. In February she had opened the lunch counter, in March cases of typhoid had begun to appear. She quit the restaurant as soon as her condition was found, and from that time till almost two years later the city was absolutely free of typhoid, as compared with a case a month during the time she ran it.

It is not often that a pair of overalls can cause typhoid, yet just such a thing happened a few years ago. On a few streets in a small manufacturing settlement typhoid began to appear. The only thing in common was the fact that the cases all lived on adjoining streets, and they were scattered over several weeks. Apparently the conditions that caused the first cases were still present and causing the later ones. The streets on which the cases occurred were so located on the end of a water main that had there been pollution of the supply as it passed a certain factory it would have accounted for the peculiar distribution of the cases. Careful search of this factory revealed a cross connection between the public water supply and a polluted supply intended for fire purposes. A hinged check valve between the two was so arranged that when the fire pumps were started it was to close automatically to keep the polluted water out of the town supply. The theory was all right, but who would have foreseen that in some way a pair of overalls would have been sucked up from the river and lodge in the check valve. Whenever the fire pumps were given their weekly test the valve had failed to close, polluted water entered the mains, and the people living on these few streets were given a weekly dose of typhoid. The connection was broken, with a prompt disappearance of typhoid.

These are but a few examples of what is constantly going on to extend our protection against typhoid. The way was paved by the improvement in water supplies, to the point that today 97 per cent of the people in this State live in communities with public supplies. We will never see a return of the typhoid as it was known by our forefathers. In order to guard against possible small recurrences, and to wipe out what little remains, constant alertness and medical detective work is required.

Time does not permit further description of this work, or entrance upon other ways in which the public is being protected from disease. Let us hope that we will appreciate a bit better the fact that the doctor of today is not solely a person to get us well when we are sick, but, just as important, is one who can help us to keep well and can protect us against certain diseases.

TRICHINOSIS

JOHN J. POUTAS, M.D.

District Health Officer
Massachusetts Department of Public Health

Trichinosis is a preventable disease. The public health agencies cannot prevent this infection. Absolute protection against it will result if the citizen resolves not to eat pork or pork products unless they have been thoroughly cooked. Such a resolution involves a responsibility on the part of the consumer, but primarily does it belong to any individual who prepares meat for human consumption, inasmuch as improperly cooked pork is the cause of human cases of trichinosis.

This is a disease which occurs with great frequency in hogs, with the result that hundreds of encysted living worms, trichinae, are deposited in meat which sooner or later is sold for human consumption. If we assume, for the moment, that this infected meat is eaten without having been thoroughly cooked to kill the trichinae, what happens? The gastric juice dissolves the cyst from about the still living worms, which are liberated in the intestinal canal. Many of these pass through the intestinal tract but numerous others are absorbed into the blood and finally take up their abode in the muscles of the human victim. This chain of events was definitely established in 1860. Since that time trichinosis has been recognized as a definite disease, whereas previously the more severe cases were mistaken for typhoid fever, while the milder ones were attributed to that bogey "indigestion," even as some of them are today.

Trichinosis is not at all a rare disease. There are cases in Massachusetts at all times. Particularly is it apt to occur in outbreaks, where a group has partaken of poorly prepared pork or, what is quite common, homemade sausage. In 1938 there were 29 cases reported, with two deaths. During the past five years there have been 179 cases and 11 deaths, all of which might have been prevented. Trichinosis in the human is a reportable disease, but obviously only those who are sufficiently ill to call a physician are ever recognized and subsequently reported. Numerous studies have been described, however, in which autopsies on individuals dying from other causes show that a startling percentage of them had, at some time or other, been infected with trichinosis, but so mildly that it went unnoticed. In a definite case the onset occurs one to two weeks after the eating of trichinous pork. It is marked by fever, constipation or diarrhea, pain in the muscles, swelling about the eyes, and may last for weeks. Occasionally there is a death.

It is frequently rumored that certain shipments of pork are heavily infected—the fact is that a high percentage of all pork on the market is trichinous, which by no means calls for its being condemned. There is no method known today to meat inspectors by which infected pork can be accurately detected and for that reason there is no compulsory inspection for trichinae. By the same token do not depend on any statement that a certain lot has been found infection-free. All pork and pork products, no matter the price, must be treated with suspicion and eaten only after thorough and complete cooking. The trichinae are not resistant to heat and are easily destroyed at a temperature of 137 F. Smoking and pickling are not to be relied upon as rendering pork safe for consumption.

It is not the intention of this article to intimate that pork is not one of our most valuable and tasty foods. It rightly deserves a place in any well-balanced dietary and will continue to do so, but it must be used properly. In brief, the prevention of trichinosis is a personal responsibility, doubly heavy on the cook.

JUST A LITTLE ROUTINE

HERMANN C. LYTHGOE, S.B.

Director and Analyst
Division of Food and Drugs
Massachusetts Department of Public Health

Most of the work of the Food and Drug Division of the Department of Public Health is a matter of prearranged routine, but if specific assignments are necessary as a result of any of this work, the routine is temporarily suspended.

Once each week in the division director's office there is a conference with the chief of laboratory and the inspectors. At this conference the results of the prior seven days' work are considered, special attention being given to those violations of the law discovered either by the direct effort of the inspectors or by the results of chemical or bacteriological analyses made by the laboratory workers. Each inspector is given an assignment of such character that the inspectors as well as the laboratory force will be busy until the next weekly conference.

Naturally there must not be delivered to the laboratory more work than the chemists and bacteriologists can perform, and for this reason some of the inspectors are assigned to make sanitary inspections of food establishments, which usually do not require the collection of samples.

At one of these conferences an inspector was assigned to a certain town for the collection of raw milk intended for pasteurization, the samples to be collected for bacteriological examination only. The selection of the specific pasteurization establishment was left to the discretion of the inspector, the purpose in this instance being to collect as far as possible samples of milk produced on Massachusetts dairy farms. The collection was made, and the bacteriologist began the preparation of the plate cultures by means of which the bacterial counts are made after a two-day period of incubation. In this instance the bacteriologist also made a microscopic examination of the milk itself and found one sample to contain pus and streptococci. This combination is often associated with a milk-borne disease.

The inspector was directed to go on the following day to the farm where the milk was supposed to have been produced, and he was asked to obtain a sample of milk from each cow. He was acquainted with the farm and knew that it was one where every precaution was taken as a matter of routine, and he expressed surprise at the results of the microscopic examination of the milk. He went to the farm, obtained samples of milk from each cow, the bacteriologist made microscopic examinations of the samples and was unable to find any pus or streptococci in any of the samples. It was then assumed that when the inspector collected the samples at the pasteurization establishment he was given the name of the wrong dairy farm from which this particular sample had been received.

The inspector returned to the plant, repeated the collection of samples, and admonished the proprietor of the plant to give him accurately the names of the owners of each dairy from which the samples were obtained. Microscopic examinations of these samples showed, as in the first instance, that one dairy was delivering milk containing pus and streptococci.

The following day the inspector went to the dairy farm. The owner was absent, but the inspector saw the foreman and told him of the results of the examination. The foreman then told the inspector that he thought he could pick out the cow responsible for the trouble. He did pick out the right cow, although the inspector obtained a sample from each cow. As soon as the microscopic examination had been made, the inspector telephoned the milk dealer to stop pasteurizing any milk from that dairy until further notice.

The following morning the inspector went to the pasteurizing plant and found the owner had separated the milk from this dairy with the intention of making butter for his own use. The inspector advised the man not to take the chance on such milk unless he pasteurized it, as there was a possibility that the infection might be dangerous to health.

The inspector went back to the dairy accompanied by one of the veterinarians of the division. The veterinarian examined the cow and found that the udder was in fact diseased. The owner questioned the accuracy of our findings. The inspector then obtained two glasses and milked the sick cow into one glass and into the other glass milked a second cow and pointed out the difference to the owner of the herd. The owner was of the opinion at first that the difference in the appearance of the two samples of milk was due to a high fat content of the milk produced by the sick cow. In a short time the owner noted a decided difference between the two samples and admitted that some time prior he had fed saltpeter to the cow and believed that the condition had cleared up.

The owner of the cow stated that he did not care to take the financial loss and suggested returning the cow to the person from whom he purchased it a year prior. The inspector informed him that there might be legal difficulties if he did so, and the owner decided then to consult his own veterinarian and a representative of the Livestock Disease Control Division. Apparently he did so, and two days later the cow was slaughtered.

Fortunately in this instance the milk was pasteurized. The law provides a penalty for the sale of milk produced by a sick or diseased cow. In every instance like the above where the inspector of the Department has found that a dairyman has been producing milk from a sick cow, and the dairyman has been informed of the above law, he has voluntarily sent the cow to the slaughterhouse. In cases like the above where the lesion is localized, the meat would pass for food purposes unless for some other reason the carcass must be confiscated.

This incident illustrates that occasionally by purely routine work it is possible to locate a needle in a haystack.

OVERNIGHT CAMP SANITATION
WILLIAM H. DOGGETT, M.S.
Assistant Sanitary Engineer
Division of Sanitary Engineering
Massachusetts Department of Public Health

The overnight camp is a development of present-day life which is associated with the increasing number of automobiles. Overnight camps are located principally along the main traveled routes and are generally found outside of cities and towns, most often at some vantage point, such as on a hill commanding a view or near a pond or grove, field or other open space. The average automobile traveler probably stops at an overnight camp because it is cheaper than going to a hotel with the necessary garaging of the automobile. Again the spirit of camping out while on vacation is a factor. Most overnight camps are unheated and in this state are not operated during the cold weather.

Anyone who has done much traveling over the highways realizes the great difference in the caliber of the overnight camps. At some of them the sanitary conditions are excellent, but in many cases sanitation in some phase or other is badly neglected. Everyone is or should be interested in obtaining drinking water of good quality. At any overnight camp where the water comes from a municipal supply there is nothing to worry about. Any other source, such as a well or spring, should greatly concern the user if there is any danger or threat of pollution by reason of location near a privy, cesspool, or septic tank or if it is not protected against the entrance of surface water or foreign matter. The drinking water supply should be of good sanitary quality and of sufficient quantity and should be approved by the State Department of Public Health. Any well or spring of poor or questionable quality should be closed to use or posted as unsafe. It has been stated that "Water is the most essential commodity, other than air, to the continuation of life."

The next important aspect of overnight camp sanitation is that of proper sewage disposal. The rest room, comfort station or, as it is generally called, the toilet, should be of a standard of cleanliness that no one need hesitate to use it. In many cases the toilet or old-fashioned privy is very offensive. All sewage from the camp should be disposed of in ground that is lower in elevation than that where the water supply is obtained, and also at a considerable distance from it. Pit privies may provide a satisfactory method of disposal, but they should be so constructed that flies and other insects cannot have access. The privies should be so maintained that they will not cause odors. For small camps it is common practice to have an earth vault 4 to 6 feet in depth, disinfecting the contents effectively with chloride of lime daily and covering them also with fresh soil. Some overnight camps are provided with chemical toilets while some have modern flush toilets connected with cesspools or septic tank and subsurface disposal drain.

Another phase of overnight camp sanitation is the proper disposal of garbage and waste. It is essential that garbage and waste be kept in tightly-covered receptacles and emptied at frequent intervals.

Overnight camps should be provided with proper screens to keep out flies and mosquitoes.

Overnight camps should have signs posted indicating the location of water supplies, toilets and receptacles for garbage and refuse.

The State Department of Public Health is equipped to furnish overnight camp owners advice in regard to water supply and sewage disposal or other correlated problems which they encounter. By a more complete cooperation between the camp owner and the Department it will be possible to improve sanitation to the mutual benefit of the user of the camp and the owner.

PULMONARY TUBERCULOSIS — HOW IT SPREADS IN THE HOME AND FAMILY

DAVID ZACKS, M.D.

*Chief of Clinics, Division of Tuberculosis
Massachusetts Department of Public Health*

I want to discuss briefly this afternoon how tuberculosis spreads in the home and family.

It has long been known that tuberculosis is a disease which occurs in families. This led to the belief, which unfortunately is still prevalent, that tuberculosis is hereditary. Later, when the theory of the transmission of the disease at birth was proved to be false, the impression gained ground that children are born with some peculiar predisposition to this disease. This idea also is not true, but there are some people who still believe it.

If tuberculosis is not hereditary, and if there is no inherited predisposition, why then does tuberculosis so frequently occur in families? The answer is that tuberculosis is an infectious disease. One case of pulmonary tuberculosis comes from another case by contagion. The source of contagion is the germ of the disease, namely, the tubercle bacillus.

There is no question at all that a father or mother who has pulmonary tuberculosis is a constant source of danger to the innocent children who are born from such a union. The children are closely and constantly exposed to this danger in the intimacies of family life. The only one who is happy is the tubercle bacillus itself, for its toll of human misery and human life is appalling. Let me cite two examples picked at random: (1) Annie was the mother of four children. She knew that she had tuberculosis in 1919. In 1924 a daughter, Rose, at the age of ten years developed miliary tuberculosis and died. In 1928 a son, Tom, at the age of twelve years, was found to have tuberculosis and he died four years later in 1932. In 1929, a second son, John, came down with tuberculosis and he is now in a sanatorium. In 1935, a third son, Vincent, was found with pulmonary tuberculosis in school and he, too, is now a patient at a sanatorium. The mother is still alive, but her children are either dead from pulmonary tuberculosis or are patients in sanatoria under treatment for this disease. That she, herself, was the cause of this family tragedy, there is no doubt at all.

The second example:

(2) Amelia was the mother of eight children. She knew that she had tuberculosis in 1923 and she died in 1925. The oldest daughter, Mary, died of pulmonary tuberculosis in 1927. A son, Ben, was found with pulmonary tuberculosis in school in 1928. He died in 1932. Another son, George, had childhood-type tuberculosis in 1932. A third son, Allan, had bone and joint tuberculosis in 1928. A fourth son, David, is now under observation as a suspicious case of pulmonary tuberculosis. The three other children have escaped the disease so far. The husband, who was a stonecutter, developed pulmonary tuberculosis in 1933 and died in 1936. In this family, then, the tubercle bacillus has taken a toll of four lives— mother, father, a son and a daughter. One son has bone tuberculosis, another son probably has pulmonary tuberculosis, one son has childhood-type tuberculosis, and only three members of the family have escaped infection. The home was broken up in 1929.

There is a lesson here which the tuberculous father or mother to whom in particular I am addressing these remarks should learn thoroughly and completely. This is the lesson:

It is not fate which has so cruelly invaded your home and family. It is but a tiny bacillus which is known to you and which you can and should control by a little conscious effort diligently and persistently applied by yourself. You know, or you should know, that the tubercle bacillus is carried by you in the sputum which you raise up with your cough. Do not hide this away in a false sense of shame! You are not to blame for your disease. Have your sputum examined frequently by your family doctor or your dispensary. If the sputum no longer carries the tubercle bacillus after several examinations, your family is safe. If the sputum contains this source of contagion which is so dangerous to your children, then you should place yourself under treatment for your own sake, in a sanatorium, and arrange for your children to be brought up in an atmosphere which is free from the danger of contagion with the tubercle bacillus.

I say—"Do this"—but you need not do it unaided. There is help, much help, for your asking. Your local board of health, your local tuberculosis nurse, your county and state sanatoria, as well as voluntary agencies, are ready and willing to help you at all times. All I ask is your cooperation, your willingness to have all of these agencies help you.

PULMONARY TUBERCULOSIS—HOW ITS SPREAD IN THE FAMILY CAN BE PREVENTED

DAVID ZACKS, M.D.

Chief of Clinics, Division of Tuberculosis
Massachusetts Department of Public Health

In the first part of this talk, I stated that pulmonary tuberculosis is not a hereditary disease, nor is there a family predisposition transmitted to the offspring. I traced how pulmonary tuberculosis definitely spreads in the home and family, and pointed out that the germ which causes the disease, the tubercle bacillus, is the real source of the danger of spread. Two examples were cited of families where precaution was not taken to protect the children. The sad result of this neglect was the definite and persistent spread of tuberculosis to the other members of these families who "broke down" with the disease, one after another, at puberty or later.

In this place, I want to discuss how the spread of pulmonary tuberculosis in the family can and should be prevented. The most important fact for the patient with pulmonary tuberculosis to determine is whether his sputum is positive or negative. A positive sputum means that the tubercle bacillus is present in the sputum. This can be determined by a laboratory examination of the sputum. This examination is free. Ask the tuberculosis nurse in your community, or your own doctor, if necessary, to have your sputum examined at frequent intervals.

If the sputum which you bring up as the result of your cough is persistently negative, you are not a danger to the other members of your family or to your friends. If, however, the bacillus is present in your sputum, you should apply to your doctor for treatment immediately at one of the sanatoria with which this State is amply provided. There you will take the "cure," and, what is of equal importance, you will learn something of the nature of tuberculosis which will help you personally in your battle with the disease after you leave the sanatorium and return to your home and your community.

Above all, stay in the sanatorium until your sputum has become negative. While your sputum is still positive, do not leave the sanatorium for brief visits to your family, even if you are physically able to do so.

Have all of the members of your family examined with a tuberculin test and x-ray. This examination should follow immediately after a diagnosis of tuberculosis has been made in any member of a family. Furthermore, this examination should be repeated with x-rays at yearly intervals in the case of children under ten years of age; for the children ten years of age and over a more frequent examination is necessary. The nearer the child approaches to puberty, the more often should the examination with x-rays be given, particularly to girls.

Now, this advice to remain in the sanatorium as long as the sputum is positive and as long as the disease is still active, may seem like a long time and quite a sacrifice on the part of the patient. Unfortunately, I know of no other way that will so completely protect the other members of the family of a tuberculous patient.

It may be, furthermore, that the stay at the sanatorium until the sputum becomes negative and remains negative, need not be so long after all, for at the present time, pneumothorax treatment which is so extensively used may convert a positive sputum into a negative sputum in a very short time. Other surgical procedures are also available at the present time and are made use of in well-equipped sanatoria for the express purpose of converting positive sputum to negative, if it is at all possible to do so.

The aim of the tuberculous parent who has children at home should be to prevent his children from developing this disease at whatever sacrifice may be necessary. The best way and the safest way, to repeat, is to stay in the sanatorium as long as may be necessary in order to obtain a negative sputum and a true arrest of this disease. Once a negative sputum has been obtained as a result of the "cure" and the patient has returned to his home, it is still necessary to continue the sputum examinations at frequent intervals. This should be done as a precaution in order to have further and continued assurance that the sputum remains negative and that there is actually no danger of infecting the family.

THE HUMANITARIAN MOVEMENT

ELEANOR J. MACDONALD, A.B.

Epidemiologist, Division of Adult Hygiene
Massachusetts Department of Public Health

Every new development is completely dependent upon the events that lead up to it; a complicated algebraic formula upon elementary processes; research upon conditions that need explaining; and philanthropy upon the aggravated sociologic conditions demanding redress. In order to understand the public health measures that arose in correcting economic abuses, it is imperative that the conditions to be corrected be understood.

The fusion of the Renaissance and the Reformation in the sixteenth century gave rise to a new sequence of happenings. Following the long period of struggle for existence came the period of centralization for mutual protection in parishes. This brought about the feudal relationships where people were expected to defend their masters in times of stress, but in return for which they were clothed, fed, and given homes in which to maintain their individual and family integrity with a complete sense of protection.

The development of this fusion carried in its wake the beginnings of our present economic, as well as social problems. In the latter eighteenth and early nineteenth centuries, there were disagreements among the various sects, and it became fashionable to scoff at religion. The parishes, monasteries, and abbeys, which had been the centers of the lives of the largest class of the people, had been confiscated and turned into private homes for the rich or simply destroyed. The clergy, who had been looked upon to help those in distress and to teach the youth, were lethargic and there was no recognized authority to whom the poor could turn.

In England, as in the other countries of Europe, there was a general exodus from the country to the city. An utter disregard of the sanitary emergency that would of necessity arise in communities that were suddenly subjected to an enormous increase in population was evident in England of this period. The people went into the newly-aroused industrial pursuits which were carried on on a large and commercial scale, where the object was to turn out materials and to obtain the maximum of work from each individual. The employer, himself, took no responsibility for the welfare of his workers. Scant wages, crowded unsanitary living and working conditions, broken health, and vice followed. The period became one of such viciousness that the extremes of English society boasted of unbelief in Christianity in any form and became distinguished for the grossness and immorality of their lives. "Drunkenness and foul talk were thought no discredit to Walpole. . . . At the other end of the social scale lay the masses. They were ignorant and brutal to a degree which it is hard to conceive, for the vast increase of population which followed on the growth of towns and the development of manufactures had been met by no effort for their religious or educational improvement. Not a new parish had been created. Hardly a single new church had been built. The rural peasantry, who were fast being reduced to pauperism by the abuse of the poor laws, were left without moral training of any sort. Within the towns it was worse. There were no effective police; and in great outbreaks the mob of London or Birmingham burnt houses, flung open prisons, and sacked and pillaged at their will. The criminal classes gathered boldness and numbers in the face of the ruthless laws which only testified to the terror of society, laws which made it a capital crime to cut down a cherry tree, and which strung up twenty young thieves of a morning in front of Newgate; while the introduction of gin gave a new impetus to drunkenness. In the streets of London gin-shops invited every passerby to get drunk for a penny, or dead drunk for twopence."

There is never any history in which all is desolation. This period had its stability in the inbred piety of the middle classes. Outstanding in this group, and almost evangelical in character, were the Wesley brothers—the one an organizer, and the other a poet and preacher. The people that the Wesleys banded together called themselves "Methodists" and were the nucleus from which has grown the present Methodist organization. The greatest thing that the Wesleyan movement accomplished was the rekindling of the clergy of all the sects, from their apathy. A fresh spirit of moral zeal awakened in the hearts of the poor, and the other classes were aroused to the sorrow and tragedy that befell the less fortunate. It needed this aroused devotion in England to bring about the new philanthropic movement.

John R. Green, the famous English historian, called this movement the "New Humanity." Every branch of social and industrial life felt its influence. Those who should have been the leaders of the movement were swept into action by the humanitarians. The prisons were reformed. Their unsanitary conditions were attacked. The criminal sick were cared for. The employers who exploited labor were exposed to the censure of public scorn. Child labor was relieved. Working conditions were studied and corrected. Landlords were forced to render sanitary the homes they rented. In fact, the zealous reformers, in their turn, exploited to public resentment the many selfish interests that were delaying reform. The legislative records of the late eighteenth and nineteenth centuries are a vivid record of the rise of this "New Humanity."

Poverty came to be recognized, at last, as a misfortune that left its incumbents helpless. The realization that the illness of the very poor was the responsibility of society and not punishment for the individual threw a new light on the medical history of the time. Not only were new hospitals established, but dispensaries for treatment were opened. The movement extended to the criminal classes as well and societies were formed to work for their betterment and perhaps even their reclamation. It was this period that saw the first public efforts for the education of the children of the poor. The religious revival was peculiar to itself in one respect—that although the numerous sects were often in dispute on questions of dogma, they were generally in agreement on the spirit of brotherly love. In fact, the individuals who would be considered pagans by any of the religions were anxious to fall in line and grant help to the less fortunate. The "New Humanity" gained in momentum as it went along, and to its growth we owe our present concept of public health.

Two historical events of the greatest significance occurred in this period—the American Revolution in 1776, and the French Revolution in 1789-1790. Two other events of special significance both to the United States and to England took place in 1776—the beginning of modern political economy with the publication of the "Wealth of Nations" by Adam Smith, and the beginnings of conscious constitutional reform with the publication of "Fragment on Government," the first of a series of papers by Jeremy Bentham. The importance of these revolutions and movements did not lie in the immediate accomplishment of great objectives, but in the evidence of clear, free thinking that the debates on the various changes entailed. To hear men discuss the abstract principle of good government, to hear the clear interpretation of the rights of every man and the duty of government toward the individual—these were the important events of the era. For these were new things and would not have been possible without the "New Humanity" and its recognition of each man's right to life and "the pursuit of happiness."

The sudden realization that justice and mutual helpfulness were the problems of government, as well as of religion, was reflected in the altruistic legislation of the period. The first gesture in England was the enlargement of the electoral basis for representation in the House of Commons. Close to this change came the demand for reform laws. Sidney Smith, one of the leading reformers of the time, sketches the outstanding grievances as follows: "The Catholics were not emancipated—the Corporation and Test Acts were unrepealed—the Game Laws were horribly oppressive—Steel Traps and Spring Guns were set all over the country—Prisoners tried for their lives could have no Counsel—Lord Eldon and the Court of Chancery pressed heavily upon mankind—Libel was punished by the most cruel and vindictive imprisonments—the principles of Political Economy were little understood—the Law of Debt and of Conspiracy were upon the worst possible footing—the enormous wickedness of the Slave Trade was tolerated—a thousand evils were in existence, which the talents of good and able men have since lessened and removed."

The spirit pervaded the literature of the time and many people were reached through the genuine sincerity of Goldsmith and Burns that would never have read theological treatises on the same subjects.

This was the period in which Captain Cook of the ship "Resolution" made his trip around the world, and kept his men free from scurvy by feeding them lemons. This, too, was the period when John Howard, a squire from Bedfordshire, at his own expense, and in danger of death from disease, visited personally nearly all the gaols in England to study for himself the existing conditions and to present petitions for their reform.

The most impressive result of this remarkable study, next to the immediate and permanent reform of the prisons, was the effect of Howard's example on his fellow countrymen. Sir John Simon points out that the career of this great man "taught in a supreme degree the value of methodical or scientific, as distinguished from merely impulsive, philanthropy."

Sir John Simon said in part in his excellent summary of the period, "Society had become readier than ever before to hear individual voices which told of pain or asked for redress of wrong; abler than before to admit that justice does not weigh her balances in relation to the ranks, or creeds, or colours, or nationalities of men; apter than before to perceive that the just balances which serve between man and man may, in principle, serve between nation and nation. . . . The so-called 'masses' of mankind had come to be of interest in other points of view than those of recruiting-serjeant and the tax-gatherer. . . . And statesmen could not but acknowledge that the greatest happiness of the greatest number is at least a good security for social quiet."

THE LABORATORY FIGHTS PNEUMONIA
ELLIOTT S. A. ROBINSON, M.D.
Director and Pathologist
Division of Biologic Laboratories
Massachusetts Department of Public Health

The American Public does not have to be told that the laboratory has contributed a large share to the advancement of our knowledge of disease and how it is treated. Biographies of pioneers in this field have received wide distribution. Probably everyone listening in today has read with interest the achievements of such men as Pasteur, Lister, Reed, Gorgas and many others who have made contributions to this field. That this interest still exists is evidenced by the fact that many popular periodicals carry stories of the achievements of present day workers.

The publicity which is going out from the Massachusetts Department of Public Health in regard to pneumonia and its treatment would not be complete without discussing the part which the laboratory has played in this particular field. Those of you who see the film sponsored by the Department entitled "A New Day" which will be on the screen of many theatres in Massachusetts during the next few weeks will be forcibly impressed with the necessity of having a laboratory near at hand.

The problem of the treatment of pneumonia, in fact, was solved only when it was attacked in the laboratory. Medical men had divided pneumonias into two groups; first, those which attack only a single lobe of the lung, called lobar pneumonia; and second, those which are usually disseminated throughout both lungs and are called bronchopneumonia. Such a classification aided in selecting treatment, but was far from being the final answer and more than one-fourth of those attacked by the disease continued to die.

As far back as Pasteur it was known that pneumonias were caused by several kinds of bacteria. It was soon discovered by the laboratory men that the most important cause was a class of germs known as pneumococci. This knowledge by itself was not of much use until laboratory workers eventually discovered that by injecting animals with pneumococci, a serum could be made which would help fight the disease. The first important American contribution in solving this problem was made by workers in the Rockefeller Institute in 1915. At that time they verified the fact that all pneumococci were not exactly the same. They separated out three kinds, types I, II, and III and demonstrated that a serum made for Type I was of great benefit in saving the lives of those who were attacked by this type. On the other hand, no benefit resulted when a person ill of Type II or III was given serum for Type I. Before long they also developed a serum for Type II, but even down to the present day serums made for Type III are of very little use.

Laboratory workers were not content with the discovery of only three types of pneumococci. At the Health Department of New York City, twenty-nine other types were eventually discovered, and still other types probably yet remain to be recognized. Work was immediately begun upon the problem of providing serums for some of these other twenty-nine types. At the present time serums are being made for six of them, and, without doubt, several others will be available in the near future.

The necessity of having laboratories to assist in fighting disease was early recognized in Massachusetts. Immediately after the discovery of diphtheria antitoxin, its manufacture was begun in this State. For over forty years, this material has been distributed free of charge to physicians in Massachusetts. It was likewise one of the earliest states to begin the manufacture of pneumonia serum, the first supply becoming available in 1917. It was disappointing to see how slowly the use of serum was taken up. Year after year went by with no increase in its use even though the quality was continually improving. In 1930 the Department became dissatisfied with the slow spread and decided that something should be done about it.

A survey of the situation was begun. There seemed to be several reasons why serum was not being used. First, there was delay in determining the type of pneumococcus. It was seldom possible to conclude the examination in less than 12 hours and sometimes as long as 24 to 48 hours elapsed. Second, there were only a few typing laboratories, restricting such facilities to only a few physicians. Third, because serum tended to be low in potency large volumes had to be given to effect a cure. Fourth, reactions to serums were numerous and sometimes alarming.

A plan of action to overcome some of these difficulties was outlined. Funds for carrying out the plan were requested from one of the private foundations, The Commonwealth Fund of New York City. The request was granted and Massachusetts launched upon its five-year study of pneumonia.

Because of the pressing need for rapid determination of the type of pneumococcus, this problem received immediate attention. The methods then in use were improved and speeded up as much as possible. Fortunately, before the study had been in progress very long, a new method of typing came into use. This method made it possible to determine the type in as short a time as thirty minutes in many instances. It had the added advantage of requiring less equipment and materials, and was therefore adaptable to many of the smaller laboratories. This made it possible to overcome the second difficulty, the lack of laboratory facilities. At the present time over eighty approved typing laboratories are located at strategic points throughout the State.

Meanwhile the problem of producing a more potent serum was undertaken. Methods were found to speed up the production of antibodies in the horses which were being injected, and Doctor Felton at the Harvard Medical School was perfecting new methods of concentrating these serums so that the final product was becoming more and more potent. A study of the reactions which occurred after the injection of serum, particularly the occurrence of chills, was undertaken. It was found that the chill-producing serums could be discovered by the injection of samples into monkeys. Only those which failed to produce chills in monkeys were used in treating humans.

The five-year study came to an end two years ago, but the production of serum has continued, and its use has spread to all parts of the State. Over 1,000 physicians have now treated cases in this State.

Questions

Q. You say that Massachusetts makes its own serum; where is it made?

A. The State Laboratory is located in Forest Hills, at the edge of the Arnold Arboretum.

Q. Is it a large laboratory?

A. Well, large enough to keep 50 horses in its stables, and to employ about 50 workers.

Q. Is special training required to make serum?

A. Yes, quite special training; our laboratory when it has a full staff, has 3 physicians, 1 veterinarian, 4 men who have Ph.D. degrees in Chemistry or Bacteriology and several others who have had training in laboratory work before coming to us.

Q. Does the laboratory make serums for any other kinds of diseases?

A. Yes, indeed; antitoxins are made for diphtheria and scarlet fever, and serums for two kinds of meningitis.

Q. I suppose the laboratory makes other kinds of products?

A. Yes, we make smallpox vaccine, typhoid vaccine, toxoid and toxin-antitoxin for diphtheria prevention, to name a few.

Q. How quickly can you make serum for pneumonia, in 2 or 3 weeks?

A. Well, hardly; it sometimes takes a year or even more before a serum is ready to give to the doctor.

Q. That seems a terribly long time; what makes it take so long?

A. One of the principal reasons is that we are largely dependent on nature for the production of these serums. We begin treating horses with pneumococci in very small doses and gradually work up to large doses. Chemical substances called antibodies to fight the pneumococcus are formed in the blood of the horse.

Q. Why doesn't the horse get pneumonia when you inject the germs into him?

A. The principal reason is that we kill the pneumococci before we inject them into the horse.

Q. Do you have to have a different horse for each type of serum?

A. No, the same horse may be used to make more than one type of serum.

Q. Do you make serum for all 32 types in 1 horse?

A. That is not possible. The reaction from the injection of the pneumococci would be entirely too great if the proper dose of each of the 32 types were given at the same time. If small doses of each type were given the serum would never become potent enough against any type to be useful in treatment. We usually make only one or two types in each horse.

Q. We have been talking a good deal about serum; just what is it?

A. It is that part of the blood which remains fluid when blood is allowed to clot.

Q. How do you get serum from the horse?

A. Blood is removed from the neck vein by means of a needle connected with a rubber tube to a sterile jar. The jars are taken to a cold room and kept until the serum is expressed from the clot.

Q. How frequently can you take blood from a horse?

A. We usually get it every 3 weeks.

Q. Doesn't this frequent bleeding weaken the horse?

A. No, the horse remains in good condition and gains in weight while being bled.

Q. Did you say that serum was concentrated?

A. Yes, it has been discovered that by chemical methods the antibody can be caused to precipitate. This precipitate is collected and redissolved. The remainder of the serum does not contain antibody and is discarded.

Q. How do you test the potency of a serum?

A. Varied quantities of serum are given to mice which have received enough pneumococci to cause certain death unless serum is administered. Of course, the smaller the quantity of serum which will save the life of the mouse, the more potent is the serum.

Q. Is the typing also done in your laboratory?

A. No, these tests are done largely in the 80 laboratories scattered about the State.

Q. I suppose these are State laboratories?

A. Oh, no! these are largely hospital laboratories which are co-operating with the State Department of Public Health in the pneumonia program.

Q. Doesn't the State have any typing laboratories?

A. Yes, the Bacteriological Laboratory in the State House does typing for many of the physicians who are near enough to send specimens there. More typings are done in this laboratory than in any other single laboratory in the State.

Q. Just how is typing done?

A. A small drop of serum of each type is mixed with a small drop of sputum from the patient. The type is determined by examining the specimen under the microscope and noting which serum causes the small capsule around the pneumococcus to swell several times as large as the normal capsule.

Q. Are these laboratories open day and night?

A. Most of them attempt to observe regular hours, but usually the technician is on call so that typing can be done at night as well as during the day.

Q. When the type is determined where can the physician get serum to treat the patient?

A. The Department keeps Type I serum at most of the typing laboratories, so the physician can get it at the same place the typing is done. The supply of the higher types is limited and can be obtained at certain of the laboratories.

Q. For which of the higher types does Massachusetts have serum?

A. We are already distributing serum for Types II, V, and VII and hope to have serum for Type VIII in the near future.

Q. Do many people have pneumonia due to these types in Massachusetts?

A. It is estimated that there are about 1,500 cases due to Type I each year; about 1,000 due to Type II; and about 1,000 more due to Types V, VII, and VIII. These proportions change from year to year.

Q. How many of these cases end fatally?

A. Usually more than a quarter of them if serum is not available.

CLINICS FOR CRIPPLED CHILDREN

ARTHUR WAKEFIELD, M.D.

Supervisor of Clinics for Crippled Children
Massachusetts Department of Public Health

I think the taxpayers would be more happy if they knew how their taxes were being used. Some abuses *might* be corrected and considerable pleasure would be *gained* by knowing the fine things that are being done.

To one who travels over the State it has been distressing to note the number of crippled children seen in the schools and on the streets in small towns. In large cities such as Boston, Worcester, Springfield and New Bedford where there are orthopedic surgeons and hospitals for crippled children there are few of such cases to be seen, for these large centers have done a very great deal for their crippled children. However, in the country and smaller towns there are no orthopedic surgeons or hospitals available. No local funds can be used; in fact, the expense of hospital and operative care is so great in this type of work that only quite well-to-do people can find the money to pay for *needed treatment*.

For a crippled child to go through life handicapped, often unable to earn a livelihood because of crippling is not only bad business *economically* but from the human standpoint unendurable.

To meet the need of the country towns the crippled child clinics were established. These clinics are held in ten cities every month. The clinics are held in Haverhill, Salem, Lowell, Gardner, Pittsfield, Springfield, Worcester, Brockton, Fall River and Hyannis and so from these centers every town and village in the State is reached. These larger cities are used for clinics because each one has X-ray facilities and equipment enabling us to make a diagnosis of our crippling conditions. The clinic is primarily for people in rural areas and not for large cities where long established organizations have for years cared for their crippled children. For instance, orthopedic doctors in Worcester have for years cared for all cripples in Worcester. Large cities have Community Chests and civic organizations that enable them to provide for the crippled child. Our clinics would not possibly care for all cripples in the State but we can care for the children living in small towns and in the country places who heretofore have been without facilities for needed treatment.

These clinics are not "open" clinics where anyone, rich or poor, can come. They are "consultation clinics" and only patients who bring an application from the family doctor are seen.

This brings up the matter of clinics—good and bad. In the past there has been a great abuse of clinic facilities bringing about grave injustice to the practicing physician and the taxpayer. Lincoln said, "To do the right thing in the wrong way is as bad as to do the wrong thing." The Chinese have a proverb that it is most difficult to do good deeds, "Nine dollars is wasted to every one dollar spent rightly."

Long experience in clinic work has enabled the State Department of Public Health to avoid mistakes and to do effectively and economically the work that needs to be done.

To be fair to the medical profession only patients whom doctors refer are seen at our clinics. With a crippled child the family and friends usually do all they can for the unfortunate victim but the hospital, operating room, and surgeon's fees make expense for these cases very heavy. Further, after operations are done follow-up care by physiotherapy nurses to retain newly placed muscles, to prevent contractions that would make operations a failure, must be provided. Orthopedic surgeons do not like to correct a deformity for a child in a far distant part of the State and send him home where the necessary aftercare may not be possible. So you see our local clinics with a staff of physiotherapy nurses are meeting a very grave need through the State.

The families of some of the patients can, at times, pay in part for work we do. This is right and wholesome. Moreover, it lets us meet a very real need of the kind of family that wants to pay a part but cannot pay the whole expense.

To safeguard the work every case is checked by a social service worker after the first visit to the clinic. This check-up gives us much needed information. It tells us whether the family is really entitled to the services of the clinic and whether they can pay in part the expense of the work to be done. It tells us also whether the home conditions are such that adequate care can be given after the child leaves the hospital and whether someone in the family is capable of carrying on the muscle training under the instructions of our nurses who come once or twice a week to supervise the work.

We must not forget that a crippled child needs more than medical help and so we check up on schooling and try to train them for some occupation in order to fit the child to better meet the coming problem of self-support.

The efforts we have made and the information we have collected are given to a Medical Society of the district in which the child lives for its final approval and help.

No case we have treated in the clinic has ever been disapproved by the representatives of the medical society. This suggests that these clinics are doing the right thing in the right way. We are striving to be entirely fair both to the medical profession and to the taxpayer. There is a real joy in doing our work; a real pleasure in working with the medical men of the State—men who are keeping the tradition of serving, healing, making life more worth living.

Questions

Q. How are these crippled children found and how many crippled children have you record of in Massachusetts?

A. The schools of the State report crippled children of school age; that is the way they are found. We had a record of over 6,000 of these when we started our clinics. Our field workers see the family doctors and find from them those that are suitable for our clinics. Local nurses as well as doctors and hospitals report cases. Such groups as those at Children's Hospital and Shriners' Hospital work with us and we take over cases they have begun to treat but have not completed when the age limit set for these institutions is reached.

Moreover, we are working for a complete register of all crippled children in the State including those who have had every care possible. This register is essential if we are to get a complete picture of crippling conditions in the State.

At times people resent our inquiries—simply because they do not understand our purposes and the value of such study.

Q. Dr. Wakefield, do you have other workers besides doctors connected with these clinics?

A. Yes. We have five physiotherapy nurses. These technical workers carry on the treatments recommended by our surgeons in the clinics. In some cases their work makes operations unnecessary; often after operative treatment the training of the muscles and prevention of deformity is an important feature of their work. Every case seen in our clinics is followed up so that the greatest amount of correction may be obtained.

Then besides we have four social service workers in the field. These workers study home conditions of every child to find out whether it is going to be possible to carry on the care needed in the home after the operation has been successfully done.

They also go into problems of feeding, schooling, and vocational training, as we said. Here the help of the Welfare and school groups is enlisted in order to make the child as self-supporting as possible and to find out the type of work most suitable to his handicap. We not only do all that can be done for his crippling condition but we try to do all that can be done in getting him fitted into the world he lives in.

Q. Doctor, don't you have some hard-to-crack nuts in the clinic?

A. Of course, there are some patients for whom we can do little or nothing. Most of these are where the crippling is due to injury to brain or spinal cord. In mentally deficient children a good operation may be done only to find the child has not the will power or the ability to readjust and learn to use the new muscles that have been transplanted to take the place of muscles that are gone.

Then there is the hopelessly crippled child that is beyond all surgical help—often utterly dependent in the family. Such cases try our souls. Eventually, the State may find it possible to place such cases in a special institution where they may be cared for in a group as they cannot be cared for in a home and, at the same time, relieve the members of the family from the necessity of constant nursing and enable them to carry on a more normal productive life.

Q. What is included in your definition of a crippled child?

A. In general we mean a crippling condition that is treated by an orthopedic surgeon—infantile paralysis, clubfeet, birth injuries, humpback, for example.

Of course, any illness will, at least for a time, "cripple" a child but our work is practically limited to injuries or deformities of bones and muscles. Moreover, acute injury cases are specifically excluded. We do not attempt to take automobile accident cases away from the family doctors. Tonsil, adenoid and hernia cases are specifically excluded. Chronic heart cases and cross-eyes are not accepted. We do, on the other hand, take cleft palates and old burn injuries. We do not take chronic cases for long nursing care in a home or institution.

You see we must use our funds on cases that can be definitely helped by operation or braces or special treatment. To attempt to care for the hopelessly crippled child who would live in a hospital or home for years would use all our funds and we would be unable to help those that can definitely be helped by active operation and care.

ENDOCRINE GLANDS

JAMES H. MEANS, M.D.

The engine of your automobile requires a carefully adjusted electric timing system in order that its various parts may be kept moving harmoniously, or, as we might say, so that the action of the entire mechanism may be perfectly in tune.

Your body also, being a mechanism far more complicated and mysterious than the gasoline motor, requires regulating devices so that its various parts may work together to the good of the whole.

The nervous system, as you know, is one of the body's chief regulating mechanisms. By means of it, messages are sent over nerves from one place to another securing coordination of action, but in addition, there is another regulating mechanism which depends, not on messages sent over nerves, but through the blood stream by means of chemical messengers—the so-called hormones.

These hormones are manufactured by certain organs, known as endocrine glands, or glands which discharge the substance they manufacture inside, instead of outside of the body. Each gland makes and delivers to the blood stream one or more highly complicated chemical substances which promote certain special results in far-off parts of the body, when they arrive at these parts, by way of the circulation of the blood.

Knowledge of these glands, their hormones and their action has been, of late years, advancing very rapidly. Facts about them are piling up and a host of investigators is trying to find out what these facts mean.

Imagination, however, has outstripped knowledge in matters endocrine and the layman may well learn to be skeptical about endocrine information which reaches him through other than reliable medical channels. In short, a vast deal of nonsense has been written about endocrinology, or the glands of internal secretion, and it is the duty of the medical profession to make clear to the public what is fact and what is fancy.

Included in the group of endocrine glands are the thyroid which is situated just below the Adam's apple in the neck, the pituitary which is in the very middle of the head, the parathyroids which are directly behind the thyroid, the adrenals which are on top of the kidneys, a portion of the pancreas which is just below the stomach, and the sex glands—the testes in the male and the ovaries in the female.

We cannot, in a brief broadcast, even outline the complicated working of these peculiar glands. Let us get at once to the practical. In what ways, for example, do our endocrine glands get out of order, and what can be done about it?

In general a gland may overdo or underdo its particular job.

When it does not seem to be equal to its job, we may sometimes help it by giving the person an extract or hormone of the same kind of gland, taken from an animal. We call this "substitution treatment."

Good examples of this sort are the treatment of diabetes, by means of insulin, and the treatment of a disease called "myxedema," by means of dried thyroid gland.

Diabetes occurs when a certain endocrine gland—in this case a portion of the pancreas—is unable to make an adequate supply of its proper hormone. The result is an inability of the body properly to take care of sugar. Thanks to Banting and Best, the hormone, which we call insulin, has been separated and, if given under the skin in proper dosage, the symptoms of diabetes are completely relieved. Insulin is destroyed by the digestive tract, and so it doesn't do any good if given by mouth. The treatment, however, must be continued throughout life, because the needed substance comes from an outside source. It is not a cure of the disease, but only an artificial supply of the material which is needed for life, but which, for some reason, the person's own glands cannot provide.

The same thing happens in the disease called "myxedema," which is the disease that results when the thyroid gland fails to make its peculiar substance, or hormone. A lack of thyroid hormone produces a state of sluggishness, mental and physical, of dryness and coarseness of the skin, puffiness of the face, of chilliness, and other characteristic manifestations. Giving thyroid hormone relieves all these symptoms completely and in this case the hormone can be administered by mouth in the form of the dried thyroid of an animal put up in the form of tablets.

The relief of this disease, myxedema, by feeding thyroid, was the first substitution treatment discovered. It was discovered by Dr. Murray, of London, in 1891. My friend, Dr. Alexander Burgess, of Providence, has told of a patient of his who started thyroid treatment for myxedema in 1892 and has taken it steadily ever since. She is now 86 years old. Well treated myxedema, therefore, doesn't prevent the attainment of a ripe old age.

Other forms of this substitution treatment are gradually being discovered. Of late years, for example, several hormones of the reproductive glands, or gonads, have been separated and their chemical structures discovered. These organs, it should be stressed, not only produce the elements necessary for the propagation of the race, but also manufacture hormones which, among other things, virtually make the woman's body take on certain of its female characteristics and the man's body certain of its male characteristics. Should these organs be absent or destroyed, it is now possible to give substitution treatment for the second of these functions. For example, even without the ovaries, a woman can be made to have monthly periods regularly and avoid the symptoms of a premature change of life. Also in certain irregularities, not due to organic disease of the womb, the normal menstrual rhythm can be restored by a physician who thoroughly understands the use of these various hormones.

I wish there were time for me to tell you more about this interesting form of treatment, but we must get on to another phase of the subject.

When these glands make too much material, as for example the thyroid gland in certain kinds of goiter, the most effective method of treatment is to remove the gland in whole or in part by an operation. X-ray treatment may also stop the gland from working overtime in certain cases.

Sometimes tumors form in these endocrine glands and cause the gland to secrete too much of its peculiar hormone. Cures in such cases can often be brought about by surgical removal of the tumor. Seemingly magical cures have been made in this way. The parathyroid glands, the size of small peas, situated in the neck near the main thyroid, make a hormone which has to do with the removal of lime salts from the bones. Parathyroid tumors, by making an excess of parathyroid hormone, may cause a condition in which the bones lose their lime salts—or become decalcified—and become so soft that they break easily. This condition can be cured by an operation which removes the tumor.

Another example is a tumor arising in one of the adrenal glands, which lie on top of the kidneys. Excess of this hormone causes some remarkable changes in the character of the person. A woman suffering from such a tumor might become man-like, and develop high blood pressure and some other troublesome symptoms. Removal of the offending tumor might restore her to her proper state.

Such, in brief, are some of the high spots of the science called endocrinology. While it has advanced rapidly and far, it should also be frankly admitted that there is a great deal yet to learn. We don't yet know all about it. We know, for example, that in a certain kind of poisonous goiter the thyroid is working overtime, but we don't know why. We relieve the patient by removing a portion of his offending thyroid gland, but some day we may learn why the thyroid is overactive and be able to check its activity by a method less radical than taking it out.

Questions

Q. *Dr. Means, is excessive weight, which you call obesity, generally a result of gland trouble?*

A. No, it certainly is not. It is always the result of eating too much and usually of nothing else. There are some types of endocrine disease in which obesity occurs as a symptom, but even in these, weight will be lost if the food is cut down.

Q. *But, Dr. Means, suppose I really enjoy eating, aren't there any medicines that will make me lose weight?*

A. Yes, thyroid will, but it is not the best way to reduce. The reduction occurs because the food is burned up faster in the body, but this may also have some ill consequences, particularly upon the heart. So if you want to guard your health, what it really amounts to is food or figure—you make the choice.

Q. *Are any preparations containing extracts of, not one, but of several glands, often valuable?*

A. No. Such treatment is undesirable. It is what we call shotgun treatment. The doctor, not knowing precisely what is wrong, gives a lot of medicine at once in the hope that one will hit the mark. It is far better to give only one gland preparation at a time and watch what effect it has. In this way the diagnosis is made clear and the patient is treated intelligently. Don't experiment with these powerful substances. Have a reliable doctor find out what's wrong first and then have him find out how to make what's wrong, right.

Q. *Do babies or young children have glandular disturbances?*

A. Yes. By far the most important glandular disturbance of babies or young children is lack of thyroid function, which produces dwarfism and imbecility if not recognized early and thoroughly treated with thyroid. These unfortunate children are what are called "cretins." If they are allowed to live too long without treatment, they can never be completely relieved, but if the diagnosis is made early by an alert doctor —and by early I mean as early as within the first six months—and treatment started and continued, they can grow up to be perfectly normal adults. Please note that here, as in diabetes, which I have mentioned also, treatment must be continued throughout life.

Q. *Dr. Means, could glandular trouble make you feel tired all the time?*

A. Yes, it could. Although there are various causes for chronic fatigue, many of which have nothing to do with the endocrine glands, there are certainly cases in which the cause is traceable to one of these organs. There is a disease called Addison's disease, which is due to a failure in the function of the adrenal glands, in which fatigue is one of the outstanding symptoms. It is very rare, however. A much more common type of fatigue, traceable to endocrine glands, is that in which the thyroid is mildly underactive. Such cases are often greatly benefited by treatment.

Q. *Can a woman, who apparently is unable to have children be helped by glandular treatment?*

A. Yes. Sometimes the failure to have children is a result of the faulty action of some endocrine gland and can be corrected if a physician gives the appropriate hormone in proper dosage.

ARTHRITIS

FRANCIS C. HALL, M.D.

Arthritis is a disease of the joints. Changes take place within the joints which interfere with normal use, and the sufferer has pain, swelling, and usually stiffness of the joints. There are many causes for this disease. Thus, arthritis is not one disease, but often the evidence in the joints of several disorders of the body. Sudden, severe inflammation of a joint we call acute arthritis. A slowly developing, mild inflammation of the joints which lasts months or years, we call chronic arthritis. It is often called chronic rheumatism. A neglected or carelessly treated acute arthritis becomes chronic, and crippling may result. The chronic condition is more important because sometimes its causes little pain, and it can cripple before a person wakes up to what is happening.

Acute arthritis is usually caused by one of three things. (1) Any one of the kinds of germs or bacteria—those associated with pneumonia, sore throats, social diseases, etc. (2) It may be caused by a fall or a blow, or overwork. (3) It may be caused by chemical agents—as in gout, or gouty arthritis. Sudden, severe attacks of acute arthritis in men are occasionally due to this disease which seems to be associated with diet.

A patient suffering from acute arthritis must be put to bed. Indeed, he is so uncomfortable that he goes to bed on his own hook, and asks for relief of pain. His joints should be kept quiet in splints part of the time. Local treatment to the joints should be given and a persistent search should be made for the cause. This cause should be attacked and if possible, removed. Sometimes this means draining a joint surgically, or later removing a focus of infection like the tonsils. It may mean the use of drugs like sulfanilamide for certain types of infection, or the drug colchicine for gout. It may require a careful study of the diet as well. It certainly will mean avoidance of use of the affected joints until they have quieted down in order to prevent a chronic arthritis from developing, with resulting joint damage.

It is chronic arthritis that is especially important from a social and economic point of view. This oldest of known diseases flourishes in all the densely populated regions of the world, but especially in the temperate climates. Except for mental disease, it causes more disability than any other disease. More people are affected by chronic arthritis than the number of all the people in the United States suffering from tuberculosis, diabetes, and cancer combined. There are 140,000 people in Massachusetts alone suffering from this disease that does not kill, but often cripples. The economic loss resulting from this invalidism is enormous. Only since the war has this situation regarding chronic arthritis in the world been known, and many workers are now trying to awaken people to the realization that something must be done to correct this condition by stirring up the interest of the public, and getting further help, to lighten the suffering, and lessen the economic burden of the taxpayers.

Chronic arthritis can be divided into two main groups, (1) those types of arthritis in which the cause is known, and (2) those types in which the exact cause is not known. In addition, there are patients who have aches and pains in muscles and joints, and who think they have arthritis, but who really do not. Rather, these pains may be due to one of the five following causes: (1) Physical exhaustion, (2) Worry and unhappiness, (3) Postural joint strain, or standing in a drooping posture, (4) Thyroid gland deficiency, (5) The glandular readjustment in women at the change of life, which is associated with the characteristic symptoms of that time of life. These conditions can usually be cured by appropriate treatment.

The types of chronic arthritis of which the causes are known may arise from (1) Infections like dysentery, pneumonia, and the social diseases, (2) Gout, (3) Overuse or strain of the joints, and (4) Certain rare conditions. The infections may be present in the joints, or the joint may be inflamed from the poison produced by infections elsewhere in the body. These various infections comprise a long list of possibilities. The infection must be found, identified, and then removed, treated with drugs, or in some appropriate manner consistent with our knowledge of that particular disease. The principle of treatment is the same as in the treatment of acute arthritis. Gout may be chronic as well as acute, and needs to be recognized, and a proper diet and proper medication must be prescribed.

Mechanical irritation or trauma, as we call it, is a known cause of chronic arthritis. People who use certain joints excessively due to the nature of their work or to overweight, people who use joints incorrectly or out of line, and people who injure joints from time to time and instead of giving them proper time to heal, keep on using them, frequently develop changes in these joints which may cause chronic pain and disability. We all develop some of these changes in our joints as we get older for these very reasons. The best treatment for these conditions, and the best way to preserve these joints for long years of usefulness is to try to prevent this too early wearing out of joints by standing, walking, and sitting in a proper posture, by keeping our weight down to normal, and by taking care not to injure or overuse painful joints. Once severe damage to the joints occurs, they can never be quite brought back to normal, though much can be done to improve function. If injury of joints by these ways could be treated as early and as effectively as wounds and fractures are treated, the results in prevention of crippling would be much better than they are now. Even when crippled, the orthopedic surgeon can often do much by surgery and appliances to make these crippled and painful joints much more useful, and to relieve their pain.

There are three types of chronic arthritis whose exact cause is not known. Therefore we have no single cure for them. We do know a great deal about the nature of these diseases, and we believe that with our present limited knowledge we can help nature to arrest the disease in a large percentage of cases. These diseases are (1) Rheumatic Fever (2) Hypertrophic Arthritis, or degenerative joint disease, and (3) Atrophic or Rheumatoid Arthritis.

Rheumatic Fever is a disease of children and young adults. While arthritis is frequently present and may be severe, the arthritis usually subsides, leaving normal joints. This is partly due to the fact that the patient is in bed, is running a fever, and is not allowed to use these sore joints. The doctor's chief fear is that his patient with rheumatic fever will suffer injury to the heart, for this disease is the chief cause of heart disease. These patients often become crippled because of the damage to the heart, but not because of damage to the joints.

Hypertrophic Arthritis, or Degenerative Joint Disease, is a disease occurring most often in robust people over 40 years of age. It begins in the cartilage lining the joint which appears motheaten. It is only slowly progressive, has none of the signs of infection or inflammation, but considerable evidence that mechanical irritation or wear and tear play a major role. There are many contributing factors playing minor roles. This type causes varying degrees of pain, causes enlargement of joints, but is not the severely crippling type of disease. These patients, like others, need study, correction of all contributing factors, and proper care of the joints.

Atrophic, or Rheumatoid Arthritis, is the most dreaded type of arthritis because it *is* the severely crippling type. This type occurs in people under forty years of age, especially in women. It begins gradually, usually in people with great worries, in people who overwork, who have slept too little, or are depleted by a series of infections. This type of person works until he drops, driving himself on in spite of sore joints. At first there is mild joint inflammation (swelling, pain), and later permanent changes in the joints occur. The disease may go on for years, getting better and then getting worse. The end result is deformity or stiffening of the joint. Yet this end result is usually not necessary. Taken early, and treated wisely, many of these sufferers have the disease stopped even though we may not know the exact cause of his or her disease. Proper care of the patient, proper care of his joints, and correction of those factors which contribute to the patient's poor health are rewarding, but the treatment must go on for months. Supervision of the patient for years is necessary to prevent the disease from coming back again.

Questions

Q. *In all these different kinds of arthritis, what are the most important things for a patient to do to prevent crippling, and to get well?*

A. The patient must give up the idea of a quick, specific cure. Only a small percentage of patients have a type of disease for which a specific drug can be given with the expectation of a quick cure. Vaccines and sulphur have no proved value. If the patient does the proper things quite early in the disease, however, there may be a quick cure. He must get plenty of sleep, a good diet, and above all stop using the joints. These should be kept quiet, often for many weeks. If this is done early in the disease, before the joint is damaged, he should do well. He should keep in touch with his doctor as long as any arthritis is present.

Q. *Is nothing being done to meet this terrible scourge of chronic arthritis in the world?*

A. Yes, much is being done. Some 25 countries have formed societies for the study and control of rheumatic diseases. They have international meetings for the exchange of ideas. Our American Society has stimulated research in arthritis in hospitals, the formation of arthritic clinics, the exchange of knowledge through publications and meetings. We are trying to interest laymen and laywomen in joining and contributing money to the cause so that we may prevent serious disease from occurring, and treat it vigorously early in the disease before crippling occurs. With more money, more hospital facilities, and more cooperation we could do much to correct this condition of 140,000 sufferers from chronic arthritis in Massachusetts, even with our present knowledge, just as was done in the campaign to stop tuberculosis.

WHAT TO EAT AND WHY

SARA M. JORDAN, M.D.

Food, its selection and quantity, captivates the interest of all human beings, from the man who forages the wood and the stream, and the working man and his wife, to the health enthusiast and the modern hostess, for upon good judgment and wisdom in its use depend to a large degree the well-being and the social life of man. It is natural, therefore, that this interest has been exploited, either innocently or with mercenary motive, by food faddists who have advocated all manner of diets for all conditions and states of being, or who have ascribed to a given diet the power to cure all and correct all.

To prescribe a uniform diet for Tom, Dick, and Harry, as well as for Jane and Mary, is to ignore their differences in age, stature, mode of living, as well as their taste and tolerance for food. Every mother learns that she must serve twice as much food to her growing boy as to his father, and approximately three times as much to the boy as to his grandfather. The clerk in the office knows that on his vacation in the country when he swims and plays tennis, he can eat and enjoy eating at least one and a half times as much food as when he sits at his desk all day. And we all learn sooner or later when our neighbor persuades us to eat what he enjoys eating, that what is sauce for the goose is sometimes poison for the gander.

In spite of all these variations, however, certain facts about man's diet may be considered basic. A very brief description of the digestive apparatus may help us to understand why we want food and what we do with it. The simplest conception of the digestive tract is of a muscular tube which runs through the body, with wide and narrow parts. The widest part, designed to catch and hold food, the stomach, is an exquisitely made chemical and mechanical workshop, where secretions pour forth to create appetite for food and to reduce complicated foods to simple materials which can be absorbed by the narrowest part, the small intestine, and then passed on to the stronger and somewhat wider portion, the large intestine, where the final absorption of valuable fluid takes place, and the waste is passed on for excretion. Nervous force, emanating from the central nervous system of the individual, causes the glands which line the digestive tract, to pour out their valuable digestive juices and the muscles to contract and dilate more or less rhythmically, so that the food material can be held in certain parts and pushed along in others to produce effective digestion and assimilation. We all know how important rest and exercise and proper living are in maintaining our obvious nervous equilibrium, the temperamental serenity and good disposition which we like to present to the outside world. We must always remember that the tranquility of our digestive tract is just as dependent as our disposition upon our nervous stability, and when we are "living right," to use a favorite colloquialism, we are usually digesting right.

The habits of eating have grown up with man. By common usage for example, a three-meal-a-day schedule has been evolved, a meal with which man starts the day's work, one to support him in the middle of it, and one with which to end it. The relative strength of these meals has changed for our city population from the heavy breakfast and noon meal with the light supper, which were used by our farmer ancestors and are still in vogue in the country, to the opposite, the light breakfast and lunch with a heavy dinner. While the latter food schedule is more convenient and better tolerated by the healthy individual whose alertness of mind during the daytime hours means his bread and butter, an exception must be made in individuals whose stomach nerves are so taut that too large a burden cannot be given it at the end of the day. In those cases, a division should be made of the day's food into three meals of equal size, or with a lighter evening meal.

In these days of interest in dietetics, knowledge of the main food constituents is common: of protein as the general body builder and replacer of waste tissue, of fat and carbohydrates as the cushion builders and sources of energy, of calcium as the bone builder and the protector of beautiful teeth, of iron as the blood builder, and finally, of the important vitamins, those *sine qua nons* of bodily happiness. It is interesting to note that the usual pattern for eating, adopted by man living under normal conditions, contains enough meat, fish, eggs, and cheese to supply the protein, enough butter, olive oil and cream for the fat supply, enough bread, cereals, potatoes, and desserts for the carbohydrates, enough milk for the calcium, enough vegetables and fruits for the iron, and of all these classes of foods, enough for the vitamins from A to D. Therefore, if we adhere to the old-fashioned design for meals, evolved from man's experience, in choice of food, we shall have cereals, meats, vegetables, fruits, milk, and fats in the right proportions to maintain our health. A sample day's diet, a large glass of orange juice, a portion of cereal with cream, an egg, bacon, meat, potato, two green vegetables, fruits, a pint of milk, bread and butter, and pudding or sweets (and these foods in any desired combination) will furnish all the necessary food principles, including the necessary vitamins. Bread, potato, rice, and macaroni will provide the starches necessary for increasing or maintaining the weight of those who have a tendency to be malnourished, and an absence or minimum of these foods will help the stout to reduce. Let us not be led astray by the fancies of the faddists.

Modern concepts of diet have concerned in a beneficent way, the preparation of food and the determination of its quantity. While the frying pan and deep fat are still used by the expert cook to produce delectable concoctions which perhaps because they tickle the palate so delightfully, do not overburden the stomach, these instruments of cooking have in general given way to the broiler, the boiler, and the oven. Thus food is prepared without incorporating fat so firmly into the food particles that the stomach has difficulty in breaking them down. It is this difficulty which creates the unpleasant discomfort in the pit of the stomach, and this occurs when the food given the stomach to digest is improperly prepared, or when the stomach itself is in no condition (too tired or too nervous) to attempt its work of digestion. The quantity of food to be eaten is variable with the individual. There is probably no sphere of physiology where injustice prevails to as great a degree as in this matter of ratio between appetite and need for food. The obese usually have large appetites and don't need them, while the puny must be tempted and coerced into eating. Of course, much of this discrepancy is due to faulty habits. Instead of there being an unfair distribution of appetites, it is usually a matter of a long-continued abuse of appetite developed into a habit. When so recognized by an individual who is sincerely interested in correcting it, a new habit of under-eating for the obese and over-eating for the malnourished can be established, and after a short interval of discomfort, such a habit will be painless.

To conclude these remarks about diet, the following points might bear emphasis:

(1) The natural evolution of man's diet stands the scrutiny of modern science. Our three meals a day schedule, with adaptation of the strength of the meals to the character of the day's activities, still stands us in good stead.

(2) The pattern of the day's rations should be cereal and bread, meat or fish, cheese and eggs, vegetables, milk, fruit, cream and butter and sweets. Deduction of cereal, bread, butter, cream, and sweets for the stout, and addition of large quantities of these foods for the thin, will keep the caloric value adapted to the individual.

(3) The frying pan and the kettle of deep fat should be banished except when they are to be used by expert hands to produce delicacies to add charm to the special occasion.

(4) Through the experience of living, every normal human being learns how much and what kinds of food he needs, just as he learns how much sleep and exercise he requires, and if he regards these needs as his norm and deviates as little as possible, he will be eating right and living right.

Questions

Q. What do you consider the safest way to diet to reduce?

A. The logical way to reduce is to keep a diary of one's food intake when one is either gaining or maintaining overweight, then subtract the foods which are known to produce weight most quickly—as for example—the bread, butter, potatoes, cream, desserts, sweets, and alcoholic drinks. Then keep a diary and a weight chart and deduct still further or add, according to the results obtained. But keep meat, green vegetables, fruits, and milk in your diet always.

Q. Do you regard white bread as more or less healthful than the dark breads, the so-called health breads?

A. The caloric value is usually about the same. The rougher breads are often irritating to the digestive tract, and for people with sensitive intestines they frequently cause indigestion. The most easily digested form of bread is the thin white bread toasted very brown—the so-called Melba toast.

Q. How much attention should we pay to roughage in the diet?

A. Here again, the individual must learn by experience. He must have enough bulk and stimulating food to start intestinal activity, but he must avoid over-stimulation and irritation which causes at least 35% of all indigestion. Too much roughage over a long period of time can produce a chronic irritability of the digestive tract which may be very distressing.

Q. Is it true that some people can't eat certain apparently harmless foods without becoming ill, or having a rash break out, or is this just a coincidence and a notion on their part?

A. There is a definite group in individuals who are allergic to certain foods—which means simply that these foods poison them because they are sensitized to them. If allergy is suspected, a food diary or tests will usually determine what the offending food is, and treatment can be given to desensitize the individual.

Q. Do you think eating between meals and before retiring is harmful?

A. The poorly nourished person adds a goodly number of calories to his diet by snacks between meals, but he should be sure that his snacks are easily digestible, especially the one which he takes before retiring.

The stomach should rest at night, but a glass of warm milk or malted milk taken at bedtime often has a soothing effect on the individual, and will not keep the stomach working too long after the rest of the body begins its rest.

Q. Should a person who has persistent indigestion eliminate one food after another in order to find the diet suited to him?

A. No, because persistent indigestion is usually due to a defect of the digestive tract, not of the diet. He should have a careful examination to find the cause, which may be innocent and easily relieved. On the other hand, it may be serious and for the safety of the individual, should be diagnosed early.

NERVOUS FATIGUE

Vernon P. Williams, M.D.

Doctors frequently see people who are in sound physical health and yet who complain that they get tired very easily. Some of these people say that the least exertion beyond a very limited amount of activity may exhaust them completely. Others say that though they are able to get through their daily tasks everything is an effort and that they are conscious of feeling tired most of the time. It isn't always physical work which results in this abnormal fatigue. Sometimes the individual gets tired even if he is doing something that would ordinarily be considered a pleasure.

Now, we know that fatigue or tire is a perfectly normal thing for any healthy person. Most of us feel tired after a few sets of tennis, or after a long walk, after a day spent in seeing a world's fair, or after a day of hard work. But from this kind of fatigue we recover fairly quickly. We know, too, that certain physical diseases, such as tuberculosis, heart disease, or anemia may be characterized by fatigue, as one of the symptoms.

But the strange thing about the kind of fatigue which is the subject of this talk is that no physical disease is present; the fatigue comes on too easily and lasts too long. The amount of exercise which preceded it isn't enough to account for it, and just resting doesn't do much good. This kind of fatigue is commonly known as "nervous fatigue."

The question we should like to try to answer is, what causes nervous fatigue if there is nothing wrong with the body? There are various causes, but the question can be answered in a general way by saying that nervous fatigue is a sign that something is wrong in the individual's way of living. He is, in some way, out of tune with the environment in which he lives or there may be some strong emotional need which has not been satisfied, or something bothering him which he can't seem to settle.

One rule of thumb which will be of help in discovering the causes of nervous fatigue in an individual is to consider what there is too much of or too little of in his round of daily living. We human beings are so made that we require balance in our daily life. Is there too much monotony in the person's life? Has he, on the other hand, become too dependent upon excitement, jumping from one thing to another? Does he work too much or not enough?

The woman, whose life, year in and year out, consists of household duties and the care of growing children, with little opportunity for fun, is liable to lead a dull existence which becomes fatiguing from its very monotony. She needs the company of stimulating friends or the chance to go to the movies now and again. If she lives in the city she should be able to go out into the countryside if that appeals to her, or if she lives in the country she needs the fun of an occasional trip to the city, even a night club if it holds any interest for her.

On the other hand, the woman who leads an active social life, with numerous engagements every day and parties several nights a week, may become too dependent upon excitement and stimulation and may find herself too tired to accomplish anything that requires close attention. She has energy only for the pastimes which give her a kick, and as time goes on she may find even these fatiguing.

Change and diversion from the activities which take up the largest part of our time, whether these activities be work or so-called pleasure, are important in avoiding nervous fatigue. It is interesting, however, that the more we like what we are doing the longer we can apply ourselves before we are aware of feeling tired. In fact, when we are really interested we don't think of applying ourselves; our attention is held automatically and we don't like to stop. Unless we become "hipped" on fatigue, so that we exaggerate the feeling, we are likely to have the energy for doing what we really want to do. A boy may become sleepy and tired after an hour of study, but in some remarkable way has the energy for skating or skiing for hours at a time. And especially are we able to go on doing almost indefinitely anything in which we excel and which, at the same time, brings us praise and admiration from other people. Successful opera stars, in spite of the great expenditure of energy required of them, don't seem to collapse from fatigue.

An important consideration in avoiding nervous fatigue is to be sure that we are suited to our occupations. Too many people are misled by ambition and undertake enterprises or work for which they do not have the ability or equipment. They may struggle along for a while with determination, but as it becomes clear that their measure of success isn't and probably never will be equal to the amount of effort expended the road ahead seems endless and even temporary rest by the wayside doesn't revive them sufficiently to make them able to "carry on."

Fatigue is often the result of emotional disturbances. Human beings are at bottom emotional, and not rational and it is the emotions which are the driving forces behind most of what we do. It is the nature of our emotions to want satisfaction or fulfillment and when, for one reason or another, our emotional strivings are blocked or thwarted a situation of what we call "frustration" may occur. Energy is then not properly used and the result is often a feeling of fatigue or exhaustion. One of our greatest needs is a suitable outlet for our affections. We are attracted to other people and we fall in love because we need each other. It is a rare person who is self-sufficient in this regard. If we do not find some one who responds to our offer of affection a fundamental emotional craving in our natures goes unsatisfied. Unless we can accept this "frustration" after we reason it out we live under strain and tension which frequently are causes of fatigue.

Besides this desire for the companionship and caring of another person is the strong urge for making the most of ourselves. Not only do we want friends who like and appreciate us, but we want to feel that we exert influence and power ourselves at least in a small way. We want to feel that what we do in the world is needed and is of value to others. If we do not feel this, an adequate stimulus and interest in living is lacking and the daily round may be boring to the point of fatigue. We must be careful, however, with our selfish ambitions, that we don't ask for too much. The person who has become accustomed to success in every direction will find it difficult to call a halt when he meets a situation to which his abilities are not adapted. If the halt is not called there will be a wasteful output of energy which may lead to "frustration."

Some people get into the habit of putting off making a decision in both big and little problems. They have difficulty in making up their minds. They seem to think that waiting just a little longer will enable them to make a better decision; but it isn't so, the longer they wait the harder it is to make the decision. Such prolonged indecision is a strain and is fatiguing. Learning to say "yes" and "no" decisively, after a reasonable amount of thought, gives us a sense of well-being and we feel in command of ourselves.

If, then, we are burdened with a feeling of fatigue which isn't due to physical disease we should look inside ourselves to discover what is wrong in our way of living. If emotional problems and worries hang heavily on us we should make what changes we can in our situations. If no reasonable changes can be made we should make a clean-cut decision to accept without further brooding over it. "What can't be cured must be endured." In this way we save energy and can turn our attention to constructive interests. Our lives are like houses with many rooms and it is hardly sensible to spend all of our time in only one of the rooms. If the plaster is falling off the ceiling in one of the rooms let's do what we can to fix it but not waste time and energy wishing that the plaster weren't falling.

Questions

Q. What you say about inefficiency in living and emotional problems causing fatigue is interesting, but surely overwork or working too hard can in itself cause the kind of fatigue you have been talking about, can't it?

A. If the person really cares about his work, if it is the kind of work for which he is suited, neither too difficult nor too easy for him, and if he isn't doing it only to keep the wolf from the door, there isn't much chance that he will find it fatiguing. Some people work hard, even feverishly, to keep themselves from thinking about or facing emotional problems. This isn't a satisfactory method of escape. The problem is still there unsolved. If the problem has been faced clearly and a decision has been reached in regard to it then the person can work hard because he has decided that it will do no good to keep brooding over what might have been or might be if the world were just as he would like to have it. No matter how interesting the work, relaxation and diversion from it are necessary to prevent the individual from becoming stale. A few geniuses on fire with enthusiasm seem to be able to keep from getting stale without much of any relaxation or diversion, but these are the exceptions.

Q. Don't you think people differ in some fundamental way in the amount of energy they have at their command?

A. Yes, I think there can be little question about that. No two human beings are exactly alike in every way. We differ in temperament, in intellectual ability, in our senses of humor, in physical build, and so forth. And we probably differ in how much energy is at our disposal. But we mustn't be misled by the appearance of weakness. We often see frail-looking people who accomplish many times the amount accomplished by the well-nourished, healthy-looking people. If we want something strongly enough and if getting it seems reasonably possible, great quantities of energy are apt to be available for its attainment. It is the people who are brooding over past disappointments, who won't let the past go and who don't look at the present or future within the limits of what is possible for them who become weary of existence. As a poet said, "Rest is not quitting this busy career, rest is the fitting of self to one's sphere."

Q. Can you explain a little further what you mean by emotional disturbances and frustration causing fatigue?

A. All of us are made up of bundles of wants or desires. The closer we come to having these wants or desires satisfied the more comfortable and secure we feel. We want enough money so that we won't have to worry about food, shelter, and clothing. We want the love of someone else to satisfy the natural sex instincts and the desire for companionship which will help to keep us from feeling alone. We want friends and success in our work. If we can't get what we want in these ways we become unhappy. If nothing can be done about satisfying a particular want we do well to determine to make the best of it. Otherwise the emotional turmoil created by the dissatisfaction burns up energy in a futile way and fatigue results.

Q. I suppose we all have worries, strains and problems and yet all of us don't become tired. Why is that?

A. It depends upon how we handle the situation. That is why it is important to teach children right at the start that they shouldn't expect always to have everything their own way. If, in early years, they become used to self-control and to putting up with not getting everything they want, they will form the habit of adjusting themselves to the frustrations which we all meet throughout our lives. Another point is that because of individual differences in make-up, people react in various ways to emotional difficulties, if these difficulties aren't dealt with properly. Instead of becoming fatigued, some people get headaches, or develop digestive troubles or sleep poorly, get the "jitters," or have palpitation, and so forth.

Q. You said that sometimes people feel tired even if they are doing things that they consider a pleasure. Why would they become tired if they are doing what they want to do?

A. That often occurs when a person is paying too much attention to the way he feels. Since fatigue is an unpleasant sensation sometimes the individual is too much on the look-out for it. He thinks if he feels tired it is a sign that he needs rest. The more he watches himself the more aware he becomes of any feeling of fatigue whatever. It becomes a habit for him to detect this feeling and then he becomes so accustomed to watch himself that the feeling may come on no matter what he is doing. Any one of us can notice that oftentimes we feel tired but we know it is of no importance and go ahead with what we are doing. As William James pointed out in his excellent essay on "The Energies of Men," fatigue is apt to pass away if we work through it to the store of energy beneath.

Simply because fatigue of the nervous kind can't be cured with a pill is no reason to become discouraged about it. We wouldn't approve of a business that is run inefficiently and we shouldn't approve of living half-heartedly, when a little investigation may offer a solution. One of the oldest and wisest of sayings is that the most important thing in life is to learn to know yourself.

MASSACHUSETTS CANCER PROGRAM

HERBERT L. LOMBARD, M.D.

Director, Division of Adult Hygiene
Massachusetts Department of Public Health

Dr. Lombard:

Today I have invited my executive staff to discuss with you phases of the Massachusetts Cancer Program with which they are most familiar. They include Dr. Lila Owen Burbank, Mr. Bernard E. Bradley, Miss Eleanor Macdonald, Miss Eleanor Kelly, Miss Francis Macdonald, and Miss Mary Connor. Miss Frances Macdonald, will you briefly outline the salient facts in the history of the Massachusetts Cancer Program?

Miss F. Macdonald:

In 1896 the Massachusetts Board of Health reviewed the cancer situation in this State from 1856 through 1895 and thus recorded the need for a future cancer program. In 1899 the Harvard Cancer Commission was appointed. This group has done much in furthering cancer control throughout the past thirty-nine years. In 1913 Dr. Francis D. Donoghue represented the Commonwealth at the Third International Cancer Conference held in Brussels. On his return he recommended that the Governor appoint a committee to study the various methods of cancer therapy, to report the need of further hospitalization, and to devise means for procuring curative agents prohibitive in price to the average person. In this report he discussed radium, mesothorium, and other radio-active substances. Massachusetts was not yet ready to adopt Dr. Donoghue's suggestions and his bill was rejected. However, the interest in cancer grew. Other men worked in the interest of cancer and in 1919 a small sum of money was appropriated for cancer control. With this money an arrangement was made with the Harvard Cancer Commission so that the specimens collected by physicians in the Commonwealth would be diagnosed free of all cost for the presence of malignancy. While this was a step forward, those actively engaged in procuring adequate cancer legislation were not satisfied and continued their efforts for a more comprehensive program.

In 1925, through the efforts of many sincere workers, the most active being the late Monsignor Ambrose F. Roche, a study of the whole situation was authorized and the following year the Massachusetts Cancer program had its inception. The first eight years were a period of trial and error. Up to this time health departments had not attempted to include cancer among their activities and the methods previously used in other diseases did not apply. The eight years of experimental work furnished the necessary data on which the present cancer program is based. It enabled the Department in 1934 to reorganize its method of attack against this disease to such an extent that at the present time the world looks to Massachusetts for guidance.

Dr. Lombard:

Thank you, Miss Macdonald. The present program consists of five parts: hospitalization, State-aided cancer clinics, Tumor Diagnosis Service, cancer education, and biometric research. Dr. Burbank, will you tell us a little about the Massachusetts cancer hospitals?

Dr. Burbank:

We have two hospitals in Massachusetts that are prepared to treat individuals with cancer who cannot be adequately treated elsewhere. One of these hospitals, Pondville, is located about twenty-two miles out of Boston on the old Providence road; the other at the Westfield State Sanatorium. At both of these institutions expert service is available and the facilities equal or surpass those available in any other hospital. The major cost of maintaining these institutions is provided by the State. Individuals who are able to pay a fraction of this cost do so. Those unable to pay are freely admitted. The wealthy naturally go to the private institutions and the State hospitals cater to the poor and the low-moderate income groups. The two hospitals have a combined bed capacity of two hundred and the turnover is such that approximately two thousand patients yearly can be cared for at these institutions. The patients who attend these hospitals fall into one of three groups: those who can be cured; those who can be helped and whose lives may be prolonged; and those for whom only terminal care can be given. The years have seen an ever-increasing number in the first class and it is expected that this improvement will continue.

Dr. Lombard:

Thank you, Dr. Burbank. Mr. Bradley, will you discuss the State-aided cancer clinics?

Mr. Bradley:

The Massachusetts State-aided cancer clinics now number twenty-two. The last one was opened on November 15th in Salem, Massachusetts. These clinics are administered by committees appointed by the local medical organizations. These committees have charge of the administrative details connected with their respective clinics but in all cases they must conform with the minimum standards set by the Department. These are:

(a) *Group Diagnosis.* The group must consist of at least three men, preferably surgeon, pathologist, and radiologist. When any of these are not available, other physicians may be substituted.

(b) *Uniform Records.* Forms are furnished by the Department for this purpose as is also money for clerical service when needed.

(c) *Social Service.* All cases of cancer and precancer are referred to social service for follow-up. The follow-up continues throughout life in the case of cancer and until removal of the lesion in the case of precancer. The State either furnishes money to help defray the expenses of the social worker or furnishes the clinic the services of a part-time social worker.

Every physician in the Commonwealth may bring or send his patient to the clinic for free consultative service with the group. If the individual case requires such diagnostic procedure as gastrointestinal series this must be paid for by the patient if he is able to do so, but if he is not able to do so funds are available for this service.

Each case is returned to the physician who sent him to the clinic, and this physician decides whether or not he desires the assistance of social service in securing treatment for his patient.

The clinics must meet at least twice a month. At intervals determined by the clinic committee, but in no instance less than once a year, some form of teaching for the physician in the community is required. Some clinics perform this service by having consultants come to the clinics at stated intervals; others have adopted the plan of having all the physicians in the community serve on the clinic staff; while still others confine their activities to having an address on cancer by some surgeon from another city.

The clinic itself is furnished the following services by the State: (1) advice, information, and literature; (2) funds for or services of social worker; (3) funds for travel of social worker; (4) funds for X-ray diagnosis for those unable to pay; (5) funds for teaching clinics; (6) funds for clerical assistance in clinics; (7) funds for postage, telephone, stationery, etc.; (8) special clinics for the staffs of the clinics; and (9) reference of cancer cases to hospital through social service.

The purpose of the clinics is to furnish to physicians and the public, group consultation service in cancer, as well as to improve the knowledge of cancer among the medical profession and the laity. The group furnishes a diagnosis and outlines a plan of treatment for any person suspected of having cancer, regardless of financial status. Every effort is made to have the family physician either come with his patient to the clinic or send the patient with such information as he cares to furnish. Any individual is admitted to the clinic, although it is preferred to have the patients referred by physicians so that any tendency to use the cancer clinic in order to establish a diagnosis of a condition originally not suspected of being cancer may be eliminated.

Dr. Lombard

Thank you, Mr. Bradley. Miss Kelly, Mr. Bradley has just mentioned social service in the cancer clinics. Will you give us a little more detail on this subject?

Miss Kelly:

The medical social worker in the cancer clinic aids the doctor in securing for his patient the utmost that medical facilities have to offer. Various terms are used by the professional worker in this field to describe these activities, but the general term "service" seems best understood by those outside her profession.

The experience of the Massachusetts Cancer Program has, I believe, shown the value and need of such service.

In some cases the service is completed at the clinic or in the patient's home through an interview with the patient, or member of his family. In other cases, further study is indicated and more complex social problems may be found with a bearing upon the health problem.

The patient coming to the clinic is met by the social worker who attempts to obtain some idea of the motivating causes that brought the patient. The physician is seen and the diagnosis and methods of treatment are told the patient either by the clinic physician or by his family physician.

The social worker again sees the patient and when necessary reinforces the physician's explanation. Sometimes when the patient has returned home he decides against treatment. A woman has been told she has breast cancer and needs radical operation. At home, however, a neighbor reminds her that Mrs. A died under operation or that Mrs. B was cured by a salve. The patient decides that perhaps she is better off without operation or that she may not have cancer anyway, and that besides, a radical operation will mean disfigurement. The social worker's task is to make the patient realize her condition and the possibilities inherent in prompt following of the doctor's orders. The patient may have been distraught upon hearing the diagnosis at the clinic and many questions which she did not ask the physician then can be presented to the social worker; the answers received usually result in acceptance of the physician's advice.

In many cases, it is necessary for the social worker to interpret to the patient's family his medical social need and help them work out with the patient his problem. An attitude of fear or hopelessness on their part, whether expressed or not, may discourage the patient to the point of his refusing treatment. I think now of one patient who lost her chance for cure because, although she was ready to accept treatment, the daughter could not bear to have her mother subjected to an operation.

Many patients can, of course, make all their own plans; others are unable, without assistance, to overcome difficulties which stand in the way of treatment. The mother who must leave her children alone may refuse hospitalization; the children must then be cared for until her return. Often just talking the matter over will enable a patient to see the solution to his own problem. Sometimes, however, the social worker will herself need to initiate some plan. A man refused treatment because he had just secured work after many months of unemployment, and feared to lose time from work. With his consent, the social worker explained the situation to his employer. The employer recognized its urgency and agreed to hold the man's job during the few weeks he would be under treatment.

Sometimes transportation to the clinic or hospital must be arranged. When it is the breadwinner who is incapacitated financial aid may have to be secured for his family.

Patients in an inoperable condition may need help in securing hospitalization, or in making some temporary plan if the chronic hospital has a waiting list. Adequate home arrangements for this patient who cannot benefit by hospital care may also mean that hospital bed can be given to a patient who does need treatment.

For the patient to whom the physician offers no hope of cure, the social worker can often do much in helping him to accept the truth and make the most of the remaining months. Work commensurate with his strength may be found, recreation suggested, or perhaps a changed attitude brought about on the part of his family or friends whose discouragement does not escape him.

In a rooming house, a patient whose condition is offensive may be unwelcome and other plans will need to be made for him.

At work, a cured patient whose face has been seriously disfigured, may no longer be acceptable, and not only must other work be sought, but the patient helped to accept this new attitude of people toward him.

In following up patients after their treatment the social worker urges prompt return to the doctor when there seem to be recurrent symptoms. Precancerous conditions are also kept under observation, and here again the follow-up visit is the means of sending the patient more promptly to his doctor at the slightest sign of trouble.

Many other types of social problem accompany, or are caused by, a patient's illness, and in each case the social worker studies the particular need. She then utilizes existing community resources—social and other agencies—as well as the resources within the patient's own group, or within himself, in an effort to meet his need.

Thus the medical social worker is aiding the physician in his fight against a disease in which prompt carrying out of his orders is of such vital importance. She acts in conjunction with the doctor and is an auxiliary rather than an independent unit in the combat of disease.

The family physician of earlier days often acted as doctor, spiritual adviser and friend. The advancement of medical science and the trend of the times has forced him to relinquish, in many cases, some of his former activities. While he still stands as the original social worker, he is greatly aided by the professional medical social workers of today.

Dr. Lombard:

Thank you, Miss Kelly. Miss Connor, will you discuss the Tumor Diagnosis Service?

Miss Connor:

The Massachusetts State Tumor Diagnosis Service examines the tissues sent in by any physician in the State provided there is a suspicion of malignancy. It endeavors to send out its report within thirty-six to forty-eight hours from the time the specimen is received. Containers are supplied by the State as well as cards for the necessary information accompanying the specimen. The work of the Tumor Diagnosis Service has steadily increased and over three thousand specimens are examined annually. In addition to first furnishing a diagnosis for the specimen, the laboratory is making special studies of tumors which are adding to the sum total of knowledge of the disease.

Dr. Lombard:

Thank you, Miss Connor. Miss Eleanor Macdonald, for a number of years you have been closely affiliated with our work in cancer education. Will you tell us something about it?

Miss E. Macdonald:

In the first eight years of the Massachusetts Cancer Program it was demonstrated that in order to teach individuals to act without delay in the presence of physical abnormality which might be malignant, education by personal discussion must be disseminated through the agency of the family physician. Every individual must have an equal opportunity to know exactly what is the present status of knowledge of cancer, so that he may protect himself by the avoidance of delay and the application of this information. It was realized fully that this plan was almost Utopian in scope, and that the minuteness of its execution would take tremendous planning and effort. It was realized also that if the physicians of the State would assume this new burden and the individuals in the State would cooperate, after the first two or three years the momentum of this basic form of control would sweep away every vestige of an excuse for failure to secure the best treatment without delay and would result in the restoration to health or the saving of the lives of approximately two thousand individuals annually in Massachusetts alone with the present knowledge.

There are nearly four and one-half million individuals, seven thousand physicians, and three hundred and fifty-five communities in Massachusetts. If every family averaged four members and every physician was interested in this plan, it would be too great a task for the seven thousand physicians to instruct separately each of the more than a million families. In place of this, the organization into Cooperative Cancer Control Committees of the whole State, community by community, was planned so that small groups might meet with local physicians for the purpose of discussing cancer. Each community, regardless of its size, is analyzed carefully before work is begun in it. Its population structure is ascertained by a study of the census figures. Its organized clubs, churches, industries, schools and general characteristics are understood and recorded from its directory or from a reliable local source. Each of its physicians confers concerning the whole plan with a member of the staff of the Cancer Division, and in more than 90 per cent of all cases gives immediate promise of full and sympathetic cooperation. Representative members of the local community give counsel as to whom to approach in order to obtain the most satisfactory response. At this point several trained surveyors of the Cancer Division start to make personal calls on representatives of every group in the population—social, fraternal, political, religious, service, labor, military and racial. This plan is not for a cross section of the State; to work, it must reach everyone. Each individual contacted is told the plan briefly and asked to come to an official organization meeting or to send a substitute. The newspapers carry articles of local interest in connection with the whole plan. A physician gives a talk on cancer, the disease, at the organization meeting and a member of the Cancer Division details the plan, again going into the reasons for its efficient operation. The plan is accepted in every town and city, and the community, through its committee and medical profession, assumes its prerogative of local autonomy in the cancer program.

Everyone is asked to go back to the groups he represents and to urge them to have at least one meeting a year at which cancer is discussed and to which a local physician is invited to speak. The nature of the group determines the type of the talk. Whether the group prefers a formal talk or merely an opportunity to ask questions is a matter for it to decide. The discussion of cancer is the important fact. Groups are strongly urged to give individuals an opportunity to ask questions. No question is too unimportant for the physician's consideration. It is only by the erasure from the minds of thousands, of the confusion brought about by misconceptions concerning causation and prevention, that the ground may be prepared for the reception of the real story of cancer and its control. The clubs with large memberships are asked to divide up into small units for cancer talks, as it is felt that large groups fail in accomplishing their purpose, because their size precludes the possibility of a question period. In small communities there are usually at least ten clubs; in medium-sized towns they number dozens; and in the cities they number hundreds.

Each representative visited is a member of the large Cooperative Cancer Control Committee. A central committee of several members is usually elected, after nomination by a group of local individuals appointed by the chairman at the public meetings. This committee coordinates the larger local group and keeps in contact with the Cancer Division of the State Department of Public Health. It sends in notices, provided for the purpose, of every meeting, stating the date, the name of the organization, the name of the community, the physician who spoke, and the number in attendance.

The limited staff engaged in this work has retarded the speed of organization. Experience has shown that there is a seasonal period for contact work. Planning for the fall and winter, combined with intensive follow-up occupies the workers during periods inauspicious for the introduction of new community projects. Of the total 355 communities in this State, 300 are organized and are carrying on with enthusiasm. This does not mean that every club in every community is complying with alacrity to this appeal to help itself. The majority of clubs are having their meetings. Those that are not, need and receive more active follow-up. Experience obtained from observations of the clubs organized in the first years shows that in many instances one individual holds back group approval, and once this individual is apprised of the importance and need of cancer education, support is obtained and the group is reached. The physicians are showing more and more interest as they note the obvious increase in the number of individuals who are coming to seek advice as soon as they notice an abnormal symptom.

Dr. Lombard:

Thank you, Miss Macdonald. In order to make a rounded program it was found necessary that a large amount of time be devoted to biometric research. It is necessary to learn as much as possible regarding the many exciting causes of cancers as well as to try to ascertain the root cause of the disease. Studies have been made on the trend in the cancer death rate, the relationship of Massachusetts to other states, the cancer rates among various nativity groups, the geographic location of cancer patients, the percentage of cures, the effects of the various daily habits of living on cancer, and other factors. By biometric methods, certain ideas regarding cancer have been proven false while others have been substantiated. Another important activity of this phase of the work is periodic appraisal of the value of cancer activities. Too often one is tempted to adopt a procedure and continue it indefinitely without just appraisal as to its worth-whileness. Throughout the cancer program the attempt has been made to continue an activity only so long as its use seems justifiable. This analytical approach was responsible for the major change in the program in 1934 and for minor changes at other periods. At the present time we are delighted at the results of the recent efforts. The combined activity of the physicians in Massachusetts, the representatives of over ten thousand organizations, and the Massachusetts Department of Public Health has resulted in a reduction in the age adjusted cancer death rate for women. This reduction began in 1935, is still continuing, and has not been duplicated in any other part of the world as far as can be ascertained. In fact, increases have been noted in nearby states compared to our decreases. While the male trend has not yet begun to decline, it gives indications of doing so within a very short period.

The delay between the first recognizable symptoms of the disease and the time when the patient presents himself to a physician is one measure of the effectiveness of public education in cancer. Between 1927 and 1935 this period of delay fluctuated in the neighborhood of 6.0 months—the highest figure being 6.5 months and the lowest 6.0 months. In 1936 it dropped to 5.0 months, held this rate through 1937, and dropped to 4.8 months in 1938. Five months is too long a period for an individual with cancer to delay before consulting a physician, but it is a decided improvement over six and a fraction months.

Another estimate of a similar nature is the percentage of individuals who go to their physicians within the first month of recognizable symptoms. In 1933 this percentage was 12.4. In 1938 it had risen to 21.1, the highest figure since the inception of the Massachusetts Cancer Program.

More and more the physicians of Massachusetts are taking the lead in referring patients to the cancer clinics. In the early days of the movement many patients came to the clinics because of newspaper publicity, and the percentage referred by physicians was relatively small. In the first year of the clinics the physicians referred 44.8 per cent of all cancer patients attending the clinics. In 1938 this figure increased to 86.2 per cent.

The total individuals with cancer attending the clinics has steadily increased. In the first year there were 302; in 1938 there were 1,685. The total attendance at the cancer clinics in 1938, including new and old cancer patients as well as noncancer patients, was 16,346. Of the new patients, about one-third had cancer. Of the old patients, a much larger percentage had cancer. Many of the visits of the old patients were repeat visits of the same individuals.

Of the group of 302 cancer patients who came in 1927, 23.5 per cent were alive eleven years after coming to the clinic. This does not necessarily mean that all of them were cured cases. Some of them were not, but it is felt that years of longevity may well be a measure of success in a cancer program.

At this time I desire to thank the thousands who have helped us in perfecting this program. Without their aid, the results which I have just mentioned could not have been realized. The Massachusetts Cooperative Cancer Control Program is well named.

GONORRHEA AND SYPHILIS — NOTIONS VERSUS FACTS

NELS A. NELSON, M.D.

Director, Division of Genitoinfectious Diseases
Massachusetts Department of Public Health

Someone has said that it isn't our ignorance that does the most harm; it's that we know so much that ain't so. Someone else has said that a little knowledge is a dangerous thing. Certainly, a little knowledge may be dangerous if it leads to conclusions that ain't so.

We are all often amused at the silly things, and shocked at the tragic things, which people do before they learn the truth. No civilized person today believes in witches; yet people once did sincerely believe in witches, and put them to torture and to death. Not so many years ago a Boston physician dared to experiment with the inoculation of people against smallpox. He was so persecuted and abused that he was obliged to hide to save his life. Our grandmothers used to hang little bags of sulphur around our necks to protect us against disease. Chloroform and ether, now used in every hospital to deaden pain during operations, were once looked upon as instruments of the devil. It was argued that if God had not intended that people should suffer pain, He would not have created pain. Hence, to use an anesthetic was to go contrary to the will of God.

Although we smile at the folly and weep at the cruelty of our ancestors, in the light of our greater knowledge of some things, it may be worth our while to pause and consider whether we may not sometimes be guilty of equal folly and cruelty in other things. How much do we know that ain't so? How likely are we, having a little knowledge, to come to silly or harmful conclusions in the belief that we know it all?

Less than two years ago, the American public had little, if any, knowledge concerning two extremely prevalent communicable diseases. The reason for this ignorance was due to the fact that people knew so much about gonorrhea and syphilis that wasn't so that they would not listen to anyone who wished to tell them the truth. The notion was so fixed in the public mind that these were diseases of only those who misbehave that no one was allowed to talk long enough about them to point out that hundreds of thousands of persons were infected innocently every year.

In July, 1936, Surgeon General Parran, of the United States Public Health Service, was able, with the help of the *Reader's Digest*, to bring the subject forcibly to the attention of the American people in one overwhelming article. Millions of Americans read that article and found it impossible to ignore the facts which it contained. Today, thanks to the flood of information which followed, most people know something about syphilis and gonorrhea. They know that these are among the most prevalent of communicable diseases; that nearly half the infections are acquired through no fault of those who acquire them; that most infections occur in young people between the ages of fifteen and thirty years; that babies are born with syphilis and may be blinded by gonorrhea. They know that blood tests are used in the detection of syphilis; that smears from infected areas may be examined for the germs of gonorrhea; that the treatment of syphilis in prospective mothers can prevent infection of the baby. They know that the adequate treatment of syphilis requires many months and sometimes years; that the sooner treatment is begun for either gonorrhea or syphilis, the better it will be for the patient and the less likely it is that the infection will be spread; that neglect of treatment leads to complication and disaster.

All this is necessary knowledge. It is good that the people of this country have awakened, at last, to the situation. But it is not enough that they have awakened, for it is precisely at this point that a little knowledge may be a dangerous thing for it may lead to conclusions that ain't so.

It is just as silly to think that gonorrhea may be acquired from doorknobs or from shaking hands or from food, as it was for grandmother to hang little bags of sulphur around our necks to ward off disease. Both are silly because they have no foundation in fact. They are the product of a little knowledge and a lot of wild imagination. It is just as cruel to drive a person with gonorrhea or syphilis from his job as it was to torture a witch. Both are cruel because they are unnecessary and unjust and the product of a little knowledge and a lot of knowing what ain't so.

It is worth repeating what we have said from this station upon other occasions;—that every disease has its own peculiar characteristics, and that the control of one disease may depend upon procedures which cannot be applied to the control of another disease. It is of the utmost importance that each disease be thoroughly understood if ridiculous and even harmful measures are not to be undertaken for its control. Smallpox is controlled by vaccination and only by vaccination. Typhoid fever is controlled by protection of water supply, pasteurization of milk and guarding certain other foods from contamination. Tuberculosis is controlled by case finding, hospital care for the infected and improvement in the standards of working and living. Each of these diseases is spread in a different way, and different measures must be taken for the control of each. Ignorance of the nature of a disease and the manner of its spread gives rise to panic and hysterical slashing about in the dark. Pesthouses for smallpox patients disappeared when it was discovered that safety lay in vaccination. The tuberculous were no longer shunned when it was learned that they could be cured and hospitals were built for their care during the open stages of the disease. Whole populations fled from their homes when typhoid appeared, until it was discovered that typhoid fever could be controlled.

There is no need for fear of gonorrhea and syphilis. It is well known how they are spread, and there is no need for either panic or hysterical slashing here and there in the hope that somehow the enemy will be hit. There is no need of firing people from their jobs because of infection with either of these two diseases, or of avoiding the infected in the ordinary walks of life. The sooner the now aroused public learns the truth concerning the nature of gonorrhea and syphilis and the manner of their spread, the sooner some of the foolish things now being done for their control will be stopped.

Gonorrhea is a communicable disease, but it is not spread through food or water or through such ordinary contacts as might lead to infection with a cold or measles or diphtheria. Although many of those with whom we work or otherwise associate have gonorrhea, we need have no fear of acquiring their infections so long as we avoid sexual contact with them. If people ceased having promiscuous sexual relationships, if those who cannot be persuaded to behave sexually would take care to avoid infection, if those who do expose themselves would seek competent medical attention, and if the infected would carefully avoid exposing others either through promiscuous sexual relationships or marriage, there would be no more gonorrhea.

Syphilis is also a communicable disease, and under certain circumstances it can be spread through other than sexual contacts. Those contacts must be reasonably intimate, however, such, for instance, as occurs in kissing. Furthermore, the infected person must have the disease in its early stages and there must be open sores with which to come into contact if accidental infection is to occur. Not more than five per cent of all infections occur through nonsexual contacts, if congenital syphilis is left out of consideration for the moment. The rest are acquired in exactly the same manner as gonorrhea.

Syphilis becomes less communicable with time, even though it is not treated. Although the disease may do more and more harm to the person who has it, it becomes less and less communicable even in sexual contacts. A person who has had the disease for many years is rarely dangerous, so far as spread of the infection is concerned, except that an infected woman may give the disease to her unborn child unless she is treated properly during pregnancy. We need not go about our ordinary business, therefore, fearing infection with syphilis at every turn. It is not to be found on doorknobs or street car straps or in a handshake or in food or on tools or books or other such objects. Few people use common drinking cups or swap pipes or lipsticks these days. Even those objects would have to be used almost immediately after having been in contact with on open sore of early syphilis to be dangerous.

Blood tests for syphilis are of the utmost importance in the diagnosis and control of the disease, but the public has an entirely wrong notion of their significance. Blood tests have no relationship whatsoever to the communicability of the disease. A person may have a negative blood test and still have communicable syphilis. A little treatment may change a positive test to negative, yet the patient may still have communicable syphilis. A patient who has had syphilis for many years, even one who has had excellent treatment, may never have a negative test, yet his infection may be completely noncommunicable.

Blood tests are indispensible in the control of syphilis, but they must be understood and used intelligently, or they may lead to disastrous conclusions. The maid in your home may have a positive blood test, but she may be the safest person you could possibly employ, if her infection is an old one or is under proper medical control. The school child with congenital syphilis is a danger to nobody, so far as spread of infection is concerned. Some newborn babies with congenital syphilis may be dangerous to handle. If an infected infant is not treated for syphilis, it may, in some cases, continue to be dangerous up to two years or so of age. Therefore, no matter how much damage the disease may do to the one who has it, it will not be spread by any occupational or social contact.

These, then, are the facts: Those who have gonorrhea will not spread their infections through any ordinary social or occupational contact, except that young girls may acquire the disease from infected members of their household. Syphilis is dangerous so long as the open sores of the early stages of the disease are present, or may appear because of neglect of treatment. Otherwise, syphilis in its late stages, or syphilis in any stage, properly treated, is not dangerous in any ordinary, everyday, nonsexual relationship. Although blood tests usually detect the presence or absence of infection with syphilis, they do not always do so, and they never indicate whether the disease is in a communicable or noncommunicable stage.

Both syphilis and gonorrhea are extremely prevalent diseases. They are dangerous diseases and they are no respecters of person, wealth, social standing or morals. The sons and daughters of the best families are marrying into gonorrhea and syphilis. Every effort should be put forward for their control, but the effort should be intelligently directed in full knowledge of the facts. Otherwise we may make ourselves as ridiculous as grandmother with her little bags of sulphur to drive away disease, or just as cruel as our forefathers who burned witches at the stake.

Book Notes

TEACHING PROCEDURES IN HEALTH EDUCATION by Howard L. Conrad and Joseph F. Meister. $1.75. 160 pp. Philadelphia. Saunders. 1938.

It is gratifying that health education in the secondary schools is today sufficiently recognized to the extent that there has appeared a much-needed book on modern methods of teaching as particularly applied to the classroom teaching of health. Conrad and Meister's *Teaching Procedures in Health Education* published by the W. B. Saunders Company in 1938, is such a text.

The authors have, throughout their entire development, realized that there is no magic panacea for the teaching of health. They are sound in assuming that the teacher of health must study the entire field of educational methods and measure her health teaching by the general criteria for all aspects of the school curriculum. The chapter headings, such as: "Health and Education"—"Planned Learning"—"Types of Planning in Health Instruction"—"The Question and Answer Phase of Instruction"—"Visual Aids to Health Education"—"Vitalizing Health Instruction"—and "Testing Outcomes in Health Education"—reveal the wide background of the authors.

However, in one respect it is disappointing—in that the laws of learning as stated by the authors would seem to be too narrowly confined to the psychology of Thorndike, without giving enough emphasis to some of the newer schools of psychology.

HOW TO CONQUER CONSTIPATION by J. F. Montague, M.D. $1.50. 244 pp. Philadelphia. Lippincott. 1938.

In a book of 244 pages, the author discusses a field which is usually covered in far less space. He goes into detail on every phase of the subject, devoting chapters to such titles as "Is Mineral Oil Harmful?" "Good Old Castor Oil!" "What about Yeast?"

Dr. Montague states that constipation affects every organ of the body and is the cause of nervousness, irritability, and mental depression.

For treatment the author stresses the use of enemas as against cathartics, the necessity of establishing regularity in evacuating the bowels, and urges again and again not to delay in consulting a physician with regard to any abnormality in the rectum or anus, particularly bleeding stools which are often the symptoms of cancer. He advises consultation with a physician with regard to the proper diet and exercise. Repeatedly he advocates the drinking of plenty of water, and cites three quarts a day as sufficient.

In places it would seem that the author was engendering phobias. An example of this is his discussion of milk of magnesia which he admits is among the least harmful of the salines. "Where it has been used for long periods in the large doses which one is obliged to employ to produce a cathartic effect in an adult, 'stomach stones' or alvine concretions sometimes form. These remain in the gastric cavity, for magnesium is a mineral, and the formation of stones by deposit of salts can take place here as in any other part of the body." Inasmuch as stones formed in the stomach by the use of milk of magnesia would be a most rare medical curiosity, it might have been better to have eliminated this statement.

There is some inconsistency in the book. It is stated in one chapter that the enema should be between 95 to 110 degrees, whereas in a former chapter it is stated that the water for the enema should be around 80 degrees.

The work is intended for lay consumption and has much to commend it, but it would seem the material could have been more condensed and certain parts omitted.

REPORT OF DIVISION OF FOOD AND DRUGS

(As required by General Laws, Chapter 111, Section 25.)

During the months of March, April, and May, 1939, samples were collected in 254 cities and towns.

There were 1,778 samples of milk examined, of which 225 were below standard, from 8 samples the cream had been in part removed, and 29 samples contained added water. There were 1,982 bacteriological examinations made of milk, 1,804 of which complied with the requirements. There were 146 bacteriological examinations made of cream, 32 of which did not comply with the requirements. There were 3 bacteriological examinations made of chocolate milk, 1 of which did not comply with the requirements; 2 bacteriological examinations of skimmed milk, which were marked, all of which complied with the requirements; 1 bacteriological examination of an empty bottle which did not comply with the requirements; there were 5 bacteriological examinations of tonic, and 1 bacteriological examination of canned soup, all of which complied with the requirements; and 53 bacteriological examinations of mattress fillings, 22 of which did not comply with the requirements.

There were 718 samples of food examined, 149 of which were adulterated. These consisted of 1 sample of butter which was rancid; 28 samples of clams, 27 of which contained added water, and 1 sample was decomposed; 1 sample of oysters to which water had been added; 2 samples of fish which contained formaldehyde; 3 samples of fillet wash water which contained formaldehyde; 2 samples of cream, 1 of which was low in fat for this grade, and 1 sample showed a positive phosphatase reaction; 6 samples of cream cheese all of which did not conform to the legal standard; 1 sample of decomposed eggs; 1 sample of cooked pickled products which was slimy on the outside of the cellophane casing; 1 sample of maple syrup which contained cane sugar; 38 samples of sausage, 2 samples of which contained starch in excess of 2%, 5 samples contained a compound of sulphur dioxide not so labeled, 30 samples were decomposed, and 1 sample was both decomposed and contained a compound of sulphur dioxide not so labeled; 1 sample of keilbassa which was decomposed; 2 samples of lamb patties, and 1 sample of veal patties, all of which were decomposed; 9 samples of hamburg, 8 of which were decomposed, and 1 contained a compound of sulphur dioxide not properly marked; 2 samples of turkey sandwiches which were decomposed; 4 samples of relish which contained benzoic acid not so labeled; 8 samples of soft drinks, 5 of which contained benzoic acid not so labeled, 2 samples contained saccharin, and 1 sample was misbranded; 21 samples of soft drink wash water which were deficient in caustic alkali; 10 samples of bedding and upholstering material, 4 of which contained secondhand material not so labeled, and 6 samples contained a mixture of new and secondhand material not so labeled; and 7 samples of feathers and down which were labeled as containing a certain percentage of different kinds of feathers and down which samples did not contain the materials as specified.

There were 30 samples of drugs examined, of which 8 were adulterated. These samples were samples of silver nitrate solution which contained less silver nitrate than specified on the label; of these 8 samples 1 sample contained no silver nitrate.

The police departments submitted 104 samples of liquor for examination. The police departments also submitted 40 samples to be analyzed for poisons or drugs, 30 of which contained heroin, 1 contained cannabis, 2 contained strychnine, 3 contained morphine, and 4 samples were examined for narcotics with negative results.

There were inspected 410 plants operated for the pasteurization of milk; 75 restaurants; 190 soft drink plants; 38 ice cream plants; 64 bakeries; 352 mattress establishments; 1 candy factory; 1 hotel kitchen and icebox; 106 stores; and 10 sausage factories.

There were 170 hearings held pertaining to violations of the laws.

There were 99 convictions pertaining to violations of the laws, $2,440 in fines being imposed.

Alek Byko of Middleton, and Rasmus F. Peterson of Bedford, were convicted for violations of the milk laws.

Harold Fletcher of Mansfield; Hazen K. Richardson of Middleton; John W. Grandell of North Weymouth; Frank Lola, 3 cases, of Franklin; Benjamin Mendelson of Malden; Ubald Robbillard of Westminster; and Jacob Davidson of Chelsea were convicted for violations of the pasteurization laws and regulations. Frank Lola of Franklin appealed all 3 cases.

Abraham Glass and Arthur Shulman of Worcester; East Smithfield Farms, Incorporated, of Philadelphia, Pennsylvania; the Economy Grocery Stores Corporation, of Lynn; Frank Astuti, 2 cases, Harry Gillis, 2 cases, Harry Krivitsky, Arnold Scheu, Benjamin Shuffani, M. F. Foley Company, Nature Food Centres, Incorporated, Waldorf System Incorporated, Guiffre's Fish Market, Incorporated, United Markets, Incorporated, Henry Bialsky, 2 cases, and Saul Diamond all of Boston; Alex Pappas of Webster; Central Meat and Grocery Company, Incorporated, 2 cases, of Southbridge; Harry Rabinovitz, Benjamin Gross, 2 cases, Hyman Paul, Ida Bernstein, 2 cases, and Stark Supply, Incorporated, of Roxbury; The Atlantic and Pacific Tea Company, Incorporated, Henry Beach, and Antonio Fratoni of Attleboro; Northampton Public Market, Incorporated, of Northampton; Charles F. Pease of Warren; Louis Zionts, Harris Tillman, and Anna Klys, 2 cases, of Springfield; the Atlantic and Pacific Tea Company, Incorporated, John Presto, and Hubert Abraham, all of Holyoke; Peter Fertig, and Bernard Roberts of West Springfield; Samuel Calabano and Economy Grocery Stores Corporation of Lawrence; the Food Centre, Incorporated, Austin L. Robinson, and the Thomas Fish Market, Incorporated, of Brookline; John B. Gorton of Fall River; Alfred Costa of New Bedford; Alexander Beaudry of Lowell; William Brenner, and Harry Terrio of Chelsea; Alfonso Caslagnola of Revere; Joseph Maziarz of Chicopee; Sam Cimini, and Francisco Gai of Pittsfield; and the Big Four, Incorporated of North Adams were all convicted for violations of the food laws. Abraham Glass of Worcester, and John B. Gorton of Fall River appealed their cases.

The Johnson Wholesale Perfumery Company, Incorporated, 2 cases, of Boston; and the S. Pfeiffer Manufacturing Company, Incorporated of St. Louis, Missouri, were convicted for violations of the drug laws. The Johnson Wholesale Perfumery Company, Incorporated, appealed both cases.

John Kilkus of Brockton, and George W. Milbery of Saugus were convicted for violations of the bakery laws. George W. Milbery of Saugus appealed his case.

The Crescent Star Beverage Company, Incorporated, of Charlestown; Julius Lipovsky of Springfield; Cox J. Warren of Waltham; Castle Rock Springs, Incorporated, of Saugus; J. Louis Wasserman, 2 cases, of Millis; Michael Wojtowicz of Fall River; Wasil T. Pauk, and Andrew P. Wisniewski of Lawrence; Louis Paulauskas, 2 cases, and Walter Paulauskas, 2 cases, of Lowell; and Alfred Roccuzzo of Everett were convicted for violations of the soft drink regulations. Wasil T. Pauk of Lawrence, and Alfred Roccuzzo of Everett appealed their cases; Walter Paulauskas of Lowell appealed 1 of his cases.

The Diamond Mattress Company, Incorporated, of Woonsocket, Rhode Island; Charles J. Ehrlich, 2 counts, of New Bedford; the Franklin Furniture Company, Incorporated, of Norwood; Spero Brothers, Incorporated, of Wakefield; Albert Geffner, 2 cases, of Fall River; the Sunset Bedding Company, Incorporated, of Boston; and Walter S. Tkacyzk, 2 cases, of Gardner were convicted for violations of the mattress laws. The Sunset Bedding Company, Incorporated, of Boston, appealed its case.

Aaron Mandelbaum of Chelsea was convicted for the obstruction of an inspector.

In accordance with Section 25, Chapter 111 of the General Laws, the following is the list of articles of adulterated food collected in original packages from manufacturers, wholesalers, or producers:

One sample of butter which was rancid was obtained from Harry Rabinovitz of Roxbury.

One sample of heavy cream which was low in fat for the grade specified was obtained from Robert Hare of Sharon.

Cream cheese not conforming to the legal standard was obtained as follows:

One sample from Vermont Farm Cream Cheese of Lyndonville, Vermont; and 2 samples each, from Conestaga Cream Cheese Manufacturing Corporation of New York City, and Abbott's Dairy, Incorporated, of Philadelphia, Pennsylvania.

One sample of maple syrup which contained cane sugar was obtained from the Home Restaurant, Incorporated, of Boston.

One sample of pickled beets and 3 samples of relish all of which contained benzoic acid not so labeled were obtained from the Hi Hat Food Products Company of Providence, Rhode Island.

One sample of clams which was decomposed was obtained from the Quality Fish Market, Incorporated, of Worcester.

Clams to which water was added were obtained as follows:

Six samples were obtained from the Ipswich Shellfish Company of Ipswich; 3 samples were obtained from M. F. Foley Company of Boston; and 1 sample each, from Guiffre Fish Market, Incorporated, United Markets, Incorporated, and Albert Landsman of Boston; Food Centre, Incorporated, Austin L. Robinson, Thomas Fish Market, Incorporated, and Economy Grocery Stores Corporation of Brookline; Brockton Public Market, Incorporated, of Brockton; United Markets, Incorporated; Economy Grocery Stores Corporation and the Great Atlantic & Pacific Tea Company of Cambridge; John B. Gorton of Fall River; Albert J. McCarthy and the First National Stores of Newton; and Philip S. Mogul of Somerville.

One sample of watered oysters was obtained from the J. C. Coulbourne Company of Baltimore, Maryland.

One sample of veal patties which was decomposed was obtained from Max Jacobson of Holyoke.

Two samples of decomposed turkey sandwich were obtained from the Waldorf Lunch of Boston.

Lamb patties which were decomposed were obtained as follows: One sample each from the Grand Union Market, Incorporated, of Pittsfield; and the Fall River Public Market, Incorporated, of Fall River.

One sample of hamburg steak which contained a compound of sulphur dioxide not properly labeled was obtained from the Terminal Market, Incorporated, of Roxbury.

Hamburg steak which was decomposed was obtained as follows: One sample each from the Grand Union Market, Incorporated, of Pittsfield; Fred Karl of Chicopee; J. Rienholtz, Incorporated, of Boston; Grand Cash Market, Incorporated, of Gardner; Alfred Costa of New Bedford; Hyman Paul, and Benjamin Gross of Roxbury.

One sample of sausage which contained starch in excess of 2% was obtained from Aaron Mandelbaum of Chelsea.

Sausage which contained a compound of sulphur dioxide and was not so labeled was obtained as follows:

One sample each from the Italian and Greek Grocery, Incorporated, of Boston; and Walter H. Terrio, William Brenner, Charles Delheim, Julius Cohen, and Nathan Needleman of Chelsea.

One sample of sausage which was decomposed and also contained a compound of sulphur dioxide not so labeled was obtained from Ida Bernstein of Roxbury.

Sausage which was decomposed was obtained as follows: One sample each from Alfonso Sastagrola of Revere; Arthur Shulman of Worcester; Charles Cohen, Louis Zais, and the Public Market, Incorporated, of Fall River; Alex Pappas of Webster; Growers' Outlet Incorporated, Abraham Houdas, and Benjamin Solomon of Greenfield; Harry Newman, J. Rienholtz, Incorporated, Edward Iandolis, and Hymon Alpert & Company, Incorporated of Boston; Milton Miller of New Bedford; Stark Supply, Incorporated, and Benjamin Gross of Roxbury; May Phillips of South Deerfield; Mary Babel of South Norwood; Central Market, Incorporated, of Southbridge; Armand Davignon and Joseph

Maziarz of Chicopee; John Presto and Gus Schwartz of Holyoke; Francisco Gai and Sam Cimini of Pittsfield; Bernard Roberts of West Springfield; Big Four, Incorporated, of North Adams; and Agnes Klys of Southbridge and Webster.

Two samples of soft drinks which contained saccharin were obtained from Louis Paulauskas of Lowell.

Soft drinks which contained benzoic acid not so labeled were obtained as follows:

One sample each from Adrien Vanasee of Northampton; Lewis Newman of Malden; John E. Daly of North Attleboro; London Seal Bottling Company of Waltham; and American Beverage & Seltzer Company of Beverly.

There were 14 confiscations, consisting of 10 pounds of decomposed butter; 165 pounds of mouldy chickens; 350 pounds of mouldy turkeys; 3 pounds of decomposed beef; 2 pounds of decomposed salt pork; 3 pounds of decomposed veal chops; 44 pounds of decomposed hamburg steak; 925 pounds of meats contaminated and decomposed by fire; 3 pounds of decomposed sausage; 18 pounds of decomposed sausage meat; and 1200 pounds of groceries contaminated and decomposed by fire.

The licensed cold storage warehouses reported the following amounts of food placed in storage during February, 1939: 47,280 dozens of case eggs; 692,083 pounds of broken out eggs; 159,737 pounds of butter; 1,826,154 pounds of poultry; 1,997,506 pounds of fresh meat and fresh meat products; and 2,798,883 pounds of fresh food fish.

There was on hand March 1, 1939: 6,360 dozens of case eggs; 1,131,182 pounds of broken out eggs; 1,808,239 pounds of butter; 6,812,390 pounds of poultry; 5,130,262 pounds of fresh meat and fresh meat products; and 9,124,249 pounds of fresh food fish.

The licensed cold storage warehouses reported the following amounts of food placed in storage during March, 1939:—244,680 dozens of case eggs; 775,420 pounds of broken out eggs; 270,659 pounds of butter; 1,255,903 pounds of poultry; 2,036,196 pounds of fresh meat and fresh meat products; and 4,462,307 pounds of fresh food fish.

There was on hand April 1, 1939: 218,400 dozens of case eggs; 1,130,936 pounds of broken out eggs: 1,107,949 pounds of butter; 5,496,264 pounds of poultry; 4,715,376 pounds of fresh meat and fresh meat products; and 5,927,527 pounds of fresh food fish.

The Massachusetts cold storage warehouses reported the following amounts of food placed in storage during April, 1939: 1,585,890 dozens of case eggs; 1,464,156 pounds of broken out eggs; 438,371 pounds of butter; 1,017,978 pounds of poultry; 1,897,137 pounds of fresh meat and fresh meat products; and 7,424,312 pounds of fresh food fish.

There was on hand May 1, 1939:—1,775,160 dozens of case eggs; 1,765,163 pounds of broken out eggs; 443,536 pounds of butter; 4,176,473 pounds of poultry; 4,161,700 pounds of fresh meat and fresh meat products; and 7,146,240 pounds of fresh food fish.

MASSACHUSETTS DEPARTMENT OF PUBLIC HEALTH

Commissioner of Public Health, PAUL J. JAKMAUH, M.D.

Public Health Council

PAUL J. JAKMAUH, M.D., *Chairman*

GEORGE D. DALTON, M.D.
FRANCIS H. LALLY, M.D.
CHARLES F. LYNCH, M.D.
RICHARD M. SMITH, M.D.
RICHARD P. STRONG, M.D.
JAMES L. TIGHE

Secretary, FLORENCE L. WALL

Division of Administration . . Under direction of Commissioner
Division of Sanitary Engineering . Director and Chief Engineer,
ARTHUR D. WESTON, C.E.
Division of Communicable Diseases Director, ROY F. FEEMSTER, M.D.
Division of Biologic Laboratories . Director and Pathologist,
ELLIOTT S. ROBINSON, M.D.
Division of Food and Drugs . . Director and Analyst,
HERMANN C. LYTHGOE, S.B.
Division of Child Hygiene . . Director, M. LUISE DIEZ, M.D.
Division of Tuberculosis . . . Director, ALTON S. POPE, M.D.
Division of Adult Hygiene . . Director,
HERBERT L. LOMBARD, M.D.
Division of Genitoinfectious Diseases Director, NELS A. NELSON, M.D.

State District Health Officers

The Southeastern District . . HAROLD W. STEVENS, M.D., Middleborough
The South Metropolitan District . HENRY M. DE WOLFE, M.D., Braintree
The North Metropolitan District . ———
The Northeastern District . . ROBERT E. ARCHIBALD, M.D., Melrose
The Worcester District . . OSCAR A. DUDLEY, M.D., Worcester
South Connecticut Valley District . CHARLES E. GILL, M.D., Westfield
North Connecticut Valley District . WALTER W. LEE, M.D., Greenfield
The Berkshire District . . FRANK B. CARROLL, M.D., Great Barrington.

PUBLICATION OF THIS DOCUMENT APPROVED BY THE COMMISSION ON ADMINISTRATION AND FINANCE
7500. 8-'39. Order 7866.

THE COMMONHEALTH

Volume 26
No. 4

Oct.—Nov.—Dec.
1939

PNEUMONIA

MASSACHUSETTS
DEPARTMENT OF PUBLIC HEALTH

THE COMMONHEALTH

QUARTERLY BULLETIN OF THE MASSACHUSETTS DEPARTMENT OF
PUBLIC HEALTH

Sent Free to any Citizen of the State
Entered as second class matter at Boston Post Office

M. LUISE DIEZ, M.D., DIRECTOR OF DIVISION OF CHILD HYGIENE, EDITOR.
1 Beacon Street, Boston, Mass.

CONTENTS

	PAGE
Foreword	223
Important Considerations in Serum Treatment of Pneumococcus Pneumonia, by Frederick T. Lord, M.D.	224
Chemotherapy and Serum Therapy of Pneumonia, by Frederick T. Lord, M.D.	232
The Use of Specific Serums in the Treatment of Pneumonias Associated with Pneumococci of the "Higher Types," by Maxwell Finland, M.D.	245
Pneumococcal Meningitis and Its Treatment, by Maxwell Finland, M.D.	248
Pneumococcus Pneumonia in Infants and Children, by John A. V. Davies, M.D., and Edward C. Curnen, M.D.	257
Special Problems in the Typing of Pneumococci from Infants and Young Children, by Arthur P. Long, M.D.	262
Nursing the Pneumonia Patient in the Home, by Dorothy J. Carter, R.N.	264
Types of Pneumococci in Massachusetts, by Edith A. Beckler, S.B.	268
The Work of the Collaborating Pneumococcus Typing Laboratories of Massachusetts, by Ernest J. Vogel, M.D., and Roy F. Feemster, M.D., Dr.P.H.	270
The Use of the Term "Group IV" Pneumococcus, by F. Randolf Philbrook, M.D.	273
Instructions to Laboratories Doing Pneumococcus Typing and Distributing Antipneumococcic Serum	275
Regulations Relative to the Payment for Certain Laboratory Tests on Specimens from Cases of Pneumonia	276
Report of Division of Food and Drugs, June, July and August, 1939	277
Book Note:	
Pneumonia with Special Reference to Pneumococcus Lobar Pneumonia, by Roderick Heffron, M.D.	280
Index to Volume 26	282

FOREWORD

PAUL J. JAKMAUH, M.D.

Commissioner of Public Health

Massachusetts Department of Public Health

The pioneer work of this Department in formulating and putting into effect a practical pneumonia program to combat the most deadly communicable disease of the present decade stimulated a far-reaching interest in the problem throughout the country. The five-year study under grants from the Commonwealth Fund of New York City came to an end on January 1, 1936, but the interest in the problem has not decreased, and the services to physicians have been gradually expanded since that time so that typing service and serum depots are now within easy reach of every physician in the state.

Most of the papers in this issue of *The Commonhealth* were prepared late in 1938. Due to the introduction and the rapidly increasing use of chemotherapy, the publication of the papers was purposely delayed until more information in regard to the usefulness of the new drugs became available. The authors have made revisions in the papers to bring them up to date, and additional information in regard to chemotherapy has been included. It is hoped that this issue will be useful to Massachusetts physicians in choosing the best treatment for patients who fall victims to the ever-prevalent pneumococcus.

Much effort has been expended in building up the typing service in the State to its present efficiency. It will be unfortunate if physicians do not make full use of this service as there is much to learn about the most effective method of treating pneumonia due to the different types of pneumococcus, and little information on this point can be obtained unless every case of pneumonia is properly typed.

IMPORTANT CONSIDERATIONS IN SERUM TREATMENT OF PNEUMOCOCCUS PNEUMONIA

By FREDERICK T. LORD, M.D.

*Clinical Professor of Medicine, Emeritus, Harvard Medical School
Member Board of Consultation, Massachusetts General Hospital*

It may be helpful to consider certain matters of importance in reaching an attainable goal in the specific treatment of pneumococcus pneumonia.

Classification of the Pneumonias

The distinction between lobar pneumonia and bronchopneumonia is at times difficult not only clinically, but also at the post-mortem table. Both lesions may be present in the same patient.

It has become customary clinically to refer to the pneumonias which do not conform to the lobar variety as atypical and include the bronchopneumonias under this term, but the classification into lobar and atypical or bronchopneumonia is not of practical importance and the pneumonias should so far as possible be classified in accordance with the inciting agent and not with respect to the pathologic anatomy.

• It may, in general, be said that pneumococcus pneumonia is usually lobar and that infection with other organisms results in bronchopneumonia.

The mistake has frequently been made of regarding lobar pneumonia only as amenable to antipneumococcic serum therapy and dismissing bronchopneumonia from consideration. It should be appreciated, however, that any one type of pneumococcus may cause either lobar or bronchopneumonia. To be sure, the individual types of pneumococci vary in the frequency with which they are responsible for one or the other form of pneumonia. Thus, Type 1 and Type 2 pneumococci cause lobar pneumonia in a large proportion of the cases, but may also cause bronchopneumonia. The proportion of those with bronchopneumonia rises among pneumococcus pneumonias due to other types and, as shown by Finland (*Annals Int. Med.* 10:1531, April, 1937) may reach one-third to one-half of the cases.

Early Diagnosis of Pneumonia

In view of the importance of the pneumococcus as a cause of both lobar pneumonia and bronchopneumonia, the differentiation of the one from the other has lost much of its significance. Labor pneumonia is, however, of greater relative importance, because of the infrequency with which other than pneumococci are the cause and the high incidence of Types 1 and 2 as inciting agents.

It is fortunately easy to recognize lobar pneumonia at its inception in a large proportion of the cases. In typical instances there is often the history of a preceding cold. The onset is commonly abrupt with coincident pain in the side, cough and chill or chilliness, rapid elevation of temperature and rusty sputum. This complex of initial symptoms is incomplete in a small proportion of cases. Definite physical signs are not to be expected early in the disease and two to three days may elapse before there is definite evidence of consolidation. In rare instances, examination by other means than X-ray may be negative throughout the illness.

Bronchopneumonia as a pneumococcus infection, is usually due to Type 3 and still higher types of the pneumococcus. Primary bronchopneumonia is for the most part a disease of infancy and the first four years of life. After this age, primary bronchopneumonia is uncommon but may be expected in a proportion not exceeding ten per cent. The essential factor in the production of secondary bronchopneumonia is the extension downward of an infecting agent and the types of penumococci or other organisms normally present in the upper parts of the respiratory tract are concerned in the production of the disease. Pneumococci are found in the upper respiratory tract in a large proportion of normal persons. The carrier state may be transient, intermittent or chronic. Among normal individuals without a history of recent exposure to a patient with lobar pneumonia, the pneumococci harbored in the upper respiratory tract are rarely Type 1 or Type 2 and more often Type 3 and still higher types.

In primary pneumococcus bronchopneumonia, there is, as with lobar pneumonia, usually the history of an acute respiratory infection such as accompanies a cold. The onset is less abrupt than with lobar pneumonia. An initial chill and pain are less often present. The sputum is usually mucopurulent, occasionally rusty. In cases in which pneumococcus bronchopneumonia is secondary and occurs in the course of other serious illnesses, after childbirth, during the puerperium, or after surgical operation, the onset may be insidious and the pneumonia discovered only in the course of a routine physical examination. The usual occurrence of bronchopneumonia as a complication of an existing respiratory infection, the insidious onset, irregular course and frequent absence of definite physical signs make the diagnosis of the disease difficult and at times impossible without resort to X-ray examination. In the absence of this means of examination, it often happens that for a time it can only be regarded as probable from the attendant circumstances and the symptoms or signs. It should be appreciated that bronchopneumonia practically always complicates capillary bronchitis and may be assumed to be present in the disease even in the absence of more definite indications. Bronchopneumonia should also be suspected, in the course of an acute bronchitis, when the fever persists longer than a few days, or when râles are localized and persist in one place longer than elsewhere, or when, without change in the local signs, there is an abrupt increase in toxic symptoms and elevation of temperature, pulse and respiration. As there are no distinctive features of the different types of pneumococcus infection, resort must be made to the laboratory for the determination of the type of pneumococcus infection in each case of pneumonia.

Types of Pneumococci in Pneumococcus Pneumonia

The incidence of the various types of pneumococci vary at different times and different places. In adults under ordinary circumstances, infection with Type 1 pneumococcus is more common than with other types.

Among 3,066 cases of pneumococcus pneumonia (including both lobar pneumonia and bronchopneumonia) in adults, investigated by Bullowa and Wilcox (*Arch. Int. Med.* 59:394, March, 1937) the average incidence of the types most frequently encountered in adults was as follows:

Pneumococcus type	Percentage distribution in 3,066 cases
1	23.7
3	9.7
2	8.4
5	7.5
8	7.3
7	6.3
4	5.8
14	2.8
9	2.2
18	2.1

Typing of Pneumococci

In view of the importance of early specific treatment, determination of the type of infection should be made at the earliest possible moment.

Type determination is more readily made by the examination of sputum than by other means. The specimen of sputum should come from the lung with as little admixture of saliva or nasal secretion as possible. Rusty or blood-streaked material is most likely to show the inciting agent. Small amounts of sputum suffice for typing by the Neufeld method, culture on blood agar and, if necessary, mouse inoculation. It is no longer necessary to obtain the large amounts which were required for typing by the precipitation method. A fresh specimen should be sent at once to the nearest laboratory equipped for typing. It should be collected in a small, clean, dry and preferably sterile, widemouthed bottle. Clear glass facilitates the selection by the technician of suitable portions of the specimen. As drying is to be avoided, cardboard sputum boxes are less serviceable and it is best to collect the sputum in the special containers available through local boards of health. No antiseptic should be added to the specimen, as the determination of type may depend on the presence of living organisms. Tuberculosis sputum outfits should not be used as they contain carbolic acid.

Sputum can be obtained from adults in most cases if the physician is sufficiently insistent. When no sputum is available, the type of pneumococcus infection may be determined by the examination of material obtained from the pharynx on a sterile cotton swab. This is replaced in the sterile tube and sent at once to the laboratory where particles of sputum may be removed by twirling the swab rapidly back and forth in a small amount of broth. Application of the Neufeld method to the sediment obtained by centrifuging at high speed may permit identification of the type of pneumococcus at once or incubation of the broth or mouse inoculation with the sediment may give a positive result after the lapse of some hours.

The limited distribution of Types 1 and 2 pneumococci with rare exception to patients with pneumonia or their contacts may be taken to indicate that the finding of one or the other in the sputum of a patient with pneumonia means that the organism is almost certainly the cause of the infection. On the other hand, the finding of one of the higher types commonly present in the normal mouth may mean that the causative organism has been missed and the typing should at once be repeated on another specimen of sputum.

Importance of Blood Cultures

A blood culture should be taken as a routine in all cases and may be the means of making a diagnosis of type when other methods fail. Blood cultures are, however, positive in only a minority of cases. In general, about one-quarter of those with Type 1 and one-third of those with Type 2 pneumococcus pneumonia develop bacteriemia. The blood culture is, thus, more likely to be negative than positive and there is the further disadvantage in the necessity of making the diagnosis of type by this means that it entails loss of time in waiting for the growth of organisms.

In specifically treated cases, a blood culture should be taken immediately preceding the first injection of serum and as occasion may require throughout the illness. The information derived from the blood culture is of great importance in treatment. In Type 1 and Type 2 cases, not treated with serum, the fatality rate is four to five times as high in those with, as in those without, bacteriemia. The high death rate in bacteriemic cases may be much reduced by serum treatment, but much larger doses are required. If the blood cultures taken before serum is given are positive, or, if negative, and the progress of the case is unsatisfactory, it is important to continue to take blood cultures at intervals of twenty-four hours or more often.

Failure to determine the presence of bacteriemia in serum-treated cases deprives the physician of one of the most important guides to dosage. In the earlier Massachusetts cases, of 1,341 Type 1, 2 or 5 cases (1931-37) blood cultures were taken in only 635 or 47.4 per cent. During the period in which these cases occurred, facilities for taking blood cultures were for the most part available only in the larger hospitals. In February, 1938, Chadwick (Serum Treatment of Pneumonia, *N. E. J. of Med.* 218: 366, Feb. 24, 1938) announced that blood culture outfits could be obtained from laboratories approved by the State Department of Public Health. After the addition of the patient's blood to the culture medium, the outfit should be returned at once to the same laboratory. Postal regulations do not permit the mailing of these blood cultures, and the outfits must therefore be sent by messenger.

It is encouraging to note that in the later Massachusetts experience* (1937-38) of 550 Types 1, 2, 5, 7 and 8 cases, blood cultures were taken in 326, or 59.3 per cent. In this group, though the proportion of those on whom blood cultures were taken has risen about twelve per cent over that in the earlier group (1931-37), lack of information regarding bacteriemia in 40 per cent of the cases and consequent uncertainty regarding the necessary dosage of serum may be regarded as a serious obstacle to adequate specific treatment.

In consequence of the importance of determining the presence or absence of bacteriemia, blood culture medium is part of the necessary equipment for the treatment of pneumonia. With the patient in a hospital and the laboratory nearby, culture medium in cotton-plugged flasks can be used. For use in the home, culture media in rubber-stoppered bottles covered with a gauze cotton hood are available through approved laboratories. Five cubic centimeters of the patient's blood should be added to the 50 c.c. of culture fluid. Caution should be exercised to avoid contamination of the medium in handling. Before blood is obtained, the stopper should be loosened without removing the hood. For the introduction of blood, the bottle is inclined at an angle of about 45 degrees, the hood and stopper together lifted directly upward, blood ejected from the syringe and the hood and stopper replaced. Contamination especially with staphylococci is likely to occur if the stopper itself is handled or if the fringe of the hood is drawn across the mouth of the bottle. In the presence of pneumococci in the sample of blood, growth may be expected after eight to twelve or more hours, and the type determined by the Neufeld method.

Results in the Massachusetts Series

The case fatality rate of Type 1 pneumococcus pneumonia untreated with serum is approximately 30 per cent and of Type 2 about 43 per cent. Of 1,451 Type 1 cases in the Massachusetts Pneumonia series, which were treated with serum within the first four days of the illness, 194, or 13.3 per cent died. Of 368 Type 2 cases similarly treated, 80, or 21.7 per cent died. The experience in Massachusetts and elsewhere has demonstrated that specific treatment can be successfully used by physicians in general practice.

The importance of the time element is emphasized by the experience in Massachusetts. Of 1,205 Type 1 cases treated during the first three days, 145 (12 per cent) died, and of 246 treated on the fourth day, 49 (20 per cent) died. If patients with Type 1 pneumococcus pneumonia are treated within the first twenty-four hours, the fatality rate may be reduced to 5 per cent.**

*For this and other data dealing with the 1937-38 series, I am indebted to Dr. Frank R. Philbrook.

**Cecil, R: J. A. M. A. 108:689, Feb. 27, 1937.

Results and Dosage of Serum

It should be appreciated that variation in individual requirements make it impossible to treat patients by rule of thumb. In estimating the required dosage, reliance must be placed chiefly on the results obtained in large groups of cases. Decrease in the fatality rates in serum-treated cases below the rates to be expected without such treatment, is the most important index of the degree of success in estimating dosage. The experience in Massachusetts has an important bearing on this problem. Owing to the small number of cases due to infection with other than Types 1 or 2 pneumococcus, the results in these two groups only will be considered.

In 956 Type 1 cases (1931-37) treated with serum of known potency during the first four days of the illness, there were 134 deaths, or 14 per cent. The average total dosage for each case in this group was 87,569 units. In 408 later (1937-38) Type 1 cases treated with serum of known potency during the first four days, 49, or 12 per cent died. The estimated average total dosage of serum in these cases was 109,900 units.

In appraising these results in Type 1 cases in the Massachusetts series, it is encouraging to note that there has been a reduction from an expected death rate of 30 per cent to 14 per cent and 12 per cent, respectively, as noted above in the two groups, or well over a half.

In 259 Type 2 cases (1931-37) treated with serum of known potency during the first four days, there were 57 deaths, or 22 per cent. The average total dosage for each case in this group was 92,718 units. In 87 later (1937-38) Type 2 cases, 17, or 19.5 per cent died, and the estimated average total dosage was 110,800 units. As the expected fatality rate in Type 2 cases without serum treatment is 43 per cent, there has been a reduction of well over half.

Changes of Policy with Respect to the Distribution of Serum

The results presented in Type 1 and 2 cases are based on cases treated within the first four days of the illness. This restriction in the use of serum supplied by the State Department of Public Health was removed in March, 1937 (Chadwick, J. A. M. A. 109:1926, Dec. 4, 1937). Though the benefits of serum diminish as the days go by after the onset, no time limit can be set beyond which serum is ineffective. Patients should not be deprived of specific treatment even though its use is begun late in the illness.

The amount of serum dispensed by the Department of Public Health for the treatment of a patient with pneumonia is no longer restricted. (Circular, Department of Public Health, Division of Biologic Laboratories, May 3, 1937.)

Dosage of Serum

It is not to be expected that even under the most favorable circumstances every patient with pneumococcus pneumonia can be saved, but the reduction in the fatality rate in the Massachusetts Series falls short of an attainable goal. Among the avoidable causes of failure in specific treatment are a delay in beginning treatment, insufficient dosage, too long intervals between doses, and lack of attention to the requirements of individual patients.

Regarding delay in treatment, it is encouraging to note that while in the first 1,043* Type 1 cases, 17.5 per cent were treated on the first day, 36.8 per cent on the second, 28 per cent on the third and 17.4 per cent on the fourth, in the last 408 cases (1937-38) the corresponding percentages were 23, 40, 21 and 15.6 per cent.

It is to be hoped that in subsequent cases, a very much larger proportion will be treated on the first day of the disease.

It is desirable to give the necessary amount of antibody not only as early as possible, but within as short a time as is consistent with safety. The fatality rate in Type 1 cases of 12 per cent, as in the 1937-38 series, can doubtless be lowered by more careful attention to the individual needs of the patients.

Suggestions regarding dosage are given in detail on the blue sheet which is distributed with the serum. The importance of certain of those recommendations may be emphasized. At present, in Massachusetts, it is recommended, subject to the precautions which must be exercised with respect to treatment with alien serum, that patients with Type 1 pneumococcus pneumonia be given an *initial dosage* of *at least* 60,000 units, with Types 2, 5, or 8 *at least* 100,000 units, and with Type 7 *at least* 60,000 to 90,000 units. This is only *the initial course of injections* and does not constitute the *full initial dosage* in all cases.

To secure the initial dosage indicated above, all the serum is not given at one time. The serum is usually administered at two-hour intervals until the dosage decided upon has been given. The customary amount of the first injection is 2 cc., the second the remainder of the contents of the vial, the third the contents of two vials, and subsequent injections the contents of three or more vials. The amount of serum injected at one time should not exceed 50 cc. The introduction of the words *at least* before each amount in the paragraph above is to be regarded as a warning to give a larger initial dosage in severe cases and to err rather on the side of too much than too little serum. Then, too, it must be appreciated that these figures refer only to the dosage in the initial course of injections and do not imply that the specific treatment should stop here. In fact, the use of the term *initial dosage* is of itself an intimation that further dosage may be desirable.

In the scheme outlined, it is recommended, furthermore, that under certain unfavorable circumstances, such as the inauguration of treatment after the third day, with a patient over 40, with pregnancy or during the first week of the puerperium, multilobar involvement and pneumococcus bacteriemia, that the dosage of serum in the initial course of injections be at least doubled.

---

*Including 956 cases treated with serum of known potency and 87 cases with serum of unknown potency.

Having followed the directions thus far, in many cases only a beginning has been made in treatment and subsequent dosage must be estimated in accordance with the needs of each case. Here again it is better to err on the side of safety and give too much rather than too little serum. Additional individual injections of 40,000 to 60,000 units

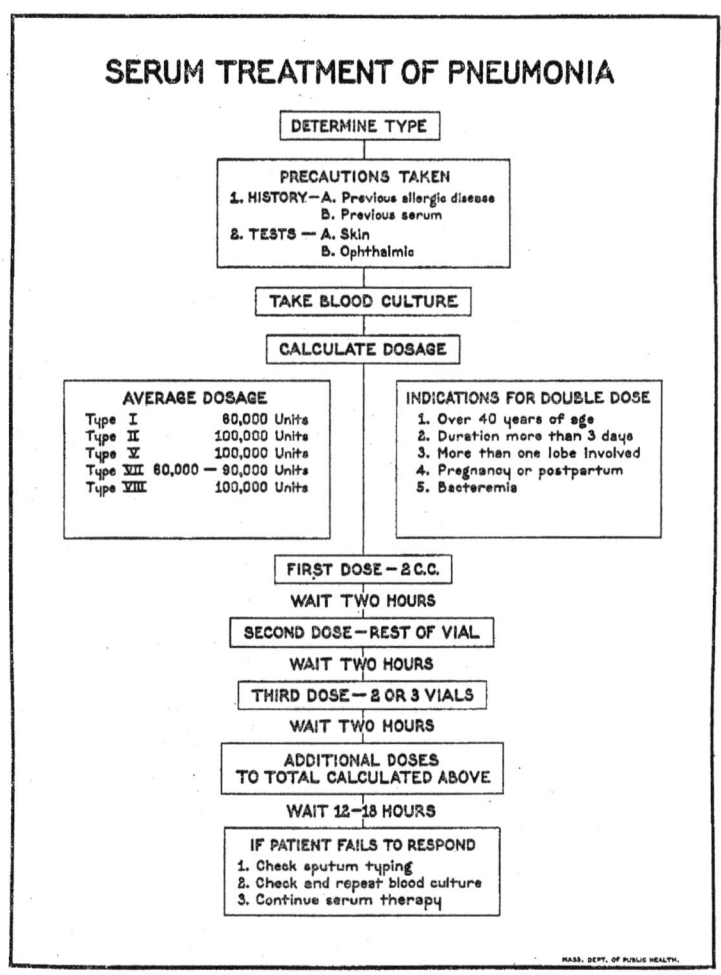

should be given at intervals of every three to four hours, in all severe cases and in any case if the temperature does not fall below 102 degrees F. by rectum within twelve hours of beginning serum treatment, or having fallen, it again rises above this level, if bacteriemia has been demonstrated regardless of the clinical course, or if there is evidence of a spreading lesion. In this group, it is desirable that the serum be given in the larger doses and for a longer period in the presence of two or more of the circumstances mentioned above.

The amount of antibody necessary for successful specific treatment varies within wide limits in different cases. The suggestions with respect to dosage should be taken to indicate that there is wide latitude in the schedule and that the dosage must be adjusted to the needs of the individual patient.

If the patient fails to improve within twenty-four to forty-eight hours after beginning specific therapy, it is desirable to send another specimen of sputum for typing, as a mistake in bacteriologic diagnosis is possible.

Failure to improve after seventy-two hours suggests the presence of some complication such as empyema.

CHEMOTHERAPY AND SERUM THERAPY OF PNEUMONIA
By FREDERICK T. LORD, M.D.

Clinical Professor of Medicine, Emeritus, Harvard Medical School
Member Board of Consultation, Massachusetts General Hospital

Synthesis of the azo dyes in the dye industry is responsible for the production of para-aminobenzenesulfonamide, for which the nonproprietary name "Sulfanilamide" was adopted(1). Encouraging results against pneumococcus infection with sulfanilamide led to the development of the pyridine derivative 2-(p-aminobenzenesulfonamido) pyridine. In May, 1938, Whitby(2) demonstrated its therapeutic value against experimental hemolytic streptococcic, meningococcic and pneumococcic infection in mice. The designation "Sulfapyridine" has been adopted(3).

In Vitro and Animal Experiments

In vitro experiments indicate that sulfanilamide and sulfapyridine are capable of inhibiting the growth of pneumococci and that this bacteriostatic action is enhanced in the presence of specific antipneumococcic serum.

Sulfanilamide and sulfapyridine are capable of delaying death and in some instances saving the life of animals inoculated with otherwise fatal doses of pneumococci. Sulfapyridine is more effective in this respect than sulfanilamide. In animal experiments, the combined use of sulfanilamide and specific antipneumococcic serum has proved more effective against pneumococcus infection than either alone.

Sulfanilamide in Pneumococcus Pneumonia

The controlled series of cases of pneumococcus pneumonia treated with sulfanilamide by Price and Myers(4) is of special significance. An attempt was made to maintain the blood concentration between 7 and 15 mg. per cent and preferably above 10 milligrams. Of 115 treated cases, 18, or 15.7 per cent, died, and of 94 controls, 29, or 30.8 per cent, died. Comparison of the treated cases with the controls suggests that the favorable results are to be ascribed to the sulfanilamide.

A severe hemolytic anemia developed in 6, or 5.2 per cent, and a modrate secondary anemia in an additional 21, or 18.2 per cent, of the patients treated with sulfanilamide. Toxic hepatitis developed in one patient.

Of 81 collected cases of Type 3 pneumococcus pneumonia treated with sulfanilamide[4]-[12] 24, or 29.6 per cent died. Though this fatality rate is considerably lower than the expected rate of about 50 per cent in this type of infection, a larger series will be necessary before the merit of the drug in the treatment of Type 3 pneumococcus pneumonia can be regarded as established.

Though there is merit in the use of sulfanilamide in the treatment of pneumococcus pneumonia, it is less effective and more likely to produce toxic effects than sulfapyridine.

Sulfapyridine in Pneumonia

Reports on the use of sulfapyridine in a large number of cases of pneumonia have been published. In the reports by Telling and Oliver[13]; Evans and Gaisford[14]; Christie[15]; Dyke and Reid[16]; Lawrence[17]; Anderson and Dowdeswell[18]; Agranat, Dreosti and Ordman [19]; Flippen, Lockwood, Pepper and Schwartz[20]; Whittemore, Royster and Riedel[21]; Meakins and Hanson[22]; Plummer and Ensworth[23]; Graham, Warner, Dauphinee and Dickson[24]; Alsted[25]; Gaisford[26]; Finland, Spring, Lowell and Brown[27]; Pepper, Flippin, Schwartz and Lockwood[28]; and Cutts, Gormly and Burgess[29] there is a total of 1,512 cases, with 98 deaths, or 6.5 per cent. The series as a whole includes cases classed as lobar pneumonia and pneumonia without specification as to the form of the disease. Various types of pneumococci were demonstrated as the inciting agent in a considerable proportion. In certain cases, pneumococci were found, but were not typed, or were nontypable. In some, no pneumococci were found. In a small proportion, other organisms may have been the cause of the process.

The expected death rate in treated cases must be estimated at a somewhat higher figure than 6.5 per cent, and probably between 7 and 8 per cent, owing, as noted later, to unusual conditions in the African cases reported by Anderson and Dowdeswell[18], and by Agranat, Dreosti and Ordman[19].

Though the 1,512 cases cover only about one year's experience, the large size of the series and the widely separated sources suggest that it may, with the exception of the African cases, be regarded as representative. Excluding these from consideration, the expected death rate in similar cases without drug treatment, may be estimated at about 25 per cent. Comparison of the results in drug-treated cases with those in simultaneous controls without the drug, but otherwise similar, confirms the merit of the method.

Favorable results in controlled cases of pneumonia treated with sulfapyridine have been reported from England, Africa and Canada. Pneumococci were not demonstrated as the cause in all cases. In the combined series of Evans and Gaisford (Birmingham) (14); Anderson and Dowdeswell (Nairobi) (18); Agranat, Dreosti and Ordman (Johannesburg) (19); and Graham, Warner, Dauphinee and Dickson (Toronto) (24) there are 480 cases treated with sulfapyridine with 22 deaths, or 4.6 per cent, against 450 not so treated with 69 deaths, or 15.3 per cent. Comparison of the treated and control groups suggests that the age distribution and the type of pneumococcus infection is not the explanation of the more favorable result in the treated cases. The treated and control groups, as a whole, do not, however, represent random samples of the population and equally favorable results are not ordinarily to be expected. The unusually low death rate in both groups is due to the inclusion in the series of a large number of African patients; i. e., 330 in the treated and 320 in the control groups, a very large proportion of whom were selected males 20-40 years of age and some of whom had been previously vaccinated against pneumococci.

Sulfapyridine in Pneumococcus Pneumonia

In the series of 1,512 cases, there are 1,051 of pneumococcus pneumonia,* with 68 deaths, or 6.5 per cent. In general, it may be estimated that the expected death rate in pneumococcus pneumonia without drug or antiserum is 25 to 30 per cent. In Bullowa and Wilcox's series (30), of 1,515 cases of pneumococcus pneumonia (including lobar and bronchopneumonia) there were 379 deaths, or 25 per cent.

Sulfapyridine in Pneumonia Due to Specific Types of Pneumococcus Infection

Variation in the efficiency of chemotherapy against experimental pneumococcus infection in animals has been attributed to individual strain (31, 32) rather than type differences of the organism. The results with sulfapyridine in the treatment of pneumococcus pneumonia appear to be favorable with all types of pneumococcus infection. The number of treated cases due to individual types is, however, sufficiently large for separate consideration in only two types. Of 312 treated Type 1 cases, there were only 18 deaths, or 5.8 per cent, against an expected death rate of about 30 per cent. Of 204 Type 3 cases there were only 19 deaths, or 9.3 per cent, against an expected rate of about 50 per cent. The results with Type 3 are especially significant, owing to the ineffectiveness of specific antiserum in the treatment of pneumonia due to this type. Further evidence is desirable regarding the merit of the drug in statistically significant numbers of other specific types of pneumococcus pneumonia. Of 90 Type 2 cases, there were 4 deaths, or 4.4 per cent, against

---

*In this group are included all cases in which pneumococci were found. In certain instances, other organisms which may have been of significance were also found.

an expected rate of about 43 per cent. More information should also be obtained regarding variations in the resistance of different strains of pneumococci to sulfapyridine.

Causes of Failure in Chemotherapy

In reviewing the reports of the findings in fatal cases, it is obvious that many were inevitable failures. In some, cardiac or renal complications played an important part in the death of the patient. In some, chemotherapy was inaugurated late in the course of the disease and the infection already involved the pleura or meninges, or had progressed to such a stage that the patient was moribund on admission.

The age of the patients influenced the results to an important degree. Of 1,125 collected, drug-treated cases, 675 were 39 years of age or under with 11 deaths, or 1.6 per cent, and 450 were 40 years of age and over, with 62 deaths, or 13.7 per cent. The greater seriousness of the disease as age advances may be ascribed to diminished resistance against the pneumococcus and a greater tendency in consequence toward generalization of the infection at this period of life.

Blood cultures were taken in only a small proportion of the reported cases and on the whole the percentage with bacteriemia was low. Of 81 cases with positive blood cultures, 19, or 23.5 per cent died.

It may be assumed that the results with sulfapyridine in the treatment of pneumococcus pneumonia fall short of an attainable goal. Earlier drug therapy would probably have saved a still larger proportion. The higher fatality rate in patients in the older age group, and especially in bacteriemic cases, suggests that reliance on sulfapyridine alone is undesirable when the outlook is known to be relatively poor and that, in severe cases due to specific types of pneumococcus infection for which antiserum is available and contraindications are absent, treatment with antiserum should be combined with chemotherapy.

Influence of Sulfapyridine on the Clinical Course of Pneumonia

One of the most impressive effects of treatment of pneumococcus pneumonia with sulfapyridine is the fall in the temperature, usually to normal within 24 to 36 hours in a large proportion of cases. Not infrequently, the temperature again rises to a low grade of fever. The fall in the temperature is accompanied by an improvement in the patient's general condition, but this improvement is more gradual than after a normal crisis. Failure of the temperature to fall suggests the presence of a complication or some other inciting agent than the pneumococcus.

No immediate change in the physical signs is to be expected and the area of consolidation runs its usual course. Some extension of the pulmonary process occurs in a small proportion of cases.

The length of stay in hospital is less in drug-treated than in control cases.

The influence of sulfapyridine on the occurrence of serofibrinous effusion and empyema as a complication is uncertain.

On the whole, the evidence suggests some reduction under chemotherapy in the proportion of cases with empyema.

Toxic Effects of Sulfapyridine

The most common toxic effect of sulfapyridine is nausea and vomiting, which are more troublesome in adults than in infants and children. In adults, anorexia and nausea are likely to be present in almost all cases. Vomiting occurs in about two-thirds of the cases and is sufficiently troublesome to interfere with the treatment in about ten per cent. Mental and physical depression and delirium occur in some cases. Cyanosis is much less often observed with sulfapyridine than with sulfanilamide. Dermatitis has occurred in rare instances.

Severe blood changes in the course of treatment of pneumonia with sulfapyridine are much less frequent than with sulfanilamide. Agranulocytosis is reported in one of 50 cases by Graham, Warner, Dauphinee and Dickson(24). The patient had been treated for 19 days with a total of 79 grams of sulfapyridine. Interruption of the drug was followed by improvement and at the time of the report the patient was making a satisfactory recovery. Agranulocytosis is reported in one of 27 Europeans in the Johannesburg series by Agranat, Dreosti and Ordman(19). Marked leucopenia developed in two of Pepper, Flippin, Schwartz and Lockwood's(28) 400 cases, but no instance of agranulocytosis was observed. One fatal case of agranulocytosis in a nineteen-year-old boy is reported by Finland, Spring, Lowell and Brown(27), but the case is not included in their series as no pneumococci were found in the sputum.

A moderate fall in hemoglobin and red count may be expected in severe cases of pneumonia in consequence of the infection. Pepper, Flippin, Schwartz and Lockwood(28) observed in several instances a drop in the red cell count of over two million with reduction in hemoglobin of as much as 40 per cent. In their series of 400 typed cases treated with sulfapyridine there was one instance of acute hemolytic anemia, with apparent recovery.

The formation of uroliths in the urinary tract of animals fed with sulfapyridine was observed by Antopol and Robinson(33) and by Gross, Cooper and Lewis(34). Gross hematuria, usually with ureteral pain, was noted in four of the 50 cases reported by Graham, Warner, Dauphinee and Dickson(24). The blood disappeared in a few days without residual damage to the kidney. Gross hematuria was noted in three of 381 cases by Pepper, Flippin, Schwartz and Lockwood(28). Southworth and Cooke(35) report three cases of hematuria, one with visible blood, under treatment with sulfapyridine. In two of the three there was severe abdominal pain and, in two, nitrogen retention due to renal insufficiency. Further information is desirable regarding the frequency and possible seriousness of this complication.

Administration of Sulfapyridine

In cases of pneumonia, in which chemotherapy is under consideration, it is desirable to obtain material with which to determine the inciting agent before the administration of the drug. The sputum should be examined by Gram's method of staining to determine the presence and number of organisms. Pneumococci should be typed by the usual procedures. Owing to the difficulty at times of making a distinction between pneumococci and streptococci by morphology and staining reaction, cultures should be made on blood agar plates and, if necessary, the organism tested for bile solubility. If no sputum is available, the inciting agent may be determined by the examination of material on a pharyngeal or laryngeal swab.

Owing to the bacteriostatic effect of chemotherapy, the growth of organisms present in the blood may be prevented and it is therefore desirable to take a blood culture as a routine before sulfapyridine is administered. In cases in which the response to drug treatment is not favorable, other blood cultures should also be taken.

In view of the possibility of toxic reactions after chemotherapy, the blood should be examined before the treatment is begun and at suitable intervals thereafter. The examination should include estimation of the hemoglobin, red and white and differential counts. The urine should also be examined before and during the treatment. Sulfapyridine should not be given in the presence of hemolytic anemia or agranulocytosis. Other precautions are not yet fully known, but it may for the present be considered undesirable to administer the drug in the presence of jaundice or impaired liver or kidney function.

For adults, the initial dosage of sulfapyridine is two grams followed by one gram every four hours. It is desirable to continue this dosage until the temperature has been normal for thirty-six to forty-eight hours. Cessation of treatment at this time may be followed by a lighting up of the infection and it is desirable after the afebrile period to continue with one gram every six hours until resolution is well under way and to give 0.5 grams four times daily until the lungs are clear. The total amount necessary is likely to vary in different patients within rather wide limits, but in general, from 16 to 25 grams may be expected to be sufficient. With a spreading lesion or with bacteriemia, from 25 to 50 grams may be necessary.

Sulfapyridine appears to be better tolerated if the tablets are crushed and taken with water, milk or fruit juice and with 0.6 gram (10 grains) of sodium bicarbonate. With troublesome nausea and vomiting, phenobarbital or barbital may be helpful, and to prevent dehydration and maintain a balance of electrolytes, intravenous physiologic salt solution and glucose are desirable. The drug should, if possible, be continued in spite of vomiting. If a dose is vomited, it should be repeated. Though there is no evidence that cyanosis is due to the formation of sulf-hemoglobin, it is suggested that sulphur-containing drugs be avoided during the administration of sulfapyridine. Owing to the development of dermatitis following exposure to ultraviolet irradiation in a case under treatment by Hallam(36), further evidence should be obtained regarding the influence, if any, of exposure to sunlight or any form of artificial sunlight during administration of the drug.

Other than oral administration of sulfapyridine is not practical, because of the very slight solubility of the drug. The soluble sodium salt of sulfapyridine described by Marshall, Bratton and Litchfield(37) and investigated in experiments in dogs and patients with pneumonia by Marshall and Long(38), may be given intravenously. Dosage is calculated on the basis of 0.05 gm. per kilogram body weight and the drug, dispensed in sterile ampoules, is made up in a 5 per cent solution in sterile distilled water. If the solution gets outside the vein, a bad slough may result. The injection should be made slowly at the rate of 5 cc. per minute. Intravenous therapy may be used to supplement administration of sulfapyrdine by mouth, if absorption from the gastrointestinal tract is poor or the patient severely ill. If may also be used in the treatment of patients who cannot retain sulfapyridine because of vomiting. Nausea and vomiting follow intravenous as well as oral therapy, but effective blood concentrations may thus be obtained. The intravenous dose may be repeated at intervals of six to eight hours.

Gaisford, Evans and Whitelaw(39) find from an experience with over 200 injections that the sodium salt of sulfapyridine can be given intramuscularly in a 33 1/3 per cent. solution (1 gram in 3 cc.) with only slight risk of ulceration at the site of injection. The solution should be injected deeply into the gluteal muscles with as little escape along the needle tract as possible. In their experience, intramuscular is preferable to intravenous injection, being easier for general use, less likely to cause vomiting, and equally satisfactory with respect to blood concentration of the drug.

Blood Concentration

Greey, MacLaren and Lucas(40) find that in the treatment of pneumococcus infection of mice with sulfapyridine, a high percentage of survivors was obtained only when the blood concentration was kept above 10 mg. per cent for several days. In man, lower concentration may be expected to be effective, in consequence of greater natural resistance to pneumococcus infection.

The blood concentration of the drug is found to vary widely among pneumonia patients on the same schedule of dosage. Individual variation in the rate of absorption, in the rate of formation of the inactive conjugated p-acetylaminobenzenesulfamidopyridine and in the rate of excretion may be responsible for this lack of uniformity. There appears to be no definite correlation between the blood concentration and the results thus far obtained, and further evidence concerning this matter is desirable.

Relative Merits of Sulfapyridine and Antiserum

Considering only pneumococcus pneumonia, the death rate under treatment with sulfapyridine alone is lower than with specific antiserum alone. Of the various types of pneumococcus pneumonia treated with the drug, Type 1 cases only comprise a sufficient number to warrant comparison. As already noted, 233 Type 1 cases have been treated with sulfapyridine with a death rate of 5.6 per cent. By contrast, in Cole's(41) 462 Type 1 cases treated with antiserum, the death rate was 10.5 per cent, the lowest attained in any large series of cases. The data given are insufficient to compare the two series with respect to age grouping, bacteriemia, duration before treatment, alcoholism and extent of lung involvement, but it is unlikely that there are significant differences in these respects in the two series, and the results are more favorable with the drug than with antiserum. Comparison of the results in Type 1 cases with drug treatment and in the Massachusetts Series with antiserum is even more favorable to the drug, as the fatality rate in 1,451 cases treated with antiserum within the first four days of the illness was 13.3 per cent(42).

Sulfapyridine has the additional advantage that it is applicable to all types of pneumococcus infection and can be administered by mouth. Precautions in its use involve the application of relatively simple procedures and serious toxic effects are rarely observed.

Sulfapyridine and Antiserum in Pneumococcus Pneumonia

There is, thus far, little information with respect to the results in the combined use of sulfapyridine and antiserum. Plummer and Ensworth(23) treated 48 cases with 2 deaths; Pepper, Flippen, Schwartz and Lockwood(28) 12 with 2 deaths; and Cutts, Gormly and Burgess(29) 13 with 3 deaths, making a total of 73 cases with 7 deaths, or 9.5 per cent. Details regarding the cases are lacking, and the possibility cannot be excluded from the data given that in certain instances a combination of the two types of therapy was used in the more severe cases. Of the 80 cases selected for treatment with the drug and antiserum in Finland, Spring, Lowell and Brown's(27) series, 81 per cent were over the age of 40, and 34 per cent over 60. Bacteriemia was present in 40 cases, or 50 per cent. The pneumonia was due to Type 1 pneumococcus in 33, Type 2 in 17, Type 3 in 16, Type 5 in 4, Type 7 in 3, Type 8 in 3, and other specific types in 4. Of the 80 cases, 21 died, or 26 per cent. These results with combined sulfapyridine and specific antiserum are not comparable with their results in cases treated with sulfapyridine alone in which of 95 cases, 14 died, or 15 per cent. Only the milder cases were first chosen for treatment with the drug alone. The expected death rate in similar cases without specific serum or drug is estimated at from 75 to 90 per cent and with specific serum alone at 50 to 60 per cent. In the combined use of antiserum and sulfapyridine they find that the drug can be dispensed with in periods varying from 12 to 36 hours and that with probability much smaller doses of serum are needed than in cases treated without the use of the drug.

In view of the established merit of sulfapyridine in pneumococcus pneumonia and of specific antiserum in certain types of pneumococcus infection, it may be assumed that the combination of the two methods of treatment will prove more effective in certain cases than the drug alone, and it is unfortunate that there is, thus far, no series of cases available with statistically significant numbers for comparison of drug-treated cases alone with cases otherwise similar and treated with the combination of the drug and specific antiserum.

Mechanism of Recovery in Treated Cases

Though no satisfactory explanation of the therapeutic effectiveness of sulfapyridine in the treatment of pneumococcus pneumonia can be offered, an interplay of two factors may be assumed in the mastery of the invading organism; i. e., the effect of the drug, and the defenses of the host on the pneumococcus.

Regarding the effect of the drug on the pneumococcus, in vitro experiments suggest that, in the absence of leucocytes, there is an inhibition of growth or bacteriostasis and no bactericidal action. With sulfanilamide and with sulfapyridine in vitro, there is a short latent period during which no effect is produced and it seems probable that in the infected host there is first an action on the pneumococcus. This action, as suggested by MacIntosh and Whitby (43) may be due to interference with the metabolic or enzymatic activities of actively growing organisms.

The defenses of the host play a necessary part in recovery. The most significant factors are specific antibodies and free and mobile phagocytic cells. Specific antibodies in the patient's blood have an important bearing on the outcome. With them, a large proportion of patients recover and without them a large proportion die. The manner in which they act is imperfectly understood, but they may be assumed to alter the protective covering or capsule and thus prepare the organism for destruction by phagocytic cells.

Until the advent of chemotherapy, the outcome of pneumococcus pneumonia was largely dependent on the natural resistance of the patient, his power during the course of the disease to elaborate and utilize specific antibodies reinforced by the use of specific antiserum, and his capacity to withstand the ill effects of pneumococcus toxemia. The favorable results with sulfapyridine alone are to be ascribed to the combined effect of the drug and the defenses of the host. Animal experiments indicate, however, that chemotherapy is enhanced in the presence of specific antibody and the experience in man suggests that better results are to be expected in certain cases with the combined use of sulfapyridine and specific antibody.

Summary and Recommendations

Advances of great importance have been made in the development of sulfonamide derivatives for the treatment of bacterial infections and especially in the discovery of the merit of sulfanilamide and sulfapyridine in pneumonia. Of these substances, sulfapyridine is more effective and less likely to give rise to toxic effects than sulfanilamide.

There are reports on the use of sulfapyridine in the treatment of a large number of cases of pneumonia including those classed as lobar pneumonia and pneumonia without specification as to the form of the disease, and a reduction in the fatality rate from about 25 per cent to between 7 and 8 per cent may be expected.

In pneumococcus pneumonia treated with sulfapyridine, the fatality rate has been reduced from 25 to 30 per cent to between 6 and 7 per cent. The drug appears to be effective irrespective of the type of pneumococcus infection. The fatality rates in drug-treated Type 1 pneumococcus pneumonia cases is between 5 and 6 per cent as against an expected rate of about 30 per cent, and in Type 3 cases between 9 and 10 per cent as against an expected rate of about 50 per cent.

The results in the treatment of pneumococcus pneumonia with sulfapyridine alone are more favorable than with specific antiserum alone. Drug therapy earlier in the course of the disease would probably have saved a larger proportion of cases.

The combined use of sulfapyridine and antiserum in certain cases will doubtless prove more effective than either alone. The favorable results with sulfapyridine in man are to be ascribed to the combined effect of the drug and the defenses of the host, and it may be assumed that in certain drug-treated cases the production of specific antibody by the patient is not sufficient to overcome the infection and that under such circumstances the administration of specific antiserum will also be necessary.

In cases in which sulfapyridine is under consideration, it is desirable to obtain material with which to determine the inciting agent before the administration of the drug. If no sputum is available, examination may be made of material obtained on a pharyngeal or laryngeal swab. Owing to the bacteriostatic effect of sulfapyridine, the growth of organisms present in the blood may be prevented and it is, therefore, desirable to take a blood culture as a routine before the drug is administered and at suitable intervals thereafter.

In view of the established merit of sulfapyridine in pneumococcus pneumonia, it is desirable to begin treatment with the drug as soon as the diagnosis is established, provided there are no contraindications to its use. In view of the possibility of toxic reactions, the blood should be examined before the treatment is begun and at suitable intervals thereafter. This examination should include estimation of the hemoglobin, red and white and differential counts. The urine should also be examined before and during treatment. It is undesirable to administer sulfapyridine in the presence of hemolytic anemia or agranulocytosis. Of other precautions, it may for the present be considered undesirable to give the drug in the presence of jaundice or impaired liver or kidney function.

In some cases, vomiting is sufficiently severe to require discontinuance of the drug.

With pneumonia due to specific types of pneumococci in which sulfapyridine cannot be used, specific antipneumococcic serum, with due precautions in the use of alien serum, is desirable.

Specific antiserum may well be held in reserve and given, with due precautions, in cases in which chemotherapy is begun early in the disease if the pulse, respiration and temperature fail to fall essentially to normal within 24 to 36 hours. The more immediate resort to combined drug therapy and specific antiserum is desirable under such relatively unfavorable circumstances as in patients with pneumococcus pneumonia over forty years of age, in the known presence of bacteriemia, with multilobar involvement, a spreading lesion, pregnancy, or during the first week of the puerperium.

References

(1) Report of the Council on Pharmacy and Chemistry of the American Medical Association. *J. A. M. A.* 108:1340, 1937.

(2) Whitby, L. E. H.: "Chemotherapy of pneumococcal and other infections with 2-(p-aminobenzenesulfonamido) pyridine," *Lancet* 1:1210-1212, 1938.

(3) Council on Pharmacy and Chemistry: Preliminary Report of the Council. *J. A. M. A.* 112:538, 1939.

(4) Price, A. E., and Myers, G. B., "Treatment of pneumococcic pneumonia with sulfanilamide." *J. A. M. A.* 112:1021-1027, 1939.

(5) Bullowa, J. G. M., *Management of the Pneumonias.* Oxford University Press, N. Y., 1937, page 201.

(6) Heintzelman, J. H. L., Hadley, P. and Mellon, R. R.: "Use of P-aminobenzenesulphonamide in Type 3 pneumococcus pneumonia." *Am. J. M. Sc.* 193:759-763, 1937.

(7) Millett, J.: "Sulphanilamide; report of case." *New York State J. Med.* 37:1743-1744, 1937.

(8) Louis, D. J.: "Treatment of pneumonias with sulfanilamide." *Illinois M. J.* 73:422-425, 1938.

(9) Sadusk, J. F., Jr.: "Observations on sulfanilamide therapy in pneumonia and meningitis due to Type 3 pneumococci." *New England J. Med.* 219:787-790, 1938.

(10) Garrett, R. T. and Twiss, J. R.: "Treatment of pneumococcus Type 3 pneumonia with rabbit serum and sulfanilamide." *New York State J. Med.* 39:345-350, 1939.

(11) Ottenberg, R.: "Clinical experiences with sulfanilamide therapy, with special reference to toxic effects." *New York State J. Med.* 39:418-430, 1939.

(12) Finland, M. and Brown, J. W.: "Treatment of pneumococcus Type 3 pneumonia with specific serum and sulfanilamide." *New England J. Med.* 220:365-372, 1939.

(13) Telling, M. and Oliver, W. A.: "Case of massive pneumonia, Type 3, with massive collapse, treated with 2-(p-aminobenzenesulphonamido) pyridine." *Lancet* 1:1391-1393, 1938.

(14) Evans, G. M. and Gaisford, W. F.: "Treatment of pneumonia with 2-(p-aminobenzenesulphonamido) pyridine." *Lancet* 2:14-19, 1938.

(15) Christie, J. M.: Chemotherapy of Pneumonia. Correspondence, *Lancet* 2:281-282, 1938.

(16) Dyke, S. C. and Reid, G. C. K.: "Treatment of lobar pneumonia with M. & B. 693." *Lancet* 2:1157-1159, 1938.

(17) Lawrence, E. A.: "Type 3 pneumococcus pneumonia; effect of para-aminobenzenesulphonamidopyridine in treatment." *New York State J. Med.* 39:22-25, 1939.

(18) Anderson, T. F. and Dowdeswell, R. M.: "Treatment of pneumonia with M. & B. 693, with bacteriological observations." *Lancet* 1:251-254, 1939.

(19) Agranat, A. L., Dreosti, A. O., and Ordman, D.: "Treatment of pneumonia with 2-(p-aminobenzenesulphonamido) pyridine (M. & B. 693)." *Lancet* 1:309 and 380, 1939.

(20) Flippen, H. F., Lockwood, J. S., Pepper, D. S., and Schwartz, L.: "Treatment of pneumococcic pneumonia with sulfapyridine; progress report on observations in 100 cases." *J. A. M. A.* 112:529-534, 1939.

(21) Whittemore, W. L., Royster, C. L., and Riedel, P. A.: "Treatment of lobar pneumonia with sulfapyridine." *New York State J. Med.* 39:540-543, 1939.

(22) Meakins, J. C. and Hanson, F. R.: "Treatment of pneumococcic pneumonia with sulfapyridine." *Canada M. A. J.* 40:333-336, 1939.

(23) Plummer, N. and Ensworth, H.: "Preliminary report on the use of sulfapyridine in the treatment of pneumonia." *Bull. New York Acad. Med.* 15:241-248, 1939.

(24) Graham, D., Warner, W. P., Dauphinee, J. A. and Dickson, R. C.: "Treatment of pneumococcal pneumonia with Dagenan (M. & B. 693)." *Canad. M. A. J.* 40:325-332, 1939.

(25) Alsted, G.: "Type 3 pneumococcus pneumonia; effect of M. & B. 693." *Lancet* 1:869-871, 1939.

(26) Gaisford, W. F.: "Experience with M. & B. 693; Report of Societies: Meeting Medical Society of London on March 27, 1939." *Brit. M. J.* April 8, 1939; "Results of Treatment of 400 cases of lobar pneumonia with M. & B. 693." *Proc. Roy. Soc. Med.* 32: 1070-1075, July, 1939.

(27) Finland, M., Spring, W. C., Lowell, F. C. and Brown, J. W.: "Specific serotherapy and chemotherapy of the pneumococcus

pneumonias." *Ann. Int. Med.* 12:1816-1829, 1939.

(28) Pepper, D. S., Flippin, H. F., Schwartz, L., and Lockwood, J. S.: "The results of sulfapyridine therapy in 400 cases of typed pneumococcus pneumonia." *Am. J. M. Sc.* 198:22-35, 1939.

(29) Cutts, M., Gormly, C. F. and Burgess, A. M.: "The Treatment of lobar pneumonia with sulfapyridine." *New England J. Med.* 221:263-266, 1939.

(30) Bullowa, J. G. M. and Wilcox, C.: "Endemic Pneumonia." *Arch. Int. Med.* 59:394-407, 1937.

(31) Rosenthal, S. M.: "Studies in chemotherapy; Chemotherapy of experimental pneumococcus infections." *Pub. Health Rep.* 52:48-53, 1937.

(32) Maclean, I. H., Rogers, K. B., and Fleming, A.: "M. & B. 693 and pneumococci." *Lancet* 1:562, March 11, 1939.

(33) Antopol, Wm. and Robinson, H.: "Urolithiasis and renal pathology after oral administration of 2-sulfanilylaminopyridine (sulfapyridine)." *Proc. Soc. Exper. Biol. and Med.* 40:428-430, 1939.

(34) Gross, P., Cooper, F.B., and Lewis, M.: "Urinary concretions caused by sulfapyridine." *Proc. Soc. Exper. Biol. and Med.* 40:448-449, 1939.

(35) Southworth, H. and Cooke, C.: "Hematuria, abdominal pain and nitrogen retention associated with sulfapyridine." *J.A.M.A.* 112:1820-1821, 1939.

(36) Hallam, R.: "Severe skin and general reaction following administration of sulfapyridine and exposure to ultraviolet light." *Brit. M.J.* 1:559, 1939.

(37) Marshall, E. K., Jr., Bratton, A. C. and Litchfield, J. T., Jr.: "Toxicity and absorption of 2-sulfanilamidopyridine and its soluble sodium salt." *Science* 88:597-599, 1938.

(38) Marshall, E.K., Jr., and Long, P.H.: "The intravenous use of sodium sulfapyridine." *J.A.M.A.* 112:1671-1675, 1939.

(39) Gaisford, W.F., Evans, G.M., and Whitelaw, W.: "Parenteral Therapy with M. & B. 693 soluble." *Lancet* 2: 69, July 8, 1939.

(40) Greey, P.H., Maclaren, D.B. and Lucas, C.C.: "Comparative chemotherapy in experimental pneumococcal infections." *Canad. M.A.J.* 40:319-324, 1939.

(41) Cole, R.: "Treatment of Pneumonia." Ann. Int. Med. 10:1-12, 1936.

(42) Boston Health League Letter: "Specific treatment for pneumococcus pneumonia." *New England J. Med.* 219:932-933, 1938.

(43) MacIntosh, J. and Whitby, L.E.H.: "Mode of action of drugs of sulphonamide group." *Lancet* 1:431-435, 1939.

THE USE OF SPECIFIC SERUMS IN THE TREATMENT OF PNEUMONIAS ASSOCIATED WITH PNEUMOCOCCI OF THE "HIGHER TYPES"

By MAXWELL FINLAND, M.D.

Associate in Medicine, Harvard Medical School
Assistant Physician, Thorndike Memorial Laboratory
Assistant Visiting Physician, Boston City Hospital

The problem of the specific treatment of pneumonias due to the less frequent or "higher" types of pneumococci is a difficult one to discuss with any degree of finality at the present time. This can be easily appreciated when one considers that it took more than a quarter of a century to persuade any large body of physicians to use specific serums in cases of Type 1 pneumonia, in spite of the facts that this organism caused 30 per cent of all cases of primary lobar pneumonia and that an overwhelming body of experimental and clinical evidence supported the therapeutic efficacy of antipneumococcal serum in pneumonia due to this type.

It is best to consider the most frequent of the "higher" types, namely Types 5, 7 and 8, separately. Each of these is sufficiently prevalent so that significant numbers of cases may be accumulated within a reasonable time, enough to indicate the efficacy of any therapy. The data thus far available, both at the Boston City Hospital and elsewhere, already indicate the general character of the results attainable and the difficulties that may be expected. First of all, pneumonias due to the "higher" types may be quite atypical both in their symptomatology and in the character of the pulmonary lesions produced. This is in sharp contrast to Types 1 and 2, which are associated, except in rare cases, with typical lobar pneumonias. Thus a small percentage of cases of Type 5 pneumonia are atypical, but among those due to Types 7 and 8, particularly the latter, the disease may be atypical in a considerable proportion of cases.

The experience of all observers who have treated any appreciable number of cases of Type 5 pneumonia has been uniformly favorable. In most clinics, including the Boston City Hospital, the results as judged by the reduction in mortality and the occurrence of rapid clinical improvement have been comparable with or even better than those obtained in Type 1 cases. Experiences with Type 7 and Type 8 cases, on the other hand, have varied widely; most of them have been favorable, and the mortality in specifically treated cases has been lower than that of non-serum-treated cases. One may also include Type 14 pneumonia in infants and young children among those which have given favorable results in clinics where serum has been used extensively.

There are many fundamental reasons underlying the differences in result, and these are in no way different from the circumstances previously encountered in Type 1 and Type 2 cases. Most vital, perhaps, is the lack of adequate experience; that is, the number of cases of the "higher" types in any one observer's experience is too small to make it possible to sift out the necessary important factors, particularly if the data in individual cases are incomplete. Moreover, experience with the production and standardization of these serums, and as a consequence the opportunities for obtaining accurate criteria concerning dosage are extremely meager.

In dealing with pneumococci of the "higher" types, the difficulties of forming sound opinions multiply enormously. There is great variability among these types with respect to their pathogenicity for man. Very diverse clinical pictures result when they produce pulmonary infections. It is frequently difficult to distinguish in any given patient the type of pneumococcus which is the causative agent in the disease from those which may be habitual or transient residents in the respiratory tract without causative relation to the infection. With a number of these types even material obtained from lung taps, as employed in some clinics, is seldom helpful, since negative results are the rule. Such material is a help in picking out some of the commoner types occasionally missed in the typing of sputum. These and the many unknown factors concerning the serums all contribute to the complexity of the problem. Perhaps the only redeeming feature in this respect has been the recent introduction of the use of rabbit serums, which are making available potent antibodies against most of the types. These products and the development of methods for their standardization may help to solve some of the problems.

What should be our present attitude? In the first place, every effort should be made to acquire the necessary basic information with regard to the frequency of the various types in pneumonia, the bacteriemic incidence, the death rates among the various types of pneumonia and the occurrence of the same types of pneumococcus in the respiratory tract under other conditions. For this purpose the present resources may be utilized with only minor expansion. Our state laboratory and several other clinical and bacteriological laboratories are equipped to carry out complete typing of all pneumococci. It is highly desirable that all, or at least most, laboratories offering typing service be equipped to do likewise. The benefits from such a system accrue to all cases, particularly those actually caused by the more frequent and so-called "treatble" types. Errors, and particularly failures, in typing are much less likely to occur if it is required to ascertain the type of pneumococcus in a positive manner, rather than to report negative results when characteristic pneumococci are seen in a specimen and no reaction occurs with the four or five serums at hand. The work and expense entailed may be somewhat more than doubled (group serums are used first, and then the types within the positive group), but this is more than offset by the satisfaction of obtaining positive results on which to base a plan of action. To be sure, one may decide only to obtain another specimen and determine whether the "higher" type predominates, or whether another type is also present which can be identified. Frequently one of the commoner types is found, and may even predominate in the second specimen, particularly if better sputum is available. If this is the case, specific treatment is directed against the frequent type, since it is much more likely to be the causative organism.

The same argument applies, but with considerably greater force, to the advisability of using mouse inoculation* to supplement direct typing whenever adequate numbers of pneumococci of the commoner types are not seen with the latter method. Examination of the peritoneal exudate of the mouse by the Neufeld method from three to six hours after the inoculation of such sputum or of the early growth from a throat culture will yield a homogeneous suspension of pneumococci with little extraneous material; this considerably diminishes the chances for errors and omissions.

Positive results of blood cultures are of the greatest help. Physicians have been repeatedly and urgently recommended to take frequent blood cultures during the acute stage of pneumonia. The results of such cultures are the best available guides to proper diagnosis and prognosis and the conduct of serum therapy, and serve as the best safeguard for the interpretation of the results of the typing of sputum. In any patient with pneumonia, the discovery in the blood culture of a growth of pneumococci which are identified with any of the "higher" types is the best available indication for specific treatment, provided serum for that type can be obtained. The probable mortality in bacteremic cases is extremely high without serum, and specific antibody offers perhaps the best hope of obtaining a cure.

In cases with sterile blood cultures, or before the results are available, it is best to consider all the facts at hand. The severity of the disease, the age of the patient, the character of the material from which the sputum was obtained, the number of organisms of that type seen and the relative number and character of other organisms present (as seen in the Neufeld preparation and in a Gram stained smear) will all influence the decision. If an infrequent type, or a common mouth inhabitant, such as Type 3 or Type 6, is obtained in small numbers from a poor specimen, or if other organisms predominate, it is best to obtain a second and better specimen in order to ascertain the relative numbers of the pneumococcus in question. At times, if part of the same specimen is sent to a second laboratory, it may be discovered that a common type was missed owing to errors in technic or interpretation or to deterioration of the typing serum. In acutely sick patients with good sputum raised from the bronchi, particularly if it is rusty, the discovery of a given type as the only or definitely predominating organism is adequate indication for specific serum, and its proper employment will probably increase the chances of rapid recovery.

Further experience may reveal that certain of the types are more regularly and intimately related to pneumonia than are others. Already it appears that a greater proportion of Types 4, 12 and 18 pneumococci, for example, are causative agents in pneumonia than are those of Types 6, 10, 20 and types "higher" than Type 20. This is only relatively true, however, since probably every type may cause severe and even fatal

---

*The Massachusetts Department of Public Health is requiring laboratories approved for typing pneumococci to use either mouse inoculation or a satisfactory culture method to supplement direct Neufeld typing.

pneumonia under the proper circumstances or in a particular individual. What has been said refers to the employment of specific serums. As for the use of the newer chemotherapeutic agents, their field of usefulness has not been thoroughly explored. There are so many difficulties and even dangers associated with their use, and the data concerning the exact limits of their value are so inadequate, that one is justified in refraining from utilizing them in cases of pneumonia except under ideally controlled conditions. Exact clinical and bacteriological studies, including blood cultures, and the complete typing of pneumococci and even cultures of sputums, should be made in order to be able to define the merit of such agents or to detect the conditions under which they fail, and in order to be prepared to cope with such conditions. Such data, obtained at the earliest moment, will place the physician in a position to use specific serum as soon as it becomes apparent that the patient is not responding to or cannot tolerate the chemotherapeutic agent.

PNEUMOCOCCAL MENINGITIS AND ITS TREATMENT

By MAXWELL FINLAND, M.D.

Associate in Medicine, Harvard Medical School;
Assistant Physician, Thorndike Memorial Laboratory;
Assistant Visiting Physician, Boston City Hospital.

While not a very common disease, pneumococcal meningitis occurs frequently enough in certain types of medical and surgical practice to be quite disturbing, particularly since it is considered to be almost universally fatal. In untreated cases, or in cases treated by most of the methods recommended, the course of this disease is fulminating and death usually occurs two to five days after the appearance of the first symptom. Individual reports of recoveries from this disease have appeared in the literature from time to time, but the vast majority of these cases lack adequate bacteriological data to warrant their inclusion in this etiological category without reservations. Furthermore, it is difficult to judge the case fatality rate in this disease since most writers have limited their reports to the particular case at hand and have usually mentioned only that all previous cases have been fatal. The largest recent authentic individual experience is that from the Meningitis Division of the Bureau of Laboratories of the New York City Department of Health in which no recoveries occurred in over 250 cases observed over a number of years prior to 1936. At the Boston City Hospital, there were no recoveries among 125 consecutive cases of typed pneumococcus meningitis in the eight years prior to October, 1937, and at the Children's Hospital in Boston only one recovered among 74 cases occurring before this year.

Among the recovered cases reported prior to the last few months, the treatment most commonly used included frequent or forced drainage through the lumbar or the combined lumbar and cisternal routes supplemented by either specific antipneumococcic serums or by drugs, notably optochin derivatives, or by combinations of serums and drugs given intravenously, intraspinally, or by both routes. Occasional recoveries have occurred spontaneously or after drainage carried out in various ways. In many of the cases recovery occurred only after the surgical drainage or eradication of foci of infection in the mastoids, accessory sinuses, or brain abscesses. Since the introduction of sulfanilamide, reports of recoveries have been more frequent. Some of the recent recoveries have followed the use of this drug or of sulfapyridine alone, and in others they followed the use of combinations of these drugs and specific serum given in various ways. The response to treatment in some of the recent cases has been very dramatic. At the Boston City Hospital, prior to July, 1938, sulfanilamide alone was used in the treatment of 18 cases of meningitis due to pneumococci of specific types, and various combinations of specific antibody and sulfanilamide were used in six cases, with recoveries in two of the former and four of the latter. Since that time there have been three more recoveries and eight deaths with the combined treatment, some of these deaths occurring under the most unfavorable circumstances. In the last six of these cases, including one who recovered, sulfapyridine was used instead of sulfanilamide. Six other patients treated with sulfapyridine alone all died.

Materials are now available which, when properly used, offer the prospect of a higher percentage of recoveries than has ever before been attained in this disease. It is important, therefore, that physicians become familiar with the clinical features of this disease, the conditions under which it may arise, the methods of establishing the diagnosis rapidly and accurately, and the application of the available therapeutic measures to the greatest advantage.

Predisposing Factors.

The disease occurs at all ages but is most frequent before adult life, about 60 per cent of the cases being under 20 years of age. The commonest predisposing factors in the order of their frequency are: (1) otitis media, mastoiditis, and nasal sinusitis; (2) pneumonia, usually with other focal complications, notably empyema and endocarditis; (3) injuries or operations on the head, particularly those involving the mastoid cells, the nasal sinuses, and the cribriform plate; and (4) other acute respiratory infections. In a considerable number of cases, the disease appears to be "primary" inasmuch as no other focus of pneumococcal infection is discoverable clinically or at autopsy.

Relative Importance of the Pneumococcus as a Cause of Acute Purulent Meningitis.

This is best shown in Table 1, which lists the results of a large experience reported from New York City and from the Children's Hospital in Boston.

Table I. — Causes of Meningitis

	New York City	Children's Hospital
Meningococcus	1,566	83
Streptococcus	274	50
Pneumococcus	255	61
Influenza bacillus	164	76
Tubercle bacillus	1,010	91
Miscellaneous organisms	233	44
Total	3,502	405

Meningitis due to the tubercle bacillus can be easily differentiated by its less fulminating course, and particularly by the character of the cells found in the cerebrospinal fluid, which are predominately or entirely lymphocytes, in contrast to the almost pure polymorphonuclear response in meningitis due to pyogenic organisms. Meningococcus meningitis may occur in epidemic form, which explains its high incidence in the figures from New York City. In endemic periods, its incidence is not far in excess of the other common organisms, as shown in the Children's Hospital figures. In such periods pneumococci, streptococci and, in infants and children, influenza bacilli are the other common causes of acute purulent meningitis, and all occur with about the same frequency.

Types of Pneumococci Causing Meningitis.

Almost every one of the known specific Types, 1 to 32, have been found in cases of pneumococcal meningitis. The most frequent types among the cases complicating pneumonia are the same as those most frequently found in the latter disease; viz., Types 1, 2, 3, 5, 7, and 8, although they vary in their relative frequency. Type 3 is by far the most common in cases complicating otitis media and mastoiditis.

Clinical Features.

In otorhinological cases, and in cases with head injuries, the symptoms may appear early or late or, in some instances, only after surgical intervention. In pneumonia, meningitis occurs usually as a late complication in bacteremic cases, often accompanies other focal purulent complications, such as empyema or pericarditis, and, when the course is protracted, may be the terminal feature following the development of vegetative endocarditis. In certain cases with empyema the meningitis may develop even as long as several weeks after surgical drainage has been established. During the early stages of pneumonia it is uncommon, but simulating symptoms (meningismus) may be manifested, particularly in children.

The most frequent symptoms are: continuous and severe headache, fever, retraction of the head, delirium, vomiting, and later convulsions and coma. The classical signs are the stiff neck, positive Kernig's sign, fever, and relatively slow pulse. Later on, various neurological signs and symptoms may be manifested. The course in untreated cases is usually fulminating, with deepening coma, the development of very high fever, and death in two to five days.

Diagnosis.

The diagnosis depends on the identification of pneumococci in purulent cerebrospinal fluid. It is necessary to perform a lumbar puncture as soon as meningitis is suspected. The fluid obtained is turbid in early cases, and later becomes thick and fibrinopurulent in character. The cells are almost all polymorphonuclear leukocytes, numbering a few hundred to several thousand, and there may be a varying number of red blood cells. The protein content is very high and the sugar content very low. A fibrin clot may form on standing in the late cases. One of the important features in the cases due to pneumococci is the large number of organisms, all extracellular, which are usually recognizable with ease in a smear of the fluid made either directly or from the sediment after centrifugation at relatively high speed. A Gram stain preparation should be made, taking great care to decolorize the smear thoroughly. The organisms appear characteristically as Gram-positive diplococci, usually somewhat elongated, with lancet shaped ends. Often a small capsule can be seen and, in cases with Type 3 pneumococci, the organism may be somewhat larger, more rounded, and the typical large capsule may be visualized. Where the characteristic organisms are seen, the type of pneumococcus may be determined by direct examination of the fluid or sediment and the demonstration of the typical capsular swelling (Neufeld typing) when mixed with diagnostic rabbit serum of the proper type. If organisms cannot be seen in the direct smear or Neufeld preparations, the fluid should be inoculated into proper fluid media, preferably broth containing rabbit serum or blood, and also streaked on the surface of blood agar plates. If Gram-positive organisms are not seen, it is best to culture some of the fluid under increased carbon dioxide tension (in a candle jar) and also on chocolate agar in order to detect the presence of meningococci or influenza bacilli. Pneumococci usually will grow out luxuriantly in six to twelve hours (or sooner if present in large numbers) in proper fluid media and they can then be identified and typed. *Culture of fluids obtained during sulfanilamide or sulfapyridine therapy are often unsatisfactory since growth may be inhibited or markedly delayed. The culture and typing should be considered as an emergency measure so that specific serum therapy may be instituted as soon as possible.* In addition, *blood.cultures* should be made in every case where turbid fluid is obtained. This should be done as soon as possible *and before any specific treatment or drugs are administered.* From 3 to 10 c. c. of fluid is inoculated in 50 to 100 c. c. of broth.

The care and study of the fluid obtained at the time of first diagnostic puncture is most important for diagnosis. After various therapeutic measures are undertaken the diagnostic characteristics of the fluids may be altered materially. After the parenteral administration of glucose which is often undertaken because of vomiting, dehydration, or pulmonary edema, the sugar content of the spinal fluid may be deceivingly high. This may also occur after the use of sulfanilamide alone, even while organisms are still present in large numbers in the fluid, and the growth of these organisms may be inhibited. It may be mentioned at this point that whenever turbid fluid is found under increased pressure in a case of meningitis, it is important to allow the fluid to escape very slowly, but it is equally important to remove as much fluid as possible, taking as much time as may be necessary to do this. If the flow stops, abdominal or jugular compression may be applied before withdrawing the needle, or if the fluid is thick and there is likelihood of the needle being plugged, the gentlest suction may be applied or a small amount of saline may be introduced and then gently withdrawn through the syringe. However, suction should not be used to hasten removal of fluid or to remove fluid that is under decreased pressure. These procedures may often yield a large amount of fluid without ill effects and often increase the period of symptomatic relief obtained from the tap. It should always be possible to obtain an ample supply of fluid the first time, even in small infants, to carry out all the necessary tests unless the patient is excessively dehydrated.

At the present time it is no longer necessary, indeed it is unwise, to adhere to the principle that antimeningococcus serum should be available when a lumbar puncture is done in a case suspected of meningitis and the serum given as soon as turbid fluid is obtained. The prompt and proper use of sulfanilamide or sulfapyridine permits a delay, even in cases due to meningococcus, until the etiological diagnosis is established by proper smears or culture. The intrathecal use of antimeningococcus serum in cases due to other organisms may prove definitely harmful. On the other hand, the use of the drugs is not contraindicated but may be beneficial in all cases with turbid fluid except, perhaps, in cases of tuberculous meningitis. Their efficacy in the treatment of cases due to streptococci and meningococci is already fairly well established and in cases due to pneumococci they are highly essential for the most successful therapy, even when specific serum is used.

Principles Involved in the Treatment of Pneumococcal Meningitis.

It is now known that sulfanilamide, in amounts used in human therapy, exerts a powerful bacteriostatic effect on the pneumococcus. Sulfapyridine is also bacteriostatic even in low concentrations, and greater concentrations are also bactericidal for most strains and types of pneumococci. This is evidenced by the decrease in the numbers of bacteria and corresponding increase in the sugar content of the cerebrospinal fluid after the use of these drugs. They are not equally effective against all types of pneumococci and may not influence all strains of the same type to the same degree. The complete destruction of pneumococci in the living host usually requires phagocytosis and intracellular digestion of the organisms, and for that purpose it is essential to have type-specific antibodies. Such antibodies are often present in the blood of cases of meningitis and presumably it is only under such conditions that patients recover when they are treated with sulfanilamide alone, unless one is fortunate enough to maintain adequate bacteriostatic action for a long enough period to permit the patient to develop his own antibodies. In most cases, however, it is necessary to administer the type-specific antibodies in order to produce the desired effect. Another factor usually missing in the spinal fluid and which may be necessary in addition to antibodies to obtain complete sterilization of the cerebrospinal fluid is complement — a heat-labile factor which can be readily obtained from fresh normal human serum and is almost always present in the circulating blood of the patient except, perhaps, late in the disease if the blood is heavily invaded. Sulfapyridine alone may be effective in destroying pneumococci, but its action is considerably enhanced by the additional use of homologous antibodies.

Practical Aspects of the Treatment Recommended.

1. It is essential that the management of the case be centered in the hands of a single individual who should bear in mind the objectives to be attained, keep informed immediately of the results of all procedures carried out, follow the clinical course, and direct all the therapy.

2. Frequent and complete drainage is done by the lumbar route, as noted above, or by the cisternal route if necessary. Fluid should be withdrawn about every six or eight hours while the pressure remains elevated and the fluid is still turbid. The interval between punctures is lengthened gradually as the pressure and the cellular content drops but only after sterile fluids have been obtained. It is advisable to use progressive lumbar interspaces for successive taps so as to minimize the local trauma, and for the same reason, adequate assistance should be available to keep the patient from moving excessively during the tap. Mild sedation may be used in hyperirritable patients. It is important to examine fluids frequently (at least once a day at first) for the cellular content and preferably also for chemistry, including the concentration of the drug being used.

3. Adequate fluids should be given (3,000 to 4,000 cc. daily for the average adult) so as to maintain a free flow of cerebrospinal fluid but not sufficient to cause excessive elimination of the chemical being administered. This is given by mouth or stomach tube, or normal saline is given by slow, constant, intravenous drip. It is usually necessary, at first, to use the latter method and give 1,000 to 2,000 cc. of fluid containing 5 or 10 per cent glucose in the saline when the patient is dehydrated due to vomiting.

4. Treatment with sulfapyridine or sulfanilamide should be started immediately after the turbid fluid is obtained. If the patient has been vomiting, sulfanilamide should be used and the first few doses may be

given subcutaneously in an 0.8 per cent solution in physiological saline. It should be allowed to go in by gravity, under low pressure, taking from one to two hours to administer each dose. This first dose may contain about 500 cc. (4 grams) and later doses, given at five- to eight-hour intervals, containing 250 to 400 cc. (2 to 3.2 grams). Sodium lactate (one-sixth molar) should be given with the saline in the injections if it is not possible for the patient to retain bicarbonate of soda by oral administration or through the stomach tube. If the sodium salt of sulfapyridine is available, this may be used to begin sulfapryidine therapy. Four or five grams of this compound may be injected *intravenously*, either in 5 per cent solution with a syringe or diluted to one per cent in physiological saline and given intravenously by a slow drip. This material is very alkaline and extravasation may result in bad sloughs. As soon as possible, the oral or stomach tube route should be started and nourishing fluids as well as the drug given in that way. Absorption from the oral route may vary widely and the dosage will have to be adjusted by measuring the concentration attained in the spinal fluid. In general, it is desirable to have a level of 5 mgm. or more of sulfapyridine or 10 mgm. per 100 cc. of spinal fluid or higher if sulfanilamide is used. In some cases recoveries have taken place when the only recorded levels for sulfanilamide were from 5 to 7 mgm. per 100 cc. or when sulfapyridine levels were 3 mgm. per 100 cc. of blood or spinal fluid. There is reason to believe that levels as high as 20 mgm. per cent of sulfanilamide are sometimes necessary, at least for short periods. It is usually sufficient, after the large initial dose of 4 grams, to give from 1 to 2 grams of sulfanilamide, or 1 gram of sulfapyridine, every four hours during the period of active infection in the average adult. It is probably essential for the optimum effect to give these drugs at regular intervals so that no more than four or five hours elapse between doses. The dosage is best controlled by frequent determinations of the concentration of the drug in the spinal fluid, and adjustments made or the route altered according to the results of these determinations. The dose may be diminished gradually after sterile fluids have been reported and the spinal fluid cell count has dropped to a low level (2 to 400) and lymphocytes begin to appear in the fluid. It may be discontinued after a week or ten days of sterile fluids. Bicarbonate of soda in about half the amounts of the drug are given with each oral dose of sulfanilamide. This is not necessary with sulfapyridine, although its use is said to reduce the chances of renal irritation. Any dose that is vomited is repeated within an hour, or an equivalent amount is given subcutaneously if sulfanilamide is used. Unless it is not feasible to use other routes, it is probably not desirable to use the drugs intravenously because of the greater danger of toxic effects and because of the more rapid excretion when given by this route. It is to be borne in mind that fever is likely to persist as long as the drug is being given and this symptom alone cannot, therefore, be used as a guide for continuing its use. Persistent negative cultures, constant reduction in cell content, maintenance of high sugar level, and the appearance and increase in relative proportion of lymphocytes in the spinal fluid are better guides for discontinuing the use of the drug.

Many writers have used prontosil subcutaneously and intrathecally and others have recently advocated the use of similar material in capsules by mouth. Thus far there has been no convincing evidence to indicate any advantage of the intrathecal route while many have advised against its use. Likewise most writers have preferred to use sulfanilamide mainly because it is far less expensive, its properties are better understood, and its action may be superior in some respects. Sulfapyridin is probably preferable to sulfanilamide on experimental grounds and should be the drug of choice. Practically, while its superiority in the treatment of pneumonia is beyond question, the same has not been proved decisively with respect to meningitis. When sterilization of the spinal fluid does not occur in three or four days, it may be advantageous to change over to the use of sulfanilamide.

5. Specific antipneumococcus horse or rabbit serum is given intravenously as soon as the type is determined unless it can be shown that the antibodies for the infecting organisms are already present in the blood. When there are numerous organisms visible in the smear of the spinal fluid, they can be used directly to test for the presence of antibodies by merely mixing thoroughly a loopful of the fluid or sediment with a drop of the patient's serum on a microscopic slide, and staining the preparation. If the organisms clump (agglutinate) in regular patterns with typical surroundings precipitate, it may be inferred that adequate antibodies are present. The same procedure may be carried out with the growth from the spinal fluid in the liquid media or from growth in the blood culture when that is positive. In cases where the blood culture is positive, antibodies will not be found before serum treatment, except in cases with vegetable endocarditis.

If antibodies are not found, then the type-specific serum should be given with the usual precautions and in a manner similar to that used in the treatment of cases of pneumonia. The total amount given at first is such as to insure an adequate balance of antibodies. Usually 200,000 or 300,000 units in divided doses are sufficient, but larger amounts may be needed if the blood culture is positive. Since most of the cases will be of higher types and the effective dose is not known, it is best to test for the presence of agglutinins in the manner already indicated. If rabbit serums are used, the patient's serum may be tested for its ability to cause capsular swelling of freshly grown or heat-killed organisms. The method is the same as that used in typing. For that purpose it is wise to save a small amount of a culture of the spinal fluid after exposing it to 80° C. for one-half an hour so as to kill the organisms and prevent their autolysis.

6. Since the antibody probably does not readily penetrate in sufficient amounts into the subarachnoid space and since complement cannot usually be demonstrated in the spinal fluid it may be necessary to introduce small amounts of both intraspinally in order to provide the necessary components to enable the cells to phagocytize and destroy the bacteria still present. This is done only after sulfanilamide and the intraven-

ous antibody have already been given, usually after the completion of the second or third lumbar drainage. The combination of antibody and complement may be obtained by separating the serum from about 20 cc. of venous blood drawn from the patient just before the lumbar drainage, or 0.5 to 1.0 cc. of therapeutic serum is added to freshly separated serum from about 20 cc. of normal human blood, and the mixture injected slowly into the spinal canal or into the cistern. It may be helpful to raise the foot of the bed after the serum has been introduced intraspinally. The whole procedure may be repeated after each subsequent drainage, but in the successful cases it has not been found necessary to give more than two or three intraspinal injections. The cisternal route has been found preferable in some cases where the first fluid obtained during lumbar drainage is sterile while that obtained at the end of the procedure shows growth. Some writers have felt that this entire procedure is superfluous. Others feel that antipneumococcus rabbit serum should be injected directly without additional complement. We have reason to believe from our experience to date, that the method recommended is the preferable one.

7. The two dangerous untoward reactions from both sulfanilamide and sulfapyridine are hemolytic anemia and agranulocytosis. Every patient receiving these drugs, therefore, should have complete blood counts done every day or two and suitable donors should be "matched up" and ready to give blood for transfusions if necessary. Slowly but constantly progressing anemia occurs, however, in almost every patient receiving these drugs over a period of a week or longer. It is best to give transfusions beginning the fourth or fifth day of treatment. It has been found satisfactory to take 500 to 600 cc. of blood in citrate from the donor and give this in two or three installments twenty-four hours apart, giving it in a slow intravenous drip. In young children, of course, smaller amounts are used. The procedure is repeated after a three- to five-day interval. In certain septic cases, transfusion may be used to advantage on the first or second day of treatment as a general supportive measure. When sulfapyridine is used, the urine should be watched for the appearance of hematuria and the blood analyzed to detect nitrogen retention. If found, this drug should be discontinued or its dose reduced—or sulfanilamide may be substituted and the fluid intake temporarily increased and supplemented by intravenous injections of physiological saline. The appearance of a drug rash also indicates either discontinuing the drug, if the spinal fluid has already been sterile for a few days, or changing over to another drug.

8. The proper surgical treatment of infected mastoids, sinuses, brain abscesses, or other foci of infection is essential. Most workers are agreed that no lasting improvement can be expected, as a rule, until this is done. The surgical aspects are outside the province of this paper, but there can be little doubt that the success in some of the recovered cases reported from the Boston City Hospital was due, in large measure, to the thorough and skillful handling of those cases by the neurological and otological surgeons.

Failures are to be expected, but that is natural in such a disease. In persons in whom thick fibrinous exudate has already accumulated at the base of the brain, in those with thromboses or hemorrhages from cerebral vessels, or where osteomyelitis of the cranial bones or other foci of infection persist and remain unrecognized, in cases of endocarditis and in others, particularly infants and aged individuals, who are already in too poor general condition to tolerate vigorous treatment, the treatment outlined is not likely to meet with frequent success. No doubt the skill in carrying out the measures outlined, the meticulous and intelligent handling of the general supportive and symptomatic measures, the proper use of stimulants and sedatives, and the quality of the nursing care, all contribute and may spell the difference between success and failure in a large majority of the cases. One unfortunate aspect of many of the failures has been the prolonged period during which those patients in whom only bacteriostasis is attained have survived with marked improvement in their general and mental condition, only to die after two to six weeks with overwhelming infection. In our experience, all the cases who failed to respond by sterilization of the spinal fluid after the treatment outlined had been carried out for two or three days eventually died in spite of persistent treatment.

Most of the aspects of the treatment outlined are still relatively new and much remains to be learned. Many new drugs are being studied by various workers which may prove more efficacious. In the meantime, it is best to use the available agents with due consideration for their possible toxic effects.

PNEUMOCOCCUS PNEUMONIA IN INFANTS AND CHILDREN

By JOHN A. V. DAVIES, M.D.

Associate in Pediatrics, Harvard Medical School
Staff Bacteriologist, Infants' and Children's Hospitals

and

EDWARD C. CURNEN, M.D.

Assistant in Pediatrics, Harvard Medical School
Resident in Pediatrics, Infants' and Children's Hospitals

Ample evidence is now at hand to show that pneumococcus pneumonia in infants and children, although not so highly fatal as in adults, may be a severe, prolonged, and often disabling disease. Complications, such as otitis media, mastoiditis, empyema, pericarditis, peritonitis, and meningitis, are common and reflect the widespread invasion by the organism in the course of the disease.

During the first two or three years of life, pneumonia is usually the sequel of a common cold. In these young patients the onset of pneumonia is characterized by a rise in fever, a more prostrated, pallid or flushed appearance, cough, and the development of grunting respirations with dilatation of the alae nasi. Vomiting, abdominal pain, or convulsions may occur at this time. In older children the onset may be accompanied by a shaking chill. Rusty or bloody sputum is practically never seen. Physical signs in the child may be equivocal at first, the earliest and most important to appear being usually suppression of breath sounds over the affected area.

Types of Pneumococci

Studies in various clinics during the past few years have revealed that the distribution of types of pneumococci in infants and children is not identical in frequency or significance with that of adults. In consequence, new importance has been attached to certain of the so-called "higher types" (4 to 32) formerly classified as a heterogeneous "Group IV" and regarded from earlier observations in adults as relatively unimportant. In this region, for example, Types 14, 1, 6, 19, 9, 5, 4, 3, 7, and 8, in about that order, are the ones most commonly found in the throats of infants and children. Type 14 is fairly closely associated with infancy, its incidence and pathogenicity appearing to fall off sharply after the third year. It carries a relatively high case fatality rate. Type 1 occurs infrequently in infants, but in children over three, as in adults, it assumes the predominating role. While the case fatality rate of Type 1 in children is relatively low, this type often produces bacteriemia and is the organism of highest incidence causing pneumonia. These two most frequent types, when found in the throats of infants and children, are usually significant of active or recent infection of the host by these organisms. In one hospital series, about one-fifth of the infants with Type 14 pneumonia died and about one-fifth of the Type 1 patients developed empyema.

Type 6, like Type 14, a rare cause of pneumonia in adults, is the third most frequent pneumococcus occurring during pneumonia in infants and children. Unlike Type 14, however, which when found in the presence of pneumonia is usually considered the responsible agent, Type 6 may merely be present as an apparently innocuous inhabitant of the upper respiratory passages, although it can, on occasion, cause severe pneumonia and fatal complications. A characteristic of Type 6 is its frequent association with other more or less invasive types, so that its relative importance is sometimes difficult to evaluate. Type 19 and Type 9 are similar to Type 6 in the latter respect, although they occur less frequently. Type 3 occurs quite often in infections of the sinuses, middle ears, mastoids, and meninges, even in the absence of pneumonia. Type 5 is likely to produce purulent complications, especially empyema. Type 2, so frequent in adults, is a rare but serious etiologic agent of pneumonia in infants and children.

Recognition of the relationship of these higher types of pneumococci to the pneumonia of infants and children has led to the development of corresponding antipneumococcic sera. Growing experience has shown them to be of definite therapeutic value, especially when employed early in the disease. With the recent development of sulfapyridine another effective means of treating pneumonia due to the pneumococcus has been provided.

Neufeld Typing and Cultures

In order to obtain the optimum benefit from specific therapy, whether serum or sulfapyridine, prompt clinical diagnosis and accurate determinations of the pathogenic organism or organisms associated with the disease are important. Various methods have been employed for obtaining material for culture and pneumococcus typing from infants and children. Nasal swabs and washings; lung punctures, aspirated stomach contents, and laryngeal swabs obtained through a laryngoscope have been advocated. One of the simplest and most effective techniques is to obtain sputum in the form of mucoid material caught on a throat swab from the posterior pharynx as the child's tongue is depressed and he is made to gag or cough. If at the bedside the swab is immediately placed in a suitable medium, such as ascitic fluid or rabbit blood broth, and the specimen brought promptly to a typing laboratory, good growth of any pneumococci present is usually obtained after four to six hours' incubation, and from this the type can be identified by the Neufeld method.

When typing is carefully done, more than one type of pneumococcus is often found in the throat of the same patient. One clinic found 30 per cent of the infants and over 40 per cent of the children sick with pneumococcus pneumonia had from two to six types of pneumococci in their throats. The occurrence of more than one type of pneumococcus in the same patient may render the choice of a specific antiserum difficult.

Inasmuch as other organisms besides pneumococci may, alone or with pneumococci, cause pneumonia, it is important to inoculate a blood agar plate with the same or a similar "deep throat swab." The hemolytic streptococcus, B. influenzae, or staphylococcus aureus, for example, may each impose its characteristic features on the disease process and influence the plan of therapy.

Sources of organisms other than the throat, nose, or sputum may indicate which organism has actually invaded. Thus, though blood cultures are probably less frequently positive in infants and children than in adults, they may on occasion contribute valuable information. Empyema pus usually yields the organism responsible for the pneumonia. A pneumococcus obtained from aural discharge may, however, represent merely an invader of the upper respiratory passages.

General Treatment

In the treatment of pneumonia of infants and children due to the pneumococcus, ample rest, suitable diet, fluid and vitamin intake, proper nursing care, use of oxygen and discreet administration of sedatives are procedures of fundamental importance. In the presence of anemia the patient may derive benefit from a blood transfusion. From the standpoint of prevention, it is well to point out that pneumococcus pneumonia is a contagious disease, as many studies of family and institutional epidemics have shown. Too much attention cannot be paid towards protecting the sick child from other members of the family, especially from adults who may carry pneumococci harmless to themselves but dangerous to the susceptible patient. In the home as well as in hospitals strenuous efforts are justified to avoid cross infections not only from patient to patient but also from attendant to patient and the reverse.

Specific Treatment

Specific therapy of pneumococcus pneumonia in infants and children advanced on a broad front with the relatively recent development of antipnuemococcic rabbit sera against many of the more important higher types (4 to 32). The advent of sulfapyridine in 1938, however, seems to have relegated antipneumococcic serum to a less important role, which further experience may show to be limited to its use in conjunction with the new drug or to the treatment of infants and children who react unfavorably or fail to respond to it. In general, there are several cogent reasons for considering sulfapyridine the therapeutic agent of choice:

1. It is effective against all types of pneumococci, so far as present experience goes. It is also effective against hemolytic streptococci.

2. It is easily administered by mouth, without the need of intravenous injection.

3. There is no special hazard for serum-sensitive patients.

4. It obviates immediate thermal reactions and the development of serum sensitivity so common after serum therapy. It may be given repeatedly. Only a few patients, as noted below, cannot tolerate it.

5. Its effectiveness is not especially limited to the first few days after the onset of the disease.

6. It is much less expensive than serum.

Sulfapyridine is relatively insoluble and almost tasteless. If not already powdered, the drug should be crushed finely and mixed with a palatable semisolid food, such as applesauce. An effective dose for infants is usually one-half grain per pound as an initial dose, followed by one and one-half grains per pound per day, divided into four or six doses. For children over two years of age, an initial dose of one-half grain per pound, followed by a dose of one grain per pound per day divided into four or six doses, is recommended.

Since most infants and children with uncomplicated pneumonia due to the pneumococcus respond to the above dosage within forty-eight hours with a fall of temperature to nearly normal levels, it is usually sufficient to administer the drug only three or four days. Delay in response is an urgent indication for careful search for complications, such as empyema. For the treatment of localized collections of pus within the body cavities, sulfapyridine apparently cannot take the place of surgery, and its continued use should not be allowed to mask the indications for surgical drainage.

Failure of the patient to respond favorably to a standard dose of sulfapyridine may be the result of inability of the patient to retain the drug or to inadequate or irregular absorption. A blood level of 4 to 8 mg. per cent is desirable. A laboratory equipped with a photo-electric colorimeter can easily determine the blood level by a micro-method requiring a small amount of blood obtained from a finger or toe.

Rectal administration of sulfapyridine cannot be recommended, inasmuch as the resultant blood levels are usually too low to be effective.

For intravenous use, the very soluble sodium salt of sulfapyridine, dissolved in a 2 to 5 per cent concentration in physiologic saline, is a valuable adjunct. An initial dose of one-half to one grain per pound, given slowly, is recommended. After one or two doses intravenously, the patient's condition may improve sufficiently so that one may change to ordinary sulfapyridine by mouth. Since solutions of the sodium salt are quite alkaline, they are not suitable for subcutaneous administration.

Toxic Manifestations of Sulfapyridine

As a rule, infants and children tolerate sulfapyridine remarkably well, but certain toxic manifestations of the drug should be borne in mind in any consideration of its usefulness. Of these, nausea and vomiting are by far the commonest. When severe enough to interfere with the absorption of the drug, resort may be made to the intravenous route of administration. This should not be done before determining the blood level, since the latter may be unnecessarily high (above 10 mg. per cent).

General irritability of the patient is quite common. The development of gross hematuria, anuria and hemoglobinuria, and agranulocytosis and severe anemia are definite indications for the immediate discontinuance of the drug. They occur often enough to call for an examination of the urine every day (at least for albumin and red blood cells) and of the blood every other day (at least a white blood count and hemoglobin determination) for as long as the drug is administered and for three or four days thereafter. Cyanosis due to the drug at ordinary blood levels is scarcely noteworthy and a drug rash is unusual.

It remains to be seen whether the addition of enough sodium bicarbonate by mouth to maintain the urine at an alkaline reaction will reduce the incidence of toxic reactions, such as nephritis. Most of the toxic effects of sulfapyridine clear up within a day or two after the discontinuance of the drug. When anuria is present, intravenous fluids, such as glucose and saline, should be given promptly.

Indications for Sulfapyridine

Because of these toxic hazards, the use of sulfapyridine should at present be limited to the treatment of patients with definite, well-defined pneumonia of moderate or severe degree caused by the pneumococcus or the hemolytic streptococcus. Usually it is practicable to await the results of Neufeld typing. When the urgency for treatment appears to justify the immediate employment of sulfapyridine, the clinical impression of a pneumococcus (or hemolytic streptococcus) pneumonia should be verified within twenty-four hours by Neufeld typing or sputum culture. This precaution may help clarify an otherwise puzzling therapeutic failure.

One of the most satisfying rewards of diligent care of infants and children is the speed with which they are capable of responding to well-directed treatment. In the hands of intelligent and careful physicians, general supportive measures can usually be combined with specific therapy so as to diminish the chances of complications and cut short the period of illness with extraordinary regularity.

SPECIAL PROBLEMS IN THE TYPING OF PNEUMOCOCCI FROM INFANTS AND YOUNG CHILDREN

By ARTHUR P. LONG, M.D.

Assistant Director, Division of Biologic Laboratories
Massachusetts Department of Public Health

It has been shown by a number of workers that a large proportion of the pneumococcal pneumonias in infants and young children have as their etiological agent pneumococci classifiable in the so-called "higher types." This is especially true in children under six years of age and to an even greater extent in infants under two. The types most commonly encountered in the latter age group are 14, 6, and 19. Of these, Type 14 is the most common offender and likewise the most virulent.

With the advent of specific sera for the treatment of pneumonia due to these types there has come the problem of the typing of the pneumococci causing the infection in these small patients. It should also be emphasized that chemotherapy in pneumonia does not preclude the necessity for typing. From the evidence available at present there is every reason to believe that specific therapy will continue to play an important role in the treatment of pneumonia. A specific type of pneumococcus should, therefore, be sought in all cases of suspected pneumococcal pneumonia.

This problem of typing differs from that of the typing of organisms causing pneumonia in adults chiefly in the manner of collecting a satisfactory sputum specimen from an infant, satisfactory typing in these cases demanding even greater co-operation between the physician and the technician than typing in adult cases. Further, it requires somewhat more care, equipment, and materials.

The most satisfactory method in current use for obtaining material from infants and children or others who are unable to deliver a satisfactory sputum specimen is the "gag swab" method. The materials required for this procedure are: sterile throat swabs, tongue depressors, and sterile broth in test tubes or small centrifuge tubes containing 3 to 5 cc. each. The broth used may be any nutrient broth known to support good growth of pneumococci. Two such broths are: A. alkaline (pH 7.8) beef infusion broth containing 0.5 per cent glucose and 2 to 4 per cent sterile defibrinated rabbit, horse, or sheep blood; B. alkaline (pH 7.8) beef infusion broth containing 0.1 per cent glucose and 0.5 per cent sterile rabbit serum. (Sterile ascitic fluid has also been used for this purpose with a reasonable degree of success.)

If white mice are available, their use is a helpful adjunct to the method and will, on occasion, result in the typing of a specimen which otherwise would go untyped.

The technique employed is as follows:

(1) Have an assistant stand at the head of the bed or crib and hold the patient's arms firmly alongside of his head. This serves the dual purpose of immobilizing the patient's head and keeping his hands out of the way. A tongue depressor is then inserted well back on the patient's tongue and moderate pressure is exerted downward and forward. This procedure alone will usually suffice to induce gagging, and material rising from the bronchial tree may be collected on the swab which is held in the other hand. However, if the patient does not gag, further efforts to make him do so may be made by rubbing the posterior pharyngeal wall with the swab, reaching as far down toward the larynx as possible. It is well to collect material on at least two swabs by this method, inserting them immediately into separate tubes of broth which are at hand. In placing the swabs in the broth, twirl them several times in order to distribute the material clinging to them into the broth.

If possible, material should be obtained by this method not less than one hour after the feeding of an infant. This is to prevent loss of food through vomiting as a result of the gagging induced and also to prevent the mixture and, hence, dilution of the material from the bronchial tree with stomach contents.

(2) The tubes with swabs in place are taken as quickly as possible to the laboratory and incubated 4 to 6 hours at 37-38° C. The time of incubation may be extended if growth is slight or if no pneumococci are found. However, as a general rule, pneumococci will be difficult to demonstrate after periods much in excess of eight hours due to overgrowth by other organisms and the production of an acid reaction in the medium with resultant autolysis of the pneumococci.

(3) The treatment of the culture obtained is then the same as that of any other culture in which pneumococci are suspected; i.e., the Neufeld reaction test is set up and a search made for swelling of the capsules of pneumococci in a serum homologous with the organisms present. In making the Neufeld set-up, a ratio of one small loopful of culture and two medium-sized loopfuls of serum is usually adequate. It is often advisable, however, to make a preliminary smear and Gram stain of the culture to determine the approximate numbers of organisms resembling pneumococci that are present. If they are quite infrequent, the culture may be centrifuged and the typing done using the sediment. If there appear to be somewhat more than ten to twenty per field, the culture may be diluted with broth for more satisfactory swelling reactions. It is probably unwise to discard a culture without doing a Neufeld

test if no organisms are seen that are morphologically typical of pneumococci, since certain of the types of pneumococci do not always present the so-called typical morphology by Gram stain.

(4) If no satisfactory type is determined from the culture, 0.5 to 1 cc. of the culture should be injected intraperitoneally into a white mouse and further search made in the peritoneal exudate and heart's blood from the mouse in the same fashion as in mice injected with ordinary sputum specimens.

One other method which has been described but which does not appear to be as practical and simple as the one given above is that of aspiration of stomach contents. For this purpose a 50 centimeter stomach tube 4 mm. in diameter with a 2 mm. bore, a 20 cc. Luer syringe, 10 cc. sterile normal saline solution, and a clean Petri dish are needed in addition to the broth and mice as noted above. To carry out this procedure the child should be wrapped in a mummy binder. The tube is passed into the stomach either through the mouth or the nose, and suction applied with the syringe. If material is successfully aspirated, it is expelled into 5 cc. normal saline in a Petri dish, the tube and syringe being rinsed out with another 5 cc. of saline and this added to that in the dish. The material thus obtained is examined and any fleck of sputum found may be examined directly for pneumococci. In addition, broth and a mouse should be inoculated and a search for a typable pneumococcus carried on as above.

In addition to the typing of pneumococci from specimens thus procured from children, it should be borne in mind that blood cultures are just as valuable and important in these patients as in adults. A blood culture should always be taken just before the administration of the first dose of serum if specific therapy has been decided upon, and one should be taken in any case to determine the presence or absence of bacteriemia and to serve as a check on the type of pneumococcus isolated from the sputum. It is worth while to point out in this connection that the external jugler vein is readily accessible in small children and in many instances provides an easy source of blood for culture purposes.

NURSING THE PNEUMONIA PATIENT IN THE HOME

By Dorothy J. Carter, R.N.

General Director
Boston Community Health Association

There is probably no disease that offers such a challenge to the nurse as pneumonia. Whether she is a floor nurse on the ward of a hospital, or a "special" in the private patient division, or a visiting nurse in the home, the pneumonia patient demands the utmost in nursing skill and care.

If the patient in the hospital, with physicians immediately at hand and all facilities available, still presents a nursing problem, how much more so does the patient ill with pneumonia in the home, where the nurse must often work with inadequate equipment, and where family and friends so often prove to be a handicap as well as invaluable aids?

What is the nurse who enters a home on a first visit to a pneumonia case apt to find, and what steps does she take in planning nursing care for her patients? We assume that she has kept in touch with the latest scientific developments in the knowledge and treatment of pneumonia and is informed in regard to the program and resources of the state and of her own community.

Early in her plans will be the provision for collecting a specimen of sputum for typing to have it ready for the physician with the least possible delay. This is particularly important in the event that the nurse chances to arrive on the scene in advance of the physician.

She may have been able to reach the physician in charge of the case before she makes her visit and to secure his specific orders for treatment and care, or she may find the orders waiting for her in the home. In pneumonia, as in all her nursing program, the nurse gives special care only with the physician's orders.

One of her first steps may be to calm and reassure an alarmed family and to give them some explanation of what needs to be done in providing adequate care for the patient. Her second step may sometimes have to be ridding the house, as diplomatically as possible, of well-meaning relatives and neighbors who have gathered, often in the patient's room, to sympathize with the patient and the family and offer suggestions and advice.

With these preliminary steps taken, the nurse proceeds in her plan for care, first selecting a responsible member of the family who will take charge of the patient in the nurse's absence and to whom she can demonstrate the necessary treatment.

Since pneumonia is considered a communicable disease, the fundamental principles of communicable disease technique should be followed, including the isolation of the patient, in so far as this can be carried out under some of our crowded living conditions, proper care of respiratory secretions, and thorough washing of the hands after caring for the patient. Through demonstration and instruction, the family is taught the importance of carrying out these procedures in the nurse's absence.

In considering the actual nursing needs of the patient, one is impressed with the increasing emphasis that is being placed on the cardinal factor of rest. How often in the past, and even sometimes today, have some of us, with the best intentions in the world, in our efforts to do all we could for our patients, flagrantly neglected this principle. We have insisted on forcing fluids, and carrying out "q4h" orders for medication, treatment and care, regardless of whether the patient were awake or sleeping. We can at least try to plan the schedule so that as far as possible the major treatments are given at one time, and the minor ones, such as taking temperatures, giving fluids, etc., during the intervals when the patient is awake. The patient should be disturbed as little as possible, and the test of the good nurse lies just as much in her imaginative discrimination in planning care as it does in her skill in giving it.

An important factor in securing as much rest as possible for the patient is the nurse's observation and treatment of those symptoms which add to his discomfort and handicap his fight to overcome the infection. Pleurisy, dyspnoea, and distention are frequently present during the height of the disease, and the nurse will do well to secure in advance from the physician orders for alleviating these conditions.

Chest binders, strapping and the application of heat are used most frequently to help alleviate painful respiration, while enemas or colonic irrigations and adequate fluid intake help to lessen the distention. Turning the patient frequently and encouraging him to cough and raise sputum aid in clearing out the respiratory passages. The care of the mouth and nose is particularly important in keeping the mucous membrane clear and moist. A clean mouth also helps to preserve the patient's sense of taste—an important factor when it is necessary to give large amounts of liquid nourishment.

A daily sponge bath is usually given, unless it tires the patient too much, and special attention is directed toward preventing pressure sores. While the patient should be kept warm and protected from chilling, he should not be burdened with too much or too heavy bedding—a point that is sometimes difficult for our foreign-born families to understand.

"Keep all unnecessary persons and articles out of the sickroom at all times"* is a good maxim to follow. In the congested districts where families are large and space is at a premium, this is difficult to carry out. The nurse can be insistent with the adults, however, and it is frequently possible to have small children in the family placed temporarily with relatives or friends.

Just as important as keeping the environment free of external unessentials is it to relieve the patient's mind of any worries and anxieties. While it is almost impossible to eliminate entirely physical strain during pneumonia, one can at least see to it that there is no cause for mental strain.

The room should be kept at a temperature of 65 to 70 degrees, with an adequate supply of fresh air and moisture, but the patient should be protected from draughts.

A fluid diet, high in carbohydrates, and up to an amount of 3,000 cc. or more in 24 hours is usually recommended if the patient can take that amount. And here again, the nurse's skill is called into play in enticing the patient to take as much nourishment as possible without actually forcing it.

In following the acute course of the disease from day to day, the nurse, whether she is on private duty or a visiting nurse making but one or two visits a day, brings to the patient and family not only her nursing skills but also a strengthening of morale that is vitally important both to the patient in helping him keep up the fight and to the family in their

---

*Handbook on the Nursing Care of Pneumonia. Reprinted by permission of the New York State Department of Health by the Metropolitan Life Insurance Company, New York, New York. This pamphlet has been made available to nurses in Massachusetts by the Massachusetts Department of Public Health.

responsibility for his care. The quiet assurance of the professional worker in maintaining an atmosphere of calm and hopefulness is not the least important part of her contribution.

The nurse should be familiar with oxygen treatment, and if it is given, should take all of the precautions necessary to prevent fire and explosion.

One of the most important factors in the treatment of pneumonia today is serum therapy, and no nurse can neglect to make herself proficient in her knowledge of this treatment and the part she plays in it. Massachusetts has been one of the pioneer states to develop a state-wide program for the reduction of the pneumonia death rate by the use of serum. Every nurse in the State, if she is not already familiar with it, should know about the pneumonia study conducted by the Department of Public Health and the present State program. The State is making every effort to promote the use of serum among the physicians of the Commonwealth, and to make facilities for typing and an adequate supply of serum easily accessible. There are several ways in which the nurse can aid in this program:

1. She can make every effort to secure a specimen of sputum as soon as she goes in on a case.

2. She can learn where the approved laboratories for pneumococcus typing and serum distribution are situated in her community.

3. She can bring this to the physician's attention and offer her assistance in getting the sputum typed.

4. She can assist the physician in the actual administering of the serum.

It may often seem difficult to the busy physician to give the serum treatment in the home, particularly if the facilities and equipment are meager. The public health nurse, a fundamental part of whose training consists in the adaptation of hospital techniques to the home situation, should be able to demonstrate to the physician that this treatment can be given aseptically and safely. By setting up trays with the necessary hypodermics, solutions, etc., standing by and assisting in the actual administration of the serum, reassuring the patient and family, and watching for serum reactions, she can do much in making serum treatment in the home a comparatively simple procedure.

Also because of her close contact with the family, she can supplement the physician's instructions in regard to the milder reactions that frequently occur and to cases of delayed serum sickness which, while not serious, are sometimes distressing to the patient and upsetting to the family.

Practically every nurse is familiar with the pneumonia crisis and the special care that is necessary during that period and immediately following. Here, too, the emphasis should be on allowing the patient as much rest as possible.

Fully as important as rest during the acute stage of the disease is rest during convalescence and a carefully planned program of progressive activity. Here again it will sometimes take the best efforts of the physician and nurse to make the patient and family realize the importance of the convalescent period not only in preventing complications but also in the eventual restoration of the patient to complete health and activity. To suggest ways and means to a harassed mother of amusing a restless child, or to try to find a convalescent home for a wage earning adult, taxes one's ingenuity to the utmost besides consuming a vast amount of time, but are often necessary adjuncts to the convalescent period and are factors in our follow-up nursing care that we are too often prone to neglect. It is as important to "follow through" on a pneumonia case as in any other case of serious communicable disease.

Nor can we discuss the role of the public health nurse in the care of pneumonia without emphasizing her specific contribution to the prevention of the disease. In her general health teaching of daily hygiene, the building up of resistance and the importance of taking care of the "common cold," and in her insistence on proper medical care for suspicious symptoms, the nurse can do much in the preventive program.

Important is it, too, for the nurse who expects to come into contact with pneumonia to keep herself in the best physical condition. She, most of all, must obey "the rules of the game" if she is to contribute her share in the control of pneumonia.

TYPES OF PNEUMOCOCCI IN MASSACHUSETTS

By EDITH A. BECKLER, S.B.

Chief of Bacteriological Laboratory
Massachusetts Department of Public Health

In planning pneumonia programs it is important to know the prevalence of various types of pneumococcic pneumonias. Until laboratory facilities are available so that every case of pneumonia can be typed through the thirty types, such information will not be available through morbidity reports. However, some information can be obtained by studying the typings done in a large laboratory. It must be understood that such figures do not represent actual cases of pneumonia because specimens are sent in from cases of various respiratory diseases, the symptoms of which might suggest an early pneumonia. It is inevitable, therefore, that certain casual inhabitants of the throat not responsible for infections of the lung will be included in such tabulations. For these and other reasons it is dangerous to draw too final conclusions from figures of this kind, but they are given for whatever may be learned from them.

During the past three years and six months (January 1936 to June 1939) the Bacteriological Laboratory of the Massachusetts Department of Public Health has examined 10,043 specimens for type of pneumococcus. The specimens received were principally sputums, but blood cultures, spinal fluid, throat swabs, ear cultures, etc. are included in the total. Similar figures have been collected from the approved laboratories in the State. The tabulations are given in another paper in this issue. The results of the examinations in this laboratory are tabulated below:

Incidence of Pneumococci by Type
For Period of 42 Months Ending June 30, 1939
Bacteriological Laboratory, State House.

Type	1936	Per Cent	1937	Per Cent	1938	Per Cent	(6 mos.) 1939	Per Cent	Total	Per Cent
1	189	21.1	201	20.0	236	12.2	240	13.4	866	15.4
2	52	5.8	49	4.9	58	3.0	45	2.5	204	3.6
3	95	10.6	120	11.9	248	12.9	280	15.7	743	13.2
4	32	3.6	50	5.0	84	4.4	81	4.5	247	4.4
5	142	15.9	77	7.6	85	4.4	60	3.4	364	6.5
6	33	3.7	32	3.2	127	6.6	83	4.7	275	5.0
7	58	6.5	68	6.8	107	5.6	106	5.9	339	6.0
8	82	9.2	106	10.5	147	7.6	126	7.1	461	8.2
9	10	1.1	19	1.9	50	2.6	47	2.6	126	2.3
10	10	1.1	5	0.5	49	2.5	37	2.1	101	1.8
11	16	1.8	18	1.8	51	2.6	52	2.9	137	2.4
12	7	0.8	5	0.5	21	1.1	13	0.7	46	0.8
13	8	0.9	9	0.9	37	1.9	37	2.1	91	1.6
14	16	1.8	23	2.3	49	2.5	47	2.6	135	2.4
15	13	1.4	14	1.4	43	2.2	45	2.5	115	2.1
16	10	1.1	16	1.6	35	1.8	34	1.9	95	1.7
17	9	1.0	26	2.6	42	2.2	40	2.2	117	2.1
18	18	2.0	27	2.7	79	4.1	48	2.7	172	3.1
19	22	2.5	41	4.1	84	4.3	85	4.8	232	4.1
20	13	1.4	20	2.0	53	2.8	56	3.1	142	2.5
21	20	2.2	6	0.6	24	1.2	23	1.3	73	1.3
22	4	0.4	8	0.8	31	1.6	22	1.2	65	1.2
23	7	0.8	18	1.8	56	2.9	44	2.5	125	2.2
24	1	0.1	9	0.9	19	1.0	26	1.5	55	1.0
25	3	0.3	3	0.3	19	1.0	17	0.9	42	0.8
27	2	0.2	1	0.1	11	0.6	3	0.2	17	0.3
28	8	0.9	6	0.6	19	1.0	14	0.8	47	0.8
29	3	0.3	20	2.0	41	2.1	44	2.5	108	1.9
31	6	0.7	2	0.2	22	1.1	11	0.6	41	0.7
32	0	0.0	2	0.2	1	0.1	3	0.2	6	0.1
Unclassified	7	0.8	3	0.3	1	0.1	17	0.9	28*	0.5
Subtotal	896	100.0	1,004	100.0	1,929	100.0	1,786	100.0	5,615	100.0
No Pneumococci	545		946		1,800		1,420		4,711	
Total	1,441		1,950		3,729		3,206		10,326**	

It will be observed that the ten commonest types of pneumococci are 1, 3, 8, 5, 7, 6, 4, 19, 2, and 18 in the order of their frequency. These ten types represent 69.5% of the specimens showing pneumococci. From year to year the relative importance may shift. As the higher types have been recorded in increasing numbers, the percentage of the lower types has appeared to drop. In 1936 the cases which could have been treated with serums for Types 1, 2, 5, 7, and 8 represented 58.5% of the total. In 1938 this percentage had dropped to 32.8% and yet the total number of positive specimens was higher than for 1936.

As is inevitable in a public health laboratory, a high percentage (45.6) of specimens examined showed no pneumococci. This is explained partly by the fact that many specimens are sent from cases of respiratory disease other than pneumonia and partly because many poor speci-

---

*Sixteen of the unclassified pneumococci belonged to one serological type as yet unnumbered.

**Specimens showing more than one type of pneumococcus are recorded under each type. This accounts for the total being larger than the number of specimens examined.

mens are sent from cases of lobar pneumonia. Negative blood cultures contribute to the number of specimens showing no pneumococci. Although the specimens containing no pneumococci are time-consuming to examine and unsatisfactory to the laboratory worker, the yearly incidence of such specimens would appear to indicate that the general practitioner is thinking of pneumococcus typing for all cases of respiratory disease in which the symptoms might represent an early case of pneumonia. Such interest increases the likelihood of the receipt of more specimens from cases of pneumococcic pneumonia.

With the introduction of sulfapyridine in the treatment of pneumonia, new problems have arisen in the pneumococcus typing laboratories. Conflicting reports have been published concerning the effect of the drug upon the pneumococcus capsule; some writers claim that the capsule is disintegrated while others state that the capsule is unchanged in appearance and that the type of pneumococcus can be determined by the Neufeld method as readily after drug therapy as before.

Data collected having been insufficient to ensure certainty in this matter, it is advisable to obtain a specimen of sputum from the patient before the administration of the drug and to have the type determined early without waiting, necessarily, for the laboratory report before using sulfapyridine.

Since it is likely that serums will be used also in many cases, the early typing of pneumococci is important; but even if there is no thought of serum therapy it would seem advisable to collect data on the types of pneumococci found in cases treated with sulfapyridine alone.

THE WORK OF THE COLLABORATING PNEUMOCOCCUS TYPING LABORATORIES OF MASSACHUSETTS

By ERNEST J. VOGEL, M.D., *Epidemiologist*, and

ROY F. FEEMSTER, M.D., Dr.P.H., *Director*

Division of Communicable Diseases, Massachusetts Department of Public Health

In 1938, there were 79 hospital and other laboratories approved to do pneumococcus typing in Massachusetts. The majority of these reported only on the types of organism for which the Department supplied homologous therapeutic serum. This meant only Types 1, 2, 5, 7, and 8 pneumococci were reported by most technicians. As a result, less information is available in regard to most of the remaining 25 types because most of the laboratories were unable to classify them by type.

Since the disadvantages of this incomplete laboratory diagnosis were many, both theoretically and practically, an important addition to the Pneumonia Program was made in February, 1939. At this time all approved laboratories were supplied by the Department with all the pools (Mixtures A to F, inclusive). While the purpose of combining the 30 types into 6 groups is principally to decrease the labor of typing, swelling of the capsule in any of the pools gives evidence that a pneumococcus is present in the specimen. This additional information is valuable even though complete identification is not possible.

By this time there were 89 laboratories approved for doing typings. Twenty of those distributing the higher types of therapeutic serum were provided with monovalent typing serum for all of the types. At the same time, 24 others purchased the monovalent serum for the additional types not supplied by the Department. One-half of the typing laboratories, therefore, are now prepared to make complete identification of all the pneumococci usually encountered.

Since January 1, 1938, the Department has requested quarterly reports of typings done in each collaborating laboratory. With a few exceptions, reports have been received from each for the six quarters since that date. However, no figures are available from one large hospital performing hundreds of typings. The information on these quarterly reports has been compiled in Table I.

Table I. Incidence of Pneumococci by Types
in the Collaborating Local Laboratories
by three month periods.

Type	1938					1939		
	1st	2nd	3rd	4th	Total	1st	2nd	Total
1	234	159	36	121	550	336	226	562
2	57	59	8	39	163	60	33	93
3	168	74	44	113	399	322	219	541
4	21	20	27	35	103	59	24	83
5	61	30	9	30	130	74	45	119
6	27	17	11	28	83	45	36	81
7	82	31	11	38	162	110	76	186
8	73	38	11	56	178	133	84	217
9	6	0	2	14	22	26	9	35
10	5	3	3	9	20	11	23	34
11	5	6	3	9	23	23	11	34
12	5	2	0	3	10	9	2	11
13	1	1	1	6	9	10	12	22
14	37	32	10	30	109	42	28	70
15	2	4	5	7	18	20	23	43
16	1	2	3	12	18	24	10	34
17	9	1	0	16	26	17	20	37
18	8	6	1	19	34	22	22	44
19	14	14	5	39	72	41	36	77
20	10	0	1	10	21	15	10	25
21	1	1	1	3	6	10	12	22
22	5	4	0	8	17	17	9	26
23	7	6	4	9	26	15	21	36
24	1	0	0	2	3	9	4	13
25	1	1	2	2	6	8	7	15
27	1	0	2	2	5	7	3	10
28	1	1	1	3	6	4	4	8
29	3	1	2	5	11	20	11	31
31	2	1	0	2	5	3	4	7
32	0	0	0	0	0	1	4	5
Total	848	514	203	670	2,235	1,493	1,028	2,521
*Unclassified	1,123	539	296	576	2,534	289	153	442
No Pneumonia	252	174	153	481	1,060	967	815	1,782
Grand Total	2,223	1,227	652	1,727	5,829	2,749	1,996	4,745

*Pneumococci present, Neufeld negative.

Attention is called to the fact that these figures do not represent the total number of patients examined because several specimens are often sent from one individual. Neither should it be inferred that the numbers listed horizontally opposite "No pneumococci" indicate that patients submitting these specimens did not have pneumonia because in many instances succeeding specimens sent in showed the presence of pneumococci. Finally because the significance of the higher types is still problematical it must not be concluded that the higher types as reported in the table indicate pneumococcic pneumonias. In short, these figures represent the volume of work done by typing laboratories in Massachusetts exclusive of the State Bacteriological Laboratory and any conclusions drawn from them must be made with reserve.

An analysis of this table suggests the following comments:

1. The ten most common types are 1, 2, 3, 4, 5, 6, 7, 8, 14, and 19. This list differs from the typings at the State Bacteriological Laboratory only in that Type 14 is included instead of Type 18.

2. These ten types represent 87.1% of the total in 1938 and 80.5% of the total during the first 6 months of 1939.

3. Type 1 remains the most frequently reported pneumococcus, even though it has decreased in relative importance.

4. Type 3 is next in frequency. Since it is commonly agreed that this type is found in healthy persons more frequently than Type 1 the figures probably represent a smaller proportion of pneumonias.

5. Types 7 and 8 now surpass Type 2 in prevalence and Type 5 has increased in importance.

6. The "Unclassified" (Pneumococci present, Neufeld negative with typing sera on hand) decreased very markedly in 1939 because of the increase in the number of laboratories prepared to do complete classification. However, it must be noted that there was an increase in specimens in which "No pneumococci" were reported, indicating that organisms morphologically resembling pneumococci which might previously have been included among the "Unclassified" are now being found not to be pneumococci.

7. A total of 4,745 examinations were made in the first 6 months of 1939 in contrast to 3,450 in a similar period in 1938, an increase of 37.5%.

In Table II, totals for both the collaborating laboratories and the State Bacteriological Laboratory are brought together for 1938 and 1939. The 1938 figures, exclusive of the one large hospital mentioned above, amount to almost 10,000 typings. The figure for 1939 will undoubtedly approach 15,000 as the total number for the first 6 months was probably nearer 9,000 than the 7,951 given in the table. What the trend will be with the increase in the popularity of chemotherapy is difficult to predict. It is hoped, however, that physicians will continue to have all cases of pneumonia typed so that the comparative effectiveness of the drug in pneumonias due to the various types will become apparent.

Table II—Total Typings of Pneumococci in Massachusetts
by three month periods.

Quarters	1938			1939		
	State Laboratory	Hospital	Total	State Laboratory	Hospital	Total
1st	1,253	2,223	3,476	2,118	2,749	4,867
2nd	1,191	1,227	2,418	1,088	1,996	3,084
3rd	369	652	1,021			
4th	907	1,727	2,634			
Total	3,720	5,829	9,549	3,206	4,745	7,951

The Department has made every effort to assist the local laboratories in increasing the accuracy of their typings. Visits have been made to every collaborating laboratory by a representative of the Department. Opportunity has been given to newly appointed members of personnel to spend time in the State Bacteriological Laboratory to gain additional experience in typing. Repeat visits have been arranged for many who have been to the Laboratory in previous years. Hundreds of specimens have been re-examined to verify the type observed in the local laboratory. The splendid cooperation of these laboratories has done much to popularize the use of the typing service and to make it possible to extend the use of antipneumococcic serum.

A fund has been made available to reimburse local laboratories for typings done on patients treated in the home who are unable to pay laboratory fees, which fund has relieved the laboratories of a burden borne largely by them in previous years.

A list of the laboratories for pneumococcus typing and serum distribution is available from the Department on application.

THE USE OF THE TERM "GROUP IV" PNEUMOCOCCUS

By F. RANDOLF PHILBROOK, M.D.

Epidemiologist, Division of Communicable Diseases
Massachusetts Department of Public Health

The name of Georgia Cooper will always be outstanding on any list of those bacteriologists or technicians doing research with pneumococci. Her great contribution was the separation of pneumococci of Types 4 to 32 from "Group IV."

When she started her work with these organisms only three type-specific or definite strains had been universally recognized; they were called Types 1, 2, and 3. It was known that there were other varieties of pneumococci and that a few of these were type-specific, but all of those which did not belong to the three types were placed, for lack of properly correlated immunological work, into a "wastebasket" category called "Group IV." By April, 1932, she had retrieved from the "wastebasket" some twenty-nine type-specific pneumococci, and had given each of them a number, beginning at Type 4 and going through Type 32. This was a tremendously important contribution to the field of pneumonia research.

It happens that recently Types 26 and 30 have been dropped out of her classification because of their close relationship to or identity with Types 6 and 15, respectively.

There still remain a few as yet unclassified pneumococci but they are not encountered with great frequency. Only eleven specimens in the last six thousand received at the Bacteriological Laboratory at the State House, Boston, have contained pneumococci which could not be classified. However, no exhaustive attempt has been made to ferret out those which could not be identified with the thirty typing sera now available, and the incidence may actually be somewhat higher than the two-per-thousand as found in that laboratory. It is probable that the identification of a few more strains of pneumococci will be reported eventually, and that typing serums for these types will be available.

The present widespread use of the term "Group IV" to describe a pneumococcus which is not a Type 1, 2 or 3 is obviously obsolete. Serving no useful purpose except in discussion of pneumococcus history, the term may be strongly objected to, if for no other reason than the frequent confusion with "Type 4." This is true particularly now that commercial Type 4 therapeutic serums are available. Some few technicians have on occasion reported a specimen as Type 4 instead of Group IV; and, on the basis of such a report, one physician is known to have given Type 4 therapeutic serum to a patient. Some technicians have been in the habit of reporting as Group IV any specimen in which no capsular swelling is observed with the use of only six or seven typing serums, and whether or not pneumococci are observed. Such a report is valueless and misleading.

It is suggested that technicians definitely avoid the use of the term "Group IV" and report their findings on specimens examined for pneumococci as follows:

(1) If no pneumococci are found, report that none were found.

(2) If pneumococci are present and a capsular swelling is obtained with a monovalent typing serum, report the type of pneumococcus found.

(3) If a pneumococcus is found and capsular swelling occurs in a pool for which part or none of the monovalent components are on hand, the report should enumerate the types included in the pool and state which, if any, of its monovalent components had been used without obtaining capsular swelling and should specify which are not on hand.

(4) If organisms resembling pneumococci are observed and all thirty-two types of typing serum are used without obtaining capsular swelling, the report should be negative for Types 1 to 32, but mention should be made of the fact that organisms resembling pneumococci were present. However, if a bile solubility, inulin fermentation or other test confirms that the organism, which has failed to swell with any of the thirty-two types of potent typing serum, is a pneumococcus, then report an unclassified pneumococcus found.

INSTRUCTIONS TO LABORATORIES DOING PNEUMOCOCCUS TYPING AND DISTRIBUTING ANTIPNEUMOCOCCIC SERUM

1. *Do typing* for at least all the pools of typing serum unless no organisms resembling pneumococci are present.
2. *Culture* or *inoculate into mouse* each specimen which is *apparently negative* on direct Neufeld typing and Gram stained smear. Examination of such culture or of material aspirated from mouse peritoneal cavity should be made at 4, 8, 12, and 24 hours.
3. Certain therapeutic serums for higher types of pneumococcus pneumonia are available commercially. Accordingly, in the event a pneumococcus is observed and *capsular swelling* occurs *in a pool* of typing serum for which you *do not have* the component *monovalent typing serums*, it is well to properly report your results to the physician and at the same time, to learn from him whether or not he wishes to arrange to *buy therapeutic serum* for a higher type should it be available. If so, it is important that the technician tell him the location of the *nearest laboratory* where *complete typing* is done.
4. *Send sample* of each specimen in which an organism resembling pneumococcus is observed, but which for any reason you are *not able to identify* as a definite type, to the State Bacteriological Laboratory, State House, Boston. Enclose with such specimen the *colored card* properly filled out. Report will be returned directly to you. Do not enclose white card with such specimen. (Regular pneumonia sputum mailing outfits are to be used for forwarding such specimens.)
5. *Report results* of examination in one of the *following manners*:
    I. Organisms resembling *pneumococci present*:
        A. Identified as Type ...(Types and .. , Type predominating.)
        B. Capsular swelling in Pool , composed of Types... ; no capsular swelling for Types ; monovalent typing sera for Types not on hand.
        C. No capsular swelling. Not Types 1 to 32.
    II. Organisms resembling *pneumococci not present*:
        A. Specimen still under examination. No pneumococcus found as yet. Another sputum requested.
        B. No pneumococci found on direct Neufeld typing or after culture and/or mouse inoculation.
6. Give to physician or his messenger:
    A. Serum of appropriate type in appropriate dose. (To determine appropriate dose refer to the green serum circular. Request immediate return of any unused serum.)
    B. Serum *sensitivity outfit*.
    C. *Blood culture* outfit.
    D. *History* sheet.

7. Fill out and *mail* to Antitoxin and Vaccine Laboratory *post cards* for all *serum when issued*, showing lot number and number of vials of serum issued.
8. Report on post card *return of unused serum* to you by physician.
9. Return all serum *unused at expiration date.*
10. *Request supplies* of typing serum, history sheets, and serum sensitivity outfits as needed. (Therapeutic serum and post cards are sent automatically if our records show they are needed.)
11. *Keep record* in laboratory of:
    A. Sputum typings done, by type and patient's name or number chronologically.
    B. Blood cultures done on pneumonia patients—same classification.
    C. Serum issued or received, by patient's name, lot number and number of vials issued or returned.
12. All specimens typed by persons "covering" at night or at other times should be checked for type at the earliest possible time by the bacteriologist or technician responsible for typing.
13. Serum is not to be issued on the basis of typings done by a laboratory not approved by the Department, unless the typing has already been checked by an approved laboratory.

REGULATIONS RELATIVE TO THE PAYMENT FOR CERTAIN LABORATORY TESTS ON SPECIMENS FROM CASES OF PNEUMONIA

Payments will be made for pneumococcus typing of sputum and for blood cultures at rates specified in the table below on material from persons having, or suspected of having, pneumonia under the following conditions:

1. If the tests are done for patients outside the hospital in which the typing laboratory is situated.
2. If the laboratory requesting payment is approved by this Department for doing such tests; if the tests are performed or checked by an approved technician; and if the laboratory certifies that payment for the tests has not been made.
3. If the physician when submitting the specimen certifies over his signature that the payment of the charges would be an undue hardship on the patient.
4. If the number of examinations on a single patient is reasonable and satisfactory explanation for repeated tests accompanies the bill.

5. If the pneumococcus typing has covered all the types for which typing serum is provided by the Department.
6. If the bill is submitted for approval by the 10th of the next succeeding month after the tests are performed.

RATES OF PAYMENT

(Depend upon reagents used)

	Polyvalent Pools A to F Monovalent Types 1, 2, 3, 5, 7, 8, 14.	Polyvalent Pools A to F Monovalent Types 1 to 32
Sputum Typing	$1.50	$2.00
Blood Culture*	2.00	2.50

*Pneumococci in blood culture must be identified by Neufeld Typing.

REPORT OF DIVISION OF FOOD AND DRUGS
(As required by General Laws, Chapter 111, Section 25.)

During the months of June, July and August, 1939, samples were collected in 200 cities and towns.

There were 1,343 samples of milk examined, of which 128 were below standard, from 6 samples the cream had been in part removed, and 1 sample contained added water. There were 1,553 bacteriological examinations made of milk, 1,163 of which complied with the requirements. There were 133 bacteriological examinations made of cream, 63 of which did not comply with the requirements; 371 bacteriological examinations of ice cream, 77 of which did not comply with the requirements; 1 bacteriological examination of chocolate drink, 1 bacteriological examination of chocolate milk, 1 bacteriological examination of buttermilk, and 1 bacteriological examination of an empty soft drink bottle, all of which complied with the requirements; 2 bacteriological examinations of coffee cereal special, and 1 bacteriological examination of an empty milk bottle, all of which did not comply with the requirements; and 19 bacteriological examinations of mattress fillings, 10 of which did not comply with the requirements. There were bacteriological examinations also made of a ham beans and 6 samples of flour.

There were 746 samples of food examined, 117 of which were adulterated. These consisted of 2 samples of butter, 1 of which was rancid, and 1 sample was oleomargarine colored with coal tar dye; 14 samples of clams, 13 of which contained added water, and 1 sample was decomposed; 7 samples of cranberries, a considerable number of which were rotten; 4 samples of fish, 2 of which contained formaldehyde, and 2 samples were decomposed; 1 sample of lamb patties, 1 sample of veal patties, 1 sample of pork chops, 1 sample of duck, 2 samples of fowl, 1 sample of kielbassa, 1 sample of chicken croquettes, and 1 sample of frozen eggs, all of which were decomposed; 9 samples of hamburg steak, 7 of which were decomposed, 1 contained sodium sulphite in excess of one tenth of one per cent, and 1 sample contained a compound of sulphur dioxide not so labelled; 22 samples of sausage, 21 of which were decomposed, and 1 sample contained starch in excess of 2 per cent; 1 sample of cider which contained sodium benzoate not so labeled; 1 sample of macaroni which was wormy and infested with larvae; 1 sample of lima beans which contained worm excreta; 1 sample of split peas which contained dead worms and also worm and mouse excreta; 1 sample sold as olive oil which was adulterated and misbranded and found to consist of cottonseed oil; 5 samples of soft drinks, 2 of which contained saccharine, and 3 samples contained benzoic acid not so labeled; 16 samples of soft drink wash water which were deficient in caustic alkali; 13 samples of misbranded cream substitute, 1 of which also contained sediment (hardened casein); 7 samples of cream, 4 of which were low in fat for the grade specified, and 3 samples contained sediment (hardened casein); 2

samples of upholstering material, 1 of which did not contain the materials as specified, and 1 sample contained secondhand material; and 2 samples of feathers and down which were labeled as containing a certain percentage of different kinds of feathers and down, which samples did not contain the materials as specified.

There were 62 samples of drugs examined, of which 15 were adulterated. These consisted of 2 samples of silver nitrate solution, 1 sample of milk of bismuth, 1 sample of camphorated oil, 4 samples of distilled water, 1 sample of lime water, 1 sample of sweet oil, 3 samples of spirit of nitrous ether, and 2 samples of carbolic acid solution, all of which did not conform to the requirements of the U. S. Pharmacopoeia.

The police departments submitted 109 samples of liquor for examination. The police departments also submitted 19 samples to be analyzed for poisons or drugs, 12 of which contained heroin, 1 contained caffeine, 1 sample of crystals contained chloral hydrate, and 5 samples were examined for poison with negative results.

There were inspected 295 plants operated for the pasteurization of milk; 271 restaurants; 124 soft drink plants; 170 ice cream establishments; 379 bakeries; 153 stores; 2 sausage factories; 1 tapioca factory; and 544 mattress establishments.

There were 178 hearings held pertaining to violations of the laws.

There were 61 convictions pertaining to violations of the laws, $1,620 in fines being imposed.

Frank J. Pomphret of Methuen, and Parke Chapman of Montgomery, were convicted for violations of the milk laws.

Frank R. Spofford, 2 cases, of Groveland; John Borges, 2 cases, of Fall River; Dwight A. Ware, 2 cases, of Abington; Lewis Pedercini of North Adams; James M. Daly of Pittsfield; United Dairy System of Northampton; Parke Chapman of Montgomery; and Bellows Falls Cooperative Creamery, Incorporated, of Bellows Falls, Vermont, were convicted for violations of the pasteurization laws and regulations. Frank R. Spofford, 2 cases, of Groveland, appealed.

Harry Newman, 2 cases, J. Reinholtz, Incorporated, 2 cases, Holland Butter Company, and Edward Iandoli, all of Boston; George Pappas and Joseph Sikora of Ipswich; Economy Grocery Stores, Incorporated, of Newtonville; Fall River Public Market, Incorporated, 2 cases, and Charles Cohen of Fall River; Armour & Company of Salem; Ted Posovsky, 2 cases, of Orange; Leo Feinstein, 2 cases, of Quincy; Milton Miller of New Bedford; Guiseppe Marinelli of North Adams; Economy Grocery Stores Corporation of Lynn; Great Atlantic & Pacific Tea Company, and Francis Donelan of Athol; Samuel Levy and Grand Union Stores, Incorporated, of Pittsfield; Arthur Laro of Chester; United Meats, Incorporated, 2 cases, and Joseph M. Levi of Springfield; William W. Taylor of Provincetown; and Agnes Klys of Webster, were all convicted for violations of the food laws. J. Reinholtz, Incorporated, 2 cases, and Holland Butter Company of Boston; Economy Grocery Stores, Incorporated, of Newtonville; and Milton Miller of New Bedford, appealed their cases.

Pocassett Bottling Company, Incorporated, 2 cases, and Michael Wojtowicz of Fall River, were convicted for violations of the soft drink regulations.

Abraham Cohen, Eugene Cohen, Abraham Azoff and Bertha Weintraub of Malden; Carolina Tenczar, Steve Wronski, Morris Lesser, and Jacob Pikul of Holyoke; and Thomas Stadnicki of Chicopee, were all convicted for violations of the bakery laws.

Guiseppe Marinelli of North Adams was convicted for misbranding.

Edward Milstone of Lawrence; William Goldberg of Roxbury; George L. Gershman of Worcester; and Wayland Manufacturing Company of Providence, R. I., were all convicted for violations of the mattress laws.

Albert Waterman of Rehoboth was convicted for a violation of the slaughtering laws.

In accordance with Section 25, Chapter 111 of the General Laws, the following is the list of articles of adulterated food collected in original packages from manufacturers, wholesalers, or producers:

One sample of butter which was rancid was obtained from Holland Butter Company of Boston.

One sample of frozen eggs which was decomposed was obtained from Roy J. Robarge of Pittsfield.

One sample of cider which contained sodium benzoate not so labeled was obtained from Northboro Cider Mills of Northboro.

One sample of macaroni which was wormy and infested with larvae was obtained from The Great Atlantic & Pacific Tea Company of Wollaston.

One sample of dried lima beans which contained worm excrete was obtained from Economy Grocery Stores Corporation of Quincy.

One sample of split peas which contained dead worms, also worm and mouse excreta, was obtained from Economy Grocery Stores Corporation of Quincy.

One sample of olive oil which was adulterated and misbranded was obtained from Joseph Marinelli of North Adams.

Soft drinks which contained saccharine were obtained as follows:

One sample each, from Chicago Dietetic Supply House of Chicago; and Loeb's Dietetic Supply House of New York.

Soft drinks which contained benzoic acid not so labeled were obtained as follows:

One sample each, from White Eagle Bottling Company of Chicopee; and Bowles Brothers of Brockton.

Cream which was low in fat for the grade specified was obtained as follows:

One sample each, from Braley's Creamery, Incorporated, of Fall River; United Dairy System of Springfield; and Shawmut Dairy Company, Incorporated, of East Boston.

Cream which contained sediment was obtained as follows:

Two samples from William J. Burbeck Company of Lowell; and one sample from Braley's Creamery, Incorporated, of Dartmouth.

One sample of clams which was decomposed was obtained from Stop & Shop (Economy Grocery Stores Corporation) of Lynn.

Clams to which water was added were obtained as follows:

Two samples each, from Harold Arrington of Lynn, and Veto Amerio of Ipswich; and 1 sample from Jean Amerio of Ipswich.

One sample of duck which was decomposed was obtained from Charles E. Goldman of Norwell.

One sample of chicken croquettes which was decomposed was obtained from Growers Outlet, Incorporated, of Northampton.

One sample of kielbassa which was decomposed was obtained from Athol Cooperative Stores of Athol.

One sample of pork chops which was decomposed was obtained from Alexander's Market of Lowell.

One sample of lamb patties which was decomposed was obtained from First National Stores, Incorporated, of Wollaston.

One sample of veal patties which was decomposed was obtained from Samuel Levy of Pittsfield.

Fowl which was decomposed was obtained as follows:

One sample each, from Charles E. Goldman and Lyonal Forkey of Norwell.

One sample of hamburg steak which contained sodium sulphite in excess of one tenth of one per cent was obtained from Leo Feinstein of Quincy.

One sample of hamburg steak which contained a compound of sulphur dioxide not so labeled was obtained from Blair's Market of Roxbury.

Hamburg steak which was decomposed was obtained as follows:

One sample each, from Economy Grocery Stores Corporation of Newtonville; Joseph M. Levi and First National Stores, Incorporated, of Springfield; Ted Posovsky of Orange; John Soja of Easthampton; and Ruth Richton of North Adams.

Sausage which was decomposed was obtained as follows:

Two samples each, from United Meats, Incorporated, and David Levine of Springfield; and Leo Feinstein of Quincy; and 1 sample each, from Harry Kronick & Son, Simon Kronick, and Ruth Richton of North Adams; The Great Atlantic & Pacific Tea Company, and Francis Donelan of Athol; Rose Weiss of Ware; John Moskal of Northampton; Anna Klys of Palmer; Grand Union Service Market, Incorporated, of Pittsfield; Edward & George Abdalla of Great Barrington; Arthur Laro of Chester; Ted Posovsky of Orange; Brockelman's Market of Lawrence; and John S. Andrade of Fall River.

One sample of sausage which contained starch in excess of 2 per cent was obtained from Armour & Company of Salem.

There were 20 confiscations, consisting of 80 pounds of decomposed chickens, 89 pounds of decomposed fowl, 70 pounds of decompsed beef, 5 pounds of decomposed ham, 4 pounds of decomposed Scotch ham, 1 pound of decomposed liver, 25 pounds of decomposed calves' livers, 20 pounds of decomposed pork scraps, 79 pounds of decomposed frankforts, 1½ gallons of decomposed clams, and 125 pounds of decomposed halibut.

The licensed cold storage warehouses reported the following amounts of food placed in storage during May, 1939:—2,210,040 dozens of case eggs; 2,002,160 pounds of broken out eggs; 1,439,395 pounds of butter; 1,465,862 pounds of poultry; 2,266,217 pounds of fresh meat and fresh meat products; and 10,403,647 pounds of fresh food fish.

There was on hand June 1, 1939:—3,904,140 dozens of case eggs; 2,645,441 pounds of broken out eggs; 1,439,010 pounds of butter; 3,647,553 pounds of poultry; 3,914,163 pounds of fresh meat and fresh meat products; and 11,420,240 pounds of fresh food fish.

The licensed cold storage warehouses reported the following amounts of food placed in storage during June, 1939:—569,400 dozens of case eggs; 1,807,824 pounds of broken out eggs; 3,760,865 pounds of butter; 1,891,269 pounds of poultry; 2,260,227 pounds of fresh meat and fresh meat products; and 13,396,148 pounds of fresh food fish.

There was on hand July 1, 1939:—4,292,400 dozens of case eggs; 3,233,326 pounds of broken out eggs; 4,598,626 pounds of butter; 3,673,491 pounds of poultry; 3,826,469 pounds of fresh meat and fresh meat products; and 18,854,557 pounds of fresh food fish.

The licensed cold storage warehouses reported the following amounts of food placed in storage during July, 1939:—187,620 dozens of case eggs; 909,718 pounds of broken out eggs; 2,019,711 pounds of butter; 1,693,698 pounds of poultry; 2,102, 998 pounds of fresh meat and fresh meat products; and 13,649,351 pounds of fresh food fish.

There was on hand August 1, 1939:—3,916,170 dozens of case eggs; 3,022,262 pounds of broken out eggs; 5,865,813 pounds of butter; 3,695,946 pounds of poultry; 3,180,685 pounds of fresh meat and fresh meat products; and 25,781,841 pounds of fresh food fish.

Book Note

PNEUMONIA WITH SPECIAL REFERENCE TO PNEUMOCOCCUS LOBAR PNEUMONIA by Roderick Heffron, M.D.

($4.50. 1086 pp. New York. The Commonwealth Fund, 1939.)

The appearance of Heffron's Pneumonia, with Special Reference to Pneumococcus Lobar Pneumonia, completes the triad of volumes planned as part of the Massachusetts Pneumonia Study and Service. It discusses thoroughly all aspects of the disease in man including not only the clinical manifestations, therapy, and pathology, but also the epidemiology of pneumonia and a description of methods currently employed for its control. As Dr. Heffron was Field Director of the Massachusetts program, much of the material was drawn from his experience there but to this has been added much more obtained from the literature and from his contacts with others interested in the pneumonia problem.

Not the least interesting chapter is that devoted to a statement of the problems still unsolved, of which there are many. It is to be hoped that this volume may serve to stimulate investigation along lines which will fill in some of the gaps in our knowledge.

The book is well written and beautifully printed. Doubtless it contains typographical errors and perhaps even mis-statements, but this reviewer has not found any. Instead, he wishes to repeat the last sentence of Dr. Lord's Foreword to the volume, "It is with profound satisfaction that I commend this book to the medical profession."

MASSACHUSETTS DEPARTMENT OF PUBLIC HEALTH

Commissioner of Public Health, PAUL J. JAKMAUH, M.D.

Public Health Council

PAUL J. JAKMAUH, M.D., *Chairman*

GEORGE D. DALTON, M.D.   RICHARD M. SMITH, M.D.
FRANCIS H. LALLY, M.D.   RICHARD P. STRONG, M.D.
CHARLES F. LYNCH, M.D.   JAMES L. TIGHE

Secretary, FLORENCE L. WALL

Division of Administration . . Under direction of Commissioner
Division of Sanitary Engineering . Director and Chief Engineer, ARTHUR D. WESTON, C.E.
Division of Communicable Diseases Director, ROY F. FEEMSTER, M.D.
Division of Biologic Laboratories . Director and Pathologist, ELLIOTT S. ROBINSON, M.D.
Division of Food and Drugs . . Director and Anaylst, HERMANN C. LYTHGOE, S.B.
Division of Child Hygiene . . Director, M. LUISE DIEZ, M.D.
Division of Tuberculosis . . . Director, ALTON S. POPE, M.D.
Division of Adult Hygiene . . Director, HERBERT L. LOMBARD, M.D.
Division of Genitoinfectious Diseases Director, NELS A. NELSON, M.D.

State District Health Officers

The Southeastern District . . . HAROLD W. STEVENS, M.D. Middleborough
The South Metropolitan District . HENRY M. DE WOLFE, M.D. Braintree
The North Metropolitan District . JOHN J. POUTAS, M.D., Newton
The Northeastern District . . ROBERT E. ARCHIBALD, M.D., Melrose
The Worcester District . . . OSCAR A. DUDLEY, M.D., Worcester
South Connecticut Valley District . CHARLES E. GILL, M.D., Westfield
North Connecticut Valley District . WALTER W. LEE, M.D., Greenfield
The Berkshire District . . . FRANK B. CARROLL, M.D., Great Barrington.

INDEX

Adaptation of public health education to the radio, The, by Lila Owen Burbank, M.D. 161
Anderson, Gaylord W., M.D., Control of typhoid 167
Arthritis, by Francis C. Hall, M.D. 190
Augustine, Donald, Sc.D., Trichinosis, a preventable disease . . 56
Beckler, Edith A., S.B., Types of pneumococci in Massachusetts . . 268
Book Notes:
   How to conquer constipation, by J. F. Montague, M.D. . . . 213
   Maternity care in a rural community, by Maxwell E. Lapham, M.D. . 152
   Teaching procedures in health education, by Howard L. Conrad and Joseph F. Meister 213
Brauer, John C., D.D.S , The Iowa plan for dental health education . 106
Burbank, Lila Owen, M.D., The adaptation of public health education to the radio 161
Cady, F. C., D.D.C., Recent studies point the way to better dental health . 123
Cancer, Massachusetts program, by Herbert L. Lombard, M.D. . . 201
Carter, Dorothy J., R. N., Nursing the pneumonia patient in the home . 264
Chemotherapy and serum therapy of pneumonia, by Frederick T. Lord, M.D. 232
Chicken pox, by Olive S. Feemster, M.D. 10
Clinics for crippled children, by Arthur Wakefield, M.D. . . . 183
Coffin, Susan M., M.D., Prenatal dental service 131
Control of communicable diseases, by Roy F. Feemster, M.D. . . 4
Control of typhoid, by Gaylord W. Anderson, M.D. 167
Curnen, Edward C., M.D., and Davies, oJhn A. V., M.D., Pneumococcus pneumonia in infants and children 257
Daffinee, Ralph W., M D., Infantile paralysis 20
Davies, John A. V., M.D., and Curnen, Edward C., M.D., Pneumococcus pneumonia in infants and children 257
Dental extractions by Frank W. Rounds, A.B., D.D.S. 108
   Health exhibits, by Albertine P. McKellar, B.S. 148
   Needs and the supply of dentists, by Fred W. Morse, Jr., M.D. . 136
Dental Health:
   Developments in dental education, by Howard M. Marjerison, D.M.D. . 119
   Diploma in her hand and twenty-one cavities in her teeth, A, . 97
   Extension of dental facilities, by William Hayes Hoyt, D.D.S. . 117
   Importance of an adequate dental program, The, by Arthur E. Westwell, D.M D. 138
   Iowa plan for dental health education, The, by John C. Brauer, D.D.S., M.Sc., F.A.C.D. 106
   Is sugar the lone factor in producing dental caries? by Mary Spalding, M.A. 111
   New Jersey State Dental Society Program—Dental Health Education, by J M. Wisan, D.D.S. 121
   Oral hygiene, report of the special Commission to Study and Investigate Public Health Laws and Policies 98
   Pediatrist looks at children's teeth, A, by Merritt B. Low, M.D. . 104
   Prenatal dental service, by Susan M. Coffin, M.D. 131
   Preparation and training of dental hygienists, The, by Evelyn B. Morse 126
   Progress in school dental health, by Jean V. Latimer, B S., A.M. 133
   Promotion of dental internships in general hospitals, The, by Richard H. Norton, D.D.S., D.M.D. 114
   Public health nursing and its relation to dental hygiene, by Ann W. Dinegan, B.S., R.N. 135
   Recent studies point the way to better dental health, by F. C. Cady, D D S , C.P.H. 123
   Structural and nervous effects of thumb-sucking, by Earl W. Swinehart, D.D.S. 41
   Teeth in congenital syphilis, The, by Florence B. Hopkins, M.D., D.M.D. 52
Developments in dental education, by Howard M. Marjerison, D.M.D. . 119
Dinegan, Ann W., B.S., R.N., Public health nursing and its relation to dental hygiene 135
Diphtheria, by Edwin H. Place, M.D. 14
Diploma in her hand and twenty-one cavities in her teeth, A, . . 97
Diseases, Control of communicable, by Rov F. Feemster, M.D. . . 4
   Reportable, rare in Massachusetts, by Roy F. Feemster, M.D. . 74
Doggett, William H., M.S., Overnight camp sanitation . . . 172
Don't say "Serum" When you mean "Vaccine," by Laura A. Thorpe . 8
Dysentery, Bacillary, by Walter W. Lee, M.D. 11
Education, adaptation of public health, to the radio, The, by Lila Owen Burbank, M D. 161
Endocrine glands, by James H. Means, M.D. 187
Extension of dental facilities, by William Hayes Hoyt, D.D.S. . . 117
Feemster, Olive S., M.D., Chicken pox 10
Feemster, Roy F., M.D., Control of communicable diseases . . . 4
   Reportable diseases rare in Massachusetts 74
   Smallpox 50
Feemster, Roy F., M.D., and Vogel, Ernest J., M D., The work of the collaborating pneumococcus typing laboratories of Massachusetts . 270
Finland, Maxwell, M.D., The use of specific serums in the treatment of pneumonias associated with pneumococci of the "higher types" . 245
   Pneumococcal meningitis and its treatment 248
Food and Drugs, Report of the Division of:
   October and November, 1938 91
   December, 1938, January and February, 1939 153
    215
   March, April, May, 1939 277

Foreword (Communicable Disease Number), by Paul J. Jakmauh, M.D. . . 3
  (Pneumonia Number), by Paul J. Jakmauh, M.D 223
Fothergill, LeRoy D., M.D., Meningitis 26

Gill, Charles E., M.D., Typhoid fever 64
Gilman, B. Barrett, M.D., Paratyphoid fever 31
  Rabies 42
Gonorrhea, by Ernest B. Howard, M.D. 18
  Syphilis—Notions versus facts, by N. A Nelson, M D. . . . 209
Gordon, John E., M D., Scarlet fever 46
Green lights to health, Sample of 179

Hall, Francis C, M.D., Arthritis 190
Health Review, Sample of 176
Higgins, Harold L., M.D., Mumps 29
Hopkins, Florence B., M.D., D.M.D., The teeth in congenital syphilis . 145
Howard, Ernest B., M.D., Gonorrhea 18
  Syphilis 54
Hoyt, William Hayes, D.D S., Extension of dental facilities . . . 117
Humanitarian movement, The, by Eleanor J. Macdonald, A. B. . 176

Importance of an adequate dental program, The, by Arthur E Westwell,
  D.M.D. 138
Important considerations in serum treatment of pneumococcus pneumonia
  by Frederick T. Lord, M D. 224
Infantile paralysis, by Ralph W. Daffinee, M D. 20
Instructions to laboratories doing pneumococcus typing and distributing
  antipneumococcic serum 275
Iowa plan for dental health education, The, by John C. Brauer, D.D S . 106
Is sugar the lone factor in producing dental caries? by Mary Spalding, M A. 111

Jordan, Sara M., M D, What to eat and why 193
Just a little routine, by Hermann C. Lythgoe, S.B. 170

Laboratory fights pneumonia, The, by Elliott S. Robinson, M.D. . . 179
Latimer, Jean V., B.S., A.M., Progress in school dental health . . . 133
Lee, Walter W., M.D., Dysentery, Bacillary 11
Lombard, Herbert L., The Massachusetts cancer program . . . 201
Long, Arthur P, M.D., Special problems in the typing of pneumococci from
  infants and young children 262
Lord, Frederick T., M.D., Important considerations in serum treatment of
  pneumococcus pneumonia 224
  Chemotherapy and serum therapy of pneumonia 232
Low, Merritt B., M.D, A pediatrist looks at children's teeth . . . 104
Lythgoe, Hermann C., S.B., Just a little routine 170

Macdonald, Eleanor J., A.B, The humanitarian movement . . . 176
Marjerison, Howard M., D M D., Developments in dental education . . 119
Massachusetts cancer program, The, by Herbert L. Lombard, M D. . . 201
Massachusetts saves prematurely born babies, by Florence L McKay, M.D. . 165
Maternal deaths in Massachusetts, 1933-1937 90
McKay, Florence L., M.D., Massachusetts saves prematurely born babies 165
McKellar, Albertine P., B S., Dental health exhibits 148
McKhann, Charles F., M D., Measles 23
Means, James H., M D, Endocrine glands 187
Measles, by Charles F. McKhann, M.D. 23
Meningitis, by LeRoy D. Fothergill, M D. 26
Morse, Evelyn B., The preparation and training of dental hygienists . 126
Morse, Fred W., Jr., M D., Dental needs and the supply of dentists . 136
Mumps, by Harold L. Higgins, M D. 29

Nelson, N. A., M.D., Gonorrhea and syphilis—Notions versus facts . . 209
Nervous fatigue, by Vernon P. Williams, M.D 197
New Jersey State Dental Society Program—Dental health education, by J.
  M. Wisan, D.D.S. 121
News Note:
  Vocational-placement service to public health nurses . . . 153
Norton, Richard H., D D S., D.M.D., The promotion of dental internships in
  general hospitals 114
Nursing the pneumonia patient in the home, by Dorothy J. Carter, R.N. . 264

Oral hygiene, report of the Special Commission to Study and Investigate
  Public Health Laws and Policies 98
Overnight camp sanitation, by William H. Doggett, M.S. . . . 172

Paratyphoid fever, by B. Barrett Gilman, M.D. 31
Pediatrist looks at children's teeth, A, by Merritt B. Low, M.D . . 104
Philbrook, F. Randolf, M D., Pneumonia 32
  The use of the term "Group IV" pneumococcus 273
Place, Edwin H., M.D., Diphtheria 14
Pneumococcal meningitis and its treatment, by Maxwell Finland, M.D. . 248
Pneumococcus pneumonia in infants and children, by John A. V. Davies, M.D.,
  and Edward C. Curnen, M.D. 257
Pneumonia, by F. Randolf Philbrook, M.D. 32
  Chemotherapy and serum therapy of, by Frederick T. Lord, M.D. . 232
  Important considerations in serum treatment of pneumococcus pneu-
    monia, by Frederick T. Lord, M.D. 224
  Instructions to laboratories doing pneumococcus typing and distributing
    antipneumococcic serum 275
  Nursing the patient in the home, by Dorothy J. Carter, R.N. . . 264
  Regulations relative to the payment for certain laboratory tests on
    specimens from cases of pneumonia 276

Special problems in the typing of, from infants and young children, by
    Arthur P. Long, M.D. 262
Types of pneumococci in Massachusetts, by Edith A. Beckler, S.B. . . 268
Use of specific serums in the treatment of, associated with pneumococci
    of the "higher types," The, by Maxwell Finland, M.D. . . . 245
Use of the term "Group IV" pneumococcus, The, by F. Randolf Philbrook,
    M.D. 273
Work of the collaborating pneumococcus typing laboratories of Massa-
    chusetts, The, by Ernest J. Vogel, M.D., and Roy F. Feemster, M.D.,
    Dr. P.H. 270
Pollock, Madelen P., R.N., The prematurely born baby needs specialized nurs-
    ing care 166
Pope, Alton S., M.D., Tuberculosis 60
Poutas, John J., M.D., Trichinosis 169
Prematurely born baby needs specialized nursing care, The, by Madelen P.
    Pollock, R.N. 166
Prenatal dental service, by Susan M. Coffin, M.D. 131
Preparation and training of dental hygienists, The, by Evelyn B. Morse . 126
Progress in school dental health, by Jean V. Latimer, B.S., A.M. . . 133
Promotion of dental internship in general hospitals, The, by Richard H.
    Norton, D.D.S., D.M.D. 114
Public health nursing and its relation to dental hygiene, by Ann W. Dine-
    gan, B.S., R.N. 135
Pulmonary tuberculosis—How it spreads in the home and family, by David
    Zacks, M.D. 173
    How its spread in the family can be prevented, by David Zacks, M.D. . 175
Rabies, by B. Barrett Gilman, M.D. 42
Radio Health Forum, Sample of 165
Recent studies point the way to better dental health, by F. C. Cady, D.D.S.,
    C.P.H. 123
Regulations:
    Funeral 89
    Governing the control of gonorrhea and syphilis 85
    Relative to diseases dangerous to the Public Health 79
    Relative to the conveyance of bodies dead of any disease dangerous to
        the Public Health 88
    Relative to the payment for certain laboratory tests on specimens from
        cases of pneumonia 276
Report of Division of Food and Drugs:
    October and November, 1938 91
    December, 1938, January and February, 1939 153
    March, April, May, 1939 215
    June, July, August, 1939 277
Reportable diseases rare in Massachusetts, by Roy F. Feemster, M.D. . 74
Robinson, Elliott S., M.D., The laboratory fights pneumonia . . . 179
Rounds, Frank W., A.B., D.D.S., Dental extractions 108
Rubenstein, A. Daniel, M.D., Undulant fever 68
Scarlet fever, by John E. Gordon, M.D. 46
Smallpox, by Roy F. Feemster, M.D. 50
Spalding, Mary, M.A., Is sugar the lone factor in producing dental caries? . 111
Special problems in the typing of pneumococci from infants and young chil-
    dren, by Arthur P. Long, M.D. 262
Structural and nervous effects of thumb-sucking, by Earl W. Swinehart,
    D.D.S. 141
Swinehart, Earl W., D.D.S., Structural and nervous effects of thumb-sucking 141
Syphilis, by Ernest B. Howard, M.D. 54
Teeth in congenital syphilis, The, by Florence B. Hopkins, M.D., D.M.D. . 145
Thorpe, Laura A., Don't say "Serum" when you mean "Vaccine" . . 8
Trichinosis, by John J. Poutas, M.D. 169
    A preventable disease, by Donald Augustine, Sc.D. 56
Tuberculosis, by Alton S. Pope, M.D. 60
Types of pneumococci in Massachusetts, by Edith A. Beckler, S.B. . . 268
Typhoid, Control of, by Gaylord W. Anderson, M.D. 167
Typhoid fever, by Charles E. Gill, M.D. 64
Undulant fever, by A. Daniel Rubenstein, M.D. 68
Use of specific serums in the treatment of pneumonias associated with pneu-
    mococci of the "higher types," The, by Maxwell Finland, M.D. . 245
Use of the term "Group IV" pneumococcus, The, by F. Randolf Philbrook,
    M.D. 273
Vogel, Ernest J., M.D., and Feemster, Roy F., M.D., Dr.P.H., The work of the
    collaborating pneumococcus typing laboratories of Massachusetts . 270
Wakefield, Arthur, M.D., Clinics for crippled children 183
Wesselhoeft, Conrad, M.D., Whooping cough 70
Westwell, Arthur E., D.M.D., The importance of an adequate dental program 138
What to eat and why, by Sara M. Jordan, M.D. 193
Whooping cough, by Conrad Wesselhoeft, M.D. 70
Williams, Vernon P., M.D., Nervous fatigue 197
Wisan, J. M., D.D.S., New Jersey State Dental Society Program—Dental
    health education 121
Work of the collaborating pneumococcus typing laboratories of Massachu-
    setts, The, by Ernest J. Vogel, M.D., and Roy F. Feemster, M.D. . 270
Zacks, David, M.D., Pulmonary tuberculosis—How it spreads in the home and
    family 173
    How its spread in the family can be prevented 175

PUBLICATION OF THIS DOCUMENT APPROVED BY THE COMMISSION ON ADMINISTRATION AND FINANCE